PRINCIPLES OF FINANCIAL REGULATION

T0323688

Principles of Financial Regulation

JOHN ARMOUR, DAN AWREY, PAUL DAVIES,
LUCA ENRIQUES, JEFFREY N. GORDON,
COLIN MAYER, AND JENNIFER PAYNE

OXFORD
UNIVERSITY PRESS

OXFORD

UNIVERSITY PRESS

Great Clarendon Street, Oxford, OX2 6DP,
United Kingdom

Oxford University Press is a department of the University of Oxford.
It furthers the University's objective of excellence in research, scholarship,
and education by publishing worldwide. Oxford is a registered trade mark of
Oxford University Press in the UK and in certain other countries

Published in the United States of America by Oxford University Press
198 Madison Avenue, New York, NY 10016, United States of America

British Library Cataloguing in Publication Data
Data available

ISBN 978–0–19–878648–1

Printed and bound by
CPI Group (UK) Ltd, Croydon, CR0 4YY

Preface

How We Came to Write This Book

On Monday, 15 September 2008, Lehman Bros entered Chapter 11 bankruptcy proceedings. That afternoon, two of us were running a class on comparative corporate law in New York. As we arrived in class, one of us passed a note to the other: 'I withdrew $500 before class. Don't know if ATMs will still be working after.'

The class, ironically, was about 'bubbles'. But when a student asked us how we could explain what was happening downtown, we realized we had no convincing answers.

We began reading about banks and banking regulation; the more we read, the more unhappy we became. In a paper written a number of years earlier, Charles Goodhart and colleagues had forcefully criticized the then new Basel II accord—which by 2008 was the centrepiece of banking regulation around the world—on the basis that it would make the financial system more 'procyclical'—that is, more prone to boom and bust. They observed prophetically:[1]

> [The Basel II] proposals, taken together, will enhance both the procyclicality of regulation and the susceptibility of the financial system to systemic crises, thus negating the central purpose of the whole exercise. Reconsider before it is too late.

Why had no one listened? We turned next to literature on banking regulators. In the US, we found that oversight of investment banks—like Lehman—under the Basel II framework was being undertaken by the Securities and Exchange Commission ('SEC'). The SEC was a 'market regulator', and had no mandate to care about 'financial stability'. But why should 'market regulators' not care about financial stability? And if they did not, why should investment banks be allocated to a 'market regulator'?

In the UK, the Financial Services and Markets Act 2000 had, to great fanfare, recently merged the oversight of all aspects of financial regulation in the UK, including banking. The legislation did not include 'financial stability' amongst the goals the new Financial Services Authority was required to pursue. Why was this not thought relevant?

The more we thought about it, the more we felt convinced that the breadth and depth of the currents in the financial system had simply flowed past and around regulators tied to particular islands of jurisdiction and expertise. The lack of appreciation of the wider picture was startling. The starkness of the errors, and the gravity of the consequences, meant that financial regulation became a major research interest for us, in a way that it had not previously been.

Financial regulation soon became a huge growth industry. Others had had the same reaction as us. Everyone had an opinion, it seemed, and everything was being changed,

---

[1] J Daníelsson, P Embrechts, C Goodhart, C Keating, F Muennich, O Renault, and HS Shin, 'An Academic Response to Basel II', LSE Financial Markets Group Special Paper No 130 (2001), 5.

all at once. But if there were problems with the coordination of ideas before, how could these possibly be solved by proceeding in this way?

The following year, a group of us in Oxford decided to launch a new course, 'Principles of Financial Regulation', for our graduate students—including those taking our new MSc in Law and Finance. We felt that people entering the professional world who might work in, or with, the financial sector would value the chance to engage critically with what was going on. It would also give us a chance to try to organize our thinking in a systematic way.

There were two central challenges to this undertaking, however. The first was the breadth of potentially relevant material and the range of interconnection. The second was the pace of change. The breadth of material meant that it would be very difficult to offer a course that would provide detailed engagement with regulatory measures to the level needed to advise about compliance. The pace of change meant that, even if it had been possible to offer such detail, it would have been futile, because the content stood a high chance of being outdated before students actually got to put it into practice. Besides, large law firms have tremendously sophisticated in-house teams who aggregate and analyse the latest information at a highly detailed level. There would be little comparative advantage to us trying to replicate this in a university.

So we decided instead to develop what we think of as a 'macro' approach. Just as we think of the discipline of economics as split into macro and micro branches, so too might we approach legal scholarship.[2] A macro project is one that looks at the level of the system as a whole, and understands the interrelation of the various components at the aggregate level. In particular, we thought it was important to offer a treatment that could comprehend the regulation of both securities markets and banks, which had traditionally been treated as entirely different, despite the increasing functional over-laps. Of course, a macro system must be built on sound micro foundations. But in order to give an understanding of how things work at the macro level, it is not necessary to convey all the detail of the micro foundations. What we wanted to do was to give a roadmap to the regulation of the financial system, which students could use to situate their understanding of the rules.

In particular, we thought it would be helpful to present substantive rules from the major jurisdictions involved in the financial crisis—the US and the EU (and especially, within the latter, the UK, given our base)—as exemplifying policy choices. This allows for a treatment that presents large-scale principles, upon which examples of particular policy choices are hung. The approach emphasizes the interaction of policy choices and the consequences one piece of the jigsaw has for the others. But it is of course not comprehensive.

Soon after we had launched the course, we decided it would be worthwhile to combine our research and pedagogical endeavours in the field and produce a book that would seek to deliver the ambitions of our course to a wider readership. Looking around, we found no existing book that offered the sort of roadmap we felt was necessary: an understanding of how financial regulation relates to the economic goals

---

[2] There is in fact a very venerable tradition of studying 'macro law', in the form of Roman Law.

of the financial system, and how it can be improved. The idea of a 'holistic' approach proved very appealing to people with whom we discussed the idea, including our publisher.

Unfortunately, there was a reason why no such book existed. And it was not that no one had previously thought it would be a good idea. It was rather that the project was so big as to be (nearly) unmanageable. There followed several years of intense meetings amongst the co-authors, at which we discussed and tore up each other's drafts. Frustratingly, the more progress was made in understanding, the less progress seemed to be made towards completion. Fortunately, our publisher was very patient. Gradually, we inched towards a framework that we all felt we could subscribe to, at least at the macro level. (Of course, given the number and contentiousness of the issues, there are surely particular matters on which each of us may disagree with the book's aggregate line.)

How to Read This Book

We hope this book will be of use for a wide range of readers: students and academics (in law, business, public policy, and economics), regulators, and practitioners. With this breadth of potential readership in mind, we think it helpful to offer some guidance on how it is structured.

The book is divided into six Parts. Part A is foundational material. Parts B, C, and D then consider, respectively, financial markets, consumer finance, and banking regulation. Part E—entitled 'Banks and Markets'—builds on the preceding Parts to see how interconnections between different components create new regulatory challenges. Part F deals with institutional issues—the architecture of regulatory authorities—both within jurisdictions and at the international level, the challenges of supervision and enforcement, and the politics of financial regulation.

Parts B, C, D, and E each begin with an overview chapter that is more theoretical in orientation than the rest of the chapters in the respective sections. In each case, the introductory chapter identifies the main underlying principles for the section; the following chapters then frame the regulatory norms around these principles.

A general course on financial regulation can simply follow the whole book. To give a more institutional flavour, Part F could be set immediately after Part A rather than left to the end. If time is short, then the coverage could be abbreviated in various ways. Chapters 7 (Market Infrastructure), 11 (Financial Advice), 12 (Financial Products), 17 (Bank Governance), and 18 (Payment and Settlement Systems) are each relatively self-contained, as are most of the chapters in Part F.

The book can also be used as a supplement for more traditional courses on securities or banking regulation, on either side of the Atlantic. In this case, the relevant material would be Part A, then Part B or D (for securities or banking, respectively), then Part E (to appreciate cross-sectional issues). Chapter 10 (theory of consumer financial regulation) is likely to be relevant insofar as behavioural finance forms any part of a securities law course.

For students in business schools or economics departments, the theory chapters—all of Part A's Chapters and then Chapters 5 (markets), 10 (consumers), 13 (banks), and

20 (market-based credit intermediation)—would be the most natural points around which to hang a course. Substantive chapters could then be used as case studies. In this respect, the topics in Chapters 6 (information intermediaries), 7 (market structure), 14–16 (bank capital, liquidity, and resolution), 19 (macroprudential oversight), 21 (market makers), 22 (collective investments and financial stability), and 23 (structural regulation of financial institutions) will probably be of most interest.

For those already working in the field of financial regulation, we hope that the book will provide some generalist insights about linkages between fields. So, for example, a specialist in banking will, we hope, find the material on other aspects of financial regulation, as well as the general framing, useful.

Acknowledgements

The book grew out of the course we teach to graduate students in Oxford under the same name. It is impossible to acknowledge fully the degree to which development of these ideas has been strengthened and focused over a period of several years through intense debate with the exceptionally talented group of students—and latterly alumni— with whom we have been fortunate enough to interact.

We also owe a significant debt to the reviewers who read and commented on the book outline for OUP; in particular, Niamh Moloney, whose patience and generosity in this regard went far beyond the course of duty.

In the course of writing, many of the individual chapters have benefited from comments and feedback from seminar and workshop presentations, as well as colleagues who generously read drafts. In particular, we thank Johnathan Chertkow (Chapter 10), Mathias Dewatripont (Chapter 15), Stavros Gadinis (Chapter 8), Zohar Goshen (Chapter 10), Ed Greene (Chapters 8 and 9), Kevin Haeberle (Chapters 8 and 9), Mathias Lehmann (Chapter 3), Ronald Mann (Chapter 18), Geoff Miller (Chapter 17), Joseph Raz (Chapter 10), Roberta Romano (Chapters 19 and 23), Chuck Sabel (Chapter 10), Michel Tison (Chapter 11), Andrew Tuch (Chapters 8 and 9), Peter Zimmermann (Chapters 19 and 27), and especially Bill Williams, who read and commented on the entire manuscript and saved us from many errors. All remaining errors are exclusively our responsibility.

We also thank participants in the following for helpful feedback and questions on presentations of, or drawing on, particular chapters: a Staff Seminar at the University of Edinburgh Law Department (Chapter 1); Seminars at the Oxford-Man Institute for Quantitative Finance (Chapters 1, 19, and 27); a lecture at Norton Rose (now Norton Rose Fulbright) in London (Chapter 3); a Faculty Seminar at Columbia Law School (Chapter 10); Business Law Workshops in Oxford (Chapters 10 and 17); a Cambridge/ LSE conference on 'New Legal Thinking in Financial Regulation' (Chapter 15), a seminar at the National Bank of Belgium (Chapter 15), Commonwealth Central Bank Governors' Meetings at the World Bank in Washington DC (Chapters 16 and 28); an ETH/NYU Banking Regulation conference in New York (Chapter 17); a Blue Sky Workshop at Columbia Law School (Chapter 23); and a conference on European Banking Regulation at the Centre for Advanced Studies at the Ludwig Maximilian University of Munich (Chapter 23).

The ideas in the book have also benefited from thoughtful comments from and discussions with many others, including Franklin Allen, Mads Andenas, Patrick Bolton, Ryan Bubb, Charlie Calomiris, John Coates, Veerle Colaerts, Matthew Conaglen, Luis Correia, Eilís Ferran, Julian Franks, Xavier Freixas, Merritt Fox, Simon Gleeson, Talia Gillis, Ron Gilson, Joanna Gray, Gerard Hertig, Elizabeth Howell, Howell Jackson, Robert Jackson Jr, Kate Judge, Reinier Kraakman, Marco Lamandini, Rosa Lastra, Iain MacNeil, Ignacio Mas, Nicholas Morris, Andrea Polo, Eric Posner, Roberta Romano, and Michael Taylor.

In addition, in working on this project we have been extremely fortunate in the assistance, engagement, support, and critique provided to us by our colleagues at Oxford, including Paul Craig, Horst Eidenmueller, Stefan Enchelmaier, Timothy Endicott, Joshua Getzler, Roy Goode, Louise Gullifer, Chris Hare, Chris Hodges, Angus Johnston, Emily Jones, Walter Mattli, Alan Morrison, Tom Noe, Jeremias Prassl, Georg Ringe, Richard Salter, Oren Sussman, Peter Tufano, John Vella, John Vickers, David Vines, Rebecca Williams, Ngaire Woods, and Kristin van Zwieten.

We have also benefited from the opportunity to explore, vicariously, many of these issues in more depth, and with greater energy, through our doctoral students, including Martin Bengtzen, Antonios Chatzivasileiadis, Jonathan Greenacre, Kosmas Kaprinis, Wande McCunn, Katrien Morbee, Natalie Mrockova, Javier Solana, and Thom Wetzer. We are grateful in particular for research assistance so ably provided by Martin Bengtzen, Antonis Chatzivasileiadis, and Wande McCunn.

We are enormously grateful for the exceptional patience and steadfast support provided to us in this project by Alex Flach at OUP. We also thank Carla Hodge, Nicole Leyland, and Sarah Cheeseman for their excellent work in producing such a large manuscript in so short a time.

Finally, we owe an immeasurable debt of gratitude to our families, for their patience, support, and encouragement over the many years this project has taken to come to fruition. Without you it would have been impossible.

New York
Oxford
7 January 2016

Contents

PART F THE MIX OF INSTITUTIONS

List of Abbreviations

ABCP	asset-backed commercial paper
ABS	asset-backed security
AFME	Association of Financial Markets in Europe
AIM	Alternative Investment Market
AMEX	American Stock Exchange
APR	annual percentage rate
ASIC	Australian Securities and Investment Commission
AT1	Additional Tier 1
ATM	automated teller machine
ATS	alternative trading system
BaFin	Bundesanstalt für Finanzdienstleistungsaufsicht (German Federal Financial Supervisory Authority)
BAML	Bank of America Merrill Lynch
Basel I	First Basel Accord
Basel II	Second Basel Accord
Basel 2.5	Basel Accord 2.5
Basel III	Third Basel Accord
BBA	British Bankers Association
BCBS	Basel Committee on Banking Supervision
BHC	bank holding company
BIS	Bank for International Settlements
BoE	Bank of England
BRRD	Bank Recovery and Resolution Directive
CAMEL	Capital, Asset quality, Management, Earnings, and Liquidity
CB	central bank
CCB	Capital Conservation Buffer
CCCB	Counter-Cyclical Capital Buffer
CCP	central counterparty
CDO	collateralized debt obligation
CDS	credit default swap
CET1	Core Equity Tier 1 Capital
CEO	Chief Executive Officer
CFPB	Consumer Financial Protection Bureau
CFTC	Commodity Futures Trading Commission
CHIPS	Clearinghouse Interbank Payment System
CLO	collateralized loan obligation
CLS	continuous linked settlement
CMA	Competition and Markets Authority
CoCo	contingent convertible bond
CoVar	conditional value at risk
CPMI	Committee on Payments and Market Infrastructures
CPSS	Committee on Payment and Settlement Systems
CRA	credit rating agency
CRD III	Capital Requirements Directive III

CRD IV	Capital Requirements Directive IV
Credit CARD Act	Credit Card Accountability, Responsibility, and Disclosure Act
CRR	Capital Requirements Regulation
CSD	central securities depository
CSE	Consolidated Supervised Entities
CTRF	Contingent Term Repo Facility
DB	defined benefit
DC	defined contribution
DGS	deposit guarantee scheme
DNS	deferred net settlement
D&O	directors and officers
DOJ	US Department of Justice
D-SIB	domestic systemically important bank
DTC	Depository Trust Company
DTCC	Depository Trust and Clearing Company
DTI	debt service-to-income ratio
DvP	delivery-versus-payment
EAD	exposure at default
EBA	European Banking Authority
EBF	European Banking Federation
EBITDA	earnings before interest, taxes, depreciation, and amortization
EBU	European Banking Union
ECB	European Central Bank
ECMH	efficient capital markets hypothesis
EDIS	European Deposit Insurance Scheme
EEA	European Economic Area
EIOPA	European Insurance and Occupational Pensions Authority
ESFS	European System of Financial Supervision
ESM	European Stability Mechanism
ESMA	European Securities and Markets Authority
ESRB	European Systemic Risk Board
ETF	exchange traded fund
EU	European Union
FCA	Financial Conduct Authority
FD	Fair Disclosure
FDIA	Federal Deposit Insurance Act
FDIC	Federal Deposit Insurance Corporation
FDICIA	Federal Deposit Insurance Corporation Improvement Act
Fed	Federal Reserve
FHFA	Federal Housing Finance Agency
FINMA	Eidgenössische Finanzmarktaufsicht (Swiss Financial Market Supervisory Authority)
FINRA	Financial Industry Regulatory Authority
FIO	Federal Insurance Office
FIRREA	Financial Institutions Reform, Recovery, and Enforcement Act of 1989
forex	foreign exchange
FPC	Financial Policy Committee
FSA	Financial Services Authority

FSAP	Financial Sector Assistance Program
FSB	Financial Stability Board
FSMA	Financial Services and Markets Act
FSOC	Financial Stability Oversight Council
FTC	Federal Trade Commission
FTT	financial transaction tax
G20	Group of Twenty
GAAP	Generally Accepted Accounting Principles
GDP	gross domestic product
GSE	government-sponsored enterprise
G-SIB	global systemically important bank
G-SII	global systemically important insurer
HFT	high frequency trading
HoldCo	holding company
HQLA	high quality liquid assets
IAIS	International Association of Insurance Supervisors
IASB	International Accounting Standards Board
ICB	Independent Commission on Banking
ICE	Intercontinental Exchange
IFRS	International Financial Reporting Standards
ILTR	Indexed Long-Term Repos
IMF	International Monetary Fund
IOSCO	International Organization of Securities Commissions
IPO	initial public offering
IRA	Individual Retirement Account
IRB	internal ratings-based
ISCD	international central securities depository
ISDA	International Swaps and Derivatives Association
JOBS Act	Jumpstart Our Business Startups Act
KIID	Key Investor Information Document
LCR	Liquidity Coverage Ratio
LEI	legal entity identifier
LGD	loss given default
LIBOR	London Interbank Offered Rate
LOLR	lender of last resort
LR	Leverage Ratio
LSE	London Stock Exchange
LTI	loan-to-income ratio
LTV	loan-to-value ratio
MacroPru	macroprudential
MBS	mortgage-backed security
MD&A	management discussion and analysis
MiFID	Markets in Financial Instruments Directive
MiFID II	Markets in Financial Instruments Directive II
MIFIR	Markets in Financial Instruments Regulation
MMF	money market fund
MOU	memorandum of understanding
MPA	macroprudential authority

MPC	Monetary Policy Committee
MTF	multilateral trading facility
NASDAQ	National Association of Securities Dealers Automated Quotations
NAV	net asset value
NBFI	non-bank financial institution
NCA	national competent authority
NMS	National Market System
NR	Northern Rock
NRSRO	Nationally Recognized Statistical Rating Organization
NSFR	Net Stable Funding Ratio
NTNI	non-traditional or non-insurance (activities)
NYSE	New York Stock Exchange
OCC	Office of the Comptroller of the Currency
OEIC	open-ended investment company
OFR	Office of Financial Research
OFT	Office of Fair Trading
OLA	Orderly Liquidation Authority
OTC	over-the-counter
OTF	organised trading facility
OTS	Office of Thrift Supervision
P2P	peer-to-peer
PCBS	Parliamentary Commission on Banking Standards
PD	probability of default
PI	product identifier
PPI	payment protection insurance
PRA	Prudential Regulation Authority
PRIIP	Packaged Retail and Insurance Investment-Based Product
RBS	Royal Bank of Scotland
repo	repurchase agreement
RFB	ring-fenced body
RMBS	residential mortgage backed securities
RRP	recovery and resolution plan
RTGS	real-time gross settlement
RWAs	risk-weighted assets
SAP	Special Administration Process
SCP	Synthetic Credit Portfolio
SEC	Securities and Exchange Commission
SIFI	systemically important financial institution
SIFMA	Securities Industry and Financial Markets Association
SIPC	Securities Investor Protection Corporation
SIV	structured investment vehicle
SMEs	small and medium-sized enterprises
SMR	Structural Measures Regulation (proposed)
S&P	Standard and Poor's
SPE	special purpose entity
SPOE	Single Point of Entry
SPV	special purpose vehicle
SRB	Single Resolution Board (in Chapter 23: systemic risk buffer)

SRM	Single Resolution Mechanism
SRMP	Systemic Risk Management Plan
SRO	self-regulatory organization
SRR	Special Resolution Regime
SSM	Single Supervisory Mechanism
STWF	Short-Term Wholesale Funding
T2	Tier 2
TALF	Term Asset-Backed Securities Loan Facility
TARP	Troubled Asset Relief Progam
TCF	Treat Customers Fairly
TLAC	Total Loss Absorbing Capacity
TRACE	Trade Reporting and Compliance Engine
UCITS	undertaking for collective investment in transferable securities
UNCTAD	United Nations Conference on Trade and Development

Table of Cases

UK

AUSTRALIA

EU

US

Table of Legislation

TABLE OF BASEL ACCORDS

Guide to the Companion Website

This book is accompanied by a Companion Website that provides you with various resources to reinforce your learning, help your revision, and prepare you for essay or exam assessment. These resources are all free of charge and designed to maximize your learning experience.

www.oup.co.uk/companion/pfr

PART A

FOUNDATIONS

1

Introduction

> Over the course of this crisis, we as an industry caused a lot of damage. Never has it
> been clearer how mistakes made by financial companies can affect Main Street, and we
> need to learn the lessons of the past few years.
>
> Brian T. Moynihan, CEO and President, Bank of America
> (Testimony to Financial Crisis Inquiry Commission)

The financial crisis of 2007–9 was the most serious economic disturbance in the post Second World War era. It caused a major contraction in economic activity in developed countries around the world with estimated losses of more than $15 trillion— approximately one-fifth of the value of total world annual production.[1] Firms cut investment and laid off workers, causing substantial increases in unemployment and significant economic hardship from which many economies are only just now beginning to recover. National efforts to mitigate the financial crisis triggered a follow-on sovereign debt crisis in the Eurozone, which even now is a source of economic instability.

The questions that many people have been thinking about since the crisis are why it happened, and what can be done to prevent it happening again. One of the underlying causes is widely thought to have been a failure of financial regulation—a failure to control the misconduct and excesses in which financial institutions were indulging prior to the crisis. Financial regulation was comprehensively outmanoeuvred by financial markets and institutions, leaving it exposed to the failures and contagion that occurred in 2008. While this book is about financial regulation, rather than the financial crisis itself, the fact that there was a serious failure of prevailing wisdom provides a strong motivation for writing it. A reconsideration of the nature and conduct of financial regulation is required, which is what this book seeks to do. Its goal is to articulate a framework within which financial regulation can be analysed in a coherent and comprehensive fashion.

1.1 The Changing Financial System

Traditionally financial regulation has distinguished between banks and securities markets. *Bank regulation* has a long history, and in many countries developed out of informal central bank oversight. Its development was rather more explicit in the US, reflecting political compromises in a large federal system. Three key steps were: first,

---

[1] See eg A Yoon, 'Total Global Losses from Financial Crisis: $15 Trillion', *Wall Street Journal, Real Time Economics Blog*, 1 October 2012; World Bank, *The World at a Glance*, http://data.worldbank.org (World GDP estimate $77.87 trillion) (accessed 18 August 2015).

Principles of Financial Regulation. First Edition. John Armour, Dan Awrey, Paul Davies, Luca Enriques, Jeffrey N. Gordon, Colin Mayer, and Jennifer Payne. © John Armour, Dan Awrey, Paul Davies, Luca Enriques, Jeffrey N. Gordon, Colin Mayer, and Jennifer Payne 2016. Published 2016 by Oxford University Press.

the national bank chartering and regulation that arose as a by-product of the Civil War; second, the establishment of the Federal Reserve System in 1913; and third, the New Deal reforms in response to the banking crises of the Great Depression. In particular, the Banking Act of 1933 created federal deposit insurance and the Federal Deposit Insurance Corporation ('FDIC') to resolve failed banks, and the contemporaneous Glass–Steagall Act separated commercial from investment banking.

This separation of 'banking' and 'market' activity was accompanied by the advent of securities regulation as a separate field. The Wall Street Crash of 1929 prompted the Securities Act of 1933 and the Securities Exchange Act of 1934, which regulated the interstate sale and trading of securities, respectively, and created the Securities and Exchange Commission ('SEC') to implement and enforce the regulatory scheme. So from the 1930s onward, there was a clear partition between the two fields in the US.

The intellectual framework of these discrete categories of regulation has been very influential internationally. At the end of the twentieth century, another group of states embarking on a project of building a single market—the European Union (EU)—likewise produced distinct streams of banking regulation and securities regulation, although there was never—at least not yet—any formal separation of banking and securities activity.

Securities law and banking regulation have undergone significant reform over the subsequent eighty years (not least with the repeal in 1999 of the Glass–Steagall Act's separation requirements), but the fundamental regulatory divide between securities markets and banking remains intact and is the basis of modern financial regulation in the US and many countries around the world.[2] Yet while the conceptual framing of financial regulation has remained the same, the financial system has not. There have been profound changes, most significantly over the last few decades.

First, there has been a significant shift in the way funds are channelled from suppliers to users of capital. Commercial banks have been and remain a fundamental route through which this occurs via the channelling of bank deposits from savers to borrowers. Banks remain a particularly important source of finance for small and medium-sized firms[3] and for the funding of certain types of activities, most notably large projects. But developed securities markets allow investors to enjoy the liquidity of bank deposits (ie the ability to convert their investments rapidly into cash) through selling their securities to other investors rather than through repayments of deposits from banks. While the relative size and significance of banks versus securities markets

---

[2] The UK sought to make a far-reaching change to the structure of its financial regulation at the turn of the century, by creating a single 'super-regulator' with responsibility for all aspects of financial regulation—the Financial Services Authority ('FSA'). This was done in explicit recognition of the increasing level of interconnection in the financial system. Unfortunately, while the regulators were merged, the intellectual frameworks of banking and securities regulation were not. See text to nn 17–18. The case of the FSA is discussed further in Chapter 27, section 27.2.3.

[3] See AM Robb and DT Robinson, 'The Capital Structure Decisions of New Firms' (2014) 27 *Review of Financial Studies* 153. See also Chapter 2.

varies appreciably across countries,[4] many countries have witnessed a substantial growth in the proportion of market-based finance over the last twenty years.[5]

This secular growth in the importance of financial markets has been driven by several factors. The first is demography. People have been living longer—average life expectancy at birth today in the developed world is 80,[6] as compared with 68 in 1950.[7] When state retirement provision was introduced in the UK, it was typically paying for just a few years of retirement; now, it must cover on average more than a decade. At the same time, with people having fewer children, the capacity to maintain or improve retirement payouts from traditional state-run pension schemes funded out of current taxes has been undermined. Instead, people have increasingly turned to the private sector for pension provision through collective savings vehicles offered by pension funds and insurance companies and, especially in the US, mutual funds. These financial intermediaries substitute for banks in the provision of credit to the real economy. Instead of 'bank loans', they purchase debt securities issued by borrowers. Thus the demand for pension provision has created both a new class of financial intermediaries that operate through securities markets and a new supply of funds available to market-based finance.

Second, for most of the twentieth century, investments in equities (shares) greatly outperformed investments in debt (bank deposits and bonds).[8] There are several reasons for this, one of which was the erosion of the value of fixed interest investments in periods of high inflation during the twentieth century and the high real returns earned on corporate investments during a period of rapid (re)industrialization and the introduction of mass production.[9] The higher returns on equity encouraged a shift from saving via bank deposits into equity markets, which in turn further fuelled the increase in equity values.

Third, there have been substantial technological advances that have reduced the costs of financial transactions. In particular, the development of computers and new communications media has dramatically enhanced the power and speed with which investors can trade on financial markets. In many cases, these developments have also improved the transparency of market trading and increased information flows to market participants. However, there are concerns that the private benefits that institutions derive from trading (sometimes milli- or nano-seconds) faster than others may exceed the benefits to society as a whole from the increasing speed of trades.

Fourth, globalization has had a transformative impact on finance. Thirty years ago 'the financial system' would have been interpreted by most readers as relating to domestic

---

[4] See F Allen and D Gale, *Comparing Financial Systems* (Cambridge, MA: MIT Press, 2000).

[5] See L Gambacorta, K Tsatsaronis, and J Yang, 'Financial Structure and Growth', *BIS Quarterly Review*, March 2014.

[6] OECD, *Health: Key Tables from OECD*, Table 1.1, Life Expectancy at Birth, Total Population.

[7] Office for National Statistics (UK), *Mortality, 2010-based NPP Reference Volume* (2012), 2 (UK life expectancy at birth 68 in 1950); US Census Bureau, *Statistical Abstract of the United States: 1999*, Table 1421, Expectation of Life at Birth (US life expectancy at birth 68 in 1950).

[8] For example, $1 invested in a deposit account in 1926 was worth $22 in 2012; $1 invested in investment grade bonds was worth $84; $1 in large market capitalization US stocks was worth $3,189; and $1 in small market capitalization US stocks was worth $14,370—653 times the investment in a deposit account!

[9] See eg B Eichengreen, *The European Economy Since 1945: Coordinated Capitalism and Beyond* (Princeton, NJ: Princeton University Press, 2006).

institutions and markets; today it is typically regarded as referring to a global network. Relaxation of national capital controls has contributed to this process but so too have ambitious programmes of economic integration, such as those undertaken by the EU. The result has been larger financial systems, greater competition, and accelerated processes of change with wider potential ramifications for national and international economies.

International capital flows have encouraged the emergence of new markets for managing associated risks in currencies and interest rates. Firms are now able to raise capital on markets around the world, which has promoted new instruments and institutions for managing risks and raising finance on a global basis. Differential growth rates have generated global imbalances, with some countries having large surpluses and others large deficits that have contributed to substantial capital flows.

Globalization has also created particular regulatory challenges because global spill-overs and linkages mean that states can no longer authoritatively regulate even their own financial system, let alone the global financial system as a whole. International financial regulation depends upon a unique set of agreements and understandings among governments, central banks, and financial regulators that, with some exceptions (for example, within the EU), are legally unenforceable.

We argue in this book that these changes in the nature of financial systems—the growth of markets in relation to financial intermediaries and the internationalization of markets—have had profound effects on the risks inherent in these systems. These changes in risks in turn require a different structure of financial regulation from that which was established in the first half of the twentieth century and, in particular, a rethink of the historical separation between securities markets and banking regulation and between the domestic activities of national regulators.

1.2 The Genesis of the Financial Crisis

The growth in international financial markets meant that globalization fostered an appearance of greater diversification in risk bearing. Alan Greenspan, then Chairman of the Board of Governors of the US Federal Reserve, opined in 2004 that:

> [n]ot only have individual financial institutions become less vulnerable to shocks from underlying risk factors, but also the financial system as a whole has become more resilient.[10]

Such sentiments were widely shared at the time. When Raghuram Rajan, then a Professor of Finance at Chicago's Booth Business School (and currently Governor of the Reserve Bank of India) suggested at a central bankers' conference in 2005 that financial globalization might have entailed costs as well as benefits, his presentation was ridiculed.[11]

As we now know, the complacency was misplaced. The changes in the global financial system sowed the seeds of a number of problems. First, the consolidation, and global

---

[10] A Greenspan, Remarks at American Bankers Association Annual Convention, New York, 5 October 2004 (available at http://www.federalreserve.gov/BOARDDOCS/Speeches/2004/20041005/default.htm).
[11] RG Rajan, 'Has Financial Development Made the World Riskier?' (2005) *Proceedings, Federal Bank of Kansas City* 313.

reach, of large financial institutions meant that their individual stability became more important for the global system as a whole. Second, financial institutions' response to competition from markets was to refocus their business on market activities, in particular, the provision of underwriting services to firms accessing capital markets, the maintenance of inventories of financial assets to provide market-making (dealer) services, and engaging in trading on their own account ('proprietary' trading). Third, the development of new markets for risk failed to go hand in hand with any market or regulatory mechanism to identify the ultimate risk bearers within the system. Policymakers assumed that market finance implied diversification. But fourth, although these new interactions were market-based, they operated quite differently from the stock markets that policymakers understood. Stock markets transfer securities to investors who value them most highly and, in the process, aggregate information about their value. The new markets, such as over-the-counter (OTC) derivatives, did not work in the same way, because they were characterized by incomplete transfer of risk. In periods of extreme stress, these incomplete risk transfers operated to link the fortunes of significant participants. As a consequence, global financial institutions not only failed to disperse risk through the financial system, but also aggregated it amongst themselves. Fifth, the scale of conflicts of interest, manipulation, and outright deceit far exceeded what anyone had thought conceivable in institutions and markets that previously had been held in high regard.

Matters were further compounded by the influx of capital triggered by both global demographics and trade imbalances. Together, these created a powerful demand for high yielding but safe assets. To meet demand, financial and legal innovation delivered new types of financial contract. Amongst these, the best known was 'securitization': the transfer of packages of bank loans, especially mortgages, to free-standing 'special investment vehicles', which issued securities that were then sold to investors.

In principle, the parcelling together of a diversified portfolio of loan assets helped to lower investment risk; but the really important innovation lay in the marketing of a series of different 'tranches' of securities in the relevant entities, each carrying a different priority. Cash flows received from all the loans in the portfolio could be rearranged to give structural priority to payments owed to the senior tranche, creating a 'waterfall' that shifted the default risks within the portfolio to the junior tranches. These techniques permitted financial alchemy: the transformation of high-risk loan assets into low-risk senior securities.[12]

Reliance on financial innovations that promise much, through mechanisms that no one understands, has a history of ending badly. Securitization massively increased the complexity involved in calculating the risk profiles of ultimate securities.[13] This meant that even sophisticated investors were unable to undertake meaningful risk assessments. Instead, they relied on specialist risk assessors—the credit rating agencies (CRAs)—whose ratings turned out in many cases to be seriously in error.

---

[12] E Benmelech and J Dlugosz, 'The Alchemy of CDO Credit Ratings' (2009) 56 *Journal of Monetary Economics* 617.

[13] See R Bartlett, 'Inefficiencies in the Information Thicket: A Case Study of Derivatives Disclosure During the Financial Crisis' (2010) 36 *Journal of Corporation Law* 1; K Judge, 'Fragmentation Nodes: A Study in Financial Innovation, Complexity, and Systemic Risk' (2012) 64 *Stanford Law Review* 657.

In part this was due to conflicts of interest: credit rating agencies were paid by the very firms—the underwriters—that packaged and promoted the securitizations. The business of rating such securitizations was lucrative and the underwriters could shop among the rating agencies for the best rating.[14] Moreover, the banks setting up securitized portfolios had incentives to offload loans that were of lower quality than those they retained on their own balance sheets.[15]

One of the reasons securitization played a major role in the financial crisis was the unanticipated feedback effects of an influx of capital on underlying real estate markets.[16] Alongside a US Government policy of seeking to extend home ownership to previously excluded individuals, securitization facilitated a significant increase in mortgage lending, especially to riskier borrowers. This was because the 'alchemy' meant that even investors seeking safe investments could nevertheless supply funds to risky markets.

The influx of funds stimulated a historically unparalleled nationwide rise in housing prices.[17] By shifting mortgages from regional to national markets, securitization changed property price movements from being local to being national. As a consequence, the conventional wisdom that geographical distributions of residential real estate investments were an effective way of lowering overall risk proved inaccurate. But investors did not appreciate this, with the result that risk in securitized real estate transactions was significantly mispriced. In short, securitization, which purported to add stability through diversification, instead *intensified* risk by creating a new source of correlation. Moreover, the securities were bought by yield-hungry, safety-seeking investors around the world, especially in Europe, which elevated the significance of problems in this market to a global level.

It was a fall in US real estate that put a spark to this combustible mixture. At the end of 2006, investors began to realize that the scale of defaults on US subprime mortgages greatly exceeded expectations. For several months, everything proceeded in a state of suspended animation, rather like Wile E Coyote, the children's cartoon character who runs off a cliff but continues to spin his legs mid-air—until, that is, he looks down. Market participants began to appreciate the gravity of their situation in July 2007, when bank stock prices fell dramatically as Bear Stearns, the US investment bank, announced it was closing two funds it had promoted, which had invested heavily in subprime assets.[18] In August 2007 the French Bank BNP Paribas halted withdrawals from three

---

[14] See generally LJ White, 'Markets: The Credit Rating Agencies' (2010) 24 *Journal of Economic Perspectives* 211.

[15] BJ Keys, T Mukherjee, A Seru, and V Vig, 'Did Securitization Lead to Lax Screening? Evidence from Subprime Loans' (2010) 125 *Quarterly Journal of Economics* 307. Interestingly, this problem appears to have been avoided in relation to securitizations of corporate loans (so-called 'CLOs'): E Benmelech, J Dlugosz, and V Ivashina, 'Securitization without Adverse Selection: The Case of CLOs' (2012) 106 *Journal of Financial Economics* 91.

[16] See BS Black, CK Whitehead, and JM Coupland, 'The Nonprime Mortgage Crisis and Positive Feedback Lending', Working Paper, Northwestern University School of Law/Cornell Law School (2015).

[17] See R Shiller, *The Subprime Solution* (Princeton, NJ: Princeton University Press, 2008).

[18] Highly readable accounts of the events surrounding the financial crisis include T Geithner, *Stress Test* (New York, NY: Crown Publishers, 2014); N Irwin, *The Alchemists* (New York, NY: Penguin, 2013); M Lewis, *The Big Short* (New York, NY: Norton, 2010); H Paulson, *On the Brink* (New York, NY: Business Plus, 2010); and AR Sorkin, *Too Big to Fail* (New York, NY: Penguin, 2010).

investment funds because various securitized assets could not be priced, which brought investors to the sudden realization that the fall in subprime values could have global dimensions.

At this point, many financial institutions that had developed close ties to financial markets found themselves in difficulty. Securitization markets froze when the credit ratings attached to mortgage-backed securities were cast into doubt. This stranded the vendor banks that held large inventories of freshly originated subprime mortgages 'warehoused' pending securitization. The supposedly 'off balance sheet' entities used in the securitizations ran into trouble: they relied on short-term capital market financing to meet short-term liquidity needs arising from mismatches between cash flows from the underlying mortgage borrowers and cash flows promised to investors. Short-term debt investors, such as money market funds, now refused to 'roll over' their loans. Major underwriting banks were called upon to prop up troubled securitization vehicles, either under explicit or implicit guarantees. Such overt action brought the special investment vehicles onto visibly damaged bank balance sheets.

The trouble spread far beyond those underwriting the securitizations. Many banks and other financial institutions, both in the US and elsewhere around the world, held substantial volumes of mortgage-related securities, the values of which were compromised. This triggered large balance sheet write-downs, although no one knew whether they were sufficient. Doubtful valuations meant that a bank that had financed large holdings substantially through wholesale short-term markets now faced the risk of a 'run'. British bank Northern Rock fell to such a run in September 2007.

Other financial institutions financed their holdings of mortgage-related and other exotic securities with short-term funding that was often collateralized by these very same instruments. The funders—concerned about risks to their own viability from these counterparty exposures—insisted on more collateral and/or higher-quality, less exotic collateral. Thus financial institutions found themselves under pressure to sell exotic securities to obtain more prosaic assets, such as cash. Yet because of the uncertainty surrounding the value of the exotic securities, no one wanted to buy them.[19]

Markets simply dried up, leaving the financial institutions facing a squeeze that was terminal in some cases. Bear Stearns narrowly survived failure in March 2008 when a rescue merger was facilitated through a loan from the Federal Reserve. When the far larger Lehman Brothers reached crisis point in September 2008, potential merger partners were unwilling to take on the much greater risks given the limits on the Fed's capacity (or willingness) to backstop losses. Lehman's subsequent bankruptcy became the defining moment of the financial crisis.

One of the striking features of the mechanics of securitization is the extent to which the process operated outside the regulated arena, or at least outside the regulatory provisions designed to respond to the kinds of risks it created. A central goal of banking regulation is to ensure the stability of financial institutions. To this end it imposes prudential constraints on the balance sheets of banks intended to ensure that these

---

[19] GB Gorton, *Slapped by the Invisible Hand: The Panic of 2007* (New York, NY: OUP, 2010).

firms are able to withstand an unexpected slump in the value of their assets. However, during the go-go years of financial globalization, it had widely been thought that the encroachment of markets onto banking terrain would lessen the need for such regulation. It was thought that where assets were marketable or 'liquid', a troubled institution could extricate itself from problems by converting the assets into cash. Consequently, institutions such as investment banks—whether stand-alone or part of a larger financial conglomerate—which held assets in the form of marketable securities were subject to far less stringent capital regulation than traditional commercial banks, which held assets in the form of loans. The widespread freezing of wholesale markets demonstrated that this policy was based on a misapprehension: just when the ability to sell marketable securities was needed most, it evaporated.

1.3 The Intellectual Framework

Why were these problems not spotted previously? The changes we have sketched here transformed financial sectors into more market-oriented, and more international, arenas than they had previously been. Part of the problem, though, was that thinking about financial regulation remained largely within the same intellectual silos it had inhabited for three-quarters of a century. The intellectual division between the regulation of securities markets and the regulation of banks introduced in the 1930s as part of the New Deal had made sense at that time, because of the structural separation of the two sectors. Moreover, there were always sound pragmatic reasons for focusing on a limited set of issues in order to gain more analytic traction. The resulting intellectual partition has continued to frame debates in US law schools and policy circles ever since. Not only that, but other jurisdictions, seeking to implement reforms to stimulate securities markets, looked to the well-developed institutions and scholarship in the US for guidance. Consequently, the idea of the partition was exported to frame the structure of financial regulation in the EU and elsewhere, and continues to do so even post-crisis.

The scope of these regimes is incomplete. Banking issues are covered by 'banking regulation', the domain of which is determined by the question, 'what is a bank?'. And securities-related issues are covered by 'securities regulation', the domain of which is determined by the question, 'what is a security?'. Moreover, the goals of these sectoral regulatory regimes are parochial. Banking regulation is concerned with the protection of bank deposits and the stability of banks, in part because bank depositors are not expected to monitor the quality of bank assets. Securities regulation is concerned with the facilitation of trading markets and the protection of investors via mandatory disclosure that enables investors to fend for themselves in assessing the risks of particular securities. Safety-and-soundness oversight of institutions in securities markets was traditionally far more limited than for banking institutions, which became problematic when such institutions took on bank-like functions, just as banks' use of securities markets (through securitization most notably) to substitute for traditional means of credit extension had been an afterthought for bank regulation.

The financial crisis highlighted the costs of these limitations. Even in terms of their own parochial goals, the scope of such regimes does not make sense unless defined in functional terms. The appropriate question is therefore not, 'what does the applicable legislation cover?', but rather, 'what sorts of organizations give rise to the problems regulation is seeking to address?'. That is, the question is not so much, 'what is a bank?' but, 'what ought to be regulated as a bank?'. Likewise, what activities can be left to disclosure regimes on the grounds that the relevant actors can knowledgeably evaluate and manage risks themselves and what activities require active intervention because they cannot?

More fundamentally, however, the parochial goals of sectoral regulation are limited and incomplete from the perspective of the stability of the system as a whole, and quite often in tension with one another. This was illustrated all too painfully by the case of the UK's FSA. The FSA, which was inaugurated at the turn of the century with great fanfare, operated as a unified financial regulator, encompassing securities, banking, insurance, and pensions. The idea was that the problems of sectoral regulatory incompleteness would be avoided by putting responsibility for all regulation under the same roof. The effect of this was to push the challenge onto the way in which the FSA was organized internally and the organization's priorities were defined.[20] The FSA's objectives were articulated as a list under the Financial Services and Markets Act 2000, most of which were derived from the pre-existing goals of institutional regulators. Unfortunately, the list was incomplete, because it did not include 'financial stability'.[21] Moreover, it left the FSA substantial discretion as to how to prioritize amongst the goals. Of the goals that were included, the FSA arguably over-invested in promoting consumer protection, seemingly at the expense of other goals.

1.4 This Book's Foundations

The rest of Part A sets out the foundations for the book's analysis, developing the key building blocks. The first of these is where we begin our account of financial regulation: not with regulatory instruments, but with the financial system. We ask first, what the financial system does, and second, how regulation can help it to function better. The enquiry as to the scope of regulation is therefore as much a normative as a positive exercise. In so doing, we consider a series of substantive topics in financial regulation in a comparative way, explaining differences in how the rules are structured in the EU and the US. These provide the opportunity to compare different policy solutions to a series of common underlying problems.

To this end, Chapter 2 gives an overview of the way in which the financial system functions. It explains the role the sector as a whole performs in mediating between suppliers and users of capital in the economy, and why this matters for economic growth. It then describes the principal components within the sector. In so doing, it describes how the significance of finance that has been intermediated via firms—that is, banks and other financial institutions—has declined over time, relative to that which has been allocated via markets. This trend has not, however, resulted in a lessening of the significance of financial institutions within the sector. Rather, their role has

---

[20] See further Chapter 4, section 4.4 and Chapter 27, section 27.2.3.
[21] This was added, after the crisis, by the Financial Services Act 2010.

evolved such that their functions in relation to the operation of financial markets—underwriting, market-making, and proprietary trading—have grown to be at least as significant as the traditional roles of deposit-taking and lending.

The functioning of the financial system is an economic matter. The second building block on which the book is premised is that the goals of financial regulation have to be considered from a perspective grounded in economics. In Chapter 3, we present an account of the goals of financial regulation in economic terms, namely to improve the functioning of institutions and markets. Economists have a well-developed understanding of the circumstances and ways in which regulatory intervention can do this. Chapter 3 maps these onto the self-styled goals of legislative instruments underpinning financial regulation.

Our understanding of 'regulation' is also grounded in this economic approach. We conceive of financial regulation as measures imposed by government on the financial sector. Consequently, private agreements between parties are not regulation on this view, except insofar as regulators mandate their terms.[22] While outcomes may doubtless be shaped by private law—in particular, the degree to which property law facilitates the partitioning of assets—the focus of this book is on the mandatory rules of regulation. This means we do not generally consider the private law of finance per se, but rather to the extent that it interacts with, or is shaped by, mandatory rules, such as when private parties voluntarily create groups or networks for the purpose of resolving common problems and, in some instances, often supported by public regulation, establish more formal self-regulatory frameworks.

Three further building blocks may be seen as corollaries of the first two. They are so important, and so frequently overlooked, that we set them out here separately. Applying an economic analysis of market failure to the financial system presupposes that we think about the financial system in functional rather than institutional terms. This is the third building block informing the book, namely that our analysis of the financial system will be functional in orientation. This means we are not so much concerned with the question, 'what is a bank?', but rather with, 'what functions do banks perform?'. The latter question emphasizes that the set of firms performing these functions are not necessarily limited to those firms categorized by current regulation as 'banks'. The way in which securitization performed many of the same economic functions as conventional banks while residing outside the ambit of bank prudential regulation is a good case in point.

The way in which the financial system performs its functions is not static. As the account in Chapter 2 makes clear, the system is subject to continuous change. Our fourth building block is that the financial system is dynamic—that is, continuously changing—in the way it operates, in response to changes in markets and in regulation itself, and that regulatory responses should be calibrated accordingly. A failure to recognize this was an important underlying cause of the inadequacy of financial regulation in the run-up to the financial crisis.

---

[22] For a more expansive view of the regulatory nature of private law, see H Collins, *Regulating Contracts* (Oxford: OUP, 1999). We consider 'enforced self-regulation' in Chapter 24, section 24.4.

One of the drivers of financial systems' dynamism is market players' continuous effort to find and exploit the best regulatory environment available to them. In other words, whenever there is scope for market players' choice with regard to regulations, they can be expected to make use of it and engage in regulatory arbitrage. Within a given jurisdiction, regulatory arbitrage is a possibility whenever the regulatory system provides for two different regimes of two formally different products or services that perform the same economic function (for example, a bank deposit and units in a money market mutual fund): market players may then choose, and in fact often create *ex novo*, the contractual form allowing them to gain the highest profits. Financial firms may choose or devise the less-regulated or unregulated product because compliance costs are lower or, more generally, because it makes it easier for them to exploit market failures to their advantage. But they may do so also because existing rules for the more heavily regulated product are just inefficient and make both financial firms and their clients worse off than if they use the unregulated or less-regulated product.

Another oft-overlooked aspect of financial regulation is that the goals it seeks to further sometimes come into conflict. We suspect that the partition of regulation fostered a false sense of security about this issue. If one focuses only on a particular sector of the financial system, one likely fails to see the costs a particular regulatory intervention may have on other sectors. Making use of the first four building blocks helps to avoid that kind of mistake. A functional account implies that particular market failures do not neatly match up to particular types of institution, instead, rather that the picture is somewhat messier. Consequently, there is a need to prioritize which failures are to be addressed. Our fifth building block, which follows from this, is a normative claim: one should prioritize according to the scale of losses that particular failures can inflict, while at the same time aiming to minimize the costs of regulation itself. A theme we develop throughout the book is that this places particular significance on systemic risks.

Simply identifying the economic problems to which financial regulation can—or should—respond is, of course, not the same as solving them. For a variety of reasons, real-world regulation and regulators fall short of their goals, even if these goals are appropriately set. In particular, the inherent dynamism of the financial system, coupled with its complexity, means that it forms a fleeting target for regulatory intervention. It is hard for regulators to keep abreast of developments. Matters are not helped by the fact that inside the system are players who stand to profit from working around whatever structures are put in place, and who—in particular, the global financial behemoths—have vastly greater resources to throw at undermining the rules than regulators do at designing them.

What is more, the relationship between politicians and regulation is often unhelpful: electorates are only interested in financial regulation in times of crisis. This gives politicians incentives to be too lax in good times, and too interventionist in bad times. Chapter 4 considers these problems in the round. The goal is to ground policy discussion within a realistic sense of what is possible: we should be under no illusions that perfect regulation can be implemented. At the same time, we should be careful not to allow ourselves to become defeatist: while perfection is not possible, there are many feasible opportunities for improvement of financial regulation simply through better understanding of its functions and how it interacts with the financial system. Our two final 'building blocks' also provide examples of how this has already taken place since the financial crisis.

The sixth building block for the book's analysis is that the effects of the actions of financial firms and regulators in one jurisdiction may spill over to others and that firms may engage in cross-border regulatory arbitrage—that is, deliberately choose to relocate in order to achieve more favourable regulatory treatment.[23] Such phenomena have become more salient after financial systems have become ever more interconnected due both to globalization and international agreements, including EU regulations, which have allowed financial firms to conduct their activities across borders.

Interjurisdictional spillovers have long been understood by economists to be problematic.[24] What has proved truly difficult has been making progress on their resolution through international cooperation. Yet the post-crisis era has seen a remarkable impetus for multilateral engagement with this challenge, as exemplified by the establishment of the G20's agenda-setting organization for international financial regulation, the Financial Stability Board ('FSB').

A final corollary, and our seventh building block, is that while the dichotomy between securities markets and bank regulation might once have served a valuable purpose, it is becoming increasingly untenable as securities markets and their associated institutions progressively perform banking functions and banks embrace securities markets activities. Instead of thinking in compartmentalized forms, we should adopt a holistic approach. The interface between banks and markets has become so complex that an approach to maintaining systemic stability at the level of the system as a whole is required. So-called macroprudential policy is intended to do just this. The key insights of Parts D and E, which are reflected throughout the rest of the book, are that measures seeking to protect the integrity of the system as a whole generally must be targeted at that level. The establishment of macroprudential authorities, endowed with extensive powers to intervene in the functioning of the financial sector, has been one of the major intellectual achievements, and its practical implementation one of the major intellectual challenges, of the post-crisis era.

While this holistic approach is an underlying theme of the book, we have sought to embed it and the other ideas in a more conventional framework, which starts from the traditional view of the financial system in which securities markets, consumers, and banks are the basic building blocks. We then explain the regulation of each of these areas in Parts B, C, and D, respectively, before turning in Part E to consider how the reframing of the financial system through interactions between markets and banks poses new challenges for regulation. We have chosen to present things in this way, rather than through a series of new categories derived directly from functions of the financial system, for two reasons. First, it makes the structure easier to navigate for those already familiar with the subject. Second, it creates a dynamic aspect to the

---

[23] Note that, as in the case of domestic regulatory arbitrage, firms may relocate because the chosen jurisdiction allows them to reap higher profits by failing to control externalities and address market failures or because the rules and their enforcement in that jurisdiction are better (from private parties' as well as society's perspectives) than in their country of origin.

[24] For example, see J Eatwell and L Taylor, *Global Finance at Risk: The Case for International Regulation* (New York, NY: New Press, 2000).

treatment, as we see how the constituent components are regulated, before examining how well these measures fare—or do not fare—in relation to their combination.

1.5 An Overview of the Rest of the Book

Parts B to E of the book present a series of topics in substantive financial regulation. These are discussed first from a policy perspective, then with an overview of the relevant regulatory provisions as implemented in the US and EU. In Parts B and D, we consider the regulation, respectively, of financial markets (primarily securities markets) and of bank-based credit intermediation. These two sections perhaps most closely track the scope of traditional law school courses, in securities regulation and banking regulation, respectively. Rather than abandon these well-understood and widely used categories, we have chosen to present material falling squarely within them accordingly. However, the treatment involves significantly less coverage of legal detail, and rather more coverage of policy underpinnings, than would be the case in a standard law course. This makes it feasible to cover both sets of topics in the same book or course. The advantage of this approach is that readers who have understood the basic issues in relation both to markets and credit intermediation are then able to understand better the distinct issues raised in Part E, which deals with 'crossover' issues spanning both markets and banks. More specifically, Part E deals with the regulation of the new intersection between banks and financial markets described here and in Chapter 2. We take a central lesson of the financial crisis to be the importance of better understanding, and regulation, of this intersection.

We discuss the regulation of consumer finance in Part C. This comes immediately after the consideration of securities markets in Part B, because consumers buying financial products or advice are subject to similar information asymmetries as are purchasers of securities. However, there is an important difference. Securities market mechanisms, in particular mandatory disclosure, do not work nearly as well for consumer financial products. Stock prices on well-developed secondary markets trade at 'fair' prices; financial products issued by a financial institution typically come without that assurance. Part C in turn comes *before* our consideration of banks—in Part D— because the most effective techniques for regulating financial products—which focus on controlling the behaviour of financial firms—are precursors for the way in which bank regulation controls the behaviour of these institutions in relation to depositors.

1.5.1 Financial markets

Part B, 'Financial Markets', begins with an account—in Chapter 5—of the economic theory of financial markets. Financial markets function both to mobilize savings and to allocate capital to firms. More than this, they serve to aggregate information about the future prospects of issuers, which helps monitor the way in which firms use the funds they have raised, and also ensures that savers who want to exit their investments get the best available price. Markets which perform this aggregation function well are said to be *informationally efficient*—and assisting them to do this is the key regulatory goal for the law of financial markets. In considering how markets come to impound new information, we review where the information comes from. Regulation can help to stimulate the production and verification of new information. The next four chapters are, in essence, concerned with the regulation of a succession of such mechanisms.

Chapter 6 discusses *information intermediaries*: core market participants who specialize in conveying and/or processing information, such as underwriters, analysts, rating agencies, auditors, and lawyers. They share a general challenge: how to generate incentives to disseminate high-quality unbiased information. In Chapter 7, we turn to *market infrastructure*. This is concerned with the means by which the infrastructure of financial markets is organized—exchanges, market makers, counterparties, clearing and settlement, and the like. Two key themes emerge from the discussion: the impact of competition and the significance of the way in which pricing information is disclosed.

In Chapter 8, we discuss the regulation of *issuer disclosure*—that is, by firms that have raised capital from public markets. Central questions here concern the scope and timing of both initial disclosures surrounding an initial public offering (IPO) of shares (that is, the prospectus) and subsequent disclosures (for example, information having a material impact on pricing). This chapter explains why—and to what extent—mandating such disclosure may be desirable even if many investors do not actually read the announcements. Finally, Chapter 9 is concerned with regulation of the conduct of participants in the market—in particular, *market manipulation*, *insider trading*, and *short selling*. We see that a principal concern of these aspects of market regulation is to rule out types of conduct that may impede stock market efficiency, although this struggles to explain restrictions on short selling.

1.5.2 Consumers and the financial system

Part C, 'Consumers and the Financial System', begins, in Chapter 10, with a discussion of the theory of the regulation of consumer finance. This differs from the economic bases for regulation advanced elsewhere in the book, in that here we incorporate insights from behavioural economics. Chapter 10's central enquiry is the extent to which these behavioural considerations—bounded rationality and the like—justify more intensive regulatory intervention than in relation to other aspects of the financial system. The answer turns out to be a qualified yes, but more qualified than we might at first think. While the problems that behavioural biases introduce into consumer decision-making are very real, the extent to which regulatory intervention can actually succeed in ameliorating matters—as opposed simply to introducing an additional layer of costs that ultimately must be borne by consumers—is far from clear. We draw two clear conclusions about regulatory strategies: first, disclosure is much less effective at protecting consumers who deal with financial firms than is commonly thought to be the case. Second, controls on the behaviour of financial firms in dealing with consumers ('conduct regulation') are far more readily justifiable than are restrictions on the terms of consumer financial products ('product regulation').

Chapters 11 and 12 then consider applications of the theory to two of the most important contexts in which consumers accessing the financial system may need protection: the giving of financial advice (Chapter 11) and the purchase of financial products from financial institutions (Chapter 12). We see the difficulties regulators encounter in crafting effective disclosure techniques for consumers. We also consider the use of product regulation, using as an example the UK's recent introduction of a rate cap on short-term high-interest loans. A third approach, currently in vogue with regulators in Europe, focuses not on the outcomes in terms of disclosures or contract terms, but on the firm's internal processes regarding product design and testing. This technique, which is known as 'product governance', harnesses the superior information of financial services firms to help weed out problematic consumer financial products early in their development.

Finally, we consider the application of prudential regulation in relation to firms offering consumer investment products. These rules serve to control agency costs—to restrict financial firms from taking on increased risk in a way that benefits their owners but harms the interests of their investors. Such regulation is generally *micro*prudential, in that it is concerned with the protection of the interests of investors in particular firms through ensuring the soundness and viability of these firms. The idea of the prudential regulation as a consumer protection mechanism carries across into Part D, where we turn to banks.

1.5.3 Banks

Part D, 'Banks', addresses the goal of banking regulation, namely the prudential regulation of institutions, as it has come to be reinterpreted, post-crisis, as including maintenance of financial stability. Chapter 13 sets out the economic theory of banking. Banks perform a number of similar functions in the financial system to markets: they mobilize savings and allocate capital to projects. But they do so in a very different way. We explore the rationale for intermediation via banks, rather than directly via markets. Rather than the aggregation of information that characterizes markets, banks gather and analyse their own information. At the same time, they offer liquidity to depositors. However, in so doing, banks are exposed to potential runs. Because banks are connected to one another via the payments system and inter-bank lending, the failure of one bank may bring down others.

If bank managers and shareholders underprice the risks attached to the bank's business model, there is a potential role for regulation to address this market failure. Chapters 14 and 15, respectively, deal with the prudential regulation of bank capital and liquidity, noting the way in which the regulatory standards have been strengthened in light of financial stability concerns. The financial crisis also brought renewed attention to the safe 'resolution' of a troubled bank (Chapter 16) and the distinctive governance needs of financial institutions (Chapter 17). One response to the question, 'why are banks special?' is their role in the payment and settlement systems, the arteries of the real economy; thus Chapter 18 is devoted to the regulation of such systems.

In Chapter 19, 'The Macroprudential Approach', bank regulation is refocused and enlarged by the post-crisis lens. In contrast to a narrowly microprudential approach, aimed at safeguarding financial *firms* in order to protect depositors—rather like the consumer protection rules we saw in Part C—and through that, safeguard financial stability, the macroprudential approach focuses on how the dynamics of the overall financial *system*, with its interconnections, correlation of risks, and so on, affect its overall stability, sweeping away individual institutions that would look safe and sound in isolation. This brings an approach to regulation of bank balance sheets that emphasizes resiliency at times of systemic financial stress, that worries about financial activity occurring outside the regulatory perimeter of the traditional banking system, and that devises strategies to effect the macro-economic environment, as through the constraining of credit-fuelled asset bubbles.

1.5.4 Markets and banks

Macroprudential oversight is concerned with systemic risk not just within the banking system, but also outside it. This provides a natural segue to Part E, 'Markets and Banks', which forms the fulcrum of the book. It explores the challenges posed by the developments charted in the financial system, and what was revealed by the financial crisis, for regulation at the intersection of institutions and markets.

Because banks have fragile capital structures and can be a source of contagion, financial stability is an important goal of banking regulation. However, this was not traditionally a concern of market regulation. Market regulation instead focused on disclosure and the conduct of market participants, with a view to ensuring the speed and accuracy of the price formation process. Based on such thinking, regulators' initial response to the shift away from banks was to assume that overall systemic risk had reduced, because the work done by the banking sector—the perceived locus of systemic risk—had become smaller.

But the shift in the financial system did not so much reduce systemic risk as change the ways in which it arose. As a result, a regulatory framework that focused its search for systemic risk on 'banks' was not apt to spot, and still less control, emergent varieties of that risk. Regulators were stuck in a framework that did not contemplate the migration of systemic risk, and there was consequently no serious attempt to monitor this from a macroprudential perspective. As a result, the new sources of systemic risk slipped cleanly under the radar.

Understanding how the changes in the financial system brought with them new sources of systemic risk goes to the heart of current regulatory endeavours, and of this book's project. Obviously, it matters a great deal that we understand what happened in order to be sure we can prevent a recurrence. To preserve financial stability, regulators need to understand the new cross-section of systemic risk. The same is true for anyone who wants to evaluate, or even understand, the new strategies regulators have deployed in response. In Part E, we consider how the changes in the structure of the financial system altered the incidence of systemic risk and how regulators have responded.

The following four topics are considered. Chapter 20 discusses market-based credit intermediation—the rise of institutions that perform credit intermediation services functionally equivalent to traditional banks, but falling outside the ambit of traditional banking regulation. The central question of this chapter is to determine what is 'functionally equivalent' to a bank: that is, what should be the domain of banking regulation? Chapter 21 deals with 'Making Markets'. Market makers hold inventories of financial assets with a view to being able to meet demand for both sales and purchases. If the volume of trade is large enough, it may not be necessary to have market makers who hold inventory at all: order-driven markets simply provide a technological route to the connection of buyers and sellers. Where volumes of trade are low, having market makers hold inventories on their own balance sheets may be crucial for ensuring that trade can occur at all. However, this in turn depends on the ability of the market makers themselves to weather sudden swings in prices.

As has been discussed, the rise of institutional investors has been a key trend over the past thirty years. These investment vehicles are regulated in order to protect consumers, issues that have been treated in Chapter 12. But this regulation intended to protect consumers may have unintended consequences for the system as a whole. Chapter 22, 'Asset Managers and Stability', discusses these issues. In particular, many regulatory regimes place substantive restrictions on the types of asset into which institutional investors can put their funds, motivated by a desire to protect end-investors from excess risk. With the massive growth in funds invested through collective investment vehicles, such restrictions come to impose an artificial constraint on (or stimulus for) certain types of asset class. To the extent that there are no substantive restrictions, a related issue concerns the process by which managers of such collective investment vehicles go about selecting the types of asset class into which they will invest their funds.

Chapter 23, 'Structural Regulation', considers an important set of regulatory initiatives geared towards the preservation of the system as a whole. Specifically, the chapter is concerned with rules limiting the types of business activity that may be carried on by entities engaging in particular types of core services within the financial system. The nature and motivation for such restrictions are varied. Historically the best-known example was the Glass–Steagall Act of 1933, which mandated the separation of investment and commercial banks in the US. The original rationales were largely concerned with consumer protection and market integrity. In particular, during the 1920s, US banks had encouraged their depositors to invest in the stock market, with brokerage services supplied by the banks themselves. The concern was that they had aggressively supplied 'margin' lending to their customers, causing the latter to become over-indebted and the stock market prices to be driven up inappropriately. Structural separation, it was thought, would put an end to this. Only secondary was the concern that losses on margin lending could endanger the soundness of the commercial banks themselves. This latter concern has resurfaced in the more recent iteration of interest in structural regulation. Proposals in both Europe and the US are concerned with insulating 'safe' commercial banking from 'risky' investment banking activities, especially proprietary trading in financial markets. Unfortunately, the appropriate positioning of market-making activity within these frameworks is not obvious. There is therefore a close relationship between this material and Chapter 21.

1.5.5 The mix of institutions

This concludes the book's discussion of substantive topics. Part F then turns to what we term 'The Mix of Institutions': questions of the design of regulatory institutions themselves. Chapter 24 begins by presenting an overview of the terrain covered in

Part F. These chapters then proceed as follows. Chapter 25 is about the political economy of regulation. It discusses the way in which regulators are appointed and appraised, and mechanisms of accountability to democratically elected politicians. It also discusses the tensions between electoral cycles, volatility of public interest in financial regulation, and technocratic expertise in agencies. It then goes on to consider the problems of interest group lobbying, in particular by financial sector firms. A range of mechanisms is considered that may serve to ameliorate these problems.

Chapter 26 discusses supervision and enforcement. Supervision is an ongoing dialogue with regulated firms; enforcement is action taken to punish (and deter) non-compliance. Perspectives differ on the appropriate allocation of resources as between the two activities, as techniques for eliciting good conduct. The chapter identifies the types of issues for which supervision-led and enforcement-led regulatory strategies, respectively, are likely to be successful.

Chapter 27 is concerned with the appropriate structure of regulatory agencies. The old 'institutional' structure, as practised in the US, was shown to be problematic for the reasons already discussed. Yet it is unfortunately not obvious what should be done instead.[25] The limitations of the institutional model are well known, and indeed underlay its abandonment in the UK at the turn of the century in favour of a single integrated regulator, the FSA. Yet the FSA too failed spectacularly in its role, apparently because its goals and priorities were, respectively, poorly defined and set.

The lesson seems to be that integrating regulation should simply shift attention from the structure of regulators to the process of goal and priority setting. Perhaps because of the loss of credibility of the integrated model, or perhaps because of political disagreement about where it should be based, the EU has simply proceeded to implement a 'new' federal regulatory structure of the 'old' institutional variety in the immediate aftermath to the financial crisis, with separate regulators for banks (the European Banking Authority), markets (the European Securities Market Authority) and insurance companies, and pension schemes (the European Insurance and Occupational Pensions Authority).

There is a third model for the structure of financial regulation, which has not been discredited by the crisis. This goal-oriented model posits that for each (functional) goal of financial regulation, there should be a regulatory champion. The best-known version of this approach is the so-called 'twin peaks' model, whereby there is a separate prudential and conduct regulator. This was in effect in Australia, which weathered the financial crisis very successfully, and has now been implemented in the UK. Post-crisis reform in the US, while not dismantling the old institutional structure of regulation, purports to create a financial stability champion through creation of the Financial Stability Oversight Council, a college of financial regulators that is tasked with responsibility to monitor systemic risk throughout the financial system.

Chapter 28 rounds off Part E with a discussion of the problems posed by the international context of financial regulation. The chapter discusses three techniques by which international cooperation has been furthered. The first is by legal multilateral

---

[25] See D Awrey, 'The FSA, Integrated Regulation and the Curious Case of OTC Derivatives' (2010) 12 *University of Pennsylvania Journal of Business Law* 101.

binding agreements, such as the EU. The second is through 'soft law' multilateral agreements, such as the G20 and the guidance issued by the Financial Stability Board as well as international standard setting by agreement among bank supervisors, the work of the Basel Committee on Banking Supervision. And the third is through bilateral agreements between leading states. A cause for optimism, despite the limitations of financial regulation announced in Chapter 4 and echoed throughout Part F, is how much progress has been made in the direction of international cooperation since the financial crisis.

Chapter 29 concludes the book as a whole by reviewing and restating the core messages, along with providing the outlook for the future.

1.6 Conclusion

As will be clear, this book seeks to cover a vast amount of substantive terrain. To do this, it is necessary to fly at a higher altitude than is normally the case with a legal text. What we do might be termed macro, rather than micro, legal analysis. As should by now be clear, our aim in doing this is also different from a typical text. We are not seeking to give the reader a sufficient knowledge of the relevant rules so as to be able to give a client legal advice about compliance. This would require many thousands of pages. What is more, the pace of change in financial regulation is such that it would likely be out of date before it even hit the bookshelves.

Rather, our goal has been to present a set of principles with which readers can be equipped to understand better the detail of substantive regulation. Because they are cross cutting, these principles are rarely articulated in a general way; hence the benefit to our generalist approach. The shape of the financial system is subject to continual change, and technology may well be accelerating its pace. While we may not be able to predict all the ways in which these changes *will* affect the cross-section of systemic risk, having the analytic tools to understand how such changes *can* be linked will surely put us in a better position to do so.

2

The Financial System

2.1 Introduction

To understand what financial regulation is and should be doing, we need to begin by understanding the object of regulation—that is, the financial system. We are all familiar with some aspects of the financial system. As savers we deposit our money in banks or special savings institutions. As purchasers we use cheques and cash drawn from banks and borrow money from banks and specialized lenders. As investors we buy shares on the stock market and give our money to fund managers who invest on our behalf. But each of us is only exposed to a tiny fragment of the financial system. Behind what we see is a massive engine of individuals and institutions that keep it functioning.

Why is the financial system so large and complex? Everyone needs finance in some form or another, but the needs of individuals and companies differ appreciably and the facilities that are required to satisfy their needs are diverse. Yet this diversity alone is not enough to explain the complexity we see. The complexity is multiplied by the need to relate the future to the present. The financial system does more than simply keep capital flowing round the economy today. It is also a time machine, linking the economy of today to the economy of tomorrow. That is a Herculean task and it demands a measure of sophistication that is the source of both its successes and failures.

The financial system is often distinguished from the so-called 'real' economy—the firms who make things or provide services and the people who consume them. The significance of the financial system lies in the functions it performs in relation to the real economy. It does these through intermediating between the personal sector of an economy comprising individuals and households and the corporate sector consisting of start-ups, small entrepreneurial firms, medium-sized enterprises, and large corporations. We will see how as companies expand the nature of their financing needs alters, and how the financial system responds by providing funding in a variety of different forms.

This chapter will guide you through the structure and functions of the financial system. Its purpose is not to describe in precise detail the role of all of the different components, but to give you a sufficient understanding to appreciate what it does, why it matters, and what can go wrong. This will in turn give you a sense of the activity that financial regulation seeks to cover. With that, you should be equipped to understand why, where, and how we seek to regulate and control its functioning.

We begin in section 2.2 with five fundamental roles of financial systems. These are: (i) providing a secure mechanism for *payments* at a distance; (ii) *mobilizing capital* from savers who have more financial resources than uses for them; (iii) *selecting projects* from amongst those seeking investment to capital; (iv) *monitoring* the performance of those executing projects in which investment has been made; and

Principles of Financial Regulation. First Edition. John Armour, Dan Awrey, Paul Davies, Luca Enriques, Jeffrey N. Gordon, Colin Mayer, and Jennifer Payne. © John Armour, Dan Awrey, Paul Davies, Luca Enriques, Jeffrey N. Gordon, Colin Mayer, and Jennifer Payne 2016. Published 2016 by Oxford University Press.

(v) *managing risk*. There are institutions and financial instruments that monitor and manage risk and there are others that assist investors with taking risks.

In section 2.3 we introduce the institutional components of financial systems. Traditionally, these have been broken down into two components: first, financial *intermediaries* such as banks, savings and lending institutions, pension funds, mutual funds, and insurance companies; and second, financial *markets* such as equity markets, bond markets, derivative and options markets, futures and commodity markets, and ancillary actors which facilitate the production and dissemination of information that enable markets to operate. We will see that each of these traditional institutional 'pockets' is capable of performing most, if not all, of the core functions. This begs the question as to whether there is an optimal mix, or whether one has comparative advantage over the other.

That question is taken up in section 2.4. The structure of financial systems, understood as bundles of financial intermediaries and financial markets, has varied markedly across countries. This naturally provokes reflection as to why it should be the case, and whether particular aspects have comparative advantages in certain contexts. In particular, we emphasize the size of financial markets in relation to domestic economic activity, the role of intermediaries as against markets, and the way in which financial systems interact with their corporate sectors.

The structure of financial systems is far from static, however. Over the past few decades, two secular trends have reshaped financial systems beyond recognition. The first is the impact of globalization—in this context meaning the removal of barriers to international trade and capital flows—which has transformed the functions performed by, and the way we conceive of, the financial system from a mainly domestic to an increasingly international web of activities. This has resulted from international flows of capital through banks and financial markets, the internationalization of financial intermediaries themselves, and, relatedly, the interconnections that have occurred as a result of the transmission of risks between actors from different domestic financial systems.

The second trend has been the growing blurring of the boundaries between the 'intermediated' and the 'market' components of the financial system. On the one hand, market actors have begun to encroach on activities traditionally performed only by institutions; this has been mirrored by a growth in intermediaries' investment in markets and reliance upon them for fundraising. The implication—that the traditional institutional divisions are increasingly difficult to draw—is a central theme of the book. We sketch this process in section 2.5, and treat the issue more fully in Chapter 20.

Finally, in section 2.6 we consider pathologies in the operation of financial systems. Why have financial crises occurred repeatedly in history, up to and including the global crisis that began in 2007? We will consider some of the main causes of failure, in particular, problems of information, problems of contractual failure and bankruptcy, and system-wide failures that arise from the interconnections that are described in section 2.5.

By the end of the chapter, you should have a sense of what financial systems do, how they do it, how they differ, how they interact with each other, and how and why they are subject to failure. You should be aware of the interconnectedness of the financial system as a whole and how different financial institutions and instruments perform similar roles. In particular, the chapter will suggest that the boundaries between institutions and markets are increasingly blurred and that the conventional distinction that is drawn between financial institutions and securities markets is becoming less relevant. As subsequent chapters of the book suggest, this has important implications for the design and limitations of financial regulation. By the end of this chapter you should therefore have an initial appreciation of the subject-matter to which financial regulation applies, and hence the issues that lie at the heart of this book.

2.2 The Functions of Financial Systems

Financial systems perform at least five fundamental roles in the economy.[1] First, and most obviously, they facilitate *exchange* through the payments system. By providing secure mechanisms for payments conducted over large geographic distances, the payments system facilitates arm's length transactions across the entire economy.

Second, they *mobilize savings* from households who have funds surplus to their requirements for current consumption, permitting them to earn a return on their capital and thereby to enjoy greater consumption in the future. Financial systems provide the channel through which financial resources in an economy can be allocated between those individuals and institutions that need them and those that have them. Typically, companies need resources to invest in plant, equipment, buildings, people, research, and the development of new ideas. Individuals save during their working lives to have money when they retire, are in ill-health, or wish to make large-scale purchases such as houses or cars. In practice it is not as straightforward as that, as some individuals need to be able to borrow to meet their family commitments or to purchase housing and some companies generate more earnings and profits than they can employ themselves and so lend to others.[2]

We can illustrate this function by reference to the UK. Figure 2.1 shows the balance sheet of UK households and corporations between 1994 and 2007. It reveals several striking features of the composition of both groups' assets and liabilities. First, the dominant form of asset holding of UK households is housing. Much of the debt that households raise is used to finance the purchase of houses through mortgages. The second most important asset is pensions. Saving for retirement is a critical element of household saving. Finally, a significant fraction of household assets is bank deposits. Direct holdings of equity and other financial instruments are relatively modest for households, reflecting the fact that these are primarily, in the case of the UK, owned by financial institutions.

On the liability side of the corporate balance sheet, the primary source of corporate capital is equity. Most of this does not come from raising new equity on the stock

---

[1] R Merton and Z Bodie, 'A Conceptual Framework for Analyzing the Financial Environment', in DB Crane, KA Froot, SP Mason, A Perold, RC Merton, Z Bodie, ER Sirri, and P Tufano (eds) *The Global Financial System: A Functional Perspective* (Cambridge, MA: Harvard Business School Press, 1995), 3.

[2] For further descriptions of financial systems see F Allen and D Gale, *Comparing Financial Systems* (Cambridge, MA: MIT Press, 2001) and S Gurusamy, *Financial Services and Systems* (Noida: McGraw-Hill Education, 2008).

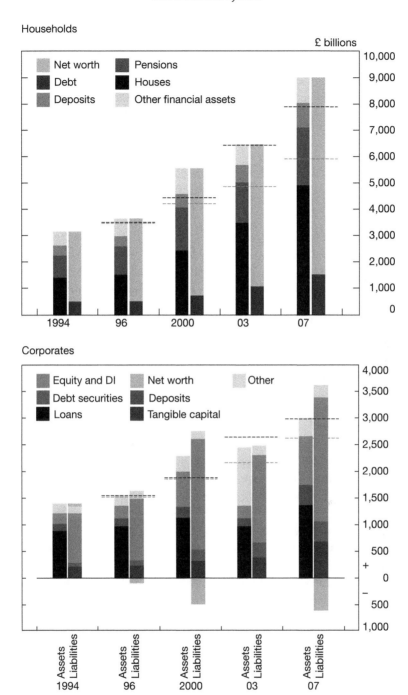

Households

£ billions

Corporates

Fig. 2.1 The Balance Sheet of UK Households and Corporations, 1994 to 2007

Source: R Barwell and O Burrows, 'Growing Fragilities? Balance Sheets in the Great Moderation'
Bank of England Financial Stability Paper 10 (2011).

market but from the profits that companies retain in their businesses and do not distribute to their shareholders in the form of dividends or repurchases of shares. Loans from banks are the most significant source of debt finance for companies. Debt securities, primarily bonds, are a comparatively modest (although still significant in absolute terms) part of the overall capital that corporations raise. On the assets side, companies primarily invest in tangible capital, plant and equipment, and buildings. They also hold a significant amount of shares in other companies, some of which they purchase in the process of acquiring controlling stakes in other firms. Like households, corporations also hold substantial deposits at banks to finance their day-to-day working capital.

In terms of changes over time, the graphs show how the accumulation of household assets increased in the UK up to the time just before the start of the financial crisis in 2007. In particular, there was an explosion in the value of housing reflecting the property booms that occurred over this period. The 'net worth' of the household sector therefore increased appreciably. The assets and liabilities of the corporate sector also grew appreciably and on the liabilities side there was a significant increase in both equity (predominantly retained earnings) and debt, especially loans. In particular, there is evidence of a substantial build-up of debt in the corporate sector prior to the financial crisis. Once the financial crisis unfolded, this acted as a significant burden on the corporate sector, prompting a substantial decline in corporate investment and activity that exacerbated the post-crisis recession across Europe as a whole.[3]

In channelling capital mobilized from savers to fund projects that require investment,[4] financial systems perform further crucial tasks. Their third function is to *select* those projects that will yield the best return. Done well, there is a virtuous circle. Getting project selection right generates more returns for savers—and hence encourages further mobilization of capital, while at the same time ensuring that the most valuable projects are the ones that get funded. Closely related to this is a fourth function, *monitoring* the performance of those projects which have received funding, ensuring that they remain true to their original promise and that those who manage their execution do not divert resources to other goals. We can also identify a fifth function, which has grown in importance in recent years—the facilitation of *risk management* by firms and individuals.

These functions are in turn of vital importance to the functioning of the real economy. A well-functioning financial system is associated with overall economic growth, as illustrated by Figure 2.2.[5] Of course, to simply point to this association does not establish the direction of causation. It might not be that the availability of finance stimulates growth, but rather that economic growth stimulates demand for finance. However, the better view is that development in the financial system is causally important for economic growth. As a matter of theory, we have seen that the functions

---

[3] European Central Bank (2013), 'Corporate Finance and Economic Activity in the Euro Area: Structural Issues', Occasional Paper, No 151.

[4] Some part of this is for households who prioritize present over future consumption, but the more important component is to fund business projects that will yield goods and services for consumption.

[5] See eg R Levine, 'Financial Development and Economic Growth: Views and Agenda' (1997) 35 *Journal of Economic Literature* 688, 688–703.

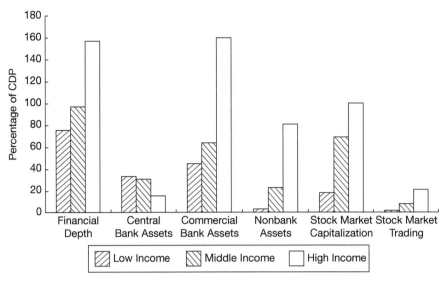

Fig. 2.2 Financial Structure in Low-, Middle-, and High-Income Economies, 1990

Source: R Levine, 'Financial Development and Economic Growth: Views and Agenda' (1997) 35 *Journal of Economic Literature* 688, 716.

of the financial system include the selection of good projects and the monitoring of their execution. These are crucial steps to get right to secure economic growth. And as a matter of evidence, studies document a robust association between financial system development in 1960 and economic growth over the following thirty years.[6] It seems implausible that subsequent economic growth should have generated prior demand for finance.

The importance of the financial system for the economy generally can also be framed in a negative way. The Great Depression of the 1930s was preceded by a stock market crash and coincided with a collapse of the US banking system. Ben Bernanke's early work as an academic economist identified the channels through which banking collapse led to economic contraction.[7] This is consistent with the key role banks played in selecting which projects should receive credit. Bankers specialized in making these difficult decisions; their failure resulted in both a contraction in the supply of capital for investment, and in the less effective allocation of such capital as was still available through other channels. This is echoed in the dramatic contractions of economic growth that followed the financial crisis of 2007–9.[8]

[6] RG King and R Levine, 'Finance, Entrepreneurship and Growth: Theory and Evidence' (1993) 32 *Journal of Monetary Economics* 513.

[7] BS Bernanke, 'Nonmonetary Effects of the Financial Crisis in the Propagation of the Great Depression' (1983) 73 *American Economic Review* 257. See also M Friedman and AJ Schwartz, *A Monetary History of the United States, 1867–1960* (Chicago: NBER, 1963).

[8] However, new monetary policy measures deployed by central bankers during and after the 2007–9 financial crisis—stimulated by a desire to avoid repeating earlier errors—helped ensure the economic consequences were generally not as severe: see B Eichengreen, *Hall of Mirrors: The Great Depression, the Great Recession, and the Uses—and Misuses—of History* (New York, NY: OUP, 2015).

2.3 The (Traditional) Components of the Financial System

We have traditionally understood the financial system as being comprised of a mixture of financial intermediaries and financial markets, with a range of supporting institutions that facilitate the effective operation of markets. As we will discuss in section 2.5 and subsequent chapters, this neat partition no longer holds. However, it is nevertheless useful to review these respective components, and how they each perform the functions described in section 2.2. This helps to explain the historical evolution of the financial system, and—of crucial importance for this book—the structure of the financial regulation that has been applied to it. It provides a solid foundation for understanding the subsequent developments in the financial system, and for framing current debates about how regulatory initiatives should best respond to them.

2.3.1 Direct intermediaries: banks

Commercial banks act as intermediaries between savers and borrowers. Lenders deposit money in banks in checking deposit and time accounts, and borrowers are lent money for a variety of terms. Banks lend and borrow at fixed and variable rates of interest.[9]

To give a sense of the extent of this intermediation activity, Figure 2.3 presents a snapshot of the balance sheets of the world's thousand largest banks in 2011. It shows that loans accounted for approximately 40 per cent of the assets of large banks and deposits and short-term funding for nearly 60 per cent of liabilities. So a big part of what banks do is to take in deposits and lend them out as loans to the corporate and the household sectors.

In so doing, banks also perform most of the functions we described the financial system as a whole as performing for the real economy. Transactions between banks effected as agents for savers in respect of their funds on deposit with the bank perform the function of *payment services*.

Second, banks mobilize capital by providing depositors with both a return on their investment and *liquidity*.[10] Savers want to be able to convert (some part of) their investments to cash at short notice, in case they suffer a financial shock—loss of employment, illness, divorce—or decide to change their consumption patterns. Many investments in business projects, however, are *illiquid*, meaning that investors could not get their money back in the short run without a significant loss.[11] By pooling savings from many different households, bank intermediation enables savers to get

---

[9] There are many other institutions that perform similar functions, most notably specialist savings institutions that lend to particular types of borrowers, for example, to small and medium-sized enterprises and home owners. Some institutions such as pension funds raise money from individuals at one stage in their life, while they are working, to pay out to them when they retire. Similarly, insurance funds raise money when savers have a surplus and provide a payout based on the occurrence of some pre-specified event in the future.

[10] DW Diamond and PH Dybvig, 'Bank Runs, Deposit Insurance, and Liquidity' (1983) 91 *Journal of Political Economy* 401.

[11] Imagine that a firm decides to invest in a new product, for example. Funds must be spent upfront on the manufacturing equipment, before sales revenue is generated. If the project were liquidated in the short run, then this would compromise its value—the machinery is unlikely to be worth as much in any other use.

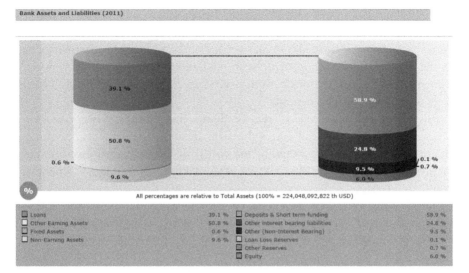

Fig. 2.3 Aggregate Balance Sheets of the Largest Thousand Banks in 2011
Source: Bankscope.

access to the higher returns offered by illiquid investments, but still to have access to liquid funds. This works if savers' needs for liquidity are not correlated with one another—that is, only a fraction at any time need to have access to their funds. The bank simply maintains a portion of its assets as cash or near-cash, which can be used to repay those who need funds.

Banks also perform *project selection* and *monitoring* functions. To this end, their personnel develop considerable expertise in assessing the quality of credit decisions and in monitoring borrowers' performance. Why does this need an intermediary, as opposed to investors performing this function directly? The answer has to do with economies of scale. If we assume (plausibly) an asymmetry of information between borrowers and investor—that is, borrowers know more about the quality of their projects and the actions that they take to execute them than do their investors—then investors must incur costs to *screen* and *monitor* borrowers in making effective lending decisions. If individual savers only have small amounts of capital to invest, it is not economic for them each to perform these screening and monitoring functions. Rather, it is efficient for them to delegate this function to an intermediary who can then specialize in performing these functions.[12] Astute readers will see that the tricky part of this analysis lies in the fact that the savers now need to worry about whether the intermediary performs its job effectively, but we defer detailed discussion of this until Chapter 13.

That banks' specialized screening and monitoring have value is evidenced by the fact that when a bank re-finances a loan, other investors become more willing to advance funds to the firm. Similarly, if a bank fails, its corporate borrowers suffer a loss in value reflecting the fact that it will be costly for another lender to acquire the same private

---

[12] DW Diamond, 'Financial Intermediation and Delegated Monitoring' (1984) 51 *Review of Economic Studies* 393. See also G Gorton and A Winton, 'Financial Intermediation', in G Constantinides, M Harris, and R Stulz (eds), *Handbook of the Economics of Finance: Corporate Finance* (2003).

knowledge about its business that its original lender did, and consequently that it will become more costly for the firm to raise capital in the short run.[13]

Banks can in turn be divided into *commercial banks*, which are concerned primarily with the taking and investing of deposits and other funds which they raise, and *investment banks*, which provide similar services to commercial banks but using sources of funds other than deposits.

Finally, banks can *manage risks* associated with investment at lower cost than the investors themselves. They can derive the diversification benefits from investing in a large array of assets which it would be too costly for the individual investors to hold themselves. They can hedge risks of investment in a form which might be infeasible for the ultimate investors.

For all these reasons, there are significant benefits of credit intermediation through banks that cannot be derived from direct investment and as a consequence, a substantial amount of financial activity is undertaken via credit intermediaries.

Examples of a Small Regional Bank and a Large Commercial Bank in the US

Folsom Lake Bank is a small regional bank in California. As at September 2012 it had total assets worth about $130 million. In order to acquire those assets it utilizes deposits which are about 85% of its total assets, has shares worth about 12% of its total assets, and the residual 3% comes from mortgage indebtedness and capitalized leases. The bank keeps about 5% of its assets in cash, 35% in securities most of which are issued by Freddie Mae and Fannie Mac, and 56% in loans most of which are secured by real estate.

On the other hand, Bank of America Merrill Lynch ('BAML') is a large commercial bank in the United States. As at September 2012 it had total assets worth about $1.45 trillion. In order to acquire those assets it utilizes deposits which are about 75% of its total assets, money market funds worth 7% of total assets, and shares worth 12% of total assets. The residual 6% of funding is raised from bond markets. The bank keeps about 8% of its assets in cash, 23% in securities which are predominantly government securities, and 50% in loans for real estate, commercial and industrial use, individuals, and leases.

Clearly there are a number of similarities between the two banks. However, they differ in some important respects. Most evidently, BAML utilizes money market funds and owns a broader range of assets. Other differences which are not apparent from a comparison of their balance sheets include the significant amounts of off-balance sheet liabilities and the use of derivatives by BAML.

2.3.2 Financial markets

Alongside financial institutions such as banks are financial markets that allow savers and borrowers to connect directly with each other. There are a large number of such markets but the most important are those for equities, bonds, commodities, derivatives, and currencies.

---

[13] MB Slovin, ME Sushka, and JA Polonchek, 'The Value of Bank Durability: Borrowers as Bank Stakeholders' (1993) 48 *Journal of Finance* 247.

Equity markets are markets where companies sell their shares to investors, thereby raising equity capital ('primary' markets), and investors then trade shares, usually on a stock exchange ('secondary' markets). Typically companies are established as private organizations in which the shares of the firm are held by a small number of, often family and closely related, shareholders. The shares will not be much exchanged and may be held for lengthy periods of time. Some of the shares may be held by venture capital firms which will look to sell their shares either to other companies, in what are known as trade sales, or on stock markets. If the latter is the exit route of the family or outside investors, then the company will access the primary market via an Initial Public Offering ('IPO') of its shares on a stock exchange both to sell some of the shares of the owners and to raise new capital for the company. Once listed on the exchange, the company may also raise further capital through seasoned issues.

In addition to raising money in the form of equity, companies also borrow in the form of debt, which in contrast to equity pays a return as interest payments and repayment of capital. As discussed, under financial intermediation, banks play a critical role in lending to companies. However, companies can also borrow directly from investors by issuing bonds or commercial paper. These are issued for particular periods of time—in the case of commercial paper, for less than a year—and over that period pay interest at a pre-agreed but not necessarily constant rate. In some cases the interest rate may vary in line with other interest rates in the market and in other cases they are fixed for the duration of the bond. At the end of the period when the obligation matures, the principal (the amount borrowed) is repaid.

In contrast, equity does not offer a pre-set return but only pays shareholders a dividend if there are sufficient earnings (profits) to do so. Furthermore, equity is typically permanent capital in the sense that it is never repaid to its shareholders but is retained in the company. Shareholders are merely rewarded from the uncertain dividends that they receive and the possibility of being able to sell their shares at a profit (a capital gain) to other investors at some stage in the future.

As in the case of equities, there are often secondary markets on which bonds are traded. This allows bondholders to sell their bonds or to purchase other bonds after they have been issued. In addition to companies, governments, international agencies, and other organizations issue bonds.[14] Bond markets provide what is termed liquidity to the bonds that are traded, allowing those who hold the bonds to be able to sell their holdings easily and at low cost. They may wish to do so to invest in other bonds or other financial instruments or because they need to make a purchase of a good or service.

In both equity and bond markets, the investors are a mixture of private individuals and institutional investors. Historically, individuals were important investors on both markets but increasingly they have been replaced by institutions such as banks, insurance companies, mutual funds, and pension funds. As we will discuss later, one of the reasons for the growth of institutional holdings has been the knowledge and the

---

[14] Governments in particular are important issuers of bonds to fund the public sector deficit, which is the difference between the amounts that governments raise in the form of taxation and the amount that they spend in the form of government expenditure on public goods and services such as defence, education, and health care.

expertise that institutions have developed in determining which financial instruments to buy and sell.

Commodity markets are the markets for trading a range of primary commodities such as foods (soya beans and wheat), metals (gold and copper), and energy (oil and gas). They are the markets in which those countries that are rich in natural resources sell their commodities to those who have a need for the commodities as part of their production and supply activities.

Derivatives markets are markets on which financial instruments based on other financial instruments are traded. The financial instruments are described as 'derivatives' to reflect the fact that their payoffs are derived from movements in other financial securities or assets (the 'underlying'). What these do is to allow investors to hold and trade financial instruments whose value fluctuates in line with movements in the underlying equities, bonds, commodities, or currencies without them actually having to hold the equities, bonds, commodities, and currencies themselves.

Options are a type of derivative, the value of which is dependent on the price of shares or bonds being above or below certain levels. So for example, a 'call' option is the right to purchase a share in a company at or prior to some date in the future (the 'expiration' date) for a fixed price (the 'exercise' or 'strike' price) in exchange for a sum usually paid upfront (the 'premium'). The right will be exercised if the share price rises above the strike price.

There are several advantages of trading derivatives as against the underlying securities. First, it is possible to produce a richer array of financial profiles than the underlying securities themselves offer. For example, a call option which gives a right to invest in a security at a particular strike price is only of value if the underlying security is worth more than the strike price. Otherwise the option will remain unexercised at the expiration date. It therefore offers an upside gain for strong performance of the underlying security while protecting the investor from losses in the event of weak performance to which those holding the security are subject.

Second, it allows investors to earn returns from securities at low cost. Since the holder of a call option only has to pay if they decide to exercise the option, the purchase of an option involves small initial costs (the premium) in relation to those that would be incurred in buying the underlying securities themselves.

Third, markets in derivatives may be more liquid than the underlying securities, in the sense that there is an active market in them which allows investors to buy and sell them easily. In particular, the difference between the purchase and sale prices (the 'bid and offer' or 'bid and ask' prices) can be low for derivatives in relation to those of the fundamental equities and bonds. One reason for this is the low cost at which derivatives positions are bought and sold, thereby allowing the trading of larger volumes of securities than would otherwise be the case.

Another example of derivative markets are 'futures' markets, where contracts are traded under which parties agree to exchange securities, commodities, or currencies at a future date for a pre-set price. They thereby allow some investors to 'hedge' their risks by purchasing or selling futures that relate to the underlying risks of their portfolios. For example, companies seek to hedge the exchange rate risks to which they are exposed as a consequence of their trading or investment activities. Financial

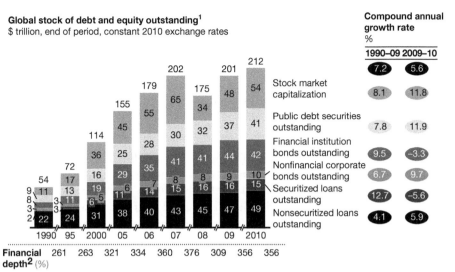

Financial depth[2] (%) 261 263 321 334 360 376 309 356 356

1 Based on a sample of 79 countries.
2 Calculated as global debt and equity outstanding divided by global GDP.
NOTE: Numbers may not sum due to rounding.

Fig. 2.4 Global Debt and Equity Markets

Source: McKinsey Global Institute.

institutions seek to hedge interest rate risks and commodity producers offset commodity price fluctuations. On the other side of the market, when the counterparty does not itself hedge the risk it is taking by similarly buying protection against adverse price movements, futures markets allow investors to speculate on movements in the underlying asset price.

The currency (or foreign exchange—'forex') market is the market in which parties exchange one currency for another, say US dollars for British pounds. It is by far the largest market in the world and is dominated by international banks acting as dealers—that is, trading on their own account, often with each other. The forex market includes the spot market, in which currencies are traded at the current market price and transactions are immediately executed, and the derivatives forex market, which has currencies as the underlying asset.

Figure 2.4 shows that the world's stock of debt and equity outstanding amounted to over $200 trillion in 2010. That compares with a total world Gross Domestic Product (GDP) of approximately $60 trillion. So the stock of outstanding debt and equity is more than three times global GDP. Within that, Figure 2.4 shows that global stock markets accounted for approximately $50 trillion in 2010 and the remainder is bonds and loans. Bonds, including public sector debt securities, amounted to around $100 trillion and the remainder is loans. The figure shows that there was a particularly rapid growth in securitized lending (namely, loans that were sold on to other institutional investors in securitized forms) from the beginning of the 2000s.

Interestingly, well-functioning financial markets are capable of performing the same functions as traditional bank intermediation. Where firms issue securities that are traded in liquid markets—that is, there is a lot of trading activity, meaning that investors who wish to sell their shares in a particular company can readily find a buyer—then investors can achieve liquidity. Rather than pooling their savings with other investors in the hands of a bank, they exit the investment by selling their claim to another investor. There is no need to liquidate the underlying project. Offering investors liquidity means that markets can mobilize savings effectively.

Markets can also perform project screening and monitoring functions. They do this through the price mechanism. As Chapter 5 will explain in more detail, in a well-functioning capital market, the price serves to aggregate information about the expected value of the activities of securities issuers. In making investment decisions, savers and speculators are making assumptions about the likely prospect for economies, firms, and markets. They invest where they hold a positive view about future prospects and they withdraw funds and sell financial instruments where they hold a negative view. These flows in and out of financial instruments, institutions, companies, and markets affect the prices at which they trade and these prices in turn reflect the information that individuals have about their likely future prospects. Buoyant expectations result in high prices and negative sentiment in low prices.

If corporate managers use the stock price as a guide to their investment decisions, which corporate governance practices have increasingly encouraged them to do,[15] then the market's aggregation of public information serves to guide project selection and monitoring. In essence the market is a large machine for collecting the information of everyone participating in markets and producing prices that reflect that information. In some markets, such as stock exchanges and bond and commodity markets, there are computers which do exactly that. In many cases the prices reflect the trades of a large number of individuals that do not necessarily pass through a central computer. Whatever the mechanism, financial markets are potentially a vital source of information about individuals' views of future financial performance.

This brief survey suggests that there is an important degree of substitution between banks and financial markets in performing the basic functions of the financial system. Indeed, the only one of the core functions of the financial system that cannot readily be performed by markets is payments.

2.3.3 Market-facilitating institutions

Markets are generally complemented by a number of institutions that assist in their functioning. A uniting theme is the production and analysis of information that assists in the pricing process. Most obvious amongst these are equity analysts and credit rating agencies (CRAs), which facilitate price formation by analysing information about the performance and valuation of equities and bonds, respectively. Credit rating agencies evaluate the financial soundness of companies, financial institutions, and governments that issue bonds and other fixed-income securities. Equity analysts evaluate the likely future prospects of shares of individual companies and make recommendations of whether investors should buy or sell the shares. We discuss these intermediaries further in Chapter 6.

---

[15] See Chapter 17, especially section 17.2.

Example of Credit Rating Agency and Equity Analyst

Standard & Poor's (S&P) is one of the three big credit rating agencies. The other two are Moody's Investor Service and Fitch Ratings. In the United States an institution is able to provide a credit rating after being designated a Nationally Recognized Statistical Rating Organization (NRSRO) by the Securities and Exchange Commission (SEC). There are currently ten firms, including the big three, with the NRSRO designation. S&P is paid by issuers of public and private debt to provide a rating (which is an opinion) on debt instruments on a scale from AAA to D. The ratings are used by investors to determine the credit risk of issuers. They are both a simple and a standardized way to convey information about the credit risk of the issuer. The ratings are also used in capital and liquidity requirements for financial and institutional investors.

Equity analysts are not institutions but individuals within an institution. They provide a recommendation to investors to buy, sell, or hold a share, frequently focusing on particular sectors of the market, such as engineering and construction. They are generally distinguished on the basis of being buy-side or sell-side. Sell-side analysts are employed by an investment bank, while buy-side analysts are employed by an institutional investor or an independent research firm that sells its reports to investors.

Perhaps the most important information intermediaries, however, are investment banks. Investment banks help companies to raise money when they come to stock markets for the first time (IPOs) and when they are raising additional equity capital (so-called 'seasoned' issues) and debt. They assist governments and public sector organizations to issue bonds on primary markets. They organize the creation and distribution of new securities, such as derivatives, which allow investors to hedge risks, for example, from foreign currency or interest rate fluctuations. The key role performed by the investment bank in all these instances is that of setting the price for the security on the primary market—that is, establishing the market price before the standard information-aggregation mechanism that is secondary trading has begun.[16]

Activities of Investment Banks

Investment banks have historically performed four main activities that generate fees or result in speculative earnings. First, their traditional function is providing advisory and underwriting services to firms. This activity involves investment banks identifying or assisting firms to issue equity or debt securities. It also involves identifying potential investors and generating information to ascertain a market price for the securities. Finally, an investment bank underwrites (guarantees) that the securities will be sold at a particular price to give comfort to the issuing firm that the securities will be sold.

A second activity of investment banks that is also related to the functioning of securities markets is brokerage: when acting as a broker, the investment bank executes trades on the market on behalf of its customers. Sometimes, investment banks also execute clients' orders by entering into the contract themselves on the other side, in which case they act as dealers.

The third activity of investment banks consists of asset management. Asset management generates fees from the investment advice and portfolio management services provided to

---

[16] AD Morrison and WJ Wilhelm Jr, *Investment Banking: Institutions, Politics, and Law* (Oxford: OUP, 2007), Ch 1.

retail and institutional clients. It includes funds management services to retail and institutional clients and acting as prime brokers for institutions such as hedge funds.[17]

Fourth, from the 1980s onwards, investment banks increasingly began to engage in trading and principal investment using their own funds. This activity requires the investment bank to either speculate or hedge its exposure. For instance, an investment bank might speculate as a limited partner in a private equity firm. Similarly an investment bank might own a hedge fund management company. Another example of speculation is an investment bank acting as counterparty in an over-the-counter derivatives arrangement. The investment bank could be approached by a Brazilian agricultural exporter wanting to eliminate fluctuations between the real and the US dollar. The investment bank may act as counterparty to the exporter. It might then eliminate its exposure to the US dollar by entering itself into a currency swap with another counterparty.

Proprietary trading can also take the form of market making, by which the investment bank declares itself ready at the same time to buy and sell a given securities at two different prices, one lower (the bid price) than the other (the ask price), thus providing liquidity to the market for that security. This is often done by posting 'quotes' on an exchange.

Since the financial crisis, policymakers have sought to distinguish between market-making, which is vital for the functioning of securities markets, and 'pure' proprietary trading, which involves simply participating in such markets. As we will see in Chapter 23, this distinction is far from straightforward to apply.

Secondary trading itself requires institutions that facilitate the matching of buyers and sellers. This was for centuries the exclusive job of exchanges. Historically, these were organized as physical locations (trading floors) on which individuals made of flesh and blood (its 'members') traded the securities. Over the last few decades trading floors have been replaced by computers that automate the process by which the prices of shares are determined and the markets are 'cleared' (demands for shares are brought into line with the supply by finding a price at which the two are equated).

Nowadays, a number of intermediaries similarly contribute to facilitating secondary trading: other liquidity services providers, such as alternative trading systems, compete with exchanges in the supply of liquidity services, while central depositories and clearing and settlement institutions provide ancillary services. As reported in the text box above, investment banks also contribute to secondary market liquidity by acting as market makers, dealers, and brokers. We discuss these intermediaries further in Chapters 5 and 7.

2.3.4 Asset managers

Finally, some intermediaries specialize in the management of retail investors' financial assets by investing in publicly traded securities on their behalf. They also qualify as market-facilitating institutions, in that they facilitate retail investors' access to securities markets in three ways: first, they let them benefit from diversification, however small the amounts they have to invest; second, they choose investments on their behalf based on their supposedly superior expertise; finally, they execute investment decisions at a lower cost given their larger size.

---

[17] Prime brokers are investment dealers which offer brokerage, lending, clearing and settlement, custody, and other services to hedge funds and other institutional investors.

The core examples of this type of intermediary are collective investment management schemes. In particular, mutual funds—or, in EU parlance, 'UCITS' (Undertakings for Collective Investment in Transferable Securities)—pool the capital of investors and invest it collectively. There is little or no investment risk borne by the asset manager itself—all the risk is borne by the ultimate investors.

Mutual Funds

Mutual funds are investment companies that pool investors' capital to invest it collectively as a single portfolio. Total worldwide assets invested in mutual funds in 2011 amounted to US $23.8 trillion.

The mutual fund industry offers investors a number of benefits. First, investors can quickly liquidate their positions. Liquidity intermediation is a recent development that differentiates the modern open-end mutual funds from their closed-end predecessors. Second, by pooling the resources of different investors, mutual funds allow them to access securities they may not have otherwise had the capital to invest in. Third, mutual funds provide a way for investors to diversify their portfolio of securities. Fourth, because of the size of mutual funds they may incur lower transaction costs for executing trades than an individual investor. Finally, retail and institutional investors display a preference for having a professional money manager make their investment decisions. This preference exists despite empirical evidence that suggests that mutual fund managers frequently underperform the market.

BlackRock is an asset management firm and operates one of the largest mutual fund complexes in the world. In 2012 BlackRock had US$3.8 trillion in assets under management and generated revenue of US$9.3 billion. BlackRock mutual funds pool the assets of investors to purchase a number of different securities. There are four primary classes of mutual funds: equity funds, bond funds, hybrid funds, and money market funds. BlackRock generates its revenue from management fees and advisory, administration, and securities lending agreements.

Other financial intermediaries, such as pension funds and insurance companies, also have significant asset management functions. Pension funds invest for the long term in assets that will benefit employees on retirement and insurance companies offer protection to the insured against risks of loss sustained on their property and themselves. They do so by investing contributions, fees, and premiums levied in assets that yield returns and in this regard act in a similar fashion to asset management firms. Unlike these, however, they bear of course the risks they ensure their policyholders against.

The combination of markets and intermediaries specializing in asset management poses a fundamental question. If markets serve to aggregate information for investors, what role do these institutions play in monitoring and screening investments? The answer depends on how well the market in question functions. For highly liquid markets—such as shares in large companies on the FTSE100 or the S&P 500—there is probably little that asset managers' expertise can add that the market price does not already 'know'. In this case, by pooling their funds in the hands of an asset manager, investors mainly aim to benefit from diversification and gain economies of scale on the transaction costs of buying and selling shares. On the contrary, expertise regarding investment decisions is less likely to yield any gains for investors in such asset class. That is why passively managed funds, which limit themselves to replicating a market index, have become increasingly popular in the last twenty years, especially in their exchange traded variety (exchange traded funds or 'ETFs').[18]

How Mutual Funds Assist Savers with Diversifying Risks

A mutual fund is able to pool the savings of a broad range of savers in a wider range of investments than any individual investors on their own could make. For instance, in order to purchase shares in a company, a saver might need to spend a minimum of £100. In order to purchase company debt, the minimum cost might be £10,000 and to purchase a commodity it might be £500. A saver who only has £300 is unable to invest in securities other than shares. However, by investing in a mutual fund he can get access to these other asset classes. This is because a mutual fund is able to pool the savings of other savers such that a proportion of our saver's £300 can be invested in shares, company bonds, and commodities.

On the other hand, where the securities are in less liquid markets, then the markets cannot be expected to price them so accurately. In this case, specialist asset managers can add value for investors (so-called 'alpha') through the screening and monitoring of the investments in question. At the extreme, specialist asset managers focus on particular types of market, or on particular types of risk. These offer investors the opportunity to share the costs of buying into the expertise of the manager in question. Some of these funds have traditionally marketed themselves to sophisticated investors only and thereby avoided the regulatory regime otherwise applicable to collective investment schemes. Such funds are known as 'hedge funds' or 'alternative investment funds'.[19]

A Hedge Fund

Greenlight Capital is a hedge fund founded by David Einhorn in 1996. It described itself as a value oriented, research driven investment management fund. Hedge funds are usually established as partnerships or limited liability companies with the funds managed by individuals such as Mr Einhorn. By the end of 2012 the fund had earned an annual 8.3 per cent on invested capital.

Hedge funds like Greenlight obtain funding from savers such as sophisticated retail investors and institutional investors and channel those funds into a broad range of securities. Greenlight invests primarily in company shares and debt. It is particularly well known for taking short positions in stocks (ie betting that the stock price will decrease once the market price reflects unfavourable information that Mr Einhorn and his team will have unearthed based on their own research) and for seeking change in how companies are managed as an active investor. Before Lehman Brothers' collapse in September 2008, Greenlight had held a short position on its stock for months and Mr Einhorn had repeatedly attacked Lehman for having fudged its numbers and being seriously undercapitalized.

---

[18] See further Chapters 11 and 22.
[19] See generally, RM Stulz, 'Hedge Funds: Past, Present, and Future' (2007) 21 *Journal of Economic Perspectives* 175.

2.4 International Differences in Financial Systems

One of the striking features of financial systems around the world is the extent to which they differ across countries. First the size of financial systems varies appreciably across countries. Table 2.1 shows the level of savings and investment as a proportion of GDP in Australia, Canada, China, the EU, Hong Kong, India, Japan, Singapore, the UK, and the US. It also shows the stock of financial assets held by individuals as a proportion of GDP.

Of the world's $200 trillion of financial assets in 2010, $60 trillion of them are held by US residents, $50 trillion by European residents, just under $50 trillion by Japanese and Chinese residents, and the remaining $40 trillion spread around citizens of the rest of the world. In total, households hold nearly $90 trillion of the world's financial assets, pensions and life insurance companies around $50 trillion, and the corporate sector about $40 trillion. Households in the US, Europe, and Japan, pension funds in the US, and banks in Europe are particularly significant investors in financial assets, holding more than $10 trillion each.

More striking than the variation in the size of savings and holdings of financial assets are the differences in the mix of components discussed in section 2.3. Figure 2.5 shows the capitalization of stock markets, compared with the size of the economy—represented by GDP—for several major economies in 2011.

As can be seen, the market capitalization in the US and UK is larger than GDP, whereas in the EU as a whole, and in important growth markets such as China, India, and Brazil, stock market capitalization is much lower relative to the size of the economy. This implies that less capital is channelled to business through the stock market, with correspondingly more being intermediated by banks.[20]

Not all financial transactions take place on exchanges. Some are done directly between traders in bilateral 'over-the-counter' (or 'OTC') transactions. Figure 2.6 shows that in 2011 around two-thirds of OTC derivatives transactions were associated with interest rate contracts on debt instruments; 10 per cent of trades were related to foreign exchange (currency) trades and the remainder were credit default swaps (used to exchange the risks on the underlying credits), equity, and commodity linked contracts. In total, outstanding OTC derivatives trades amounted to around $700 billion.

One reason for the pronounced variation in the size and nature of financial systems is the different functions that they perform. In particular, the way in which corporate sectors finance themselves varies appreciably among countries. For example, stock markets play an important part in corporate financing in some but not all countries, whereas banks tend to be of considerable significance in most countries. Similarly, the significance of bond markets for the financing of corporations varies from the US, where it is critically important, to some Continental European countries, where it remains of modest importance. Table 2.2 shows the way in which corporations funded their activities over thirty years to the end of the last century in four countries:

---

[20] See F Allen and D Gale, *Comparing Financial Systems* (Cambridge, MA: MIT Press, 2001).

Table 2.1 Savings and stocks of financial assets held by individuals, as proportion of GDP

Financial assets owned by residents, 2010 ($ trillion)

	United States	Western Europe	Japan	China	Other developed	Other Asia	Latin America	MENA	Rest of World	Total
Households	27.0	23.0	11.6	6.5	4.1	5.4	3.5	3.7	1.4	**85.2**
Institutional investors										
· Pensions	15.0	5.3	3.3	0.5	2.4	0.6	0.7	0.4	0.1	**28.3**
· Insurance	6.6	9.6	3.5	0.6	0.7	1.0	0.3	0.1	0.3	**23.0**
· Endowments & foundations	1.1	0.2	0.0	–	0.1	–	0.0	0.0	–	**1.5**
Corporations										
· Banks	4.0	11.9	6.7	3.9	1.4	0.9	0.9	0.5	0.5	**30.7**
· Nonfinancial corporations	2.0	1.7	1.2	3.8	0.3	1.3	0.3	0.2	0.2	**11.0**
Governments										
· Central banks	2.3	1.7	1.0	2.5	0.2	1.9	0.5	0.4	1.5	**12.0**
· Sovereign wealth funds	0.1	0.6	–	0.7	0.1	0.9	0.1	1.7	0.2	**4.3**
· Other government	–	–	–	1.1	–	0.4	0.5	0.3	0.1	**2.4**
Total	**58.1**	**54.0**	**27.3**	**19.8**	**9.3**	**12.4**	**6.8**	**6.3**	**4.3**	**198.1**

Notes: 'Other developed' countries include Australia, Canada, and New Zealand. 'Other Asia' countries include both developed countries and emerging markets. 'Pensions' include defined contribution plans and individual retirement accounts. Total numbers may not sum due to rounding.

Source: McKinsey Global Institute.

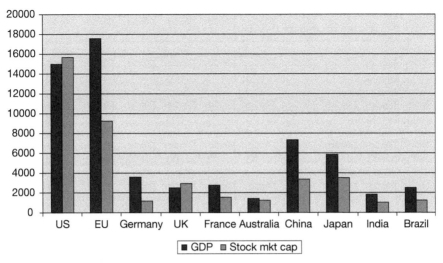

Fig. 2.5 Stock Market Capitalization and GDP for Leading Economies, 2011 ($bn)
Source: World Bank, *World Development Indicators*.

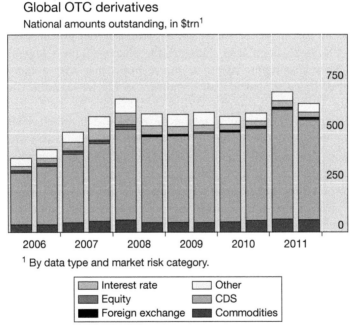

Fig. 2.6 Size of Global OTC Derivative Markets
Source: Bank for International Settlements.

Germany, Japan, the UK, and the US. It records that the dominant source of finance is internal, namely the profits of businesses that are not distributed as dividends. These account for between three-quarters of corporate funding in Japan and Germany and over 90 per cent in the UK and the US. Most of that goes towards funding the replacement of the existing capital stock.

Table 2.2 Net sources of finance for corporations in Germany, Japan, the UK, and the US, average 1970–98

	Germany	Japan	UK	US
Internal	78.9	69.9	93.3	96.1
Bank finance	11.9	26.7	14.6	11.1
Bonds	−1.0	4.0	4.2	15.4
New equity	0.1	3.5	−4.6	−7.6
Trade credit	−1.2	−5.0	−0.9	−2.4
Capital transfers	8.7	—	1.7	—
Other	1.4	1.0	0.0	−4.4
Statistical adjustment	1.2	0.0	−8.4	−8.3

Source: J Corbett and T Jenkinson, 'How is Investment Financed? A Study of Germany, Japan, the United Kingdom and the United States' (1997) 65 *The Manchester School* S69.

Of external sources of funding, loans from banks are the most important in all countries. However, bond markets play a significant role in North America and increasingly in Europe since the development of the corporate bond market at the end of the 1990s and the first decade of this century. New equity is a small and in some cases negative source of finance for firms. The negative figures reflect the fact that corporations purchase as well as sell equity. In particular, they purchase equity in other firms when they take them over and buy the shares of the companies they are acquiring.[21] They also repurchase their shares from their shareholders. Takeovers and share repurchases are particularly significant in the UK and the US—hence the negative figures in those two countries. While stock markets are not in aggregate a large net source of capital for corporate sectors in developed economies, they are very important for two particular groups of firms: first, new equity is a vital source of funding for start-ups and small companies; and second, they are a much larger source of funding of enterprises in developing and emerging markets than in developed economies.[22] In other words, large well-established firms in developed economies tend to buy a lot of shares in acquisitions and repayment of capital whereas small start-up companies, particularly in developing and emerging economies, tend to raise a large amount of capital.

An important source of finance for firms in their early stages of development is their own capital and that of families and friends. Informal sources of finance are the primary way in which firms get going. In some cases, they raise funding from wealthy private individuals, business angels that are often actively involved in the development of the firm. External early stage funding may come from venture capital firms that raise money from a variety of sources including institutional investors such as pension funds, life insurance companies, and university endowments. These investors frequently

---

[21] See J Franks, C Mayer, P Volpin, and HF Wagner, 'The Life Cycle of Family Ownership: International Evidence' (2012) 25 *Review of Financial Studies* 1675.

[22] See eg M Isakssob and S Çelik, 'Who Cares? Corporate Governance in Today's Equity Markets', OECD Corporate Governance Working Paper No 8 (2013).

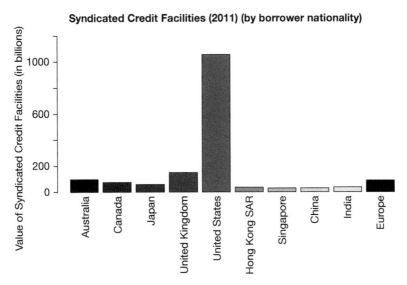

Fig. 2.7 Syndicated Bank Finance

Source: Bank for International Settlements.

seek a way of exiting from the investments within a period of five to seven years by selling the firms on stock markets as IPOs or trade sales to other firms.[23]

Once established, the main external source of finance for firms is bank borrowing. In evaluating the creditworthiness of a borrower, loan officers use several sources of information. These relate primarily to: (i) accounting data—balance sheets, profit and loss statements, and financial ratios of, for example, leverage, and earnings coverage of interest payments; (ii) projections of cash flows; (iii) information about the sector in which the firm is operating; (iv) the firm's customers and suppliers; (v) the account history of the borrower; (vi) judgemental information on the quality of management; and (vii) collateral and personal security of the directors that can be provided in the event of a firm default.

The other source of debt finance for companies is bonds, which are usually underwritten by commercial and investment banks, often acting as a 'syndicate' coordinated by one or more lead managers, and then placed directly or via other banks among institutional and retail investors. Figure 2.7 shows the value of syndicated credit facilities outstanding in 2011 across various countries.

Another important cause of differences in the nature of financial systems is the way in which pension provisions for retired employees are structured. In some countries they are primarily provided by the state and the state uses tax revenues to fund retirement schemes. In other countries, such as Germany, corporations fund their own pension schemes. In contrast, in the UK and the US, pension funds are established

---

[23] See generally, P Gompers and J Lerner, *The Venture Capital Cycle*, 2nd ed (Cambridge, MA: MIT Press, 2004).

independently of both companies and the government, and invest contributions in financial assets, such as equities and bonds. Given the scale of pension funds, a funded scheme that is invested through financial markets augments the size of bond and stock markets appreciably.

2.5 Changes in the Financial System

The structure of the financial system is not static, but subject to near-continuous evolution. In this section, we highlight two of the biggest changes of the past thirty years. These are the impact of globalization and consequent growth of international connections between domestic financial systems, and the blurring of the boundaries between banks and markets.

2.5.1 International flows of financial services

While the foregoing discussion has placed a great deal of emphasis on national financial markets and the differences that exist across countries, increasingly financial markets are becoming integrated across borders. There are three principal drivers for this development. The first is the scale of international flows of capital across borders, especially after most states abandoned capital controls and embraced global trade in the 1970s and 1980s. The second is developments in information and communication technology, which have greatly facilitated financial transactions among parties in distant locations. The third, which follows from the other two, is the internationalization of financial institutions and the multinational nature of their operations.

Table 2.3 provides data on companies cross-listed on US exchanges (NYSE, NAS-DAQ, and AMEX). It shows that in the forty-six countries surveyed, approximately 5 per cent of the companies are cross-listed in the US. Cross-listing clearly gives firms access to US investors because as can be seen from the table, the average holding by US investors of the cross-listed firms is appreciably higher than of non-cross-listed firms. By cross-listing, companies may therefore have access to deeper overseas capital markets.

One reason for cross-listing may therefore be to gain access to larger and more liquid foreign markets which assist companies with raising finance at lower cost. A second motivation could be that the quality of regulation of foreign stock exchanges is greater than that of domestic ones and companies may seek overseas listings as a way of demonstrating their quality. For example, it has been argued that companies have cross-listed on the New York Stock Exchange and NASDAQ as a way of demonstrating that they can meet the exacting standards of these exchanges and, as importantly, of the US regulatory framework.[24]

---

[24] See eg C Doidge, GA Karolyi, and RM Stulz, 'Why Are Foreign Firms Listed in the US Worth More?' (2004) 71 *Journal of Financial Economics* 205.

Table 2.3 Cross-listing of shares in 1997

	Firm Market Capitalization Available	Firm Market Float Available
Number of firms available	12,236	8,528
Number of countries	46	46
Total market value of equity ($bn)	11,080	5,927
Value of US holdings ($bn)	1,020	802
Implicit share held by US investors	9.2%	13.5%
Firms cross-listed on a US exchange	498	293
Average share held by US investors	17.5%	26.3%
Average share held in ADR form	6.4%	12.4%
Firms not cross-listed on US exchange	11,738	8,235
Average share held by US investors	2.9%	5.6%

Note: This table reports aggregate US holdings, the number and market capitalization of the sample firms, and US holdings in cross-listed and non cross-listed firms. Data on the value of US holdings are from the US Treasury/Federal Reserve Board survey of US holdings of foreign securities. Market capitalization figures are from Worldscope. Market float is calculated by scaling market capitalization by the figure given in Worldscope's closely held share field. A non-US firm is labelled as cross-listed if its shares are listed on the NYSE, AMEX, or NASDAQ. Level I ADRs trade only on OTC markets and are not considered to be cross-listed on a US exchange.

Source: J Ammer, SB Holland, DC Smith, and FE Warnock, 'Why Do US Cross-Listings Matter?' FRB International Finance Discussion Paper No 930, 26 (2008).

Table 2.4 Foreign bond issuance ($bn), and as a percentage of GDP, 2011

Region/Exchange	Foreign	GDP	% of GDP
Americas			
NYSE Euronext (US)	0.00	2,517.90	0%
TMX Group	0.04	1,758.70	0%
Asia-Pacific			
Hong Kong Exchanges	15.52	246.90	6%
National Stock Exchange India	0.09	1,843.40	0%
Osaka Securities Exchange	0.00	5,855.40	0%
Shanghai Stock Exchange	0.00	6,988.50	0%
Shenzen Stock Exchange	0.00	6,988.50	0%
Tokyo Stock Exchange Group	0.00	5,855.40	0%
Europe			
Deutsche Börse	21,722.18	3,628.60	599%
Luxembourg Stock Exchange	8,085.25	62.90	12854%
Oslo Børs	0.86	479.30	0%
SIX Swiss Exchange	312.94	665.90	47%
Weiner Börse	103.31	425.10	24%

Notes: GDP is IMF estimated data for 2011. TMX Group owns and operates Toronto Stock Exchange and TSX Venture Exchange.

Source: World Federation of Exchanges.

International flows of bond finance are particularly significant. In the face of regulations on bond finance in the US in the post Second World War period, many US companies raised bond finance from overseas, in particular European, bond markets. The 'Eurobond' market emerged as a way of satisfying the demand for

Table 2.5 Number of Countries of Operation of Leading Multinational Banks

Bank Group Name	Home Country	No of Subsidiaries	Host Country
Banco Bilbao Vizcaya Argentaria SA	ES	12	AR, CL, CO, MX, PE, PT, US, VE
Banco Santander SA	ES	13	BR, CL, DE, MX, PT, GB, US, VE
Bank of America Corp	US	2	BR, GB
Barclays Bank plc	GB	2	ES, ZA
Bayerische Hypo- und Vereinsbank AG	DE	9	HR, CZ, HU, PL, RU, AT
BNP Paribas	FR	3	IT, US
Citicorp	US	5	BR, CA, MY, MX, PL
Commerzbank AG	DE	3	NL, PL, SK
Deutsche Bank AG	DE	6	AU, IT, ES, US
HSBC Holdings plc	GB	12	BR, CA, FR, DE, HK, IND, MY, MX, SA, US
Royal Bank of Scotland plc	GB	3	IE, US
Société Générale	FR	4	AU, CA, CZ, DE
Standard Chartered plc	GB	5	HK, KE, KR, MY, TH
UBS AG	CH	2	GB, US
UniCredit SpA	IT	10	BG, HR, CZ, DE, HU, IE, PL, RU
WestLB AG	DE	6	BE, BR, FR, IE, PL, RU

Country names are according to ISO 3166-2 classification.

Source: R De Haas and I Van Lelyveld, 'Multinational Banks and the Global Financial Crisis: Weathering the Perfect Storm?' (2014) 46 *Journal of Money, Credit and Banking*, 333, 337, 358 (identifying as 'significant' subsidiaries those accounting for at least 0.5 per cent of parent-bank assets and that are at least 50 per cent owned by the parent).

overseas bond finance. International capital flows of bond finance have grown markedly since then, with governments, international agencies, as well as companies raising finance on international capital markets. Table 2.4 shows the scale of foreign bond issuance on various exchanges.

In addition to international flows of capital, financial institutions have become increasingly internationally global in their operations. Table 2.5 shows the number of countries in which some of the leading international banks have a significant presence. The significance of international flows of capital and the internationalization of banks comes in terms of the international linkages that these create among the financial systems of different jurisdictions. Whereas at one stage it was possible to insulate a country's financial system from the effects of failures elsewhere in the world, that has become increasingly difficult to achieve. Shocks in one country are rapidly transmitted to institutions and markets abroad. A clear example of that was the failure of Lehman Brothers in the US. Its failure and the refusal of the US authorities to rescue it had widespread repercussions around the world. The process of untangling the complex set of obligations that Lehman Brothers had to investors and other institutions from all over the world is still in process and will continue for many more years. We explore the consequences of inter-linkages between financial institutions and markets in the next section.

> ### The International Consequences of the Failure of Lehman Brothers
>
> The Lehman Brothers (Lehman) failure had international consequences in at least five ways. First, it affected international clients of the institution. For instance, hedge fund clients were unable to exit positions with Lehman. Second, international credit markets reassessed the existence of an implicit guarantee behind institutions like Lehman which were thought to be too-big-to-fail. The market had previously priced a credit discount for institutions such as Lehman that were believed to be beneficiaries of implicit government guarantees. The repricing (temporarily) removed that discount. Cash-poor institutions found it very difficult to borrow. Third, institutions that were unable to obtain credit were forced to sell their assets in order to satisfy their debts. Fourth, because of the pressure to hold liquid assets, financial institutions had neither the capacity nor the willingness to provide credit to companies with investment projects. Fifth, fearing the failure of more institutions and the detrimental effect of financial institutions providing credit to institutions in the real economy, governments around the world borrowed funds to bail out financial institutions. Many European countries were forced to bail out their largest institutions. Irish and Icelandic institutions had to receive significant bail-outs which in turn threatened the solvency of their governments. The solvency of governments across Europe is now constantly being scrutinized by investors as the consequences of the failure of Lehman continue to be felt.

2.5.2 Interconnections between banks and markets

Collective investment schemes and asset managers have grown dramatically around the world. This has meant that banks have been responsible for a declining share of the total amount of funds intermediated. This change has been driven in part by tax incentives to save for retirement, but also by growing efficiency of stock markets, meaning that collective investments offer comparable liquidity and higher returns than bank savings accounts. As a result, banks have been under competitive pressure. We describe this phenomenon in more detail, and analyse its consequences, in Chapter 20.

At the same time, banks have become more directly reliant on financial markets themselves. Banks increasingly raise funds from the money markets in which banks lend and borrow from each other (inter-bank markets) and from bond markets in which they raise funds over longer periods from individual and institutional investors. And, through investment banking arms, they have invested directly into markets.

Relatedly, non-bank institutions—often linked to, or sponsored by, banks—have stepped into the credit intermediation role traditionally performed by banks. Most significant amongst these are 'shadow banks' and special purpose vehicles used for securitization.[25] Shadow banks—discussed in detail in Chapter 20—perform many of the functions of banks—lending and savings—without being deposit-taking institutions or being regulated as banks by the central authorities. Examples of shadow banks include money market funds, which provide investors with similar savings and transaction functions to banks, but rather than lending their assets to companies and individuals invest in liquid money markets, and finance companies, which originate

---

[25] See section 1.2.

loans to borrowers, funded through wholesale finance markets.[26] These shadow banks extend the range of services offered to savers and borrowers, make the market for these services more competitive, and allow banks to delegate some of their activities such as mortgage lending to these institutions.

2.6 Where Financial Systems Go Wrong

This chapter has described the structure and functioning of financial systems. But really the focus of the book is on the malfunctioning of financial systems and what needs to be done to avoid and correct it. What we have described as the strengths of financial systems are also often the source of their weakness. For example, financial markets are far from a perfect mechanism for aggregating and disseminating information. The contractual provisions of financial contracts and instruments, which make them sophisticated forms of investing, make them prone to opportunistic behaviour and fraud. The interrelations between investors and firms that financial markets establish are a cause of the transmission of risks and disturbances. Financial systems are therefore prone to the failure of precisely those characteristics that are in theory their main contributions.

In principle, the value at which financial instruments trade should reflect the present value of the earnings associated with holding those instruments. So for example, a share yields financial benefits in the form of dividends paid to its investors and capital gains. The price of the share should reflect the amount at which shareholders value today the stream of dividend which will accrue in the future. However, this process of deriving a value of future dividends is complex and prone to mistakes.

For one thing, forecasts have to be made of the likely future earnings of a firm from which the dividends will be paid. Second, an assessment has to be made about the way in which the future dividends should be discounted back to the present. Third, and most serious of all, the future dividend stream will be of little interest to those shareholders who are intending to sell their shares in the near future. They will be more concerned about the price at which they will be able to sell their shares to other investors. In principle that too should reflect the future dividend stream but prices might move out of line with these 'fundamental' determinants of valuation. Instead, investors might start to try to determine the amount at which they believe that other investors value the shares. This can lead to 'bubbles' when shareholders are over-optimistic about likely future prices at which they will be able to trade shares and 'crashes' when they mark down their assessments substantially. We will be discussing information problems a great deal in this book.

A second cause of problems is contractual failure. Financial institutions contract to deliver certain services at particular prices. They are required to pay returns on savings, to hold securities, to manage assets in their clients' interest, and to execute trades with them or on their behalf. If they fail to do so, then they are liable for their failure. They should pay their customers' compensation and correct as far as possible the errors that they have made. However, if the institutions incur financial problems, then they may

---

[26] The scope of the shadow banking sector is considered further in section 20.5.

not be in a position to pay compensation—they may not have the funds to do so. In particular, investors are exposed not just to risks of mistakes but to opportunistic behaviour and, in the worst-case scenario, fraud. Money is a very fungible commodity which can readily be transferred to activities for which it was not intended. As a result, customers of financial institutions are particularly vulnerable to fraud.

Finally, there are risks that result not from the failure of a particular institution but as a consequence of the interrelations between institutions and markets that exist in a financial system. Financial institutions lend to and borrow from each other. They issue securities that are held by other financial institutions. When one institution fails, it can have repercussions across the entire financial system. Financial institutions are particularly prone to these systemic risks because of the interactions that exist between them and the fact that they depend on the confidence of their investors. If investors are concerned about the likely solvency of an institution in which they have invested they may seek to withdraw their investments at the earliest possible opportunity. Those withdrawals in turn threaten the solvency of the financial institution and make it prone to collapse, which in turn may make investors at *other* institutions similarly concerned about solvency, given the (likely) existence of credit relationships between the troubled institution and their own.

For information, contractual, and systemic reasons, financial institutions and markets are particularly prone to failure and collapse. This is the rationale for their regulation and attempts to protect customers and investors from certain types of risks. The nature of the failures of financial institutions and markets will be examined in depth in this book and it will form the basis for evaluating the regulations that have been put in place to correct these failures.

2.7 Conclusion

This chapter has described the functions that financial systems perform, the components of a financial system, the differences that exist across countries in the nature of financial systems, the internationalization of financial markets and institutions, and the failures to which financial systems are prone.

Several striking features emerge. The first is the scale of financial markets and the range of forms in which individuals, institutions, companies, and governments save and raise finance. Traditionally, a distinction is drawn between the role of financial institutions and capital markets, and regulation is currently categorized in terms of financial institutions and securities markets. However, as this chapter has suggested, that distinction is becoming increasingly untenable as borrowers look to both institutions and markets to raise finance and financial markets perform roles traditionally undertaken by financial institutions. Furthermore, while financial intermediation has traditionally been associated with banks, their activities have been replicated by non-bank intermediaries that employ financial markets to raise capital and spread risks.

There are two consequences of failing to take adequate account of the blurring of the distinction between financial intermediaries and markets. First, equivalent activities are regulated in different ways, which encourages market participants to arbitrage between the resulting different costs of transacting. Second, regulation fails to recognize the alternative ways in which similar activities are undertaken and thereby does not provide comprehensive protection for investors and customers.

What this suggests is that the traditional distinction that is drawn on the basis of institutional form is misplaced and should be replaced by a focus on function rather than form. The book will explore the implications of these developments for the way in which regulation should be designed and respond in the future.

3

The Goals and Strategies of Financial Regulation

3.1 Introduction

Financial regulation governs one of the most important systems in an economy—the financial system. The primary purpose of financial regulation is to improve the functioning of that system. The design of financial regulation is thus ultimately an exercise in economics—applying the analytic tools of economics to determine the legal and regulatory framework best suited to correcting the failures of a financial system.

The standard starting point of economics for regulation is 'if it ain't broke, don't fix it'. In other words, if there is no clear evidence of a failure of markets, do not interfere with them. To understand why, consider the 'welfare properties' of competitive markets. The invisible hand of competition guides participants in well-functioning market economies to allocate resources in ways that achieve economically efficient outcomes. They use information on prices to determine where to sell their products and where to purchase their inputs. They make employment decisions on the basis of wages and salaries and investment decisions in relation to the cost and returns on different forms of capital. Instead of relying on a large bureaucratic machine, capitalist economies run on the basis of decentralized markets that determine prices, wages, interest rates, and cost of finance on the basis of decisions made by a large number of individuals and institutions acting independently.[1]

It is a remarkable feature of market economies that the invisible hand helps guide them towards efficient outcomes where resources are allocated appropriately, production is efficiently undertaken, and savings and investment reflect future as well as current benefits. For the most part, they work pretty well and attempts to interfere with them are often counterproductive, leading to worse rather than better outcomes.[2]

While the desirability of competitive markets is well established and the alternative of central planning has now been firmly discredited, it is not always the case that free markets yield appropriate outcomes. Particular features of *financial* markets make them especially prone to malfunction. So long as the consequences of individual purchases and sales are rapidly and readily observable, it is comparatively easy to ensure the smooth functioning of markets. But when, as in the case of finance, the consequence of actions may not be revealed for extended periods of time, perhaps years or decades, then the potential for failure and the complexities of correcting it are much greater.

This gives rise to what economists describe as 'market failures'—the failure of markets to achieve the economically efficient outcomes with which they are generally

---

[1] We leave aside for present purposes the effects of central bank intervention through monetary policy.
[2] For a counterview that markets are subject to endemic failure see GA Akerlof and RJ Shiller, *Phishing for Fools: The Economics of Deception and Manipulation* (Princeton, NJ: Princeton University Press, 2015).

Principles of Financial Regulation. First Edition. John Armour, Dan Awrey, Paul Davies, Luca Enriques, Jeffrey N. Gordon, Colin Mayer, and Jennifer Payne. © John Armour, Dan Awrey, Paul Davies, Luca Enriques, Jeffrey N. Gordon, Colin Mayer, and Jennifer Payne 2016. Published 2016 by Oxford University Press.

associated. Where such failures arise, there is a *prima facie* case for actions to be taken to correct the failures. However, the case is only *prima facie*—and not definitive—because the costs of remedying the deficiency may be greater than the benefits.

There are therefore at least three stages involved in designing a regulatory system. The first is to determine the nature and extent of any market failures that exist. The second is to establish the set of possible regulatory interventions and to identify the appropriate combination required to remedy each failure. The third is to evaluate the costs or side effects of such remedial intervention and to determine whether they are so great as to outweigh the benefits. If the costs of a particular intervention exceed the benefits, then either an alternative remedy needs to be sought or the failure in question may be permitted to remain uncorrected.

It is a central proposition of this book that not only are financial systems particularly prone to failures, but their remedies are also often subject to unintended and undesirable consequences. In fact, the design of financial regulation is not just about the identification of market failures and appropriate remedies, but also their translation into law (an imperfect instrument to guide human behaviour) via the (no less imperfect) political process. We will come back to the political and legal challenges of designing an effective regulatory system in Chapter 4.

Like the regulatory process just described, this chapter will proceed by stages. It will begin in section 3.2 by setting out the economic theory of the efficiency of markets. It will describe how competitive markets yield economically efficient outcomes and the conditions under which they possess these properties.

Section 3.3 describes common market failures that can arise in financial markets and the ways in which they can justify regulation to correct them. It will discuss the primary sources of market failures arising from asymmetries of information, negative externalities, public goods, imperfect competition, and behavioural biases in consumer decision-making.

Section 3.4 considers the goals of financial regulation, as described by regulators and policymakers. It reviews seven areas often listed by governments and public-sector bodies as being major goals of financial regulation: protection of investors and other users of the financial system (especially consumers of retail financial products), financial stability, market efficiency, competition, the prevention of financial crime, and fairness. The goals of financial regulation are frequently in conflict. In particular, the book points to the conflict that may arise between goals such as investor or consumer protection and the stability of the financial system as a whole. The goals of financial regulation must therefore be traded off against each other, and to do that, governments and regulators need to have clearly defined objectives and preferences amongst the goals.

The final stage is to identify the various strategies and tools that are available to regulators and relate them to the achievement of the goals of regulation. In section 3.5, we will outline seven regulatory strategies—which we term entry, conduct, information, prudence, governance, insurance, and resolution—denoting various ways in which regulatory intervention can be structured.

This framework of market failures, goals, objectives, and strategies will underpin the analysis of the rest of the book. The book will elaborate on how the translation of market failures into regulatory strategies is undertaken in different areas of the financial system and how conflicts in the attainment of goals should be resolved through a regulatory objective function. By the end of this chapter, you should have a basic understanding of the framework of financial regulation and the combination of economic analysis and public law in its design—an understanding that will prepare you to appreciate the more detailed descriptions in the subsequent chapters of the book.

3.2 The Efficiency of Markets

The purpose of regulation is to assist markets in functioning better than they would do in its absence. The most important criteria by which economists judge how well an economy is functioning relate to the efficiency with which the economy produces and allocates resources. The starting point is that most resources such as commodities, raw materials, labour, and capital are scarce. They are therefore expensive to employ and need to be utilized as efficiently as possible.

Efficiency in this sense has three meanings. The first is that resources have to yield as much output as is possible from the given set of scarce resources—the inputs. The more output that is produced from a given level of input, the greater is what economists term the level of 'productive efficiency'. However, this does not in itself ensure that resources are well deployed because they may be employed in activities that are not particularly highly valued. The second criterion is therefore that they are not only as productively efficient as possible but also allocated as well as they could be to those activities and individuals that value them the most. This is correspondingly termed 'allocative efficiency'.

The guiding determinant of the value associated with different activities and products is the price that customers are willing to pay for them. The greater the price that individuals are willing to pay for goods and services relative to the cost of producing them, the higher is the level of the 'surplus' associated with them. That surplus may go to the consumers in the form of what is termed their consumer surplus—the amounts that they would be willing to pay for the goods and services that they consume, over and above the price that they actually have to pay for them. Alternatively, the surplus may go to producers in the form of profits—the difference between the revenue that they earn from selling the products and the costs of producing them.

The combination of 'allocative' and 'productive' efficiency together ensures that resources are allocated to their most valuable activities in the lowest-cost way. However, there is a third dimension, which is particularly relevant to the financial markets discussed in this book. It concerns the allocation of resources over time as well as between activities and individuals. Resources should be allocated as efficiently as possible between different points of time—between this year and next year, or between the current generation and future generations—as well as within years and generations. This is termed 'dynamic efficiency'. It is particularly relevant to the subject of this book because, as described in Chapter 2, one of the distinguishing and complex features of financial markets is their role in promoting savings and investment over extended periods of time. The financial system is therefore central to the achievement of dynamic efficiency.

One of the most significant insights of economics is to demonstrate how markets contribute to the attainment of allocative, productive, and dynamic efficiency. Markets indeed have this property, provided several conditions are fulfilled: there must be a large number of well-informed producers and consumers of goods and services, acting independently, in markets in which everything is priced. The remarkable feature of such markets is that large numbers of individuals acting entirely independently in pursuit of their own self-interest can achieve the three aspects of efficiency to a degree that bureaucrats in centrally planned economies could only dream. The so-called 'invisible hand' of the market acts through these self-interested individuals to deliver efficient production and consumption decisions.

This is sometimes known as the 'Pareto-optimal' property of competitive markets after Vilfredo Pareto, an Italian economist who defined efficiency as existing if there was no alternative allocation of resources that could make at least one person better off while making no one else worse off.[3] In other words, competitive markets are efficient in achieving outcomes in which there are no alternative allocations and employment of resources across activities, individuals, and time under which anyone would be better off.

It is an almost magical feature of competitive markets that they possess this property, and it underpins the hallowed status they command in modern economies. However, there are two important caveats associated with this result which make it much more complex than it at first seems. The first caveat is that it only holds if the various conditions associated with the existence of perfectly competitive markets are fulfilled. If they are not and there are 'market failures', then it may be possible to achieve superior allocations of resources than those associated with unencumbered markets and the intervention of governments and regulators may be required to achieve them.

The second caveat is that to say that the allocation of resources resulting from perfectly competitive markets is 'Pareto optimal'—that is, no one can be made better off without someone else being made worse off—does not necessarily ensure that the allocation of resources is desirable. It may involve a disproportionate allocation of resources to a small number of people, with the vast majority of people having access to very little. Such an outcome might be Pareto efficient in the sense that there is no alternative allocation that makes a majority of the population better off without the minority being made worse off, but it is not a socially desirable outcome. In other words, it does not satisfy the second set of criteria by which economists judge the merits of markets, that is, 'distribution'. An efficient allocation may not involve a fair distribution of resources and the intervention of government may be required to ensure that resources are allocated in a fair as well as an efficient manner.

Fairness is normally associated with the degree of inequality of income and wealth in an economy. A highly competitive economy may be a highly unequal one, which may justify government intervention to redistribute resources to the most needy even when market failures do not require it. The neediest include the most vulnerable members of society—the sick, old, and uneducated—as well as the poorest. As respects financial

---

[3] V Pareto, 'Il Massimo di Utilità Dato dalla Libera Concorrenza' (1894) 9 *Giornale degli Economisti* 48, 58.

regulation, fairness underpins measures to protect the vulnerable from the unscrupulous. Complexity makes financial markets particularly prone to high and extensive levels of relative vulnerability on the part of large numbers of individuals. Even some of the healthiest and best-educated members of society are at risk of being exploited by others when they invest in complex financial instruments.

The starting point for our analysis of the regulation of financial markets will therefore be the efficiency properties of competitive markets. It is a benchmark against which to judge the performance of markets. But it is only a starting point, because we then have to determine how well they match up against it, the extent to which there are market failures that undermine efficiency, and—in turn—the extent to which they can be corrected by regulation. We will on occasion also consider the role that regulation can play in achieving distributionally fair, as well as economically efficient, outcomes and protecting the most vulnerable from the most unscrupulous.

Having introduced the idea of perfect markets, in section 3.3 we now consider five types of market imperfections that can lead to market failures.

3.3 Market Failures

3.3.1 Asymmetric information

As a consumer of financial products, one of the most serious problems you face is that the products on offer are often complex and difficult to evaluate. For example, distinguishing between different investment funds is complicated by the fact that it is hard to observe the financial assets that are purchased by the fund, or the charges that are levied. These sources of uncertainty are particularly serious in the case of large transactions such as home mortgages or pension plans. These involve substantial borrowing and investment decisions over long periods of time, such that even relatively small mistakes can cumulate into large losses by the time the product matures.

The problems of uncertainty are made worse by the fact that consumers of such products are less well informed than the sellers. There is what in the parlance of economists is described as an 'asymmetry of information' between buyer and seller, with the buyer in general being less well informed about a particular financial product than a seller. It is costly for purchasers to educate themselves sufficiently to be as well informed about the financial products they are being offered as the sellers.

One of the consequences of asymmetries of information is that purchasers are particularly vulnerable to unscrupulous sellers offering financial products that are not as good as they are claimed to be or as appropriate for an individual purchaser as other products available on the market. Consumers may thus face the problem of 'adverse selection' of what are termed 'lemons'.

George Akerlof first described the problem in the context of the market for second-hand cars.[4] Sellers of second-hand cars know more about the defects of their vehicles than purchasers and, as a consequence, they tend to offload defective cars onto

---

[4] GA Akerlof, 'The Market for "Lemons": Quality Uncertainty and the Market Mechanism' (1970) 84 *Quarterly Journal of Economics* 488.

unsuspecting purchasers. But the problem is actually worse than that, because purchasers who are unable to ascertain the quality of a product will offer no more than the prevailing price for a product of *average* quality. Knowing this, sellers will only offer purchasers cars whose real value is at best equal to, and likely less than, the average price that they are being offered, driving the average quality of cars on the market, and therefore the price purchasers are willing to pay, further down. When that is the case, purchasers face a systematic adverse selection problem, such that the only available cars on the market are 'lemons'. Adverse selection therefore not only disadvantages buyers, but also causes the market for second-hand cars to collapse. Asymmetries of information have similar effects on financial markets. Not only do they result in the unfair treatment of buyers, they may also cause financial markets to shrivel or implode.[5]

The response of the market is to seek ways of mitigating problems of asymmetry of information and to provide signals of reliable quality that purchasers can trust.[6] One such signal is a warrant or guarantee of the quality of the product. The second-hand car salesman may offer to buy back the car if it is shown to be defective within a particular period of time. The seller of financial investments may guarantee performance over certain periods of time. Alternatively, there may be agencies that certify the quality of the car by undertaking independent inspections and evaluating the reliability and creditworthiness of sellers of financial products.

The information asymmetries in financial markets are often intense, and the time lapse between the parting of investors from their money and when they are to get it back can be long. As a consequence, it may take too long before investors understand that the 'signals' of quality and reliability originally provided were actually worthless. Market mechanisms may, in other words, be too weak to discourage attempts to exploit vulnerable customers.[7]

To explore this point further, we can use heuristically distinctions drawn by economists according to how easy it is for consumers to determine the characteristics of goods and services. First, there are 'search goods', whose characteristics can be identified before they are purchased. So for example, one can go to a market and determine the quality of fruit and vegetables that are being bought by inspecting them.

---

[5] Information asymmetry is of course also problematic after a product has been purchased. To the extent that the consumer's payoffs depend on actions to be taken by the supplier—for example, the selection of investments—and it is costly for the consumer to observe which actions the supplier does take, then the supplier has an incentive to take actions that benefit itself, rather than the consumer. The losses associated with such hidden actions are known as 'agency costs' (see MC Jensen and WH Meckling, 'Theory of the Firm: Managerial Behavior, Agency Costs and Ownership Structure' (1976) 3 *Journal of Financial Economics* 305). In the context of the current discussion, the anticipated level of agency costs for a particular product—and the likely efficacy of any contractual solutions offered—can be understood as simply another dimension of the things understood less well by the consumer than the financial firm at the outset.

[6] A 'signal' in this context means a way of credibly conveying information about quality. A good signal is something that it is materially more costly to do for a vendor of a low-quality product than for a high-quality product vendor.

[7] For example, Bernard Madoff, an investment adviser who committed one of the largest frauds in history, developed an exceptional reputation for his services by for many years paying clients steady 'returns' on their investments, regardless of the vicissitudes of the market. These payments were made from funds subscribed to Madoff by subsequent clients: see DB Henriques, *The Wizard of Lies: Bernie Madoff and the Death of Trust* (New York, NY: Times Books, 2011). Such a strategy can only be followed for so long as income from new clients is no less than returns due to existing clients.

However, in some cases it may not be possible to assess the quality of the product until one has actually consumed the good. These are termed 'experience goods'. Even more problematically, in some cases, it may not be possible to ascertain quality even after consumption. For example, the success of a medical intervention or surgery may be hard to assess after it has happened because the counterfactual of what would have happened had a different procedure been followed is almost impossible to assess. These are known as 'credence goods', where their quality has to be taken on trust or faith.

Financial products and services frequently fall into the credence category because there are no reliable benchmarks against which to evaluate performance. How well a collective investment fund 'should have' performed over a particular period is difficult to judge. It may have underperformed relative to a benchmark index, such as the FTSE or S&P index, but was that because it was lower risk than the benchmark, because the fund manager made poor stock selections (due to incompetence or conflicts of interest), or simply because of bad luck? For such products, information asymmetries are particularly pronounced.

3.3.2 Negative externalities

The interconnection of financial institutions and markets means that the actions of one actor, or group of actors, can have an adverse impact on other actors—a 'domino effect'. This in turn can have powerful adverse implications for the economy as a whole. In particular, the failure of financial institutions can upset the payments system, with the result that ordinary transactions become difficult or impossible to process. Moreover, the failure of banks leads to the loss of their specialist expertise in selecting and monitoring business projects for financing.[8] The failure of one or more important banks in which depositors or other creditors suffer losses can lead to 'runs' on other banks and cash-hoarding by still other banks, all of which will dramatically reduce the flow of credit to non-financial firms. A financial sector crisis can rapidly become a general economic crisis.

In economic terms, we can understand these effects as negative externalities. Externalities arise when a person or institution takes actions that impose costs (benefits) in the case of negative (positive) externalities on other parties for which that person is not fully charged (compensated). They occur when prices and incentives do not adequately reflect the consequences of actions taken.

A divergence of this kind may arise between the interests of those who own and operate financial institutions, and the interests of society at large. To be sure, the shareholders of a financial institution suffer if it fails. However, because losses are distributed so widely, the shareholders may bear only a fraction of the overall loss to society associated with failure. What is at issue are actions that increase the risk of

---

[8] BS Bernanke, 'Nonmonetary Effects of the Financial Crisis on the Propagation of the Great Depression' (1983) 73 *American Economic Review* 257; MB Slovin, ME Sushka, and JA Polonchek, 'The Value of Bank Durability: Borrowers as Bank Stakeholders' (1993) 48 *Journal of Finance* 247; JK Kang and RM Stulz, 'Do Banking Shocks Affect Borrowing Firm Performance? An Analysis of the Japanese Experience' (2000) 73 *Journal of Business* 1.

failure. Where financial institutions are paid to take on risks, this money can be paid out to shareholders as dividends during good times, but is not repayable by them should the institution fail. Consequently, shareholders take the profits associated with risk-taking, but do not bear more than a fraction of the costs associated with failure, in cases where failure has systemic consequences. As a result, shareholders may push institutions to take on more risk—that is, to tolerate a higher probability of failure—than is desirable from the viewpoint of society as a whole.[9] Indeed, a growing body of empirical research finds that those banks in which the board of directors was most closely aligned with the interests of shareholders—that is, had the 'best' corporate governance on conventional measures—took on the greatest level of risk prior to the financial crisis, and suffered the greatest losses during the crisis.[10]

There is a remarkable theory in economics, known as the 'Coase theorem', after Ronald Coase who first described it in a 1960 paper.[11] The Coase theorem states that bargaining between the various parties affected by externalities will always lead to efficient outcomes provided that the costs of negotiation and bargaining are sufficiently small. To illustrate, if investors in one bank are potentially adversely affected by the risk of failure of another bank, then they can offer a sufficient inducement to the latter bank to reduce its risk-taking to the point that at the margin, the cost of reducing it further is just equal to the benefits that investors in the first bank thereby derive.

Coase demonstrated that this same efficient outcome is derived irrespective of whether the investors in the first bank have to bribe the second bank to reduce its risk-taking or the second bank has to compensate the investors in the first bank for accepting the effects of its risk-taking. In other words, it does not matter whether the second bank has the right to take whatever risks it sees appropriate or the first bank has the right to operate without the second bank imposing risks of failure on it. Provided that these 'property' rights are clearly specified, it does not matter who holds the entitlements at the outset—bargaining and negotiation will lead to the same efficient outcome.

The Coase theorem rests critically on the assumption that negotiation or bargaining costs are small. If they are not, then the efficient outcome will not be achieved and the result of negotiation depends on how property rights are allocated: in the foregoing example, to the first or the second bank. In particular, if, as in the case of the financial crisis, there are a large number of individuals (for example, investors in our first bank discussed above) that are affected by the failure of particular institutions, then it is difficult or costly for them to coordinate in negotiation with the banks. Furthermore, it

---

[9] See J Armour and JN Gordon, 'Systemic Harms and Shareholder Value' (2014) 6 *Journal of Legal Analysis* 35. Armour and Gordon develop a distinction between diversified shareholders, whose entire portfolio is damaged by the failure of a systemically important firm, and concentrated shareholders, whose losses are limited to write-off of own-bank share values. The shareholders who are significant for corporate governance purposes tend to be concentrated shareholders who are under-diversified and who will thus fail to internalize systemic losses.

[10] See eg A Beltratti and R Stulz, 'The Credit Crisis Around the Globe: Why Did Some Banks Perform Better?' (2012) 105 *Journal of Financial Economics* 1; DH Erkens, M Hing, and P Matos, 'Corporate Governance in the 2007–2008 Financial Crisis: Evidence from Financial Institutions Worldwide' (2012) 18 *Journal of Corporate Finance* 389. These issues are discussed further in Chapter 17.

[11] RJ Coase, 'The Problem of Social Cost' (1960) 3 *Journal of Law and Economics* 1.

may be even harder for these individuals to identify in advance which banks are taking risks that might endanger their solvency and what the consequences of their failure would be.

In these cases where private negotiation is expensive or infeasible, the government may be able to 'internalize' externalities better than the private parties involved by setting taxes and subsidies which reflect their costs and benefits, or by regulating the activities of financial institutions in such a way as to prevent them from creating damaging negative externalities. Systemic risks are classic examples of negative externalities that individuals and institutions cannot effectively internalize and which governments need to correct through taxation or regulation.

3.3.3 Public goods

Banks also create *positive* externalities when they contribute to the liquidity of financial markets. For example, the provision of a payments system that allows customers to use their deposits to undertake transactions creates what is termed a 'public good'—a good or service from which everyone can benefit, even if they have not contributed to, or paid for, the provision of that good or service. The classic examples of public goods outside of the financial sector are the provision of a nation's defence or national and local public parks.

The economic problem with public goods is that since people can enjoy the benefits of them without paying for them—what is termed 'free-riding'[12]—the revenue that they generate falls short of the sum total of the benefits that they create. The result is under-provision of public goods that are privately provided.

There are a number of possible solutions to the public good problem. The first is that the providers of public goods can be in public ownership. The scale of provision of public goods is then determined, not by market processes, but through the stated preferences of the public at large for the provision of these goods and services. For example, the government can be responsible for the provision and operation of a country's payment system.

A second possibility is that the consumers of the public goods or the government subsidize private providers of public goods to the extent that the revenue the providers raise falls short of the value that consumers derive from them. For example, other market participants or the government may subsidize those providing liquidity to securities markets ('market makers') for the services that they provide.

Third, if the providers of public goods are granted a monopoly licence to be the sole providers in their respective markets, then they may be able to set prices at levels which reflect the benefits that consumers derive from them. The problem with this solution is that charges will then be well in excess of the—essentially zero—cost of giving consumers access to the public good (for example, admitting them to a public park) and their use of the public good will then fall well below what it should be.

---

[12] The term 'free-rider' originally derives from the practice, common in the early days of rail transportation, of riding a train without paying a fare.

Since public good problems are endemic in financial markets, we will see examples of a variety of methods for trying to resolve the markets failures they create.

3.3.4 Imperfect competition

In section 3.2, we described the efficiency properties of competitive markets over three distinct dimensions: productive, allocative, and dynamic efficiency. Competitive markets rely on the existence of a large number of small producers, the free entry and exit of firms into and out of markets, and a large number of well-informed consumers who can switch costlessly between producers and suppliers. If these conditions are not fulfilled, then producers will be able to charge prices in excess of the cost of provision of the goods and services, and resources will not be appropriately allocated to where they yield the greatest benefit.

Market imperfections are endemic in financial markets. For example, four large banks have traditionally dominated the retail commercial banking market in the UK. The UK competition authorities regularly scrutinize them for possible monopoly abuse.[13] Entry into the retail banking market in particular is very expensive, so long as a branch network is needed to establish a sufficient customer base, and provides incumbent retail banks with a considerable competitive advantage. And, as described in section 3.3.1, asymmetric information is pervasive in financial markets, so incumbents can exploit their market power without consumers even noticing it. As a consequence, competition in many parts of financial services is far from perfect and the distortions associated with imperfectly competitive markets, compounded by information asymmetries, are widespread: excessively high prices, poor quality service, and the sale of defective or inappropriate products.

Competition authorities, such as the Office of Fair Trading ('OFT') in the UK, the Department of Justice ('DOJ') and the Federal Trade Commission ('FTC') in the US, or the European Commission in the EU, are responsible for protecting customers against the effects of anti-competitive practices and monopoly abuses. In the case of regulated markets, such as financial services, it has also increasingly become the responsibility of regulators, as well as competition authorities, to promote competition and police competitive abuses.

3.3.5 Biases in individual decision-making

Up to this point, we have considered market failures in the context of parties who act rationally in relation to the information that is available to them. So, for example, to the extent that purchasers of financial services are at an informational disadvantage relative to sellers (as discussed in section 3.3.1), their rational response is to desist from engaging in trades that are likely to be overpriced or inappropriate. But investors who cannot process information rationally may not respond in this way. Their beliefs

---

[13] For example, in 2014 the UK's Competition and Markets Authority ('CMA') launched an investigation into the supply of personal current accounts and services to small and medium-sized enterprises (SMEs) in the UK.

about the value of financial products and services may be biased, prejudiced, swayed by crowds and herd mentality, and/or derived from the application of simple rules of thumb that are inaccurate.[14] The result can be that they buy products that they do not need, should not possess, and come to regret.

Irrational beliefs do not just create disappointed investors. They also lead to a misallocation of resources. The rational response of producers to irrational preferences of consumers is often not to seek to correct them but to pander to them. The response of banks to customers' concerns about their inability to service loans due to ill-health or unemployment led to the promotion of a new form of insurance in various European countries—payments protection—which was unnecessary for customers but hugely profitable for providers. Concerns amongst small and medium-sized companies in various European countries about possible increases in interest rates prompted the mis-selling of interest rate swaps. In both cases, banks profited from pandering to customers' irrational concerns by selling them unnecessary and/or overpriced products.

Biases in consumer behaviour pose a substantial challenge to regulators. If purchasers of financial services behave rationally, then the role of the regulator is to protect them from deceptive or inappropriate conduct on the part of sellers and to ensure that what they get is what they wanted. However, if consumer preferences are subject to biases, then the function of regulation potentially becomes a much more complex one, not aligning financial services so much with what (distorted) consumer preferences actually are, but with what analysis suggests that they should be, but for the bias in question. So for example, the appropriate pricing of payments protection insurance and interest rate swaps in the UK should then have been based not on customer perceptions of the associated risks but on unbiased expectations. This potentially involves regulators in much more paternalistic intervention in the operation of markets than a rational view of consumer behaviour would warrant.

3.4 The Goals of Financial Regulation

Having described the merits and defects of markets, the next stage is to determine what policymakers can legitimately be seeking to achieve through regulation—namely, the *goals* of regulation. While the goals of regulation are not always articulated in economic terms, an underlying thesis of this book is that considerable insights are provided by so doing. Economics starts from market efficiency (and distribution) as the defining considerations and derives a set of goals based upon these. Regulation is then understood as the means of rectifying relevant market failures.

Characterizing the goals of regulation in this way helps to develop focused criteria for assessing the merits of particular regulatory strategies. The criteria are linked to the underlying functioning of the financial system which the regulation is seeking to improve and are independent of the legal system within which the regulation is

---

[14] For reviews, see T Gilovich, D Griffin, and D Kahneman (eds), *Heuristics and Biases: The Psychology of Intuitive Judgment* (Cambridge: CUP, 2002); D Kahneman, *Thinking, Fast and Slow* (Cambridge: CUP, 2011); C Sunstein, 'Empirically Informed Regulation' (2011) 78 *University of Chicago Law Review* 1349. These issues are treated in more detail in Chapter 10.

operating. Consequently, these criteria provide a framework that can in principle be used to understand and assess financial regulation in any jurisdiction.

In this section, we review the goals of financial regulation, as articulated by regulators, and relate them to the economic rationales we have discussed. We identify six discrete goals and argue that each of these can helpfully be understood as responding to a particular type of market failure.

3.4.1 Protection of investors and other users of the financial system

The protection of users of the financial system is an important goal of financial regulation. That said, regulators do not typically refer to the category of persons to be protected as 'users' generically, but rather by a series of sector-specific names. The use of different names in the regulatory framework obscures the fact that they each respond to similar economic concerns, and so it is useful to group them together.[15]

Perhaps the best known of these goals is 'investor protection'. This is an explicit goal of securities regulation. The US Securities Act 1933 and Securities Exchange Act of 1934 were introduced with the express goal of protecting investors from fraud and other malpractices associated with securities issuance and trading during the bubble of the 1920s.[16] 'Investor protection' now also features at the centre of European securities regulation, the importance of which is emphasized by the preambles to the principal Directives.[17] In relation to issuers of securities, investor protection is understood largely in terms of mandating the disclosure of relevant information. The concern is that without this information, would-be investors will be unable to assess clearly the risks they are taking on, and will consequently be unwilling to advance funds. If we relate this back to the economic rationales for regulation, the underlying concern is asymmetric information giving rise to an adverse selection problem.

Problems stemming from asymmetric information also arise in relation to situations where an investor relies on a financial firm for judgements about investment choices or execution of trades, and/or for safe custody of assets. In this case, the regulatory goal is described as 'client protection',[18] or where the financial firm is a US broker-dealer,

---

[15] An attempt was made in the UK to overcome this balkanization of terminology through the adoption in the Financial Services and Markets Act 2000 ('FSMA 2000') of the term 'consumer protection' as an umbrella concept encompassing the protection of all the users of the financial system for the purposes of defining regulatory objectives (see now FSMA 2000, s 1G). However, this terminology has not been more widely adopted: in the US or EU, and indeed in other contexts in the UK, the term 'consumer' more usually refers only to individuals acting in a personal capacity: see section 3.4.1, especially n 28. Moreover, even in the UK, the unification of terminology is no longer comprehensive, as the Prudential Regulation Authority has since 2013 been tasked with the discrete goal of 'policyholder protection' in relation to insurance firms: FSMA 2000, s 2C(2).

[16] See eg J Seligman, 'The Historical Need for a Mandatory Corporate Disclosure System' (1983) 9 *Journal of Corporation Law* 1. See also Commodity Exchange Act of 1936 (US), 7 USC §5(b); Trust Indenture Act of 1939 (US), §302)(a) (expressing investor protection rationale).

[17] See eg Directive 2003/71/EC (Prospectus Directive) [2003] OJ L345/64, recitals 10, 12, and 16; Directive 2014/65/EU (Second Markets in Financial Instruments Directive or 'MiFID II') [2014] OJ L173/349, recitals 7, 39, 45, 57, 58, 97, and 133; Directive 2004/109/EC (Transparency Directive) [2004] OJ L390/38, recitals 1, 5, and 7.

[18] See Investment Advisers Act of 1940 (US), §201(1); MiFID II, n 17, recitals 5 and 80; Art 4(1)(9) and Annex II.

'customer protection'.[19] Here the risks for the client or customer are not only those inherent in the investments selected, but also that the financial firm may make poor investment choices, or may fail to segregate, or—worse still—misappropriate assets. These risks arise from actions the financial firm may take during the life of the relationship, which are very difficult for the client to monitor. Once again, the economic problem is asymmetric information, in this case giving rise to agency costs. A number of regulatory measures seek to reduce these risks. These include licensing requirements, custodial requirements, and measures to control conflicts of interest and enhance competence. A large part of these measures governs how the intermediary must operate its business and so they are called 'conduct of business' rules. Functionally, they can be thought of as mandatory terms of the contractual relationship between the client and the intermediary, responding to agency costs.

Agency problems are also present in relation to financial intermediaries such as banks, insurance companies, and mutual funds. Bank depositors, insurance policy holders and mutual fund investors each transfer funds to such financial intermediaries in return for claims against the intermediary's balance sheet. The value of these claims depends on how the intermediary invests the funds thereby raised. In each case, there is the potential for agency costs stemming from the difficulty of monitoring the intermediary's actions. Regulations seeking to control these agency costs are framed in terms of 'depositor protection',[20] 'policy holder protection',[21] and 'investor protection',[22] respectively. Together, the body of regulation that governs the risks associated with the business model of a financial intermediary is often referred to as 'prudential' regulation, the idea being that it instils prudence in the regulated firm so as to protect those who rely on the firm.

It is worth asking why information asymmetries between end users of the financial system and financial intermediaries should be thought to justify extensive regulation, when functionally similar problems arise in relation to many other services. A short answer is that most important non-financial services that involve extensive information asymmetries—and consequent agency costs—are in fact subject to regulation: witness for example the cases of doctors and lawyers. A more nuanced response asserts that the problems are particularly severe in relation to finance: the business model of financial firms is unusually opaque,[23] and the business of financial firms, namely money, is particularly prone to abuse. For example, the notorious fraudster Bernie Madoff maintained his investment scheme for nearly thirty years because his consistent

---

[19] See eg Securities Investor Protection Act of 1970 (US), §5.

[20] See eg Directive 2013/36/EC (Capital Requirements Directive IV or 'CRD IV') [2013] OJ L176/338, recital 47; Federal Deposit Insurance Act (US) §3(l), 12 USC §1813(l).

[21] See eg Directive 2009/138/EC ('Solvency II') [2009] OJ L335/1, recital 16 and Art 27.

[22] See eg Investment Company Act of 1940 (US), §1; Directive 2009/65/EC, as amended by Directive 2014/91/EU (Undertakings for Collective Investment in Transferable Securities Directive, or 'UCITS V') [2009] OJ L302/32, recitals 8 and 10.

[23] For example, ratings agencies disagree much more about the credit rating of bonds issued by financial institutions than for non-financial firms: see DP Morgan, 'Rating Banks: Risk and Uncertainty in an Opaque Industry' (2002) 92 *American Economic Review* 874. See also RP Bartlett, 'Making Banks Transparent' (2012) 65 *Vanderbilt Law Review* 293.

out-performance attracted increasing sums that in turn funded the payouts to his clients.[24]

3.4.2 Consumer protection in retail finance

'Consumer protection' is an express goal of the new US Consumer Financial Protection Bureau, established by the Dodd–Frank Act of 2010.[25] Similarly, it is also the express goal of certain EU consumer financial legislation, which forms part of the corpus of European consumer protection law more generally.[26] 'Consumers' in these contexts are defined as individuals acting outside the course of their business,[27] a definition we generally adopt throughout this book.

For transactions involving consumers, the rationale for regulation is significantly broader than for most types of user of the financial system, encompassing not only asymmetric information but also behavioural considerations. There is a potential role for regulation to protect consumers from exploitation of their biases and inaccurate judgements. The types of regulatory intervention calculated to further the goal of consumer protection might therefore be quite different from those aimed at assisting more sophisticated users. We discuss the particular issues relevant to the regulation of consumer finance in Chapter 10.

Although the definition of 'consumer' as an individual acting in their personal capacity is widely used in consumer law, financial regulation includes some more idiosyncratic usage.[28] In US and EU financial regulation, the term 'consumer' is principally used in the regulation of consumer credit—that is, referring to consumer users of the financial system who are also *borrowers*. This is an artefact of the continued sectoral division of regulation, in which consumers so defined form just one of many categories. In other contexts, individuals investing modest sums on their own account are referred to as 'retail' investors, clients, customers, and so on. Throughout the book, we refer to 'consumers' and 'retail' users of the financial system largely interchangeably.[29]

3.4.3 Financial stability

The financial crisis has highlighted the central importance of another goal of financial regulation, namely the stability of the financial system as a whole. In section 3.3.2 we

---

[24] See n 7.

[25] Dodd–Frank Act of 2010 (US), §1001 (short title of Title X is 'Consumer Financial Protection Act of 2010').

[26] See eg Directive 2008/48/EC on Credit Agreements for Consumers ('Consumer Credit Directive') [2008] OJ L133/66; Directive 2011/83/EU on Consumer Rights ('Consumer Rights Directive') [2011] OJ L304/64.

[27] See Dodd–Frank Act of 2010 (US) §1002(4)–(5); Consumer Credit Directive, Art 3(a); Consumer Rights Directive, Art 2(1).

[28] For example, in UK financial regulation, the term 'consumer' is used in a much broader sense, to refer to all users of regulated financial services or investors in financial instruments (see n 15). However, this sits awkwardly alongside English law's more conventional use of the term 'consumers' for the purposes of consumer contract law: see eg Consumer Rights Act 2015 (UK), s 2(3). See also Chapter 10, section 10.1.

[29] Minor differences between the two definitions are discussed in Chapter 10, sections 10.1 and 10.5.

considered how the failure of one institution can have a 'domino effect' on the entire financial sector and repercussions for the economy as a whole.

The unpredictable and extensive nature of the losses inflicted by a systemic failure makes it practically impossible for parties who might suffer losses to contract in advance with financial institutions whose choice of activities will affect their probability of failure.[30] Consequently, it is desirable for financial regulation to address this type of externality.

Prior to the financial crisis, there was thought to be almost complete overlap between the goals of user protection and financial stability, at least as regards banks. Prudential regulation designed to minimize the probability that a bank should fail was thought to be adequate to protect both the bank's depositors and the rest of the financial system. Most obviously, capital adequacy requirements, already referred to in the investor protection discussion, were thought of as being necessary to preserve financial stability as well.[31] Similarly, deposit insurance schemes, initially introduced in the US after the Great Depression to protect depositors, had the serendipitous consequence of making bank runs less likely, as depositors had little to fear from bank failure.[32] Perhaps for this reason, the UK's financial regulatory regime did not at the time of the financial crisis mention financial stability as a goal at all: it was believed that maintaining market confidence and protecting users of the financial system would necessarily entail financial stability.[33]

This equation of goals has been undermined by events leading up to the financial crisis. First, as respects bank runs, sophisticated investors proved themselves just as capable as unsophisticated consumers of engaging in 'run'-like behaviour.[34] Yet insurance schemes protect only retail depositors—that is, consumers. Second, it is unnecessary for an institution to fail for a systemic shock to be triggered. The 'domino effect' model of transmission of contagion focuses on the way in which liabilities on the balance sheet of the failed institution are assets on the balance sheet of other institutions, which transmits a shock following its failure. However, a shock may also be transmitted through correlated investment strategies. Where one institution suffers a liquidity shock and needs to sell assets quickly, this sale may depress the market price (especially if the assets are illiquid) and reduce the value of these assets on other institutions' balance sheets. This in turn might trigger a need for these institutions to liquidate assets in order to deleverage or to hold back cash that otherwise might have

---

[30] Moreover, the law of tort, which may be understood as a private law mechanism for controlling externalities, fails to be effective in relation to the financial sector, because the losses inflicted are exclusively economic, for which recovery is generally unavailable in tort. See Armour and Gordon, n 9, 46–7.

[31] See eg CRD IV, n 20, recitals 47 and 91 ('protection of depositors'). See also SG Hanson, AK Kashyap, and JC Stein, 'A Macroprudential Approach to Financial Regulation' (2011) 25 *Journal of Economic Perspectives* 3.

[32] DW Diamond and PH Dybvig, 'Banks Runs, Deposit Insurance, and Liquidity' (1983) 91 *Journal of Political Economy* 401. On the history of deposit insurance, see CW Calomiris and EN White, 'The Origins of Federal Deposit Insurance', in C Goldin and GD Libecap (eds), *The Regulated Economy: A Historical Approach to Political Economy* (Chicago: University of Chicago Press, 1994), 145.

[33] See now Bank of England Act 1998 (UK) (as amended by the Banking Act 2009 and the Financial Services Act 2012), s 2A; Financial Services and Markets Act 2000 (UK) (as amended by the Financial Services Act 2012), s 2B(3).

[34] GB Gorton, *Slapped by the Invisible Hand* (Oxford: OUP, 2010).

been lent out either to other financial firms or non-financial firms. Third, it has become clear that techniques designed to mitigate the risk of failure at a single institution are inadequate to mitigate systemic risk.

The most striking lesson of the financial crisis was the inadequacy of contemporary prudential regulation for preserving financial stability. This has resulted in a host of new measures: special regulation for institutions which are deemed to be 'systemically important', and even a new type of regulation—so called 'macroprudential' regulation—which is intended to focus on the stability of the system as a whole. This is discussed in detail in Chapter 19.

3.4.4 Market efficiency

Legislators and regulators view the facilitation of 'efficient capital markets' as part of their goal.[35] However, and rather confusingly, this term is often used in a way that does not relate to the efficiency of capital markets in the more conventional senses discussed in section 3.2, but what is called their 'informational' efficiency. We therefore need to understand what this latter concept is, and how it is related to other senses of efficiency.

Capital markets serve to allocate funds to projects which firms wish to pursue, most obviously when new securities are issued to fund a new project. However, there is a puzzle. Many markets in the financial system are secondary—that is, the trade occurs between investors. To be sure, such trade reallocates the assets between investors, with the asset ending up in the hands of someone who values it more than the original owner. However, unlike primary markets for capital, secondary markets do not affect directly the actions of the firms who have issued the claims. Such trades do not affect the capital available to firms, and consequently do not affect managers' resource constraints.

The existence of secondary markets, as we have seen in Chapter 2,[36] has the benefit of providing liquidity for investors—that is, they can exit the investment quickly if they need cash for whatever reason. The availability of this liquidity will in turn make investors more willing to buy securities in the primary market, because they know that should they suffer a financial shock, they will be able to liquidate their investment quickly. Moreover, the existence of a secondary market in which lots of trading occurs—said to be a 'liquid' market—enables capital markets better to perform the function we described of aggregating information about the value of activities.

The value of most physical assets depends on the attributes of the asset, which can be determined by examination (consider residential real estate, for example). Consequently, such an asset market can in principle achieve allocative efficiency. However, the value of financial assets—stocks or bonds, for example—depends on the resolution of many uncertainties regarding the firm's investment policy and on the control of agency costs associated with the firm's management. In short, these values, rooted in the firm's expected revenue stream, are affected by uncertainties and thus will evolve

---

[35] See eg Prospectus Directive, n 17, recitals 10 and 46 ('market efficiency'); MiFID II, n 17, recital 164 ('efficiency…of the overall market'); Transparency Directive, n 17, recital 1 ('market efficiency').

[36] Chapter 2, section 2.3.2.

over time as uncertainties are resolved. Each new piece of information will affect valuations. If there are no secondary markets, then we must rely on primary markets to assess the expected value of a firm's investment strategy at the outset. This will be difficult to do. Secondary markets allow for an exchange of financial assets where, on the announcement of new information, a different investor to the one holding the asset now values it more highly.[37]

This not only ensures that the financial assets are in the hands of the investors who value them most highly, but it also allows the market price to act as a real-time estimate of the present value of the firm's expected future revenue streams, given its current management and investment policy. The speed and accuracy with which the market price responds to the release of new information is said to be its 'informational efficiency'.[38] The informational efficiency of public securities markets is much debated and the subject of an extensive literature. It is discussed in Chapter 5.

Why is informational efficiency desirable in terms of the functioning of the financial system? Informationally efficient markets stimulate liquidity. To see this, consider a market that is known not to be informationally efficient. In such a market, some parties will assume that their counterparty is buying/selling on the basis of superior information and thus would shade the price at which they will transact. (This is called 'widening the bid-ask spread'.) Other parties would prefer to delay trading until they believe all relevant information has been incorporated into the price. Both scenarios will reduce the number of parties willing to trade and consequently will impede liquidity. Greater liquidity in turn helps to mobilize investors to participate in the market.

Informationally efficient secondary markets also open up new possibilities for monitoring the performance of firms' investment policies. In particular, the market price acts as a continuous-time assessment of the value of the firm under the current investment policy. If managers' actions can be guided by the market price, then this can help to ensure that the firm's investment decisions are allocatively efficient.[39] For this to work well, however, not only must the market incorporate new information rapidly into the price but as much information as possible.

Regulation can help to facilitate the production of such information. Although good firms would benefit from credible disclosure of their attributes, through a lower cost of capital, managers would also be concerned about revealing details of their business model to competitors. Managers may also be reluctant to subject their performance to evaluation by fully informed stock prices. Thus, left to their own devices, corporate managers would likely make less information public than is socially desirable. Corporate information is, in other words, a public good. Mandatory disclosure can thus be

---

[37] This helps us understand why secondary trading in stocks is robust while secondary trading in bonds much less so. Bondholder returns are capped at repayment of principal and interest and for most firms that issue public debt, repayment risk is stable. Bond prices are therefore less 'information sensitive' than those of stocks.

[38] See the discussion in Chapter 5, section 5.2.

[39] J Dow and G Gorton, 'Stock Market Efficiency and Economic Efficiency: Is There a Connection?' (1997) 52 *Journal of Finance* 1087.

understood as subsidizing the production of this information.[40] There is some empirical support for the assertion that increasing the scope of mandatory disclosure is associated with more accurate pricing of securities in public equity markets.[41] This in turn helps advance allocative efficiency, for the reasons we have seen.

3.4.5 Competition

Financial regulation is also concerned with promoting competition in the sector. While there are specialist competition (antitrust) laws and regulators in most jurisdictions, the task of promoting competition in the financial sector is also partly dealt with by financial regulators.

The most obvious example of the promotion of competition concerns the removal of barriers to international competition. In the European Union in particular, much of the legislative policy concerning the financial system has been concerned with establishing pan-European markets in which firms can compete with others throughout the EU.[42] This has been achieved in two steps. First, Member States have been required to drop restrictions on international firms within the EU and to give credit to the regulatory regimes in place in other Member States. As a result, a financial services firm that is licensed to operate in any EU member state is treated as having a 'passport' to market its services throughout the EU, without the imposition by other Member States of any additional regulatory burdens. This freedom is premised upon equivalence of domestic regulatory safeguards. In order to guarantee this, the associated second regulatory step has been to agree on minimum standards that have then been harmonized throughout the EU by European legislation.

There are also a number of instances where competition has actively been promoted within a jurisdiction or series of jurisdictions other than by the development of cross-border markets. For example, in the field of banking, competition can be promoted by the relaxation of prudential regulation, which effectively creates a barrier to entry, or by permitting mutual societies to convert to shareholder ownership in order to raise greater capital. Similarly, in the field of securities trading, the abolition of ties between brokers, dealers, and exchanges creates greater possibilities for competition between venues for trading securities. Each of these initiatives is motivated by the desire to increase the penetration of the relevant financial services through removing anti-competitive practices. One of the most striking examples of where deregulation was used to promote competition was 'Big Bang' in the UK in 1986, which removed the prohibitions to the free entry of new participants and the restrictive practices that previously existed in UK financial markets. Similarly, in the US, fixed commissions for

---

[40] JC Coffee, Jr, 'Market Failure and the Economic Case for a Mandatory Disclosure System' (1984) 70 *Virginia Law Review* 717.

[41] MB Fox, R Morck, B Yeung, and A Durnev, 'Law, Share Price Accuracy, and Economic Performance: The New Evidence' (2003) 102 *Michigan Law Review* 331.

[42] This is recognized in legislative measures: see eg Prospectus Directive, n 17, recital 41; Transparency Directive, n 17, recital 36; UCITS V Directive, n 22, recital 3; see also National Securities Market Improvement Act 1996 (US) §106, requiring the SEC, when exercising rulemaking powers under US securities legislation, to consider, 'in addition to the protection of investors, whether the action will promote efficiency, *competition*, and capital formation' (emphasis added).

stock trading were eliminated on 1 May 1975, 'May Day', and in 2000 the SEC ended a market rule that confined trading of securities listed on the New York Stock Exchange ('NYSE') to the NYSE itself. Thus, the way was opened for new entrants and new forms of stock market trading.

3.4.6 Preventing financial crime

The prevention of financial crime is a primary goal of financial regulation in many countries. It is mentioned explicitly, for example, as a matter to which the UK's Financial Conduct Authority must have regard in performing its general functions.[43] This goal is also implemented elsewhere by specific legislation.[44] However, there is a question mark as to the extent to which this is genuinely an independent goal of financial regulation or merely a means of achieving other goals.

In a loose sense, 'financial crime' might be understood as any criminal act associated with the financial system.[45] This would then encompass many instances of criminal liability imposed in order to further the goals of financial regulation we have already considered—for example, liability for insider trading or fraudulent misstatements in disclosures to investors. Preventing crimes of this type is not an independent goal of financial regulation; rather, it is simply an instrument for achieving the regulatory goals that criminal sanctions support.

However, we can distinguish a particular sense of 'financial crime', the prevention of which is not parasitic on other goals of the financial system. Such prohibitions are concerned with preventing the financial system from being used for ends judged to be socially harmful, namely public bads (negative externalities)—the opposite of public goods. It includes: (i) the use of financial services by criminal and terrorist organizations, justifying prohibitions on money laundering and terrorist financing; (ii) the making of payments designed to influence a decision-maker improperly—that is, bribery and corruption; (iii) the making of payments associated with trade which is in prohibited goods (such as slavery, weapons, endangered species) or with countries on which economic sanctions have been imposed; and (iv) the use of the financial system to hide assets from tax authorities and creditors.

3.4.7 Other goals of financial regulation?

Financial regulators cite a number of other goals, some of which are simply restatements of the foregoing. For example, a number of regulatory pronouncements speak of the desirability of 'lowering the cost of capital' for firms,[46] or of promoting 'capital

---

[43] Financial Services and Markets Act 2000 (as amended by the Financial Services Act 2012), s 1B(5)(b).

[44] In the EU, the Anti-Money Laundering Directive 2005/60/EC [2005] OJ L309/15, and the US, the Bank Secrecy Act (Currency and Foreign Transactions Reporting Act of 1970) and the Patriot Act (Uniting and Strengthening America by Providing Appropriate Tools Required to Intercept and Obstruct Terrorism (USA PATRIOT) Act of 2001).

[45] See eg Financial Services and Markets Act 2000 ('FSMA') (UK), s 1H(3) ('financial crime' defined as including fraud or dishonesty, misconduct in, or misuse of information relating to, a financial market, handling the proceeds of crime, or the financing of terrorism).

[46] See eg Prospectus Directive, n 17, recital 41; Transparency Directive, n 17, recital 36.

formation'.[47] These may be expected to flow from the achievement of the goals of investor protection and enhancement of market efficiency we have described.

Others are implicit in the way in which an economic case for regulation is framed. For example, the recitals to a number of the relevant EU Directives speak of the need to 'balance costs and benefits', and the need to 'encourage innovation in financial markets'.[48] Making an economic case for regulatory intervention presupposes not only that there is in principle a failure in the market, but also that regulatory intervention can put it right (or at least improve on the status quo).

In assessing this question, the fact that regulation brings with it costs must be taken into account, so that the case for regulation focuses on establishing the existence of *net* benefits where the benefits to society from intervention exceed the costs. This is not so much an independent goal of financial regulation, as a statement of the appropriate process to be followed in reaching the goals.[49] One important challenge is that assessing the costs and benefits of a financial regulatory change is often very difficult in practice,[50] particularly because important rule changes may result in considerable change to the financial system itself, in ways that are not readily predictable.[51] But cost-benefit analysis can still provide a valuable check on the rationality of policymaking, if applied insofar as the quantitative evidence will permit. Thus, a modest enquiry in the face of pervasive uncertainty might simply seek to articulate what sorts of benefits and costs a proposed rule might have (without necessarily quantifying them).[52] Or, if a range of possible estimates can be produced, policymakers can seek to satisfy themselves that the benefits of a measure are at least likely to *exceed* the costs (a 'breakeven' test).[53] The extent to which these sorts of refinements can be deployed may depend on whether cost-benefit analysis is seen simply as a tool for good policymaking,[54] or whether—as is sometimes the case in the US—it is subject to scrutiny in judicial review of the authority of regulatory action.[55]

Throughout this book we will often argue for the importance, indeed priority, of financial stability as a regulatory goal. Pursuit of this goal raises particular challenges for a decision procedure like cost-benefit analysis. The sums involved are vast—tens of billions, even trillions. In a thoughtful recent critique of the use of cost-benefit analysis

---

[47] National Securities Market Improvement Act 1996 (US) §106.

[48] See sources cited in n 42.

[49] See eg Financial Services Authority (UK), *Practical Cost-Benefit Analysis for Financial Regulators Version 1.1* (2000), 5–6.

[50] JC Coates IV, 'Cost-Benefit Analysis of Financial Regulation: Case Studies and Implications' (2015) 124 *Yale Law Journal* 882; cf EA Posner and EG Weyl, 'Benefit-Cost Analysis for Financial Regulation' (2013) 103 *American Economic Review* 393.

[51] JN Gordon, 'The Empty Call for Benefit-Cost Analysis for Financial Regulation' (2014) 43 *Journal of Legal Studies* 351. A classic example is Glass–Steagall's divorce of commercial banking from investing banking.

[52] See Coates, n 50, 891–8 (distinguishing 'conceptual' from 'quantified' cost-benefit analysis).

[53] CR Sunstein, 'Financial Regulation and Cost-Benefit Analysis' (2015) *Yale Law Journal Forum* 263.

[54] For example, in the UK, financial regulators are required to produce a 'detailed cost-benefit analysis' as part of their consultation process over new rules, but in order to exercise their powers validly are held only to the lesser standard of 'hav[ing] regard to' the principle that 'burdens' should be 'proportionate' to their expected benefits: FSMA 2000, ss 3B(1)(b), 138I, 138J.

[55] See *Business Roundtable v SEC* 647 F.3d 1144 (CADC, 2011); SEC Memo, *Current Guidance on Economic Analysis in SEC Rulemakings*, 16 March 2012.

in financial regulation, John Coates argues that the regulators' efforts to quantify in this domain are inevitably based on arbitrary choices and do not serve as an independent check on the regulators' decision-making.[56] The regulators need decision tools, however, and framing policy choices as regards financial stability in terms of trade-offs and immediate and foreseeable consequences, while marshalling whatever quantitative or qualitative evidence is available, may be the most that our limited foresight will permit.

The justifications we have discussed all have in mind the over-arching goal of enhancing efficiency. A final category of policy goals, which are based on distributional outcomes, stands distinct from this. It is not uncommon for policymakers to seek to further distributional goals through the financial system. For example, during the opening years of the twenty-first century, policymakers in the US sought to facilitate house purchases by large numbers of Americans who previously would not have been considered wealthy enough to do so. This was associated with an increase in the extension of mortgage credit. Similarly, in many developing countries, the extension of the availability of credit to citizens is viewed as a goal in its own right, regardless of their quality as borrowers. And we shall see in Chapter 10 that the regulation of consumer financial services may also be understood as furthering distributional, as well as efficiency-related, goals.

3.4.8 The regulatory objective function

We have articulated six goals of financial regulation that respond to distinct market failures and which regulators are tasked with implementing. A key challenge they pose is that the goals are often in tension and sometimes in conflict with one another. It is necessary to understand how the goals may conflict and to develop a framework for resolving such conflicts to arrive at an 'objective function' for regulators.

Investor and consumer protection may conflict with financial stability by reducing diversity in the financial system. Microprudential rules designed to reduce agency costs in financial institutions may have the effect of channelling large pools of capital into a restricted number of investment types and strategies. The application of restrictions on the types of investment in which consumers may participate increases the correlation of investment strategies at the level of the system as a whole, and reduces its resilience to systemic shocks.

Such restrictions may also have implications for informational efficiency. Restrictions on the ways in which institutional investors can trade in the market may increase the possibility of herding, which makes it more difficult for arbitrageurs to act to correct pricing anomalies and distortions.[57]

The promotion of competition amongst providers of financial services may also be in tension with other goals. Most obviously, excessive competition amongst financial

---

[56] See Coates, n 50.

[57] There may also be a tension with financial stability. In times of crisis, the short selling of financial institution shares may contribute to so-called 'equity runs'. If creditors of these institutions look to the share price for an indication of expectations, then this may become self-fulfilling. Consequently, a number of jurisdictions saw fit to impose restrictions on the short selling of financial institution stock during the financial crisis. This, however, makes it harder to control any upward price pressure.

institutions results in lower profitability and consequently an urge to engage in more risky activities.[58] This is inimical to financial stability. Eliminating interest rate caps on consumer savings accounts encourages a competition for deposits that benefits consumers, but it may also lead banks to favour riskier loans with high yields. This too can threaten financial stability. Competition also encourages firms to focus on the dimensions of their products most salient to consumers, cutting costs along other dimensions. If consumers cannot assess those other dimensions, inferior products may result.[59]

In thinking about how the pursuit of these goals should be prioritized, regulators need to think about the corpus of financial regulation in the round, and whether the various aspects combine to maximize overall efficiency of the financial system without undercutting one another. This has two important implications. The first relates to the relative size of the stakes as among different regulatory goals. The Sarbanes–Oxley Act of 2002, which targeted investor protection, is estimated to have had an impact ranging somewhere between a net cost of $289 billion and a net benefit of $317 billion.[60] The UK FSA's introduction of 'affordability' checks for mortgage borrowers in the UK, intended as a consumer protection measure, was associated with a net benefit estimated by the FSA at around $9 billion.[61] These are all large numbers. Yet the introduction of Basel III, a measure primarily seeking to further financial stability, has cost estimates in trillions, and benefit estimates in tens of trillions, of dollars:[62] orders of magnitude larger than the numbers discussed in relation to any of the other measures. This implies that the amounts at stake in relation to financial stability, at least for mature financial systems, significantly outweigh the amounts at stake as regards other regulatory goals.

The second implication is for the design of regulatory institutions: at least one agency needs to be tasked with thinking about these issues and determining a regulatory objective function. This agency should have access to information on a system-wide basis and the power to tell other agencies when to rein in (or expand) their activities in accordance with the regulatory objective function. In our view, the agency best placed to perform this function is the one tasked with macroprudential oversight of the system as a whole.[63]

3.5 The Strategies of Financial Regulation

Financial regulation around the world employs a discrete number of techniques to achieve the goals we have outlined. We group these into seven 'strategies', which are set

---

[58] X Vives, 'Competition and Stability in Banking: A New World for Competition Policy?', Working Paper (2009), IESE Business School.

[59] Competition amongst trading platforms can also undermine the goal of promoting informational efficiency. This is because price formation only operates on the basis of trades actually occurring and announced in a given marketplace. Trading in smaller venues may result in lower costs for participants, but will make price aggregation less effective: see RA Schwartz and R Francioni, *Equity Markets in Action* (2004), 318–28.

[60] Coates, n 50, 946.

[61] Ibid, 989 (citing FSA, *Mortgage Market Review: Proposed Package of Reforms*, Consultation Paper 11/31, 2011).

[62] Ibid, 959–74.   [63] See further Chapters 19 and 27.

Table 3.1 Strategies of Financial Regulation

Scope of obligations: Regulatory strategy	User	Firm	Sectoral
Ex ante strategies			
Entry regulation	Participation Profiling	Licensing Qualification requirements Product regulation Structural restrictions	Market power
Conduct regulation	Trading rules	Trading restrictions Conduct of business	
Information regulation	Education	Disclosure	
Prudential regulation		Balance sheet	Macroprudential
Governance regulation		Board structure Compensation regulation Risk management Ownership restrictions	
Ex post strategies			
Insurance	Insurance	Lender of last resort Bail-outs	Lender of last resort Bail-outs
Resolution		Resolution procedures	

out in Table 3.1.[64] The exercise of grouping is undertaken so as to facilitate an overview, from a high level, of the different mechanisms employed in financial regulation. This enables us to think about their interrelationships with each other, and with the financial system. In particular, it helps us to escape from the 'silos' approach that afflicts many other treatments of financial regulation. The classification is therefore not intended to be definitive: it is offered simply as a heuristic device rather than a traditional legal taxonomy.[65]

We categorize these seven core strategies of financial regulation in two ways. First, we classify the strategies according to the timing of their application. *Ex ante* strategies apply from the moment at which the investment is made or the activity carried out. There are five *ex ante* strategies described in this section: entry, conduct, information, prudential, and governance regulation. *Ex post* strategies apply only if something goes wrong. Insurance and resolution are examples of *ex post* strategies. This division is set out in the rows of Table 3.1.

Second, we classify the strategies by the *scope* of the obligations they impose. This is shown in the columns in Table 3.1. 'User'-based obligations restrict the actions of investors, consumers, and customers of financial products or services.

---

[64] Analysing regulatory techniques in terms of generic strategies has an influential pedigree within legal scholarship: see eg RC Clark, 'The Soundness of Financial Intermediaries' (1976) 86 *Yale Law Journal* 1; R Kraakman, J Armour, P Davies, L Enriques, H Hansmann, G Hertig, K Hopt, H Kanda, M Pargendler, WG Ringe, and E Rock, *The Anatomy of Corporate Law*, 3rd ed (Oxford: OUP, 2016), Ch 2.

[65] Questions of taxonomy are traditionally very important for legal scholars because the categorization of an obligation can affect the chances of a successful claim, through the application of defences, procedure, limitations, etc. None of these consequences flows from the classification offered here. It is simply offered as an expository device. This means that the test of its utility is whether it helps you to understand the field.

Firm-based obligations apply to firms offering, or advising upon, financial products. Sector-based obligations apply to firms offering, or advising upon, financial products conditional on the behaviour of other firms in the sector.

3.5.1 Entry

Entry regulation affects the ability of (would-be) participants in the financial system to engage in financial transactions with other participants. From the user's perspective, this means participation restrictions.[66] These inhibit the ability of market players to engage in particular sorts of financial transaction. For example, many types of security and investment product may only be offered to 'sophisticated' investors. Formally, the legal obligation to abstain from offering is imposed on the putative offeror, but the effect is primarily felt by the unsophisticated investor, who consequently may not participate in markets for securities of this type.[67]

The entry of financial firms is subject to licensing requirements: regulators must grant approval to the firm prior to it opening its doors for business. To a large degree, licensing regimes are simply a means of enforcing the other firm-based regulatory techniques. Initial and continuing compliance is made a condition of the grant of a licence, with the consequence that the sanction for non-compliance could be the cessation of the firm's business. However, licensing also entails independent requirements, especially depending on the identity and character of the owners and managers of the firm. In particular, this seeks to weed out those with a history of having committed fraud or other serious violations of financial regulations.

Another version of entry regulation affects the ability of firms to offer particular types of product to (particular types of) investors.[68] We term this 'product regulation', although in the US it is often referred to as 'merit regulation'. Because the 'products' offered by financial services firms are in fact contracts, this type of regulation is really the substantive regulation of the relevant contractual terms.

Structural restrictions, which impose limitations on the nature or scope of the business that may be carried on by certain types of financial firm, are another form of entry regulation: policymakers segment the financial sector to reduce systemic risk, conflicts of interest, or both. Examples of structural restrictions are the separation between commercial and investment banking, in force for decades in the US during the twentieth century, the distinction between brokers and jobbers in force for centuries in the UK, and the US Volcker Rule precluding banks from engaging in proprietary trading, which came into force in 2015.[69]

Finally, at the level of the sector, regulators are concerned with whether the market power of particular players creates a barrier to entry by other firms who might wish to offer similar products. In contrast to the individual and firm-level application of entry regulation, at the sector level, this strategy applies not to restrict entry, but to foster it. While the explicit goal of each of the other examples of entry regulation so far

---

[66] See Chapter 8, section 8.4.2.
[67] The offeror remains free to market such securities to 'sophisticated' investors.
[68] See Chapters 12, section 12.3.2.   [69] See Chapter 23.

considered is geared towards protecting users, such as investors and consumers, entry regulation based on market power is concerned with fostering competition.

Clearly, there may be tension between the different types of entry regulation: licensing requirements create barriers to entry, whereas the regulation of market power seeks to overcome barriers. Entry regulation can also have unintended implications for the other regulatory goals. Encouraging entry into the banking sector will reduce the extent to which banks can earn supracompetitive profits ('rents') from their activities. This in turn may stimulate them to engage in more risky activities, as the consequences of failure—loss of the ability to participate in their current market—will be less costly to their owners.[70] And encouraging entry into the provision of financial market services can result in the fragmentation of trading venues with less effective information aggregation. Conversely, restricting the entry of financial products reduces the diversity of financial contracts deployed and may thereby have adverse implications for financial stability.[71]

3.5.2 Conduct

Conduct regulation dictates appropriate standards of conduct to participants in the financial system. From the perspective of both users and firms, there are trading restrictions, which affect the way in which trades in securities may be conducted.[72] Specifically, actions taken to manipulate market prices are generally prohibited, as is trading on the basis of inside information. These restrictions are geared towards promoting market liquidity.

For financial firms, the most extensive category of conduct regulation comprises conduct of business rules.[73] These direct the way in which firms are expected to carry on their businesses. Three sets of issues are particularly important: first, the ways in which firms deal with clients and/or customers, focusing on marketing, advertising, and sales techniques; second, the handling of client assets, focusing on custody and segregation requirements; and third, the management of conflicts of interest by financial firms. These restrictions are most clearly concerned with the protection of users such as clients, customers, and consumers.

Regulators are also concerned with financial firms' conduct from the perspective of competition. In particular, collusion between firms so as to support prices or restrict supply is universally prohibited as a matter of antitrust law, which also applies to the financial sector. The regulation of collusive behaviour is concerned with the promotion of competition in the financial sector.

3.5.3 Information

This category of regulation comprises rules intended to secure the dissemination and comprehension of information about financial firms and products. From the user's

---

[70] See Vives, n 58.
[71] Roberta Romano, 'For Diversity in International Regulation of Financial Institutions: Critiquing and Recalibrating the Basel Architecture' (2014) 31 *Yale Journal on Regulation* 1.
[72] See Chapter 9.   [73] See Chapter 11; see also section 12.3.3.

perspective, an important technique is education.[74] Strictly speaking, this does not impose any legal obligation on users—rather, legal obligations to provide education are imposed on public bodies.[75] However, if education is provided, the onus is upon users to make use of it to improve their understanding. Consequently, users of the financial system who do not make use of educational provision are likely to find themselves at a disadvantage. In this sense, they are subject to practical obligations by the provision of education.

From the standpoint of firms, the principal technique of information regulation is disclosure.[76] This compels the provision of information to customers, investors, and regulators about financial products and firms' investment strategies. Specifically, it comprises: first, mandatory pre-contractual disclosure as a means of informing investors and consumers about financial products and securities; second, the imposition of initial, periodic, and event-driven disclosure requirements on issuers of securities so as to promote the informational efficiency of markets for securities; and third, obligations on financial firms to report details of their balance sheets and investment strategies to regulators charged with maintaining an overview of risk in the financial system as a whole.

Information regulation, especially disclosure, serves a number of goals. Disclosure to contractual counterparties can be understood in terms of investor or consumer protection; public disclosure can be understood as seeking to enhance the informational efficiency of financial markets, and reporting to regulators can be seen as assisting in their task of maintaining financial stability.

3.5.4 Prudence

The fourth form of regulation comprises rules that direct how financial firms shall manage their assets and liabilities.[77] It includes: first, rules on capital adequacy which require banks and other financial institutions to maintain a minimum level of net assets and to ensure a certain proportion of their liabilities are subordinated;[78] second, rules on assets requiring a certain proportion of asset holdings to be of a liquid character;[79] and third, rules restricting the riskiness of investment and insurance firms' asset portfolios, including prohibitions on the purchase of particular asset classes and procedural obligations regarding portfolio management and risk allocation.[80]

Prudential regulation has principally been understood as imposing obligations on individual firms with the goal of ensuring their safety and soundness, independently of

---

[74] See Chapter 10, section 10.4.1.

[75] See eg FSMA 2000 (UK) s 3S (obligation on FCA to establish a 'consumer financial education body' to educate members of the public about financial matters and how to manage their financial affairs); Dodd–Frank Act of 2010 (US), §1021(c)(1) (one of the functions of the newly established Consumer Financial Protection Bureau is 'conducting financial education programs'). See also European Commission Communication on Financial Education, COM(2007) 808 final, 8 (exhorting Member States to ensure financial education is 'actively promoted').

[76] See Chapter 8 and Chapter 12, section 12.3.1.

[77] Clark terms this 'portfolio regulation' (Clark, n 64, 44), but 'prudential' is much more a part of the regulatory lexicon.

[78] Chapter 14.   [79] Chapter 15.   [80] See Chapter 12, section 12.4 and Chapter 22.

the actions of other firms. Such firm-level or 'microprudential' rules are best understood as being concerned with the protection of users, such as investors and consumers. However, since the financial crisis, it has become clear that this approach is not itself sufficient to ensure stability of the financial system as a whole. Prudential regulation may in fact have unintended consequences for financial stability. By imposing substantive restrictions on which types of asset may be purchased, and/or procedural obligations regarding the ways in which risks must be managed, rules of this kind may artificially stimulate demand for particular types of asset class and increase the overall correlation of investment strategies.

Interconnectedness of firms' assets and liabilities, and correlations in their investment strategies, significantly affect the stability of the system as a whole. Consequently, the new technique of 'macroprudential' regulation imposes portfolio restrictions on firms, classes of firm, or whole sectors, according to how investment strategies interrelate.[81]

3.5.5 Governance

This strategy is exclusively focused on financial firms. It relates to the way in which such firms are organized and managed.[82] Most obviously, this strategy includes rules about executive compensation, board structure, and directors' duties for certain financial firms. These sorts of rules comprise the traditional domain of 'corporate governance'. Governance requirements have traditionally been understood as investor protection measures. However, the negative externalities associated with risk-taking by large financial institutions mean that their governance has implications for the stability of the financial system as a whole. There may also be unintended consequences. The regulation of the compensation of money managers, for example, affects their incentives regarding trading behaviour, and consequently may have implications for the effectiveness of financial markets—where trading is dominated by such money managers—at aggregating new information.

Governance also relates to combination restrictions, which deal with mergers and acquisitions by financial firms of one another. Such restrictions are concerned both with the promotion of competition in financial services and with financial stability.

3.5.6 Insurance

Each of the foregoing five strategies can be understood as operating *ex ante*; that is, at the time that an investor parts with her money (or a consumer borrows it), regulation is already shaping the investor's relationship with the financial firm and how that firm may deal with the funds. The penultimate strategy we identify, which we term 'insurance', operates *ex post*. It is triggered by the failure, or financial distress, of a financial firm. The strategy operates to provide a backup provision of liquidity at this point.

---

[81] See Chapter 19.   [82] See Chapter 17.

From the user's standpoint, the insurance strategy is implemented through investor and depositor insurance regimes. The most obvious example of these is deposit insurance schemes, which provide (retail) depositors in failed banks with compensation.[83] However, there are other insurance schemes. Best known of these is the lender of last resort ('LOLR') function played by the central bank. Traditionally, this was seen as a way of providing emergency liquidity assistance—or 'liquidity insurance'—to a temporarily troubled financial institution.[84] However, in recent years LOLR has evolved into a way in which the central bank can assist in restructuring the balance sheets of troubled entities, through lending against inferior collateral. This might be characterized as a type of 'asset insurance'.

Another form of 'insurance' for financial institutions tends to be offered through the provision of state bail-outs. These have been characterized as 'capital insurance' for financial firms, because, through such schemes, the taxpayer effectively insures investors in the troubled firm against loss of their capital through its failure.[85] Both the extension of LOLR and the provision of bail-outs create problems of moral hazard for individual firms. Consequently, the deployment of these techniques is only justified by reference to the adverse impact of the failure of financial firms on the economy at large.

3.5.7 Resolution

Finally, the post-financial crisis environment has seen much interest in *resolution* mechanisms, designed to operate more quickly and effectively than ordinary insolvency law so as to avoid the destructive loss of value associated with a bank failure.[86] These seek to introduce private capital to troubled financial institutions, rather than rely on state support. One version involves the sale of the troubled entity to a competitor; another anticipates an automatic reduction of its liabilities. In the former case, the purchaser effectively becomes guarantor for the troubled firm's liabilities; in the latter case, the existing creditors are forced to take a haircut and thereby insure protected creditors who do not participate in the restructuring.

Each of these examples of insurance and resolution strategies in financial regulation is usually understood in terms of promoting financial stability: reducing the probability of bank runs and bank failure, or the severity of the consequences of bank failure. However, they could also be understood in terms of user protection, as each one—most clearly deposit insurance—has the effect of protecting a particular class of user against loss. The provision of insurance for troubled financial firms also has competition-related implications where public support provided to an institution enables it to continue in business where others, without support, would not. This could constitute illegitimate state aid under EU competition law rules.

---

[83] See Chapter 15, sections 15.4–15.5 and Chapter 16, section 16.2.

[84] P Alessandri and AG Haldane, 'Banking on the State', Bank of England (2009) (speech given at 12th Annual Federal Reserve Bank of Chicago International Banking Conference, September 2009), 4.

[85] Ibid, 6.   [86] See Chapter 16.

3.6 Conclusion

This chapter has provided an economic analysis for financial regulation. It has started from the efficiency properties of markets and the allocative, productive, and dynamic efficiency of competitive markets. It has then considered the market failures that may undermine the achievement of these properties of markets and the adverse distributional as well as efficiency consequences that may result.

The chapter then discussed the goals of regulation and argued that each of the goals can be related to a particular type of market failure. It considered the potential conflicts that can arise in pursuit of different goals and the way in which these should addressed through the derivation of a regulatory objective function. Finally, the chapter has examined seven strategies that are available to regulators and related these to the attainment of the goals of regulation.

You should come away from this chapter with an understanding of the economic basis of financial regulation and how it can help guide the formulation of regulatory policy. This will provide the underpinnings for the discussion of regulation of different parts of the financial system in the remainder of the book.

4

The Limits of Financial Regulation

4.1 Introduction

The last chapter provided a stylized description of financial regulation and its economic foundations. There are market failures that need to be corrected to promote market efficiency and desirable distributional outcomes. There are a range of goals of regulation and a set of tools available to the regulator. The regulator then selects the regulatory tools that are best suited to achieving the goals and correcting the market failures. It is analogous to flying a plane or driving a car. There is a destination, a starting point, and a route to navigate using rudders and steering wheels to go from where we are to where we want to be.

If only it were actually so simple: financial regulation would be straightforward and protection of the financial system would have been largely solved. Unfortunately, it is not. The process of identifying market failures, determining appropriate regulatory instruments, and seeing to their implementation is fraught with difficulties. The 'dynamics' of regulation by which the content of regulation changes over time (rule-making) and is translated from 'rules on the books' into 'rules in action' (supervision and enforcement) is highly complex. Financial services and financial institutions are in a continuous state of flux, making it difficult for regulators to keep pace.[1] It is as if the ultimate destination of the plane and car is continuously moving and the pilot and driver are peering through a fog to see where they are supposed to be going. These dynamic aspects of regulation are extremely important in determining its efficacy. To this end, we devote the whole of Part F to their consideration. The present chapter serves simply to introduce these topics, with a view to grounding some of the subsequent discussion in the following sections.

For the regulator, the evolving nature of financial markets poses substantial *informational challenges*. These are introduced in section 4.2 and considered in more detail in Chapter 27. Plane-flying or car-driving analogies break down because regulators are dealing with people rather than mechanical objects. A car does not in general have a mind of its own. In contrast, financial firms respond to regulation and modify their business practices to minimize its impact on them.[2] These sorts of adjustment, the more aggressive forms of which are known as *regulatory arbitrage*, can cause regulation to fail to achieve its purpose. We discuss these issues in section 4.3.

Another area of complexity relates to the *institutional structure* of the regulators. In Chapter 3, we saw the difficulty a social planner might face in specifying an 'objective

---

[1] See eg D Awrey, 'Complexity, Innovation and the Regulation of Modern Financial Markets' (2012) 2 *Harvard Business Law Review* 235.
[2] M Brunnermeier, A Crocket, C Goodhart, AD Persaud, and H Shin, *Fundamental Principles of Financial Regulation*, Geneva Reports on the World Economy 11 (Geneva: ICMB/CEPR, 2009), 63–9.

Principles of Financial Regulation. First Edition. John Armour, Dan Awrey, Paul Davies, Luca Enriques, Jeffrey N. Gordon, Colin Mayer, and Jennifer Payne. © John Armour, Dan Awrey, Paul Davies, Luca Enriques, Jeffrey N. Gordon, Colin Mayer, and Jennifer Payne 2016. Published 2016 by Oxford University Press.

function' for regulation.[3] Even if this could be specified, there follows a very difficult set of issues regarding implementation. What should be the relationship between regulatory goals and the structure or 'architecture' of the regulatory agencies? These questions are reviewed briefly in section 4.4 and treated in more depth in Chapters 24 and 27.

The problems of implementation are, however, not simply questions of regulatory architecture. Rather, there are continuous 'frictions' in rule-making and enforcement. At the simplest level, these are 'principal–agent' problems that are characteristic of any large organization, whether a corporation[4] or a government bureaucracy.[5] 'Principals', whether legislators or shareholders, find that their 'agents'—such as corporate managers (for shareholders) or the staff at regulatory agencies (for legislators)—pursue their own goals rather than their principal's goal. The goals of agency staffers can include personal career objectives within the agency as well as the possibilities in the 'revolving door' to private-sector employment.[6]

There are also particular problems that flow from the fact that critical actors in the system, legislators, are focused on re-election, a kind of self-interest that may result in deviations from optimal regulation from a public interest perspective—as would emerge from the kind of analysis discussed in Chapter 3—and that may produce sub-optimal enforcement of existing regulations as well. These problems, which we outline in section 4.5 and discuss in more depth in Chapter 25, fly under the flag of 'political economy'. As with the analysis of market failures reviewed in Chapter 3, section 3.3, there is now a well-developed framework for analysing the frictions that emerge in public goods provision, of which regulation is a subset.[7] As we shall see, what is particularly pernicious about the political economy of financial regulation is that it is likely to weaken regulation precisely when it is needed most.

The international character of the financial system raises particular problems of political economy, which are outlined in section 4.6 and considered more fully in Chapter 28. Financial firms are highly mobile, and nations may compete with one another to attract them. This imposes an additional constraint on the ability of domestic politicians and regulators to implement rules that further the public interest.

It bears emphasis that real-world challenges to the adoption and enforcement of regulation do not undermine the usefulness of the idealized economics of financial regulation described in the previous chapter. To the contrary: the economic analysis provides a basis for understanding the purpose of regulation and the direction in which it should be heading. What this chapter introduces are the real-world complexities that arise in the implementation of the economic roadmap. Clearly defined economic analysis generates ideas and initiatives that have the power to make a real difference to the way in

---

[3] Chapter 3, section 3.4.8.

[4] M Jensen and W Meckling, 'Theory of the Firm: Managerial Behavior, Agency Costs and Ownership Structure' (1976) 3 *Journal of Financial Economics* 305.

[5] T Moe, 'The New Economics of Organization' (1984) 78 *American Journal of Political Science* 739.

[6] See L Enriques and G Hertig, 'Improving the Governance of Financial Supervisors' (2011) 12 *European Business Organization Law Review* 357, 361–5 (more broadly describing the 'bundle of incentives' that drives supervisory agency staffers and executives).

[7] See eg T Besley, *Principled Agents? The Political Economy of Good Government* (Oxford: OUP, 2006).

which the financial system functions, even against the backdrop of this chapter. In section 4.7, we consider two post-crisis examples: first, the new intellectual framework for 'macroprudential' regulation; and second, the advances in international cooperation that led to the establishment of the Financial Stability Board, the most remarkable example of international financial regulation since the post-World War II settlement.

4.2 The Informational Challenge

The financial system is very complex. Understanding this complexity creates an enormous challenge for regulators. The size of the problem can be crudely illustrated by numbers. Table 4.1 describes the size of the economy in terms of Gross Domestic Product (GDP) and the size of the domestic financial system (the sum of domestic deposit bank assets, domestic bonds, and domestic stock market capitalization) for four developed economies—the UK, the US, Germany, and Switzerland. In each case, the measures of the value of claims in the financial system add up to more than national GDP. This implies an enormous number of contractual arrangements supporting these financial claims as well as the internationalization of finance.

Table 4.1 also sets out summary data about the resources available to financial regulators in each of these countries. In Germany, for example, BaFin is charged with the supervision both of banks and financial markets. BaFin spent $0.2 billion on its operations in 2011, to supervise a financial system with claims totalling approximately $7,300 billion ($7.3 trillion). To accomplish this supervision, BaFin employed 2,151 personnel. A crude calculation suggests that each of these employees must therefore supervise the production of financial claims worth on average $3.4 billion. This seems to be asking rather a lot of staff paid an average of $65,000 per annum. The challenge facing regulators in the UK, the US, and Switzerland is of a similar order of magnitude.

Moreover, large international financial institutions have grown to a scale which puts them in an order of size and complexity equivalent to the financial systems of many

Table 4.1 Size of economies, resources of domestic financial regulators and major financial institutions, 2011

Country			Global bank headquartered in country				Domestic regulators	
Name	GDP ($tn)	Financial system depth ($tn)	Name	Assets ($tn)	Net income ($bn)	Employees	Budget ($bn)	Employees
UK	2.4	8.4	Barclays	2.5	4.8	149,700	0.8	3,439
US	15.1	42.0	Citigroup	1.9	11.1	226,000	5.5	21,735
Germany	3.6	7.3	Deutsche Bank	2.8	5.6	100,996	0.2	2,151
Switzerland	0.6	4.0	UBS	1.5	4.5	64,820	0.1	396

Sources: Financial institutions and regulators' annual reports for 2011/12, World Bank, *Global Financial Development 2010*. 'Domestic regulators': for UK, includes FSA; for US, Federal Reserve, OCC, FDIC, SEC, CFTC; for Germany, BaFin; for Switzerland, FINMA.

nation states. Table 4.1 also illustrates this by identifying four international financial institutions which have their respective headquarters in each of the countries represented in the table. For example, Barclays plc, headquartered in the UK, has global assets which at the end of 2011 were valued at $2.5 trillion, almost a third of the size of the entire stock of UK domestic financial assets and larger than the UK's GDP for the year.

The enormous scale of operations of such institutions has two implications for the informational challenge faced by regulators. First, and most obviously, the regulators will find the internal organization of such institutions at least as hard to comprehend as the structure of the external claims in the financial system at large. In the case of Barclays, the firm's global net revenues for 2011 were $4.8 billion, six times the total operating budget of the UK's then-unified financial regulator, the FSA. Another way to measure the complexity of the regulators' task is simply to count the number of discrete business units within large banking organizations. As of 2007 Barclays, for example, operated through 1,003 subsidiaries in 73 countries.[8]

Second, and more perniciously, global financial institutions have far greater resources they can devote to understanding the financial system than do regulators. In 2011, for example, Barclays employed 149,700 people worldwide, compared to the FSA's 3,439. The clear implication is that large financial institutions have a running advantage over regulators in understanding the financial system at large.

The informational challenge is made yet more pronounced for regulators by the continual *change* in the financial system. Much of this change is driven by innovation in financial products and processes. Such innovations are fostered by a range of things, including technological advances that enable more rapid transmission of information and more complex calculations, macroeconomic instability creating demand for ways to manage volatility, and the introduction of new regulations itself.[9] 'Financial innovations' generally mean new ways of structuring financial contracts. Those firms which introduce such innovations typically enjoy excess profits for a period afterwards.[10] However, this period is very short because innovation in contract design generally receives very limited intellectual property protection.[11] This means that competitors can quickly replicate new contractual innovations, fear of which in turn stimulates the

---

[8] And Citibank operated through 2,435 subsidiaries in 84 countries: R Herring and J Carmassi, 'The Corporate Structure of International Financial Conglomerates: Complexity and Its Implications for Safety and Soundness', in N Berger, P Molyneux, and JOS Wilson (eds), *The Oxford Handbook of Banking* (Oxford: OUP, 2010), Table 8.1. For a more detailed account of organizational complexity, see N Cetorelli and LS Goldberg, 'Measures of Global Bank Complexity' (2014) FRBNY *Economic Policy Review* 107.

[9] P Tufano, 'Financial Innovation', in GM Constantinides, M Harris, and R Stulz (eds), *Handbook of the Economics of Finance* (New York, NY: Elsevier, 2003), 307, 313–22; WS Frame and LJ White, 'Empirical Studies of Financial Innovation: Lots of Talk, Little Action?' (2004) 42 *Journal of Economic Literature* 116, 120–2.

[10] P Tufano, 'Financial Innovation and First-Mover Advantages' (1989) 25 *Journal of Financial Economics* 213; E Schroth, 'Innovation, Differentiation, and the Choice of an Underwriter: Evidence from Equity-Linked Securities' (2006) 19 *Review of Financial Studies* 1041.

[11] This changed in the US in 1998, when it was confirmed that 'business process patents' could be awarded for certain financial innovations: see *State Street Bank and Trust v Signature Financial Group* 149 F.3d 1368 (Fed Cir 1998). As might be expected, this provoked a significant uptick in the number of patents sought of this type: J Lerner, 'Where Does *State Street* Lead? A First Look at Finance Patents, 1971 to 2000' (2002) 57 *Journal of Finance* 901. The US Supreme Court has recently cut back the ease of obtaining such a patent. See *Alice Corp. Pty. Ltd v. CLS Bank Int'l*, 135 Sup Ct. 2347, 573 US (2014).

production of new innovations. As a result, the product cycle is very short and regulators are continually racing to catch up to the 'new thing'.

4.3 Regulatory Arbitrage

Financial regulation often imposes costs on actors in the financial system (see Figure 4.1). This is particularly the case with regulation designed to control external-ities by bringing the private costs of an activity for firms into line with the social costs. Such regulation purposefully makes the activity more costly from the firm's perspec-tive. Private firms are generally run in the interests of their shareholders. The interests of the shareholders will be in minimizing the costs experienced by the firm.

There are two basic ways in which firms subject to regulation can seek to reduce regulatory costs for their business. Both involve innovation. The first seeks to reduce the social costs of a regulated activity. A regulation designed in such a way as to let the firm bear the otherwise externalized costs of its business will prompt the firm to lower those costs to the extent that it is in its power to do so. The second route is to restructure an activity so that it no longer falls within the domain of regulation or so that it falls under a different, less costly regulation. This need not result in any lowering of social costs; rather it lowers the firm's costs by moving the activity outside the scope of the regulation.[12] Consequently, financial regulation is itself a stimulant to financial innovation.[13]

The challenge this creates for regulators, when combined with the information gap identified in section 4.2, is profound. Financial firms may be expected to innovate rapidly in response to new regulation. Regulators must then determine whether the innovation is consistent with, or undermines, the regulatory goals. This assessment is made more difficult by large financial firms' greater capacity to understand the financial system. Moreover, financial firms can exploit this differential in capacity by making the innovation unnecessarily complex simply so as to make its true effect more opaque to counterparties and to regulators.[14] Large financial firms therefore seem well positioned to outmanoeuvre regulators at every turn.

Examples abound of financial innovations which were motivated at least in part by the desire to evade regulatory or tax requirements. Here we consider three in particular:

(1) *Derivatives* can be used to create an economic exposure to the underlying asset that is equivalent to ownership, but which legally does not involve ownership.

[12] EJ Kane, 'Interaction of Regulation and Financial Innovation' (1988) 78 *American Economic Review* 328.

[13] See M Ben-Horim and WL Silber, 'Financial Innovation: A Linear Programming Approach' (1977) 1 *Journal of Banking and Finance* 277, 278–80; MH Miller, 'Financial Innovation: The Last Twenty Years and the Next' (1986) 21 *Journal of Financial and Quantitative Analysis* 459, 461–2; Tufano, n 9, 318–20. Note that, as hinted at in Chapter 1, section 1.4, market participants may also engage in regulatory arbitrage to avoid inefficient rules, for example those granting oligopoly rents to incumbents or unnecessarily restricting (eg because they are outdated) value-creating products or services. Financial innovation so motivated can be beneficial to society.

[14] F Partnoy, 'Financial Derivatives and the Costs of Regulatory Arbitrage' (1997) 22 *Journal of Corporation Law* 211, 220–3; D Awrey, 'Toward a Supply-Side Theory of Financial Innovation' (2013) 41 *Journal of Comparative Economics* 401.

"*These new regulations will fundamentally change the way we get around them.*"

Figure 4.1 Regulatory Arbitrage
Source: The New Yorker, 9 March 2009.

This technique may readily be employed to avoid tax, accounting, and regulatory restrictions. For example, an 'equity derivative' is a contract whereby the parties replicate the economic exposure of an investor in stock, without any transfer of the underlying stock. One advantage of using equity derivatives rather than buying the actual stock is that any taxes—such as stamp duty—triggered by transactions in stock are avoided. In the UK, for example, a charge of 0.5 per cent of the value of the transaction is levied as 'stamp duty' on sales of shares. This is high by international standards: there is no equivalent tax in the US, for example. It is perhaps unsurprising that the UK should be a worldwide centre for equity derivatives trading.[15]

(2) *Securitization* is a technique used whereby assets are transferred to a special purpose entity ('SPE'), which raises money by issuing securities to investors that promise future payment streams associated with the asset. The SPE uses the proceeds of the securities issuance to pay the original owner of the asset for its transfer. The asset is thereby said to have been 'securitized'. Banks have securitized their loan portfolios extensively. One motivation for this activity was a desire to minimize the impact of bank capital adequacy regulation. The Basel II framework imposed 'risk-weighted' capital requirements for banks, under

---

[15] TheCityUK, *Key Facts about the UK as an International Financial Centre*, June 2014, 14 (49 per cent of global OTC derivatives turnover occurs in London); BIS, *Derivatives Statistics*, Table 22B, http://www.bis.org/statistics/derstats.htm (OTC equity-linked derivatives in Europe account for 45 per cent of global total).

which loans held to term were judged to be more risky than tradable securities, as the latter could always be sold. Securitization could thus be used to enable a 'trading' unit in a bank to buy securities which were backed by loans that a 'banking' unit (perhaps of another bank) had sold to the SPE. This would reduce the overall amount of capital the organization would be required to hold, while still being exposed to very similar credit risks.[16]

(3) *Financial conglomerates* are firms which combine both banks and non-bank financial intermediaries. Banks are able to raise funds more cheaply when deposits are insured by a public insurance scheme than are uninsured financial intermediaries. Financial conglomerates may enable the non-bank components of the business to get access to cheap insured capital through the bank component.[17]

4.4 Design Challenges

A number of structural issues, other than the substantive content of regulation, affect its success. One such matter is the *mode* (or 'style') *of regulation*—for example, whether it should comprise a detailed list of rules specified in advance, or whether it should simply outline a shorter and more general set of principles, with operational details being left for market participants, regulators, and ultimately courts to determine on a case-by-case basis as issues emerge. Using principles economises on regulatory effort. While our intuition may be that rules, by being more precisely specified, make for greater certainty in application than do open-ended principles,[18] this may not be the case where the subject-matter of regulation is fast-changing and highly complex.[19] In a world where, as we have seen, the regulator's resources are less than those of the regulated firms, the latter may be expected to regard crystalline rules simply as a blueprint for avoidance; open-ended principles may be more difficult to evade *ex ante*. Clearly the trend is in favour of rule-based financial regulation, as reflected in the Dodd–Frank Wall Street Reform and Consumer Protection Act of 2010, with 847 pages of official text, and 290 mandated rule-makings.[20] An even lengthier body of relevant legislative measures has been passed by the EU since the crisis. In part this is an effort by legislators to control erosion of regulatory safeguards from regulatory accommodation in the 'low visibility' part of the economic cycle.

[16] D Jones, 'Emerging Problems with the Basel Capital Accord: Regulatory Capital Arbitrage and Related Issues' (2000) 24 *Journal of Banking & Finance* 35; CW Calomiris and JR Mason, 'Credit Card Securitization and Regulatory Arbitrage' (2004) 26 *Journal of Financial Services Research* 5; BW Ambrose, M Lacour-Little, and AB Sanders, 'Does Regulatory Arbitrage, Reputation, or Asymmetric Information Drive Securitization?' (2005) 28 *Journal of Financial Services Research* 113.

[17] This depends on rules governing the flow of funds between the bank and non-bank units of the conglomerate. X Freixas, G Lóránth, and A Morrison, 'Regulating Financial Conglomerates' (2007) 16 *Journal of Financial Intermediation* 479.

[18] J Raz, 'Legal Principles and the Limits of Law' (1972) 81 *Yale Law Journal* 823, 841.

[19] J Braithwaite, 'Rules and Principles: A Theory of Legal Certainty' (2002) 27 *Australian Journal of Legal Philosophy* 47. Similar analyses might be drawn from the 'rules/standards' debate. See L Kaplow, 'Rules versus Standards: An Economic Analysis' (1992) 43 *Duke Law Journal* 557.

[20] Davis Polk, 'Dodd–Frank Five Year Anniversary Progress Report' (16 July 2015).

Another structural issue is the *architecture* of regulators. The architecture of regulatory institutions relates to the identity of the regulator(s), the scope of their jurisdiction, and their accountability. The way in which regulatory institutions are organized can affect their ability to implement the regulatory objective function described in Chapter 3.[21] In addition, it can influence the ability of regulators to gather information, to anticipate and respond to regulatory arbitrage, and to resist lobbying by political and other interest groups. The current structure of the agencies responsible for financial regulation in the US and the UK, and at EU level, is described in Chapter 24, and the normative question of how such agencies should best be structured is addressed in Chapter 27. However, a quick preview of the issues is helpful at the outset.

For many years, it was thought normal to organize regulators on 'institutional' lines, which mapped onto the financial sector's own institutional boundaries. This model would yield a banking regulator for the banking sector, a securities regulator for securities markets, an insurance regulator for insurance firms, and possibly a pension regulator for pension funds. The best-known example of this sort of model in practice is the US, where securities markets and securities market intermediaries are regulated by the Securities Exchange Commission ('SEC'); markets in commodities, futures, and derivatives and associated intermediaries are regulated by the Commodities Futures Trading Commission; banks are regulated by the Federal Reserve, the Office of the Comptroller of the Currency, the Federal Deposit Insurance Corporation, and fifty state banking regulators; insurers are regulated by fifty state insurance regulators; and pension plans are regulated by the Internal Revenue Service and the Department of Labor. An institutional approach is also reflected in the EU's creation in 2011 of three new financial regulatory authorities on a sectoral basis: the European Banking Authority ('EBA'), the European Securities Markets Authority ('ESMSA'), and the European Insurance and Occupational Pensions Authority ('EIOPA').[22]

The institutional model was traditionally defended as ensuring that regulators with relevant expertise oversee the appropriate sectors of the financial system. However, it struggles with two increasingly serious problems. First, different financial institutions can produce functionally equivalent financial products, yet the associated regulators may differ in their regulatory tools and approach. This produces strong incentives for regulatory arbitrage. As a concrete example, securities market participants in the 1990s and 2000s were able to use securities markets to engage in credit intermediation and the creation of deposit-like short-term credit claims, replicating the functions of banking, but the SEC did not have the safety-and-soundness tools or regulatory culture of a bank regulator. Indeed, the SEC's interests would have been served by growth in its regulatory clients, who could deliver credit products at a lower cost than banks because of the lesser regulatory burdens.

Second, the institutional model struggles to cope with the oversight of systemic risks, which cut across different sectors of the system. Monitoring and controlling systemic risk requires a regulator to have oversight of the financial system as a whole.[23]

---

[21] Chapter 3, section 3.4.8.
[22] See Regulations (EU) No 1093/2010, 1094/2010, and 1095/2010, OJ [2010] L331/12.
[23] Brunnermeier, Crocket, Goodhart, Persaud, and Shin, n 2, 23–8, 53–8.

Moreover, the institutional model is poorly placed to deal with changes in the structure of the financial sector.[24] If, as happened in the 1990s and 2000s, large financial institutions increasingly spanned the various sectors, then they would be subject to a patchwork of regulatory oversight in which the appropriate expertise might not be delivered, and which relied heavily on regulators to coordinate between themselves about priorities.

The institutional model's difficulty in responding to the changing structure of the financial system did not go unnoticed. At the turn of the century, the UK launched a bold experiment in regulatory design, which was explicitly intended to respond to this challenge. The inauguration of the UK's Financial Services Authority ('FSA') as a single comprehensive regulatory authority was motivated by the desire to ensure that the regulator was able to coordinate its responses and allocate resources without being hampered by artificial jurisdictional boundaries.[25] One might imagine that this model would solve the problems experienced by the US structure. Far from it: it appears the FSA was blind-sided by the financial crisis just as much as US regulators.

A single regulator still has to trade off the various regulatory goals. If that trade-off is made erroneously, then there is little scope for corrective action from any other source. The FSA was subsequently found to have failed to devote sufficient resources to its prudential supervision of banking groups, most notoriously Northern Rock.[26] Even the FSA's own internal enquiry produced a damning report, which suggested amongst other things that it had focused resources on protecting consumers at the expense of prudential supervision.[27] The implication is that a single unified regulator is not necessarily superior to the institutional model.[28] In particular, a single regulator may suffer from some of the classical problems of centrally planned economies: if a mistake is made about the allocation of resources, or the prioritization of goals, then the effects are universal. Disenchantment with the unified model of regulation led the UK to abandon it—and abolish the FSA—in 2013.

There is yet another model for regulatory architecture. This posits the configuration of regulators according to regulatory goals. For example, the UK has replaced the FSA with two new agencies: the Financial Conduct Authority ('FCA'), tasked with consumer protection and ensuring market integrity, and the Prudential Regulation Authority ('PRA'), charged with implementing prudential regulation. Proponents of goal-defined regulatory architecture argue that this model has advantages over both the institutional and the unified regulatory models. In contrast to institutional regulators, goal-defined regulatory agencies will necessarily be able to cut across the scope of the

---

[24] See CK Whitehead, 'Reframing Financial Regulation' (2010) 90 *Boston University Law Review* 1.

[25] C Briault, 'The Rationale for a Single National Financial Services Regulator', FSA Occasional Paper No 2, 12–17 (1999).

[26] House of Commons Treasury Committee, *The Run on the Rock: Fifth Report of Session 2007–08*, HC 56-II, January 2008.

[27] See FSA Internal Audit Division, *The Supervision of Northern Rock: A Lessons Learned Review—Report* (2008), 108–12 ('The quality of resource devoted to the prudential supervision of high impact deposit-takers is insufficient, if the level of focus on other existing FSA priorities [such as "Treating Customers Fairly"] remains at the time of our review').

[28] See D Awrey, 'The FSA, Integrated Regulation, and the Curious Case of OTC Derivatives' (2010) 13 *University of Pennsylvania Business Law Journal* 1.

financial system, deploying the appropriate skills necessary to implement their tasks wherever they are required. And in contrast to a unified regulator, goal-defined agencies will not have to make internal decisions about prioritization, but will simply focus on achieving their particular objective.

Given the tensions we have identified between regulatory goals, organizing regulators on this basis may be expected to lead to inter-agency frictions. Proponents argue, however, that these would be productive, spurring regulators on to compete with one another and making it more difficult for financial services firms to enter into cosy arrangements with agencies. Nevertheless, it seems essential if such a system is to work for some degree of hierarchy of regulatory objectives to be articulated in the framing legislation.

Since the financial crisis, a consensus seems to be emerging that the goal of managing systemic risk should be capable of trumping other financial regulatory objectives where conflicts arise. To this end, a partial version of the objective-based model has been implemented in many countries, by establishing 'macroprudential' authorities. These agencies—such as the Financial Stability Oversight Council ('FSOC') in the US, the European Systemic Risk Board ('ESRB') in the EU, and the Financial Policy Committee ('FPC') in the UK—are tasked with high-level oversight of the financial system at large, and—in some cases—given a set of tools that may be implemented to affect particular sectors, or the entire economy. The idea is that, to the extent that the implementation of their measures conflicts with the programmes of other financial regulators, these new agencies should prevail. The tools of macroprudential policy are considered in Chapter 19, and the structure of the agencies responsible for implementing them, in Chapters 24 and 27.

Closely related to these two sets of issues is a third: the question of *enforcement*.[29] Compliance with regulation may be secured in a variety of ways, with interventions initiated by public or private actors, inside or outside formal legal process. The standard technique for financial regulators is a threat to de-license a regulated firm. This typically operates against a general background provision under which carrying on a regulated activity without a regulatory licence is a crime. The regulator thus screens entry to the market, and also sets and polices continuing conditions (regulations) with which the firm must comply if it is to remain in the market. The regulator's ultimate sanction is therefore the threat of removal of a firm's licence. The regulator also has power to levy penalties on firms, or to request payments of compensation, or changes in business practices, all of which the firm will be willing to do provided the cost is less than the value of its licence. This value is a function of the firm's expected future profits.

For the systemically consequential firms, however, the threat of licence revocation is largely illusory. The disruption to third parties that depend upon the firm for various sorts of financial services could be substantial and the lay-off of employees, most of whom would have been far removed from the objectionable behaviour, would cause too much political controversy.

---

[29] Discussed further in Chapter 26.

Regulators can, however, penalize firms through other channels. One is reputational harm. The simple fact of an announcement that a firm has been caught violating applicable rules may have an adverse impact on customers' and counterparties' willingness to trade with the firm, because they expect it might also try to cheat them. Consequently, the firm's profits will suffer. The market anticipates this adverse shift in the firm's terms of trade when the breach is announced. This could take the form of a simple announcement—with no financial penalty—or of an announcement coupled with a financial payment.[30] One study of reactions to announcements by the UK's FSA regarding penalties levied reports that the reputational loss was in the order of eight times the amount of the financial payments.[31]

Another channel is through the levying of penalties. In the case of financial institutions, this means fines, although incarceration may be an option for individuals. In general, criminal prosecutions are difficult to achieve in relation to misconduct in the financial system. The facts are complex, and moneyed defendants tend to be able to access good legal advice. This makes it hard to convince a jury to the standard of proof required in a criminal trial, namely 'beyond reasonable doubt'. Two techniques have greatly increased the efficacy of financial penalties levied by regulators. The first has been to reclassify them from 'criminal' to 'civil penalties'. This has been done in the UK and several other jurisdictions. It has the effect of withdrawing the proceedings from the constitutional guarantees afforded to defendants in criminal trials, and from withholding the stigmatization of a 'criminal record' to those successfully penalized. At the same time, it greatly facilitates the imposition of financial penalties, and the associated deterrence of misconduct that generates.

The second technique is to use plea-bargains in criminal cases. This is largely a US phenomenon.[32] The prosecutor threatens the defendants with a very heavy sanction if the matter goes to full trial, or permits payment of a (large) fine to settle the claim, often without admission of wrongdoing. Even if the prosecutor might find it hard to win a full trial, defendants do not want to take that risk, not least because it would result in loss of licences and the fine might be excluded from coverage under their liability insurance policy. Penalties levied against banks and other financial institutions through such settlements have grown at an extraordinary pace since the financial crisis: by the end of 2014, sixteen of the largest banks in the world had reportedly paid out over $240 billion in this way and made provision for a further $68 billion.[33]

There is concern in some quarters that extensive sanctions may lead to over-deterrence—that is, undermining the functioning of the financial system by driving firms out of the sector. Two arguments are often made. First, prosecutors have excessive incentives to pursue criminal charges against large firms, because they increasingly may be able to

---

[30] See eg BL Liebman and CJ Milhaupt, 'Reputational Sanctions in China's Securities Market' (2008) 108 *Columbia Law Review* 929.

[31] J Armour, C Mayer, and A Polo, 'Regulatory Sanctions and Reputational Damage in Financial Markets' (forthcoming 2016) 51 *Journal of Financial and Quantitative Analysis*.

[32] See eg BL Garrett, *Too Big to Jail: How Prosecutors Compromise with Corporations* (Cambridge, MA: Harvard UP, 2014).

[33] These figures rely on data from the Conduct Costs Project ('CCP') Research Foundation (http://www.ccpresearchfoundation.com).

use part of the payments in their budgets.[34] That said, without any direct incentive, we might worry that public prosecutors would have too little incentive to enforce. For this reason some scholars have argued in favour of private litigation as a primary enforcement mechanism for breaches of securities laws, because private plaintiffs have a direct stake in the outcome.[35] The second argument is that—as we have seen—reputational sanctions are also significant, such that adding criminal penalties will lead to 'too much' deterrence. However, an important feature about reputation is that it appears only to relate to expectations of performance by trading partners—that is, those with whom a firm is in contractual privity. Thus, harms committed by a firm against third parties—those that do not deal with it—may not be expected to affect its reputation.[36] Consequently, the deterrence of externalities may need the imposition of financial penalties by regulators.

4.5 The Political Economy of Financial Regulation

Before financial regulations can be enforced, they must be written and made binding. In a democracy, we might hope that this would be done by our elected politicians. However, legislatures normally face demands for far more measures than they have time to pass. Politicians, who wish to be re-elected, consequently tend to prioritize the issues voters care about.[37] And voters, generally, do not take much interest in financial regulation. The topic has a low salience with the public, owing to its complexity.[38] Consequently, the task of writing regulations is generally delegated by the legislature to specialists—usually the regulatory agencies we discussed in section 4.4. The regulatory agencies are staffed with experts appointed usually with an understanding of the industry they oversee. However, it seems unrealistic to assume that every employee of these agencies always acts purely in the public interest, and with selfless disregard for their own interests. If we assume (not implausibly) that like other economic agents, regulators pursue their own interests to a lesser or greater degree, what consequences should we expect this to have for the production of financial regulation?

Regulators will be in frequent contact with the firms they regulate. They will be unlikely to be in contact with the public at large, and politicians will not generally be much concerned with what is happening in a low-salience sector. Consequently, regulators may be open to 'capture' by the industry they regulate—that is, to writing and enforcing regulation in a way that is biased towards the interests of the industry, likely at the expense of society as a whole. Such capture in some countries could take the form of overt bribes. In the financial systems on which we focus—the EU and the

---

[34] See eg MH Lemos and M Minzner, 'For-Profit Public Enforcement' (2014) 127 *Harvard Law Review* 853; 'Criminalising the American Company: A Mammoth Guilt Trip', *The Economist*, 30 August 2014.

[35] JR Hay and A Shelifer, 'Private Enforcement of Public Laws: A Theory of Legal Reform' (1998) 88 *American Economic Review* 398.

[36] See Armour, Mayer, and Polo, n 31.

[37] Non-democratically elected legislators may be expected to respond to the concerns of any group whose goodwill is necessary for continuation of their office: powerful elites in the first instance, and the general populace only to the extent that revolution may be a possibility. See generally, D Acemoglu and J Robinson, *Economic Origins of Dictatorship and Democracy* (Cambridge: CUP, 2006), 118–71.

[38] PD Culpepper, *Quiet Politics and Business Power* (Cambridge: CUP, 2011).

US—outright regulatory corruption is to our knowledge mercifully rare. However, there are a variety of other more subtle ways in which the regulator's agenda may be captured by the industry. One is through 'revolving doors': regulators are often recruited from the industry so as to ensure they have the relevant expertise, and will often want to return to the industry after their tenure. The concern about such arrangements is that prior ties and the expectation of future consulting fees will lead regulators to be less hard on industry practices than they ought to be. A second is that the regulator's budget (or prestige) is likely linked to the size of the sector she oversees. The regulator will therefore not want the industry to contract, because her budget (or prestige) will follow it. Hence she may feel that her interests are aligned with those of the industry. A third, and particularly pernicious, problem stems from the informational challenge discussed in section 4.2. The size of the information differential is so large that regulators must necessarily rely on firms to understand what is happening. The concern is therefore that firms strategically cooperate to bias the information the regulator receives from them. The ability of the industry to coordinate in this way is a function of their resources and organizational structure. Consequently, if we think the financial system is prone to periods of boom and bust, then the very time we might most want regulation to step in—during a boom—is when the industry has the greatest resources available to deflect this.

As regulators are public bodies, the prospect of judicial review might be one way to ameliorate problems of regulatory capture. Yet the procedural safeguards likely to be required by a typical judicial review procedure are easily met—consultation with affected parties can be formally performed by announcing proposed rules on the agency's website and then soliciting responses. The fact that the responses come predominantly from one industry or sector does not undermine the formal appropriateness of the consultation, although it does impair its practical utility.

A more invasive form of judicial review is invited by legislative guidelines to regulators that cost-benefit analysis should be performed in preparing new rules. This sounds at first blush like a useful process constraint: requiring agencies to justify their actions by reference to data should lead to better-reasoned decision-making, shouldn't it? But there are significant problems. First, a rigorous cost-benefit analysis requirement introduces a status quo bias, especially when the starting point is one of no regulation, because the regulator has the burden of providing the evidence justifying a change.[39] Second, when a regulation is already in place, cost-benefit analysis may support calls for its repeal, because its compliance costs are relatively easy to prove, while its benefits are much harder to quantify. Third, scrutiny of cost-benefit analysis is left to the courts, where judges lack training in how to interpret the requirement for such an analysis. This then devolves into a 'battle of the expert witnesses', with

---

[39] This was notoriously illustrated by the case of *Business Roundtable v SEC* 647 F.3d 1144 (2011, DC Cir), in which a well-reasoned SEC proposal was successfully challenged on the basis that the SEC had failed to produce sufficient economic evidence that proposed reforms would add value on net. Somewhat ironically, a subsequent empirical study showed that the DC Circuit's decision to strike the proposed rules down itself caused a significant loss of value to the firms which would have been affected: B Becker, D Bergstresser, and G Subramanian, 'Does Shareholder Proxy Access Improve Firm Value? Evidence from the Business Roundtable's Challenge' (2013) 56 *Journal of Law & Economics* 127.

somewhat unpredictable results.[40] Fourth, 'significant' regulation will change the underlying financial system in a way that will make the *ex ante* calculation of costs and benefits infeasible.[41]

Obviously, there are some circumstances under which the public at large do become concerned about financial regulation: during a crisis or following a scandal. The more widespread the losses, the greater the clamour for 'something to be done', which will push politicians, keen not to lose votes, to be seen to take legislative action.[42] This predicts legislation reforming financial regulation will come as a response to a crisis. It fits well with the history of financial regulation: the two greatest financial crises of the last 100 years, namely the 1929 crash and the financial crisis of 2007–9, both triggered extensive reform of the legislative frameworks for financial regulation. Thus the modern structure of US federal banking and securities laws was established in the 1930s by the Roosevelt administration responding to popular outcry. And the period since the recent financial crisis has been one of remarkable legislative fecundity for the sector.

Unfortunately, the sort of legislation that responds to populist concerns—those of the ordinary person in the street—is not necessarily aligned with the steps needed to optimize the functioning of the financial system, which we discussed in Chapter 3.[43] That policy challenge is very complex, but the average voter does not understand its details. Politicians may be motivated to espouse measures simply because they are popular, rather than because they are efficacious. More generally, politicians will support a process that is publicly styled as 'fixing the problem'. This will require an enquiry or expert report into what went wrong, and a set of recommendations detailing how a repetition could be prevented. The recommendations are likely to be backwards-looking, because the question is framed in terms of 'how could this have been prevented'. Unfortunately, this often neglects the dynamism of the financial system: the next set of problems is likely to be different from the last.

These elements combine to form a general picture of regulatory activity that is likely to be *procyclical*: that is, there is *insufficient* regulation during periods of boom and perhaps *excessive*, or at least misguided, regulation in the wake of crises. The general story has been one of political disinterest bred from low public salience, save during times of crisis. This in turn leaves rule-making to technocratic regulators, who are susceptible to the influence of the industry. Indeed, some argue that this cycle has already restarted since the financial crisis: popular legislation having been passed,

---

[40] See JC Coates, 'Cost-Benefit Analysis of Financial Regulation: Case Studies and Implications' (2015) 124 *Yale Law Journal* 882.

[41] JN Gordon, 'The Empty Call for Benefit-Cost Analysis in Financial Regulation' (2014) 43 *Journal of Legal Studies* S351 (arguing that financial system is an 'artificial' system, created by man-made rules, unlike a 'natural system', constrained by laws of nature, and that cost-benefit quantification methodology, drawn from health and safety regulation, is therefore unlikely to be useful in the context of financial regulation).

[42] This effect is compounded by another truism: that many malpractices which occurred during 'boom' years become apparent only later during a contraction. This may be because investors who are being paid healthy returns do not ask as many questions as those who suffer losses; it may alternatively be because agencies feel more pressure to devote resources to investigation during periods of contraction. See E Gerding, 'The Next Epidemic: Bubbles and the Growth and Decay of Securities Regulation' (2006) 38 *University of Connecticut Law Review* 393.

[43] See R Romano, 'Regulating in the Dark and a Postscript Assessment of the Iron Law of Financial Regulation' (2014) 43 *Hofstra Law Review* 25.

politicians move on to other projects. But the implementation of the detail of the legislation is left to rules which must be agreed by regulators with the industry, which results in their impact being diluted.[44]

The cycle we have described for the production of regulation applies similarly in the case of enforcement. Boom times lead to cutbacks in enforcement, in part because of the responsiveness of legislators to industry lobbying against enforcement activity. Enforcement budgets shrink and legislative support for proactive enforcement recedes almost inversely to growing aggressiveness under applicable law.[45]

The account thus far has portrayed politicians as too slow to react during boom periods because they are disinterested. There are hints, however, of a more disturbing possible account. On some views, politicians have a positive interest in weak regulatory controls during credit booms. One such account points to the preferences of those who fund political campaigns. Those working in the financial sector tend to be both wealthy and able to organize at relatively low cost through their firms and trade associations. Consequently, their preferences—which tend to favour less regulation or regulation that lowers competition—are likely to be particularly salient to politicians.[46] Ability to provide such funds is a function of individual wealth, the costs of coordinating like-minded individuals, and perhaps, most importantly, the legal environment surrounding political financing. US campaign finance laws are notoriously lax in this regard compared to their European counterparts. The issue has been intensified by the 2010 Supreme Court decision in *Citizens United*,[47] which held that corporations were legal 'persons' under the constitution and hence entitled to the same safeguards regarding free speech as natural persons. This invalidated campaign finance laws prohibiting the use of corporate funds in political action. Empirical research suggests that the decision has led to a jump in corporate lobbying and political funding, and that more spending on these activities benefits shareholders in firms in regulated industries.[48]

While this first account is most relevant to the US, a second account of misalignment of politicians' interests is more general. This points to the centrality of real estate markets to financial crises. In almost all financial crises around the world since the middle of the nineteenth century, excess credit to real estate—coupled with an asset price boom in the sector—has been an important component of the problem.[49] Politicians benefit in the short run from real estate booms. Citizens have easier access to credit if their houses are worth more, and feel richer. In the short run, this greatly

[44] JC Coffee, 'The Political Economy of Dodd–Frank: Why Financial Reform Tends to be Frustrated and Systemic Risk Perpetuated' (2012) 97 *Cornell Law Review* 1019.

[45] Gerding, n 42.

[46] A point made forcefully by S Johnson and J Kwak, *Thirteen Bankers: The Wall Street Takeover and the Next Financial Meltdown* (New York, NY: Pantheon Press, 2010).

[47] *Citizens United v Federal Electoral Commission* 558 US 310 (2010).

[48] JC Coates IV, 'Corporate Politics, Governance, and Value Before and After *Citizens United*' (2012) 9 *Journal of Empirical Legal Studies* 657.

[49] See CM Reinhart and KS Rogoff, *This Time is Different: Eight Centuries of Financial Folly* (Princeton, NJ: Princeton University Press, 2009). Compare the 'dotcom' bubble of 1999–2000, in which collapse of asset prices did not produce a financial crisis precisely because valuations were not heavily reliant on credit expansion.

assists chances of re-election. In the medium to long run, it results in overheating and a shock to real estate prices—or worse. But if politicians have only a short time horizon—no longer than a single electoral cycle—then this sort of unsustainable growth strategy may look very appealing.[50]

4.6 The International Context

The international context provides a third source of potential mismatch between the interests of politicians and the public interest. Politicians may wish to attract financial services firms to do business in their country. Financial services professionals are notoriously well paid, and so generate large amounts of income tax revenue. They also generate significant employment opportunities, both for highly skilled 'knowledge workers' within the firms and for an army of services and secondary occupations that provide support facilities for these highly paid financial professionals.

One way to attract financial firms is to make the regulatory environment more appealing to them. Whether this is a good thing or not depends on the rationale for the regulation in question. If it is concerned with overcoming asymmetries of information, then the interests of business and of society are likely aligned. Financial firms will want to attract as many investors as possible, and cost-justified regulatory mechanisms that help firms overcome information asymmetry will serve the interests of both firms and their investors. However, many financial regulatory measures are directed at promoting the production of information as a public good and controlling the externalities associated with systemic risk. In these cases, a regulatory approach with greatest appeal to business is likely to be harmful for society. Financial firms would rather not internalize the social costs of their activities; they can surely make greater profits if they do not. Hence, reducing the burden of regulatory measures that are intended to do this will be attractive to them. The problem is that this can result in a 'race to the bottom', whereby states compete to reduce their control of externalities in order to attract tax revenue.

Of course, to some degree this is a self-defeating strategy, because the externalities will be borne by voters as well. Thus, if financial firms are attracted by low regulation and generate jobs and tax revenues in the short run, these beneficial effects must be traded off against the costs incurred by citizens should there be a subsequent financial crisis. How appealing the strategy will be therefore depends on the size of the country's finance sector relative to its economy at large. Politicians in countries with small finance sectors relative to the economy at large have far more to lose, and far less to gain, from competitive relaxation of financial regulation.

Conversely, those in countries with financial sectors that are large relative to the economy as a whole will find the trade-off most appealing. The problem, however, is that the countries with large financial sectors relative to their economy are also those exporting financial services, through larger, internationally active, and interconnected

[50] VV Acharya, 'Governments as Shadow Banks: The Looming Threat to Financial Stability' (2011) 90 *Texas Law Review* 1745. See also A Mian and A Sufi, *House of Debt: How They (and You) Caused the Great Recession, and How We Can Prevent It from Happening Again* (Chicago: UC Press, 2014).

financial institutions. The costs of their financial system collapse will be borne not just by their own citizens, but also by those in countries whose financial systems are connected to it. In other words, regulatory competition over measures promoting financial stability leads to international externalities.

Such spillover effects are very hard to control, because of the lack of any binding framework for international financial regulation. Until the financial crisis, there was not even a coordination mechanism for aligning states' regulatory activities in relation to stability. And international law does not enjoy the ordinary enforcement mechanisms of domestic law.

4.7 Overcoming the Limitations?

This chapter might make depressing reading to an idealist bent on saving the world from future financial crises. We hope, however, that it serves a less negative purpose. The aim is not to put readers off the enterprise of financial regulation, but to ensure that we understand the practical constraints to which it is subject. We should be under no illusion as to the significance of the challenges these pose.

Nevertheless, there are grounds for optimism. The financial crisis has stimulated serious academic and regulatory reflection on the goals and methods of financial regulation in a way that has not been undertaken for many years. The amount of energy invested in working out how to improve matters—not just how to fix the last problem, but how to improve things going forward—is impressive. And the wildfire spread of contagion across the globe in 2008–9 has given nation states a renewed imperative to work together to find common solutions. Each of these developments has yielded tangible benefits and has the potential to improve significantly the functioning of financial regulation going forward.

The intellectual energy that has gone into thinking about financial regulation has yielded many new insights. In our view the most profound of these is the recognition of the importance of thinking about the financial system at the macro level—that is, the system as a whole. This idea predates the crisis—it was first advocated by the Chief Economist of the Bank for International Settlement, Claudio Borio,[51] in 2003—but its widespread adoption did not occur until the events of the financial crisis proved its importance.

As we shall see in Chapter 19, there are many different ways we might define the scope and goals of macroprudential oversight ('MacroPru'). Effectively pursuing these goals requires a new institutional arrangement, with an authority tasked with macro-prudential matters at the apex of other regulators. It should be in receipt of information on an industrial scale from participants in the financial sector, and be equipped with talented personnel and data processing power with which to analyse it. It should follow fast-growing financial innovations and seek to understand their motivations and likely risks. It should have priority in inter-agency disputes so as to be able to avoid

---

[51] C Borio, 'Towards a Macroprudential Framework for Financial Supervision and Regulation?' (2003) 49 *CESifo Economic Studies* 181.

conflicting policies that increase systemic risk, and piggy-back off their enforcement capabilities as regards firms. Most importantly, however, it should be independent from politicians so as to be capable of putting a check on policies that are stimulating or permitting risky overheating of bank balance sheets or real estate markets.

As we have seen, a well-implemented macroprudential authority can go a significant way to mitigating the kinds of problems we have described in this chapter so far. The financial crisis has stimulated the inauguration of bodies that may, to a lesser or greater degree, be described as macroprudential authorities ('MPAs') in many jurisdictions—from the US FSOC, to the EU's ESRB and the UK's FPC. These do not each implement every desideratum in the previous list, but their establishment is a move in the right direction. This illustrates the importance of new ideas in financial regulation.

The second positive development has been the inauguration of a permanent international organization tasked with promoting financial stability, the Financial Stability Board ('FSB'). The FSB was established in 2009[52] and charged with responsibility for coordinating the design and implementation of much of the G20's post-crisis policy agenda. The FSB's mandate includes: (i) assessing vulnerabilities affecting the global financial system and reviewing regulatory actions needed to address them; (ii) promoting coordination and information exchange among national authorities responsible for financial stability; (iii) monitoring and advising on market developments and their implications for regulatory policy; (iv) coordinating the policy development work of international standard setters; and (v) promoting Member States' implementation of agreed-upon commitments, standards, and policy recommendations through monitoring, peer review, and disclosure.[53] The FSB has been extremely active in coordinating a reform agenda. A particularly significant innovation is the peer review mechanism, which subjects countries' implementation of relevant protocols to scrutiny by a cross-national team of regulators from other Member States. This is potentially an extremely effective way of bringing about regulatory change. The reviewers are experts who are free from both domestic political affiliations and domestic industry lobbying, and hence will be free from many of the failings of the domestic rule-making process we have discussed.

These two examples are indicative of the possibilities for enhancement of financial regulation: we consider that despite the limitations discussed in this chapter, real improvements in outcomes are capable of being achieved. Making such achievements possible, however, requires an understanding not only of the appropriate regulatory intervention but also of the political economy of its execution.

---

[52] Technically, it was a re-launch of a prior 'talking shop' for national finance ministers and central bank governors of the G7, the Financial Stability Forum. See JR Barth, DE Nolle, T Li, and C Brummer, 'Systemically Important Banks (SIBs) in the Post-Crisis Era: "The" Global Response and Reponses Around the Globe for 135 Countries', in AN Berger, P Molyneux, and JOS Wilson (eds), *The Oxford Handbook of Banking*, 2nd ed (Oxford: OUP, 2015), Ch 26 (describing G20–FSB interaction and initiatives); DE Nolle, 'Who's in Charge of Fixing the World's Financial System? The Under-Appreciated Lead Role of the G20 and the FSB' (2015) 24 *Financial Markets, Institutions & Instruments* 1.

[53] FSB Charter, Art 2(1).

4.8 Conclusion

In this chapter, we have introduced the idea that those writing, applying, and enforcing financial regulation—politicians and regulators—may not be motivated entirely by the pursuit of the public interest. We then explored a range of limitations on what we might realistically expect financial regulation to achieve. The financial system changes rapidly as actors engage in financial innovation that often aims at evading the application of regulatory provisions. Regulators must distinguish the 'good', welfare-enhancing innovation from the 'bad' one that aims to avoid beneficial regulations, but it is a daunting task. Not only is the financial system extremely complex, but also its largest participants have far greater resources to understand it than do its regulators. Matters might be made easier by appropriate design of regulatory institutions. We suggest that a goal-based model is likely to be best.

Regulations must be written and implemented against the background of political economy—that is, the negotiation process that goes on over the benefits of new economy-wide rules. Politicians seeking to pursue policies popular with voters are at best disinterested and sometimes may even be opposed to effective regulation where it would slow economic growth from overheating. At the same time, the financial sector uses its information advantage to influence regulatory policy in subtle and not-so-subtle ways. When things go wrong, voters do care about financial regulation, and politicians become energized, but the resulting legislation may be wide of the target. What is more, states may engage in harmful 'races to the bottom' in financial regulation in order to attract financial services firms.

These limitations are indeed significant, but they do not rule out beneficial changes in financial regulation. We have considered two examples in the post-crisis milieu: namely the shift to macroprudential regulation, and the inauguration, at the international level, of the FSB. Financial regulation is subject to real limitations, but equally real possibilities for meaningful change remain.

PART B

FINANCIAL MARKETS

5

Theory of Financial Markets

5.1 Introduction

At the heart of a financial system lie its financial markets—stock, bond, options and futures markets. They perform the function of all markets of bringing buyers and sellers together and establishing prices that ensure their demands equate with available supply. In this case, the relevant items being bought and sold are financial instruments, for example shares in companies and bonds issued by companies, financial institutions, and local and national governments.

While they differ in detail, the structure of financial markets is broadly similar. There is a system by which purchasers and sellers register their demands and supplies and there is a mechanism by which orders are matched and transactions executed. Traditionally, most financial instruments were traded in a physical location, an exchange. Some of the finest buildings in financial centres around the world are their stock and commodity exchanges on the floors of which traders would exchange bids and offers to buy and sell securities. Those physical locations have been replaced by electronic trading mechanisms on computer systems.[1] Physical interactions between traders now only take place, if at all, on over-the-counter ('OTC') markets—that is, markets where securities are bought and sold by an individual dealer in the absence of any third-party organization of the marketplace such as an exchange.

In many respects, the exchange of financial securities is no different from that of other physical commodities, such as fruit and vegetables or antiques and paintings, which underpin the operation of an economy. However, there is one respect in which markets for financial securities differ from other markets. Fruit and vegetables will in general be consumed shortly after purchase. Antiques and paintings may be enjoyed for a long period thereafter but the benefits that they confer are largely known. In the case of financial securities, the underlying 'goods' are prospects for earnings in the distant future that are only known or predictable very imprecisely.

This is the basis of one of the most important functions of financial markets and that is to provide information about investors' projections of future prospects: financial market participants are continuously updating their beliefs about expected payouts in response to new information. Financial markets, or better, the *prices* at which trades occur in such markets, *aggregate* information about the expected value of traded securities.

In this chapter we explore the process by which financial markets function and the principles by which information about future prospects is incorporated into market prices. We begin in section 5.2 by describing the fundamental theorem of financial market pricing, the efficient markets hypothesis. We discuss the conditions under

---

[1] The structure of exchanges and other trading platforms is discussed in more detail in Chapter 7.

Principles of Financial Regulation. First Edition. John Armour, Dan Awrey, Paul Davies, Luca Enriques, Jeffrey N. Gordon, Colin Mayer, and Jennifer Payne. © John Armour, Dan Awrey, Paul Davies, Luca Enriques, Jeffrey N. Gordon, Colin Mayer, and Jennifer Payne 2016. Published 2016 by Oxford University Press.

which it holds, the implications for prices when it does hold, and the circumstances under which it fails. In section 5.3 we describe the different types of investors who participate in financial markets and how they contribute to the price setting process. We will describe what they do, how they contribute to the price setting process, and how they potentially distort it as well. Section 5.4 then considers the different processes involved in price setting, namely market making, limit orders and quote driven systems, the way in which they function, their respective merits and deficiencies, and the significance of clearing and settling. The chapter should give you a good understanding of the principles of financial markets and price formation, the reasons why these markets matter so much, and why they may be subject to failures.

5.2 Efficient Markets

5.2.1 The concept of 'informational efficiency'

People and institutions buy securities for the earnings that they yield.[2] Earnings comprise two components: interest or dividend payments and capital appreciation on the value of the securities. The amount that an investor is willing to pay for these financial instruments depends on their expectations of the future returns, or to be precise, the present value of the future benefits that they anticipate from holding them. The price of a security should therefore reflect the sum of the present values of the stream of future interest or dividend payments and the price of the security at the date at which the investor anticipates selling it.

Critical to the determination of the price is the information on which investors form their expectations of the future returns on securities. According to the efficient capital markets hypothesis ('ECMH'), financial markets incorporate all available information in the setting of prices. It is described as a 'hypothesis' because it is formulated as an empirically testable prediction about the behaviour of financial markets.[3] To see the logic, note that if financial markets did not incorporate all available information, then there would be profitable trading opportunities available to investors. For example, if there were negative (positive) information about the quality of the management of a firm, not reflected by the market in the pricing of that firm's securities, then investors would be able to exploit that information in selling (buying) those securities. If that

---

[2] We focus in this chapter on the most basic types of securities—shares (equity claims) and bonds (debt claims). The issues that we discuss here are equally relevant to many other types of security. However, for a particular type of financial market—namely, *money markets*—securities are deliberately designed *not* to change in value over the course of their lifetime, so that they can function as a means of exchange: see B Holmstrom, 'Understanding the Role of Debt in a Financial System', BIS Working Paper No 479 (2015); K Judge, 'Information Gaps', Working Paper Columbia Law School (2016). And for markets in OTC derivatives, the information aggregation process can break down in times of great stress: see D Awrey, 'The Mechanisms of Derivatives Market Efficiency' 91 *NYU Law Review* (forthcoming 2016). These markets feature heavily in the intersection between banks and markets discussed in Part E, and their differences from ordinary financial markets—under-appreciated before the financial crisis—are considered in Chapters 20 and 21.

[3] However, early statements of the ECMH were noticeably thin on detail regarding the *mechanisms* by which information would come to be incorporated. It is the functioning of these mechanisms that determines the degree of informational efficiency, and on which regulation can gain useful traction: RJ Gilson and RH Kraakman, 'The Mechanisms of Market Efficiency' (1984) 70 *Virginia Law Review* 549.

information about the management were public, then there should be a general rush to sell (buy) the firm's shares, up to the point where the price of the shares correctly reflects information about the management. The practical criterion employed to assess this is often framed as whether it is possible to make money by trading on a piece of price-relevant new information.[4]

Three types of information are potentially relevant to the setting of share prices. The first is the past performance of the shares—historical information on whether share prices are currently high or low in relation to their historic average. There are said to be periods during which share prices are high relative to their historic average—what are termed 'bull' markets—and low—'bear' markets. There would therefore appear to be straightforward opportunities for making money by selling shares during bull markets when they are apparently overvalued and buying them in bear markets when they are undervalued.[5] But if that were the case, then investors would systematically sell shares during bull markets, thereby driving down their prices until the point at which the shares were no longer overvalued and purchase shares during bear markets, thereby driving up the prices to the point at which they were no longer undervalued. In other words, the information on which investors can apparently make profitable trades would be eliminated by the very possibility of the trading opportunities themselves.

This suggests that past information about the performance of shares can provide no guide to the likely profitability of holding those shares in the future. This is the basis of what is termed the 'weak form' of the efficient markets hypothesis, namely that historical information about share prices or past trades in shares provides no information about the return on holding those shares in the future.[6] The notion that it is possible to identify periods of overvalued and undervalued shares is illusory and while people talk routinely about bull and bear markets, such statements offer no guide to whether those bull or bear markets will persist into the future or indeed become even more pronounced.

The weak form of market efficiency gives rise to the well-known feature of share prices, that they follow a 'random walk'.[7] That means that the movement of share prices today is unrelated to their movement yesterday and their movement tomorrow is unrelated to that today. So any seemingly systematic movement in share prices is again illusory.

While the absence of historic patterns in share price movements is important, it does not establish what happens when new information is made available. How, for example, does the stock market react to dividend or earnings announcements by

---

[4] See eg BG Malkiel, 'The Efficient Market Hypothesis and its Critics' (2003) 17 *Journal of Economic Perspectives* 59, 60.

[5] The difficulty here is that, as we have seen, the pricing of securities depends on expectations of *future* profits, which cannot yet be known. Consequently, if a firm's share price is 'high' relative to its current profits, as compared with its historic price to earnings ratio, this could mean *either* that investors anticipate the firm's profits will increase in the future *or* that the shares are overvalued.

[6] E Fama, 'Efficient Capital Markets: A Review of Theory and Empirical Work' (1970) 25 *Journal of Finance* 383.

[7] B Malkiel, *A Random Walk Down Wall Street*, 6th ed (New York, WW Norton, 1973); E Fama, 'Random Walks in Stock Market Prices' (1965) 21 *Financial Analysts Journal* 55.

firms or statements about changes in management or new investments? Can one profit by trading on the announcement of new information, selling shares when bad information is revealed and buying those where there is positive information? The answer is no, at least not in the many markets around the world where the efficient markets hypothesis has been tested. Share prices move almost instantaneously in response to the arrival of new information. This is the second or 'semi-strong' form of the efficient market hypothesis.

Again, were this not the case, then there would be trading opportunities. Investors who were quick off the mark could make profits by buying or selling in response to corporate announcements. However, that very possibility causes the price of shares to adjust immediately in response to the arrival of the new information, thereby eliminating any trading opportunities. There is no money left on the table for investors generally.

Some traders may gain access to information before it is made public. Such traders are termed 'insiders'. They have access to privileged or private information that is not generally available. So for example, people working within a corporation might have access to information about critical managerial changes or new investments. They may know that an announcement is about to be made about disappointing earnings. Since this information is not publicly available, most investors are not in a position to trade on it and will not therefore influence the price at which shares are being traded. As a consequence, it would be surprising if, in contrast to 'weak' and 'semi-strong' market efficiency, markets exhibited 'strong' form efficiency, namely that share prices reflect all the information available to insiders as well as outsiders. Indeed, the predictions of strong-form market efficiency are violated, as insiders could—were such trading not prohibited—trade to their advantage on the basis of the privileged information which is available to them.[8]

In summary, markets are efficient in impounding all information that is available from the history of past movements of share prices (weak form) and public announcements (semi-strong form) but not the information to which insiders have privileged access in relation to other investors (strong form).

Similar principles apply in relation to other markets, in particular bond, commodity, and derivatives markets.[9] The price at which these securities trade should reflect all available information that derives from historically observing past movements in the prices of these securities and from the arrival of new information about the determinants of their underlying value. So, for example, in relation to government bonds, their prices should reflect all information that is available about macro-economic policy, the level and changes in government deficits, the tax revenue that governments expect to

---

[8] See eg M Jensen, 'Some Anomalous Evidence Regarding Market Efficiency' (1978) 6 *Journal of Financial Economics* 95. Prohibitions on insider trading are discussed in Chapter 9, section 9.3.

[9] See generally ES Hotchkiss and T Ronen, 'The Informational Efficiency of the Corporate Bond Market: An Intraday Analysis' (2002) 15 *Review of Financial Studies* 1325; L Norden and M Weber, 'Informational Efficiency of Credit Default Swap and Stock Markets: The Impact of Credit Rating Announcements' (2004) 28 *Journal of Banking & Finance* 2813. OTC derivatives markets may be subject to a breakdown in the pricing function during times of extreme stress, because parties' payoffs depend not only on underlying securities, but also on the quality of collateral and dealers' creditworthiness. See Awrey, n 2, and Chapter 21, section 21.4.

earn, and international factors such as the setting of interest rates by overseas governments. A failure to incorporate all such information into bond pricing would create
profitable trading opportunities.

5.2.2 Anomalies

Do financial markets behave like the ECMH predicts? Even in markets with features
that make them good candidates to validate the theory, such as equity markets in highly
developed economies, deviations from the theory's predictions, or 'anomalies', can be
observed.

First of all, market prices have a tendency to overreact to new pieces of relevant
information. In other words, there is evidence that share prices are excessively 'volatile'
in the sense that they fluctuate more than can be justified by the underlying earnings
streams that should determine the valuation of shares.[10]

Second, it appears that financial markets also react to information that is plausibly
irrelevant to future earnings.[11] There are well-known systematic relations between the
size of companies, the ratio of their book (accounting) to market values, and their
equity returns. Small companies outperform larger companies. Companies with high
book to market ratios (or earnings to price or dividend to price ratios) outperform
companies with low ratios. There are month of the year and day of the week effects.
Share price returns tend to be closely associated with the month of January. Stock
markets appear to suffer from Monday morning blues insofar as the returns over
weekends from Fridays to Mondays are lower than at other times in the week.

These results together constitute a substantial body of evidence of anomalies in
financial markets that are difficult to reconcile with traditional market efficiency
propositions.[12] Furthermore, the overall returns on equities appear high in relation
to those on fixed interest investments, such as government bonds. The difference
between the two should reflect the greater volatility of shares than bonds and the
degree of risk aversion of investors. But neither the volatility of shares nor the investors'
risk aversion can readily explain the scale of the 'equity risk premium'. It appears to be
too large to be justified by conventional explanations.

These anomalies raise the question of exactly what is meant by the ECMH. Does it
mean that today's price is the best estimate of the firm's expected future cash flows,
meaning that stock market prices are 'allocationally efficient'? Or does it mean only
that today's price is the best estimate of tomorrow's price, meaning that stock market
prices are 'informationally efficient'? The evidence of some disconnect between the
stability of dividends and the volatility of prices suggests that prices may deviate from
the 'fundamentals' of the firm's business. Yet the extraordinary difficulty that even

---

[10] See eg JY Campbell and RJ Shiller, 'Stock Prices, Earnings, and Expected Dividends' (1988) 43 *Journal
of Finance* 661.
[11] Whether information is (or is not) relevant to future earnings cannot of course be known at the outset.
Thus how these findings are interpreted depends on how plausible one finds it that the information in
question should be relevant to future profitability.
[12] For a review, see RJ Shiller, *Irrational Exuberance*, 2nd ed (Princeton, NJ: Princeton UP, 2005).

professional investors have in consistently outperforming the market (at least in developed markets) indicates that there is a strong degree of informational efficiency.[13]

5.2.3 Implications of market (in)efficiency

What are the implications of either market efficiency or market anomalies for the regulation of financial markets? It is helpful to begin by considering what is at stake. The cost of mispricing in financial markets comes in two forms. First, the failure of markets to reflect accurately available information about the value of underlying earnings results in a misallocation of resources. Too much investment goes to activities that markets mistakenly identify as generating high returns and too little to those with earnings streams that markets underestimate.[14] Mispricing therefore leads to real costs of *misallocation of resources*.

Second, there are net transfers between those who trade unwittingly at incorrect prices to those who are informed about the mispricing—that is, information asymmetries. These transfers discourage potential losers from investing in markets in which they anticipate that they will systematically suffer at the hands of better-informed investors. There is, in other words, a participation problem of uninformed investors abstaining from investing in markets in which they believe that they are at an informational disadvantage. A reduction in the level of investment means that *liquidity* in the market as a whole is reduced, which as we will see increases costs for those who continue to participate.

If markets can process new information appropriately, then one may think that the disclosure of more information will be wholly beneficial. The more information that is made public, the more accurate will be the price, and the better the allocation of resources. However, this begs the question of how information is generated, and by whom.[15]

Price-relevant information is costly to produce, meaning market participants will not produce it unless they can benefit from doing so. Consider, for example, that developing a new product is costly and risky. If an issuer is required fully to inform the market about its research and development ('R&D') activities, its competitors would gain insights into its achievements and free-ride on its efforts, making it harder for the issuer to profit from R&D investment. Hence, a market where all information needs to be publicly disclosed as soon as it is produced may well reflect all available information, but at the cost of reducing the amount, breadth, and insightfulness of the information pool, not to mention the impact of required disclosures on value creation. The

---

[13] Paradoxically, they cannot be *perfectly* informationally efficient: someone needs to be trading to keep markets informationally efficient, but if there are no gains to be made from trading, no informed person will trade, until such gains can be made again. See SJ Grossman and JE Stiglitz, 'On the Impossibility of Informationally Efficient Markets' (1980) 70 *American Economic Review* 393.

[14] This occurs most obviously in primary markets such as Initial Public Offerings (IPOs) where firms raise new funds. However, prices in secondary markets will also affect the investment of corporate assets where managers have incentives to maximize the stock price, as for example generated by equity-linked compensation. See J Dow and G Gorton, 'Stock Market Efficiency and Economic Efficiency: Is There a Connection?' (1997) 52 *Journal of Finance* 1087.

[15] See Gilson and Kraakman, n 3.

remaining chapters in this Part will further explore how policymakers deal with these kinds of trade-offs.

In the absence of regulation, information might become public indirectly through insiders trading on privileged information.[16] Other investors would then have to 'decode' the relevant information from the price movement. However, in carrying out such trades, insiders benefit from their knowledge at the expense of other investors. This might discourage these uninformed investors from participating in financial markets— reducing liquidity—because they are aware of the extent to which they might be exploited by insiders.[17] That is, while insider trading might help achieve accurate prices, it would do so at the cost of increasing information asymmetries. Prohibiting insider trading reduces these information asymmetries, but—provided the information is made public by other routes—need not harm price accuracy. We consider the prohibition of insider trading and related market misconduct in Chapter 9.

Assuming no insider trading (broadly defined) takes place, prices will incorporate new information as soon as it becomes publicly available, be it following an inadvertent leak, as a choice of the issuer, or in compliance with a mandatory disclosure require- ment: the new information will move prices almost instantaneously up or down, depending on whether the news is good or bad. Nowadays, these movements are chiefly the outcome of algorithmic traders' programs that are capable of automatically detecting new information, estimating the ensuing price movements, and instantan- eously trading accordingly. Other traders may intervene to 'refine' the price adjustment based on their ability to process information. Such informed traders will be supported by a host of other actors—whom we refer to as '*information intermediaries*'—perform- ing important roles in conveying and/or interpreting information for market partici- pants.[18] Yet once trading begins, the cat is out of the bag—other investors can decode the significance of the information from the price movement and free-ride on the analysis of the information. The extent to which knowledge about the value of new information can trickle down in this way and be reflected in prices therefore affects incentives to engage in analysis in the first place. A crucial factor in determining this is the level of *price transparency* in the marketplace—that is, whether parties are required to make public their trades, or even their orders. We consider price transparency in Chapter 7.

All of this discussion has proceeded on the assumption that markets do process new information appropriately. If there are market inefficiencies—anomalies and excess volatility—then the case for prohibiting insider trading remains, as such activity will

---

[16] Henry Manne famously made the case for insider trading by arguing that it would improve price accuracy: HG Manne, *Insider Trading and the Stock Market* (New York, NY: Free Press, 1966). For an unusual case study of such movement in action, see S Chakravarty and JJ McConnell, 'An Analysis of Prices, Bid/Ask Spreads, and Bid and Ask Depths Surrounding Ivan Boesky's Illegal Trading in Carnation's Stock' (1997) 26 *Financial Management* 18.

[17] This is problematic for at least two reasons. First, the presence of many potential traders in the market ensures liquidity, which facilitates the incorporation of new information into prices. Second, investors who specialize in analysing new information may have a comparative advantage to insiders in determining the extent of the impact of a new piece of information on a firm's valuation. If insider trading is permitted, other investors may be deterred from engaging in such analysis.

[18] We consider the functions and regulation of a range of information intermediaries in Chapter 6.

harm liquidity for the reasons we have discussed. There may also be a role for regulation in seeking to correct the deviations of share prices from fundamentals. However, the extent of the required correction and the best way to achieve it are far from obvious. For example, if the source of excess volatility is excessive response to the arrival of new information, then disclosure of more information—whether in the form of trade transparency or issuer disclosure—might actually serve to exacerbate the mispricing. This sort of concern underlies much of the current debates about whether disclosure is linked to short-termism and excessive trading.

5.3 Market Participants

Chapter 2 described the different types of investors in financial markets. They participate in order to make a return on their investment, but there are diverse ways in which they seek to do this, and many different motivations for trading at a particular point in time. For expository purposes, we group these into four categories of traders.[19]

5.3.1 Informed traders

The key players to ensure informationally efficient markets are informed traders, ie those who trade based on information. Such information may be about the issuer or about other market participants' trading, including across different trading venues. Informed traders seek to make money from changes in the values of securities. This implies the trader has a basis for differing from the assessment of information impounded in the current market price. Traders may analyse firm-specific information differently, they may independently generate information that they believe is relevant to pricing, or they may have their own view about the future pricing of some critical input that will affect the firm's profitability (for example, the price of fuel for airlines, or the capacity of battery cells for electric cars). This is 'speculation', in the sense that the trader runs the risk that her assessment of the information may be wrong, and will lose money.[20]

Traders go 'long' in securities that they believe will appreciate in value and 'short' in those that they believe will decline. Going long simply means purchasing the security, whether with one's own funds or with borrowed money (which is known as 'margin trading'). Going short involves borrowing a security and selling it on the promise of buying it back at a lower price in the future.

---

[19] This categorization is intended neither to be exhaustive nor definitive, and the categories are not mutually exclusive. It draws on prior such categorizations offered in the literature: see eg Gilson and Kraakman, n 3; RJ Gilson and R Kraakman, 'The Mechanisms of Market Efficiency Twenty Years Later: The Hindsight Bias' (2002) 28 *Journal of Corporation Law* 715; Z Goshen and G Parchomovsky, 'The Essential Role of Securities Regulation' (2006) 55 *Duke Law Journal* 711.

[20] What distinguishes it from gambling, which is the domain of 'noise' traders—discussed in section 5.3.4, section 9.3—is that the value investor has a rational basis supported by evidence for believing her pricing theory. Clearly, this boundary has a substantial area of no man's land.

Short Sale Example

Assume a trader, A, thinks that the shares in X plc are overpriced. They are trading at £2 a share, and A wants to profit from the expected future fall in the share price. A borrows 100 shares in X plc from an institutional investor, B, paying B a fee (say £10). A immediately sells the shares in the market for the market price (£200), then waits for the price of shares in X plc to fall. If the shares do fall (say, to £1 a share), A buys 100 shares in the market and returns them to B. A's profit (£90) is the difference between the sale price (£200) and the purchase price (£100) less the fee paid to B (£10). Obviously, if A bets wrongly, and the price of the securities rises in this period, then A will incur a loss as he will have to pay more to purchase the shares he needs to return to B than he received when he sold them initially.

There is an asymmetry to long and short positions. With a long position, the maximum a trader can lose is the amount originally invested (because of limited liability) whereas with a short position, the trader can continue to lose money as far as the share price continues to rise. For this reason, long positions tend to lend themselves more to long-term investment, in the form of 'buy and hold'.

Traders who seek to make short-term profits on the basis of their analysis, particularly if they are taking a short position, often try to engage in 'arbitrage'. Strictly speaking, *arbitrageurs* are traders who seek to identify pricing discrepancies between securities and markets and to trade in principle at zero risk by exploiting these discrepancies. They are therefore a subset of the category of 'informed' traders. To understand how arbitrageurs function in the stock market, it is useful to distinguish two cases, arbitrage across geographic distances and arbitrage across temporal distances.

Inter-market arbitrage. If the shares of companies are quoted on more than one trading platform, differences in the prices create riskless arbitrage opportunities in the form of selling (or short selling) stocks on the markets on which the shares are trading at high prices and buying on markets where they are trading at lower prices.[21] Putting aside operational issues and settlement risk, this arbitrage can be achieved at zero risk, because the purchase and sale can be simultaneously executed at known prices. Such arbitrage assures that all traders of the security benefit from the law of one price.

Inter-temporal arbitrage. An arbitrageur whose analysis suggests, for example, that a stock is overpriced relative to its growth prospects, can seek to profit by selling that stock short *today* in anticipation that the market price will fall in the future to the price that correctly impounds the firm's growth prospects. Although the arbitrageur can eliminate certain risks in this trade,[22] the lack of simultaneity in the 'buy' and the 'sell'

---

[21] Because the derivatives of shares should trade at prices that reflect the value of the underlying shares, a share can be replicated as a combination of the purchase of a call option to purchase a share at a particular exercise price and the sale of a put option to sell the share at the same exercise price. Arbitrageurs can realize riskless profits by purchasing call options and writing put options while short selling the underlying stock when the combination of the derivatives costs less than the sale value of the shares.

[22] For example, in order to avoid bearing risks associated with a general improvement in the overall economy or in the industry sector, the arbitrageur will 'hedge' by taking a long position in a 'substitute'—a company that is as similar as possible save for the difference in growth prospects or a portfolio of companies

inevitably puts the arbitrageur at risk. First, the arbitrageur bears the risk that his/her assessment of growth prospects is incorrect; prices may never adjust down. Second, the time period necessary for corrective market pricing is not predetermined; meanwhile, the arbitrageur bears the financing costs of the position (including hedges) and faces unlimited downside risk if the firm's price should increase. Many arbitrageurs went broke while correctly forecasting the demise of the dot.com bubble but too soon.

Arbitrageurs perform an important role in promoting market efficiency and eliminating anomalies in markets. Their capacity to do this depends on the resources that are available for them to perform these functions and on limitations which may be imposed on their capacity to execute the relevant trades. For example, the arbitrageurs were required to short sell stocks that they did not possess. If limitations are imposed on the ability of traders to short sell securities because of concerns about the downward pressure that such sales might exercise in depressed bear markets, then the capacity of arbitrageurs to eliminate pricing discrepancies will be restricted.[23] Likewise, limitations on the capacity of arbitrageurs to use credit to finance profitable trades will have similar effects.

This observation points to the potential detrimental effect of imposing regulation that restricts the capacity of market participants from undertaking market transactions. These rules might be introduced for sound prudential and stability reasons but might have significant unintended consequences in weakening the self-correcting mechanisms that would otherwise operate in financial markets. If traders can go 'long' but not 'short,' positive sentiments will be over-represented in market prices.[24]

But in addition to regulatory impediments, the foregoing suggests that there will be limits to the extent to which arbitrage can extinguish pricing discrepancies because of wealth and borrowing constraints that traders face. In light of the huge volumes of trades and the vast amounts of money invested in markets, there may be serious limitations to arbitrage.[25]

5.3.2 Liquidity traders

A second reason for trading is to convert an investment into cash for liquidity needs. For example, the ability to sell equities or bonds might be important for the financing of the purchase of a consumer durable like a car or house or the making of a tuition payment. Uncertainty about the precise timing of such expenditures makes the ability to realize the value of an asset at short notice an important characteristic of it for liquidity traders.

---

in the same industry. Thus, if something happens while the position is open that will increase (decrease) the value of firms in the sector generally, the arbitrageur will gain from his long position (short position), offsetting his corresponding losses from the other position. The only unhedged aspect will be changes in value of the original security owing to adjustment of the firm's growth prospects.

[23] Chapter 9 discusses the rationale behind the imposition of restrictions on short selling.
[24] See the discussion in Chapter 9, section 9.6.
[25] See A Shleifer and RW Vishny, 'The Limits of Arbitrage' (1997) 52 *Journal of Finance* 35.

5.3.3 Momentum traders

Both informed and liquidity traders have good reasons for trading shares, based on their beliefs about market movements and pricing relationships or their needs to meet their consumption requirements. Others may, however, be less well informed or motivated. A third category is what are termed *momentum* traders, who rather than following the flow of new information about a firm, simply follow the movement of stock prices. As soon as they observe unusual trading volume in a stock, they will pile in or out, hoping to profit from the difference between the price at which they entered the trade and the ultimate price at which the security settles. Like arbitrage, this is an inherently short-term trading strategy. But unlike arbitrage, it is not based on any independent analysis of information regarding the value of the securities being traded. Rather, momentum traders are free-riding on others' analysis that is revealed through price movements.

5.3.4 Noise traders

A fourth category of market participant is termed *noise* traders, capturing the idea that they trade not on real information but on 'background noise'.[26] This actually encompasses a very heterogeneous group of traders. Some are looking at potentially relevant information but mistake what is *salient*—that is, widely reported—for what is *news* to the market. Such traders typically come too late to the information to make any money from trades. Others are trading on the basis of information that is not, or is unlikely to be, relevant to prices—or on no information at all. Many trades are made on the basis of intuition and hunches. Some financial institutions may engage in trades to exploit the charges that they can impose on their customers. In particular, these customers might find themselves unwittingly the victims of trading that has served them no purpose and cost them significantly in terms of the fees that they have incurred.

Ordinarily, these noise traders' assessments of stock price valuations will not be correlated with one another. Thus, their trading behaviour will not usually affect market prices, with any minor deviations simply creating opportunities for arbitrageurs to earn a profit. However, if for whatever reason noise trading becomes correlated, then this can affect prices. Momentum traders will add themselves to a price bandwagon whatever its cause, and the resulting level of price pressure may be beyond the resources of arbitrageurs to correct, giving rise to what is sometimes known as 'noise trader risk'.[27]

---

[26] See J Dow and G Gorton, 'Noise Traders', in SN Durlauf and LE Blume (eds), *The New Palgrave: A Dictionary of Economics*, 2nd ed (New York, NY: Palgrave Macmillan, 2008).

[27] A Shleifer, *Inefficient Markets* (Oxford: Clarendon Press, 2000). Indeed, professional investors like arbitrageurs may take a 'if you can't beat them, join them' approach to a growing bubble, planning to jump off the wave before it crashes. As with short selling, timing may be everything. For evidence of this with respect to the 'tech bubble' at the turn of the century, see M Brunnermeier and S Nagel, 'Hedge Funds and the Technology Bubble' (2004) 59 *Journal of Finance* 2013. The discussion about market efficiency assumes that noise traders do not dominate informed traders to the point where they cause violations of efficient markets.

Unless noise traders dominate the market and systematically succeed in moving prices, they will lose money, first, as a consequence of the payment of unnecessary fees and, second, from being at the other end of trades that benefit well-informed counter-parties. Noise traders can therefore expect systematically to lose to the intermediaries who execute the trades on their behalf and to informed traders.[28]

Much of the regulation of financial markets is framed as seeking to protect less well-informed market participants. However, as we shall see repeatedly in Chapters 6–9, rules governing issuer disclosure and insider trading actually do not always further their cause. Rather, the regulatory interventions that genuinely serve the interests of uninformed market participants are those we categorize under the heading of 'con-sumer protection' in Part C. These include rules that require institutions to disclose the terms on which they are engaging with their customers, such as the fees that they levy for transactions, and to manage conflicts that might arise from their relations with other institutions—all of which are examples of attempts to reduce the scale of exploitation of vulnerable consumers. Likewise, conduct of business rules that require brokers to undertake trades on behalf of their clients at the best available prices ('best execution' rules) are designed to serve a similar purpose. Chapters 11 and 12 discuss these types of measure.

There are of course costs to such rules. First, they encourage intermediaries to circumvent regulatory rules by engaging in activities that are not prohibited or res-tricted. Second, they raise the cost of providing financial services by requiring institu-tions to employ people who are responsible for implementing rules. Third, they restrict what might otherwise be commercially beneficial relations and activities. For example, there might be good reasons for fund managers and brokers to have close relations and undertake repeat business with each other. Regulation might therefore interfere with the efficient operation of markets and institutions.

As a consequence, some regulation focuses on particular classes of investors distin-guishing between professional and institutional investors, which are presumed to be informed, and individual investors, which are presumed to be uninformed, and provide for more stringent rules when the latter are involved. We examine in greater detail in Chapter 8 and Part C the extent to which such market segmentation for regulatory purposes is both observed and desirable.[29]

5.4 Price Setting

One of the remarkable features of financial markets is the insight they provide into the ways in which prices are set. In the stylized world of traditional economic theory, prices are determined by auctioneers who call out prices and raise them when demand exceeds supply and lower them when the reverse holds until markets clear with demand equalling supply. In practice, few markets other than those for antiques and paintings are organized like this. In most, the process of arriving at prices is much more

---

[28] See BM Barber, T Odean, and N Zhu, 'Do Retail Trades Move Markets?' (2009) 22 *Review of Finance* 151.

[29] See Chapter 8, section 8.4.2 and Chapter 10, section 10.5.

decentralized, and the key intermediary, if there is one, is not the 'auctioneer' but rather the 'dealer', a party in the business of holding financial instruments ready to trade.

5.4.1 Price setting through market-making

Where the intermediary is the auctioneer, there is one price, the price at which all bidders except one drop out. Where the intermediary is the dealer, there are two prices: first, the price at which the dealer as *seller* is willing to sell the financial instrument, the 'offer' or 'ask' price, and second, the price at which the dealer as *buyer* is willing to purchase, the 'bid' price. The ask price is higher than the bid price and the difference between the two is known as the 'bid–ask spread'. The dealer, who is said to be 'making a market' in the securities or commodities in question, buys from sellers at the bid price, and sells to buyers at the ask price. The difference between the two prices is the gross profit earned by the dealer.

A spread is conventionally observed in all markets. For example, the price at which you can sell a second-hand car (the dealer's *bid* price) is less than the price at which you would purchase it (the dealer's *ask* price). This is attributed to the costs incurred by the dealer, whether it is making a market in used cars or securities. A dealer faces three sorts of costs: order processing, inventory holding, and asymmetric information costs. Order processing costs are the administrative and overhead costs necessitated by standing ready to trade with large numbers of counterparties—the equipment, the connection to the dealing system, and the personnel employed. Inventory holding costs are the costs to the dealer of having to buy and hold the security, which cover financing costs as well as the risk that the security will decline in value.[30]

Perhaps the most serious cost arises from the risk of asymmetric information. Dealers will be exposed to systematically adverse trades if the trading counterparties are better informed about the underlying value of the security. So a dealer that stands ready to buy a security at the bid price faces the risk that the seller knows that this price overstates its true value and that the price is likely to fall before the dealer is able to sell it. In anticipation, the dealer will offer to pay *below* the estimated true value to reflect this possibility; the bid will be shaded *down*. Conversely, when the dealer sells a security the sale might be to investors who know that the price is likely to rise. So again, by way of self-protection, the dealer deviates from the estimated true value, here with an offer that shades the ask *up*. The bid goes down; the ask goes up. Together the effect of asymmetric information is to widen the bid–ask spread and thereby to raise the cost of transacting in markets. A wider bid–ask spread will reduce market liquidity, because fewer sellers will sell at the reduced bid price and fewer buyers will buy at the elevated ask price.

Taking the order processing costs and the inventory holding costs as given, the bid–ask spread is determined by the possibility of asymmetric information between the dealer and the trader. The spread reflects the exposure that the dealer faces from interacting with the possibly more informed parties on the other side of the transaction.

---

[30] Since in an efficient market it is as likely that the price will go up as down, identifying this risk as a 'cost' assumes that the dealer is risk averse, a plausible assumption given the likely financing arrangement.

During periods in which there is more uncertainty in the market, spreads will widen partly because of risk aversion on the part of the dealer (it has to finance its inventory, so it might want to shrink the balance sheet to reduce the risk of loss) but partly also because of the greater concern that the seller has information that this particular security will be adversely affected. The costs of transacting in a market are therefore a function of uncertainty and information asymmetries as well as the pure costs of operations.

Regulators seek to improve the functioning of markets by increasing the information available to market participants. The mandatory issuer disclosure system (discussed in Chapter 8) is certainly one way of protecting dealers against information asymmetries. Countries with robust disclosure systems have narrower bid–ask spreads in trading markets.[31] For a given market, large capitalization stocks followed by many analysts and/or by the media generally have tighter bid–ask spreads than small capitalization stocks.[32] Another mechanism for reducing the information asymmetries is through reporting on transactions. Timely reporting of trades in terms of their prices and volumes allows market participants to determine the nature of transactions and to infer how the underlying value of securities is changing. The shorter the delay in reporting transactions, the less that informed traders will be able to exploit their informational advantage to the detriment of other traders and dealers. There is no free lunch, of course, because reducing the profitability of informed trading will also reduce the incentives to engage in the securities research that increases the efficiency of market prices. Chapter 6 considers problems with the revenue models of information intermediaries and Chapter 7 discusses the organization of markets and rules regarding the disclosure of trading information.

Early reporting of trades also makes it harder for liquidity-seeking investors to dispose of significant holdings without moving market prices. Rapid reporting of trades thus has cross-cutting effects on market liquidity. Early disclosure may move prices against a (large) liquidity trader and thus reduce returns from holding securities. On the other hand, reporting delays work to the benefit of informed traders and will therefore raise bid–ask spreads—to the detriment of (small) liquidity traders. There is therefore a balance to be struck in the speed with which trades should be reported. In some cases, where large blocks of securities need to be traded it can be more convenient to transact them off markets where suppliers and purchasers can negotiate directly with each other without being subject to the same trade disclosure rules.[33]

---

[31] See eg R La Porta, F Lopez-de-Silanes, and A Shleifer, 'What Works in Securities Laws?' (2006) 61 *Journal of Finance* 1, 17.

[32] See eg H Hong, T Lim, and JC Stein, 'Bad News Travels Slowly: Size, Analyst Coverage, and the Profitability of Momentum Strategies' (2000) 55 *Journal of Finance* 265; BJ Bushee, JE Core, W Guay, and SJW Hamm, 'The Role of the Business Press as an Information Intermediary' (2009) 48 *Journal of Accounting Research* 1.

[33] The trading venues that specialize in matching the orders of informed and/or large (institutional) investors are known as 'dark pools'. For a discussion of the effect of dark pools on price discovery see H Zhu, 'Do Dark Pools Harm Price Discovery?' (2014) 27 *Review of Financial Studies* 747.

5.4.2 Alternative ways of price setting

There are two ways in which equities are traded on stock markets. The first is a 'quote driven' system and the second an 'order driven' system. A *quote driven* system displays only the bids and asks of 'market makers', financial intermediaries who undertake the obligation to continuously quote the prices at which they are willing to buy and sell securities on the exchange. Traders place orders for the immediate execution of deals at the quoted price.

In contrast, in an *order driven* system, all traders' buy and sell orders are displayed and executed through an auction process, whether on a continuous basis or periodically (such as at the end of the trading day). In order driven markets, traders usually post maximum prices at which they are willing to buy or minimum prices at which they are willing to sell securities and then wait for corresponding offers to sell at below their bid prices and bids to purchase at above their offer prices. These are known as 'limit orders' because they specify the limits of the range at which the participant is willing to trade. Elements of the two systems can be combined. For example, an order driven system often also employs market makers to ensure higher liquidity.[34]

The advantage of the quote driven system for traders is that it provides immediacy and certainty that the transaction will be executed. The drawback is lack of certainty about the price at which the transactions will take place. The advantage of the order driven system is that, by using a limit order, there is certainty about the prices at which transactions occur and transparency in the sense that all bids and offers for a security are observable. The drawback is that there is no certainty about when the transaction will be executed and indeed whether it will be executed at all. A quote driven system therefore creates immediacy but not price certainty. An order driven system creates price certainty for those placing limit orders, but not immediacy.

In essence, similar to market makers, limit order traders provide liquidity to the market insofar as they offer to purchase or sell securities at particular prices and the larger the volume of limit orders, the greater the degree of liquidity. Traders who seek immediate liquidity and place 'market orders'—orders to transact at whatever the current market price—absorb or 'use up' liquidity provided by limit order traders. The liquidity of a market therefore depends on the number of traders willing to provide limit orders, the amount of capital that they have to do this, and the maximum size of the trades that they are willing to transact. Like dealers, limit order traders are exposed to volatility in share prices arising both from random movements and informed traders. In essence, those placing a limit order to sell securities are granting a call option to potential purchasers to buy the security when its intrinsic value rises above the posted ask price. Conversely, those placing a limit order to purchase securities are providing a put option to potential sellers to sell the security when its intrinsic value falls below the posted bid price. Therefore, for the reasons described before, bid–ask spreads will widen and liquidity will diminish when there is increased uncertainty or a

---

[34] Quote driven arrangements may also be used exclusively at the beginning (and/or end) of the trading day, in order to clear markets before the (next) day's trading starts.

larger presence of informed traders. The liquidity of markets is therefore vulnerable to intensified uncertainty and asymmetries of information. Insider trading therefore imposes a public cost insofar as it causes a widening of spreads on security prices. Regulation therefore seeks to increase transparency and control insider trading to avoid the public good costs that they would otherwise impose.

The provision of information has traditionally given stock exchanges and other markets such as commodity markets an element of a natural monopoly, namely that there are significant cost disadvantages to having more than one provider. The natural monopoly element in exchanges derives from the information advantage of having all information concentrated in one location. Being able to observe limit order prices and to seek quotes from all traders and dealers allows investors to make full comparisons of the available bids and offers. To the extent that transactions occur on other exchanges, they are not able to do this. On the other hand, exchanges are like other service providers. They vary in terms of the quality and costs of services that they provide and some are more efficiently run than others. Conferring a monopoly on a provider introduces inefficiencies which competition between exchanges can diminish. Recently, many new exchanges have therefore emerged that compete with the established exchanges and seek to take transactions away from them. This competition promotes efficiency in the operation of the exchanges and innovation in the delivery of new services. However, it also fragments markets and imposes information costs on investors. Unlike other services, it is therefore not clear whether there is a net advantage or drawback to competition between exchanges and the entry of new exchanges tends to be followed in short order by their absorption into or purchase of other exchanges to solidify the gains to consolidation of information on a small number of them. Chapter 7 discusses the emergence of new forms of markets and trading.

5.4.3 Clearing and settling trades

While stock markets execute transactions, they do not actually complete them. They merely establish the contractual basis on which transactions will then be settled. There are two further stages. The first is 'clearing', which occurs when transactions are reported, margins associated with the trades are posted, different transactions are netted so that purchases are subtracted from sales and the net positions of traders are determined, associated tax payments are established, and failed transactions are managed. In particular, 'clearinghouses' stand behind transactions and may use their own capital to protect traders from failures of their counterparties to pay or deliver. The second stage is 'settlement', which is the actual transfer of title to securities and payments in exchange. There is typically a delay of some days between the execution of a trade and the date on which it is agreed that it will be settled to allow the parties to clear their respective bank balances and arrange for corresponding transactions to be completed. Shortening the settlement period reduces counterparty risk on a trade and is thought, therefore, to reduce systemic risk.

As with exchanges, there are trade-offs between consolidating clearing and settling in a small number of locations and promoting competition between providers. As in the case of exchanges, there is an element of natural monopoly in clearing and settlement insofar as the processes of netting trades is most efficiently done when all trades on a particular security or by a particular trader pass through one clearinghouse. However, there are corresponding inefficiencies in stifling competition. Regulatory and competition authorities have attempted to identify the underlying sources of the natural monopoly and seek ways of promoting competition through establishing relations between clearing houses. Alternatively, since both exchanges and clearing-houses have natural monopoly elements, competition can be promoted between vertically integrated exchanges and clearinghouses so that they can compete in terms of the full range of services from execution to clearing. Settlement rules are discussed in Chapter 18.

5.5 Conclusion

This chapter has provided a basis for understanding the organization and operation of financial markets and the degree to which they fulfil the functions that they are supposed to perform of facilitating trades and investments and incorporating relevant information on the values of the underlying securities. We have noted the extent to which financial markets are efficient in pricing securities and how they sometimes deviate from efficiency by displaying various anomalies and discrepancies from the predictions of the ECMH.

In particular, the chapter has concluded that there are potential defects of markets that may justify regulatory responses. Greater transparency and disclosure enhances public information and is generally thought to enhance price accuracy.[35] However, it may have a negative impact on the incentives to produce and process information. For instance, requirements to disclose trades rapidly may increase the costs of undertaking large-volume transactions, consequently discouraging the acquisition of new information. This may drive trading off exchanges and into dark pools and OTC markets. Likewise, competition in markets may lead to fragmentation at a cost to consolidation of information and clearing of trades. Transparency, disclosure, and competition policy therefore have to be used with caution in securities markets, but nevertheless they appear to have all in all facilitated the development of liquid markets. The four subsequent chapters in this second part of the book discuss these trade-offs in more depth.

---

[35] For further discussion see Chapters 7 and 8.

6

Information Intermediaries

6.1 Introduction

Securities market prices incorporate new information thanks to the trading activity of those who, unlike liquidity and noise traders, buy and sell based on the available price-relevant information. Hence, the efficiency of securities markets is a function of the market for information: the more quickly new information is gathered, processed, verified, and distributed among informed traders, the more efficient the securities markets.[1] 'New information' that is relevant to the price of a particular firm's securities can include information about:

(i) *Trading in the firm's securities*: access to information about existing market orders (pre-trade) and executed trades (post-trade) may enable the detection of informed trading patterns before the information content underlying them is fully reflected in prices;

(ii) *The issuer*, its financial condition, its earnings, its business developments, and its governance, including its ownership patterns;

(iii) *The issuer's industry* more generally, and developments concerning competitors or 'comparable companies';

(iv) *Macroeconomic conditions and policies*; and

(v) *Other significant events*, whether natural (catastrophes) or human (political news), which have a potential impact on the whole economy, an industry, or an issuer specifically.

Informed market participants have to make sense of at least some of that information before they trade. The larger ones, or those specializing in a given information source (such as high-frequency traders who exploit order flow information), will do most of the processing work themselves, building the capacity and the technology to analyse and act upon information in-house. Other traders will rely on the processing and the analysis performed by other market participants. Virtually all informed traders have to acquire information from outside sources before they can use it. In order to execute their trades all kinds of traders (informed, liquidity, and noise traders) rely on a trading system, such as an exchange, that aggregates information about existing orders.

In the broadest sense, trading systems and other 'sources' of financial information are all 'information intermediaries'. Under this heading we group together a variety of information providers and processors performing very different functions within the financial market. Chapter 7 will show how exchanges and other trading venues such as

---

[1] RJ Gilson and RH Kraakman, 'The Mechanisms of Market Efficiency' (1984) 70 *Virginia Law Review* 549, 593.

Principles of Financial Regulation. First Edition. John Armour, Dan Awrey, Paul Davies, Luca Enriques, Jeffrey N. Gordon, Colin Mayer, and Jennifer Payne. © John Armour, Dan Awrey, Paul Davies, Luca Enriques, Jeffrey N. Gordon, Colin Mayer, and Jennifer Payne 2016. Published 2016 by Oxford University Press.

alternative trading systems, by giving access to information on market orders and executed trades, aggregate, process, and distribute that information. Similarly, 'trade repositories', such as Bloomberg, are in the business of aggregating information about executed trades in less centralized markets (such as over-the-counter derivatives markets), and selling it to other market participants.

Securities analysts, in turn, focus on issuers' disclosures, whether mandatory or voluntary: they put those disclosures into context alongside developments in the issuer's industry more generally and the economy at large, evaluate the implications for an issuer's future cash flows of the disclosures and all other material pieces of information, and synthesize their findings in (usually) short reports that even hurried traders can understand and act upon. Other information intermediaries help investors understand an issuer's risks based on their specialized skills and standardized methodologies (like credit rating agencies: hereafter, 'CRAs') or make issuers' disclosures more valuable to their users by credibly verifying them (here we think of auditors and lawyers). Still others, in addition to processing and vouching for all relevant information about a prospective listed firm, gather information about the demand for its shares and determine their price before a liquid market exists for them, as underwriters do at the initial public offering ('IPO') stage.

Underwriters, auditors, lawyers, CRAs, and analysts are the information intermediaries we focus on in this chapter. Although they comprise only a subset of information intermediaries, they perform key functions in securities markets. In addition, these intermediaries' contributions to market efficiency, their business models, and the market imperfections affecting them are so diverse that our focus on them will be sufficient to give you a good idea of the market functions of information intermediaries in general and the policy issues arising from their activities.

We begin in section 6.2 by reviewing key issues relating to the production, processing, and distribution of information in capital markets. In section 6.3, we focus on the specific roles played by our selected information intermediaries, and the particular difficulties they face in performing them. The potential need for regulation is therefore discussed in each case. In section 6.4 we briefly examine the regulation of these groups in the context of the range of regulatory techniques utilized in this area: disclosure, rules designed to ameliorate the conflicts of interest that arise, regulatory oversight, qualification requirements, intermediaries' liability for losses incurred by investors, and other techniques designed to increase the intermediary's incentive to maintain its reputation. By the end of this chapter you should have a clear idea of the functions performed by information intermediaries in general and the particular intermediaries discussed in this chapter. You should be aware of the potential difficulties associated with these roles, and the regulation that has been put in place to address them.

6.2 The Role of Information Intermediaries: General Considerations

Were one to design a securities market from scratch, one would have to address (at least) five key issues relating to the production, processing, and distribution of the set of information needed to attain the goals of informational efficiency and liquidity.

Property in price-relevant information. First, property rights in information should be allocated and defined: will someone *own* that information? If so, should the owner be allowed to profit freely from it in all possible forms (such as by trading on it, and/or by selling it to selected counterparties)? Should she perhaps be allowed to sell it to whomever she pleases, but not to trade on it? Or should she be required to let anyone willing to pay a reasonable price have access to it, on a non-discriminatory basis? Or indeed should no one be granted ownership rights in relation to information, meaning that no one can trade on it or selectively pass it on, the information instead having to be disclosed to the public?

As this and the other chapters in Part B illustrate, jurisdictions make different choices regarding property rights in information for different information items and producers. In some cases an information owner exists (usually its producer) and is free to profit from it: that is the case for buy-side analysts' employers, who can both trade on their analysts' reports and sell them to selected counterparties.[2] In other cases, the information owner may profit from it by trading, but may not grant access to it to others so that they can also trade on it. In Europe, for example, this is the case with a hedge fund manager building a position in a company to start an activist campaign: she will violate EU insider trading laws if she lets fellow hedge fund managers know about her intentions.[3] In Chapter 7, we consider some cases where the information owner may grant selective access to information, but may not trade on it himself and, in addition, has to grant access to anyone willing to pay a fair price on a non-discriminatory basis (that is, stock exchanges with regard to orders and trades, according to pre- and post-trade transparency rules). Finally, in some cases regulators assign 'negative property rights' on information to the market as a whole:[4] in those cases, information has to be disclosed to the public once it is produced or, possibly, kept confidential, but subject to a trading ban and/or a prohibition on selective disclosure. Issuer information that is subject to mandatory disclosure, our focus in Chapter 8, is a good example. Such property allocation rules can be understood as the ground rules of securities market law.

Incentives to produce price-relevant information. Second, because of its character as a public good, information may be under-produced—or under-disclosed. That, in turn, will negatively affect market efficiency. This chapter will show how this problem underlies revenue models for information intermediaries that give rise to conflicts of interest, potentially reducing their effectiveness as information conduits, and will provide illustrations of the attempts by policymakers to tackle such problems. Chapter 8, in turn, will show how issuers may disclose less information about themselves than would be optimal for the market as a whole, justifying mandatory disclosure regulation.

Intuitively, to ensure that information intermediaries distribute a reliable product to their users, a direct relationship will be preferable, whereby investors select and pay for the intermediary's services. However, this model faces severe collective action

---

[2] See section 6.3.2.   [3] See Chapter 9, section 9.3.
[4] Z Goshen and G Parchomovsky, 'The Essential Role of Securities Regulation' (2006) 55 *Duke Law Journal* 711.

problems, because it will be hard to exclude others from information, once this has been produced and passed on to investors: each investor will try to free-ride on other investors' efforts to gather information and no one will be willing to pay for it. In other words, many information intermediary services are in the nature of public goods. As a result, other funding models have arisen, where intermediaries are paid by the issuer or the intermediary cross-subsidizes its role as information intermediary with other services offered to issuers or investors. These funding models inevitably increase the chances that conflicts will arise, and a recurring theme in this chapter is the entrench-ment of incentives for intermediaries, and the way in which incentives can distort the role of information intermediaries.

Verification of information. Third, there is the matter of how readily users—including other information intermediaries—can rely upon information produced by self-interested actors. This is the question of *verification*. Think of issuers' disclosures. Companies may be tempted to misinform investors in order to inflate the market price: at the IPO stage, because those in control are selling; or later, perhaps because their managers may have equity-linked compensation. This is obviously problematic for investors seeking to rely on these disclosures, but it is a problem for the issuers too, since it can lead to investors discounting the value of investments (because they cannot distinguish good from bad investments), or declining to invest at all: the by now familiar lemons market scenario. So, is there a better way to ensure that such infor-mation is relied upon than having each user bear the cost of verifying it?

In addition to relying on criminal sanctions against fraudulent statements,[5] markets may make use of professional agents to monitor the company's management and the quality and dependability of the information they produce.[6] Various professionals fulfil this role, including underwriters, analysts, auditors, and lawyers. Similarly, CRAs help investors understand debt issuers' information, including the non-public information to which issuers usually give them access, by translating it into assessments of their default risk compared to other debt issuers based on the CRAs' specialized expertise and methodologies.

Together, such professionals can be labelled as 'reputation intermediaries': in the broadest sense, because each of them provides a useful service to the users of the information they produce, so long as their track record makes them reliable sources (think of CRAs); in some cases also because these intermediaries pledge their reputa-tion, built up over time, to vouch for the issuer (eg underwriters). The idea is that investors can trust these intermediaries more than the issuer because they have less of an incentive to deceive. Unlike unknown issuers who might have nothing to lose from a fraud, especially if they expect only to raise money from investors once and have little to fear from *ex post* enforcement measures (for instance, because they are judgement-proof), reputation intermediaries are repeat players and some of them (underwriters,

---

[5] Discussed in Chapter 9, section 9.5 and Chapter 26, section 26.3.

[6] See eg RH Kraakman, 'Gatekeepers: The Anatomy of a Third Party Enforcement Strategy' (1986) 2 *Journal of Law, Economics and Organization* 54; S Choi, 'Market Lessons for Gatekeepers' (1988) 92 *Northwestern University Law Review* 916; J Coffee, *Gatekeepers: The Professions and Corporate Governance* (Oxford: OUP, 2006).

auditors, and lawyers, as we shall see) 'repeat certifiers'. The intermediary shares none (or very few) of the gains of fraud to which it may be party, and is exposed to a large risk if the fraud is exposed, namely the loss of its reputation into the future, and possibly legal liability. In theory, as long as the intermediary has reputational capital at risk whose value exceeds the expected profit that it will receive from the individual client relationship, it should be faithful to investors, and not provide false certification. Reputational capital will therefore work effectively where incentives for the intermediary to maintain its reputation are strong.

Gatekeepers. A fourth issue is whether, for markets to work efficiently (or, as policymakers usually think about it, to protect investors), the law should *mandate* the use of any of these information intermediaries or at least incentivize their use by providing for a more favourable regulatory framework in case they are used. In this chapter we use the term 'gatekeeper' to refer to these information intermediaries.[7] The term 'gatekeeper' means literally someone that controls access to an activity, in this case the capital markets. For example, an issuer will need to make use of an auditor's services to access the market, since audited accounts are a key component of the mandatory disclosure obligations imposed on issuers, both at the IPO stage and after. By contrast, the services of a securities analyst are not a *necessary* part of the issuer's offer of securities to the public or their admission to trading on an exchange. The securities analyst is, in effect, a volunteer in this regard. This distinction between information intermediaries and gatekeepers is heuristic: for instance, there is no requirement to use lawyers in an IPO. *De facto*, however, rules for public offers are such that it is almost impossible for someone to implement one without a lawyer's assistance. However, the distinction may help us to better understand various features of the intermediaries in this chapter (for example, their models of compensation), and may also cast light on the regulatory issues that arise.

There is a potential moral hazard problem with putting information intermediaries in a gatekeeping role. The existence of a legal mandate or incentive to use a gatekeeper may lull other market participants into a false sense of security, causing them to rely on the intermediary and seek out less information on their own. In other words, there might be an expectation gap between what gatekeepers can actually achieve with their services and what investors think they can achieve.

Role of regulation. This leads to the fifth policy issue: do the markets for information intermediaries' services work well if unfettered by regulation, or will they perform their information distribution and verification role effectively only if they are regulated? And, if so, how should they be regulated? Later sections will explore the reasons why each of these intermediaries may fail to perform its role in the absence of regulations. In general, we can note that reputation alone may be insufficient to ensure that they process and verify information as independently as theory would predict. In concentrated markets with high barriers to entry, for example, it may not be

---

[7] In doing so, we provide a narrower definition of the term than others have. See eg Coffee, n 6, 2–3 (using the term more extensively to cover all reputation intermediaries as defined here).

necessary for the intermediary to maintain an unblemished record, just one that is not significantly worse than that of its rivals.[8]

6.3 The Roles of Information Intermediaries: Specific Cases

6.3.1 Underwriters

Underwriters provide a clear example of an information intermediary that also operates as a reputation intermediary. When a firm decides to issue securities to the public, it almost always hires an intermediary, typically an investment bank, as its 'underwriter'.[9] In such capacity, the bank advises the issuer on its governance, the offered securities, the offering amount, and the price,[10] and assists it in preparing the prospectus and in selling the securities to the public.

The exact role of the bank in the underwriting process will depend on the structure of the offering. In a 'firm commitment' offering, the underwriter guarantees the sale of the offering—that is, the underwriter (or syndicate of underwriters) will purchase the entire offering from the issuer before reselling the securities to investors. The underwriter will purchase the shares at a discount to the price at which the shares will subsequently be offered to the public. By contrast, in a 'best efforts' offering, the investment bank does not purchase the securities, but instead acts purely as a selling agent, receiving a commission on each security sold. This generates less risk for the underwriter, and therefore more risk is retained by the issuer. The underwriter only bears the opportunity cost of commissions not earned. This is often used for smaller, more speculative companies. A distinction can also be drawn between a fixed price issue (in which the price of the offering is determined upfront) and one in which the issue price is not given in the beginning, but the bids are made in a range and the issue price depends upon the demand for the securities. One common underwriting technique is book-building. An underwriter 'builds a book' by accepting orders from fund managers indicating the number of shares they desire and the price they are willing to pay, and the issue price is only determined after the close of the book-building period.

Underwriters have an important role in bringing companies to the market at the IPO stage, or helping a company to raise capital via a seasoned equity offering such as a rights issue. They serve as distributors for the issuer, providing the facilities and sales force necessary to sell the securities to the public. They may also provide a form of risk sharing or insurance for issuers, at least in connection with firm commitment

---

[8] See generally, Coffee, n 6, 3.

[9] It is possible for an issuer to sell securities directly to the public without an underwriter, in a direct public offering, but this has traditionally been rare. Issuers often lack the knowledge and expertise to structure the offer, and price the securities properly. They tend to lack the connections that investment banks have, eg with institutional investors, that can help to make the issue a success. They also find it hard to signal their quality overall and especially the trustworthiness of their disclosures. As a result, direct public offerings only tend to occur where the issue involves a rights issue of a company offering securities to its existing shareholders or for securities issued by financial institutions with their own sales networks, such as bonds issued by commercial banks to their clients. Note, however, that for 'crowdfunded' issues, it is normal not to have an underwriter: see Chapter 8, section 8.4.3.

[10] See AD Morrison and WJ Wilhelm, Jr, *Investment Banking: Institutions, Politics, and Law* (Oxford: OUP, 2007), Ch 1.

underwriting, since this relieves the issuer of some of the risks inherent in the offering of a security. However, the most significant benefit that the underwriter can provide is to lend its reputational capital to the issuer.[11]

For investors faced with a company issuing securities for the first time, the concerns are clear, namely how to gauge the value of the securities, given the informational asymmetry problem. Underwriters can address these concerns in two ways. First, their verification role helps convince buyers of the accuracy of the information the issuer provides. Absent the ability of insiders to communicate credibly their beliefs, or the ability of outsiders to access inside information, the lemons problem discussed earlier in this book may result in market failure.[12] The investment banker represents to the market that it has evaluated the issuer's product in good faith, and that it is prepared to stake its reputation on the accuracy of the information. Its credibility derives from having invested its time and capital in building its reputation, and from being a repeat player in the capital markets, unlike the issuer, a new entrant with little or no reputation: the underwriter's incentive to use false or misleading information is thus much lower than that of the issuer. Effectively, an underwriter can be employed to 'certify' that the issue price is consistent with information about the future earnings prospects of the firm.[13] Second, as repeat players with expertise in the book-building process, underwriters have the skills and the incentives to determine an offer price that reflects sophisticated investors' collective assessment of the value of the offered securities.[14]

From the investors' point of view, the use of underwriters as information intermediaries appears to be a success. The empirical evidence suggests that any concerns about the pricing of IPOs and seasoned equity offerings relate to underpricing rather than overpricing.[15] However, we do see evidence of a conflict of interest on the part of the investment bank. Investment banks take on a number of roles in addition to underwriting functions, principally corporate finance, brokerage services, and proprietary trading. Conflicts between the corporate finance arm and the brokerage arm are likely to be particularly acute when it comes to IPOs. Part of this arises because it is implicit in the issuer–underwriter relationship that the investment bank's analysts will follow the newly issued security in the aftermarket and it will provide (presumably positive) coverage. This is important to most new firms, as they are often unknown in the marketplace, and they want investors, especially institutional investors, to hear about them.

Underwriting is a regulated activity. For example, only certain players—in Europe, banks and investment firms—can engage in it. In contrast to the other information

---

[11] Gilson and Kraakman, n 1, 613–21.　　　[12] See Chapter 3, section 3.3.1.

[13] JR Booth and RL Smith, 'Capital Raising, Underwriting and the Certification Hypothesis' (1986) 15 *Journal of Financial Economics* 261.

[14] It helps retail investors, of course, that public offer regulations or best practices usually ensure that underwriters determine the same price for institutional investors as for retail ones. See Morrison and Wilhelm, n 10, 85.

[15] See eg RP Beatty and J Ritter, 'Investment Banking, Reputation, and the Underpricing of Initial Public Offerings' (1986) 15 *Journal of Financial Economics* 213; K Rock, 'Why New Issues Are Underpriced' (1986) 15 *Journal of Financial Economics* 187; R Carter and S Manaster, 'Initial Public Offerings and Underwriter Reputation' (1990) 45 *Journal of Finance* 1045.

intermediaries examined in this chapter, underwriting has been left almost unscathed by the post-scandal and post-crisis regulatory reforms of the last fifteen years. However, US regulators have addressed some of the practices that may contribute to IPO underpricing, for instance with a ban on 'spinning'—namely, the practice of allocating underpriced 'hot' IPOs shares to top managers of listed companies as a way to secure investment banking business with such companies.[16]

6.3.2 Securities analysts

Securities analysts are crucial in capital markets, where they test and interpret corporate disclosures, and make their own predictions as to a company's future prospects. They collect information about issuers, the securities they sell, and the industries in which they operate, along with general market factors, evaluating and synthesizing the information they obtain. They then disseminate their research in the form of reports and recommendations. In their reports analysts offer facts and opinions about the subject company and its securities. They will describe the company, but also provide predictions, most importantly predictions of the company's future earnings. Finally, they will provide a recommendation: although there is no industry standard in this regard, the most common categories are 'strong buy', 'buy', 'hold', 'underperform', and 'sell'. Analysts therefore synthesize raw information into more readily digestible pieces for investors.[17]

Just as IPOs are possible without underwriters, so input from analysts is not a necessary step for an issuer seeking access to the market, but their coverage of an issuer has a beneficial impact on its share price both in primary and secondary markets: it can help traders to become more informed and thus can result in a more informative share price.[18] In turn, this improves liquidity, as it encourages uninformed traders into the market, lowering trading costs and raising the share price.[19]

Analysts help reduce the cost of gathering, processing, and disseminating information across the market: resources would be wasted if each individual investor were to process the same commonly available information in parallel with all other investors.[20] But a public good problem also exists for analysts' products. Intermediaries may attempt to sell their services to only a subset of investors, but some investors may free-ride on the payments by other investors. That is why much securities research is in fact conducted in-house by large or specialized institutional investors employing internal 'buy-side' analysts. Indeed, buy-side analysts represent a significant proportion

---

[16] See FINRA Rule 5131(b).

[17] IOSCO *Report on Analyst Conflicts of Interest*, September 2003 and *Statement of Principles for addressing sell-side securities analyst conflicts of interest*, September 2003, 2.

[18] See Gilson and Kraakman, n 1. For evidence that the recommendations analysts make in relation to securities can move the prices of those securities in the market see KL Womack, 'Do Brokerage Analysts' Recommendations Have Investment Value?' (1996) 51 *Journal of Finance* 137.

[19] There is a significant and positive price reaction at the time of the announcement of analyst coverage; see eg N Dhiensiri and A Sayrak, 'The Value Impact of Analyst Coverage' (2010) 9 *Review of Accounting and Finance* 306.

[20] See eg F Easterbrook and D Fischel, 'Mandatory Disclosure and the Protection of Investors' (1984) 70 *Virginia Law Review* 669, 681–2.

of securities research. They engage in private proprietary research for their employers. By contrast, 'sell-side' analysts work for large investment banks. The remainder of the market comprises 'independent' analysts—that is, those working for brokerage firms that do not provide investment banking services or by specialized equity research firms. In the first instance sell-side and independent analysts' reports are available only to their employers and their clients, traditionally as a *quid pro quo* for channelling order flows to them. They are often later disseminated to the public at large.

There are a number of difficulties with this model. First, on a practical level, in contrast to other intermediaries in this chapter, such as auditors, where every company is monitored by a single gatekeeper, some companies will be monitored by multiple analysts, whereas others will not be covered by an analyst at all.[21] So, if analysts perform a useful function for investors, that role is not being performed in relation to a large number of companies.[22] Second, where analysts do act, their role is bedevilled by conflicts of interest. While buy-side analysts are less vulnerable to conflicts, as they are more closely aligned with their clients (the institutional investors for whom they work), significant conflicts arise for sell-side analysts,[23] and even for 'independent' analysts employed by brokerage firms. Most of these arise from the nature of the revenue model.[24] We highlight three in particular.

Brokerage revenue. First, it is clear that sell-side analysts are more likely to generate brokerage commissions for their employer with 'buy' recommendations than 'sell' recommendations. This is because the audience for buy recommendations is any investor, while for sell recommendations it is only those currently holding the stock, that is, the audience for buy recommendations is wider and therefore likely to generate more commissions.[25]

---

[21] See eg JL Orcutt, 'Investor Skepticism v Investor Confidence: Why the New Research Analyst Reforms Will Harm Investors' (2003) 81 *Denver University Law Review* 1, who estimated that in 2003 only 6,000 of the 14–15,000 publicly traded companies in the US at the time were regularly covered by even a single analyst.

[22] It is usually the most liquid stocks (namely, those that need analysts' reports least) that analysts will cover. This is because sell-side and independent analysts' reports are used to support brokerage services, and there will be little trading on illiquid stocks. According to industry estimates, as of 2009, roughly 40 percent of listed companies worldwide had no analyst coverage. See J Canivet, 'Small Cap Analyst Coverage: An "Under the Radar Dilemma"' (2009) 194 *Focus* 4.

[23] The scope of the conflicts on sell-side analysts in the early years of this century were such that once they came to light in the US, ten major firms entered into a Global Settlement with various US regulators in 2003 under which they paid a collective penalty of $1.3875 billion: Joint Press Release, SEC, New York Attorney General's Office, North American Securities Administrators Association, National Association of Securities Dealers and New York Stock Exchange, 'Ten of Nation's Top Investment Firms settle Enforcement Actions involving conflicts of interest between research and investment banking' (28 April 2003). Under this settlement the ten firms also agreed to a number of conflict of interest prevention arrangements.

[24] Another conflict, which does not arise from the revenue model, is that analysts may have personal conflicts. In a 2001 SEC study it was found that nearly one-third of analysts surveyed had made pre-IPO investments in a company that they later covered after the IPO (see RW McTague 'Unger Says Securities Firms Complied Poorly with Rules Relating to Analysts' Investments' (2001) 33 *Securities Regulation & Law* 1136).

[25] Because engaging in short selling is a much riskier activity than going long in a stock, as explained in Chapter 9, retail investors cannot be expected to act upon 'sell' recommendations by shorting the relevant stock as frequently as they follow 'buy' ones. Further, regulation may prevent some categories of fund managers, such as mutual funds, from engaging in short selling.

Underwriting revenue. Second, many investment firms make much of their money from their investment banking arm, and there is evidence that analyst ratings are sensitive to the identity of the firms' investment banking clients, namely analysts at underwriting firms appear to inflate their estimates of firm clients and demonstrate a reluctance to publish negative comments or reports about those clients.[26]

Issuer relations. A third conflict that can also push analysts in favour of an optimistic recommendation is the need for the analyst to maintain access to the issuer to perform her job. Regulation Fair Disclosure in the US and insider trading prohibitions in Europe have made selective disclosure of inside information illegal,[27] ruling out the most blatant forms of favouritism to reward-biased analysts. Yet, those rules do not extend to 'soft' (generic) information from managers, which is still a valuable source for analysts. In addition, they appear to have made sell-side analysts' forecasts less accurate.[28]

These conflicts tend to mean that there will be a preponderance of optimism and buy recommendations made by sell-side analysts. However, empirical research suggests that independent analysts at brokerage firms are no less optimistic.[29] To the extent that such analysts are not subsidized by investment banking they are often subsidized by brokerage commissions, and brokerage firm analysts tend to make the most optimistic forecasts, suggesting that trading fees considerations are an important factor underlying analyst research optimism. All of these issues tend to lead to an inflation of evaluations regarding securities. Indeed, research suggests that accuracy does not improve analysts' career prospects as much as do predictions that err on the side of optimism.[30]

6.3.3 Credit rating agencies

CRAs operate in the bond markets, in contrast to securities analysts, who generally operate in the equity markets. CRAs provide opinions on the creditworthiness of issuers of debt instruments, and the likelihood of default. These ratings are based on public disclosures relating to the issuer and, usually, also on non-public information provided to the CRA by the issuer. The ratings, which are based on complex methodologies, provide an alphabetical 'grade', usually ranging from AAA to D. Ratings below BBB are generally designated as sub-investment grade, although the grade scales are not harmonized among CRAs. Ratings are not an assessment of the quality of the

---

[26] R Michaely and KL Womack, 'Conflict of Interest and Credibility of Underwriter Analyst Recommendations' (1999) 12 *Review of Financial Studies* 653; BM Barber, R Lehavy, and B Trueman, 'Comparing the Stock Recommendation Performance of Investment Banks and Independent Research Firms' (2007) 85 *Journal of Financial Economics* 490; DJ Bradley, BD Jordan, and JR Ritter, 'Analyst Behaviour Following IPOs: The "Bubble Period" Evidence' (2008) 21 *Review of Financial Studies* 101.

[27] See Chapter 8, section 8.5.1 and Chapter 9, section 9.3.

[28] Coffee, n 6, 264.

[29] A Kowan, B Groysberg, and P Healy, 'Which Types of Analyst Firms are More Optimistic?' (2006) 41 *Journal of Accounting and Economics* 119.

[30] See eg I Welch, 'Herding among Security Analysts' (2000) 58 *Journal of Financial Economics* 369; H Hong and J Kubik, 'Analysing the Analysts: Career Concerns and Biased Earnings Forecasts' (2003) 58 *Journal of Finance* 313.

investment, but merely an assessment of the probability that the debt security will perform in accordance with its terms. In contrast to securities analysts, therefore, CRAs produce opinions rather than recommendations.

The ratings produced by CRAs are used in a number of ways. First, ratings potentially allow investors to assess the relative risk of the issuers or financial instruments that have been rated, thereby reducing information asymmetries. Distilling information about an issuer or its securities into an easily digestible piece of information (a single symbol) can allow issuers to send a credible signal that its securities are of a particular quality. There is a clear consensus in the empirical literature that information provided by CRAs has an effect on price.[31] How cheaply a firm can raise debt finance will generally depend on the rating of the debt: the rating determines the interest rate. Ratings are also sometimes incorporated into covenants in private debt contracts so that the borrower is required to maintain a particular rating, with the result that rating downgrades may give lenders an opportunity to accelerate debt repayments.

In addition, for some time CRAs have been hardwired into the regulatory system, and to a considerable degree still are, although efforts are being made to address this issue. For example, ratings have long been important for institutional investors, as for decades they have been subject to restrictions on the debt securities they can hold by reference to their ratings. Another example of their regulatory role is the fact that the Basel regime for regulating bank solvency places considerable weight on the credit ratings applicable to each bank's investments.[32] It is clear that CRAs have an important and powerful role to play, in rating both the debt securities of corporate issuers and sovereign debt.[33]

There are a number of reasons to doubt how effectively CRAs operate as information intermediaries. First, there is currently very little competition amongst CRAs. There are only three major ratings agencies worldwide, and two of them, Moody's and Standard and Poor's, dominate the market.[34] This lack of competition is attributable both to high barriers to entry[35] and to the regulatory licence granted by regulators. The concentration

---

[31] J Hand, R Holthausen, and R Leftwich, 'The Effect of Bond Rating Agency Announcements on Bond and Stock Prices' (1992) 47 *Journal of Finance*, 733; D Kliger and O Sarig, 'The Information Value of Bond Ratings' (2000) 55 *Journal of Finance* 2879; I Dichev and J Piotroski, 'The Long-Run Stock Returns Following Bond Ratings Changes' (2001) 56 *Journal of Finance* 173. The effect of ratings changes on price is complex, as the impact of ratings changes is different for firms with low ratings than for firms with high ratings. Note, however, that there is asymmetry between downgrades and upgrades: downgrades have a significant negative impact on price, but there is virtually no price change following an upgrade.

[32] See Chapter 14, section 14.4.1.

[33] Thomas Kirschmeier's statement in this regard has become well known: 'There are two superpowers in the world today in my opinion. There's the United States and Moody's Bond Rating Service. The United States can destroy you by dropping bombs, and Moody's can destroy you by downgrading your bonds. And believe me, it's not clear sometimes who's more powerful' (see F Partnoy, 'The Siskel and Ebert of Financial Markets? Two Thumbs Down for the Credit-Rating Agencies' (1999) 77 *Washington University Law Quarterly* 619, 620).

[34] The third is Fitch.

[35] The high barrier to entry is caused partly by the requirement for CRAs to develop complex rating methodologies, and partly by the fact that the value of a rating rests upon providing investors with a comparison between a single issuer's credit risk and that of other debt issuers and thus CRAs need to rate a high number of issuers for this form of comparative service to be valuable, see eg RJ Rhee, 'Why Credit Rating Agencies Exist' (2015) 44 *Economic Notes* 161.

in the market for CRAs is more severe than for most other information intermediaries, and this reduces the pressure to protect reputational capital: these firms do not need to have an unblemished reputation, as long as it is not significantly worse than the other major players in the market.

If the risk of a loss of reputation does not incentivize information intermediaries to act appropriately, then an alternative incentive is the threat of litigation. However, CRAs are almost never legally liable for their ratings, because they provide only an opinion, and do not verify the disclosures they receive.[36] CRAs simply suggest the likelihood of default based on assumed facts and they expressly state that they do not engage in any due diligence. These issues also diminish their effectiveness at dealing with information asymmetry. CRAs are reactive to information published, rather than proactive. For example, major rating agencies famously rated Lehman Brothers' commercial paper investment grade on the day that it declared bankruptcy.[37] Downgrades at this late stage 'resemble more an obituary than a prophecy'.[38] On one view therefore, CRAs present an unusual paradox: ratings are important but they possess potentially little informational value.[39]

A further reason for us to be wary of the effectiveness of CRAs as information intermediaries arises from the revenue model adopted. Since the 1970s, CRAs have operated under an 'issuer pays' model, by which it is the issuers who request CRAs to provide ratings in exchange for a fee.[40] This raises the potential for conflicts to arise. The severity of those conflicts may vary according to the circumstances. In markets where the big two CRAs are completely dominant, there may be little incentive for CRAs to inflate ratings to gain or retain an issuer, especially as many issuers obtain ratings from both Moody's and Standard & Poor's. However, this might change where significant new players enter the field, or where CRAs offer lucrative ancillary services and use inflated ratings to keep clients happy in highly lucrative and concentrated markets on the issuer side, such as the market for securitized products.[41]

However, one of the most significant reasons to doubt the effectiveness of CRAs as information intermediaries is their decade-long assimilation into the regulatory system. Regulations attaching positive consequences to the presence of a credit rating enable CRAs to confer a 'regulatory licence' on its customers. These benefits might accrue from the fact that a rating enables issuers to escape costly regulatory burdens or prohibitions to which it would be subject otherwise. This hardwiring potentially undermines the CRAs' information role, which ultimately relies on their reputation. To the extent that the rating can reduce the cost to the issuer or to the investor, the CRA sells regulatory licences to reduce these costs.[42] As a result, the CRA may be less concerned with preserving its reputation than the reputational capital model would predict. The regulatory licence model is not based on trust and reliance being placed in

---

[36] For an example of a CRA being held liable for a misleading and deceptive AAA rating see the decision of the Federal Court of Australia in *Bathurst Regional Council v Local Government Financial Services Pty Ltd (No 5)* [2012] FCA 1200.

[37] LJ White, 'Markets: The Credit Rating Agencies' (2010) 24 *Journal of Economic Perspectives* 211, 218.

[38] Coffee, n 6, 285.   [39] Partnoy, n 33.

[40] The original revenue model, prior to the 1970s, was a subscriber pays model.

[41] White, n 37, 221. See also Chapter 20, section 20.4.   [42] Partnoy, n 33.

the CRA by investors, but rather on the cost savings of those benefiting from the regulatory licence. The focus for the CRA will simply be on protecting its ability to issue regulatory licences.

Unlike securities analysts, where the pressure to regulate arose as a result of Enron and similar scandals in the early years of this century, it was the role of CRAs in relation to structured products, which came to light as a result of the financial crisis, that led to their comprehensive regulation. CRAs played a big part in the development of these structured products, such as collateralized debt obligations ('CDOs'), the success of which depended heavily on the rating assigned by the rating agency. However, the utility of CRAs in this regard was questionable. In particular, CRAs developed methodologies for rating CDOs which allowed the combination of tranches to be worth more than the underlying assets.[43] There were particularly acute conflict issues at work, as the CRAs were often involved in the development of the structured finance product, providing advice on the ratings that a structure might receive. Conflicts also arose as a result of the value of this work to the CRAs. With these structured products the CRAs acted as gate *openers* rather than gatekeepers. Or, as Frank Partnoy put it, '[n]o other gatekeeper has created a dysfunctional multi-trillion dollar market, built on its own errors and limitations'.[44]

6.3.4 Auditors

Companies are under an obligation to draw up annual accounts and reports. The information so produced is generally regarded as the bedrock of corporate disclosure obligations, as we discuss in Chapter 8. All companies are required to make some level of disclosure about their financials, but the amount of disclosure varies according to the size and nature of the company. Accountants have been at the forefront of the task of enabling the company to meet its statutory obligations, but legislation has also intervened, to create rules designed to deal with the presentation of accounts, the use of accounting standards, and the provision of non-financial information.[45]

These statements are likely to be important to investors in determining the value of the company's securities. Indeed, the importance of this information for accurately pricing companies' securities is such that publicly traded companies are now subject to extensive disclosure obligations that operate throughout the company's financial year.[46] As with other forms of disclosure made by companies, the issuer needs to assure investors of the credibility of its financial statements. Auditors can act as information intermediaries in this context, attesting the reliability of the statements. Indeed, issuers are legally required to retain auditors' services to do so. Given that auditors are repeat certifiers, they should act well in this capacity: rational auditors

---

[43] See E Benmelech and J Dlugosz, 'The Alchemy of CDO Credit Ratings' (2009) 56 *Journal of Monetary Economics* 617.

[44] F Partnoy, 'How and Why Credit Rating Agencies are Not Like Other Gatekeepers' (2006) University of San Diego Legal Studies Research Paper Series No 07-46, 2.

[45] In Europe much of this has been harmonized at EU level: see Directive 2013/34/EU [2013] OJ L182/19; Regulation (EC) No 1606/2002 [2002] OJ L243/1.

[46] See Chapter 8, section 8.5.

should have no incentive to sell off their reputation to a particular client by compromising their reputation for an increased reward, since if they do the lost income from existing and future clients will far exceed the gain from that single client.[47]

Since the 1930s in the US, public companies have been required to provide independently audited financial statements to the public.[48] Within the EU, the same requirement is imposed on companies whose securities are traded on a regulated market.[49] The annual accounts and report must be accompanied by an auditor's report in which the auditor states, *inter alia*, whether the annual financial statements give a 'true and fair view' of the company's financial position and results, whether the annual financial statements comply with statutory requirements, and whether the management report is consistent with the annual financial statements of the company.[50] In principle, therefore, auditors have a significant role in verifying the financial statements of the issuer, and it is the mandatory nature of this role which makes auditors not just information intermediaries, but also gatekeepers.

However, a number of matters might lead us to doubt the ability of auditors to act effectively in this role. First is the fact that, like CRAs, auditors are paid by the issuer. The issuer-pays model leads to inevitable potential conflicts.[51] Although companies are required to employ auditors, there is no regulation as to which auditor to employ, or how much to pay them. A factor intensifying the possibility of conflict is the well-documented rise in the sale of ancillary services such as tax planning, corporate finance, and IT consulting from the 1990s onwards. In the UK, for example, non-audit fees amounted to 73 per cent of audit fees in 1991, and 300 per cent ten years later.[52] The provision of these services increases the economic bond between the auditor and its client.[53] At the same time there is little by way of credible threat facing auditors. In practice changes of auditor have traditionally been rare.

The litigation risk facing auditors has been argued to be a potentially significant tool to ensure auditor independence.[54] However, whether litigation will operate in this way will depend upon the probability of a suit being brought, and the liability exposure should that suit prove successful. Auditors are generally liable to their client (the

---

[47] See eg LE DeAngelo, 'Auditor Size and Audit Quality' (1981) 3 *Journal of Accounting and Economics* 183.

[48] Securities Act 1933 15 USC 77aa, Securities Exchange Act 1934 15 USC 78m(a)(2).

[49] Directive 2004/109/EC, Arts 4 and 5, as amended by Directive 2013/50/EU.

[50] Directive 2013/34/EU, Arts 34 and 35.

[51] LE DeAngelo, 'Auditor Independence, "Low Balling", and Disclosure Regulation' (1981) 3 *Journal of Accounting and Economics* 113.

[52] V Beattie and S Fearnley, 'Auditor Independence and Non-Audit Services: A Literature Review' (London: Institute of Chartered Accountants in England and Wales, 2002). The position in the US was very similar: see eg US Gen Accounting Office, 'Public Accounting Firms: Mandated Study on Consolidation and Competition', July 2003.

[53] See D Kershaw, 'Waiting for Enron: The Unstable Equilibrium of Auditor Independence Regulation' (2006) 33 *Journal of Law and Society* 388.

[54] TA Farmer, LE Rittenberg, and GM Trompeter, 'An Investigation of the Impact of Economic and Organization Factors on Auditor Independence' (1987) 7 *Auditing: A Journal of Practice & Theory* 1; H Falk, B Lynn, S Mestelman, and M Shehata, 'Auditor Independence, Self-Interested Behaviour and Ethics: Some Experimental Evidence' (1999) 18 *Journal of Accounting and Public Policy* 395.

company being audited) in the event that the audit report is misleading or inaccurate as a result of a lack of care, skill, and diligence on the part of the auditor, and this causes loss to the company. However, there are various ways in which this litigation risk might be reduced.[55] For example, it may be possible to limit the amount of liability owed to the company by its auditor by agreement,[56] or the liability might be proportionate rather than joint and several.[57] Auditors may also be liable to third parties. In the US, auditors are potentially liable to third parties for fraud, although they are generally absolved from liability for negligence unless the relationship between the auditor and the third party approached privity.[58] In the UK, a tort action is possible if auditors act negligently in performing their role, but the scope of this duty of care has been defined narrowly.[59]

How the Houston Office Brought Arthur Andersen Down

At the beginning of the 2000s, Arthur Andersen had 2,300 clients and was one of the (then) Big Five audit firms worldwide. It expected revenues of $100 million from Enron, but its global revenue was $9 billion in 2001. The reputational capital model would suggest that Arthur Andersen should not risk its reputation with 2,299 clients in order to cover up the fraud at one client, Enron, to secure 1.1 per cent of its revenues. Yet, its acquiescence to Enron's demands led, ultimately, to Arthur Andersen's downfall, as its reputational capital became, effectively, negative and its other clients deserted it. How was that possible?

The problem at Arthur Andersen was that Enron accounted for all of the turnover of the individual lead partner assigned to it and for much of the turnover of the Houston office. The fraudulent accounting practices at Enron had been spotted as improper by Arthur Andersen's specialists at the Chicago headquarters, but bad internal control mechanisms meant that the Houston lead partner was able to override such calls and sign off Enron's accounts. In other words, bad governance of agency problems at the audit firm brought Arthur Andersen down.[60]

Another serious factor is the lack of competition in the audit profession. At the time of writing there are four main audit firms (the 'Big Four'), which dominate the market. In a market this concentrated, implicit collusion can develop among the firms. In addition, as we saw with CRAs, this tends to mean that as long as they are not spectacularly worse than the other main players, investors will find it difficult to discriminate meaningfully among them.

---

[55] For example, the auditor might also choose to deliver the audit services through a limited liability vehicle rather than through a traditional partnership, in order to limit the size of its exposure to litigation.

[56] This is possible in the UK, eg, Companies Act 2006, ss 534–8.

[57] See eg the Private Securities Litigation Reform Act of 1995 (US).

[58] *Ultramares Corp v Touche* (1931) 174 NE 441. Litigation reforms in the US in the 1990s, however, including the introduction of proportionate liability for auditors, have reduced the litigation risk faced by this profession in real terms: Coffee, n 6, 152–6.

[59] *Caparo Industries plc v Dickman* [1990] 2 AC 605; *Morgan Crucible Co plc v Hill Samuel & Co Ltd* [1991] Ch 295.

[60] JR Macey, 'Efficient Capital Markets, Corporate Disclosure, and Enron' (2003) 89 *Cornell Law Review* 394, 408–10.

Auditors do engage in reputation-depleting behaviour in a manner which the reputational capital theory would not predict,[61] as the demise of Arthur Andersen following its role in Enron's debacle illustrates.

6.3.5 Lawyers

Lawyers can act in a number of capacities, only some of which may lead them to be characterized as information intermediaries. Lawyers sometimes act as advocates for their client. On other occasions they can simply be regarded as the 'transaction engineer' on a deal.[62] These roles, which are client-facing, involve the lawyer advising its client in a way designed to achieve the client's ends, rather than to uncover wrongdoing. In these roles they have been characterized as morally neutral risk engineers for the client, rather than as representatives of the public more generally.[63]

However, in other circumstances lawyers might be regarded as lending their professional reputations to a transaction. Take, for example, an IPO. Lawyers will be hired to vet the disclosure statements being made in the prospectus by the issuer, and the role of the lawyer is to reduce the risk of liability for its clients by verifying the essential facts. In such circumstances investors may look to the issuer's lawyers to assure full disclosure by the company. This is a more modest role than auditors potentially perform. There is no equivalent of auditors signing off the company's annual report. Lawyers do not report to the company's investors. Nevertheless, they can be thought to have some form of information intermediary role. This role has been slower to develop than that of auditors.

There are some difficulties with relying on lawyers as reputation intermediaries. As with auditors, lawyers are paid for by the issuer or the underwriter. This inevitably gives rise to a potential conflict, although there are reasons to doubt that this leads to quite the same level of risk as with auditors. The market for legal services is much less concentrated than is the market for auditing services: there are dozens of large law firms that can be hired by an issuer or underwriter to provide legal services, in contrast to the Big Four audit firms discussed in the previous section. In addition, although a company is likely to have a long-term relationship with just one audit firm (and indeed one audit partner within a firm), large companies are likely to have their own in-house legal team for general purposes and may make use of many different law firms for specialist advice in different areas. Competitive bidding of law firms to win this work is common. Consequently, the relationship is likely to be less susceptible to capture. Of course, the flip side is that lawyers may know their clients less well, and therefore may be less likely to spot wrongdoing.

[61] BW Mayhew, JW Schatzberg, and GR Sevcik, 'The Effect of Accounting Uncertainty and Auditor Reputation on Auditor Objectivity' (2001) 20 *Auditing: Journal of Practice and Theory* 49.

[62] RJ Gilson, 'Value Creation by Business Lawyers: Legal Skills and Asset Pricing' (1984) 94 *Yale Law Journal* 239.

[63] A Alfieri, 'The Fall of Legal Ethics and the Rise of Risk Management' (2006) 94 *Georgetown Law Journal* 1909.

6.4 The regulation of information intermediaries

Since the turn of the century, there has been a growing consensus about the need for more regulatory control of information intermediaries. This has been given particular impetus, first, by the wave of scandals in the early years of the century, such as Enron and Parmalat, and then by the global financial crisis. Although reforming the regulation of underwriters has largely been absent from this regulatory agenda, the other information intermediaries in this chapter have all become subject to increased regulatory oversight, albeit to different degrees. The scandals of Enron, Worldcom, Parmalat, and others prompted regulatory measures to be put in place for sell-side analysts and auditors, and to a much lesser extent for lawyers. CRAs largely escaped the regulator's gaze at that point, but the financial crisis turned attention firmly in that direction and prompted significant reforms for CRAs as well as for other information intermediaries.

A range of tools is available to regulate information intermediaries.

6.4.1 Disclosure

As we shall see in Chapter 8, disclosure plays a significant role in regulating issuers in the primary and secondary markets. It also has a potential role to play in relation to regulating information intermediaries. Information intermediaries can potentially be required to disclose not merely the fact that they are subject to conflicts, but also more specific items, such as the source and amount of their compensation, or the methodology behind a recommendation.

We see disclosure being used to regulate sell-side analysts and CRAs in particular.[64] As regards CRAs, for example, rules in the US require rating agencies to use standardized forms, so as to facilitate comparisons among CRAs' performance by ratings users, and to publicly disclose their rating methodology[65] together with the degree of accuracy of their prior credit ratings. Similarly, in the EU, CRAs are required to disclose certain key information, for example on conflicts of interest, methodologies, and key rating assumptions.[66]

However, there are weaknesses with the use of this regulatory technique to deal with information intermediaries. At best, disclosure can only be of limited utility, given that the demand for many information intermediaries derives from investors' collective action problems in interpreting publicly available information.[67] What is more, simply accepting that intermediaries are inherently conflicted tends to undermine the potentially valuable role of these intermediaries and distort the information they present.[68]

---

[64] In relation to analysts see eg (in the EU) Market Abuse Regulation (EU) No 596/2014 [2014] OJ L173/1, Art 20(1) and (in the US) FINRA Rules 2241(relating to equity) and 2242 (relating to debt).

[65] Dodd–Frank Act, §932(a)(8) and see SEC Final Rule, Release No 34-72936.

[66] Regulation (EU) No 1060/2009 [2009] OJ L302/1 as amended, Arts 8 and 10–12.

[67] Thus mandatory disclosure by issuers, for example, functions as an input to information intermediaries, rather than an output from them.

[68] J Fisch and H Sale, 'Securities Analyst as Agent: Rethinking the Regulation of Analysts' (2003) *Iowa Law Review* 1035.

Research suggests that those to whom information about conflicts is disclosed tend to assume that the intermediary will then deal with them fairly, whereas the intermediary, having disclosed, may feel free to pursue its own interests aggressively.[69] As a result, it is not surprising that disclosure has only a minor role to play in controlling information intermediaries, when compared to its key role in the regulation of issuers.[70] The heavy lifting in the regulatory regimes for these intermediaries is done by other regulatory measures.

6.4.2 Management of conflicts

As described in section 6.3, the revenue models for sell-side analysts, CRAs, auditors, and lawyers lead to the potential for significant conflicts of interests to arise, since the ultimate principal (the investor) does not pay directly for the agent's services. Auditors, CRAs, and lawyers are all paid by the issuer (or the underwriter) and sell-side analysts are paid for largely through cross-subsidization of the other services being provided to clients by the investment bank.

For sell-side analysts, CRAs, and auditors, both the US and the EU focus on attempting to ameliorate the resulting conflict of interest problem as a significant aspect of their regulatory response. Lawyers have not been the focus of this concern. There still appears to be significant ambivalence as to whether lawyers can or should operate as effective information intermediaries at all.[71]

Both general and specific rules are put in place to try to regulate the conflicts that arise for sell-side analysts. For example, EU provisions require that firms take all reasonable steps to identify relevant conflicts of interest arising out of the provision of investment or ancillary services, and require the firm to put in place arrangements with a view to preventing conflicts of interest from adversely affecting the interests of clients.[72] In addition, rules are in place to try to ensure objectivity on the part of the analyst, for example, by separating sell-side analysts from the rest of the investment firm for which they work, via the introduction of firewalls between analysts and investment banking.[73]

No attempt has been made to tackle the underlying revenue model for sell-side analysts, however. This is not, perhaps, surprising. To reduce the link between sell-side analysts and investment banks would also be likely to reduce the preparedness of those banks to fund research that would otherwise be unprofitable, and there is a danger that this research would not then occur at all. Given the valuable role that securities analysts perform in the market, some academics have proposed alternative funding mechanisms to try to ensure that this role is performed, but without the conflict of interest apparent in the existing model. One model suggests a voucher

---

[69] DM Cain, G Loewenstein, and DA Moore, 'The Dirt on Coming Clean: Perverse Effects of Disclosing Conflicts of Interest' (2005) 34 *Journal of Legal Studies* 1.

[70] See Chapter 8.

[71] For discussion see eg Coffee, n 6, Ch 6.

[72] See Directive 2014/65/EU [2014] OJ L173/349 (MiFID II), Arts 16(3) and 23, and ESMA's Technical Advice to the Commission on MiFID II and MIFIR, Final Report, ESMA/2014/1569, December 2014.

[73] In the US, see FINRA Rules 2241 and 2242.

system, whereby issuers distribute vouchers to their shareholders, and those share-holders then use the vouchers to purchase securities research from their preferred analyst, with the analyst subsequently redeeming the voucher for cash from the issuer.[74] An alternative model suggests they piggyback on exchanges, which could be required to appoint an analyst in relation to each listed company that lacked a minimum level of analyst coverage.[75] There are significant practical difficulties with each of these models.[76] Nevertheless, the ideas are valuable for focusing on tackling the underlying cause of the conflict rather than simply the resulting conflicts.

For CRAs and auditors the problem is simpler in the sense that, at present, there is an obvious source of revenue for these services: the issuer is required to pay, in order to access the market. However, the resulting conflict of interest issue still needs to be managed. For CRAs we again see a focus on tackling the conflict, rather than the underlying cause of the conflict. The US and EU regulations regarding CRAs do not question the issuer-pays model. This is, again, unsurprising. Although preferable, a change in the revenue model from issuer-pays to one that restores the principal–agent relationship would not be straightforward. Finding someone other than the issuer to pay for the ratings would be problematic, given the free-rider issue.

Instead, the reforms focus on managing the conflicts, in a manner akin to the regulations introduced for sell-side analysts. A very significant body of regulation is put in place, including entry regulation, structural restrictions, operational rules, and disclosure obligations. Only a small sample is provided here. In the US, for instance, CRAs are required to take steps to prevent sales and marketing considerations from influencing ratings, to establish procedures to evaluate possible conflicts of interest, and to establish internal controls to monitor adherence to credit rating policies and procedures.[77] The EU similarly requires CRAs to identify, eliminate, or manage and disclose any actual or potential conflicts of interest.[78]

For auditors we see rules put in place that aim to ensure independence by excluding a person from acting as an auditor if there is some significant link between the auditor and client.[79] Rules are also put in place to ensure that conflicts do not arise at the level of the individual audit partners within firms. This is to deal with the concern that, although firms may take a long view on maintaining reputational capital, individual

---

[74] S Choi and J Fisch, 'How to Fix Wall Street: A Voucher Financing Proposal for Securities Intermediaries' (2003) 113 *Yale Law Journal* 269.

[75] Coffee, n 6, 345.

[76] Eg in the voucher financing model, there are practical difficulties in issuing vouchers to thousands of shareholders on a continuing basis, and the proposal does not create a strong principal to monitor the analyst as agent. A joint-venture between NASDAQ and Reuters was created in 2005 to experiment with the exchange-based model, but it shut down only two years later for lack of issuer demand, see S Markov and E-J Tan, 'Intermediation in the Market for Equity Research' (2014) 37 *Journal of Financial Research* 405, 406.

[77] Dodd–Frank Act, §932. See SEC Final Rule, Release No 34-72936. Dodd–Frank also encouraged the SEC to adopt rules designed to reduce conflicts of interest by placing restrictions on the ability of rating agencies to provide services other than credit ratings (§939).

[78] Regulation (EU) No 1060/2009 as amended, Art 6 and Annex I, Section B. For detailed discussion see N Moloney, *EU Securities and Financial Markets Regulation*, 3rd ed (Oxford: OUP, 2014), VII.2.

[79] Within the EU see Directive 2006/43/EC [2006] OJ L157/87, as amended by Directive 2014/56/EU [2014] OJ L158/196, Art 22. In the US see American Institute of Certified Public Accountants, Code of Professional Conduct, Rule 101, and SEC Rules, 17 CFR §210.2-01b (2006).

audit partners within the firm might take a much shorter-term approach.[80] So, rules in the US require rotation of the audit partner every five years.[81] EU rules for 'public interest entities' (which term includes companies whose securities are traded on a regulated market[82]) go further and require rotation of the audit firms themselves every ten years.[83] While the market for auditing services remains so concentrated, however, it is difficult to see what requiring companies to rotate around the Big Four audit firms will achieve in terms of increased independence.

Finally, given the dangers presented by non-audit services being provided to clients, structural restrictions have been introduced to reduce this area of conflict. The Sarbanes–Oxley Act of 2002 in the US introduced a list of services that public accounting firms are prohibited from providing to audit clients, such as bookkeeping or accounting services, investment banking services, financial information systems design, and legal services or expert services not related to audit.[84] Sarbanes–Oxley stopped short of a complete ban on non-audit services, although the EU has now introduced for 'public interest entities' a list of non-audit services that may not be provided by the statutory auditor or audit firm to the audited entity.[85]

In contrast to sell-side analysts and CRAs, an attempt has been made to counter the conflict issue arising in relation to auditors, by restoring the principal–agent relationship. The problem is that auditors, in certifying the financial position of the company, can be regarded as taking on a public responsibility not only to shareholders, but also to investors and the public more generally, which transcends the contractual relationship they have with the company. Both the EU and the US have made use of the concept of an audit committee of the board to address this issue. In the EU, the audit committee has an important role within public interest entities, including a direct role in the appointment of the statutory auditor or the audit firm, as well as in the monitoring of the audit.[86] In the US, auditors must receive pre-approval by the client's audit committee for any audit or non-audit services.[87] Auditors must also submit reports detailing the execution of their audit services and submit those reports to the audit committee.[88]

6.4.3 Regulatory oversight

Both the US and the EU have opted for enhanced regulatory oversight as a mechanism for tackling the perceived concerns regarding CRAs and auditors, through the creation of supervisory powers for national, or supranational, bodies, as the case may be. This is distinct from the regulatory response regarding analysts.

---

[80] As in the case of Arthur Andersen: see section 6.3.4.   [81] Sarbanes–Oxley Act, §203.
[82] Directive 2006/43/EC as amended, Art 2(13).
[83] Regulation (EU) No 537/2014 [2014] OJ L158/77, Art 17.
[84] Sarbanes–Oxley Act, §201(a) codified at 15 USC §78j–1.
[85] Regulation (EU) No 537/2014, Art 5.   [86] Ibid, Arts 16 and 10–11.
[87] Sarbanes–Oxley Act, §202.
[88] Ibid, §204. Rules are in place to attempt to ensure that this committee is sufficiently independent from management: §301.

CRAs were subject to a largely self-regulatory regime until 2006. In the US (the home of the largest CRAs), rating agencies were managed through the 'NRSRO' (Nationally Recognized Statistical Rating Organization) system. Under this system CRAs were not regulated but were designated as NRSROs, which were then eligible to provide ratings. Designation was based on an assessment of whether agencies were of national repute rather than any formal assessment by the SEC. This model of market monitoring is also observable in the Code developed by IOSCO in 2004 to deal with CRAs.[89] In the last decade, both the US and the EU have opted for significant regulatory oversight of CRAs. In the US, the 2006 Credit Rating Agency Reform Act gave oversight to the SEC and made entry into the market easier by reducing the SEC's discretion in granting NRSRO status.[90] CRAs are required to submit annual compliance reports to the SEC.[91] The SEC is permitted to suspend or revoke a rating agency's registration for a particular class of securities for failure to satisfy certain requirements. Similarly, the EU has put in place a regime for registering and regulating CRAs and subjecting them to supervision by the European Securities and Markets Authority (ESMA).[92]

As regards auditors, for much of its history the auditing profession has regulated itself, imposing ethical standards that are enforced through the rule books of the professional bodies of accountants. However, post-Enron, the scope for professional self-regulation has been substantially reduced. In the US, for example, the Public Company Accounting Oversight Board was established under the Sarbanes–Oxley Act. Its remit is, *inter alia*, to register public accounting firms, to create rules relating to independence and other issues, and to conduct inspections and investigations of those firms.[93] The UK has also moved away from self-regulation for the legal profession, albeit driven by a desire to promote competition rather than any sense that the prior standards had been too low.[94]

6.4.4 Qualification requirements

Qualification requirements can be used to control the quality of information intermediaries. This technique has been used both in relation to lawyers and auditors for some considerable period, well before the various scandals and crises of this century emerged. We see this technique being developed for regulating the quality of ratings produced by CRAs in the aftermath of the financial crisis. The Dodd–Frank Act, for

---

[89] IOSCO, Code of Conduct Fundamentals for Credit Rating Agencies, 2004. IOSCO has conducted reviews of this Code, and a Final Report was published in March 2015.

[90] Dodd–Frank created a new office of the SEC, the Office of Credit Ratings at the SEC, to supervise rating agencies: Dodd–Frank Act, §932(a)(8).

[91] Ibid, §932(b).

[92] This change was made in 2011: Regulation (EU) No 513/2011 [2011] OJ L145/30 amending Regulation (EC) No 1060/2009. Previously, the 2009 Regulation had established a mechanism for CRAs to be registered with their home Member States' competent authorities.

[93] Within the EU, auditor oversight is left to Member States. In the UK, for example, the Financial Reporting Council supervises auditors, following the Companies (Audit, Investigation, and Community Enterprise) Act 2004.

[94] Under the Legal Services Act 2007, control was transferred to the Legal Services Board from the beginning of 2010. For background, see D Clementi, *Review of Regulatory Framework for Legal Services in England and Wales: Final Report* (London: DCA, 2004).

example, requires the SEC to take steps to guarantee that any person employed by an NRSRO meets the standards of training, experience, and competence necessary to produce accurate ratings for the categories of issuers whose securities the person rates, and is tested for knowledge of the credit rating process.[95] This technique has not been adopted in relation to securities analysts in most jurisdictions. While it is common for analysts to have some combination of a post-graduate degree, certain professional qualifications, and some experience in the industry they cover, there seems little appetite for imposing mandatory professional qualifications. For example, when the EU looked at the issue of analyst regulation in 2006, the Commission did not propose mandatory registration of analysts linked to qualifications. The reason for this was that there was felt to be insufficient evidence linking the problems of analyst bias to lack of qualifications.[96]

6.4.5 Liability

As described in section 6.2, in theory the value of reputation intermediaries lies in their preparedness to pledge their costly to build, easy to lose reputation to vouch for an issuer's disclosures or their own information products. However, if the market for information intermediaries is highly concentrated, or their services are mandated, then the reputational consequences may be quite modest.[97] One way to encourage information intermediaries to focus on their role and to acquit themselves properly is therefore to increase their liability risk.

Reform efforts of this kind have focused on one of the information intermediaries in this chapter, namely CRAs. This can perhaps be explained by the fact that the prior liability risk was almost non-existent for a CRA, even if it performed its role negligently. Lawyers are liable to their clients. Auditors are liable to their clients, and to third parties in certain circumstances. The litigation threat facing analysts is relatively low,[98] but again it does exist, and in discussions on the regulation of analysts there has been little or no focus on changing the current litigation model in an attempt to increase the quality of intermediary services. This perhaps reflects a concern that imposing a significant threat of litigation would reduce the willingness of analysts to undertake their tasks.

By contrast, both the US and the EU now recognize the need to increase the litigation risk facing CRAs for the ratings they provide. However, the process has not been straightforward. One of the reforms put forward in the Dodd–Frank Act,[99] designed to remove an exemption from liability for CRAs under the Securities Act 1933, had to be

---

[95] Dodd–Frank Act, §936. Within the EU see Regulation (EU) No 1060/2009 as amended, Art 7.

[96] European Commission, 'Investment Research and Financial Analysts' COM (2006) 789 final.

[97] See JD Cox, 'The Oligopolistic Gatekeeper: The US Accounting Profession', in J Armour and JA McCahery (eds), *After Enron: Improving Corporate Law and Modernizing Securities Regulation in Europe and the US* (Oxford: Hart Publishing, 2006), 295.

[98] In the US, for example, analysts are generally exempt from the Investment Advisers Act 1940, and are protected by the doctrine of 'loss causation' from liability in securities class actions: eg *Lentell v Merrill Lynch & Co Inc*, 396 F.3d 161 (2d Cir 2005); *Demarco v Lehman Bros*, 222 FRD 243 (SDNY 2004).

[99] Dodd–Frank Act, §939G, repealing Rule 436(g) promulgated under the Securities Act of 1933, as amended.

rescinded by the SEC when CRAs refused to allow their ratings to be included in asset-backed bond-offering documents, and the market effectively shut down (a clear example of the importance of the regulatory licence role of CRAs). However, Dodd–Frank does confirm that the Securities Exchange Act 1934 provisions regarding civil remedies apply to CRAs in the same way as to registered public accountants and analysts,[100] and the EU has introduced a harmonized civil liability regime.[101] It remains to be seen whether these reforms can put pressure on CRAs to improve the quality of their ratings, and to increase investor protection.

6.4.6 Increasing the incentives to maintain reputation

As well as, or as an alternative to, increasing the litigation risk facing information intermediaries, another possibility for regulators is to seek to increase the incentives on the intermediary to maintain its reputation. For auditors and CRAs an issue raised in this chapter that undermines their potential role as information intermediary is the lack of competition in each market. As a result, an intermediary need not maintain an excellent reputation as long as their reputation is not materially worse than that of the dominant players in the market.

This issue is particularly acute for CRAs where the market is so concentrated. For a long time, entry regulation in the US reinforced their dominance: various regulatory licensing measures required that ratings be issued by NRSROs, with recognition to be granted by the SEC. For decades, the criteria to obtain such recognition were never made public and no CRA ever obtained it. Post-Enron, the US Congress managed to make entry into the credit ratings market easier by requiring the SEC to establish clear guidelines for the recognition of NRSROs,[102] which has subsequently led to the recognition of additional CRAs as NRSROs.

EU provisions regarding CRAs seek to ensure their independence by requiring debt issuers to rotate every four years between the agencies that rate them, and to require ratings from two different rating agencies for complex debt investments.[103] However, with only two big players in the market, requiring firms to rotate between CRAs, and to obtain ratings from both of them in certain situations, is unlikely to improve matters. Competition alone is unlikely to solve the difficulties inherent in ratings. Indeed, competition among CRAs may reduce investor protection if issuers can then shop for ratings.[104]

The audit market is dominated by the Big Four, and a similar issue arises. Within the EU the rotation of audit firms for some companies is required every ten years.[105] However, while the market for auditing services remains so concentrated, it is difficult

---

[100] Ibid, §933(a).
[101] Regulation (EU) No 1060/2009 as amended by Regulation (EU) No 462/2013 [2013] OJ L146/1, Art 35a.
[102] See Credit Rating Agency Reform Act of 2006.
[103] Regulation (EU) No 1060/2009 as amended, Arts 6b and 8c.
[104] P Bolton, X Freixas, and J Shapiro, 'The Credit Ratings Game' (2012) 67 *Journal of Finance* 85.
[105] Regulation (EU) No 537/2014, Art 17.

to see what requiring firms to rotate, in practice, among the Big Four firms will achieve in terms of increased independence.

In relation to CRAs, regulators might also incentivize the intermediary to maintain its reputation in another way. One of the unique aspects of CRAs is the 'regulatory licence', that may make CRAs more concerned about protecting their ability to issue regulatory licences than about preserving their reputational capital. The regulatory licence point is addressed in the reforms in both the US and the EU. In the US, for example, the Dodd–Frank Act requires all federal agencies to delete references to credit ratings, or requirements for reliance on such ratings, from their regulations.[106] The EU has likewise introduced a number of measures designed to reduce the reliance on ratings,[107] including an obligation on the European Supervisory Authorities not to refer to ratings in their guidelines, recommendations, and similar documents where such a reference has the potential to trigger mechanistic reliance by national regulators and financial market participants.[108] This is an ongoing issue and it remains to be seen whether these policies will have their desired effect.

6.5 Conclusion

Information intermediaries play an essential role in capital markets. They gather, process, reorganize, analyse, and distribute information so as to grease the wheels of the mechanisms by which market prices reflect it. However, a number of significant problems arise regarding their ability to perform this role effectively.

The public good nature of information gives rise to particular difficulties for information intermediaries. One way to deal with the lack of incentives for anyone to pay for the services of an information intermediary is to hardwire intermediaries into the system so that, for example, an issuer cannot access the capital markets without making use of those services. This casts the intermediary into the role of a gatekeeper, and also provides a clear incentive for the issuer to pay for the intermediaries' services. The downside is the potential for a conflict of interest to arise. Of the intermediaries described in this chapter, auditors and CRAs clearly occupy this gatekeeper role as a result of a regulatory warrant (in the case of auditors) or the 'regulatory licence' deriving from various prudential regulations. There is no similar requirement to hire underwriters or lawyers to conduct an IPO, but this is practically always done. Securities analysts are, by contrast, neither mandated by law nor *de facto* necessary to do an IPO or list on a stock exchange; as a result, we see that difficult issues arise regarding who funds their activities.

In practice, a number of significant issues threaten to undermine the role of the information intermediaries identified in this chapter. Regulators have sought to impose rules to address this issue in recent years. A number of regulatory techniques have been utilized. Disclosure certainly plays a part, but not as important as when regulating

---

[106] Dodd–Frank Act, §939A.   [107] Regulation (EU) No 1060/2009 as amended, Arts 5a–5c.
[108] Ibid, Art 5b.

issuer access to the market. Neither do we see much emphasis on incentivizing intermediaries to maintain their reputation by increasing litigation risk. Instead, we see a focus on providing additional oversight by regulatory agencies, particularly for CRAs and auditors, and on the imposition of rules designed to address the significant conflicts that arise in this area.

7

Market Structure

7.1 Introduction

As explored in Chapter 5, financial markets bring together buyers and sellers looking to trade equity and debt securities, currencies, derivatives, and other financial claims. In the process, they establish prices that ensure supply meets demand and facilitate the efficient allocation of resources within an economy. Chapter 6 has shown how information intermediaries support the functioning of markets by conveying and processing price-relevant information. This chapter moves from the conceptual principles described in the previous chapters to examine the institutional arrangements—the private contracts, self-regulatory rules, and other governance mechanisms—and the intermediaries—exchanges and other trading venues—that specialize in aggregating and disseminating trading-related information. These institutions are what enable financial markets to perform these functions: together with laws and regulations, they make up the 'structure' of financial markets.

Securities are traded in a wide variety of venues. We describe the structure of secondary markets for public equity securities, from traditional exchanges such as the New York Stock Exchange ('NYSE'), the London Stock Exchange ('LSE'), and Euronext (section 7.2) to various 'alternative' trading platforms (section 7.3). Section 7.4 then examines the structure of secondary markets for corporate bonds. These exchanges and trading platforms are not public utilities; rather, they are businesses seeking to make a profit. In each case, the discussion shows how these structures have evolved over time, to give a sense of how they are affected by technology and regulation.

Two key themes emerge from this discussion: the impact of competition and the significance of disclosure of pricing and other trading information. Competition—fostered in part by technology and in part by regulatory changes—has shaken up the environment in which financial markets operate, with an influx of new platforms now competing with traditional exchanges. This has shifted the focus of market operators' attention from protecting commissions to implementing measures necessary to attract order flow. In other words, competition has tilted the environment towards the interests of the investor.

The production and processing of pricing information are two of the most important functions of market structure institutions. Timely disclosure not only helps investors see they are getting the best price, but also serves as an indicator regarding the revelation of price-relevant information. In this way, we should understand market structure institutions as operating alongside the information intermediaries discussed in Chapter 6—another mechanism supporting the efficiency of equity markets. In particular, the earlier in the trading process price-relevant information is made public, the easier it is for other investors to 'decode' it. This could plausibly result in more rapid

Principles of Financial Regulation. First Edition. John Armour, Dan Awrey, Paul Davies, Luca Enriques, Jeffrey N. Gordon, Colin Mayer, and Jennifer Payne. © John Armour, Dan Awrey, Paul Davies, Luca Enriques, Jeffrey N. Gordon, Colin Mayer, and Jennifer Payne 2016. Published 2016 by Oxford University Press.

price-adjustment to new information, but at the expense of reduced incentives to acquire new information.

Section 7.5 considers the circumstances in which it may be desirable to introduce regulatory oversight of these private market structures. In theory, regulation can help address market failures. Moreover, the threat of regulatory intervention can spur market participants to address these failures on their own initiative. However, the distinction between regulation and private ordering in this area is fuzzy: one important tool that policymakers around the world have used to regulate private market structures, and exchanges more precisely, is securities regulators' approval of their all-important self-regulatory rules. As a consequence, it is now very hard to disentangle self-regulation from public regulation of exchanges, given that regulators can use their veto power on exchanges' self-regulatory rules to shape the contents of what may in fact be only in form an expression of market players' private choices.

It is of course impossible to explore every financial market structure in a single short chapter. Nevertheless, this chapter sets out a framework which will be helpful in analysing the structures of other markets we will encounter later in this book. In Chapter 18, for example, we consider the function of central securities depositories and other institutions in clearing and settling trades in various financial claims. And in Chapter 21, we see how financial intermediaries make markets in over-the-counter ('OTC') derivatives, structured finance products, and other sophisticated financial instruments.

7.2 Stock Exchanges

7.2.1 The rationale for stock exchanges

The origins of public equity markets can be traced back to the Netherlands. As early as the seventeenth century, shares in Dutch commercial ventures were traded in designated trading houses (or 'bourses'). For example, trading records for shares in the Dutch East India Company exist going as far back as 1602.[1] This innovation was introduced to England following the Glorious Revolution of 1688, in the form of a modest establishment in the City of London known as Jonathan's Coffee House. The story of Jonathan's is illustrative of both the potential economic benefits of market structure and, simultaneously, some of the obstacles to its successful emergence and development.

In 1698 a group of stockbrokers and jobbers (dealers)[2] began conducting their business out of Jonathan's. These brokers and jobbers would post prices for various

---

[1] LO Petram, 'The World's First Stock Exchange: How the Amsterdam Market for Dutch East India Company Shares Became a Modern Securities Market, 1602–1700' (2011) at 81, available at http://dare.uva.nl/document/2/85961.

[2] The distinction between stock 'brokers' and 'jobbers' dates back at least to prior to 1697, when the Act to Restrain the Number and Ill Practice of Brokers and Stock Jobbers (8&9 Wm III, c 32 (1697)) was enacted. Brokers effected transactions on behalf of the public and were prohibited from trading on their own account. Jobbers, meanwhile, acted as market makers—providing liquidity to brokers and other jobbers. The distinction between brokers and jobbers was finally abolished only by the Financial Services Act 1986.

stocks and commodities on the coffee house's walls and conclude transactions. While those who failed to honour their commitments were branded 'lame ducks' and banned from the premises,[3] there was nothing particularly exclusive about being permitted to trade there in the first place.[4] So in 1761, 150 brokers and jobbers formed a private club and contracted with the owner of Jonathan's for exclusive use of the establishment,[5] with each member contributing towards the annual rent.[6] After an expelled broker successfully sued for admission, the brokers and jobbers next purchased a nearby building and began charging a daily admission fee.[7] Over time, the proprietors established membership requirements and, in 1801, adopted a formal constitution governing the conduct of members. A codified rulebook was created in 1812. The LSE had been born.

Over time, early exchanges such as the LSE and NYSE—itself founded in 1792—developed detailed rules governing the relationships between market participants, issuers, and the exchange itself. Many of the trading rules were designed to ensure that the property rights of buyers and sellers were sufficiently protected: articulating, for example, procedures for the transfer of title and remedies for non-performance. This was essentially a body of private contract law—with the threat of being expelled as an exchange member serving as the primary mechanism to induce compliance.[8] Eventually, exchange rules were expanded to encompass matters such as fraud, market manipulation, the creditworthiness of exchange members, and the segregation of client assets. Exchanges also began to compel disclosure from issuers: first of their outstanding share capital and, subsequently, of their financial statements.[9]

The emergence and development of organized markets such as the LSE and NYSE offer a number of important insights into the economics of stock exchanges. First, the most valuable assets of an exchange are its reputation (a function of the quality of its issuers and members), its rules (shaping expectations about the behaviour of its members), and the trading information it produces. Prior to the advent of modern information technology, location was also extremely important. Crucially, however, it was often difficult to prevent non-members from enjoying some of the benefits generated by these assets. Non-members can congregate and conduct their business near the exchange, copy the exchange's rules, and make use of the information it produces.[10] Such competitors will attract at least some business away from the

---

[3] E Morgan and W Thomas, *The London Stock Exchange* (New York, NY: St Martin's Press, 1969).

[4] More particularly, there was little to distinguish its participants from expelled brokers and jobbers, who could simply congregate outside Jonathan's, or in nearby establishments.

[5] London Stock Exchange, 'Our History', available at http://www.londonstockexchange.com.

[6] Morgan and Thomas, n 3, 67–8.

[7] Ibid; P Mahoney, 'The Exchange as Regulator' (1997) 83 *Virginia Law Review* 1453.

[8] Indeed, this threat was sufficiently powerful that exchange members would continue to perform their contractual obligations even where the underlying transactions were otherwise unenforceable: see S Banner, 'The Origin of the New York Stock Exchange' (1998) 27 *Journal of Legal Studies* 113.

[9] Mahoney, n 7, 1461–2; see also J Armour and BR Cheffins, 'Stock Market Prices and the Market for Corporate Control' (forthcoming 2016) *University of Illinois Law Review*.

[10] H Mulherin, J Netter, and J Overdahl, 'Prices are Property: The Organization of Financial Exchanges from a Transaction Cost Perspective' (1991) 43 *Journal of Law and Economics* 591.

exchange, undermining the benefits to members of participation, and in turn reducing their willingness to invest in developing the exchange's assets.[11]

One potential response to this problem is to adopt restrictive rules designed to preserve the value of the exchange members' investments. Indeed, this is what must have motivated the patrons of Jonathan's to reconstitute themselves as a private club, to relocate to private premises and charge a daily admission fee, and to adopt a formal constitution and rulebook governing their conduct. Both the LSE and the NYSE also introduced rules prohibiting exchange members from publicly disclosing the prices at which trades were executed in an attempt to prevent the uncontrolled 'leakage' of information from the exchange.[12] For the same reason, NYSE rules prohibited members from trading otherwise than on the exchange during its regular hours of operation.[13] These rules were designed to protect the value—largely intangible—of the exchange's assets. In the absence of competition from other market participants, such rules also allowed exchange members to operate as a cartel and to reap excess profits—'rents'.

At the same time, exchange members also want to promote confidence in the exchange amongst potential traders.[14] This creates a countervailing incentive for them to ensure disclosure to non-members of information about issuers and trading activity. In particular, exchanges may impose screening and disclosure requirements on issuers, in order to signal the quality of the stocks traded. Exchanges may also impose transparency obligations on members regarding the prices of completed trades (post-trade transparency) and of offers to trade (pre-trade transparency) so as to reassure non-members they will be offered the best available price. Exchanges must therefore strike a balance between protecting their valuable information and generating sufficient interest from investors.

7.2.2 The functions of exchanges

Today, the World Federation of Exchanges lists over sixty stock exchanges amongst its membership.[15] Table 7.1 lists the ten largest exchange groups in 2013, as measured by the domestic market capitalization of their listed securities. These exchanges can be understood as providing market participants with a bundle of related products.[16]

---

[11] Indeed, even exchange members may be incentivized to divert business away from the exchange. Ultimately, while members have a *collective* interest in ensuring that all trades take place on the exchange, *individual* members are indifferent in respect of any given trade and will seek to trade off the exchange where it is more profitable to do so: see Mahoney, n 7, 1490–1.

[12] Ibid.

[13] In the UK, the distinction between stock brokers and jobbers performed a functionally equivalent role.

[14] D Fischel and S Grossman, 'Customer Protection in Futures and Securities Markets' (1984) 4 *Journal of Futures Markets* 273; Mahoney (n 7). Whether members possess similarly powerful incentives to enforce these rules vigorously is another matter. See Chapter 26.

[15] See http://www.world-exchanges.org.

[16] See generally, J Macey and H Kanda, 'The Stock Exchange as a Firm: The Emergence of Close Substitutes for the New York and Tokyo Stock Exchanges' (1990) 75 *Cornell Law Review* 1007; J Macey and M O'Hara, 'Regulating Exchanges and Alternative Trading Systems: A Law and Economics Perspective' (1999) 28 *Journal of Legal Studies* 17; J Macey and M O'Hara, 'The Economics of Stock Exchange Listing Fees and Listing Requirements' (2002) 11 *Journal of Financial Intermediation* 297.

Table 7.1 Ten largest exchange groups (by market capitalization), 2013

Exchange	Mkt Cap ($bn)
NYSE Euronext (US)	15,913
NASDAQ OMX	5,282
Japan Exchange Group—Tokyo	4,126
London Stock Exchange Group	3,863
NYSE Euronext (Europe)	3,120
Hong Kong Exchanges	2,803
Shanghai Stock Exchange	2,426
TMX Group	1,978
Deutsche Börse	1,593
SIX Swiss Exchange	1,378

Source: World Federation of Exchanges, http://www.world-exchanges.org.[17]

Reputation. First, exchanges historically acted as reputational intermediaries for listed firms.[18] Listing on a stock exchange—and by implication having complied with the relevant listing requirements—sends a positive signal about the issuer's quality to the marketplace. The fact that the exchange, unlike the issuer, is necessarily a repeat player in the market makes this signal more credible. If the exchange permitted low-quality firms to list with it, this would harm its future ability to attract investors. Exchanges therefore have incentives to impose minimum quality standards on firms they admit to listing.

In recent decades, the value of this signalling function has declined. Regulators, rather than stock exchanges, mandate increasing amounts of information to be disclosed by issuers. Advances in technology mean this information can be disseminated at lower cost than in the past. While many investors are unable to digest all the information directly, the emergence of other informational intermediaries (such as underwriters and securities analysts, discussed in Chapter 6) has ensured that investors now have alternative routes to assess the quality of listed firms. These developments notwithstanding, the screening of issuers via admission to listing is still what largely distinguishes traditional 'exchanges' from other trading platforms.

Liquidity. In addition to listing, exchanges provide liquidity services: they operate a physical (or, nowadays, electronic) and legal infrastructure that facilitates the meeting of demand and supply for listed securities.[19] In light of the decline of their role as reputational intermediaries, liquidity has become exchanges' most important product. For issuers, secondary market liquidity lowers the cost of raising equity capital. For investors, liquidity generates trading opportunities and improves the process of price

---

[17] Note that in 2014, after being taken over by the Intercontinental Exchange, NYSE spun off Euronext (with which it had merged in 2007). Euronext is now a stand-alone company, as it was before 2007.

[18] For a discussion of the role of reputational intermediaries within financial markets, see Chapter 6.

[19] Historically, exchanges also provided clearing and settlement services. Today, these services are provided by centralized securities depositories such as the Depository Trust and Clearing Company ('DTCC') in the US, discussed in Chapter 18, specialized intermediaries such as LCH.Clearnet in Europe, or, as once, 'vertically integrated' exchanges themselves (like the Deutsche Börse through Clearstream, a wholly owned subsidiary).

discovery. For exchange members, meanwhile, liquidity means higher trade volume, which in turn means more income from the provision of brokerage services.

Rules. A key component of an exchange's infrastructure, in addition to the physical premises (in the past) and the IT platform (now), is the set of rules under which orders are conveyed and matched, and trades executed. Amongst other matters, these rules define and protect market participants' property rights, constrain fraud and market manipulation, and ensure that exchange members—through whom trades must be executed—are sufficiently creditworthy. Collectively, these rules can be understood as creating a standard form contract between market participants, thereby reducing the drafting, negotiation, and other costs of documenting a trade.[20] However, the significance of exchange-sponsored rules is gradually decreasing over time, as regulators increasingly prescribe matters that were formerly dealt with by exchange rules.

The most important rules that remain designed and implemented by exchanges are those governing market microstructure—namely, rules governing the trading activities of buyers and sellers in the marketplace. Most exchanges are order driven markets, in which—as described in Chapter 5—trades are executed directly between participants without the assistance of a dealer. In order to facilitate this, order driven markets employ 'order precedence rules' to match buyers and sellers and 'trade pricing rules' to price the resulting trades.[21] Exchanges also control the conduct of trading sessions. Most stock exchanges, for example, offer so-called 'continuous' markets, enabling market participants to trade at any time during their regular hours of operation. These continuous markets are sometimes supplemented by 'call market' auctions at the start of trading sessions or following a halt in trading.[22]

Exchanges also use 'backstops' to try to ensure a minimum level of liquidity even at times when order flow is low. For example, exchanges often oblige designated exchange members—'market makers' or 'specialists'—to maintain fair and orderly markets in particular securities listed on the exchange. These specialists use their own balance sheets to intervene in the marketplace: buying where there is a scarcity of demand, selling where there is a scarcity of supply. Their presence thus enables exchanges to offer continuous two-way markets in listed securities even in the presence of volatile order flows.

Formerly, exchange rules also established who had access to information about existing orders (pre-trade transparency) and to information about executed trades, such as price, size, and possibly the identity of the transacting parties (post-trade transparency). However, as sections 7.3 and 7.4 illustrate, this is an area where policymakers have been deferring less and less to exchanges' own choices and increasingly imposed their own vision of what is optimal for the market as a whole.

---

[20] The standardization of these rules may also generate significant network benefits, thereby attracting market participants.

[21] L Harris, *Trading & Exchanges* (New York, NY: OUP, 2003), 90–3.

[22] Call market auctions facilitate the accumulation of buy and sell orders for a specified period of time before they are matched, priced, and executed. By allowing orders to build up, call market auctions can thus be understood as aggregating market liquidity. For this reason, some stock exchanges also use call market auctions to conduct trading sessions in thinly traded (illiquid) stocks: ibid.

Enforcement. Traditionally, exchanges also monitored compliance with the rules and managed their enforcement using the threat of expulsion. Together, the bundle of rulemaking, monitoring, and enforcement was designed to promote market integrity, thereby attracting investor order flow at a time when regulators maintained a hands-off approach towards market infrastructure matters. With the increase in regulatory surveillance of these markets, such as in the areas of market manipulation and insider trading, the scope and added value of exchanges' self-regulation and oversight have decreased.

7.2.3 Trade-offs

In designing their bundle of products, exchanges face a number of trade-offs. Historically, their role as reputational intermediaries, for example, implied that their trading should be restricted to the securities the exchanges themselves admitted to listing.[23] Yet this required exchange members to forgo fee revenues they might generate from trading other securities. The decline in importance of the exchange's reputational intermediary function makes such a limitation less important today. Moreover, developments in IT and competition—both between exchanges and with other liquidity services providers (to which we turn in section 7.3)—have led exchanges to abandon the limitation altogether. Indeed, by setting up separate trading systems, exchange operators now routinely offer liquidity services in connection with securities for which they do not provide listing services.[24]

Exchanges must also balance the benefits of transparency against market participants' incentives to invest in seeking out and analysing new information. This is most pronounced with respect to pre-trade transparency. By revealing to market participants the prices at which others stand willing to trade, the exchange signals its integrity by allowing potential traders to see that they are getting the best price. This in turn attracts order flow. But requiring market participants to disclose their *pending* orders also permits other participants to 'decode' new information before it has been impounded into security prices, thereby reducing returns to ferreting out and analysing new information.

To be sure, different market participants have different preferences regarding the mix of products offered by an exchange. Some, for example, prefer low execution costs to rapid execution. Others may be willing to sacrifice the liquidity associated with more transparent markets in exchange for greater anonymity. As a result, different markets adopt different institutional arrangements with the objective of catering to different clienteles, leading to the 'unbundling' of the traditional package of products offered by exchanges. Perhaps nowhere is this more evident than in connection with the rise of alternative trading systems.

[23] If they did not—namely, if issuers which had not submitted to an exchange's screening and monitoring could still list and trade their securities on it—there would seem little benefit in listing.

[24] For example, LSEG, the firm operating the London Stock Exchange, has acquired Turquoise, a non-exchange trading system that, according to its website, 'offers a broad universe of 4,300 stocks with uniform access to 18 major European and emerging markets as well as US stocks, IOB Depositary Receipts, ETFs and European Rights issues'. See http://www.lseg.com/turquoise/products-services.

7.3 Off-Exchange Trading Systems

7.3.1 Exchanges and off-exchange platforms compared

The idea of off-exchange trading is not new. Institutional investors used to trade listed securities off-exchange in so-called 'upstairs' markets.[25] However, all trades in these upstairs markets were negotiated face-to-face. What is new about the modern variants is the use of technology to facilitate such trading from a distance. Modern alternative trading systems ('ATSs'), as they are known in the US—or multilateral trading facilities ('MTFs') as they are known in Europe—are a heterogeneous group of electronic trading platforms—including electronic communication networks, crossing networks, and so-called 'dark pools'—that provide traders with liquidity services in competition with traditional exchanges.[26] In recent years, ATSs and MTFs have attracted an increasing percentage of equity trade volumes.[27]

Operationally, ATSs and MTFs are very similar to traditional exchanges. Market participants utilizing such off-exchange platforms enter orders directly into an electronic order book. Orders are then matched using automated execution algorithms. Many platforms also enable market participants to engage in anonymous negotiation via quote screens. But, as a matter of practice, ATSs and MTFs can be distinguished from traditional exchanges in three important respects.[28] First, the bundle of products these platforms provide does not usually include the listing of issuers' securities.[29] That is, they do not offer any reputational intermediation. Where they offer liquidity in stocks that are listed on exchanges, ATS/MTFs therefore free-ride on the reputational intermediation of exchanges, to the extent that this retains value.

Second, ATSs and MTFs generally provide less pre-trade transparency than exchanges. Both Regulation ATS in the US, and the Markets in Financial Instruments Directive ('MiFID') in Europe, contemplate the non-application or waiver of pre-trade transparency requirements for ATS/MTFs in certain circumstances.[30] Trading without pre-trade transparency involves a higher degree of information asymmetry between participants, although they are still able to take pricing cues from regular exchanges.

---

[25] So named because trades were concluded in the rooms which overlooked the exchange floor. These block trades, given their size, were exempted from members' obligation to execute trades on the market.

[26] Macey and O'Hara, 'Regulating Exchanges', n 16.

[27] See L Tittle, 'Alternative Trade Systems: Description of ATS Trading in National Market System Stocks', report prepared for the SEC Division of Economic Risk and Analysis (October 2013); M Gentile and S Fioravanti, 'The Impact of Market Fragmentation on European Stock Exchanges', CONSOB Working Paper No 69 (2011).

[28] As a matter of law, nothing prevents a European MTF from displaying all of the features that are typical of an exchange. Compare the definitions of regulated market and MTF in Art 4, Directive 2004/39/EC ('MiFID') [2004] OJ L145/1. The same is true for a US ATS, with the only exception of self-regulatory/disciplining powers vis-à-vis members, which only exchanges may grant themselves. See Regulation ATS, 17 CFR §242.300(a)(2).

[29] One exception is the LSE-operated Alternative Investment Market ('AIM'), which specializes in admission to trading of small and medium-sized firms that are unwilling to bear the costs of a stock exchange listing.

[30] Summarized in Table 7.2. See SEC, Regulation of Exchanges and Alternative Trading Systems, 17 CFR 202, 240, 242, and 249 (21 April 1999); MiFID, Art 29(2); Regulation (EC) No 1287/2006 [2006] OJ L241/1, Art 18. Post-trade transparency, however, is still required.

ATSs and MTFs thus free-ride on the greater trading information that exchanges generate in relation to listed securities.[31]

Reduced pre-trade transparency is particularly attractive for those who wish to trade large blocks of shares, because the price impact associated with the disclosure of large orders can dramatically increase trade execution costs.[32] Announcing such orders indirectly conveys valuable information to the marketplace: information which the investor placing the large trade may have expended significant resources in gathering and analysing. By executing such trades in a reduced-transparency trading environment, institutional traders ensure they capture all the returns to their investments in this information, rather than letting them be captured by other market participants who infer the significance of a large order before it is executed.[33]

A third significant difference is that, unlike exchanges, ATSs and MTFs do not generally utilize 'specialists'. Consequently, their liquidity is solely a function of the volume of existing buy and sell orders and the spread between bid and ask prices.[34]

7.3.2 Implications of growth in off-exchange liquidity

The emergence and growth of ATSs and MTFs raise a number of potentially important issues. First, by attracting order flow away from the exchanges on which securities are listed, these platforms fragment market liquidity. Where trades are not subject to pre-trade transparency rules, they also fragment trading information. It is possible, at least in theory, that such fragmentation could impede price discovery, as fewer market participants come together at any one venue.[35] However, cross-platform arbitrage is likely to ensure any such differences are only momentary.

Second, ATSs and MTFs institute a two-tier market structure under which favoured participants may secure better terms of trade. Most obviously, many such platforms restrict access to selected institutional investors. Some observers suggest this may reduce small investors' willingness to trade on exchanges, and thereby harm liquidity.[36] In response to this concern, both the US and EU regulatory regimes require ATSs or MTFs to have transparent and non-discriminatory rules regarding access.[37]

---

[31] C Di Noia, 'The Stock Exchange Industry: Network Effects, Implicit Mergers and Corporate Governance', CONSOB Working Paper No 33 (1999). ATS/MTFs can of course also be used for trading unlisted securities.

[32] Macey and O'Hara, 'Regulating Exchanges', n 16, 45–7.

[33] Ibid.

[34] Macey and O'Hara, 'The Economics of Stock Exchange', n 16, 304.

[35] SEC Release No 34-61358, 'Concept Release on Equity Market Structure' (2010).

[36] Technical Committee of the International Organization of Securities Commissions (IOSCO), 'Consultation Report: Issues Raised by Dark Liquidity' (2010).

[37] Regulation ATS, 17 CFR §242.301(b)(5); MiFID, Art 14(4). See also Directive 2014/65/EU on markets in financial instruments ('MiFID II') [2014] OJ L173/349, Art 18(3). Investors who do not have direct access—retail investors, for example—may still be able to access off-exchange liquidity indirectly via a broker. This makes retail investors more reliant on the expertise of brokers to ensure they are getting the best terms of trade. In response to this, both the US and EU impose 'best execution' obligations on brokers, requiring them to take reasonable steps, when executing orders, to obtain the best result for their client: see Chapter 11, section 11.3.7.

Table 7.2 Scope of pre-trade transparency obligations for off-exchange platforms

	US (ATSs)	EU (MTFs)
Regulation	Regulation ATS, 17 CFR §242.301.	MiFID; MiFID Implementing Regulation 1287/2006 ('IR'). [From 2018: MiFIR.]
Scope of obligation	Any National Market System ('NMS') stock (quoted elsewhere) for which the ATS carried >5% of mean daily trading volume for >4/last 6 months: §242.301(b)(3)(i).	Any equity security admitted to trading on a regulated market (exchange): MiFID Art 29(2); IR, Art 17. [From 2018—any security traded on a regulated market or an MTF: MiFIR, Arts 3 and 8.]
Exemptions		*Referential pricing*: Prices determined by reference to 'reliable reference price' generated by another system: IR, Art 18(1)(a) [MiFIR, Art 4(1)(a)]. *Negotiated transaction*: Order is negotiated privately but executed via MTF: IR, Art 18(1)(b) [MiFIR, Art 4(1)(b)]. *Large orders*: Order large in scale compared to normal market size (1–10% of average daily trading volume): IR, Art 20, Annex II Table 2 [MiFIR, Art 4(1)(c)].

Finally, the existence of ATS/MTFs may undermine the ability of exchange specialists to maintain fair and orderly markets. For specialists, the *quid pro quo* for providing liquidity during periods of market volatility is the additional order flow and income they derive under normal market conditions. However, where off-exchange platforms attract significant order flow—only to dry up during periods of volatility and thereby precipitate a return of order flow to the exchange—the economic calculus for specialists will change.[38]

Of course, ATSs and MTFs also bring with them significant benefits. First, these platforms can be understood as imposing a degree of competitive discipline on exchanges, which otherwise enjoy something close to a natural monopoly in the trading of listed securities.[39] This delivers lower trading costs for market participants. Second, as we have seen, the anonymity associated with some ATSs and MTFs serves to preserve the incentives of institutional investors to ferret out and trade on new information.

The regulatory regimes in the US and Europe attempt to strike a balance between these costs and benefits by imposing market access requirements on platform operators, and selective pre-trade transparency obligations where ATS/MTF trading in a given security is likely to be capable of having an impact on price formation overall. Table 7.2 summarizes these pre-trade transparency requirements, which exempt low-volume trading (in the US), securities not listed on any exchange (in the EU), trading

---

[38] Macey and O'Hara, 'The Economics of Stock Exchange', n 16, 304–5.

[39] That said, it would be extremely problematic were this competition to undermine the viability of the exchange model, given that ATSs do not typically offer listing services. See the discussion in nn 16–18, and in Chapter 5, section 5.4.

structured to occur at prices that refer to exchange prices (in the EU), and trades that execute transactions negotiated off-platform (in the EU).

However, a regulatory approach that permits non-exchange platforms to offer lower levels of pre-trade transparency than exchanges may bias the competitive landscape against exchanges, at least as regards large block trading. In order to avoid this type of distortion, the EU's MiFID regime makes available the same exemptions from pre-trade disclosure to regulated markets (exchanges).[40] However, by excluding securities that are not listed on exchanges, it still leaves open the possibility of bias in issuers' decisions about where to have their shares traded. From January 2018, this assimilation will be taken a stage further, as MTFs will be required to offer pre-trade transparency on all equity securities that are traded in their systems (subject to very similar exemptions to the current regime).[41]

7.3.3 Changes in exchange organization

The increase in competition from off-exchange trading platforms put pressure on the traditional organization of stock exchanges as mutual societies: that is, member-owned cooperatives, with each member (a broker-dealer or, in current EU parlance, an investment firm) typically having an equal say in the governance of the firm.[42] This structure had worked well in the era when exchanges were insulated from competition, and so the interests of exchanges and their members were largely aligned.[43]

However, competition exposed a conflict of interest between investors in traded securities and exchange members in relation, first, to investments in technologies designed to reduce trading costs, and, second, to pricing rules. While IT investments are likely to generate benefits for investors (and for profit-maximizing operators of exchanges), their impact on mutually owned exchanges' *members* was rather more ambiguous.[44] This conflict manifested itself in the opposition of many 'floor traders' to electronic trading. Similarly, 'fractional pricing', or the practice of using a fraction, such as one-eighth or one-sixteenth of a dollar, to quote prices, widened market makers' margins, allowing them to reap higher profits than competition would have commanded. As member-owned companies, US stock exchanges were not in a good position to move in the direction of decimal pricing to gain a higher share of trading fees, because such a move would directly cut into their members' profits. It took the threat of legislative action and an order from the SEC to implement the switch from fractional pricing to 'decimalization', as late as 2001.[45] In the context of a member-owned

---

[40] MiFID, Art 44; MiFID Implementing Regulation 1287/2006, Arts 17–20.

[41] Regulation (EU) No 600/2014 on markets in financial instruments ('MiFIR') [2014] OJ L173/84, Arts 3–5.

[42] O Hart and J Moore, 'The Governance of Exchanges: Members' Cooperatives Versus Outside Ownership' (1996) 12 *Oxford Review of Economic Policy* 53.

[43] See H Hansmann and M Pargendler, 'The Evolution of Shareholder Ownership Rights: Separation of Ownership and Consumption' (2014) 123 *Yale Law Journal* 948.

[44] Such investments may precipitate an increase in trade volume, but they may also reduce the informational and other rents enjoyed by exchange members.

[45] See SEC Staff Report to Congress on Decimalization (2012) at 4, available at https://www.sec.gov/news/studies/2012/decimalization-072012.pdf.

cooperative, such conflicts made it harder for exchanges to adapt to IT developments and to react to competitive pressures.

Against this backdrop, many exchanges converted from member-owned cooper-atives or not-for-profit organizations to publicly owned corporations around the turn of the century.[46] The principal benefits of such 'demutualization' were twofold. First, the cooperative structure had effectively prohibited external capital raising.[47] By converting to corporations and raising outside equity finance, exchanges have been able to fund major new technological investments and, via mergers and acquisitions, to consolidate the industry. Second, the ordinary corporate voting structure, which accords control rights on the basis of capital invested, as opposed to the one-member, one-vote structure of a mutual—better enables exchanges to make hard decisions about what will maximize profits.[48] In an era of growing competition, this increasingly requires exchanges to focus on the interests of investors, as opposed to (former) members'.

These competitive dynamics also made it much more difficult for exchanges to continue to perform their historical listing and self-regulatory functions. In an era where reputational intermediation is less important to exchanges, and reduced market power means they have less ability to enforce quality controls in any event, they are increasingly less willing or able to impose obligations on issuers. In response to such conflicts, the UK in 2000 reallocated responsibility for setting and enforcing listing requirements from the LSE itself to the Financial Services Authority (FSA) (now the Financial Conduct Authority or FCA). Similarly, the EU has invested considerable resources in developing securities market regulation since the turn of the century, both as regards issuers (with the Prospectus, Transparency, and Market Abuse Directives) and trading platforms (with MiFID and now MiFID II).[49]

7.4 The Structure of Corporate Bond Markets

On 17 May 1792, twenty-four brokers met under a buttonwood tree outside 68 Wall Street in lower Manhattan. This historic meeting—which concluded with the brokers signing what has come to be known as the 'Buttonwood Agreement'—is often associ-ated with the birth of the NYSE and thus identified as the origin of organized equity trading in North America. It is worthwhile observing, however, that the NYSE was actually created largely for the purpose of trading US Government *bonds*.[50] Indeed, the

---

[46] R Karmel, 'Turning Seats into Shares: Implications of Demutualization for the Regulation of Stock and Futures Exchanges', Address to the American Association of Law Schools (2001); R Aggarwal, 'Demutualization and Corporate Governance of Stock Exchanges' (2002) 15 *Journal of Applied Corporate Finance* 105; A Mendiola and M O'Hara, 'Taking Stock in Stock Markets: The Changing Governance of Exchanges', Working Paper (2003).

[47] Mendiola and O'Hara, n 46.

[48] See Hansmann and Pargendler, n 43.

[49] Prospectus Directive 2003/71/EC [2003] OJ L345/64, as amended; Transparency Directive 2004/109/EC [2004] OJ L390/38 (both discussed in Chapter 8); MiFID, n 28; MiFID II, n 37.

[50] B Biais and R Green, 'The Microstructure of the Bond Market in the 20th Century', IDEI Working Paper No 482 (2007). Of the first five securities listed on the NYSE, three were bonds.

NYSE supported an order driven market in many corporate and municipal bonds until well into the twentieth century.[51]

Today, by contrast, most bonds trade in dealer-intermediated, quote driven markets.[52] The structure of these markets is characterized by a loose-knit group of financial intermediaries—dealers—who buy and sell bonds on a bilateral basis as both principals and agents. Investors looking to buy or sell bonds typically solicit quotes from one or more dealers. These dealers then act as true market makers: standing ready to buy or sell a given bond at the quoted price, with the dealer's compensation being embedded within the spread between the bid and ask prices.[53] Dealers typically support this investor (or 'buy-side') market by maintaining an inventory of bonds on their own balance sheets. This market is also supported by a relatively active inter-dealer market.[54] Dealers can thus be seen as the primary source of both trading information and liquidity within corporate bond markets.

One of the most striking features of public bond markets relative to stock exchanges is the lack of pre-trade transparency. Specifically, dealers have historically refrained from publicly disseminating 'firm'—that is, binding—quotes. Instead, they have generally published 'indicative'—non-binding—quotes on selected bonds. These quotes are often obtained through information vendors such as Bloomberg, which typically only provide them to the institutional investors who subscribe to their services. This structure—combined with the fragmentation of information and liquidity associated with the decentralized nature of dealer-intermediated markets—has historically imposed high search costs on investors looking to obtain the best possible price. It has also generated potentially acute asymmetries of information between investors and the dealers upon which they must rely for prices and liquidity, opening the door to potential opportunism.[55]

Until recently, public bond markets were not subject to post-trade transparency requirements. Since 2002, however, the US has imposed extensive post-trade transparency requirements in connection with publicly issued corporate, agency, and asset-backed debt securities through the Trade Reporting and Compliance Engine ('TRACE') system. A similar system has been established for municipal bonds. In Europe, meanwhile, MiFID permits Member States to impose trade transparency requirements in public bond markets,[56] but only Italy has so far done so.[57] However,

---

[51] The NYSE's market for municipal bonds dried up by the late 1920s, its market for corporate bonds by the 1940s: ibid.

[52] Although many bonds continue to list, if not necessarily trade, on exchanges. One reason for that is regulatory: regulations often require collective investment funds and insurance companies to hold securities that are admitted to trading on an exchange.

[53] We will encounter this dealer-intermediated market structure again in connection with our examination of OTC derivatives, structured finance, and wholesale funding markets in Chapter 21.

[54] Notably, recent regulatory initiatives—including Basel III (see Chapter 14) and the Volcker Rule (see Chapter 23)—have made it more costly for dealers to perform this function. Going forward, therefore, it remains to be seen whether dealers will continue to play a central role in the structure of many bond markets.

[55] R Green, B Hollifield, and N Schurhoff, 'Financial Intermediation and the Costs of Trading in an Opaque Market' (2007) 20 *Review of Financial Studies* 275; D Duffie, N Garleanu, and L Pedersen, 'Over-the-Counter Markets', NBER Working Paper 10755 (2004).

[56] MiFID, n 28, Recital 46.

[57] CFA Institute, 'An Examination of Transparency in European Bond Markets' (2011), 1.

from 2018 a part of the successor regime to MiFID—the so-called 'MiFIR'—will impose mandatory pre-/post-trade transparency requirements on European corporate bond markets (albeit with an exemption for large orders).[58]

Given their prevailing structure—and specifically the lack of pre-trade transparency—investors in public bond markets predictably experience higher trading costs than for equivalent-sized trades in public equity markets.[59] Notably, a number of empirical studies report that trade execution costs fell following the implementation in the US of the TRACE system.[60] A 2007 study by Michael Goldstein, Edith Hotchkiss, and Eric Sirri also found that the post-trade transparency introduced by TRACE was generally associated with smaller bid–ask spreads.[61] Interestingly, however, such transparency and tighter spreads were not associated with a decrease in trade volume. These findings serve as a rebuttal to claims that greater post-trade transparency—namely, real-time publication of the price, size, and parties to an executed trade—will undermine the incentives of dealers to act as market makers, thereby precipitating a decrease in trade volume, wider spreads, and reduced liquidity. Whether the same is true of *pre*-trade transparency is a different question—one which the EU's step of imposing such transparency from 2018 will allow us to test.[62]

Ultimately, of course, it is difficult to distinguish whether the relatively high trading costs observed within public bond markets are the product of the prevailing market structure or, conversely, whether the structure of these markets simply reflects underlying transaction costs. As a preliminary matter, trade volume within bond markets is far lower than in public equity markets. To give a feel for how much lower, consider that a 2007 study reported that euro-denominated bonds in the authors' dataset traded an average of four times per day.[63] In contrast, the average stock on the LSE trades more than 450 times each day.[64] From one perspective, this lack of trade volume might be seen as undermining the economic viability of the exchange model as a platform for bond trading.[65]

---

[58] See MiFIR, n 41, Arts 8–11.

[59] L Harris and M Piwowar, 'Secondary Trading Costs in the Municipal Bond Market' (2006) 61 *Journal of Finance* 1361; A Edwards, L Harris, and M Piwowar, 'Corporate Bond Market Transaction Costs and Transparency' (2007) 62 *Journal of Finance* 1421.

[60] M Goldstein, E Hotchkiss, and E Sirri, 'Transparency and Liquidity: A Controlled Experiment in Corporate Bonds' (2007) 20 *Review of Financial Studies* 235; H Bessembinder, W Maxwell, and K Venkataraman, 'Market Transparency, Liquidity Externalities, and Institutional Trading Costs in Corporate Bonds' (2006) 82 *Journal of Financial Economics* 288; Edwards, Harris, and Piwowar, n 59.

[61] Goldstein, Hotchkiss, and Sirri, n 60 (this did not hold for very large trades and very infrequently traded bonds).

[62] Unlike post-trade transparency, pre-trade transparency—and specifically any obligation to provide firm quotes—would expose dealers to the risk that they may be forced to trade at prices which no longer reflect the most up-to-date information. To mitigate this risk, dealers would be forced to engage in potentially costly monitoring in an effort to ensure that their quotes reflected available information at all times. Rather than incur these costs, dealers might instead curtail market-making activities or withdraw altogether.

[63] B Biais and F Declerck, 'Liquidity, Competition and Price Discovery in the European Corporate Bond Market', Working Paper (2007). Sterling-denominated bonds in the same dataset only traded an average of one and a half times per day.

[64] CFA Institute, n 57.

[65] Even this, however, is not clear-cut. For example, the LSE launched a new (exchange-based) bond-trading platform called ORB (M Stothard, 'UK Retail Bond Market to Top £1bn of Issues', *Financial Times*,

At the same time, the shift from exchange trading to dealer intermediation in US corporate and municipal bond markets roughly corresponded with the rise in importance of institutional investors.[66] These market participants—by virtue of their sophistication, greater bargaining power, status as repeat players, and the size of their trades—may be relatively impervious to the costs of a more opaque, dealer-intermediated market structure.[67] They have also benefited from the emergence of electronic platforms—such as those provided by MTS, MarketAxess, Tradeweb, and ICAP—designed to bring together institutional investors and dealers. These platforms, many of which were the product of dealer-led initiatives, lower search costs for investors seeking quotes from multiple dealers and, thereby, enhance competition for trade execution services.

7.5 The Role of Regulation

As we have seen, market participants possess powerful incentives to develop institutional arrangements that reduce the information, agency, coordination, and other transaction costs encountered in connection with the trading of financial assets. For a variety of reasons, however, privately generated rules governing a particular market structure may not be socially desirable. Perhaps most importantly, these arrangements can result in monopolistic/oligopolistic competition and the under-provision of public goods such as information and liquidity. In theory, therefore, there exists a potentially compelling case for regulatory intervention to prevent or ameliorate these market failures. At the same time, of course, regulators face a number of trade-offs that potentially undermine the desirability of their intervention.

First, regulation can mandate or subsidize the production of trading, issuer, and other information. Information is a public good. As discussed in section 7.2.1, it is also one of the most important assets of organized exchanges. Moreover, market makers such as exchange specialists and bond dealers enjoy informational rents from their privileged market positions. As a result, we might expect unregulated market structures not to ensure that enough information is disclosed. Regulators can respond by imposing trade reporting requirements. They can also coordinate larger infrastructure projects such as the US NMS, which is designed to integrate the information generated across different equity trading platforms. These regulatory strategies can alleviate asymmetries of information, attract volume and liquidity, and promote more informationally efficient markets. Simultaneously, however, regulators must be careful not to blunt the incentives of market participants to invest in the creation of market structures or the acquisition of information.

Second, regulators can help overcome problems of under-provision of private rules—and their associated enforcement—by market participants. Exchanges, ATSs/

---

29 October 2012). It may be that the costs of dealer intermediation have been increased by regulatory initiatives such as Basel III (discussed in detail in Chapters 14–15), which has raised the capital costs of holding bonds on dealer trading books.

[66] Biais and Green, n 50. See also Chapter 2, section 2.3.4.
[67] Ibid; Edwards, Harris, and Piwowar, n 59.

MTFs, and other private institutions may be reluctant to write, monitor, or vigorously enforce compliance with private rules governing misconduct by market participants. This is especially so where such institutions face meaningful competition. Regulators can address this problem by introducing fraud, market manipulation, and other regulatory requirements designed to ensure a high standard of conduct across the marketplace (see Chapter 9). They can also devote public resources towards monitoring and enforcement (see Chapter 26).

Finally, regulators can work with market participants to ensure that the introduction of new trading technologies does not disrupt the smooth and efficient operation of

---

High Frequency Trading

HFT involves the use of state-of-the-art information and communication technologies and computer algorithms to identify minute pricing discrepancies and trade in and out of the relevant securities extremely rapidly, often in a matter of microseconds. HFT is a subset of algorithmic trading, but it is HFT that has attracted the most attention in recent years. In particular, debate has arisen as to whether HFT is beneficial or harmful to market efficiency. Proponents of HFT claim that it enhances market liquidity and improves price discovery. However, HFT can also put significant stress on market and institutional infrastructure. For example, the role of algorithmic trading in the 'Flash Crash' on US trading venues on 6 May 2010 was recognized in a joint report of the SEC and the Commodities and Future Trading Commission. In the Flash Crash the Dow Jones Industrial Average plunged more than 1,000 points (9 per cent) within minutes as a reaction to an aggressive automated sell order in the market for E-mini S&P 500 stock index futures. It was the biggest-ever one-day point decline for the Dow. During a twenty-minute period, over 20,000 trades, across more than 300 securities, were executed at prices which were on average 60 per cent off their prices at the start of the period. High frequency traders have been held to contribute to the crash both by adding downward pressure in the futures market by similarly entering sell orders and for their conspicuous absence on the spot market for individual stocks, most of them having just withdrawn from the market during the crash. While the effect was limited in one sense (the market was restored to normality within minutes), according to some, the new trading environment, in which HFT plays a central role in providing liquidity and thousands of orders are inserted and cancelled every second, is more prone to crashes. Crashes, in turn, while so far limited in their effects, may in the future lead other traders to lose trust in the integrity and resilience of securities markets.

Regulators are starting to tackle this issue. In the EU, for example, a mixture of operating requirements and disclosure obligations are imposed on the firms that engage in HFT trading. MiFID II requires firms engaged in HFT to ensure that their trading systems are resilient, do not operate in a way that will create a disorderly market, and cannot be used for a purpose contrary to the market abuse regime (discussed in Chapter 9).[68] Firms are required to have procedures in place to deal with trading system failures and to disclose to regulators the fact that they are engaged in HFT. They must also keep a record of all their trades, which regulators may request.

---

[68] See MiFID II, n 37, Arts 2(1)(d)–(e) and 17. US Regulators are also considering how best to regulate this issue. See MJ White, 'Focusing on Fundamentals: The Path to Address Equity Market Structure', speech to the Securities Traders Association (2 October 2013).

financial markets. As we have seen, technological advances have played an important role in enhancing the informational efficiency of public equity and debt markets. At the same time, the emergence of new technologies can pose significant risks. High frequency trading ('HFT') provides a good example.

7.6 Conclusion

The smooth and efficient operation of financial markets depends greatly on how these markets are structured. For the most part, financial market structures are created by private market participants with a view to reducing transaction costs and generating gains from trade. In addition to these private benefits, these market structures also generate potentially significant social benefits insofar as they contribute to the more efficient allocation of society's resources. Simultaneously, however, these market structures can be understood as the source of potentially significant private and social costs. As a result, there is potential scope for valuable regulatory intervention. In determining the desirability of such intervention, however, we must successfully navigate a number of important and complex trade-offs.

8

Issuer Disclosure Regulation

8.1 Introduction

Previous chapters have emphasized the importance of information in making markets work. We have seen that informationally efficient markets should ensure that at any given time even uninformed investors buying a given security pay no more than an unbiased estimate of its value. That, in turn, should have a positive effect on market liquidity, feeding again into informational efficiency. As an outcome, firms' cost of capital will decrease, and managers can find guidance in market prices when deciding how to allocate corporate resources, which can enhance allocative efficiency. We have also seen how market players, including information intermediaries, can move markets closer to informational efficiency and how they may fail to do so.

This chapter starts from the observation that policymakers all over the world require issuers of securities to disclose a wealth of information, on the (often implicit) premise that in the absence of disclosure requirements, issuers would undersupply information, leading to market prices that would not accurately reflect an issuer's projected profitability. The ensuing information asymmetry between investors and issuers could in turn lead to a lemons market dynamic—that is, to the collapse (or underdevelopment) of securities markets with serious harm for the economy as a whole.

As highlighted in Chapter 3, the explicit regulatory objective of issuer mandatory disclosure for primary as well as secondary markets is investor protection.[1] Yet, it is a widely recognized fact that retail investors do not read issuers' mandated disclosures, whether in primary markets, where prospectuses of hundreds of pages, often in highly technical language, discourage them from doing so, or in secondary markets, where, in any case, the market price has already incorporated any relevant information that the disclosure may contain before the investors have the opportunity to read and trade upon it.

This chapter aims to reconcile policymakers' investor protection goal with the behaviour of market players, including investors, in the real world, based on an understanding of the reasons why market forces alone may be insufficient to attain informational efficiency and how they may nevertheless put mandated disclosure to good use. Thus, we first ask ourselves what the *regulatory objectives* are for mandating disclosures and how they can be reconciled with economic theory (section 8.2). Next, we answer the question of why *mandatory* disclosure is needed at all (section 8.3). Then, we provide an overview of disclosure regimes, taking those of the US and the EU as examples. Section 8.4 considers the scope of disclosure obligations, and section 8.5 their content. Section 8.6 then briefly discusses the role of enforcement in ensuring adequate disclosure.

---

[1] Chapter 3, section 3.4.1.

Principles of Financial Regulation. First Edition. John Armour, Dan Awrey, Paul Davies, Luca Enriques, Jeffrey N. Gordon, Colin Mayer, and Jennifer Payne. © John Armour, Dan Awrey, Paul Davies, Luca Enriques, Jeffrey N. Gordon, Colin Mayer, and Jennifer Payne 2016. Published 2016 by Oxford University Press.

Unlike the previous chapter, which discussed the markets for both debt and equity securities, this chapter predominantly focuses on equity securities, unless otherwise indicated. This is justified by the fact that—other than for issuers in the vicinity of insolvency—debt securities are less informationally sensitive than equities.[2] But much of what we say about equity securities can be intuitively extended to debt securities markets, the disclosure regimes for the two being broadly similar.

By the end of the chapter, you should have an understanding of the justifications, functions, and role of mandatory disclosure in securities markets. You should also have a sense of the content of the disclosure obligations imposed in the US and the EU, the boundaries of those obligations, and the role of enforcement in this regard.

8.2 The Use of Disclosure to Protect Investors in Securities Markets

We have seen that the goal of lawmakers in regulating securities markets is investor protection. Historically, the first public regulation tool to achieve this goal was a very intrusive form of *entry regulation*, known as 'merit regulation', whereby public offers of securities could only be made if the issuer and/or the securities offered passed certain quality tests applied by a public regulator. This was the main regulatory response in the US prior to federal intervention in 1933–4.[3] Although elements of this approach still survive today,[4] few would defend it as an effective way to screen out bad-quality (and only bad-quality) issuers from securities markets.[5] However, entry regulation is still used to some degree to screen access to the higher-end segment of the equity market, such as via exchange premium listing requirements.[6] In addition, the idea that any security newly offered to investors should undergo a screening process still characterizes securities regulation: even today securities regulators are called on to authorize public offers. Yet, the only ground for denying authorization is that the offering document lacks the required disclosures.

As anticipated, the predominant regulatory tool adopted in the US and the EU to protect investors is *information regulation* in the form of mandatory disclosure. This approach in relation to capital markets stands in contrast to other aspects of financial regulation, in particular rules governing consumer financial products and services— discussed in Chapters 10–12—where regulation of entry and conduct has been used more extensively.

---

[2] See G Gorton and G Pennacchi, 'Financial Intermediaries and Liquidity Creation' (1990) 45 *Journal of Finance* 49.

[3] SEC, Report on the Uniformity of State Regulatory Requirements for Offerings of Securities That Are Not Covered Securities (1997).

[4] Many US states still undertake some form of vestigial merit review (ibid).

[5] Infamously, back in 1980 Massachusetts' securities officials did not allow its residents to participate in the offering of Apple Computer stock, having judged that the offering price was too high relative to its earnings and book value. See eg SS Guzik, 'Regulation A+ Offerings–A New Era at the SEC' (2014), 10–11 (http://ssrn.com/abstract=2385115).

[6] In the UK, for example, premium listed companies are required to demonstrate a 'free float' of a minimum of 25 per cent of the shares for which application for admission is made: FCA Handbook, LR 6.1.19.

To understand how disclosure can offer protection to investors we first distinguish between primary and secondary markets. This will allow us better to connect the explicit goal of investor protection with our economic perspective and, in the process, to expose how the lens of investor protection is insufficient to fully appreciate the economic functions of mandatory disclosure. In this section, for exposition's sake we assume, as policymakers usually do, that markets alone would not provide investors with all the information they need to make the right investment decisions. We defer critical discussion of that issue until section 8.3.

8.2.1 Primary markets

To understand how mandatory disclosure can benefit investors when an issuer offers new securities to the market, consider that primary markets have traditionally been comprised of three main segments.[7] The most important one is the Initial Public Offering (IPO) market, where issuers retain underwriters to place their securities with retail as well as institutional investors and list the securities on an exchange. A second segment, much less relevant for equity securities but quite large for debt issues, at least in some jurisdictions, comprises 'captive' markets, where financial institutions, such as banks, rely on their ongoing relationships with clients to place securities, often with no prospective liquid secondary market. Together, these two segments have traditionally comprised much of the overall primary market. Finally, somewhat marginal, but most dangerous from the perspective of investor protection, are what we may call 'fringe' direct offerings markets, where the risk exists that, in the absence of prior vetting by established intermediaries such as underwriters and stock exchanges, gullible investors may be duped into buying worthless or overpriced securities directly marketed by crooks or unscrupulous market players.

The starting point for our analysis is a reality that policymakers and regulators are still reluctant to admit: before making their investment decisions, most retail investors do not read the prospectus—namely, the document which securities regulation requires issuers to publish and make available to them.[8]

In the IPO market, retail investors' reticence to read prospectuses is unlikely to harm them: they can free-ride on the efforts of underwriters, analysts, and sophisticated buyers such as institutional investors to determine an IPO price that reflects all available information.[9] In other words, the protection of investors and the benefits they derive from mandatory disclosure will be mediated by the interactions of underwriters, analysts, and other informed participants in the primary market.

---

[7] We are leaving aside here equity offerings by issuers that already have shares listed on an exchange. Although, as a general matter, the law treats such offerings as public offers requiring a prospectus, the mechanisms of incorporation by reference and shelf registration (see eg Prospectus Directive 2003/71/EC [2003] OJ L345/64, as amended, Arts 9 and 11) make their regulation a hybrid of the regimes for primary and secondary markets.

[8] O Ben-Shahar and CE Schneider, *More Than You Wanted to Know* (Princeton, NJ: Princeton University Press, 2014) 68–9. See also Chapter 10.

[9] Of course, underwriters and sophisticated buyers can get it wrong. But even if they had read the prospectus, retail investors would not be in any better position to avoid such errors than underwriters and sophisticated buyers.

In 'captive' markets where issuers/intermediaries, like banks, have a strong placing power, most investors will, once again, be oblivious to the required prospectus. They will base their decision mainly on their bank's advice. Yet, should their trust in the bank be misplaced and lead them to buy the wrong securities, they may find the prospectus useful to support their claims based on conduct of business rules violations on the part of the intermediary, which we discuss in Chapter 11: it will be easier, for example, to prove that the investment was unsuitable to the client if a truthful prospectus highlights its risks.

Things may not work out so well on the fringes of primary markets, where unscrupulous players and outright fraudsters, bypassing intermediaries such as underwriters, might, in the absence of any regulation on public offers, more easily lure naïve investors into buying overpriced securities. Here, mandatory disclosures and especially regulators' vetting of prospectuses more directly protect investors. Not only should the regulator be able to catch at least the most blatant cases of fraud before investors are swindled, but even when entry regulation fails to spot fraud, mandatory disclosure detailing required information makes it easier to punish fraudulent behaviour *ex post* via criminal prosecutions and to bring successful liability suits. Given that crooks are likely to omit or falsify required information, it will be easier to prove wrongdoing arising from the simple fact of its absence than if investors and the regulator, in the absence of mandatory disclosure, had to prove that a given piece of information was material and therefore its omission fraudulent.[10] Even in this case, the point is not that investors, after reading the unscrupulous issuer's prospectus, will refrain from buying: very few of them will read the prospectus anyway and most of those who decide not to invest will do so without reading the prospectus. But, again, it will be easier for investors to enforce their rights against the fraudster.

The tension between a reality in which investors ignore prospectuses and securities laws that assume the opposite, pretending that prospectuses are there for retail investors to read, explains policymakers' efforts to make prospectuses more user-friendly, such as when they require that prospectus summaries be published and that disclosures are in 'plain' language.[11] In the US, for example, the Securities and Exchange Commission (SEC) requires that the prospectus disclosure comply with the principles of 'plain English',[12] including using short sentences, everyday words, and no legal or highly technical business terminology.

8.2.2 Secondary markets

Retail investors in the secondary market also, in theory, need information in order to determine whether to buy, hold, or sell securities that are trading in the market. Yet,

---

[10] Should a fraudulent offer be made without an authorized prospectus, public enforcement against perpetrators will be even easier if such a conduct is itself a crime or calls for administrative sanctions.

[11] See FSMA 2000 s 87A(3), implementing Prospectus Directive 2003/71/EC, Art 5(1). In addition, issuers need to provide a summary as part of the prospectus in order to further this aim: FSMA 2000 s 87A(5). Such measures have recently also been adopted, with uncertain success, in relation to collective investment vehicles: see Chapter 12, section 12.3.1.

[12] Rule 421 of the Securities Act of 1933, as amended ('1933 Act'), 17 CFR 230.421.

when markets are informationally efficient, they can enter and exit markets based on their liquidity needs without analysing all available information and asking themselves whether they are paying or being paid the 'right' price for their securities.[13] The analysis function is performed instead by informed traders such as stock-picking institutional investors, who specialize in acquiring and evaluating information regarding issuers and their securities.[14] Informed trading by these professionals moves the market price, thereby allowing new information to be assimilated. Mandatory disclosure, assuming regulation of its contents and timing is optimal, serves retail investors' interests by making sure that, at any given time, all relevant information to evaluate securities is publicly available and therefore, thanks to informed trading, swiftly incorporated into prices.[15]

Empirical work by financial economists provides evidence that the prices of securities, at least in the US, have become more informative over the last sixty years. These studies report that individual share price movements have become increasingly decoupled from overall market movements, suggesting that firm-specific information has become more influential.[16] This has coincided with a significant increase in the amount of disclosure made by issuers, both in terms of the volume of disclosure and its content.[17] In light of the theory of efficient markets, it seems plausible that these two developments are linked—that is, that greater disclosure has resulted in increased price accuracy. But one should not jump to the conclusion that, since over this period the amount of *mandatory* disclosure has increased, regulation can be credited for the change: we cannot rule out that an increase in the demand for information from institutional investors would have been matched by issuers' voluntary disclosures in the same period. Yet, empirical papers more specifically looking into the market effects of changes in mandatory disclosure regimes report that increased disclosure appears to enhance liquidity and reduce volatility.[18]

8.3 Why is Mandatory Disclosure Mandatory?

We have so far considered why disclosure is important, but we have assumed that it needs to be compulsory. Now we ask: why should it? Even in the absence of regulation,

---

[13] Chapter 5, section 5.2.

[14] See Chapter 6, section 6.3.2 for a discussion of the performance of this function by securities analysts.

[15] For detailed discussion of how information becomes 'fully reflected' in the prices of securities, see R Gilson and RH Kraakman, 'The Mechanisms of Market Efficiency' (1984) 70 *Virginia Law Review* 549.

[16] MB Fox, R Morck, B Yeung, and A Durnev, 'Law, Share Price Accuracy, and Economic Performance: The New Evidence' (2003) 102 *Michigan Law Review* 331, 333–43. For discussion, see JN Gordon, 'The Rise of Independent Directors in the United States 1950–2005: Of Shareholder Value and Stock Market Prices' (2007) 59 *Stanford Law Review* 1465, 1541–5.

[17] Gordon, ibid, 1545–57.

[18] See eg M Greenstone, P Oyer, and A Vissing-Jorgensen, 'Mandated Disclosure, Stock Returns and the 1964 Securities Acts Amendments' (2006) 121 *Quarterly Journal of Economics* 399; A Ferrell, 'Mandated Disclosure and Stock Returns: Evidence from the Over-the-Counter Market' (2007) 36 *Journal of Legal Studies* 213; L Hail and C Leuz, 'International Differences in the Cost of Equity Capital: Do Legal Institutions and Securities Regulation Matter?' (2006) 44 *Journal of Accounting Research* 485; HB Christensen, L Hail, and C Leuz, 'Capital-Market Effects of Securities Regulation: Prior Conditions, Implementation, and Enforcement' (2013), ECGI Finance Working Paper No 407/2014 (http://ssrn.com/abstract= 1745105).

there are strong incentives for issuers to disclose relevant information voluntarily. Faced with the lemons problem described in Chapter 3,[19] issuers with above-average quality securities have an incentive to disclose facts relevant to their company's true value to investors in an accurate and timely manner, in order to distinguish their securities from average ones and receive a higher price for them. Average quality issuers will want to reveal information so as to distinguish themselves from low-quality issuers, and so on: if markets have reasons to assume the worst from silence, incentives to speak should be strong enough.

Consider, however, the incentives of insiders—that is, managers and controlling shareholders—who ultimately decide how much to disclose voluntarily. The benefits to insiders of revealing private information about their firms are likely to be less than the benefits to investors as a class, that is, to the market as a whole. Managers' compensation and dominant shareholders' returns are typically tied to the performance of their particular firm. Disclosure can impose significant costs on issuers, for example by revealing commercially sensitive matters to their competitors. Especially where the issuer is not looking to raise fresh capital from investors, there may be little obvious benefit to the issuer from additional disclosures. In fact, disclosure benefits *diversified* investors, by more accurately pricing *all* firms' expected returns, and also helps ensure the appropriate allocation of corporate resources. But undiversified insiders will focus more on the costs to their particular firms and disclose less than diversified investors might wish.

Insiders will also tend not to disclose information which, while useful to markets and the firm's investors, will negatively affect them directly.[20] Think of disclosure of executive compensation and related party transactions, which may reveal expropriation by insiders. Think also of 'bad news', which will devalue equity-linked managerial compensation and increase the risk of a hostile takeover.

Similarly, insiders may be reticent in order to profit personally from new information. Although insider trading is prohibited, as we will see in Chapter 9, the prohibitions are imperfect, and violations are hard to detect and punish. Moreover, the prohibition on insider trading is also linked to mandatory disclosure from another perspective. Together, mandatory disclosure and insider trading bans reduce information asymmetries and enhance market efficiency, acting as a sort of subsidy to informed traders and securities analysts in the market.[21] To understand why, consider an alternative, laissez-faire securities law regime of legalized insider trading and no mandatory disclosure. Under such a regime, prices would incorporate new information largely owing to insider trading. The problem would be that, compared to informed trading by outsiders, insider trading is a costly way to convey new information to the market. First, insiders are not as good as informed outsiders at understanding the value of new information: informed outsiders' greater objectivity and professionalism give

---

[19] Chapter 3, section 3.3.1.

[20] See eg M Fox, 'Retaining Mandatory Securities Disclosure: Why Issuer Choice is not Investor Empowerment' (1999) 85 *Virginia Law Review* 1335, 1355–6.

[21] Z Goshen and G Parchomovsky, 'The Essential Role of Securities Regulation' (2006) 55 *Duke Law Journal* 711.

them an edge in evaluating the price impact of new information. Second, liquidity-constrained insiders may not be able to move the market with their trading as much as the new information would warrant. Third, and relatedly, other market participants may have a harder time detecting insiders' informed trading from market movements that are just as likely to be due to liquidity or noise traders' activity. Finally, informed outsiders would stand to lose money systematically to insiders and therefore there would be less (informed) trading activity on the market. To conclude, legalized insider trading would not be an efficient substitute for mandatory disclosure as a tool to enhance informational efficiency.

Another difficulty with purely voluntary disclosure is that the formatting would be idiosyncratic. Different firms would choose different ways to present their results, probably selecting the one that most flatters their performance. Mandatory disclosure imposes a degree of standardization, which improves comprehensibility and comparability, thereby increasing the value of the information to investors. It is of course possible for standardization to arise through private ordering, but there may be some advantages to a system imposed by regulation, for example it may be easier for the state to implement changes and improvements to the disclosure rules, as compared to a private system.[22]

Finally, it may be hard to commit credibly to an optimal voluntary disclosure strategy across time: how can investors know that, after the IPO, insiders will not renege on promises of full and timely disclosure? Securities regulation provides a credible commitment device: once a company is subject to it, it is usually hard to 'go dark' without buying back investors' shares.[23]

Of course, there are also disadvantages to disclosure rules. Dissemination of the required information is costly, to the extent that the mandated disclosure exceeds that which they would have disclosed voluntarily, or requires issuers to disclose the information earlier than they would otherwise have chosen to disclose it. Perhaps more importantly, whether a mandatory disclosure system has net benefits for society also depends on the scope and extent of mandated disclosure: there can clearly be too much of a good thing. For instance, an obligation to inform the market of an issuer's R&D investments and achievements in a timely fashion would clearly allow for market prices to better reflect a company's profitability. But it may also reduce the value of those investments by attracting competition. There can be a trade-off, in other words, between price informativeness—plausibly tending to enhance allocative efficiency—and dynamic efficiency.[24]

---

[22] Note, however, that this is a very limited rationale for mandatory disclosure: it simply justifies mandatory rules about *how* disclosures should be made, and says nothing about *what* should be disclosed. See L Enriques and S Gilotta, 'Disclosure and Financial Market Regulation', in N Moloney, E Ferran, and J Payne (eds), *The Oxford Handbook of Financial Regulation* (Oxford: OUP, 2015) 511, 524–5. On the other hand, regulator-dictated formats may have the effect of retarding innovation, and may not be the best way of ensuring that those reading and analysing the disclosures receive the information which they would demand for themselves.

[23] E Rock, 'Securities Regulation as a Lobster Trap: A Credible Commitment Theory of Mandatory Disclosure' (2002) 23 *Cardozo Law Review* 675.

[24] See the discussion of the dimensions of efficiency in Chapter 3, section 3.2.

To conclude, although some question the benefits of mandatory disclosure,[25] there is broad consensus that mandatory disclosure is an essential feature of capital markets regulation and contributes to market efficiency. This is certainly the accepted position in the EU and the US. Yet, whether these legal systems' mandatory disclosure regimes have net benefits for society crucially depends on the scope and the contents of disclosure obligations, to which we now turn, and on how effective such rules are 'in action'—that is, whether they are properly enforced, as we briefly discuss in section 8.6.

8.4 The Scope of Issuer Disclosure Obligations

Disclosure obligations do not apply to all securities issued by all companies to all investors in all markets. Nor does every single piece of issuer-related information need to be disclosed. It is therefore important to consider the scope and content of these rules. In general, the *scope* of mandatory disclosure can be much better understood in light of policymakers' perception that these rules are needed to protect (retail) investors rather than to enhance informational efficiency. And their *content*, which we consider in section 8.5, is the sedimentation of what policymakers across decades have held to be relevant for investment decisions made by a reasonable investor.

8.4.1 Initial triggers for disclosure obligations

What triggers disclosure obligations varies across jurisdictions. However, it is generally the case that 'private' sales of securities are beyond the reach of securities regulation. Take the example of a private company issuing shares, whether to existing shareholders or to specified new shareholders such as a venture capitalist. In general, the law does not impose mandatory disclosure obligations on these transactions. Private company share sales and purchases are treated as a matter for private negotiation. Investors purchasing a significant stake in a private company are expected either to have the relevant information already or to be able to contract for their own protection, including necessary disclosure. Where investors are able to do so, the need for investor protection that policymakers pursue does not arise. The extensive documentation typically used in venture capital financing attests to the possibility that sophisticated prospective investors can contract for the necessary protective structures.

On the other hand, in both the US and the EU, offering securities to the 'public' will trigger disclosure obligations, unless an exemption applies.[26] More precisely, it triggers disclosure rules centred upon the idea of a single document—the prospectus—

---

[25] Note that the empirical studies that do provide evidence of benefits (in terms of higher liquidity and lower cost of capital: n 18) rarely measure mandatory disclosure's costs, some of which are simply impossible to quantify. One study that does measure such costs shows that the extension of mandated disclosure to a previously unregulated market segment drove out smaller issuers. See BJ Bushee and C Leuz, 'Economic Consequences of SEC Disclosure Regulation: Evidence from the OTC Bulletin Board' (2005) 39 *Journal of Accounting and Economics* 233.

[26] See Prospectus Directive, Art 2(1)(d): '"offer of securities to the public" means a communication to persons in any form and by any means, presenting sufficient information on the terms of the offer and the securities to be offered, so as to enable an investor to decide to purchase or subscribe to these securities'. For the US, see 1933 Act, §§2–5.

containing all the relevant information for investors, which apply at this stage and until the end of the offering period.

In addition, in both systems prospectus obligations apply if an issuer wants its securities to be admitted to trading on a regulated market—that is, an exchange.[27] Having securities traded on an exchange also triggers ongoing disclosure obligations,[28] some of which, in Europe, also extend to securities admitted to trading on a multilateral trading facility ('MTF').[29] The US, however, provides for a broader scope of ongoing disclosure rules. First, companies having triggered prospectus requirements are subject to ongoing disclosure rules unless the number of securities holders falls below a minimum.[30] Second, the wider set of ongoing disclosure obligations also applies to 'large' issuers—namely, those that have more than 2,000 shareholders (or 500 persons who are not accredited investors)[31]—and satisfy other size requirements,[32] even if their securities have not been offered to the public and are not listed on an exchange. That said, in practice it is common for companies that become 'reporting companies' for size reasons also to undertake these steps, and so to have shares traded on an exchange.

Despite these differences, the rationales for disclosure triggers in the EU and the US appear to be the same, namely that once the number of shareholders passes a certain threshold it is unreasonable to expect outside investors to bargain individually for the information they need, or to be prepared to bear the costs required to do so. Or, more in line with the idea that mandatory disclosure has the goal of supporting informational efficiency, another explanation is that if a secondary market exists (securities are traded on an exchange), or is likely to exist (an issuer is large and has many shareholders), mandatory disclosure will be useful to foster its informational efficiency.

Despite these established boundaries for disclosure obligations, there are a number of situations that may at first sight look as though they should fall within the disclosure regime discussed in this chapter, but which, as a result of exemptions, nevertheless fall outside it. We will first discuss two such categories, which revolve around either the identity of the investors to whom the offer is made or their number.

8.4.2 Investors who do not require the law's protection

If the justification for mandatory disclosure is investor protection, as policymakers believe, then, if no need for their protection exists, the rationale drops away. That is the case where investors can be assumed to be capable of acquiring for themselves any information they need to evaluate the merits and risks of the potential investment. While the concept of a 'sophisticated' investor may be easily stated, determining the boundaries of this category is not straightforward.

[27] Prospectus Directive, Art 3(3); 1933 Act, §5.
[28] Securities Exchange Act of 1934 ('1934 Act'), §12(b). In the EU see eg Transparency Directive (Directive 2004/109/EC; [2004] OJ L390/38) Art 1; Market Abuse Regulation (EU) No 596/2014; [2014] OJ L173/1, Art 17.
[29] See Chapter 7, section 7.3.
[30] 1934 Act, §15(d).
[31] 1934 Act, §12(g), as amended by the JOBS Act of 2012.
[32] See DC Langevoort and RB Thompson, '"Publicness" in Contemporary Securities Regulation after the JOBS Act' (2013) 101 *Georgetown Law Journal* 337.

One rather crude proxy for 'sophistication' in this context is wealth-based. Restricting an issue of securities to the wealthy could be tackled via the manner of the issue itself, for example by imposing a high minimum payment on the part of investors.[33] Alternatively, wealth-based criteria could look at investors' characteristics. Both the EU and the US, for example, designate categories of investors—termed, respectively, 'qualified investors'[34] and 'accredited investors'[35]—that manifest certain qualities, including a substantial level of wealth, which deem them to be sophisticated. Companies offering their securities exclusively to these types of investors can— broadly—escape the mandatory disclosure rules to which they would otherwise be subject when issuing their shares.[36] The purpose of these provisions is clear: sophisticated investors should be capable of negotiating for the provision of any information they need in order to assess whether to invest. This seems reasonable as regards criteria focusing on the expected knowledge of the person: for example, the definition of qualified investors for EU purposes includes fund managers and investment banks.[37] However, investor wealth is a less obvious basis for distinction. Just because investors are wealthy does not mean that they are capable of bargaining for the information they need themselves, or appropriately evaluating investment risks. The assumption, presumably, is that such investors can pay for appropriate advice from agents.[38]

One of the boundaries to the mandatory disclosure rules in this chapter, therefore, is that they apply differently to different kinds of investors. The effect is that sophisticated investors have a choice: they can engage in the public markets where disclosure is mandatory, or they can contract with private companies for the information they require. However, pinning down exactly what it is about these investors that justifies removing the mandatory disclosure requirements needs some thought. While it seems sensible that investors who already possess the relevant information do not need mandated disclosure, the provisions go further, including investors who do not have the information but are expected to bargain for it. In this context, rulemakers sometimes struggle to define exactly which investors can be expected to have the knowledge and sophistication to bargain in this manner.

---

[33] For example, EU regulations state that offers of securities where each investor is to pay at least €100,000 in response to the offer are exempt from the mandatory disclosure rules (Prospectus Directive, Art 3(2)(c) as amended by Directive 2010/73/EU, although proposed changes to the Prospectus Directive may result in the removal of this exemption: see COM(2015) 583 final, 30 November 2015).

[34] See Prospectus Directive, Art 2(1)(e) as amended by Directive 2010/73/EU.

[35] See Regulation D, Rule 501.

[36] Note, however, that these exemptions relating to the sophistication level of investors generally only remove the (primary market) requirements of mandatory disclosure regarding the 'offer to the public' requirements. The (secondary market) disclosure obligations may well still bite, for example if these shares are then listed on the public markets. In addition, US anti-fraud rules, which we cover in Chapter 9, apply also to private offerings to accredited investors. Traditionally, such offerings were also subject to rules on how to conduct the offering itself, such as a ban on general solicitations, eg via advertisement campaigns. Importantly, the JOBS Act 2012 removed this ban. See also the box on crowdfunding.

[37] Prospectus Directive, Art 2(1)(e), as amended.

[38] See the discussion in Chapter 10, section 10.3.3.

8.4.3 Small offerings

The second category relates to small offerings. In the EU, for example, there is no requirement for mandatory disclosure where the offer is addressed to fewer than 150 persons (natural or legal) per EEA state.[39] Small offerings are also designated in other ways; for example, the Prospectus Directive does not apply where the total amount to be raised in the offer is no more than €100,000 over a period of twelve months, an amount that Member States may raise to up to €5 million.[40]

Crowdfunding

Crowdfunding ('CF') is a process by which companies can fund small-scale projects from a large number of people, each contributing a small amount, without the need for an IPO. Investors are typically recruited via the Internet and contribute to the project via a variety of means including donations, loans, and—which is most relevant here—equity investments. It is potentially valuable to start-ups and entrepreneurs as a mechanism for accessing capital at low cost, in particular avoiding the costs associated with mandatory disclosure requirements. As we have seen, in the US, firms have for a long time been able to avoid those costs by raising funds solely from 'sophisticated' investors and subject to a ban on 'general solicitation'. However, even there regulators are experimenting with permitting equity CF from retail investors through exemptions from mandatory disclosure for small-scale capital-raising.

In the EU, the Prospectus Directive allows Member States to exempt offers to the public of up to €5 million over a twelve-month period. Many Member States (including the UK) have done so, thus facilitating equity CF. Moreover, ongoing disclosure requirements do not apply to CF companies, as they do not seek admission to trading on an exchange. In contrast, the US mandatory disclosure regime has traditionally had no *de minimis* exemption. The Jumpstart Our Business Startups (JOBS) Act of 2012 legitimized equity CF in the US. But while the immediate removal of the ban on general solicitations for offerings to accredited investors spurred a number of equity CF platforms reserved to such investors, it has taken more than three years for the SEC to finalize the implementation rules for CF addressed to the general public, Regulation CF. The delayed implementation reflects the inherent tension between the investor protection rationale underlying US securities regulation and the idea of an exemption from prospectus requirements for what would arguably be one of the riskiest asset classes to which retail investors have access. Regulation CF permits companies to raise up to $1 million per year through SEC-approved CF platforms. In contrast to the EU approach, the US framework still mandates the disclosure of a significant amount of information (including financial statements, details about management and shareholders, and a discussion of the company's financial situation). Such firms will also have to file annual reports with the SEC on an ongoing basis.

According to industry data, around $1.1bn was raised by way of equity crowdfunding worldwide in 2014. It remains to be seen whether the proposed US framework will augment this or whether the associated disclosure obligations will prove prohibitive for small firms.[41]

---

[39] Prospectus Directive, Art 3(2)(b) as amended by Directive 2010/73/EU. Qualified investors do not count against this number.

[40] Ibid, Art 1(2)(e) and 1(2)(h).

[41] See J Armour and L Enriques, 'The Promise and Perils of Crowdfunding', Working Paper Oxford University (2016).

The rationale for waiving mandatory disclosure in the context of small offers is that compliance involves fixed costs. Consequently, as a proportion of the amount of capital raised, the costs decrease with the size of the issue—that is, there are economies of scale. Without exemptions for small issues, it is argued that capital-raising on this scale would be prohibitively costly. Moreover, the benefits to the investor class of disclosure may be expected to vary with the size of the issue, which indicates how much capital they collectively stake. Consequently, it is plausible that below a certain threshold, the costs of mandatory disclosure may exceed the benefits. The problem for regulators is that no one can be sure precisely where this threshold should lie.[42]

8.4.4 Differentiation based on characteristics of the issuer

Another class of exemption from mandatory disclosure obligations is delineated by characteristics of the issuer. Two examples are discussed here: small (and 'high-growth') issuers and foreign issuers.

Small (and 'high growth') issuers. As we have seen, exemptions for small *offers* are justified on the basis that the costs of mandatory disclosure fall disproportionately heavily on issuers raising a small amount of capital. Very similar reasoning can be used to justify exemptions for issuers that are small in size.[43] However, an additional consideration in relation to small issuers (but not necessarily in relation to small offers per se) is that smaller companies are likely to have less information already in the public domain than larger companies—precisely because of the higher relative costs of disclosure they face. As a consequence, it could be argued that disclosure is *especially* desirable from such issuers in order to allow investors to assess the value of the securities being offered. In other words, the benefits to investors of disclosure would seem to be disproportionately high for smaller issuers.

A plausible trade-off is to permit a *partial* exemption from mandatory disclosure obligations for smaller issuers. Thus, the US permits smaller companies (defined as those either with less than $75 million in public equity float or with revenues less than $50 million in the previous fiscal year) to elect to be 'smaller reporting companies' when fulfilling their disclosure obligations. This entitles them to reduced disclosure obligations, such as an entitlement to include two rather than the usual three years of audited financial statements in the IPO.[44]

As we have hinted, a newly established firm's desire to raise public equity capital will usually be associated with a trajectory of, or ambitions for, rapid growth. It is argued that such high-growth firms are disproportionately associated with innovation, job creation, and economic growth generally. This implies that facilitating their growth through raising equity finance will be especially beneficial to society. Investors who take

---

[42] It certainly seems more plausible that this threshold would be captured by a rule conditioning on the amount raised, as opposed to the number of investors.

[43] Indeed, where issuer 'size' is determined for these purposes by the amount of equity capital raised from the public, there is overlap with the small offers category of exemptions.

[44] See SEC Release No 33-8876, Release No 34-56994, Smaller Reporting Company Relief and Simplification, 73 Fed Reg 3 (4 January 2008).

diversified positions in such firms will be well placed to share in these benefits. Such reasoning has been used to justify exemptions from US mandatory disclosure requirements—including a need to provide two, as opposed to three, years of audited accounts—for 'emerging growth companies' undergoing IPOs.[45] An additional justification is that for high-growth companies with innovative products or business strategies, more disclosure is not only directly but also, and more importantly, indirectly costlier, because providing information about their innovative business may reduce or even destroy the value of their innovations by attracting imitators and alerting incumbents to the competitive threat they face.

Controversially, however, the identification of such companies is simply by reference to size: the exemption applies to all issuers with revenues less than $1bn. Thus, although the exemption is apparently linked to special characteristics of high-growth companies, in fact it is simply an across-the-board extension of the existing exemptions for small issuers.

While many commentators would agree that some form of policy trade-off is appropriate in relation to these issuers, a recurring problem for regulators is how to determine which exemptions to waive, and for which firms. One approach is to permit some market differentiation and experimentation based on the venue where securities are traded. We have seen that EU rules define the ongoing disclosure obligations for issuers by reference to their having securities admitted to trading on an exchange. The emergence of alternative trading systems (ATSs)/multilateral trading facilities (MTFs) has meant that trading venues could be set up for issuers that would not be subject to mandatory disclosure rules: rather, disclosure requirements would be left to the self-regulatory choices of the market operators setting up the ATSs/MTFs.

An example of an MTF of this kind is the Alternative Investment Market ('AIM') organized by the London Stock Exchange Group. In practice, the disclosure rules designed for it are very similar to the obligations facing issuers seeking to list on a regulated market, such as the London Main Market.[46] But there are two notable exceptions: first, issuers are exempt from filing and obtaining regulators' approval for the prospectus before admission to trading, so long as they offer their securities only to qualified investors; and second, while companies that wish to be admitted to a regulated market must produce three years of audited accounts,[47] companies with a shorter history need not do so for admission of their securities onto AIM. This is clearly intended as a benefit to newer companies. However, the rules are unlikely to reduce materially the costs to smaller issuers in other respects. In addition, EU policymakers have recently extended some of the obligations previously only applying to issuers with

---

[45] JOBS Act of 2012, Title I. The exemptions reduce the disclosure obligations to which such issuers are subject.

[46] LSE, *AIM Rules for Companies*, Schedule 2. In addition, issuers on this market continue to be subject to the same anti-fraud regime (the market abuse rules discussed in Chapter 9) as issuers on the main market.

[47] Directive 2001/34/EC [2001] OJ L184/1, Art 44, Commission Regulation (EC) No 809/2004 Annex 1, 20.1.

securities traded on regulated exchanges to MTF-traded securities: most significantly, the Market Abuse Regulation ad hoc disclosure requirements.[48]

Foreign issuers. Jurisdictions sometimes distinguish between foreign and domestic issuers regarding the application of disclosure obligations. They may do so with a view to attracting foreign issuers to list on their stock exchanges, that is, for reasons of regulatory competition. In the US, for example, certain requirements of securities regulation are modified for foreign issuers, so that they face a lower disclosure burden.[49] Foreign issuers do not need to disclose as much information about their various lines of business, executive compensation, and material transactions as domestic issuers.[50] The company's accounts can be compiled either in accordance with US Generally Accepted Accounting Principles (GAAP) (as per domestic issuers) or alternatively can be compiled in accordance with International Financial Reporting Standards (IFRS) or with home country generally accepted accounting principles, although in the latter case the issuer will need to explain any deviations between such principles and US GAAP. In contrast to domestic issuers, foreign issuers are not required to supply quarterly financial statements.

8.5 The Content of Issuer Disclosure: Initial and Ongoing Disclosures

Whether explicitly (as in the US) or implicitly (as in the EU), disclosure regimes for primary and secondary markets are 'integrated':[51] an issuer on the primary market has to give all the information that will then have to be provided on an ongoing basis once securities are traded on the secondary market. In addition, of course, it will have to provide some historical background on itself, so as to give prospectus users some perspective when analysing the most recent information.[52] The overall content of required information reflects policymakers' convictions about what a reasonable

---

[48] See Market Abuse Regulation, Art 2(1)(b).

[49] This change was introduced in 1982 (see Securities Act Release No 6437, 19 November 1982), prior to which foreign issuers faced the same disclosure requirements as domestic issuers in the US. This kind of differentiation also existed in the UK until 2010: a distinction was drawn between 'primary' and 'secondary' listings, with higher disclosure standards required of issuers opting for primary listings. Both UK and foreign companies could opt for primary listings but only foreign companies could opt for the lower standard of disclosure available under a secondary listing. Since 2010, although differentiation still exists, the distinction is between 'premium' and 'standard' listings: see FSA, *Listing Regime Review*, CP09/24, October 2009. All issuers, both domestic and foreign, can choose between these options.

[50] See Forms F-1, F-2, and F-3. For example, in relation to executive compensation this information may be supplied on a group basis (in contrast to domestic issuers) unless individual disclosure is required by the foreign issuer's home country or it is otherwise made public. See generally, MB Fox, 'The Political Economy of Statutory Reach: US Disclosure Rules in a Globalising Market for Securities' (1998) 97 *Michigan Law Review* 696.

[51] See eg SJ Choi and AC Pritchard, *Securities Regulation: Cases and Analysis*, 3rd ed (New York, NY: Foundation Press, 2012) 176.

[52] For a good idea of the nature of the initial disclosure requirements in the EU see the minimum disclosure requirements for a share registration document imposed by the Prospectus Directive as amended and its accompanying Regulation: Commission Regulation (EC) No 809/2004, Annex 1, as amended. For the US, see eg Regulation S-K.

investor would consider material in deciding whether to buy or sell the relevant securities.[53] In both the US and the EU, regulators articulate the broad categories of facts (such as the identity of the directors) and documents (such as financial statements) that need to be disclosed. However, as we discuss in the next section, the EU also has a sweeping provision to make sure that any new price-moving information will be promptly disclosed.

8.5.1 Periodic and event-driven disclosures

Ongoing disclosures can be divided into two types: *periodic* and *event-driven* (or 'ad hoc'). EU and US ongoing disclosure requirements of these two kinds are summarized in Table 8.1. Periodic disclosures are those that must be made at set times. Both the US and the EU require issuers to publish annually a significant amount of information about the company, including their audited financial statements.[54] In addition to these annual disclosures, both the US and the EU require additional information to be disclosed periodically during the financial year. In the EU the obligation is to disclose half-yearly reports.[55] In the US, issuers must file a Form 10-Q on a quarterly basis. The amount of information disclosed in these interim reports is much less than for the annual reports and there is no need for the financial statements filed under these disclosure obligations to be audited.

Event-driven disclosures focus primarily on providing updates to the market about material changes in issuers' fortunes—such as changes in the company's governance, financial condition, or operations—as they occur, *between* periodic disclosure obligations. This keeps investors informed about developments which may affect their decisions to buy or sell securities. Depending on the nature of the changes being disclosed, event-driven disclosures may also be valuable for shareholders in a corporate governance context.[56]

Event-driven disclosures are sometimes also explained—particularly in the EU—as helping to prevent insider trading: by ensuring that relevant information is known to the market generally, any temptation for corporate insiders to trade on it will be removed.[57] They closely complement the insider trading prohibition for another

---

[53] Regulators have recently displayed a tendency to use disclosure requirements to achieve other goals that have arguably little to do with investor protection or informational efficiency, such as ending the humanitarian crisis in the Democratic Republic of the Congo by forcing disclosure on whether an issuer uses 'conflict minerals' from there (SEC Conflict Minerals disclosure obligation, Release No 34-67716 (22 August 2012)). See generally L Enriques, H Hansmann, R Kraakman, and M Pargendler, 'The Basic Governance Structure: Minority Shareholders and Non-Shareholder Constituencies', in R Kraakman, J Armour, P Davies, L Enriques, H Hansmann, G Hertig, K Hopt, H Kanda, M Pargendler, G Ringe, and E Rock, *The Anatomy of Corporate Law*, 3rd ed (Oxford: OUP, 2016), Ch 4.

[54] For the EU see Transparency Directive, Art 4 as amended by Directive 2013/50/EU; [2013] OJ L294/13 (applicable to companies with securities traded on regulated markets). See also Directive 2013/34/EU; [2013] OJ L182/19. For the US see Form 10-K (the financial data required to be disclosed is specified in Regulation S-X).

[55] Transparency Directive, Art 5 (as amended by Directive 2013/50/EU which abolished the requirement for quarterly reporting).

[56] For example, obligations to disclose related party transactions, major shareholdings, and directors' share ownership.

[57] Market Abuse Regulation, recital 49.

Table 8.1 Summary of ongoing disclosure requirements for issuers listed in the EU and the US

	EU	US
Periodic disclosures		
Annual report and accounts	Transparency Directive, Art 4	Form 10-K (filed annually)
Interim accounts	Transparency Directive, Art 5 (half-yearly)	Form 10-Q (quarterly)
Event-driven disclosures		
Internal information	Market Abuse Regulation, Art 17	Form 8-K: disclose 'on a rapid and current basis' material changes to a company's financial condition or operations, plus additional disclosures on specific events (Form 4).[58]
Directors' trading	Market Abuse Regulation, Art 19	Securities Exchange Act of 1934, §16
Major shareholdings	Transparency Directive, Art 9 (Some Member States super-add requirements, eg in the UK, see FCA Handbook, LR 10–11).	Securities Exchange Act of 1934, §13(d)

reason. As discussed in Chapters 5 and 9, the prohibition of insider trading is justified economically on the basis that doing so reduces the risk for 'outsider' (non-insider) traders of systematically trading with better informed counterparties, thereby reducing bid–ask spreads and increasing liquidity. But a potential cost of banning insider trading is the loss of a potential channel for revelation of non-public information, as other investors 'decode' price movements triggered by insiders' trades.[59] Mandating disclosure of material changes on an ongoing basis ensures that information is transmitted to the market in a timely manner.

This complementarity is seen most clearly in the EU, which has a 'continuous disclosure' regime, placing an obligation on issuers to disclose non-public (that is, inside) information that is likely to have a significant effect on the price of their securities to the market 'as soon as possible'.[60] In contrast, disclosure obligations in the US have been described as a system of periodic disclosure, rather than continuous disclosure.[61] US issuers are required to disclose 'on a rapid and current basis' material information regarding *specified* types of changes in an issuer's financial condition or operations.[62] The specified events include the issuer filing for bankruptcy or receivership, a material modification to the rights of its security holders, or significant acquisitions or dispositions.

The distinction between the two regimes at first blush appears to be that the US mandates ongoing disclosure in relation to any of a specified list of events, whereas the EU does not specify the events which trigger disclosure, rather looking to the *consequence* of events on the stock price. However, the distinction in practice may be rather

---

[58] For a full list of the event-driven disclosures see http://www.sec.gov/info/edgar/forms/edgform.pdf.
[59] See Chapter 9, section 9.3. See also Gilson and Kraakman, n 15, 573–8.
[60] Market Abuse Regulation, Art 17(1).
[61] See eg *Gallagher v Abbott Laboratories, Inc* 269 F.2d 806 (7th Cir, 2001), *per* Judge Easterbrook.
[62] Form 8-K.

more modest. For instance, US issuers are permitted to disclose other events that would be of interest to security holders, and many choose to make such optional disclosure between quarterly Form 10-Q filings. It is obviously in issuers' interests to do so where the information is positive, although less so for negative information. Further, day-to-day circumstances can impose an affirmative obligation to disclose on the issuer, stemming from inquiries from the investment community for information, and the issuer's motivation to keep that community apprised of current developments. If an issuer wishes to communicate an answer to a particular analyst query, Regulation FD ('Fair Disclosure') requires that it make the information available to the market generally at the same time.[63] In order to minimize compliance costs, many issuers consequently adopt an affirmative policy to disclose material information, subject to exceptions such as when it is necessary to keep the information confidential or when the issuer has a legitimate business interest for not disclosing. In addition, while the European Court of Justice has broadly interpreted the obligation to provide timely disclosure of material new developments, so that an obligation to disclose may arise even when the relevant event is still in the process of materializing,[64] European issuers do keep even highly material information, such as on R&D milestones, confidential as long as they reasonably can. That may be the only way to preserve the value of their R&D investments. Not to mention that it may be much harder for companies with solvency or liquidity problems to solve them if they have to inform the market of their exact situation on an ongoing basis, as the financial crisis has shown.[65] That, of course, leads to wasteful uncertainty on how the European rule applies, which should be weighed against its advantages in terms of facilitating informed trading on the market and reducing opportunities for insider trading.

8.5.2 Historical versus forward-looking disclosure

An important distinction amongst mandated disclosures is that between historical and forward-looking information. For decades, securities regulators' approach was to focus on 'hard', historical information about the company, such as descriptions of current or completed activities and financial statements covering past financial periods. The advantage of this approach is that a recitation of specified objective facts is a relatively cheap form of disclosure for issuers. Historical facts are also easy to compare across companies. Verification is relatively cheap, and an anti-fraud liability system works best where it is relatively simple, and cheap, to verify the accuracy, or inaccuracy, of statements made by issuers. The disadvantage is that historical data of this kind may be relatively unhelpful for investors. As a security's value to investors is determined by its future potential, information relevant to the issuer's likely *future* performance is of much greater interest to investors.

---

[63] Regulation FD, 17 CFR 243.100–243.103.

[64] ECJ Case C-19/11 *Geltl v Daimler* (28 June 2012).

[65] That is why there are now special rules for financial institutions, exempting them from the ad hoc disclosure obligation when that is necessary 'to preserve financial stability', see Market Abuse Regulation (EU) No 596/2014, Art 17(5). However, non-financial companies enjoy no such discretion.

We can observe some divergence of approach between the US and the EU on this issue. The US SEC has gradually recognized that providing only hard historical information about the company may not be the most useful for investors, and has sought to encourage the inclusion of 'soft' information such as appraisals of property and estimates of future earnings.[66] One of the difficulties of this approach is in persuading issuers and their directors and advisers to provide this information, given their fear that such statements may subsequently prove inaccurate, and that liability may then attach to the statement-makers. As a result, the US regime has put in place safe harbour rules that aim to encourage such 'forward-looking' statements by speci-fying circumstances in which such statements will be deemed not to be fraudulent.[67] In addition, issuers are required to include in their registration statements and periodic disclosures a statement from management, known as 'management discussion and analysis' (or 'MD&A'), which must provide a narrative discussion of those matters necessary to an understanding of the issuer's 'financial condition, changes in financial condition and results of operations'.[68] This goes beyond mere explanation of the (historical) financial statements, and permits inclusion of forward-looking data, such as trends or issues that may affect the issuer's business, prospects, future operating results, and/or financial conditions.[69] This should improve investors' and analysts' interpretation of the hard information in issuers' registration statements and Form 10-K.

By contrast, the EU's approach has to date been more cautious. For primary markets, it has focused on the dangers associated with the inclusion of forward-looking infor-mation in prospectuses, particularly the concern that such statements will be presented in an over-optimistic manner. Consequently, the information that EU regulations require the prospectus to contain is predominantly historical in nature.[70] Where forward-looking information is allowed at all, it is tightly constrained. For example, issuers are permitted to include profit forecasts in their prospectuses.[71] But because of concerns about the salience such profit forecasts may have for unsophisticated invest-ors, their presentation is tightly regulated. Thus, for example, profit forecasts must include a statement of underlying assumptions, distinguishing between those which directors can influence and those outside their control.[72] In addition, European law provides for no safe harbour on forward-looking information, which likely discourages issuers from making other statements of this kind. However, given that enforcement of mandatory disclosure rules in the EU is much less intense than in the US,[73] the

---

[66] See Regulation S-K, Item 10.

[67] Various safe harbours have been put in place, including statutory safe harbours (eg 1933 Act, §27A; 1934 Act, §21E; Rule 175 under the 1933 Act, 17 CFR 230.175) and common law defences (see eg *Kaufman v Trump's Castle Funding*, 7 F.3d 357 (3d Cir, 1993)).

[68] Regulation S-K, Item 303.

[69] See Regulation S-K, Item 305.

[70] The prospectus must describe the issuer, its managers, shareholders, and financial situation up to the date of application for admission, and the securities being offered for sale. See n 52 for references.

[71] Commission Regulation, Annex 1, para 13.

[72] The assumptions must be specific, precise, and readily understandable by investors. Moreover, the company's auditors or accountants must confirm that the forecast has been properly compiled, that its basis is compatible with the issuer's general accounting policies, and that its contents are compatible with company's historical accounts: ibid, paras 13.1–13.3.

[73] See section 8.6 and Chapter 26, section 26.3.

unavailability of safe harbours in the EU is not as crucial as it was in the US before the safe harbour came into force.

While there is no equivalent requirement in the EU-level continuing disclosure regime, Member States are permitted to impose such obligations. The UK has chosen to do so to some extent. The strategic report and directors' report which accompany the annual accounts of UK companies must contain a wide variety of information, including 'soft' information about the prospects of the company.[74] In order to encourage directors to provide such information, the UK has also introduced 'safe harbour' provisions in relation to these statements.[75]

8.6 Enforcement of Mandatory Disclosure Obligations

The mandatory disclosure obligations we have described are only valuable if issuers actually make timely and accurate disclosures. One way to achieve this is to use information intermediaries to lend their reputation to the issuer in order to signal to investors the accuracy of the information. This latter technique has been discussed in Chapter 6, and we have shown that, unsurprisingly, it is an imperfect mechanism. Legal enforcement of disclosure obligations is therefore essential for mandatory disclosure to achieve its goals.

Enforcement will only be valuable if it is effective. In this context it has been suggested that it is not just 'law on the books' but also the level of enforcement of those laws in practice that is important in determining the quality of a jurisdiction's regulatory regime.[76] On this analysis, the level of enforcement practised within a regime will depend both on the existence of rights to enforce, for example the rights of private citizens to bring an action, or the extent of the regulator's powers to enforce, and on the intensity or frequency with which enforcement occurs in practice. These issues are discussed in detail in Chapter 26. However, a brief overview may be helpful here, if only because private enforcement, at least in the US, features unusually strongly in relation to issuer disclosure, in comparison to most other aspects of financial regulation.

In the EU, while the content of disclosure obligations is set at EU level, their enforcement is left to Member States. There is no EU-level enforcement regime. For these purposes, therefore, the UK is taken as an example, and compared with the US position.

Both the UK and the US provide civil remedies to investors who suffer losses as a result of a defective prospectus,[77] or who suffer loss as a result of errors in ongoing

---

[74] Companies Act 2006 ss 414A, 416 (see Companies Act 2006 (Strategic Report and Directors' Report) Regulations 2013, SI 2013/1970). There are exemptions for certain small companies. For quoted companies the strategic review must deal with certain additional matters (see Companies Act 2006 s 414C).

[75] Companies Act 2006 s 463 (excluding all liability for directors in relation to statements in such reports, save liability to their company for fraud).

[76] JC Coffee, 'Law and the Market: The Impact of Enforcement' (2007) 156 *University of Pennsylvania Law Review* 229.

[77] In the UK, the main mechanism available to deal with misstatements in a prospectus is FSMA 2000 s 90. There are also common law actions available to investors seeking a remedy for misstatements, but these are largely inferior to the statutory action: L Gullifer and J Payne, *Corporate Finance Law, Principles*

disclosures.[78] In general, the remedy for misstatements in the prospectus is more generous to investors. So, for example, at the IPO stage in the UK an investor-friendly form of negligence liability is imposed (it is for the defendants to prove they were not negligent rather than for the investor to demonstrate that they were), whereas in the US the issuer is strictly liable. Regarding errors in ongoing disclosures, the investors must demonstrate fraud (including that any false and misleading statement be made with scienter or recklessly).

In addition to these private enforcement mechanisms, public enforcement measures are also available. For example, *ex ante* both the UK Financial Conduct Authority ('FCA') and the US SEC have power to refuse to approve a prospectus where it does not contain the required information.[79] *Ex post*, the FCA has the ability to impose a monetary penalty,[80] or simply a statement of censure.[81] Similarly, the SEC has a range of administrative proceedings available to address securities laws violations, including administrative proceedings against persons and issuers registered with it and the power to issue 'cease and desist' orders.[82] Criminal enforcement is also possible.[83]

8.7 Conclusion

This chapter has discussed mandatory disclosure as a tool to protect investors mainly by ensuring that market prices reflect all available information. We first provided a framework to reconcile policymakers' views that mandated disclosures protect retail investors and are addressed to them with the fact that the latter almost never read prospectuses and financial statements. We have seen that mandated disclosures are used at the IPO stage by sophisticated market players to determine the IPO price and that in 'fringe' and 'captive' markets, mandated disclosures may help investors enforce their rights vis-à-vis fraudsters and self-serving financial advisors. In secondary markets, mandated disclosures serve the objective of informational efficiency, which in turn should make it more attractive for uninformed retail investors to participate in them.

We then discussed the reasons why there is a need for *mandatory* disclosure, or in other words *how* mandatory disclosures serve the objective of informational efficiency. We have focused on the divergence of interests of insiders versus diversified

---

and Policy, 2nd ed (Oxford: Hart Publishing, 2015) 10.6.2. In the US, §§11 and 12 of the 1933 Act potentially provide a remedy to investors in these circumstances, and §10(b) of the 1934 Act may also come into play if there are fraudulent statements in the prospectus.

[78] In the UK see FSMA 2000 s 90A. In the US the courts have used a general anti-fraud provision found in 1934 Act Rule 10b-5 to fashion a broad-based remedy for investors (*Kardon v National Gypsum*, 69 F Supp 512 (ED Pa 1946)) although §18 of the 1934 Act may also provide a remedy. One consequence of this broad fraud-on-the-market private cause of action may be that issuers will be hesitant to disclose more on the margin. Consequently, the role of mandatory disclosure may be to ensure a 'floor' in such a regime.

[79] FSMA 2000 s 87A; 1933 Act, §8.

[80] FSMA 2000 s 91. The FCA may also impose a restitution order.

[81] Ibid. Public censure is likely to have adverse reputational consequences for the issuer: see Chapter 26, section 26.3.

[82] See 1934 Act, §15(c) (4) (disclosure violations), §21(a) (authority to investigate violations), §21C (cease and desist), and §12(j) and (k) (trading suspensions). See also 1933 Act, §17(a).

[83] 1934 Act, §32 (which makes it criminal to engage in any wilful violation of any provision in the Act).

shareholders as one important explanation: insiders have no interest in making information public that is also relevant to determining the value of other issuers' securities. Further, they may want to postpone disclosure of bad news and provide as little information as possible about self-dealing. We have also seen how a mandatory disclosure system coupled with a ban on insider trading is superior to a laissez-faire approach relying on insider trading to ensure informational efficiency. Finally, mandatory disclosure may facilitate the standardization process that helps investors compare issuers and solve the time-inconsistency problem that arises where issuers voluntarily commit to disclosure. Because there is arguably an optimal amount of mandatory disclosure and its costs may not be evenly distributed among the recipients of mandatory disclosure rules, we have provided an illustration of mandatory disclosure rules' scope and contents in both the US and the EU.

The use of mandatory disclosure is subject to boundaries. Limits are imposed according to the nature of the investors and of the issuer. The disclosure rules themselves focus largely on the provision of 'hard' information about the company, such as descriptions of current or completed activities and financial information covering past financial periods, although disclosure obligations targeted at the secondary markets also require issuers to keep the market updated about their fortunes. The US has been more proactive than the EU in seeking to introduce more 'soft' information into its disclosure regime. Enforcement also has an important role to play in ensuring that timely and accurate disclosures are actually made by issuers.

9

Trading and Market Integrity

9.1 Introduction

In Chapter 8, we explained the reasons why issuers and their agents may disclose less information than would be optimal and how mandatory disclosure may help achieve the objective of enhancing informational efficiency, thereby protecting investors. In this chapter, we examine other potential sources of market inefficiency that have attracted regulation. In particular, we examine various forms of potential misconduct in the market, namely market manipulation, insider trading (or insider dealing as it is also known), and short selling.

It is notable that, unlike the disclosure rules we saw in Chapter 8, both market abuse and short selling regulations involve placing obligations on a broader range of market participants than just issuers. In terms of the regulatory strategies discussed in Chapter 3, we are concerned here not with information regulation, but with conduct regulation.[1] As with Chapter 8, the focus in this chapter is misconduct in the public equity markets, since this has been the focus of regulatory intervention, but this is not to suggest that misconduct does not occur in other markets, such as in debt, derivatives, and commodities markets, and indeed some of the regulatory measures discussed in this chapter in relation to public equity markets also apply more widely.[2]

In section 9.2, we discuss the nature of market manipulation and insider trading and the rationale for prohibiting these activities. We consider them together, as they have important similarities; indeed, some jurisdictions bundle them together for regulatory purposes,[3] although some key distinctions also need to be drawn between them. In sections 9.3 and 9.4, we review the regulation of insider trading and market manipulation, respectively, and in section 9.5, the enforcement of these rules. In section 9.6, we consider the regulation of short selling. In each case, the rules put in place to restrain these activities will be examined critically in light of the reasons justifying the

---

[1] See generally, Chapter 3, section 3.5, especially section 3.5.2.

[2] For example, the Market Abuse Regulation (Regulation (EU) No 596/2014, [2014] OJ L173/1) covers financial instruments admitted to trading on a regulated market, those traded on a multilateral trading facility ('MTF') (such as the Alternative Investment Market ('AIM') in London) but also those traded on an Organised Trading Facility (as defined under Directive 2014/65/EU): Art 2(1). The Regulation also affects financial instruments (including derivatives) that are traded over-the-counter and have an effect on the price or value of financial instruments subject to the Regulation (Art 2(2)), thereby bringing commodity futures and derivatives potentially within the regime. This is wider than the range of instruments falling within the US regime.

[3] In the EU, the term 'market abuse' is used to cover both insider dealing and market manipulation, and the justification for regulating these two forms of activity is the same (namely to facilitate the 'smooth functioning of securities markets': Market Abuse Regulation, recital 2). By contrast, in the US the two concepts retain their separate identity to a greater extent, as the justifications for regulation have tended to differ somewhat.

Principles of Financial Regulation. First Edition. John Armour, Dan Awrey, Paul Davies, Luca Enriques, Jeffrey N. Gordon, Colin Mayer, and Jennifer Payne. © John Armour, Dan Awrey, Paul Davies, Luca Enriques, Jeffrey N. Gordon, Colin Mayer, and Jennifer Payne 2016. Published 2016 by Oxford University Press.

imposition of regulation. In particular, we will ask whether regulation is necessary in order to promote market efficiency.

By the end of this chapter you should understand what market manipulation, insider trading, and short selling are, and any potential danger that they might pose to market efficiency. You should have a sense of the arguments for and against their regulation, and of the regulations that have been put in place in the EU and the US to deal with them.

9.2 Market Manipulation and Insider Trading

9.2.1 What are market manipulation and insider trading?

Market manipulation involves actions intended to cause an artificial movement in the market price, so as to make a profit or avoid a loss.[4] One common example involves a situation where false information is released into the market, such as a rumour that a takeover offer is about to be made for the company, in order to move up the price of the securities and let the manipulator profit from the price change. Another common example involves artificial trades designed to move the price of the security, such as 'wash sales', where a trader simultaneously buys and sells the same securities (that is, trades with himself) to give the appearance of a legitimate transfer of title or risk, or both, at a price outside the normal trading range for that investment, in order to move the price of those securities artificially.

Insider trading can be broadly defined as the use of inside information (namely, 'price-sensitive' information that has not been made available to the public) about a company or its securities, in order to make a profit or avoid a loss through trading activity. For example, a director may know that the company is about to announce that it has made substantial losses, and he sells his shares in the market in advance of the disclosure of that information and the inevitable drop in share price that will result from it. A common example is where a director knows, as a result of his position, that a takeover offer is about to be made for the company at a substantial premium to the current market price for the shares. Once this information is made public the share price is likely to rise, but before this occurs the director buys a block of the company's shares in the market in order to profit from that subsequent rise in value. Target firm stock prices do in fact almost invariably increase following the announcement of a takeover bid. We also often observe a price run-up in the days immediately preceding the public announcement of the bid, which most likely reflects profit-seeking activity by knowledgeable insiders.

It is worth distinguishing insider dealing from *selective disclosure*—that is, where price sensitive information is disclosed to only a limited number of investors or

---

[4] A note on terminology: in the US, 'market manipulation' refers only to actions aimed at artificially moving prices via trading activity, while in the EU 'market manipulation' includes both those actions (known as 'trade-based manipulation') and 'information-based manipulation' which a US lawyer would refer to as securities fraud. We use the broader, EU wording of market manipulation to cover both kinds of behaviour because 'securities fraud' in the US is a very broad legal category that, in fact, includes not only information-based manipulation, but also trade-based manipulation and even insider trading (the prohibition of which is also derived from the generic ban on securities fraud).

potential investors, for example to some institutional investors. In some ways these two forms of behaviour are closely linked: insider trading is the use of inside information without the firm's consent whereas selective disclosure is the use of inside information with the firm's consent. Selective disclosure can be viewed as problematic for the efficient operation of the market, and jurisdictions do often seek to prevent this form of activity.[5]

Insider Trading on Wall Street

A number of recent high-profile prosecutions have raised the question whether insider trading is part of the fabric of Wall Street. One such prosecution involved Rajat Gupta, an iconic Wall Street figure. Gupta, who was described as someone who 'rose to the pinnacle of Wall Street',[6] was sentenced in 2012 to twenty-four months in prison and fined $5 million for his part in insider trading activity.

On Sunday, 21 September 2008, Gupta came across a valuable piece of information as a result of his position on the board of Goldman Sachs. He learned that Berkshire Hathaway chairman Warren Buffett was going to invest $5 billion in Goldman, barely a week after the collapse of Lehman Brothers. The next morning, according to the SEC, Gupta 'very likely' had a telephone conversation with Galleon Hedge Fund founder Raj Rajaratnam. Not long after that call, Galleon bought more than 80,000 shares of Goldman Sachs. The following day, before any announcement of the Berkshire deal had been made public, Rajaratnam called Gupta for fourteen minutes. According to the SEC, less than a minute after the call began, Galleon bought 40,000 more Goldman shares. While Gupta didn't profit personally, ultimately Galleon made a profit of more than $14 million and avoided more than $3 million in losses as a result of the inside information. Other prosecutions also flowed from these events, including Raj Rajaratnam, who was sentenced to eleven years' imprisonment for trading on tips from Gupta and others.

9.2.2 Why regulate market manipulation and insider trading?

It might seem obvious that market manipulation and insider trading should be regulated. In each case, one party profits at the expense of the counterparty to their trades, who has less information. This is reflected in the common idea that permitting such activities will cause investors to 'lose confidence' in the market, believing it to be unfairly rigged against them.[7] However, the impact on investors' willingness to trade in the market is actually rather less direct than it at first seems. A peculiar feature of both activities is that the profit is made by transacting *on a market*—through a price that is

---

[5] See eg Regulation Fair Disclosure (Regulation FD), introduced in the US by the Securities and Exchange Commission (SEC) in August 2000, which requires the disclosure of material information by public companies to be made available to all investors at the same exact time when first disclosed beyond the firm. Selective disclosure to analysts is prohibited in the EU as well: Market Abuse Regulation, Art 17(8).

[6] *Bloomberg*, 25 October 2012.

[7] In the first successful criminal conviction for insider dealing brought by the UK's financial regulator, Lord Judge CJ stated that investor confidence is at the heart of the justification for prohibiting insider dealing in the UK: *R v McQuoid* [2009] EWCA Crim 1301, [8].

known by the more informed party to be inaccurate. Consequently, the inaccuracy of the market price will have consequences not only for the informed party and their immediate counterparty, but also for any other persons trading on the market contemporaneously. If the price is high relative to what it should be, then anyone buying will suffer a loss, but anyone selling will enjoy a windfall gain, and *vice versa*. For investors who participate in the market as liquidity traders—buying when they have savings and selling when they need cash—it is hard to say on average whether they will win or lose from such activity.

Nevertheless, as was explained in Chapter 5, section 5.4, the presence of such information asymmetries is likely to cause systematic losses to market-makers (dealers in quote-driven markets and those placing limit orders in order-driven markets). As a consequence, market-makers will increase their bid–ask spreads in order to compensate themselves. *These* costs will in turn be passed on to investors, making it more expensive for them to buy and sell securities. This will correspondingly reduce investors' willingness to participate in the market, meaning issuers will face a higher cost of capital. Although the empirical literature is not conclusive, several studies report associations between the enforcement of insider trading prohibitions and more liquid stock markets and lower cost of equity capital.[8]

A different type of investor protection rationale was traditionally articulated for rules governing insider trading in particular. This viewed inside information as a corporate asset, which agents of the firm—directors, officers, and employees—might appropriate for their own benefit through trading. This could harm the firm's interests in a variety of ways—for example through the revelation of confidential information to its competitors. On this analysis, rules governing insider trading are a subset of corporate law rules seeking to reduce agency costs between those running the firm and its investors.[9] From a policy perspective, this rationale has become somewhat less significant with the growth of ongoing disclosure obligations for issuers.[10] In particular, the EU's requirement for issuers to disclose price-relevant information as soon as possible means that there is less scope for its retention so as to benefit the issuer.

In addition to effects on issuers' cost of capital, market manipulation and insider trading have implications for the accuracy of market prices.[11] As we saw in Chapter 5, section 5.2, inaccurate stock prices distort the efficient allocation of corporate resources. The adverse impact on market pricing is obvious in the case of market manipulation. Market manipulation generally involves the dissemination of misleading

---

[8] U Battacharya and H Daouk, 'The World Price of Insider Trading' (2002) 57 *Journal of Finance* 75; L Beny, 'Do Insider Trading Laws Matter? Some Preliminary Comparative Evidence' (2005) 7 *American Law & Economics Review* 144. Paradoxically, a prohibition on insider trading makes the potential rewards higher for those still willing to do so, by reducing competition from other insiders. Consequently, the intensity of enforcement is very important for the efficacy of insider trading regulation: A Bris, 'Do Insider Trading Laws Work?' (2005) 11 *European Financial Management* 267; H Bhattacharya and H Daouk, 'When No Law is Better Than a Good Law' (2009) 13 *Review of Finance* 577.

[9] See eg R Kraakman, J Armour, P Davies, L Enriques, H Hansmann, G Hertig, K Hopt, H Kanda, and E Rock, *The Anatomy of Corporate Law*, 2nd ed (Oxford: OUP, 2009), 170–3. The investors protected on this view are thus the firm's shareholders.

[10] See Chapter 8, section 8.5.1; see also P Davies, 'The European Community's Directive on Insider Dealing: From Company Law to Securities Markets Regulation' (1991) 11 *Oxford Journal of Legal Studies* 92.

[11] See Beny, n 8.

information about an issuer or its securities, or artificial transactions intended to convey false information regarding the supply and demand for investments. The core of market manipulation is an interference with the market's normal price-forming mechanisms. The false information imparted to the market—whether effected by misstatements or artificial transactions—once assimilated into the price of the securities, will by definition mean that the price does *not* reflect all the genuine information relevant to the firm's value that is publicly available. Market manipulation therefore undermines informational efficiency.

The relationship between insider trading and market efficiency is a little more subtle. As discussed in Chapter 8, there are some who suggest that if informational efficiency is the goal of securities regulation, we would do better to allow insider trading to take place without interference.[12] It has been suggested that insider trading provides a good method of channelling information to the market, including information that companies would not disclose publicly, perhaps because it would be too expensive to do so, or because disclosing it publicly would destroy the value of the information. Without insider trading, it is suggested, this information will not be factored into the price, since in the semi-strong form of the efficient capital markets hypothesis only publicly available information is fully reflected in the price of the securities. Therefore, allowing insiders to trade on that information would increase informational efficiency, since the inside information would then be reflected in the price of the securities.

This contention needs some thought. In particular, we need to consider how the dealing by an insider in securities might have an impact on the price of securities. Dealing alone is a relatively slow way to impart information to the marketplace. In general, price movements in securities are affected by securities analysts and other market professionals acquiring and assessing information about a company, and then acting upon that information.[13] Insiders' trading itself will move the price, but the effect may be limited or inaccurate by reason of the fact that, first, insiders may be liquidity-constrained and, second, their understanding of the effects of new information may be biased compared to that of securities analysts, who have the additional advantage of using valuation metrics based on comparisons with many other firms in the market and, in general, a better grasp of macroeconomic factors. In addition, it is true that securities analysts and other professionals may themselves act upon price movements as an indicator of new information.[14] Determining whether price movements are due to noise traders, liquidity traders, or insiders is difficult, however;[15] even harder is for securities analysts and others to decode the underlying inside information from the fact of other market participants' dealing.

---

[12] The argument that insider trading might be beneficial to investors was first raised by H Manne, *Insider Trading and the Stock Market* (New York, NY: Free Press, 1966). See also D Carlton and D Fischel, 'The Regulation of Insider Trading' (1983) 35 *Stanford Law Review* 857, who argue that insider dealing prohibitions slow down the rate at which securities prices adjust to new information.

[13] See also Chapter 5, section 5.4 and Chapter 8, section 8.3.

[14] See eg RJ Gilson and R Kraakman, 'The Mechanisms of Market Efficiency' (1984) 70 *Virginia Law Review* 549, 573–8.

[15] Z Goshen and G Parchomovsky, 'The Essential Role of Securities Regulation' (2006) 55 *Duke Law Journal* 711.

The law imposes obligations on some (not all) insiders to disclose their dealings in their company's securities, but this disclosure only occurs after the trade has taken place (in some cases quite some time after the trade occurs).[16] However, even if analysts knew in advance of a trade that the person intending to deal is an insider, and the size of the intended trade, this decoding process would not be straightforward. Take the fact that Facebook's chief operating officer, Sheryl Sandberg, took the first opportunity offered to her after the company's stock market flotation in May 2012 to sell some of her shares. What should analysts make of the fact that she was selling 353,000 of her shares for just over $7 million? Should this be interpreted as evidence that the company was doing poorly, or that there was inside information about the company which would suggest that the securities were overvalued? Was it relevant that Ms Sandberg retained $420 million of shares in the company? How could an analyst assess whether this was evidence of inside information about the company (and if so what that inside information might be)? The point is that although insider trading has the potential to release information to the market that can be impounded into the price, this creates a very noisy signal, and consequently can be viewed as a less attractive option than the alternative, namely mandatory disclosure plus an insider trading ban.[17]

Further, we should bear in mind that the effects of restricting insider trading on informational efficiency are also closely related to the extent of mandatory disclosure obligations. The more price-relevant information issuers are required to disclose in a timely manner, the less potential there is for insider trading to transmit new information to the market in any event.[18] Moreover, prohibiting insider trading in conjunction with expansive disclosure requirements increases the returns to professional investors who expend resources analysing the contents of these disclosures.[19] This in turn encourages more investors to engage in such analysis, and means that they—rather than insiders—will be the ones whose trade causes prices to move in response to new information. Plausibly, for the reasons outlined, this will result in more accurate prices than were the movements to flow from insider trades.[20] Consistently with this account, two empirical studies report a positive association between well-enforced insider trading restrictions and stock price accuracy.[21]

---

[16] In the US, Securities Exchange Act 1934 ('1934 Act') §16 requires disclosure of trades by beneficial owners of more than 10 percent of the shares, directors, and officers, but generally no sooner than two business days after the trade. The EU requires the disclosure to the market of dealings by those discharging managerial responsibilities for companies within three business days of the transaction occurring: Market Abuse Regulation, Art 19(1).

[17] A third alternative was the system in place in the US until Regulation FD came into force: an insider trading ban plus mandatory disclosure and no ban on selective disclosures to analysts. As some have argued, for less liquid, smaller companies which may otherwise have no analyst coverage, such a system may be preferable to the one currently in place in the US and the EU. See Z Goshen and G Parchomovsky, 'On Insider Trading, Markets, and "Negative" Property Rights in Information' (2001) 87 *Virginia Law Review* 1229, 1269–72.

[18] See Chapter 8, section 8.3.

[19] See eg C Tighe and R Michener, 'The Political Economy of Insider-Trading Laws' (1994) 84 *American Economic Review* 164; A Ellul and M Panayides, 'Do Financial Analysts Restrain Insiders' Informational Advantage?', Working Paper University of Indiana (2012).

[20] See text accompanying nn 14–15.

[21] Beny, n 8; N Fernandes and MA Ferreira, 'Insider Trading Laws and Stock Price Informativeness' (2009) 22 *Review of Financial Studies* 1845. However, these results are not especially robust, because neither study takes into account differences in ongoing disclosure obligations.

9.3 The Regulation of Insider Trading

Both the EU and the US impose significant restrictions on insider trading. The principal regulatory approach is to prohibit trading on inside information. There are a number of similarities between the two regimes. While both adopt a similar conception of 'inside information'—effectively, 'material' information[22] which is non-public—there are significant differences in other respects. The current US regime is the outcome of decades of case law developed by courts based on the very generic wording of SEC Rule 10b-5. Targeting securities fraud generally rather than dealing specifically with insider trading, that rule allows for much judicial discretion in drawing the boundaries of the prohibition: despite efforts by public prosecutors and the SEC to include all cases of trading on the basis of material non-public information, no matter how acquired,[23] the courts have tended to stick to a narrower approach. In contrast, the EU rules, first introduced in the early 1990s, provide for a statutory offence that deals specifically with this issue and, reflecting the market-oriented rationales considered in section 9.2, bans trading by anyone in possession of material non-public information.[24] The two largest consequent differences between the two regimes are the breadth of the concept of an 'insider' and the relevant knowledge requirement for liability.

9.3.1 Who is an 'insider'?

In the US, the SEC and the courts will find a relevant 'fraud' not only when a director or officer uses inside information to trade in the company's securities in order to make a profit or avoid a loss,[25] but also where persons more generally in a relationship of trust and confidence with the source of information, such as accountants, consultants, investment bankers, and lawyers, use material private information received via that relationship in breach of their duty.[26] They have also expanded the reach of insider trading in other ways. Thus it constitutes 'fraud' for an outsider 'tippee' to trade on information communicated to her in breach of another's relationship of trust and confidence, so long as the knowledge requirements are met.[27] In addition, the SEC has

---

[22] In the US, 'materiality' is judged according to whether it is the kind of information that might affect the judgement of reasonable investors, including speculative as well as 'conservative' investors: *SEC v Texas Gulf Sulphur* 401 F.2d 833 (2d Cir, 1968). In the EU it is information of a precise nature, which has not been made public, which relates directly or indirectly to one or more issuers or to one or more financial instruments, and if made public would be likely to have a significant effect on the prices of those financial instruments or on the price of related derivative financial instruments: Market Abuse Regulation, Art 7(1)(a).

[23] See eg SM Bainbridge, 'Regulating Insider Trading in the Post-Fiduciary Duty Era: Equal Access or Property Rights?', in SM Bainbridge (ed), *Research Handbook on Insider Trading* (Cheltenham: Elgar, 2013) 80, 86–9.

[24] For discussion see E Greene and O Schmid, 'Duty-Free Insider Trading' (2013) *Columbia Business Law Review* 369.

[25] See eg *Speed v Transamerica* 99 F Supp 808 (Del, 1951).

[26] *United States v O'Hagan*, 521 US 642 (1997) (partner in law firm advising company).

[27] *Dirks v SEC* 463 US 646 (1983); *United States v Newman*, 733 F.3d 438 (2nd Cir, 2014). A counterintuitive outcome of this framework can be found in the decision in *SEC v Dorozhko*, 574 F.3d 42 (2nd Cir, 2009), in which a hacker gained access to information and traded on it. The hacker was clearly neither an insider nor a tippee, and the court held that, because Rule 10b-5 covered misrepresentation, if the hacker had misrepresented his identity to hack into the system, the insider dealing ban would apply, but if

introduced a more general prohibition on trading on non-public information about a tender offer originating with the target or the acquirer,[28] and has deemed that relationships of trust and confidence arise in certain circumstances.[29] Nevertheless, although there has been a move away from the narrow view of insider trading as an offence committed by a director dealing in the securities of her own company, the focus is still on a relationship between the inside trader and, ultimately, the issuer.

In contrast, in the EU regime, one's status or relationship to an issuer is irrelevant to the definition of insider: what counts is the information one holds. That is, an insider is someone with inside information, however obtained.[30] The Market Abuse Regulation establishes an offence of insider dealing and of improper disclosure of inside information.[31] An offence is committed where an insider enters into transactions involving financial instruments on the basis of inside information.[32] In addition, an insider will be liable if he improperly discloses inside information to third parties (so-called 'tipping') and, to prevent easy avoidance of the insider trading prohibition, if he recommends or induces transactions involving financial instruments on the basis of inside information.[33]

9.3.2 Knowledge necessary for liability

In the US, the basis of the regime in Rule 10b-5 means that the offence of insider trading requires 'scienter'.[34] The insider must have knowledge that the information in question is *inside* information. A tippee will only be liable if he knows or has reason to know that it is material and non-public information and has been obtained improperly;[35] the tipper, in turn, will only be liable if she breaches her duty to keep material non-public information confidential. Whether the tipper must obtain a tangible benefit, and whether the tippee must be aware of that benefit, is a matter of some debate.[36] By contrast, under the current EU provisions, in only one instance is a state of mind necessary to establish the offence: if the insider obtains the information otherwise than as a result of being part of the management of the company, a shareholder in the company, through the exercise of his profession or employment, or as a result of criminal activities, then he will only be liable if he knows, or could be expected to know,

---

he were silent (and could gain access without a misrepresentation) it would not. (Needless to say, unauthorized access to computer systems and data theft are per se severely punished in the US.)

[28] SEC Rule 14e-3.

[29] SEC Rule 10b5-2 (persons receiving confidential information; and family members).

[30] Market Abuse Regulation, Art 8.

[31] Ibid, Arts 7–10. In the UK see Financial Services and Markets Act ('FSMA') s 118(2)(3).

[32] Market Abuse Regulation, Art 8(1).

[33] Ibid, Art 8(2), 8(3).

[34] For discussion of this concept and the extent to which it may encompass recklessness, see Donald C Langevoort, 'What Were They Thinking? Insider Trading and the Scienter Requirement', in SM Bainbridge (ed) *Research Handbook on Insider Trading* (Cheltenham: Elgar, 2013).

[35] *Investors Management* 44 SEC 633 (1971).

[36] *United States v Newman*, 773 F.3d 438 (2d Cir, 2014), cf *United States v Salman*, 792 F.3d 1087 (9th Cir, 2015), which has prompted the Supreme Court to re-examine this issue.

that the information is inside information.[37] Otherwise, there is no *mens rea* element for the offence.[38] Of course, many Member States also have in place criminal penalties for insider dealing, and the Market Abuse Directive 2014 requires them to do so.[39] It is common for these criminal provisions to require more to be demonstrated by way of knowledge on the part of the insider before criminal liability will be imposed.[40]

9.3.3 Other regulatory controls

A number of other regulatory techniques may be used to control insider trading. First, disclosure rules can be used—for example, requiring potential inside traders to disclose their dealings in the company's securities. This technique is used to a limited extent in both the EU and the US, for example requiring directors and officers to disclose their dealings in their company's securities after the trade has occurred.[41] The aim of this is presumably that if directors know that their dealings will be made public they are less likely to trade on the basis of inside information. The aim does not seem to be to provide information to the market in order to inform the price of securities.

Second, potential insiders might be required to disgorge profits from their trades. Thus, for example, directors, officers, and significant shareholders of US issuers are liable to disgorge any 'short swing' profits made in trading their company's shares within a period of less than six months.[42] Third, and more invasively, regulators might prohibit any trading by potential insiders in their company's shares, irrespective of whether they are in possession of inside information. A version of this approach is taken by the UK Corporate Governance Code, which provides that directors should not deal in the securities of their company in the two months preceding the issuance of any of the company's periodic reports.[43]

---

[37] Market Abuse Regulation, Art 8(4).

[38] Ibid. Note, however, that the state of the mind of the defendant may be relevant when the regulatory authority determines whether to impose a penalty and the appropriate size of penalty (eg FSMA, ss 123(2) and 124(2), which allow the FCA to reduce the penalty or not to impose one at all if it is satisfied that the person believed on reasonable grounds that he was not acting in breach of the insider dealing provisions, or had taken all reasonable precautions and exercised due diligence to avoid the prohibition).

[39] Directive 2014/57/EU [2014] OJ L173/179. The UK has announced its decision not to opt into this Directive at the present time, as existing UK provisions already cover the offences within the Directive (see in particular the Criminal Justice Act 1993, Part V and the Financial Services Act 2012, ss 89–91).

[40] See eg the UK's criminal law provisions regarding insider dealing which require (for the offence of actual dealing in securities) that the insider knows that the information is inside information and that he has it from an inside source (Criminal Justice Act 1993, s 57(1)). There are similar knowledge requirements for the offences of encouraging another person to deal and the offence of disclosing inside information to another person (ss 52 and 53).

[41] See sources cited in n 16. The US regime extends further, encompassing also disclosure of trades by beneficial owners of more than 10 per cent of any class of equity securities: 1934 Act §16(a).

[42] 1934 Act §16(b).

[43] FCA Handbook, LR 9.2.7, 9.2.8 (applicable on a comply or explain basis to companies with a premium listing in the UK). See also Market Abuse Regulation, Art 19(11) which prohibits those discharging managerial responsibilities trading in the company's securities in the thirty-day period prior to the announcement of interim financial reports or year-end accounts.

9.4 The Regulation of Market Manipulation

Both the EU and the US impose a general ban on market manipulation. In the EU, the Market Abuse Regulation creates a number of offences, including effecting transactions that give, or are likely to give, a false or misleading impression about the supply of, or demand for, or the price of securities, employing fictitious devices in those transactions, and disseminating information that is likely to give a false or misleading impression about the price of a security.[44] In the US, in addition to the general anti-fraud provision in Rule 10b-5, it is an offence to engage in a series of transactions in any security registered on a national exchange creating actual or apparent active trading in such security or raising or depressing the price of such security.[45]

Although it is relatively easy to justify the imposition of rules designed to constrain market manipulation, defining the precise ambit and boundaries of those rules is less straightforward.[46] One reason for this is the potentially complex nature of this offence. Although some forms of market manipulation may be relatively straightforward (such as the spreading of false rumours), this offence can also encompass highly sophisticated and complex practices designed to increase or decrease artificially a security's trading volumes and/or distort its price. Coupled with this is the fact that market manipulation practices are constantly evolving as new products are developed, new participants enter the market, and markets become more interconnected. One recent regulatory concern, for example, has been market abuse in the context of dark pools and high frequency trading.[47] So, formal, detailed definitions are unlikely to capture the full range of manipulative activity, and are likely to become outdated rapidly.

However, attempting to devise a more general definition of market manipulation can be difficult, as it requires the regulator to pin down the circumstances in which engaging in conduct that has the purpose, or the effect, of moving the market price is manipulative.[48] Some aspects of market manipulation are clearly fraudulent (for example, where an insider deliberately discloses misleading information), but not all forms of manipulation can be easily categorized in this way. Take the example of the company that decides to purchase its own shares in order to push up the price of those shares. What is the harm involved in this activity? Is it deliberately distorting the price of the security? What if managers believe in good faith that the shares are undervalued and the company's actions are intended to signal that fact? If trading then moves the price in the correct direction, the resultant price change should not be labelled 'artificial', and indeed such a price change is something to be valued rather than

---

[44] Market Abuse Regulation, Art 12, implemented in the UK via FSMA, s 118. In addition, the UK has a criminal offence of market manipulation: ss 89–91 Financial Services Act 2012.

[45] 1934 Act §9(a)(2).

[46] DR Fischel and DJ Ross, 'Should the Law Prohibit "Manipulation" in Financial Markets?' (1991) 105 *Harvard Law Review* 503.

[47] See eg Market Abuse Regulation, Art 12(2)(c) which specifies the behaviours regarding algorithmic and high-frequency trading strategies that will amount to market abuse. Algorithmic and high-frequency trading are discussed further in Chapter 7, section 7.5.

[48] For discussion see E Avgouleas, *The Mechanics and Regulation of Market Abuse* (Oxford: OUP, 2006), Ch 4.

discouraged, from an informational efficiency perspective. Is the wrongful aspect of manipulation therefore that the manipulation moves the price further away from its 'correct' level? The difficulty with this approach is that ascertaining the 'correct' level for the price of a security is simply impossible. For this reason some commentators suggest that although some aspects of market manipulation should be prohibited (especially those where some evidence of fraud is present), other aspects of market manipulation (particularly those controls based on price-distorting effects) should be deregulated.[49]

It is certainly true that establishing indicators of when a security price is artificial—as evidence of manipulative conduct—presents a significant challenge for regulators. Regulators tend to look at effects-based criteria in this context, such as whether the trades undertaken represent a significant proportion of the daily trading volume of a security, whether changes in beneficial ownership occur, whether the orders are undertaken by those with a significant buying or selling position, and whether the trades result in a significant movement in the price of the securities. However, these signals are clearly imperfect—the activities in question may be evidence of entirely proper behaviour—for example, a large, legitimate trade in a particular security. Given the difficulty in establishing objective criteria for manipulation, one regulatory approach is to adopt a subjective test, focusing on the improper intent of the trader. In the US, therefore, in addition to the foregoing objective criteria, the person accused of market manipulation must be shown to have 'scienter'—that is, a legally sufficient intent to commit the manipulation—and it must be shown that the defendant trans-acted with the purpose of inducing the purchase or sale of such security by others.[50] By contrast, the EU provisions relating to misleading conduct require no such intent, although where the defendant is accused of disseminating misleading information it must be shown that the person knew or could reasonably be expected to have known that the information is false or misleading (that is, a negligence standard).[51] This latter approach, focused more directly on effects than intention, presumably reflects the view that even without an intention to manipulate, if the market's normal price-forming mechanisms are impeded, market efficiency will be affected.

It might be thought that market manipulation could be defined simply as activity that involves an interference with the market's normal price-forming mechanisms. However, this formulation also runs into difficulties, since there are some instances of interfering with the market that are regarded as acceptable, and even desirable. An example is the price stabilization rules. These rules allow underwriters to support the prices of new issues for a limited period during the offering, by buying those securities in the secondary market. The injection of a large new block of securities may exert a temporary depressing influence on market price. The price stabilization rules allow the underwriters to 'stabilize' the price by creating demand for the securities. The

---

[49] Fischel and Ross, n 46.

[50] This is the case in the US under both §§9 and 10(b) of the 1934 Act. This is similar to the *mens rea* element required for the criminal offence of market manipulation in the UK (see Financial Services Act 2012 ss 89–90).

[51] Market Abuse Regulation, Art 12(1)(c)(d). Note also that an important defence is where the person who entered the transactions can prove that his reasons are legitimate and the transactions in question conform to 'accepted market practices' on the market concerned (Art 12(1)(a)).

economic justification for allowing this to occur is that it facilitates new issues and thus supports the raising of capital. Both the US and the EU allow price stabilization to take place, although given its potential to distort the market, it is regulated in both jurisdictions.[52] So, for example, those seeking to stabilize must disclose this fact, and the stabilization price cannot be greater than the offering price.

Forming a workable definition of market manipulation in practice is therefore not straightforward. It needs to capture those activities which, if left unregulated, will impede market efficiency, while excluding price-moving activity that is valuable from a market efficiency perspective (such as price stabilization, market making, and arbitrage activities).

9.5 Enforcement

As discussed, empirical studies suggest that regulating insider trading can have a beneficial effect on companies' cost of capital, but only if the provisions are enforced.[53] An enforcement regime is therefore an important aspect of the regulation of both insider trading and market manipulation. There are various reasons why *public* enforcement is needed to ensure that market abuse is not rampant in a given jurisdiction.

First, financial transactions are frequently complex, making the allocation of responsibility for losses to individual investors a challenge. The theft of a car is fairly straightforward. The thief either took it or didn't, and you as owner either have it or you don't. Determining whether a trader has suffered a loss because of market manipulation is not so straightforward. To establish that, it will be necessary to answer a counterfactual question of what would have happened if the alleged misconduct had not occurred. In some cases—for example, where the abuse was to subject the trader to higher than anticipated risk—it may be hard to show that the misconduct occurred, or that it caused any actual loss to the relevant trader. In other cases it may be hard to demonstrate that the trader would not have entered into the same transaction but for a particular misrepresentation. Establishing responsibility for losses in financial markets is rarely straightforward, and that may lead to under-enforcement by private parties.

Second, fraud in financial markets is frequently 'victimless'. Misrepresentation of trades and false reporting may not impose losses of any magnitude on one particular investor but may have significant costs across the market as a whole. As a consequence, no one is particularly on their guard to prevent it or indeed particularly concerned from a personal perspective when it happens.

Market manipulation is a good illustration of this problem. If by posting false information traders can drive up or down the prices of securities, they may be able to realize profits by selling or purchasing them at a profit. The costs of such manipulations are borne by the market as a whole, not by any particular investor. Nevertheless, the

---

[52] In the US see 1934 Act, Rule 104 of Regulation M; in the EU see Market Abuse Regulation, Art 5 and see ESMA Consultation Paper ESMA/2014/809 (in the UK see FSMA, s 118A(5)(b)).

[53] See n 8. See also D Del Guercio, ER Odders-White, and MJ Ready, 'The Deterrence Effect of SEC Enforcement Intensity on Illegal Insider Trading', Working Paper Wisconsin School of Business (2015).

social costs in terms of damage to the integrity of markets can be substantial. From a public perspective the benefits of deterring market manipulation may therefore be considerable but the private incentives of enforcement may be small. As a consequence, public law and public enforcement are needed to discourage this type of abuse.

Until recently there was no effective harmonization of enforcement of market abuse at EU level, but the Market Abuse Regulation 2014 takes a first step in this direction by imposing detailed minimum standards in relation to sanctions. Member States are required to have the power to force those culpable of market abuse to disgorge their profits, the power to withdraw or suspend the authorization of a firm, and the power to impose bans on those performing management functions.[54] The enforcement itself will still take place at Member State level. For this section the comparison will therefore focus on the US and the UK regimes. Both have well-developed public enforcement regimes. The UK has mechanisms in place to impose both criminal and administrative sanctions on those who manipulate the market, or engage in insider trading. Its administrative sanctions are now largely a result of the UK's implementation of the EU Market Abuse regime.[55] The UK also has criminal sanctions in place, which predate the EU regime.[56]

In the US, public enforcement is possible as a result of the SEC's power to enforce the 1934 Act,[57] under which, as we have seen, the substantive liabilities for insider trading and market manipulation arise. In addition, the SEC has powers to impose a civil penalty of up to three times the profits made by insider trading—in addition to disgorgement of the profits—and to impose vicarious liability on those who controlled the insider or tipper.[58] Moreover, the US Department of Justice has power to bring criminal prosecutions against inside traders.[59]

The US also allows for private enforcement, expressly for market manipulation under section 9 of the 1934 Act, and through judicial recognition of an implied private right of action for breaches of Rule 10b-5.[60] In contrast, the UK regime has no mechanism available to allow private enforcement of insider trading or market manipulation.

As we see in Chapter 26, there is a significant difference in the overall intensity of public enforcement observed in the UK and the US.[61] During the 2000s, the number of enforcement actions brought, and value of monetary penalties imposed, by the UK's Financial Services Authority (FSA) (the predecessor of the Financial Conduct Authority (FCA)) was a fraction of those brought by the US SEC, even with adjustment to

---

[54] Market Abuse Regulation, Art 30, see also Arts 31–4.

[55] See FSMA, s 118.

[56] See Financial Services Act 2012, ss 89–91 (and previously FSMA, s 397) and Criminal Justice Act 1993, Part V.

[57] 1934 Act §21(d) (power to bring enforcement actions in a federal district court).

[58] Ibid, §21A (as amended by Insider Trading Sanctions Act of 1984 and Insider Trading and Securities Fraud Enforcement Act of 1988 ('ITSEA')).

[59] Ibid, §32.

[60] *Kardon v National Gypsum Co* 69 F Supp 512 (ED Pa, 1946). Under 1934 Act, §20A, introduced by ITSEA in 1988, a person trading opposite an inside trader now also has an express private right of action for disgorgement of gains.

[61] Chapter 26, section 26.3.

reflect differences in market size.[62] However, since the financial crisis, the UK regulator has taken a markedly more aggressive approach to enforcement. There is some suggestion that this has had an impact on insider trading activity: according to the FCA, the level of unusual price movements prior to takeover announcements for UK listed firms has declined steadily since 2009.[63]

9.6 Short Selling

9.6.1 Why regulate short selling?

As discussed in Chapter 5, section 5.3, short selling is a trading technique used by investors who believe that the price of securities will fall. There are two types of short selling: 'covered' short selling and 'naked' short selling. In a covered short sale, the party wishing to go short ('S') borrows the shares from another person ('B') before selling them into the market: S uses the borrowed shares to settle his sales.[64] In naked short selling, S sells the shares before he identifies where he will obtain them in order to settle the sales to which he commits. This is possible because of settlement periods in securities transactions—that is, the time gap between the *agreement* to transfer the securities for a particular price, and the *actual* payment and transfer. Depending on the type of security traded, the exact length of the settlement period will differ. The settlement period is often quoted as 'T+1', 'T+2', or 'T+3', meaning that the buyer must transfer cash to the seller, and the seller must transfer ownership of the stock to the buyer, respectively, one, two, or three days after the trade was made. This gives S the opportunity to find shares to borrow in the market in order to deliver them to the purchaser before the expiry of the settlement period.

Historically, some jurisdictions have been disinterested in regulating short selling.[65] However, the panic generated by Lehman Brothers' bankruptcy in September 2008 and the collapse in market prices of listed financial company securities that ensued prompted many market regulators across the globe to introduce a ban on short selling as an emergency measure.[66] After the crisis, both the US and the EU implemented permanent restrictions on short selling.

---

[62] JC Coffee, Jr, 'Law and the Market: The Impact of Enforcement' (2007) 156 *University of Pennsylvania Law Review* 229, 263–8.

[63] FCA, 'Why Has the FCA's Market Cleanliness Statistic for Takeover Announcements Decreased since 2009?', Occasional Paper No 4 (2014).

[64] Technically, a 'loan' of shares is actually structured as a sale and agreement to repurchase, plus a fee. Otherwise, S could not give good title to the shares to the persons to whom he sells them. B is content to receive other shares when the time comes to close out the 'loan' transaction, because shares are fungible— that is, economically identical.

[65] Eg the UK had no short selling regulation in place until 2008. In contrast, the US has a long history of such regulation, starting with the introduction of an uptick rule in 1938: Securities Exchange Act 1934, Rule 10a-1 (repealed in July 2007).

[66] Eg SEC, Emergency Order Pursuant to Section 12(k)(2) of the Securities Exchange Act of 1934 Taking Temporary Action to Respond to Market Developments, Release No 34-58592 (18 September 2008) (which expired 17 October 2008); FSA, Short Selling (No 2) Instrument 2008 (relating to UK Financial Sector Companies), FSA 2008/50 (18 September 2008) (which expired 17 January 2009).

The fact that short sellers profit by selling something that they do not own is felt by some to be morally dubious, as is the fact that short sellers profit through the failure, rather than the success, of issuers. However, the popular distaste for short sellers is at odds with their role in financial markets. As we saw in Chapter 5, far from being villains, short sellers are actually very important in the price-formation process in securities markets.[67] If a security is overvalued by the market, then it is only through taking short positions that arbitrageurs can restore the price to a level consistent with publicly available information.[68] Empirical studies suggest that short sales do contribute to more efficient price discovery.[69] Indeed, some studies suggest that short sellers' contribution to the market's informational efficiency is superior to that of securities analysts.[70] In particular, short sellers can exert a useful downward pressure on a market, given the tendency of securities analysts to be overoptimistic with their buy recommendations.[71]

Short selling, as we have seen, exposes investors to greater potential losses than taking long positions. The difference in potential losses and gains means that investors are usually uncomfortable about keeping a short position open for a long period of time.[72] It may also be difficult to find securities to borrow for short selling purposes. As an outcome, one would expect short selling volumes to be often lower than price levels would warrant even in the absence of regulation.[73] Adding regulatory constraints on short selling can be expected to further limit the practice, with the effect of increasing the likelihood of overvalued asset prices.[74] If regulators were motivated by market efficiency concerns, they would then seek to *encourage* short selling, rather than restrict it. Indeed, this is precisely the course of action prescribed by many economists, including Nobel laureate Robert Shiller, in order to counter the build-up of asset bubbles. They argue that the inability of investors to take a short position in many

---

[67] Chapter 5, section 5.3. IOSCO's Technical Committee has recognized that short selling can bring efficiency gains: IOSCO Technical Committee, *Regulation of Short Selling—Consultation Report* (March 2009), 5, 22.

[68] EM Miller, 'Risk, Uncertainty and Divergence of Opinion' (1977) 32 *Journal of Finance* 1151; K Diether, K-H Lee, and IM Werner, 'Short-Sale Strategies and Return Predictability' (2009) 22 *Review of Financial Studies* 575; JE Engleberg, AV Reed, and MC Ringgenberg, 'How are Shorts Informed? Short Sellers, News, and Information Processing' (2012) 105 *Journal of Financial Economics* 260. Research suggests that short sellers may in fact discover and anticipate financial misconduct in firms, and as a result may convey beneficial information to the market: JM Karpoff and X Lou, 'Short Sellers and Financial Misconduct' (2010) 65 *Journal of Finance* 1879; M Fox, LR Glosten, and PC Tetlock, 'Short Selling and the News: A Preliminary Report on an Empirical Study' (2010) 54 *New York Law School Law Review* 646.

[69] Eg CM Jones and OA Lamont, 'Short-Sale Constraints and Stock Returns' (2002) 66 *Journal of Financial Economics* 207; A Bris, WN Goetzmann, and N Zhu, 'Efficiency and the Bear: Short Sales and Markets Around the World' (2007) 62 *Journal of Finance* 1029; E Boehmer, CM Jones, and X Zhang, 'Which Shorts are Informed?' (2008) 63 *Journal of Finance* 491; PAC Saffi and K Sigurdson, 'Price Efficiency and Short Selling' (2008), available at http://www.ssrn.com/abstract-id=949027.

[70] MS Drake, L Lees, and EP Swanson, 'Should Investors Follow the Prophets or the Bears? Evidence on the Use of Public Information by Analysts and Short Sellers' (2011) 86 *The Accounting Review* 101.

[71] See Chapter 6, section 6.3.2.

[72] The median duration of a securities lending agreement in the US for short selling is eleven days: Diether, Lee, and Werner, n 68, 578.

[73] According to a study using data from 2005, on average only 24 per cent of New York Stock Exchange (NYSE) and 31 per cent of NASDAQ trades are short sales: Diether, Lee, and Werner, n 68, 584.

[74] See eg EM Miller, 'Risk, Uncertainty and Divergence of Opinion' (1977) 32 *Journal of Finance* 1151; RJ Shiller, *Irrational Exuberance*, 2nd ed (Princeton, NJ: Princeton UP, 2005), 182–3.

markets, such as housing or subprime securities, may help explain these markets' pre-crisis booms.[75]

Bursting the Subprime Mortgage Bubble in 2007

Goldman Sachs was able to profit from the collapse in subprime mortgage bonds in the summer of 2007 by short selling subprime mortgage-backed securities. Two Goldman traders, Michael Swenson and Josh Birnbaum, are credited with being responsible for the firm's large profits during the crisis. The pair, members of Goldman's structured products group in New York, made a profit of $4 billion by 'betting' on a collapse in the subprime market, and shorting mortgage-related securities. They did this via the ABX index, which Wall Street had introduced in 2006. ABX became a way to invest in the direction of mortgage securities. The index allowed traders to bet on or against pools of mortgages with different risk characteristics, just as stock indexes enable traders to bet on whether the overall stock market, or technology stocks or bank stocks, will go up or down. Many believe that Goldman's actions (together with those of other traders who similarly found ways to bet on the collapse of the subprime market, such as John Paulson and the asset managers described in Michael Lewis' *Big Short*) contributed to the bursting of this particular asset bubble. Short selling therefore prevented the asset bubble developing further, which would have led to an even larger crash at a later point in time.

Short selling is also used for hedging purposes by those taking long equity positions. Consider the case of an investor planning to buy shares in an individual company, based on his own research showing that they are currently underpriced. If he just buys the shares, he runs the risk of losing money should the entire market or sector go down.[76] More likely, he will hedge against market risk by going short either on a basket of shares in the same sector or on one other stock whose price is highly correlated to the one in which he is taking the long position. That will not be a possibility in the presence of a ban on short selling. Restrictions on this practice thus make it riskier for people to take *long* positions in individual stocks. At the margin, that will harm informational efficiency and liquidity.

The financial crisis brought to the fore a popular belief that short selling destabilizes orderly markets and increases market volatility. This was felt particularly strongly in September 2008, following the collapse of Lehman Brothers and of other financial institutions, such as AIG. The failure of these institutions signalled to creditors and shareholders in other financial sector firms that there was a significant possibility of large losses to their investments. The prices of these securities began to fall, and stock markets in September 2008 witnessed a huge increase in short selling of these financial sector shares. This increase in short selling was perceived as a significant cause of the downward price pressures affecting these securities. This popular belief, however, confuses causes and effects. The appearance of many short positions is the normal *effect* of the release of significant negative information about a firm or sector. This is

---

[75] RJ Shiller, *The Subprime Solution: How Today's Global Financial Crisis Happened, and What to Do about it* (Princeton, NJ: Princeton UP, 2008). See also RJ Gilson and R Kraakman, 'Market Efficiency after the Financial Crisis: It's Still a Matter of Information Costs' (2014) 100 *Virginia Law Review* 314, 369.

[76] See Chapter 5, section 5.3.

precisely how markets operate to impound that information into prices. Nevertheless, as anticipated, temporary bans on the short selling of financial firm securities were introduced in the US, the UK, and many other jurisdictions in September 2008.[77]

Subsequent studies of the effects of these bans—comparing the trading of securities within the temporary ban and those outside it—bore out the criticisms of economists that such bans would harm market efficiency. The studies report that although the share prices of the financial companies in question received a temporary boost, in the medium term the stocks subject to the ban suffered a significant deterioration in market quality as measured by spreads, price impact, and intraday volatility, and a considerable loss of liquidity.[78] Nevertheless, both the US and the EU introduced further permanent restrictions on short selling of financial and non-financial firms, the content of which we will shortly consider.

It is easy to explain the post-crisis regulation of short selling as a primarily political phenomenon. Politicians looked for scapegoats during a period of rare public interest in financial regulation. The riskiness of short selling means that it is rarely practised by retail investors, but rather confined to professional arbitrageurs. Most voters, even if they are themselves investors in the stock market, do not fully understand short selling and view it as an alien, if not morally dubious, activity. Short sellers therefore became a convenient scapegoat.

Yet perhaps we should not dismiss out of hand the potential merits of regulating short selling. Notwithstanding the adverse impact on market efficiency, temporary restrictions on short selling of financial firms may potentially be justified on the basis of concerns about financial stability, which during a crisis regulators should sensibly prioritize. The firms in question were banks and other financial institutions, the failure of which could impose high externalities—in the form of contagion—onto the rest of the financial system. While reductions in the value of their shares could not directly bankrupt these firms, it could nevertheless have a powerful indirect effect on their viability.[79] Counterparties would look to movements in the share price as an indicator of new information about the valuation of the firm's assets.[80] The period during the financial crisis was one of extraordinarily high stock market volatility, as investors were unsure how to quantify the price effects of new information.[81] If investors

---

[77] See n 66.

[78] M Clifton and M Snape, 'The Effect of Short Selling Restrictions on Liquidity: Evidence from the London Stock Exchange' (2008); A Bris, 'Short Selling Activity in Financial Stocks and the SEC July 15th Emergency Order' (2008), available at http://www.imd.ch/news/upload/Report.pdf; E Boehmer, CM Jones, and X Zhang, 'Shackling Short Sellers: The 2008 Shorting Ban' (2013) 26 *Review of Financial Studies* 1363. For a broader, international, study on the effect of the temporary regulatory constraints imposed in 2007–9 see A Beber and M Pagano, 'Short Selling Bans Around the World: Evidence from the 2007–09 Crisis' (2013) 68 *Journal of Finance* 343. Yet, it is fair to say that no study will ever be able to demonstrate that in the absence of the temporary short selling bans equity market dynamics would have been no worse and financial stability at no higher risk.

[79] For a model, see MK Brunnermeier and M Oehmke, 'Predatory Short Selling' (2013) *Review of Finance* 1.

[80] A rapid decline in the share price might also result in inadvertent triggering of obligations to convert subordinated debt to equity, if these are conditioned on the market price: see Chapters 14 and 16.

[81] EG Fox, MB Fox, and RJ Gilson, 'Economic Crisis and the Integration of Law and Finance: The Impact of Volatility Spikes', Columbia Law and Economics Working Paper No 468 (2015).

*over*reacted in the short run to the negative information associated with Lehman's failure, then this could trigger negative feedback. Banning short selling could thus be justified as a way of protectively straitjacketing the pricing mechanism. This rationale would only be applicable in limited circumstances: to systemically important firms, during periods of high market volatility.

Two further concerns are raised about short selling. The first relates to the use of such sales to manipulate the market in a stock. Short selling can be abused to create misleading signals about the real supply, or the correct valuation, of a stock. The potential for abuse is particularly strong where short sales occur before a rights issue.[82] In evaluating this as a rationale for regulation, it is important to be clear as to what is the perceived ill. Is the problem simply market manipulation? As we saw in section 9.2.2, market manipulation is regarded as harmful because of its adverse impact on market efficiency. It is far from obvious that it is desirable to restrict short selling—with a predictably adverse impact on market efficiency—in order to enhance market efficiency by making manipulation harder.[83] If, on the other hand, the problem is rather that manipulators may use short selling to harm the prospects of financial firms, thereby precipitating contagion, then this concern merges with the systemic risk rationale discussed in the previous paragraph.

A final concern is the issue of settlement risk—that is, there may be settlement default if the short seller does not have a strong incentive to settle, or the share lending market has become illiquid, not allowing the seller to fulfil his settlement obligations. This concern arises particularly strongly in relation to naked short selling. Indeed, in relation to the concerns about financial stability and market manipulation, naked short selling is also regarded as being potentially more problematic than covered short selling, since it can be conducted more aggressively. Securities to borrow may be hard to find and naked short selling allows this difficulty to be bypassed. The requirement to borrow first can, therefore, be seen as inhibiting both the speed and extent of short selling. For this reason concerns about the need to regulate short selling often focus particularly strongly on the need to regulate naked short selling. However, it is hard to see that settlement risk justifies general restrictions on short selling, as opposed to specific safeguards in relation to settlement.[84]

9.6.2 Possible regulatory techniques

If a decision is taken to regulate short selling, a number of regulatory techniques can be deployed. These options are not mutually exclusive.

A ban on short selling. The most radical option is to prohibit short selling altogether. There are various forms that such a ban could take. First, it could be temporary or permanent. A temporary ban could respond to a particular set of market conditions,

---

[82] See FSA, Short Selling, Discussion Paper 09/1 (2009), para 3.7; A Saffieddine and W Wilhelm, 'An Empirical Investigation of Short Selling Activity Prior to Seasoned Equity Offerings' (1996) 51 *Journal of Finance* 729.
[83] See V Fotak, V Ramen, and PK Yadev, 'Fails-to-Deliver, Short Selling, and Market Quality' (2014) 114 *Journal of Financial Economics* 493.
[84] See CL Culp and JB Heaton, 'The Economics of Naked Short Selling' (2008) 31 *Regulation* 46, 49–50.

such as those that arose in the immediate aftermath of the Lehman bankruptcy.[85] The EU Short Selling Regulation enables Member States to make use of temporary bans in response to specific market conditions.[86] Alternatively, permanent bans could be put in place, designed not to respond to specific market conditions, but more generally to deal with the perceived legal and economic concerns arising in relation to short selling.

Second, the ban could relate to naked short selling, covered short selling, or both. Although the temporary bans put in place in September 2008 did not differentiate between covered and naked short selling, the more permanent bans that have been put in place subsequently have tended to focus on banning only naked short selling. Some jurisdictions have introduced a 'locate' rule to regulate this issue. This requires the short seller to be able to 'locate' the security to be sold short, for example by having put in place arrangements to borrow it, before the short selling can proceed.[87] The precise parameters of the 'locate' arrangements determine how close this rule comes to an absolute ban on naked short selling. The provisions in place in the EU Short Selling Regulation, for example, amount to a *de facto* ban on naked short selling.[88]

Third, a ban could cover short selling per se or relate to net short positions, which would allow any long position held by a person to be taken into account in determining whether and to what extent short selling has occurred. If defined broadly, as is the case under the EU Short Selling Regulation, the net short position approach also allows regulators to include positive and negative economic interests arising from derivatives positions.[89]

Finally, a ban might cover all shares or only some shares. For example, one of the significant drivers behind the temporary bans put in place in September 2008 arose from the special nature of the financial sector on which attention was focused in that period, and in particular, the potential financial stability concerns that were perceived to exist. However, many of the more permanent measures implemented in the wake of the financial crisis have not made this distinction, and apply to all shares within the ambit of the particular legislative provisions.[90]

'Uptick' and 'circuit breaker' rules. The idea of a circuit breaker or uptick rule is to prevent short sales being used as a tool to accelerate price falls in a declining market. An uptick rule is a trading restriction that disallows the short selling of securities except on an 'uptick'. For the rule to be satisfied, the short must be either at a price above the last traded price of the security, or at the last traded price, if that price was higher than the price in the previous trade. The US first introduced an uptick rule in 1938. This uptick rule was repealed in 2007, but a modified version was introduced in 2010.

The modified version added a circuit breaker into the equation. As a result, restrictions are placed on short sales of a share whose price has fallen by more than 10 per

---

[85] See n 66 and accompanying text.

[86] Regulation (EU) No 236/2012 of the European Parliament and of the Council of 14 March 2012 on short selling and certain aspects of credit default swaps, [2012] OJ L86/1 (EU Short Selling Regulation), Arts 20–1.

[87] See eg US Regulation SHO (introduced before the crisis, in July 2004, which requires broker-dealers to have reasonable grounds to believe that a security to be sold short can be borrowed); see EU Short Selling Regulation, Art 12.

[88] See Commission Implementing Regulation (EU) No 827/2012, [2012] OJ L251/11.

[89] See Commission Delegated Regulation (EU) No 918/2012, [2012] OJ L274/1, Arts 5–6.

[90] Eg EU Short Selling Regulation, Art 12.

cent compared to its closing price the previous day.[91] Once the circuit breaker is triggered, this rule applies to short sale orders in the affected security for the remainder of the day as well as the following day, allowing short sales to occur only where the price is above the current national bid price. The EU Short Selling Regulation also allows the use by Member States (or by the European Securities and Markets Authority (ESMA) in the last resort) of temporary powers, including the use of circuit breakers, in exceptional circumstances.[92]

The uptick rule in the US was heavily criticized before its repeal in 2007,[93] and empirical studies conducted after its repeal suggest that although the volume of short selling increased as a result, there was no increase in the volatility of the US markets, and that, further, the uptick rule had no meaningful role in halting price declines.[94] In 2004 the SEC initiated a year-long pilot that eliminated short sale restrictions for approximately one-third of the largest stocks. The purpose of the pilot was to study how this removal impacted the market for those securities. The SEC's conclusion was that the uptick rule should be repealed because it reduced liquidity, however modestly, and did not appear necessary to prevent manipulation.[95]

The financial crisis prompted the reintroduction of the modified version of this rule. However, it remains unclear what benefit this modified uptick test will bring. Indeed, the evidence from the previous version of this rule suggests that it may reduce the efficiency of the market by reducing liquidity.

Reporting/Disclosure. Another option is to require greater transparency of short positions. This can involve reporting to a regulator and/or disclosure to the public. The rationale for reporting to the regulator is to allow it to monitor and regulate potentially abusive positions.[96] Disclosure of short selling to the public, in turn, can provide data to the market about the impact of short selling on prices, and therefore can contribute to more efficient pricing of stocks.

Yet, fearing that other players in the market may take opposite positions to frustrate a short selling strategy, potential short sellers may seek to avoid public scrutiny of their actions, and as a result might want to stay below the relevant threshold and therefore engage in less short selling than they otherwise would. Depending on one's view of short selling, this might be a good or a bad thing.[97] But another potential effect of such

---

[91] SEC, Amendments to Regulation SHO, Release No 34-61595 (February 2010) (Final Rule).

[92] EU Short Selling Regulation, Arts 23 and 28.

[93] J Macey, M Mitchell, and JM Netter, 'Restrictions on Short Sales: An Analysis of the Uptick Rule and its Role in View of the October 1987 Stock Market Crash' (1989) 74 *Cornell Law Review* 799.

[94] Eg E Boehmer, CM Jones, and X Zhang, 'Unshackling Short Sellers: The Repeal of the Uptick Rule', Working Paper Columbia Business School (2008). For further criticism of the uptick rule see eg GJ Alexander and MA Peterson, 'Short Selling on the New York Stock Exchange and the Effects of the Uptick Rule' (1999) 8 *Journal of Financial Intermediation* 90; K Diether, K-H Lee, and IM Werner, 'It's SHO Time! Short-Sale Price-Tests and Market Quality' (2009) 64 *Journal of Finance* 37.

[95] SEC, 'SEC Votes on Regulation SHO Amendments and Proposals; Also Votes to Eliminate "Tick" Test', Press Release 2007-114 (2007).

[96] See eg FSA, n 82, para 5.28. Yet, if manipulation is the concern, it is hard to understand why there should be no reporting requirements for margin trading, which is bound to create the same risk of manipulative behaviour as short selling but in the opposite direction.

[97] See eg CM Jones, AV Reed, and W Waller, 'Revealing Shorts: An Examination of Large Short Position Disclosures' (2015), available at http://ssrn.com/abstract=1910372.

disclosure obligations is troublesome whatever one thinks of short selling: public disclosure may actually facilitate predatory short sellers' coordination and contribute to herding behaviour, exacerbating the downward spirals that these regulations are designed to prevent.

The EU Short Selling Regulation has adopted a two-tier approach. Investors must report significant net short positions to regulators once these amount to 0.2 per cent of the issued share capital of a company,[98] and must disclose to the market at a higher 0.5 per cent threshold.[99] All changes of position should be reported at increments of 0.1 per cent, first to the regulator (at 0.3 per cent and 0.4 per cent) and then to the regulator and the market at 0.5 per cent.[100] In order to make such disclosures meaningful, 'short' positions are broadly defined to include derivative positions as well.[101] By contrast with the EU, reporting and disclosure do not play a large part in the US short selling regime.[102]

Settlement rules. Settlement failure is potentially problematic, as it can cause disruption to the orderly operation of the market in the securities concerned. However, a number of measures can be put in place to try to reduce the risk. First, this problem is caused in large part because of the need for settlement periods. Given the nature of securities, some kind of settlement period is necessary (unlike buying apples from a market stall, the buyers and sellers of securities are not physically present in the stock market to exchange the cash and securities and some jurisdictions do not yet have the infrastructure to facilitate delivery against payment on a daily basis). However, keeping settlement periods to a minimum can be beneficial. For stocks in the US, the settlement period is T + 3, whereas the settlement period for transferable securities executed on trading venues across the EU is T + 2.[103] In addition, penalties can be put in place for failure to settle in order to provide incentives for traders. The EU, for example, requires daily fines for settlement failures.[104] Obligations can also be placed on trading venues to make good any failure. For example, the EU requires trading venues to ensure that there are adequate arrangements in place for the buy-in of securities where there is a settlement failure (or for cash compensation to be paid in the event of a buy-in proving impossible), with reimbursement from the seller.[105]

---

[98] EU Short Selling Regulation, Art 5.   [99] Ibid, Art 6.

[100] Ibid, Arts 5(2) and 6(2).   [101] Ibid, Art 3(1).

[102] The US rules contain no requirement to notify individual short positions to either the regulator or the market. Rather they include requirements to 'mark' all orders of equity securities as 'short' or 'long' (Regulation SHO, Rule 200(g)) and the rules provide for more general transparency obligations, such as general order and reporting requirements. The Dodd–Frank Act of 2010 set out proposals concerning short sale reporting and required the SEC to conduct studies in this regard (§417(a)(2)), but the SEC's report ultimately determined that none of the options was likely to be cost-effective: SEC, Short Sale Position and Transaction Reporting Report, 5 June 2014.

[103] Regulation (EU) No 909/2014 on Improving Securities Settlement and on Central Securities Depositaries [2014] OJ L257/1, Art 5(2).

[104] Ibid, Art 7(2).

[105] Ibid, Arts 7(3)–(8). In the US see SEC, Amendments to Regulation SHO, Release No 34-58572 (September 2008) and Release No 34-60388 (July 2009), which introduce new rules designed to reduce the number of fails to deliver. Studies suggest that tightening up these rules regarding settlement has reduced the number of fails to deliver: Office of Economic Analysis, Memorandum, Impact of Recent SHO Rule Changes on Fails to Deliver (April 2009).

9.7 Conclusion

As in Chapter 8, this chapter has considered whether capital market regulation requires a public regulatory response to supplement private ordering. In Chapter 8 we analysed mandatory disclosure as a tool to enhance informational efficiency and, by doing so, to protect investors. In this chapter we have considered whether it is necessary to regulate other forms of market conduct, in order to ensure the efficiency of the market. We have explored a number of different forms of such conduct that have attracted regulation, namely insider trading, market manipulation, and short selling. The regulation of all these activities has been justified, to some extent, by the need to safeguard market efficiency. However, these arguments do not always stand up to scrutiny. In terms of the behaviour described in this chapter, there is a hierarchy of the ease with which it is possible to justify regulation on market efficiency grounds, with market manipulation regulation being easiest, then insider trading, and last short selling. In fact, general bans or restrictions on short selling most likely have a deleterious effect on market efficiency.

PART C

CONSUMERS AND THE FINANCIAL SYSTEM

10

Regulating Consumer Finance

10.1 Introduction

Part C is concerned with financial regulation protecting the interests of consumers. Who is treated as a 'consumer' varies depending on the regulatory context.[1] In US and EU financial regulation, as in consumer contract law generally, 'consumers' are taken to be individuals transacting in a personal capacity—that is, outside the course of their trade, business, or profession.[2] This is also the definition generally adopted in this book.[3] While the basic regulatory thesis is that consumers are deserving of special regulatory protection above and beyond other users of the financial system, it will be obvious that, especially where a broad definition of 'consumers' is employed, it is often necessary to draw finer distinctions within that category. Hence the regulatory treatment typically also distinguishes between 'sophisticated' clients or investors and 'retail' clients or investors.[4] The latter are generally individuals acting in a personal capacity or small businesses, in each case dealing with relatively modest sums—criteria that largely follow the narrower definition of 'consumer'.[5] So we can begin our discussion with the idea in mind that 'consumer protection' measures are deployed most strongly in favour of individuals who participate in the financial system on their own account, on a modest scale.

In the guise of 'retail investors', individuals are the ultimate suppliers of much of the liquidity in the financial system, through their *savings*. Consumers are also an important source of demand for funds from the financial system, *borrowing* against future income to fund the purchase of real estate and other present consumption. The financial system also provides *payment services* to consumers, offers *insurance products* in order for consumers to manage risk, and provides *advice and information* to consumers about transactions in the preceding categories.

From an economic perspective, we can distinguish between two related—and partially overlapping—justifications for regulatory intervention vis-à-vis consumers.[6] The

---

[1] We use this chapter's analysis to address this question from a normative perspective in section 10.5.

[2] See eg Directive 2008/48/EC [2008] OJ L133/66 on Credit Agreements for Consumers, Art 3(a) ('consumer' is defined as a 'natural person…acting for purposes which are outside his trade, craft or profession'); Directive 2011/83/EU on Consumer Rights [2011] OJ L304/64, Art 2(1) (same); Truth in Lending Act of 1968 (US), 12 CFR 226.2, §226.2(a)(11), (12); Dodd–Frank Act of 2010 (US) §1002(4)–(5) ('consumer financial products' or 'consumer financial services' defined as those entered into by 'individuals' for 'personal, family or household purposes').

[3] However, in UK financial regulation, 'consumers' are taken to be all users of the financial system—that is, all parties who use financial services or transact in financial instruments without being themselves regulated financial firms: Financial Services and Markets Act 2000 (UK), s 1G.

[4] See Chapter 8, section 8.4.2.

[5] See n 2.

[6] JY Campbell, HE Jackson, BC Madrian, and P Tufano, 'Consumer Financial Protection' (2011) 25 *Journal of Economic Perspectives* 91.

Principles of Financial Regulation. First Edition. John Armour, Dan Awrey, Paul Davies, Luca Enriques, Jeffrey N. Gordon, Colin Mayer, and Jennifer Payne. © John Armour, Dan Awrey, Paul Davies, Luca Enriques, Jeffrey N. Gordon, Colin Mayer, and Jennifer Payne 2016. Published 2016 by Oxford University Press.

first is concerned with asymmetries of information between consumers and the persons with whom they transact. Regulatory measures implemented in this spirit might, for example, encourage the transmission of information during the process of entering into a financial contract, or bond financial firms to act in a way consistent with consumers' interests over the life of a contract. However, if asymmetric information were the only market imperfection, private parties should, in theory, be expected to understand its consequences. Rational consumers, aware of their predicament, would be unwilling to transact. Persons seeking to attract such consumers' custom might be expected voluntarily to adopt measures designed to ameliorate their concerns. In this milieu, regulation would be useful only if it could do a better job of overcoming the problems of information asymmetry than private parties could do for themselves. This rationale is therefore not as strong as it at first appears.

A second and seemingly more potent justification is grounded in the behavioural characteristics of consumers. It is now widely understood that individual cognitive processing has limited capacity, and that the human brain deploys many mechanisms to economize upon such processing. The resulting decision-making processes, while saving time, also generate errors: predictable deviations from what might otherwise be in an individual's best interests. For example, many engage in transactions in the face of manifest asymmetries of information, owing perhaps to excess optimism or other biases in their decision-making processes. The propensity of individuals to make such errors can provide a rationale for regulation. However, this rationale also requires careful calibration. If such biases distort consumers' behaviour, it may be hard to discern their 'true' preferences. Consequently, there is a risk that well-meaning regulatory intervention may actually make consumers *worse* off.

The most promising case for intervention focuses on the activities of financial *firms* given the presence of asymmetric information and/or behavioural biases on the part of consumers. Where consumers predictably focus on certain 'salient' attributes (most obviously, price), firms have incentives to design and market products so that they appear appealing on those dimensions.[7] The more competitive the market, the greater the firms' incentive to showcase 'good' salient characteristics while slipping unappealing features into less visible places. Recent advances in data capture and processing technology mean that large financial firms have enviable capacity to analyse consumer behaviour. As financial 'products' are simply contracts, they can be tailored with ease to increase sales. While it may not be easy to assess whether any given *product* enhances consumer welfare, it is clearly undesirable that financial firms deliberately design a product in such a way as to exploit consumers' ignorance or biases. The firms' resources spent on this activity are wasted, and the outcomes, from a distributional point of view, are highly unappealing.

The rest of this chapter articulates these rationales more clearly. Section 10.2 begins by outlining the theory of consumer choice, focusing in particular on the imperfections introduced by behavioural biases. The principal implication we draw from this research is that consumers predictably make mistakes in selecting financial products. This poses

---

[7] Of course, this is nothing new: the entire history of advertising is motivated by this simple insight.

the question—considered in section 10.3—why suppliers or third-party accreditation services do not seek to improve consumers' choices, since this would obviously be valuable to consumers. Section 10.4 then considers the extent to which regulatory intervention in consumer financial markets may be justified. Section 10.5 then asks how broadly we should understand the scope of 'consumer' finance, in the sense of contexts where intervention may be justified on the foregoing grounds.

Chapters 11 and 12 then turn to the substantive content of the regulation of consumer finance. Chapter 11 considers the regulation of financial advice—a service which has the potential to improve consumers' decision-making about financial products, but which is itself subject to many of the same market failures. Chapter 12 reviews common financial products offered to consumers, and then considers the regulation of their direct sale to consumers by financial firms.

10.2 Imperfect Consumer Choice

10.2.1 Evidence of mistakes in consumer financial planning

Orthodox economic theory presupposes that individuals make choices in a way that rationally furthers their own self-interest. Individuals' own assessments of their interests—their *preferences*—are consequently revealed by their choices. However, there appear to be significant constraints on consumers' ability to make choices that accord with their financial interests.

An extensive body of research suggests that consumers make financial decisions that result in their receiving a lower return with no conceivable compensating benefit. In technical terms, such consumers pass up a Pareto improvement for themselves; colloquially, they 'leave money on the table'. We can (loosely, for now) characterize such decisions as 'mistakes'. Let us quickly review some examples, two involving borrowing and three more involving saving and investing.

- *Mortgages.* Many individuals holding fixed-rate mortgages misunderstand the interest rates they are paying. Survey results suggest that around 7 per cent (that is, approximately 8 million) of US households believe their mortgage interest rates are lower than they actually are. Linked to this, a significant proportion of individuals with fixed-rate mortgages fail to lower their interest costs by refinancing when long-term interest rates fall.[8]

- *Credit cards.* Survey evidence suggests only a third of the US population understand how basic features of standard consumer lending agreements such as compound interest and credit card charges operate. 'Financial illiteracy', so defined, is correlated with costly borrowing behaviour, such that up to a third of the charges paid by such individuals might be attributable to their ignorance of the implications of their actions.[9]

---

[8] JY Campbell, 'Household Finance' (2006) 61 *Journal of Finance* 1553, 1579–84.
[9] A Lusardi and P Tufano, 'Debt Literacy, Financial Experiences, and Overindebtedness' (2009) NBER Working Paper No 14808.

- *Retirement saving.* Individuals routinely fail to take steps towards retirement saving, even where there are generous tax and employer incentives to do so. Of course, pension saving usually involves a loss of current liquidity, because employee contributions are deducted from wages. But underutilization is revealed most strikingly by studies of employees' behaviour in relation to pension schemes that involve no cost to the employee. For example, a study of twenty-five UK defined benefit pension plans, which were fully funded by the employer and required no employee contribution, found that only half of eligible employees actually signed up.[10]

- *Diversification.* Despite the fact that investors are not compensated for bearing diversifiable risk, many individuals who invest directly in stocks tend to be poorly diversified. For example, the mean number of stocks held by those who invest directly in the US stock market is somewhere between four and seven.[11] Similarly, individuals tend to diversify their allocation of savings within defined contribution retirement schemes very poorly.[12]

- *Trading.* Retail investors who are customers of discount brokerages tend to trade according to the short-term movements of stocks. Because this usually only reflects volatility, the transaction costs of such trades eat up the investors' returns.[13]

We might wonder whether these are in fact mistakes at all, or whether they simply reveal something about the preferences of the individuals concerned. Many of these cases turn on consumers' failure to take steps that would have resulted in a higher return—for example, opting into a generous pension scheme, meeting a payment date so as to avoid charges, refinancing a mortgage, or learning more about diversification. All these steps take time. Might we not infer from this that the consumers in question simply placed a relatively high value on their time? If this were true, we would expect the consumers who make such 'mistakes' the most to be those whose time has the highest value. However, the reality seems to be the opposite. 'Mistakes' of the sort we have described are more likely to be made by consumers who are in less well-paid employment, unemployed, or who are retired—all categories of people for whom the value of time might be expected to be relatively low.[14] These cases therefore pose a puzzle.

---

[10] S Benartzi and RH Thaler, 'Heuristics and Biases in Retirement Savings Behavior' (2007) 21 *Journal of Economic Perspectives* 81, 82. Similarly, a study of US employees over 60, whose pension schemes enjoyed matching employer contributions and who were permitted to withdraw their investments at any time without tax penalty, found that 40 per cent did not sign up (ibid).

[11] WN Goetzmann and A Kumar, 'Equity Portfolio Diversification' (2008) 12 *Review of Finance* 433. Moreover, investors tend to concentrate their investments in domestic firms (A Karlsson and L Nordén, 'Home Sweet Home: Home Bias and International Diversification Among Individual Investors' (2007) 31 *Journal of Banking & Finance* 317) and many employees invest a significant part of their portfolio in their employer's stock (S Benartzi, 'Excessive Extrapolation and the Allocation of 401(k) Accounts to Company Stock' (2001) 56 *Journal of Finance* 1747).

[12] Benartzi and Thaler, n 10, 87–8.

[13] BM Barber and T Odean, 'Trading is Hazardous to Your Wealth: The Common Stock Investment Performance of Individual Investors' (2000) 55 *Journal of Finance* 773.

[14] See in particular sources cited in nn 8–9.

10.2.2 Why do consumers make mistakes?

How do we explain these patterns of consumer financial behaviour? We might think the answer lies in asymmetry of information between consumers and financial institutions. If consumers cannot at sufficiently low cost acquire information about the range of options open to them, or monitor the performance of their investments, then this restricts their range of choices. We have already described asymmetric information as a form of market failure in Chapter 3,[15] and we will not repeat that discussion here. Suffice it to say, however, that this does not fully explain the examples we have described. Rational consumers faced with information asymmetry would realize that trade is likely to make them worse off, and so avoid entering the market altogether (hence, market *failure*). Yet, consumers do purchase financial products. In many cases, they do so in ways that cost them more money than available alternatives. This pattern can be explained if consumers' ability to *process* information rationally is compromised in some way. Advances in economics, psychology, and neuroscience are exploring the way in which individuals actually process information and make decisions. These provide a fruitful source of potential errors in consumer decision-making.

A well-known body of experimental research investigates the decisions that individuals actually make under particular sets of circumstances. This behavioural research has typically been presented as identifying 'anomalies' or 'biases' in decision-making, relative to how individuals seeking to maximize their own welfare might be expected to make decisions.[16] However, this literature lacks robust accounts as to *why* these results obtain and what exactly *are* the processes that guide decision-making (as opposed to what the processes are that do *not* guide it). This makes it difficult to know when any particular bias or anomaly—as opposed to another bias, or no bias at all—is likely to be in operation. In turn, this makes it hard to discern policy implications from the experimental results.

A novel field of research known as *neuroeconomics* seeks to link neuroscience with the social-scientific study of decision-making, the goal being to understand the cognitive foundations of choice.[17] Using MRI scans showing the activation of subjects' brains during different experimental activities, researchers working in this field aim to shed light on the neurological processes associated with human decision-making. Although this field is still in its early stages, this work may have the potential to ground experimentally observed behavioural effects on 'hard-wired' features of the brain. Two such features in particular—on which some consensus seems to be emerging—can explain many of the mistakes described in section 10.2.1. We will consider them in turn.

---

[15] Chapter 3, section 3.3.1.

[16] For a review of how this approach is applied by the UK's FCA, see FCA, 'Applying Behavioural Economics at the Financial Conduct Authority', Occasional Paper No 1 (2013).

[17] For introductions, see C Camerer, G Loewenstein, and D Prelec, 'Neuroeconomics: How Neuroscience Can Inform Economics' (2005) 43 *Journal of Economic Literature* 9; G Loewenstein, S Rick, and JD Cohen, 'Neuroeconomics' (2008) 59 *Annual Review of Psychology* 647; P Politser, *Neuroeconomics: A Guide to the New Science of Making Choices* (Oxford: OUP, 2008); PW Glimcher, *Foundations of Neuroeconomic Analysis* (Oxford: OUP, 2011).

(1) *Instantaneous gratification.* Standard economic theory assumes that agents discount the value of future goods relative to the present at a constant discount rate. In experiments, however, individuals act as though their discount rate were very high when comparing the present moment with the future, but smaller when comparing two periods in the future.[18] In short, individuals seem to exhibit a strong preference for 'instantaneous gratification'.[19] Moreover, this appears to have neurological foundations: different parts of the brain are triggered in relation to decisions involving short-term rewards than for those assessing longer-term options.[20] It seems plausible that, in making decisions about the present moment, a 'fast' or an 'intuitive' process gets deployed, presumably because such decisions may need to be made very quickly.[21] In contrast, decisions about matters at some point in the future are more readily susceptible to conscious deliberation. Not only this, but the intuitive process appears to yield outputs that trump the conscious process, when the two run in parallel to compare outcomes over time.

Instantaneous gratification can explain the empirically observed phenomena of inertia and procrastination in individual choice. Where doing something—including making a decision—involves an investment of time, individuals put off the cost of so doing until 'later' because they perceive a cost that must be paid today as much greater than one payable tomorrow. When tomorrow comes, the same process is repeated to delay the cost for another day. Consequently, complexity in problems tends to delay choice, because of the upfront costs. This tends to push individuals towards procrastination and the selection of default options.[22]

This aspect of decision-making could help to explain a significant part of the pattern of consumer financial mistakes. The empirical literature reports that those who are less well-educated tend to be more likely to make financial mistakes, as are those who are older (retired).[23] For such persons, the amount of time required to understand a new financial product is likely to be relatively large. Consequently, we might expect such individuals to be more likely to view a decision based on such understanding as something which would better be taken 'later', and hence act on the basis of an uninformed decision 'now'.

(2) *Reference dependence.* The human nervous system has to perform many complex operations to transform sensory data into perceptions upon which choices and actions may be based. However, most of the objective sensory data are in fact discarded:

---

[18] See G Ainslie, 'Specious Reward: A Behavioural Theory of Impulsiveness and Impulse Control' (1975) 82 *Psychological Bulletin* 463; RH Thaler, 'Some Empirical Evidence on Dynamic Inconsistency' (1981) 8 *Economics Letters* 201. This pattern could be explained by a discount rate that is a *hyperbolic* function: D Laibson, 'Golden Eggs and Hyperbolic Discounting' (1997) *Quarterly Journal of Economics* 443.

[19] See C Harris and D Laibson, 'Instantaneous Gratification' (2013) 128 *Quarterly Journal of Economics* 205.

[20] See SM McClure, DI Laibson, G Loewenstein, and JD Cohen, 'Separate Neural Systems Value Immediate and Delayed Monetary Rewards' (2004) 306 *Science* 503; SM McClure, KM Ericson, DI Laibson, G Loewenstein, and JD Cohen, 'Time Discounting for Primary Rewards' (2007) 27 *Journal of Neuroscience* 5796.

[21] D Kahneman, *Thinking, Fast and Slow* (New York, NY: Farrar, Strauss and Giroux, 2011).

[22] J Beshears, JJ Choi, D Laibson, and BC Madrian, 'How Are Preferences Revealed?' (2008) 92 *Journal of Public Economics* 1787, 1788.

[23] See sources cited in nn 8–9.

rather, what is principally relied upon is evidence of *changes*, rather than objective values. This economizes hugely on the necessary processing power. The mechanism used to do this is to compare observations to a shifting benchmark that reflects recent measurements. That is, observations are compared to a 'reference point' in the recent past.[24] This means that our perceptions of events are inevitably coloured by our recent experiences. A good example is an experiment in which subjects are asked to put one hand in cold water and the other in hot water for a period of one minute. They must then put both hands into the same bowl of lukewarm water. Subjects report feeling that the *same bowl of water* is simultaneously hot (via the hand that was in cold water) and cold (via the hand that was in hot water).[25]

Although the neurological underpinnings are more conjectural than for instantaneous gratification, it seems highly plausible that this general reference-dependence of sensory data feeds over into reference-dependence in experienced utility.[26] In particular, experimental results show that people care more about losing something they have than about gaining something they do not have. This result is observed in experiments where some subjects are given an object, such as a mug, and others money. At the outset each is asked how much they would be willing to pay to purchase the mug. Then mugs and modest sums of money are randomly distributed amongst subjects. Those subjects who are given the mug exhibit what has been termed an 'endowment effect': they now demand a higher price to sell than they would have been willing to offer had they not possessed the mug.[27] The reference point has changed once subjects have possession of the mug. Similarly, a well-known body of evidence shows convincingly that decision-making under uncertainty is different as regards potential gains and losses, regardless of total wealth. Subjects appear to behave in a risk-averse fashion as regards potential gains, but in a way that seems risk-*seeking* as respects losses.[28] Reference-dependence of this sort can help to explain, for example, the observation that retail investors tend to sell stocks that have done well, but retain stocks that have done poorly, over a particular period.[29]

The observation that the brain uses only a small part of the information it is fed from the senses is general. The brain makes associations and draws cues from limited information. This is simply because individuals face constraints on their information-processing capacity. Rather, they use *heuristics*; that is, rules-of-thumb that yield approximately accurate results, but require radically less processing power.[30] However, a consequence of this is that the way in which information is presented or *framed* makes a difference to perceptions, and to choices.

---

[24] Glimcher, n 17, 273–89.

[25] N Wilkinson, *An Introduction to Behavioural Economics* (London: Palgrave Macmillan, 2008), 103–4.

[26] See eg B Knutson, GE Wimmer, S Rick, NG Hollon, D Prelec, and G Loewenstein, 'Neural Antecedents of the Endowment Effect' (2008) 58 *Neuron* 814.

[27] D Kahneman, JL Knetsch, and RH Thaler, 'Experimental Tests of the Endowment Effect and the Coase Theorem' (1990) 98 *Journal of Political Economy* 1352.

[28] D Kahneman and A Tversky, 'Prospect Theory: An Analysis of Decision Under Risk' (1979) 47 *Econometrica* 263.

[29] H Shefrin and M Statman, 'The Disposition to Sell Winners Early and Ride Losers Too Long: Theory and Evidence' (1985) 40 *Journal of Finance* 777.

[30] A Tversky and D Kahneman, 'Judgment under Uncertainty: Heuristics and Biases' (1974) 185 *Science* 1124.

Many authors characterize the processes we consider here as evidence of 'irrationality' on the part of individuals. However, viewed in evolutionary terms, sacrificing a little accuracy for speed seems perfectly rational given finite mental processing capacity.[31] Rather than delve into a philosophical enquiry as to the meaning of 'rationality', we limit our concern to the potential unreliability of individuals' choices as indicators of their actual preferences.[32] Given this observation, what then matters is whether the choice-making environment can be modified so as to ameliorate these problems.

10.3 Can Markets Supply Solutions?

Before considering the case for regulatory intervention, it is apposite to reflect on whether market solutions might present themselves. If consumers habitually make mistakes, then economists are naturally inclined to ask why the market does not supply them with services that help them to avoid errors. If people are happier not making these mistakes, the reasoning goes, then there will be money to be made by supplying such services. Unfortunately, as we shall see, there is often more money to be made by exploiting such mistakes.

10.3.1 Financial products

Financial 'products' are nothing more than contracts with financial firms. In entering into such transactions, consumers face not only the risk that they will make a mistake, for the sorts of reasons described in the previous section, but also that financial firms design contracts to take advantage of such mistakes. Where only certain aspects of a contract are salient to consumers, competition gives financial firms strong incentives to make their contracts appealing along the salient dimensions. Competitive advantage can be gained by introducing unappealing features into low-visibility aspects of the contract, which consumers do not take into account when making their choice. Because consumers do not focus on non-salient features, firms have incentives to pursue this cross-subsidization approach well beyond the point at which it reduces the net value of the contract to the consumer. What matters, from the standpoint of sales, is how the contract *appears* to a consumer facing the operative decision-making biases.

This type of problematic outcome has long been studied in relation to consumer contracts.[33] Schwartz and Wilde, in a classic article dealing with asymmetric information in consumer markets, articulated a mechanism through which private ordering could supply a solution.[34] They argued that even if consumers generally have imperfect

---

[31] See eg G Gigerenzer, *Rationality for Mortals* (Oxford: OUP, 2008), 3–19.
[32] See Beshears, Choi, Laibson, and Madrian, n 22.
[33] See eg V Goldberg, 'Institutional Change and the Quasi-Invisible Hand' (1974) 17 *Journal of Law & Economics* 461.
[34] A Schwartz and LL Wilde, 'Intervening in Markets on the Basis of Imperfect Information: A Legal and Economic Analysis' (1979) 127 *University of Pennsylvania Law Review* 630. See also A Schwartz and LL Wilde, 'Imperfect Information in Markets for Contract Terms: The Examples of Warranties and Security Interests' (1983) 69 *Virginia Law Review* 1387.

information about contract terms, provided a subset of consumers *is* informed, sellers will respond to the preferences of the informed consumers. This is because the informed consumers will be the *marginal* consumers—that is, the ones who will be most sensitive to movements in price or term quality. Consequently, producers have incentives to adjust their prices or terms so as to attract the informed consumers away from their competitors' products. Consumers may become informed either through investing effort, or by purchasing subscriptions to third-party reports, such as *Which?* or *Consumer Reports*, which offer detailed advice on and comparative analysis of, amongst other things, simple consumer financial products.

A similar analysis could be applied to behavioural biases. If individuals frequently make impulsive decisions in relation to the consumption of particular goods, then one might expect the market to supply mechanisms that facilitate pre-commitment. Such mechanisms are in fact observed. A well-known example is gym membership, which typically involves a significant upfront payment coupled with low per-use fees. This can be understood as encouraging consumers, once they have joined, to maximize attendance so that they get the best value from their membership.[35]

Unfortunately, there are significant limitations on the success of these market mechanisms. The ability of informed consumers to move market prices depends on: (i) the existence of a sufficiently large group of informed consumers who understand the non-salient terms; and (ii) the products in question being homogeneous—that is, the informed and uninformed consumers buying the same thing. Neither condition is likely to be satisfied in most consumer finance markets.

As regards the first condition, let us consider how consumers might become informed. One route would be to study contract terms themselves. The evidence suggests that few, if any, do this. In a recent study, Bakos, Marotta-Wurgler, and Trossen tracked Internet browsing behaviour of consumers purchasing software online, and found that only one or two of every thousand purchasers actually opened the contract terms; even those one or two did not keep the window open long enough to read more than a fraction.[36] There is no reason to think that behaviour should be any different as respects financial products.

These difficulties are compounded if individuals not only do not understand the terms of the product, but also wrongly anticipate their own future behaviour.[37] For example, consumers are likely to overestimate their ability to extricate themselves from financial contracts that begin on attractive terms but change to be less attractive—so-called 'teaser rates' in savings and borrowing products.[38]

---

[35] S DellaVigna and U Malmendier, 'Contract Design and Self-Control: Theory and Evidence' (2004) 119 *Quarterly Journal of Economics* 353. However, such contracts will *reduce* the welfare of consumers who misperceive their own future behaviour: see n 38.

[36] Y Bakos, F Marotta-Wurgler, and DR Trossen, 'Does Anyone Read the Fine Print? Testing a Law and Economics Approach to Standard Form Contracts' (2014) 43 *Journal of Legal Studies* 1.

[37] O Bar-Gill and E Warren, 'Making Credit Safer' (2008) 157 *University of Pennsylvania Law Review* 1, 11–17.

[38] Similarly, consumers who select annual gym membership plans (which can be understood as a pre-commitment device) appear to overestimate the effectiveness of the commitment, and on average use the gym so infrequently that it would have been cheaper for them to pay a per-visit fee: S DellaVigna and U Malmendier, 'Paying Not to Go to the Gym' (2006) 96 *American Economic Review* 694.

A second way in which consumers could become informed about complex products might be through experience. Indeed, economists speak of 'experience' goods to refer to instances where quality parameters cannot be assessed in advance, but only through the process of consumption.[39] However, while consumers may plausibly learn about quality attributes of financial products they regularly purchase (such as travel insurance), this channel of learning is not open where the product is only bought once.[40] Many important consumer financial decisions, such as choice of pension savings scheme, mortgage, or life insurance, are made very infrequently, offering consumers strictly limited opportunities for learning.[41]

Credit Card 'Teaser Rates'

It is commonplace for credit card issuers to offer attractive—or even zero—interest rates for an introductory period, especially on balances transferred from other cards. This highly salient benefit to consumers generally comes with less-visible costs attached. Here we highlight two.

(1) *Costs hidden in the small print.* The credit card agreement may, for example, contain a low-visibility fee for 'administering' the balance transfer. Or a condition that payments will be applied to the prior balance before current spending, which means the entire transferred balance has to be paid off before any current spending can be paid for. A very high interest rate might then be charged on any such new balance.

(2) *Costs underestimated due to biases in future behaviour.* A consumer may transfer a balance in the belief that, at the end of the (fixed) period of low interest, she will transfer any remaining balance to a similar introductory deal with another provider. However, when the end of the introductory period arrives, many consumers either forget or procrastinate the task of switching providers. The interest rate after the end of the introductory period may be very high.

The US Credit Card Accountability, Responsibility, and Disclosure Act of 2009 (the 'Credit CARD Act') responded specifically to these features of credit card agreements. Credit card issuers are now prohibited from increasing interest rates at the end of teaser periods unless they disclosed to the consumer at the outset, 'in a clear and conspicuous manner', what the later, higher rate would be.[42] The UK's Financial Conduct Authority ('FCA') has recently launched a study of the credit card market, with the proliferation of teaser rates also being a key issue.[43]

---

[39] This terminology is due to Nelson, who contrasted 'experience' with 'search' goods, for which quality may be established in advance through search efforts: P Nelson, 'Information and Consumer Behavior' (1970) 78 *Journal of Political Economy* 311. The provision of financial advice may have characteristics even less favourable to the consumer, such that it is impossible to determine the quality of advice even by experience—a so-called 'credence' good: U Dulleck and R Kerschbamer, 'On Doctors, Mechanics and Computer Specialists: The Economics of Credence Goods' (2006) 46 *Journal of Economic Literature* 5.

[40] Schwartz and Wilde (1979), n 34, 662.

[41] There is of course a market for services designed to assist consumers in making financial choices: the market for financial advisers. But see section 10.3.3.

[42] Credit CARD Act of 2009, Pub L No 111-24, 123 Stat 1734 (2009), §101.

[43] FCA, 'Credit Card Market Study: Interim Report', November 2015, 50–68.

Even if some consumers understand the impact of low-visibility terms, this is unlikely to affect product terms generally. This is because many financial products and services are customized according to the individual consumer's needs, making price and quality comparison difficult.[44] This product tailoring can be used to accommodate informed consumers in a way that is differentiated from uninformed or myopic consumers, meaning that their behaviour has no general impact on product terms.

In fact, firms in a competitive market may face incentives to cross-subsidize more attractive terms for informed consumers by introducing yet more unappealing hidden features—or 'shrouded costs'—in packages sold to uninformed or myopic consumers.[45] Firms have little incentive therefore to offer products with costs that are both salient to consumers and indicative of the true expected lifetime cost of the product. These will be unattractive to both types of consumer. Informed consumers will rightly reason they are better off with the product carrying an artificially low upfront cost and then taking steps to avoid the hidden costs. Uninformed or myopic consumers will wrongly reason they are better off with the product carrying the low upfront cost, because they do not take the hidden costs into account.[46]

10.3.2 Financial markets

On a more positive note, many of the foregoing difficulties may be ameliorated by the presence of a deep and liquid *secondary* market for particular financial contracts. The paradigm case is public equity markets. Here retail investors trade anonymously alongside many sophisticated and better-informed parties. As we have seen in Part B,[47] such a market serves to aggregate the information of private parties and impound it into the market price. In an informationally efficient capital market, the price reflects the best available estimate of the value of the securities being traded. This means that from the standpoint of retail investors who buy and sell securities according to their liquidity needs, there is unlikely to be much information asymmetry between them and their counterparties. In an informationally efficient market, the prices will fairly reflect the expected long-term value of the assets purchased.

Of course, this feature of deep and liquid secondary markets can only be of benefit to consumers who wish to *invest*. It does little to assist those who wish to borrow, or who need payment services. Moreover, many retail investors in efficient capital markets often overlook two further features of such markets, to the detriment of their financial

---

[44] Bar-Gill and Warren, n 37, 15–16.

[45] X Gabaix and D Laibson, 'Shrouded Attributes, Consumer Myopia, and Information Suppression in Competitive Markets' (2006) 121 *Quarterly Journal of Economics* 505; M Armstrong and J Vickers, 'Consumer Protection and Contingent Charges' (2012) 50 *Journal of Economic Literature* 477. 'Shrouded' attributes are ones that are deliberately hidden by the producer, even though they could be revealed almost at no cost. The costs the sophisticated consumers incur to avoid the add-on prices are part of the welfare loss of this equilibrium. For evidence that this sort of 'shrouded' pricing structure is used in the European market for structured retail investment products, see C Célérier and B Vallée, 'Catering to Investors through Product Complexity', Working Paper University of Zurich/Harvard Business School (2015).

[46] Seeking to educate the uninformed consumers about hidden costs will not necessarily bring about any change, as this may simply convert them into informed consumers who will still then prefer the product with low upfront costs and hidden fees.

[47] See especially Chapter 5, section 5.2.

well-being. The first is that the price of securities is set without reference to idiosyncratic risk, which can be diversified away. This means that investors with poorly diversified portfolios are bearing idiosyncratic risk for which they are not compensated: the risk-adjusted returns from their portfolios are likely to be lower than necessary. Despite the fact that investors are not compensated for bearing diversifiable risk, many individuals who invest directly in stocks tend to be poorly diversified.[48]

The second commonly overlooked feature of efficient capital markets is that precisely *because* the price already impounds relevant information, it is not generally possible for retail investors to make money by engaging in short-term trading. Unfortunately, many investors have biased beliefs in their own ability to 'pick winners' and engage in multiple trades that do not improve their gross portfolio returns. Rather, these significantly reduce net returns through incurring trading costs.[49] Moreover, such trading is asymmetric: retail investors exhibit a pattern of selling 'winners'—stocks which perform well over a short period—but holding 'losers'—stocks which perform badly over the same period—when both might be expected to have an equivalent impact on the performance of their portfolio as a whole.[50]

10.3.3 Financial advice

An obvious potential market solution to the problems faced both by consumers in relation to financial products and by retail investors in relation to equity markets, is financial advice. A financial adviser can provide a consumer with guidance about appropriate choices regarding financial products and investment strategies. This can help consumers to overcome asymmetric information and limitations in their own decision-making capacity.

Unfortunately, choosing an adviser is itself a decision characterized by the same problems as the choice of underlying financial contracts. By definition, there is an asymmetry of information between the consumer and the adviser. What is worse, it may be impossible for the consumer ever to determine whether less-than-expected performance from their financial contract is due to risks they intended to take under the contract or to poor advice from the advisor regarding the selection of the contract.[51] Consumers aware of this issue will likely discount what they are willing to pay for advice. Furthermore, many of the behavioural biases discussed in section 10.2.2 can lead consumers further to undervalue financial advice that must be paid for upfront. Consumers subject to an instantaneous gratification effect will tend to overweight any upfront cost that must be paid to an investment adviser, relative to the (future) benefit of better investment returns. And consumers who are seeking to borrow money are likely to be wealth-constrained and so unable to pay an upfront fee for financial advice.

As a response to these problems, a common practice has been for advisers to offer services for which no fee is taken from the consumer at the point of use and to be

---

[48] See n 11 and accompanying text.
[49] Barber and Odean, n 13. See also the discussion in Chapter 5, section 5.3.4.
[50] Shefrin and Statman, n 29.
[51] Financial advice, in other words, is a 'credence good': see n 39.

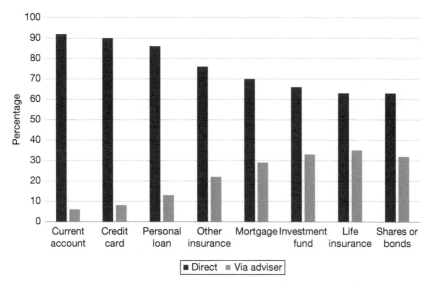

Fig. 10.1 Distribution channels used to purchase financial products by EU citizens, 2011

Source: Eurobarometer, 'Retail Financial Services: Report', *Special Eurobarometer* 373 (2012), 44. 'Direct' distribution channels include face-to-face, online, and telephone.

compensated through commissions paid by financial product suppliers whose products consumers select upon the adviser's recommendation. Of course, on this model, the adviser is subject to an intense conflict of interest. Where the consumer is unaware of the conflict, or—more problematically—of the extent to which it biases the advice offered, then such 'advice' will become less a service for the consumer and more a part of financial firms' marketing.[52] A closely related version of this problem also afflicts markets for retail investment in securities. Sell-side analysts, whose reports are funded by underwriters, are generally optimistic in their assessments.[53]

In light of these difficulties, it is perhaps not surprising that many consumers simply forgo financial advice. As Figure 10.1 shows, direct contracting with the financial firm is by far the most common route for the purchase of financial products.[54] The problem here is that the boundary between 'advice' and 'adverts' becomes very blurred, as evidenced by the common framing of marketing information as an opportunity to 'learn more'. Similarly, much 'educative' material that is provided to retail investors may be subtly geared towards encouraging them to trade more frequently, which generates brokerage revenues.

---

[52] The authors of a well-known text on the marketing of financial services make the following observation: '[t]he ubiquity of the term *financial adviser* is a relatively recent phenomenon having displaced the earlier, and nowadays less acceptable, term of *insurance salesman*' (emphasis added) (C Ennew and N Waite, *Financial Services Marketing: An International Guide to Principles and Practice*, 2nd ed (London: Routledge, 2013), 36).

[53] See Chapter 6, section 6.3.2.

[54] However, these data apparently do not capture cases where consumers seek advice and then enter the market directly, as opposed to purchasing a product via the adviser.

There is, of course, *some* market for financial advice that is paid for upfront and offered on an independent basis, free from commission or conflict of interest.[55] Paying for financial advice through upfront fees has clear economies of scale, so it is likely to be seen as relatively more valuable to high, than low, net-worth individuals. Similarly, those with experience of financial markets are likely to be better able to distinguish between high-quality and low-quality advisers. These considerations suggest that the principal clients of independent financial advisers are unlikely to be retail customers.

10.4 Justifying Regulatory Intervention in Consumer Finance Markets

We have learned that consumers routinely make mistakes in relation to financial transactions, and that markets do not provide robust solutions. Consequently, consumer choice may reflect inconsistent preferences over time or from different frames of reference. Can—and should—regulation assist in improving outcomes? We shall see that the strength of the case depends on the mode of intervention.

10.4.1 Facilitating improved consumer choice: information-based strategies

A seemingly straightforward response is to focus not on intervening to rule out 'bad' choices, but on *facilitating* the consumer's own achievement of good (or at least, better) choices. Classic examples of this approach are to mandate the disclosure of relevant information in relation to particular transactions, or to subsidize the provision of financial education for consumers generally. These might be effective responses were the problem simply one of asymmetric information—that is, if consumers do not understand the consequences of their choices. However, disclosure will do little to change behaviour driven by biases or instantaneous gratification. Such consumers may know perfectly well *ex ante* that there will be subsequent costs associated with their choices; the issue is simply that their assessment of the utility consequences of these costs changes over time. What is worse, some of the behavioural considerations thought to underlie many poor financial choices will also tend further to undermine the utility of disclosure and education.[56] In particular, those individuals who have the highest propensity to instantaneous gratification are likely to benefit the least from education or disclosure of information, as they will be least capable of investing the necessary time.[57]

---

[55] Since January 2013 in the UK, and from January 2018 throughout the EU, financial advisers who offer 'independent' advice have been (will be) prohibited from accepting any sales commissions or other benefits from third parties in relation to their advice. See Chapter 11, section 11.3.5.

[56] O Ben-Shahar and CE Schneider, 'The Failure of Mandated Disclosure' (2010) 159 *University of Pennsylvania Law Review* 659, 704–28.

[57] See eg KN Kirby, GC Winston, and M Santiesteban, 'Impatience and Grades: Delay-Discount Rates Correlate Negatively with College GPA' (2005) 15 *Learning and Individual Differences* 213. An FSA literature review of outcomes from financial education programmes reinforces this idea, suggesting that such programmes have greatest impact where they are least needed—in relation to consumers who have

10.4.2 Restricting poor choices? Product regulation

Does the lack of efficacy of information-based strategies justify intervention that has the effect of *precluding* 'bad' choices? This might include, for example, prohibitions on certain types of term in financial contracts, or on the offer of certain types of contract to consumers. US scholars Oren Bar-Gill and (now, Senator) Elizabeth Warren have famously argued, by analogy with physical products, that financial products should be subject to 'safety' regulation.[58] Just as poorly designed or manufactured physical products are subject to precautionary regulation because they are capable of causing physical harm to consumers, so too, these authors argue, financial products should be regulated because they are capable of causing financial harm.

Unfortunately, the divergence between neoclassical choice theory and actual human decision-making creates a conceptual problem when it comes to efforts to improve outcomes.[59] If consumers' actual choices do not necessarily reflect consistent preferences, what does it mean to 'improve' a consumer's welfare? To see this, imagine a consumer borrower, Brian, who has a strong bias towards instantaneous gratification. Brian borrows £100 for three weeks from a 'payday' lender. He agrees to repay £120, meaning that it will cost him, at the end of the loan, £20 for the benefit of having been able to spend £100 three weeks sooner than otherwise.[60] At the time Brian enters into the contract, his bias to instantaneous gratification means he discounts the future very heavily relative to the present, and so this (then, future) cost seems trivial relative to the benefit he will obtain from immediate enjoyment of whatever he plans to purchase with the £100. However, when the time comes for repayment, Brian is forced to forgo consumption of £20-worth of (by then) immediate enjoyment, and at this point he may greatly regret his earlier decision.[61]

How can regulatory intervention improve Brian's welfare? Imagine an interest rate cap is introduced.[62] This would increase Brian's welfare *ex post*, but would also likely reduce the amount of credit he would be able to borrow, thus reducing his welfare *ex ante*. The problem for policymakers is that where biases such as instantaneous gratification distort choice, there is no *a priori* reason to assert the superiority of the later point in time as a measure of the individual's welfare. Both reflect his own assessment of his welfare, just at different points in time.

Now we might reasonably assume that the amount Brian will be better off *ex post* (whatever utility he can obtain with £20) is greater than the benefit he will forgo *ex ante*

---

self-selected for programmes having identified weaknesses in their own knowledge: FSA, 'Evidence of Impact: An Overview of Financial Education Evaluations', Consumer Research Paper 68 (2008).

[58] Bar-Gill and Warren, n 37.

[59] However, for an attempt to derive welfare criteria applicable in the presence of biased choices, see BD Bernheim and A Rangel, 'Beyond Revealed Preference: Choice-Theoretic Foundations for Behavioral Welfare Economics' (2009) 124 *Quarterly Journal of Economics* 51.

[60] This level of interest charge is not uncommon in payday lending: see Chapter 12, section 12.3.2.

[61] This problem of temporally inconsistent choices is sometimes referred to by economists as one of 'internality': the current self imposes a (subsequently unwanted) cost on the future self. See eg S Levmore, 'From Helmets to Savings and Inheritance Taxes: Regulatory Intensity, Information Revelation, and Internalities' (2014) 81 *University of Chicago Law Review* 229.

[62] As has indeed happened in the UK: see Chapter 12, section 12.3.2.

(the time taken to make an application to another lender, or perhaps a delay of three weeks in getting his £100, or whatever he purchases with the money). Yet because Brian's assessment of his own welfare is inconsistent across time we have no obvious way of determining which of these is subjectively more important to him. If it was just a case of visiting a couple more websites to find a better deal, he would surely be better off following such an intervention. But if he needed the money to pay for an urgent unexpected outgoing, and could not in fact obtain credit elsewhere, he might feel very differently. In short, the finding that consumers do not *in fact* behave as neoclassical theory predicts makes it problematic to assert that they *ought* to do so.[63]

Indeed, the very idea of comparing *ex ante* losses with *ex post* gains implies some sort of privileged perspective that the consumer never actually achieves, precisely because his preferences are temporally inconsistent. Yet this is surely no different in principle from the problem faced by a policymaker who wishes to implement a policy on the standard basis that the benefits *across persons* outweigh the costs. Indeed, policymakers would need to combine the two to reason about the welfare effects of product regulation across a heterogeneous body of consumers. Because of these difficulties, policymakers are generally hesitant to regulate product terms directly, and increasingly concerned to examine evidence regarding welfare effects before intervening. Nevertheless, there are still some examples of this type of intervention, including—as we shall see in Chapter 12, section 12.3.2—in relation to payday loans.

We will now consider three types of rationale that regulators may use to deflect these concerns and better justify intervention in circumstances of this kind.

10.4.3 'Nudging' consumers

One widely touted possibility is to seek to influence consumer decision-making through adjustments to the 'choice architecture'—features of the environment surrounding entry into a financial contract that affect the terms ultimately selected. The best-known version is concerned with *default rules*. These are the baseline rules which apply in a particular contractual context unless the parties stipulate otherwise. Structuring the default in a way that avoids a common mistake will 'nudge' consumers towards better outcomes.[64]

Other aspects of the choice architecture, apart from default rules, can also be modified. One such strategy, which we term 'structured' disclosure, involves mandating not just *what* information must be disclosed, but *how* it must be presented to the consumer. This can assist consumers by at once making the information easier to comprehend—thus reducing difficulties caused by the desire for instantaneous gratification—and also framing the information so as to facilitate less biased decisions.

Designing behavioural bias-sensitive defaults can be a useful intervention in situations where the only impediment to the consumer making a 'rational' choice concerns over-weighting the immediate value of the time spent in researching, or signing up for,

---

[63] Gigerenzer, n 31, 6–7.
[64] RH Thaler and CR Sunstein, *Nudge* (New Haven, CT: Yale University Press, 2008).

a programme. A well-known example concerns voluntary contributions to tax-subsidized occupational pension schemes. Many employees do not sign up for these even where they represent exceptionally good opportunities or even 'free money'.[65] A plausible explanation is that, each month, employees overweight the value to them of the time it will take to complete the sign-up, and discount greatly the value of the opportunity. Each month, the process is repeated, leading to indefinite procrastination. If the scheme is framed as opt-out, rather than opt-in, the employees do not lose any time in signing up and enjoy the benefits of participation. Where employees do not wish to participate in the scheme for reasons other than procrastination, they can still choose not to do so.

This position, dubbed 'libertarian paternalism' by its proponents,[66] must walk a delicate line. The 'stickier' the default—that is, the less is consumers' propensity to change it—the more effective a nudge delivered through the content of the default. Yet, that self-same stickiness also dictates how great a practical restriction the default may pose for consumers who wish not to participate for other reasons.[67] The selection of a sticky default may therefore be more akin to a mandatory rule than it at first appears,[68] with the need to face the difficulties discussed in section 10.4.2. Moreover, the conditions for efficacy of nudges may be very context-dependent, meaning that intervention should be preceded by a careful programme of evidence-gathering.

10.4.4 Welfare safety nets

In societies that operate a social safety net—for example, state pensions, welfare payments for the unemployed, free medical care for those on low incomes, and the like—financial contracts that predictably harm consumers' future financial well-being can be understood as imposing externalities on the rest of society. Failure to save for retirement increases the size of payouts demanded under state pensions, excessive borrowing increases the likelihood of calling on welfare support, and the like. This may be thought to justify intervention. The UK, for example, operates a state-run mandatory savings scheme known as 'National Insurance' into which all working employees are required to pay in return for access to benefits.

In addition to these externalities, there may also be incentive effects as respects individual consumers. In a country where there is a generous social safety net, consumers are likely to discount the future consequences of poor financial outcomes

---

[65] See n 10 and text thereto.

[66] RH Thaler and CR Sunstein, 'Libertarian Paternalism' (2003) 93 *American Economic Review Papers and Proceedings* 179. This approach is also styled as 'asymmetric' or 'soft' paternalism: see CF Camerer, S Issacharoff, G Loewenstein, T O'Donaghue, and M Rabin, 'Regulation for Conservatives: Behavioral Economics and the Case for "Asymmetric Paternalism"' (2003) 151 *University of Pennsylvania Law Review* 1211.

[67] G Mitchell, 'Libertarian Paternalism is an Oxymoron' (2005) 99 *Northwestern University Law Review* 1245; DM Hausman and B Welch, 'Debate: To Nudge or Not to Nudge' (2010) 18 *Journal of Political Philosophy* 123.

[68] R Sugden, 'On Nudging' (2009) 16 *International Journal of the Economics of Business* 365, 369–70; see also Gigerenzer, n 31.

more heavily than in a society with no safety net, and therefore the case for intervention may be more wide-ranging.[69]

10.4.5 Rent-seeking by financial institutions

A regulatory strategy that is easier to justify than mandating terms for financial contracts in order to improve consumer welfare is to focus on the *conduct* of financial firms contracting with consumers. There are three reasons why intervention to improve such conduct is easier to justify than regulation that focuses on terms.

First, while we may not be sure where the consumer's subjective best interests lie, it is clearly undesirable for parties contracting with them actively to seek to confuse the consumer or to trigger biases.[70] As we saw, in competitive markets where consumers exhibit biases in decision-making, firms have incentives to design products that consumers will find attractive *due to these biases*. Moreover, it is a small step from here for firms to seek to activate, or enlarge, the biases consumers bring to bear on the decision. From the point of view of society, effort expended by financial firms in analysing consumer data in order to exploit consumer biases is wasteful: these resources are spent to bring about a mere transfer of wealth from consumers to firms, which makes society worse off overall because it is costly to do.[71]

Second, the distributional consequences of such rent-seeking are particularly unappealing. As we saw in section 10.2, individuals who are older, less wealthy, or less well-educated are statistically more likely to make mistakes that result in them paying unnecessarily high costs for financial services. As we saw in section 10.3, in competitive markets, financial firms have incentives to offer products with low upfront fees and high hidden costs. 'Sophisticated' consumers—perhaps wealthier and better-educated, or better able to afford good financial advice—find these products attractive because they are able to avoid the hidden costs and so simply enjoy the low upfront fees. But in so doing they are enjoying a cross-subsidy from the 'naïve', and marginalized, consumers. This is a deeply unappealing result.

As we shall see more clearly in Chapters 11 and 12, there is also a third, pragmatic, reason for focusing on restrictions on firms' conduct, as opposed to terms of contracts or disclosures. Prescribing particular features in contracts offered to unsophisticated consumers is like trying to get water to flow uphill. There are any number of ways in which a contract can be designed to the advantage of a sophisticated party. Proscribing a few of these will simply cause sophisticated firms to redesign their contracts, achieving at best a short-term improvement in outcomes for consumers.[72] However,

---

[69] E Posner, 'Contract Law in the Welfare State: A Defense of the Unconscionability Doctrine, Usury Law, and Related Limitations on the Freedom to Contract' (1995) 24 *Journal of Legal Studies* 283.

[70] It seems that firms which are owned by consumers, as opposed to shareholders, are less likely to offer financial contracts containing 'shrouded costs': see R Bubb and A Kaufman, 'Consumer Biases and Mutual Ownership' (2013) 105 *Journal of Public Economics* 39.

[71] See eg, PG Mahoney, 'Precaution Costs and the Law of Fraud in Impersonal Markets' (1992) 78 *Virginia Law Review* 623, 630–31.

[72] For example, the Credit CARD Act of 2009 (n 42) sought, amongst other things, to restrict the extent to which issuers could exploit consumers by offering low short-term 'teaser rates' followed by a substantial hike in rates once the introductory period was over. In an empirical study of the Act's impact, Bar-Gill and

a focus on firms' *conduct* can, as we shall see, encompass a dynamic engagement by the regulator with the firm over the life cycle of the product, including design, testing, and marketing—at each of which stages the firm can be required to meet standards of good conduct. This approach has been adopted in the UK, and will be implemented across the EU from 2018.[73]

We can now summarize the discussion in section 10.4 with three broad propositions. First, interventions designed to facilitate improved decision-making by consumers—disclosure, education, and the like—are relatively easy to justify, but unlikely to be effective. Second, interventions designed to structure the terms of financial contracts, while likely to change outcomes, give no certainty that the changes will improve the subjective well-being of consumers. Third, interventions designed to restrict the deliberate exploitation of consumer biases by financial firms are easier to justify.

10.5 Who Should be Treated as a 'Consumer'?

In this chapter, we have reviewed the case for intervention grounded on behavioural frailties of consumers. However, we have so far adopted a rather uncritical position on the important question of who should be treated as a 'consumer' for the purposes of regulatory intervention; that is, who should benefit from regulatory intervention intended to protect consumers. Having reviewed the issues in this chapter, we are now in a position to understand what is at stake.

The behavioural biases discussed in section 10.2 are features of human decision-making. Their actual incidence is unevenly distributed across individuals, and in ways that are difficult to identify in advance. Surely professional investors are also humans, and so they too may be subject to biases? This is true, but we should remember that professional investors are not drawn randomly from the population. They are carefully screened for their ability to make good investment decisions, and educated about how to improve them. Moreover, they are paid according to incentive compensation schemes that can be designed to de-bias agents making investment decisions. Not surprisingly, a number of studies report that professional investors are less subject to behavioural biases than individuals acting on their own account.[74] This provides a justification for a distinction in treatment between individuals acting as professional investors, and those acting for their own account.

But should all individuals acting on their own account be offered the same protection? Here, the discussion in section 10.3 can help to justify three other policy lines that

---

Bubb report that while it has reduced low-visibility costs across those terms directly regulated by the Act, it has done nothing to restrict the loading of costs onto low-visibility terms not covered by the Act: O Bar-Gill and R Bubb, 'Credit Card Pricing: The CARD Act and Beyond' (2012) 97 *Cornell Law Review* 967.

[73] See Chapter 12, section 12.3.3. This is an example of what has been termed 'principles-based' regulation, which is explained in Chapter 24, section 24.4.2. See also N Moloney, *How To Protect Investors: Lessons from the EC and the UK* (Cambridge: CUP, 2010), 108–14.

[74] See eg Z Shapira and I Venezia, 'Patterns of Behaviour of Professionally Managed and Independent Investors' (2001) 25 *Journal of Banking & Finance* 1573; L Feng and MS Seasholes, 'Do Investor Sophistication and Trading Experience Eliminate Behavioural Biases in Financial Markets?' (2005) 9 *Review of Finance* 305.

are drawn regarding the scope of intervention.[75] First, the line between individuals of modest, as opposed to wealthy, means (relevant especially in the US, and to a lesser extent in the EU): although wealth *per se* will not improve individuals' financial decision-making, it will greatly increase their ability to access independent financial advice. Second, the line between individuals with little or no experience of the financial system as opposed to those who do have such experience. Professional involvement in the financial system is relevant to the determination of an investor's status as 'professional' in the EU, a distinction supported by evidence that experience does improve decision-making.[76] And third, a distinction between individuals buying financial products in purely primary markets with financial firms, as opposed to those buying securities in (secondary) financial markets. Financial firms have economies of scale in the design of financial contracts and may use these to exploit individuals' decisional errors; however, such contracts will fare less well where they are traded in secondary markets with sophisticated as well as unsophisticated investors.[77]

A final set of questions concerns the treatment of market participants acting in the course of a business. While we might expect behavioural biases in this context generally to be more limited than for individuals acting in a personal capacity, they are not necessarily absent, and there is still potential for significant asymmetries of information. Here, we can make three further points. First, we might distinguish between non-financial and financial businesses. Finance firms are likely to be better informed about financial products than non-financial firms, leading to asymmetries of information over the terms of transactions, should they trade together.[78]

Second, within the category of non-financial firms, we might distinguish between large and small businesses. While financial transactions are not the primary business of non-financial firms, large firms have sufficient amounts at stake in raising finance and hedging risks to make it more worthwhile for them to develop financial expertise in-house, or to buy in external advice. In contrast, small non-financial firms do not enjoy these economies of scale, and may face a similar set of challenges to those faced by wealth-constrained individuals acting in their own capacity.[79]

Third, even as between 'sophisticated' financial firms, less-informed parties may underestimate the degree of information asymmetry. One example concerns investment in private equity funds by pension funds, insurance companies, and other institutional investors. Private equity investment agreements are extremely complex. While sophisticated parties like to have well-prepared terms governing relevant eventualities, if one party (eg the general partner of a private equity fund) has economies of

---

[75] See Chapter 8, section 8.4.2 and Chapter 11, section 11.3.2.

[76] See Feng and Seasholes, n 74.

[77] See generally N Moloney, 'The Investor Model Underlying the EU's Investor Protection Regime: Consumers or Investors?' (2012) 13 *European Business Organization Law Review* 169.

[78] This is consistent with the distinction drawn in EU financial services law between 'professional investors'—who merit most of the conduct of business protections we will discuss in Chapter 11—and 'eligible counterparties'—that is, financial firms—for whom most of these protections are waived. See Directive 2014/65/EU [2014] OJ L173/349 (MiFID II), Art 30. See also Chapter 11, section 11.3.2.

[79] Consistently with this account, EU financial services law treats large non-financial firms as automatically being 'professional' investors, whereas small non-financial firms are only so treated if they *in fact* have sufficient experience and/or loss-bearing capacity. See MiFID II, Annex II, Schedule I(2) and Schedule II.

scale in drafting a term sheet that is then offered to a number of others, there may still be a significant differential in understanding of the terms. It was recently reported, for example, that many private equity funds had been charging substantial 'service fees' to the companies they control, a practice that was at once poorly controlled by their investment agreements, opaque, and likely harmful to their (supposedly sophisticated) investors.[80]

10.6 Conclusion

In this chapter, we have reviewed the special challenges for regulators in relation to consumer financial products. You should now have an awareness of the sorts of factors that lead consumers to make 'mistakes' in selecting financial products, and the circumstances under which market forces cannot be relied upon to correct these biases. You should also understand the difficulties inherent in justifying regulatory intervention, particularly in the form of mandatory rules.

---

[80] See L Phalippou, C Rauch, and M Umber, 'Private Equity Portfolio Company Fees', Working Paper Saïd Business School (2015). In recognition of these sorts of issues, MiFID II imposes a core minimum set of conduct obligations as regards dealings with eligible counterparties (see MiFID II, recital 104 and Art 30 (1)), and excludes municipalities and local public authorities from the list of persons deemed automatically to be professional investors: ibid, recital 104 and Annex II Schedule 1(3).

11

Financial Advice

11.1 Introduction

Individuals who want to access the financial system face a bewildering range of potential choices. In selecting amongst financial products, they may either act on their own initiative and based on their own knowledge and experience of the financial system, or seek professional advice. Such advisers may be associated with originators of financial products (for example, a bank or pension fund provider) or operate on a stand-alone basis. Stand-alone advisers may have distribution agreements in place with a range of originators, or they may be independent and give advice without any special relationship with any of the product originators. In this chapter, we consider the regulation of all these forms of investment advice and, in particular, the relationship between the financial adviser and the investor.[1] The range of consumer products, and the various channels of regulation applicable where they are marketed without professional advice, are discussed in Chapter 12. The regulation of securities issuance and trading—another context in which individuals might invest directly—was covered in Part B.

For consumers, faced with large asymmetries of information in most financial transactions, recourse to a financial adviser may seem like a sensible option. However, as discussed in Chapter 10,[2] there are two significant problems for consumers in relying on advisers, which interact in a problematic way. The first is that choosing an adviser is itself a decision characterized by the same types of asymmetry of information as the underlying decision of which financial contract(s) to enter. The second problem is how to pay for such advice. Consumers who are borrowing money, or who have limited funds, will generally not be able to afford advice. And many consumers who can afford to pay choose not to do so, because of the adverse selection problem they face: it is rational to discount the value of advice in the face of asymmetric information about its quality. Consequently, consumers directly pay for the financial advice they get in only a minority of cases. More frequently, they pay for it indirectly (and in the absence of regulation, often unwittingly) in the form of the commissions paid by product originators to the advisers, in which case the advice is inherently biased by a conflict of interest.

Financial advice can be offered either on a free-standing basis or bundled with execution services. For those investors who seek financial advice, the central concern can be understood in terms of agency costs. The nature of financial products means that it is difficult for investors, particularly retail investors, to compare investment

---

[1] The term 'financial adviser' in this chapter is intended to capture all those providing advice to investors, and in the US context encompasses both investment advisers and broker-dealers. See section 11.3.1.

[2] Chapter 10, section 10.3.3.

Principles of Financial Regulation. First Edition. John Armour, Dan Awrey, Paul Davies, Luca Enriques, Jeffrey N. Gordon, Colin Mayer, and Jennifer Payne. © John Armour, Dan Awrey, Paul Davies, Luca Enriques, Jeffrey N. Gordon, Colin Mayer, and Jennifer Payne 2016. Published 2016 by Oxford University Press.

services and products and to assess long-term performance.[3] Information risks also flow from the significant potential for incentive misalignment in the relationship between investors and intermediaries. An investor dealing with a financial adviser faces various potential dangers. For example, the adviser could engage in *fraud* (such as absconding with the investor's money), be *negligent* (for instance, by misunderstanding the investor's wishes and selling her something unsuitable), or, as hinted already, suffer from a *conflict of interest* (such as choosing a product that suits the adviser rather than the client, because it earns him a larger commission). Because the investor has less information than the adviser about the products, services, or investments the adviser selects, it is difficult for the investor to tell whether less-than-expected returns are the result of poor performance of the adviser or simply the adverse materialization of an underlying investment risk. Moreover, behavioural biases on the part of consumers (discussed in Chapter 10) may affect their selection of, and reliance on, advisers, causing them in some cases to underestimate the size of the agency problems they face. It is consequently not surprising that there are numerous examples of poor advice or mis-selling occurring in practice, a recent one being the mis-selling of Payment Protection Insurance ('PPI').

The PPI Mis-Selling Scandal

Payment Protection Insurance ('PPI') is an insurance product that enables consumers to insure repayment of loans against the risk that the borrower dies, becomes ill, loses her job, or faces other circumstances that may prevent her from earning income to repay the debt. PPI has been widely sold by banks and other credit providers as an add-on to the loan or overdraft product. A survey of forty-eight major lenders by *Which?* found that the price of PPI was 16–25 per cent of the amount of the debt.

In recent years PPI has been mis-sold, and complaints about it mishandled, on an industrial scale, with this mis-selling being carried out by not only the banks or providers, but also by third-party brokers. The sale of such policies was typically encouraged by large commissions, as the insurance would commonly make the bank/provider more money than the interest on the original loan, so that many mainstream personal loan providers made little or no profit on the loans themselves; all or almost all profit was derived from PPI commission and profit share. Some companies developed sales scripts that guided sales-people to say only that the loan was 'protected' without mentioning the nature or cost of the insurance. When challenged by the customer, they sometimes incorrectly stated that this insurance improved the borrower's chances of getting the loan or that it was mandatory. A consumer in financial difficulty is unlikely to question the policy and risk the loan being refused. Other consumers were unaware that they even had (and were paying for) this insurance for the loans they obtained.

Regulators in the UK have stepped in to ensure that consumers mis-sold PPI are compensated. Between 2007 and 2014, it is estimated that financial firms made compensation payments to more than 10 million consumers in relation to PPI and the total amount of compensation paid out as at October 2015 is estimated to exceed £20 billion.[4]

---

[3] See Chapter 10, section 10.3.1.
[4] FCA, 'The Financial Conduct Authority's Statement on Payment Protection Insurance (PPI)', 2 October 2015.

This is not a trivial problem. Many investors follow the advice of a banker or an agent when making investment decisions, and some directly delegate such choices to their adviser, who then acts as their portfolio manager. All countries with developed financial markets have therefore sought to regulate advisers. This chapter examines these rules. In terms of the regulatory strategies discussed in Chapter 3, we are concerned here predominantly, although by no means exclusively, with conduct regulation.[5]

In section 11.2 we explore the need for regulation, along with the options available to regulators. The main focus of the regulation, namely a set of rules aimed at addressing the imbalance in the relationship between the financial adviser and the investor, is explained. In section 11.3, we discuss the various rules put in place by regulators to address this imbalance, and consider their advantages and disadvantages. The focus here is on the regulations put in place in the EU and the US to regulate this issue. By the end of this chapter you should have an understanding of the rules that are put in place between financial firms and investors in the EU and the US to regulate the situation where financial advice is provided, together with a sense of the strengths and weaknesses of the regulatory strategies that have been adopted.

11.2 Regulatory Strategies for Financial Advice

11.2.1 The range of regulatory strategies

A wide range of regulatory strategies could in principle be deployed to provide consumers with protection when they make financial decisions in reliance on advisers. Amongst these, the least interventionist are information strategies, such as disclosure and consumer education. At the other end of the scale are entry regulations, which restrict who may offer advice (qualification requirements) and the terms on which it may be offered (product regulation). Falling between these, in terms of the extent to which they seek to alter parties' behaviour, are conduct regulation (in particular, conduct of business rules) and—although less relevant in this context—prudential regulation.

Entry regulation. This strategy involves regulators using criteria designed to screen entry into the field, and minimum standards criteria—that is, making use of authorization rules.[6] The extent of the protection provided by this technique will depend to a large extent on the criteria imposed by the regulator and the level of scrutiny applied. In the US, for example, federal securities law requires intermediaries providing financial advice and recommendations and other securities-related services to register with the Securities and Exchange Commission (SEC), unless an exemption applies,[7] but any adviser is able to register and therefore this is not an effective quality barrier. Providing

---

[5] See Chapter 3, section 3.5.2.

[6] In the EU, see Directive 2014/65/EU on markets in financial instruments and amending Directive 2002/92/EC and Directive 2011/61/EU, [2014] OJ L173/349 ('MiFID II'), Arts 5–9 (to be implemented by the beginning of 2018).

[7] See Investment Advisers Act of 1940, §203 (as regards investment advisers) and Securities Exchange Act of 1934, §15(a) (as regards broker-dealers). Broker-dealers that deal with the public must also register with the Financial Industry Regulatory Authority ('FINRA'), a self-regulatory body to which the SEC has delegated much of its authority in this area.

a perimeter of this kind can be valuable, but only when used in conjunction with other rules designed to police the provision of services within the perimeter.

Prudential regulation. The provision of financial advice, by itself, is not usually thought of as giving rise to concerns about systemic risk. However, where advice is combined with custody of client assets—for example, if custodianship services are also offered—it is possible to imagine scenarios where investment firms may be associated with systemic risk. Presumably for this reason, the EU subjects investment firms that accept custody of client assets to capital adequacy requirements, but not those merely providing stand-alone investment advice.[8] While the control of systemic risk in relation to asset managers is considered in Chapter 22, we should note in passing that capital rules also enable firms to commit credibly to the payment of compensatory damages to investors who are given misleading advice.[9]

A further body of prudential rules are those imposed to ensure the segregation and safe custody of investors' funds, for intermediaries that assume responsibility for the safekeeping of investments as part of their role. Dangers clearly arise where the client's assets are co-mingled with the adviser's assets, particularly where the assets are then used by the adviser without the client's consent, or where the firm subsequently goes into insolvency and the client's assets are at risk of being treated as firm assets as regards claims by the firm's creditors.[10] Asset protection rules are therefore important protective devices to counter these risks.[11] These rules aim to protect client assets from being lost, misused, misappropriated, or subject to the advisers' financial reverses, such as insolvency.

Governance. Firm-based obligations can also include the imposition of particular organizational requirements.[12] For example, EU reforms due to come into effect in 2018 aim to address a concern about poor risk management of financial sector firms at board level and thus seek to strengthen the oversight of risk management officers within the firm.[13] Governance rules imposed in this context might involve requirements as to the quality of the managerial body (to tackle concerns that they possess the knowledge, skills, and experience to perform their role well),[14] as well as provisions regarding those areas over which the management body is required to have oversight.[15]

---

[8] See Directive 2013/36/EU [2013] OJ L176/338, Art 3(1)(2) and Regulation (EU) No 575/2013 [2013] OJ L176/1, Art 4(1)(2); MiFID II, Art 15.

[9] J Franks, C Mayer, and L Correia da Silva, *Asset Management and Investor Protection: An International Analysis* (Oxford: OUP, 2003), 15–16.

[10] In the EU, rules are put in place to restrict co-mingling and to prevent the firm's use of the client's assets without that client's consent and otherwise to protect the client's funds (see MiFID II, Art 16(8)–(10)). In the US, investment advisers are also subject to rules that aim to prevent co-mingling (Investment Advisers Act 1940, Rule 206(4)-2). Broker-dealers are subject to a slightly different regime: Securities Exchange Act 1934 Rules 15c3-1, 15c3-2, 15c3-3.

[11] See Franks, Mayer, and Correia da Silva, n 9, 17–18, 88.

[12] Some provisions relating to governance and organizational structure may also have an investor-facing aspect, for example if the purpose of the structure is to ensure that the firm's activities focus on clients' interests.

[13] MiFID II, Art 9.

[14] See eg MiFID II, Art 9(4). In some instances the suitability of certain shareholders within the firm may also be taken into account: Art 10.

[15] Ibid, Art 9(3).

Relevant provisions can also require firms to have adequate policies and procedures in place to prevent misbehaviour and to ensure the compliance of the firm, its managers, and employees with relevant regulatory provisions, including having effective organizational arrangements in place to prevent conflicts of interest.[16] More generally, firms can be required to have in place sound administrative and accounting procedures, internal control mechanisms, effective procedures for risk assessment and effective arrangements for information processing, record keeping, and the safeguarding of client assets.

Disclosure. The techniques identified above are important, but the focus of the primary regulatory effort in this area is intuitively more on the relationship between the firm and the investor, and on rules designed to determine how the adviser interacts with its clients. At the heart of this regime are disclosure rules imposed on the adviser. This approach is based on the idea of empowering investors, including retail investors, to make better decisions for themselves.[17] As discussed, information asymmetry is at the core of the problem facing investors and it is therefore unsurprising that regulators make use of disclosure as an important strategy in this context. However, as discussed in Chapter 10,[18] retail investors are subject to behavioural characteristics that cast doubt on the use of disclosure as a regulatory tool. A regulatory strategy based on choice and investor empowerment may not do enough to prevent investors from falling prey to opportunistic investment advisers and inappropriate products, even where disclosure is made available.

Conduct. As a result, disclosure has been coupled with other regulatory tools that seek to regulate the relationship between the adviser and the investor. These rules aim to regulate how the firm carries out its role, including regulation of the quality of the services being provided. They impose standards of good behaviour (conduct rules) on intermediaries, which are designed to protect the investor against the imbalances in the relationship. These principally include suitability rules, best execution rules, and rules designed to manage the conflicts of interest that arise in the adviser–investor relationship.

Insurance. Finally, jurisdictions can put in place insurance schemes or similar structures to provide mechanisms of last resort to investors who suffer loss at the hands of investment firms.[19]

---

[16] See eg MiFID II, Arts 16 and 23. In the US, both investment advisers and broker-dealers must eliminate or disclose material conflicts of interest.

[17] See N Moloney, *How To Protect Investors: Lessons from the EC and the UK* (Cambridge: CUP, 2010), 53–8.

[18] Chapter 10, section 10.4.1.

[19] See eg in the EU, the Investor Compensation Schemes Directive 97/9/EC [1997] OJ L84/22 (and the Proposal to amend this Directive: COM (2010) 317) and MiFID II, Art 14; in the UK, see Financial Services and Markets Act 2000, Part XV (establishing the Financial Services Compensation Scheme). In the US, a scheme does exist to protect investors (Securities Investor Protection Corporation ('SIPC'), established pursuant to the Securities Investor Protection Act of 1970, 15 USC §78aaa–lll) but the focus of this scheme is the protection of cash and securities in the event of the failure of a firm rather than as a protection against misconduct.

11.2.2 The role of private and public law in conduct regulation

The relationship between an investment firm and its client is predominantly contractual and will be governed both by contract and by any general, common/private law principles that apply in this context,[20] such as potential liability in tort law for fraud or negligence.[21] An investment firm's private law obligations arising from its relationships with clients will be supplemented by its obligations arising from conduct regulation. Some of these obligations may just duplicate the content of the general common/ private law ones, others will articulate and contextualize them, and still others will complement them by spelling out additional obligations. It is therefore common to see both private law rules and regulatory obligations governing the relationship between the parties. In the US and the UK, for example, both general law (contract law and fiduciary duties) and regulatory obligations (such as conduct of business rules) apply to regulate the conduct of financial intermediaries towards their clients.[22] Similarly, the EU regulatory regime places a core obligation on intermediaries to act in the best interests of their clients,[23] coupled with specific obligations dealing with how the firm should conduct itself in relation to its client,[24] which supplement relevant national private law obligations.

This invites the question why a twin-track approach should be necessary. Why can matters not be left simply to general private law? Three distinct answers can be provided. The first is that ordinary contract law is premised on the idea of an agreement between two parties with approximately equal understanding of the terms of the transaction. As we have seen in Chapter 10, this fails to capture the reality of consumer financial transactions, meaning that the contracts consumers agree to, if they are not offered additional protection, will not secure their interests. A market failure may result.

However, this answer understates the scope of what private law can do for consumers, at least in common law countries with a tradition of fiduciary duties.[25] Such duties apply, in addition to contract and tort obligations, depending on the characterization of the adviser's relationship with the client. In essence, fiduciary obligations are duties to act in the interest of one party because of that party's dependence on the other for a particular service.[26] So, for example, where an intermediary acts as a trustee of a pension fund it will have fiduciary status, and where a financial intermediary is holding itself out as an expert on financial matters and undertakes to perform a financial

---

[20] See eg G McMeel and J Virgo (eds), *McMeel and Virgo on Financial Advice and Financial Products*, 3rd ed (Oxford: OUP, 2014), Chs 5–7.

[21] In the UK, see *South Australia Asset Management Corp v York Montague Ltd* [1997] AC 191.

[22] See I MacNeil, 'Rethinking Conduct Regulation' (2015) 30(7) *Butterworths Journal of International Banking and Financial Law* 413.

[23] MiFID II, Art 24(1).

[24] The European Commission has described MiFID as entailing 'reinforced fiduciary duties': European Commission, Green Paper on Retail Financial Services in the Single Market, COM(2007) 226 final, Brussels 30 April 2007, 12.

[25] MacNeil, n 22.

[26] See eg PD Finn, *Fiduciary Obligations* (Cambridge: CUP, 1977); D DeMott, 'Beyond Metaphor: An Analysis of Fiduciary Obligation' (1988) 37 *Duke Law Journal* 879; MD Conaglen, *Fiduciary Loyalty: Protecting the Due Performance of Non-Fiduciary Duties* (Oxford: Hart Publishing, 2010).

advisory role for the client, then that relationship can be characterized as fiduciary in nature. In the UK, the common law imposes various duties on a fiduciary, stemming from a core principle of loyalty, including an obligation not to place itself in a position where its own interests conflict with those of the customer (the 'no conflict' rule), and an obligation not to profit from its position at the expense of the customer (the 'no profit' rule). Generally, fiduciary duties restrict the intermediary's freedom to act in ways inconsistent with the interests of the client without the informed consent of the party to whom the duty is owed.

Fiduciary obligations can therefore serve as a powerful mechanism for protecting the interests of a vulnerable party. However, an important determinant of their utility in this respect is whether parties are permitted to exclude or disclaim the existence of fiduciary duties by contract. In the UK, it is generally accepted that this is possible,[27] which justifies the presence of overlapping but unwaivable conduct of business obligations under financial services law. In contrast, most US states hold to the idea of 'mandatory' fiduciary obligations that, once invoked, cannot be waived by contract.[28]

A second rationale for specific regulatory obligations for consumer finance has to do with problems of enforcement. Private law obligations are ordinarily enforced by the right-holders: in our case, this would be the consumers. However, just as with the contracting process itself, consumers seeking to launch litigation against financial firms face overwhelming asymmetries of information. A financial firm is able to spread its legal costs over many disputes, and to diversify legal risk, neither of which is open to a consumer. In contrast, regulatory obligations are public law and thus enforceable by the regulator. The regulator can monitor and enforce far more effectively than individual consumers. Compensation of consumers can be separated from enforcement through the establishment of an insurance scheme.

The third rationale concerns the contents of the relevant obligations. General consumer (or fiduciary law) rules are applicable across a wide range of potential transactions. Having financial regulators promulgate specific rules relating to consumer finance enables firms to understand their obligations more clearly, and the rules to be updated more frequently in response to new developments. It also facilitates private and public enforcement by reducing judicial discretion in evaluating the adviser's behaviour and by easing the enforcer's burden of proof.

This next section provides an overview of the main conduct of business obligations that are put in place in the US and in the EU to address the perceived imbalance in the relationship between intermediaries and their clients. The rules in this area predominantly focus on two particular risks that investors face, namely mis-selling risks, and conflicts of interest between the intermediary and its client, both of which impact the quality of advice received by investors. The rules impose duties on intermediaries when dealing with investors.

---

[27] See eg *Citibank v MBIA Assurance SA* [2007] EWCA Civ 11; [2008] 12 BCLC 376. See also J Getzler, 'Financial Crisis and the Decline of Fiduciary Law', in N Morris and D Vines (eds), *Capital Failure: Rebuilding Trust in Financial Services* (Oxford: OUP, 2014), Ch 9.

[28] The US approach to this issue is more restrictive: Restatement (Third) of Agency, §8.06. This more mandatory treatment of fiduciary obligations in the US may substitute for the absence of general consumer contract protections of the sort encompassed in EU law.

11.3 Regulating the Relationship between the Adviser and the Investor

11.3.1 The regulatory framework

The EU. Within the EU, the relationship between financial advisers and their clients is governed by the Markets in Financial Instruments Directive ('MiFID II') adopted in 2014, which applies from the beginning of 2018 and replaces and recasts the earlier Directive governing these issues (now known as 'MiFID I').[29] Within the EU framework, the foundational duty is a broad, fiduciary-like obligation: when providing investment services to professional clients and retail clients, a firm must act honestly, fairly, and professionally in accordance with the best interests of its client.[30] A matrix of rules is then put in place to govern the relationship between the adviser and the investor: regulation covers every stage of that relationship, starting from the initial marketing phase in which the adviser might engage to attract the client in the first place.[31] Rules are in place to ensure that the advice provided is suitable for the client and untainted by conflict, that clients' orders are handled fairly and executed in a way consistent with clients' interests, that advisers exercise discretion in managing clients' assets without abusing their position, and so on. In addition to ensuring that they comply with these EU provisions, Member States may supplement these requirements either with general law (so that in the UK, for example, advisers may be fiduciaries and subject to private law-imposed fiduciary obligations) and legislation that may 'gold-plate' the EU provisions.[32]

The US. In the US, those providing financial advice to investors are divided into two broad categories: investment advisers and broker-dealers.[33] *Investment advisers* are in the business of providing advice—which may include discretionary portfolio management—and/or issuing reports about securities.[34] They advise both retail and institutional investors and they are regulated by the SEC pursuant to the Investment Advisers Act 1940. By contrast, *broker-dealers* are regulated by the Securities Exchange Act 1934, and while they can—and increasingly do—give advice or make recommendations about securities,[35] they are predominantly regarded as performing other functions,

---

[29] See Directive 2004/39/EC [2004] OJ L145/1 ('MiFID I'); MiFID II and Regulation (EU) No 600/2014 [2014] OJ L173/84 ('MiFIR').

[30] MIFID II, Art 24(1). For a discussion of the disadvantages of such a potentially vague rule see N Moloney, *EU Securities and Financial Markets Regulation*, 3rd ed (Oxford: OUP, 2014), 215–24.

[31] In the EU, for example, all communications sent to clients must be 'fair, clear and not misleading' (MiFID II, Art 24(3)).

[32] For an example of such gold-plating see the outright prohibition of the taking of commissions by persons offering independent financial advice introduced by the UK from 1 January 2013, which gold-plated the MiFID I provisions in place at that time: FCA Handbook, COBS 6.1A.

[33] For a discussion of the historical origins of this division see eg B Black, 'Brokers and Advisers—What's In a Name?' (2005) 11 *Fordham Journal of Corporate and Financial Law* 31; A Laby, 'Reforming the Regulation of Broker-Dealers and Investment Advisers' (2010) 65 *Business Lawyer* 395.

[34] See Investment Advisers Act 1940, §202(a)(11).

[35] Laby, n 33. Importantly, broker-dealers who do provide advice will not be regarded as investment advisers so long as the advice provided is 'solely incidental' to the conduct of their business as a broker-dealer and they receive no 'special compensation' for that advice: 15 USC s 80b–2(a)(11)(C). If they don't satisfy these requirements, they must dual-register as an investment adviser. Only about 5 per cent of

specifically carrying out securities transactions for others (as brokers) or buying and selling securities on their own behalf (as dealers).[36] Broker-dealers are typically paid by way of commissions and other transaction-based compensation, whereas investment advisers are generally remunerated on the basis of funds under management.

Different regulatory regimes affect investment advisers and broker-dealers. Both are subject to SEC regulation and enforcement (although broker-dealers are regulated by a separate SEC division from that which regulates investment advisers) but, in addition, broker-dealers that deal with the public must register with the Financial Industry Regulatory Authority ('FINRA').[37] While some rules apply equally to both types of intermediary (both are subject to the anti-fraud provision of section 10(b) of the Securities Exchange Act 1934, for example), one very significant difference between them is that investment advisers are regarded as fiduciaries, and thus subject to fiduciary duties,[38] whereas broker-dealers are not generally regarded as such.[39]

Although some similarities exist between the conduct duties to which investment advisers and broker-dealers are subject, there are clearly differences in the way that these conduct obligations operate in practice.[40] One of the most fundamental distinctions at present is that investment advisers are subject to duty of loyalty obligations that flow from their status as fiduciaries. Broker-dealers are not regarded generally as fiduciaries (and thus not subject to this duty of loyalty), although the courts do sometimes deem them to be fiduciaries where the circumstances require such an outcome. For example, the courts have held that where broker-dealers exercise discretion or control over the customer's assets (that is, deal on a discretionary basis) or have a relationship of trust and confidence with the client, they may well owe that client fiduciary duties,[41] although the cases are not always easy to reconcile on this point.

The obligations to which broker-dealers are subject are expressed in different terms. Under FINRA rules, broker-dealers must observe 'high standards of commercial honor and just and equitable principles of trade'.[42] Furthermore, they have been held to owe an obligation to deal fairly with their customers.[43] Although the aim may be broadly

---

investment advisers are dual registered as broker-dealers: see A Tuch, 'Conduct of Business Regulation', in N Moloney, E Ferran, and J Payne (eds), *The Oxford Handbook of Financial Regulation* (Oxford: OUP, 2015), 548.

[36] See Securities Exchange Act 1934, §3(a)(4)(A), §3(a)(5)(A).

[37] An assessment carried out by the SEC revealed large differences in the regulatory oversight applied to investment advisers and broker-dealers: SEC, 'Staff Study on Enhancing Investment Adviser Examinations as required by section 914 of the Dodd–Frank Wall Street Reform and Consumer Protection Act' (2010).

[38] The US Supreme Court has construed the Investment Advisers Act of 1940, §206(1) and (2) as establishing a federal fiduciary standard governing the conduct of advisers: *SEC v Capital Gains Research Bureau, Inc* 375 US 180 (1963). Note, however, that the concept of fiduciary obligation for this purpose has been developed in a way that is distinct from the common law fiduciary standard, in order to accommodate the particular factual matrix that applies to financial intermediaries: *Steadman v SEC* 603 F.2d 1126 (5th Cir, 1979).

[39] For discussion see T Hazen, 'Are Existing Stock Broker Standards Sufficient? Principles, Rules and Fiduciary Duties' (2010) *Columbia Business Law Review* 710.

[40] See SEC, n 37.   [41] See eg *US v Skelly* 442 F.3d 94, 98 (2d Cir 2006).

[42] FINRA Rule 2010. They are also regarded as owing a duty of fair dealing in relation to their clients: *Charles Hughes & Co v SEC*, 139 F.2d 434.

[43] See R Karmel, 'Is the Shingle Theory Dead?' (1995) 52 *Washington and Lee Law Review* 1271. Broker-dealers may, however, avoid the imposition of this obligation through disclosure.

similar it is not clear that the outcome will always be the same. In particular, this does not appear to hold broker-dealers to the same high standards of loyalty as are imposed on fiduciaries.[44]

These differences in regulatory treatment are hard to justify, particularly given the fact that increasingly broker-dealers are performing many of the same functions as investment advisers in terms of providing advice and recommendations to investors. This dichotomy is confusing and unhelpful for investors.[45] The Dodd–Frank Act required the SEC to evaluate whether the current fiduciary standards applied to investment advisers should also be applied to broker-dealers when they provide personalized investment advice about securities to retail customers.[46] The resulting study recommended that a uniform fiduciary standard be adopted for both broker-dealers and investment advisers,[47] and there are some signs of movement in this direction.[48]

11.3.2 Client identification and classification

One of the difficulties facing a regulatory framework for the relationship between investors and intermediaries is whether and how to deal with different kinds of investors. Those purchasing financial products can potentially range from private, financially unsophisticated, individuals purchasing a one-off financial product, to highly sophisticated investors, such as investment firms, credit institutions, and institutional investors. The average private retail customer will need more protection from the law in this regard than a sophisticated professional investor, and not surprisingly most regulators attempt to calibrate the regulatory regime in this context to take account of these issues.

The EU puts in place an obligation on intermediaries to 'know their client' at the account opening stage. This is similar to the obligation imposed on broker-dealers in the US, although that obligation is specified in relatively general terms.[49] In the EU, by contrast, detailed legislative provisions classify investors based on their levels of knowledge and experience.[50] In the EU regime, a three fold classification system is created, involving eligible counterparties (in effect financial institutions), professional investors, and retail investors. Firms must inform clients of their categorization and

---

[44] A recent SEC study confirms that there are differences in practice between the obligations imposed on broker-dealers and those imposed on investment advisers: SEC, n 37.

[45] See Rand Institute for Civil Justice, 'Report on Investor and Industry Perspectives on Investment Advisers and Broker-Dealers: Sponsored by the SEC' (2008); A Laby, 'Selling Advice and Creating Expectations: Why Brokers Should be Fiduciaries' (2012) *Washington Law Review* 707.

[46] Dodd–Frank Act of 2010, §913.

[47] SEC, n 37. It is anticipated that this fiduciary standard will overlap with existing investment adviser and broker-dealer regimes, thereby increasing the overall complexity of the picture.

[48] For example, in June 2015 SIFMA (the Securities Industry and Financial Markets Association), the trade association for the US securities industry, announced a proposed 'Best Interests of the Customer Standard for Broker Dealers' to replace the current suitability standard imposed by FINRA.

[49] See eg FINRA Rule 2090: 'every member shall use reasonable diligence, in regard to the opening and maintenance of every account, to know (and retain) the essential facts concerning every customer and concerning the authority of each person acting on behalf of such customer'. See further section 11.3.4.

[50] See MiFID II, Annex II.

give them the right to request a different categorization. This classification has consequences for the level of protection provided to investors by the EU regime. For example, eligible counterparties are not owed certain duties such as suitability, appropriateness, and best execution,[51] and the duty owed to professional investors is somewhat reduced as compared to that owed to retail investors.[52] While the US regime does not engage in this formal categorization, it does adjust the obligations placed on firms in some circumstances, reducing the obligations that firms owe towards institutional clients.[53]

It is notable, however, that both regimes do provide a level of protection for institutional investors as well as retail investors. The action of the SEC against Goldman Sachs in 2010 in relation to a collateralized-debt obligation called Abacus 2007-AC1 is a reminder that it should not be assumed that institutional investors can look after themselves in this regard. This is a trend that looks set to continue. In the US, for example, two new categories of participant in derivatives markets (swap dealers and major swap participants) were created by the Dodd–Frank Act and conduct of business standards are imposed on them despite the fact that their counterparties are virtually never non-professional retail investors.[54] In the EU, one change introduced by MiFID II is the imposition of a standard of fair dealing on investment firms in their dealings with eligible counterparties.[55]

Goldman Sachs and the ABACUS Deal

In 2007 Goldman Sachs was approached by Paulson & Co, a hedge fund, to assemble a synthetic CDO (dubbed ABACUS 2007-ACI) in exchange for a $15 million fee. Goldman brought in an outside asset manager (ACA Capital) to select the underlying assets for this CDO, which consisted primarily of subprime mortgages. However, in reality, Paulson played a significant role in selecting the reference securities for this purpose. Paulson then took a short position in ABACUS.

Goldman sold ABACUS to institutional investors, including German-based bank IKB. When the CDO's underlying assets defaulted as a result of the subprime market meltdown, those invested in the CDO lost substantial sums (with IKB losing approximately $150 million) while Paulson netted approximately $1 billion. In April 2010 the SEC brought a civil action against Goldman alleging that Goldman had misled investors into believing that ACA Capital was solely in charge of picking the reference securities, and had not disclosed Paulson's role in this regard. It was also argued that Goldman should have revealed both to investors and to ACA Capital that Paulson was taking a significant short position against this CDO (ACA Capital having lost approximately $900 million in the deal).

---

[51] MiFID II, Art 30(1). However, there are some exceptions: for example, as regards Art 25 (suitability) the requirements under Art 25(6) continue to apply.

[52] This is the case at present under the MiFID I regime which, for example, applies more intensive rules to investment firm disclosures in the retail market (see MiFID Implementing Directive 2006/73/EC [2006] OJ L241/26) and a similar approach is expected under MiFID II (see eg MiFID II, Art 24(13) and Art 25(8) which require the Commission to take into account the retail or professional nature of investors when adopting delegated acts under Arts 24 and 25), although the detail will only become clear once the Level 2 measures are finalized.

[53] See eg FINRA Rule 2111(b).   [54] Dodd–Frank Act, Title VII.

[55] MiFID II, Art 30(1).

In July 2010 Goldman agreed a $550 million settlement with the SEC under which it acknowledged it should have revealed Paulson's role in the ABACUS transaction and, in particular, the 'incomplete information' it provided to its (sophisticated) clients. Robert Khuzami, director of the SEC's division of enforcement, said: 'This settlement is a stark lesson to Wall Street firms that no product is too complex, and no investor too sophisticated, to avoid a heavy price if a firm violates the fundamental principles of honest treatment and fair dealing.'

However, note that if an investor wishes to sell a security short on a stock exchange, another investor has to take a long position against them, by buying the shares that the short investor sells. There is no obligation for the short investor, or their broker, to disclose their trading strategy to the party buying the shares. Why should the treatment of sophisticated parties to an OTC market transaction such as the ABACUS deal be any different?[56]

ACA launched a suit against Goldman, alleging that they had relied on fraudulent misrepresentations made in an email—responding to questions from ACA—that Paulson was taking a long position in the transaction. However, Goldman brought a motion to dismiss the claim, pointing out that the offering circular under which ACA had entered the transaction specified that (i) Paulson was not taking a long position, and (ii) investors were not relying on any representations that might be made by Goldman, in deciding whether to enter the transaction. An intermediate New York appellate court granted Goldman's motion to dismiss, but this was reversed by a divided New York Court of Appeals on the ground that the question of ACA's 'justifiable reliance' was too fact-laden to be decided in a preliminary hearing.[57]

11.3.3 Disclosure

Both the EU and the US make use of disclosure as a significant tool in regulating the relationship between the intermediary and the investor. Disclosure is used at every stage in the investor–intermediary relationship, starting with marketing and advertising, pre-contract and contract disclosure, and disclosure in order execution. In addition, intermediaries are generally required to provide appropriate information to clients and potential clients about the investment firm and the services being provided.

Both the EU and the US impose numerous rules in this regard. The EU tackles the issue of disclosure by putting in place a number of overarching principles-based obligations.[58] So, for example, all information addressed by an investment firm to its clients or potential clients must be 'fair, clear and not misleading'[59] and the information provided to clients and potential clients must be in a comprehensible form.[60] In

---

[56] See SM Davidoff, AD Morrison, and WJ Wilhelm, Jr, 'The SEC v. Goldman Sachs: Reputation, Trust, and Fiduciary Duties in Investment Banking' (2011) 57 *Journal of Corporation Law* 529, 539–40.

[57] *ACA Financial Guaranty Corp v Goldman, Sachs & Co* (2015) NY Slip Op 03876, (NYCA, 7 May 2015).

[58] MiFID II, Art 24(4).   [59] Ibid, Art 24(3).

[60] Ibid, Art 24(5). In addition, the EU rules require disclosure to be made about the order execution policy employed by the intermediary with a view to informing investors and enabling them to compare such services across firms: Art 27(3).

addition to these general provisions, there is a host of more detailed provisions.[61] Risk warnings tend to form a key part of the disclosure strategy: a general description of the nature and risks of the financial instrument in question must be provided and must be detailed enough to enable the investor to understand those risks.[62]

This is similar to the approach in the US, where both investment advisers and broker-dealers are subject to disclosure obligations, although these arise from different sources. Investment advisers' fiduciary duty imposes a general duty on intermediaries to provide full and fair disclosure and not to mislead their clients,[63] and more specific disclosure obligations are imposed by legislation.[64] Despite the absence of a fiduciary duty, broker-dealers are also subject to a disclosure obligation, although this obligation stems from the anti-fraud provisions of federal securities laws,[65] and the different regimes to which they are subject mean that the disclosure obligations operate differently, with investment advisers tending to disclose conflicts more often and in greater detail than broker dealers.[66]

This technique assumes a rational, competent investor and seeks to provide that investor with the information necessary to make an informed choice. Whether the assumption inherent in a disclosure-based strategy (that investors are indeed rational and capable of understanding and acting appropriately on the disclosures made to them) is a sound one was discussed in Chapter 10.[67] As regards retail investors, in particular, their behavioural characteristics suggest that we should be sceptical of their ability to do so.

11.3.4 Suitability rules

In both the US and the EU, suitability rules operate alongside disclosure and seek to ensure that the advice received and products recommended are suitable for the client. These rules are associated with a more paternalistic approach to regulation and in recent years have become associated with an attempt to minimize the behavioural defects under which investors operate.

The approach to this issue adopted in both the EU and the US is process based. Suitability rules require the firm to obtain required information regarding the investor's knowledge and experience in the investment field relevant to the specific type of product or service being offered, together with the investor's financial situation and

---

[61] These disclosure requirements are subject to delegated *rule-making* which is likely to generate substantial rules relating to the form and content of disclosures: ibid, Art 24(13).

[62] MiFID II, Art 24(4)(5).   [63] *SEC v Capital Gains Research Bureau Inc*, n 38.

[64] Eg Investment Advisers Act of 1940, Rule 204-3 (investment advisers must provide prospective clients with a 'firm brochure' that details information about the firm, including levels of fees and client referral details, before or at the time of entering into the advisory contract, and then annually thereafter). Depending on the nature of the product being provided, the investment adviser also falls under disclosure obligation in relation to that product, for example for mutual funds the investment adviser is under an obligation to deliver a prospectus containing mandated information, and to provide periodic disclosures thereafter: Investment Advisers Act of 1940, Rule 204-3, 204-3(b).

[65] *In the Matter of Richmark Capital Corp*, Exchange Act Release No 48758 (7 November 2003).

[66] SEC, n 37, 106. For discussion see Tuch, n 35, 552.   [67] Chapter 10, section 10.4.1.

investment objectives.[68] Crucially, this duty cannot be satisfied simply by disclosing the risk, or by ensuring that the investor understands the recommendation and has decided to follow it. This duty exists in relation to both retail and institutional investors, although it is more readily satisfied in relation to the latter category.

In both the EU and the US, therefore, intermediaries need to conduct an investigation of their clients to provide a reasonable basis for believing that the advice they give to the client is suitable.[69] However, there are clearly limits to the investor protection that these suitability rules can provide. Suitability is necessarily personalized and context-specific, and as a result, the line between suitable and unsuitable advice will often be difficult to determine.[70] While a process-based regulatory approach makes it easier to determine when firms have complied with their obligations, this raises its own issues as to whether process-based regulation can support the exercise of judgement. The evidence so far is not particularly encouraging. In mystery shopping tests carried out by the FSA in 2006, for example, only one-third of recommendations satisfied the suitability requirement.[71]

Another potential difficulty with suitability rules is that they seem to envisage an independent adviser delivering a personalized, specific, tailored service to the investor. However, the reality of the financial services market is that the industry encompasses many other forms of intermediary, in particular tied agents in product providers' distribution networks and bank-based advisory/sales services. As a result, rules geared towards dealing with conflicts of interest might be more relevant and effective if they recognize and manage the incentive misalignment that arises where an investor buys a product from a product provider or from an adviser operating on commission. These issues are discussed further in section 11.3.5.

11.3.5 Conflict of interest and remuneration-based risks

Numerous potential conflicts exist in the relationship between financial intermediaries and investors. First, there is the possibility that soft commissions and bundling arrangements raise costs. Second, client portfolios may be inappropriately churned (namely, there will be excess trading of securities) in order to increase portfolio fees. In

---

[68] In the EU see MiFID II, Art 25 (which specifies that the adviser must provide a statement to the client specifying the advice given and how it meets the preferences and objectives of the client: Art 25(6)). In the US, for broker-dealers see FINRA Rule 2111, for investment advisers see discussion in SEC, n 37, 27–8.

[69] In the EU, the suitability regime applies in relation to the provision of financial advice and portfolio management services; a lighter 'appropriateness' regime applies to other investment services, unless the non-advised execution-only regime applies: see section 11.3.6. The suitability duty is well developed in relation to broker-dealers in the US via the FINRA rules, in particular, FINRA Rule 2111, and they are subject to a specific 'know your client' duty which requires them to gather and record a wide range of information about their clients at the time of opening the account (FINRA Rule 2090). By contrast, although investment advisers are subject to both a duty of care and a separate suitability duty, requiring advisers to take account of the client's investment objectives and financial situation these obligations are less well developed than those that exist in relation to broker-dealers.

[70] D Langevoort, 'The Behavioural Economics of Corporate Compliance with Law' (2002) *Columbia Business Law Review* 71, 95.

[71] FSA, 'Quality of Advice Process in Firms Offering Financial Advice: Findings of a Mystery Shopping Exercise', Consumer Research No 52 (2006); see also FSA 'Measuring Outcomes', November 2007.

addition, proprietary products might be inappropriately allocated to the investors' portfolio. Commissions offered to advisers could lead to the investor being offered unsuitable advice or being sold inappropriate investments. Furthermore remuneration structures inside firms have very considerable potential to misalign incentives.[72]

The need to ensure that intermediaries avoid conflicts of interest is well understood. Despite these foundations, it is notable that the relevant duties do not amount to the strict standards that have been imposed by private (fiduciary) law in this regard. Rather than a straightforward 'no conflict' rule (requiring the informed consent of the person to whom the duty is owed to release the fiduciary), the approach to regulating this issue in the context of financial intermediaries in both the EU and the US has been to put in place disclosure obligations coupled with rules designed to place specific obligations on the intermediary to regulate the conflict issues that arise.[73] So, for example, the EU rules state that where firms cannot prevent a conflict arising, they must disclose the conflict to the client before undertaking business on its behalf.[74]

US courts have imposed a similar obligation on investment advisers, as part of their fiduciary duty, requiring them to disclose to their clients all material information that is intended 'to eliminate, or at least expose, all conflicts of interest, which might incline an investment adviser—consciously or unconsciously—to render advice which was not disinterested'.[75] So, for example, if an adviser recommends another adviser to a client, it must disclose any compensation arrangements or other business relationships between the advisory firms, along with the conflicts created, and explain how it intends to address them.

These regimes aim to make use of rules designed to prevent conflicts of interest *ex ante* rather than to make use of *ex post* review and disclosure. However, built into the system is an acceptance of disclosure as a 'last resort' option where firms judge that conflicts cannot be prevented.[76] However, as discussed in Chapter 10, the value of

---

[72] M Krausz and J Paroush, 'Financial Advising in the Presence of Conflicts of Interest' (2002) 54 *Journal of Economics and Business* 55.

[73] In the US, while disclosure is used to tackle conflict of interest concerns regarding both broker-dealers and investment advisers, the timing and the nature of the disclosure obligations differ, with investment advisers generally required to make fuller and more frequent disclosure of conflicts of interest than broker-dealers: see SEC, n 37.

[74] MiFID II, Art 23(2).

[75] *SEC v Capital Gains Research Bureau Inc*, n 38, 194. In relation to broker-dealers the standard of disclosure required to alert clients to potential conflicts of interest has been held to be more limited: see eg *Shivangi v Dean Witter Reynolds Inc*, 825 F.2d 885 (5th Cir, 1997). This distinction is often felt to be one of the most significant differences in the standards facing broker-dealers and investment advisers in the US. While this reduced standard may be acceptable where the broker-dealer is acting on an execution-only basis, it is difficult to justify if this standard is applied to the provision of investment advice: see A Laby, 'Fiduciary Obligations of Broker Dealers and Investment Advisers' (2010) 55 *Villanova Law Review* 701.

[76] Disclosure may not completely absolve the firm of liability or be sufficient for compliance purposes, however. First, recital 27 of MiFID Implementing Directive 2006/73/EC [2006] OJ L241/26 clarifies that 'an over-reliance on disclosure without adequate consideration as to how conflicts may appropriately be managed is not permitted'. In addition, the duty to act in the client's best interest applies even when all prophylactic measures have failed. See L Enriques, 'Conflicts of Interest in Investment Services: The Price and Uncertain Impact of MiFID's Regulatory Framework', in G Ferrarini and E Wymeersch (eds), *Investor Protection in Europe. Corporate Law Making, the MiFID and Beyond* (Oxford: OUP, 2006), 326.

disclosure in regulating conflicts of interest can be questioned.[77] Merely providing information to retail investors may not help them understand and appreciate the impact this is likely to have on the advice they receive. Even if a customer knows that advice is biased, knowing how much to discount that advice is problematic.[78] Empirical research also suggests that requiring disclosure influences the behaviour of those doing the disclosing to bias their advice more than they would without making the disclosure.[79] This use of disclosure, even as a last resort, allows the possibility that retail clients will be left unprotected by firms that judge conflicts to be unresolvable and choose disclosure as the option, with all its attendant risks. The obligation amounts not to a requirement to avoid conflicts of interests, or even to manage them, but ultimately only to disclose those conflicts that exist.

These rules may be criticized on the basis that this approach fails to recognize the complexity of the services being offered to investors by intermediaries.[80] In a world where independent fee-based advice is relatively rare, this approach does not grapple sufficiently with the idea of product 'sales' by banks and commission-based advisers. These issues of intermediary remuneration and incentives are fundamental. Although the possibility of conflict in this regard is recognized by regulators, the approach until relatively recently was one of accepting that these remuneration structures give rise to conflict, requiring the intermediary to put rules in place to avoid conflicts, and, if this is not possible, to disclose the conflict to the investor. In other words, a focus on the symptoms arising from the conflict, rather than tackling the root cause.

The nettle has recently been gripped by the EU, and MiFID II introduces a number of measures designed to deal with this issue. Investment firms are required to inform clients and potential clients whether their advice is provided 'on an independent basis'[81] and, where it is, the firm will be prohibited from accepting fees commissions or other benefits from a third party in relation to the service to clients.[82] This follows similar reforms in some of the Member States.[83] In the UK, where the ban on commissions was introduced in January 2013, while there is little evidence to date to suggest that cost is a major deterrent to seeking advice, nevertheless the use of non-advised channels 'appears set to grow'.[84] In addition, MiFID II introduces a requirement that independent investment advice be based on an assessment of a sufficiently

---

[77] See eg D Schwarz, 'Beyond Disclosure: The Case for Banning Contingent Commissions' (2007) 25 *Yale Law and Policy Review* 289.

[78] DM Cain, G Loewenstein, and DA Moore, 'Coming Clean but Playing Dirtier: The Shortcomings of Disclosure as a Solution to Conflicts of Interest', in DA Moore, DM Cain, G Loewenstein, and MH Bazerman (eds), *Conflicts of Interest: Challenges and Solutions in Business, Law, Medicine and Public Policy* (Cambridge: CUP, 2005), 104.

[79] DM Cain, G Loewenstein, and DA Moore, 'The Dirt on Coming Clean: Perverse Effects of Disclosing Conflicts of Interest' (2005) 34 *Journal of Legal Studies* 1.

[80] N Moloney, *supra* n 30, 244–7.   [81] MiFID II, Art 24(4).

[82] MiFID II, Art 24(7). Of course, these provisions do nothing to protect those who do not receive 'independent' advice.

[83] In the UK, for example, an outright prohibition of the taking of commissions by persons offering independent financial advice was introduced in 2013: FCA Handbook, COBS 6.1A.

[84] NMG Consulting, 'Impact of the Retail Distribution Review on Consumer Interaction with the Retail Investments Market: A Quantitative Research Report' (2014) (a research project carried out for the FCA), 11.

diverse range of financial instruments and not be limited to proprietary products.[85] Unfortunately, this remains a notable lacuna in the US regime.[86] Little meaningful regulation of these issues exists at present and although the Dodd–Frank Act empowers the SEC to create rules to prohibit or restrict compensation schemes for broker-dealers,[87] the US approach remains much more piecemeal than the EU approach.

11.3.6 Appropriateness obligations in the EU

Many, indeed most, customers purchase financial products without personalized advice. Non-advised transactions include a wide range of circumstances that may involve greater or lesser reliance on the financial firm by the client. At one extreme, a pure 'execution only' transaction involves a client approaching the financial firm with a particular product in mind, the risks of which they understand, and asking the firm to help the client undertake the transaction. At the other extreme, the financial firm may circulate information as part of marketing literature, which has the effect of encouraging clients to enter into transactions of particular types. Retail clients' unwillingness to pay upfront for personalized advice, coupled with the fact that marketing literature is usually designed to be as salient as possible to actual and potential customers, creates a real risk that unsophisticated investors will rely on this information *as though it were advice*.

Clearly, the size of this problem is in part a function of the scope of what counts as 'advice'. On this point, the EU takes a significantly narrower approach than do regulators in the US. In the EU, 'investment advice' is defined as a personal recommendation that a financial transaction is suitable for a particular client; for these purposes, recommendations issued generally to the public do not count.[88] In the US, the question is simply whether the statement amounts to 'advice' or a 'recommendation' about the desirability of particular investments or investment strategies.[89] This is treated as an objective inquiry, in which the communication's content, context and presentation are reviewed to determine whether it 'reasonably would influence an investor' to proceed.[90]

---

[85] MiFID II, Art 24(7).

[86] See eg H Jackson and L Burlingame, 'Kickbacks or Compensation: The Case of Yield Spread Premiums' (2007) 12 *Stanford Journal of Law, Business and Finance* 289; D Johnsen, 'Property Rights to Investment Research: The Agency Costs of Soft Dollar Brokerage' (1994) 11 *Yale Journal on Regulation* 75. This lacuna applies to both investment advisers and broker-dealers, but broker-dealers appear to face particularly acute conflicts as a result of their commission-based remuneration structure (see section 11.3.1).

[87] Dodd–Frank Act, §913(g).

[88] See eg MiFID II, Art 4(1)(4). See also MiFID Implementing Directive 2006/73/EC [2006] OJ L241/26, Art 52 (although this implements MiFID, it appears that MiFID II's implementation will not differ materially on this point: ESMA, 'Consultation Paper: MiFID II/MiFIR' (2014), 16–17).

[89] See Investment Advisers Act of 1940, §202(a)(11) ('investment advice' triggering requirement to register as adviser); FINRA Rule 2111 ('recommendation' triggering obligation to determine suitability by broker-dealer exempted from registration as investment adviser).

[90] FINRA, 'Know Your Customer and Suitability', Regulatory Notice 11-02 (2011), 2–3; *Michael Frederick Siegel*, SEC, Securities Exchange Act Release No 58737 (2008), 9–11.

The EU's narrower approach to what constitutes 'advice' is paired with a two-tier approach to the obligations of investment firms. Even where EU investment firms do not give personal recommendations to clients, they are still under a general obligation to ask their clients to provide information regarding their knowledge and experience in the investment field so as to assess whether a product or service is appropriate for the client.[91] This is a similar, but much less onerous, obligation to the suitability requirement applicable where advice is given. In particular, if the firm concludes that the product is unsuitable, or that it has insufficient information to assess this, it is only obligated to warn the client of this and not prohibited from completing the transaction.[92]

Clearly, imposing obligations to determine the appropriateness of transactions for clients who actually understand what they are doing will simply increase costs unnecessarily. With this in mind, the basic obligation is subject to two principal exceptions. First, professional clients are deemed to understand the appropriateness of products offered to them.[93] Second, for 'non-complex' instruments sold in 'execution only' mode, there is no obligation to determine appropriateness, even for retail clients.[94] An 'execution only' transaction is one that is initiated by the client, and 'non-complex' financial instruments are simple and liquid financial products, such as publicly traded shares or bonds, money market funds, and UCITS.[95] These share the feature of having their prices determined in a liquid market, or (in the case of UCITS) being subject to extensive product regulation, either of which may be expected to offer retail investors protection.

11.3.7 Best execution

In addition to focusing on the advice provided by intermediaries, conduct of business rules also recognize that there is a need to ensure investor protection in relation to the trading process itself—that is, when the intermediary actually executes the client's trade. The aim of the best execution rules is to require intermediaries to seek the best possible result for their clients in that scenario. The origins of this rule are in ameliorating the agency problems that arise between the intermediary and investor rather than concerns about behavioural biases. These rules apply whether the intermediary is acting on a discretionary or non-discretionary basis for the client or whether the client is a retail or professional investor. As we saw in Chapter 7, trading is increasingly fragmented across competitive order-execution venues. In this milieu, best execution is an important investor protection device.

Both the EU and the US have best execution requirements.[96] These rules are based on a core obligation that firms take reasonable steps, when executing orders, to obtain the best possible result for their clients. The rules are flexible enough to require

---

[91] MiFID II, Art 25(3).

[92] Ibid; see also MiFID Implementing Directive, Art 36. Consequently, if the intermediary chooses not to sell a particular product to retail clients, the screening performed by the intermediary may be much more pro forma, geared simply to determining that users are professional clients.

[93] MiFID Implementing Directive, Art 36.   [94] MiFID II, Art 25(4).

[95] Ibid. See also MiFID Implementing Directive, Art 38.

[96] See MiFID II, Art 27. In the US, for broker-dealers see FINRA Rule 2320, for investment advisers see Investment Advisers Act 1940, Rule 206(3)-2(c).

intermediaries to take account of a range of factors, not just price, when determining how to obtain the best possible result for their client. These include the impact of trading costs, the speed and likelihood of execution and settlement, and other relevant considerations.[97] However, for retail investors price will generally be key, so that other factors (speed, likelihood of execution and settlement, etc) will generally only be given precedence if they can be shown to be instrumental in delivering the best possible result for the retail investor. In general, this is about process from the firm's point of view. It requires the firms to take reasonable steps to obtain the best result, and predominantly this is about them having effective arrangements in place in order to achieve that result.

11.4 Conclusion

Both the EU and the US put in place a range of rules designed to regulate the relationship between financial advisers and investors. Many of the techniques adopted in the EU and the US are broadly similar, although inevitably some differences of approach emerge.[98] Most rules in this context are designed to ameliorate the information asymmetry problems arising from the principal–agent relationship. The disclosure rules do so directly, since they mandate firms to provide the information that investors could not cheaply discover for themselves. The conflict of interest rules clearly seek to address this issue by attempting to mitigate the difficulties that arise in this context. However, other rules are more concerned with the behavioural characteristics of investors. The suitability rules are the clearest example of this approach, since they require the adviser to know its client and its client's investment objectives before providing advice. It is interesting to note that these regimes encompass both retail and professional investors, both as regards those rules designed to deal with asymmetry problems and those that tackle behavioural issues, albeit that the duties imposed on the intermediaries tend to be lower as regards professional investors. This trend is one that seems likely to continue. Although these rules are most readily associated with retail investors, there is a growing understanding that professional investors need protection too.

Increasingly the rules in this area seem designed to regulate the firm's duties to the investor rather than to focus on the investor's ability to make disclosure-based decisions for itself. Disclosure alone is insufficient to protect investors in this context, and therefore there is a sharper focus on supply-side reforms and a more interventionist approach by regulators, such as increased regulation of the intermediary–investor relationship (such as specific provisions regulating the remuneration structure of the relationship). Where disclosure is used it tends to reinforce the focus on conduct of business rules, by providing investors with the information they need to understand the nature of the investor–firm relationship. These changes go hand in hand with an increased focus on issues of product regulation, discussed in the next chapter.

---

[97] See eg MiFID II, Art 27(1); FINRA Rule 2320(a); Interpretive Release Concerning the Scope of Section 28e of the Securities Exchange Act of 1934 and Related Matters, Exchange Act Release No 23170 (23 April 1986).

[98] See World Bank, 'Comparing European and US Securities Regulations: MiFID versus Corresponding US Regulations', World Bank Working Paper No 184 (2010), 22.

12

Financial Products

12.1 Introduction

A financial product is a contract or package of contracts—typically offered by a financial institution as part of business activities—that allows the other party to satisfy a financial need.[1] The most common such needs include investing savings, increasing one's purchasing power via borrowing, storing value that can then be used to make payments, and insuring against a given risk. Some financial products also fall under the legal concept of a 'security' or 'financial instrument', in which case the relevant regulations[2] will apply in addition or, less frequently, as an alternative to consumer finance laws, depending on individual jurisdictions' choices. In keeping with the orientation of Part C, we focus in this chapter on retail financial products (that is, those offered to consumers), although a number of the issues discussed are capable of generalization beyond this context.

Financial products range from the quite simple to the very complex, as when they combine the basic consumer financial needs that have been outlined. For example, 'term' life insurance, which promises a lump sum payout upon premature death of the insured, is a simple financial product. However, life insurance can also be sold bundled with a savings component, which converts at a future point into a payment stream tied to stock market returns, a so-called 'variable annuity'. This is a much more complex financial product.

Some financial products are highly liquid, such as the shares of a mutual fund—redeemable by the fund at proportional net asset value—or the freely tradable shares of an exchange traded fund ('ETF'), designed to follow a market index. Other financial products have considerable lock-in, such as a variable annuity life insurance product, which can be exited only upon significant cost to the purchaser, or a fixed-rate home purchase loan, which may stipulate a significant charge for early repayment.

Financial products may be either standardized—in the sense that the terms are offered by the financial firm as a standard form, over which there is little or no negotiation—or 'bespoke', in which key terms are negotiated between the parties.

---

[1] Jurisdictions do not usually provide a comprehensive definition of 'financial products'. The EU's recent Packaged Retail and Insurance Investment-Based Products Regulation (the 'PRIIPs Regulation') falls short of that by defining a packaged retail investment product as one where 'regardless of the legal form of the investment, the amount repayable to the retail investor is subject to fluctuations because of exposure to reference values or to the performance of one or more assets which are not directly purchased by the retail investor': Regulation (EU) No 1286/2014 [2014] OJ L352/1, Art 4(1). This therefore leaves out simple investment products and all loan products.

[2] See generally Chapter 8.

Principles of Financial Regulation. First Edition. John Armour, Dan Awrey, Paul Davies, Luca Enriques, Jeffrey N. Gordon, Colin Mayer, and Jennifer Payne. © John Armour, Dan Awrey, Paul Davies, Luca Enriques, Jeffrey N. Gordon, Colin Mayer, and Jennifer Payne 2016. Published 2016 by Oxford University Press.

Generally speaking, the greater the asymmetry of expertise between the parties, the more likely the product is to be offered on a standardized basis. Financial firms that offer such standardized products are commonly referred to as 'manufacturers'.[3] Although it may at first sound jarring to use this terminology to describe a party to a *contract*, the term is not inapt to describe a firm that captures economies of scale in contract design by offering the same terms to a large number of customers.

With financial products, the obvious concern is that customers may enter into contracts (that is, 'purchase products') that do not meet their actual needs. In the case of consumers, the potential market failures here relate, as we saw in Chapter 10, to information asymmetry and behavioural biases in consumer decision-making. In response to these concerns, a range of regulatory strategies are used to govern the manufacturer's relationship with consumers—that is, the information provided, the terms of the contract, and the firm's behaviour. These focus primarily on risks of mismatch between consumers' needs or expectations and the obligations assumed by the financial firm under the contract.

Traditionally, regulation of manufacturers' dealings with consumers has focused on the provision of *information*, intended to enable consumers to make better decisions. However, we saw in Chapter 10 that disclosure alone is often insufficient to improve consumers' financial decision-making, as the information often simply does not get taken into account. A more interventionist approach to this concern is to regulate the terms of the product directly: *product regulation*. However, this is fraught with difficulties, owing to the heterogeneity of consumer preferences and the context-sensitivity of prescriptions for improving outcomes. In short, there is a risk that well-meaning intervention will make at least some consumers worse off, a risk the extent of which is hard for regulators to measure before they take the plunge.

As we also saw in Chapter 10, there are good reasons to prefer a third approach, which focuses on the behaviour, or *conduct*, of the firm in relation to the consumer. The goal is not for the regulator to try to improve outcomes for consumers directly, or even to get consumers to improve outcomes for themselves, but simply to prevent firms from seeking to exploit—that is, take advantage of and make things worse for— consumers. By co-opting manufacturers' considerable expertise about consumer behaviour, this approach can *indirectly* facilitate better consumer choice and generate products that improve consumer welfare—an approach coming to be known as *product governance*.

A related—but conceptually distinct—concern, which is specific to investment products, is that the customer relies on the manufacturer to make payments by way of return on the investment. Even if the product itself is a perfect fit with the customer's needs, the customer is still exposed to the financial firm's *credit risk*. This may be a problem if uninformed, optimistic consumers underestimate the size of that risk. Even

---

[3] See eg PRIIPs Regulation, Art 4(3) and recital (12).

where the credit risk is appropriately assessed, there remains an agency problem regarding actions the financial firm might take to increase its credit risk over the life of the product. In response to this concern, investment product manufacturers are subjected to various types of *prudential regulation*. This is 'microprudential' regulation in the narrowest sense, in that it is concerned solely with the protection of the interests of investors in the specific firm.

In this chapter, we focus on the way in which these regulatory strategies are employed in relation to financial products as such—that is, to their manufacture and distribution, regardless of the channels that are used. If financial advice is sought, or given, as part of the process, then the regulation we described in Chapter 11 will apply, usually in addition to the rules we cover in this chapter. Section 12.2 briefly reviews the structure and function of common consumer financial products. In section 12.3, we consider the regulation of the consumer's relation with the manufacturer. Section 12.4 considers prudential regulation of investment product manufacturers.

12.2 An Overview of Retail Financial Products

12.2.1 Simple financial products

The most commonly used forms of retail financial products are bank accounts, accident and life insurance, credit cards, and mortgages (Figure 12.1). Coming slightly behind are personal loans and investment products. Consumers generally purchase most of these products directly from the provider, whether face-to-face, over the telephone, or, increasingly, online.[4] We will now consider common types of investment product.

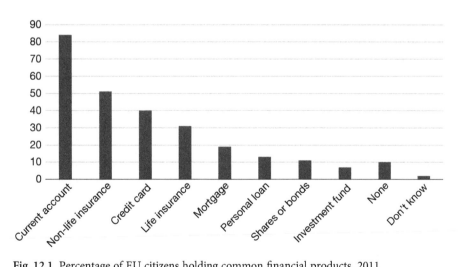

Fig. 12.1 Percentage of EU citizens holding common financial products, 2011

Source: Eurobarometer, 'Retail Financial Services: Report', *Special Eurobarometer* 373 (2012), 13.

---

[4] See Chapter 10, section 10.3.3.

12.2.2 Retirement savings and pensions

In an era of ageing populations and declining state pension provision, private pension saving is of considerable—and still growing—significance. The vast majority of private pension provision occurs through occupational schemes—that is, sponsored by employers. A fund is set up, overseen by trustees, into which both employees and employer make regular payments. These payments are made before tax, so as to give participants an incentive to save. The fund is invested by managers appointed by the trustees. Employees are then able to draw on the fund when they reach retirement age.

Defined benefit vs defined contribution. In a traditional defined benefit ('DB') plan, the employees' entitlement is contractually determined in advance; typically, it is an annuity, set with reference to the employee's final wage. The employer bears shortfall risk. The principal risk borne by the employees is that of employer insolvency or fraud, meaning that the scheme is not sufficiently funded to pay out when the time comes. DB plans used to be very common, but in the last twenty-five years there has been a secular shift in employer-sponsored pension plans away from the DB model towards defined contribution ('DC') plans. In a DC scheme, the employer will pay a defined amount into an employee-specific separate retirement account; commonly the employee will contribute as well. The employee is entitled to whatever return has been achieved on his individual account over the years. This places shortfall risk on the employee, rather than the employer. In recognition of this, employees are generally offered more freedom over investment and distribution decisions in DC plans. A version of this type of pension plan, known as a '401(k) plan' by virtue of the tax legislation that established it in 1978, has become particularly popular in the US.[5]

Many countries also offer tax incentives to encourage citizens to save for their retirement on an individual basis.[6] Such schemes are attractive for self-employed persons or others not entitled to the benefits of a corporate pension plan, those who change employers frequently, and those who wish to top up the benefits provided by their workplace scheme. In the US, for example, savings paid into an Individual Retirement Account ('IRA'), from which distributions may not be made until the saver is nearly 60, are tax-deductible.

Individual pension accounts, on the other hand, put all the responsibility onto the saver to choose a product that will prove appropriate for her needs. Because of the long time-horizon, these are particularly difficult choices to make. Where individuals are selecting products themselves for their retirement savings, they typically choose amongst collective investment schemes of the sort discussed in the next subsection. Depending on the tax treatment, these will sometimes be held in vehicles described as 'retirement accounts', and in other cases simply held as savings. As can be seen in Figure 12.2, the use of discretionary

---

[5] Internal Revenue Code §401(k). See D Rajnes, 'An Evolving Pension System: Trends in Defined Benefit and Defined Contribution Plans' (2002) *Employee Benefit Research Institute Issue Brief* No 249.

[6] This leads to considerable differences in *off balance-sheet* national liabilities for future pension obligations: see R Holzmann, R Palacious, and A Zviniene, 'Implicit Pension Debt: Issues, Measurement and Scope in International Perspective', World Bank Social Protection Discussion Paper No 0403 (2004).

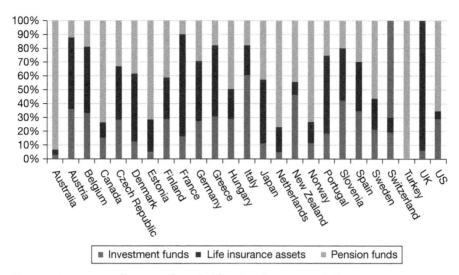

Fig. 12.2 Proportion of aggregate household savings by savings vehicle, 2010

Source: OECD.

Notes: Data for Italy are from 2009. Data for UK do not differentiate between pensions and life insurance.

savings vehicles varies considerably across countries. Much of this variation has to do with domestic tax incentives associated with retirement saving.

12.2.3 Insurance

Non-life insurance. Classically, insurers engage in risk-pooling: they underwrite risks from an exposed group of persons and spread over that population the costs of meeting the consequences of those risks that materialize. Non-life insurance fits this description well. Individuals and businesses insure against the risks of loss or damage to their property (household and vehicle insurance) or themselves (personal injury insurance), against liability for losses they may inflict on others (car or workplace liability insurance). Insurance thus raises squarely the two issues described in section 12.1: that the insurance contract may not be appropriate for the customer's needs (mismatch risk) and that the insurance company may not be able to meet the payments if and when the insured risk materializes (credit risk).

Life insurance. Originally, life insurance also fitted this model. A sum of money became payable on the death of an insured to a person who relied financially on the deceased, known as a 'dependant'. While life insurance is still used for this limited purpose (so-called 'term' life insurance), it has increasingly also become a way of saving for retirement.[7] To achieve this, policies are structured so that funds accumulated during the savings stage of the policy are paid out to the insured (in case of survival) during his or her retirement, for example through an annuity. Although life insurance policies have sometimes carried guarantees as to the rates at which the accumulated

---

[7] More than half the total premiums of $4.1 trillion received by insurers globally in 2009 were paid to life insurers: International Association of Insurance Supervisors ('IAIS'), *Insurance and Financial Stability* (2011), para 4.1.

savings may be turned into an annuity,[8] the total amount of the savings pot at retirement is rarely guaranteed. Often, policyholders are given the option to link their retirement payouts to market-based performance measures. In consequence, a life insurance policy, at least during the accumulation period, is a discretionary savings product functionally similar to a defined contribution pension scheme.[9]

12.2.4 Investment funds

Retail investment vehicles are so called because they raise money from retail investors. A retail investment 'fund' is typically structured as a corporate entity (or a trust, or simply a contract), in which investors buy shares or 'units'. Investor contributions are invested in financial assets, the investment choices being made for the fund by an investment adviser. Legally speaking, the fund 'contracts with' the investment adviser—and, at least in theory, could switch to another adviser. In practice, the investment advisor usually sets up and markets the fund. Advisers to retail funds generally receive fees based on the volume of assets under management, rather than the fund's performance.[10] In the US, such investment companies are generally known as 'mutual funds'. In Europe, they are known as 'UCITS' (pronounced 'you-sits'), short for 'undertakings for collective investment in transferable securities'.[11] The US terminology is used internationally in a colloquial sense to mean equivalent retail investment funds. Indeed, the worldwide industry is heavily dominated by the US, where fully half the sector's $30 trillion of global assets under management is located.[12]

Investment funds have been around since the early days of public equity markets.[13] So, too have controversies about their performance. During the stock market boom of the 1920s, investment companies became very popular in the US.[14] These were so-called 'closed-ended' funds, meaning that investors were not permitted to redeem their shares at any time. Investors obtained liquidity—the ability to exit their investments—by selling their shares in these companies in the secondary market. These companies

---

[8] Sometimes with disastrous consequences for the solvency of the insurer, as in the case of UK insurer Equitable Life. See Lord Penrose, 'Report of the Equitable Life Enquiry' HC 290 (2004).

[9] Health insurance policies, which are based on many of the same actuarial models that are used in life insurance, can be thought of as a third member of this group.

[10] Because superior performance draws in more assets and investment management costs are largely fixed, the overall fee structure has strong performance-based incentives.

[11] See Directive 2009/65/EU [2009] OJ L302/32, as amended by Directive 2014/91/EU [2014] OJ L257/186 ('UCITS V Directive'), Art 1(2). This is overlaid onto a wide range of pre-UCITS terms for investment funds. For example, in the UK, 'unit trusts' and 'open-ended investment companies' (or 'OEICs') are domestic funds using, respectively, a trust and a corporate structure, which may or may not be UCITS: see generally, J Armour, 'Companies and Other Associations', in A Burrows (ed), *English Private Law*, 3rd ed (Oxford: OUP, 2013), 115, §§3.84–5, 3.119. There are also 'investment trusts', which confusingly are actually structured as companies. These differ from the others in that they are 'closed-ended': investors are not permitted to redeem their shares to achieve liquidity (because of this feature, they cannot be UCITS): see text to n 18.

[12] Investment Company Institute, *2014 Investment Company Fact Book*, 54th ed (ICI, 2014), 2. See also A Khorana, H Servaes, and P Tufano, 'Explaining the Size of the Mutual Fund Industry Around the World' (2005) 78 *Journal of Financial Economics* 145.

[13] Investment companies, known as 'investment trusts', first became popular in the UK in the late nineteenth century: LR Robinson, 'Investment Trusts' (1930) 3 *Journal of Business* 279, 286; J Newlands, *Put Not Your Trust in Money* (London: Association of Investment Trust Companies, 1997).

[14] See generally, JK Galbraith, *The Great Crash of 1929* (Boston, MA: Houghton Mifflin, 1988), 43–65.

used high levels of leverage, boosting returns to their shareholders during the growth years of the stock market. However, this also compounded their shareholders' losses when the underlying securities fell in value. While investment company stocks traded at an average of 136 per cent of the value of their underlying assets in 1928, eight years later they languished at only 75 per cent of the (by then much lower) value of those assets.[15] Many investors found themselves 'locked in' as a result. It also emerged that investment advisers to such companies had engaged in widespread fraud upon their investors.[16]

As part of the package of 'New Deal' legislation that defined US securities laws, in 1940 the US enacted both the Investment Company Act and the Investment Advisers Act. These were intended to protect investors against the sort of misfeasance that had occurred in the 1920s. The revelation of the frauds committed in the 'roaring twenties' left a lasting scar on the collective consciousness of investors, who shunned investment companies for many years. Fund promoters experimented during the 1930s with fund designs intended to protect investors against some of these risks. A new variety of investment company, known as 'open-ended', had its debut.[17] Shares in such companies were redeemable (that is, could be sold back, or 'put', to the company) each day at a price calculated as a *pro rata* share of its net asset value at the end of the day. This ensured that investors would always be able to exit their investment at a price that reflected the value of the underlying assets. This innovation rapidly became a common feature of collective investment vehicles, and is required for open-ended US mutual funds and EU UCITS.[18]

Mutual funds have become a very important route by which individual investors engage with the stock market. This is partly because of the economies of scale in acquiring stocks and bonds offered by such pooled investment vehicles relative to an individual investment account at a broker-dealer.[19] More powerfully, the rise of mutual funds reflects the triumph of 'portfolio theory',[20] according to which: (i) diversification improves risk-adjusted returns; (ii) the broader the portfolio, the greater the diversification; and (iii) since secondary markets in seasoned equities are highly efficient,

---

[15] SEC, *Report on the Study of Investment Trusts and Investment Companies: Part 2* (1939), 323, 814 (average ratio of market price to asset value of sample of diversified closed-end management investment companies with more than nominal asset values was 136 per cent in 1928, but had fallen to 86 per cent by 1930 and 75 per cent by 1936).

[16] Investment bankers acting as advisors had used their captive investment companies as a convenient repository for stock they had underwritten but which had not been taken up in IPOs, and to buy influential stakes in companies they wished to 'steer' towards themselves for advisory work. Advisors had even engaged in covert buying of investment company stock to support the price. See US Congress Senate Committee on Banking and Currency, *Hearings on Investment Trusts and Investment Companies, Part 1* (1940), 228–9.

[17] The term 'open-ended' reflects the fact that the number of shares issued by the investment company is not fixed: it varies depending on investor redemptions. This means that the fund managers must actively manage the fund's asset portfolio so as to have sufficient liquid assets available to be able to meet anticipated demand for redemptions.

[18] WJ Baumol, SM Goldfeld, LA Gordon, and MF Koehn, *The Economics of Mutual Fund Markets: Competition Versus Regulation* (Kluwer, 1990), 28 (detailing declining proportion of total mutual fund assets under management in closed-ended funds: 95.4 per cent closed-ended in 1929, 57.5 per cent in 1940, 25.8 per cent in 1950, 10.9 per cent in 1960, 7.8 per cent in 1970, and 5.5 per cent in 1980).

[19] See generally, Chapter 10, section 10.3.2.

[20] HM Markowitz, *Portfolio Selection: Efficient Diversification of Investments* (New York, NY: Wiley, 1959), 3.

research that adds value is expensive and its fixed cost is best spread across large portfolios. Mutual funds offer diversified portfolios at very low cost.

12.2.5 New financial products

Financial firms are continually developing and marketing new financial products. These innovations often respond to changes in the tax and regulatory framework, or to opportunities created by new technology.[21] We discuss here three types of new consumer financial product that have seen recent rapid growth. Where new products are offered to consumers, the risk of mismatch between consumer preferences and product terms is a particular concern, because consumers are more likely to misunderstand the product terms.

'Structured' or 'packaged' investment products. Financial firms can fashion 'structured' or 'packaged' products that purport to reshape the risk and return profile of traditional investments or financial products, such as securities, insurance, or even deposit accounts, by reference to fluctuations in the value of other assets not owned by the consumer.[22] For example, a product could be offered that is described and marketed (or 'wrapped', to use the industry terminology) as a deposit, but offers a return that is linked, at least in part, to the performance of a reference portfolio of securities. The most obvious form of structured investment product is an investment fund. Others include structured insurance products and structured deposits.[23]

Structured products offer consumers cheap access to diversification of investment risk. However, what is less clear is why they should be offered in such a seemingly bewildering array of different forms—not just as investment funds, but as insurance and deposit products with similar risks embedded. One possible explanation has to do with marketing and differential consumer awareness. While consumers who know they want cheap access to diversification might be inclined to shop for investment funds, other consumers will be unaware of these products and their benefits. This creates an opportunity for manufacturers of products for which such consumers do shop—such as insurance or deposits—to package more complex features as part of those more 'familiar' products and then persuade their consumers of the package's benefits.[24]

Clearly, there is a possibility of cynical exploitation by manufacturers, using the features of established products as a Trojan horse within which to package investment risks that may be poorly understood by, and not beneficial to, consumers. There is evidence suggesting that manufacturers do this. A study of one such product marketed in the US, 'Stock Participation Accreting Redemption Quarterly-pay Securities' (or

---

[21] See eg WL Silber, 'The Process of Financial Innovation' (1983) 73 *American Economic Review* 89; P Tufano, 'Financial Innovation', in GM Constantinides, M Harris, and RM Stulz (eds), *Handbook of the Economics of Finance* (Amsterdam: Elsevier, 2003), 307.

[22] See eg PRIIPs Regulation, n 1, Art 4(1).

[23] See generally, Europe Economics, 'Study on the Costs and Benefits of Potential Changes to Distribution Rules for Insurance Investment Products and other Non-MIFID Packaged Retail Investment Products: Final Report' (2010), Ch 2 (survey of environment in Europe).

[24] A related story has to do with regulation: to the extent that different types of product are subject to different regulation, certain investment risks may only be marketed to consumers if they take the form of one type of product rather than another.

'SPARQS'), found that prices at which they were issued to investors were, on average, 8 per cent more than the fair value of the claims, assessed using option pricing methods.[25] Similarly, a study of structured retail investment products marketed in Europe reported that products with more complex payoff formulas offered better 'headline' rates of return, but at the cost of higher risks of complete loss of the investment. Correspondingly, these more complex products offered retail investors lower realized performance, but yielded higher profits for banks.[26]

Exchange-traded funds ('ETFs'). A new structured product that has seen massive recent growth is the ETF. ETFs are investment funds that, unlike mutual funds, issue shares that retail investors can trade in the stock market. Thus, investors can exit immediately, rather than having to wait until the end of each day for redemptions, as with traditional mutual funds.

The first ETF was offered to US retail investors in 1993.[27] Since then, the sector has grown very quickly, reaching approximately $2 trillion in assets under management by 2014 in the US alone.[28] One driver of the growth of ETFs is lower fees than for comparable mutual funds; moreover, ETFs do not bear the administrative overhead of retail accounts, and the costs of trading ETF shares on exchanges tend to be lower than the costs of redeeming them for a traditional mutual fund.

Of course, the idea of relying on trading, rather than redemptions, for exit is not new: this underpinned the old-style closed-ended investment fund.[29] However, ETFs cleverly make use of an open-ended structure to avoid the potential for mismatch between the price of ETF shares and its net asset value ('NAV'). ETFs do in fact issue redeemable shares: the catch is that redemptions must be in very large batches, such as 50,000-plus. These batches are issued to market-makers, who then trade the individual shares in their bundle with retail investors. The possibility of redemption ensures 'price-NAV parity', meaning that the market price does not become significantly divorced from net asset value, because an arbitrageur can always buy a large block of shares and demand redemption. One way to understand ETFs is therefore a modern synthesis of the features of traditional open-ended and closed-ended investment fund structures, in an attempt to have the best of both.

As new products that have grown rapidly, ETFs carry with them concerns that their downsides may not yet be fully understood. One potential issue is that during periods of market turbulence, the exit mechanism may fail to operate effectively. Because maintaining price-NAV parity relies on redemptions of large batches of shares at the

---

[25] BJ Henderson and ND Pearson, 'The Dark Side of Financial Innovation: A Case Study in the Pricing of a Retail Financial Product' (2011) 100 *Journal of Financial Economics* 227. See also FCA, 'Two Plus Two Makes Five? Survey Evidence that Investors Overvalue Structured Deposits', FCA Occasional Paper No 9 (2015) (surveyed UK consumers typically overestimated absolute returns from structured deposit products by 9.7 per cent over a five-year period, a factor of almost 100 per cent compared to returns predicted by the FCA's model).

[26] C Célérier and B Vallée, 'Catering to Investors through Product Complexity', Working Paper, University of Zurich/Harvard Business School (2015).

[27] See AI Weinberg, 'Should You Fear the ETF?', *Wall Street Journal*, 6 December 2015, citing A Raghavan, 'Amex to Set "Spiders" on Small Investors', *Wall Street Journal*, 22 January 1993.

[28] SEC, 'Request for Comment on Exchange-Traded Products', Release No 34-75165 (2015), 4. In comparison, the traditional mutual fund sector had $13 trillion in assets under management.

[29] See nn 13–18 and text thereto.

end of each day, this may break down intraday if the market fears the funds may be unable to obtain sufficient liquidity to meet demand for redemptions. Thus, for example, on 24 August 2015, a fall in Chinese stock markets triggered a rollercoaster in US stock prices. During this period, many ETF shares traded at a significant discount to their underlying NAVs.[30]

A more fundamental concern relates to the types of investment strategy adopted by ETFs. ETF portfolios are typically designed to mimic the return on a specified bench-mark portfolio, which can vary from a broad-based market measure, like the S&P 500, to a narrow sectoral portfolio, such as a health care stocks index. However, with the growth of excitement about the sector, promoters have started to bundle increasingly esoteric and risky investment strategies into ETF wrappers, raising concerns about the consumer's ability to understand the products on offer.[31]

Peer-to-peer lending. The imposition of greater capital controls on traditional lenders since the financial crisis has coincided with a dramatic growth of 'peer-to-peer' ('P2P') lending.[32] In essence, this involves retail savers lending to retail (and business, usually small and medium-sized enterprises—'SMEs') borrowers, without the interposition of a bank intermediary. There is a range of different business models for P2P lending. These differ according to the way in which borrowers are selected—in some models, lenders scrutinize borrowers' applications directly, whereas in others, they rely on credit scores and algorithms offered by the P2P 'platform'. They also differ by whether the P2P platform acts as an intermediary, taking funds from investors onto its own balance sheet and then on-loaning them to borrowers, or simply brokers a series of loans made directly by investors to borrowers.[33] What these share in common is that they fall outside conventional regulation of banking, because the P2P platforms, even where they are intermediaries, do not engage in deposit-taking. This means that there is no need to comply with regulatory capital requirements or to pay deposit insurance premia, but leaves retail investors with less liquidity and far greater investment risk than in a deposit account.

What is as yet unclear is whether the credit-screening techniques used have any advantage over traditional banks in making investment decisions. A sceptic might suggest that the growth of P2P lending does not reflect any comparative advantage, but rather a contraction in traditional bank lending caused by the sudden imposition of higher capital requirements after the financial crisis. A more positive view would be that platforms can use similar screening algorithms to banks themselves, at least as respects retail borrowers, but deploy them in a way that has far lower administrative

---

[30] Weinberg, n 27.

[31] SEC, n 28, 45–8. Especially in such instances, it may be the case that ETFs are not physically invested in the benchmark assets, but rather enter into derivatives that give exposure to them, which means that ETF shareholders also bear (often unwittingly) counterparty risk.

[32] See eg P Baeck, L Collins, and B Zhang, *Understanding Alternative Finance: The UK Alternative Finance Industry Report 2014* (Nesta/University of Cambridge, 2014), 28, 40 (P2P business and consumer lending in the UK grew annually by an average of 250 per cent and 108 per cent, respectively, over the period 2011–14).

[33] To the extent that the platforms are simply brokers, P2P lending does not fit our general description of a 'financial product', because the transactions are directly between lenders and borrowers, neither of which need be a financial firm. In such a case, lenders and borrowers are technically purchasing brokerage services from the platform.

costs. However, as respects SME lending, it seems implausible that retail investors can make lending decisions as effectively as bank lending officers, making such markets prone to adverse selection problems. Perhaps for this reason, the business borrowing component of P2P has seen a shift towards institutional, rather than retail, lenders.[34]

We now turn to a review of the various strategies employed to regulate consumer financial products.

12.3 Regulating Consumer Financial Products

Regulation of retail financial products comes in at least three different varieties, reflecting differing conceptions of the rationales for intervention. Traditionally, regulation focused on seeking to improve consumers' ability to make choices by giving them more *information*. This idea underpins a wide number of rules mandating the disclosure of relevant information to consumers prior to entry into the contract, which we consider in 12.3.1. However, we saw in Chapter 10 that disclosure alone is often insufficient to improve consumers' financial decision-making, as the information often simply does not get taken into account. A more interventionist approach to this concern is to regulate the terms of the product directly: *product regulation*, our focus in section 12.3.2, is problematic too, because of the difficulty for regulators in identifying what consumers actually want, and the context-sensitivity of solutions.

A more promising approach is to focus not so much on consumer choice (as with information) or welfare (as with product regulation) directly, but rather on the behaviour or *conduct* of the manufacturer, distributor, or adviser. The goal is not for the regulator to try to improve outcomes for consumers, or even to get consumers to improve outcomes for themselves, but rather at a minimum to prevent firms from seeking to exploit—that is, make things worse for—consumers. In Chapter 11, we considered the conduct obligations imposed on financial advisers and, in the EU, distributors of complex financial products, to determine the suitability or appropriateness of these products for clients. A more expansionist version of this approach, which has recently found favour with the UK's FCA and EU authorities, is to seek to co-opt the considerable expertise available to financial product *manufacturers* about consumer choice and preferences in order to facilitate the manufacture of products that improve consumer welfare. In this guise, the regulatory strategy is coming to be known as 'product governance'. In effect, it seeks to cover the same set of issues as the more traditional information and product regulation strategies. The difference is that it is the manufacturers, and not the regulator, that are in charge of the design choices. The regulator's role is not to direct outcomes in the relationship between manufacturers and consumers, but rather to oversee the firm's process in approaching that relationship. We analyse this potentially more effective way of overcoming the practical and philosophical problems with traditional regulatory strategies in section 12.3.3.

---

[34] See K Judge, 'The Future of Direct Finance: The Diverging Paths of Peer-to-Peer Lending and Kickstarter' (2015) 50 *Wake Forest Law Review* 603.

12.3.1 Information regulation: disclosure and beyond

The idea of disclosure. The traditional paradigm of information regulation involves seeking to ensure that relevant information is disclosed prior to entry into a financial contract. While the efficacy of disclosure as a means of improving outcomes in consumer financial product markets is doubtful, it continues to be heavily relied on by regulators. This in part reflects the relatively recent growth of research into behavioural economics, and continuing uncertainty about its implications. It likely also reflects the fact that disclosure is politically easier to mandate than many of the other regulatory strategies we shall discuss.[35]

But what exactly is meant by 'disclosure'? On a narrow view, 'disclosure' might mean only that the discloser has in some way *communicated* the relevant information. On this view, all the terms of a financial contract are necessarily 'disclosed', because under ordinary contractual principles parties must have an opportunity to see the terms in order to be bound. Disclosure in this narrow sense would need only to be mandated for matters that would not otherwise be presented to the consumer—for example, the existence of conflicts of interest on the part of an adviser.[36]

The problem with this narrow, or literal, conception of 'disclosure' is that the mere presentation of information is insufficient to ensure that consumers actually understand it, or that they process it effectively.[37] The complexity of contracts for even what might seem a simple financial product, such as a bank account, can be very high.[38] This makes it costly for a consumer to become informed. As a consequence, very few consumers actually read such contractual terms, nor will they be likely to read additional mandated disclosures.[39] Indeed, simply mandating the provision of more information—without any attention paid to how it is presented—may actually make it harder for consumers to discern what is important.[40] Coupled with the fact that disclosures are costly to produce, the regrettable conclusion is that rules mandating disclosure in this fashion may actually be *worse* than useless in the context of consumer finance.

By way of an aside, we should note that the objective discussed here—that of making it easier for consumers to understand details of the financial contract into which they are entering—is quite different from the objective of 'disclosure' in relation to equity securities, discussed in Chapter 8. In that setting, disclosure is simply about communicating information to market participants that would otherwise have been private to

---

[35] See O Ben-Shahar and CE Schneider, *More Than You Wanted to Know: The Failure of Mandated Disclosure* (Princeton, NJ: Princeton UP, 2014), 138–50.

[36] See Chapter 11, section 11.3.5.

[37] Ben-Shahar and Schneider, n 35, 14–32.

[38] For example, HSBC's 'General Terms and Conditions for Current Accounts and Savings Accounts' (10 November 2014) runs to forty-four pages of single-spaced text. This is for what is generally thought to be one of the simplest types of financial product available.

[39] Online purchasing environments provide a good way to test the impact of disclosure, as the time spent on particular pages can be logged precisely. Florencia Marotta-Wurgler reports that making contract terms more prominently available has no impact on readership of these terms: F Marotta-Wurgler, 'Does Contract Disclosure Matter?'(2012) 168 *Journal of Institutional and Theoretical Economics* 94.

[40] See eg M Wheatley, 'Making Competition King—the Rise of Behavioural Economics at the FCA', speech to Australian Securities and Investments Commission (ASIC), 25 March 2014.

insiders. Because of the way secondary markets operate to impound information into the price through trading, all that matters in that context is that the information is communicated, not that it be understood by retail investors.

For information-based strategies to have an impact on consumers, it seems that attention should be paid not only to the fact of communication, but its *manner*.[41] In theory, rules prescribing the format in which disclosed information is presented could help consumers overcome information asymmetries, especially as regards the terms of the contract. Spelling things out more clearly, or highlighting certain types of term, can assist comprehension. So too, one might think, would additional time to reflect on the meaning of complex terms. Moreover, because the way in which information is conveyed to a consumer can affect the point of reference used in evaluating it, prescribing the presentation of information in a particular way can, in principle, respond to biases generated by framing effects.

However, the *effective* implementation of these techniques is highly contingent on both the specific decisional frailties of the consumer and the precise nature of the financial contract in question.[42] Correctly calibrating disclosure regulation is therefore hugely challenging, and potentially subject to constant change as financial firms evolve their products. We illustrate these challenges in the following three examples.

Extending time: the 'cooling-off' period. A well-known early example of an attempt to make it easier for consumers to process relevant information is the 'cooling-off' period. This is a mandated period during which a consumer may elect to rescind an agreement *ab initio*, without offering any explanation or paying a fee. In theory, this could be a useful response either to asymmetric information or myopic consumer decision-making. Giving the consumer additional time, along with the relevant information, could allow him to inform himself better about the merits of the contract.[43]

The idea of a cooling-off period has been widely implemented in consumer transactions, following its initial introduction in the UK in the early 1960s.[44] Thus, for example, the US Truth in Lending Act of 1968 mandates a three-business-day cooling-off period on entry into a mortgage agreement secured by the borrower's principal dwelling.[45] Similarly, the EU's Consumer Credit Directive and Consumer Mortgage

---

[41] Although not strictly 'disclosure' in the narrow sense discussed above, rules prescribing the presentation of information are meaningfully part of 'disclosure regulation' more broadly defined: in this broader sense, 'disclosure' is taken to mean not simply presentation of information, but *effective* communication to consumers in a way they may reasonably comprehend. Moreover, nothing turns on whether we call this 'disclosure' or 'information presentation'. What matters is whether it helps ameliorate the problems, described in Chapter 10, sections 10.2 and 10.3, of consumers not being able to make sense of complex terms.

[42] See TB Gillis, 'Putting Disclosure to the Test: Toward Better Evidence-Based Policy' (forthcoming 2016) 27 *LUC Consumer Law Review*.

[43] BD Sher, 'The "Cooling-Off" Period in Door-to-Door Sales' (1968) 15 *UCLA Law Review* 717; P Rekaiti and R Van den Bergh, 'Cooling-Off Periods in the Consumer Laws of EC Member States: A Comparative Law and Economics Approach' (2000) 23 *Journal of Consumer Policy* 371.

[44] Hire-Purchase Act 1965 (UK), s 11 (four-day cooling-off period).

[45] Truth in Lending Act of 1968 §125, 15 USC §1635. This does not begin until the consumer has received mandated disclosures from the lender.

Directive give consumers a seven- or fourteen-day right of withdrawal, respectively, from unsecured credit agreements or mortgages,[46] and under the Distance Marketing of Financial Services Directive, EU consumers have a fourteen-day cooling-off period for any financial services agreement concluded otherwise than face-to-face.[47]

However, although the idea of cooling-off periods has been around for more than fifty years, there is little evidence that they contribute to improving outcomes.[48] Indeed, as a matter of theory, consumers who suffer from a strong bias towards instantaneous gratification are no more likely to take time to learn about complex contract terms the day after they have signed than the day before. Consistently with this, such experimental evidence as there is finds that cooling-off periods make only a very marginal difference to outcomes.[49]

Summary disclosure of 'key features'. A related technique is to seek to facilitate consumers' comprehension of relevant information by mandating the presentation of 'key features' in a prescribed format. In theory, this can help reduce the cost to consumers of becoming informed about relevant provisions, and thereby facilitate better decision-making. In relation to consumer borrowing, the idea has a similarly long pedigree to cooling-off periods. For example, the US Truth in Lending Act of 1968 and the UK Consumer Credit Act 1974 have long mandated disclosure of key provisions of a loan agreement at the points of application for, and agreement on (or 'closing' of), a loan.[50] Regulators have also recently begun to make use of this approach in relation to investment products. Unfortunately, this technique exhibits all the problems of specificity that have been described, as can be illustrated by two well-known examples.

(1) *Annual Percentage Rate ('APR').* In relation to consumer credit, regulation stipulates formulae for standardizing the overall cost of a credit arrangement to the consumer, which must be prominently displayed so as to allow comparison. This is done through the concept of the Annual Percentage Rate ('APR'), intended to reflect the annualized cost of the credit agreement to the consumer, as a percentage of the sum borrowed.[51] The APR takes into account all charges and fees that will be levied, including interest, and converts this into an annual percentage. However, the calculation requires that a number of assumptions be made where the contract allows for flexibility—in particular, about the timing of drawdowns and repayments; this is especially true in relation to open-ended credit facilities such as credit

---

[46] Directive 2014/17/EU (the 'Consumer Mortgage Directive') [2014] OJ L60/34, Art 14(6); Directive 2008/48/EC (the 'Consumer Credit Directive') [2008] OJ L133/66, Art 14.

[47] Directive 2002/65/EC (the 'Distance Marketing of Consumer Financial Services Directive') [2002] OJ L271/16, Art 6.

[48] They were originally introduced simply on the basis of diagnoses of the problems of consumer decision-making, as opposed to the prescription of particular solutions: See Committee on Consumer Protection, *Final Report*, Cmnd 1781 (London: HMSO, 1962); Sher, n 43, 721–5.

[49] See J Oechssler, A Roider, and PW Schmitz, 'Cooling Off in Negotiations: Does it Work?' (2015) 171 *Journal of Institutional and Theoretical Economics* 565.

[50] See Truth in Lending Act of 1968 (US), §4; Consumer Credit Act 1974 (UK), s 55.

[51] See Directive 2008/48/EU, Art 19 and Annex II; 15 USC §1606 and CFR Title 12, Part 1026, Appendix J.

cards.[52] This gives lenders scope to design their products such that they are 'flattered' by the APR figure generated by the formula.

(2) *Key investor information.* Regulators in both the US and the EU have recently moved to require highly abbreviated investor disclosures aimed at facilitating consumer understanding.[53] Investment fund promoters must now, in addition to the ordinary (full-length) prospectus, communicate key provisions to potential investors in a prescribed format—known as a 'summary prospectus' in the US and a 'key investor information document' (or 'KIID') in the EU. These are intended to be very short summaries that potential investors should be able to parse more rapidly than the full prospectuses, which can run to hundreds of pages. This immediately raises the question how such reams of information are to be summarized in just a few pages. As regards investment funds, US and EU policymakers have opted for similar-looking packages, requiring disclosure of matters such as details of the fund's investments and its objectives, past performance and prospective risks, and fees and charges levied.[54]

Unfortunately, experimental research suggests that these innovations have done little to assist retail investors. A group of experimental subjects provided with summary prospectuses and asked to make an investment decision made statistically indistinguishable choices from a group who were given only the full prospectuses.[55] In both cases, investors appeared to misunderstand the effects of fees and chose funds that did not maximize their expected returns net of fees.[56] Nevertheless, regulators' enthusiasm appears undimmed. For example, a current major initiative of the European Commission in relation to consumer finance is to roll out abbreviated disclosures for all packaged retail investment products.[57]

---

[52] See D Miles, *The UK Mortgage Market: Taking a Longer-Term View* (HM Treasury: London, 2004). Difficulties with the stipulation of appropriate assumptions required the modification of the APR formula used in the EU Credit Agreements Directive just months after it became effective: see Directive 2011/90/EU [2011] OJ L296/35.

[53] SEC Rule 498(b); UCITS V Directive, Art 78.

[54] In addition, the SEC mandates a description of the management of the fund.

[55] J Beshears, JJ Choi, D Laibson, and BC Madrian, 'How Does Simplified Disclosure Affect Individuals' Mutual Fund Choices?', in DA Wise (ed), *Explorations in the Economics of Aging* (Chicago: University of Chicago Press, 2011), 75.

[56] There are two components: first, the operating expenses charged on an annual basis by the fund manager; and second, any sales commission paid to a financial adviser who has recommended the fund to the investor. It was traditionally the case that commission would be charged to the investor as a one-off fee for buying into the fund, known as the 'sales load'. However, over time the use of such 'front-end load' arrangements has declined. Over the same period, the average operating expense, as a proportion of assets under management, has risen. One interpretation is that this is because the one-off front-end fee is salient, whereas a fee that is annualized over the life of the investment is not: front-end sales loads predict lower investment flows, but operating expenses are uncorrelated with investment flows: BM Barber, T Odean, and L Zheng, 'Out of Sight, Out of Mind: The Effect of Expenses on Mutual Fund Flows' (2005) 78 *Journal of Business* 2095. Under SEC Rule 12b-1, mutual fund managers are permitted only to charge the fund fees for the costs of marketing and selling shares insofar as the fund has adopted a plan authorizing their payment. This rule prohibits funds from giving brokerage business to advisers in return for marketing the fund, but otherwise imposes no restrictions on the amount of sales costs which may be charged to the fund.

[57] PRIIPs Regulation, Arts 5–14, in force from the beginning of 2017. At the time of writing, the details of the relevant KIDs were under consultation: see ESMA/EBA/EIOPA, *Joint Consultation Paper: PRIIPs Key Information Documents* (2015).

In response to these challenges, consumer financial regulators such as the UK's FCA and the US Consumer Finance Protection Bureau ('CFPB') have begun to conduct observational and experimental research into ways of modifying the content and presentation of information to consumers.[58] For example, the UK's FCA conducted a field experiment on bank savers regarding the communication of information about a decrease in interest rates. Rates of switching accounts increased significantly when customers were sent an additional letter explaining how much they would 'lose' under the new, lower, interest rate, and how much they could 'gain' by switching to an alternative account.[59]

Advertising. Even if regulators are well informed as to the appropriate framing of communications, a significant constraint on the efficacy of disclosure-based intervention remains, at least as regards the point of entry to consumer financial contracts. That constraint is the presence of advertising. Advertising is explicitly designed to induce consumers to choose a particular brand of product, both in relation to other products and instead of no product at all. Advertising agencies may be expected to seek to exploit consumers' behavioural biases in order to stimulate demand for their clients' products.[60] Moreover, advertising clearly influences consumers of financial products. Advertising spend by US mutual funds is associated with higher subsequent inflows of funds.[61] In light of this, advertising for financial contracts deserves close scrutiny by regulators.

In the UK, the FCA's regulation of advertising has three principal aspects. First, there is an overarching standard that financial promotions be 'fair, clear and not misleading'.[62] Second, there are specific rules relating to particular information that must be included in promotional communications to consumers and warnings regarding performance information.[63] Third, certain channels of communication are ruled out: specifically, the cold-calling of consumers is prohibited.[64] Under this regime, promotions of most financial products are in principle subject to prior scrutiny. In most cases, an FCA-authorized person must review the communication to ensure its compliance with the FCA's regime on financial promotions.[65]

---

[58] See generally, FCA, 'Applying Behavioural Economics at the Financial Conduct Authority', Occasional Paper No 1 (2013); J Niemann, 'Behavioural Economics and the CFPB', *CFPB Journal*, 22 September 2015.

[59] FCA, 'Stimulating Interest: Reminding Savers to Act When Rates Decrease', Occasional Paper No 7 (2015).

[60] For example, consumer research studies find that US mutual fund adverts typically do not contain information about 'sales loads' (charges covering sales commission): MA Jones and T Smythe, 'The Information Content of Mutual Fund Print Advertising' (2003) 37 *Journal of Consumer Affairs* 22; B Humann and N Bhattaharyya, 'Does Mutual Fund Advertising Provide Necessary Investment Information?' (2005) 23 *International Journal of Bank Marketing* 296.

[61] See eg Barber, Odean, and Zheng, n 56. Furthermore, the number of investors holding a US public company's stock and its liquidity are correlated with the firm's advertising spend in product markets: G Grullon, G Kanatas, and JP Weston, 'Advertising, Breadth of Ownership, and Liquidity' (2004) 17 *Review of Financial Studies* 439.

[62] COBS 4.2. This standard is applied across the EU to all information provided to clients by investment firms: see eg Directive 2014/65/EU ('MiFID II') [2014] OJ L173/349, Art 24, but the FCA's rules are more broadly applicable, covering non-MiFID manufacturers as well.

[63] COBS 4.5–4.6.   [64] COBS 4.8.

[65] FSMA 2000 s 21. However, the FCA maintains a list of safe-harbour exemptions; communications falling into any of the listed categories do not require specific approval.

In the US, advertising regulation is applied in a more sectoral way, reflecting the compartmentalization of financial regulation. The CFPB applies Dodd–Frank Act's broad-sweep standards prohibiting unfair, deceptive, or abusive acts or practices in connection with, *inter alia*, the advertising of consumer financial products and services.[66] Meanwhile, the SEC deems advertising for mutual funds to be misleading (and consequently unlawful) unless, first, performance data are presented in a prescribed format to aid comparability and comprehension, and, second, a prescribed warning is introduced stating that past performance does not guarantee future results.[67] Unfortunately, experimental research suggests that a warning in this format makes no difference to retail investors' choices about mutual fund investments.[68]

The general theme emerging from this discussion is that for regulators to ensure that consumers have the right information to make a 'good' decision regarding product selection is a complex and multifaceted problem, involving both the content and presentation of useful information, and—it would seem—the control of false or, more tendentiously, 'distracting' information.

12.3.2 Product regulation

The complexity involved in getting disclosure right may mean that in many cases the potential of information-based interventions may go unfulfilled. Moreover, some biases may still be operative even in the presence of the clearest information. Regulators may therefore consider an alternative approach, based not on regulating the process of contracting but on the substantive terms of financial contracts.

Such restrictions might be framed as applying to the terms of specific types of financial contract—requiring (or restricting the effect of) particular provisions. Alternatively, they may be framed as permitting (or not permitting) certain types of financial contract to be offered to consumers. In either case, the difficulty faced by regulators is that, just as with disclosure-based intervention, the relevant restrictions probably require careful calibration to be effective. However, the stakes are higher with product regulation: if imperfectly calibrated, restrictions on the range of enforceable contracts can make consumers worse off by impeding their access to contracts they in fact would have wanted. Moreover, it is often quite straightforward for financial firms to evade such restrictions by altering other terms of the contract, or by re-framing the product that is offered. For these reasons, regulators are generally chary of imposing mandatory rules, traditionally relying on information strategies and increasingly moving towards regulating the conduct of financial firms, as we shall see in the next section. Nevertheless, there are examples of mandatory rules in consumer financial products. For instance, credit card agreements in the US and the UK, and latterly across the EU, have long been subject, in addition to the information-based strategies discussed in the

---

[66] See Dodd–Frank Act §1031; see also 12 CFR Part 1026 (Regulation Z: Truth in Lending), §1026.24(i) (listing prohibited acts or practices in advertisements for credit secured by a dwelling).

[67] 1940 Act §34b-1, SEC Rule 482.

[68] M Mercer, AR Palmiter, and AE Taha, 'Worthless Warnings? Testing the Effectiveness of Disclaimers in Mutual Fund Advertisements' (2010) 7 *Journal of Empirical Legal Studies* 429. However, a more extensive warning—'past returns usually do not persist'—did have an effect on investors' decisions.

previous section, to a modest number of mandatory terms.[69] More generally, recent legislative changes in the UK, and similar measures to be rolled out across the EU by 2018, give regulators the power to prohibit the offering for sale of financial products if necessary to achieve regulatory goals including—most obviously in this context—the protection of consumers.[70]

We will consider in detail a recent example of the application of this strategy in the UK, to so-called 'payday loans'. Payday loans are short-term credit made available at very high interest rates. The name shows the origins of the sector, which was to provide finance to tide a consumer over 'until payday', where they had suffered a temporary liquidity shock in the interim and needed immediate funds. The sector began in the US through physical premises, but grew rapidly internationally in the early years of the twenty-first century, making heavy use of the Internet as a distribution channel.

Example of a Payday Lender: Wonga.com

Wonga.com is a well-known British payday lender. It makes loans of up to £400 available to consumers via its website for a maximum of one month (thirty days). The website makes very clear to potential customers that the borrowing will be very expensive. A loan of £400 for thirty days will cost, for example, £96 in interest, meaning that £496 will be repayable at the end of the month. It also explains that the typical APR for this type of loan would be in excess of 4,000 per cent. One may ask why a borrower would find this type of credit appealing. It is interesting that both the website and Wonga's advertising emphasize heavily the speed with which the funds will be made available: 'in your bank account within five minutes'. One plausible explanation is that this re-frames the borrowing decision for many consumers: rather than a comparison of two times in the future (when the funds are advanced versus when they must be repaid) it becomes a comparison between immediate funds versus when they must be repaid at some point in the future.

In principle, a source of short-term available liquidity could be welfare-enhancing. Many consumers on modest incomes might find it difficult to meet basic payments, such as mortgage or home rental, or car instalment payments, following a sudden liquidity shock such as unemployment, illness, or divorce. Many of these consumers would also find it difficult to get access to traditional forms of credit, especially if they had impaired credit histories. The payday lending sector offers such individuals access to emergency liquidity in order to cover their necessary payments until they are paid. Thus, the maximum loan duration is usually a month, in keeping with the idea of being

---

[69] See eg Truth in Lending Act of 1968, Pub L 90-321 (15 USC 1601), as amended (US) (implemented through Regulation Z, 12 CFR 1026), §1026.12(b) (limit on liability of credit cardholder for unauthorized use); Consumer Credit Act 1974, as amended by Consumer Credit Act 2006 (UK), ss 94 (right to complete payments ahead of time) and 140A–140D (control of 'unfair' creditor–debtor agreements or creditor behaviour thereunder); Consumer Credit Directive 2008/48/EC [2008] OJ L133/66 (repealing Consumer Credit Directive 87/102/EEC [1987] OJ L42/48) (EU), Art 16 (right to early repayment).

[70] Financial Services and Markets Act 2000 (UK) ('FSMA 2000') (as amended by Financial Services Act 2012), ss 137C, 137D, and 138N; MiFID II, Art 69(2)(s); Regulation (EU) No 600/2014 (MiFIR) [2014] OJ L173/84, Arts 40–2.

'until payday'. Because payday loans involve only small sums, advanced for short periods of time, and at very high interest rates, payday lenders are willing to extend credit with only the most minimal of checks about their borrowers. This makes the product very quick and easy to obtain for consumers.

The potential market failures in the payday lending model track our general discussion in Chapter 10. First, there may be a problem of asymmetric information: borrowers may not understand the terms and conditions on which the loans are advanced. Second, and more subtly, the 'no questions asked' nature of the applications process may be particularly appealing to consumers with a bias towards immediate gratification.[71]

The typical payday borrower has very low, but positive, income—barely above subsistence, but with a steady income nonetheless. To put this in context, a CFPB study found that 68 per cent of US payday borrowers reported their annual income as below $30,000,[72] compared with a US household median income of $52,000.[73] Moreover, such borrowers are generally of below-average financial literacy.[74] Contrary to the idea that payday loans are offered as a means of tiding borrowers over liquidity difficulties, it appears that over 75 per cent of funds advanced by US payday lenders— and the associated fee revenues raised—were in transactions with borrowers taking out upwards of eleven payday loans per year.[75] This suggests that borrowers frequently have difficulty repaying an initial loan and find themselves in a cycle of rollovers, re-borrowing, and paying further fees and interest every month. Consistent with this interpretation are the results of several studies of the impact of access to payday loans. A representative example is a study by Melzer, who exploited the fact that payday lending is prohibited in some US states to develop a measure of access to payday lending based on the physical distance an individual in a 'prohibition state' lives from the border with a state where the activity is permitted.[76] Using data from the mid-1990s, before Internet payday loans became common, this gives a good indicator of the effort—in terms of miles driven—required to take out a payday loan. Melzer found that easier access to payday loans was correlated with *greater* delinquency rates on mortgages, rent, car repayments, and medical bills—precisely the opposite one would

---

[71] By focusing on speed and ease of access, the loan providers make the choice a very immediate one for the borrower. An ordinary bank loan involves an immediate cost—an invasive scrutiny of finances, followed by an intermediate benefit (advance of funds) and a subsequent cost (repayment with interest). In contrast, an Internet-delivered payday loan promises an upfront benefit—money in the borrower's account almost immediately—and a subsequent cost (repayment of interest). For consumers whose brains place emphasis on immediate satisfaction, the payday loan may seem very appealing, because these individuals overemphasize immediate payoffs. If this is the case, then we would expect to see payday lending being used by such individuals as a general form of credit, and not simply to meet sudden and unanticipated liquidity needs.

[72] CFPB, 'Payday Loans and Deposit Advance Products' (2013), 18.

[73] US Census Bureau, 'Household Income: 2013', 3.

[74] A Lusardi and C de Bassa Scheresberg, 'Financial Literacy and High-Cost Borrowing in the United States', NBER Working Paper No 18969 (2013).

[75] CFPB, n 72, 22.

[76] BT Melzer, 'The Real Costs of Credit Access: Evidence from the Payday Lending Market' (2011) 126 *Quarterly Journal of Economics* 571.

expect if the product was confined to its stated use.[77] However, this is not to say that *all* payday loans are harmful—another study, for example, reports that access to payday loans helped citizens smooth liquidity shocks following natural disasters such as earthquakes.[78]

The picture emerging from this evidence is of a product that is offered ostensibly for one purpose—emergency liquidity—but in practice is used heavily to finance ongoing lifestyle expenses by consumers lacking in basic financial literacy (which as we have seen is likely to be correlated with a bias towards instantaneous gratification).[79] This appears to have outcomes that are on average harmful for these consumers, reducing their already limited resources.

In 2013 the UK Parliament required the FCA to make rules capping the charges applied by lenders in 'high-cost short-term credit',[80] which the FCA duly implemented from the beginning of 2015.[81] Specifically, the FCA's new rules cap the maximum interest rate payable to 0.8 per cent per day, the maximum fee payable on default to £15, and—perhaps most significantly—capped the total cost of borrowing to 100 per cent of the amount borrowed. In their cost-benefit analysis that preceded the regulations, the FCA assessed the risk that some such restrictions would impede access to emergency liquidity by borrowers who needed this product. They concluded that the fee caps would 'bite' on the most marginal borrowers, who would be the ones most exposed to misuse of the product.[82] Since the cap has been introduced, supply has contracted in the sector, which is in line with the FCA's expectations.[83] In light of the analysis, this is probably to be welcomed.

12.3.3 Conduct regulation

We have so far considered interventions targeting the process of entering into financial contracts, and the terms of those contracts. A recurring theme has been the need for very precise calibration in order for interventions to be effective. However, it is problematic if these measures are linked only to particular types of financial contract.[84] Financial firms may seek to evade such interventions by reframing their offering as a

---

[77] Similarly, other studies report that access to payday lending is associated with increased likelihood of involuntary closure of consumers' bank accounts (D Campbell, F Asís Martínez-Jerez, and P Tufano, 'Bouncing Out of the Banking System: An Empirical Analysis of Involuntary Bank Account Closures' (2012) 36 *Journal of Banking & Finance* 1224) and deterioration in job performance and decreased employment retention amongst US military personnel: S Carrell and J Zinman, 'In Harm's Way? Payday Loan Access and Military Personnel Performance' (2014) 27 *Review of Financial Studies* 2805. See also the review of earlier literature in JY Campbell, HE Jackson, BC Madrian, and P Tufano, 'Consumer Financial Protection' (2011) 25 *Journal of Economic Perspectives* 91, 100–3.

[78] A Morse, 'Payday Lenders: Heroes or Villains?' (2011) 102 *Journal of Financial Economics* 28.

[79] See Chapter 10, section 10.2.2.

[80] Financial Services (Banking Reform) Act 2013 s 131(1), amending FSMA 2000 s 137C.

[81] FCA Handbook, CONC 5A. See also FCA, 'Detailed Rules for the Price Cap on High-Cost Short-Term Credit', PS14/16 (2014).

[82] FCA, 'Proposals for a Price Cap on High-Cost Short-Term Credit', CP14/10 (2014), 23–9, 60–96.

[83] E Dunkley, 'Payday Lender Numbers Shrink By a Third in Response to New Rules', *Financial Times*, 11 June 2015.

[84] See V Colaerts, 'European Banking, Securities and Insurance Law: Cutting through Sectoral Lines?' (2015) 52 *Common Market Law Review* 1579, 1594–607.

different type of product. More fundamentally, the nature of demand may evolve such that the product structure changes, upsetting the calibration of the intervention.

An alternative regulatory approach is to focus not so much on the content of information that is disclosed to the consumer, but on the behaviour of the financial firm. 'Conduct regulation' for consumer products focuses on the activities of the financial firm in relation to its customers. Relevant 'conduct' can encompass the entirety of the sales and marketing process, including advertising and marketing literature, sales communications, pre-contractual information, advice and recommendations, ongoing behaviour during the life of the contract, and even the way in which the product has been designed.

The financial firm can be required to comply with high-level, open-ended standards of conduct—for example, 'treat customers fairly', or 'manage conflicts of interest'. These high-level principles must then be interpreted and applied by the firm through their internal management channels. Successful interpretation and implementation require extensive supervisory oversight by the regulator.[85] However, this approach holds out the promise that the content of the regulation—the principles, as applied by firms—will be more dynamic, as firms' application of the general principles must move with the evolution of their business. The regulatory supervision is typically at the level of the firm's systems and processes—governance mechanisms put in place in order to secure compliance. Conduct regulation of this type holds out the promise of more effective control over both the provision of information and product design than does 'direct' regulatory prescription of the type considered in section 12.3.2. We focus here on product design.[86]

Product governance. The UK's FCA, following on from an initiative launched by its predecessor, the FSA,[87] has recently been developing a conduct-based intervention strategy known as 'product governance'. This has subsequently been adopted by EU-level authorities.[88] The core idea is regulatory oversight of the systems and processes in place regarding product quality throughout the 'lifecycle' of the product.[89]

This begins with the design and marketing of new products. Here firms are expected to ensure that for each new product, a case is developed that explains the target market they see for the product in question, and what steps they have taken in the design and

---

[85] See the discussion in Chapter 24, section 24.4.

[86] As regards information, general standards that communications must be 'fair, clear and not misleading', as applied in the UK, and the EU under the MiFID regime—see n 62 and text thereto—are examples of conduct regulation, which articulate broad open-ended standards regulators can then apply to specific contexts.

[87] On the background, see FSA, 'Treating Customers Fairly (TCF) in product design' (2007); FSA, 'Retail Product Development and Governance—Structured Products Review', Finalised Guidance (2012).

[88] The EU sectoral authorities have each consulted on product governance frameworks to be implemented under corporate governance rules for firms under their jurisdiction. See ESMA, 'Structured Retail Products—Good Practices for Product Governance Arrangements', March 2014; EIOPA, 'Consultation Paper on the Proposal for Guidelines on Product Oversight and Governance Arrangements by Insurance Undertakings', October 2014; EBA, 'Draft Guidelines on Product Oversight and Governance Arrangements for Retail Banking Products', November 2014. It is also to be rolled out through MiFID II to all investment firms across Europe by 2018: see MiFID II, Arts 16(3) and 24(2).

[89] The following discussion is drawn from the principles articulated in FCA, 'Structured Products: Thematic Review of Product Development and Governance', March 2015. This is representative of the positions in the sources cited in n 88.

marketing process to ensure that the products are appropriate for the needs of members of the target groups. This process requires firms' senior management to identify a target market at the outset during product design, which should then inform each subsequent part of the product development and distribution strategy. The design progress should include stress testing of the product to ensure that it has a reasonable chance of delivering value to consumers. Firms should also monitor the uptake of their products, to ensure that it is reaching the target market and not being sold inappropriately. Governance concerns in relation to this might include the way in which distributors' incentives are affected by their compensation regarding sales.

What is to ensure that firms take these obligations seriously? Combined with the regulatory expectations about these internal processes are (in the case of the FCA), or will be (in the case of other European regulators), powers to implement 'product bans' for products where the firm has failed to develop or apply an effective product approval process.[90] Product governance is a potentially effective regulatory strategy in light of the analysis in Chapter 10, because it harnesses the informational advantage that the financial firm has in order to ensure better outcomes for consumers. In particular, a financial firm with 'big data' regarding consumer preferences is in a good situation to design a genuinely useful product, or alternatively a product that will be effective at transferring rents from consumers to the firm. If the regulator simply tries to impose structured disclosures, or product regulation, onto the terms of the agreement or onto the pattern of the contacting process, it is doomed to be outsmarted by the firm. But product governance co-opts the firm's talent and information to work to the consumer's advantage, in a process that cleverly shifts the onus of proof. If the regulator wants to ban something using its product intervention powers, it has to produce a cost-benefit analysis to show this is in the public interest, or at least build a case that a court may find persuasive in a potential judicial review. But with product governance, the regulator is framing the firm's obligation as a procedural one. The evidence that must be produced is to demonstrate that the firm is meeting its obligations to put consumers first. And it is *the firm* that is to have in place a product approval process to weed out those that do not serve consumers' interests.

This strategy may prove to be a neat solution to the problems identified in Chapter 10, section 10.4. From the standpoint of principle, it targets firm rent-seeking, not consumer harm directly. From the standpoint of pragmatism, it harnesses the firm's superior information and resources.

The limitation underlying all this is how the target market is to be identified. If consumers suffer from behavioural problems, how is the firm to go about determining that the product will make consumers better off? Of course, there is no easy answer— but notice that the difficulties are rather less where firms seek to make these determinations than where regulators do—as with the case of direct product regulation. It is the firm, not the regulator, that must put in place the design and approval process. Consequently, different firms may be expected to identify different target markets,

---

[90] See MiFID II, Art 69(2)(t) and sources cited above n 70. This is a product regulation strategy contingent upon the finding of a product governance failure.

and run different stress tests. So, competition in the marketplace might ensure that there will be a variety of choices open to the consumer. This will be less restrictive than a policy set by the regulator.[91]

12.4 Prudential Regulation

Many firms offering consumer financial products are also subject to prudential regulation. Such rules relate to the balance sheet and governance of financial firms, and can readily be rationalized in terms of agency costs.[92] After a consumer has advanced her funds under a financial contract, a number of agency problems arise vis-à-vis the firm on whose balance sheet they rely for payment. The longer the time horizon, the greater the discretion granted to the firm, its managers, or advisers, and the more complex the investment portfolio, the greater the associated agency problems will be.

What is the difference between prudential regulation and product regulation? Legally, the distinction is crystalline: product regulation implies terms into (or outright prohibits) consumer financial products, whereas prudential regulation applies restrictions to the firm itself. From an economic or functional perspective, however, there is little difference. Both impose mandatory rules on firms involved in selling certain types of products, which restrict the extent to which the firm can profit at the expense of the consumer. They have similar consequences for the consumer, in that they are likely simultaneously to increase the high-visibility costs of the contract, but reduce the low-visibility risks. Indeed, from an economic perspective, prudential obligations are best understood as akin to covenants that well-informed and advised parties negotiating with the financial firm would seek in order to protect their interests.[93]

We will now—briefly—consider the case for, and scope of, such regulation in relation to insurers and investment funds.

12.4.1 Insurance

In the case of an insurance company, the crucial financial decision is the determination of the likely profile of future payout obligations under the promises it has made against

---

[91] Of course, a less prescriptive regulatory strategy (in the form of procedural requirements as opposed to a ban on a specific product) entails the risk that regulators will be unable to spot inadequate product governance processes at individual firms and therefore, that inappropriate products still make it to the market.

[92] These are the costs of hidden action by the firm—that is, actions that the consumer finds it hard to observe—after the contract is on foot, which promote the firm's interest at the expense of the consumer's.

[93] The difference between the legal and economic perspectives is brought into relief when we consider the case of collective investment funds. As we have seen, these are often structured as companies. These corporate entities are subject to a range of balance sheet restrictions (discussed in section 12.4.2). Legally these are restrictions on the firm, rather than terms of the contract between investor and firm. However, while legally a separate firm, the investment fund has no real independence from its manager. This reality is reflected in EU law by placing the conduct of business obligations as regard fund investors onto the manager directly, as opposed to the fund. This effectively treats the investment fund offered to the consumer as a 'product' offered by the fund manager, and not as a separate financial firm (N Moloney, *How to Protect Investors: Lessons from the EC and UK* (Cambridge: CUP, 2010), 134–52). On this view, the restrictions on the way in which the fund may invest its assets are not prudential regulation of a financial firm, but rather regulation of the structured product that the collective investment vehicle represents. From the standpoint of investors, it makes no difference as regards the balance sheet restrictions on the fund.

the income it has or will receive (by way of premiums and investment income on premiums not immediately needed to meet claims). Likely payout obligations appear on the liability side of the insurer's balance sheet as 'technical provisions' (in the EU) or 'reserves' (in the US) and constitute on average some three-quarters of insurers' liabilities.[94] Determining whether the technical provisions or reserves are adequate requires considerable actuarial expertise, which is a core attribute of an insurance company, just as assessing the creditworthiness of borrowers is a core function of banks. However, there are three reasons why insureds might be concerned about agency costs.

First, in a version of the shareholder/bondholder conflict in all companies benefiting from limited liability, directors responding to the interests of risk-neutral shareholders have an incentive to increase the riskiness of the insurer's assets and liabilities. Risk-averse insureds will reap no benefit from the increased riskiness but will suffer from the higher probability of insolvency and thus obtain reduced value for their premia.[95] Regulation of, for example, the level of an insurer's technical provisions will address this problem of the committed insured, but it will also have the *ex ante* effect of encouraging more persons to take out insurance. Regulation can act as a form of pre-commitment on the part of insurers to treat insureds fairly and thus facilitate the expansion of the insurance industry. Regulation here constitutes a form of bonding by insurers which allows high-value sellers credibly to convey to potential insureds the value of their products. Thus, regulation of this type is not necessarily contrary to the interests of shareholders in insurance companies.[96]

Second, the insurer's management, while not aiming to increase the riskiness of the insurer's assets and liabilities, may achieve this result, perhaps through pure incompetence but more likely as a result of a desire to expand the size of the insurer. As the IAIS has remarked:

> [M]ajor impairment factors both for life and non-life insurers are deficient loss provisioning[,] inadequate pricing...and rapid growth, which in many cases was coupled with deficiencies in risk management as well as in sound and balanced governance. These causes tend to be interrelated.[97]

The classic case of an aggressively expanding insurer that under-reserved, under-priced, and later collapsed is HIH, the Australian insurer whose collapse in 2001 was the largest corporate failure in Australian history. Again, regulation addressing these issues may benefit both well-conducted insurers and their clients: insurance companies

---

[94] IAIS, n 7, Figure 2. Since the contingency which will trigger the payout obligation has not yet occurred, there is no current obligation to pay.

[95] D Filipovic, R Kremslehner, and A Muermann, 'Optimal Investment and Premium Policies under Risk Shifting and Solvency Regulation' (2015) 82 *Journal of Risk and Insurance* 261.

[96] An alternative approach, often adopted before the rise of effective insurance regulation, was to remove the shareholders and to form insurance companies as mutuals, ie companies owned by their policyholders. The capital constraints of mutuals, however, have induced many to demutualize in recent years. See O Erhemjamts and JT Leverty, 'The Demise of the Mutual Organizational Form: An Investigation of the Life Insurance Industry' (2010) 42 *Journal of Money, Credit and Banking* 1011.

[97] IAIS, n 7, 9–10.

that engage in inadequate provisioning may gain at least a temporary advantage over competitors that provision properly, thus driving down provisioning standards across the industry.

Third, even if the management of insurers does not increase the riskiness of their assets and liabilities, it may not act fairly in respect of all insureds of the same class. This is a particular danger with life insurance companies, which have incentives not to treat existing insureds as well as new customers.[98] New customers have to be wooed with attractive promises; existing customers are locked in. The insurance company thus has an incentive to make non-legally enforceable promises to the new customers, which it subsequently reneges on when they become existing customers (a 'time-inconsistency' problem). To be sure, this is to put the issue a little crudely. There are constraints on the power of this incentive: at some level, information about the treatment of existing customers will deter new customers, but this information may not be readily apparent to outsiders.

12.4.2 Investment funds

Investment funds are, as we have seen, a ubiquitous retail financial product. There are many mandatory rules governing the way in which retail investment funds must be structured and managed, most of which address agency problems. Each of these restrictions is designed to reduce the risks of opportunistic behaviour on the part of the fund manager that retail investors who buy into the fund bear. Here we consider, by way of example, a series of such restrictions imposed on typical retail funds, namely UCITS in the EU and diversified mutual funds in the US.

- *Liquidity.* Retail funds are restricted to investing in liquid assets. The lists of eligible assets are quite similar for both EU UCITS and US diversified mutual funds.[99] These comprise cash (bank deposits) and market-traded securities (including both equity and debt), money market instruments, and exchange-traded derivatives.[100] The idea is to prevent open-ended retail funds from engaging in liquidity transformation, thereby ensuring the credibility of their commitment to redeem investors' shares on demand. This approach is in sharp contrast to that taken in relation to deposit-taking institutions.

- *Diversification.* There are also restrictions on how much of a fund's portfolio may be invested in a single security, issuer, or counterparty. Generally no more than 5 per cent of a fund's portfolio asset value may be invested in securities and money-market instruments issued by a single body.[101] The rules governing

---

[98] A Morrison, 'Life Insurance Regulation as Contract Enforcement' *Economic Affairs*, December 2004, 47.

[99] UCITS funds must invest all of their assets subject to this restriction; US diversified mutual funds may invest 25 per cent of their assets in other ways.

[100] UCITS V, Art 50; Investment Company Act of 1940 ('1940 Act'), §5(b)(1). UCITS are also permitted to invest in other regulated retail investment funds and in OTC derivatives for which the underlying are on the list of eligible assets: ibid.

[101] UCITS V, Art 52(1)(a); 1940 Act, §5(b)(1). For UCITS, this may be raised by Member States to 10 per cent, provided that no more than 40 per cent of the overall portfolio is placed in such 'overweight'

UCITS provide that a greater asset allocation may be made into bonds issued by EU credit institutions (up to 25 per cent of the fund's asset value) and to sovereign instruments (up to 35 per cent of the fund's asset value).[102] A related set of rules restricts exposure not by reference to the fund, but by reference to the investee entity. For US diversified mutual funds, this cap is set at 10 per cent of the outstanding voting rights, whereas UCITS are prohibited from acquiring sufficient voting shares to exercise a 'significant influence' over an issuer's management.[103]

- *Capital structure.* Restrictions on leverage prevent or inhibit funds from using leverage to boost equity risk and return. UCITS are prohibited from using leverage, and US mutual funds may borrow no more than one-third of the value of their assets.[104]

- *Short selling.* US mutual funds are also prohibited from engaging in short selling.[105] This is intended to protect investors from the risk of uncapped losses associated with short sales.[106]

Arguably, the most fundamental aspect of investor protection in relation to retail funds is mandatory redemption rights, used for UCITS and for open-ended US mutual funds.[107] These require the fund to permit investors to redeem their shares (sell them back to the fund) at the firm's (*pro rata*) net asset value. This ensures liquidity for retail investors at all times. It marks a continuing point of sharp differentiation from practice in relation to hedge funds, where it is commonplace to manage concerns about maturity mismatch by locking up investors' money for a minimum notice period of three months. The need to ensure sufficient liquidity to meet demand for redemptions at any time surely creates an opportunity cost for mutual funds, which is probably part of the explanation why, despite having professional managers, mutual fund returns persistently underperform market benchmarks.[108]

---

investments: UCITS V Art 52(2). UCITS are also restricted to holding no more than 20 per cent of their assets on deposit with a single body; as regards derivatives, UCITS permitted to take on a risk exposure of no more than 5 per cent of their assets in a single transaction, or 10 per cent where the counterparty is a regulated credit institution (Art 52(1)).

[102] UCITS V, Art 52(3)–(4). Such investments are exempted from the overall limit of 40 per cent invested in a single counterparty. Moreover, Member States have the option to permit UCITS to invest up to 100 per cent of their assets in sovereign securities: Art 54. These rules—which echo the more relaxed treatment of OTC derivative exposure where the counterparty is a regulated credit institution—seem hard to justify unless sovereign and bank bonds are more liquid, and carry less idiosyncratic risk, than other types of security. The events of the last few years belie this. These provisions may be better explained as attempts to ensure a ready market for EU bank and sovereign debt.

[103] UCITS V, Art 56, 1940 Act, §5(b)(1). UCITS are also prohibited from holding more than 10 per cent of non-voting shares, bonds, or money market instruments of a single issuer.

[104] UCITS V Art 83; 1940 Act, §18(f).   [105] 1940 Act, §12(a)(3).

[106] See eg Chapter 5, section 5.3.1.   [107] UCITS V Art 84; 1940 Act, §5(a)(1).

[108] RM Edelen, 'Investor Flows and the Assessed Performance of Open-End Mutual Funds' (1999) 53 *Journal of Financial Economics* 439.

12.5 Conclusion

In this chapter, we have considered the range of consumer financial products, and the principal regulatory strategies used in relation to them. There are two potential market failures: asymmetric information and behavioural limitations in consumer decision-making. There is a real risk that unscrupulous financial firms may exploit consumers through marketing products designed to appeal to consumers' biases, rather than to improve their welfare.

As regards the relationship between manufacturers and consumers, there are three broad regulatory strategies in play. The first—disclosure or 'information-based' regulatory strategies—suffers from the limitation that consumers often do not understand the information presented to them. While regulators can prescribe short, targeted, disclosures, their success is highly sensitive to the starting circumstances. This problem of context-specificity is even more significant in relation to product regulation, where the regulator steps in and directs to firms whether or not they may market a particular product.

A better approach to the management of product effects may be found under the banner of 'product governance'. This reverses the onus of proof attaching to legislative intervention, ensuring that the firm's information and expertise are harnessed in designing and marketing projects that are fit for purpose.

Financial firms that manufacture investment products also retain obligations regarding the prudential management of their balance sheets. The latter respond to agency costs and impose a range of restrictions on the types of asset in which such firms may invest, the extent of leverage they may take on, and so forth. These are microprudential rules in the sense that they serve to reduce the likelihood of excessive risk-taking in the manufacturer firm in order to protect its investors. As such, they provide a natural segue into Part D.

PART D

BANKS

13

Theory of Banking

13.1 Introduction

The term 'bank' derives from the tables or benches of moneylenders who kept money in safekeeping for depositors and lent surpluses to borrowers.[1] The principle underlying this is what is termed 'fractional reserve banking'. On the assumption that a fraction of depositors need to withdraw their funds on any one occasion, banks only have to hold a fraction of the money that is deposited with them in reserve to meet withdrawals. The remainder can be lent out to borrowers.

Economies in holding deposits are clearly of immense benefit in funding productive activities. Individually, people have to set aside a significant fraction of their monetary holdings to meet possible expenditures in the future. Collectively, they can pool their deposits and set aside a much smaller fraction because when one person needs to withdraw, another does not. The principle of fractional banking is simple, powerful, and of considerable economic significance. It has driven much economic activity over a long period of time.

It is also a source of financial disaster. The principle of fractional reserve banking relies on withdrawals by individuals not being closely correlated. If, however, many people—or, still worse, everyone—wants to withdraw their money at the same time then a bank that has only set aside a fraction of its deposits to meet withdrawals may find itself short of funds with which to pay them. Furthermore, the very possibility of this occurring will itself prompt depositors to withdraw their funds for fear of not being able to do so. It creates the phenomenon of bank runs that has occurred repeatedly in history and reared its head again in the most recent financial crisis.

This is one illustration of the magic and manias of banks. They are the source of both remarkable economic prosperity and spectacular collapses, and appreciating their role and fragility in financial systems is critical to an understanding of their regulation. However, their purpose extends well beyond fractional lending. They play a critical role in the monetary system of countries and one reason that governments attach such significance to their stability is the damage that their failures can inflict on not only their depositors but also a country's monetary system as a whole. They are, in other words, part of a country's monetary payments system and as such, they underpin all transactions that occur in an economy.

Even this fails to capture the full function of banks. In lending their depositors' money, banks assess the quality of their borrowers and the investments that they are

---

[1] *Oxford English Dictionary* (Oxford: OUP, 2015), http://www.oed.com.

Principles of Financial Regulation. First Edition. John Armour, Dan Awrey, Paul Davies, Luca Enriques, Jeffrey N. Gordon, Colin Mayer, and Jennifer Payne. © John Armour, Dan Awrey, Paul Davies, Luca Enriques, Jeffrey N. Gordon, Colin Mayer, and Jennifer Payne 2016. Published 2016 by Oxford University Press.

making. The depositors could do this directly themselves, but they lack the expertise, the time, and the information to do this. Banks not only economize on their holding of deposits to meet withdrawals but they also economize on evaluations of the quality of investments that they make on behalf of their depositors. They are often described as 'delegated monitors'—delegated on behalf of their investors to evaluate and monitor the quality and activities of their borrowers.

Again this is a very powerful economic function but it too is prone to failure, for in the very process of accumulating information that is not directly available to their investors, banks introduce a degree of opacity into their transactions that can be subject to abuse. That opacity makes it easier for owners and managers to misdirect funds to activities that benefit them at the expense of depositors' safety, thereby making banks more vulnerable to failure.

Of course, some of the most important functions of banks—mobilizing savings and selecting projects for investment—are also performed by markets, as we saw in Chapters 2 and 5. These thus represent alternative channels within the financial sector through which funds can be transferred from savers to firms. These functions are assisted by firms, including investment banks. Later in the book—in Part E—we will consider the implications of the blurring of the boundaries between these two channels.

In this chapter we focus solely on the economics of ordinary, or 'commercial', banks: we shall examine banks' potential contributions and exposures and their implications for the regulatory discussions of the subsequent chapters. In section 13.2 we begin by considering what a bank is, and its role as provider of liquidity. We discuss how a bank creates liquidity, is exposed to runs, and mitigates risks through holding reserves. In section 13.3 we describe the role of banks in the payments system, the regulatory implications of the payments function, and alternatives to banks as providers of payments. Section 13.4 then discusses banks as delegated monitors, the way in which they economize on information, and the potential failures to which this gives rise. In section 13.5 we consider the implications of this analysis of banking for regulation and in particular, the way in which regulators set entry requirements, conduct rules, and prudential (balance sheet) requirements.

By the end of the chapter you should be clear about the purpose and functions of banks, how and in what different forms they perform these functions, the risks and failures to which they are exposed, and some of the implications of all this for the regulation of banks. This serves as an introduction and roadmap to the issues covered by the other chapters in Part D: Chapter 14 considers capital requirements in more detail; Chapter 15 focuses on liquidity requirements; Chapter 16 discusses the resolution of failing banks; Chapter 17, the appropriate governance of banks; Chapter 18, the regulation of the payments system, and Chapter 19, an approach to financial regulation that looks to overall financial stability, the macroprudential approach. All of these chapters reflect the way in which the financial crisis has changed our understanding of how banks operate and thus what regulatory measures are necessary for safety and soundness of individual banks and, more importantly, for the stability of the financial system.

13.2 What is a Bank?

13.2.1 Functions of banks

Three functions are central to the operation of banks: liquidity transformation, maturity transformation, and credit transformation.[2]

Liquidity transformation. A primary function of banks is to provide liquidity which allows its investors to access money of known value for consumption purposes, a 'sum certain'. It does this in two ways: by providing access to notes and coins, and by allowing its liabilities, in the form of cheques drawn on the bank, to be used as a means of payment. There are two aspects of this liquidity. The first is certainty—knowledge about the value of assets available for transaction purposes—and the second is immediacy.

What makes the role of the bank particularly interesting is that its assets are predominantly illiquid—corporate and personal loans and mortgages. While the bank cannot quickly convert its assets to cash, it allows its depositors to do so. It can do this by holding some cash reserves to meet withdrawals. These are only a fraction of the total assets and liabilities of the bank because in general, at any one time, only a small fraction of depositors wants to withdraw their deposits, and most often only in part. If the bank has many depositors, each with a small fraction of the bank's total deposits, then it can predict from the 'law of large numbers' the likely level of withdrawals at any one time with a reasonably high degree of confidence. So, while individually each depositor would have to hold a significant fraction of their savings in money to meet their consumption needs, collectively they only have to set aside a much smaller proportion because the withdrawals of some depositors are matched by the continuing holdings of others. Meanwhile, the deposited amounts (less cash reserves) can be lent out; the interest received defrays the bank's cost of maintaining the deposit accounts and providing transaction services, and, depending on the nature of the account, providing a yield. There is therefore an economy which comes from the pooling of deposits.[3]

This aspect of banking, known as 'fractional reserve banking', is the most basic function of banks and, as was described at the beginning of the chapter, dates back to the earliest days of banking. In essence, what banks are doing is to perform a 'liquidity transformation function'—they are allowing the liquid assets of depositors to be converted into investments in illiquid assets and they are doing this on the basis of the law of large numbers.

Maturity transformation. A related but distinct function of banks is known as 'maturity transformation'. Not only are the assets of banks illiquid, but they are also long term in nature. For example, banks may extend home mortgage loans of twenty-five years or fund infrastructure projects with even longer maturities. On the other side of the balance sheet, they take deposits that can be withdrawn instantaneously, or after

---

[2] See eg X Freixas and J-C Rochet, *Microeconomics of Banking*, 2nd ed (Cambridge, MA: MIT Press, 2008).

[3] DW Diamond and PH Dybvig, 'Bank Runs, Deposit Insurance, and Liquidity' (1983) 91 *Journal of Political Economy* 401.

one, two, or three years. So they translate short-term deposits into long-term investments. By so doing banks can offer depositors part of the benefits of the higher returns that long-term investments earn.

This works well in normal circumstances, but it is fragile. Its fragility stems from a confidence trick that is vulnerable to failure. The confidence trick works so long as depositors believe that (a) the bank's investments are safe and will yield the returns that they promise, and (b) other depositors will not withdraw more than their customary amounts. If, on the other hand, there are doubts about the performance of the bank's investments, then depositors will justifiably be concerned about the safety of their deposits. Furthermore, since the investments of the bank are in long-term, illiquid assets the depositors know that there is only a limited amount that the bank can pay back today. Since, in the absence of other arrangements, the bank will pay out to those who demand their deposits back earliest, those who delay will perceive a risk that the bank will run out of money and become incapable of servicing all its depositors. The rational response of depositors who are concerned about the performance of the bank's assets is to rush to the bank and withdraw their deposits as quickly as possible ahead of other depositors. In other words, because in this scenario 'first movers' *may* be better off than those who delay, and are never worse off, there will be a run on the bank.

Credit transformation. The third function of banks is credit transformation. Banks invest in risky assets. In particular, banks are critical to the financing of individuals and small and medium-sized companies. These have traditionally had limited access to alternative sources of finance because of the risks that are inherent in their operations. Banks transform these low-risk liabilities into risky investments and allow their investors to hold deposits in banks that are of certain value.

The way in which banks do this is through monitoring and controlling the risks of their investments, pooling risks across a large number of investments, and holding capital themselves to provide protection against the failure of their investments. Banks screen and monitor the quality of the individuals and companies to which they lend and they monitor their subsequent performance, withdrawing funds where risks of investment intensify and requiring companies to take actions that mitigate the bank's exposure.

While investment in any one individual or company is risky, the failure of one is only imperfectly correlated with that of another. In particular, by investing in different sectors of the economy in geographically distinct parts of the country or the world, banks can reduce their exposure to specific industry or local risks. By pooling a large number of less than perfectly correlated risks—diversification—banks reduce the overall risk of their portfolio of investments.

Finally, banks hold their own capital—representing the claims of their shareholders, not their depositors—which acts as a cushion against the failure of their investment portfolios. This reduces the exposure of their depositors and other creditors to their loan portfolios and makes shareholders and other providers of capital the risk-takers of first instance. Only in the event that equity is insufficient do depositors and other creditors bear risks of failure. Screening, monitoring, pooling, and their own capital together allow banks to convert low-risk deposits into individually high-risk investments.[4]

---

[4] DW Diamond, 'Financial Intermediation and Delegated Monitoring' (1984) 51 *Review of Economic Studies* 393.

13.2.2 Fragility of banks

The fragility of banks derives from two features. The first is that the bank is performing maturity and liquidity transformation so that in the event of a large number of depositors withdrawing their investments, the bank is unable to meet their demands by liquidating assets and cashing in long-term investments.[5] A problem of liquidity—the inability to convert long-term assets into cash except at a discount to 'hold to maturity' values—will rapidly morph into a problem of 'solvency'—assets being worth less than debts—if left unchecked. The second feature is the obligation of the bank to service its depositors so long as it is solvent, thereby creating an incentive on depositors who are concerned about the viability of the bank to withdraw their deposits ahead of other people.

The risk of runs arises not only because of justifiable concerns about the performance of the firm's assets, but also simply in response to a belief, perhaps irrational, that other savers are about to withdraw their deposits. Even if the bank's investments are performing well, the fact that in the event of other depositors seeking the return of their savings it would be unable to service them will alone create a risk of the bank failing. So any event that might trigger such a belief, for example the failure of another bank or a false rumour that other depositors are seeking to withdraw their funds, might prompt a run that the bank will be unable to stop.

13.2.3 The idea of banking regulation

Banks' fragility, combined with the important functions they perform, engenders a belief that they need to be regulated and offer insurance to depositors against the risks of failures. Four types of regulatory tool are commonly observed. The first is to impose capital requirements on banks to maintain balance sheet reserves, so as to meet any shortfall in the value of the bank assets in relation to their liabilities, the capacity for 'loss absorbency'. The second is to require banks to hold some of their assets in a liquid form, which is available to meet withdrawals by depositors. The third is to set up a 'lender of last resort' ('LOLR') that stands ready to make short-term loans to banks against illiquid assets, and the fourth is insurance against risks of losses on deposits.[6] In terms of our taxonomy of regulatory strategies in Chapter 3,[7] the first two of these are

---

[5] Bear in mind that the core assets of a bank are its loan portfolio. The bank cannot usually demand immediate repayment from its borrowers, but rather must 'liquidate' such assets by transferring—assigning—its entitlements to a purchaser. There is an adverse selection problem, because the vendor bank knows more about the quality of its borrowers—and hence the value of its loans—than does a purchaser. The purchaser will worry that the vendor will be offloading lower quality loans first. Ordinarily a vendor would grant a warranty to a purchaser to signal the quality of assets sold, but if the vendor's financial health is doubtful—as with a bank subject to a run—then any warranties it grants will not be credible. Consequently, the purchaser will discount the value of the loans significantly.

[6] Interestingly, recent work by Charles Calomiris and co-authors demonstrates that in the nineteenth century, before creation of the Federal Reserve or federal deposit insurance, US banks privately adopted the first two of these measures, presumably in order to attract depositors. CW Calomiris and M Carlson, 'Corporate Governance and Risk Management at Unprotected Banks: National Banks in the 1890s', NBER Working Paper 19806 (2014).

[7] Chapter 3, section 3.5.

examples of the 'prudential' strategy, and the last two are examples of the 'insurance' strategy.

Capital adequacy requirements focus on maintaining the value of the stake held by shareholders (and other junior claimants) in the bank. The simplest measure is the bank's net assets—the value of its assets minus its debt liabilities. This represents a 'buffer' of asset value, and reduces the risk of a bank becoming insolvent as a consequence of a decline in the value of its investments. The larger the capital reserves, the more losses—for example, through defaults on loans—the bank can sustain before being unable to pay its debts. Capital adequacy requirements, which are discussed in detail in Chapter 14, may be set so as to address the problem of disturbances in the real economy that could undermine the safety of deposits, not just to protect depositors from mistakes in the bank's issuance and monitoring of loans.[8] In other words, a bank with extensive capital reserves is better placed to weather a deep recession: more borrowers can default before its ability to pay its debts is called into question.

However, capital requirements do not by themselves mitigate the risk of—perhaps irrational—bank runs. The bank may have very valuable assets, but because these assets are generally illiquid, if a significant part of its depositors demand their money back immediately, the bank will not be able to meet their demands. Raising cash would require asset sales at 'fire sale' prices, meaning a significant discount to the 'hold to maturity' value of the asset on the bank balance sheet. But registering such losses would soon make the bank actually insolvent. To mitigate this concern, *liquidity requirements*—discussed in Chapter 15—prescribe that banks maintain a proportion of liquid assets. This reduces the likelihood of the bank's being unable to meet demands for cash withdrawals. However, because these requirements do not increase the overall value of the bank's assets, they do not eliminate the risks banks run from real economic shocks. Capital and liquidity requirements are thus commonly deployed together.

Liquidity requirements only reduce, but do not eliminate, the possibility of depositors suffering losses in the event of bank runs: if a sufficiently large proportion of depositors demand repayment, the liquid assets will still be exhausted and the bank will be caught in the Hobson's choice of asset sales. If depositors see the draining of the bank's required liquidity, they may still take fright and seek the premature withdrawal of their deposits. An LOLR—ordinarily a central bank—can mitigate this concern by standing ready to provide short-term loans to a bank that is in need of liquidity but which has adequate capital reserves—that is, for which the problem is one of 'liquidity' rather than 'solvency'. Failure to distinguish between these cases would see central banks making loans that simply keep the troubled bank afloat—in effect, the LOLR would be bailing out the bank.[9]

---

[8] In other words, the performance on a loan will depend on factors particular to the borrower ('idiosyncratic risk') as well as the state of the general economy ('systematic risk'). In making loans, banks will generally not be fully diversified. This is because the core bank lending function, which entails screening and monitoring, is costly, and there may be advantages in specialization in lending to particular industry sectors or types of borrowers.

[9] As we discuss in Chapter 15, a central bank will generally provide LOLR support only if the loan is supported by adequate collateral so that even upon the bank's default, the central bank will be made whole. In this regard, even support of an insolvent bank would not generally expose the LOLR to credit risk. Nevertheless, LOLR lending to an insolvent bank (or banks at a time of systemic crisis) is discouraged

Even with an LOLR in place, there is still a risk of mishap: if the central bank does not respond with alacrity to liquidity problems, then these may degenerate into solvency problems, with consequent losses for depositors. *Deposit insurance* is the only complete protection against such losses, and even then, it has to satisfy a number of conditions for it to avoid the risk of runs. First, it must to be 100 per cent insurance in the sense that depositors are fully compensated for losses in the event of bank failures. During the financial crisis a number of countries had deposit insurance schemes that only provided partial coverage, for example for 90 per cent of the amount of deposits up to a certain maximum amount of deposits.[10] A less than complete insurance scheme (or one that will not pay out immediately) will not prevent a run on a bank, because depositors will still appreciate that if they can withdraw their funds ahead of others, then they will receive all of their money now, as against 90 per cent of it or a particular maximum later on. As a consequence, many countries have since moved to a more comprehensive system of deposit insurance that provides full rather than partial coverage; ceilings on the amount recoverable were also raised and the smooth operation of the guarantee was ensured.

Second, depositors will need to be confident that the insurance scheme will be able to meet demands for payments when they arise. In the event of a single bank failure, the question of the solvency of the insurance scheme is unlikely to be in question. But faced with the simultaneous failure of many banks in a financial crisis, it may be impossible for a private or mutual scheme organized by banks themselves to be able to meet all the claims on its funds. In that case, concerns about the consequences of bank failures will remain.

13.3 Payments

Important though liquidity, maturity, and credit transformation are to the functioning of banks, they do not distinguish banks from other institutions. As we will describe in Part E of the book in particular, there are many financial institutions that perform one or more of these functions but are not banks as such. These 'shadow banks' replicate the three transformation functions of banks that are discussed in section 13.2, while remaining outside the formal banking system. What distinguishes banks from these other institutions is that banks are *deposit-takers*. They take in deposits that form part of a country's payment system. So a cheque drawn on the account of a bank is a

---

because the consequence would be to keep alive a 'zombie' bank that is unlikely to provide credit support to firms in the 'real economy'. If the bank is insolvent (in the balance sheet sense) it will be unable to raise additional equity from shareholders, because it will suffer from 'debt overhang': any new equity investment would immediately go to shore up the value of creditors' claims. The only way for such a bank to re-establish solvency (positive value for its shareholders) is to let its loans gradually pay down, holding onto interest and principal repayments as retained earnings. A bank pursuing this course will not make new loans. This means that the loan origination infrastructure that the bank had assembled will be allowed to dissipate, which is an unnecessary cost, thereby undermining a valuable credit channel. This is a permanent loss to the real economy. For a real-world example of this phenomenon, see T Hoshi and AK Kashyap, 'Japan's Financial Crisis and Economic Stagnation' (2004) 18 *Journal of Economic Perspectives* 3.

[10] This was the case, for example, in the UK. The Northern Rock debacle showed conclusively that partial (90 per cent in the UK at the time) deposit insurance was insufficient to prevent runs.

claim against the assets of the bank that can be used for the payments of goods and services provided by other parties. In other words, it is the nature of the liabilities of banks, their deposits, which distinguish banks from shadow banks.[11]

The element of deposit-taking is important for a number of reasons. First, because the liabilities of banks are to a large extent part of the monetary system, the cost to banks of servicing these liabilities—in terms of the interest rates that have to be paid on them—is lower than for other institutions that raise non-deposit finance. The fact that deposits can be used as 'money'—that is, for transaction purposes—makes them valuable to customers in their own right and holders of deposit do not therefore require as high a return on their deposits as they do on their other investments. In effect, the depositors are paying the bank for the provision of liquidity services.

Second, because deposits are part of the payments system, the failure of a formal bank is of particular social and political as well as economic significance. The failure of a large bank or many banks might well threaten a country's payment system and as such is potentially a source of considerable turmoil.[12] We will discuss the mechanics of the payment system that would be disrupted, but in the simplest sense, when a bank fails, its depositors lose the capacity to make and receive payments. A company may have a zero balance on the day the bank fails, and thus suffer no loss, but what happens the next day when it was expecting to receive a customer payment that would in turn fund wage payments to its employees (many of whom may be depositors in the failed bank) and payments to its suppliers? Disruption to the 'payment channel' is immediately apparent and costly. Countries seek to avoid the risk of failures of their banks and they do so by offering protection in a number of forms. They more frequently and readily bail out banks than other institutions and corporations, and they provide insurance to depositors to protect them from risks of failure of their banks.

Banks are therefore able to raise finance more cheaply than non-bank institutions on several scores. First, they can raise funds more cheaply as a consequence of the use of deposits as a medium of exchange, through the cheque-drawing system.[13] Second, their depositors benefit from insurance—further lowering the bank's cost of deposit finance. Third, they tend to get bailed out by central banks and national governments in the event of failures, certainly if they are sufficiently large to threaten the functioning of a country's payment system. The costs of bail-outs, and to a lesser degree deposit insurance, are typically borne by the state rather than the banking sector. Banks thus benefit from implicit subsidies, which increase with size.[14] They are therefore particularly significant and favoured parts of an economy.

---

[11] US money market funds (and some asset management groups) offer retail customers cheque-drawing privileges that are in some respects equivalent to the monetary liabilities of banks. These accounts offer customers liquidity but not necessarily the safety of a sum certain in their account balances. Often the privileges are constrained by minimum amounts so they are not necessarily a full substitute for a bank account.

[12] See eg Independent Commission on Banking, *Final Report* (2011), para 4.10 ('A major disruption to the payments system could have a catastrophic social and economic impact').

[13] Or through wire-transfers and, more recently, debit cards.

[14] See J Noss and R Sowerbutts, 'The Implicit Subsidy of Banks', Bank of England Financial Stability Paper No 15 (2012).

By virtue of being a recognized deposit-taking institution, a bank has the ability to utilize its deposits as part of the payments system. Other financial institutions may perform very similar functions to banks but do not have the same ability to provide and create means of exchange. That confers a particular value on bank deposits over and above any interest and repayment characteristic that they might have.

As a provider of payment services, banks are members of systems for the clearing and settlement of transactions. When a cheque is drawn on one bank for payment into a customer in another bank, there is a centralized system of crediting the account and bank of the recipient customer and debiting the payee's account and bank. For example, in the UK, the Bank of England operates a Real-Time Gross Settlement system which provides for real-time irrevocable posting of debt and credit entries to individual accounts. We describe the payment and settlement system more fully in Chapter 18.

The payments system is vulnerable to failure. In the event of bankruptcy, transactions that are in the process of being settled are at risk of failing to be completed. Recipient banks may therefore not be in receipt of payments due which in turn might make them vulnerable to failure. The payments system is therefore one medium through which financial institutions and banks in particular are interconnected so that the failure of one impacts on the solvency of others.[15]

In the presence of such interconnections there are systemic concerns over and above those relating to the solvency of the institution in question. There is an externality in the sense that the exposure of one bank to failure may threaten the viability of a second, through correct and incorrect depositor inferences about its own solvency. The first bank may take account of the impact of its activities on its own customers but might well not take account of the effect on the customers of other financial institutions. The care that the first bank takes will therefore be insufficient in relation to what is required from a systemic perspective. For example, the chosen level of equity capital reserves and liquidity will be inadequate in relation to what the bank should hold to provide adequate protection for the system as a whole.

This is one of the justifications for the imposition of regulation to protect against systemic risk. In the absence of it, the payments system will be vulnerable to failure to the detriment of the citizens of a nation or a monetary union as a whole. We discuss 'macroprudential' regulation later in the chapter and in more detail in Chapter 19. At this stage it is just worth noting that the level of capital and liquidity required to protect against this will in general be well in excess of what is needed to safeguard depositors in the bank itself.

New technologies are raising questions about the degree to which it is really necessary to associate payments with banks. Like elsewhere, one of the most widely used payments systems in the UK for some time was run by the postal services. More recently, PayPal has provided an alternative electronic form of payments and mobile banking has begun to emerge, in particular in developing and emerging markets where bank branch networks are often sparse and banking services far from widely accessible.

---

[15] There are many other forms of interconnection—see eg the discussion in Chapter 3, section 3.4.3.

In a mobile money transaction, individuals make payments directly to other network customers by sending a text message. Mobile money accounts are credited with receipts from others and debited when payments are made. Cash can be paid into accounts and withdrawn from them. The payments system in mobile money therefore bypasses the banking system and any centralized system altogether.[16] Signals are sent directly by the mobile phone company.

In essence, then, it is possible to take payments outside of banks and have payments operating in parallel with the banking system. The implications of this are twofold. First, there is no *necessary* interrelation between banks via the payments system, which exacerbates systemic risks. Second, with mobile money, the protection of the payments system does not necessarily justify protection of banks.[17]

So, while payments are traditionally regarded as a central function of banks and a justification for their regulation, this is not *necessarily* the case. It is *possible* to imagine an economy in which the two are separated and the protection of banks is not necessary to uphold the security of the payments system. Is there anything else special about banks?

13.4 Monitoring and Screening

To this point, we have mainly focused on the liability side of banks' balance sheets and in particular, their deposits. As previously noted, a distinguishing feature of banks is the mismatch between the short-term, liquid nature of their liabilities and their long-term, illiquid assets. We now turn to the asset side and in particular, the loan book of banks. Table 13.1 presents a stylized bank balance sheet to help illustrate the discussion.

A primary function of banks is to lend money to individual and corporate borrowers. Of course, many other institutions and investors do that, not least bondholders who invest in corporations through markets rather than financial intermediaries. However, what distinguishes the lending activity of banks is the screening and monitoring role that they perform in evaluating prospective borrowers and overseeing the performance of the loans.[18] Of course, bondholders also screen their loans, often taking advantage of information intermediaries' services such as underwriters and credit rating agencies ('CRAs'),[19] but when it comes to monitoring loans performance they suffer from coordination costs, which mean they cannot perform this function as efficiently as banks.

---

[16] Of course, to the extent that cross-network payments are facilitated, this necessitates either routing via the banking system or the creation of an inter-network payment settlement system. Consortia of banks started MasterCard and Visa. Visa is still owned by 22,000 member banks, which compete for customers and yet cooperate. Visa's worldwide customer base is 750 million, clearing $125 trillion annually. MasterCard became a public company in 2006. It describes itself as operating a network that links a cardholder, a merchant, the card issuer (the cardholder's financial institution), and the 'acquirer' (the merchant's financial institution).

[17] It may instead justify the protection of non-bank payment system providers: see J Armour and D Awrey, 'Prioritizing the Implementation of International Financial Regulation', Commonwealth Secretariat Economic Paper No 95 (2015), 24. In developed countries, the embedded transaction account structure is likely to make banks central to the payments system for the foreseeable future. Not so in emerging market economies in which many savers are not 'included' in the traditional banking system.

[18] Diamond, n 4.   [19] See Chapter 6, sections 6.3.1 and 6.3.3.

Table 13.1 Stylized example of a bank balance sheet

Assets	$m	Liabilities	$m
Federal funds sold and securities purchased under resell agreement	170,000	Interest-bearing deposits	
		Savings	40,000
		Now and money market	220,000
Residential mortgages	170,000	CDs and time deposits	130,000
Credit cards	90,000	Federal funds purchases, securities sold under repurchase agreements	120,000
Consumer loans	110,000	Long-term debt	
Commercial loans and leases	100,000		
		Non-interest-bearing liabilities	130,000
Other assets	40,000		
Cash and cash equivalents	30,000	Shareholders' equity	70,000
Total assets	**710,000**	**Total liabilities and equity**	**710,000**

The intense screening and monitoring that banks perform are particularly signifi-cant in relation to small and medium-sized companies.[20] For such firms, there is only limited information in the public domain.[21] For example, in the absence of mandates to this effect, most private companies in the US do not publish accounts at all. Moreover, such companies are often younger, and so have no established reputation. This makes careful scrutiny—of the sort in which banks specialize—particularly important. The nature of the risks involved in investing in a small company will be dependent on the nature of the individuals involved as well as the investments that will be made with the loans.

Typically, loan officers evaluate bank loans according to a standard set of proced-ures. In the case of individual borrowers, those focus on credit-scoring techniques by which the creditworthiness of prospective borrowers is evaluated by reference to the characteristics, financial condition, and past record of the borrowers. In the case of corporate borrowers the information is more complex, involving an assessment of a variety of factors.

A system that has been conventionally employed is known as the 'CAMEL' procedure—Capital, Asset quality, Management, Earnings, and Liquidity. *Capital* relates to the equity available to provide protection against fluctuations in performance along the lines described in section 13.2. *Asset quality* relates to the nature and value of the assets that the company holds. What condition are the assets in? What is their serviceable life? To what extent are assets impaired in the sense that their economic

---

[20] See AM Robb and DT Robinson, 'The Capital Structure Decisions of New Firms' (2014) *Review of Financial Studies* 153 (observing that principal source of outside finance for newly formed firms in the US is bank debt).

[21] As discussed in Chapter 8, sections 8.4.3–8.4.4, the fixed costs of disclosure fall disproportionately heavily on smaller firms.

value falls below their purchase price or historic cost? The enquiry continues by asking what is the quality of top *managers*? What is their track record and how well are they suited to the purpose of the business? What are the current and projected *earnings* of the business and what are the anticipated cash flows? By how much do the projected earnings provide the firm with cash—*liquidity*—to cover interest payments and repayment of loans?

The screening of loans is an extensive data-collection exercise. So too is the process of monitoring the performance of loans. Loan officers are responsible for ongoing evaluation of their loan portfolio and identifying cases where there is a risk of loan impairment in the sense of companies not being able to service their loans. Increasingly, sophisticated software is used to assist in the processing of initial borrower characteristics and subsequent borrower behaviour.

Where there are doubts about the viability of corporate borrowings, the loan officers will seek remedial action. The loan contracts that are signed with companies will contain detailed covenants, promises made by the borrower in addition to repaying the loan.[22] These typically relate, for example, to the maintenance of assets, maximum levels of leverage, and payment of dividends. They include restrictions on new borrowings and on significant changes in the nature of the business. They confer rights on banks to intervene in the event of a company violating any of these covenants.

The types of remedial action that a bank might require of a troubled company include changes in the company's financial structure—the issue of new equity or reductions in dividend distributions and shares buy-backs, the curtailment of plans to invest or acquire other companies, and changes in the firm's management.[23] The covenants restrict the freedom of a company to pursue activities that might be detrimental to the solvency of the firm.

In the event that such restrictions fail to prevent the firm from getting into difficulty, the bank has two options. The first is to work with the company in restructuring its activities, liabilities, and assets by putting together a 'work-out' plan to restore the firm to financial health. Such informal restructurings will be the first response of banks to financial distress of their borrowers.[24] If that fails, banks will seek to recover their loans or as much of them as possible through formal bankruptcy and insolvency procedures.

The whole process from initial screening to subsequent monitoring and, where necessary, work-outs and bankruptcies of borrowers is costly and time-consuming. A substantial fraction of a commercial bank's resources will be devoted to the lending function. It differs appreciably from bond markets where in place of loan officers, creditors mainly rely on CRAs to perform some of these functions. We have discussed

---

[22] See generally, CW Smith, Jr and JB Warner, 'On Financial Contracting: An Analysis of Bond Covenants' (1979) 7 *Journal of Financial Economics* 117; L Gullifer and J Payne, *Corporate Finance Law: Principles and Policy* (Oxford: Hart Publishing, 2011), Ch 5; M Bradley and MR Roberts, 'The Structure and Pricing of Corporate Debt Covenants' (2015) 5 *Quarterly Journal of Finance*.

[23] See eg SC Gilson, 'Management Turnover and Financial Distress' (1989) 25 *Journal of Financial Economics* 241; J Franks, C Mayer, and L Renneboog, 'Who Disciplines Management in Poorly Performing Companies?' (2001) 10 *Journal of Financial Intermediation* 209.

[24] See J Armour and S Frisby, 'Rethinking Receivership' (2001) 21 *Oxford Journal of Legal Studies* 73, 91–5; J Franks and O Sussman, 'Financial Distress and Bank Restructuring of Small to Medium Size UK Companies' (2005) 9 *Review of Financial Studies* 65, 74–5.

the role of CRAs in relation to information in markets in Chapter 6, but suffice it to say here that the amount of resources per dollar of loan that is devoted to loan evaluations is far less within CRAs than within banks. Typically, a CRA may employ a handful of people to evaluate all the corporations in a particular industry in comparison to the allocation of a small portfolio of loans to a particular loan officer in a bank.

As a result, the administrative cost of bank lending is large relative to bond finance. Furthermore, intermediation by the bank would appear to create a layer between investors (depositors) and borrowers (companies), which itself needs monitoring. Can depositors be sure that banks are performing their screening and monitoring functions adequately? In one respect the answer may be yes. In comparison to evaluating the performance of individual loans, evaluating the performance of banks might be relatively straightforward. Since they are investing in a large number of companies and the largely unpredictable returns of individual borrowers should average out to a predictable average return of the bank's portfolio as a whole, the bank's predicted performance should be comparatively easy to evaluate. So, for example, if the average return on loans in a bank's portfolio is 5 per cent, then the bank should be able to earn a return of 5 per cent across all its loans. By investing in a portfolio of a large number of loans, the performance of banks should be less volatile than the individual loans.[25]

In practice, monitoring bank performance is complicated by the myriad of activities in which banks engage. In addition, there are so many depositors in any bank that none of them has any incentive to engage in its monitoring. Furthermore, they in general lack the confidential information and expertise required to do so.

As a consequence, the regulation of banks is a critical and necessary function, and regulators (supervisors) with access to confidential information are employed to evaluate the quality of banking activity.[26] Regulators frequently deploy similar types of monitoring tools to the ones that banks use. So, for example, in the US the CAMEL classification was used by bank regulators in evaluating banks as well as by banks in evaluating their own loans.

13.5 The Regulation of Banks

The market failures stemming from the asymmetries of information and externalities described in the previous sections give rise to the need for a variety of forms of bank regulation. There are four in particular that are widely employed: entry requirements, governance rules, prudential requirements, and resolution.

Entry requirements relate to the structural feature of banks at the time that they apply for banking licences. They have to demonstrate that they have appropriate personnel in charge of the bank and adequate systems for managing their operations and their portfolio. The board of directors and the senior management have to be 'fit and proper' for the functions that they perform. They have to be persons of good

---

[25] Diamond, n 4.

[26] See M Dewatripont and J Tirole, *The Prudential Regulation of Banks* (Cambridge, MA: MIT Press, 1994).

repute, with a sound record of management in the past. They have to be appropriately qualified for the functions that they perform and to have training and experience that is suitable for their roles in the bank.

Governance rules focus on the structures and processes that are fit for a bank's functions. They require boards to have an adequate number of independent members from sufficiently diverse and appropriate backgrounds, to give them a proper induction and to evaluate their performance on a regular basis.

In addition, the bank has to have operating systems that are sound and reliable and fit for their intended purposes. It has to have appropriate methods of screening and monitoring prospective and existing borrowers. It has to be able to contain and manage the scale of its loan losses and to remedy failing loans. An essential tool to achieve this is internal and external systems of risk management that are capable of identifying the main risk exposures of the bank and the ways of mitigating its risks. Risk officers reporting to the board and risk committees that have sufficient authority in the bank to ensure that they can adequately control the bank's risks are regarded as key elements of such risk management systems.

After the crisis, another focus of governance rules has been managerial compensation, which is now heavily regulated. We discuss it further in Chapter 17, together with other bank governance requirements.

Prudential rules require banks to hold appropriate levels of capital and liquidity. They have to monitor the risks of their loans and relate their level of capital and liquidity to the scale and nature of the bank's risks. Chapters 14 and 15 discuss capital and liquidity requirements that are imposed on banks.

Finally, precisely because the failure of a bank may impose significant externalities, special 'resolution' procedures have been devised to minimize the cost of these failures. One of the major post-financial crisis policy questions has been the search for a resolution strategy that minimizes the knock-on effects of failure of systemically important financial institutions while avoiding a taxpayer bail-out. This is the subject of Chapter 16.

13.6 Conclusion

This chapter has discussed the role of banks in a financial system. It has emphasized their importance in relation to provision of liquidity, payments, and lending. It has noted their role in relation to performing liquidity, maturity, and credit transformation in converting illiquid, long-term, risky assets into liquid, short-term, low-risk liabilities. This is quite a feat and it is not surprising that banks are regarded as so special.

However, we have also noted that there are other operators that perform very similar functions to banks. Liquidity, maturity, and credit transformation are therefore neither the sole nor unique functions of banks.

What does distinguish banks from other institutions, however, is the nature of their liabilities, which are part of the monetary system and can be used as a means of payment. Insofar as monetary systems are critical to the functioning of economies then so, too, are their banks. A failure of banks has repercussions well beyond savings and lending to the core process of exchange in an economy.

It is no wonder then, that the financial crisis generated considerable concern about the robustness of countries' banking systems and the ways in which this should be strengthened. These debates have raised fundamental questions about the nature and purpose of banking and the way in which regulatory authorities should seek to protect banks. It is a topic that will in particular concern us when we discuss the macroprudential supervision of banks in Chapter 19.

14

Capital Regulation

14.1 Introduction

14.1.1 The role of capital and liquidity regulation

In Chapter 13, we outlined the basic business model of commercial banks: taking on liabilities by way of short-term debt provided by retail depositors and the wholesale money markets and using them to make medium- and long-term loans to businesses and households (the principal component of the bank's assets). The core of the bank's business thus expresses itself in the transformation it effects between the liability and the asset sides of its balance sheet. This transformation process has three facets. The bank turns short-term funding into medium- and long-term loans (maturity transformation), liquid liabilities (demand or short-notice debt) into much less liquid loans (liquidity transformation), and riskless[1] deposits into risky loans (credit transformation). Or, looking at it the other way around, the bank provides short-term, liquid, and riskless deposits (and other short-term liabilities) on the back of medium-term, illiquid, and risky assets.

This is a very valuable societal function. Without this process of transformation, the supply of investment funds to the productive economy would be reduced and households would be less able to manage their financial needs. Yet, the risks attached to such transformation are stark. The bank may misjudge the creditworthiness of its borrowers (credit risk) so that the value of its assets sinks below its liabilities and the bank becomes insolvent in the balance sheet sense. Or the bank may suffer an unexpected withdrawal of funds by short-term lenders, which exhausts its liquid assets. Here the risk is of inability to pay debts as they fall due.[2] In short, the lack of 'fit' between assets and liabilities means that banks' financial structure is inherently fragile.

The standard mechanisms for addressing these risks are also well established. The higher the level of the bank's capital (sometimes referred to as the 'shareholders' equity'—that is, funding contributed by the shareholders either by way of purchase of shares from the bank or retention by the bank of profits earned), the less the risk of balance sheet insolvency, because any losses the bank incurs on its assets will first fall on the shareholders. So long as the bank's losses do not exceed its equity, it will still have positive net assets (that is, assets less liabilities). Thus, 'leverage'—the ratio of the bank's debt funding to its funding through equity or capital—is always a central issue

---

[1] 'Riskless' not in the sense that the depositor is sure to be repaid (indeed the risk to depositors of non-payment is central to this chapter) but in the sense that the value of the deposit is not expected by the depositor to vary with the creditworthiness of the bank in the way that the value of a bond does. In the jargon, this liability is expected to be 'information insensitive'.

[2] In relation to non-financial firms, inability to pay current debts and a shortfall of assets against liabilities are both referred to as 'insolvency'. In the context of banks, however, the term is generally used only for the latter, with the former being referred to as 'illiquidity'.

Principles of Financial Regulation. First Edition. John Armour, Dan Awrey, Paul Davies, Luca Enriques, Jeffrey N. Gordon, Colin Mayer, and Jennifer Payne. © John Armour, Dan Awrey, Paul Davies, Luca Enriques, Jeffrey N. Gordon, Colin Mayer, and Jennifer Payne 2016. Published 2016 by Oxford University Press.

in bank regulation. The more equity, the safer the bank; but a bank funded entirely by equity would achieve no transformation. Equally, the higher the level of liquid assets the bank holds (that is, cash or assets easily convertible into cash), the easier it will be to meet demands from depositors, thus reducing the risk of liquidity crises. Again, however, a bank with wholly liquid assets would do no transformation.

It would be wrong to conclude that capital regulation addresses only the risks on the asset side of a bank's balance sheet (such as making bad loans), while liquidity regulation addresses only the risk of an unexpected withdrawal of short-term deposits. Problems on one side of the balance sheet quickly spread to the other side. Consequently, both types of regulation have an impact on both sets of problems; and both are central to promoting the safety and soundness of banks.

Take an unexpected and extensive withdrawal of deposits (a 'bank run'). This risk is addressed through the bank's holding of liquid assets. However, if the withdrawal demand exceeds the bank's store of liquid assets, it will turn to selling its illiquid loans or to using them as collateral for loans to the bank from third parties. It is unlikely to realize the full value of its loans in this way: it will obtain low prices in a sale or suffer large 'haircuts' if the assets are used as collateral.[3] First, the bank will be under greater pressure to sell than buyers will be to buy (in other words, it will be a 'fire sale'). Second, bank loans are notoriously difficult for outsiders to value, so the principle of adverse selection will mean buyers (or lenders) will treat the loans as having a lesser value than they may in fact have. However, a bank will be better able to absorb the losses on a forced sale of its assets or the implicit marking-down of the value of its assets when borrowing against them, if it has a high level of capital. So, in terms of the bank's capacity to survive a run, a very high level of capital could function as a substitute for a very high level of liquidity.

Similarly, a problem on the asset side of the balance sheet may—in fact is very likely to—have its first impact on the bank through a withdrawal of funds by either retail or wholesale funders, as the asset problem becomes known outside the bank. A bank with a high level of liquid assets may thus secure enough time to fix the problem with its assets, even though it holds only a modest level of capital.

None of this is news to those who manage or invest in banks. Thus, the question arises, why not leave it to bank boards and shareholders to decide how much equity capital the bank should hold and what percentage of its assets should be in liquid form? This is the approach corporate law adopts towards these issues in non-financial companies.[4] The answer, by and large, is to be found in the prediction that bank boards and shareholders will under-price the risks of failure, because only some of the negative consequences of bank failure will be borne by them.[5] As we noted in

---

[3] A common form of borrowing is the 'repurchase' agreement ('repo') in which the assets serve as collateral for loans. Valuation uncertainties will induce lenders to insist on greater discounts (or 'haircuts') to ensure that the repo loans are fully secured. Repos are more fully described in Chapter 20, section 20.3.2, and Chapter 21, section 21.2.

[4] Even in those jurisdictions which have minimum capital requirements for public companies, these are normally set at a trivial level; and constraints on distributions rarely go beyond setting profits earned as their outer parameter.

[5] This is not to say that bank managers and shareholders suffer no losses if a bank fails. In fact, the more valuable the bank franchise, the greater the losses they are likely to suffer. Consequently, competition policy

Chapter 13, a substantial proportion of the costs of bank failure are externalities, accruing beyond the failing bank itself and indeed outside the financial sector.[6] If, for example, the failure or prospective failure of a bank causes other banks to hoard cash and not to lend, the resulting 'credit crunch' may severely restrict the flow of funds to businesses and households and thus contribute to a significantly lower level of economic activity, as the aftermath of the recent financial crisis showed only too well.

If bank managers and shareholders under-price the risks attached to the bank's business model,[7] there is a potential role for regulation to address this market failure. That is, regulation could aim to mimic the capital and liquidity decisions which would be taken by bank controllers fully exposed to the costs of bank failure and thus to internalize the full costs of banks' activities. In terms of our typology of regulatory strategies, this is *prudential regulation*.[8] However, it may not be wise for regulation to go so far as full internalization of the costs of bank failure. Ordinarily, banking generates positive externalities—that is, the benefits from lending to businesses, households, and society in general (for example, higher employment and higher tax revenues), and these too are not fully captured by the banks' shareholders and managers. Regulation should take account of the positive as well as the negative externalities of banking activity.

More generally, this argument for regulation shows that it is the 'systemic' consequences of bank failure which provide the most powerful rationale for regulation, to minimize the impact of bank failure on the 'real' economy. This has important implications for how the regulation of banks should be perceived, the implications of which were not fully appreciated until the recent financial crisis. The aim of regulation should be to promote the safety and soundness of the banking system, not necessarily of individual banks. Individual banks can—and should—be allowed to fail, if the systemic consequences of failure can be contained.[9] Ensuring the survival of all banks, but at the cost of a severe impairment of their transformation potential, cannot be regarded as the achievement of systemic health.

This insight has two further important implications for capital and liquidity regulation of banks. First, it may be appropriate to have more demanding capital and liquidity requirements for banks which are systemically important—assuming such can be effectively identified. Second, the impact of capital and liquidity regulation on the capacity or incentives of banks to lend to the real economy needs to be carefully considered, both in relation to their overall capacity to lend and in relation to their capacity or incentives to lend at different points in the business cycle. We will see both

is a double-edged sword here. It may reduce costs to consumers but may also reduce the incentives to run the bank safely.

[6] Of course, the failure of a large non-financial corporation may also give rise to externalities (think of its trading partners or the local community in which it operates), but the scale of the problem is far larger with the collapse of a large financial company.

[7] Diversified shareholders might be less prone to under-price these risks because they may bear the externalities of bank failure through a diminution in the value of their non-financial holdings, yet the governance set-up of banks undercuts the pursuit of this set of interests: see J Armour and JN Gordon, 'Systemic Harms and Shareholder Value' (2014) 6 *Journal of Legal Analysis* 35.

[8] See Chapter 3, section 3.5.

[9] See Chapter 16 on ways of resolving failing banks.

these factors at play throughout this chapter. The role of regulation in providing systemic protection will be discussed further in Chapter 19.

14.1.2 What is a bank?

What is a 'Bank'? Legal Definitions

EU: '"Credit institution" is an undertaking the business of which is to take deposits or other repayable funds from the public and to grant credits for its own account...' Regulation (EU) No 575/2013, Art 4.1(1).

US: 'An institution...which both—(i) accepts demand deposits or deposits that the depositor may withdraw by check or similar means for payment to third parties or others; and (ii) is engaged in the business of making commercial loans. Bank Holding Company Act 1956 (US), §2(c).

So far, we have treated the definition of a bank as non-contentious. Legal definitions of a bank focus on precisely the elements we have identified as generating the central risks of the bank's business model. These are funding via short-term deposits and the making of loans.

These definitions are based on function, so it does not matter what the institution is called if in fact it engages in the activity described. For example, a 'building society' in the UK or a 'savings and loan association' in the US borrows short from depositors and lends long to individuals who wish to purchase living accommodation and so is to be regarded as a bank within the definitions.[10]

A more significant feature of these definitions of the banking function is that they omit a substantial proportion of what large banks actually do. Small banks may not discharge much more than the core functions of taking deposits and making loans to households and businesses, but as we saw in Chapter 2, large universal banks, such as Barclays, Citigroup, Deutsche Bank, and HSBC, do a great deal more. They provide services such as underwriting to companies seeking access to the capital markets, provide advice to companies seeking to carry out mergers or acquisitions, act as market makers in various securities markets, create derivative instruments, and even trade in securities on their own account—that is, proprietary trading. The safety and soundness of deposit-taking banks that engage in this wider range of activities are obviously important for the stability of the financial system. But how can capital and liquidity regulation reach such activities, given the narrow legal definition of a bank?

A large part of the answer is that, once a company engages in activities which qualify it as a bank, *all* its activities are taken into account in assessing its capital and liquidity requirements. Equally, the parent company of a group containing a bank is subject to capital and liquidity requirements that reflect the financial activities of the group as a

---

[10] Perhaps for this reason, the EU definition does not claim to be a definition of a 'bank' but of a 'credit institution'.

whole. On this approach, investment banking (or 'broker-dealer') activities are assessed when setting the capital and liquidity requirements of the bank or banking group, even though those activities are not relevant to the legal definition of a bank. Thus, the Basel rules apply to the holding company of a banking group so as to take into account all group financial activities.[11]

However, this extension of banking regulation gives rise to a further puzzle. Should a financial institution or group which engages in the same range of activities as a large bank, but is not funded by deposits, be subject to the same capital and liquidity requirements as a deposit-taker that engages in this wider range of activities? We might be prepared to give a negative answer if such non-bank financial institutions were free of the mismatch between assets and liabilities at the heart of the standard commercial bank model. But this is not the case. As we shall see in Chapter 21, non-deposit-taking broker-dealers (as well as ones that are members of a banking group) fund themselves extensively in the short-term credit market, especially the 'repo' market, thus using short-term loans to finance the acquisition of assets. Those assets may typically be tradable but, in a crisis, may quickly lose their liquidity. Their value as collateral in repos is substantially reduced in consequence, thus giving rise to a 'repo run' not dissimilar from a retail depositor bank run. Non-bank broker-dealers are, in general, even more highly leveraged than commercial banks.[12] And their capacity for the transmission of contagion is high.

A good example of the issue was the collapse of Lehman Brothers, a non-deposit-taker, in late 2008, which considerably intensified the financial crisis.[13] However, this particular problem of non-bank broker-dealers has largely been resolved since the crisis: the large US broker-dealers either failed, were forced into mergers with commercial banks, or their parents chose to reconfigure themselves as bank holding companies. The problem was largely a US phenomenon in any event, probably a result of the banking legislation of the 1930s. Elsewhere in the world, the 'universal' banking model prevailed, whereby investment banks also functioned as, or were members of groups which contained, deposit-takers.

The takeaway is that, although deposit-taking and granting loans are the key constituents of the definition of a bank, prudential regulation—in the form of bank

---

[11] On the significance of the Basel rules see section 14.1.3. They state as follows: 'The scope of application of the Framework will include, on a fully consolidated basis, any holding company that is the parent entity within a banking group to ensure that it captures the risk of the whole banking group. Banking groups are groups that engage predominantly in banking activities and, in some countries, a banking group may be registered as a bank....To the greatest extent possible, all banking and other relevant financial activities (both regulated and unregulated) conducted within a group containing an internationally active bank will be captured through consolidation.' BIS/BCBS, *International Convergence of Capital Measurement and Capital Standards: A Revised Framework—Comprehensive Version*, bcbs128 (2006), paras 20 and 24. This document contains the Basel II rules, but the same scoping provisions apply to Basel III. There is a separate question, which we discuss in Chapter 23, as to whether restrictions should be placed, for financial stability reasons, on the range of financial activities that banking groups may carry on. In this chapter we discuss the capital and liquidity consequences of the set of *permitted* activities.

[12] Even after the crisis, the US Financial Stability Oversight Council (FSOC) reports that broker-dealers operate on aggregate at twenty-two times leverage, more than the typical commercial bank: FSOC, *Annual Report 2013* (2014), 82.

[13] Discussed in more detail in Chapters 1 and 21.

capital and liquidity rules—needs to take account of the fact that the largest banks engage in a much wider range of activities. In this chapter, when we refer to a 'bank', we mean a firm which takes deposits and makes medium- and long-term loans, no matter what else it may do or what its formal title may be. When we want to refer to a firm which does not fall within the statutory definition of a bank, we will use the term 'financial institution' or qualify the term 'bank' in some way, for example by using the phrase 'investment bank'.

14.1.3 The Basel Committee on Banking Supervision

For the purposes of the discussion in this chapter, we will focus primarily on the rules developed by the Basel Committee on Banking Supervision (the 'Basel Committee' or 'BCBS')—*de facto*, the global standard-setter in this area. The Basel Committee, through its Accord of 1988 ('Basel I') and its successors (Basel II (2004) and Basel III (2010)—although the latter is not yet fully in force),[14] has become 'the dominant power in banking regulation' despite being, initially, an informal creation of central bankers lacking 'powers, constitution or even legal existence'.[15] Its rules on banks' capital and liquidity are widely followed, not only by the thirty or so states represented on the Committee, but also by a much wider range of countries. While the Basel rules have no legally binding force at national level—even in states represented on the Committee— there is a system of peer pressure, organized by the Basel Committee, to promote compliance.[16] The Basel rules are also expressed to be minimum standards, so that more demanding standards may be set in national implementation, consistently with the Basel framework. Substantial lobbying efforts over national implementation of particular aspects of the Basel rules are thus common. In particular, the Accords apply formally only to internationally active banks, but some jurisdictions (for example, the US and the EU) apply them to all banks. However, from our point of view the crucial thing about the Basel rules is that they illustrate the policy dilemmas that any set of capital and liquidity standards will have to resolve. By understanding how to analyse the Basel choices, you will be able to analyse any different set of choices made by national and regional regulators.

Today, the Basel rules deal with both capital and liquidity regulation (though initially they left out liquidity). We will deal with capital regulation in this chapter and liquidity regulation in the following one. Besides avoiding an over-long chapter, this approach can be justified on the grounds that the two regulatory strategies have different impacts on banks' transformation processes—liquidity requirements being potentially much more intrusive but also arguably more useful in providing a safety net for banks in financial crises.

---

[14] In fact the timetable for the introduction of Basel III is an elongated one. The capital and liquidity requirements of Basel III are not required to be fully implemented until January 2019. The analysis in this chapter generally assumes they are fully in force.

[15] S Gleeson, *International Regulation of Banking*, 2nd ed (Oxford: OUP, 2012), 33. We discuss the Basel Committee in the context of international financial regulatory coordination in Chapter 28.

[16] Within the EU, implementation is largely a matter for Union law.

These minimum capital and liquidity rules constitute just one of the three 'pillars' of the Basel regime, though we will analyse the other two pillars less deeply. Pillar 2 deals with the role of national or regional supervisors. Supervision is considered more fully in Chapter 26, but we should note here that supervisors under Pillar 2 may add to the capital and liquidity requirements of particular banks which cause them concern. Such additions are often made after 'stress tests' which reveal that a particular bank or banks would not have a good chance of survival in the stressed scenario, despite their compliance with the Basel minima. Or the Pillar 2 powers may be used to implement the Basel III requirements more quickly than is formally required.[17] Pillar 3 requires banks to disclose to the market data on how they approach capital adequacy, in order to co-opt market discipline to the regulator's goals.

The rest of the chapter proceeds as follows. We examine in turn the fundamental choices made by the Basel Committee when designing the capital rules and consider various critiques of those choices which have been advanced. By the end of the chapter you should have a good understanding of the potential and limits of capital regulation to reduce the fragility of banks.

14.2 Setting Capital Rules: The Main Issues

The core idea behind capital rules for banks is that shareholders' equity should fund a minimum proportion of the current value of the bank's assets, in order to increase the chances that a bank will be able to absorb losses on the assets side of its balance sheet without becoming insolvent and, more importantly, without triggering a run on its deposits or other short-term funding. This requirement is imposed, not only at formation, but on a continuing basis. Moreover, it is adjusted as the amount and quality of the bank's assets varies.[18] It is a restriction on the bank's leverage—that is, it constrains the extent to which the bank can finance itself through debt. Thus, a 10 per cent capital requirement would require the bank to hold capital equivalent to 10 per cent of the value of the bank's assets. The other 90 per cent of the value of the assets could be financed by debt. A 10 per cent capital requirement would imply a debt-to-equity ratio of 9:1.

The implementation of this simple idea requires, however, a series of further questions to be answered. The main ones, since inception, were as follows.

- Against which risks should capital be held?
- Should the capital requirement be formulated as a percentage of the face value of the assets or should that value be risk weighted?
- How should capital be defined?
- How much capital should be required?

---

[17] See 'Global Banks Reach Almost All 2019 Capital Standards' (*Financial Times*, 15 September 2015), reporting that at the end of 2014 the 100 largest internationally active banks met the 2019 Basel requirements for CET1 capital, but less progress had been made in relation to liquidity requirements and the leverage ratio.

[18] It is thus very different from the minimum capital requirement known to some corporate laws. That is aimed at undercapitalized start-ups and is calculated only once—on formation—and, typically, is specified as an amount of money rather than as a proportion of the assets.

After the financial crisis, an answer was given to these additional questions.

- How to avoid the procyclical impact of capital requirements, namely that they are too lax in an economic upswing and too constraining in the downswing?
- Is the same ratio appropriate for all banks, no matter what their systemic importance?
- Should the ratio vary depending on factors that increase the bank's risk of failure (eg a greater fraction of 'wholesale' short-term liabilities)?

In the following sections we shall examine how the Basel Committee decided these central policy questions and how those decisions changed over time as the limitations of the initial policy choices became apparent. We shall also examine the arguments in favour of different choices.

14.3 Against Which Risks Should Capital be Held?

The commercial banking model suggests that the main risk against which capital should be held is credit risk—that is, the risk that borrowers will not repay. This indeed is the basis upon which Basel I approached this question. Banks were required to hold capital only against *credit risk*. As we discuss in Chapter 20, significant amounts of credit intermediation have moved from commercial banks to market intermediaries, a transition initially spurred by free-standing investment banks. Commercial banks have followed into market intermediation, if only for competitive reasons. With the expansion of the investment banking activities of large banks (or banking groups), however, it became clear that *trading risk* was an important source of fragility for such banks. Trading risk is the risk that securities which banks hold, for market-making or proprietary-trading purposes, suffer a decline in market value.

With the 'market risk amendment' of 1996 (coming between Basel I and Basel II), the Committee moved to bring trading risks explicitly within the Basel Framework. At this time, banks' non-loan assets consisted principally of relatively simple positions taken in relation to equity or debt securities that traded on liquid markets. The potential loss the bank faced was conceived as continuing for a relatively short time, only until the securities could be disposed of in the market. The task was thus to calculate the possible loss on the portfolio in this period and apply the capital charge as a percentage of the resulting number.

By the time of the crisis, however, large banks had moved beyond holding simple positions in traded securities into large holdings of credit instruments that often did not trade in deep and liquid markets. The largest losses in the crisis resulted from mortgage trading, trading in asset-backed securities, credit derivatives, loan origination and syndication, and securitization warehousing.[19] In all these cases the assumption of

---

[19] BIS/BCBS, *Fundamental Review of the Trading Book*, bcbs219 (2012), Annex 1, Figure 2.

an always-available liquid market was inappropriate. Absent an effective market, the holders of such instruments faced the risk of a default by, or credit-downgrade of, the counterparty (counterparty credit risk). This risk, although central to risk assessment in the banking book, was not part of the risk assessment in the trading book.

Both gaps were plugged by measures introduced immediately after the financial crisis (usually referred to as 'Basel 2.5') and, more fully, in Basel III.[20] Referring to the latter, the Committee has estimated that, 'the revised trading book framework, on average, requires banks to hold additional capital of around three to four times the old capital requirements'.[21] Despite these patches being applied, with apparently increasing desperation, to the machinery for the assessment of market risk, the regulatory structure for market risk does not inspire a high level of confidence, even in the Basel Committee itself. Risk weightings for market risk vary very widely across banks, the variations not being fully explained by variations in banks' holdings but seemingly by their choice of model for assessing market risk.[22] In its recently completed 'fundamental review'[23] of the trading book the Committee pointed out that the division between the banking book and the trading book (which currently turns on the bank's intentions—to hold or to trade—in relation to the asset) is very difficult to police and yet of fundamental importance in the light of the different risk-assessment methodologies deployed in the two areas. Overall in relation to market risk, the Basel rules have been playing 'catch up' with what banks actually do.

In addition to credit risk and trading risk, *operational* risk has been identified as a third capital-triggering category. With the growing complexity of investment banks and the opacity of their trading operations even to insiders, the risk of large losses from employee fraud has risen (as notoriously happened in the cases of Barings Bank in 1995 and Société Générale in 2008). Operational risk embraces a number of internal risks beyond employee fraud, including, for example, the breakdown of computer systems or even simple failure of different parts of complex organizations to coordinate their activities effectively (the problem of 'silos'). This risk was recognized for capital purposes in Basel II. The capital charge for operational risk is set, essentially, as a percentage of the bank's gross income rather than its assets. In light of the now-critical importance of IT for bank operations and the growing intensity of malware attacks, it seems likely that this calibration will also become viewed as too coarse.[24]

---

[20] See generally, BIS, *International Regulatory Framework for Banks (Basel III)*, http://www.bis.org/bcbs/basel3.htm (accessed 25 August 2015).

[21] BIS/BCBS, *The Basel Committee's Response to the Financial Crisis: Report to the G20*, bcbs179 (2010), 5.

[22] BIS/BCBS, *Regulatory Consistency Assessment Programme (RCAP): Analysis of Risk-Weighted Assets for Market Risk*, bcbs240 (2013); BIS/BCBS, *Regulatory Consistency Assessment Programme (RCAP): Second Report on Risk-Weighted Assets for Market Risk*, bcbs267 (2013).

[23] BIS/BCBS, *Fundamental Review of the Trading Book*, bcbs219 (2012). For the resulting reform see *Minimum Capital Requirements for Market Risk*, bcbs352 (January 2016).

[24] BIS/BCBS, *Operational Risk—Revisions to the Simpler Approaches: Consultation Document*, bcbs291 (2014).

14.4 Risk-Weighting of Assets

14.4.1 The idea of risk-weighting

The Basel Committee can thus be said to have been rather slow at identifying the full range of risks to which internationally active banks (the Basel constituency) are subject and in setting capital requirements to match that range. However, much more controversial has been the question of how the amount of required (or 'regulatory') capital should be calibrated, once the risks have been identified. There are two sub-issues in the calibration debate: how much capital should be required and should that capital requirement be risk-weighted? In this section we deal with the second issue and again we shall see that trading risk posed the most difficult issues. We then turn to the first issue in the next section.

The capital requirement is set as a percentage of the bank's assets. It is not a fixed monetary amount. It is a ratio and so it can be adjusted by changing either of its two elements: the numerator—the bank's capital—or the denominator, its assets. In particular, a higher ratio can result from increasing capital or lowering the value of the assets.

Even after all the classes of risky assets held by the bank have been identified, there remains the question of whether the percentage capital charge should be applied equally across all the bank's assets. Although the Basel headline charge is presented as a single figure (8 per cent), only a modest amount of investigation into the Basel rulebook reveals that the value of the denominator in the ratio varies according to the perceived riskiness of different classes of asset. This is achieved by risk-weighting different types of asset, so that the 8 per cent capital charge is applied to a *notional* valuation of the asset, which may be greater or lesser than the face value of the asset. The capital charge in consequence may be either greater or less than 8 per cent of face value.

For example, if the loan is weighted at 100 per cent and the amount of the loan is $200, the capital charge is $16 (0.08 x 200). However, if the loan is weighted at 50 per cent, the capital charge is reduced by half to $8 (0.08 x 100), whereas if the weighting is 150 per cent, then the capital charge is increased by half to $24 (0.08 x 300). So, depending on the composition of the bank's loans, its effective capital charge may be significantly different from the headline figure of 8 per cent. In particular, if the loans are concentrated in the less risky half of the rating distribution, the effective charge will be significantly lower.

The Basel Accords have always adopted a risk-weighted approach but, over time, the risk-weighting methodology has become more sophisticated and responsibility for risk-weighting has moved increasingly from the regulators to the banks themselves.

The intuition behind risk-weighting is obvious enough: a bank which, for example, lends $10 billion to the German government is running less risk than a bank which lends a similar amount to a company set up for the purpose of searching for oil in a part of the world that is geologically and politically challenging. A non-risk weighted requirement would not capture this risk differential and would therefore incentivize banks to engage in the latter type of lending.

Table 14.1 Standardized approach—claims on corporates

Credit Assessment	AAA to AA−	A+ to A−	BBB+ to BB−	Below BB−	Unrated
Risk Weight	20%	50%	100%	150%	100%

Table 14.2 Claims on sovereigns and central banks

Credit Assessment	AAA to AA−	A+ to A−	BBB+ to BBB−	BB+ to B−	Below B−	Unrated
Risk Weight	0%	20%	50%	100%	150%	100%

Source: BIS/BCBS, *International Convergence of Capital Measurement and Capital Standards: A Revised Framework—Comprehensive Version*, bcbs128 (2006), paras 53 and 66.

However, the decision to risk-weight still leaves open the question of how granular the risk assessment is to be. Under Basel I, bank loan assets were divided into a small number of different types ('buckets') and risk-weights were assigned to each bucket by the rules themselves. This was a rather unsophisticated approach, taking no account of varying risks within each bucket. Under Basel II, the process became more sophisticated and complex. Within each bucket, the capital requirement is adjusted upwards or downwards according to the riskiness of the asset. Tables 14.1 and 14.2 set out two examples of the results of this process, relating to bank exposures to corporate borrowers (the vast majority of the claims owned by any bank) and to sovereigns or their central banks. These loans are risk-weighted according to the borrower's credit rating.

Loans to retail customers (another big chunk of banks' business) are more simply risk-weighted. A well-diversified portfolio of unsecured loans to individuals and small businesses is typically risk-weighted at 75 per cent, and claims secured on residential property at 35 per cent.

14.4.2 Using banks' internal models to produce risk weights

While the risk-weighting approach has roused some controversy, still more controversial has been the migration of the risk-weighting exercise to the banks themselves. The market risk amendment of 1996 introduced the principle that banks, subject to supervisory permission, could do the risk-weighting on the basis of their own historical data relating to losses and on the basis of their own evaluation models. This permission was extended to credit risk assessment in Basel II. Since that time, there have been two general approaches to risk weighting: one embodied in the rules (the 'standardized' approach), and one carried out by the banks themselves (the 'internal ratings-based' approach or 'IRB' for short).[25]

---

[25] The IRB approach comes in two forms: a foundation IRB, in which the bank's internal system sets only some of the elements of the risk-weighting, and an advanced IRB, in which the bank's internal system does the whole job. Thus, in relation to loans, under foundation IRB, the bank sets only the probability of default ('PD') but not the loss given default ('LGD') or exposure at default ('EAD'); under advanced IRB, the bank sets all three. LGD takes account of the fact that the bank may recover something even in default, for

The intellectual justification of the IRB approach is that the standardized approach, by adding up risk assessments on a class-of-asset by class-of-asset basis, gives no value to the spread of the bank's overall portfolio of assets across the different classes, the risks of which may be uncorrelated. The IRB approach also allows the bank to benefit from investment in superior systems for evaluating risks. Since the bank uses its own internal data to compute the risk-weighting, the bank's actual historical experience with losses is reflected in the result.

14.4.3 Critiques of IRB approach

Large banks enthusiastically embraced the IRB approach. This approach involved only marginal extra expenditure, since the banks had elaborate risk-assessment systems in place for their own purposes, and it produced the welcome (to the banks) result that the capital charge was significantly reduced below the level demanded by the standardized approach. From the point of view of financial stability, however, the system worked poorly in the run-up to the crisis.[26] This was particularly true of the risk-weighting of items in the trading book. As the Basel Committee later commented:

> One of the underlying features of the crisis was the build-up of excessive on- and off-balance sheet leverage in the banking system. In many cases, banks built up excessive leverage while still showing strong risk based capital ratios.[27]

The left-hand graph in Figure 14.1 shows that the assets of ten of the world's largest banks approximately doubled in the decade prior to the crisis, whereas their risk-weighted assets increased by only one-third. This would have made sense if the banks had been shifting into less risky assets as well as expanding their total assets. But hindsight suggests this was not the case in the decade before the crisis, as does the right-hand graph. The two core activities of these banks—taking deposits and making loans—both fell as a proportion of total assets, while securities holdings ('investments') increased. The most plausible explanation is that the assessed risk-weights on bank assets were falling at the very time that the risks to which banks were exposed were increasing. This casts considerable doubt on the utility of the IRB approach.

Three arguments competed to explain the pre-crisis data. First, there was a widespread suspicion—but no proof—that banks were able to manipulate the IRB approach. What is clear is that banks' risk assessments under IRB vary significantly from bank to bank. In relation to credit risk, the largest component in a typical bank's overall risk-weighting, the Basel Committee found that up to three-quarters of the variation could be explained by variation in the asset profile—a variation the IRB approach is designed to produce—while the rest was due to variations in either bank or

---

example where the loan is secured; EAD takes account of the fact that, for example, the loan might not be fully drawn down at default.

[26] The IRB approach may also create a barrier to entry, since new banks will not have the historical data to feed into their model.

[27] BIS/BCBS, *Basel III: A Global Regulatory Framework for More Resilient Banks and Banking Systems*, bcbs189, rev'd June 2011, para 151.

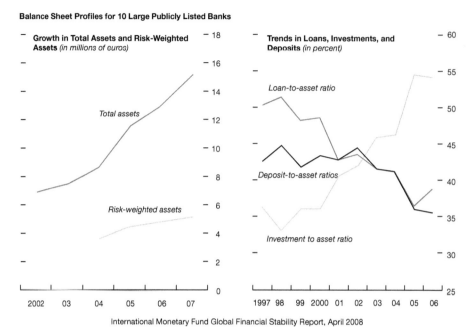

Fig. 14.1 Balance sheet profiles for ten large publicly traded banks

Source: IMF, *Global Stability Report* (April 2008) 31.

supervisory practice.[28] Greater variation was found in relation to trading book assessments, of particular significance for institutions active in investment banking.[29]

The second argument questioned the quality of the internal data available to the banks. These data did not go back very far and so related to an unusually benign economic period. In particular, they failed to capture crisis risks (or 'tail' risks—risks that are very unlikely to eventuate, but which will have a major impact on the bank if they do). The banks' models thus failed to allow for the financial crisis, which was a tail risk event.

The third argument related to the models the banks used. This criticism builds on the distinction between 'risk' and 'uncertainty' drawn by economist Frank Knight in the 1920s.[30] In his terms, the probability distribution of a *risky* event occurring is known or at least knowable, and so risk can be modelled, priced, and traded. More information is a good thing, because it brings the model closer to the actual distribution of the risk. The probability of an *uncertain* event, such as a major financial crisis, is not in principle knowable. Consequently, there is no reason to suppose that more data and

---

[28] BIS/BCBS, *Regulatory Consistency Assessment Programme (RCAP): Analysis of Risk-Weighted Assets for Credit Risk in the Banking Book*, bcbs256 (2013).

[29] BIS/BCBS, *Analysis of Risk-Weighted Assets for Market Risk*, n 22. This paper is coy in assigning percentages to the possible explanations for the divergences.

[30] F Knight, *Risk, Uncertainty and Profit* (Boston: Houghton Mifflin, 1921). The modern application of this distinction to financial markets is associated above all with Gerd Gigerenzer: see G Gigerenzer, *Risk Savvy* (New York, NY: Viking, 2014), esp Ch 11.

more sophisticated models will improve the reliability of predictions. However, at least for some uncertain events, experience shows that simple indicators ('heuristics'), while imperfect, are reasonably good predictors.[31] This approach raises the question whether such heuristics exist in relation to bank failures. If they do, they present a fundamental challenge to the IRB approach and perhaps to the whole policy of risk-weighting banks' capital requirements.[32]

14.4.4 Responses to the critiques

International and national authorities have developed responses or proposed responses, addressing each of the critiques. The first is to rein in the IRB, by making the criteria for access to the IRB approach more stringent, by specifying the qualities the IRB must display, or by setting a floor below which the IRB approach cannot reduce the capital charge set on the standardized approach.[33]

A second and more important response, developed by national and regional authorities, is the 'stress test'. A stress test involves the generation of a hypothetical situation by the regulator that is aimed at reproducing tail risk. The amount of capital needed to survive the hypothetical situation is then calculated and if it is more than the existing level of the bank's regulatory capital, then that requirement is adjusted upwards.[34] Although stress tests, at least in the EU, were initially undemanding (and found to be unconvincing in the market), they have improved over time. The 2014 stress test run by the Bank of England—a domestic version of the test run by the European Central Bank (ECB) at the same time—required banks to imagine an economic downturn which has occurred only once in the UK in the past century and a half, namely at the end of the First World War.[35]

The stress test is a major qualification of the IRB approach, since it implies that banks are no longer able to rely exclusively on their own historical loss data when setting capital requirements. Given the stress test requirement, one may wonder whether the IRB approach still has substantial advantages for the bank. It appears that it does, because the bank still uses its internal model to compute its capital requirements in the stressed scenario. Nevertheless, effectively executed stress tests constitute a significant shift of capital-setting power back into the hands of the regulators. They also demonstrate the increased importance of Basel 'Pillar 2' (supervisory review) supplementing 'Pillar 1'. The minimum, uniform capital requirements

---

[31] Gigerenzer, n 30. The role of heuristics in decision-making is discussed more fully in Chapter 10, in relation to consumer financial decision-making.

[32] Over one-quarter of the pages of Basel II (ignoring annexes) are devoted to this topic.

[33] BIS/BCBS, *Reducing Excessive Variability in Banks' Regulatory Capital Ratios: A Report to the G20*, bcbs298 (2014). The revised market risk framework (n 23) requires internal models to be calibrated to periods of stress (so that the bank cannot rely wholly on its own historical data) and makes regulatory approval of internal rating systems more granular (it operates at the level of the regulatory trading desk, not the whole bank). In the US, Dodd–Frank Act §171 (the so-called 'Collins Amendment,' after Sen. Susan Collins) specifies that the Basel I capital requirements are to serve as a floor to regulatory capital.

[34] Stress tests are more fully discussed in Chapter 19 (section 19.6) as part of the macroprudential approach to financial regulation that has emerged post-crisis.

[35] Bank of England, *Stress Testing the UK Banking System: Key Elements of the 2014 Stress Test* (2014), 9.

of Pillar 1 are supplemented by institution-specific capital requirements resulting from the stress test carried out by national or regional regulators.

The stress test generates a capital requirement which is still formulated on a risk-weighted basis. The third, and potentially most radical, approach is to develop a non-risk-weighted capital test and to use that to set a floor below which the risk-weighted requirements cannot fall. The non-risk-weighted capital requirement is referred to as a leverage ratio. The Basel Committee has moved, cautiously, in this direction with proposals for a 'backstop' leverage ratio (LR) of 3 per cent.[36] The term 'backstop' refers to the role of the LR in constraining the activity of banks in economic upswings, when banks' historical internal data are likely to indicate that borrowers are less likely to default and that markets are more benign, so that the same amount of capital can support a higher level of activity. But a larger role for the LR could be envisaged, for example, to combat 'model risk' (that is, the risk that banks' internal models are defective) or to deal with events which are uncertain in the Knightian sense.[37] Some major financial jurisdictions have moved more quickly than the Basel regulators to impose an LR.[38]

Even with a broader role for the LR, however, it does not displace, but rather supplements, the risk-weighted approach. The rationale for this twin-track approach is that a leverage ratio can easily be manipulated: a bank that increases the riskiness of its activities but not the value of associated assets leaves its unweighted leverage ratio unchanged. Regulators in at least some major countries can be said to be moving towards an approach to capital regulation in which both risk-weighted and non-risk-weighted elements play a significant role in setting regulatory capital. Firm believers in heuristics might argue that the risk-weighted elements could be removed entirely from the regulation. However, a simulation of capital requirements of various types against known default rates on one core class of corporate assets (loans to corporates) showed that the standard Basel approach to risk-weighting worked well. Moreover, the performance of the IRB approach was substantially improved if the number of prior years' data fed into the model was significantly increased, and the IRB approach had the virtue of minimizing the need to hold 'surplus' capital (that is, more than required to meet losses).[39] If the stress test is regarded as the functional equivalent of feeding more

---

[36] BIS/BCBS, *Basel III Leverage Ratio and Disclosure Requirements*, bcbs270 (2014). A leverage ratio of 3 per cent would have constrained the level of UK bank activity in the two to three years prior to the crisis: Bank of England, *Financial Stability Report* (December 2011), chart 2.4.

[37] Bank of England, *The Financial Policy Committee's Review of the Leverage Ratio* (2014) (proposing leverage ratio mimicking standard capital requirements, save for absence of risk-weighting).

[38] Dodd–Frank Act of 2010 §171 (the Collins amendment) in the US. In the case of large banking groups (more than $700bn assets or $10,000bn under custody), this provision imposes a leverage ratio of 6 per cent on the deposit-taking member of the group and a 5 per cent leverage 'buffer' at group level. The aim is to maintain the impact of the leverage ratio, given the higher risk-weighted capital requirements imposed on such groups, rather than to expand the function of the leverage ratio. See (2014) 79 *Federal Register*, 84, 24528. For the UK see the previous note. On buffers and global systemically important banks, see section 14.5.2. The leverage ratio consists of a numerator (CET1 [Common Equity] and Additional Tier 1 capital) and a denominator, designed to pick up on-balance sheet assets and off-balance sheet exposures. The definition of the denominator has been controversial.

[39] D Aikman, M Galesic, and G Gigerenzer, 'Taking Uncertainty Seriously: Simplicity versus Complexity in Financial Regulation', Bank of England Financial Stability Paper No 28 (2014), 13–14.

years of data into the internal models, this study is some support for the twin-track approach to setting regulatory capital standards.

14.5 What Counts as Capital? Basel III Requirements

The most controversial debate in relation to the Basel capital requirements concerns the level of capital required. The Basel III requirements have been widely criticized by academics and some policymakers as too low. At the same time, banks have resisted any increase on the ground that increased capital requirements are expensive for them and will raise the cost of lending, thus depriving marginal business projects of funding they would otherwise receive. In order to assess this debate we need to proceed in stages, starting with the apparently simple question: what level of capital does Basel III require?

At first sight, this seems a question to which an uncomplicated answer can be given. The remarkable thing about the amount of minimum capital which is required under the Basel rules is that the headline figure—8 per cent of Risk Weighted Assets (RWA)—was set in Basel I and has remained the same ever since. However, Basel III has done two significant things: it has altered the composition of the 8 per cent minimum figure, and it has introduced capital 'buffers' to supplement the minimum capital requirements.

14.5.1 Composition

The Basel minimum capital requirement is made up of two, or more accurately three, components. The first is indeed shareholders' equity—funds contributed to the company by investors through ordinary share subscriptions and undistributed profits held within the bank. This is core equity tier 1 capital ('CET1') in the Basel nomenclature. Under Basel II, only one-quarter of the 8 per cent (that's right, 2 per cent) had to be contributed through CET1. Under Basel III that requirement is raised to 4.5 per cent.

The remainder of the 8 per cent is made up of Additional Tier 1 (AT1) or Tier 2 (T2) capital. This further capital may be shareholders' equity (or some types of non-cumulative preference share), but, remarkably, it may also be supplied by subordinated debt. This seems wrong in principle, since although the issue of debt securities brings assets into the company, it increases the liabilities of the bank by exactly the same amount. The ratio of shareholder equity to assets is thus not improved; in fact, it falls slightly.[40] It can be argued that subordinated debt will protect creditors higher up in the ranking against loss once the bank is in insolvency, but importantly, debt in its standard form has no loss-absorbing capacity outside insolvency. As we shall see in Chapter 16, governments in the financial crisis proved unwilling, probably rightly, to allow banks to fall into insolvency. Instead they were bailed out without entering insolvency. So, subordinated debt offered banks no loss-absorbing capacity in this

---

[40] If a bank has $100 in assets funded by $10 of equity, and then purchases $10-worth of additional assets funded by subordinated debt, the proportion of its assets funded by equity falls from 10 per cent to ≈ 9 per cent.

Table 14.3 Composition of Basel III minimum capital requirement

Core Equity Tier One (CET1)	4.5%
Additional Tier One (AT1)	1.5%
Tier Two (T2)	2.0%

situation, leaving them with only their—very thin—layer of equity as genuine protection. The Basel response was not to remove subordinated debt entirely from counting against minimum capital requirements. Instead, a form of hybrid subordinated debt, which converts into equity or is written off at or before the resolution of the bank, was permitted to continue as AT1 or T2 capital.[41] Moreover, the more than doubling of CET1 to 4.5 per cent reduced the scope for utilizing hybrid subordinated debt significantly. The resulting numbers are shown in Table 14.3.

Many analysts and commentators concerned with the safety of banks focus solely on the CET1 position of the bank. So too do the new Basel buffers, discussed in section 14.5.2. The new CET1 minimum implies a permitted leverage ratio of over 20:1, based on risk-weighted assets[42]—before, however, the buffers are added on.

14.5.2 Buffers

The persistence of the Basel '8 per cent' requirement is misleading because it relates only to the *minimum capital requirement* for banks. Basel III introduced a number of additional *capital buffers*, which—when applicable—require banks to increase CET1 capital. The formal difference between buffers and minimum capital requirements concerns the consequences of failure to meet their requirements. The minimum capital requirement is a condition for continued operation: a bank which falls below its minimum capital requirement, or even gets near to it, is likely to be closed down by regulators. In contrast, the sanction for falling below a buffer requirement is that distributions to shareholders and managers (by way of bonuses) are constrained, so that the bank's CET1 can be rebuilt. There may be a complete prohibition on distributions or a cap, depending on how far below the buffer requirement the bank has fallen. Although less draconian than closure, a distribution constraint is still a powerful incentive to comply with the buffer requirement.

There are three principal buffers introduced by Basel III, which we now consider in turn. One applies to all banks all of the time. A second applies to some banks all of the time. The third applies to some or all banks some of the time. These buffers are each to a greater or lesser degree 'macroprudential' in their orientation, and are discussed in this context in Chapter 19.[43]

---

[41] AT1 hybrid debt must be perpetual; T2 debt must have a minimum maturity of five years.

[42] However, some assets, permitted under normal accounting rules, are excluded when computing the bank's CET1. Examples are intangibles, goodwill, and deferred tax assets. This makes the 4.5 per cent figure slightly more constraining than it appears at first sight. Eliminating classes of assets has a proportionately bigger impact on the bank's capital (assets less liabilities) than it does on the bank's assets considered on their own.

[43] Chapter 19, section 19.3.1.

Capital Conservation Buffer ('CCB'). This buffer applies to all banks all of the time. It addresses a criticism made of the previous rules that they were procyclical. Applied to the downswing of the economic cycle, the argument was that banks maintained their capital ratios despite poorer borrower performance and more volatile markets, not by adjusting the capital side of the ratio (raising more capital), but by adjusting the asset side of the ratio (reducing their assets, especially by making fewer loans). This preserved banks' regulatory capital yet worsened the impact on the real economy, as bank loans became harder to obtain.

Basel III introduces a 2.5 per cent CET1 capital conservation buffer. The CCB is 'designed to ensure banks build up capital buffers outside periods of stress which can be drawn down as losses are incurred'.[44] In theory, banks will be able to maintain their previous levels of lending in the downturn by allowing the CCB to absorb the temporarily higher level of losses. In practice, it is doubtful whether the CCB will work in this simple way. Given the restrictions on distributions, both management and shareholders will prefer to restore the buffer as soon as possible and so are likely to eschew a routine policy of going below the buffer in hard times. So, the private interests of bank shareholders and managers will probably still favour the traditional policy of reducing assets in a downturn. Indeed, early empirical studies of the operation of such measures suggest they have the potential to in fact exacerbate the problems they are supposed to cure.[45] Supervisory pressure on the banks to behave differently will be needed if the rationale of the CCB is to be realized.

Systemically important banks. The Global Systemically Important Bank (G-SIB) buffer is an additional CET1 requirement that applies to only some banks, but all of the time. It addresses the argument that the Basel rules are focused on the safety and soundness of individual banks rather than on the banking system as a whole.[46] Before Basel III, the rules were based on the assumption that the negative externalities of bank failure are linearly related to the size of the bank's assets. If that relationship is non-linear or if matters other than the size of the bank's assets are relevant in determining the likely externalities of bank failure, then it might be appropriate to impose a higher capital requirement on those banks likely to generate disproportionate externalities. The importance of a risk depends not only on the chances of its materializing but also on its impact if it does. The Basel III rules respond to this point by differentiating within the Basel population between 'systemically important' and other banks.

The Basel criteria for the G-SIB capital surcharge focus on the size, interconnectedness, complexity, scale of cross-border operations, and the non-substitutability of the services provided by a bank to determine its status as a G-SIB.[47] By 2015, these criteria, as applied by the Financial Stability Board (FSB), had produced a list of thirty G-SIBs,

---

[44] BIS/BCBS, *Basel III*, n 27, para 122.

[45] E Cerutti, S Claessens, and L Laeven, 'The Use and Effectiveness of Macroprudential Policies: New Evidence', IMF WP 15/61 (2015).

[46] For this argument applied to bank regulation as a whole see J Gordon and C Mayer, 'The Micro, Macro and International Design of Financial Regulation', Working Paper Columbia Law School/Oxford University (2012), available at http://www.ssrn.com. See also Chapter 19.

[47] BIS/BCBS, *Global Systemically Important Banks*, bcbs207 (2011), para 15.

with differing top-up requirements. Depending on the predicted impact of failure, the potential top-up varies from 1 to 3.5 per cent CET1, though no bank has received the maximum top-up of 3.5 per cent and only six have top-ups of 2 per cent or more.[48, 49]

The Basel rules extend the system to domestic SIBs (D-SIBs) from 2016. The identification of banks which are systemically important within a national jurisdiction and the size of the buffer to be imposed are a matter for national regulators, acting within principles set by the Committee.[50] This is consistent with the notion that the Basel rules are minima and that states have 'Pillar 2' powers to add to these minima as appropriate. Thus, under the Dodd–Frank Act in the US, the Federal Reserve is required to apply 'enhanced prudential supervision', including potentially higher capital standards, to banks with assets in excess of US$50bn, whether they appear on the FSB's list of global systemically important banks or not.[51]

Counter-cyclical capital buffer ('CCCB'). This buffer may be applied to all or some banks, but only applies some of the time. Like the CCB, it aims to address concerns about procyclicality, but this time in an economic upswing, where existing capital will support a higher level of bank activity because of better borrower performance and more benign markets. In other words, the CCCB is designed to constrain lending by banks during an economic boom and to prepare banks for the coming 'bust'. The CCCB operates only when a (national) regulator decides to impose it, and may be set at any level up to 2.5 per cent CET1. In the case of the US, the current (2016) rate is 0, whilst in the UK it will be 0.5% from 2017.

The relationship between the minimum CET1 requirement and the three buffers discussed in this section can be presented schematically as shown in Figure 14.2. The cycle neutral buffer can be equated with the CCB and the G-SIB buffer, if one applies. The overall CET1 level can be seen as varying over time as the CCCB is imposed on banks or removed and as banks fall below and then restore their buffers.

Overall. Taking account of the buffers, the minimum CET1 requirement is actually raised from 4.5 to 7 per cent for all banks, potentially to 10.5 per cent for G-SIBs (though it is unlikely to reach this level since there is no G-SIB in the 3.5 per cent category at present), with the possibility of macroprudential authorities adding up to a further 2.5 per cent if an asset bubble is developing, as Figure 14.3 shows. Whether the 'real' CET1 requirement is 4.5 or 13 per cent, or indeed somewhere in between,

---

[48] The 30 G-SIBs, with their applicable top-ups, are: HSBC, JP Morgan Chase (2.5 per cent); BNP Paribas, Barclays, Citigroup, Deutsche Bank (2 per cent); Bank of America, Credit Suisse, Goldman Sachs, Mitsubishi, Morgan Stanley (1.5 per cent); Agricultural Bank of China, Bank of China, Bank of New York Mellon, China Construction Bank, Groupe BPCE, Groupe Crédit Agricole, Industrial and Commercial Bank of China, ING Bank, Mizuho FG, Nordea, Royal Bank of Scotland, Santander, Société Générale, Standard Chartered, State Street, Sumitomo Mitsui FG, UBS, Unicredit Group, Wells Fargo (1.0 per cent) (FSB, November 2015).

[49] The Federal Reserve has recently proposed to augment the Basel Framework for US G-SIBs by assessing an additional charge based on a measure of the bank's 'short-term wholesale funding'. Such funding, which can materially increase run-risk, adds to a bank's susceptibility to failure. The Federal Reserve's proposed implementation of Basel III would produce a G-SIB surcharge with a 4.5 per cent cap.

[50] BIS/BCBS, *A Framework for Dealing with Domestic Systemically Important Banks—Final Document*, bcbs233 (2012).

[51] Dodd–Frank Act of 2010 §115. See also n 38.

Capital requirements (per cent of risk-weighted assets)

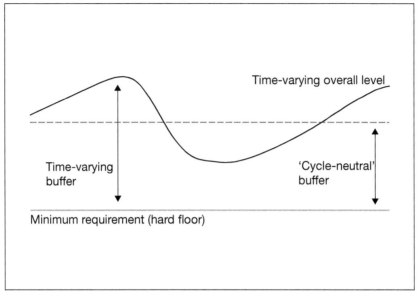

Fig. 14.2 CET1: Minimum requirement plus buffers (constant and varying)
Source: Bank of England, *Financial Stability Review* (June 2010), 11.

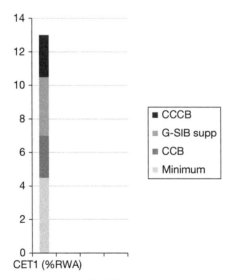

Fig. 14.3 Basel III CET1 Requirements

depends on (i) the strength of incentives to maintain buffers intact, (ii) how authorities set the CCCB and the buffer for systemic importance, and (iii) how they classify the large international banks.

14.6 Are Basel III Capital Levels High Enough?

14.6.1 Is equity more expensive than debt?

We are now in a position to move on to the second part of the answer to the question: are the CET1 requirements, as laid down in Basel III, correctly set? Most commentators see the answer to the question as a trade-off: equity is somewhat more expensive than debt to banks—opinions differ as to how much—and so more equity risks raising the costs of borrowing, against which the benefit of higher equity is that bank stability is promoted. However, one view, closely associated with Professors Admati and Hellwig, holds that equity is not more expensive than debt, implying that no trade-off is required.[52] Even they do not propose that banks should be required to be financed with 100 per cent equity. This would destroy the transformation function of banks, which would be prohibited from channelling pools of short-term excess cash into term loans through the deposit mechanism or other forms of short-term funding. The result would likely be a reduction in the supply of loans to firms and households—paradoxically, the very result the capital requirements are ultimately aimed at avoiding.[53] Consequently, it is better to think of the 'how-much-equity?' question as one about the balance between funding via equity versus long-term debt, such as bank bonds. Nevertheless, Admati and Hellwig (A&H) propose an equity requirement of 20–30 per cent of non-risk-weighted assets (in other words, a leverage ratio),[54] equivalent to over 50 per cent RWA, very substantially bigger than the current Basel requirements and bigger than UK and US banks have actually achieved over the past 150 years.[55]

In support of A&H, the Modigliani–Miller theorem shows that, under strong assumptions, the value of a firm is not increased or decreased by its funding structure.[56] The firm's value depends upon its earnings, not how its business is financed. Modigliani and Miller accept that, in most states of the world, debt is cheaper than equity because debt holders rank ahead of equity holders and so take less risk. Nevertheless, they show that the gains to firm value from any increase in the proportion of debt in the funding structure will be exactly counterbalanced by an increased cost of the equity, which has been made more risky by the firm's increased leverage. Conversely, any costs resulting from decreased debt will be matched by the gains from now cheaper, because less risky, equity.

However, there are three real-world frictions which plausibly support the suggestion that debt is more expensive than equity for banks. Indeed, A&H do not dispute their existence. Their counterargument is that these costs are private costs to banks, not

---

[52] A Admati and M Hellwig, *The Bankers' New Clothes* (Princeton, NJ: Princeton UP), 2013.

[53] This is, however, precisely what supporters of 'narrow banking' advocate. On their view, deposit insurance should be available only to banks whose assets consist wholly of high-quality and highly liquid assets; that is, mainly cash and cash-like instruments.

[54] See n 52, 179.

[55] P Alessandri and A Haldane, 'Banking on the State', Bank of England (2009), Chart 2.

[56] F Modigliani and M Miller, 'The Cost of Capital, Corporation Finance and the Theory of Investment' (1958) 48 *American Economic Review* 261.

social costs: in other words, costs to banks are balanced by equivalent gains to society at large. This may not be an adequate response, however, if the private cost to the bank causes it to take action which is socially costly. Consider the first friction: in many jurisdictions debt interest benefits from a tax shield which is not available for dividends. A shift from debt to equity increases the bank's tax costs, all else being equal, but the state benefits by an equivalent amount from increased tax revenues. However, banks may pass these increased costs on to borrowers, with the result that marginal projects are no longer funded—potentially a social cost. In theory, the state could redress the balance by using the additional tax revenues to subsidize the financing of marginal projects. More plausibly, it could alter the tax system so as to be neutral between debt and equity. However, in the absence of state action of some sort, the social cost may not be redressed.

The second friction is the debt-overhang problem.[57] A financially constrained company will be able to raise new equity only at a significant discount to the current market price because investors understand that part of the benefit of the new funds will be captured by the company's creditors, whose position is thereby strengthened. New shareholders protect themselves through the price mechanism, so what actually happens is a transfer of wealth to the bank's creditors from its existing shareholders (and managers). This makes shareholders and managers reluctant to raise new equity when the bank is performing poorly. They may instead prefer to raise capital ratios by reducing assets, thus reducing the supply of funding to business projects. Again, regulatory solutions are available, such as mandatory share issues or increasing capital through constraints on distributions (including distributions by way of share repurchases).

A third friction is the loss of the implicit state guarantee of bank debt,[58] arising from the expectation that the bank will be bailed out rather than allowed to go into insolvency. In this situation debt-holders (normally) will not bear losses, so that bank debt becomes less risky and investors will lend to banks at lower rates than in the absence of the implicit guarantee. A shift from debt to equity thus reduces the value of the implicit guarantee to the bank and is a private cost to the bank. However, in this case the private cost is socially beneficial. The implicit guarantee amounts to a state subsidy of banking activity (as against other forms of economic activity financed by debt where no implicit guarantee is in place) for which no obvious rationale exists, at least for the extent of the subsidies enjoyed prior to the financial crisis. As we shall see in Chapter 16, since the financial crisis states have been engaged in concerted efforts to reduce or even eliminate such implicit guarantees, so that in this case a shift from debt to equity would complement, rather than cut across, other policy initiatives.

However, there is an argument that capital is costly for banks, which goes beyond such 'frictions', to question the basic Modigliani–Miller hypothesis as applied to banks. For a bank, unlike a non-financial firm, the composition of the balance sheet is essential to its value. The business of a bank is not just about screening and monitoring when extending credit to firms and households but also about extending liquidity services to

---

[57] See J Tirole, *The Theory of Corporate Finance* (Princeton, NJ: Princeton UP, 2006), 3.3.
[58] There is, of course, an explicit guarantee in the case of deposits (see Chapter 15) but, as stated, we assume in this section that the equity would replace long-term bank debt.

depositors in the form of claims that are sum certain and continuously redeemable. One might go so far as to say that the *business* of a bank is financing medium- and long-term credit claims *with deposits*. This means that an all-equity bank will be a less valuable bank than one funded at least in part by deposits. The idea of the 'irrelevancy' of financing to business project value does not hold where the business project *itself* is a particular form of financing.[59]

14.6.2 Costly equity vs financial security?

If capital is not only privately but also socially costly, the trade-off question cannot be avoided, though the calculations are fearsomely difficult because of the assumptions which have to be made.[60] Most simulations suggest that non-trivial additions to the Basel requirements would put banks' lending rates up by only modest amounts, and that these higher lending rates would in turn lead to only moderate reductions in economic output, compared with the world based on the Basel III minima.[61] Nevertheless, any loss to output is a cost. As to the benefits, since the costs of a large-scale crisis in terms of economic output forgone are very large, the estimated benefit of more rigorous capital requirements can be a very large number, even if the reduced chance of a crisis is only modest. The results of these analyses can be sense-checked against the actual experience with recent financial crises. The Independent Commission on Banking in the UK did this and suggested that CET1 figures in the range of 16 to 24 per cent of RWA would have enabled 95 per cent of banks to survive recent crises.[62]

14.6.3 Are we stuck with a debt/equity dichotomy?

The debate referred to in the previous section has been carried on by reference to a dichotomy between debt and equity: only equity absorbs losses short of insolvency; debt absorbs loss only in insolvency; the costs of bank insolvency are too high for society to bear; so the solution is more bank equity. But it is perfectly possible, by legislative fiat, to make bank debt bear loss short of insolvency. As we shall see in

---

[59] A thought experiment shows the limited relevance of the Modigliani–Miller hypothesis for bank regulation. For a given level of equity, the value of the bank, and separately, the fragility of the bank, will be critically affected by the make-up of the liabilities: deposits, short-term wholesale claims, and term debt. For example, at a given level of equity, a bank that can readily obtain short-term wholesale finance will probably be more valuable because it can readily acquire assets, but it will also be more fragile because of the heightened run-risk. For a given level of equity and given level of deposits, a bank that additionally finances its assets with term debt rather than short-term wholesale claims will probably be less valuable and less fragile. These trade-offs are part of the Basel III liquidity regime that we discuss in Chapter 15.

[60] See J Gordon, 'The Empty Call for Benefit-Cost Analysis in Financial Regulation' (2014) 43 *Journal of Legal Studies* S351.

[61] A Santos and D Elliott, 'Estimating the Costs of Financial Regulation', IMF Staff Discussion Note 12/11 (2011) (adding 3 per cent to Basel III equity requirements would add seven to twenty basis points to banks' lending rates); D Miles, J Yang, and G Marcheggiano, 'Optimal Bank Capital', Bank of England Discussion Paper 31 (2011) (doubling Basel III RWA requirements would increase UK banks' lending rates by about eighteen basis points). Santos and Elliott discuss and discount some of the literature which comes up with much larger effects. This literature largely ignores a bank's lower cost of debt funding if there is less debt in the bank's funding structure.

[62] Independent Commission on Banking ('ICB'), *Final Report* (2011), para 4.109.

Chapter 16, this process is usually referred to as 'bail in': some categories of the debt of a failing bank are written off or converted into equity when the bank is in financial distress but before it is bailed out by the state, so that debt bears loss at that point. Only debt which has this characteristic now counts, as we have seen, towards AT1 or T2 capital under the Basel rules. Or a bank may choose to issue debt on terms that it will be written off or converted upon some 'trigger' event short of resolution.

If the focus is on the loss-absorbing capacity of financial instruments issued by banks rather than on their equity characterization, then some of the private costs to banks associated with higher equity can be made to disappear. Hybrid debt may carry the tax shield of debt (depending on local tax rules) and no immediate debt-overhang issue exists, since equity is not being issued (though a debt-overhang problem may be created for the future). Hybrid debt will not benefit from the implicit state guarantee—the whole purpose of its creation is that it should not—and, as we have seen, removal or reduction of this guarantee is the aim of many post-crisis reforms. Long-term debt capable of bearing losses in resolution will certainly be more costly to the bank than debt likely to be bailed out, but that is what removal of the subsidy entails.

Thus, the route to increasing banks' loss-absorbing capacity beyond the Basel III minima and buffers may be less troublesome than had initially been thought. Taking advantage of the concept of writing off and converting debt in resolution, the Independent Commission on Banking (ICB) in the UK proposed that banks should have a minimum 'total loss absorbing capacity' ('TLAC') of 17 per cent for a retail bank or 20 per cent for an investment bank, well above the Basel minima. The difference would be made up by 'bail-inable' bonds—that is, bonds capable of being written off (or converted into equity). And this approach has now been recommended by the FSB for all global systemically important banks.[63] We examine it in Chapter 16. However, the extent to which debt capable of bail-in is a substitute for equity is still highly controversial.[64]

14.7 Conclusion

That the Basel Committee has been, and continues to be, active in its responses to the financial crisis is not open to doubt. We can identify the following major changes:

- *Risk-weighting*, although still at the centre of the Basel rules, has been supplemented by an unweighted *leverage ratio* and banks' own rating mechanisms have been subject to greater controls (for example, stress tests).

[63] Ibid, para 4.118ff; FSB, *Adequacy of Loss-Absorbing Capacity of Global Systemically Important Banks in Resolution: Consultative Document* (2014). See P Davies, 'The Fall and Rise of Debt' (2015) 16 *European Business Organization Law Review* 491.

[64] See the public disagreement between Sir John Vickers, formerly chair of the ICB, and the Bank of England over the levels of CET1 proposed for UK D-SIBs, where the Bank's proposals, criticized by Sir John as too low, were defended partly on the grounds of the availability now of a framework for bail-in. See 'The Bank of England Must Think Again On Systemic Risk' (*Financial Times*, 14 February 2016) (Vickers); 'Proposals Designed to Fulfil BoE's Core Mission' (*Financial Times*, 16 February 2016) (Bank of England); 'Equity Buffers Are In the Public Interest' (*Financial Times*, 17 February 2016) (Vickers); see also Chapter 23, section 23.6.

- The sophistication of the Basel approach to *market risk* has been substantially increased as a result of the current 'fundamental review' of the trading book.

- The requirements for *CET1 capital* have been substantially increased.

- Efforts have been made to reduce the *procyclicality* of the capital rules through the introduction of two buffers (CCB and CCCB).

- *Systemic importance* has been recognized through the introduction of a further buffer for systemically important banks.

Yet, the overall levels of capital required, even after Basel III, seem small compared with the actual losses banks have suffered in financial crises. As we have noted, the UK's ICB concluded that a requirement of 24 per cent of RWA would have been needed to absorb the losses suffered by 95 per cent of the banks involved in the crises.[65] Of course, some states have gone further through the exercise of their Pillar 2 powers, especially in relation to large banks. Nevertheless, in neither the UK nor Switzerland—the two countries with the biggest banking sectors relative to GDP and therefore most at risk from a banking crisis—has the CET1 requirement actually been raised much beyond about 10 per cent of RWA.

Why have the changes been so modest? Part of the answer is that movement to higher levels of capital is thought to require long transition periods. Another concern is the competitive advantage thought to be given to banks from other countries if an individual jurisdiction goes ahead alone with very much higher CET1 requirements while other jurisdictions remain with the international standard and foreign banks cannot be required to operate through local subsidiaries.[66] Both answers imply that policymakers do not accept the proposition that equity is not expensive.

More important, high levels of CET1 only increase the chances that a bank will survive an external or internal shock. Only at very high equity levels, which might interfere with the bank's transformation function, will equity provide something approaching a guarantee of survival. Thus, the question becomes whether higher levels of equity in the 25 per cent range are likely to appear persuasive to short-term funders (depositors and short-term wholesale market funders) on an *ex ante* basis, so as to induce them to keep their money in the bank if a bank is suspected of having incurred heavy losses. We do not know the answer to this question. It may well be possible to say, *ex post*, that equity equivalent to 24 per cent of RWA would have allowed 95 per cent of banks to survive recent crises. However, even this does not guarantee survival, and a short-term investor in any individual bank is unlikely to wish to hang around in order to discover the outcome.

In short, it appears that capital requirements, at any acceptable level, are not likely to provide by themselves a sufficient inducement for short-term funders not to withdraw from the bank in the case of serious uncertainty about the value of its assets, while a capital requirement that did do this job might seriously inhibit bank transformation. Other mechanisms to promote the safety and soundness of banks are needed to

---

[65] Even this figure would not have saved all banks: Anglo-Irish Bank would have needed a capital of 39 per cent of RWA to survive.

[66] ICB, n 62, para 4.35.

supplement the capital mechanism. In terms of surviving a shock, liquidity regulation—considered in the next chapter—has an important part to play. Effective resolution mechanisms—considered in Chapter 16—may help to prevent the spread of contagion from a failing bank, aided possibly by structural regulation (Chapter 23), while better bank governance (Chapter 17) and macroprudential policy (Chapter 19) may make it less likely that the bank will suffer a shock in the first place.

15

Liquidity Regulation

15.1 Introduction

As discussed in Chapters 13 and 14, banks perform the socially useful function of a three-sided transformation: credit transformation, liquidity transformation, and maturity transformation. Roughly, this means converting short-term funds supplied by depositors and other funders into loans and other credit assets that individually may carry significant risk, may remain outstanding for a substantial time period, and whose immediate sale price would likely be substantially below the 'hold to maturity' value. Because of the liquidity mismatch, the bank is exposed to a serious risk of a run—a sudden withdrawal of funds in excess of the cash reserves the bank retains or could quickly raise—which could bring down the bank, even if its balance sheet was solvent before the run. We discussed in Chapter 14 the role that 'capital' plays in protecting bank stability, by reassuring short-term funders that any losses experienced by the bank from bad loans or from 'fire sale' valuations on forced asset sales will be absorbed by the bank's shareholders, not its short-term funders. Now we turn to explicit regulation of the bank's 'liquidity': that is, its capacity to respond to a sudden withdrawal of short-term funds without having to sell off illiquid assets. Liquidity regulation obviously reduces the risks associated with runs for individual banks, but it also protects the financial system as a whole, since a fire-sale at one significant bank can affect the balance sheet valuation of many other banks, raising solvency questions that can also trigger runs at those banks.

The risk of ill-advised or unfortunate use of corporate assets—in the case of a bank, poor lending decisions, for example—is one shared by any commercial company. However, the liquidity risk that a bank faces arises out of the structural mismatch between its liabilities and its assets. A firm which borrows short term (from whatever source) and uses those funds to create illiquid assets runs a *funding liquidity risk*.[1] It was funding illiquidity, rather than balance sheet insolvency, which was the dominant risk for banks in the recent crisis. As the Basel Committee later remarked:

> During the early liquidity phase of the financial crisis starting in 2007, many banks—despite meeting the existing capital requirements—experienced difficulties because they did not prudently manage their liquidity…The rapid reversal in market conditions showed how quickly liquidity can dry up and also how long it can take to come back.[2]

---

[1] See T Geithner, 'Liquidity and Financial Markets' (February 2007), http://www.bis.org/review/r070301b.pdf: 'Liquidity can mean many different things. One dimension of liquidity is the availability of credit or the ease with which institutions can borrow or take on leverage. This is generally referred to as funding liquidity. Another dimension of liquidity is the ease with which market participants can transact, or the ability of markets to absorb large purchases or sales without much effect on prices. This is what is generally called market liquidity.'

[2] BIS/BCBS, *Basel III: The Net Stable Funding Ratio, Consultative Document*, bcbs271 (2014).

Principles of Financial Regulation. First Edition. John Armour, Dan Awrey, Paul Davies, Luca Enriques, Jeffrey N. Gordon, Colin Mayer, and Jennifer Payne. © John Armour, Dan Awrey, Paul Davies, Luca Enriques, Jeffrey N. Gordon, Colin Mayer, and Jennifer Payne 2016. Published 2016 by Oxford University Press.

For example, Northern Rock in the UK, Bear Stearns in the US, and Lehman Brothers International (Europe) were probably balance-sheet solvent in the period immediately before they were bailed out or went into bankruptcy, but they could not continue in the face of liquidity shortages. Of course, once lack of liquidity turns into a fire-sale of assets, whether outside or within a formal bankruptcy process, the bank is likely to become balance-sheet insolvent as well.

Banks' short-term funding comes in two main forms. The bigger category is retail deposits. Most of these will be individually small but some deposits, although retail in character, are large in terms of the depositor's overall wealth, perhaps representing someone's life savings or the proceeds of the recent sale of a house or other major personal asset. The proportion of deposits, in aggregate, in banks' total funding (including equity) varies from region to region in the world and over time. It is usually high in Japan and in Asia generally (over 70 per cent), lower in the US (about 55 per cent), and even lower in the Eurozone (below 40 per cent).[3] The second and smaller category is short-term wholesale funding. This may be either secured or unsecured. Secured short-term funding takes the form mainly of repos and swaps.[4] Unsecured funding is mainly interbank deposits, commercial paper, and certificates of deposit. The importance of this second category of funding also varies by region, being in 2012 about 2 per cent in Japan, 10 per cent in the rest of Asia and the US, and 15 per cent in the Eurozone.[5] It also varies according to the type of banking activity: investment banks and broker-dealers (which may not be deposit-taking institutions at all) rely more heavily on short-term secured wholesale funding (mainly repos) and less on other forms of short-term funding than do commercial banks. It might be thought that short-term funding which is secured is less at risk of being withdrawn and will instead be rolled over, precisely because it is secured. However, in a systemic crisis in which the value of banks' assets has become uncertain, a bank will have to pledge more collateral to secure the same amount of lending,[6] or may even find that the assets it previously put forward as collateral are no longer acceptable. In sum, all short-term funding, retail or wholesale, secured or unsecured, is in danger of being withdrawn if the bank's capacity to repay the loan comes into question. If

---

[3] IMF, *Global Financial Stability Report* (2013), Figure 3.1. The figures are for 2012.

[4] Because 'repos' played an important role in 'funding liquidity', a brief explanation is warranted here (they are discussed in more detail in Chapter 20, section 20.3.2, and Chapter 21, section 21.2). A 'repo' is a sale of a security with an agreement to repurchase at a later date—usually the next day. The difference between the sale and repurchase prices reflects the interest paid by the 'seller' of the security for enjoying the overnight liquidity. Functionally, the transaction is a collateralized loan; legally, it is a sale and repurchase. The market value of the security typically exceeds the value of the cash the borrower receives. This difference, normally expressed as a percentage, is called the 'haircut' (or 'margin') and reflects the extent to which the transaction is over-collateralized. If the borrower (seller) defaults, the lender (purchaser) retains the security. Laws of most jurisdictions protect the lender (purchaser) from otherwise applicable insolvency laws that would 'stay' a secured party's foreclosing on the borrower's collateral. Repo, then, provides a short-term wholesale credit supplier with the functional equivalent of deposit insurance. Indeed, perhaps better, because there are no caps on repo finance supplied by a particular lender.

[5] Ibid.

[6] In the jargon, this means the borrowing bank will suffer a larger 'haircut' on the value of collateral used to secure the loan.

all or most short-term funders seek to withdraw their money, then the bank is said to face a 'run'.[7]

Some types of collective withdrawal are easy to predict and thus to handle. The bank will know, for example, that the level of retail and wholesale deposits declines around major holiday periods or when the demands of the taxing authorities have to be met. It will ensure that it has liquid assets on hand (by managing the size of its so-called 'fractional reserves') to meet such expected demand. By contrast, a funder's idiosyncratic decision to consume (and so withdraw funds) need not concern the bank, because, assuming the bank has a large funding base, that decision will be balanced by another funder's decision to save rather than consume. This is the law of large numbers.

What the bank has most to fear is an unexpected and widespread withdrawal of short-term funding. As discussed in Chapter 13, this is most likely to occur for reasons connected with the (depositors' perception of the) bank's financial position.[8] Because the value of the bank's loans is difficult for third parties to assess, a short-term funder who receives what is thought to be an adverse signal about the bank's solvency will withdraw those funds and put them elsewhere, rather than attempt to establish the true position. This is normally an inexpensive form of self-help for the funder—even if it has the unfortunate result that, if all short-term funders behave in this way, the feared insolvency will inevitably be brought about. As the recent financial crisis showed, if fears about the solvency of banks and other financial institutions are widespread (that is, they are driven not by worries about the idiosyncratic risks of a particular institution but by fears about risks faced by all institutions), then short-term funding may be withdrawn on a systemic basis—a so-called 'banking panic'. This may cause the failure of a number of institutions and a widespread reduction in lending by banks to the real economy, as each bank hoards liquid assets in order (partly) to replace the external funding which has been withdrawn. At this point, there is a feedback loop. Banks refuse to lend to other banks, not only because of fears about those other banks' insolvency but also because they have a better use for the cash: to protect themselves against a reduction in their own funding liquidity.

Consequently, those in charge of public policy might take the view that funding liquidity is a bigger risk to the bank (and the real economy) than balance-sheet insolvency (despite their interconnectedness) and that measures which directly address that liquidity risk have a greater salience than capital rules, which address it only indirectly.[9] In this chapter, we will first analyse more fully the risk of an unexpected, large-scale withdrawal of short-term funding (the 'bank run') and then look at three different regulatory techniques for addressing this risk. The first technique is an extension of the strategy of prudential regulation, which we introduced in the previous chapter. Here, however, the rules aim not to require the bank to have a minimum

---

[7] For example, repo lenders can run by refusing to renew, or rollover, their financing arrangements when they expire. If the repo collateral is risk-free (eg US Treasury bills), there should be no incentive to run. But if the collateral is subject to value deterioration—as was the case, for example, with purportedly 'AAA' mortgage-backed securities in 2007–8—then a repo run could become established.

[8] Chapter 13, section 13.2.2.

[9] By putting the bank in a better position to absorb losses in a fire sale.

proportion of equity funding backing its assets but rather to hold a certain proportion of those assets in a liquid form (no matter how they are funded). In other words, liquidity rules (in general) constrain the composition of the asset side of the bank's balance sheet, whereas capital rules constrain the liabilities side.[10]

The second and third techniques are different forms of insurance provision, the second technique involving the provision of insurance to the bank and the third the provision of insurance to the short-term funders. The second technique seeks to address the illiquidity of the bank's assets. If a bank could deal with its assets at full value, by way of sale or as collateral for loans (that is, if the bank had full 'market liquidity' in respect of its assets), then its funding liquidity risks would be much less significant. The first type of insurance aims to provide the bank with something approaching market liquidity. Small banks sometimes engage in buying such insurance privately, by arranging lines of credit (backed by the small bank's assets) with larger banks, to be drawn down in times of loss of funding liquidity. However, for larger banks and in times of systemic uncertainty, the only bank capable of fulfilling this role on the required scale is a central bank. The role of the central bank as lender of last resort ('LOLR') can be traced back at least as far as the second half of the nineteenth century. In the recent crisis, the LOLR functions of the central banks of both the US and the UK expanded dramatically. The central bank facilities grew more and more to be an arrangement banks could rely on to provide liquidity in a crisis, and the Bank of England, for one, now uses the term 'liquidity insurance' to describe what was formerly termed its LOLR function.[11]

The third technique is the provision of insurance directly to the short-term funders. Here, if the bank fails to fulfil its obligations to the short-term funders, the state steps in and performs them and is then subrogated (sometimes with enhancement) to the position of the short-term funders as against the bank. One class of short-term funders—retail depositors—have benefited from such insurance in the US since the Banking Act of 1933. The body set up to administer the scheme, the Federal Deposit Insurance Corporation ('FDIC'), does not simply collect premiums and pay out compensation but has become in addition the central body in the resolution of failing banks. It took nearly half a century for this form of insurance to spread to Europe, but it is now mandatory for all Member States of the EU and is widely found around the world. But the insurance bodies outside the US often play only a minor role in the resolution of failing banks.

Both of the insurance techniques have obvious costs as well as clear benefits. The benefits stem mainly from the fact that, unlike prudential regulation, insurance has little impact on the transformation function of banks. Assets held in liquid form on the bank's balance sheet under prudential regulation cannot be lent out to the productive economy. However, insurance has potential costs, both moral hazard and subsidy costs. As with any insured, a bank may take a higher level of risk in relation to the

---

[10] As we will discuss, liquidity rules can also touch the liabilities side by limiting the bank's funding of its assets through sources that are not 'stable', such as short-term wholesale credit claims. Term debt, for example, presents negligible run risk compared to overnight repo.

[11] Bank of England, *The Bank of England's Sterling Monetary Framework*, June 2015 (the 'Red Book').

insured loss than it would without the insurance—precisely because the loss will not fall on it. Subsidy has two aspects: insured lenders will lend to the bank at lower rates of interest because they bear less risk (funding subsidy), and the bank may use those cheap funds to take more risks in the hunt for higher returns than if the lender carried the full funding costs (activity subsidy). This will mean the bank may be larger and riskier than otherwise, but not necessarily more efficient. With insurance, therefore, the question is how to design the scheme so as to maximize its benefits while minimizing its costs.

15.2 Bank Runs

The idea of a bank run is usually analysed by reference to retail depositors who have deposited funds with the bank on a demand or short-notice basis. However, the analysis applies to all short-term funders who share the same information asymmetries and coordination costs as retail depositors. The Northern Rock run of 2007 is usually presented as a retail run story—with the public queuing around the block to withdraw their deposits. This was indeed part of the story. But the Rock's decline was precipitated by a withdrawal of short-term wholesale money, through the unwillingness of holders of the Rock's short-term commercial paper to roll it over. The retail run was triggered only when news leaked out that the Rock had obtained LOLR funds from the Bank of England to replace the commercial paper funds. Moreover, the immediate cause of the failure of Lehman Brothers was also a funding liquidity crisis, even though that institution had no depositors.

For the reasons explained in Chapter 13, section 13.4, depositors know much less about the state of the bank's assets, especially its loans, than do bank insiders, but they also know that the insiders have every incentive not to reveal bad news in a timely manner. Further, individual small depositors have little incentive to invest in obtaining that information. Finally, retail depositors face overwhelming coordination costs which deter them from producing a collective response to fears about the bank's solvency. The low-cost and potentially effective step is for the individual depositors to withdraw the deposited funds if presented with a signal which, they believe, suggests that the bank is facing a solvency problem. So, the position is not, as is sometimes said, that retail depositors do not monitor the bank, but rather that their capacity to monitor is limited and their response to signals is a simple 'stay or run' decision.[12] The signals to which they react may be so 'noisy' that they are taken to identify as insolvent a bank that is in fact solvent—for example, a bank whose business model appears similar to that of another bank that is in difficulties, but whose financial position is in fact much stronger. A particularly pernicious feature of depositor flight is its tendency to create feedback. Even depositors who do not believe the signal indicates insolvency nevertheless have an incentive to run if they believe a sufficient number of other depositors will do so: no one wants to be the last depositor to seek to withdraw.

---

[12] Arguably, this is a case where it is better to have no monitoring than imperfect monitoring. Deposit insurance in effect brings about this situation by removing the incentive to monitor entirely and (if effective) replicating the benefits of running.

From the point of view of the depositors as a whole, a bank run may be self-defeating, because the run ensures the bank's insolvency. However, because the depositors cannot agree effectively, *ex ante* or *ex post*, to maintain their normal deposit and withdrawal behaviour when the bank's assets are impaired or might be so, running is an entirely effective strategy for those who remove their funds first. They get their money back whole and avoid any consequential losses which non-recovery might entail, such as inability to discharge personal debts falling due in the short term.

The influential model of the bank run put forward by Diamond and Dybvig presents the depositors' position as having two principal equilibria ('stay' or 'run'), with the depositors' inability to coordinate their actions meaning that the 'stay' equilibrium is always precarious and may at any time shift to a 'run' equilibrium.[13] However, the model tells us very little about the propensity of depositors to shift from the one equilibrium to the other. This is a matter of psychology (or 'confidence') rather than anything else.

It might be thought that the above analysis does not apply well to short-term wholesale funders. These are sophisticated investors, who could respond to an adverse signal by adjusting the terms of their investments rather than running. However, it appears that wholesale funders treat commercial paper and other short-term funding instruments as, in the words of Dang, Gorton, and Holmström, 'information insensitive'.[14] This means that even these investors do not regard it as worthwhile to incur the cost of obtaining private information about the likelihood of default by the bank on the security. Instead, they rely in normal times on the public rating attached to the commercial paper by rating agencies. If they ever have reason to doubt the bank's solvency, then, like retail depositors, they run—in this case by refusing to rollover the paper. It is probably true that wholesale funders are less likely than retail depositors to engage in a pure 'panic run' by making egregious errors about whether the bank is facing a solvency risk.[15] On the other hand, they are also likely to pick up instances of solvency risks more quickly since they are 'closer to the bank' than retail depositors.[16]

We now turn to the principal regulatory techniques that might sustain confidence on the part of depositors and other short-term funders, even in the face of adverse signals.

---

[13] D Diamond and P Dybvig, 'Bank Runs, Deposit Insurance and Liquidity' (1983) 91 *Journal of Political Economy* 401. This models a 'pure panic' run. For a model incorporating both panic and fundamentals runs see F Allen, E Carletti, I Goldstein, and A Leonello, 'Government Guarantees and Financial Stability', Working Paper CEPR (2014).

[14] T Vi Dang, G Gorton, and B Holmström, 'Ignorance, Debt and Financial Crises', Working Paper (2015), earlier version discussed in G Gorton and A Metrick, 'Regulating the Shadow Banking System' (2010) *Brookings Papers on Economic Activity* 261.

[15] In a 'pure panic' run, the bank is not balance-sheet insolvent at the outset, but becomes so when short-term funders withdraw and trigger a fire sale of assets. Consequently, if the panic can be stopped, the bank should continue merrily on. In a 'fundamentals' run, the bank does indeed face balance-sheet insolvency. If such a run can be prevented, this may give the bank time to achieve a 'workout'—a recapitalization without going into resolution—or, even if it falls into resolution, there will be a more equal impact on its creditors.

[16] In the case of Northern Rock, the wholesale funders seem to have put together two facts: the liquidity crunch the financial crisis was generating and the bank's heavy reliance on wholesale funding.

15.3 Regulating Banks' Balance Sheets for Liquidity

Despite the salience of liquidity requirements, they were until recently a matter solely for national regulators. The Basel rules contained nothing on this topic until the Basel III revisions (and even now the Basel III liquidity rules have yet to come into force). The Basel rules now contain two liquidity constraints on a bank's portfolio: the Liquidity Coverage Ratio ('LCR') and the Net Stable Funding Ratio ('NSFR'). The former is designed to promote banks' short-term resilience to liquidity shocks, whilst the latter aims to give banks an incentive to fund themselves on an ongoing basis with more stable sources of funding.[17] These two constraints are different sides of the same coin, in that more 'stable funding' reduces immediate liquidity requirements.

15.3.1 The Liquidity Coverage Ratio ('LCR')

The LCR requires banks to recalibrate their liquidity reserves in order to take account of tail risks. The LCR requires banks to hold a stock of high-quality liquid assets ('HQLA') which must be at least equivalent to the likely net cash outflows from the bank over thirty days in a specified stress scenario.[18] The stress scenario incorporates many of the shocks experienced during the crisis that started in 2007. To model likely outflows, the rules stipulate minimum 'run-off' rates for different classes of bank liabilities—that is, the percentage of the liability class which, it is estimated, would be withdrawn during a thirty-day stress period. The details need not concern us.[19] However, it is worth noting that the Basel Committee on Banking Supervision (BCBS), fearful of the impact the LCR might have on the availability of funds for loans to the real economy, watered down elements of the calculation in the adopted rules, relative to what had been initially proposed. So, whereas HQLA had initially only embraced cash, treasuries, and high-quality corporate bonds, the adopted version of the LCR allows any investment grade bond, and some securitization issues, to count towards a proportion of the HQLA. Moreover, the run-off rates were reduced for some classes of bank liabilities.[20]

Two features of the LCR need to be stressed. First, it imposes potentially socially wasteful restrictions on bank assets. The bank is required to hold at all times liquid assets sufficient to meet an eventuality which is unlikely to occur but which will have a significant impact on the bank if it does. The cost of this arrangement is that the transformation function of banks is impeded and the benefit is that banks are more likely to be able to survive liquidity crunches induced by financial crises. By contrast, requiring a bank to hold capital to meet tail risks does not have an impact on the composition of the bank's assets; it is purely a funding requirement. It is thus less

---

[17] BIS/BCBS, *Basel III: The Liquidity Coverage Ratio and liquidity risk monitoring tools*, bcbs238 (2013), para 4.

[18] The assumption is that either the problem or the bank will be resolved within the 30-day period.

[19] They are set out in BIS/BCBS, n 17, and are analysed in P Davies, 'Liquidity Safety Nets for Banks' (2013) 13 *Journal of Corporate Law Studies* 285, 298–300.

[20] Full implementation of the LCR was also postponed until 1 January 2019. See 'Big Banks Have Liquidity Wishes Granted', *Financial Times*, 11 January 2013.

constraining of the transformation function.[21] Second, the LCR is a novel form of liquidity regulation. It is not a simple requirement that a certain percentage of the bank's assets be held in liquid form. Rather, the liability and asset sides of the balance sheet are linked up: the amount of HQLA required to be held at all times is a function of the predicted stability (or otherwise) of short-term funding in a stressed scenario.

In terms of our discussion in the previous chapter, the LCR is a 'buffer', not a hard minimum, such that banks are permitted to fall below a 100 per cent ratio of liquid assets to expected cash outflows in times of actual stress.[22] The rules leave it to national supervisors to work out the consequences for banks that eat into their buffers of liquid assets.

15.3.2 The Net Stable Funding Ratio ('NSFR')

The objective of the NSFR is to discourage banks from relying heavily on short-term funding from the wholesale markets, in the belief that such funders are comparatively more likely to run than other funding sources as financial stresses mount. This ratio focuses on the notion of 'stable funding' and requires banks to have *available* stable funding at least equivalent to its *required* stable funding over a one-year time period.[23] The ratio involves, on the requirements side, weighting the bank's assets according to the likelihood of the bank being able to liquidate them at face value (in a stressed market) and, on the availability side, weighting the bank's liabilities according to the likelihood of the funding being withdrawn in the same situation. Rather obviously, long-term liabilities (more than one year) are regarded as more stable than shorter-term liabilities. But stability also turns on the type of funder: short-term funding provided by retail and business customers is regarded as more stable than short-term wholesale funding. As to assets, their liquidity characteristics are again obviously important, but so also is the tenor of the asset (for how long is the bank committed to the loan, for example).[24]

Once again, we see the linking up of the asset and liability sides of the bank's balance sheet: the bank can achieve the required ratio by holding more liquid assets or more stable funding (or some of both). As with the LCR, in moving towards the final rules for the NSFR the Basel Committee softened their impact.[25] Nevertheless, the thrust of the mechanism is still clear. Thus, on the asset side, long-term commercial loans require stable funding equivalent to 65–85 per cent of the face value of the loan (depending on their riskiness), but claims on central banks of less than six months' duration require

---

[21] See Chapter 14, section 14.3. But capital requirements may raise the costs of borrowing to some degree.

[22] Otherwise Charles Goodhart's famous taxi anecdote would apply: a traveller arrives on a train late at night and is relieved to see a taxi waiting in the station car park. The driver, however, refuses to take the tired traveller to her destination. When asked to explain, the driver points to the local ordinance which states that 'at all times one taxi must be waiting at the station'.

[23] BIS/BCBS, *Basel III: The Net Stable Funding Ratio*, bcbsd295 (2014). 'The NSFR is defined as the amount of available stable funding relative to the amount of required stable funding. This ratio should be equal to at least 100% on an ongoing basis. "*Stable funding*" is defined as the portion of capital and liabilities expected to be reliable over the time horizon considered by the NSFR, which extends to one year' (para 9).

[24] Tenor needs to be assessed on a business basis, not just formally. Preserving customer relationships (and thus future business) may require the bank to roll over some loans it formally could call in.

[25] See n 2. The changes are summarized in Annex 1 to that document and the final weightings proposed are set out in Tables 1 and 2 (In force, 1 January 2018.).

no stable funding. On the liability side, equity contributes 100 per cent of its issue price to the required available funding, retail and business deposits contribute 90 or 95 per cent of face value, while unsecured short-term funding from non-financial companies contributes only 50 per cent and the same funding from financial companies, nothing at all.[26] The incentives generated for the banks by the NSFR are thus to lengthen the maturities of ('term out') their liabilities (and in the case of short-term funding from financial institutions to avoid it entirely) or shorten the maturities of their assets.[27] The former pressure constrains banks' access to cheap short-term funding from wholesale markets, the latter their incentives to make long-term loans.

Taken together, the two new liquidity requirements are likely to have a bigger impact on banks' costs than the revised capital rules,[28] as the Basel Committee implicitly recognized in its attenuation of the LCR and NSFR.

15.4 Insuring the Bank

15.4.1 The idea of lender of last resort ('LOLR')

The idea behind the LCR mechanism is a requirement that a certain proportion of the bank's assets should be constituted at all times by instruments that will retain their liquidity in private markets even in a period of market stress (which is expected to occur infrequently). The core instruments will be cash and treasuries; to the extent that anything else is allowed in, there is a risk that in a crisis these lesser instruments will in fact lose their liquidity. Insuring the bank, in this context, involves finding a way of restoring to the bank in a crisis the liquidity its assets have in private markets in normal times—without the bank having at all times to hold those assets in HQLA form.[29] The mechanism is, essentially, that the bank in a period of market stress is able to shift some of its (now) illiquid assets to a third party in exchange for liquid assets. This alternative way of proceeding potentially allows the bank to rely on a wider range of assets to provide the liquidity it needs in times of stress. In particular, it opens up the possibility of the bank using at least its more highly rated loans as collateral to obtain cash from third parties. Note that the bank's transformation function is less inhibited with an arrangement of this type than by the LCR, because its need for HQLA is reduced. It also renders the NSFR less important—perhaps even unnecessary—because the bank now has an alternative way of countering withdrawals of short-term funding. Such an arrangement may be particularly important in relation to 'tail risks'—low-frequency, high-impact risks. For a bank always to hold liquid assets on its balance sheet against

---

[26] 'Short-term' means a maturity of less than twelve months.

[27] Going in the same direction, the run-off rate stipulated under the LCR for wholesale money from financial institutions is 100 per cent.

[28] D Elliott, S Salloy, and AO Santos Sr, 'Assessing the Cost of Financial Regulation', IMF Working Paper 12/233 (2012). However, R Banerjee and H Mio ('The Impact of Liquidity Regulation on Banks', Bank of England Staff Working Paper 536, 2015) found that a UK predecessor of the LCR brought about a shift away from short-term funding from financial lenders and an increase in central bank reserves on the part of UK banks, but without an increase in the cost of lending to the real economy, the implication being a decrease in banks' profitability.

[29] More prosaically, this might be called 'contingent liquidity provision' by the central bank, rather than insurance, but we have noted in section 15.1 that the Bank of England now uses the term 'liquidity insurance'.

such risks may seem particularly inefficient, making a mechanism that provides liquidity against illiquid assets only at the point of need especially attractive.

For liquidity insurance to work, the third party providing liquidity in times of stress must be an institution which stands outside the private markets. The obvious candidate for this role is a central bank under a scheme in which it exchanges liquid assets (central bank reserves, gilts, treasury bills) for illiquid bank loans. As long ago as 1873, Walter Bagehot described and critiqued the role of a central bank (in his case the Bank of England) in providing LOLR facilities to banks in periods of stress.[30] Under Bagehot's prescription, in banking panics the central bank should lend to solvent banks within its jurisdiction freely but at a high interest rate and on good collateral.[31] Only by lending freely can the central bank end the panic. The level of the interest rate should be set slightly above what the relevant private market charged *in normal times*, so as to provide an incentive for the bank to return to the private markets when normal times return, thus preserving the central bank's last resort status.[32] A central bank is ultimately in a position to lend freely when private markets are frozen because its formal powers to create money are unlimited, but it should lend only on good collateral in order to reduce the risk to its own balance sheet. Despite the injunction to lend freely, a further component of traditional LOLR is that advancing support is a discretionary decision of the central bank, taken for the purposes of preserving financial stability, and not an entitlement of the bank. On this approach, LOLR cannot truly be presented as insurance for the banks. Hedge funds discovered the uncomfortable nature of this 'constructive ambiguity' aspect of LOLR when they litigated in the aftermath of the temporary nationalization in the UK of the mortgage bank Northern Rock.

SRM Global Master Fund LP v The Commissioners of Her Majesty's Treasury

[2009] EWCA Civ 788, Court of Appeal (England)

The claimant, a hedge fund incorporated in the Cayman Islands, acquired 11.5 per cent of the ordinary share capital of Northern Rock (NR), after NR had been advanced LOLR support by the Bank of England (and its deposits had been guaranteed by the UK government). NR was later nationalized under the Banking (Special Provisions) Act 2008 (the precursor of the current special resolution regime discussed in Chapter 16). In valuing the bank's shares for compensation purposes, section 5(4) of that Act required the valuer to assume, contrary to the facts, 'that all financial assistance provided by the Bank of England or the Treasury to the deposit-taker in question has been withdrawn'. On this basis the shares were probably worthless. The claimant challenged the valuation provisions as contrary to the guarantee of private property contained in Article 1 of Protocol 1 to the European Convention on Human Rights.

---

[30] W Bagehot, *Lombard Street: A Description of the Money Market* (London: Henry S King & Co, 1873), 51 ('In wild periods of alarm, one failure makes many, and the best way to prevent the derivative failures is to arrest the primary failure which causes them').

[31] Ibid, 197–8.

[32] Charging at the rate demanded in the private market in a panic would clearly defeat the object of the exercise. Chapter 13 discusses the additional desideratum in LOLR practice of lending only to solvent institutions.

In rejecting the claim the Court relied heavily on the financial stability rationale for LOLR support, as explained by previous governors of the Bank of England. Laws L J, for the court, stated: 'If the shareholders had received more favourable treatment than was furnished by these arrangements, the LOLR operation would (through the prism of the government's exit strategy, the company's nationalization) have been the source of a specific benefit conferred on them. That would not be consistent with a governing principle of LOLR, namely its deployment only in the interest of the financial system as a whole. And it would encourage for the future—at least this would be the risk—the very moral hazard which the LOLR scheme is carefully constructed to avoid.'

An appeal to the European Court of Human Rights also failed: *Grainger v UK* [2012] ECHR 1675.

15.4.2 LOLR in the recent crisis

In the recent financial crisis, there was a veritable explosion of new (but generally temporary) LOLR initiatives from central banks, especially the Federal Reserve in the US and the Bank of England (the European Central Bank followed along in the later Eurozone crisis). As Cooley and Phillipon remark, in the crisis the Fed 'created a dozen new vehicles to provide liquidity to the financial sector'.[33] These reactions suggest that, while the principle of LOLR was well established on both sides of the Atlantic, it needed significant extension to cope with the financial crisis. We do not intend to go through these (often temporary) schemes in detail, though three central examples are set out in the text box. Compared to the Bagehotian template for LOLR, the following points are significant:

(i) Although the facilities were (usually) formally confined to solvent banks, the distinction between solvent and illiquid banks proved difficult to draw. This should not surprise us. As we have seen, an illiquid bank will quickly become insolvent if it cannot quickly acquire the liquidity it needs. The test of solvency thus has a somewhat hypothetical character and in practice it is not clear how rigorously it was adhered to.

(ii) The quality of the collateral which central banks demanded in exchange for the liquid assets provided by them tended to degrade. As banks' demands for liquidity exceeded the banks' stock of traditional high-quality assets, central banks lowered their collateral requirements rather than choke off the supply of liquidity.

(iii) In order to maximize the supply of loans to the productive economy, central banks did not always insist on penal rates of interest for borrowings from them. Instead, they relied on the temporary nature of the schemes to secure return to the private markets post-crisis.

---

[33] TF Cooley and T Philippon, 'The Role of the Federal Reserve', in VV Acharya and M Richardson (eds), *Restoring Financial Stability: How to Repair a Failed System* (New York, NY: John Wiley & Sons Inc, 2009), 277. For a table of the central bank initiatives, see VV Acharya and DK Backus, 'Private Lessons for Public Banking: The Case for Conditionality in LOLR Facilities', in Acharya and Richardson (eds), 305, 312–18. The range of facilities reflected the fact that the Federal Reserve used emergency powers to create LOLR mechanisms for various non-bank financial market actors who were not eligible to use the discount window and to devise facilities whose use would not carry a negative signal of solvency, 'stigma'.

(iv) The institutions eligible to participate in at least some of these facilities were not restricted to banks, as technically defined. This was particularly so in the US because of the growth of market-based credit intermediation provided through the investment bank/dealer bank model.

However, Bagehot's injunction to 'lend freely' was certainly observed. For example, the Fed's balance sheet moved from $874bn to $2,058bn between 1 August 2007 and 14 January 2009.[34]

LOLR Initiatives in Response to the Financial Crisis

Special Liquidity Scheme (Bank of England)

This was a temporary scheme open to all banks which was available for less than a year from spring 2008. Its aim was to deal with the overhang of loans in the course of securitization which burdened banks' balance sheets with the freezing of the wholesale money markets in the previous year. The Bank offered to swap Treasury bills for bank-generated asset-backed securities (ABS) or covered bonds for periods of up to three years, thus giving the banks a significant period of time to refinance the loans. But the scheme did not apply to future securitizations. The scheme was a success: the Bank of England provided £185bn against collateral with a face value of £287bn; there were no defaults; and the Bank made a profit of £2.26bn. This was handed over to the UK government, which had agreed to indemnify the Bank against any losses incurred under the scheme.

Term Auction Facility (Federal Reserve)

This scheme was open to banks as legally defined ('deposit institutions') and allowed them to swap for Treasury bills a variety of bank assets for periods of up to three months. In particular, the bank assets included asset-backed commercial paper, whether existing or newly created, which the market no longer wanted. The interest rate was set through an auction. The scheme operated between December 2007 and March 2010. Nearly $4 trillion was advanced under the facility. There were no defaults.

Term Securities Lending Facility (Federal Reserve)

This was a scheme, introduced in March 2008, which was open to the Federal Reserve's primary dealers, a group of some twenty international banks, some of which were purely investment banks/dealer banks. The Fed would swap Treasury securities for debt securities held by the dealers (meaning, ultimately, any investment grade debt security) for periods of up to twenty-eight days. The aim was to provide the dealers with collateral (treasuries) which was still acceptable in the secured funding markets (notably the repo market) even in the stressed conditions of the financial crisis. The Fed in effect took as collateral for its loan to the dealers the securities which the dealers had previously been able to use as collateral directly in the repo markets. Thus, these investment banks were able to continue to fund their assets in the secured lending markets and not be pushed into a fire-sale of those assets. The programme was structured as a series of monthly auctions. Over $2 trillion was advanced over the period the facility remained active; at its peak in late 2008, the amount outstanding under the facility was over $250 billion.

---

[34] Cooley and Philippon, n 33, 281, though some of this increase was due to increased deposits by banks with the Fed, now regarded as one of the few safe havens for excess cash.

15.4.3 LOLR in the future

After these temporary schemes were wound up, central banks moved to reflect on what they had learned in the scramble to provide effective LOLR mechanisms at the height of the crisis. One result was that central banks sought to supplement the traditional bilateral LOLR mechanisms, which had existed before the crisis, with explicit multi-lateral schemes of the type introduced in the crisis. Banks in difficulty, such as Northern Rock, had always been free to approach their central bank and seek liquidity for that particular bank on a bilateral basis, through what is usually referred to as the 'discount window'. At the height of the crisis, a wide variety of general schemes were put in place, albeit only for a limited time. Post-crisis, central banks moved to have permanent multilateral schemes in place in addition to the discount window, while not excluding the possibility of supplementing them in times of general panic.

For example, the Bank of England now has two LOLR schemes in addition to the discount window. One is a standing scheme and the other a contingent scheme which needs to be triggered by the bank; both now accept the 'widest' set of collateral in exchange for central bank reserves.[35] The 'widest' set of collateral includes mortgage and corporate bonds, securitizations, own-name securities, and, perhaps most signifi-cant, portfolios of loans. The standing scheme is based on monthly auctions of central bank reserves for a term of six months; the additional scheme is triggered by the bank in times of market stress. It could be debated whether a standing facility for the provision of central bank liquidity against publicly announced classes of collateral is in fact a LOLR facility at all. Indeed, the Bank of England's current description of its money-market operations does not refer to LOLR. Revealingly, it uses instead the phrase 'liquidity insurance'.[36]

These recent moves by the Bank of England raise the question of whether there should be a further development away from the traditional discretionary approach to LOLR, to the point where banks enter into formal contracts for liquidity support from their central bank in times of stress, just as small banks do—or did—contract for lines of credit with larger banks as a method of meeting their liquidity needs. Even standing liquidity schemes do not give a contractual level of assurance to banks, since the schemes can be withdrawn or amended unilaterally by the central bank. A particular advantage of this further step is that, subject to conditions, the contractual rights could be used to meet the banks' regulatory liquidity requirements under the LCR, thus further enhancing the banks' transformation function.[37]

The potential benefits of this new approach, whether or not it extends to formal contracting, are those already noted: bank lending will be facilitated if the proportion of

---

[35] See Bank of England, *Liquidity Insurance at the Bank of England: Developments in the Sterling Monetary Framework* (2013). The forbidding titles of the two schemes are, respectively, Indexed Long Term Repos (ILTR) and Contingent Term Repo Facility (CTRF). The predecessor of the CTRF was triggered in June 2012 at the height of the Eurozone crisis.

[36] Bank of England, *The Bank of England's Sterling Monetary Framework* (2015), 5.

[37] For such a proposal, see B Winters, *Review of the Bank of England's Framework for Providing Liquidity to the Banking System* (2012). The Basel Committee accepts that 'committed use' facilities at the central bank can count as liquid assets under the LCR: BCBS, *Revisions to Basel III*, bcbs274 (2014).

bank assets required to be held in liquid form is reduced and instead market liquidity is provided by shifting bank loans to the central bank in times of stress. The principal objections to this extension of LOLR are: (a) it will be unattractive to banks for stigma reasons; (b) it involves a significant moral hazard risk; and (c) it will amount to subsidizing banks.

15.4.4 Stigma

'Stigma' refers to the risk that banks discovered to be using LOLR facilities will be assessed by the market as posing a solvency risk. Even if insurance is available only to formally solvent banks, the market might doubt the central bank's ability to distinguish between illiquid and insolvent banks or its willingness to apply the access criteria rigorously in a period of financial stress. Stigma is particularly associated with access to bilateral LOLR (such as the discount window), where the process is initiated by the bank seeking to shift its assets. However, even a market-wide liquidity offer, initiated by the central bank, can attract stigma, if it is in fact used by only a small number of banks, since it suggests that only some banks have been adversely affected by the market-wide stress. It may be possible to hide information about the use of a general scheme for some time, but public accountability considerations suggest that disclosure will eventually be required.[38] Even if the scheme is widely used initially, stigma may attach to banks which repay later than others.[39] One way forward might be to make it attractive for banks at all times to purchase liquidity options from the central bank, the terms of which options would be set so as to provide a further incentive for banks actually to exercise routinely some of the options purchased.[40] This might reduce stigma by equating the central bank's liquidity insurance provisions with contractual entitlements and the routine exercise of the options might also reduce stigma.

---

[38] Under the Dodd–Frank Act (disclosure with a two-year lag) the Fed recently released individual institution access data in respect of the various liquidity programmes it put in place in the crisis. It will be interesting to see if the market reacts adversely in a future situation of market stress to those institutions reported to have made heavy use of the crisis mechanisms. See MJ Fleming, 'Federal Reserve Liquidity Provision During the Financial Crisis' (2012) 4 *Annual Review of Financial Economics* 161, Tables 2 and 3. Barclays Bank was the biggest user of the two largest liquidity programmes instituted by the Fed in the crisis. Former Fed Chair Ben Bernanke has underlined the dilemma: '[Disclosure] provisions serve the important purposes of advancing transparency, accountability, and democratic legitimacy, and I am not advocating that they be changed. But we should be aware that, by increasing the risk of early disclosure of borrowers' identities, these requirements will probably reduce the willingness of firms to borrow from the Fed in a panic and thus potentially impair the effectiveness of the government's crisis response.' Available at http://www.brookings.edu/blogs/ben-bernanke/posts/2015/12/03-fed-emergency-lending.

[39] As is said to have been an issue recently in relation to the ECB's longer-term refinancing operation, where prompt repayment by some banks put all banks under pressure to pay back at least a proportion of their drawings: 'Fears Over ECB's Longer-Term Refinancing Operation', *Financial Times*, 24 January 2013.

[40] Winters, n 37. The setting of the level of the fee for taking out the option and the terms of their exercise would be crucial. The—somewhat conflicting—goals are to induce routine take-up and exercise of some of the options, while not replacing the private markets for liquidity provision in normal times or providing a high level of subsidy to banking activities.

15.4.5 Moral hazard and subsidy

'Moral hazard', in this context, refers principally to the incentive that access to central bank funds gives to banks to take more risks with their own liquidity provision, relying on liquidity provided by the central bank to get them out of trouble. However, this is a concern only if central bank liquidity provision is not properly priced. A somewhat separate worry is that central banks might have concerns about the size and quality of their own balance sheets, if they became routine providers of liquidity to the banking system, and they might also worry that, in such a case, central bank fiat rather than the market would begin to determine the allocation of resources. However, the central bank can control for such behaviour by setting standards for the quality of the assets it is prepared to accept as collateral, and there will always be the prudential capital and (now) enhanced supervisory and macroprudential controls in the background. Indeed, as Acharya and Backus have suggested,[41] access to central bank liquidity provision could be made conditional upon adherence to capital standards (not necessarily just the Basel minima), thus providing an additional incentive for banks to observe those standards and removing any incentive to seek central bank liquidity rather than recapitalize the bank in times of stress. In short, the discretionary element of LOLR no longer has to carry the full weight of deterring moral hazard and so it need not be a central element of general liquidity schemes. The potential subsidy to banks arising out of the willingness of short-term funders to lend to the bank at lower rates of interest because of the central bank insurance also disappears if the central bank liquidity provision is properly priced.

15.4.6 Non-banks

In Chapter 14, section 14.1, we noted the potential disadvantages of confining the legal definition of a bank to, in effect, deposit-taking institutions. Any institution that borrows short and buys illiquid assets runs a liquidity risk, whether or not the short-term funding takes the form of retail deposits, and in some cases those non-bank institutions may be systemically important. It is a striking fact that, at the beginning of the crisis, none of the major investment banks in the US had access to LOLR, and all failed (Bear Sterns, Lehman Brothers), were merged away (Merrill Lynch), or converted into bank holding companies (Goldman Sachs, Morgan Stanley) so as to obtain that access. As we have seen, some of the general schemes developed by the Fed in the crisis were designed to provide liquidity support to non-banks.[42] The Bank of England has now extended its standing liquidity facilities to broker-dealers.[43] In principle, there is

---

[41] See n 33.

[42] See the Term Securities Lending Facility, described in section 15.4.2—applicable to the Fed's 'primary dealers', which includes broker-dealers/investment banks. The Fed still appears to have authority under Dodd–Frank to develop general schemes which apply to non-banks: Dodd–Frank Act §716(b); and the Bank of England's 'Red Book' (n 36, 5) explicitly contemplates a role for the Bank as 'market maker of last resort'.

[43] See n 36, Part 1.VI. See also the speech by WC Dudley, President and Chief Executive Officer, Federal Reserve Bank of New York, *Fixing Wholesale Funding to Build a More Stable Financial System*, 2013 (available at http://www.ny.frb.org/newsevents/speeches/2013/dud130201.html).

an argument from the point of view of financial stability that all systemically important institutions should have access to the central bank's liquidity arrangements and that such an opening is a counterpoint to the subjection of some non-banks to capital requirements.

15.4.7 Providing liquidity to the market

It was a short, but significant, step for central banks to move from swapping treasuries for the bank's assets to swapping treasuries for securities issued by banks but held by investors. Both the Bank of England and the Fed took this step in the crisis, not primarily to solve banks' liquidity problems, but to restart credit markets which had become frozen. Under the Fed's Term Asset-Backed Securities Loan Facility ('TALF') programme, any US citizen holding asset-backed paper issued by banks could use it as collateral for treasuries in swaps, which could last as long as three to five years (to match the maturities of notes issued by banks in securitizations). The scheme operated in 2008–9 and $75bn was advanced under it. The aim of the programme was:

> to provide liquidity in the form of term loans to investors in the least risky part—the AAA tranches—of particular types of asset-backed securities, including those backed by consumer loans, student loans, small business loans, and commercial real estate loans. The hope was that, by providing loans directly to investors against asset-backed collateral, the TALF would help stabilize and improve the prices at which those securities could be sold, thus reducing lenders' costs of funds. With lenders' funding strains alleviated, the extension of credit to consumers and other borrowers could occur on more favorable terms.[44]

This scheme (and others like it) addressed the problem that strains on the banks' liquidity were likely to induce them to reduce lending to the real economy, but addressed it not by allowing banks to swap assets for central bank liquidity, but by allowing the holders of bank securities to do so. By targeting securities issued by banks on the back of particular types of lending, those types of lending could be encouraged.[45] The Bank of England's Asset Purchase Facility began life with a similar objective, though it has lived on as a way of delivering the Bank's policy of quantitative easing— that is, it moved beyond providing liquidity to particular markets to providing liquidity to the economy as a whole and thus is to be seen today as an instrument of monetary policy. With the provision of liquidity to particular markets or to the economy as a whole, however, central banks moved beyond the more limited goal of providing a liquidity safety net for banks, and we do not consider such schemes further.

---

[44] BP Sack, Executive Vice President, Federal Reserve Bank of New York, speech, 9 June 2010.

[45] Prior to the crisis, much consumer lending (eg automobiles and credit-card receivables) in the US had migrated from banks to specialized non-bank lenders, which financed themselves through securitization. Unlike residential mortgage securitization, underwriting standards for these mortgage-based securities did not decline, in part because originators took a first-loss position. Nevertheless, after Lehman's failure, investor demand for all asset-backed securities collapsed. See A Ashcraft, A Malz, and Z Pozsar, 'The Federal Reserve's Term Asset-Backed Securities Loan Facility' (2012) *FRBNY Economic Policy Review* (November) 34.

15.4.8 Central bank support vs LCR

We come back, then, to the question of why we should have a binding Liquidity Coverage Ratio regime that is complex to administer and may be socially costly if liquidity can readily be provided at time of financial stress by LOLR or, more broadly, central bank liquidity insurance? There are three interlinked answers. First, a fundamental principle is that central bank support should go only to solvent institutions. The liquidity self-insurance of the LCR gives the central bank time to determine whether the institution is solvent or not. As Chapter 13, section 13.2.3 explains, liquidity support for an insolvent bank (or banks) actively works against recovery from a financial crisis because it keeps alive 'zombie banks' that will be hoarding cash, rather than lending to the real economy. Second, the many ways that an institution could, in the absence of liquidity self-insurance, find itself facing a liquidity crisis will not always perfectly match the legal authority of central banks to lend. In reaction to large Fed loans to AIG and various other Fed-associated rescues the Dodd–Frank Act cut back the Fed's authority to make emergency loans (that is, outside normal discount window activity) except through generally available programmes.[46] Under current arrangements, Eurozone provision of 'Emergency Liquidity Assistance' needs to be routed through a national central bank, rather than extended by the ECB,[47] though the implications of the consolidation of supervisory and resolution authority in the European Banking Union may eventually point to a different outcome. Liquidity self-insurance is protection against those gaps. Third, at least in the US context, central bank support has been broadly read as 'bail-out' of the affected financial institutions. Public disclosure of the recipients is required (though purportedly with lag to mitigate the strongest 'stigma' effects); public opprobrium (political stigma) is likely to follow. This will make institutions reluctant to seek Fed support and the Fed will be cautious in its response. Although only the first rationale is a principled argument in favour of the LCR, it can be argued that, by reducing the demand for central bank support, liquidity self-insurance will mitigate the practical, legal, and political risks associated with pinning financial stability on the availability of timely and adequate central bank support.

15.5 Insuring Short-Term Funders

15.5.1 The idea of deposit guarantee schemes ('DGS')

In the previous section we analysed mechanisms for offering solvent *banks* something close to an assurance that they will retain market liquidity in a crisis. An alternative approach is to address the bank's funding liquidity problem directly by providing

---

[46] Dodd–Frank Act, §1101. See generally, K Judge, 'The First Year: The Role of a Modern Lender of Last Resort' (2016) 116 *Columbia Law Review* 843.

[47] See ECB, 'ELA Procedures', available at https://www.ecb.europa.eu/mopo/ela/html/index.en.html. See also G Illing and P König, 'The European Central Bank as Lender of Last Resort' (2014) 9 *DIW Economic Bulletin* 16. As the ECB in principle stands as LOLR for Eurozone governments, National central bank LOLR is effectively indirect ECB support.

assurance to short-term *funders* that their claims on the bank will be met by a third party in case the bank defaults. If short-term funders' claims are assured in this way, they have no incentive to run, even in a panic. Clearly, the third party must be of impeccable financial standing (it must be the state, or a state-backed fund)[48] and the mechanism whereby the third party is substituted for the bank must operate very smoothly. Such mechanisms to protect retail depositors—within limits—are well established across jurisdictions, in the shape of deposit guarantee schemes ('DGS').[49] The extension of short-term funding sources for banks beyond traditional retail deposits into the wholesale markets raises the question whether the guarantee should be widened.

Whether it is desirable to extend DGS beyond depositors turns partly on how one sees the function of the DGS. If the DGS is seen as a form of consumer protection with redistributive goals, then this would be an argument against extending it beyond 'poor' retail depositors to 'rich' wholesale funders. However, those with substantial sums of money in bank accounts are not the poorest members of society and so any such redistributive rationale looks weak in this case. Alternatively, a consumer protection rationale may be based on asymmetry of information between depositor and customer, which, as we saw in section 15.2, is an important element in their propensity to run. However, the difficulty of evaluating the loans made by banks applies to all short-term funders. This suggests an argument for extending guarantees beyond retail depositors.

On the other hand, it is far from clear that guarantees, even for retail depositors, are a necessary element in an effective policy for maintaining depositor confidence in the banking system. The UK had no deposit bank run between the City of Glasgow Bank failure in 1878 and Northern Rock in 2007, despite the fact that it had no effective DGS in place during the whole of that period and no DGS at all until 1982. In the absence of good information about the bank's solvency, depositors' decisions to remain in or leave a bank turn on the general level of confidence they have in that bank or banks generally. If good capital regulation and effective supervision—and good luck—in fact produce a situation in which banks do not fail over a period of time, then the sensitivity of depositors to adverse signals about the bank's solvency will also decrease.[50] Non-failure and a reduction in the propensity to run are mutually re-enforcing, so that, even in the absence of a DGS, depositors may prove 'sticky' in the face of adverse news. By contrast, frequent bank failures will increase the sensitivity of depositors to bad news about their bank or banks in general, perhaps producing a situation in which only a state-backed guarantee will restore depositors' trust.

This is illustrated by the legislative history of the Banking Act 1933, which introduced the DGS in the US. Henry Steagall successfully promoted the introduction of deposit insurance in order to preserve the then dominant but idiosyncratic US 'unit

---

[48] And not all states will do, as the UK and Dutch depositors in the Icelandic banks which failed in the crisis will know.

[49] See A Demirgüç-Kunt, E Kane, and L Laeven, 'Deposit Insurance Around the World: A Comprehensive Analysis and Database' (2015) 20 *Journal of Financial Stability* 155.

[50] 'An old-established bank has a "prestige", which amounts to a "privileged opportunity"; though no exclusive right is given to it by law, a peculiar power is given to it by opinion' (Bagehot, n 30, 244).

banking' system.[51] US banks were normally confined to only one place of business and were in consequence highly fragile because they could not diversify their loan portfolios. If the crops in the area had a bad year, the bank went down. Some 5,700 banks failed in the US in the period 1921–9—before the Great Depression—thus creating a powerful argument for either reforming bank structure or introducing deposit insurance. The latter policy won out. The crucial point is that, assuming unit banking stayed, the regulatory reform had to deal with a banking system which was not only fragile but which had abundantly demonstrated this fact to depositors over previous decades.[52] In that situation, a state guarantee of the deposit was perhaps the only credible reform available to the legislator, though it was very controversial at the time and is still not universally accepted.

We will look first at the conditions for the success of a DGS, then at the potential costs, then at their possible extension beyond retail depositors.

15.5.2 Designing an effective DGS

An effective DGS—effective, that is, from the point of view of the depositor—must pay out quickly if the bank defaults, and pay out in full; moreover, the promise to do these things must be credible to depositors. The last requirement means that the scheme must normally have state backing. However, as we shall see, the cost of the scheme need not ultimately fall on the taxpayer. A mutual insurance scheme run by the banks themselves is conceivable, especially in jurisdictions with few but large banks, so that coordination costs are reduced, but it must be doubtful whether such schemes would be credible in a global crisis. In any event, DGS are invariably state-run or state-backed today.

Paying out quickly and in full are essential constituents of effectiveness. Since withdrawal is easy for the depositor, even the risk of a slight loss or temporary deprivation of liquidity will be enough to dispose the depositor to run. An effective model for achieving these ends has been developed by the Federal Deposit Insurance Corporation ('FDIC') over the years, though it is to be noted that it depends on the FDIC's powers in bank resolution, which many DGS operators do not have. Under this core model, the FDIC seizes control of the failing bank after close of business on a Friday night and over the weekend transfers the bank's deposit liabilities (with sufficient assets to cover them) and perhaps some other assets and liabilities to another existing bank, so that the depositors wake up on Monday morning as depositors in a new bank, but with exactly the same balances as on Friday.[53]

---

[51] C Calomiris, 'The Political Lessons of Depression-Era Banking Reform' (2010) 26 *Oxford Review of Economic Policy* 540. The DGS was opposed by the 'money center' banks, whose businesses were more diversified and whose competitive position was threatened by the DGS. For many years the compromise was that the guarantee was set at a low level.

[52] It is not the case, however, that, where the bank went down, the depositors lost everything. They seem to have recovered 80–90 per cent of their deposits, after a wait.

[53] They may then move those balances to another bank, if they wish. A bare transfer of deposits (and assets to cover) is used in about one-third of cases ('insured deposit transfer') and additional assets and liabilities (that is, viable bank businesses) are transferred in one-half ('purchase and assumption'). D Skeel, *The New Financial Deal: Understanding the Dodd–Frank Act and Its (Unintended) Consequences* (New

By contrast, the UK's pre-crisis DGS was a model of how *not* to design an effective DGS. It capped the insured deposits at £35k per institution (ie to cover all accounts held by single depositor in that institution), insured only 90 per cent of deposits above £2k (so that a depositor holding at the £35k level would receive £31.7k), and paid out only at the end of the insolvency process. It is perhaps unsurprising that the depositors in Northern Rock were not dissuaded from running by this scheme. Under domestic pressure and EU reforms, the cap has been raised to the equivalent of €100k, the element of co-insurance removed and payout promised within seven days.[54]

15.5.3 Minimizing the costs of the DGS

When the DGS was introduced in the US in 1933, it was very controversial and was not in fact supported by President Roosevelt. It has remained controversial ever since. Some take the view that, without DGS, bank regulation would be substantially unnecessary. This argument is based on the premise that uninsured depositors would monitor the bank so as to avoid failure. This seems implausible. For the reasons given above, retail depositors are in a poor position to monitor the bank's activities and have no incentive to invest substantial resources in so doing. Without the DGS, they would indeed monitor and react in the way they traditionally have done, namely by running when they detected what they thought was a risk of insolvency. The DGS certainly removes the incentive for depositors to monitor in this way, but it is precisely because such monitoring proved destabilizing that financial stability is promoted by removing the need for it.

However, the argument from monitoring might support the cap, which is to be found in nearly all DGS schemes, on the amount insured. The withdrawal of large deposits might act as a warning signal to banks that they were taking on unacceptable risks and large uninsured depositors might be willing to devote more resources to monitoring. In fact, however, these caps—€100,000 in the EU; $250,000 in the US—are largely cosmetic. They are applied not to depositors' total holdings but to the amounts deposited in an insured institution (EU) or an insured account (US). No wealthy depositor, who is moderately well informed, need fail to have the whole of his or her deposits covered by spreading them over a number of locations.[55]

There is, therefore, the risk of some loss of monitoring capacity through the *de facto* extension of DGS coverage to very large depositors. However, for this to be a significant loss to financial stability, one would have to assume that uninsured large depositors would remain depositors in the bank but engage in monitoring. It might be that such depositors would regard it as less costly to move their deposits to a state bank or to find a deposit opportunity in the private market that provided them with collateral against

---

York, NY: John Wiley & Sons, 2011), 122–3. The FDIC has traditionally saved all depositors in this way (not just insured ones).

[54] See FSA, *Banking and Compensation Reform*, PS09/11 (2009); Directive 2014/49/EU (OJ L173/149).

[55] Equally, most schemes extend beyond individual depositors to embrace companies and other institutions (sometimes with exclusions).

their deposit (perhaps via a money market mutual fund which specialized in repo operations).[56]

While the proposition that, without DGS, bank regulation could be substantially scaled down is doubtful, DGS do generate a case for some additional regulation in order to minimize their costs. Those costs are, again, moral hazard and subsidy. Effective DGS turn deposits into riskless investments, for which the bank will pay a lower interest rate than if the DGS were not there. That subsidy to banks in the form of cheap lending is an undesirable subsidy to the banking industry—as against industries whose short-term funding is not subsidized in this way—and also encourages banks to grow bigger (and take more risks) than they would do without the cheap funding that is largely risk-insensitive. Since scale in banks beyond a certain level seems not to be cost-minimizing, this is also undesirable. Moral hazard, as already identified, is the risk that banks will engage in more risky activities than they would in the absence of insurance of their funding sources.

In principle, the solution to both problems is to put the costs of the DGS onto the industry, by requiring the compensation to be funded by the banks and for the levies on the banks to be adjusted according to the riskiness of each bank's activities. A debate can be had as to whether the scheme should be pre- or post-funded. Under post-funding the state is recompensed by industry only after paying out through the scheme. This means that the compensation costs are borne by the banks which survive, which may have been the more prudent ones. If the payout occurs in a crisis, the obligation to fund becomes an additional, procyclical constraint on the surviving banks' liquidity. The balance of argument seems to favour pre-funding: the US scheme has been designed in this way since its inception and the EU now requires this.[57]

Relating the funding, whether pre or post, to the riskiness of each bank's activities is in principle correct, for both anti-subsidy and combating moral hazard reasons. Again the US scheme has been risk-related from its origins, and the EU now requires this— but with the risk-weighting left to the Member States. Accurate calibration of the risk-related premiums is technically difficult, in any event.[58]

15.5.4 Extending guarantees to other forms of short-term funding?

Given the shift in banks' funding in the direction of raising short-term funds in the wholesale markets—for example, by issuing commercial paper with maturities measured in months—the question arises whether the guarantee should not be extended to

---

[56] See Chapters 21 and 22.

[57] *Ex ante* funding necessarily involves determining the percentage of covered deposits which the fund shall hold. Since such funds are lost to the banking industry, the level is necessarily modest (0.8 per cent in the EU). Oddly, it would seem, the 'Orderly Liquidation Fund' established to facilitate resolution under Dodd–Frank was not pre-funded, on the argument that the availability of such a fund would make 'bail-out' more likely than 'liquidation', presumably because it was thought that to draw down from a Treasury line of credit would seem less palatable to the FDIC than the use of a pre-existing fund. For further reflections on this point, see J Gordon and C Muller, 'Confronting Financial Crisis: The Case for a Systemic Emergency Insurance Fund' (2011) 28 *Yale Journal on Regulation* 151, 193.

[58] F Allen, E Carletti, and A Leonetto, 'Deposit Insurance and Risk Taking' (2011) 27 *Oxford Review of Economic Policy* 464, §IV, show that designing the optimal charging scheme is not straightforward.

such short-term funders as well. If adopted, this would be the opposite strategy from that underlying the NSFR, which, as we saw in section 15.3, discourages the banks from raising short-term wholesale funding ('STWF'). This alternative strategy would leave levels of short-term funding to be determined by the market. Regulatory action would be directed at avoiding runs on STWF, of the type seen by the holders of commercial paper at the outset of the Northern Rock event. This would amount to a significant extension of the state-backed insurance system for banks.

There are two main constraints on proposals for such an extension of the DGS. First, it is probably only a few, super-wealthy states (or wealthy states with small banking systems) that are capable of making a credible commitment of this type.[59] The ring-fence proposals we discuss in Chapter 23 suggest that European states, even large ones, do not want to take on this obligation. The second is whether the funding and moral hazard issues generated by the extended guarantee can be addressed in the same way as in relation to DGS; that is, by requiring *ex ante*, risk-related funding of the scheme which pays out to STWF and by supervision of the banking industry.[60] The main proponent of the extension, Morgan Ricks, while not confining his proposals to deposit-taking banks, would confine it to financial institutions that were subject to apparently tough portfolio restrictions on their assets, while 'money claims' would not be permitted to be issued by non-guaranteed institutions. In consequence of the extended guarantee, short-term funding, whether retail or wholesale, would be available to support only a constrained range of activities.[61]

15.6 Conclusion

In this chapter we have discussed three techniques for regulating the liquidity of banks, the lack of which turned out to be so destabilizing in the financial crisis. The technique favoured by the Basel Committee is a substantial requirement on banks as to the levels of liquid assets which they hold. We have indicated the downside of such a policy, in terms of its sterilization of the uses to which bank assets may be put and, in particular, its hindrance of the transformation function of banks. The implication of this argument is that the other two techniques, expanded central bank facilities and DGS (perhaps also expanded), are to be preferred. In fact, however, the Basel liquidity

---

[59] It is true that the guarantee is, in fact, costless if the threatened run is a pure 'panic' run, such that the bank is not in danger of insolvency. Provided the run is stopped by the *promise* of the guarantee, the guarantee will not be called on. If, however, the bank run is driven by accurate fears of insolvency, the extended guarantee is potentially very expensive for the state backing the scheme and it might not promote economic recovery for the state to seek to recover the amount expended from the banking sector—either at all or quickly.

[60] Loss of monitoring capacity might be thought to be more of an issue with wholesale funders, but if, as argued, STWF is regarded as information-insensitive, then there is no loss of monitoring capacity through this scheme.

[61] M Ricks, 'A Regulatory Design for Monetary Stability' (2012) 65 *Vanderbilt Law Review* 1289, esp s IV.B; M Ricks, *The Money Problem: Rethinking Financial Regulation* (Chicago: Chicago UP, 2016). It is not entirely clear how constraining the asset restrictions would be. However, it does appear that, unlike the retail ring-fence, discussed in Chapter 23, the flow of wholesale as well as retail funds to non-permitted activities would be constrained, but, on the other hand, the range of assets permitted to the guaranteed institution would be wider than those permitted to the ring-fenced retail bank.

rules seem designed to replace to a significant extent the other two techniques. If a bank does in fact hold enough liquid assets of its own to survive a thirty-day stressed scenario, it will, by definition, be able to meet the withdrawal demands made on it in this period. By the end of the period, the bank will, likely, either have taken substantial steps towards rehabilitation or will be put into resolution.[62] In short, the Basel scheme is to require banks to become internal sources of their own liquidity.

Since we may assume the impact on banks' lending capacity of the new rules was something of which the Basel Committee was all too aware, it must be that the Committee thought this was a cost worth bearing in order to further some alternative goal. That goal may simply have been an improvement in the chances of banks surviving a future crisis, but, while that may explain the Committee's new focus on liquidity, it does not explain their choice of technique. An alternative explanation may be that the Committee thought that the other two techniques were likely to cause the fragility risk at bank level to reappear at sovereign level, a risk which was avoided by throwing the liquidity burden onto the banks themselves. We know that in the financial crisis the Icelandic deposit guarantee fund failed and the Icelandic government declined to bail it out fully; that Ireland needed to be bailed out by its Eurozone partners in part because of the extended guarantees it had offered on the liabilities of the Irish banks; and that later on in the Eurozone crisis the Cypriot and Greek governments could not sustain their banking systems without a Eurozone bail-out. Central bank facilities may appear at first sight to be less troublesome than state guarantees, since the assets the central bank advances are secured on collateral put in place by the bank.[63] Nevertheless, there may be a fear that under pressure of the crisis the central bank will put its own balance sheet in danger by accepting suboptimal collateral; and even if this is not the case, the central bank's balance sheet may balloon under the pressure of the demand from banks to swap assets. The complicated operation of the European System of Central Banks, in which 'Emergency Liquidity Assistance' requires cooperation of the ECB and the national central bank of the bank's domicile (which bear much risk), may also have been a factor for the Basel Committee. It is possibly no accident that the only two really active central banks in the financial crisis in creating new central bank facilities were from large states—the US and the UK, which also had unambiguous control over their own currencies—though it is also true that these were the two countries most heavily hit by the crisis.

Why should sovereign risk have become so prominent in the recent crisis, not having been so before? It may be that central bank facilities or state-backing of DGS works well in the case of a failure of a bank or a group of banks for idiosyncratic reasons. In the case of a systemic crisis, especially a global systemic crisis, the risk of the sovereign being overwhelmed by the liquidity demands of the banks operating in its jurisdiction becomes substantial, at least in small and medium-sized states. Although the cost to the state of guarantees of bank liabilities may ultimately be recouped from the industry, in the meantime they fall on the sovereign; and if the central bank over-

---

[62] Of course, liquidity provision and depositor protection may continue to be important in resolution. See Chapter 16.

[63] Since the collateral is subject to a haircut, the swap is in fact overcollateralized.

extends itself, only the sovereign can rescue it. The Basel Committee is designing rules for the banking world as a whole and might reasonably have concluded that, even though bank-provided liquidity is socially costly, it is less costly than the financial failure of states. This leaves just one loose end. Sovereign risk arising out of a financial crisis is not likely to be salient for economies that are large in relation to their banking systems. The US can be said to fall into this category; beyond that, it is not so clear. Should such states have to accept, under Basel rules, a reduction in the lending capacity of their banks, in order to diminish a risk which for them is not substantial? As we have seen, a way forward may be to allow banks in states which are prepared to give their banks a contractual guarantee of central bank facilities to use those commitments to meet the Basel rules, thus reducing the bank's need to hold liquid assets on its books.[64]

However that issue is resolved, liquidity is an area where bank risk meets sovereign risk; and, equally, sovereign risk feeds back into the appropriate choice of regulatory technique for banks.

---

[64] See section 15.4, especially text attached to n 37.

16

Bank Resolution

16.1 Introduction

Incurring losses is an inescapable risk of running any business, whether financial or non-financial. Those losses may be limited and/or temporary, or they may be sufficient to put the viability of the business in jeopardy. In the private sector, for the general run of corporate businesses, losses are absorbed in the following stylized way.

(a) So long as the company is a going concern, the losses are borne by the shareholders.

(b) If the company enters a bankruptcy (insolvency) procedure, the shareholders are likely to be wiped out and the remaining corporate losses are borne by the company's creditors, according to their priority ranking.

(c) Some costs of corporate failure are not borne by the company but are externalized onto third parties. However, these costs are normally (but not always) modest.

As to (a), the shareholders' equity in the company consists of the excess of corporate assets over liabilities. If a company incurs a loss in a particular year, the value of the company's net assets (assets less liabilities) will be reduced, to the detriment of its shareholders. Thus, shareholders bear going-concern losses seamlessly and automatically. However, a fall in the value of the shareholders' equity (assuming a continuing positive value for net assets) does not constitute an event which puts the continuation of the company in question as a matter of law—though the shareholders may respond with various forms of self-help, such as selling their shares, replacing the management, or selling the company to an acquirer.

As to (b), once the shareholders' equity is exhausted or the company is close to that position, it is likely to default on at least some of its obligations to its creditors, entitling the latter to put the company into a bankruptcy procedure or, even without default, the board of directors may be required to initiate a bankruptcy procedure.[1] Often, more than one type of bankruptcy procedure is available, depending on whether the emphasis is on the liquidation of the company or its reorganization so that it can return to going concern status on a restructured basis. Either way, the pre-bankruptcy creditors will bear the losses, after the shareholders have been wiped out, according to the intra-creditor priorities which were established by contract when the debt was raised or which are imposed by legislation. Secured creditors will be able to make claims against specific corporate assets, which are therefore taken out of the company's

---

[1] A company with negative net assets may still have sufficient cash to meet the claims on it for a period of time. Legal systems vary in the extent to which they permit balance-sheet insolvent companies to continue trading so long as they are solvent in cash-flow terms.

Principles of Financial Regulation. First Edition. John Armour, Dan Awrey, Paul Davies, Luca Enriques, Jeffrey N. Gordon, Colin Mayer, and Jennifer Payne. © John Armour, Dan Awrey, Paul Davies, Luca Enriques, Jeffrey N. Gordon, Colin Mayer, and Jennifer Payne 2016. Published 2016 by Oxford University Press.

estate. Because of the unpalatable consequences of (b) for both shareholders and creditors, they have some incentive to negotiate an alternative private solution in the shadow of this second step (a 'workout')—and in some jurisdictions the formal bankruptcy procedures facilitate private agreements.

As to (c), a variety of costs are borne by persons other than shareholders and creditors of the company when a company fails, especially if it is a large company. Employees may find that there is no outlet for the firm-specific skills acquired when working for the now bankrupt company and so have to accept alternative jobs at a lower wage, businesses whose customer base was the employees of the defunct company may do less well or even collapse, local and central government may collect less tax, or the domestic economy may lose capacity to produce certain goods or services. Bankruptcy law generally does not recognize such losses. These costs of corporate failure are handled through other mechanisms (such as state-subsidized job-search facilities) or left to lie where they fall.

Occasionally, however, these externalities of corporate failure are thought to be so large that they constitute a reason for not allowing the company to fall into bankruptcy. Instead, the company is saved by an injection of state financing—it is 'bailed out'. The political pressures on government to bail-out large manufacturing companies can be intense. Sometimes the bail-out is successful in the sense that the company returns fully to private ownership and flourishes. A good example is the bail-out by the UK government of the aero-engine manufacturer, Rolls Royce, in the early 1970s. Others can be found in the US Government's bail-out and forced restructuring of GM and Chrysler in the depth of the financial crisis. More often, state financing simply postpones the inevitable, as with the UK government's successive bail-outs of the domestically owned car industry over a period of decades. Even when state financing is successful, it will often be difficult to rebut the contention that the same result could have been achieved more cheaply through a reorganization-focused bankruptcy procedure.

16.1.1 The special position of banks

How does the foregoing analysis map onto banks? It is commonly thought that bank bankruptcy is different from that of other companies, for three reasons. First, the prospect of bankruptcy is very damaging to a bank, since the value of the bank's franchise dissipates very rapidly once doubts are raised about its financial viability. Second, the typical mechanics of bankruptcy are not well suited to a bank. In the bankruptcy of a non-financial firm, value is conserved by the imposition of an 'automatic stay' that limits creditors' rights to obtain payment of their claims. Since a core business of the bank is honouring depositors' cheques, this would put the bank out of business. Third, the negative externalities of bank failure can be very significant, depending on the size of the bank and the number of banks that simultaneously fail.

Once a bank's solvency is in doubt, its short-term lenders will withdraw their funding and borrowers will look elsewhere for their loans, as we saw in Chapter 13. In short, the bank is pushed into 'run-off'—simply receiving payments due under the loans it has already made, rather than originating new business. It is virtually impossible to restructure a bank's balance sheet in a standard bankruptcy procedure while keeping its business going. As the UK Parliamentary Commission on Banking Standards (PCBS) observed, 'for banks the balance sheet *is* the operating business: its creditors are its customers'.[2] This is another consequence of the fragility of the banks' funding model which we analysed in Chapters 13 to 15. To put the point another way, the bankruptcy costs of a bank failure are far higher than those incurred in the failure of a non-financial firm (perhaps 40 per cent, as opposed to 20 per cent, of the pre-bankruptcy firm value).[3]

However, by itself this is not a compelling reason for taking banks out of the standard bankruptcy procedures. One might even argue that the costs to shareholders and creditors of bankruptcy will lead bank managers to be careful to avoid this state. A stronger argument for separate resolution procedures for banks (and other similar financial institutions) rests on the contagion effects of bank failure, which we analysed in Chapter 13. We there saw that these include not simply the 'domino' impact of the failure of one bank upon the solvency of other banks but also, and more important, the potential loss of access to the payments system and of lending capacity to households and businesses through a contraction of the banking system, as confidence evaporates. The 'real' economy may suffer significantly if banks go down, but those costs are not usually borne by the bank's shareholders, managers, and creditors.

The contagion effects of bank failure give states a powerful incentive to bail-out the bank if the only alternative is a standard bankruptcy mechanism and it is not thought to be feasible to contain the impact of the failure. A bail-out uses state resources to keep the bank out of bankruptcy and minimize negative externalities. However, by saving the bank from bankruptcy, the bail-out stymies the mechanism for imposing losses on creditors (see Figure 16.1).[4] Although banking regulation aims to save retail depositors (and perhaps other short-term funders) from the costs of bank failure there is no good reason for doing the same for the long-term creditors of banks, notably its bondholders. Under the terms of their contracts, bondholders cannot run, so there is little reason to bail them out. Moreover, bailing them out involves considerable costs. If bondholders expect to be bailed out, this will degrade their incentives to monitor the bank. Moreover, they will accept a lower interest rate, so that an (anticipated) bail-out constitutes an unjustified state subsidy to those banks most likely to attract a bail-out.[5] Yet, in the financial crisis, bank bondholders typically did get paid in full under various state rescue packages (discussed in section 16.2), the costs of which fell entirely on the taxpayer.

---

[2] Parliamentary Commission on Banking Standards (PCBS), *First Report* (2012), 16.

[3] C James, 'The Losses Realised in Bank Failures' (1991) 46 *Journal of Finance* 1223, 1228.

[4] Shareholders probably do somewhat better under bail-out than liquidation. In both cases they suffer losses up to the point of liquidation or bail-out, but they avoid the costs of bankruptcy in a bail-out (likely to be high in the case of a bank for the reasons given in the text). On the other hand, the capital injected by the state may be at discount to the current market price of the shares, so that the shareholders are significantly diluted.

[5] The Independent Commission on Banking (ICB) estimated the subsidy to UK banks' funding costs of the implicit guarantee of bondholders to be in the order of £10bn per year: ICB, *Interim Report* (2011), 162–3.

Liquidation vs Bail-out

Liquidation	Bail-out
• Shareholders suffer losses	• Shareholders suffer losses
• Creditors bear losses according to their hierarchy—subordinated, unsecured, preferred, secured	• Creditors typically bear no losses
• Societal losses uncompensated	• Societal losses minimised
• Taxpayers contribute nothing	• Taxpayers absorb most of the resolution costs

Fig. 16.1 Bank Liquidation versus Bail-out

16.1.2 Bank resolution procedures

The case for a 'third way' with banks—neither standard bankruptcy nor bail-out—is potentially a strong one.[6] An ideal bank resolution procedure achieves the objective of minimizing the negative externalities of bank failure but allocates the costs of so doing primarily to the bank's shareholders and bondholders and only thereafter, if at all, to the taxpayer. Two principal resolution mechanisms are discussed in this chapter: one involves the rapid transfer to a solvent acquirer of the bank's insured deposits and possibly other viable businesses of the bank, with the liquidation of the rump of the bank which is not transferred. In this mechanism, therefore, standard bankruptcy retains a residual role, but the force of the procedure lies in the rapid transfer of the failing bank's assets and liabilities to a new owner, which is effected much more rapidly than standard bankruptcy procedures allow.

Such a transfer mechanism, which we discuss in section 16.3, is not a new invention. A tolerably successful version of it, known as 'bank receivership', was developed by the Federal Deposit Insurance Corporation ('FDIC') in the US in the last century. It was adopted by the UK, which previously had no special procedure for insolvent banks, in the Banking Act 2009. It is also central to the EU's Bank Recovery and Resolution Directive (the 'BRRD').[7] However, FDIC bank receivership was developed in the

---

[6] The argument depends somewhat on the sophistication of a jurisdiction's standard reorganization procedure for bankrupt companies. Some have argued that the Chapter 11 bankruptcy procedure in the US could handle bank insolvencies with relatively minor amendments: see DA Skeel, Jr, *The New Financial Deal: Understanding the Dodd–Frank Act and its (Unintended) Consequences* (Hoboken, NJ: John Wiley & Sons, 2011), 155–74; JF Bovenzi, RD Guynn, and TH Jackson, *Too Big to Fail: The Path to a Solution—A Report of the Financial Resolution Task Force of the Financial Regulatory Reform Initiative of the Bipartisan Policy Center* (2013), 70–2. Formally, the Orderly Liquidation Procedure of Dodd–Frank (discussed in section 16.4) is to be used only when Chapter 11 will not do the job. The core problem with Chapter 11 for a systemically important financial institution is that private liquidity provision through 'debtor in possession' financing is likely to be unavailable in a time of intense financial distress and Congress will be unwilling to supply such a facility (involving $billions) for a proceeding run by a bankruptcy judge with the standard bankruptcy mandate of maximizing returns solely for creditors.

[7] Directive 2014/59/EU ([2014] OJ L173/190) establishing a framework for the recovery and resolution of credit institutions and investment firms. It should be noted that the BRRD applies to all Member States of the EU and not just to the Eurozone members, as is the case with the rules we analyse in section 16.8.

context of the resolution of commercial banks—and generally simple ones at that. Thus, both the EU's BRRD and the Dodd–Frank Act in the US have sought to develop 'stretched' versions of the basic procedure which, conceivably, could cope with the resolution of complex commercial and investment banks and, indeed, other systemic financial institutions.

The second procedure, generally referred to as 'bail-in', consists of reorganizing the failing bank so that it emerges as a restored, viable entity, without either being put into standard bankruptcy or a transferee being found for its viable businesses. This can be achieved through voluntary agreement among the banks' creditors and shareholders,[8] but, post crisis, statutory procedures have been created which will impose it in the absence of agreement (thus, perhaps, providing an incentive to voluntary agreement). The central element of these new procedures is that losses are inflicted, by regulatory decision, on long-term creditors, as in a bankruptcy, but without the company being put into bankruptcy. The debt may either be written down or converted into equity. In this scenario, which we discuss in section 16.4, the bank is recapitalized but remains in existence as the entity conducting the banking businesses.[9]

So far we have presented transfer and reorganization as two independent resolution mechanisms. But they may be linked. Most obviously, the regulator may start with a reorganization involving bail-in, but discover that this step does not resolve the bank, so that a transfer has to be arranged. But there may be more complex interrelationships between the two forms of resolution.[10]

Moreover, the bank might seek to mimic contractually the statutory reorganization procedure—or something like it. This we discuss in section 16.7. Thus, a bank might issue debt whose terms provide for it to be written down and possibly converted into equity on some pre-defined trigger point ahead of non-viability.[11] This type of debt instrument is usually called a 'contingent convertible' (or 'coco' for short). A number of European banks have issued significant amounts of cocos in recent years. The new capital rules, discussed in Chapter 14, give them a substantial incentive to do so. Subject to certain conditions, not only will this form of debt count as additional Tier 1 or as Tier 2 capital under the Basel rules[12]—and possibly under additional national regulation—but it also has tax advantages over equity as a way of meeting these requirements.

In section 16.6 we discuss a resolution strategy, Single Point of Entry ('SPE'), which is closely linked to bail-in and seems particularly well suited to the United States, because of the holding company structure of its large financial firms. We also discuss the FSB's and

---

[8] In 2013 the UK's Cooperative Bank, which was facing financial distress, reached an agreement with its long-term creditors under which the latter swapped their debt for equity and the previous 100 per cent shareholder was diluted to about a 30 per cent ownership stake. This raised some eyebrows because the debt was at the time held largely by hedge funds, while the diluted former shareholder was a left-leaning mutual society with its origins in the self-help movement of the nineteenth century. They were thought to be odd bedfellows.

[9] Of course, it is likely that those businesses would need to be reduced or re-modelled in some way, but that would be done by the bank, not the transferee.

[10] The technical requirements of the Dodd–Frank Act require the FDIC to start with a receivership proceeding before initiating its favoured form of bail-in resolution, 'Single Point of Entry'. See section 16.6.

[11] Or, as a halfway house, regulation might require banks to issue contingent capital, but the trigger would be automatic and defined in the contract rather than pulled by the regulator.

[12] See Chapter 14, section 14.5.1. See also BIS, Press Statement, 13 January 2011, Annex.

Fed's proposals for Total Loss-Absorbing Capital ('TLAC') and the way that TLAC can facilitate an orderly, minimally disruptive resolution of a large financial firm.

In the midst of the Eurozone financial crisis of 2010–12, which linked a sovereign debt crisis to a banking crisis, the members of the Eurozone agreed to form a Banking Union to break the links between sovereign and bank financial distress. The Banking Union project includes a particular procedure for triggering a bank resolution, a mechanism for prescribing the resolution strategy, and provision of facilitative financial support that was not meant to be loss-absorbing. We discuss this resolution mechanism in section 16.8.

By the end of this chapter you should have a good idea of how bank resolution—that is, ultrafast transfer and recapitalization—mechanisms work, how they interrelate, and how they differ from standard bankruptcy procedures. You should be aware of the potential value of these procedures beyond banks as legally defined. Finally, you should be aware of the residual value of bail-outs.

16.2 Bail-Outs

Bailing out a bank because of contagion fears did not occur for the first time during the recent financial crisis. The accolade of being the first bank which was officially identified as too big or too interconnected to fail is often awarded to the Continental Illinois Bank.[13] This was bailed out by the US Government (through the FDIC), which in 1984 guaranteed the deposits of all depositors (not just those within the insurance limits) and all the bank's general creditors and took a large ownership position in the bank. In consequence of the FDIC action the bondholders in the bank's parent company suffered no losses. The rescue was mounted because it was feared that this bank's collapse would lead to the collapse of a number of smaller banks that held substantial uninsured deposits in Continental Illinois. The US Government thus wished to avert a feared cascade of bank failures.

However, bank bail-outs reached spectacular levels in the recent financial crisis. Figure 16.2 shows the extent, year by year, of public-sector interventions in the first three years of the crisis, in the Eurozone, the UK, and the US, as percentages of GDP. Although the US devoted four to five times more resources in cash terms to bank bail-outs than the UK, bail-out resources represented a higher proportion of GDP in the UK than the US.

The bail-outs were implemented in three principal ways. First, and most obviously, state funds were injected into the bank in exchange for shares (capital injections), often preference shares in order to ensure that any dividend payments went first to the state rather than the prior shareholders in the bank.[14] The banks' prior shareholders were

---

[13] See eg GB Gorton, *Misunderstanding Financial Crises: Why We Don't See Them Coming* (Oxford: OUP, 2012), 143–6. Like Northern Rock in 2007 (see Chapter 15, section 15.2), Continental Illinois was particularly vulnerable to a liquidity crisis because of its extensive short-term wholesale funding, relying especially on foreign funders.

[14] On the other hand, the dividend priority of the state made raising further ordinary share capital from the financial markets more difficult. Successful recapitalization of the bank often required conversion of the government's preference shares into ordinary (or 'common') shares.

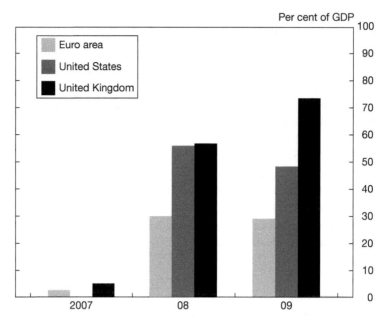

Fig. 16.2 Public Sector Interventions to Support Financial Institutions, 2007–9

Source: Bank of England, *Financial Stability Report*, December 2009, 6.

thus heavily diluted but not necessarily wiped out.[15] Second, the state might, in addition or instead, guarantee to third parties some or all the liabilities of the bank beyond the normal limits of the deposit guarantee scheme, including non-deposit liabilities. Third, the state might guarantee to the bank (in whole or in part) the value of certain of the bank's (now doubtful) assets.

It follows that the ultimate cost to a state of a bail-out cannot be established at the point the aid is advanced. Figure 16.2 therefore refers to actual cash expenditures (on capital injections) and exposures under the guarantees. However, it might be that the shares the state acquired through its capital injection can be sold to the market subsequently at a profit.[16] Or the guarantee is never called on because third parties refrain from withdrawing their funds or asset prices recover, in part precisely because of the bail-out, while the state hangs onto the fees payable for providing the

---

[15] Even if the state decided to nationalize the bank (as happened with Northern Rock), the shareholders received compensation for whatever their shares were worth. See Chapter 15, section 15.4.1.

[16] For the Troubled Asset Relief Progam ('TARP') bank investment scheme, the US Treasury invested approximately $240 billion, and has thus far received $29.9 billion more than that. See US Department of Treasury, 'Bank Investment Programs', available at https://www.treasury.gov/initiatives/financial-stability/TARP-Programs/bank-investment-programs/Pages/default.aspx (last accessed 2 January 2016). On the government's $180 billion investment in AIG (made by the Fed and the US Treasury), the government earned a $22.7 billion profit: see MJ De La Merced, 'Treasury Earns $7.6 Billion from Sale of Last Shares in A.I.G.', *New York Times*, 11 December 2012. Of course these are nominal returns, not risk-adjusted.

guarantees.[17] In the medium term, therefore, the state may come out ahead on the aid provided.

On the other hand, for a small state with a large banking system the initial funding needed for the bail-out may be more than the public finances can sustain.[18] Even for large states, however, the immediate costs of a large-scale bail-out are significant and public expenditure may be skewed for a number of years thereafter. One can reasonably ask why even states that can afford it engage in bail-outs, given the harsh adjustments to the public finances that normally follow. The answer is that the costs to the economy of not bailing out the banks are feared to be larger than the costs of the bail-out. We know that banking crises produce heavy costs, in terms of lost output from the economy and all that this entails. These costs will not be incurred if the banking system remains stable—but then no bail-out is required either. The bail-out question arises only once the banking system has become unstable. The question then is: are the overall costs of instability reduced by a bail-out or not? Governments around the world viewed the costs of bailing out the banks as likely to be less than the costs of letting them fail. Minimizing contagion from bank failure through bail-out, it was argued, was the less costly way of dealing with the given fact of loss of banking system stability.[19]

It is likely that the debate over the merits of bail-outs will never be satisfactorily resolved, since it turns on building a convincing counter-factual. In the financial crisis, the debate focused on the failure of the US Government to bail-out Lehman Brothers in September 2008. The dominant view is that this was a policy mistake: Lehman Brothers' entry into bankruptcy intensified the crisis and the costs of bailing it out most likely would have been less than the losses in fact caused to the economy by its failure,[20] but not everyone agrees.[21]

Despite this economic rationale for the bail-out, it is not surprising that, after the crisis, attention focused on developing resolution mechanisms that could match the advantages of the bail-out but at a lower or no cost to the taxpayer. However, often strong political objection 'in principle' was expressed to the idea of a bail-out precisely because it preserved the jobs and activities 'which got us into this mess in the first place'. So, there was a tide of opinion in the financial crisis that bail-outs should be

---

[17] For an example of a highly successful guarantee programme of this type see box text in Chapter 15, section 15.4.2.

[18] See the examples given in Chapter 15, section 15.6.

[19] For making it less likely that the banking system would become unstable, one should look to other devices than the bail-out, such as the capital and liquidity regulation discussed in Chapters 14–15, or the governance regulation discussed in Chapter 17 or to macroprudential policies (Chapter 19) or structural constraints (Chapter 23).

[20] Gorton, n 13, 147–50; A Admati and M Hellwig, *The Bankers' New Clothes: What's Wrong with Banking and What to Do About It* (Princeton, NJ: Princeton UP, 2013), 74–8; V Acharya and M Richardson, *Restoring Financial Stability* (Englewood Cliffs, NJ: John Wiley & Sons Inc, 2009), 6, 298.

[21] Skeel, n 6, Ch 2. There seems to be no serious case that AIG should have been left to fail, however. See R McDonald and A Paulson, 'AIG in Hindsight' (2015) 29 *Journal of Economic Perspectives* 81. At the time of the rescue, AIG had $20 billion in commercial paper outstanding and $50 billion in counterparty exposure to banks via loans, lines of credit, and derivatives. As a point of comparison, Lehman Brothers had $5.7 billion in outstanding commercial paper, default on which all but brought down the money market fund sector.

prohibited or severely controlled in the future, even in situations where no alternative effective resolution mechanism is available and even if it is economically rational (that is, it reduces society's costs overall) to bail out the banking system.

The UK and the US reacted differently, post-crisis, to the question of how the role of the bail-out should be identified in the future. The UK, having had previously no formal statutory authority to bail out banks, moved to put one in place in the Banking Act 2009. Section 228 of this Act confers a broad power to provide financial assistance to banks and other financial institutions and legitimates any payments made before the Act came into force as well as subsequent ones. Normally, payments are to be approved by Parliament but in case of urgency the executive can act alone, reporting to Parliament *ex post* the amount spent, though not the identity of the recipients. No doubt, this power is intended to be one of last resort, where the resolution powers discussed in the remainder of this chapter have failed on their own to restore stability. However, the UK's freedom to act under section 228 is constrained by EU-level legislation, the Bank Recovery and Resolution Directive (BRRD),[22] which permits bail-outs only with restrictive pre-conditions.[23]

By contrast, in the US the Dodd–Frank Act is full of provisions preventing the agencies operating under that Act from using resources to bail-out systemically important banks and other financial institutions.[24] For example, under the new Orderly Liquidation Authority ('OLA') provisions for dealing with large financial institutions, the FDIC is prohibited from using taxpayer funds to prevent the liquidation of any covered institution or from taking an equity position in any covered institution.[25] The Fed's emergency authority, which was used to rescue Bear Stearns and AIG, was cut back to prevent such future rescues.[26] Similarly, the FDIC's issuance of loan guarantees outside an OLA proceeding was made subject to advance Congressional approval.[27] These provisions do not mean that bail-outs cannot occur in the

---

[22] In particular, Art 37(10) requires a contribution of 8 per cent of total liabilities to be provided by shareholders and/or bail-in debt-holders before state resources can be devoted to the resolution of the bank. Ironically, in the Greek crisis of 2014/15 the EU raced to complete the recapitalization of the Greek banks through state (in this case, EU) resources before this provision came into force, for fear that its impact would be to bail-in uninsured depositors: 'Eurozone Races to Restructure Greek Banks as Bail-In Looms', *Financial Times*, 16 September 2015.

[23] The EU's state aid rules also require equity and subordinated debt to be written off before state aid is provided to failing banks. See *Communication from the Commission on the application, from 1 August 2013, of State aid rules to support measures in favour of banks in the context of the financial crisis*, OJ C 216/1, 30.7.2013, para 3.1.2. Any form of state aid given by a Member State to a firm requires Commission approval. Without such approval the aid is unlawful and must be repaid by the recipient. In the financial crisis the main impact of the state aid rules was to require eventual disposal of parts of the rescued banks' businesses on the grounds that the bail-out was a form of unfair competition whose competitive effects should be reversed.

[24] The Dodd–Frank Act did not cut back the FDIC's prior authority with respect to banks under its existing resolution authority.

[25] Dodd–Frank Act of 2010 §§214(a) and 206(5).

[26] Ibid, §1101 (amending §13(3) of the Federal Reserve Act, under which many lender of last resort (LOLR) programmes were constructed (see Chapter 15)). The objective instead is to channel a failing firm into either bankruptcy or Orderly Liquidation under Title II of the Dodd–Frank Act.

[27] Dodd–Frank Act of 2010, §§1105 and 1106. For discussion of the possible implications of the various cutbacks in emergency authority, see JN Gordon and C Muller, 'Confronting Financial Crisis: Dodd–Frank's Dangers and the Case for a Systemic Emergency Insurance Fund' (2011) 28 *Yale Journal on Regulation* 151, 194–204.

future, but rather that they will need Congressional approval. Given the history in the US of not allowing banks to fail in a crisis, it seems likely that these provisions will mean slower (and possibly more expensive) bail-outs rather than no bail-outs at all. Nevertheless, as we explain in section 16.6, the FDIC has shaped its authority under Dodd–Frank to minimize the knock-on effects of such a 'liquidation.' Moreover, the FSB has mandated that all Global Systemically Important Banks ('G-SIBs') construct balance sheets that include sufficient TLAC, a form of self-insurance, so as to permit orderly resolution that does not depend on bail-outs.

16.3 Special Transfer Procedures for Banks and Other Financial Institutions

Whatever view is taken on the merits of bail-outs, it is obviously desirable to remove the incentive for states to bail-out banks just because the only alternative is an inappropriate standard bankruptcy procedure. This was the situation faced by the UK in 2007 in relation to Northern Rock, which the UK government opted to take into government ownership—and later sold back to the private sector—and the US Government in relation to Lehman Brothers in 2008, which it allowed to fail. If an effective resolution procedure can be designed for such institutions, the use of state funds to bail out banks can be very substantially reduced, though probably never eliminated.[28]

16.3.1 Core characteristics of a resolution procedure

In this section we analyse the central characteristics of a resolution procedure based on the transfer of the deposits and viable businesses of the failing bank to a solvent third party, with the rump of the failing institution being liquidated. Those key attributes have been identified by the FSB.[29] The FSB's ideal clearly reflects in many ways the powers and procedures developed in the US by the FDIC in relation to bank receivership.[30]

Speed. Owing to the loss of franchise value and the risk of contagion associated with bank failure (see section 16.1), an effective procedure must operate very quickly indeed—as the UK PCBS put it, it must be 'ultrafast'.[31] Ideally, the main elements of

---

[28] Where the use of public funds is unavoidable, they might be provided either via a bail-out entirely outside the resolution procedure or within the resolution procedure, so as to facilitate a transfer of liabilities to a third party.

[29] Financial Stability Board, *Key Attributes of Effective Resolution Regimes for Financial Institutions*, October 2011 and the preceding consultative document, *Effective Resolution of Systemically Important Financial Institutions*, July 2011.

[30] The FDIC, as both the operator of the deposit guarantee scheme (DGS) and administrator of the resolution procedure had a natural interest in developing a resolution procedure which minimized losses to the insurance fund. In most countries, the operator of the DGS and the administrator of the resolution procedure are different bodies.

[31] See n 2, para 233.

the resolution plan should be implemented between bank closure on one business day and its reopening on the next business day.[32]

Purpose. The purpose of resolution is to promote financial stability by securing uninterrupted availability of core banking services—such as access to the payments system and the protection of insured depositors—while maximizing the value of non-core aspects of the bank's business. For both these reasons, a number of departures from standard bankruptcy procedures are indicated.

Administrative process. In the interests of speed, the role of courts in overseeing the process is minimized—indeed, virtually excluded—except for some form of limited judicial review of the decisions of the administrator of the resolution procedure. The process is driven by an administrative body, for example, in the US the FDIC, and in the UK the Bank of England.

Creditor and shareholder rights subordinated. The administrator's goal is to preserve financial stability, not to maximize payouts to creditors, in contrast to classical bankruptcy procedures. Creditor control of the process is thus inappropriate. In particular, in order to secure swift transfer of parts of the bank's business to viable third parties, the rights of creditors and shareholders which might impede such transfers may be overridden.

However, creditors must not be expropriated. Constitutional protections of property rights might otherwise be infringed.[33] The market cost would be that the prospect of expropriation at the resolution stage would increase the cost of debt financing for banks. A standard response to these considerations is to guarantee to creditors the amount they would have received if the bank had been put through a standard bankruptcy procedure. Given the loss of franchise value in a standard bankruptcy procedure, this may be a small amount. Or there may be special protection for particular classes of creditors.[34]

Range of resolution tools. There are three core tools available to the administrator of the transfer procedure. The first is to transfer parts of the bank's business to a third-party purchaser. The administrator will want to transfer insured deposits and current accounts, at a minimum. A purchaser may also be available for the failing bank's loan book or other assets—or at least part of them. This tool is referred to in the US as 'purchase [of assets] and assumption [of liabilities]'. The second is to transfer parts of the bank's business to a 'bridge bank' operated by the administrator. This bank provides a 'bridge' to some permanent solution for the part of the business transferred, ideally a purchase by a third party. This may be appropriate for saleable parts of the bank's business for which an immediate purchaser is not available, for example, because those parts are difficult to value quickly.

---

[32] Hence the popularity of weekend resolution with the FDIC.

[33] Avoiding interference with property rights as defined in the European Convention on Human Rights thus appears as one of (now) seven objectives of the Special Resolution Procedure introduced in the UK by the Banking Act 2009.

[34] For example, the UK Banking Act 2009 provides that the security for a debt may not be transferred to a third party unless the debt is transferred as well.

The non-transferred rump of the bank can be liquidated, either in a standard liquidation procedure or some close analogy thereto, having received whatever proceeds third parties are prepared to pay for the businesses transferred. At this point, those creditors who have not gone over with the businesses transferred will bear losses if the assets of the rump bank are insufficient to cover their claims on it, as is likely to be the case. The pre-liquidation transfers may well mean that the asset-to-liability ratio is worse in the rump entity than it was before the transfers took place. The 'no creditor worse off' principle will provide compensation to creditors,[35] if the ratio in the rump is worse than it would have been had (hypothetically) the bank been put into a standard bankruptcy procedure. However, distribution of the benefits of resolution (as against liquidation) may still be unequal across different creditors of the same class—as between those transferred and those not.

Thus far, we have assumed two classes of asset: those saleable within a short timetable to a third party and those not so saleable which will be liquidated, equally within a short timetable. Conceivably, there is a third category—that is, assets the value of which is maximized if they are disposed of over a longer timetable. The EU's BRRD makes explicit provision for the 'bad bank' concept, or in the Directive's terms, an 'asset separation tool'. This takes the form of an asset management vehicle whose role is eventually to sell the impaired assets transferred to it or to liquidate them. This vehicle is to be used, for example, where selling the assets in the liquidation of the rump might have an adverse impact on the overall value of assets of that class (to the detriment of other financial institutions) or where liquidation proceeds will be enhanced through the bad bank mechanism. This resolution tool is not envisaged in the BRRD as a freestanding one: it can be used only in conjunction with (in the transfer context) a transfer to a third party or a bridge bank. In principle, a bridge bank could be used to hold 'bad bank' assets, but the BRRD separates out the 'bad bank' mechanism, probably because the bridge bank is seen as the repository for a functioning business with a potentially viable future, while the asset management vehicle is seen as the holding entity for a collection of assets which need to be disposed of—but not just yet.[36]

Public ownership. There can be no guarantee that a third party will be interested in buying the business of a failing bank. The administrator may choose to liquidate it, but that may be unattractive if core banking functions will then disappear. Consequently, the third tool is to nationalize the bank (that is, transfer it to the state), for which different jurisdictions employ different euphemisms—'temporary public ownership' in the UK, and 'conservatorship' in the US. This takes us back to the bail-out discussion in section 16.2.

---

[35] Probably promised by the state but recouped by the state via a preferential claim over the proceeds of the liquidation or from the industry more generally. For problems of unequal treatment in resolution of creditors of the same class see *Goldman Sachs International v Novo Banco S A* [2015] EWHC 2371 (resolution of the Portuguese *Banco Espirito Santo*); 'Fourteen asset managers sue Portuguese central bank', *Financial Times*, 4 April, 2016.

[36] The asset separation tool is defined in Art 42 of the BRRD. It may also be relevant that the maximum life of the bridge bank is set in Art 41 at two years from the last transfer to it from the failing institution, extendable for one further year in exceptional circumstances, whereas no such limit applies to the asset management vehicle.

16.3.2 Financing the resolution process

The transfer process may require an injection of resources to make it work. For example, the transferee will be prepared to take on more liabilities than assets from the failing bank only if the gap is met from elsewhere. The obvious source of such funding is the deposit guarantee fund. If resolution is successful, the fund will not have to pay out to the (now transferred) insured depositors. Consequently, it is commonly provided that the fund shall contribute to the costs of the resolution an amount not greater than the payouts avoided. If the bank's liabilities consist mainly of deposits, this source of funding will normally be enough. We discuss in section 16.4 funding provision where the bank's liability structure is more complex.

UK Bank Resolution in Action: Dunfermline Building Society

The Bank of England used the Special Resolution Regime ('SRR') provisions of the Banking Act 2009 for the first time in the resolution of Dunfermline Building Society ('Dunfermline').

Over the weekend of 28–29 March 2009, the Bank of England led an auction process for certain of Dunfermline's assets and liabilities. This process saw Nationwide, as the successful bidder, acquire both liabilities—Dunfermline's retail and wholesale deposits—and assets—branches, head office, and originated residential mortgages, other than social housing loans and related deposits which were thought to be difficult to value.

Since the value of the assets acquired was less than the liabilities assumed, the Nationwide received £1.6bn from the Treasury.

Dunfermline's social housing portfolio (together with related deposits) was temporarily transferred to DBS Bridge Bank Ltd, owned and controlled by the Bank of England, to provide time to reach a permanent solution. On 17 June it was announced that Nationwide had been selected as the preferred bidder for the social housing loans and related deposits held by DBS Bridge Bank Ltd. After the transfer to DBS Bridge Bank Ltd, the social housing business was carried on in the usual course for its customers, until its disposal to Nationwide. The Bridge Bank was then liquidated and some £356m was paid to Dunfermline (essentially the sale price of the assets held by the Bridge Bank less the costs of running it and winding it up).

The remainder of Dunfermline's business, including commercial loans, acquired residential assets, subordinated debt and most treasury assets, was placed into the Special Administration Process ('SAP')—essentially a liquidation. The Treasury was an unsecured creditor in this process for the £1.6bn advanced to Nationwide.

As at the end of July 2015, with the SAP still incomplete, some £1.075bn had been repaid to the Treasury. If the Treasury fails to recover in the SAP the full amount of its funding, it is entitled to claim against the UK DGS for the amount that DGS was better off as a result of the use of the SRR. However, this was determined by an independent adjudicator to be only £11m, on the grounds that, if Dunfermline had gone into ordinary bankruptcy (administration), the UK DGS would have recovered in that process all but £11m of the amount it would have paid out to insured depositors. This was a controversial decision. Thus, it may well be some of the public funds injected to facilitate the transfer will not be recovered.

Even if the assets and liabilities taken on by the transferee are of roughly equal value, the assets may currently lack liquidity. So, liquidity will be an immediate concern. Provided the transferee is solvent, however, liquidity should in principle be available, either from private markets (such as the repo market) or, if those private markets are temporarily disrupted, via standard central bank liquidity provision (as discussed in Chapter 15), in both cases using the transferred assets as collateral for the required liquidity.

The text box illustrates a simple use of the transfer tools in the case of the Dunfermline Building Society, a small mortgage bank, in 2009.

16.4 Resolution and Large Banks/Non-Financial Institutions

In Chapters 14 and 15, we noted two central questions in the drafting of modern banking rules: should there be enhancements of the rules for systemically important banks, and should those enhanced rules be applied to large, bank-like financial institutions financed otherwise than by taking deposits? Similar questions arise in relation to resolution procedures. In the crisis, the US Government found it politic to bail out Bear Steans, an investment bank (and broker-dealer), which was not a deposit-taking institution and thus not a bank as legally defined. It also bailed out AIG, an insurance company, because of fear of the impact of its failure on its bank and broker-dealer counterparties and on money market funds. And, as we have noted, its failure to bail out Lehman Brothers, again a non-deposit-taker, is thought to have contributed to the severity of the crisis.

However, it is debated whether the transfer procedure is appropriate for such institutions.[37] There is some reason to be sceptical. Although the FDIC, the main exemplar in this field, has resolved some large banks in recent years (for example, Continental Illinois), the main staple for its resolution activities has been small banks and banks that are relatively simple businesses, both on the liabilities side (mainly deposit funding) and the assets side (mainly retail and commercial loans). There is therefore a serious question about how effectively a FDIC-type procedure will work in relation to large and complex banks.

Nevertheless, on both sides of the Atlantic a great deal of faith has been placed on the application of the transfer procedure to large banks and bank-like financial institutions. Title II of the Dodd–Frank legislation creates an 'Orderly Liquidation Authority' (OLA) for large bank holding companies (which are not themselves 'banks') and large non-bank financial institutions,[38] while the EU's BRRD applies to 'financial institutions', not just to banks.[39] Under Dodd–Frank, where any covered institution is determined (through a complex mechanism involving several regulators or government agencies) to be in danger of default and that default is determined to threaten the financial stability of the United States, OLA will be invoked. Despite the separateness of this piece of legislation, it is the FDIC which administers the procedure and the Act

---

[37] See J Armour, 'Making Bank Resolution Credible', in N Moloney, E Ferran, and J Payne, *The Oxford Handbook of Financial Regulation* (Oxford: OUP, 2015), 453, 466 (characterizing transfer procedures as 'first generation' resolution mechanisms).

[38] For insurance companies the procedure is somewhat more complex because insurance companies are regulated at state level.

[39] By a complex set of legislative cross references one ends up with a list of activities for a 'financial institution' which covers pretty well anything an investment bank might wish to undertake, plus asset management. See Directive 2013/36/EU, Annex 1.

gives the FDIC similar tools to the ones it has under the Federal Deposit Insurance Act ('FDIA') to deal with smaller banks (sale of assets, assumption of liabilities, establishment of a bridge bank). A notable feature of OLA is the legislature's insistence that public funds are not to be used under this procedure to bail out large financial institutions. The OLA name suggests that 'liquidation' of the financial institution is the principal objective of the procedure, but it is clear that the FDIC expects, if all goes well, that it is only the rump of the failing institution that will be liquidated and that the viable parts of the failing institution's business will be transferred to a new owner, probably via a bridge bank—just as under the FDIA.[40]

In the UK, which before the crisis had lacked a special resolution procedure for banks, the transfer procedure based on the FDIC precedent proved overwhelmingly attractive. This is what was introduced in the UK Banking Act 2009. Yet its applicability to the large banks which dominate the UK market must be questionable. It is difficult to imagine, for example, that a purchaser could have been found over the weekend for most of the business of the Royal Bank of Scotland (RBS) which was bailed out in 2008, in which the UK government eventually took an equity stake of over 70 per cent. Or even that, in such a short timescale, a complex bank like RBS could have been split effectively into 'good' and 'bad' bank elements and the former transferred to a bridge bank.[41] If this is so, then substantial public funding would have been required to keep the bank operational while it was divided and sold off, probably over a lengthy period, judging by the fact that in 2016 the state still held its 70 per cent share in that bank. Perhaps some degree of scepticism about the likelihood of the transfer mechanism rendering bail-out unnecessary underlies the introduction in the UK of the ring-fence structure we discuss in Chapter 23. That structure makes it easier to separate out and, if necessary, to bail out the retail bank, while conceivably leaving the non-retail part of the bank to be liquidated, if no buyer can be found.

One obvious issue arising out of the extension of resolution procedures to complex banks and non-banks is funding. For non-banks, there is no DGS that can be used to fund the resolution; and even for complex banks, deposits may constitute only a small fraction of the short-term funding which needs to be replaced in the resolution procedure.[42] For example, the repo funding of the failing bank's assets may dry up entirely, leading to the risk of a fire-sale of those assets, unless the wholesale short-term funding is replaced. The Dodd–Frank legislation addresses this issue by permitting the FDIC to borrow money from the Treasury to provide liquidity support (but only liquidity) to the bridge bank transferee in the OLA, the money being claimed back from the industry *ex post* if the institution's collateral proves insufficient for the amount borrowed. The FDIC can also guarantee the issuances of the bridge institution, which should permit it to turn to private capital markets for financing.

---

[40] See eg FDIC, *The Orderly Liquidation of Lehman Brothers Holdings Inc under the Dodd–Frank Act* (2011) 5 *FDIC Quarterly* (No 2). Given the FDIC's creative interpretation of its powers, the OLA might have been better termed an 'Orderly Resolution Authority'.

[41] However, see the discussion of living wills in section 16.4.1.

[42] See Chapter 15, section 15.1 for a discussion of banks' sources of short-term funding.

The EU's BRRD, by contrast, envisages the creation of a system of 'financing arrangements' to support resolution, on the lines of the deposit guarantee fund—that is, financed by *ex ante* contributions from covered financial institutions, by *ex post* levies (if necessary) and, probably, by government subvention if the funding arrangements should prove insufficient in a crisis. The purposes of the fund under the EU rules are particularly widely stated but, even so, it may not be used 'directly' to absorb the losses of the failing institution or to recapitalize it.[43] As to 'indirect' use of the resolution fund there is a cap on the amount of the contribution as well as a precondition that some loss is imposed on shareholders and creditors before resort to the fund.[44] Further, as we noted in section 16.2, the BRRD does not remove Member States' powers to engage in straightforward bail-out in a systemic crisis, subject to state aid rules. One might say that in the EU, the desire to minimize the societal costs of bank failure has been given a higher priority than the policy of complete avoidance of bail-outs. Resolution by transfer plus an element of bail-out is likely to be the EU pattern, should a large and complex financial institution ever enter resolution.[45]

A second criticism of the 'freewheeling' administrative process in resolution—as against court-controlled bankruptcy—is that creditors may be unfairly treated in resolution. In traditional FDIC resolution of small banks, there is only one significant creditor class—the depositors—which the FDIC in practice acted to protect, whether insured or not. With multiple classes of creditor in a large financial institution, their treatment in the OLA is much more difficult to predict. It is standard to provide creditors with the 'no worse off' guarantee (as compared with ordinary bankruptcy) but that may not be worth very much if the bank would lose a substantial part of its value in standard bankruptcy.[46]

Overall, then, the FDIC-type resolution-by-transfer process can be seen as the big winner in the post-crisis reforms, as it has been extended to an ever-widening range of financial institutions in a wide range of countries. As we have seen, however, some doubt it will be successful in this broader role. David Skeel has put these doubts powerfully, commenting that 'the resolution process is spectacularly ill-suited to large institutions',[47] partly because of the likely unavailability of purchasers and partly

---

[43] Art 101.

[44] The minimum figure is a contribution from shareholders and debt-holders equal to 8 per cent of the failing institution's liabilities and the cap is 5 per cent of total liabilities: Arts 101(4) and 44.

[45] Thus, Art 31(2)(c) of the BRRD sets a resolution objective of 'minimizing' (but not avoiding) 'extraordinary public financial support' for the bank and gives that objective no greater priority than the five other objectives, which include ensuring continuity of critical functions and avoiding significant adverse impact on financial stability.

[46] For example, investors in Northern Rock, complaining that the transfer to public ownership for no compensation had amounted to an unjustified expropriation, were told that they had confused 'a legislative provision that provides for the payment of no compensation…with a provision that provides for compensation to be determined by a valuer on specified assumptions….[T]he fact that no, or negligible, compensation is payable results not from any unfairness in the statutory provisions, but from the lack of any value attributable to the asset in question' (*SRM Global Master Fund LP v HM Treasury* [2009] EWHC 227 (Admin) at [89], *per* Stanley Burnton LJ).

[47] See n 6, 125. The case against OLA is developed in chapters 7 and 8 of that work, which was written before the FDIC had developed its 'Single Point of Entry' plan discussed in section 16.6.

because non-depositor creditors may not be fairly treated in the discretionary FDIC process.

16.4.1 Living wills

The first of Skeel's objections is at least partly addressed by a widespread regulatory novelty, the recovery and resolution plan ('RRP'), colloquially termed the 'living will'. Living wills are an integral part of the FSB's Key Attributes.[48] They are required to be produced for systemically important banks and other financial institutions under the Dodd–Frank legislation, under the BRRD and under national legislation. Under the Key Attributes, production of the recovery plan is the primary responsibility of the firm and the resolution plan of the regulator (with mandatory firm cooperation). The regulator can ultimately impose structural sanctions in order to arrive at a credible RRP.[49]

As its name indicates, RRPs comprise both a 'recovery' and a 'resolution' plan—respectively, a plan the institution itself might implement after a financial reverse (for example, to exit certain risky activities), and steps to facilitate resolution. Concentrating here on the latter, a central purpose of the RRP is to facilitate the speedy break-up of the bank's various activities in resolution, so that core functions can be maintained, saleable activities preserved, and the rest liquidated.[50] The problems the RRP seeks to address are two fold. First, the business activities of groups of companies rarely map onto the legal entities within the group in a simple manner. Single business lines may spread across a number of legal entities, while single entities may engage in (parts of) a number of business lines. For the purposes of the transfer of particular activities to purchasers or a bridge bank, a simpler mapping of activities onto corporate structures would be immensely helpful. Second, some crucial services, such as information technology, may be provided centrally or outsourced to a third party, so that the RRP has to indicate how they would continue to be supplied to a part of the business which has been transferred.

Although the RRP comes into effect only when the bank faces financial difficulty, it generates a potentially significant *ex ante* impact on the way the bank is run as a going concern. Although certain elements of the plan may be triggered only at the resolution stage (for example, continued provision of information technology services), better alignment of business activities and corporate structures would need to be put in place in advance. Insofar as the lack of fit between activities and structure is the result of the historical happenstance, such reorganization, while expensive in one-off terms, may carry no continuing costs. But, if there are good cost reasons for the existing complexity, banks may be expected to resist the change (for example, the centralized management of cash in Lehman Brothers, which meant that its UK subsidiary was without

---

[48] See n 29, Consultative Document, Annex 6. The FSB's concern is more with the 'resolution' than the 'recovery' of the financial institution.

[49] That is, restrictions on the range of activities the bank may engage in, so as to reduce its systemic riskiness.

[50] The RRP would have value, therefore, even if the institution were being dealt with in a standard bankruptcy procedure.

cash when the parent collapsed). The RRP could thus operate as an indirect way of undermining the universal or investment banking model, if regulators take a tough line on what an acceptable RRP must contain. Perhaps for these reasons, progress towards agreeing RRPs with regulators appears to be slow.[51]

16.4.2 Regulatory forbearance and prompt corrective action

No matter whether the resolution procedure covers only simple banks or more complex financial institutions as well, the procedure comes into operation only when it is triggered by a regulator. Can one be sure that the regulator will pull the trigger at the appropriate time? Too early intervention (to the potential detriment of share-holders and creditors other than insured depositors) is normally controlled by speci-fying resolution as a procedure available only where the bank is likely to breach the regulatory conditions necessary for its continued operation, for example, its minimum capital requirements. The opposite risk of regulatory forbearance (that is, unjustified delay) may particularly arise if the regulator responsible for the trigger is also the regulator which carries prudential responsibility for the industry. Pulling the trigger may be thought to reveal the failure of prudential regulation and so the regulator will have an incentive to delay in the hope the institution will recover (even if delay makes subsequent resolution more costly and potentially exposes the regulator to more intense criticism). This might be thought of as the public sector equivalent of 'gambling for resurrection' in the case of insolvent private companies.

The classic example of regulatory forbearance occurred in the crisis that engulfed the savings and loan ('thrifts') industry in the United States in the 1980s, where the primary prudential regulator had charge of the trigger and was thought to have delayed unduly in pulling it.[52] This led in 1991 to a substantial revision of the legislation under which the FDIC operates, responsibility for thrifts being transferred at the same time to the FDIC.[53] For present purposes the most important changes were two fold. First, if a bank fails and causes substantial loss to the insurance fund, the bank's prudential regulator has to undergo a public enquiry into the effectiveness of its regulatory

---

[51] 'US Rejects "Living Wills" of Five Banks', *Financial Times*, 13 April 2014. The US has a particular problem, which is the result of the tension in Dodd–Frank between the bankruptcy/'liquidation' propon-ents and the resolution/'reorganization' proponents. The test for a successful living will is whether the firm can achieve an 'orderly resolution' *under the Bankruptcy Code*, and a firm that cannot make such a showing is subject to divestiture orders and constraints on activities and profit-distributions, Dodd–Frank Act, §165(d). Even the proponents of bankruptcy instead of OLA believe that the Code would need significant revision to make possible such an orderly resolution of a systemically important financial firm. See n 6.

[52] Skeel, n 6, 118–22. An additional problem was that the deposit insurance fund for thrifts was insufficiently funded to provide protection for insured thrift depositors. A Congressional appropriation would have been required to close down insolvent thrifts because many were insolvent. In the effort to break runaway inflation in the 1970s, the Fed (under Chairman Volcker) pushed short-term rates to record levels. Since thrifts' assets were almost entirely long-term fixed-rate mortgages, the interest rate mismatch with deposits was devastating. The alternative was to expand the thrifts' powers beyond housing finance. Regulatory forbearance, insured deposits, and new powers created an industry that 'gambled for resurrec-tion' on commercial real estate and junk bonds, which multiplied the ultimate losses.

[53] On the Federal Deposit Insurance Corporation Improvement Act 1991, see R Carnell, 'A Partial Antidote to Perverse Incentives' (1993) 12 *Annual Review of Banking Law* 317.

procedures. This 'cost' of delay for the regulator is aimed to counteract the incentives otherwise operating in favour of delay.

Second, as the bank declines, the law increasingly constrains the regulator's discretion over the handling of the bank and eventually mandates the pulling of the resolution trigger. This process, usually termed 'prompt corrective action', is set out in what is now section 38 of FDIA. The points at which regulatory action have to be taken are defined by reference to the bank's capital, using capital and leverage ratios of the type discussed in Chapter 14. Any bank which becomes 'undercapitalized' by reference to the criteria set under section 38 is required to produce a capital restoration plan, which requires regulatory approval. Regulators must normally require 'significantly undercapitalized' banks to issue fresh capital or to be acquired by another bank, and may impose a range of other restrictions. For 'critically undercapitalized' banks the regulator must normally pull the resolution trigger. None of this is very different from what one would expect a good regulator to do; the point about section 38 is that it makes it less likely that the regulator will refrain from taking the appropriate action.

Prompt corrective action (known in that Directive as 'early intervention') is part also of the EU's BRRD,[54] which requires Member States to give their competent authorities early intervention powers, but the EU guidelines on early intervention are less prescriptive than the FDIA rules.[55] Title II of the Dodd–Frank Act does not apply section 38 to the systemically important financial institutions within its scope, being more concerned to control the process by which the resolution procedure is triggered by reference to a standard that permits consideration of the likelihood of capital depletion.[56] The 'Enhanced Prudential Supervision' by the Federal Reserve of large financial institutions that is required by Title I of Dodd–Frank should produce pressure on these companies to repair diminished capital or face the risk of triggering a resolution proceeding.

16.5 Bail-In

Given the doubts, analysed in 16.4, about the feasibility of applying the transfer tool to large and complex financial institutions, it is not surprising that other resolution techniques have been examined. In particular, measures to make bank creditors bear losses (or 'bail them in') have become very popular in policy circles.

---

[54] Art 27.

[55] EBA, *Guidelines on Triggers for the Use of Early Intervention Measures Pursuant to Article 27(4) of Directive 2014/59/EU* (2015).

[56] Dodd–Frank Act of 2010, §§203(a)(2)(A) and 203(c)(4). The test is whether the financial company is 'in default or in danger of default'. One of the permitted criteria is whether the 'financial company has incurred, or is likely to incur, losses that will deplete all or substantially all of its capital', similar to the prompt corrective action test. Such a determination requires the consent of the Treasury, the Federal Reserve, and the FDIC, except that in cases in which the major financial entity is a broker-dealer, the SEC replaces the FDIC, and for an insurer, the Director of the Federal Insurance Office replaces the FDIC, ibid, §203(a)(1).

One might say that bail-in occurs whenever creditors bear some share of the bank's losses which they would incur in a standard bankruptcy procedure, even though the bank has not entered into such a procedure, for example, because it has been bailed out.

We will analyse bail-in in the following way. In section 16.5.1, we will look at how bail-in operates as a free-standing resolution tool—that is, where it is not used in conjunction with any other resolution tools. In section 16.5.2, we will look at its use in conjunction with the resolution-by-transfer tools. In section 16.6 we examine the role of bail-in the context of the resolution of banking groups through the SPE technique. Finally in section 16.7, we will look at the contractual arrangements banks might put in place to provide bail-in mechanisms which might operate before the point is reached at which a regulator would impose bail-in.

16.5.1 Bail-in as a free-standing resolution tool

For the purpose of analysing bail-in as a free-standing resolution tool we will focus on the BRRD, which clearly envisages that the bail-in tool will be used in this way (as well as in conjunction with the transfer tools).[57]

When used by itself, the bail-in tool seeks to bring about a recapitalization of the bank or other failing institution by writing off the debt, wholly or partially, and by converting debt into equity. This has both financial and governance consequences for the bank. On the financial side, the bank's liabilities are reduced by the amount of the write-off or conversion and the demands on the bank's cash flows are reduced by the removal of the requirement to pay interest on the debt written off or converted. Depending on the size of the write-off or conversion, it is conceivable that this single step could be enough to restore the bank's balance sheet so that the bank has a positive net asset value and is no longer balance-sheet insolvent or in danger of becoming so. The reduction of the demand on the bank's cash flows may also be such that it is no longer in danger of being unable to meet its debts as they fall due (that is, no longer cash-flow insolvent). If there is conversion of debt into equity, the amount of the bank's capital is increased and this may help the bank meet its regulatory capital requirements.[58] At the end of the day, the economic result of bail-in may replicate the transferor/transferee arrangement, but without the need to transfer assets and liabilities between legal entities. The bailed-in bank will hold the good assets and maintain the liabilities which are to be preserved (such as deposits), while the liabilities supporting bad assets, which would have remained with the transferor, will have been written down to reflect the true value of those bad assets.

On the governance side, where the former debt-holders become equity holders, control of the bank may pass into new hands. This consequence is particularly likely to occur because the BRRD requires that the first step in the implementation of the

---

[57] Art 43(2).
[58] This may be regarded as a somewhat artificial exercise because (a) shares count towards regulatory capital at their book value (par plus share premium), not their market value, and (b) the consideration provided in a debt/equity swap is usually calculated as being the face value of the debt written off, not its market value. In distress, both book values are likely to exceed the market values.

bail-in procedure should be the cancellation or heavy dilution of the shares held by the existing shareholders.[59] This change of control will operate, *ex ante*, to induce the pre-crisis shareholders to monitor the management more carefully and, *ex post*, to substitute for the previous shareholders a set of presumably risk-averse investors whose main aim is to secure the repayment of the principal initially lent to the bank. Again, this result may mirror the transfer arrangement, in that the owners of the transferor lose control of the 'good' assets which go across to the transferee.

In order for there to be a real prospect that bail-in will achieve resolution of the bank by itself, a number of conditions must be met.[60] First, there must be enough debt in the failing bank for bailing it in to constitute a significant relief for the bank. Ironically, therefore, the more leveraged the bank, the more bail-in alone is likely to be effective. The BRRD requires banks to hold at all times a certain minimum amount of 'eligible' liabilities (debt particularly suited to bail-in).[61] How much bail-in debt is a regulator likely to require? A senior Bank of England (BoE) official has estimated that a UK bank should have an amount of debt capable of bail-in equal to the bank's minimum capital requirement plus the amount X, where X is an estimate of the loss a bank could suffer in a stressed scenario which would not be absorbed by its existing equity. Bailing in that amount of debt would permit the bank to absorb the losses not absorbed by the prior equity and then to be recapitalized at the minimum required level.[62]

Second, not all debt-holders are suitable for bail-in. For example, the BRRD excludes insured deposits from bail-in.[63] The reasoning behind this exclusion is clear enough: deposit insurance is there to render the bank run unnecessary (as we saw in Chapter 15). The risk of a bail-in undercuts that function of the deposit guarantee: there is now a good reason to run, namely to avoid a bail-in.[64] By extension, there is a good argument for not bailing in any short-term funder, precisely because they are also able to run, and for confining bail-in to long-term creditors only. The BRRD, however, does not take this step.[65] So, the commercial paper holders of Northern Rock[66] would not be exempted from bail-in and would still have an incentive to run (as would large depositors, to the extent of their excess over the €100,000 guarantee limit). Perhaps aware of this risk, the Directive gives resolution authorities power to exempt particular categories of debt-holders where this is necessary to avoid widespread contagion. Insofar as this power turns on a case-by-case determination *ex post* by the resolution authority once the bail-in

---

[59] Art 47. Thus, under the Directive bail-in normally involves conversion, not just write-off.

[60] Keeping the bank solvent in the future is likely to require fundamental changes to the bank's businesses in addition to the bail-in. Those changes might already be envisaged in the RRP. In any event, the BRRD permits the use of the bail-in tool as a stand-alone mechanism only if there is a 'reasonable prospect' that the bail-in, coupled with a reorganization of the businesses, will restore the bank to long-term viability (Art 43(3)).

[61] Art 45. The European Commission is to adopt 'technical standards' on the amount of eligible liabilities.

[62] Bank of England, 'Resolution and the Future of Finance', speech by Paul Tucker, 20 May 2013.

[63] Art 44(2). Secured liabilities are also excluded.

[64] Despite this, the Eurozone authorities came close to bailing-in the insured depositors in the Cypriot banks in the crisis of 2013: W Münchau, 'Europe is Risking a Bank Run', *Financial Times*, 17 March 2013.

[65] Art 44(2). However, only debt with a remaining maturity of a year counts towards the eligible liabilities a bank must at all times maintain: Art 45(4).

[66] See Chapter 15, section 15.2.

process is initiated, as the wording of the relevant legal instruments strongly suggests,[67] it hardly reduces the *ex ante* incentive for non-exempt short-term funders to run. Why would a normally bailed-in short-term funder wait around to discover whether, exceptionally, it was to be exempted in this particular case?

Bail-in is likely, therefore, to help resolve the bank, without precipitating the very financial distress the mechanism is there to avoid, if it is confined to long-term debt, the holders of which cannot run. That debt may be subordinated or senior, but, either way, it is long term.[68] However, even some holders of long-term debt appear to be poor candidates for bail-in. Bail-in worsens the financial position of the debt holders. This, of course, is the object of the exercise, since it gives long-term debt holders an incentive to monitor the management of the bank *ex ante*. However, if the holder of the debt is another bank or fragile financial institution, the effect of bail-in *ex post* may simply be to transfer the problem to another bank in the system.[69]

The legal effectiveness of the resolution authority's exercise of the bail-in power may also be in doubt where the debt has been issued in a jurisdiction outside the EEA. The BRRD requires banks in such cases to include in the debt contract a term recognizing the power of the home resolution authority to implement a bail-in and a legal opinion that this clause will be effective under the law of the foreign jurisdiction.[70] The absence of these steps does not deprive the resolution authority of its power to bail-in, but will leave open the question of whether the foreign jurisdiction will recognize the legal efficacy of the actions of the domestic regulator.

The implementation of the bail-in mechanism necessitates a valuation of the bank, to work out how much debt needs to be bailed in. This is a difficult calculation and one which standard bankruptcy avoids. In standard bankruptcy the creditors are paid out only after the company's assets have been sold off, either on a going-concern or a break-up basis. So, the company's worth is represented by cold cash in the liquidator's hands. In a bail-in, where the objective is to keep the company as a going concern, valuation ought to occur in principle as the first step in the process. Valuation as a first step is what the BRRD envisages—to be carried out by an independent valuer.[71] Perhaps appreciating the unreality of this requirement in an emergency situation—it cuts against the need for speed which we have identified as a necessary ingredient of a good resolution procedure—the Directive permits a 'quick and dirty' provisional valuation to be done at the outset, with a full valuation by an independent person to

---

[67] Art 44(3) and, in particular, Commission Delegated Regulation C(2016) 379 final, Art 4: exclusions 'shall be based on a case-by-case analysis of the institution under resolution and shall not be automatic'. If the exclusion would throw an extra burden on the resolution financial arrangements, the approval of the Commission is required for the exclusion: Art 44(12).

[68] Which we may think of, roughly, as having an initial maturity of one year or more. The debt is to be bailed in, of course, in accordance with its seniority in normal bankruptcy procedure.

[69] The Directive requires Member States to limit holdings of bail-in debt by other banks and financial institutions covered by the Directive: Art 44(2).

[70] Art 55. On the legal difficulties in this area see M Lehmann, 'Bail-In and Private International Law: How to Make Bank Resolution Measures Effective Across Borders' (2016) available at ssrn.com/abstract=2759763.

[71] Art 36.

be carried out *ex post*, with the necessary adjustments being done then also. This is more complex but also more realistic.

As to the conversion of debt into equity, the resolution authority is given discretion as to the conversion rate and may apply different conversion rates to different classes of liability. However, it is clear that the BRRD does not see conversion as a form of punishment of the debt-holders. The conversion of the debt into equity rather is designed to provide 'appropriate compensation' for the loss the debt-holders have incurred through the removal of their contractual rights under the debt issue.[72] But this may not mean shares will be issued of exactly equivalent value to the face value of the debt converted. Such a conversion rate could be considered as over-compensation, since the bonds might have been trading at less than par before the conversion. On the other hand, face-value conversion promotes one of the other objectives of the Directive: substantial dilution of the existing shareholders.[73]

16.5.2 Bail-in in conjunction with the transfer tool

If one of the main aims of the bail-in tool is to ensure that creditors' claims against the bank (other than the exempted classes) do not emerge unscathed from the bank's distress because it has been bailed out by the taxpayer, then it is not immediately obvious why the bail-in tool is needed as a supplement to the transfer mechanism. When the rump of the bank is liquidated after the transfer, its creditors will necessarily bear losses at that point, just as in a standard bankruptcy. However, we have noted that the BRRD (unlike the OLA in the US) contemplates that taxpayer money may be used to subsidize the transfer. That money may come either from taxpayer subvention to the resolution fund or from direct use of bail-out mechanisms. Creditors whose liabilities are transferred in such circumstances will have claims against a new and solvent owner, whose ability to meet those claims has been supported by the taxpayer.

Consequently, the BRRD contemplates a role for bail-in to convert or write down debt which is to be transferred to a bridge bank, a new private-sector owner or to an asset-management agency.[74] Where the debt is simply written down, the value of the transferred claim is reduced; where it is converted into equity in the transferee, it helps to capitalize the transferee (for example, a bridge bank). Even under OLA there is a role for bail-in to facilitate a transfer. The FDIC contemplates the use of the bail-in to promote the capitalization of the transferee. The value of the claims of the creditors in the liquidation of the rump, instead of being paid out in cash, will be converted into equity of, or subordinated debt claims on, the transferee (both of which can count as capital).

---

[72] Art 50(2). Senior creditors must not have conversion rates applied to them which are less favourable than those applied to junior creditors.

[73] Art 47(1). It also reduces the incentives for debt holders to monitor the bank. Overall, the BRRD is ambiguous whether its provisions are aimed to enhance shareholder or debt holder monitoring of the bank in advance of resolution.

[74] Art 43(2)(b).

16.6 Bail-in and Single Point of Entry Resolution

Despite the novelty of the bail-in tool, it has been adopted enthusiastically by the Bank of England and, even more so, by the FDIC in the US as the preferred method of resolving internationally active banks. The BoE envisages that it will use a statutory bail-in power to recapitalize the parent company rather than operate by transferring assets to a bridge bank and using the liquidation of the rump to inflict losses on the creditors. The parent's debt would be written down and ownership of the equity would be transferred to the former creditors—though the recapitalized bank would probably have to raise fresh equity, thus diluting the creditors' equity.[75] Bail-in of the parent company debt has been facilitated by the FSB's proposals for debt to be a significant part of a bank's 'total loss absorbing capacity' (TLAC).[76]

Surprisingly, at first sight, bail-in at the parent company level has been promoted also by the FDIC under OLA - the Orderly *Liquidation* Authority. To a much greater extent than in Europe, the US has been concerned about banks that are 'Too Big To Fail'.[77] Perhaps this is because, historically, the US banking system has been highly fragmented. The elimination in the early 1990s of federal statutory hindrances to interstate mergers triggered a massive consolidation wave; the repeal of Glass–Steagall's limit on commercial bank/investment bank affiliation in 1999 triggered further financial sector consolidation. Finally, the too-big banks got even bigger as a result of purchase and assumption acquisitions of failing banks during the financial crisis and other crisis-related consolidation. Thus the largest US banks and the FDIC have convergent interests in devising a credible resolution strategy. The banks have been concerned that they faced break-up if they remain 'too big to fail'. The FDIC of course wants to show it can make effective use of its newly delegated authority. This convergence has produced a resolution strategy under OLA known as Single Point of Entry ('SPOE').[78]

The approach takes advantage of the fact that the largest US financial firms are organized as holding companies, in which the holding company ('HoldCo') is the only publicly traded entity; its assets consist principally of the shares of its operating subsidiaries, and its liabilities are generally long-term debt. Short-term debt claims, whether deposits or commercial paper or repo, are issued by the operating subsidiaries.

---

[75] FDIC/Bank of England, *Resolving Globally Active, Systemically Important, Financial Institutions* (2012). Successful bail-in of the parent company of the group (known as 'single point of entry' resolution) avoids the need to resolve other group entities, a particular advantage if these entities are located in other jurisdictions. See generally, JN Gordon and WG Ringe, 'Bank Resolution in the European Banking Union: A Transatlantic Perspective on What it Would Take' (2015) 115 *Columbia Law Review* 1297.

[76] FSB, 'Principles on Loss-Absorbing and Recapitalisation Capacity of G-SIBs in Resolution: Total Loss-Absorbing Capacity (TLAC) Term Sheet' (November 2015).

[77] See eg GH Stern and RJ Feldman (eds), *Too Big to Fail: The Hazards of Bank Bailouts* (Washington DC: Brookings, 2004).

[78] For more detail, see Gordon and Ringe, n 75; JN Gordon and WG Ringe, 'Bank Resolution in Europe: The Unfinished Agenda of Structural Reform', in D Busch and G Ferrarini (eds), *European Banking Union* (Oxford: OUP, 2015), Ch 15; P Davies, 'Resolution of Cross-border Groups', in M Haentjens and B Wessels (eds), *Research Handbook on Crisis Management in the Banking Sector* (Cheltenham: Edward Elgar, 2015), Ch 11.

Under SPOE, losses at a depository bank subsidiary, for example, would be upstreamed to the holding company, first to be charged against HoldCo's capital and then, if necessary, to trigger a resolution in which only HoldCo is put into resolution—the 'single point' of entry to resolution—so that further losses can be charged to unsecured term debt held at the HoldCo level. This unsecured term debt, which is structurally subordinated to credit claims against the subsidiaries because held by HoldCo, is thus 'bailed-in' and either written off or converted into equity as necessary to recapitalize the firm. The great advantage of this SPOE strategy is that only HoldCo is put into resolution: the operating subsidiaries are untouched; their short-term claims are shielded by the subordinated term debt (which cannot run) issued at the HoldCo level.[79] By reducing run risk, this should substantially reduce systemic knock-on effects of the resolution and thus make bail-in, rather than bail-out, a credible approach to a failing systemically important financial firm. Moreover, the FDIC also contemplates that foreign subsidiaries will be protected in the same manner, avoiding the risk of disruptive foreign resolution proceeding, as occurred with Lehman UK.[80]

A key part of the regulatory strategy is to require HoldCo to issue sufficient TLAC so as to make such a resolution feasible under most circumstances. The FSB proposal that was ratified at the 2015 G20 Leaders Summit calls for TLAC of equity plus subordinated term debt that is greater than twice the amount of required equity capital on both risk-weighted and leverage measures.[81] This means TLAC equal to the greater of 18 per cent of risk-weighted assets (plus additional regulatory capital buffers as appropriate), and, when fully phased in, a minimum Basel III leverage ratio of 6.75 per cent. It bears emphasis that the TLAC requirement will apply to all G-SIBS, which includes the largest EU banks. The FSB proposal permits higher levels, and the Fed has obliged. In its current (October 2015) proposal, the required TLAC for US G-SIBs will be the greater of 18 per cent of risk-weighted assets or 9.5 per cent of total leverage. The TLAC must include a long-term debt amount of the greater of 6 per cent (plus the G-SIB surcharge) of risk-weighted assets and 4.5 per cent of total leverage. Under the proposed rule TLAC would be as high as 23.5 per cent of risk-weighted assets for JP Morgan Chase.[82] Six of the eight US G-SIBs fall short of the requirements and will need to raise a total of $120 billion in TLAC, including the required long-term debt. The Fed explains further:

---

[79] Because the Dodd–Frank Act speaks in terms of 'orderly liquidation' rather than 'orderly resolution' (or 'orderly reorganization'), the US variant of SPOE has a twist: the FDIC will impose a receivership on the failed systematically important financial institution ('SIFI') (HoldCo) and then transfer its assets to a successor bridge bank, 'BridgeCo'. HoldCo will disappear into the FDIC's receivership while BridgeCo continues. HoldCo's shareholders will almost surely be wiped out. (Perhaps an equity stub remains, depending on the initial level of capital.) Based on the FDIC's estimate of losses, HoldCo's unsecured debt will be partly written off (to cover losses in the transferred subsidiaries not already covered by the write-down of HoldCo's capital) and partly converted into equity in a fully recapitalized BridgeCo.

[80] We discuss the international aspect of resolution in Chapter 28, section 28.6.

[81] FSB, 'Principles on Loss-Absorbing and Recapitalisation Capacity of G-SIBs in Resolution: Total Loss-Absorbing Capacity (TLAC) Term Sheet' (November 2015).

[82] See D Tarullo, 'Memo to the Board of Governors, Proposed rule establishing total loss-absorbing capacity, long-term debt, and clean holding company requirement for US globally systemically important banking organizations' (October 2015) (with attachments).

To further facilitate an orderly resolution, the proposal also would require the parent holding company...to avoid entering into certain financial arrangements that would create obstacles to an orderly resolution. These 'clean holding company' requirements would include bans on issuance of short-term debt to external investors and on entering into derivatives and certain other types of financial contracts with external counterparties. These requirements will reduce the risk of destabilizing funding runs at the holding company, reduce holding company complexity, and enhance the resiliency of operating subsidiaries during an orderly resolution.[83]

One critical element to the scheme is that the TLAC debt should be held outside the banking system, so that a bail-in will not have contagion effects. This will be achieved by requiring an onerous capital charge for any such debt holding.

SPOE seems to provide a credible mechanism for implementation of a bail-in strategy.[84] It requires firms to 'self-insure' a smooth path in resolution rather than rely on a taxpayer bail-out, or even a mutual risk-sharing scheme funded within the banking sector like the Single Resolution Fund in the Eurozone. Bail-in may be harder to implement in the EU (including the Eurozone) than in the US because firms are not organized in holding-company form, so it may not be possible to keep operating entities entirely outside the resolution procedure and questions of the subordination of TLAC debt may arise. Moreover, the operations of firms are geographically dispersed, and it may seem appropriate to invoke 'Multiple Points of Entry' in some cases. Some have nevertheless strenuously argued for structural reform of G-SIBs in the EU to take advantage of the way in which SPOE makes bail-in resolution genuinely credible.[85]

16.7 Contingent Capital

In section 16.1, we noted that the costs of standard bankruptcy provide an incentive for creditors and debtors to reach a voluntary agreement outside bankruptcy (a 'workout'). The same is true of bank resolution procedures. Indeed, some have argued that the OLA is so draconian and shot-full of regulatory discretion that its main impact will be to induce workouts.[86] However, effecting a workout may be more difficult in the case of a financial company, precisely because of the loss of franchise value if knowledge of the workout becomes public (as it likely will).[87] Consequently, a private recapitalization of a financial institution needs to be triggered well in advance of the point at which resolution threatens. It also needs to be clear in advance of the trigger event what the nature of the work-out will be.

One such mechanism for a work-out is contingent convertible bonds (commonly referred to as 'cocos')—that is, subordinated debt issued on the contractual basis that it

---

[83] Federal Reserve Press Release (30 October 2015).

[84] See Armour, n 37, 469–71. It has been argued, however, against bail-ins that, in principle, taxpayers are better able to absorb the costs of bank failure that the holders of even long-term bank debt: C Goodhart and E Evgouleas, *A Critical Evaluation of Bail-Ins as Bank Recapitalisation Mechanisms* (Centre for Economic Policy Discussion Paper 10065, 2014), who refer to the holders of such debt as 'pensioners and savers'.

[85] See Gordon and Ringe, n 78.

[86] Skadden, Arps, Slate, Meagher & Flom LLP, *The Dodd–Frank Act: Commentary and Insights* (2010), 102.

[87] In terms of speed and secrecy, a regulator is likely to do better than multiple private parties.

will be written off or converted into equity if the institution suffers a financial decline but before the point at which the institution is likely to be unable to satisfy the regulatory requirements for continued existence. Such a trigger point might be identified by reference to a substantial decline in the share price (say, 20 per cent or more) or a decline in the bank's capital. Even before the financial crisis such a scheme had been proposed by Professor Mark Flannery.[88] His scheme, besides providing for recapitalization, was designed to provide substantial incentives for the existing shareholders of the bank to monitor bank management, in the expectation that they would wish to prevent the trigger point being reached. At the trigger point the existing shareholders were to suffer extensive dilution, while the holders of the hybrid debt would suffer little financial loss, though the nature of their investment in the bank would change. Consequently, the trigger point would be set well in advance of resolution and by reference to the market value of the bank's shares (not its book value, as with regulatory capital triggers), while conversion would be from the face value of the debt to the market value of the shares at the trigger point.

Post-crisis, substantial amounts of contingent capital have been issued by European banks, but it is far from clear that the aim is to follow the Flannery model. As we noted in Chapter 14, there is a regulatory incentive to issue convertible subordinated debt because, even under Basel III, it can count as Additional Tier 1 or as Tier 2 capital for regulatory purposes, while still retaining the tax shield of debt. In order to meet the Basel requirements, cocos need to be capable of being written down or converted by the regulator in resolution (Chapter V of the BRRD provides for this), but the features of the Flannery model which alter existing shareholder incentives are not part of the regulatory requirements. Many recent cocos do not in fact have these features. Sometimes there is no conversion at the trigger point, only write-off, so that the debt-holders receive no compensation and the existing shareholders are not diluted. In the jargon, these are 'sudden death' cocos. They are like conventional bank bonds, but run the risk of reduced or non-repayment in adverse circumstances short of bankruptcy. At other times, the conversion ratio is so unfavourable to the debt-holders that conversion still transfers wealth to the shareholders. In both cases, the monitoring incentives lie on the debt-holders rather than the shareholders.

A second interesting feature of recent issues is that they have been tied to a trigger point which is not very remote from resolution. Thus, Barclays has issued cocos where the trigger is common equity Tier 1 capital falling below 7 per cent. Since the Basel minimum is 4.5 per cent and there is a systemically important addition for Barclays of 2 per cent (not yet in force but *de facto* applied by the national regulator), it is difficult to believe that the UK resolution authority would not be actively engaged in monitoring the bank and would perhaps already have triggered resolution before or at the time the contractual trigger was pulled. In effect, a coco of this type is likely to operate not so

---

[88] MJ Flannery, 'No Pain, No Gain? Effecting Market Discipline via "Reverse Convertible Debentures"', in HS Scott (ed), *Capital Adequacy beyond Basel: Banking Securities and Insurance* (Oxford: OUP, 2005), Ch 5. See also JC Coffee Jr, 'Systemic Risk after Dodd–Frank: Contingent Capital and the Need for Regulatory Strategies beyond Oversight' (2011) 111 *Columbia Law Review* 795 (proposing conversion into cumulative voting preference shares in order to make bank's post-conversion corporate governance more cautious).

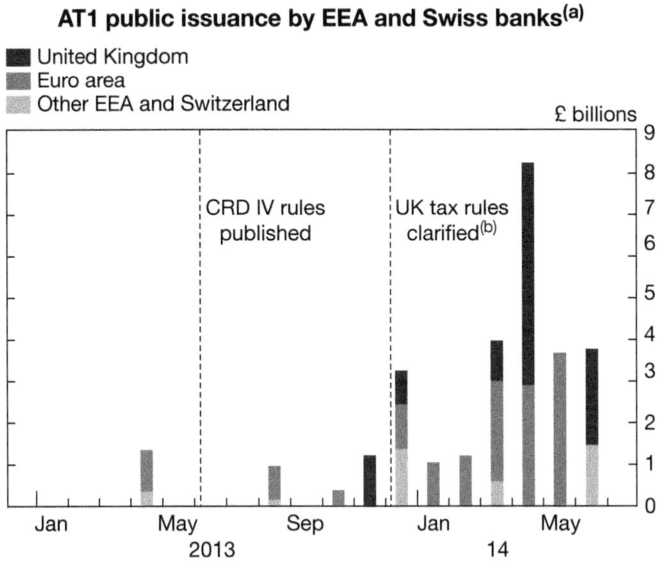

AT1 public issuance by EEA and Swiss banks[a]

■ United Kingdom
■ Euro area
▨ Other EEA and Switzerland

£ billions

CRD IV rules
published

UK tax rules
clarified[b]

Jan   May   Sep   Jan   May
        2013   14

Fig. 16.3 Coco Issuance by EEA and Swiss Banks, 2013–14

Source: Bank of England, *Financial Stability Report*, June 2014, 34.

as to produce a contractual recapitalization before resolution authority intervention, but as a way of determining the order of write-off in resolution. A sudden-death coco triggered at resolution is in effect a form of super-subordinated debt. It may also be that, in the current state of banks' equity levels, a 'high trigger' coco would be a very expensive instrument for the bank to issue (in terms of the interest rate it would have to offer to attract investors).[89] Figure 16.3 suggests that regulatory, rather than governance, incentives have been driving coco issuance to date.

There are two main uncertainties with cocos. First, purchasers of cocos may not be able accurately to price the risks attached to bail-in bonds. This will depend in part on how predictable the trigger point is and the consequences of pulling it are. Second, under the Flannery model, the very prospect of bail-in may hasten the financial distress of the bank. If bail-in is tied to share price and will lead to substantial dilution of the existing shareholders, then the price of the shares will fall and trigger bail-in as the bail-in point approaches, providing an incentive to short the shares. These concerns may explain why banks have predicated bail-ins of cocos on loss of regulatory capital alone and have often attached to the triggers consequences which are unfavourable to the debt-holders.

16.8 Resolution in the European Banking Union

Under the pressure of the Eurozone financial crisis of 2010–12, the Eurozone Member States agreed to form the European Banking Union as a means to disentangle the

---

[89] Switzerland is an interesting jurisdiction in terms of cocos. Not only has it made the issuance of cocos mandatory for G-SIFIs, but also a certain proportion of the mandated issue must consist of 'high trigger' cocos. For analysis see Swiss Finance Institute, *The Extra Cost of Swiss Banking Regulation* (2014), esp 8–9.

dangerous links between sovereigns and their banks.[90] At the most basic level, the objective is to ensure a level playing-field for the Eurozone banking industry and remove any national biases or supervisory forbearance.[91] But the ambition of the Banking Union goes well beyond that: its objective is to eliminate the asset and liability matching on a national level that has been a driver of the EU sovereign debt crisis. The Banking Union at the moment stands somewhat uncertainly on two legs, the Single Supervisory Mechanism ('SSM') and the Single Resolution Mechanism ('SRM'), with hopes for a complementary third, the European Deposit Insurance Scheme ('EDIS').[92]

The SRM is an effort to lodge the decision whether to put a bank into resolution at the Eurozone-level, not the member-state level, and to have key decisions about the terms of resolution made at the Eurozone level as well. Thus, the decision to shut down a bank involves the European Central Bank, the new Single Resolution Board ('SRB') (comprising permanent members, the European Commission, the Council, the ECB, and national resolution authorities), and the European Commission. National authorities will execute the resolution, not the SRB or the Commission (although under instruction by the latter). This may also create some leeway for national regulators to influence the resolution process.

As a side agreement to the SRM, the Eurozone Member States agreed to raise a Single Resolution Fund (the 'Fund'), to be funded over time by annual contributions from the banks it will protect.[93] The target size of the Fund is 1 per cent of covered deposits of all credit institutions of the participating Member States, currently estimated at roughly €75 billion. The SRB would use the Fund to ensure the operability of the failing bank in the short run; it is not a bail-out fund designed to take losses. That was key to obtaining widespread agreement, for the Eurozone North strenuously resisted efforts to 'mutualize' losses (that is, to bail out the South). It is not altogether clear what the Fund does, since it is certainly not large enough to cover the liquidity needs of a reorganizing failed G-SIB. That would require engagement by the ECB. Potentially available in connection with a resolution is bail-out support from the European Stability Mechanism, and proposals for EDIS have been tabled.[94] In any event, the resolution scheme devised by the SRB will apply the BRRD, including the provisions requiring creditors to bear losses before any state aid is available. If the failing bank is a G-SIB, it will have been subject to

---

[90] The Eurozone is a subset of the Member States of the EU. The Banking Union is mandatory for those states but also available to non-Eurozone Member States. The UK is not a member of the Eurozone and has indicated it will not join the Banking Union. But it is governed by the BRRD (see n 7). The principal institutional features are described in Chapter 24, section 24.3.4. See also the essays collected in D Busch and G Ferrarini (eds), *European Banking Union* (Oxford: OUP, 2015). For more on resolution in the Eurozone, see also Gordon and Ringe, nn 75 and 78; Armour, n 37, 467–82; Davies, n 78; European Commission, 'Banking Union: Restoring Financial Stability in the Eurozone', updated version of memo first published on 15 April 2014 (24 November 2015).

[91] Y Mersch, Member, Executive Board of the ECB, '"Built to Last": The New Euro-Area Framework', Speech at the Barclays Research Conference, London (17 May 2013).

[92] See Chapter 24, section 24.3.4.

[93] Regulation (EU) No 806/2014, of the European Parliament and of the Council of 15 July 2014 Establishing Uniform Rules and a Uniform Procedure for the Resolution of Credit Institutions and Certain Investment Firms in the Framework of a Single Resolution Mechanism and a Single Resolution Fund and Amending Regulation (EU) No 1093/2010, [2014] OJ L225/1, Art 18.

[94] See European Commission, 'Restoring Financial Stability in the Eurozone', n 90; see also Chapter 24, section 24.3.4.

the FSB's requirement for the maintenance of sufficient TLAC to cover substantial losses through a bail-in while still remaining sufficiently capitalized to remain in business, as discussed in section 16.7.

16.9 Conclusion

Since the crisis, the inadequacy of ordinary bankruptcy for banks and analogous financial institutions has become widely accepted, even in jurisdictions, such as the UK, which previously had largely ignored the issue. The driving force behind these developments were strong political imperatives (a) to reduce, or even eliminate, the risk of large-scale injections of public resources into failing banks in future crises and (b) to make sure that long-term creditors did not emerge whole in future bank failures but absorbed losses. By and large, policymakers have been more successful with the second aim than with the first. It seems likely that in all future bank and near-bank failures, long-term creditors will absorb losses, either because their claims are left in the rump of the failing bank which is then liquidated (as in the transfer procedure) or because they are explicitly bailed-in under the reorganization procedure.

The demise of the bail-out can be less confidently predicted. If there is no ready purchaser for a large and complex institution under the transfer procedure or if, even after bail-in, the institution is not firmly solvent (on both a balance sheet and a cash-flow basis), the state will be faced with the unpalatable choice it was presented with in the financial crisis. Without an injection of state resources the bank will not survive. So, the state will have to decide again: are the negative externalities of bail-out greater or lesser than the negative externalities of bank failure? From this perspective, the EU Directive, making state resources available to supplement resolution, seems more pragmatic than the Dodd–Frank insistence that public support for insolvent banks requires Congressional approval. On the other hand, vigorous application of the TLAC requirement looks to be a kind of self-insurance that is triggered by an administrative resolution procedure that should it make it possible in all but dire circumstances for a kind of internal reorganization to take place that does not depend upon bail-out.

The great risk in all these resolution schemes is that they work best in the case of 'idiosyncratic' failure, that is, failure for reasons particular to the given firm rather than common to many such firms. Correlated business strategies and common exposure to global economic conditions seem likely, however. In such circumstances, is it really the case that the only source of relief will be through serial resolution procedures that will give banking authorities direct responsibility for (and control of) the global financial system? The test of the post-financial crisis settlement will come after the failure of a large financial firm. Has the system been strongly enough reinforced so as to withstand the shock, really an earthquake, without a liquidity and credit contraction that severely damages the real economy, and without state support?

17

Bank Governance

17.1 Introduction

So far, our analysis of the regulation of banks has focused on the imposition of rules relating to their capital structure and liquidity to reduce risks of failure and on resolution processes in the event of failure. According to a common narrative, however, in addition to inadequate capital and liquidity, the failure of banks in the financial crisis also reflected their poor corporate governance.[1] By 'corporate governance', commentators mean the mechanisms by which managers are selected, motivated, and rendered accountable to shareholders, as well as those by which managers oversee the activities of other employees. Yet empirical studies report that the banks with the 'best' corporate governance practices, as measured by ordinary standards, were the ones that did worst during the financial crisis. The weakness in pre-crisis bank governance was not that banks had ignored 'best practices' in corporate governance. Rather, it was a failure to appreciate that the ways in which banks differ from non-financial firms imply that 'best practice' for bank governance should also be different.

Banks are materially different in their financing, business model, and balance sheets from most non-financial firms. First, banks are highly leveraged institutions: shareholders may gain at creditors' expense from an increase in risk and associated returns. If things go well, shareholders keep the higher returns; if things go badly, the creditors suffer. If banks were companies like any other, depositors and other creditors would take notice of the risk of shareholder opportunism and either charge a higher interest rate (making financing through debt more expensive and therefore less predominant) or insist on having stronger governance and control rights.[2]

Yet various factors stand in the way of creditors themselves playing an important part in disciplining shareholder opportunism. Depositors have no oversight rights, are dispersed, and are protected by deposit insurance. Banking regulation and supervision are there precisely to prevent shareholder opportunism of this kind, so that (at least unsophisticated) market participants may over-rely on their effectiveness. And perhaps most importantly, as we have seen in Chapter 16, creditors of larger banks could (and perhaps still can) reasonably expect a state bail-out that will avoid them any losses should the bank become insolvent.

---

[1] See eg OECD, *Corporate Governance and the Financial Crisis: Key Findings and Main Messages* 41 (2009); European Banking Authority, *EBA Guidelines on Internal Governance* 3 (2011).

[2] On the important role of creditors in the governance of listed companies even in a highly shareholder-focused corporate governance system such as the US, see DG Baird and RK Rasmussen, 'Private Debt and the Missing Lever of Corporate Governance' (2006) 154 *University of Pennsylvania Law Review* 1209.

Principles of Financial Regulation. First Edition. John Armour, Dan Awrey, Paul Davies, Luca Enriques, Jeffrey N. Gordon, Colin Mayer, and Jennifer Payne. © John Armour, Dan Awrey, Paul Davies, Luca Enriques, Jeffrey N. Gordon, Colin Mayer, and Jennifer Payne 2016. Published 2016 by Oxford University Press.

In addition, as Chapter 16 also illustrated, bank failures have the ability to impose large costs on society at large—externalities—which are not borne by bank shareholders. Finally, a bank's assets (its loans) are hard to monitor for any outsider, which makes any external monitoring mechanism less effective.

In the period leading up to the financial crisis, the peculiarities of banks' balance sheets, their regulation, and the externalities they can create were thought not to necessitate any difference in the structure of bank governance from that of non-financial firms. Regulators, it was believed, would cause banks to internalize the costs of their activities, meaning that what maximized bank shareholders' returns would also be in the interests of society. On this view, which we might call the 'assimilation' theory of bank governance, it was thought appropriate for banks to use the same governance tools as non-financial companies to minimize shareholder-management agency costs, namely independent boards, shareholder rights, the threat of takeovers, and equity-based executive compensation.

Unfortunately, tightening the linkage between shareholders and managers in banks had the adverse effect of encouraging bank managers to test the limits of regulatory controls and take excessive risks. As we describe in this chapter, the banks that had the most 'pro-shareholder' boards and the closest alignment between executive returns and the stock price were those that took the greatest risks prior to, and suffered the greatest losses during, the crisis.

As a result, a significant rethink about the way in which banks are governed is required. The revised perspective might be termed a 'bank exceptionalism' theory of governance.[3] The structure and function of bank boards, the compensation of bank employees, and the function of risk management within banks need careful crafting if governance reforms are to address, and not exacerbate, bank failures. In the last few years, a plethora of special 'bank governance' rules have been introduced. While these initiatives recognize that assimilation was an error, we shall see that it remains unclear how effectively the new measures get to grips with the exceptional challenges of bank governance.

The rest of this chapter is structured as follows. Section 17.2 reviews the goals and mechanisms of 'ordinary' corporate governance, and explains their limitations when applied to banks. Sections 17.3–17.6 then consider, respectively, the operation of boards of directors, executive pay, shareholder rights, and directors' duties in relation to banks, reviewing empirical evidence and describing regulatory initiatives. By the end of this chapter, you should have a good understanding of why the corporate governance tools that have prevailed for listed companies generally in the last thirty years may have led to undesired consequences when applied to banks. In addition, you should have an idea of which bank governance reforms have been implemented on each side of the Atlantic and how they may support the goal of a more resilient banking system.

---

[3] To the extent that the factors differentiating banks are also relevant for other, non-bank, financial firms, then this 'bank exceptionalism' theory of governance should also extend *mutatis mutandis*.

17.2 Corporate Governance: How are Banks Different?

17.2.1 The conventional approach to corporate governance

The standard approach to corporate governance exhorts managers to run their firm in the interests of shareholders. This is because shareholders are 'residual claimants': that is, they receive what is left after all fixed claimants have been paid. Focusing on maximizing the residual surplus gives incentives to maximize the overall value of the firm: that is, to run it as efficiently as possible. Moreover, amongst those who contract with the firm—investors, creditors, employees, customers, and suppliers—the shareholders have the most homogeneous interests in the financial performance of the firm.[4] Their interests relate simply to the maximization of the value of their claims, which, in the context of a publicly traded firm, is reflected in the firm's stock price. Consequently, maximizing the stock price should be management's objective.

To implement this, shareholders are given the right to appoint directors, who in turn select the managers.[5] The significance of the directors derives from the fact that ownership of shares in large public corporations is typically widely dispersed. As a consequence, shareholders face high coordination costs in exercising their rights. A number of mechanisms are relied upon to overcome this problem.

First, the board of directors has increasingly come to be viewed as performing the function of monitoring managerial performance on behalf of the shareholders. If the shareholders are too dispersed to be able to engage in effective monitoring themselves, then the elected board of directors can do so in their stead. The problem here is that the shareholders' very lack of coordination may undermine the process of election of effective monitors. The managers may influence the list of candidates and ensure that only their friends and associates are represented on the board. In response to this concern, directors are increasingly expected to be 'independent' of the firm: that is, they should have no family, financial, or employment ties to the firm or its managers. Independent directors, it is thought, will make better delegated monitors on behalf of shareholders. The problem remains that in the absence of effective shareholder input, the 'independence' of directors means simply the absence of a conflict of interest; it does nothing to ensure the presence of the necessary qualities to be an effective monitor.

Executive pay comprises a second mechanism, which has in recent years become the most important focus of governance activity in the US. Tying managerial compensation to the stock performance gives very direct incentives. A drawback with conditioning pay on financial performance is that it requires managers to bear the risk of the firm's underperformance, even for reasons beyond their control. This may result in managers adopting an unduly risk-averse approach to decision-making, passing up valuable but risky opportunities in favour of safer, more conservative, strategies. One way to encourage managerial risk-taking and stock price maximization at the same

---

[4] H Hansmann, *The Ownership of Enterprise* (Cambridge, MA: Belknap Press, 1996).
[5] R Kraakman, J Armour, P Davies, L Enriques, H Hansmann, G Hertig, K Hopt, H Kanda, M Pargendler, G Ringe, and E Rock, *The Anatomy of Corporate Law*, 3rd ed (Oxford: OUP, 2016), s 1.2.5.

time is to pay managers by way of options. These have the potential to offer managers rewards for increasing the stock price, but with no associated loss if the share price falls. However, the incentives associated with options are highly sensitive to the way in which the strike price is set. These contracts are normally negotiated by the compensation committee of the board of directors. Their success, therefore, is a function of the quality of the board. Because of this, some influential scholars argue that the rise in option-based compensation is not so much a function of improved corporate governance, but of a combination of changes to the US tax code that made it cheaper for firms to grant options than cash compensation, and of thinly veiled managerial self-interest.[6]

Third, shareholder rights provide channels through which shareholders may exercise control, for example by voting on major business decisions or more generally by removing directors. The exercise of shareholder rights requires some concentration of ownership, so as to overcome coordination problems. It is sometimes suggested that takeovers are a mechanism by which external discipline is brought to bear on management even in the presence of dispersed shareholdings. Poorly performing management faces the threat of acquisition by another company, and the mere threat of this occurring may be sufficient to encourage management to pursue the interests of their shareholders vigorously.

Recently, we have witnessed the emergence of a second mechanism by which external discipline is brought to bear on management in the presence of dispersed shareholders. Activist shareholders, and in particular hedge funds, have acquired significant but not necessarily controlling shareholdings in firms to effect changes in corporate policy and management. They frequently act in conjunction with other institutional investors in promoting change. The rise of institutional activists has had a profound impact on the conduct of management in dispersed ownership systems in the UK and US particularly.

Fourth, directors and officers are subject to legal duties to avoid conflicts of interest and to take appropriate care in the running of their company. These may be enforced by shareholders through derivative or class actions, which enable a single shareholder or group of shareholders to represent the rest in claims against errant directors. However, it is unlikely that the shareholders who initiate such an action, or the judges called upon to adjudicate them, will know as much about the business as the incumbent managers. This makes litigation a blunt instrument. To avoid overzealous enforcement, there are typically checks on shareholder litigation in relation to good faith business decisions that grant considerable discretion to management in the running of their businesses, leaving shareholder plaintiffs to focus on more egregious cases of conflicts of interest.

---

[6] See L Bebchuk and J Fried, *Pay Without Performance. The Unfulfilled Promise of Executive Compensation* (Cambridge, MA: Harvard University Press, 2004); JC Coffee, 'A Theory of Corporate Scandals: Why the USA and Europe Differ' (2005) *Oxford Review of Economic Policy* 198, 202.

17.2.2 How are banks different?

As anticipated in the introduction, governance problems and mechanisms may play out differently in banks than in ordinary firms, reflecting how banks differ from non-financial firms in three important respects. The first difference is that banks are highly leveraged. The core of a bank's business model is to transform short-term deposits into long-term loans, implying that most of its capital is raised through debt. In addition to deposits, banks raise money via short-term and long-term debt which, together with deposits, typically make up most of the liability side of their balance sheets. As a result, shareholders may stand to benefit at creditors' expense from changes in the bank's investment projects that increase risk and associated returns. If things go well, the shareholders keep the increased returns, whereas if things go badly, the creditors suffer losses. Perversely, mechanisms that succeed in tying executives to the interests of shareholders may actually exacerbate these financial agency costs. Creditors should therefore satisfy themselves that there are strong checks in place to ensure that the riskiness of the bank's activities is kept within acceptable limits. However, depositors usually have only modest amounts at stake and are widely dispersed, so they do not wish to, or feel able to, monitor bank lending effectively.

The second difference is that bank failure imposes greater costs on society. A bank failure can trigger contagion in other parts of the financial system, and, by impeding the operation of the financial system, can harm the ability of businesses to obtain finance. Since losses are purely economic, they are not generally susceptible to compensation through the tort system.[7] Moreover, as the source of contagion is usually the failure of a financial firm, governments have incentives to throw money at troubled firms to avert such failure.[8] The more systemically important the bank, the more likely it will be able to rely on government support should it get into difficulties. This gives banks a perverse incentive to structure their operations such that they are systemically important and, in the eyes of policymakers, 'too big to fail'.[9] The implicit government guarantee means that such firms enjoy a lower cost of credit,[10] and that creditors' incentives to monitor the firms' performance is undermined. What this does is to morph the creditors' problem described in the previous paragraph into a problem for society more generally, through the implicit subsidy that creditors receive.

---

[7] This is ordinarily justified on the basis that economic harms to one party often represent opportunities to someone else: a power outage closing firm A's factory for a week (and resulting in lost profits) represents an opportunity for A's competitors to earn extra profits by selling more products instead. However, if contagion is *systemic* in the sense that it affects the entire financial sector, competitors will not profit from a bank's difficulties, nor will competitors of manufacturing firms who are unable to raise finance be readily able to profit from their circumstances. And even if the economic losses caused by contagion were in principle recoverable, the way in which they are triggered ensures they will not be visited on shareholders. Banks trigger contagion through their financial distress and there would consequently be no assets to pay tort liabilities.

[8] This is distinct from other cases of catastrophic industrial accidents, where governments intervene to ameliorate the consequences but nevertheless are content to bankrupt the firm in the process.

[9] See M Roe, 'Structural Corporate Degradation Due to Too-Big-To-Fail Finance' (2014) 162 *University of Pennsylvania Law Review* 1419.

[10] See VV Acharya, D Anginer, and AJ Warburton, 'The End of Market Discipline? Investor Expectations of Implicit Government Guarantees', Working Paper (2016).

'IBG–YBG'

To be sure, bank shareholders will lose money if their bank fails, but, because of limited liability, the shareholders' maximum loss is set by the initial value of their shares. Consequently, other than the extent to which it affects creditors' willingness to lend, shareholders have no incentive to take precautions that might reduce the total losses consequent upon failure: as far as the shareholders are concerned, they have lost everything anyway by that point. There is even a Wall Street acronym, used by market participants to reassure themselves they need not worry about marginal losses consequent upon failure: 'IBG–YBG'—'I'll be gone, You'll be gone': I'll have taken my commission, you'll have sold out to the next guy.[11] Yet the costs to society from bank failure can greatly exceed the losses to shareholders, given the risk of domino effects that may bring down the entire financial system and freeze loan markets across the economy.

The third difference is that certain types of financial assets are hard to observe and measure. The rationale for bank lending, as previously described in Chapter 13 is that banks may be able to collect information on borrowers that is not available to others. Hence, the value of their loan portfolio may not readily be subject to external scrutiny by shareholders as well as potential hostile bidders and creditors themselves.[12]

As a result of the first and second of these differences, regulators—in lieu of creditors—are tasked with monitoring and controlling bank risk-taking. However, the very difficulty of monitoring financial assets—the third of the differences described above—makes it particularly challenging for regulators, as well as investors, to perform this task effectively.[13] And the efficacy of regulatory control is further compromised by very intense managerial incentives to maximize the share price. Managers may, therefore, seek to avoid regulation and to minimize the costs of regulation by influencing regulators, rather than taking desired actions and precautions to minimize risks of failure.

17.2.3 Bank governance before the crisis

For much of the postwar period, banks were treated as utilities subject to a form of rate regulation: both entry to the sector, and profits, were restricted. This gave shareholders a steady stream of returns, and no great incentive to push managers. Managers in turn had no great incentive to push to increase the firm's performance. From the 1980s onwards, there was significant deregulation in banking in the US, the UK, and many other countries. This introduced greater competition to the sector and volatility to shareholder returns. Bank governance, therefore, became more intensely focused on

---

[11] See eg E Dash, 'What's Really Wrong with Wall Street Pay', *New York Times Economix Blog*, 18 September 2009 (http://economix.blogs.nytimes.com/2009/09/18/whats-really-wrong-with-wall-street-pay/).
[12] Banking supervisors control over banks' ownership structure also makes hostile bids more difficult. See JC Coates IV, 'Takeover Defenses in the Shadow of the Pill: A Critique of the Scientific Evidence' (2000) 79 *Texas Law Review* 271, 290.
[13] See Chapter 4, section 4.2 and Chapter 24, section 24.2.

share price maximization. To the extent that banks were different, it was thought that financial regulation could be relied upon to correct any problems. Consequently, policymakers and industry participants sought to apply ordinary 'best practice' in corporate governance to banking firms. For example, guidance by the Basel Committee concerning corporate governance in banks emphasized the monitoring role of the board of directors.[14]

Of the governance mechanisms described in section 17.1, incentive pay was perhaps the most heavily relied upon to control bank executives. This tracked the rise of executive compensation as a governance mechanism generally. Moreover, variable pay has long been a feature of employment in the investment banking sector. When the major investment banks converted from partnerships to corporations in the 1990s, profit-sharing that had previously been effected through partnership status came to be managed through variable pay for risk-takers instead. As investment banks merged with commercial banks, these pay practices were rationalized as promoting shareholder value and extended to the commercial banking divisions of the resulting financial conglomerates.

However, reliance on incentive compensation has a serious drawback in the context of financial institutions. Correctly calibrating incentive pay depends on assessments of the state of financial assets, which by definition are hard to observe. For example, consider a loan officer, who agrees to loans on the bank's behalf. The number of loans she writes, and the interest charged, are easy to observe. But the quality of the borrowers she lends to is not. If the bank were to offer her 'incentive' compensation, this should condition amongst other things on the quality of borrowers, but because borrower quality is hard to observe, the bank may only be able to make the contract conditional on loan size and interest rates, which will lead to predictably problematic results.

The failure to appreciate that the differences between banks and non-financial firms had implications for governance, and that these could not readily be solved by regulators, had unfortunate consequences. An emerging body of literature reports that the bank executives subject to the strongest incentives to maximize the value of their shares—as reflected in stock-based compensation, oversight by independent directors, and shareholder power—worked at banks that took the greatest risks and suffered the greatest losses.[15] In other words, financial firms that had the 'best' governance mechanisms, as conventionally understood before the crisis, actually did *worst* during the crisis.

We now review the application to financial institutions of each of the corporate governance mechanisms described in section 17.1. We begin with boards of directors, then consider compensation practices, then shareholder rights, and conclude with a discussion of legal duties. In each case, we consider first what we have learned from pre-crisis practices, and then review critically recent regulatory initiatives.

---

[14] BCBS, *Enhancing Corporate Governance for Banking Organisations* (1999), 6–7; ibid (2006), 6–15.
[15] See section 17.3.1 for references.

17.3 Bank Boards of Directors

17.3.1 Before the crisis

Historically, bank boards in the UK and the US were typically larger, and had more independent directors, than non-financial firms.[16] However, the size of bank boards around the world had been shrinking during the decade prior to the financial crisis, making these boards look more like those in non-financial firms.[17] Yet banks' compliance with general norms of 'good' corporate governance was associated with their failure during the financial crisis.[18] Two studies of banks around the world report that those with more 'shareholder-oriented' boards had greater levels of risk prior to the crisis and experienced greater losses subsequently.[19] There are at least two, likely complementary, explanations for these results. The first is that independent directors in banks may have assumed that regulators were exercising appropriate risk controls and consequently became less intensive in their own scrutiny. The second is that, because of the externalities associated with bank risk-taking, shareholders would have wanted banks to take greater risks. In other words, since financial gains benefit shareholders and losses that are so large as to put banks into bankruptcy are borne by others, shareholders benefit from the firm's pursuit of more risky investments.

17.3.2 Bank internal controls

An important role of the board of directors is to oversee internal controls within a firm. In most firms, these are primarily concerned with ensuring operational decisions are actually made in accordance with the firm's strategy. However, the business of financial institutions is principally concerned with the allocation of risk. As a result, these firms need to engage in risk management: that is, ensuring that the financial risks assumed by the organization are consistent with its objectives.[20] At the core of this is the need to

---

[16] RB Adams and H Mehran, 'Bank Board Structure and Performance: Evidence for Large Bank Holding Companies' (2012) 21 *Journal of Financial Intermediation* 243 (study of thirty-five bank holding companies over 1964–99, reporting a positive relationship between board size and shareholder returns, and no link between number of independent directors and shareholder returns); cf D Walker, *A Review of Corporate Governance in UK Banks and other Financial Industry Entities* (2009) 41; RB Adams, 'Governance and the Financial Crisis' (2012) 12 *International Review of Finance* 7, 27.

[17] M Becht, P Bolton, and A Röell, 'Why Bank Governance is Different' (2012) 27 *Oxford Review of Economic Policy* 437, 448. In contrast to non-financial companies, some studies report a positive association between bank board size and shareholder returns: see Adams and Mehran, n 16.

[18] For reviews, see Becht, Bolton, and Röell, n 17.

[19] A Beltratti and RM Stulz, 'The Credit Crisis Around the Globe: Why Did Some Banks Perform Better?' (2012) 105 *Journal of Financial Economics* 1, 10–11, 14–15 (sample of 503 deposit-taking banks around the world; reporting positive association between index of 'shareholder-friendliness' compiled from twenty-five ISS board variables and pre-crisis default risk, and a negative association with post-crisis performance); DH Erkens, M Hung, and P Matos, 'Corporate Governance in the 2007–2008 Financial Crisis: Evidence from Financial Institutions Worldwide' (2012) 18 *Journal of Corporate Finance* 389 (panel of 296 financial firms worldwide; reporting positive association between proportion of independent directors and pre-crisis risk-taking, and negative association with post-crisis performance).

[20] AM Santomero, 'Commercial Bank Risk Management: An Analysis of the Process' (1997) 12 *Journal of Financial Services Research* 83, 89–90; DH Pyle, 'Bank Risk Management: Theory', in D Galai, D

assess whether (a) the risks are justified by the returns associated (for particular contracts), and whether (b) the portfolio of risks taken on by the firm as a whole is appropriately constructed.

Banks' risk management systems can be subdivided into four components:[21] (i) the assimilation and communication of information about exposures, in the form of standards and reports; (ii) the application of rules governing limits on positions that employees with a given level of authority may enter into on the firm's behalf; (iii) the development of strategies and guidelines governing investment; and (iv) the design of employee compensation so as to generate appropriate incentives. Each component needs to be monitored and reviewed on a continuing basis, as does its relationship with the others.

A number of aspects of bank risk management are particularly problematic. First is the gross level of complexity. In addition to the inherent difficulty of observing financial assets, noted in section 17.2, bank risk management systems have evolved gradually over time, following different trajectories in relation to different categories of risk. Credit risk management differs from interest rate risk or liquidity risk, for example. The level of complexity involved in the management of each of these has evolved in accordance with the limit of the competence of the most highly skilled teams of experts. This makes it extremely difficult for senior management to synthesize and assess overall risks to the firm.[22]

Second, there is a particular conflict between risk management and high-powered financial incentives for employees. Employees with strongly incentive-based compensation will seek to maximize whatever performance benchmark has been set for them. The more intense the incentive to maximize a particular benchmark, the more single-minded the focus on that measure will be, which may be to the detriment of other business objectives. Worse still, intense incentives can lead employees to seek to 'game' the performance benchmark through steps that are positively harmful to the business as a whole, or even fraudulent. Given the great difficulties in monitoring financial assets, the appropriate calibration of employee compensation schemes and the policing of the way in which employees meet their performance targets are extremely important for the successful operation of the business. They therefore demand significant levels of internal oversight. This needs to be effected not just at the level of individual compensation targets and behaviour, but also at group- and firm-wide levels, ensuring that individual (group) targets are set in a way that are mutually consistent at the level of the firm as a whole.

Consistent with intuition, there is evidence that the level of resources devoted to risk management has a meaningful impact on bank overall returns. Ellul and Yerramilli constructed an index of risk management intended to capture the strength and independence of risk management functions at US bank holding companies. They

---

Ruthenberg, M Sarnat, and BZ Schreiber, *Risk Management and Regulation in Banking* (New York, NY: Kluwer, 1999), 7, 8.

[21] Santomero, ibid, 86.   [22] Ibid, 110–12.

report that bank holding companies with higher scores in this index were less risky prior to the crisis and enjoyed better returns during the crisis.[23]

17.3.3 EU Regulation of bank board structure and risk management

The EU has, under the aegis of the Capital Requirements Directive IV ('CRD IV') and the accompanying Capital Requirements Regulation ('CRR'),[24] introduced a wide-ranging and prescriptive set of guidelines for bank governance, dealing *inter alia* with board structure and risk management. In contrast, the US has steered clear of imposing prescriptive rules on bank boards, save as respects compensation committees (discussed in section 17.4) and for risk management, for which a board committee with oversight over risk management policies is required under Dodd-Frank and the implementing regulations, with heightened requirements for the largest firms.[24a]

CRD IV, which applies to credit institutions and investment firms, emphasizes the obligations of the board to monitor the performance, risk controls, compensation strategy, and integrity of disclosures of the firm.[25] It imposes regulatory duties of care and loyalty on board members.[26] It does not impose any minimum requirements for the proportion of independent directors, or the extent of their 'independence', save for separation of Chair and Chief Executive and the composition of the nomination, remuneration, and risk committees.[27] However, it does require that board members 'commit sufficient time to perform their functions in the institution', and to encourage this, mandates that not more than two non-executive roles at other organizations may be combined with one executive role, and not more than four non-executive roles in total may be held by any individual director.[28] It also requires firms to promote diversity in the boardroom, on the theory that this will assist in 'recruiting a broad set of qualities and competences'.[29] To this end, nomination committees must specifically introduce targets for representation of women on the boards, although not as regards ethnicity.[30]

CRD IV also imposes both procedural and substantive requirements regarding risk management. Procedurally, it emphasizes the importance of overall risk management functions that are proportionate to the nature, scale, and complexity of the risks inherent in the firm's business model.[31] It also requires boards to 'devote sufficient time to consideration of risks', and for large firms to establish a risk committee of the board comprised of non-executive directors.[32] Firms are also required to ensure that they have a 'risk management function', which is independent of the operational

---

[23] A Ellul and V Yarramilli, 'Stronger Risk Controls, Lower Risk: Evidence from US Bank Holding Companies' (2013) 68 *Journal of Finance* 1757.

[24] Directive 2013/36/EU of the European Parliament and of the Council on Access to the Activity of Credit Institutions and the Prudential Supervision of Credit Institutions and Investment Firms, Amending Directive 2002/87/EC and Repealing Directives 2006/48/EC and 2006/49/EC [2013] OJ L176/338; Regulation (EU) No 575/2013 on prudential requirements for credit institutions and investment firms and amending Regulation (EU) No 648/2012 [2013] OJ L176/1.

[24a] Dodd-Frank Act sec. 165(h); 12 CFR 252.22, 252.33.

[25] CRD IV, Art 88(1).   [26] Ibid, Art 91(7)–(8).   [27] Ibid, Arts 88(2) and 95.

[28] Ibid, Art 91.   [29] Ibid, Art 91(10).

[30] Ibid, Arts 88(2)(a) and 91(10). For a critical overview of the measures described in this paragraph see L Enriques and D Zetzsche, 'Quack Corporate Governance, Round III? Bank Board Regulation Under the New European Capital Requirement Directive' (2015) 16 *Theoretical Inquiries in Law* 211.

[31] CRD IV, Art 74(2).   [32] Ibid, Art 76(2)–(3).

decision-makers, reports to the board, has sufficient stature and resources to ensure that 'all material risks are identified, measured, and properly reported', and is capable of delivering a 'complete view of the whole range of risks of the institution'.[33] Turning to substantive requirements, the Directive requires regulators to specify guidelines regarding the management of various types of risk run by financial institutions.[34] Ironically, however, to the extent that these detailed guidelines adopt different measurement technologies for different types of risk, they may actually make it harder for boards and risk committees to comply with their procedural obligations.[35]

Institutions must also disclose their recruitment and diversity policies for the board and its members' relevant knowledge and expertise, whether or not the firm has a risk committee, and if so, how frequently it meets, and a description of the information flow on risk to the management body.[36]

17.4 Executive Pay in Banks

17.4.1 History and problems

Prior to the crisis, the financial sector made enthusiastic use of performance-related pay.[37] In keeping with the pattern for non-financial firms, CEOs of US banks typically received far more variable pay than base salary.[38] For example, Fahlenbrach and Stulz ('F&S'), studying compensation of US bank CEOs in 2006, report a mean base salary of $760,000, which is less than a sixth of the mean variable pay (comprising cash bonus and equity compensation) of $5.3 million.[39] This heavy weighting towards variable pay—characterized as 'performance-related'—was relatively recent. Historically, US bank executives received a greater fraction of fixed pay than was the norm in non-financial firms.[40] Following the deregulation of banking in the 1990s, the use of equity-based pay rose sharply in the sector, such that by the turn of the century, bank executive pay looked very similar to other sectors.[41]

Just as before the crisis no one questioned the application to banks of ordinary governance standards, it has now become an article of faith that high levels of variable pay for bank executives tend to encourage 'excessive' risk-taking. Yet such a

---

[33] Ibid, Art 76(5).   [34] Ibid, Arts 77–87.   [35] See nn 21–2.   [36] CRR, Art 435(2).

[37] Most is known about the compensation of US CEOs and 'top five' executives, because US disclosure rules require the most detailed information to be made public about their compensation.

[38] Nevertheless, in comparison to non-financial firms, when controlling for firm characteristics (especially size), banks typically have less CEO total and incentive compensation, and less director compensation: Adams, n 16, 27.

[39] R Fahlenbrach and RM Stulz, 'Bank CEO Incentives and the Credit Crisis' (2011) 99 *Journal of Financial Economics* 11, 16.

[40] See JF Houston and C James, 'CEO Compensation and Bank Risk: Is Compensation in Banking Structured to Promote Risk Taking?' (1995) 36 *Journal of Monetary Economics* 405; L Angbazo and R Narayanan, 'Top Management Compensation and the Structure of the Board of Directors in Commercial Banks' (1997) 1 *European Finance Review* 239.

[41] DA Becher, TL Campbell II, and MB Frye, 'Incentive Compensation for Bank Directors: The Impact of Deregulation' (2005) 78 *Journal of Business* 1753; V Cuñat and M Guadalupe, 'Executive Compensation and Competition in the Banking and Financial Sectors' (2009) 33 *Journal of Banking and Finance* 495; R DeYoung, EY Peng, and M Yan, 'Executive Compensation and Business Policy Choices at US Commercial Banks' (2013) *Journal of Financial and Quantitative Analysis* 1.

generalization might be just as misleading as the pre-crisis complacency. We need to look carefully at the details in order to understand the mechanisms in play.

Did having 'skin in the game' restrain risk-taking? First, we should note that bank executives typically held significant holdings of stock in their firms. In F&S' sample, the mean value of the stock CEOs held in their own firm was $87.5 million, approximately 0.4 per cent of the outstanding stock.[42] In part this would have been because stock awards were often 'restricted' for five years, meaning that the CEO could not sell until five years after grant. However, these very large holdings also reflected a significant degree of voluntary exposure by executives: that is, not selling their stock holdings even when they were no longer restricted. As a result, bank CEOs suffered huge losses—averaging $31.5 million—over the period 2006-8.[43] Should we conclude that because managers had such a substantial amount of 'skin in the game', they did not have incentives to indulge in 'excessive' risk-taking?

Apparently not. While managers clearly had significant downside exposure, looking solely at their holdings of stock does not take account of cash already received from bonuses and stock sales. Bebchuk, Cohen, and Spamann report that the top five executives in Bear Stearns and Lehman Brothers received aggregate cash flows of $2.4 billion over the period 2000-8.[44] Although these executives suffered losses of approximately $1.4 billion through their holdings of stock in their firms, taking cash flows into account showed they were still ahead by approximately $1 billion over these eight years.[45] In other words, even for the financial firms that failed outright, managers' payouts from good years had greatly exceeded their eventual losses when the firms failed. This asymmetry—upside returns exceeding downside—seems to generalize. Thus F&S report that, taking into account options and cash bonuses, the mean CEO in their sample would receive 2.4 per cent of the value of any increase in the stock price.[46] However, their downside losses would only be 0.4 per cent of any decrease, tracking their holdings of the firm's stock. In short, incentives on the upside were five times as strong as on the downside.

Moreover, this asymmetry of incentives appears linked to underperformance during the financial crisis. F&S report that the greater the managers' incentives to increase the stock price—as measured by the proportion of the increase in value they captured—the worse were bank shareholders' returns during the financial crisis.[47] This suggests that powerfully asymmetric financial incentives encouraged managers to pursue strategies

---

[42] Fahlenbrach and Stulz, n 39.

[43] Ibid, 23. Note that the median was only $5.1m, however.

[44] LA Bebchuk, A Cohen, and H Spamann, 'The Wages of Failure: Executive Compensation at Bear Stearns and Lehman 2000–2008' (2010) 27 *Yale Journal on Regulation* 257.

[45] Similarly, Bhagat and Bolton look at CEO payoffs in the largest fourteen crisis institutions, and find that they took $1.77bn in net stock sales plus $0.89bn in cash compensation during the period 2000–8, a total cash flow of $2.66bn. In 2008, their equity holdings suffered an aggregate loss of $2.01bn. Nevertheless, they were better off, on net, over the period by $0.65bn: S Bhagat and P Bolton, 'Financial Crisis and Bank Executive Compensation' (2014) 25 *Journal of Corporate Finance* 313, 319–23.

[46] Fahlenbrach and Stulz, n 39, 17.

[47] F&S gauge the incentive effect for managers by measuring the dollar value CEOs earn from a 1 per cent increase in stock price. (ibid). This measure—the change in managerial pay associated with a change in the stock price—is known as the 'delta' of the compensation package.

that, at least *ex post*, turned out to be harmful to shareholders. We need to understand why this may have been the case.

One answer may be that stock options gave incentives to take risks in excess of what was optimal even from the shareholders' perspective. The basic rationale for using options is that—assuming they are correctly priced (that is, 'out-of-the-money')—they provide a powerful upside incentive to take actions that will increase the stock price. But might managers be pushed too far? Could options encourage them to pursue risky projects simply for the sake of it? An increase in the volatility of a firm's stock price will increase the value of an out-of-the-money option on that stock[48] and if the incentive is sufficiently powerful, then managers may be induced to select projects with lower net present values simply because they are more risky. F&S did not find any evidence of a link between the risk-sensitivity of managers' portfolios and shareholder returns.[49] In other words, they found no evidence that option compensation led managers to select projects with lower expected values—thus harming even shareholders—simply because they are more risky. However, this does not imply that option contracts do not encourage a degree of risk-taking that is detrimental to creditors or society.

Were the risks excessive from a societal perspective? The costs of financial firm failure are not borne entirely by shareholders. Implicit or explicit government guarantees of creditors mean that these costs are only partially priced into credit agreements. As a result, shareholders as a group may stand to benefit from strategies that increase default risk but generate more positive cash flows in other states of the world. Consistently with this, Balachandran et al report a positive relationship between managerial equity compensation and default risk.[50] That is, firms whose managers had the strongest incentives to maximize share price were also those most likely to fail. However, this cynical perspective fails to explain why managers did not reduce their holdings of shares in anticipation of the financial crisis. Had managers simply been ramping up risk in order to transfer losses to the state, it would make no sense for them to remain holding shares at the time the losses crystallized. Moreover, this perspective also overlooks the fact that—in the US and the UK at least—most bank shareholders are diversified, meaning that they incur significant losses through their other portfolio firms should systemic harms materialize.[51] Such shareholders would not want bank managers to take socially excessive risks.[52]

---

[48] This is because the increase in volatility implies an increase in the states of the world in which the option will be in-the-money. The extent to which an increase in the volatility of the share price results in an increase in the value of managerial compensation is known as the 'vega' of the latter.

[49] Ibid, 18–19. But see Bhagat and Bolton, n 45.

[50] S Balachandran, B Kogut, and H Harnal, 'Did Executive Compensation Encourage Extreme Risk-Taking in Financial Institutions?', Working Paper (2011).

[51] J Armour and JN Gordon, 'Systemic Harms and Shareholder Value' (2014) 6 *Journal of Legal Analysis* 35.

[52] On the other hand, the private incentives of asset managers who control institutional portfolios may have led financial firms to engage in excessive risk taking. Recent theoretical and empirical work suggests that the riskiest firms, which generally outperformed in the pre-financial crisis period, gave the highest levels of variable pay, to compensate executives for the extra risk-taking: see I-H Chang, H Gong, and JA Scheinkman, 'Yesterday's Heroes: Compensation and Risk at Financial Firms' (2015) 70 *Journal of Finance* 839. Asset managers, who are evaluated on relative performance, would encourage risk-taking by portfolio companies that would lead to outperformance. On the corporate governance issue, see section 17.5 and Armour and Gordon, n 51, 56, 60–1.

What about more junior employees? We have so far focused on the compensation of senior managers, primarily because these are the only group for whom detailed compensation information must be disclosed. Consequently, far less is known about the compensation of less senior employees. However, such literature as exists suggests that incentive problems stemming from miscalibrated 'performance' pay may have been most egregious at the level of trading and sales staff, rather than senior executives. Shortly after the onset of the financial crisis, the FSA carried out a study of bank employee compensation practices in the UK.[53] They found that cash bonuses accounted for a large proportion of employees' pay. However, these bonuses were typically not linked to the stock price, but to *net revenues* in that financial year. Conditioning bonuses on revenues, rather than stock price, means that not even the market's (perhaps imperfect) assessment of the downside risk for shareholders of the firm's strategies was priced-in. In fact, it seems an astonishingly poor way to motivate employees, as the box text explains.

'Performance Pay' and Insurance Contracts

Where a financial firm takes on a risk under a contract, it is functionally—albeit perhaps not legally—providing insurance to the counterparty in respect of that risk. We would expect the premium for providing this insurance to be reflected in the price of the contract. It is clearly a mistake to reward people for writing insurance based only on the size of the premium they earn, without taking into account the risks insured. This simply gives them incentives to commit their firm to the biggest risks they can find, because these will attract the highest premiums. But this is precisely the effect of rewarding employees in a financial firm on the basis of revenues, without any adjustment for risk.

This disturbing picture is reinforced by Acharya et al's innovative study of the impact of employee incentive compensation.[54] These authors identify the aggregate compensation for sub-board-level employees by subtracting the (disclosed) compensation for 'top five' executives from the (disclosed) aggregate total compensation paid by financial firms, and then determine how sensitive this total compensation is to the firm's revenues (not stock price). This gives a measure of the extent to which employees are incentivized to maximize revenues in a given year. The authors go on to report that greater revenue-sensitivity of aggregate employee cash pay was associated with greater default risk for the firm. This implies that incentive contracts of the type the FSA reported—linking pay to revenues—were associated with greater default risk.

In light of our discussion in section 17.4 about the deficiencies of internal monitoring, we can offer a conjecture about the ways in which senior management may have made mistakes about risk-taking. Management with strong incentives to increase the stock price may have been more inclined to focus simply on revenues generated by

---

[53] FSA, 'Reforming Remuneration Practices in Financial Services', Consultation Paper 09/10 (2009).

[54] V Acharya, LP Litov, and SM Sepe, 'Seeking Alpha, Taking Risks: Evidence from Non-Executive Pay in US Bank Holding Companies', Working Paper NYU/University of Arizona (2014); see also SM Sepe and CK Whitehead, 'Paying for Risk: Bankers, Competition and Compensation' (2015) 100 *Cornell Law Review* 655.

employees and (mistakenly) reflected in the stock price, paying insufficient attention to appropriate risk-adjustment of returns. That is, there was likely a negative synergy between the extent to which managers were encouraged to 'manage the stock price' and the extent to which the stock price failed—owing to opacity—to take into account the true downside costs of firms' strategies.

17.4.2 The new regulation of executive compensation in banks

Bank executive compensation became an early target for regulatory reform. At the G20 summit in Pittsburgh in September 2009, member countries circulated a *Statement of Principles* regarding executive pay in the financial services sector.[55] This encompassed a programme of reform with the following three pillars: first, internal governance mechanisms were to be strengthened as regards the process of setting compensation; second, the substance of compensation packages should be more closely aligned with 'prudent risk-taking'; and third, there should be more disclosure, and effective supervisory oversight, of both the process and substance of compensation arrangements.

These principles were first implemented in Europe through CRD III,[56] and subsequently tightened considerably in CRD IV,[57] which goes significantly beyond what is envisaged by the FSB's *Statement of Principles*. In the US, the Dodd–Frank Act requires the appropriate Federal regulators to introduce rules in relation to internal governance,[58] disclosure of executive pay, and substantive regulation of compensation contracts.[59] Rules regarding internal governance, in particular the role of compensation committees, have been implemented by the Securities and Exchange Commission ('SEC'), and in 2016 there was a revised interagency rule proposal regarding enhanced disclosure of compensation in financial firms and substantive standards on compensation contracts.[60] Table 17.1 sets out the firms and executives to which the regulations apply in the EU and the US, respectively. We now turn to consider specific details of the rules that have emerged.

The Process of Setting Compensation. The FSB's first pillar proposed more active internal oversight of the setting of compensation.[61] At the centre is the idea of a remuneration committee of the board with sufficient independence and expertise to exercise appropriate judgement on remuneration policies. The remuneration committee should work with the firm's risk committee to evaluate the incentives created by the

---

[55] Financial Stability Forum, *FSF Principles for Sound Compensation Practices*, 2 April 2009.
[56] Directive 2010/76/EU [2010] OJ L329/3. In the UK specifically, this was implemented under the Financial Services Act 2010, ss 4–6, and amendments to the FSA's (now FCA's) Remuneration Code: FSA, *Revising the Remuneration Code*, Consultation Paper 10/19 (2010).
[57] Directive 2013/36/EU [2013] OJ L176/338.
[58] §952, inserting new §10C into the Securities Exchange Act of 1934.
[59] §956 (enhanced disclosure and reporting of compensation arrangements at financial institutions and provision for prohibition of 'types of incentive-based compensation arrangement, that the regulators determine encourages inappropriate risks by covered financial institutions').
[60] US Department of the Treasury et al, 'Notice of Proposed Rulemaking and Request for Commen: Incentive-Based Compensation Arrangements' 21 April 2016.
[61] FSB, *FSB Principles for Sound Compensation Practices: Implementation Standards*, 25 September 2009, 2.

Table 17.1 To which financial firms does the regulation of executive compensation apply?

	EU	US
Which firms?	CRD IV Art 3, CRR Art 4(1). '*Credit institutions*' (firms both taking deposits and granting credit); '*Investment firms*' (firms providing investment services or engaging in investment activities, including brokers, dealers, investment managers, underwriters, and market operators).	Dodd–Frank Act of 2010, §956 '*Covered financial institutions*' (firms taking deposits or their holding companies, registered broker-dealers, credit unions, investment advisors, Fannie Mae and Freddie Mac, and any other financial institution that Federal regulators jointly determine should be treated as such) with assets > $1 billion.
Which employees?	CRD IV Art 92(2) and Delegated Regulation (EU) No 604/2014. '*Material risk-takers*' (categories of employee whose professional activities have a material impact on [the firm's] risk profile). Identification based on both internal criteria developed by the firm and qualitative (functions performed) and quantitative (compensation value) criteria applied by supervisors. *Qualitative criteria*: Board and senior management; staff with the authority to commit significant credit risk exposures. *Quantitative criteria*: (i) Total gross remuneration > €500,000; or (ii) among firm's 0.3 per cent most highly paid staff; or (iii) remuneration equal to senior managers; or (iv) variable pay could exceed €75,000 and 75 per cent of fixed pay.	Dodd–Frank Act of 2010, §956 and proposed Rule 'Senior executive officers and significant risk-takers': senior executive officers, and any other executive officer or employee who received total compensation in top 5 per cent (for firms with assets >$250bn) or 2 per cent (for firms with assets >$50bn) of payroll or who can expose 0.5 per cent or more of the firm's net worth.

firm's compensation arrangements so as to ensure that these are consistent with the risk committee's assessment of the firm's financial condition and prospects, and with regulatory guidelines. It should also oversee an annual review of compensation practices which should be produced for regulators. Employees working in the firm's risk and compliance function should have their remuneration set independently of the firm's performance, at a level sufficient to attract qualified and experienced staff, and their performance should be assessed on the basis of the achievement of the objectives of their functions (that is, risk management).

This was the least controversial aspect of the FSB's proposals, and—with the addition of a nod to greater involvement by risk management officials in the process—largely reflected existing best practice.[62]

Substantive Regulation of Executive Compensation Arrangements. Much more significant are the substantive guidelines regarding the content of executive compensation, which are to be overseen by regulators. At their heart is a commitment to continued use of performance-related pay, but in a manner better aligned with the

---

[62] See eg FSA, *Revising the Remuneration Code*, Consultation Paper 10/19 (2010), 24–5.

long-term and risk-adjusted performance of the firm. There are two principal routes by which the guidelines seek to do this. First, variable compensation awards must be adjusted *ex ante* in accordance with the riskiness of the activities undertaken by the employee and/or the firm.[63] While this idea is easy to state in principle, it is harder to implement in practice, because it requires a benchmark of risk. Any such benchmark in turn creates incentives to game the system.

The second limb operates in part as a check against such gaming. It requires that performance-related pay should vary with *ex post* realizations of risk outcomes, over a sufficiently long period of time. The FSB consequently prescribes that for senior executives and other employees whose actions have a material impact on the firm's risk exposure ('material risk-takers'), a 'substantial proportion' of pay should be performance-related over time.[64] A large part of this variable pay (no less than 40 per cent, rising to at least 60 per cent for the most senior executives) should be deferred for a period of at least three years, but possibly longer depending on the risks associated with the business.[65] This is most easily done for equity-related pay (stock and options), by restricting the manager's ability to sell stock or exercise the options for a longer period. The FSB also suggests that at least half of variable pay should be awarded in equity. Some part of cash bonuses can also be deferred, with the possibility that it will not vest if negative performance is realized. This deferred compensation must then be subject to clawback—a so-called 'malus' award—if poor performance outcomes are realized within the vesting period.[66]

Although the EU first implemented these guidelines under CRD III, it then went significantly beyond them with CRD IV.[67] CRD IV imposes an outright cap on the amount of variable compensation that may be paid.[68] It may not exceed the amount of fixed pay for any individual, although with the approval of a supermajority of the shareholders, it may be up to twice the size of fixed pay. What is more, the rules regarding the identification of material risk-takers (to whom the restrictions apply) are extensive in their coverage.[69] They apply to all employees of EU-based groups, including, for example, those working in New York or Singapore.[70] Up to 25 per cent of variable compensation may be discounted (for the purposes of the cap) at a supervisor-determined rate, provided that it is deferred for at least five years.[71] Moreover, up to

---

[63] See CRD IV, Art 92(a) and (g)(ii).   [64] FSB, n 61, 3.   [65] Ibid.
[66] The FSB's guidelines also seek to ensure that the payment of variable compensation does not occur at times when the firm's capital is, or is likely to become, impaired, or when it is in receipt of government assistance.
[67] At least 50 per cent of any variable compensation must be equity-linked; at least 40 per cent of variable compensation must be deferred for more than three years; at least 60 per cent where it is 'particularly high'. And the deferral period must relate to the risks of the business: CRD IV, Art 94(1)(l)–(m).
[68] CRD IV, Art 94(1)(g).
[69] Commission Delegated Regulation (EU) No 604/2014 supplementing Directive 2013/36/EU with regard to regulatory technical standards on with respect to qualitative and appropriate quantitative criteria to identify categories of staff whose professional activities have a material impact on an institution's risk profile [2014] OJ L167/30.
[70] CRD IV, Art 92(1).   [71] Ibid, Art 94(1)(g)(iii).

100 per cent of variable compensation (not just that part which has been deferred) is subject to 'malus' or clawback provisions.[72]

In the US, implementation of the FSB *Principles* will be through an inter-agency rule made under the mandate conferred by section 956 of the Dodd–Frank Act. The current draft outlines standards as regards incentive-based compensation, such that it must not 'encourage inappropriate risks' by either providing 'excessive compensation, fees, or benefits', or 'that could lead to a material financial loss'.[73] Moreover, for institutions with assets in excess of $50 billion, there are detailed rules requiring deferral of 40–60 per cent (depending on seniority and size of firm) of variable compensation for at least three years (or four years for firms with assets of more than $250 billion), and its adjustment downwards to reflect losses realized during this period.

The EU's step of capping the ratio of variable pay to fixed pay is likely to lead to an increase in base rates of pay, given an internationally competitive market for executive talent. It may also have a counterintuitive impact on risk-taking. This is because, according to some commentators, the base pay in a traditional investment banking compensation scheme was set below the competitive rate, such that the bonus already incorporated a significant amount of downside performance sensitivity. Increasing the proportion of fixed pay will reduce this. Decreasing the proportion of variable pay will also reduce the upside payoffs. As a result, executives will have less incentive to take risks with upside components, and more incentive to take risks with downside components.[74] Moreover, incentives to increase performance will entirely dry up once the bonus has been 'maxed out'. Coupled with deferrals and realized performance contingencies, it will create incentives to 'manage' performance into subsequent periods as well. There are also likely to be employment selection effects. Making pay less performance-sensitive will select away from highly talented individuals and in favour of less talented types. Resistance to the variable pay cap has been particularly vigorous in the City of London, and various efforts have been made to camouflage elements of compensation. This has provoked serious skirmishing with the European Banking Authority, which writes the rulebook on the compensation regulation.

Disclosure and Supervision of Compensation Practices. The FSB's third pillar exhorts that information about both the process of setting compensation and the quantum of pay for top executives should be disclosed publicly, at least annually.[75] Process information should include information about the composition and mandate of the remuneration committee; the most important criteria used in setting compensation are performance measurement, risk adjustment, pay-performance linkage, deferral policy and vesting criteria, and the parameters used for choosing between cash and other forms of compensation. As regards substantive pay, there should be aggregate disclosure of the total (and the breakdown into various components) paid to all senior executives and material risk-takers. This level of disclosure was already largely in place in the US under existing rules for disclosure by public corporations of executive

---

[72] Ibid, Art 94(1)(n).   [73] US Draft Rule, n 60 (rule _.4).

[74] K J Murphy, 'Regulating Banking Bonuses in the European Union: A Case Study in Unintended Consequences' (2013) 19 *European Financial Management* 631.

[75] FSB Principles, 2009, para 3; Implementation Standards para 15.

compensation arrangements. In the EU, the relevant disclosure obligations are found in the Capital Requirements Regulation accompanying CRD IV.[76]

The FSB also called for 'rigorous and sustained' domestic supervisory engagement with the implementation of the FSB Principles.[77] In particular, compensation practices should be taken into account as part of supervisory risk review of financial service firms. Failure by firms to implement appropriate compensation policies should result in 'prompt remedial action' to offset any associated risks. This is to be implemented in the US through rules made under section 956 of the Dodd–Frank Act, and will require covered financial institutions to keep records for at least seven years of incentive-based compensation plans. In the EU, this will be implemented by Article 75 of CRD IV.

17.5 Shareholder Rights

Early responses to the financial crisis suggested that lack of shareholder oversight was part of the problem in the governance of financial institutions. For example, the Walker Review, commissioned by the UK government in 2009, concluded that greater engagement by institutional shareholders with boards of financial institutions was desirable.[78] Similarly, the Dodd–Frank Act in the US introduced powers for the SEC to strengthen shareholders' rights, in particular their ability to put forward candidates for the board not supported by incumbent management and a right to vote to approve the compensation of senior executives.[79]

It is far from clear that such proposals are appropriate. As shareholders enjoy limited liability, in the presence of imperfectly priced deposit insurance, or the expectation of a bail-out for 'too big to fail' firms, we might think they would have incentives to encourage firms to take more risk than is socially desirable.[80] Consistently with this, Ferreira et al report that US banks in which shareholders enjoy objectively greater power—in terms of shareholder rights and ability to control management—were more likely to be bailed out during the financial crisis.[81]

We might expect this concern to be ameliorated where investors hold shares in banks as part of a diversified portfolio. Such investors will internalize a large part of the costs to society of bank failure through losses to their other portfolio firms.[82] On the other hand, the problems will be exacerbated by the presence of controlling shareholders, who will be in a position to make more of a difference to the control of the firm than dispersed shareholders, and who will be less diversified and so care less about impacts on other firms. In a study of large banks from across forty-eight countries, Laeven and Levine report that the proportion of the cash-flow rights enjoyed by large

---

[76] CRR, Art 450.

[77] FSB Principles 2009 para 3, Implementation Standards para 16.

[78] D Walker, *A Review of Corporate Governance in UK Banks and other Financial Industry Entities: Final Recommendations* (2009), 12, 68–89.

[79] Dodd–Frank Act of 2010 §§951 and 971.   [80] See nn 50–1.

[81] D Ferreira, D Kershaw, T Kirchmaier, and E-P Schuster, 'Shareholder Empowerment and Bank Bailouts', ECGI Finance Working Paper No 345/2013.

[82] Armour and Gordon, n 51.

shareholders is positively correlated with bank risk-taking.[83] To this end, many regimes require regulatory approval of the identity of major shareholders as a condition of bank licensing.[84] Similar restrictions apply to changes of control, with regulators reserving the right to refuse to approve such deals.[85] A key factor as regards such approval is the reputation of the controlling shareholder.[86]

17.6 Liability Rules

Is it enough simply to moderate the 'upside' returns that those running a bank receive, by altering the terms of executive compensation? Or should we also push for the imposition of more 'downside' liability? The classic objections to liability for those controlling a business firm—at least for business decisions (as opposed to conflicts of interest)—are that judges lack the capacity to review such decisions effectively, and that fear of liability will induce undiversified managers to take less risk than diversified shareholders might want. In the case of firms whose activities have the propensity to create systemic risk, this logic might actually be reversed. Diversified shareholders may actually stand to lose proportionally more, in the case of default, than executives who have a stake in the firm through equity-based compensation. This is because systemic harms can impact negatively on their entire portfolios, not just on their holding in the bank. Consequently, for banks with diversified share ownership and managers with equity-based pay, fear of liability would not lead to undesirable risk-aversion on the part of managers. Rather, it might simply rein in undesirably risky activities such managers might otherwise take.[87]

Such liability is in principle available in the US in the case of banks entering FDIC receivership proceedings.[88] However, for other banks, directors and officers are shielded from liability for errors and omissions in relation to business judgement and oversight, unless they are so egregious as to evince a lack of good faith.[89] In the UK and many other European countries, directors and officers do in principle owe a duty of care in relation to business decisions, but this is almost never enforced. Civil procedure rules make it costly for shareholder litigation to be commenced. Enforcement by public agencies seems a more worthwhile strategy in this case. Here, the problem has been that agencies lack standing to pursue private law obligations, but rather enforce a parallel regulatory regime. Within this, there has been a lack of clarity as to individual versus organizational responsibility.[90] Upon the input of the UK's Parliamentary Commission on Banking Standards, UK supervisory authorities have approved a new regime aimed at focusing regulatory responsibility onto specific

---

[83] L Laeven and R Levine, 'Bank Governance, Regulation and Risk Taking' (2009) 93 *Journal of Financial Economics* 259.

[84] Eg CRD IV, Art 14.   [85] Ibid, Arts 22–3.

[86] Ibid, Art 23(1)(a).   [87] Armour and Gordon, n 51.

[88] See Financial Institutions Reform, Recovery, and Enforcement Act of 1989 ('FIRREA'), Pub. L. No 101-73, Title II, §212(k), 103 Stat 243, codified at 12 USC §1821(k).

[89] *Stone v Ritter*, 911 A.2d 362, 370 (Del Sup 2006); *In re Citigroup Inc. Shareholder Derivative Litigation*, 964 A.2d 106 (Del Ch 2009).

[90] Parliamentary Commission on Banking Standards, *Changing Banking for Good*, Volume II (2013), 289–90.

individuals, who should then become natural targets for regulatory enforcement.[91] Moreover, a new criminal offence for bank senior managers whose reckless misconduct causes their firm to fail has been introduced.[92]

17.7 Conclusion

In this chapter, we have explored why the corporate governance framework that is applied for most businesses, in which managers are encouraged to focus on maximizing the stock price, is less well suited to the case of banks. Financial assets are particularly hard to monitor, and so managerial agency costs are unusually high. Banks' business model makes them unusually fragile, and their failure imposes costs on society beyond those borne by their investors. As a consequence, ordinary mechanisms of corporate governance, which rely on stock market prices to incentivize managers, are liable to yield perverse results. Managers may exploit the opacity of financial assets to game the measures, and regulators will face an uphill struggle to uncover this. Maximizing the stock price may not be the right approach in any event, as shareholders' interests may diverge from those of society. Reforms since the financial crisis have gone some way to address these problems. Two particularly beneficial steps have been the push towards greater resources being deployed in risk management and internal monitoring functions, and an attempt to better calibrate incentives in relation to executive pay. The latter task will be extremely challenging for regulators to get right, but the former seems more promising.

[91] See FCA, CP15/22 Strengthening accountability in banking: Final rules (including feedback on CP14/31 and CP15/5) and consultation on extending the Certification Regime to wholesale market activities (2015).
[92] Financial Services (Banking Reform) Act (2013) s 36.

18

Payment and Settlement Systems

18.1 Introduction

On 19 June 2012, a routine software upgrade at the Royal Bank of Scotland ('RBS') triggered a massive failure of the bank's information technology systems. For several days, customers were left unable to access their account information, withdraw cash, or use their debit cards. Mortgage, credit card, and bill payments went unprocessed. One customer even spent the weekend in prison, unable to post bail.[1] In all, some 7 million account holders were affected and the incident was ultimately estimated to cost RBS nearly £125 million.[2] This figure does not take into account the inconvenience experienced by customers, nor, ultimately, any loss of confidence in the financial system that this incident may have precipitated.

Payment and settlement systems can be understood as a collection of institutional arrangements that facilitate the transfer of funds and other assets in satisfaction of financial obligations.[3] When you receive your salary deposited by your employer into your bank account, or when you write a cheque, use your credit or debit card, pay a bill, or purchase shares on a stock exchange, you are relying on one or more payment and/ or settlement systems to complete the transaction. Accordingly, while payment and settlement systems often fade into the background of the financial system, there are few parts of this system that impact more directly on our daily lives.

Payment and settlement systems form the institutional backbone that ensures the flow of funds between central banks, financial intermediaries, businesses, and households. They are also an integral component of the market infrastructure that facilitates trading in financial assets such as shares and bonds (see Chapter 7). The security, efficiency, and stability of payment and settlement systems can thus be expected to have a significant impact on the security, efficiency, and stability of the financial system as a whole. When the plumbing breaks down, the entire house is at risk of flooding.

Broadly speaking, payment and settlement systems can be divided into three categories. The first category consists of *wholesale* (or *interbank*) payment systems that facilitate the flow of funds between financial intermediaries. The second category comprises *retail* payment systems that facilitate the flow of funds between businesses and households. The third category consists of *securities settlement* systems that facilitate the confirmation, clearance, and settlement of securities trades and the safe-keeping of securities. As we shall see, these systems are highly interdependent. At the same time, the institutional arrangements and regulatory regimes governing wholesale

---

[1] BBC News, 'RBS Computer Problems Kept Man in Prison' (25 June 2012), available at http://www.bbc.co.uk/news/uk-18589280.

[2] J Treanor, 'RBS Computer Failure to Cost Bank £100m', *The Guardian*, 2 August 2012.

[3] A Haldane, S Millard, and V Saporta (eds), *The Future of Payment Systems* (Routledge: Abingdon, 2007), Introduction at 2.

Principles of Financial Regulation. First Edition. John Armour, Dan Awrey, Paul Davies, Luca Enriques, Jeffrey N. Gordon, Colin Mayer, and Jennifer Payne. © John Armour, Dan Awrey, Paul Davies, Luca Enriques, Jeffrey N. Gordon, Colin Mayer, and Jennifer Payne 2016. Published 2016 by Oxford University Press.

payment, retail payment, and securities settlement systems are often very different. These differences reflect underlying differences in the risks the respective systems pose, both to their participants and the broader financial system. For retail payment systems, the most important issues concern the balance between efficiency, security, and competition. For wholesale payment and securities settlement systems, meanwhile, the most important issues relate to operational, credit, and liquidity risks and, as a consequence, potential threats to financial stability.

Section 18.2 provides an overview of the origins, economic function, and basic mechanics of wholesale payment systems. It then traces the historical evolution of these systems from deferred net settlement ('DNS'), to real-time gross settlement ('RTGS'), to the 'hybrid' RTGS systems used extensively today. It also traces the development of the continuous linked settlement ('CLS') system used to facilitate foreign exchange transactions across a number of widely used currencies. This section concludes by examining the governance and regulation of wholesale payment systems, along with the important role played by central banks as both prudential supervisors and providers of backstop liquidity.

Section 18.3 examines securities settlement systems. These systems can be contrasted with wholesale payment systems insofar as they contemplate the delivery of financial instruments—such as shares, bonds, or derivatives contracts—in exchange for pay-ment. At the same time, securities settlement systems are highly dependent on whole-sale payment systems and, as a result, are ultimately exposed to many of the same risks. As we shall see, these risks are reflected in both the operational mechanics of securities settlement systems and in the regulatory regimes that govern them.

Section 18.4 then turns to retail payment systems. Retail payment systems are extremely diverse: encompassing cheque clearing and settlement systems, debit and credit card networks, automated teller machine ('ATM') and point-of-sale infrastruc-ture, remittance services, Web-based payment systems, and platforms such as PayPal. Although many of these systems rely on the infrastructure of wholesale payment systems, many others do not. Retail payment systems often have relatively little regulatory oversight. Instead, these systems are often governed by sophisticated private contractual and institutional frameworks. They are also supported by public laws allocating property rights—along with the risk of fraud, loss, etc—and attempting to constrain anti-competitive conduct by payment service providers.

Section 18.5 concludes by briefly canvassing several emerging issues in the regulation of payment and settlement systems. For the most part, these issues stem from the ongoing impact of technological change on various payment and settlement systems. There is little doubt that technological advances have generated significant efficiency gains. At the same time, however, the shift from paper-based to electronic payments within the retail marketplace, for example, has strained the existing payment and settlement infrastructure. Similarly, as demonstrated by the RBS example, the prolif-eration of payment systems and the increasing volume of electronic payments—both once again driven by technological advances—have put significant pressure on the back office infrastructure of banks and other financial intermediaries. Finally, the growing provision of retail payment services by non-banks raises interesting and important challenges for financial regulation. By the end of this chapter you should have an understanding of the basic functions and operations of whole payment systems, retail payment systems, and security settlement systems, along with their important roles within the financial system. This understanding will then help frame the subsequent discussion of the reasons why many large banks—as the principal institutions through which payment systems operate—are viewed as too important and interconnected to fail.

18.2 Wholesale Payment Systems

18.2.1 The basic mechanics of wholesale payment systems

It is difficult to understand the role wholesale payments systems play without understanding the development and economic function of both money and banks. Businesses and households have a natural demand for a safe and verifiable asset—such as money or gold—that can be exchanged for goods and services.[4] In turn, the existence of such an asset generates demand for low-cost means of verifying its authenticity, protecting it against theft, and transferring it in satisfaction of financial obligations.

In most jurisdictions, each of these functions has historically been performed by what we now think of as conventional deposit-taking banks. Modern banks originally developed as a place where businesses and households could deposit their gold for safekeeping.[5] As part of the deposit-taking process, banks would count and verify the authenticity of gold deposits.[6] They would then issue receipts—or 'notes'—to their customers as evidence of their deposit and the resulting obligation of the bank to return the deposited gold on demand. In many cases, these bank notes ultimately came to possess a degree of transferability—thus enabling the holder of the note to exchange it for the purchase of goods and services. Final 'settlement' would then occur when the provider of the goods or services, or a subsequent transferee, returned the note to the bank that issued it—in effect demanding that the bank make good on its obligation to deliver the deposited gold or other assets. These privately issued bank notes were the precursor to modern fiat money issued by central banks.

The most important function of banks for the present purposes, however, is the role they play in facilitating the transfer of funds between businesses, households, and, ultimately, other banks. The most straightforward case is one in which a customer (the payor) wishes to make a payment to someone (the payee) with an account at the same bank. In this example, the customer would make an 'in bank' payment, pursuant to which the bank debited the account of the payor and credited the account of the payee.

---

[4] This demand is driven by the so-called 'double coincidence of wants' problem; see W Jevons, *Money and the Mechanism of Exchange* (New York, NY: Appleton & Co, 1875); N Kiyotaki and R Wright, 'On Money as a Medium of Exchange' (1989) 97 *Journal of Political Economy* 927; C Kahn and W Roberds, 'Payment System Settlement and Bank Incentives', Wharton Financial Institutions Center Working Paper 97-32 (2006); and S Millard and V Saporta, 'Central Banks and Payment Systems: Past, Present and Future', in Haldane, Millard, and Saporta, n 3.

[5] Millard and Saporta, n 4.

[6] Ibid; see also M Kohn, 'Bills of Exchange and the Money Market to 1600', Dartmouth University Department of Economics Working Paper No 99-04 (1999).

In effect, this transaction is little more than a series of book entries on the bank's internal accounting system.

This transaction becomes somewhat more complicated where the payee does not have an account at the payor's bank. In the absence of a wholesale payment system, the payor and payee effectively have two options. First, the payee could open an account at the payor's bank. However, while this option might not initially seem all that unreasonable, imagine how costly and cumbersome it would be if you needed to open an account with the bank of every individual and firm—your state or local government, landlord, university, utilities provider, phone company, and so forth—to whom you owed a financial obligation. Second, the parties might physically transfer the money from the payor's bank to the payee's bank. This, however, could be a very costly process, raising obvious concerns about theft, inadvertent loss, or destruction of physical currency. These concerns would be particularly acute where the transactions involved large amounts or where the geographic dispersion of banks, payees, and payors was significant.

Clearly, a less costly and more secure option is for banks to develop a system—a *network*—designed to facilitate interbank transfers. When designing such a system, participating banks must answer two important questions.[7] First, what should be used as the ultimate settlement asset? While private money issued by participating banks is one possibility, these bank notes expose holding (creditor) banks to the credit risk of the issuing (debtor) institution. If the issuing bank defaults, banks holding the notes are unlikely to be able to receive full value for their holding of these claims. As a result, we would expect private money to trade at a discount to its face value. Second, what mechanism should banks use to effect settlement? One intuitively appealing answer to both questions is for all participating banks to maintain an account at the most creditworthy bank (so all interbank transfers are effectively 'in bank' payments of the variety described above) and to use the liabilities of that bank as the preferred settlement asset. Charles Calomiris and Charles Kahn describe how the privately organized Suffolk banking system performed this role in New England from the 1820s through to the 1850s.[8] In most modern economies, however, this role is performed by central banks, with the preferred settlement asset being the fiat money issued by these public institutions. The role of central banks in the operation of wholesale payment systems is examined in greater detail in section 18.2.4.

Figure 18.1 depicts the (simplified) flow of funds from payor to payee within a wholesale payment system with a central bank at its apex. Figure 18.1 simplifies the payment process in at least two important respects.[9] First, as the volume of wholesale payments has increased, it has become increasingly difficult to process all wholesale fund transfers through a central bank. As a result, many interbank transfers are now *cleared* through automated clearinghouses before being

---

[7] Putting aside the question of which banks should be allowed to participate.

[8] C Calomiris and C Kahn, 'The Efficiency of Self-Regulated Payments Systems: Learning from the Suffolk System', NBER Working Paper 5442 (1996).

[9] It also does not accurately represent the flow of payments for cheques or bankers' drafts, for example, where the payee deposits the instrument with its bank, which then in effect becomes a creditor of the payor's bank.

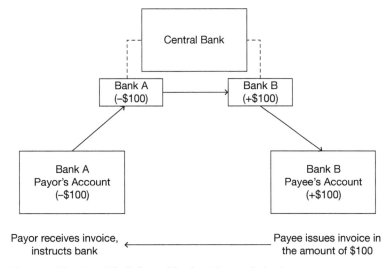

Fig. 18.1 The (simplified) flow of funds within a wholesale payment system

routed through a central bank or a private settlement agent for *settlement*. Clearing in this context refers to the process by which payment instructions are transmitted, reconciled, and, in some cases, confirmed prior to settlement.[10] Banks transmit batches of payment instructions to a clearinghouse that, after sorting them and amalgamating payments destined for the same bank, then transmits information to each participating bank regarding the details of payments to be made to their customers. As part of this process, the clearinghouse may also calculate and transmit net positions to the settlement agent. Settlement, in contrast, is the event marking the moment at which the payment obligation has been discharged.[11]

Second, for various reasons, not all banks elect to become direct participants of wholesale payment systems. These non-participating banks will typically enter into bilateral agreements with direct participants, pursuant to which the latter provide 'correspondent' banking services. In effect, non-participating institutions gain indirect access to the wholesale payment system by becoming customers of one or more correspondent banks. Systems that exhibit this hierarchical structure—with the central bank at the apex, followed by participating (correspondent) banks, and then non-participating banks—are often referred to as 'tiered' payment systems.

This overview of the basic structure of wholesale payment systems allows us to make two preliminary observations. First, when wholesale payment systems function effectively, they greatly reduce the costs of transferring funds between banks in satisfaction of their customers' financial obligations. Second, however, the failure of a wholesale payment system could generate massive externalities as businesses and households

---

[10] Committee on Payment and Settlement Systems ('CPSS'), 'A Glossary of Terms Used in Payment and Settlement Systems' (2003), available at http://www.bis.org/cpmi/glossary_030301.pdf. The CPSS has subsequently changed its name to the Committee on Payments and Market Infrastructures ('CPMI').

[11] D Rambure and A Nacamuli, *Payment Systems: From the Salt Mines to the Board Room* (Basingstoke: Palgrave, 2008).

experience widespread disruption to their expected cash flows. In the next section, we explore the evolution of the settlement mechanisms designed to mitigate these risks.

18.2.2 The evolution of wholesale payment systems

Prior to the 1990s, the vast majority of wholesale payment systems utilized what were known as deferred net settlement (or 'DNS') systems.[12] In a DNS system, individual payment instructions are collected during the course of the business day or some other predefined settlement period. At the end of this period, the aggregate amount by which each participating bank is in credit (or debit) is calculated and then netted off, typically on a multilateral basis amongst all the system's participants. The net positions are then communicated to the settlement agent—usually a central bank—for settlement. The benefits of DNS systems flow from those of multilateral netting more generally: principally the reduction in the overall number of transfers (relative to bilateral netting) and in the amount of money needed to settle a given set of obligations (relative to gross payments).

Where a participating bank fails to meet its obligations, DNS systems typically contemplate some sort of 'unwind' procedure. An unwind commences with the cancellation of all payment instructions both to and from the defaulting participant. The remaining multilateral net positions are then recalculated and settlement is once again attempted. In the event that one or more of the other participants are unable to meet their obligations as a result of the deterioration of their net positions due to their direct or indirect exposure to the defaulting participant, payment instructions involving these participants are also unwound. Theoretically, this process continues until all surviving participants are able to settle their obligations to the system. In practice, however, there has never been a settlement failure on a major DNS system.[13]

The principal drawback of DNS systems is settlement risk. More specifically, because final settlement only occurs at the end of the relevant settlement period, participating banks have no certainty that they will receive payment before this point in time. This risk was highlighted by the failure of Herstatt Bank in 1974, described in greater detail in section 18.2.3. Moreover, from a systemic perspective, if one participating bank fails to meet its obligations, a large number of payment instructions might be unwound, with the consequent risk of other banks being unable to meet their obligations, thereby potentially triggering a series of knock-on defaults. In this respect, the ability of participating banks to meet their payment obligations within a DNS system can be seen as highly interdependent.

However, it is unclear how real or pressing the risk of settlement failure actually was within wholesale DNS systems. First, as a matter of practice, central banks often provided implicit or explicit settlement guarantees to participating banks.[14] Second, as George

---

[12] M Bech and B Hobjin, 'Technology Diffusion within Central Banking: The Case of Real Time Gross Settlement' (2007) 3 *International Journal of Central Banking* 147.

[13] G Selgin, 'Wholesale Payments: Questioning the Market-Failure Hypothesis', in Haldane, Millard, and Saporta, n 3.

[14] Ibid.

Selgin has observed, banks would only be exposed to settlement risk if they credited their customer accounts before the end of the relevant settlement period.[15] Otherwise, the payments would simply be unwound, and the attendant risks passed on to the affected payees. Nevertheless, as the volume of payments processed through wholesale DNS systems around the world grew during the 1980s and 1990s, central banks became increasingly concerned about the possibility of settlement failure and its potential impact on financial stability. As a result, steps were taken to reduce the amount of settlement risk via the implementation of RTGS systems.[16] By the turn of the new millennium, traditional wholesale DNS systems had been replaced by RTGS systems within most developed economies.[17]

The defining feature of RTGS systems is that payment instructions are processed as they are received, with the system transferring credits representing the gross value of individual payment instructions. Some RTGS systems require participant banks to maintain sufficient funds in their settlement account to cover all outgoing payments. Others, however, allow participants to rely on intraday credit—often referred to as 'daylight overdrafts'—to cover payments in excess of their available balances. Participant banks drawing on these overdrafts are generally required to deposit sufficient funds into their settlement accounts by the end of each business day.

RTGS systems require participating banks to keep more funds on hand in order to execute payments on a gross (as opposed to net) basis. Put differently, RTGS systems require more liquidity than DNS systems.[18] One unfortunate by-product of this is that participating banks may seek to delay entering payment instructions into the system, ultimately in the hope that they can obtain liquidity from incoming payments.[19] That is to say, RTGS systems generate incentives for participating banks to free-ride on the liquidity of other participants. Empirical support for this can be found in James McAndrews and Samira Rajan's study of Fedwire, the RTGS system owned and operated by the US Federal Reserve System. McAndrews and Rajan report that Fedwire experiences its highest volumes in the late afternoon—around the time that the Clearinghouse Interbank Payment System (or 'CHIPS'), a privately owned and operated clearinghouse that processes a substantial proportion of US large value payments, sends its payment instructions to participating banks via Fedwire.[20]

The liquidity needs of RTGS systems put pressure on central banks to ensure the continuous flow of funds within these systems. Indeed, central banks—as the issuers of the ultimate settlement asset—are uniquely positioned to offer subsidized short-term

---

[15] Ibid—although, in practice, receiving banks often immediately credited their customer accounts.

[16] For a more detailed historical account of the migration to RTGS systems, see Bech and Hobijn, n 12.

[17] Although they continued to be used in some developing economies and in retail payment systems.

[18] Selgin, n 13; B Lester, S Millard, and M Willison, 'Optimal Settlement Rules for Payment Systems', in Haldane, Millard, and Saporta, n 3.

[19] G Afonso and HS Shin, 'Systemic Risk and Liquidity in Payment Systems', Federal Reserve Bank of New York Staff Report No 352 (2009); M Bech and R Garratt, 'The Intraday Liquidity Management Game' (2003) 109 *Journal of Economic Theory* 198; J McAndrews and S Rajan, 'The Timing and Funding of Fedwire Funds Transfers' (2000) *Federal Reserve Bank of New York Policy Review* 17.

[20] McAndrews and Rajan, n 19. See also O Armantier, J Arnold, and J McAndrews, 'Changes in the Timing Distribution of Fedwire Funds Transfers' (2008) *Federal Reserve Bank of New York Policy Review* 83.

credit to participating banks.[21] This, however, creates a moral hazard problem insofar as underpriced liquidity can be expected further to distort the incentives of participating banks.[22] Central banks have thus introduced a number of mechanisms designed to address this problem. The US Federal Reserve, for example, employs a system of net debit caps on daylight overdrafts based on an institution's creditworthiness. The Fed also imposes a fee on uncollateralized overdrafts and, since 2001, permits institutions with access to the Fed's discount window to pledge collateral to secure daylight overdrafts.[23] Both the Bank of England and the European Central Bank, meanwhile, provide 'free' short-term credit against specified collateral.

Ultimately, the costs associated with RTGS systems have stoked demand for new 'hybrid' wholesale payment systems. These hybrids seek to capture the reduced settlement risk associated with RTGS systems, while keeping the lower liquidity costs of DNS systems.[24] Although the institutional details of these systems vary widely in practice, they tend to share several common features. These include: *queue management systems* enabling participants to view, reorder, or cancel individual payment instructions; *automated algorithms* that search the queue for offsetting payments; separate *payment streams* for 'urgent' and 'non-urgent' payments; and *liquidity pooling* across affiliated entities.[25] In addition to reducing the demand for intraday liquidity, many view these features—and in particular, the greater transparency offered by queue management systems—as enabling participants to better signal their willingness to meet their obligations towards one other.[26]

18.2.3 Continuous linked settlement ('CLS') of foreign exchange transactions

To this point, we have been examining the mechanics of domestic wholesale payment systems used to facilitate payments denominated in a single currency. With the growth of cross-border trade over recent decades, however, there has been a corresponding increase in the number and size of foreign exchange transactions. Historically, foreign exchange transactions took place through a system of correspondent relationships whereby banks would open accounts (often referred to as 'nostro' accounts) with other banks domiciled in the jurisdiction in which the currency they wished to acquire was issued. Thus, for example, a UK bank looking to sell sterling and buy Japanese yen would need to open a yen-denominated nostro account with a Japanese bank. Similarly, a Japanese industrial firm looking to sell yen and buy sterling would need to open

---

[21] E Green, 'The Role of the Central Bank in Payment Systems' in Haldane, Millard, and Saporta, n 3.

[22] J Lacker, 'Payment Economics and the Role of Central Banks', in Haldane, Millard, and Saporta, n 3.

[23] See Federal Reserve, 'Overview of the Federal Reserve's Payment System Risk Policy on Intraday Credit' (July 2012).

[24] J McAndrews and J Trundle, 'New Payment Systems Designs: Causes and Consequences' (2001) *Financial Stability Review* 127.

[25] M Bech, 'The Diffusion of Real-Time Gross Settlement', in Haldane, Millard, and Saporta, n 3; McAndrews and Trundle, n 24.

[26] McAndrews and Trundle, n 24.

an account with a UK bank. Due to time zone differences, however, the different 'legs'[27] of a foreign exchange transaction—between our UK bank and Japanese industrial, for example—may not be settled at precisely the same time. This, in turn, can expose the counterparty who performs first to the risk that the other may not deliver the desired currency. A settlement failure—or 'fail'—occurs when one leg of the transaction does not settle as contemplated.

On 26 June 1974, the German Bundesbank withdrew the banking licence of Herstatt, a small private bank active in foreign exchange markets. Herstatt had entered into a number of foreign exchange transactions to sell US dollars and buy Deutschmarks in order to meet its payment obligations in Germany. However, while the counterparties to these transactions had performed their obligations, the withdrawal of Herstatt's licence—which occurred in the middle of the business day—meant it was unable to deliver US dollars in satisfaction of its obligations. This left Herstatt's counterparties bearing considerable losses. The term 'Herstatt risk' has thus become synonymous with settlement risk in foreign exchange transactions. Counterparties experienced similar problems in connection with the failures of Drexel Burnham Lambert in 1990 and BCCI in 1991.[28]

In 1996 the Bank for International Settlements published the *Allsopp Report*, which recommended managing Herstatt risk through the simultaneous and interdependent settlement of both legs of foreign exchange transactions.[29] This objective was achieved in 2002 with the creation of the Continuously Linked Settlement (or 'CLS') system.[30] The CLS system acts like an escrow agent by ensuring that payments are not released until both legs of a foreign exchange transaction have been completed. If one counterparty fails to perform, the funds are returned to the other counterparty. In this respect, CLS can be seen as substituting, in place of settlement risk, *replacement* risk: the risk that the market may have moved against the performing counterparty during the relevant timeframe. As of 2015, CLS supported trading in seventeen of the world's major currencies through direct links with domestic RTGS systems.[31]

To reduce funding demands on participants, CLS employs multilateral netting on a per currency basis and continually monitors trades to identify which are capable of settlement. While transactions processed through CLS are self-collateralizing—that is, payments into the system largely match payments out—the system also utilizes a number of other mechanisms to manage credit and other risks. These mechanisms include: short position limits for each participant; aggregate position limits across each currency; and a requirement that a participant's net position across all currencies must remain positive at all times—subject to a haircut to account for market fluctuations in the relevant currencies. Where a participant fails to perform its obligations, CLS may also call upon other designated participants—known as 'liquidity providers'—to make

---

[27] There are two 'legs' in a foreign exchange transaction because both counterparties are required to deliver the currency they are selling to the other.

[28] Rambure and Nacamuli, n 11.

[29] See CPSS, 'Settlement Risk in Foreign Exchange Transactions—A Strategy for Addressing FX Settlement Risk' (the 'Allsopp Report') (1996).

[30] For an overview of the CLS system generally, see Rambure and Nacamuli, n 11, 139–46.

[31] See 'About Us', http://www.cls-group.com.

up the shortfall.[32] As of July 2015, over a million payment instructions were submitted to CLS each day, with an average aggregate value of $4.5 trillion.[33] Perhaps not surprisingly, CLS itself has thus been designated as a systemically important Financial Market Utility by the US Financial Stability Oversight Council.

18.2.4 The governance and regulation of wholesale payment systems

In most jurisdictions, the governance and regulation of wholesale payment systems are prescribed through a combination of law and regulation and private contractual and institutional arrangements. The mechanics of wholesale payment systems described in section 18.2.2 are generally set out in the policies and procedures of the relevant clearinghouse. Compliance with these rules and procedures is then mandated under the contracts entered into between the clearinghouse and its participants. Thus, for example, the clearinghouse will: prescribe participant eligibility criteria; design and implement the mechanisms used to manage liquidity, credit, and other risks; and monitor and enforce compliance with these internal rules.[34] The clearinghouse will often perform these functions under the oversight of a governing body, typically comprised primarily of representatives drawn from participating institutions.[35]

Sitting atop this private governance and regulatory architecture are regulatory regimes typically overseen by central banks. Indeed, central banks often play a wide variety of roles within domestic wholesale payment systems. As a preliminary matter, central banks issue the ultimate settlement asset and administer the accounts through which settlement takes place. They also stand ready to provide short-term liquidity to system participants. For these reasons, they often—although not invariably—maintain some sort of direct (prudential) regulatory oversight of the financial institutions that enjoy access to these settlement and liquidity facilities. Beyond these basic functions, however, the nature and extent of central bank oversight vary considerably from jurisdiction to jurisdiction.[36] In the Eurozone, the central bank owns, operates, and oversees the wholesale payment system.[37] In the UK, the Bank of England owns and operates the RTGS system which is then linked to multiple private wholesale payment systems subject to oversight by an independent payment systems regulator.[38] In the US, meanwhile, the Federal Reserve owns and operates Fedwire while providing oversight of the privately owned and operated CHIPS.[39]

The regulatory architecture imposed by central banks and other regulators also performs a number of ancillary functions in the governance of wholesale payment

---

[32] Either through foreign exchange swaps or direct transactions.

[33] CLS Monthly Data (July 2015), available at http://www.cls-group.com.

[34] Rambure and Nacamuli, n 11. See eg the CHIPS Rules and Administrative Procedures, available at http://www.chips.org.

[35] And, in some cases, representatives from the central bank or prudential supervisor.

[36] See Millard and Saporta, n 4, 37, for an overview.   [37] Ibid.

[38] While independent, the UK payment systems regulator is required to put in place a memorandum of understanding with the Bank of England, Prudential Regulation Authority, and Financial Conduct Authority (of which the payment systems regulator is also a subsidiary). In certain prescribed circumstances, these authorities can also direct the payment systems regulator to refrain from taking specified actions.

[39] Millard and Saporta, n 4.

systems. First, together with the applicable private institutional arrangements, it defines the legal rights and obligations of system participants.[40] Second, it is often used to establish various 'housekeeping' rules: stipulating, for example, hours of operation, security measures, authorization, fees, and the timeframe within which transfers must be posted to client accounts. Finally, and perhaps most importantly, it articulates the circumstances in which the central bank will be willing to provide intraday liquidity.[41]

There are at least two potential justifications for central bank oversight of wholesale payment systems. First, the ability of central banks to perform their core monetary policy functions is contingent on a healthy and functioning wholesale payment system. It is the demand for central bank liabilities as the settlement asset, after all, that enables them to conduct monetary policy through both open market operations and the discount window. Second, where central banks provide underpriced intraday liquidity to ensure the smooth functioning of RTGS systems, we would expect privately owned and operated systems to generate socially suboptimal levels of risk management.[42] As described in Chapter 3, this may justify some sort of public regulatory intervention with a view to ensuring that payment system providers and participants internalize the attendant costs. [43]

18.3 Securities Settlement Systems

18.3.1 The basic mechanics of securities settlement systems

In Chapter 7, we examined the market infrastructure that facilitates *trading* in various financial assets. Securities settlement systems provide the infrastructure that facilitates the post-trade processes that *clear* these trades, ensure timely *settlement*, and provide for their *safekeeping*. They are also the conduits through which the vast majority of financial collateral, utilized by financial institutions and other businesses to raise capital, flows. While the mechanics of securities settlement systems vary considerably between equity, debt, derivatives, and government securities, they are all delivery-versus-payment (or 'DvP') systems. In a nutshell, DvP systems connect the two legs of a trade: namely, the transfer of *securities*, on the one hand, and the transfer of *funds* via the wholesale payment system, on the other. The key feature of these DvP systems is that they ensure that the delivery of the relevant securities occurs if, and only if, the corresponding fund transfer is completed.[44] In this way, DvP systems thus seek to ensure finality of settlement in respect of both legs of a securities transaction.

There are three types of DvP systems. The first ('gross/gross') model involves the gross settlement of both legs of a trade upon confirmation from the wholesale payment

---

[40] Federal Reserve Board Regulation J, for example, incorporates section 4A of the Uniform Commercial Code governing fund transfers.

[41] See eg the Federal Reserve Board's Payment System Risk Policy on Intraday Credit, available at http://www.federalreserve.gov/paymentsystems/psr_overview.htm.

[42] H Allen, G Christodoulou, and S Millard, 'Financial Infrastructure and Corporate Governance', Bank of England Working Paper No 316 (2006).

[43] Lacker, n 22.

[44] CPSS and Technical Committee of the International Organization of Securities Commissions ('IOSCO'), 'Principles for Financial Market Infrastructures' (2012).

system that the relevant fund transfer has been completed. The relevant securities and funds accounts are then debited/credited simultaneously, with settlement finality being achieved at this point. Overdrafts on counterparties' securities accounts are prohibited, but the settlement agent may provide intraday liquidity by lending securities to the relevant counterparty. The advantages of this model stem from the reduction in settlement, credit, and liquidity risk through simultaneous settlement of both legs of the transaction. The primary disadvantage, meanwhile, is the fact that—like RTGS systems—participants must keep cash or other highly liquid assets on hand in order to meet funding demands on a gross basis. To minimize these demands, many DvP systems based on this model have introduced liquidity savings features similar to those employed by hybrid RTGS systems.

Under the second ('gross/net') model, securities transfers are settled on a gross basis throughout the day. Funds transfers, meanwhile, are only settled net at the end of each settlement period. Under the third ('net/net') model, in contrast, both legs are settled on a net basis at the end of each settlement period. Counterparties' funds and securities accounts are thus not debited/credited until the conclusion of the relevant processing cycle. In the interim, all transfers are conditional and there is no finality of settlement. By providing for settlement on a net basis, the gross/net and net/net models thus reduce liquidity demands on system participants. Simultaneously, however, both of these models generate the securities equivalent of Herstatt risk: namely, the risk that the failure of one or more counterparties could precipitate a chain reaction of settlement failures. For this reason, the gross/gross model is generally viewed as the safest of the three.

18.3.2 The role of central securities depositories

The majority of securities settlement systems are operated by central securities depositories (or 'CSDs'), such as the Depository Trust Company ('DTC') in the US or CREST in the UK. CSDs have two main functions. The first is to maintain the accounts that record the issuance, ownership, and transfer of securities. The second is to provide for the centralized safekeeping of those securities.[45] While securities can sometimes still be held in immobilized physical form, recent years have witnessed a pronounced shift towards 'dematerialization'.[46] This shift has helped facilitate electronic trading and automated trade monitoring, reduced processing times and costs, and effectively eliminated the risk of destruction or theft.

Generally speaking, CSDs are direct participants in the wholesale payment system, thus establishing the technical links necessary to coordinate settlement of both the securities and funds legs of a trade. At the same time, however, the interdependence between CSDs and wholesale payment systems is an important source of risk. Should

---

[45] CSDs will also often provide ancillary services such as administration of corporate actions, dividends, redemptions, and taxes.

[46] Whereas *immobilization* contemplates the placement of physical certificates or other documents of title evidencing ownership of securities in a CSD, *dematerialization* contemplates the substitution of physical certificates for an electronic book-entry system.

one or more participants experience liquidity problems within the wholesale payment system, for example, this could disrupt the settlement of trades involving these participants, potentially leading to knock-on securities settlement failures by other participants.[47]

Cross-border securities settlement raises a number of additional issues and, as a result, is often considerably more costly.[48] These issues are driven by differences between the information technology platforms utilized by domestic CSDs, the domestic legal treatment of securities or other assets, the domestic legal treatment of bilateral and/or multilateral netting, and other operational parameters (such as settlement models, settlement periods, operating hours, and so forth).[49] As a result, cross-border securities settlement has historically relied on complex chains of indirect holding often involving multiple CSDs, custodians, and other financial intermediaries. Predictably, this has had a negative impact in terms of the efficiency of cross-border settlement and increased both the interdependence and risks associated with cross-border trades.

To help ameliorate these risks, centralize their cross-border operations, and streamline their portfolio management, market participants will often utilize the services of global custodians (typically specialized banks), which settle cross-border securities trades through a network of domestic sub-custodians.[50] Recent years have also witnessed the emergence of international central securities depositories (or 'ICSDs'), such as Euroclear and Clearstream, that operate alongside CSDs and establish links between domestic systems. The provision of both custodial and ICSD services is characterized by pronounced economies of scale. This is reflected in the concentration of these services in the hands of a small number of providers, often affiliated with systemically important financial institutions. This concentration raises both competition and consumer protection concerns. It also raises the prospect that ICSDs or global custodians might become conduits for the transmission of systemic risk. As a result, regulators in different jurisdictions—and in particular the EU (see section 18.3.3)—have taken an increasing interest in cross-border securities settlement.

18.3.3 The governance and regulation of securities settlement systems

The majority of security settlement systems are organized as privately owned institutions operating under the oversight of public regulators. The DTC, for example, is a subsidiary of the participant-owned Depository Trust and Clearing Company ('DTCC'). Through its subsidiaries, the DTCC provides clearing, settlement, and other services in connection with trading in equity and debt securities, money market instruments, and derivatives. The DTC—which clears and settles trades in equity

---

[47] CPSS, 'The Interdependencies of Payment and Settlement Systems' (June 2008), available at http://www.bis.org/cpmi/publ/d84.htm.

[48] In 2012, for example, the European Commission estimated that the costs associated with cross-border settlement within the EU were up to four times higher than the equivalent domestic settlement costs: see European Commission, 'Proposal for a Regulation on Improving Securities Settlement in the European Union', COM (2012) 73 final, 2.

[49] Rambure and Nacamuli, n 11.

[50] They also carry out a number of the ancillary administrative services typically provided by domestic CSDs.

securities—is a limited purpose trust under New York banking law, a member of the Federal Reserve System, and an SEC-registered clearing agency. The UK's CREST system, meanwhile, is privately owned and operated by Belgium-based Euroclear and operates under the oversight of the Bank of England.

While the substantive regulation of securities settlement systems varies from jurisdiction to jurisdiction, the Committee on Payments and Market Infrastructures ('CPMI') and the International Organization of Securities Commissions ('IOSCO') have published a set of broad principles for the regulation of financial market infrastructures—including CSDs. The principles stipulate, amongst other matters, that a CSD should be required to: have rules and procedures that ensure the integrity of securities issues and minimize and manage the risks associated with safekeeping; maintain securities in an immobilized or dematerialized form; protect assets against the CSD's own negligence, fraud, poor administration, and inaccurate recordkeeping (so-called 'custody risk'); and employ a robust system that ensures the segregation of both participants' assets and those of their clients.[51] The principles also state that a CSD should prohibit overdrafts and debit balances in securities accounts in order to avoid credit risk and reduce the potential for the 'creation' of securities as a result of double counting.[52]

If a CSD provides services other than safekeeping and administration, the CPMI–IOSCO principles provide that it should be required to identify, measure, monitor, and manage the risks associated with these activities.[53] For example, where a CSD provides securities lending facilities to help facilitate timely settlement and reduce settlement fails, it should take measures to manage the resulting liquidity, counterparty credit, and replacement risk.

The EU has also been active recently in the area of securities settlement infrastructure.[54] The Securities Settlement and CSD Regulation aims to harmonize both the timing and conduct of securities settlement within the EU, along with the rules governing domestic and international CSDs. Its stated objectives are to improve the safety of settlements (and in particular cross-border settlements), foster an internal market for the operation of CSDs, and apply higher prudential requirements to CSDs in line with international standards.[55]

Reflecting the CPMI–IOSCO principles, the Securities Settlement and CSD Regulation mandates the immobilization and dematerialization of securities with a view to increasing the efficiency of settlement and ensuring the integrity of securities.[56] It also mandates the introduction of harmonized settlement periods.[57] Participants failing to meet their obligations to deliver securities on the settlement date are then subject to a wide range of potential sanctions. They are also subject to a 'buy-in' procedure, pursuant to which the relevant securities would be purchased and delivered in a timely manner to the intended recipients.[58]

---

[51] CPSS and IOSCO, n 44.   [52] Ibid.   [53] Ibid.
[54] Regulation (EU) No 909/2014 on improving securities settlement in the European Union and on central securities depositories and amending Directives 98/26/EC and 2014/65/EU and Regulation (EU) No 236/2012 (the 'Securities Settlement and CSD Regulation'), [2014] OJ L257/1.
[55] See ibid, recitals 4, 5, and 20.   [56] Art 3.   [57] Art 5.   [58] Art 7.

The regulation confers upon issuers the right to record their securities with any CSD authorized within the EU.[59] It also enables domestically authorized CSDs to provide services in any EU Member State and grants CSDs the right to become a participant of a securities settlement system administered by another CSD.[60] CSDs, meanwhile, are required to employ non-discriminatory, transparent, and strictly risk-based criteria when determining whether a prospective participant should be granted access to the system.[61] The objective of these measures is to promote a more competitive market for securities settlement and related services within the EU. Clearly, greater competition has the potential to pose challenges for stability. To this end, the Regulation also imposes a series of additional prudential safeguards on CSDs, including governance, risk management, investment, and capital requirements.[62]

Finally, the new regulation subjects CSDs to harmonized authorization, conduct of business, and prudential standards. For example, the regulation requires CSDs to comply with common governance arrangements and capital adequacy standards, provides for the segregation of accounts of participants (and enables participants to segregate the accounts of each of their clients), and mandates that CSDs employ measures to mitigate various operational risks. CSDs are also required to seek additional authorization for the provision of ancillary banking services such the provision of intraday liquidity to system participants. CSDs authorized to provide these services are then subject to enhanced prudential requirements to manage the attendant intraday credit and liquidity risks.

18.4 Retail Payment Systems

18.4.1 Overview of retail payment systems

Broadly speaking, retail payment systems facilitate transactions between consumers and merchants involving the purchase and sale of goods and services. These transactions can be made using a wide range of payment instruments and methods: cash, cheques, credit or debit cards, stored value cards, or electronic fund transfers. The infrastructure supporting retail payments is almost universally owned and operated by private-sector payment services providers—banks, credit card companies such as Visa and Mastercard and, increasingly, non-bank intermediaries such as mobile phone operators and PayPal. This infrastructure varies considerably between different payment instruments and methods, and from jurisdiction to jurisdiction. Moreover, the way consumers make retail payments is constantly evolving. Accordingly, it is not possible to describe the mechanics of retail payment systems here in any detail. What follows, therefore, is an overview of the interactions between three important drivers underlying the development and regulation of retail payment systems: convenience, security, and competition.

For most of the twentieth century, retail payment systems were dominated by paper-based instruments: namely, cash and cheques. The primary advantage of cash is immediate

---

[59] Art 49. Whereas domestic laws in some jurisdictions dictate that equity securities, for example, must be issued through domestic CSDs.

[60] Arts 23 and 50.   [61] Art 52.   [62] Arts 42–7.

finality of settlement. At the same time, however, cash is costly to store, secure, and transport. It is also susceptible to theft. While cheques resolve some of these problems, they are extremely costly for merchants and financial institutions to handle and process. With advances in information technology, therefore, it should perhaps come as no surprise that new—electronic—payment methods have emerged and blossomed. From a consumer standpoint, electronic payment instruments and methods are inexpensive and convenient when used as a means of payment (although less so when used as a source of credit). From the perspective of merchants, electronic payments lower the costs of handling cash and cheques. By facilitating deferred payment, meanwhile, credit cards also stimulate consumer spending.

All this is not to say that electronic payments eliminate the risks associated with paper-based instruments. Electronic gift cards and other 'store of value' systems— which depend on the ability of payees to verify the authenticity of the payment instrument—are still at risk of physical appropriation. Simultaneously, 'account-based' systems such as credit cards, debit cards, and electronic fund transfers—which rely on the ability of payees to verify the identity of the payors—are susceptible to fraud and identity theft. Providers of account-based payment systems are also vulnerable to network security breaches. As a result, while electronic payment instruments and methods offer many advantages, the advances in information technology from which these advantages largely flow are also the source of potential security risks.

The rise of electronic payment instruments and methods has also changed the competitive dynamics of many retail payment systems. As purveyors of so-called 'information goods', payment service providers enjoy significant economies of scale in terms of the infrastructure used to process payment information. Retail payment systems are also characterized by pronounced network effects: with each additional participant increasing the value of the network to existing users. Consumers, for example, would see little value in a payment instrument that was only accepted by a small number of merchants. Merchants, conversely, would see little point in making investments in payment infrastructure if relatively few customers were likely to use the relevant instrument. Each of these factors tends towards monopoly service provision, with obvious implications for competition within the payment services industry.[63] Additional competition concerns arise in the context of so-called 'two-sided' payment markets such as those for credit card services.[64]

18.4.2 The governance and regulation of retail payment systems

The structure and intensity of public regulatory oversight of retail payment systems vary from jurisdiction to jurisdiction. In the UK, for example, the Bank of England has historically exerted influence on retail payment systems providers through its

---

[63] W Bolt and D Humphrey, 'Public Good Issues in TARGET: Natural Monopoly, Scale Economies, Network Effects and Cost Allocation', ECB Working Paper Series 0505 (2005).

[64] J-C Rochet and J Tirole, 'Platform Competition in Two-Sided Markets' (2003) 1 *Journal of the European Economic Association* 990. Two-sided markets are characterized by the existence of two distinct groups—consumers and merchants in the case of credit cards, for example—each generating network externalities for the other.

participation in various industry bodies. This largely informal arrangement was modified in April 2015 with the establishment of an independent payment systems regulator. The statutory objectives of this new regulator are to promote competition and innovation in payment services, and to ensure that payment systems are operated in a way that promotes the interests of their users. In the US, in contrast, the Federal Reserve Act of 1913 gives the Federal Reserve Board sole responsibility for the oversight of retail payment systems. The CPMI has identified the objectives of central bank oversight and intervention as being to address legal and regulatory impediments to market development and innovation, foster competitive market conditions, and support the development of effective standards and infrastructure arrangements.[65]

Given the ostensible absence of market failures within retail payment systems (other than those stemming from competitive distortions), there are those who see little or no justification for central bank oversight of retail payment systems.[66] Nevertheless, the safe and efficient use of cash as a medium of exchange in retail payments is one of the most important functions of a fiat currency. Moreover, public confidence in the currency could be undermined if retail payment systems were inefficient or unsafe. Accordingly, it seems reasonable to suggest that—at the very least—central banks are important stakeholders in the efficiency and safety of retail payment systems.

18.5 Emerging Issues in Payment and Settlement Systems

Payment and settlement systems are constantly evolving. While the pace and direction of this evolution often vary dramatically from jurisdiction to jurisdiction, it is generally driven by technological advances.[67] In retail payment systems, the most prominent trend in recent decades has been the gradual shift away from cash as a means of making payments and towards various electronic payment methods such as credit and debit cards, electronic fund transfers, and Web-based payments. These advances have generated efficiency gains for both consumers and businesses. At the same time, however, many of these new technologies expose users to the risk of fraud and identity theft (although, again, technological advances such as 'chip-and-pin' technology have also helped to reduce these risks). Striking the right balance between efficiency and security will continue to be an important—and difficult—task for both payment system providers and regulators.

A second emerging issue is the growing role of non-banks such as mobile telephone operators in the provision of retail payment services. The emergence of these institutions as payment service providers raises a number of intertwined questions. First, to what extent do these institutions perform the same economic functions as conventional 'bank-based' payment systems? Second, do these institutions possess the capacity and incentives to screen for and monitor the consumer credit and other risks to which they may be exposed?[68] Third, to what extent can or should existing regulatory regimes— such as prudential regulation, deposit insurance and resolution—be extended to these

---

[65] CPSS and IOSCO, n 44.   [66] See eg Lacker, n 22.
[67] CPSS and IOSCO, n 44.   [68] Haldane, Millard, and Saporta, n 3, 9.

non-bank intermediaries? Complicating matters, the pace of change in this area—to say nothing of the fact that the innovation is coming from outside the financial sector— makes it difficult for regulators to identify, monitor, and evaluate the potential benefits and risks associated with new payment innovations. Once again, while the prospective benefits are considerable—especially for under-banked developing countries—so too are the potential risks.

In terms of wholesale payment and securities settlement systems, the most signifi- cant emerging issues revolve around the growing interdependence between these systems. The eventual expansion of the CLS system to include more currencies, for example, will simultaneously serve to concentrate systemic risk within international money markets. It also risks inefficient monopoly service provision.[69] More generally, the linkages among and between payment and settlement systems—both domestically and at the international level—exacerbate the risk that liquidity or operational events could spread quickly between systems. For this reason, Richard Pattison has argued for both a global liquidity bridge and mechanisms which would render both liquidity needs and operational failures more transparent.[70]

Looking further beyond the horizon, there is the prospect of e-settlement. The basic idea behind e-settlement is that the current centralized account-based structure of wholesale payment systems would be replaced by a decentralized electronic network. The settlement asset would then be a secure digital stamp attached to electronic payment instructions sent (and received) directly by participants over a dedicated platform. In a world of e-settlement, central banks would no longer perform a direct role in clearing wholesale payments. They would, however, continue to provide the settlement asset: generating digital stamps and distributing them to participating banks.

18.6 Conclusion

Payment and settlement systems are the plumbing of the global financial system. And, like the plumbing, we tend to take the smooth and fluid operation of these systems for granted—until something breaks. Ultimately, regulating payment and settlement sys- tems involves a series of trade-offs. In wholesale payment and securities settlement systems, these trade-offs include balancing the costs and benefits of liquidity versus finality of settlement, interconnectedness versus interdependency, and private innov- ation versus public regulatory oversight. In retail payment systems, meanwhile, the principal trade-off is between greater convenience, on the one hand, and security and competition, on the other. In both realms, the optimal trade-off is a function of, amongst other things, available technology, the effectiveness of both private institu- tional arrangements and public regulatory oversight, and the nature and probability of the attendant risks.

---

[69] Millard and Saporta, n 4; R Pattison, 'Real-Time Liquidity Management in a Globally-Connected Market', in Haldane, Millard, and Saporta, n 3.

[70] Pattison, n 69.

19

The Macroprudential Approach

19.1 Introduction

Much of the discussion about regulation in this book has been focused on the protection of investors and consumers, and the efficient operation of financial markets. Regulation is concerned with the avoidance of fraud, market abuse, and misleading information that harms investors and undermines market efficiency. It is also concerned to ensure the soundness of financial institutions in which individuals place their confidence, while ensuring competition amongst such firms in order to benefit consumers. However, the financial crisis brought out the importance for regulators of the protection of financial systems as a whole. In terms of the framework articulated in Chapter 3, serious disruption in the financial sector produces spillovers—negative externalities—for the real economy. The historical evidence demonstrates that recovery from economic downturns following financial crises is much more protracted and bumpier than from an 'ordinary' business cycle recession.[1]

Prior to the recent financial crisis, it was generally thought that ensuring the soundness of individual banks—so-called 'microprudential' regulation—was sufficient to ensure the stability of the system as a whole. The common view was that systemic risk was a matter of contagion from one failing institution to the others. However, the financial crisis demonstrated the inadequacies of this perspective. One of the most significant post-crisis innovations has consequently been the advent of a distinct 'macroprudential' approach to safeguarding financial stability.[2] In contrast to microprudential regulation, which is aimed at safeguarding financial *firms*, the macroprudential approach focuses on the stability of the financial *system* as a whole. The distinction between the microprudential and macroprudential approaches can be illustrated by analogy with that between medicine and public health care. Medicine is concerned with the saving of individual lives, public health care with protecting populations and communities as a whole. Good treatment of individuals does not necessarily provide effective protection against the spread of disease. Likewise, regulation aimed at protecting individual institutions does not necessarily ensure the stability of the financial system as a whole; a distinct macroprudential approach is a necessary element of the regulatory package.

---

[1] CM Reinhart and K Rogoff, *This Time is Different: Eight Centuries of Financial Folly* (Princeton, NJ: Princeton UP, 2009).

[2] See generally, A Crockett, 'Marrying the Micro- and Macro-prudential Dimensions of Financial Stability', speech given at 11th International Conference of Banking Supervisors, Basel, Switzerland, 18 September 2000; C Borio, 'Towards a Macroprudential Framework for Financial Supervision and Regulation?' (2003) 49 *CESifo Economic Studies* 181; SG Hanson, AK Kashyap, and JC Stein, 'A Macroprudential Approach to Financial Regulation' (2011) 25 *Journal of Economic Perspectives* 3; G Galati and R Moessner, 'Macroprudential Policy—A Literature Review', BIS WP No 337 (2011).

In section 19.2, we describe the macroprudential approach to financial regulation, which we term 'MacroPru' for short.[3] As the idea of MacroPru is still novel, its operational scope is not yet as clearly specified as many other aspects of regulation.[4] Nevertheless, it is tolerably clear that the risks to be addressed by MacroPru encompass two distinct perspectives. The first, or 'cross-sectional', perspective is concerned with ensuring the resiliency of the financial system should a shock materialize at any point. This requires far more than simply ensuring the soundness of individual banks. The interconnections between banks—direct and indirect—mean they are fragile institutions *collectively* as well as individually. Moreover, as we will explore in Chapters 20 and 21, the financial system consists not only of banks but also of non-bank financial institutions linked together through financial markets. The second, or 'time-series', perspective on MacroPru is concerned with the build-up of risk in the financial system as a whole over time. A key insight from the lead-up to the crisis is that the financial sector may be subject to *cycles* involving aggregate build-up and wind-down of risk.

In section 19.3, we turn to the modes of intervention, or *tools*, associated with MacroPru. We categorize these largely according to whether they respond to cross-sectional or time-series systemic risks.[5] Three general features emerge. First, for pragmatic reasons, much of the early progress in implementing MacroPru has been with measures in Basel III, which built on existing microprudential regulation. This yields a common core of MacroPru measures across countries, but makes it difficult to distinguish between macroprudential and microprudential measures. We consequently term these core measures 'microprudential plus'. Second, beyond these core measures, there is considerable national and regional diversity in the MacroPru tools that have been made available to authorities. This likely reflects the experimental state of the field as much as local differences among financial systems. Third, the range of measures that could potentially have implications for financial stability is far broader than those expressly described as 'macroprudential' in any system. Extending the ambit of 'MacroPru' so broadly as to cover all of these is probably not politically feasible. Successful MacroPru measures must therefore be crafted to coordinate with a wide range of other regulatory and fiscal measures.

In section 19.4, we reflect on challenges facing those tasked with implementing effective MacroPru measures. First, there is the difficulty of identifying a build-up over time of genuine systemic risk—as opposed to sustainable economic growth—and of employing tools that mitigate such risks without causing general economic harm. Second, as regards cross-sectional risks, MacroPru is likely to foster regulatory arbitrage,

---

[3] This papers over a division in nomenclature—the policy literature tends to refer to 'macroprudential policy' whereas the academic literature often refers to 'macroprudential regulation'.

[4] See eg European Systemic Risk Board ('ESRB'), 'A review of macro-prudential policy in the EU one year after the introduction of the CRD/CRR' (2015), 6 ('defining what exactly constitutes a macroprudential measure remains challenging').

[5] See eg Borio, n 2, 188–92, 195–200; Bank of England, 'Instruments of Macroprudential Policy: A Discussion Paper' (2011), 10–17. For alternative sub-classifications, see eg FSB/IMF/BIS, 'Macroprudential Policy Tools and Frameworks: Progress Report to G20' (2011), 11–12; S Claessens, 'An Overview of Macroprudential Policy Tools', IMF WP/14/214 (2014), 13–15.

pushing financial activity beyond the perimeter of the channels through which the MacroPru tools are implemented. Third, MacroPru measures are likely to be hated by industry participants and politicians, both of which may have short-term interests in permitting financial growth to overheat.

Section 19.5 then sketches the new macroprudential authorities ('MPAs') that have been created to coordinate and/or execute MacroPru measures. We focus on the Financial Stability Oversight Council in the US, the Financial Policy Committee in the UK, and the Systemic Risk Board in the EU. In each case, the MPA is distinct from existing regulators, reflecting its need for greater generality of oversight, and its occasional need to adjudicate on the scope of the regulatory perimeter and the propensity of other regulators' measures themselves to contribute to systemic risk. The effective application of MacroPru tools requires the MPA to have wide-ranging access to *information* concerning activities within the financial sector and beyond, and serious capability to *analyse* these reams of data. Section 19.6 discusses how these critical ingredients are supplied to MPAs. Section 19.7 concludes, emphasizing common themes throughout the book.

19.2 Foundations of the Macroprudential Perspective

While the idea of a macroprudential perspective had been articulated prior to the financial crisis—most notably in 2003 by Claudio Borio, then Chief Economist of the Bank for International Settlements ('BIS')[6]—it was regarded as little more than an academic curiosity.[7] The financial crisis changed this completely.

19.2.1 Cross-sectional systemic risks

The financial crisis made clear the inadequacy of regulatory measures taken to ensure stability in the event of a sudden systemic shock. This can be summarized in two points. First, the channels of contagion are much more varied than was previously appreciated. Traditionally, regulators were concerned about bank failures causing losses at creditor firms and triggering depositor runs at other similar banks. However, there turned out to be many more interconnections, which traditional microprudential tools did not constrain. Financial firms' balance sheets were indirectly linked by the pursuit of correlated investment strategies.[8] Balance sheet linkages were also introduced by the run-like behaviour of short-term wholesale lenders, who were uninsured.[9] Financial instruments such as credit default swaps, which were supposed to spread risks, connected the fortunes of counterparty financial institutions, thereby serving to

---

[6] See Borio, n 2.

[7] Various sorts of credit-constraining and credit-loosening policies have been used from time to time by national financial authorities, including legislatures, but generally not as a consciously 'macroprudential' policy intervention designed to control systemic risk in the financial sector. For the US, this phenomenon is documented in DJ Elliott, G Feldberg, and A Lehnert, 'The History of Cyclical Macroprudential Policy in the United States', Office of Financial Research (OFR) Working Paper #0008 (2013).

[8] See Chapter 1, section 1.2 and Chapter 2, section 2.5.

[9] We develop this point at length in Chapters 20 and 21. See in particular sections 20.3 and 21.2.

concentrate risk in the system as a whole.[10] In each of these examples, there were externalities that markets or institutions failed to price.

Second, and relatedly, the micro orientation of prudential regulation focused on the stability of individual institutions, rather than of the system as a whole. This was a natural complement to the parochial division of financial regulation into components covering banks, markets, and insurance. This had the consequence of focusing regulatory attention on the conditions necessary for the soundness of a given (type of) institution, and each tended to conceive of 'stability' as a concern from the standpoint of investors and credit-seeking customers, who might be prejudiced by the instability of particular institutions, but not from the standpoint of the system as a whole.[11] This approach took as given the significance (or otherwise) of particular types of institution for systemic risk, meaning that banks were the focus of stability concerns. The financial crisis made clear that the institutional location of financial activity—whether intermediation takes place in regulated institutions or outside them—is not fixed.[12] Moreover, the growth in global financial conglomerates means that their teams are in a position to understand the links in the financial system—and the lack of links in financial regulation—far more effectively than any regulators. To the extent that such institutions engaged in regulatory arbitrage, this information gap proved highly problematic. Regulators concerned with the soundness of the system as a whole must consequently be prepared to monitor changes in activity and modify the scope of measures according to emergent risks to stability.

19.2.2 Time-series systemic risks

Not only were the cross-sectional safeguards against major shocks shown to be inadequate, but also regulators were generally blind-sided by the build-up to the financial crisis. As of 2006, both international financial monitors and national banking supervisors were quite positive about the prospects for continued growth in the global economy and the health of the financial sector.[13] Even in early 2007, as the subprime mortgage market began to implode, regulators expressed confidence in the resilience of

---

[10] See Chapter 21, section 21.4. The famous example is AIG. See RG McDonald and A Paulson, 'AIG in Hindsight' (2015) 29 *Journal of Economic Perspectives* 81, 90–102.

[11] See sources cited in n 2.   [12] See Chapters 20 and 21.

[13] Eg BIS, 76th *Annual Report* 3 (June 2006): 'This time last year there was both satisfaction and surprise at the continuing excellent performance of the global economy....One year later, the same sentiments could be invoked in even greater measure...Not only has the good performance continued..., but there are even indications that some aspects of the imbalances themselves might be receding.' TF Geithner, 'Risk Management Challenges in the US Financial System' (2006) *BIS Review* 14/2006: 'The rapid growth of instruments for risk transfer and risk management, the increased role played by nonbank financial institutions in capital markets around the world, and the much greater integration of national financial systems...provide substantial benefits to the financial system....These changes have contributed to a substantial improvement in the financial strength of the core financial intermediaries and in the overall flexibility and resilience of the financial system in the United States. And these improvements in the stability of the system and efficiency of the process of financial intermediation have probably contributed to the acceleration in productivity growth in the United States and in the increased stability in growth outcomes experienced over the past two decades.'

the financial sector.[14] This confidence reflected a generally shared belief that the extent of systemic risk was quite modest. While banks have inherently fragile capital structures, it was thought that both their overall risk-taking and their propensity for contagion could be managed effectively by microprudential regulation such as capital adequacy rules, which focused on ensuring the safety and soundness of individual financial firms, and by the backstop of deposit insurance and resort to lender of last resort ('LOLR') facilities. It was also believed that the growth of linkages between banks and markets served to spread risk and thereby reduce the propensity for contagion. In particular, it was thought that the 'originate and distribute' model associated with securitization had led banks to shed risk, that credit derivatives had led banks to reduce risk through hedging, and that the result was stronger banking institutions and, incidentally, a more resilient financial sector. It was also due in part to the apparent success of central bankers over the prior two decades in taming macroeconomic volatility, a period now known as the 'Great Moderation'.[15]

The tumult of 2008–9 put paid to these beliefs. Regulators and policy analysts suddenly became focused on the fact that financial crises had been a ubiquitous feature of financial history.[16] Previously, standard economic models regarded finance as a 'veil', not an independent source of risk.[17] Now attention turned to out-of-the-mainstream models that emphasized the risks of increasing levels of debt and leverage in households and financial institutions in creating financial instability, and further, to the claim that capitalist financial systems have a strongly procyclical bias that can produce highly disruptive breaks.[18] The new wisdom is that 'financial cycles' of credit and leverage are perhaps no less important to economic well-being than the business cycle.[19] These can be described as the *time-series* component of macroprudential risks.[20]

Historically, a precondition for financial crises has been a credit-fuelled asset boom, which causes widespread damage to financial institutions, and thereby to the financial system, when it collapses. Such a build-up of aggregate risk is well illustrated by the residential real estate that figured so prominently in the crisis. The short-term supply of residential real estate is fixed. So a credit expansion, whether through monetary policy or financial liberalization, increases demand for the asset—and consequently its price.

[14] BS Bernanke, *The Courage to Act: A Memoir of the Crisis and its Aftermath* (New York, NY: WW Norton & Co, 2015), 134–5 (Congressional testimony in March 2007 that 'the impact on the broader economy and financial markets in the problem in the subprime market seems likely to be contained'. This proved to be wrong 'because we did not take into account the possibility that losses on subprime mortgages could ultimately destabilize both the U.S. and global financial system').

[15] BS Bernanke, 'The Great Moderation', Remarks by Governor Ben S Bernanke at the Meetings of the Eastern Economic Association, Washington DC, 20 February 2004.

[16] C Kindleberger, *Manias, Panics, and Crashes* (New York, NY: Basic Books, 1978); Reinhart and Rogoff, n 1.

[17] See Elliott, Feldberg, and Lehnert, n 7.

[18] See H Minsky, *Stabilizing an Unstable Economy* (New York, NY: McGraw-Hill, 2008) (first published in 1986); H Minsky, *Can 'It' Happen Again? Essays on Instability and Finance* (Armonk: ME Sharpe, 1982). For further references, see JN Gordon and C Muller, 'Confronting Financial Crisis: Dodd–Frank's Dangers and the Case for a Systemic Emergency Insurance Fund' (2011) 28 *Yale Journal on Regulation* 149, 164–6.

[19] C Borio, 'The Financial Cycle and Macroeconomics: What Have We Learnt?' (2014) 45 *Journal of Banking & Finance* 182.

[20] See sources cited in n 5.

For residential real estate, price increases may paradoxically stimulate demand, as prospective buyers now queue up for properties that will meet their housing needs before prices escalate further. In an environment of rising prices, banks' assessment of the risk of loss in residential mortgage lending declines, even on a default, since mortgage loans are secured by houses that are appreciating in value. As the rate of house price growth increases, banks become willing to lend to increasingly marginal borrowers.[21] This further credit expansion in turn spurs demand and thus prices. Households may extract some of the appreciation of their homes' value through taking on debt secured by the property—'home equity loans'. Eventually, parties discover that assets are overvalued relative to the non-financial sector cash flows on which their value depends. For example, banks discover that because wages have not increased, borrowers cannot make mortgage payments, home-owners cannot repay home equity loans, and flat or declining real estate prices mean that they cannot borrow additional funds to fund loan repayments. The default rate goes up; asset values decline. Collateral is insufficient to cover the losses and collateral sales further depress asset prices—a spiral that may result in the impairment of bank capital. The damaged banks begin to ration credit, which reduces the demand for housing and thus further reduces housing prices. This is the stylized story that was an essential element of the financial crisis.

The link between housing price growth and the financial crisis was no coincidence. Bank exposure to residential real estate crashes—following booms—has been a near-universal trigger for banking crises. Real estate has high unit costs, making credit finance for its purchase ubiquitous. It is also an asset class sought by a large number of purchasers, owing to its value for consumption as well as investment. This means it is capable of attracting very large volumes of credit financing. The collapse of a *credit-fuelled* boom can produce a crisis across the system, not just the failure of a single bank or a small group.[22] The systemic distress resides in the fact that damaged credit institutions are then unable to continue to supply finance to the economy. Compare, for example, the 'dot.com' sector stock market bubble at the end of the twentieth century. Its collapse may have triggered a recession but not a financial crisis, because stock purchases on credit had been limited.[23] These factors help to explain the observed link between real estate booms and financial crises.

The real estate boom of the early 2000s that led up to the financial crisis was particularly large in historical terms.[24] It was exacerbated by financial innovation, which increased the supply of credit and thus fed the boom. The US housing boom was fed by the expansion of 'securitization', a mechanism for market-based housing

---

[21] The quality of a mortgage loan from the bank's perspective is a combined function of the borrower's ability to repay (captured by the ratio of the loan amount to the borrower's income: 'LTI' or 'DTI') and the ability of the bank to obtain repayment from repossession and sale of the mortgaged property (captured by the ratio of the loan amount to the value of the house: 'LTV'). If housing prices are rising, then a higher LTV at the outset of the loan will be tolerated. And if housing price inflation outstrips wage inflation, then property values will be likely to dominate borrower incomes in the lenders' analysis.

[22] Reinhart and Rogoff, n 1, 158–62.

[23] The need to control lending on 'margin' was one of the grim lessons of the 1929 stock market collapse. Indeed, the Federal Reserve's control over margin lending can be understood as an early macroprudential measure, introduced in response to the Great Depression.

[24] See eg R Shiller, *Irrational Exuberance*, 2nd ed (Princeton, NJ: Princeton UP, 2005), 11–25.

finance that expanded the pool of funds available for housing finance by the creation of an asset class of very safe (AAA) but yield-attractive debt securities.[25] One of the purported 'safety' strategies was the packaging of mortgages from (different) local markets into mortgage-backed securities, in order to reduce risk through diversification. The strategy proved to be self-undermining. Securitization created a national market in real estate. The additional finance was disseminated to real estate markets throughout the US; thus the idiosyncratic nature of local real estate markets was lost, and with it, much of the diversification that had been critical to the securities' design.

Securitization was heralded as an alternative to bank finance of housing, because while the bank may have *originated* the mortgage, it had *distributed* the credit risk to other risk bearers. It turned out that the securitization vehicles had received private LOLR protection from the banks ('liquidity puts') and other implicit guarantees, which meant that credit risk had been only partially, if at all, offloaded. Moreover, much of the credit expansion to real estate finance was carried out outside the official banking system, by 'non-bank banks' that used short-term wholesale funding to finance long-term assets. As mortgage defaults increased, short-term funders fled. The credit-fuelled real estate bubble ended in widespread financial distress.

The *procyclical* effects of credit bubbles undercut traditional microprudential regulatory approaches. Take capital adequacy rules, for example. In a risk-weighted capital adequacy framework, the capital charge associated with loans depends on their credit rating. This in turn is a function of their riskiness, including factors such as the probability of default and the lenders' expected loss given default. In an economic upturn, the probability that borrowers will default is relatively low. To the extent that the relevant risk-weighting tracks recent experience, capital requirements will systematically *under-charge* during periods of growth.[26] Similarly, asset booms understate the 'embedded' leverage on financial firms' balance sheets. Leverage is a function of a firm's debt-to-asset ratio; yet those assets 'embed' risks associated with the *borrower's* leverage in the bank's balance sheet, which are not shown in a simple snapshot of their value. In other words, loans made to borrowers who are themselves highly leveraged generate risk measures that understate the true build-up of risk in the system. The paradox is this: at the moment when traditional microprudential measures are flashing green, the dangers of financial instability loom just over the horizon.[27] The temptation to believe that 'this time is different' will reach regulators as well, in part because political actors, who are subject to the short-termist pressures of the electoral cycle, will celebrate the boom and are likely to be opposed to measures that could undermine it.

---

[25] We explain securitization in more detail in Chapter 20, section 20.4 and Chapter 21, section 21.3.

[26] See eg A Taylor and C Goodhart, 'Procyclicality and Volatility in the Financial System: The Implementation of Basel II and IAS 39', in S Gerlach and P Gruenwald (eds), *Procyclicality of Financial Systems in Asia* (New York, NY: IMF, 2006), 9 at 11–14; FSF, Report on the Financial Stability Forum on Addressing Procyclicality in the Financial System (2009), 11–12.

[27] C Borio, 'Implementing a Macroprudential Framework: Blending Boldness and Realism' (2011) 6 *Capitalism and Society* 1.

19.3 The Evolution of Macroprudential Tools

19.3.1 Basel III measures: 'microprudential plus'

Following the financial crisis, the Basel Committee for Banking Supervision was (rightly) concerned that the existing Basel II framework had failed to provide sufficient protection for the financial system, and had even operated in a procyclical fashion to encourage the build-up of aggregate risk during periods of credit expansion. In conjunction with the Financial Stability Forum (which soon became the Financial Stability Board, or 'FSB') they produced proposals for new measures to combat systemic risk introduced as part of Basel III,[28] discussed in detail in Chapters 14 and 15. These measures, which encompass both time-varying and cross-sectional components,[29] adapt and enhance microprudential tools. For this reason, we term this body of requirements 'microprudential plus'.

The Basel III measures employ traditional microprudential tools: balance sheet requirements for banks. This begs a fundamental question about how micro and macro prudential measures are to be distinguished. We take *microprudential* measures to be primarily aimed at investor (or 'depositor' or 'consumer') protection through controlling agency costs at financial firms, and *macroprudential* measures to be primarily aimed at the protection of the stability of the financial system as a whole. Of course, many traditional microprudential tools such as capital adequacy requirements help to mitigate systemic risk and preserve financial stability. Although such requirements are in style microprudential, in that they operate to reduce the risk of failure of individual firms, they yield macroprudential benefits by also reducing consequent risks of contagion and loss of capacity in the financial sector. There is thus an overlap between measures targeting investor protection (micro) and those targeting systemic risk (macro) in the field of traditional banking regulation.

Regulators' mistake prior to the crisis was not to assume that microprudential measures were *necessary* for ensuring financial stability—they surely are—but rather to assume that pre-crisis microprudential measures were, by themselves, *sufficient* to do so. Seen in this light, the core components of the Basel III regime—the heightened capital requirements, the additional leverage requirement, the more robust liquidity requirements, and the paired net stable funding requirement—are all measures relevant both to the microprudential concern of protecting investors in these particular firms and the macroprudential concern of mitigating systemic risk. They thus serve to enhance the financial system's resilience, as compared to its pre-crisis state. These measures are cross-sectional in orientation, a kind of extra steel added to the superstructure of the financial system to protect against earthquakes.[30]

---

[28] FSF, Recommendations for Addressing Procyclicality in the Financial System (2009); FSB/IMF/BIS, n 5, 5–6.

[29] See D Tarullo, 'Advancing Macroprudential Policy Objectives' (Federal Reserve Board, 30 January 2015) (at the time of this speech, Governor Tarullo was the Federal Reserve's leader on regulatory reform).

[30] This is so regardless of whether one characterizes these additional requirements as primarily oriented towards investor protection or systemic risk. There is, however, a good case for seeing them as the latter, because the potential systemic externalities from the financial crisis (as proxied by governments' willingness

The concern with systemic risk becomes even clearer in the context of the additional capital requirements imposed on Global Systemically Important Banks ('G-SIBs'). These impose capital surcharges of between 1 and 2.5 per cent of risk-weighted assets assessed on several tests of the potential contribution of the institution to systemic risk.[31] Similarly, national regulators are encouraged to apply additional core tier 1 equity capital ('CET1') requirements on Domestic Systemically Important Banks ('D-SIBs').[32] Again, these operate to reduce the risk of failure of individual firms, but their being targeted at systemically important institutions makes clear that their rationale is concerned with systemic externalities. A similar analysis could also be used in relation to other enhancements to bank regulation justified primarily on the basis of systemic risk—namely, bank resolution (Chapter 16) and bank governance (Chapter 17).

The Basel III reforms also introduce expressly 'time-varying' aspects of traditional microprudential requirements. These are expressly motivated by systemic risk, in particular, the concern that the Basel II requirements generated perverse procyclical incentives on the part of regulated firms. Thus, the capital requirements of Basel III, discussed in Chapter 14, section 14.5, include a 'countercyclical buffer', consisting of additional CET1 capital for banks that would be built up in flush times of credit expansion to be available for loss absorbency or credit expansion in the down part of the cycle. The current approach is to leave to home country supervisors the decisions about how much additional capital to require—up to 2.5 per cent—and similarly to give supervisors discretion as to when to release the requirement.[33]

Similar in spirit is the 'capital conservation buffer'. This is an additional capital buffer of 2.5 per cent of risk-weighted assets applied to systemically important firms. In contrast to ordinary capital adequacy requirements, however, a failure to maintain the capital conservation buffer will not attract an instruction from the regulator to repair the bank's balance sheet. Rather, the only consequence of impairment is to prohibit the bank from paying dividends, repurchasing its shares, or paying equity-related compensation until the capital conservation buffer has been replenished. The idea is that this fluctuating buffer will reduce the need for banks to improve their capital positions in the down part of the economic cycle—commonly addressed through reduced lending and balance sheet shrinking—and thus mitigate the procyclicality of an increased capital requirement.[34]

---

to engage in bail-outs to avoid them) far exceeded the extent of investor losses from the crisis. See J Armour and JN Gordon, 'Systemic Harms and Shareholder Value' (2014) 6 *Journal of Legal Analysis* 35, 43.

[31] The agreed list of G-SIBs is maintained by the FSB. See FSB, *2015 Update of List of Global Systemically Important Banks (G-SIBs)* (2015).

[32] BIS/BCBS, *A Framework for Dealing with Domestic Systemically Important Banks—Final Document*, bcbs233 (2012). This is implemented in the EU through the Capital Requirements Directive IV: see Directive 2013/36/EU [2013] OJ L176/338, Art 133.

[33] See generally, BCBS, *Basel III: A Global Regulatory Framework for More Resilient Banks and Banking Systems*, paras 136–45, 150 (rev. June 2011).

[34] Many are sceptical that countercyclical buffers or capital conservation buffers will work on the downside of the cycle. At a time when losses are mounting and market scepticism is growing, how likely is it that regulators will *encourage* banks to cut back on capital? Moreover, the experience of the financial crisis was that banks with relatively low levels of equity capital found this harmed their terms of trade—a market-driven *de facto* capital requirement. Indeed, a study by World Bank economists reports that the availability of such measures is if anything associated with higher levels of asset contraction during downturns:

The rapid implementation of Basel III around the world means that its requirements form a 'common core' of global MacroPru measures. However, because they are built on microprudential foundations, these measures share core limitations of pre-crisis financial regulation, in that their scope of application is limited to banking institutions, and their mechanisms are limited to general restrictions on bank balance sheets. Some believe that such 'microprudential plus' measures are inherently inadequate, because the collapse of a large asset bubble will trigger a tsunami that creates high correlation among risky asset classes that previously were thought to be diversified and thus will swamp firm-level protections. Thus they argue strenuously for a MacroPru approach that uses broader, more macroeconomic, tools.[35] As we shall see, national and regional authorities are simultaneously experimenting with a wide variety of other, more expansive MacroPru measures.[36] There is, however, a divergence of approach, with the US emphasizing measures responding to cross-sectional risks, and the EU experimenting more with additional time-varying measures.

19.3.2 Cross-sectional measures

To date, we can identify three significant ways in which cross-sectional MacroPru measures have been implemented by policymakers that extend beyond the Basel III framework. The first is a process of seeking to identify 'systemically important' financial institutions beyond banks. This responds to the concern, discussed in Chapters 20 to 22, that firms other than 'banks' might be sources of systemic risk. To the extent that such firms are identified as systemically important, the approach to date has been to treat them analogously to banks, by applying Basel III-type measures to them. This is useful only if such non-bank financial institutions ('NBFIs') generate systemic risk in similar ways to banks, which requires a case-by-case analysis. To the extent that they do not, then there is a concern that imposition of such cross-sectional requirements will be an expensive placebo.

Second, steps have been taken to address the incomplete and opaque risk transfer between systemically important financial institutions that characterized OTC derivative markets, discussed in Chapter 21. In particular, laws such as the US Dodd–Frank Act and the EU Market Infrastructure Regulation have mandated that, to the extent feasible, financial contracting should run through central clearing counterparties ('CCPs'), also known as 'financial market utilities'. Such CCPs will act as the counterparty to all buyers and sellers. This means, for example, that a failure of Bear Stearns would not lead to direct defaults on payments to other financial firms. But by concentrating risk in the CCP, this approach creates a new systemically important institution. It thereby implies that appropriately configured 'microprudential plus' measures—in this case heightened capital and margin requirements—should be

---

S Claessens, SR Ghosh, and R Mihet, 'Macro-Prudential Policies to Mitigate Financial System Vulnerabilities' (2013) 39 *Journal of International Money and Finance* 153.

[35] Borio, n 27.

[36] See eg ESRB, n 4; E Cerutti, S Claessens, and L Laeven, 'The Use and Effectiveness of Macroprudential Policies: New Evidence' (forthcoming 2016) 22 *Journal of Financial Stability*.

applied to CCPs to protect the resiliency of the financial sector. The *net* impact of this change on systemic risk therefore depends greatly on the incentives and capability of the CCP to control its risk-taking, given these measures.

Third, as we discuss in Chapter 23, policymakers on both sides of the Atlantic are experimenting with structural reforms to the banking sector with the express goal of mitigating systemic risk. The likely outcome of these measures is unclear. In particular, the propensity of structural separation of retail and investment banking to concentrate risks associated with domestic mortgage lending into retail banks, by reducing firm-level diversification, may potentially exacerbate, rather than reduce, the systemic risk concerns arising from these firms.

19.3.3 Time-varying measures

As discussed in section 19.2, credit-fuelled asset booms have historically been import-ant triggers of financial crises. The challenge for regulators and policymakers is how to craft measures that are sufficiently forceful so as to prevent overheating in the relevant sector, yet at once sufficiently targeted so as to avoid harming growth in the economy at large. This can be illustrated by reference to monetary policy, a set of policy instru-ments wielded by central banks to control the money supply and thus the cost of credit. Monetary policy could in principle be used to control asset booms. Higher interest rates increase the cost of buying an asset with credit finance and thus reduce demand. It is, however, a blunt instrument. Higher interest rates apply across the board, thus creating contractionary pressure throughout the economy, not just the overheating sector. Monetary policy may suppress growth overall. Given the bluntness of monetary policy, regulators have looked for more targeted policy instruments.

As we have seen in section 19.3.1, two such measures have been made available to MPAs as part of Basel III, namely the capital conservation buffer and the counter-cyclical buffer. However, these measures were largely inspired by the need to counter-act the procyclical aspect of Basel II-style risk-weighted capital rules, which *exacerbated* credit booms. Thus, it is unlikely that they alone will be sufficient to prevent the growth of future credit-fuelled asset booms. Moreover, they apply across the board to all bank activity, not just particular asset classes. Historically and on a cross-country basis, a number of other potential instruments have been deployed.[37]

Much of the innovation to date has been with time-varying measures that aim to restrict bank lending into *particular types* of asset class. In keeping with the significance of real estate in triggering financial crises, most of these measures have been imple-mented in relation to that asset class. However, restrictions have in some cases also been applied to other types of lending that have the potential for feedback onto asset prices, for example margin borrowing for stock purchases, or lending to fund leveraged buyouts.

---

[37] See C Lim, F Columba, A Costa, P Kongsamut, A Otani, M Sayid, T Wezel, and X Wu, 'Macro-prudential Policy: What Instruments and How to Use Them? Lessons from Country Experiences', IMF Working Paper (2011); A Haldane, 'Macroprudential Policy in Prospect', in G Akerlof, O Blanchard, D Romer, and J Stiglitz, *What Have We Learned? Macroeconomic Policy After the Crisis* (Cambridge, MA: MIT Press, 2014), 65; Claessens, Ghosh, and Mihet, n 34; Elliott, Feldberg, and Lehnert, n 7.

Recent Examples of Targeted MacroPru Measures to Control Time-Series Systemic Risk

---

UK: housing prices. In the low-interest environment that has prevailed since the financial crisis, residential real estate prices have appreciated considerably. This growth has been particularly strong in the UK, where there have been constraints on the supply of new housing. The Financial Policy Committee ('FPC') has monitored this closely, concerned about the potential risks to financial stability posed by banks' direct exposure to these loans, and the economy's indirect exposure through high levels of household indebtedness.[38] In June 2014, the FPC made two recommendations designed to introduce modest brakes on house price appreciation.

(1) *Mortgage affordability tests.* UK mortgage lenders are required under the Financial Conduct Authority ('FCA')'s conduct of business rules to assess whether requested loans are 'affordable' by applicants. This is primarily framed as a consumer-protection measure. However, in conducting their affordability assessments, lenders are required to have regard to any FPC recommendation about appropriate interest rate stress tests.[39] In June 2014, the FPC recommended that lenders test affordability with a stress test based on a rise in interest rates of 3 per cent above the prevailing rate at origination, at any point during the first five years of the loan.

(2) *Loan-to-income ratios.* The FPC recommended to the Prudential Regulation Authority ('PRA') and the FCA that they should ensure that large mortgage lenders do not extend more than 15 per cent of their total number of new residential mortgages at loan-to-income ratios at or greater than 4.5.

The following year saw a modest reduction in house price growth and no further overall growth of UK household indebtedness. However, the FPC concluded that the effect of its recommendations had only been marginal. Based on previous lending patterns, only 3 per cent of mortgage advances, in aggregate, would have been affected, and in any event, large mortgage lenders had already introduced loan-to-income restrictions that were more stringent than those recommended by the FPC. However, this may understate the *indirect* effect of the FPC's intervention, because it is plausible that large banks sought to 'overcomply' in order to avoid the subsequent application of more stringent measures.

In April 2015, the FPC was given new powers of Direction over the PRA and FCA to set loan-to-value and debt-to-income limits in respect of owner-occupied mortgage lending.[40]

US: leveraged loans. US banking regulators became concerned with the volume of loans originated by banks to non-investment grade companies in the post-crisis period. Such originations had collapsed in 2009, but subsequently grew rapidly, spurred by low interest rates. In 2013, originations amounted to approximately $600 billion, exceeding the 2007 peak. These loans typically went to companies engaging in leveraged buyouts or recapitalizations; the loans typically were 'covenant lite', offering minimal protections to creditors so long as payments were made.[41] The originating banks would transfer most of the credit risk in secondary markets to other banks and non-bank institutional investors. Concerned about

---

[38] FPC, 'Statement on Housing Market Powers of Direction from its Policy Meeting, 26 September 2014', 2 October 2014, 2–3.

[39] FCA Handbook, MCOB 11.6.18(2).

[40] See Bank of England, *Financial Stability Report July 2015* (2015), 23–6.

[41] This is another example of the 'embedded leverage' referred to in the case of residential mortgages in an asset booms, *supra* text accompanying nn 26–7.

the build-up of risk within the financial sector, the regulators issued 'Guidance' with respect to such loans, establishing procedural and substantive standards for origination.[42] In particular, banks were cautioned about making loans that were too highly leveraged—where the debt would be equal to or exceed 6x the operating cash flow ('EBITDA' or earnings before interest, taxes, depreciation, and amortization)—and without sufficient covenant protection. Before the crisis, 'hot' leveraged buyout markets produced leverage ratios of 7x or 8x EBITDA. The goal was plainly macroprudential—protecting not just the banking sector, but also the financial sector as a whole, against what to regulators appeared to be a boom in speculative grade credit. The jury is still out on the intervention's success. There is conflicting evidence on subsequent levels of origination, and the extent to which (any) changes reflect regulatory intervention, as opposed to market conditions. In 2014 the regulators expressed uncertainty, noting that over 45 per cent of new originations had leverage greater than 6x EBITDA, including 15 per cent with leverage ratios of 8x or higher.[43] There is evidence of greater recent determination by the regulators to reduce leveraged lending.[44] US regulators have also served notice of their determination to cool down lending to the commercial real-estate market.[45]

The way in which such restrictions can be crafted with progressive degrees of intensity can be illustrated by reference to residential real estate. The underlying idea is that credit-fuelled real estate growth can be constrained by limiting the most *marginal*, or risky, lending, as it is ordinarily activity at the margin that changes prices. 'Marginal', or 'risky', mortgage lending is calibrated by measures such as (i) loan-to-value ratio ('LTV')—the relationship between the value of the house offered as collateral and the loan secured upon it; and/or (ii) debt-service-to-income ('DTI') or loan-to-income ('LTI') ratio—the relationship between the sum borrowed and the income of the borrower.[46] This calibration can be used to apply tools such as—in progressive order of intensity—higher risk-weighted capital charges for lending to support particular types of more marginal lending, restrictions on the proportion of bank assets that may consist of marginal real estate loans, and outright prohibitions on bank lending for marginal real estate loans.

In principle, policy instruments targeting asset booms can be thought of as working on the 'supply side', affecting banks' willingness to lend, or the 'demand side', affecting borrowers' willingness (or capacity) to borrow. It is notable that all the measures so far

---

[42] See OCC/FRB/FDIC, 'Interagency Guidance on Leveraged Lending', 78 *Federal Register* 17766 (22 March 2013). See also Frequently Asked Questions for Implementing March 2013 Interagency Guidance on Leveraged Lending (7 November 2014). For discussion of the market, see Leveraged Loan, *Primer*, http:// www.leveragedloan.com/primer/#!definingleveraged; SE Kim, 'Managing Regulatory Blindspots: A Case Study of Leveraged Loans' (2015) *Yale Journal on Regulation* 89, 94–9.

[43] See OCC/FRB/FDIC, 'Shared National Credits Program: 2014 Review', available at http://www. federalreserve.gov/newsevents/press/bcreg/bcreg20141107a1.pdf; and 2014 Leverage Loan Supplement, available at https://www.fdic.gov/news/news/press/2014/pr14096b.pdf.

[44] See OCC/FRB/FDIC, 'Shared National Credits Program: 2015 Review', http://www.federalreserve. gov/newsevents/press/bcreg/bcreg20151105a1.pdf.

[45] Tracy Ryan, 'U.S. Banking Regulators Step Up Rhetoric on Commercial Real Estate Loans', *Wall Street Journal*, 18 December 2015.

[46] On the relationship with loan riskiness, see further n 21 and text thereto.

described apply only to the supply side, since they are almost exclusively mediated through restrictions imposed on banks subject to the relevant authority's jurisdiction.[47] Of course, such measures will be less effective to constrain credit-fuelled asset price growth than outright constraints on borrowers. Marginal borrowers unable to obtain finance from domestic banks may instead borrow from non-bank lenders, or from foreign banks.[48] For this reason one might think that a central lesson of the financial crisis—the growth of non-bank credit—has been missed by authorities in their design of time-varying targeted measures to date.[49]

However, there are political considerations in play regarding the non-extension of MacroPru measures to borrowers directly.[50] Measures restricting borrowers' access to credit in order to preserve systemic stability—'for the greater good'—are likely to be highly politically salient and—because they do not benefit the borrowers affected— highly unpopular. In contrast, measures affecting only lenders are likely to be less salient: from the standpoint of the borrower, the problem may (erroneously) appear to be the lender's refusal, as opposed to the regulator's imposition—a perspective that will be reinforced if borrowers are still able to access credit from non-bank sources.

19.3.4 Interaction with other regulatory and fiscal measures

At this point, it is worth noting that contiguous regulatory and fiscal measures may also affect asset booms. To date, such measures have not been deployed by any MPA in a time-varying way to control the build-up of asset booms. Rather, the relevant decisions have been made by other regulators, or politicians. However, MPAs at the very least need to understand the potential interactions, and ideally to be able to influence or direct the (timing of the) imposition of these measures.[51]

An example of a relevant regulatory measure is consumer protection rules applied to mortgage borrowing. Rules designed to 'protect' myopic consumers from financial institutions, discussed in Part C, can have the effect of restricting the aggregate supply of regulated financial products. The imposition of such restrictions in relation to mortgage lending can dampen demand for house prices by making it more difficult

---

[47] For example, as of June 2015, only one EU Member State had implemented any measure applying to non-bank entities (alternative investment funds in Ireland): ESRB, n 4, 24.

[48] See eg S Aiyar, CW Calomiris, and T Wieladek, 'Does Macro-Prudential Regulation Leak? Evidence from a UK Policy Experiment' (2014) 46 *Journal of Money Credit & Banking* 181.

[49] Note further that constraints applying only to banks will be hard for regulators to maintain in the face of escalating profits of non-bank lenders in the up-phase of an asset boom.

[50] Moreover, given our still-evolving understanding of systemic risk and the potential costs of overkill with MacroPru measures, MPAs' caution in relation to applying time-varying measures may be justified even in the absence of political considerations, at least for now. Historically, credit-fuelled asset booms have triggered financial crises via *banks' exposure* to them. Consequently, measures restricting *bank exposure* to the relevant asset class may reduce systemic risk even if the asset class continues to boom. This depends on whether exposure of non-bank lenders to the asset boom poses an independent threat to stability, and the efficacy of cross-sectional MacroPru measures in containing threats that do materialize.

[51] 'Influence' would be appropriate for fiscal measures imposed by politicians, or regulatory measures imposed by foreign regulators; 'direct' may be appropriate for measures imposed by domestic regulators. See eg Bank of England Act 1998 (UK), ss 9H, 9Q (FPC's power to give directions, and make recommendations, to FCA or PRA); Dodd–Frank Act of 2010 (UK) §1023 (FSOC's power to set aside regulations made by Consumer Financial Protection Bureau, if necessary for financial stability).

for borrowers to access credit. For example, in the UK, the FCA from April 2014 required all mortgage lenders (bank and non-bank) entering into such transactions with UK consumer borrowers to undertake a more stringent 'affordability' assessment in order to ensure that loans were not made to borrowers highly likely to be unable to repay.[52] While implemented primarily as a consumer protection measure, its introduction has coincided with a reduction in housing price growth.[53]

Serious attempts to mitigate the build-up of credit risk in the economy at large must also engage with a range of relevant fiscal measures.[54] For example, the tax deductibility of corporate interest payments creates an incentive to use debt, rather than equity, finance which arguably has undermined systemic stability by giving financial institutions strong incentives to remain as highly leveraged as possible.[55] Distortions between debt and equity could be removed by eliminating the tax deductibility of interest payments.[56] However, only a few countries, such as Belgium, have so far reduced the implicit subsidy that tax deductibility of interest provides for debt finance. Tax incentives are also highly relevant for growth in real estate prices. Homeowners generally do not pay capital gains tax on their primary residence.[57] In some countries, such as the US, they are able to deduct mortgage interest from their personal taxation. Property taxes, both on an annualized basis, and levied on sales ('stamp duty') are also likely to impact real estate prices. Again, there has to date been little movement to remove implicit subsidies or add costs to home ownership.

Nevertheless, a number of other tax-related measures have been introduced, particularly in the EU, with a view to moderating the systemically significant activities of banks. These include measures intended to increase the price of particular types of transactions thought to contribute to systemic disturbances.[58] An example of an attempt to implement such a measure is the EU's proposed financial transaction tax ('FTT').[59] This measure would apply a levy of between 0.01 and 0.1 per cent of transaction value to transactions in securities (or derivatives thereof) between financial institutions. The proposal has been immensely controversial, and has only been able to make progress

---

[52] See FSA, *Mortgage Market Review, Feedback on CP11/31 and final rules*, Policy Statement PS12/16 (2012).

[53] See eg L Warwick-Ching, 'Chart that Tells a Story—Mortgage Market Review', *Financial Times*, 24 April 2015. The measures were originally proposed by the then-FSA (before the creation of the FPC), which clearly understood them as also having implications for systemic stability. See FSA, *Mortgage Market Review*, Discussion Paper 09/3 (2009). While such measures are also politically salient, they are framed as being for borrowers' individual benefit, and so less obviously objectionable than measures explicitly restricting individuals' borrowing in the service of the greater good.

[54] See IMF, *Key Aspects of Macroprudential Policy* (2013), 9–13.

[55] See eg R de Mooij, 'Tax Biases to Debt Finance', IMF Staff Discussion Note, SDN/11/11 (2011).

[56] See eg A Admati and M Hellwig, *The Bankers' New Clothes: What's Wrong with Banking and What to Do About It* (Princeton, NJ: Princeton UP, 2013). See also the discussion in Chapter 14, section 14.6.

[57] This benefit is capped in the US at $250,000 of excludable gain for a single person; $500,000 for a married couple.

[58] The idea of such a tax has a long history, being first proposed in the early 1970s by Nobel laureate economist James Tobin in the context of currency transactions and exchange rate volatility: see J Tobin, *The New Economics One Decade Older* (Princeton, NJ: Princeton UP, 1974).

[59] European Commission, Proposal for a Council Directive implementing enhanced cooperation in the area of financial transaction tax, COM(2013) 71 final.

as an opt-in, rather than a mandatory measure.[60] A related fiscal initiative is a tax on systemically important institutions, such as the UK's bank levy.[61] This measure, introduced unilaterally from January 2011, imposes a charge (currently set at 0.21 per cent) on UK banks calculated by reference to the size of the firm's balance sheet minus its regulatory capital and insured deposits.

In theory, such measures could contribute usefully to the reduction of systemic risk. However, the calibration of such measures in order to balance systemic risk reduction goals against potential loss of capacity in the financial system and consequent harm to economic growth is an immensely complex task. It is regrettable, therefore, that the scope and calibration of these measures to date have been politically determined, rather than assessed by MPAs following a thorough process of information-gathering and analysis. Initial assessments suggest that the resulting measures are likely poorly calibrated to achieve MacroPru goals.[62]

19.4 The Challenges of MacroPru

It should be obvious from the discussion so far that the successful implementation of MacroPru measures entails significant challenges. First, the use of time-varying Macro-Pru tools requires very careful timing and targeting. To deploy these tools successfully, MPAs must identify the relevant build-up of risk—somehow distinguishing 'overheating' asset booms from a secular growth in demand—and then pick the tool that suppresses the boom without imposing constraints on other economic growth. These are non-trivial problems.[63] Perhaps for these reasons, the use of such tools has a mixed record. Analysis of the historic deployment of such tools in the US, and contemporary use across countries, suggests that such measures are more effective at tightening than easing credit, and have more effect on growth of consumer credit than bank credit.[64]

Second, cross-sectional MacroPru measures will raise the cost of credit intermediation in banks and other financial firms, by requiring targeted firms to internalize systemic stability costs. These costs in turn provide incentives to engage in credit intermediation through non-targeted firms, beyond the current regulatory perimeter. Not only will this weaken banks economically but it will also raise the risk of financial disruption for the real economy. If significant amounts of financial intermediation shift outside the official sector, a sturdy banking system may not be enough to save the real economy from systemic distress. For all the reasons that bank failures produce systemic harm by destroying credit channels, so could the failure of alternative credit providers.

---

[60] Even so, the FTT proposal attracted legal challenge on the basis of the breadth of its application to non-participating Member States. See European Council Legal Service Opinion on the legality of the counterparty-based deemed establishment of financial institutions, 2013/0045 (CNS), Brussels 6 Sept 2013; Case C-209/13, *UK v Council of the EU*, ECLI:EU:C:2014:283.

[61] Finance Act 2011 (UK), Sch 19 paras 6–7.

[62] See eg M Deveraux, N Johannesen, and J Vella, 'Can Taxes Tame the Banks? Evidence from European Bank Levies', Saïd Business School WP 2015-5 (2015).

[63] See William C Dudley, 'Is the Active Use of Macroprudential Tools Institutionally Realistic?' FRBNY, 3 October 2015.

[64] See Elliott, Feldberg, and Lehnert, n 7; Claessens, Ghosh, and Mihet, n 34.

Third, many MacroPru measures, especially sectorally targeted time-varying measures, are likely to come under attack by industry participants and politicians, for similar reasons. Both groups have shorter time horizons than the period over which systemic risk will build up and perhaps explode. For example, holding down the demand for housing will not be popular with the construction industry or tradespeople thinking about quarterly or yearly results. Actions that suppress 'growth' or make it harder for the benefits of home ownership to be widely shared will be opposed by politicians attentive to the electoral cycle. It will be the regulators' opinion that a threat is inexorably building, but the costs will be immediate, while the benefits of the individual measure in terms of systemic risk reduction are impossible to quantify. Indeed, the longer the regulators have produced financial stability, the less plausible will be the claim of necessity for stringent policy interventions.

19.5 New Macroprudential Institutions

One of the most important post-crisis financial regulatory reforms has been the creation of new MPAs, charged with identifying systemic risk and invoking or coordinating various macroprudential tools. This has occurred, amongst other places, in the US, the UK, and the EU.

In the US, the Dodd–Frank Act established the Financial Stability Oversight Council ('FSOC'). It is essentially an interagency 'apex committee', which coordinates among the heads of all the significant financial regulators and policymakers in the US. It is tasked with identifying and responding to threats to US financial stability, with a focus on the activities of systemically important banks and other financial institutions. Associated with this role, the FSOC has broad duties to monitor the financial system in order to identify potential threats to financial stability, and is assisted by a new information-gathering unit, the Office of Financial Research ('OFR'), based in the Treasury Department. The FSOC plays an important role in observing the migration of financial activity beyond the regulatory perimeter. In particular, it can designate a non-bank financial institution as 'systemically important' and thus bring the institution within the prudential oversight of the Federal Reserve Board.[65]

In the UK, a new Financial Policy Committee ('FPC') was established at the Bank of England. This was clearly modelled on the existing Monetary Policy Committee ('MPC'), which has responsibility for setting interest rates. The FPC has responsibility for identifying, monitoring, and controlling systemic risks to the UK financial system.[66] In contrast to the US FSOC, the FPC is not simply an interagency coordination council, but draws heavily on the expertise of the Bank itself (through the Governor and Deputy Governors) as well as the expert external members in formulating and setting policy. Similarly, at the EU level, the European Systemic Risk Board ('ESRB') was established

---

[65] However, the FSOC's remit is essentially only what we have here termed cross-sectional measures. The application of time-varying MacroPru measures—so far, meaning only those tools contained in Basel III—is the preserve of the banking regulators. See Chapter 27, section 27.3.

[66] Bank of England Act 1998 s 9C.

in December 2010 with responsibility for macroprudential oversight and the control of systemic risk within the EU financial system.[67]

These institutions help address some of the barriers to effective macroprudential policy by creating entities with some political insulation specifically charged with a financial stability mandate. The new institutions have a singular financial stability mission. This gives them incentives to use their information-gathering and analysis powers to identify emerging systemic risks and their operational powers to mitigate such risks. They are described in more detail in Chapter 27, section 27.3.

19.6 Information Gathering and Analysis

The ideal of MacroPru implies a decision-maker at the apex of the financial system, having an overview of everything that is going on, and making adjustments accordingly. This is nearly impossible in practice. But it yields a clear policy implication: the more information possessed by an MPA, and the better their processing capability, the better their chances of being able to make effective macroprudential policy.[68]

Wide-ranging data-gathering is only the first step to providing effective MacroPru oversight. The data must then be analysed in a meaningful way. A real problem here is the tendency for analytic work to be influenced by consultancy reports commissioned by deep-pocketed financial institutions. As we saw in Chapter 4, section 4.2, global financial institutions have vastly more resources at their disposal than even the best-resourced regulators. And global financial institutions have a breadth of understanding of interconnections around the world that the most outward-looking of domestic regulators cannot match.

19.6.1 Information gathering

The principal channel through which the new MPAs receive information is via the various agencies represented in their meetings. MPA meetings provide obvious opportunities for information-sharing amongst the regulatory agencies represented. In addition, the UK's FPC and the EU's FSRB are given powers to require represented agencies to provide them with any information needed in the pursuance of their functions.[69] And the US FSOC is subject to a duty to collect and share information between the represented agencies.[70]

This approach makes efficient use of data-collection capacities possessed by existing agencies. But its limitations are likewise a function of the scope of such authorities, which as we have seen were shown to be incomplete by the financial crisis. An important initiative responding to this limitation has been the establishment in the US of the OFR, specifically tasked with gathering aggregate data about the financial

---

[67] Regulation (EU) 1092/2010, Art 3(1).
[68] See generally, FSB/IMF, The Financial Crisis and Information Gaps: Report to the G20 Finance Ministers and Central Bank Governors (2009).
[69] Bank of England Act 1998 (UK) s 9Y (PRA and FCA); Regulation (EU) 1092/2010, Art 15.
[70] Dodd–Frank Act §112(a)(2)(A).

system. Another step forward is the introduction of confidential reporting obligations for a wide set of financial firms not previously obliged to disclose anything. These are rules requiring financial firms to report to domestic market regulators (not to MPAs directly) about various aspects of their balance sheet and business activity, with a view to facilitating effective monitoring of potential systemic risk. For example, such rules have been introduced in relation to alternative investment funds in both the EU and the US.[71] They are an attempt to meet regulators' need to have appropriate information, while preserving the competitive advantage of individual firms as regards their investment strategies.

The MPAs also have powers to require the provision of information that they deem necessary for the performance of their oversight functions. Thus, the US FSOC may require the submission of periodic reports directly from any bank holding company or non-bank financial company in order to determine whether or not the firm in question is a threat to financial stability.[72] The EU's ESRB does not have power to compel the production of information from financial firms directly, but instead has the ability to do so indirectly, by compelling represented agencies, central banks, or even Member States to gather the necessary information.[73] Similarly, the UK's FPC has power to ask the FCA or PRA to collect any relevant information from a private firm that the agency in question has power to require.[74]

19.6.2 Analysis

MPAs are employing a variety of different techniques to seek to measure and monitor systemic risk.[75] An important advance is the concept of conditional value at risk ('CoVar'), which looks at the contribution of an individual institution's risk to systemic risk.[76] There are attempts to introduce financial sectors into macroeconomic models including dynamic stochastic general equilibrium models,[77] and there are empirical analyses of the effects of macroprudential regulation on systemic stability.[78] Similarly, there are efforts to quantify the systemic risk contributed by specific institutions as well as the global financial system as a whole.[79] In addition, MPAs and central banks have strengthened their monitoring of vulnerabilities of financial systems, in particular in regard to systematically important financial institutions ('SIFIs'),

---

[71] See Chapter 22, sections 22.2.2 and 22.2.3.   [72] Dodd–Frank Act §112(a)(2)(B).
[73] Regulation (EU) 1092/2010, Art 15(5).   [74] Bank of England Act 1998, s 9Y(3).
[75] See eg D Bisias, M Flood, A Lo, and S Valavanis, 'A Survey of Systemic Risk Analytics', (2012) 4 *Annual Review of Financial Economics* 255.
[76] See eg MA Segoviano and C Goodhart, 'Banking Stability Measures', IMF Working Paper WP/09/4 (2009); T Adrian and MK Brunnermeier, 'CoVaR', NBER Working Paper 17454 (2011).
[77] See eg C Borio and H Zhu, 'Capital Regulation, Risk-Taking and Monetary Policy: A Missing Link in the Transmission Mechanism?' (2012) 8 *Journal of Financial Stability* 236; M Brunnermeier and Y Sannikov, 'A Macroeconomic Model with a Financial Sector' (2014) 104 *American Economic Review* 379.
[78] See eg C Gauthier, A Lehar, and M Souissi, 'Macroprudential Capital Requirements and Systemic Risk' (2012) 21 *Journal of Financial Intermediation* 594.
[79] See VV Acharya, LH Pedersen, T Philippon, and M Richardson, 'Measuring Systemic Risk', CEPR (2012). See also the NYU Stern Global Systemic Risk Rankings (updated periodically), http://vlab.stern.nyu.edu/analysis/RISK.WORLDFIN-MR.GMES.

shadow banking, asset markets, and the non-financial sector.[80] Various tools are used to provide early warning of impending financial crises. Models of crises have been developed that link together measures of financial fragility and the costs of financial failures in terms of bail-outs to such variables as GDP, real exchange rates, interest rates, capital flows, and trade flows.[81] The idea behind these models is to see whether there are systematic patterns behind past failures that could be used to predict the incidence of future failures.

A particularly significant methodological innovation has been the use of what have

---

Stress Testing in Action

Following pioneering work by the US Federal Reserve in implementing the requirements of the Dodd–Frank Act,[82] stress tests have become a key analytic tool used for the setting of time-varying capital requirements in relation to banks. The Fed's stress test consists of 'simultaneous, forward-looking projections of potential losses and revenues based on each bank's portfolio and circumstances' in response to supervisory models of 'sharp deterioration in economic and financial conditions'.[83] The loss estimates 'are used to project post-stress capital levels and ratios' under these adverse conditions.[84] A bank is required to restrain share buybacks or dividends—a measure similar to the imposition of a capital conservation buffer, but targeted at individual firms, rather than all banks—if the stress test shows that its capital levels would fall short of regulatory benchmarks in the stressed environment. Thus, the stress test aims to assure that in response to a general economic shock (for example, a sudden fall in housing prices) or a shock specific to the financial system (such as failure of a major institution), individual banks and the banking system as a whole would have sufficient resiliency to continue to lend to households and businesses. Thus far, the Fed has used stress test results to recalibrate balance sheet protections that would otherwise be required under the Basel III regime, in particular to require additional capital—a microprudential approach to MacroPru. For further discussion of stress tests as interacting with the Basel framework, see Chapter 14, section 14.4.4.

---

come to be known as 'stress tests'.[85] This is a technique for assessing the resilience of a particular institution, financial contract, or market sector to an exogenous shock. At its core, it is a simulation of outcomes given a hypothetical—but imaginable—set of parameters. By running a series of such tests using progressively more restrictive parameters,

---

[80] See T Adrian, D Covitz, and N Liang, 'Financial Stability Monitoring', Finance and Economics Discussion Series, Federal Reserve Board, Washington DC (2013).

[81] See eg J Bell and D Pain, 'Leading Indicator Models of Banking Crises—A Critical Review' (2000) 9 *Financial Stability Review* 113; C Borio and M Drehmann, 'Assessing the Risk of Banking Crises Revisited' (2009) *BIS Quarterly Review* 29; EP Davis and D Karim, 'Comparing Early Warning Systems for Banking Crises' (2008) 4 *Journal of Financial Stability* 89.

[82] See Dodd–Frank Act §165(i). Stress tests have gained international acceptance as an important supervisory tool in the post-crisis era. See eg BIS, Peer Review of Supervisory Authorities' Implementation of Stress Testing Principle (Basel, April 2012).

[83] D Tarullo, 'Stress Testing After Five Years', Federal Reserve Board (25 June 2014). Tarullo is an enthusiast of the stress test: 'The opportunities it provides to incorporate macroprudential elements make it, in my judgment, the single most important advance in prudential regulation since the crisis.'

[84] Ibid.

[85] See generally, TF Geithner, *Stress Test: Reflections on Financial Crises* (New York, NY: Crown, 2014).

policymakers can rapidly get an appreciation for the resilience—or fragility—of the firm, contract, or sector in question to changes in a particular variable.[86] The benefit of this approach is that it is tailored to the actual contours of the financial system. Like the use of simulations generally, it does not require a comprehensive theorization of linkages in order to predict outcomes—the policymaker simply 'sees what would happen'. Moreover, stress tests using data from all major banks simultaneously allow regulators to understand how particular risk(s) might affect the banking system as a whole.[87]

The limitations of stress testing are the flipside of its benefits. Because it is based on simulation, it only provides guidance as to outcomes emerging under the specified parameters. Policymakers do not have the resources to test every possible parameter shift, and so the usefulness of the results depends very much on the appropriateness of the parameter selection. This is an art, not a science, being based on regulators' perceptions of what sorts of changes may cause problems. This in turn is likely to be shaped by their prior experience. It follows that stress tests may be expected to be most useful in providing guidance to regulators about how to mitigate a realized systemic risk—the relevant parameters of which will be known—as opposed to providing early warnings of as-yet-unexpected vulnerabilities.[88] Moreover, stress tests thus far have led to microprudential measures, such as requiring more capital to cover higher-than-expected loan write-offs in an adverse scenario or value declines in interest-rate sensitive assets from an interest rate shock. Stress tests have not so far played a large role in the 'macro tools' side of MacroPru.

19.7 Conclusion

Four principal conclusions emerge from this and previous chapters in Part D of the book. The first is that the design of macroprudential measures to provide stability to the financial system as a whole is distinct from, albeit related to, the protection and regulation of individual institutions. Microprudential regulation alone does not sufficiently ensure systemic protection and, as was illustrated by procyclicality in Basel II, can give rise to unintended and undesirable systemic consequences.

Second, the financial system has to be considered as an integrated whole with cross-linkages and interrelations that can create feedback effects that are quite different from those observed at the level of individual institutions. We will develop this theme in Part E of the book—the next four chapters—by observing the growth of 'shadow banking' and the emergence of financial transactions outside the formal regulated sectors, 'non-bank financial intermediation', more generally. These developments are in part a consequence of regulation but they equally have significant implications for the design of regulation. It means that systemic stability has to encompass activities outside as well as within the

---

[86] See eg Bank of England, Stress Testing the UK Banking System: Key Elements of the 2015 Stress Test (2015).
[87] B Bernanke, 'Stress Testing Banks', Federal Reserve Board (8 April 2013).
[88] C Borio, M Drehmann, and K Tsatsaronis, 'Stress-Testing Macro Stress Testing: Does it Live Up to Expectations?' (2012) 12 *Journal of Financial Stability* 3.

formal banking system. A failure to do so is like providing public health management in one part of a town without taking account of the risks of infection in other parts.

Third, this reinforces one of the main messages of the book, that financial regulation should be considered on a functional rather than an institutional basis. By encouraging the emergence of activities in institutions that are regulated in different ways, an institutional approach leads to a blinkered view of the consequences and effects of regulation. However, systemic interrelations are not restricted to similar activities and both the time-series and the cross-sectional modelling discussed in this chapter have to be considered at a broad systemic, rather than a narrow sectoral or institutional, level. This is particularly important for the scope of application of MacroPru tools, which, as we saw in section 19.3, are still heavily focused on banks.

Fourth, contagion does not stop at national boundaries. The financial system has to be regulated as a globally integrated whole. This requires a high degree of international coordination and cooperation to ensure that information is transmitted between regulators, that there is consistency in approach to prevent the emergence of systemic problems, and that remedial action does not have unanticipated cross-border effects. We return to questions of regulatory architecture and international financial regulatory coordination in Part F of the book. Suffice it to say here that in the absence of effective international coordination to oversee, manage, and correct systemic disturbances, the prevention of future crises will prove extremely difficult. Political and economic interests differ across countries, and the response of uncoordinated national regulatory bodies to crises with significant domestic ramifications is hard to predict in advance.

This is exemplified by the considerable variation across systems in what MPAs are asked to do. In the US, the primary focus of the FSOC is on cross-sectional measures to reduce contagion. In contrast, EU MPAs have been more oriented towards the application of time-varying measures. To some degree this difference of function is complemented by differences in the way the MPAs are structured. The FSOC is an interagency body with a strong political steer from its chair, the Treasury Secretary. This would seem a well-suited composition for work on projects that require the reconfiguration of existing regulatory boundaries and measures. In contrast, European MPAs such as the FPC are more detached from politicians, which is probably helpful in making hard choices about the application of time-varying measures calculated to reduce the build-up of systemic risk. At the same time, a number of important cross-sectional measures in the EU—such as bank resolution mechanisms—have been taken forward by political processes running in parallel with the establishment of MPAs.

There remains a need for more effort in identifying and avoiding unintended adverse consequences for systemic risk of well-meaning regulatory interventions. Institutionally, this requires MPAs to devote resources to considering the interaction between MacroPru and other regulatory and fiscal measures. And conceptually, it implies a clear identification of systemic stability as the 'senior' goal of financial regulation, capable of trumping the pursuit of others where there is conflict. While considerable progress has been made in identifying this problem, work to solve it has been compromised by the fact that since the financial crisis a vast number of regulatory changes have been implemented largely in parallel, often motivated by political considerations. There is considerable potential for unintended consequences, as illustrated by the uncertainty over the merits of structural regulation, discussed in Chapter 23.

PART E

MARKETS AND BANKS

20

Market-Based Credit Intermediation

Shadow Banks and Systemic Risk

20.1 Introduction

So far, much of our account of financial regulation has tracked the traditional distinction between securities regulation and bank regulation, in Parts B and D respectively. In broad outline, these regulatory systems pursue different strategies: disclosure is at the core of securities regulation, whereas prudential oversight is at the core of banking regulation. (Indeed, we saw the segue from one of these strategies to the other in Part C.) This regulatory difference maps onto what has been taken to be the central function of each regime. The canonical financial claim of securities regulation is *equity*, which gives the holder a proportionate share of the firm's business success. The value of equity depends upon the profitability of the issuing firm and is assessed over time through trading in secondary markets, which provide the means for value realization. Disclosure of the firm's performance is thus central to the determination of value, both upon the initial public offering of the claim and in its subsequent trading. By contrast, the canonical claim of banking regulation is the *deposit*, issued by a bank and redeemable by that bank. The value of a deposit is designed to be invariant: a sum certain. The regulatory task, then, is taken to be the protection of the deposit claim, which requires prudential oversight of the risk-taking and balance sheet of the bank.[1]

One of the most salient developments over the past fifty years has been the growth of 'market-based credit intermediation'. By this we mean the use of securities markets to provide debt financing for firms and households, which would otherwise have been supplied by banks. The phenomenon has been particularly strong in the US,[2] but a similar trend has also been evident in the EU.[3] Indeed, the most recent FSB report on the largest economies indicates that non-bank financial intermediaries now hold $137 trillion in assets, approximately 40 per cent of total financial system assets in the

---

[1] See B Holmstrom, 'Understanding the Role of Debt in the Financial System', BIS Working Paper No 479 (2015); see also K Judge, 'Information Gaps and Shadow Banking', Working Paper Columbia Law School (2015).

[2] F Edwards and F Mishkin, 'The Decline of Traditional Banking: Implications for Financial Stability and Regulatory Policy' (1995) *Federal Reserve Board of New York Economic Policy Review*, July, 27. In the US, banks' share of total financial assets was below that of pension funds, insurers, and other financial intermediaries over the period 2004–14; the bank share percentage ranged in the low 20s over the period. FSB, 'Global Shadow Banking Monitoring Report 2015' (2015), 59.

[3] See J De Haan, S Oosterloo, and D Schoenmaker, *European Financial Markets and Institutions* (Cambridge: CUP, 2009), 181. In the UK, for example, banks' share was consistently above that of insurers, pension funds, and other financial intermediaries throughout the period 2004–14; the bank share percentage ranged mostly in the 50s: FSB, n 2, 59.

Principles of Financial Regulation. First Edition. John Armour, Dan Awrey, Paul Davies, Luca Enriques, Jeffrey N. Gordon, Colin Mayer, and Jennifer Payne. © John Armour, Dan Awrey, Paul Davies, Luca Enriques, Jeffrey N. Gordon, Colin Mayer, and Jennifer Payne 2016. Published 2016 by Oxford University Press.

surveyed jurisdictions.[4] In the US, where non-bank financial intermediation is most advanced, the bank share of financial assets has been *less* than 25 per cent for at least the last ten years.[5] As we shall explain in sections 20.2–20.4, this phenomenon has been driven in part by valuable financial innovation and in part by regulatory arbitrage.

Prior to the financial crisis, regulators generally believed that these developments had reduced the overall level of systemic risk. This is because, as we explored in Chapter 13, the banking model entails a certain level of institutional fragility and, because of its tie to the payment system, represents a locus of systemic risk in the economy. Thus, it was reasoned, the substitution of credit provision by markets rather than banks would reduce systemic risk. We know now that this view was mistaken. The shift in the financial system did not so much reduce systemic risk as change the ways in which it arose. Thus a regulatory framework that focused its search for systemic risk on 'banks' was not apt to spot, and still less to control, emergent varieties of that risk. More specifically, a regulatory framework that regarded disclosure as the principal strategy for control of market-based risks did not quickly perceive the need for prudential oversight of the forms of market-based credit intermediation that performed bank-like liquidity and maturity transformation.

In terms of the framework for understanding systemic risk articulated in Chapter 19, the change in the structure of the financial system brought with it a change in the *cross-sectional* configuration of systemic risk. Regulators were stuck in a framework that did not contemplate the migration of systemic risk, and there was consequently no serious attempt to monitor this from a macroprudential perspective. As a result, the new sources of systemic risk slipped cleanly under the radar. Understanding how the changes in the financial system brought with them new sources of systemic risk goes to the heart of current regulatory endeavours, and of this book's project. Obviously, it matters a great deal that we understand what happened in the run-up to the financial crisis in order to reduce the chances of a recurrence. To preserve financial stability, regulators need to understand the new cross-section of systemic risk. Of course, this cross-section surely will continue to evolve. Better still, then, that regulators should understand what might be called the 'primitives' of systemic risk: the basic elements that combine to create instability as the financial system reconfigures itself over time. The same is true for anyone who wants to evaluate, or even understand, the new strategies regulators have deployed in response. In Part E, we consider how the changes in the structure of the financial system altered the incidence of systemic risk and how regulators have responded.

This chapter is organized as follows. Section 20.2 explains historically (and analytically) the rise of market-based credit intermediation. This is in two parts: first, the flow of retirement and personal savings into institutional investor intermediaries that did not need the liquidity, maturity, or credit transformation services of banks; and second, the (US) story of how Glass–Steagall helped foster a set of financial firms—investment banks—with strong incentives to develop market-based alternatives to bank finance.

---

[4] FSB, n 2, 2. This is a 'broad measure' of non-bank financial institutions that includes insurance companies, pension funds, and 'other financial intermediaries' (such as bond funds and investment banks).

[5] See n 2.

Section 20.3 explores the systemic dangers in market-based finance that arose from the effort to substitute *market-based* liquidity and maturity transformation for *bank-based* transformation. We use one example for each transformation service: first, the mortgage-backed securitization structures that offered liquidity, backstopped by *private* lender of last resort ('LOLR') assurances from the sponsoring banks; and second, the funding of long-term debt securities on dealer bank balance sheets by short-term liabilities supported by a *private* form of deposit insurance, repo finance. The systemic danger is that in financial distress, private LOLR assurances and private deposit insurance may crumble, producing a massive run on the market-based system that may spill over into the banking system itself.

Section 20.4 explores the systemic dangers in market-based finance that arise from the effort to substitute *market-based* credit transformation for *banks*. The example here is mortgage-backed securitization. This purported to provide a superior form of diversification through rearrangement of cash flows to provide claims that were as safe as deposits, that were as liquid, but that offered higher yield. When the alchemy for producing superior credit transformation—tranching overseen by credit-rating agencies—was shown to be flawed, this form of market-based finance crumbled.

Section 20.5 then explores how regulators around the world have attempted to distinguish this systemically sensitive activity, 'shadow-banking'—for which more stringent regulation is required—from other, benign, forms of market-based credit intermediation. There is a methodological divide here: is the right approach to try to identify institutions that perform 'bank-like' functions, and—if they achieve sufficient scale to become 'dangerous'—then sweep them into the (prudential) regulatory perimeter? Or is it better to try to identify certain financial market practices that appear to increase systemic risk, such as the use of short-term wholesale credit to finance risky assets, and place economy-wide limits on the practice? A 'functional' approach requires regulators to understand how the various institutions operate within markets in assessing how to protect financial stability.

This chapter can be seen as an introduction to Part E. Chapter 21 provides a more institutionally detailed account of the elements of market-based finance. Chapter 22 takes a detailed look at asset managers, who are critical actors in the market-based credit intermediation system, because as famed (US) bank robber Willie Sutton once said, 'that's where the money is'. The point is to assess the potential for systemic risk in their diverse business models. Chapter 23 then asks whether seeking to break links between various components of the large banking organizations that navigate both banking and securities markets would enhance systemic stability. This poses a contemporary version of the Glass–Steagall question.

20.2 The Rise of Market-Based Credit Intermediation

The rise of market-based credit intermediation since the 1960s had two main drivers: first, the flow of funds into non-bank financial intermediaries (pension funds, life insurers, mutual funds), which did not need the transformation services that banks provided; and second, the way that regulation in the US—most notably the Glass–Steagall

Act and geographic limits on bank expansion—gave investment banks the incentive and opportunity to pursue market-based credit finance vigorously.[6]

20.2.1 The flow of savings into institutional investors not banks

Throughout the post Second World War period, increasing private retirement provision—boosted by strong tax incentives in the UK and US—has enhanced the mobilization of capital into the hands of institutional investors who manage these funds on behalf of their ultimate beneficiaries.[7] The most notable such institutions are pension funds and life insurers.[8] These institutions do not need the intermediation services that banks provide, specifically the transformation services, and thus are candidates for market-based alternatives.

Why do they not need banks? The core reason is that the beneficiaries/customers of the pension funds and life insurers, respectively, are not entitled to receive/contract for liquid claims. First, the beneficiaries of pension funds and life insurers have claims that are (in general) payable only upon contractually specified future events: retirement, and death; they are not immediately redeemable. Pension funds and life insurers can thus plan for highly predictable future needs for cash. This means that pension funds and insurers do not need the *liquidity transformation* services provided by bank deposits. Similarly, because their cash needs are predictable and can be satisfied by laddering the payout of maturing debt, pension funds and life insurers do not experience a potential maturity mismatch in holding long-term claims. Thus they do not need the bank's *maturity transformation* services. Indeed, their planning horizon means that such institutional investors can hold the longest-term debt more readily than a bank.

Second, pension funds and insurers invest on a scale that means that they can justify the expense of obtaining their own high-quality investment advice. This means that like banks, they can minimize risk through well-advised credit-selection and portfolio diversification. Indeed, the scale of the invested funds far exceeds a bank's deposit insurance ceiling, so depositing the funds in a bank would provide no greater margin of safety than the bank's own diversified asset portfolio, which such institutional investors can at least replicate, if not improve upon.[9] Moreover, by buying only investment grade bonds, a typical practice of pension funds and insurers, the institution can substantially

---

[6] An enabling factor was technological advance, particularly the increasing availability of low-cost computer power and high-speed communications, which greatly facilitated the functioning of securities markets. These advances lowered the transaction costs of trading, meaning that institutional investors could rearrange their portfolios at lower cost, and enabled the design of portfolios, indeed the debt securities themselves, that permitted institutional investors to create diversified debt portfolios and otherwise manage risk at low cost.

[7] See the discussion in Chapter 12, section 12.2.

[8] See GL Clark, *Pension Fund Capitalism* (Oxford: OUP, 2000); EP Davis and B Steil, *Institutional Investors* (Cambridge, MA: MIT Press, 2001); RJ Gilson and JN Gordon, 'The Agency Costs of Agency Capitalism: Activist Investors and the Revaluation of Governance Rights' (2013) 113 *Columbia Law Review* 863.

[9] In the US, historically the most generous provider of deposit insurance, the ceiling was $100,000 per deposit account. The current limit is $250,000. See generally Chapter 15, section 15.5.

eliminate its need for high-level monitoring and loan management. Such institutions therefore do not need the *credit transformation* services of a bank account.

A parallel development augmented the supply of funds available to market-based finance and extended the range of corporate borrowers that could obtain credit in markets rather than from commercial banks. This was the shift in pension provisioning from 'defined benefit' plans, for which the company managed a fund towards the goal of providing an employee with a fixed payout, towards 'defined contribution' plans, for which companies annually paid a fixed amount into accounts managed by the individual employee. These defined contribution accounts were typically administered by an asset manager that provided employees a menu of investment choices, including 'bond funds'. These bond funds would assemble debt securities of varying credit risk—not necessarily limited to investment grade—and would be sold on the basis of yield, reflecting risk-bearing and diversification.[10] Shares in the bond funds were redeemable daily on the basis of the proportionate share of the fund's current net asset value ('NAV'). Because a fund's obligation to the investor was to redeem at NAV, the fund was not transforming maturity or credit risk. An investor in a bond fund had what might be regarded as 'imperfect liquidity'—the right to receive cash, as with a bank deposit, but not a sum certain, because the value of the bond portfolio could fluctuate with interest rate or credit factors. In short, this was not bank-like liquidity transformation. The fund might include a certain level of cash in its portfolio to satisfy redemption requests without the need to sell credit assets into the market at possibly depressed prices, but this was principally as a matter of protection for non-redeeming investors, not to avoid the insolvency of the fund.

20.2.2 The regulatory stimulants to market-based credit intermediation

The rise of life insurers, pension funds, and bond funds thus generated a vast pool of funds looking for debt-like claims but not needing the transformation services that banks supplied. This was the precondition for the growth of market-based credit intermediation. The key institutional catalyst in the creation of this market was the investment bank, which could replace commercial banks in the 'origination' of loans, except that the form of this origination was the underwriting of debt securities of the corporate issuer. Unlike a commercial bank, which held credit claims that it originated, the investment bank would 'distribute' debt securities to willing institutional buyers, which would bear credit risk, albeit in diversified portfolios. Investment-grade companies quickly learned that they could obtain more favourable interest rates and other credit terms through securities issuance to pension funds and life insurers than through bank loans, whose interest charge would have to cover the costs of the bank's transformation services (including the cost of regulatory capital). The investment banks could earn substantial profits from the underwriting fees, while distributing the risk-bearing to the institutional buyers. Thus the key fact: market-based credit intermediation undercuts

---

[10] If an issuer fell into financial distress, the bond fund could sell the bond to a hedge fund that specialized in managing 'distressed credit' situations; in effect, the bond fund could outsource this element of credit transformation.

a core lending business of large commercial banks. The rise of institutional investor intermediaries—pension funds, life insurers, and bond funds—provided an alternative to banks in the holding of debt claims. And a particular sort of market intermediary, investment banks, provided an alternative to bank-based loan origination in the form of underwriting.

In what way did regulation play a role in stimulating this development? First, the separation of investment banking from commercial banking that followed Glass–Steagall created a set of market-focused intermediaries: the investment banks. Equity issuances are infrequent; but firms are continually raising debt—if only to roll-over maturing indebtedness. Because investment banks were blocked from conventional commercial banking, they had strong incentives to figure out how to propagate market-based credit intermediation and then pursued the cost advantages relentlessly. As European finance demonstrates, a universal bank with a strong commercial lending franchise will be reluctant to cannibalize its existing business through market-finance innovations.

Second, US banks have historically been subject to geographic restrictions on the scope of their operation. Until federal legislative change in 1994, interstate bank operations were tightly circumscribed by a mix of federal and state laws. Indeed, the most common bank had been the 'unit' bank, a single location in a single state. These restrictions may have facilitated monitoring of local bank activity by in-state regulators (or protected the local banking monopolies of local elites), but they also impeded the extent to which commercial banks were able to offer finance at a scale appropriate for large US public companies. This had the effect of steering corporate finance-raising away from bank loans and towards bond markets. To raise substantial sums through bank loans required the formation of a syndicate of dozens, sometimes hundreds, of banks, typically organized by a lead 'money centre' bank. The transaction costs were quite high, especially if a debt-restructuring proved necessary. By contrast, a small group of investment banks could readily tap into a nationwide bond market of large institutional investors to raise funds through a securities issuance. Moreover, innovations in the Bankruptcy Reform Act of 1978 that facilitated bondholder coordination on a value-conserving reorganization of a failing firm reversed the advantage that banks had previously enjoyed in restructuring the debt of a distressed corporate debtor.[11]

The rise of market-based credit intermediation provided the impetus for the steady erosion of Glass–Steagall through a process of regulatory exceptions over the 1980s and 1990s and that led to its ultimate repeal in 1999.[12] US banks were now permitted to affiliate with securities firms. An immediate consequence was that the balance sheets of the US bank holding companies that these securities firms joined became much larger and more complex—and thus more of a supervisory challenge. Nevertheless, in its origins, market-based credit intermediation looks to have been motivated by efficiency.

---

[11] On the role of reorganization law in facilitating debt restructuring, see S Djankov, O Hart, C McLiesh, and A Shleifer, 'Debt Enforcement Around the World' (2008) 116 *Journal of Political Economy* 1105; J Armour, G Hertig, and H Kanda, 'Transactions with Creditors', in R Kraakman, J Armour, P Davies, L Enriques, H Hansmann, G Hertig, K Hopt, H Kanda, M Pargendler, G Ringe, and E Rock, *The Anatomy of Corporate Law*, 3rd ed (Oxford: OUP, 2016), Ch 5.
[12] Gramm–Leach–Bliley Act of 1999, Pub L 106-102, 113 Stat 138.

The debt securities 'buy side' simply did not need the transformation services of banks. These costs, which included the bank's loan origination and monitoring infrastructure as well as the costly balance sheet constraints necessary to maintain the bank's capacity to provide liquidity transformation, could be avoided without immediately creating powerful new vectors of systemic risk.

20.3 Liquidity and Maturity Transformation through Markets: Enter Systemic Risk

Pension funds and insurers were serving beneficiaries and customers who were not seeking liquidity; bond funds served customers who were satisfied with imperfect liquidity (liquidity without a sum certain). The challenge for market-based credit finance was how to take advantage of funding sources that demanded 'perfect' liquidity (liquidity with sum certain) and that were pursuing yield. Here are two examples that show how market-based efforts to supply this product massively increased systemic risk. The first is bank-sponsored securitizations in which banks entered into private LOLR arrangements to support the liquidity of short-term payment obligations. The second is the use of repo finance to create private deposit insurance for short-term financing of long-term assets held by dealer banks. In both cases the goal was to avoid runs that would force the destabilizing sale of debt securities into unreceptive markets.

20.3.1 Securitizations, asset-backed commercial paper and bank LOLR provision

We discuss securitization in considerable detail in Chapter 21, section 21.3. For present purposes these elements are useful: securitization of residential mortgages arose in part to solve the problems revealed in the US savings-and-loan crisis of the 1970s and 1980s,[13] in particular the maturity mismatch between long-term mortgage loans and short-term deposits, and the risk of correlated defaults because of regional economic shocks.[14] Securitization was a technique to separate the *origination* of the mortgage loan from the risk-bearing function. Whole mortgage loans could be purchased by a 'special investment vehicle' ('SIV') that would in turn issue (or *distribute*) long-term 'mortgage-backed securities' ('MBS'), the proceeds of which would cover the purchase of the loans. The SIV needed to issue short-term securities as well, 'asset-backed commercial paper' ('ABCP'), both to fund initial loan purchases and to smooth out payments to MBS holders in light of the potential bumpiness of mortgage repayments. The SIVs were structured so that the ABCP was over-collateralized, meaning purchasers would take no credit risk, and so ABCP could be sold to money market funds

---

[13] We discuss this in section 16.4.2.

[14] In the US, the Government-sponsored enterprises ('GSEs') of 'Fannie Mae' (Federal National Mortgage Association) and 'Freddy Mac' (Federal Home Loan Mortgage Corporation) securitized most high-quality mortgage loans below a ceiling amount, absorbing credit risk but not early repayment risk or interest rate risk. Banks and investment banks did 'private label' securitizations of lower-quality loans (including 'subprime' loans) and 'jumbo' (very large) loans, and fashioned the complex securitization products that figured in the financial crisis.

and others as a substitute for a bank certificate of deposit. At each rollover of the ABCP as it matured, the holder could stay invested or receive payment—in effect, redeeming.

What if there came to be uncertainty about the payment streams, such as the mortgage repayment rates on which the cash flows depended? This could lead to a run on the SIV as ABCP holders refused to roll-over their investments and potential new buyers stayed away. As the run gained momentum, the SIV's liquidity reserves would be drained, forcing an asset liquidation and leading to losses for the non-redeeming ABCP holders, the anticipation of which would accelerate the run. This is a classic story of structural fragility associated with liquidity transformation.

The solution was private provision of LOLR services. The sponsoring bank would issue a 'liquidity put' to the SIV, meaning that if the market froze, the bank would provide 'liquidity' to the SIV, sufficient to pay off the redeeming APCB holders. Under the Basel rules that then applied, this obligation was regarded as a remote contingent obligation for the sponsoring bank that carried only a nominal charge. In the event, the bank's performing as a LOLR—lending against 'good' collateral—would mean taking onto its balance sheet the credit risk of the SIV's assets that had supposedly been taken off its balance sheet by the securitization. In the financial crisis, tens of billions of dollars of MBS boomeranged back onto bank balance sheets in this way, abruptly changing capital ratios and in some cases creating destabilizing solvency questions about the bank itself. Market-based credit intermediation that purported to provide liquidity transformation outside the official banking system had failed. The key point is this: the private LOLR mechanism that stabilized the structure would not scale—the banks could not substitute for the Federal Reserve as securitization came into widespread use. This form of market-based credit intermediation *added* to systemic risk.

20.3.2 Dealer banks and private deposit insurance

One element in the rise of market-based credit intermediation was the growth in the balance sheets of 'dealer banks', which held long-term debt securities financed with short-term liabilities.[15] Since legally (even after repeal of Glass–Steagall) dealer banks were not permitted to issue 'deposits', these short-term issuances were necessarily funded through the short-term wholesale credit market. The structural fragility was immediately apparent, because the dealer bank was providing maturity transformation (and liquidity transformation) without either a LOLR or deposit insurance. The private-ordering substitute that would sustain this form of market-based credit intermediation was a form of secured lending, 'repo', which could act as a kind of private deposit insurance and thus minimize the run risk of highly sophisticated counterparties who were constitutionally unable to take credit risk (money market funds) or simply unwilling to do so.

We explain 'repo' and other forms of wholesale finance in Chapter 21, section 21.2. For present purposes it is sufficient to describe repo as a collateralized loan structured as a sale and repurchase transaction in which the 'seller' (borrower) sells a security to the 'purchaser' (lender) for $x with the understanding that it will repurchase the

---

[15] Dealer banks, which Chapter 21 discusses in detail, can be regarded as the market-making and proprietary trading part of an investment bank.

security (commonly the next day) at $x + y$ B.P., the y Basis Points reflecting the interest charge.[16] Commonly, the market value of the security exceeds the loan, and the difference is called the 'haircut' (or 'margin') and reflects the extent to which the transaction is over-collateralized. If the borrower defaults on its repurchase obligation (repayment of the loan), the lender can retain the security or sell it and apply the proceeds to the loan. Laws of most jurisdictions protect the lender (purchaser) from insolvency laws that might otherwise stay a secured party's foreclosing on the borrower's collateral, a bankruptcy safe harbour. By protecting the value of the lender's 'deposit', repo provides a kind of private deposit insurance.

A key constraint on the size of a dealer bank's balance sheet was the capacity to provide such private deposit insurance because unsecured short-term lending is prone to runs. We know that before the advent of deposit insurance, commercial banks carried much higher levels of capital and much higher levels of cash and cash equivalents.[17] So in effect, the capacity of the dealer banks to provide transformation services was increasing in the extent to which they could offer 'private deposit insurance' in the way we have described. Two interrelated developments in the run-up to the financial crisis increased the extent to which they could do so. The first was the use of the securitization mechanism (discussed in the next section) to engage in a particular form of credit transformation of risky cash flows from individual mortgages into AAA-rated MBS. The second was the expansion in 2005 of the bankruptcy safe harbour to include mortgage-backed securities as collateral eligible for this special treatment.[18] The combination of such high credit ratings and access to the bankruptcy safe harbour meant that these new securities could be financed using repos.

The mortgages underlying the AAA-rated MBS were long-term obligations. These generated a stream of interest revenue that was higher than the short-term interest rates payable for overnight financing in the repo market. This meant the dealer banks had an incentive to expand the size of their holdings of these AAA-rated MBS to exploit the interest rate spread between long-term and short-term rates.[19] They did this by tapping into the unprecedented worldwide flow of funds looking for safe, liquid assets.[20] The private deposit insurance permitted the dealer banks to provide maturity and liquidity transformation services that were limited only by the ready supply of

---

[16] A 'basis point' is one-hundredth of a percentage point.

[17] AG Haldane, 'Capital Discipline', Speech to American Economic Association, Denver, 9 January 2011 (2011); CW Calomiris and M Carlson, 'Corporate Governance and Risk Management at Unprotected Banks: National Banks in the 1890s' (forthcoming 2016) 119 *Journal of Financial Economics*.

[18] The 2005 expansion is discussed in detail in ER Morrison and J Riegel, 'Financial Contracts and the New Bankruptcy Code: Insulating Markets from Bankrupt Debtors and Bankruptcy Judges' (2005) 11 *American Bankruptcy Institute Journal* 641. See 11 USC §101(47). The consequences and a call for reform are elaborated in ER Morrison, ME Roe, and CS Sontchi, 'Rolling Back the Repo Safe Harbors' (2014) 69 *Business Lawyer* 1015.

[19] The dealer banks could also profit from trading bonds if they could accurately forecast changes in long-term interest rates and from fees on trading on behalf of customers.

[20] See Z Pozsar, 'Institutional Cash Pools and the Triffin Dilemma of the US Banking System', IMF Working Paper 11/190 (2011); BS Bernanke, C Bertaut, LP DeMarco, and S Kamin, 'International Capital Flows and the Returns of Safe Assets in the United States, 2003–2007', Federal Reserve Board International Finance Discussion Paper No 1014 (2011).

AAA-rated MBS that could be financed through repo.[21] The overnight nature of repo borrowing meant the dealer banks could adjust interest rates daily to assure that 'depositors' did not withdraw funds to pursue higher yields. The availability of interest rate swaps[22] permitted the dealer banks to adjust their exposure to interest rate risk on their long-term debt holdings without selling them. Thus they could stably transform daily demandable liquidity into long-term holdings. A large and robust repo market meant that dealer banks could handle the 'withdrawal' of large sums by 'depositors' who needed funds for some other purpose, because there were ample substitute short-term credit providers attracted by the private deposit insurance of the repo system. Because this form of 'deposit insurance' was not capped, it was especially attractive to wholesale providers.

What happened next to unravel the private deposit insurance system is well known.[23] As the level of mortgage foreclosures began to increase in 2007 and 2008, the value of the AAA-rated MBS became suspect; in particular, the flaws in the credit intermediation technology (described in the next section) became manifest. Short-term credit providers, who remained reliant on private deposit insurance, demanded increasingly large haircuts on the securities used for repo, or, as valuations became extremely uncertain, withdrew altogether. This can be described as a 'run'. The point is that as the private deposit insurance capacity of the dealer banks dramatically shrank, so did their ability to draw in and hold the short-term funds necessary to finance their assets. This led to rounds of fire sales that in some cases rendered dealer banks insolvent and that had terrible knock-on effects for the commercial banks, which carried similar assets on their balance sheet. Dealer banks had purported to offer maturity and liquidity transformation services sustained by a market-based form of deposit insurance. But the stability the 'private deposit insurance' provided was only relative. It reduced run risk in a repo market on a modest scale, but eventually its capacity to control run risk was exceeded. When that point was reached, this market-based credit finance had massively increased systemic risk.[24]

20.4 Securitization and the 'Perfection' of Credit Transformation

In addition to liquidity and maturity transformation, banks engage in 'credit transformation'. This means the transformation of a collection of risky assets (and thus variable payout streams) into a safe asset with a fixed payout stream, the deposit. Banks

---

[21] This of course stimulated the product of such assets, both through mortgage origination but also through financially engineered credit transformation.

[22] See Chapter 21.

[23] See G Gorton and A Metrick, 'Securitized Banking and the Run on Repo' (2012) 10 *Journal of Financial Economics* 425; G Gorton and A Metrick, 'Who Ran on Repo?', NBER Working Paper No 18455 (2012).

[24] Note that this account of this form of market-based liquidity and maturity transformation also suggests its own corrective: limiting the bankruptcy safe harbour to risk-free assets like US Treasury issuances or other sovereign debt issuances that will hold their value even in a financial crisis. In other words, if the same balance sheet that is behind public deposit insurance is reflected in the instrument used for repo finance, then private deposit insurance will offer equivalent protection. See Chapter 21, section 21.2.3.

do this by credit screening in the origination of loans, diversification to minimize concentrated borrower, industry, and, to the extent possible, geographic risks, and then follow-on monitoring of loan performance, including intervention to minimize losses on any particular loan. An important element to this credit transformation was the bank's loss-absorbency capacity, particularly shareholder equity and, on occasion, subordinated debt. Securitization as promoted by its underwriters purported to provide a superior version of credit transformation and at lower cost. The canonical residential mortgage-backed security ('RMBS') aggregated mortgages that were geographically diverse; these mortgages were also issued to buyers of lesser creditworthiness, 'sub-prime' or just above.[25] The novel feature was to rearrange the incoming cash flows like a 'waterfall', so that the securitization vehicle could issue securities of different credit quality.[26] In the simplest version, the senior 'tranche' would have priority over all incoming cash flows until its claims were paid and thus could receive an AAA-rating. As a result of this prioritization scheme, 'many of the manufactured tranches [were] far safer than the average asset in the underlying pool'.[27] This credit transformation was thought to be superior to a bank's, because it produced AAA-rated securities from loans that would weigh down the bank's balance sheet, and without the cost of regulatory capital.[28] Moreover, the 'mezzanine' tranches could be pooled and on the same prioritization principle, the resulting Collateralized Debt Obligation ('CDO') could also issue a certain fraction of AAA-rated securities. In the hands of a financial institution, an AAA-rated MBS could also produce immediate liquidity, because as we discussed in section 20.3.2, it would be taken as collateral for a repo loan close to the face amount.

We now know that the credit transformation of securitization was in many respects inferior to a bank's. First, while a prioritization waterfall could indeed produce a layer of AAA-rated credit, the financial engineering models—used by the issuer banks and by the rating agencies—that produced a large percentage of the AAA-rated tranches were based on inadequate historical data about housing prices, including an assumption about continual price appreciation, and failed to understand that the national diversification strategy designed for risk reduction had created a national real estate market that undermined local diversity and added correlation to default risks. More-over, the relatively small number of underwriters were able to 'ratings shop' among the small number of credit rating agencies (CRAs) to squeeze more AAA ratings out of the same risk pool.[29]

Second, it was hard to value an MBS tranche. The complexity of the prescribed movement of cash within a particular securitization vehicle made their payoff

---

[25] Other multi-sector securitizations might include, for example, automobile loans, credit card receivables, and even commercial real-estate loans.

[26] In practice there were essentially three tranches: AAA, BBB (the 'mezzanine' tranche), and the 'equity' tranche, which picked up the residuals left by the higher-rated tranches.

[27] J Coval, J Jurek, and E Stafford, 'The Economics of Structured Finance' (2009) 23 *Journal of Economic Perspectives* 3.

[28] The securitizer could further enhance the credit quality of the tranche by arrange for third-party insurance in the form of a credit default swap.

[29] See LJ White, 'Markets: The Credit Rating Agencies' (2010) 24 *Journal of Economic Perspectives* 211. See also Chapter 6, section 6.3.3.

structures immensely complex.[30] To some extent this facilitated the process of liquidity and maturity transformation, since short-term credit suppliers to a dealer bank could feel that the opacity of the MBS structure protected them against potential adverse selection problems in the proffer and acceptance of collateral.[31] On the other hand, as mortgage defaults increased, real estate values went into decline, and credit rating agencies' ratings—and conflicts—came under withering fire,[32] the very complexity of the MBS—and *a fortiori*, their more exotic brethren—made value determinations difficult if not impossible. Short-term credit suppliers knew that valuation was import-ant, knew that they didn't know it, and thus pulled back from repo finance; they ran. When the method for producing superior credit transformation—tranching overseen by credit rating agencies—was shown to be flawed, this form of market-based finance crumbled.

That is the negative result on one side of the credit transformation process. On the other side, securitization seems to have exacerbated losses from increasing mortgage default rates.[33] Securitization unbundled the housing finance function through con-tracts with various agents, including servicers, who collected payments from the homeowners and forwarded them. The servicers were also supposed to manage any necessary loan renegotiation and modification with a financially constrained mortga-gee. But servicers were not paid enough to cooperate; their incentives were to foreclose, irrespective of ultimate recovery rates on the defaulted mortgage or the impact on surrounding property values. The complexity of many securitization vehicles made it very difficult to avoid irritating some fraction of loss-bearing holders. By contrast, banks, which internalize the cost of foreclosure, achieved more modifications and ultimately preserved more value. In short, securitization provided a market substitute for the bank's credit transformation, but it presented its own set of institutional frailties and showed a propensity for adding, not subtracting, systemic risk.

In sum, the commercial banks through their off-balance sheet SIVs, the dealer banks in the financing of their balance sheets, and the securitizers in their reshaping of financial claims, had each engaged in forms of transformation activity traditionally performed by banks. Because of this, and the fact that this activity was not regulated as 'banking', it has come to be known as 'shadow banking'.

---

[30] See R Bartlett, 'Inefficiencies in the Information Thicket: A Case Study of Derivatives Disclosure During the Financial Crisis' (2010) 36 *Journal of Corporation Law* 1; K Judge, 'Fragmentation Nodes' (2012) 64 *Stanford Law Review* 657.

[31] That is to say, the dealer banks offering the securities as collateral could credibly claim they did not understand the expected cash flows much better than the institutional investors taking them as such in the repo market. See sources cited in n 1. Such adverse selection as there was in securitizations was at the stage when the loans were transferred to the SIV from the originator, not in the transfer of the MBS that the SIV issued: see BJ Keys, T Mukherjee, A Seru, and V Vig, 'Did Securitization Lead to Lax Screening? Evidence from Subprime Loans' (2010) 125 *Quarterly Journal of Economics* 307.

[32] These conflicts are discussed in Chapter 6, section 6.3.3.

[33] See T Piskorski, A Seru, and V Vig, 'Securitization and Distressed Loan Renegotiation: Evidence from the Subprime Mortgage Crisis' (2010) 97 *Journal of Financial Economics* 369; S Agarwal, G Amromin, I Ben-David, S Chomsisengphet, and D Evanoff, 'The Role of Securitization in Mortgage Renegotiation' (2011) 102 *Journal of Financial Economics* 559.

20.5 Shadow Banking and Market-Based Financial Intermediation

Since the financial crisis, considerable effort has been devoted to reining in the propensity of the shadow banking sector to create systemic risk. Perhaps inevitably, what should count as 'shadow banking' has become hotly contested in this regulatory debate.[34] A functional approach calls for understanding how the institutions of market-based credit intermediation function, both separately and collectively, in assessing the best regulatory techniques to strengthen the market-based system a whole. This means that the most important regulatory initiatives may be those that target market-wide practices and behaviour, rather than particular institutions.

Initially the Financial Stability Board (FSB), the agenda-setter for post-crisis regulatory reform, pushed for the broadest conceivable definition of 'shadow banking', namely 'credit intermediation involving entities and activities (fully or partially) outside the regular banking system'.[35] This would encompass virtually all market-based credit intermediation. It would imply that asset managers are shadow bankers and that even a pass-through vehicle like a bond fund is a shadow bank, despite the limited transformation services that we have described. This definition is apt to capture the full amount of credit intermediation that may be occurring in the financial system outside the banking sector. This may be relevant for macroprudential authorities thinking about the application of time-varying macroprudential tools, for example.[36] It may be harder to make these work if a larger proportion of credit intermediation occurs outside the regulated banking sector, beyond the reach of time-varying capital controls, for example.

But simply because a firm engages in credit intermediation does not mean that it adds to systemic risk in the cross-sectional sense.[37] If we are concerned to identify those firms, or sectors, which do this, then a more restrictive definition is needed. We can think about market-based credit intermediation as potentially adding cross-sectional systemic risk in two distinct ways: (i) through linkages that render the regular banking sector less stable; and (ii) through systemic risk *within* the 'shadow banking' sector. If there are no links to the regular banking sector, then the contribution to systemic risk of any market-based financial intermediation channel depends on its size relative to the economy as a whole, and its fragility. A large but stable sector has a small risk of failure,

---

[34] A useful article is Z Pozsar, T Adrian, A Ashcraft, and H Boesky, 'Shadow Banking' (2013) *FRBNY Economic Policy Review*, December, 1.

[35] See eg FSB, 'Strengthening Oversight and Regulation of Shadow Banking: An Overview of Policy Recommendations' (2013), iv; see also M Carney, 'The Need to Focus a Light on Shadow Banking is Nigh', *Financial Times*, 15 June 2014 ('the extension of credit from entities and activities outside the regular banking system'). These sentiments were echoed in a report of the US Treasury's Office of Financial Research (the research arm of FSOC), 'Asset Management and Financial Stability' (September 2013) that proved to be highly controversial, though it did provoke the SEC to move towards greater prudential oversight of large asset managers.

[36] See Chapter 19, section 19.3.3.

[37] Indeed, if activity were to move away from the banking sector in favour of non-bank financial intermediaries that engaged only in credit transformation and not liquidity or maturity transformation, the overall cross-sectional systemic risk would likely be reduced.

but would cause a lot of harm to the real economy in the rare circumstances in which it did fail. Conversely, a smaller but more fragile sector might engender the same overall level of systemic risk. If the market-based financial intermediation channel is linked to the regular banking sector, then there may be potential for contagion from one to the other. In such a case, the consequences of instability in the sector outside the banking perimeter are greatly magnified, because they potentially encompass the regular banking system as well.

(i) Linkages to the banking sector.   Focusing on the linkages, we can understand that bank-sponsored SIVs were particularly dangerous because their usage directly threatened the stability of the official banking system through the private LOLR call on the sponsoring banks. Bank-sponsored securitization was pure regulatory arbitrage—an expansion of bank leverage permitted by a gap (now closed) in the risk-weighting rules. This was perhaps not so much 'shadow' banking as 'disguised' banking designed to fool the regulator. A specific policy approach—structural regulation of banking—aims to address the problem of linkages by separating banking from other activities. We consider this in detail in Chapter 23. Regulators have also responded to the problem indirectly by seeking to shore up the banking sector through the safeguards discussed in Chapters 14–18.

(ii) Systemic risk outside the banking sector but within the 'shadow banking' sector.   The initial question is what sort of 'shadow banking' actors exist that are not linked to the regular banking sector—what we might call a 'parallel' banking system? One example might be dealer banks, and other market actors who engage in bank-like liquidity and maturity transformation but contract for liquidity protection through back-up credit lines now provided by hedge funds rather than banks. Another example might be the finance companies that originate loans but which are not 'banks' because they are not deposit-funded. Instead, they may fund their activities through wholesale finance (issuing commercial paper, typically to money market funds) and securitization (selling their loan assets to minimize capital requirements). So-called 'fintech' firms—finance companies that make heavy use of the Internet to reach high-quality borrowers—fall into this category.

How might we think about systemic risk, then, in a 'parallel' banking system? It is easy to see how the failure of a very *large* dealer bank, or finance company, could have systemic effects. For example, the liquidation of the dealer bank is likely to affect the value of similar assets held by official banks. Moreover, a large dealer bank's disappearance could well damage the financing of important activity for the real economy. Similarly, the collapse of a large fintech company, as through the sudden 'run' of commercial paper purchasers, could destroy an important credit channel. Size, therefore, is relevant for systemic risk—a point we return to in Chapter 22.

But surely it is not simply a matter of scale. In thinking about the sources of instability within the market-based credit intermediation sector, it is helpful to look to the 'primitives' we described in the foregoing sections. Certain elements add risk: short-term finance, maturity mismatches, liquidity mismatches, reliance on a disassembled credit intermediation chain (as with some securitizations), interconnection with other financial firms that create channels of contagion, high correlation of asset types among financial firms, and size as a proxy of importance to the real economy. 'Shadow banks' are unlikely to bundle these elements in the same way as official banks. They are not monolithic and the levels of systemic risk and fragility will not present in the same way. A functional approach calls for assessment of the mechanisms or patterns of bundling and then to regulate accordingly. Regulators have so far responded to the sources of instability in the shadow banking sector through a number of measures we consider in Chapter 21. Rather than designate a growing list of institutions as systemically important (which raises the challenging question of tailoring multiple regimes suitable for diverse institutions), another approach is to designate specific *practices* or *financing strategies* as systemically sensitive and constrain them accordingly.[38] Such a functional approach is aimed at strengthening the resiliency of market-based credit intermediation as a general system.

The most recent FSB *Global Shadow Banking Monitoring Report* distinguishes between the 'broad measure' of non-bank financial intermediation and, as a subset of this, a 'narrow measure' of 'global shadow banking that may pose financial stability risks'. As of 2014, the narrow measure encompassed assets of $36 trillion globally, as opposed to $137 million under the broad measure.[39] This narrowing should usefully be understood as not simply an exercise in taxonomy, but rather as motivated by a functional assessment of the sources of systemic risk. These include the various primitives we have discussed, such as liquidity and maturity transformation, which can be performed by the interaction of firms through markets, as well as internalized within firms.[40]

20.6 Conclusion

One of the most distinctive practices that has recently emerged in developed financial systems is the rise of market-based credit intermediation. At first it was thought that market-based substitutes for bank finance would help to reduce systemic risk, because they did not seem to rely on the bank balance sheet and did not put at risk the bank-based payment system. The financial crisis showed that the market-based alternatives nevertheless created systemic risk. In part, this was because of linkages between market-based finance and the commercial banking system. One linkage came through contingent liquidity obligations—private LOLR facilities—that banks entered into with market-finance entities and firms. These facilities burdened—and at times overwhelmed—bank balance sheets, and constrained their lending capacity. Another linkage came through damage to bank balance sheets triggered by losses on assets and products originated by market-finance entities and firms.

---

[38] This is the approach taken by the EU's recent 'Securitization initiative', identifying criteria for 'simple, transparent and standardized' securitizations, which are to be accorded lower capital charges than other forms of securitization: see European Commission, Proposal for a Regulation laying down common rules on securitisation and creating a European framework for simple, transparent, and standardized securitization, COM/2015/0472 final, Brussels 30.9.2015; European Commission, Proposal for a Regulation amending Regulation (EU) No 575/2013 on prudential requirements for credit institutions and investment firms, COM/2015/0473 final, Brussels 30.9.2015.

[39] FSB, n 2, 2.   [40] Ibid, 7–8.

Quite apart from the direct and indirect effects on the banking system, the sheer magnitude of market-based credit intermediation relative to the real economy may itself threaten financial stability. It is quite possible to imagine circumstances in which a peer-to-peer lender,[41] for example, faces a run on investor confidence, which spreads to other such firms, and thus brings to a sudden stop activity that is becoming an important credit channel.

These observations have a number of implications for regulators. First, as a matter of bank supervision, it will be important for regulators to monitor a bank's exposure to market-based credit intermediation, which may attempt to free-ride on the bank's balance sheet. Second, non-bank credit institutions may themselves reach systemic size and scope quite independently of the commercial banking system and, if so, their importance to the real economy will require their designation and supervision as systemically important institutions. Third, although institutional size matters, it may also be that particular funding mechanisms, especially short-term wholesale credit practices, are especially prone to fragility and so may be most appropriate for regulatory intervention. The increasing importance of 'shadow banking' calls attention to the fact that a functional approach requires regulatory attention to the resiliency of market structures and practices as well as to institutions. We address these issues in more detail in Chapter 21.

---

[41] Outlined in Chapter 12, section 12.2.5.

21

Making Markets

21.1 Introduction

In 1869 Marcus Goldman set up a small trading firm in the basement of 30 Pine Street in Lower Manhattan. Goldman's firm specialized in providing short-term financing to local clothiers, jewellers, and other merchants. What these merchants all possessed were significant accounts receivable representing the legally enforceable promises of their clients to pay for goods and services already provided. What they—often urgently—required, however, was cash to pay for labour and raw materials. This is where Goldman came into the picture. Goldman would purchase these accounts receivable at a discount—or *haircut*—to their face value. He would then bundle the notes representing these receivables together and sell them on to uptown banks at a slightly smaller discount. These banks would then hold the notes to maturity and collect the debts from the merchants' clients.

This relatively simple form of financial intermediation generated important benefits for each of the participants. Merchants were able to transform their illiquid, longer-term assets into much needed cash; uptown banks were able to access profitable investment opportunities, and Marcus Goldman was able to capture the difference—or *spread*—between the price at which he purchased the receivables and the price at which he sold them. In effect, Goldman's profits came from using his young firm's balance sheet to make markets in financial instruments. Viewed from this perspective, the business model of the firm Goldman founded—Goldman Sachs—has changed very little in the intervening 150 years.[1] What has changed dramatically over this period, however, is the importance and diversity of the roles played by financial intermediaries in making markets.

So far, our consideration of both microprudential and systemic risks in relation to financial intermediaries have largely revolved around a single category of intermediary: the conventional deposit-taking 'bank'. These intermediaries lend to firms and households, monitor creditor and asset quality throughout the life of the loans, and typically hold the loans to maturity. These loans are financed using a combination of equity, long-term debt, and short-term deposits. As we saw in Chapter 13, this combination of illiquid, long-term assets funded by liquid, short-term liabilities makes these institutions susceptible to destabilizing depositor runs. To minimize the likelihood of such runs, many jurisdictions have introduced deposit guarantee schemes that ensure that bank depositors can access their savings on a timely basis in the event of a bank's insolvency. The central banks in these jurisdictions also stand ready to provide emergency liquidity support. To address the resulting moral hazard problems, these

---

[1] For a history of Marcus Goldman and the firm he founded, see W Cohan, *Money and Power: How Goldman Sachs Came to Rule the World* (New York, NY: First Anchor, 2011).

Principles of Financial Regulation. First Edition. John Armour, Dan Awrey, Paul Davies, Luca Enriques, Jeffrey N. Gordon, Colin Mayer, and Jennifer Payne. © John Armour, Dan Awrey, Paul Davies, Luca Enriques, Jeffrey N. Gordon, Colin Mayer, and Jennifer Payne 2016. Published 2016 by Oxford University Press.

institutions are then subject to prudential supervision by public regulatory authorities, along with capital, liquidity, governance, and other requirements designed to constrain excessive risk-taking, as discussed in Chapters 14, 15, and 17.

The business models of so-called 'investment' or 'dealer' banks such as Goldman Sachs diverge significantly from those of their conventional deposit-taking cousins. These dealers operate under different categories of registration in different jurisdictions. In the US, for example, dealers are typically registered as 'broker-dealers'. In Europe, they are typically registered as 'investment firms'. As described in Chapter 6, these non-bank financial intermediaries rent their reputations and balance sheets to firms as a means of overcoming adverse selection problems in connection with new issues of equity and debt securities. As we saw in Chapter 7, they have also historically played an important role in the dealer-intermediated, quote-driven structure of the secondary markets for sovereign, corporate, and other bonds. Today, however, arguably the most important role played by these intermediaries is in engineering new investment opportunities for their clients, and helping them manage market, credit, liquidity, and other risks. They do so by creating and marketing derivatives, structured finance vehicles, and other sophisticated financial instruments, by offering prime brokerage and other services to institutional investors, and through their participation within wholesale funding markets. Indeed, in much the same way as Marcus Goldman, these institutions make money by making markets.

Like Goldman, the intermediation performed by these dealers generates a number of important benefits. Dealers use their vast networks to match buyers and sellers in the marketplace, thereby lowering search costs for their clients. In many cases, they also quote 'bid' and 'ask' prices for various financial assets and stand ready to use their own balance sheets to take either side of the resulting trades. This, in turn, can enhance the process of price formation and, importantly, generate greater market liquidity. Finally, dealers use their considerable expertise to advise clients about how best to manage various risks which might arise in the course of their day-to-day business activities. In theory, these benefits combine to make more complete, efficient, and stable financial markets.

At the same time, however, dealer intermediation poses a number of potentially significant risks. As a preliminary matter, the market-making role of dealers gives them an informational advantage over other market participants. Combined with their often superior expertise, the resulting asymmetries of information generate acute agency problems, giving rise to significant investor and consumer protection concerns, which echo those we discussed in relation to equity markets in Chapters 6 and 7. The interests of dealers may also conflict with those of their clients: either where they are advising counterparties on both sides of a trade, or where the dealers are themselves engaged in proprietary trading. Perhaps most importantly, however, the activities of dealers involve significant levels of credit, maturity, and liquidity transformation. As a result, while the mechanisms may at first appear very different, dealers are ultimately vulnerable to the same sort of destabilizing liquidity shocks experienced by conventional deposit-taking banks, which we considered in Chapters 14 and 15.

This chapter examines the economic functions, risks, and regulation of three of the most important dealer-intermediated markets. It examines these markets from the perspective of dealers for three reasons. First, the incentives of dealers play an important role in shaping the structure of these markets. Second, many dealers are part of larger financial services groups that include conventional deposit-taking banks. Third, and as a result, dealers are one of the most important channels through which instability within these markets can spread to the broader financial system. Section 21.2 begins by examining the mechanics of wholesale funding markets and, specifically, the markets for short-term repurchase (or 'repo') agreements and commercial paper. Section 21.3 examines the mechanics of structured finance (or 'securitization') markets in which illiquid loans, mortgages, receivables, and other credit claims are restructured as marketable securities. Section 21.4 examines the mechanics of over-the-counter ('OTC') derivatives markets and, specifically, swaps. Section 21.5 then examines the intermediation 'chains' created when we combine these markets, along with how these chains effectively recreate the credit, maturity, and liquidity transformation performed by conventional deposit-taking banks. In each case, we examine the role of dealers and other financial intermediaries in making these markets, the risks these markets pose, how these risks manifested themselves during the global financial crisis, and the policy proposals that have been put forward in its wake to address potential market failures.

There are four principal takeaways from this chapter. The first is that the business of 'banking' has in some jurisdictions evolved from a deposit-funded, credit risk driven process of financial intermediation to a more wholesale-funded, market driven one.[2] Some observers have characterized this as 'financial disintermediation'.[3] Others have labelled it as 'shadow banking'.[4] Second, regardless of what we decide to call it, the risks generated within the dealer-intermediated markets for wholesale funding, structured finance, and derivatives exhibit many parallels with those posed by conventional deposit-taking banks. Most importantly, to the extent that the activities of these non-bank financial intermediaries generate maturity and liquidity mismatches, these institutions are susceptible to the functional equivalent of depositor runs: sapping them of funding liquidity and undermining their stability. Third, and as a result, the most important question from a policy perspective is the extent to which we should subject the institutions that make these markets to supervisory and regulatory regimes functionally similar to those imposed on conventional deposit-taking banks. Fourth, the market-making activities of dealer banks are an important source of interconnectedness and potential contagion within the global financial system. In the wake of the financial crisis, policymakers have thus proposed and adopted a number of reforms designed to address the potential systemic risks arising from these activities. These reforms include mandatory central clearing for many standardized derivatives, along

---

[2] See Z Pozsar, T Adrian, A Ashcraft, and H Boesky, 'Shadow Banking' (2013) 19:2 *Federal Reserve Bank of New York Economic Policy Review* 1.

[3] See S Schwarcz, 'Regulating Shadows: Financial Regulation and Responsibility Failure' (2013) 70 *Washington & Lee Law Review* 1781. Although, as Schwarcz himself notes, the term 'disintermediation' is somewhat inaccurate in this context insofar as financial intermediaries—that is, dealers, asset managers, structured finance vehicles, and even conventional banks—play a variety of important roles within these markets.

[4] Z Pozsar, T Adrian, A Ashcraft, and H Boesky, n 2 and FSB, *Strengthening Oversight and Regulation of Shadow Banking: An Overview of Policy Recommendations* (2013).

with more onerous prudential requirements for repos, structured finance markets, and bilaterally cleared derivatives. They also include the structural reforms described in detail in Chapter 23.

21.2 Wholesale Funding Markets

21.2.1 How wholesale funding markets work

As we saw in Chapter 13, conventional deposit-taking banks fund their lending activity through short-term deposits, in combination with longer-term equity and debt. Non-bank financial intermediaries such as dealers, not being regulated as 'banks', are prohibited from accepting conventional deposits. They must therefore identify alternative sources of short-term funding to meet their liquidity needs. These alternatives include 'wholesale' funding markets, where they raise short-term finance from institutional investors and other financial institutions. Wholesale funding markets have grown significantly in recent decades, reflecting the growth of both dealers and institutional investors. As a measure of the growing importance of dealers, Figure 21.1 charts the growth in the total assets of US broker-dealers between 1990 and 2008 relative to the total assets of US commercial banks. It has been estimated that as of 2008 over 40 per cent of the assets of the five largest US dealers were financed through wholesale funding markets.[5] By way of comparison, the equivalent figure for US commercial banks was approximately 2.7 per cent.[6]

Two important sources of wholesale funding for dealers and other financial intermediaries are *commercial paper* and *repos*. Commercial paper is unsecured short-term debt, typically issued with a maturity of between one and nine months. In most cases, commercial paper is issued at a discount to face value, with the difference between the issue price and face value then determining the interest rate. Importantly, firms using commercial paper as a source of short-term funding will often pay off maturing commercial paper through the issuance of new paper. This gives rise to the risk—often referred to as 'rollover' risk—that the funds raised will be insufficient to meet the obligations owed to existing commercial paper holders. As Figure 21.2 shows, US commercial paper markets grew dramatically in the years leading up to the global financial crisis. By the beginning of 2007, there was almost $2 trillion of commercial paper outstanding in the US, approximately 92 per cent of which had been issued by firms in the financial services industry.[7] Money market mutual funds, which restrict their assets to highly liquid, short-term obligations, are major investors in commercial paper.[8]

A repo is effectively a form of short-term secured debt collateralized by financial assets. While repos can thus functionally be understood as a form of secured lending,

---

[5] See M King, 'Are the Brokers Broken?', Citi European Quantitative Credit, Strategy and Analysis (5 September 2008). This figure includes repurchase agreements but excludes other sources of wholesale funding such as commercial paper.

[6] See G Afonso, A Kovner, and A Schoar, 'Stressed, Not Frozen: The Federal Funds Market in the Financial Crisis', Federal Reserve Bank of New York Staff Report No 437 (2011).

[7] M Kacperczyk and P Schnabl, 'When Safe Proved Risky: Commercial Paper During the Financial Crisis of 2007–2009' (2010) 24 *Journal of Economic Perspectives* 29.

[8] See section 21.3.

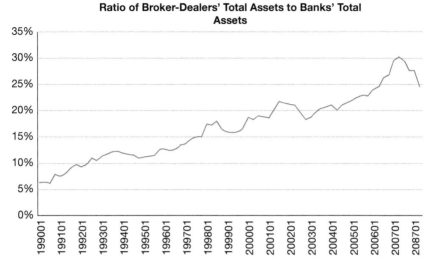

Fig. 21.1 Growth of Dealers Relative to Banks

Source: G Gorton and A Metrick, 'Securitized Banking and the Run on Repo' (2012) NBER Working Paper No 15223, Figure 7.

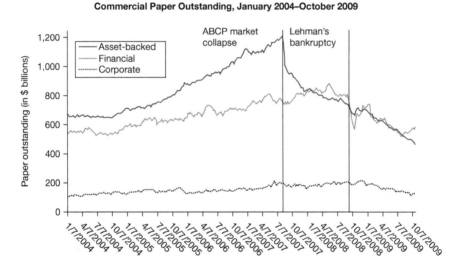

Fig. 21.2 The US Commercial Paper Market

Source: M Kacperczyk and P Schnabl, 'When Safe Proved Risky: Commercial Paper during the Financial Crisis of 2007–2009' (2010) 24 *Journal of Economic Perspectives* 29, 38.

they are often legally structured as a sale and subsequent repurchase. There are two legs to a repo transaction. In the first leg, one counterparty (the borrower) sells the collateral assets to another counterparty (the lender) in exchange for cash. This cash can then be used by the borrower to pay its liabilities or, in many cases, purchase other financial assets. In the second leg, the borrower is then obligated to repurchase equivalent collateral assets from the lender at a specified point in time: often the next business day. The price received in exchange for the collateral assets in the first leg is typically calculated at a discount or 'haircut' to these assets' fair market value. This haircut can be understood as an attempt by the lender to mitigate counterparty credit risk, along with any market and liquidity risk associated with the collateral assets. The repurchase price paid by the borrower in the second leg minus the sale price paid in the first, divided by the sale price, is the effective interest or 'repo' rate. Thus, for example, if a collateral asset has a fair market value of $100 and is sold for $95 with an agreement to repurchase an equivalent asset the next business day for $98, then the haircut would be 5 per cent ($100−$95/$100) and the repo rate would be 3.2 per cent ($98−$95/$95).

The lender takes security so as not to have to bear any risk should the borrower default. Of course, if the value of the securities taken as collateral were to fall below the amount of the debt, then this would mean the lender did bear some risk. To avoid any possibility of this, lenders only lend a maximum percentage of the value of the collateral. This haircut can be understood as an attempt by the lender to mitigate both counterparty credit risk and any market and liquidity risk associated with the collateral assets.

While many repo agreements are entered into directly between the lender and borrower, there is also a significant 'triparty' repo market. In the triparty repo market, a clearing bank stands between the lender and borrower, holding both the cash and collateral assets in escrow as a means of ensuring the performance of each counterparty's obligations. In the US, JPMorgan and BNY Mellon are the primary clearing banks for the triparty repo market. In Europe, clearing services are provided primarily by Clearstream and Euroclear.

The use of repo agreements as a source of short-term financing for dealers grew dramatically in the run-up to the global financial crisis. Between 1996 and 2007, the total amount of overnight and term repo financing used by so-called 'primary' dealers—the market makers in US government treasury securities—grew from approximately $1.7 trillion to over $6.5 trillion.[9] (To put this in context, US GDP in 2007 was $14.5 trillion.)[10] This growth can be attributed to several factors. The first is the growth in size and importance of institutional investors. Institutional investors often hold relatively large amounts of cash and, ideally, would prefer to invest it in relatively safe and highly liquid assets. The funds they have to invest are usually far in excess of the ceiling on deposit insurance. The short-term, secured nature of repo financing, in contrast, offers these investors a low-risk, flexible investment into which they can channel their excess cash.[11] Second, as we already have seen, dealers are prohibited from using conventional deposits as a source of short-term financing. The use of repos can be understood as an effective substitute for such deposits: enabling

---

[9] SIFMA, 'Financing by US Government Securities Primary Dealers—Average Daily Amount Outstanding', available at http://www.sifma.org/research/statistics.aspx. This figure includes reverse repo financing.

[10] World Bank, *World Development Indicators*.

[11] See G Gorton and A Metrick, 'Securitized Banking and the Run on Repo' (2012) 104 *Journal of Financial Economics* 425.

dealers to leverage their own balance sheets as a source of relatively cheap, highly flexible, short-term financing.[12]

A third explanation for the growth of repo markets in recent years is a consequence of the special treatment extended to repos under bankruptcy law. In general, bankruptcy laws in jurisdictions such as the US and UK impose an automatic stay upon bankruptcy filing: preventing lenders from, *inter alia*, immediately seizing and liquidating any collateral against which the obligations of the bankrupt counterparty may have been secured.[13] Bankruptcy laws in some jurisdictions also impose restrictions on the ability of lenders to terminate contracts or net out different claims with a bankrupt counterparty, along with restrictions on the ability of borrowers to make special payments to creditors or dispose of assets during the period immediately preceding the bankruptcy filing. Over the course of the last several decades, however, repo agreements have received near-universal legislative carve-outs from these important restrictions, thus enabling repo lenders to liquidate the collateral of a bankrupt counterparty, net out gains and losses on different repos, and retain any eve-of-bankruptcy payments.[14] The result is a *de facto* reprioritization of claims within the bankrupt counterparty's capital structure: repo lenders effectively enjoy a form of 'super priority' over many other creditors, thus rendering repo a more attractive form of short-term investment.

The widespread use of repo markets by dealers and other financial intermediaries raises an important question: where do intermediaries obtain the financial assets necessary to collateralize these transactions? Broadly speaking, these collateral assets derive from four sources. The first is the balance sheets of the dealers themselves; namely, their own inventories of bonds, shares, and other financial instruments. The second source is the brokerage assets of these dealers' clients. When an institutional client opens a margin account with a dealer, for example, the dealer will typically take the assets in the account as collateral against the margin loan. Because securities are fungible, the dealer is often permitted under the terms of the agreement to reuse or rehypothecate these assets as collateral within its wholesale and other financing

---

[12] See D Duffie, 'The Failure Mechanics of Dealer Banks' (2010) 24 *Journal of Economic Perspectives* 51.

[13] In some jurisdictions, the fact that repos are legally structured as a sale and repurchase means that bankruptcy laws are not applicable because the securities are in law the property of the lender unless and until the borrower repurchases them. As a result, the lender does not need to take any action to 'enforce' against the collateral. In other jurisdictions, meanwhile, the legal treatment of repos reflects their functional status as collateralized debt transactions. In these jurisdictions, the automatic stay would technically apply but for the carve-outs described here.

[14] For further information about these carve-outs under US bankruptcy law, see F Edwards and E Morrison, 'Derivatives and the Bankruptcy Code: Why the Special Treatment?' (2005) 22 *Yale Journal on Regulation* 91, and M Roe, 'The Derivatives Market's Payment Priorities as Financial Crisis Accelerator' (2011) 63 *Stanford Law Review* 539. One particular element in the expansion of repo was a 2005 amendment of the bankruptcy code to expand the collateral that could be used in a financial contract qualifying for the exemption from the bankruptcy stay to include private label mortgage-backed securities (MBS). Repo expanded because there were more assets that could be used as collateral. This in turn had the unfortunate result of encouraging the issuance of more private label MBS at the wrong time. For discussion of the equivalent carve-outs in the UK and the EU, see Louise Gullifer, 'What Should We Do About Financial Collateral?' (2012) 65 *Current Legal Problems* 377. See also Directive 2002/47/EC on Financial Collateral Arrangements [2002] OJ L168/43, as amended by Directive 2009/44/EC [2009] OJ L146/37; Directive 98/26/EC on Settlement Finality in Payment and Securities Systems [1998] OJ L166/45, also as amended by Directive 2009/44/EC.

activities. This takes us to the third source of collateral: reuse and rehypothecation. Reuse refers to the ability of a dealer to sell collateral obtained in connection with one transaction onto a third party in connection with a second, unrelated transaction. For example, a dealer might reuse collateral originally obtained in connection with a derivatives transaction as part of a collateral package sold under a repo agreement.[15] Rehypothecation, meanwhile, refers to the repledging of collateral assets the title over which remains with the original collateral provider.[16] Fourth, as described in greater detail in section 21.4, dealers can manufacture new collateral assets through the process of securitization.

Dealers and other financial intermediaries use the funds raised within repo and other wholesale funding markets for three primary purposes. First, they use the funds to purchase financial assets. These assets can then be held on the firm's balance sheet as part of the investment portfolio of their proprietary trading desk or, as we shall see, repackaged and resold via securitization. Second, dealers can use the funds to support their brokerage and market-making activities: ensuring that they are able to meet their obligations as counterparties to OTC derivatives or as sponsors of structured finance vehicles, for example. Third, dealers can use the funds to satisfy other liabilities arising in the course of their activities. These liabilities include dividends to shareholders, payroll obligations and maturing term debt or commercial paper, along with liabilities to third-party service providers.

21.2.2 Wholesale funding markets and risks to stability

As we have seen, the financing model of dealers looks functionally very similar to that of conventional deposit-taking banks. First, like conventional banks, dealers rely heavily on short-term funding to finance their investment portfolios and operations. Second, in a great many cases, the assets purchased using this short-term funding are less liquid and have a longer maturity than the financial instruments used to finance them. Accordingly, much like conventional banks, the business model of dealers can be understood as involving significant levels of credit, maturity, and liquidity transformation.

The risks to institutional and broader financial stability posed by this financing model are also broadly similar to those facing conventional deposit-taking banks. The short-term nature of commercial paper and especially repo liabilities renders these institutions vulnerable to the wholesale equivalent of depositor runs.[17] Specifically, if market participants lose confidence in the creditworthiness of a dealer—or in the market value or liquidity of the financial assets on its balance sheet or used as collateral

---

[15] See section 21.3.

[16] Notably, the availability of rehypothecation varies from jurisdiction to jurisdiction. In the US, SIFMA's model master securities lending agreement specifically contemplates rehypothecation and distinguishes it from reuse. In the UK, in contrast, the ability of a collateral taker to rehypothecate pledged collateral does not extend to securities.

[17] For a more detailed description of this risk within repo markets, see Gorton and Metrick, n 11. For commercial paper markets, see Kacpercyzk and Schnabl, n 7. See also C Calomiris, 'Is the Discount Window Necessary? A Penn-Central Perspective' (1994) 76 *Federal Reserve Bank of St Louis Review* 31.

within its wholesale funding operations—commercial paper holders and repo counterparties may demand higher interest rates and/or more collateral to compensate
them for the perceived increase in the attendant risks. *In extremis*, they may even refuse
altogether to roll over maturing instruments, effectively leaving the dealer without a
private source of short-term financing.[18]

Combining extremely short terms, full collateralization, and bankruptcy super
priority, repo transactions in particular do everything it is possible for private law to
do to protect the status of lenders. While we might thus view these as a private law
substitute for deposit insurance, they remain vulnerable to a shock to the value or
liquidity of the assets used as collateral, which for many asset classes may have much
greater volatility than would the value of a depositor's claim against a deposit insurance
fund.

The global financial crisis has provided a powerful illustration of the risk of destabilizing runs within wholesale funding markets. Gary Gorton and Andrew Metrick, for
example, document a sharp increase in repo rates and collateral haircuts during the
crisis in response to fears about the creditworthiness of dealers and other counterparties, which we reproduce in Figure 21.3.[19] This shows that the cost of borrowing
within wholesale funding markets—at least as measured by the size of repo haircuts—
was extremely low prior to the crisis. It also shows that these costs did not reflect
differences in the types of financial assets used to collateralize these transactions. As
Figure 21.3 clearly shows, the crisis triggered an increase in haircuts, but not equally for
all collateral assets. Average haircuts on subprime structured finance assets were
roughly five times more than those of other assets.[20] Once haircuts on these subprime
assets reached 100 per cent, this effectively signalled the complete breakdown of repo
markets using these particular assets as collateral.

The features of wholesale funding that protect lenders—short terms, collateralization, and super priority status—also weaken the incentives of lenders to engage in
effective monitoring of dealers.[21] Reliance on wholesale funding may thus result in too

---

[18] An analogous problem arises within the triparty repo market, where a clearing bank, known as the
triparty agent, interposes itself between the two parties to the repo. During periods of relative stability,
clearing banks will extend secured daylight overdrafts to repo counterparties in order to facilitate trading
during the business day. In response to changes in counterparty credit, market, or liquidity risk, however,
clearing banks may restrict access to these overdrafts, thereby undermining the liquidity of the dealers and
other counterparties that rely on them, and potentially exacerbating institutional and broader financial
instability. See Duffie, n 12.

[19] Kacpercyzk and Schnabl, n 7, document a similar phenomenon during the crisis within US commercial paper markets (see Figure 21.2).

[20] Amongst other things, the significant difference between the size of haircuts on subprime versus other
assets suggests that the gradual expansion of the range of collateral assets eligible for special treatment
under applicable bankruptcy laws in jurisdictions such as the US and the UK in the years leading up to the
financial crisis may have had an adverse impact on the stability of these markets. It may have also spurred
demand for structured finance assets.

[21] See Roe, n 14. From another perspective, the point of repo finance is to create 'informationally
insensitive' assets that would count as 'money' for the safety-seeking institutions on the other side of the
repo trade. See B Holmstrom, 'Understanding the Role of Debt in the Financial System', BIS Working Paper
No 479 (2015). From this perspective, the stability problem was greatly enlarged by mid-2000s legislation
that expanded the range of collateral that qualified for the special bankruptcy exception from US Treasury
securities to a class that included residential MBS. This fed the supply of credit for residential real estate,
fuelling the boom, while producing assets that could lose value when the boom collapsed. Put otherwise,

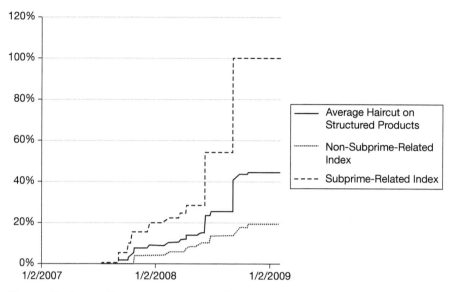

Fig. 21.3 Evolution of Repo Haircuts During the Financial Crisis

Source: G Gorton and A Metrick, 'Haircuts' (2009) NBER Working Paper No 15273, Figure 2.

few constraints on risk-taking by dealers, in turn increasing the probability of their instability. This lack of monitoring likely exacerbates contagion during periods of financial distress as lenders come to realize that they have insufficient information about the creditworthiness of their counterparties, thereby precipitating indiscriminate run-like behaviour.

Another risk associated with wholesale funding markets stems from the reuse and rehypothecation of collateral assets. As described above, dealers are often able to reuse or rehypothecate client assets as the raw material for repo and other forms of secured financing. In the process, dealers often create complex collateral chains, with the same underlying assets used to collateralize multiple transactions: for example, the original margin loan to the dealer's client, a repo transaction in which the dealer acts as borrower, and any other transactions in which the repo lender reuses the collateral. At the same time, any cash balances belonging to a dealer's clients are often commingled with those of other clients and, in many cases, with those of the dealer itself. In the ordinary course of business, this pooling of cash and collateral serves to lower dealers' cost of capital. It also gives them more flexibility to manage both their own liquidity needs and those of their clients. During periods of institutional or broader financial instability, however, where a dealer receives correlated demands from clients for cash or the return of collateral assets, extensive reuse or rehypothecation may undermine their ability to satisfy these demands on a timely basis. Indeed, commingling and collateral chains may actually incentivize counterparties to make these demands out of

wholesale funding based on collateral that can decline in value presents a greater systemic risk than that based on risk-free collateral. The systemic risk is greater still if the assets financed by this wholesale funding become the collateral for 'safe' short-term loans; this creates a self-inflating bubble.

the fear that the failure to do so may leave them with insufficient security over these assets in the event of the dealer's insolvency. Viewed from this perspective, extensive reuse and rehypothecation renders dealers vulnerable to yet another species of run-like behaviour: *collateral* runs.

21.2.3 Regulation of wholesale funding markets

Despite their susceptibility to destabilizing runs, wholesale funding markets have not historically been subject to the same type of prudential regulation and supervision typically imposed on conventional deposit-taking banks. Nor, in many cases, have the financial institutions that most heavily rely on these markets as sources of short-term funding. Drawing on the lessons of the financial crisis, however, policymakers have recently advanced a number of proposals for regulatory reform. Many of these proposals target the financial institutions that use wholesale funding. The liquidity rules introduced under Basel III,[22] for example, can be understood as an attempt to curb reliance on unstable short-term wholesale funding. The Basel Committee on Banking Supervision ('BCBS') has also proposed a new supervisory framework for measuring and controlling large exposures.[23] Once implemented, this framework will reduce the ability of dealers and other financial institutions to rely on a small number of counterparties as sources of wholesale funding, thereby limiting the potential knock-on effects in the event of a counterparty's insolvency. The Federal Reserve has targeted wholesale funding as a special systemic risk factor that should be assessed in the calculation of the extra capital charge required under the Basel framework for a global systemically important bank ('G-SIB').[24]

Other proposals more specifically target wholesale funding markets themselves. These proposals include the imposition of minimum haircuts on collateral assets used in repo and other securities financing transactions.[25] Pursuant to these proposals, the size of the haircut would be a function of both the type of collateral asset—such as corporate or sovereign debt, asset-backed securities, or equity—and the asset's remaining term to maturity.[26] Other proposals include the imposition of reinvestment constraints limiting the duration of assets that may be purchased using cash collateral, restrictions on the reuse and rehypothecation of assets, and minimum requirements for collateral quality.[27] Collectively, these proposals constrain the amount of credit,

---

[22] See Chapter 15.

[23] BCBS, Consultative Document, 'Supervisory Framework for Measuring and Controlling Large Exposures' (2013).

[24] Federal Reserve System, 'Regulatory Capital Rules: Implementation of Risk-Based Capital Surcharges for Global Systemically Important Bank Holding Companies' (2015).

[25] See FSB, 'Strengthening Oversight and Regulation of Shadow Banking: Policy Framework for Addressing Shadow Banking Risks in Securities Lending and Repos' (29 August 2013); FSB, 'Transforming Shadow Banking into Resilient Market-Based Finance' (November 2015); D Tarullo, 'Thinking Critically about Nonbank Financial Intermediation' (November 2015) (describing the Fed's plans).

[26] Ibid.

[27] Ibid. These proposals also call for better disclosure to clients regarding the reuse and rehypothecation of collateral assets in order to help them better understand their exposures in the event of an institution's insolvency. See also FSB, 'Regulatory Framework for Haircuts on Non-Centrally Cleared Securities Financing Transactions' (14 October 2014), available at http://www.fsb.org.

maturity, and liquidity transformation performed by dealers and other financial institutions. From a microprudential perspective, these proposals can thus be understood as limiting the amount of leverage these institutions may take on via their wholesale funding operations, as well as helping to insulate counterparties from the knock-on effects of institutional instability. From a macroprudential perspective, meanwhile, they can be understood as reducing the prospect of systemic underpricing within wholesale funding markets.

While many view these regulatory reforms as a step in the right direction, there are also those who advocate a more fundamental restructuring of wholesale funding markets. Morgan Ricks, for example, has proposed a system whereby issuers of repos and other 'money-claims' would be licensed and subject to portfolio restrictions and capital requirements.[28] The state would then provide a form of risk-based 'deposit' insurance guaranteeing the performance of these claims, thereby reducing the probability of run-like behaviour. In effect, Ricks' proposal is to extend the prudential regulatory regime applicable to conventional deposit-taking banks to dealers and other non-bank financial intermediaries that finance their activities within wholesale funding markets. Others suggest narrowing or even removing the bankruptcy carve-outs for repos secured by risky or illiquid collateral.[29] At present, however, policymakers have signalled that they do not intend to take forward any of these proposals for more sweeping reform of wholesale funding markets.[30]

21.3 Structured Finance Markets and Securitization

21.3.1 How structured finance works

In very basic terms, structured finance or 'securitization' is a process whereby the cash flows generated by illiquid assets are pooled together, restructured (see the discussion regarding structural subordination), and sold as more liquid asset-backed securities ('ABS'). The first ABS was issued in 1970.[31] This nascent ABS market initially revolved around the issuance of securities backed by residential mortgages—or MBS—by US government-sponsored entities (GSEs) such as the National Mortgage Association, Federal National Mortgage Association, and Federal Home Loan Mortgage Association. Between 1970 and 2013, annual issuances within this so-called 'agency' MBS market grew from approximately $452 million to over $1.9 trillion.[32] Observing this success, private-sector financial institutions—principally larger commercial and

---

[28] M Ricks, *The Money Problem: Rethinking Financial Regulation* (Chicago: Chicago UP, 2016); M Ricks, 'A Regulatory Design for Monetary Stability' (2012) 65 *Vanderbilt Law Review* 1289.

[29] D Duffie and D Skeel, 'A Dialogue on the Costs and Benefits of Automatic Stays for Derivatives and Repurchase Agreements', in K Scott and J Taylor (eds), *Bankruptcy Not Bailout: A Special Chapter 14* (Palo Alto: Hoover Institution Press, 2012); V Acharya and S Öncü, 'A Proposal for the Resolution of Systemically Important Assets and Liabilities: The Case of the Repo Market', presented at the Federal Reserve Board Conference on Central Banking Before, During, and After the Crisis (23 and 24 March 2012), available at http://www.ssrn.com. See also sources cited in Chapter 20, n 18.

[30] See FSB, n 25.

[31] S Heffernan, *Modern Banking* (Chichester: John Wiley & Sons, 2005), 46.

[32] SIFMA, 'US Agency Mortgage-Backed Securities Issued and Outstanding' (12 April 2014).

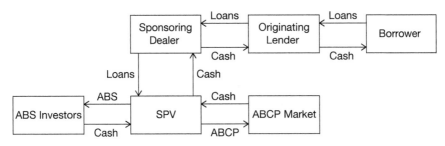

Fig. 21.4 Stylized Securitization Process

investment banks—began structuring and distributing 'private label' ABS in the mid-1980s.[33] These financial institutions employed the structures developed by the GSEs in connection with residential mortgages and adapted them to securitize a far broader range of underlying assets including: commercial mortgages; home equity and student loans; automobile, aircraft, and equipment leases; credit card receivables; corporate debt; and even other ABS. As of 2014, the aggregate size of the agency and private label ABS market in the US and Europe exceeded $10.5 trillion.[34]

Figure 21.4 depicts the basic steps in the securitization process. At one end of the process are lenders—eg commercial banks, finance companies, and other financial institutions—originating loans and other credit instruments to borrowers in exchange for the promise to make periodic payments of interest and principal. These loans are then sold to dealers, who may or may not be affiliated with the originating lenders. These dealers transfer the loans to entities known as special purpose vehicles ('SPVs'). Within an SPV, the cash flow rights associated with the loans are pooled together and restructured to create ABS. These ABS are then sold as fixed-income securities to institutional and other investors, who effectively receive interest paid out from the cash flows generated by the underlying loan pool. Sponsoring dealers may also retain ABS on their own balance sheets, either for investment purposes or as a source of collateral for use within their wholesale funding operations.

Figure 21.4 is a highly stylized depiction of the securitization process. There are several important features of this process that demand closer examination. The first is the sale of loans to *bankruptcy remote* SPVs. In theory, originating lenders could achieve many of the economic benefits of structured finance described in greater detail below simply by issuing bonds secured against the underlying assets.[35] In practice, however, securitization takes place through SPVs which both hold the loans and issue ABS to investors.[36] This has two important implications. First, the utilization of a separate entity renders the asset pool bankruptcy remote from both the originating

---

[33] Heffernan, n 31, 47.

[34] SIMFA, 'Europe Structured Finance Issued and Outstanding' (8 September 2014) and SIFMA, n 32. Of this amount, the US accounted for approximately $8.74 trillion and Europe approximately $1.85 trillion.

[35] These are so-called 'covered' bonds: S Lubben, *Corporate Finance* (New York, NY: Wolters Kluwer, 2014), 381.

[36] In many cases, SPVs actually serve as the originating lenders: with banks and other financial institutions simply referring clients to SPVs on the basis of specified underwriting criteria and performing a monitoring and administration role.

lender and the sponsoring dealer. Second, and as a corollary, the liabilities of the SPVs have historically been considered not to reside on the balance sheets of either the originating lenders or sponsoring dealers for accounting or prudential regulatory purposes.

The second important feature of securitization is *structural subordination*. Structural subordination involves the contractual allocation of losses on the underlying loan pool amongst different species—typically referred to as 'tranches'—of ABS issued by an SPV. It is often described in terms of a waterfall: with tranches higher up in the waterfall entitled to repayment before those further towards the bottom. Put differently, structural subordination contemplates that the first losses in a loan pool up to a specified threshold will be allocated to the bottom, or 'junior', tranche, while any subsequent losses will be absorbed by progressively more 'senior' tranches further up the SPV's capital structure. Each junior tranche thus serves as a form of credit enhancement for more senior tranches.[37] This is reflected in the pricing of different tranches: with junior tranches paying investors a higher return commensurate with the higher degree of exposure to default on the underlying loans.

The third and in many respects most important feature of securitization is its *financing model*. Sponsoring dealers typically finance the acquisition of loans from originating lenders via their wholesale funding operations.[38] SPVs, meanwhile, finance the purchase or origination of loans by issuing asset-backed commercial paper ('ABCP') to institutional investors such as money market mutual funds.[39] SPVs also use ABCP to bridge any liquidity mismatch between the cash flows generated by the loan pool and scheduled payments to ABS investors. To protect investors against liquidity shortfalls stemming from the breakdown of the ABCP market, sponsoring dealers then typically provide backstop guarantees to the SPV, often referred to as 'liquidity puts'. In a comprehensive survey of the US ABCP market just prior to the financial crisis, Viral Acharya, Phillip Schnabl, and Gustavo Suarez found that approximately 74 per cent of ABCP was covered by these liquidity or credit guarantees.[40] This financing model is notable in two respects. First, sponsoring dealers and SPVs rely on short-term liabilities in the form of ABCP and other wholesale funding to finance the holding of longer-term loans and payments to ABS investors. This is important because the cash flows coming in from loan assets might not match the cash flows due out to investors over the short run.[41] Second, despite historically being characterized as 'off-balance sheet' items for accounting and regulatory purposes, the provision of backstop guarantees to SPVs clearly exposes dealers to the risk of disruption within ABCP and other wholesale funding markets.

---

[37] D Jones, 'Emerging Problems with the Basel Capital Accord: Regulatory Capital Arbitrage and Related Issues' (2000) 24 *Journal of Banking and Finance* 35.

[38] Poszar, Adrian, Ashcraft, and Boesky, n 2.

[39] Jones, n 37. As the name implies, ABCP is simply a form of commercial paper collateralized by the loan pool held by an SPV.

[40] V Acharya, P Schnabl, and G Suarez, 'Securitization without Risk Transfer' (2013) 107 *Journal of Financial Economics* 515.

[41] For example, if borrowers have been given low-interest introductory or 'teaser' rates for a fixed initial period.

21.3.2 Structured finance and risks to stability

Structured finance holds out potentially significant economic benefits. In theory, it can lower information costs encountered in connection with the valuation of illiquid assets such as residential mortgages or loans to small- and medium-sized enterprises. Instead of evaluating the creditworthiness of thousands of underlying borrowers and the value of pledged collateral, securitization in principle enables investors to focus on the cash flow characteristics of the loan pool as a whole and their priority within the capital structure of the SPV. Moreover, in most cases, each ABS tranche receives an individualized rating from a credit rating agency (CRA), which proves essential, if not for its information value, for regulatory purposes.[42] Second, securitization can offer investors diversified exposure to relatively inaccessible asset classes such as residential and commercial real estate.

Structured finance also holds out a number of important benefits for both originating creditors and sponsoring dealers, which help to explain its popularity. Financial institutions involved in the securitization process typically earn sizeable fees. Notably, these fees derive not from holding financial assets, but from *intermediation*.[43] Second, securitization in principle enables financial institutions to shift the underlying assets and associated risks off their balance sheets, thereby freeing up capital for the purpose of making new investments.[44] Moreover, the assets can be more efficiently held by institutional investors such as insurers and pension funds whose liabilities are better matched, as we explained in Chapter 20, section 20.2.1. We would expect this, in turn, to lower the cost of capital for both financial institutions and, ultimately, the households and businesses to which they lend.[45] Finally, as described, the securitization process effectively creates new assets—ABS—which can be employed within the wholesale funding operations of sponsoring dealers.

Cutting against the benefits of structured finance are a number of significant risks. First, the structure of both ABS and the collateralized debt obligations ('CDOs')[46] into which they were often repackaged made it difficult for investors to understand precisely what they were purchasing. As ABS were typically not marketed to retail investors, issuers were often not required to produce extensive disclosure.[47] Conversely, when relevant information was disclosed, there were so many matters—legal, financial, creditor, asset, and other data—that could be price-relevant as to overwhelm the capacity of

---

[42] See Chapter 6 for the discussion on CRAs' regulatory licence. On the shortcomings in the methodological approach adopted by credit-rating agencies towards rating structured finance products prior to the crisis, see J Coval, J Jurek, and E Stafford, 'The Economics of Structured Finance' (2009) 23 *Journal of Economic Perspectives* 3.

[43] Gorton and Metrick, n 11.   [44] Ibid.

[45] Putting aside for the moment the question of whether cheaper credit is desirable from the perspective of financial stability.

[46] In the simplest possible terms, a CDO is simply an ABS the cash flows from which are derived from a pool of other fixed-income securities (eg bonds, swaps, or ABS).

[47] In the US, most public offerings of ABS were conducted through expedited SEC registration procedures known as 'shelf offerings'. ABS offerings were also sold as private placements exempt from SEC registration requirements.

investors to assimilate it all.[48] This tended to encourage reliance on credit ratings, themselves produced by agencies paid for by the originators and so suffering from severe conflicts of interest. What is worse, the transfer of risk from originators to investors effected by securitization appears to have undermined the incentives of originating lenders to screen for and monitor borrower and asset quality.[49] As a result, there exists the rather unsettling prospect that ABS may have been structured and marketed by financial institutions with weak incentives to constrain risk within the underlying loan pool and purchased by investors who, lacking the information or capacity to fully understand these risks, relied on credit-rating agencies with incentives to overstate quality. These same information problems also undermined the ability of financial regulators to monitor the build-up of risk within structured finance markets.

Second, structured finance has historically been used by financial institutions for regulatory arbitrage. Perhaps most infamously, tranching, remote origination, and liquidity puts were all used by dealers and originating lenders to reduce their capital requirements under Basel II.[50] In many cases, the resulting capital treatment did not reflect these institutions' economic exposures to the underlying assets. This was particularly the case where sponsoring dealers provided SPVs with backstop liquidity puts or other guarantees, thus effectively shifting the tail risk associated with the breakdown of wholesale funding markets from investors in those markets to the dealers themselves.[51]

Third, as vividly illustrated during the financial crisis, the structurally interdependent relationship between sponsoring dealers, SPVs, and ABCP and other wholesale funding markets can be a source of both institutional and systemic instability. As we have already seen, the reliance of sponsoring dealers on repo and commercial paper exposes these institutions to rollover risk. SPVs are exposed to a similar risk by virtue of their reliance on ABCP. More generally, both dealers and SPVs are vulnerable to widespread disruption within wholesale funding markets.[52] Exacerbating matters, when wholesale funding markets broke down during the crisis, the liquidity puts and other guarantees provided by dealers to SPVs put immense pressure on dealers at a time when their balance sheets were already under considerable strain. Indeed, these guarantees were one of the primary mechanisms by which the disruption within the ABCP market was transmitted to dealers and, ultimately, the broader financial system.[53]

The breakdown of wholesale funding markets during the financial crisis thus understandably raised important questions about both the stability of dealers' funding

---

[48] R Bartlett III, 'Inefficiencies in the Information Thicket: A Case Study of Derivatives Disclosures During the Financial Crisis' (2010) 36 *Journal of Corporation Law* 1. Nor was there a robust secondary market in these claims that could impound new information into prices. ABS were commonly priced in private market transactions (over-the-counter), not generally disclosed. The ABX index that aggregated ABS information was created only in 2006. Until well into 2007, the index indicated virtually zero risk on the AAA tranches and so was not a leading indicator of risk. In short, disclosure-based regulation was insufficient to anticipate and modulate risk in this market.

[49] See B Keys, T Mukherjee, A Seru, and V Vig, 'Did Securitization Lead to Lax Screening? Evidence from Subprime Loans' (2010) 125 *Quarterly Journal of Economics* 305; but see R Bubb and A Kaufman, 'Securitization and Moral Hazard: Evidence from Credit Score Cutoff Rules' (2014) 63 *Journal of Monetary Economics* 1.

[50] See Acharya, Schnabl and Suarez, n 40; Jones, n 37.   [51] Duffie, n 12.

[52] Pozsar, Adrian, Ashcraft, and Boesky, n 2.   [53] Ibid.

models and the nature and extent of their exposures to structured finance markets. Evaluating these risks in real time and in the midst of an unfolding crisis, however, proved exceedingly difficult for both market participants and regulators given the acute information problems associated with these markets and, more generally, dealer balance sheets. These information problems—along with the fact that many other market participants also needed liquidity in the wake of the breakdown of wholesale funding markets—triggered a flight of clients, capital, and collateral from those dealers deemed most vulnerable. These same information problems, as we have seen, also compelled investors to demand higher haircuts on—or refuse to accept altogether—certain types of ABS as collateral, thereby increasing the cost of short-term funding. The use of ABS as collateral within repo markets thus helped further transmit and magnify problems originating within the US subprime mortgage market to dealers and other financial institutions across the globe.[54] Together, these developments created a near-perfect storm: dramatically reducing dealers' access to private sources of funding at a time when this funding was most urgently required.

21.3.3 Regulation of structured finance

Like wholesale funding, structured finance markets attracted surprisingly little regulatory scrutiny prior to the global financial crisis. Since the crisis, however, policymakers have implemented a number of regulatory reforms in relation to securitization. These include measures designed to ensure greater transparency and standardization of ABS.[55] These measures are intended to target information problems, which it is hoped will make it easier for regulators to monitor the location, concentration, and extent of potential risks. Other reforms include risk retention requirements mandating, for example, that sponsors and originating lenders retain a specified percentage of either *each* tranche of ABS issued by an SPV (a so-called 'vertical slice') or the most *junior* tranche in the SPV's capital structure (a so-called 'horizontal slice').[56] Together with new rules imposing more stringent underwriting standards,[57] these risk-retention requirements are designed to ensure that originators and dealers have incentives to investigate and monitor both the creditworthiness of borrowers and the quality of underlying assets.[58]

Other proposed reforms target the economic interconnections between sponsoring dealers and SPVs. The FSB, for example, is developing guidance with a view to promoting the consolidation of SPVs onto dealer balance sheets for prudential regulatory purposes.[59] The FSB is also considering proposals that would impose higher

---

[54] Gorton and Metrick, n 11.

[55] See eg Dodd–Frank Act (US) §942; Capital Requirements Regulation ('CRR') (EU), Regulation 575/2013, Art 409.

[56] See eg Dodd–Frank Act §941; CRR Art 405.

[57] See eg Dodd–Frank Act §941; CRR Arts 406 and 408.

[58] This reform may not give due weight to the crisis-era phenomenon that the banks believed their own story: investment banks and commercial banks suffered serious losses because of ABS they had added to their balance sheets because they liked the yield/risk proposition.

[59] FSB, 'Strengthening Oversight and Regulation of Shadow Banking: An Overview of Policy Recommendations' (29 August 2013) and FSB, 'Shadow Banking: Strengthening Oversight and Regulation' (27 October 2011), both available at http://www.fsb.org.

capital requirements on dealers providing contingent support—such as liquidity puts or other guarantees—to unconsolidated SPVs.[60] Finally, the BCBS's proposed framework for measuring and controlling large exposures includes exposures to SPVs and other shadow banking entities.[61] If implemented, these proposals will provide regulators with better information about the nature and extent of interconnections between dealers and SPVs, along with new tools to constrain excess risk-taking and limit contagion between structured finance markets and sponsoring dealers.

Looking forward, it is difficult to predict the market impact of these reforms and thus their likely success. At present, the detailed rules implementing many of these reforms are still under development. These rules may ultimately carve out certain financial institutions, investors, and underlying assets from the application of these reforms, thereby potentially limiting their effectiveness. Moreover, emerging differences between proposed reforms across jurisdictions—particularly in relation to risk-retention requirements[62]—may in time generate new opportunities for regulatory arbitrage. Similarly, these reforms may encourage the migration of structured finance markets away from dealers and toward other, potentially even more fragile and less regulated, parts of the financial system. At the same time, however, by expanding the perimeter of prudential regulation to encompass structured finance, these reforms provide the foundation for addressing the information problems, perverse incentives, and fragility which have historically characterized these markets.

21.4 OTC Derivatives Markets

21.4.1 How OTC derivatives markets work

Derivatives are financial assets the value or expected performance of which is determined by reference to another ('underlying') asset, rate, index, or event. Common underlying include: financial assets such as equity, debt, currencies, and interest rates; physical commodities such as agricultural products, base and precious metals, and other natural resources; and more exotic assets, indices, and events such as emissions rights, the volatility of financial instruments or indices, and even Acts of God. All derivatives are engineered from two basic building blocks: options and forwards. Options represent a contingent *right* to acquire or dispose of an asset in the future at a predetermined price. Forwards, in contrast, represent an *obligation* to do so.[63] Theoretically, these basic building blocks can be combined in an infinite number of ways, each yielding a different derivative instrument.

Many derivatives are traded on organized order-driven exchanges such as the Chicago Mercantile Exchange, Eurex, or Intercontinental Exchange ('ICE'). These exchange-traded derivatives are highly standardized instruments that offer market participants a relatively limited menu of potential underlying and prescribe a narrow

---

[60] Ibid.   [61] BCBS, n 23.

[62] See Linklaters, 'Risk Retention: More Than Words', *International Financial Law Review* (November 2013), available at http://www.iflr.com.

[63] Futures, viewed by some as a third basic building block, are simply forwards executed on an organized exchange.

range of available settlement amounts, maturity dates, and strike prices. This standardization is a necessary, if not always sufficient, condition for the development of liquid markets in these instruments. Standardization also enables exchanges to clear and settle trades through centralized clearinghouses. As will be described in greater detail, clearinghouses interpose themselves between the counterparties to a derivatives transaction, in effect becoming a buyer to every seller and a seller to every buyer. In the process, clearinghouses assume the counterparty credit and other risks to which the parties would otherwise be exposed.[64]

As in public equity markets, derivatives exchanges play an important role in the governance of these markets: writing, monitoring, and enforcing rules regarding, amongst other matters, exchange membership, trading qualifications and practices, risk management, and the approval of new derivative instruments.[65] Unlike public equity markets, derivatives exchanges also play an integral role in *designing* the instruments that trade on each exchange. Derivatives exchanges perform these roles under the oversight of domestic securities regulators and are required to comply with entry, information, and conduct regulation, and other requirements.[66]

The term 'over-the-counter' or 'OTC' derivatives has historically been used to describe derivatives entered into outside the environment of an organized exchange. In sharp contrast with their exchange-traded cousins, OTC derivatives thus offer counterparties the ability to structure completely bespoke instruments. The most ubiquitous species of OTC derivative is the 'swap'. In the simplest possible terms, a swap is a series of mutual forward obligations whereby two counterparties agree periodically to exchange—or *swap*—cash flows on predetermined dates over a specified period of time. Perhaps the most straightforward example is a plain vanilla interest rate swap. Under an interest rate swap, one counterparty—for example, a borrower with fixed-rate obligations—agrees to make payments at a fixed interest rate to another counterparty who in turn agrees to pay the borrower a variable (or 'floating') rate. The fixed-rate borrower receiving the floating rate thus stands to benefit from any subsequent increase in interest rates, whereas its counterparty receiving the fixed rate will benefit from any decline. The periodic payments due under a swap are calculated with reference to what is known as the 'notional amount'.[67] The resulting obligations are then netted out against one another so that only one of the parties is required to make payment on any given date. Figure 21.5 depicts a stylized interest rate swap transaction.[68]

---

[64] Viewed differently, counterparties using exchange-traded derivatives effectively substitute the credit risk of their original counterparty for that of the clearinghouse. In this way, the identity of the original counterparty becomes irrelevant: all obligations are owed to and by the clearinghouse itself.

[65] See Chapter 7.

[66] In the US, responsibility for the oversight of exchange-traded derivatives is split between the SEC and the Commodity Futures Trading Commission. In the EU, exchange-traded derivatives are subject to oversight by national regulatory authorities within each Member State.

[67] While the notional amount provides a conventional measure of the *size* of an OTC derivatives transaction, it does not capture the attendant *risks*. A more useful measure of size is 'gross market value', which reflects the current exposures of counterparties under open contracts assuming that these contracts were all settled immediately.

[68] This depiction of an interest rate swap is stylized in several respects. Perhaps most importantly, the counterparties to a typical swap will not contract directly with one another but, rather, will enter into separate swaps with a dealer.

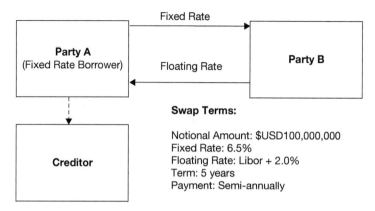

Fig. 21.5 Stylized Interest Rate Swap

A second important subspecies of swap is the credit default swap ('CDS'). A CDS is a derivative instrument pursuant to which one counterparty—often referred to as the 'credit protection seller'—agrees to compensate another counterparty—the 'credit protection buyer'—upon the occurrence of certain prescribed credit events—most fundamentally, default or restructuring—in connection with underlying debt obligations issued by one or more reference entities.[69] The economic effect of a CDS is thus to transfer some or all of the credit risk associated with the underlying debt ('reference') obligations from the credit protection buyer to the credit protection seller.

Swaps and other OTC derivatives are typically entered into within relatively opaque, quote-driven markets in which dealers perform an explicit market-making role: structuring derivatives and marketing them to clients, often on the basis that they are willing to take either side of the trade. These dealers then typically look to hedge the resulting exposures by seeking out and entering into offsetting trades with other clients or, in many cases, other dealers. In theory, dealers thus seek to maintain a 'matched' or neutral trading book: making money not by taking a view on the future direction of the market, but by charging each counterparty a fee—typically embedded in their quoted bid–ask spread—in exchange for their willingness to stand on the opposite side of the trade.

Dealers can thus be understood as performing several important economic functions within OTC derivatives markets. First, dealers use their large client networks to assist clients in identifying potential counterparties willing to take the opposite side of a trade, thereby reducing search costs. In doing so, dealers may also resolve any temporal gaps by taking risk on to their own balance sheet during the search process. Second, in our example in Figure 21.5, both the fixed-rate borrower and its counterparty are exposed to the risk that the other might become insolvent or opportunistically seek

---

[69] Credit events typically include the *insolvency* of a reference entity, its *failure to pay* its debts when due, or the *restructuring* of those debts in order to avoid insolvency. Reference entities can include corporate and sovereign debt issuers, baskets of debt instruments, or financial indices. Reference obligations, meanwhile, can include bonds, loans, or virtually any conceivable form of debt instrument. The credit protection seller provides this protection in exchange for a periodic fee—putting them in a similar position to the fixed-rate borrower under the stylized interest rate swap depicted in Figure 21.5.

to prematurely terminate the swap. Dealer intermediation can help minimize these risks for two reasons. First, insofar as their balance sheets are more diversified than those of their clients, dealers can be seen as the more efficient bearers of counterparty credit and other risks. Second, dealers are also likely to be better positioned to hedge any residual exposures. Finally, by contractually interposing themselves between counterparties, dealers can be seen as playing an important role as reputational intermediaries: in effect using their status as repeat players to enhance the credibility of the commitments underpinning derivatives trades.

Historically, the vast majority of OTC derivatives have not been cleared or settled through clearinghouses. Instead, dealers and other counterparties developed bilateral contractual mechanisms designed to mitigate the risks of counterparty credit and other risks. These mechanisms are typically embedded within standardized 'master' agreements and other documentation developed by industry bodies such as the International Swaps and Derivatives Association ('ISDA'). These master agreements are designed to incorporate multiple transactions between two counterparties under the umbrella of a single legal relationship, contemplating only the preparation of a brief and customizable trade confirmation for each individual trade.

Two of the most important contractual mechanisms used to minimize counterparty credit risk are *closeout netting* and *collateral*. Closeout netting involves the termination, valuation, and netting-out of obligations owed by a defaulting counterparty to a non-defaulting counterparty in the event of default or other specified termination events.[70] Where the netted closeout amount puts the non-defaulting counterparty in the money (that is, it is owed money by the defaulting party), closeout netting entitles this party to seize any collateral posted by the defaulting counterparty in satisfaction of this amount.[71] In contrast, where the defaulting counterparty is in the money, the non-defaulting party is entitled to set off against the amount it owes to the defaulting counterparty any amounts owed to it by the defaulting counterparty, irrespective of whether these are derived from derivatives trades or other sources. Importantly, the enforceability of closeout netting—like repo agreements—relies on a series of carveouts from national bankruptcy laws.[72]

Dealers seek to minimize their residual net exposures after closeout netting by requiring their counterparties to post collateral—typically cash or highly liquid securities—at the outset of trade. This collateral, often referred to as 'initial margin' or the 'independent amount', is intended to reflect each counterparty's exposure to the default of the other counterparty (that is, counterparty credit risk) over the duration of the trade. Thereafter, counterparties may also be required to periodically recalculate the amount of collateral one or both counterparties are required to post. This 'variation margin' is designed to reflect changes in the market price of the relevant underlying, which in turn affects the net exposure under the agreement. Changes in variation

---

[70] Events of default can include breach of the agreement itself (along with any supporting credit agreements), other specified transactions, cross default, and bankruptcy. Termination events can include certain tax and credit events, mergers, and *force majeure*.

[71] With any residual amounts owed generally being treated as an unsecured claim in the defaulting counterparty's estate.

[72] See sources cited in n 14.

margin may take place in accordance with triggers predetermined in the contract—for example, a downgrade in a counterparty's credit rating—or be negotiated on a more ad hoc basis in response to market developments. Like closeout netting, the enforceability of these collateral arrangements relies on carve-outs from applicable bankruptcy laws.

21.4.2 OTC derivatives and risks to stability

The prevailing view prior to the financial crisis was that the private contractual mechanisms that governed OTC derivatives, combined with the powerful incentives of market participants to monitor the financial health of their counterparties, were sufficient to minimize the risks associated with the use of these instruments.[73] This view was reflected in the sevenfold growth of these markets in the years leading up to the crisis.[74] In retrospect, however, this growth engendered a number of significant risks.

First, OTC derivatives are the source of often acute asymmetries of information. The ultimate financial consequences of OTC derivative agreements are exceptionally opaque, even by the standards of financial products more generally.[75] This causes problems for less sophisticated counterparties who enter into such trades as clients of dealers. There are pronounced imbalances of information and expertise between dealers and their clients with respect to the legal and economic structure of many derivatives instruments, with the result that non-financial counterparties often fail fully to understand the risks they are taking.[76] Compounding matters, the dealer-intermediated, quote-driven structure of OTC derivatives markets makes it difficult for clients to directly observe prevailing market conditions: that is, the identity and creditworthiness of other market participants, the depth and volume of trade, or the spread between bid and asking prices.

The extreme opacity of OTC derivatives also poses information problems for dealers' shareholders, counterparties, and other creditors. Specifically, the size, complexity, and opacity of dealers' derivatives portfolios can make it difficult for these market participants to meaningfully evaluate the financial condition of these institutions. Obviously, the same issues also undermine the effectiveness of supervision and enforcement by public regulatory authorities.[77]

Second, swaps and other OTC derivatives often generate high levels of (implicit) leverage. To see this, imagine that a client seeking exposure to Apple Inc's stock enters

---

[73] See eg A Greenspan, 'Financial Derivatives', remarks to the Futures Industry Association, Boca Raton, Florida (19 March 1999); A Greenspan, 'Government Regulation and Derivatives Contracts', remarks to the Financial Markets Conference of the Federal Reserve Bank of Atlanta (21 February 1997).

[74] Between December 2000 and June 2008, the outstanding notional amount of all OTC derivatives grew from approximately $95 trillion to over $683 trillion: BIS, *BIS Quarterly Review* (May 2001) and *BIS Quarterly Review* (November 2008).

[75] We characterize financial products as generally more opaque than non-financial products: see Chapter 3, section 3.2.1.

[76] See eg the UK FCA's review of interest rate hedging products; http://www.fca.org.uk/consumers/financial-services-products/banking/interest-rate-hedging-products.

[77] D Duffie, A Li, and T Lubke, 'Policy Perspectives on OTC Derivatives Market Infrastructure', Federal Reserve Bank of New York Staff Report No 424 (2010).

into five-year total return equity swap on a notional value of $10m of that company's shares, with semi-annual payments of 5 per cent. This means the client will be obligated to pay the dealer $500,000 every six months, in exchange for which it will receive payments from the dealer reflecting any capital appreciation and dividends on $10m-worth of Apple shares. Should the price of Apple's stock decline, however, the client will be required to make a payment to the dealer reflecting the deterioration in value of the notional holding of $10m. From an economic perspective, this swap is thus identical to the client simply borrowing $10 million from the dealer on margin at a 5 per cent interest rate and investing it in Apple shares.[78] The interest payable on this 'implicit' or 'synthetic' leverage (so-called because it is not formally characterized as borrowing under the agreement) means that the client actually loses money under the trade unless Apple's stock increases in value by 50 per cent over the term of the agreement![79] Like all debt financing, this implicit leverage renders the financial position of the client more fragile, in this case in relation to movements in the market price of the underlying.[80]

Third, the mechanisms that derivatives counterparties employ to mitigate counterparty credit and other risks can contribute both to distress at a particular institution and broader financial instability. Consider 'novation', a legal mechanism by which parties agree that the rights and obligations of one party to a contract will be transferred to a third party. Many of the prime brokerage clients of Bear Stearns, for example, novated their derivatives trades to other—more creditworthy—dealers in the months leading up to the firm's failure.[81] This had two effects. First, the novation of these trades required Bear to return to their counterparties any cash or posted collateral, thereby draining the firm's liquidity. (In this regard, recall the discussion of reuse and rehypothecation in section 21.2.1.) Second, the fact that a large number of trades with Bear were being novated sent a strong signal to other dealers and market participants that Bear's creditworthiness was rapidly deteriorating.[82] Conversely, had Bear refused to permit the novation of these trades, market participants may have taken this as a signal that the firm could not return the relevant cash and collateral without undermining its liquidity position. Viewed in this light, these novations can be seen as a modern-day equivalent of a long queue outside a bank: signalling its impending failure and thus precipitating further demands on its dwindling liquidity.

A second way these mechanisms contribute to instability stems from collateral calls. OTC derivatives usually contemplate that additional collateral may be required in

---

[78] The dealer will hedge their exposure to the movement of Apple's shares by entering into an offsetting agreement with a counterparty who wants a synthetic *short* exposure to Apple.

[79] The client must make ten bi-annual payments of $500,000 to the dealer, which over five years amounts to a total of $5m. Hence if the Apple stock initially worth $10m is worth anything less than $15m at the completion of the trade, the client's cash flows are net negative over the life of the swap. This example assumes that the benchmark price for Apple shares is reset to reflect the market price as at every payment date (eg every six months) over the life of the swap.

[80] While collateral can help minimize the impact of such price movements on the dealer, it will only do so insofar as the value of the collateral is not itself correlated with the price of the underlying. Thus shares in other tech companies would probably not be good collateral for this swap.

[81] Duffie, n 12.   [82] Duffie, Li, and Lubke, n 77.

certain circumstances: either specified triggering events (such as a credit rating down-grade) or in response to adverse market movements (for example, a decline in the price of the underlying or of posted collateral). This raises the prospect of large—or 'lumpy'—collateral calls precisely when the counterparties required to meet them are already facing severe liquidity constraints. JP Morgan, for example, requested billions of dollars in additional collateral from Lehman in September 2008, just days before Lehman's collapse. Goldman Sachs and other counterparties similarly demanded over $30 billion in additional collateral from AIG in the months leading up to its bail-out.[83] These collateral calls had the effect of draining liquidity from systemically important dealers during a period of extreme market dislocation. While it is unclear whether these collateral calls contributed to the failure of either firm, they likely exacerbated what was already an extremely volatile situation.

Importantly, such eve-of-bankruptcy collateral calls would probably not have been legally enforceable but for the carve-outs for derivatives from the automatic stay and fraudulent preference provisions under US bankruptcy law. In addition to pouring petrol on the fire for a troubled counterparty, these carve-outs also weaken the *ex ante* incentives of derivatives users to monitor the creditworthiness of their counterparties, leading to an underpricing of risk.[84] This could also contribute to information conta-gion: where parties lack a detailed understanding of the financial health of their counter-parties, they may be more prone to engage in an indiscriminate 'run' in response to the emergence of a negative signal.[85]

21.4.3 Regulation of OTC derivatives

In the wake of the financial crisis, policymakers have adopted a number of measures designed to strengthen the regulation of OTC derivatives markets.[86] The most signifi-cant has been to mandate the clearing and settlement of standardized swaps through clearinghouses. The main benefit of clearinghouses derives from the mechanisms they use to mitigate counterparty credit risk.[87] First, clearinghouses employ multilateral netting in order to eliminate offsetting exposures, thereby reducing the overall size and number of payment obligations and thus each counterparty's exposure in the event of counterparty default. Second, clearinghouses seek to minimize their residual net exposures after multilateral netting by requiring counterparties to post both initial and variation margin (collateral). Unlike bilateral swap markets—where, as we have seen, collateral calls are infrequent and consequently often 'lumpy', which has a tendency to exacerbate institutional instability—the variation margin demanded by clearinghouses is calculated on a daily basis, reflecting movements in the price of the

---

[83] See Congressional Oversight Panel, 'The AIG Rescue, Its Impact on Markets, and the Governments Exit Strategy' (20 June 2010), available at http://www.gpo.gov. See also Roe, n 14 and Cohan, n 1.

[84] Roe, n 14.   [85] Ibid.

[86] In the US, the majority of these reforms have been introduced under Title VII of the Dodd–Frank Act and in Europe, under the European Market Infrastructure Regulation, Regulation (EU) No 648/2012 ('EMIR'), along with relevant subordinate regulation in each case.

[87] The clearing and settlement of trades through clearinghouses obviously also resolves the 'run by novation' problem described in text accompanying n 82.

underlying.[88] Together with multilateral netting, these margin requirements can also be understood as liquidity-enhancing: facilitating faster payouts in the event of default, reducing complexity and uncertainty during periods of market turmoil, and facilitating resolution.[89] Third, clearinghouses employ a number of other loss-sharing mechanisms designed to minimize market disruption in the event of the failure of one or more dealer (or 'clearing') members. These include pre-funded default funds, clearing member capital calls, recourse to the clearinghouse's own capital, and so-called 'position portability' procedures.[90] Collectively, these mechanisms—often referred to as a clearinghouse's 'default waterfall'—can be understood as mutualizing the risks stemming from the default of a clearing member across all members of the clearinghouse.

The mandatory clearing and settlement of standardized swaps through clearinghouses has been accompanied by a number of complementary regulatory reforms. Some are designed to strengthen the governance of clearinghouses: mandating, for example, stricter capital, ownership, independent oversight, clearing member eligibility, margin, and collateral quality requirements.[91] Others target remaining bilateral swaps, which are not easily susceptible to central clearing and settlement.[92] Thus, for example, proposals have been put forward which would impose minimum standards on counterparties to bilateral swaps in relation to the calculation of margin requirements, the frequency with which they are required to post variation margin, and the quality of posted collateral.[93] In order to encourage the migration of swaps to clearinghouses, bilateral swaps are also now subject to higher capital requirements.[94]

Policymakers have also adopted a number of measures designed to enhance transparency within OTC derivatives markets. In both the US and Europe, swap dealers, other significant counterparties, and clearinghouses are now required to report all bilateral and centrally cleared swaps to so-called 'trade repositories'.[95] Both clearinghouses and trade repositories are then obligated to report granular counterparty and transaction data to regulatory authorities.[96] These measures should enable authorities to monitor the location, nature, and extent of potential risks residing within OTC derivatives markets more effectively. Clearinghouses and trade repositories are also

---

[88] Importantly, however, these variation margin requirements are not updated to reflect changes in the credit risk of the relevant counterparties.

[89] R Squire, 'Clearinghouses and the Rapid Resolution of Financial Firms' (2013) 99 *Cornell Law Review* 857.

[90] Position portability procedures obligate surviving clearing members to assume the rights and obligations of trades entered into by defaulting clearing members.

[91] See eg Dodd–Frank Act §§725, 728, 733, and 763; EMIR, Title VI.

[92] Typically because they are either insufficiently standardized or because they are too illiquid to be effectively priced and, thus, hedged.

[93] See BCBS and IOSCO, 'Margin Requirements for Non-Centrally Cleared Derivatives' (September 2013), available at http://www.bis.org.

[94] See CRD IV and CRR and Federal Reserve System, Regulatory Capital Rules: Regulatory Capital, Implementation of Basel III, Capital Adequacy, Transition Provisions, Prompt Corrective Action, Standardized Approach for Risk-Weighted Assets, Market Discipline and Disclosure Requirements, Advanced Approaches Risk-Based Capital Rule, and Mark Risk Capital Rule, 78 Fed Reg 62,018 (11 October 2013) (codified 12 CFR Parts 208, 217, and 225).

[95] See Dodd–Frank Act §§727, 729, and 766; EMIR, Art 9. In the US, 'trade repositories' are known for regulatory purposes as 'swap data repositories'.

[96] See eg Dodd–Frank Act §§725, 728, and 733.

required to make public anonymized transaction and pricing data.[97] These disclosure requirements are expressly designed to enhance price formation. They should also make it less costly for counterparties to monitor prevailing market conditions and, thus, to identify opportunistic behaviour on the part of dealers.

It remains to be seen whether mandatory central clearing and other post-crisis regulatory reforms targeting swaps will effectively address the risks to stability lurking within OTC derivatives markets. Simultaneously, central clearing may itself pose a number of potentially significant risks. Most obviously, while the ability of clearinghouses to effectively manage counterparty credit and other risks increases with each additional swap they clear, this concentration of market activity—and risk—also makes these institutions themselves systemically important.[98] Compounding matters, the mechanisms employed by clearinghouses to mitigate counterparty credit risk may in certain circumstances generate unintended adverse consequences. For example, while multilateral netting and margin requirements increase the proportion of outstanding payments that counterparties receive upon default, conferring this advantage on derivatives counterparties necessarily dilutes the claims of the defaulting counterparty's other creditors.[99] There is ultimately no guarantee that the losses thereby imposed on these other creditors will not have systemic knock-on effects.

It is also important to acknowledge the inherent limits of these mechanisms. First, while multilateral netting and margin requirements can theoretically reduce the leverage embedded within swaps and other OTC derivatives, counterparties may simply use this increased debt capacity to increase leverage elsewhere on their balance sheets.[100] The net effect of mandatory clearing and settlement on leverage at both the institutional and systemic level is thus ambiguous. Second, while variation margin requirements take into account movements in the price of the underlying, they are generally not sensitive to changes in counterparty credit risk. Moreover, where clearinghouse margin requirements are sensitive to changes in counterparty credit risk, it is often on the basis of changes to a clearing member's credit rating, thereby once again introducing the prospect of lumpy and potentially destabilizing collateral calls. Third, and most importantly, while mutualization is an effective way to mitigate *idiosyncratic* risks to clearing members, it cannot protect against the *correlated* failure of multiple clearing members. Indeed, insofar as the loss-sharing mechanisms employed by clearinghouses require dealers to contribute capital during periods of broader market disruption, they can be understood as imposing costs on clearing members at the precise moment at

---

[97] See eg Dodd–Frank Act §727. In the US, this responsibility technically falls to the relevant regulatory authorities.

[98] As reflected in the fact that many clearinghouses have been designated as systemically important financial market infrastructures or, in the language of the Dodd–Frank Act, Title VIII, a systemically important 'financial market utility'.

[99] C Pirrong, 'A Bill of Goods: CCPs and Systemic Risk' (2014) 2 *Journal of Financial Market Infrastructures* 55; Squire, n 89; Roe, n 14. This, in turn, points to another potential shortcoming of post-crisis reforms targeting OTC derivatives: their failure to address the problems generated by the bankruptcy carve-outs.

[100] Pirrong, n 99.

which they are likely to be least able to afford them.[101] These 'wrong way' risks may thus *accelerate*—rather than dampen—an emerging threat to stability.

At present, it is far from clear whether clearinghouses possess sufficiently strong incentives to monitor and manage these risks effectively. As observed by Robert Litan, the fact that clearinghouses are often owned by derivatives dealers generates potentially acute conflicts of interest.[102] In the same vein, competition amongst clearinghouses may over time lead to a deleterious 'race to the bottom' in margin, collateral quality, loss sharing, and other mechanisms designed to mitigate counterparty credit and other risks. Ultimately, of course, we might view these potential incentive problems as relatively straightforward to resolve insofar as regulatory authorities are able to provide effective oversight. In many cases, however, we might expect regulators to lack both the resources and incentives to effectively constrain socially excessive risk-taking.[103] Accordingly, a number of important questions remain over whether mandatory central clearing will effectively mitigate the systemic risks generated by the widespread use of OTC derivatives.

21.5 Interconnection and Intermediation Chains

This chapter has examined wholesale funding, structured finance, and OTC derivatives markets largely independently of one another. It is worth briefly observing that, in reality, these markets are often deeply interconnected. Repurchase agreements and commercial paper are important sources of funding for structured finance markets. Structured finance products such as ABS, in turn, are used as collateral within wholesale funding markets. Swaps, meanwhile—and in particular CDS—are used as a form of credit enhancement within structured finance markets: providing a form of insurance to ABS investors against losses on the underlying loan pool. They also provide the raw material for more complex structured finance vehicles such as so-called 'synthetic' securitizations.[104]

Together, these markets often combine with non-bank financial intermediaries to perform significant credit, liquidity, and maturity transformation. The securitization process provides an illustrative example.[105] At one end of the process, long-term, illiquid loans are sold to sponsoring dealers and, ultimately, to SPVs. To finance the acquisition and holding of these loans, the dealers and SPVs rely predominantly on wholesale funding: specifically repo and ABCP markets. At the other end of the process, then, the ABCP issued by SPVs is purchased by institutional investors, including money-market funds. Investors in these money-market funds have historically been able to withdraw their investment on demand at a fixed net asset value,

---

[101] Ibid.

[102] R Litan, 'The Derivatives Dealers Club and Derivatives Markets Reform: A Guide for Policy Makers, Citizens and Other Interested Parties', Brookings Institution (7 April 2010), available at http://www.brookings.edu. See also S Griffith, 'Governing Systemic Risk: Toward a Governance Structure for Derivatives Clearinghouses' (2012) 61 *Emory Law Review* 1153.

[103] See Chapters 24–25.

[104] In a nutshell, a synthetic securitization involves the use of CDS to replicate the cash flows generated by an underlying debt instrument.

[105] Poszar, Adrian, Ashcraft, and Boesky, n 2.

thereby completing the transformation of the long-term, illiquid loans into short-term deposit-like claims.

In many cases, wholesale funding, structured finance, and OTC derivatives markets are also highly interconnected with the formal banking system. Conventional deposit-taking banks use repo and commercial paper markets as sources of short-term funding. These banks are also important originators of the loans and other credit claims repackaged and sold via securitization, and often act as guarantors of the ABS and ABCP issued by affiliated SPVs. The dealers residing at the heart of these markets, meanwhile, are often part of larger financial services groups which include conventional banks. Indeed, as Zoltan Poszar and others have observed, these groups can span the entire range of financial markets and institutions within a given intermediation chain.[106] Thus, for example, a conventional bank within a larger financial services group can theoretically originate a loan, sell it to an SPV sponsored by an affiliated dealer, and the ABS issued by the SPV can then be purchased by the asset management arm of the same group.

What are the implications of this from a policy perspective? First, in order to identify potential threats to financial stability, financial regulators must actively monitor and seek to understand how different financial markets and institutions interact with one another and what risks these interactions might potentially pose. Given the nature and pace of change within the financial system, this monitoring and risk assessment must take place on an ongoing basis. Second, the idea that the formal and so-called 'shadow' banking systems are somehow two different systems is, in many cases, inaccurate. In reality, the two are often fundamentally intertwined. As non-bank financial intermediation supported by conventional banks grows in size, therefore, it may place pressure on the ability of the formal banking system to effectively backstop it.[107] This raises important questions about the desirable scope of both microprudential and macroprudential regulation and supervision. In general, broader is better. It also raises questions about the extent to which lender of last resort and other public backstops should be extended to financial markets and institutions other than banks. Ultimately, the answer to this question depends both on the social desirability of different forms of non-bank financial intermediation and whether it is possible to effectively insulate the formal banking system from instability generated by other markets and institutions (discussed in Chapter 23).

21.6 Conclusion

On the surface, the financial markets and institutions examined in this chapter bear little resemblance to conventional deposit-taking banks. Look deeper, however, and these markets and institutions—both alone and in combination—perform many of the same economic functions. They also pose many of the same risks. Perhaps most importantly,

---

[106] Ibid.
[107] S Luck and P Schempp, 'Banks, Shadow Banking and Fragility' (8 July 2014), Working Paper on file with authors.

the credit, maturity, and liquidity transformation performed within these markets and institutions can be the source of significant financial instability. This is especially the case where these markets and institutions are highly interconnected with the formal banking system. The challenges from a regulatory perspective are thus to identify these risks, to understand their likely effects and how they might spread through the financial system, and to design regulatory regimes capable of effectively addressing them.

22

Asset Managers and Stability

22.1 Introduction

In this chapter, we return to the subject of collective investment. The key economic function of collective investment is to reap economies of scale regarding the costs of investing. In particular, collective investment vehicles provide low-cost access to diversification, to the expertise of asset managers, and to the acquisition of market information.[1] Collective investment vehicles, and the asset managers that sponsor them, are therefore key market intermediaries in the financial system. We previously identified, in Chapters 2 and 20, the spectacular growth of this sector as one of the most important changes in the financial system in recent years. We considered the issues the sector raises regarding investor or consumer protection in Chapter 12. In this chapter, we explore the implications of its growth for the stability of the financial system.

We first ask whether these market intermediaries may possess structural fragilities similar to those affecting banks, which we discussed in Part D. The answer is, for the large part, 'no'. Most asset management vehicles pass investment risk through to end-investors. Investors thereby receive a return that varies with the value of the investment portfolio, rather than a promise of a fixed sum (as with a bank account). This removes the risk that the fund might face a shortfall of assets against liabilities to investors. At the same time, much collective investment activity is geared towards long-term saving and does not offer investors short-term liquidity (again, in sharp contrast to a bank account). This reduces the risk of a destabilizing 'run' by investors following poor performance.

Of course, there are significant exceptions to each of these generalizations. Defined benefit pension funds and insurance companies typically promise their investors fixed returns. And mutual funds (or in Europe, UCITS) typically promise their investors immediate liquidity. While it is rare to find vehicles promising immediate liquidity *and* fixed returns, there are important exceptions amongst the categories of fund that are components of the 'shadow banking' system. These include the money-market mutual funds that provide short-term financing for dealers and special investment vehicles (SIVs) (discussed in Chapters 20 and 21) and 'credit' hedge funds, which engage in bank-like lending activity (although located outside the regulated banking sector). They also include other hedge funds that are fragile simply because of high levels of leverage, and any company that has large exposure under derivative transactions, where margin calls demand immediate liquidity.

---

[1] These are discussed in Chapter 11.

Principles of Financial Regulation. First Edition. John Armour, Dan Awrey, Paul Davies, Luca Enriques, Jeffrey N. Gordon, Colin Mayer, and Jennifer Payne. © John Armour, Dan Awrey, Paul Davies, Luca Enriques, Jeffrey N. Gordon, Colin Mayer, and Jennifer Payne 2016. Published 2016 by Oxford University Press.

What turns firm-level fragility into systemic risk is the prospect of contagion to other systemically important firms. In several instances, we highlight possible contagion akin to that which happens in the banking sector—through transactions with other systemically important institutions, or by investors drawing adverse inferences about similarly situated firms. However, the activities of asset management firms also generate possibilities for contagion across markets: where one investment vehicle becomes financially distressed and has to liquidate its portfolio, this may depress assets values for other firms holding similar assets. Systemic risk is thus an issue for the regulation of asset managers despite the lower fragility of their business models, as compared to banks.

As we shall see, there lurks within this area a troubling tension between the regulatory goals of investor protection and mitigation of systemic risk. On the one hand, if those with exposure to a collective investment vehicle are themselves systemically important institutions, then pursuing investor protection also promotes systemic stability. However, an appropriate regulatory response to this concern would be targeted at the systemically important investor firms, rather than the entire collective investment sector, which would be overkill. On the other hand, regulatory measures designed to promote the protection of investors in collective vehicles may themselves engender systemic risks. The existence of regulations designed to promote the 'safety' of certain types of investment vehicle or investment instrument acts to channel consumer funds into those vehicles. Rather than randomly distributed 'noise', the investment patterns are now concentrated in whatever is designated as 'safe'.

It is easy to see that such correlation can foster contagion *ex post* through investor inferences about performance, and through fire-sale damage to asset values. Perhaps less obvious is the fact that it may also foster even more pernicious *ex ante* problems. Investor protection rules that restrict the range of 'safe' assets foster distortions. One example is the case of money-market funds, which are—for investor protection reasons—permitted to invest only in short-term, high-quality, debt securities. It happens that financial institutions produce the majority of such commercial paper. Thus these investor protection rules helped create a captive market for this commercial paper and facilitated the growth of the shadow banking sector. Other measures designed to protect investors may also generate systemic effects. Thus deficits in defined-benefit pension funds are most likely to be revealed by mark-to-market accounting at low points in the business cycle, imposing further costs on sponsor firms precisely when they can least absorb them.

The rest of this chapter is structured as follows. In section 22.2, we consider collective investment funds, in section 22.3, we discuss risks in the insurance industry, and in section 22.4, we perform the same analysis in relation to pension schemes.

22.2 Collective Investment Funds

Investment funds take many different forms, which encompass a wide range of implications for systemic risk. The general structure, however, is that the investment fund is a separate pass-through vehicle sponsored, marketed, and managed by the asset

---

Asset Managers

'Asset managers' provide investment advice and allocation services to individuals, pension funds, insurance companies, charities, and even governments. They are the interface between investors, on the one hand, and financial markets and companies, on the other, performing the functions of economizing on transaction costs, portfolio diversification, and governance.[2] A key fact is that the asset manager does not bear investment risk. This is borne by the investment vehicles receiving the asset manager's services, and terms with the public can vary. Investors in a mutual fund are subject to changes in the fund's net asset value; beneficiaries of life insurance are not. In both cases portfolio allocation decisions may be made by an asset manager. Asset managers vary in entrepreneurial stance. An asset manager may 'sponsor' (and serve as the investment advisor for) a family of mutual funds or be hired by a pension fund or an insurer. Asset managers may be in the business of creating new financial products (see Chapter 12) or managing portfolios assembled by others.

The nature of the asset management business differs appreciably across countries. While the UK dominates the European pension fund, insurance asset management, and hedge fund businesses,[3] it is a smaller player in retail investment funds (known as 'UCITS' in Europe and 'mutual funds' in the US).[4] Both the business and the type of investor differ significantly across countries. In some countries, clients of asset management firms are predominantly large institutional investors, and, in others, they are individuals.

Countries differ in the ownership of asset management firms. Outside the UK and the US, asset management firms have been predominantly owned by banks and insurance companies, many of which may be classified as parts of large financial conglomerates. While this is the case in some of the largest asset management firms in the UK, there are also a large number of small independent firms. In the US, the largest asset management firms are freestanding, some controlling assets in the $trillions, yet there are many more asset management firms than in the UK.[5] Concentration of ownership is therefore appreciably higher in Continental Europe than in the UK and the US. Furthermore, there are differences within Continental Europe, where France has seen a rapidly increasing number of small, independent asset management firms.

---

manager. Ordinary retail mutual funds or UCITS, which pass investment risk onto their investors, produce, in general, a low level of systemic risk associated with distress. Because leverage is prohibited or tightly controlled, the fund is not exposed to sharp losses in net asset value through a market decline. It will manage its liquidity risk by investing in liquid securities. Investors in mutual funds understand they are obtaining protection against idiosyncratic, not market-wide, risk. They may exercise their freely

---

[2] See generally, J Franks, C Mayer, and L Correia da Silva, *Asset Management and Investor Protection: An International Analysis* (Oxford: OUP, 2002).

[3] See European Commission, *Report of the Alternative Investment Expert Group: Managing, Servicing and Marketing Hedge Funds in Europe*, July 2006, 10–17.

[4] See A Khorana, H Servaes, and P Tufano, 'Explaining the Size of the Mutual Fund Industry Around the World' (2005) 78 *Journal of Financial Economics* 145.

[5] A recent census run by the Office of Financial Research in the US Treasury Department, using a threshold of $150 million of assets under management, counted nearly 2,700 advisors and almost 25,000 funds, holding approximately $10 trillion in assets. Adding parallel managed accounts brings the total of managed assets to approximately $12.75 trillion: SEC, 'Annual Staff Report Relating to the Use of Data Collected from Private Fund Systemic Risk Reports', 13 August 2015. US GDP was approximately $17.8 trillion as of July 2015. US Dep't of Commerce Bureau of Economic Analysis, National Income and Product Accounts (30 July 2015).

available exit right if the assets of the fund decline in value, but that is not much different from investors who have invested directly in the market deciding to exit in a bear market.

This analysis assumes mutual funds will invest in markets that will retain their liquidity even in times of financial crisis, such as the main equity markets in leading financial centres or the markets for government bonds. However, mutual funds may be offered to retail investors whose investments are in markets which do not have this feature, such as some emerging country equity markets, some high-yield debt markets, some commodity markets, or certain derivatives.[6] In such cases, those investors who exit the fund first may be treated better than later withdrawers because the former are paid out of the fund's liquid assets, while the latter are paid out of illiquid assets sold at a discount, with consequent adverse impact on the fund's net asset value. Thus, an incentive to 'run' is generated. As discussed in Chapter 20, funds that invest in corporate debt—'bond funds'—play a particular role in the credit intermediation process. An external shock, such as a sudden shift in interest rates, may lead to correlated redemption demands that extend beyond the customary liquidity provision of such funds. Funds might be forced to sell assets at 'fire-sale' prices, which could affect asset values on the books of other financial institutions that are not pass-through. Such declining values could require capital set-asides and might affect lending—a systemic effect. Policymakers continue to debate the systemic risks associated with mutual funds. The Financial Stability Board ('FSB'), which has identified some thirty banks and nine insurers as global systemically important financial institutions, recently abandoned proposals to extend this categorization to fund managers—while retaining an interest in the impact of 'fire-sales' by, and high levels of leverage in, such funds.[7] More modestly, the Securities Exchange Commission (SEC) proposes to address the central liquidity issue by requiring mutual funds to have a 'liquidity risk management program', which, among other things, would require funds to set a minimum level of holdings that could be liquidated within three days (but the SEC itself would not determine how that minimum amount should be calculated). In addition, the SEC proposes giving fund managers the freedom to spread the costs of redemption more equally across early and late redeemers.[8]

22.2.1 Money-market funds ('MMFs')

MMFs constitute a class of mutual funds where systemic risks are clear. The key is that MMFs take the legal form of mutual funds but perform the economic function of bank accounts. They promise, at least conditionally, that investments can be liquidated at any time at par. While investments legally take the form of redeemable shares, to investors they are functionally indistinguishable from bank deposits, because the

---

[6] This is particularly true of UCITS, which under recent incarnations of the Directive are permitted to offer retail investors exposure to OTC derivatives, albeit only up to 10 per cent of the fund's total assets: UCITS V (Directive 2009/65/EC, as amended by Directive 2014/91/EU), Arts 50 and 52.

[7] 'Big US fund managers fight off "systemic" label', *Financial Times*, 14 July 2015.

[8] SEC, Press Release 2015-201, 22 September 2015 and see David Grim, Remarks to the Investment Company Institute's 2016 Mutual Funds and Investment Management Conference, March 2016.

expectation is that the MMF will return the capital amount invested plus interest. The MMF generates these returns by investing in wholesale credit markets, in particular commercial paper and repos. Because they are legally structured as mutual funds, MMFs operate outside the ambit of banking regulation: they are not subject to prudential capital regulation, and their 'depositors' do not benefit from formal deposit insurance nor the funds from the lender of last resort (LOLR) facilities available to banks. This renders them vulnerable to 'runs' if investors ever fear that the fund's net asset value will decline because of defaults in portfolio securities. To underscore the point: MMFs have no capacity to recover value lost through a default in a portfolio security because, under mutual fund rules, MMFs are capitalized exclusively with redeemable shares and earnings must be paid out rather than retained—meaning that MMFs may not be recapitalized through earnings retention. Historically, defaults and other declines in portfolio value have been covered by discretionary 'swap outs' (substitution of good assets for the impaired ones) by the sponsoring asset managers (including banks).

How did such institutions become so prominent? This is largely a US story and it is one of regulatory arbitrage of a rule that had become unsustainable in light of external market conditions. Regulation Q, made under the US Banking Act 1933, prohibited banks from paying interest on transaction accounts and limited the interest payable on savings accounts.[9] The argument appears to have been that by bidding up interest rates, banks had reduced their profits on their lending activities—or had stretched to make riskier, higher-yielding loans—and this had contributed to the fragility of banks. In other words, this was an example of a policy of constraining inter-bank competition in order to preserve stability.[10] This limit on bank rates also came along with the enactment of federal deposit insurance; in light of the moral hazard problems of deposit insurance, constraints on bank competition could be seen as a complementary measure.

In the 1970s, a time of high inflation, depositors were reluctant to make bank deposits that would earn negative real returns. Competitors to banks devised securities-market-based ways to avoid the interest restrictions and thus to capture the flow of short-term retail money from the banking system.[11] This gave rise to the money market fund (MMF). Because the MMF was a mutual fund, it was not subject to the interest rate restrictions. Nor did it need to meet bank capital requirements, or pay deposit insurance premiums. The trick was to design it so that it met the expectation that, as with a bank deposit, the fund shares could be redeemed at any time at par. In the jargon, the question was, how could constant or fixed net asset value ('NAV') funds be

---

[9] US Code of Federal Regulations, Title 12 Part 217, passed under powers granted by §11 of the Glass–Steagall Act of 1933 (formerly 12 USC §371a). Interest rate ceilings on savings accounts were abolished by the Depository Institutions Deregulation and Monetary Control Act of 1980, and the provision authorizing interest rate regulation (12 USC §371a) was finally repealed in 2010, along with abolition of controls on demand deposits.

[10] On conflicts between regulatory goals, see Chapter 3, section 3.4.8.

[11] See JR Macey and GP Miller, 'Nondeposit Deposits and the Future of Bank Regulation' (1992) 91 *Michigan Law Review* 237, 256–60.

created?[12] Part of the answer was that MMFs restricted the range of assets they acquired to high-quality, short-term liabilities.[13] Some funds confined their assets to governmental securities; others included short-term liabilities of financial and non-financial issuers—for example, commercial paper—upon which a higher interest rate was generally paid. By acquiring only high-quality assets of carefully chosen maturities, MMFs could reduce the credit and liquidity risks to which they were subject, as compared with a commercial bank. Short maturities also reduced interest rate risk. However, as the financial crisis showed, when financial institutions' commercial paper lost liquidity, those risks were not eliminated even within these 'narrow asset' institutions.

Even without a financial crisis, the value of the assets of an MMF could be expected to display some volatility, albeit less volatility than the assets of a commercial bank. How could an MMF promise to redeem shares at par, since it was under the standard mutual fund obligation to use the market value of its assets as the basis for redemption? Here regulation itself came to the aid of this exercise in regulatory arbitrage. A fund that followed the SEC's rules could take advantage of a 'penny rounding' convention, namely rounding the price per share to the nearest 1 per cent.[14] With this regulatory help, since par was $1.00 per share, small decrements in value would not lead to a fund's 'breaking the buck'. Moreover, MMFs relied upon the implicit support promises of the asset managers who sponsored them and made their investment decisions. Even before the financial crisis, there were many occasions in which a sponsor would swap out (replace) a defaulted security or a security with deteriorating value so as to protect the NAV of the sponsored MMF. Such sponsor support was massive and endemic throughout the financial crisis, over $10 billion in such support, protecting more than two dozen funds from 'breaking the buck'.[15]

Money market funds began as a retail product, providing retail customers with access to higher-yielding money market instruments. Beginning in the 1990s, however, MMFs came increasingly to be used for cash management by institutions (pension funds, insurance companies) and corporates that had temporary cash surpluses that far exceeded the limits on deposit insurance.[16] MMFs could offer the treasurers of such entities a diversified pool of credit-screened short-term credit claims on financial and non-financial institutions. By 2008 institutions accounted for almost 60 per cent of the approximately $3.5 trillion in MMF assets. (In the EU, MMFs have been used almost exclusively by institutions and corporates.)

---

[12] In the US, MMFs historically were constant NAV funds. Elsewhere, funds may or may not hold out the promise of repayment at par. A non-constant NAV fund is then just a standard mutual fund which invests in a narrow range of safe assets. The focus of this section is on constant-NAV funds, although we discuss post-crisis reforms.

[13] 17 CFR §270.2a-7.

[14] Ibid. Thus it would be permitted to report that the value of its assets was at par even if that value was in fact only 0.995 per cent of par (or better).

[15] See J Gordon and C Gandia, 'Money Market Funds Run Risk: Will Floating Net Asset Value Fix the Problem?' (2014) *Columbia Business Law Review* 313, 361–2.

[16] Alternatively, the wholesale funders might lend their money out via the repo market, discussed in Chapter 21, section 21.2. The yield on MMFs was typically higher.

The need to create portfolios of short duration meant that MMFs disproportionately came to fund financial institutions. Non-financial firms found it difficult to finance long-term projects on the basis of short-term money, while, as we have seen in Chapter 13, this is precisely the function that is central to banking. Consequently, by the onset of the crisis, MMFs were acting as very significant conduits for short-term savings from both retail and wholesale funders to the financial sector, especially to banks and broker-dealers.[17] The MMF sat between the funders and the financial institution, but the exposures of those funders were not very different from those they would have incurred as direct depositors in or purchasers of asset-backed commercial paper from the financial institution. The diversification provided by MMFs was partial. First, diversification within the financial sector still exposed MMF shareholder/depositors to risks that correlated throughout the financial sector. Second, a diversified portfolio might nevertheless contain securities from a single large issuer in an amount that exceeded 0.005 per cent of the portfolio, meaning that issuer failure could result in an MMF's 'breaking the buck'.

This was demonstrated in the financial crisis. In the collapse of Lehman Brothers, the Reserve Primary Fund, which had about 1 per cent of its assets in Lehman commercial paper, could no longer report its assets at par, even with the benefit of the 'penny rounding' rule. Nor was the Reserve's sponsor able to cover the losses. There was a run by its shareholders that spread to other MMFs, even those which held no Lehman paper, because of the well-placed concern about correlated risks. The US government's reactions to this chain of events demonstrated very clearly its perception of the nature of investments in MMFs and the consequences of a run on MMFs for financial stability. A MMF run was destabilizing not so much because of losses that might be suffered by the shareholder/depositors, but because of the sudden withdrawal of funding from the banks, securitization vehicles, and broker-dealers that had depended on this funding source. The US Treasury extended the deposit insurance scheme for banks to MMF investments. The Federal Reserve set up schemes which enabled MMFs to dispose of their ABCP (see Chapter 21) on a non-discounted basis to the commercial banks, meaning that the Federal Reserve took on uncompensated-for credit risk.[18] These two steps stopped the run on MMFs.

The Treasury guarantee was never called upon, but the Federal Reserve's schemes were heavily used. After the crisis, the question naturally arose as to how the financial stability of MMFs could be maintained and their systemic risk contained without recourse to taxpayer support. As mutual funds, MMFs fell within the regulatory purview of the SEC. The SEC's initial post-crisis move was to tighten portfolio constraints, both as to maturity and quality, and to heighten liquidity requirements so as to make MMFs more resilient.[19] The Financial Stability Oversight Council

---

[17] Even post-crisis, over 40 per cent of US ABCP issuance was held by MMFs: SEC, *Money Market Fund Reform*, Release No. 33-9408, 17 September 2013, 305.

[18] More details can be found in SEC, ibid, 35. See also Gordon and Gandia, n 15, 317–18.

[19] See Money Market Fund Reform, 75 Fed. Reg. 10,060 (4 March 2010) (codified at 17 CFR pts. 270, 274). See J Fisch and E Roiter, 'A Floating NAV for Money Market Funds: Fix or Fantasy?' (2012) *University of Illinois Law Review* 1003, 1017–28. Under the SEC's 2010 Guidelines, 10 per cent of MMF assets must have a maturity of one day; an additional 20 per cent a maturity of not more than one week; and the average

(FSOC), the 'college' of US financial regulators described in Chapter 27,[20] was dissatisfied with the SEC reform. Exercising its regulatory review powers under the Dodd–Frank Act, the FSOC objected that the SEC had not addressed the core systemic risk problem for MMFs, namely, that their model depended upon continuous redeemability of MMF shares at fixed-NAV despite the absence of any loss-absorbing capacity. The FSOC promoted 'floating' NAV (that is, the customary mutual fund model) or various approaches to providing capital to absorb losses and otherwise to negate 'run' incentives.[21]

The SEC responded with a rule change that reflected the political economy of the mutual fund industry as much as straightforward policy analysis.[22] First, 'institutional' MMFs would be required to offer their shares on a floating NAV basis; moreover, when liquidity levels fell below certain critical thresholds, the funds would have the option of imposing 'gates' (meaning, temporary suspension of redemption rights) and/or 'fees' (meaning, a charge imposed on redeeming shareholders). Second, 'retail' MMFs would be permitted to continue with the present fixed NAV structure, as would 'government' MMFs. The logic of the carve-out for retail funds, apart from the political salience, was that institutions, not retail investors, had led the run on MMFs during Lehman week. Of course, that experience demonstrated only that institutional MMF shareholders are quick to run, not that retail investors will remain stolidly in place. For example, in the case of the UK bank Northern Rock in 2008, retail depositors ran after they got wind that wholesale depositors had run the week before. What stopped the MMF run in fall 2008 was intervention by the US Treasury and the Federal Reserve, not the special patience of retail investors.

The SEC 'solution' for institutional MMFs is subject to several concerns. First, it may simply lead to a dramatic shrinking of institutional MMFs, since floating NAV deprives the users of the transactional simplicity of a fixed NAV. Instead, institutions may switch to government funds, which, because they are required to hold assets backed by the US government almost exclusively, are permitted to stay with a fixed NAV.[23] Second, although floating NAV has been a favourite reform strategy because it eliminates the run dynamic associated with the possibility that the fund will break the buck, MMFs with floating NAV may nevertheless be exposed to significant run risk. This is because the short-term financial sector instruments that make up a large fraction of MMF assets are highly correlated in value and the pricing of such instruments, which are infrequently traded, is 'stale'. In the event of a significant shock to the financial

---

maturity of the assets should not exceed sixty days. Note that such liquidity rules add to systemic risk, since the constraints on asset maturity (i) make it *less* likely MMFs will be in a position to buy the liabilities of the non-financial sector and more likely to concentrate in the financial sector, and (ii) more likely that MMFs will run (by refusing to roll-over short-term credit obligations) on the financial sector that has come to depend upon its funding.

[20] See Chapter 27, section 27.3.1.

[21] Proposed Recommendations Regarding Money Market Mutual Fund Reform, 77 Fed. Reg. 69,455 (19 November 2012).

[22] See http://www.sec.gov/rules/final/2014/33-9616.pdf. In general the industry argued that MMFs were victims of the financial crisis rather than causative agents, and characterized the Federal Reserve intervention as necessary to provide liquidity in relevant debt markets, not to bail out MMFs.

[23] Some may regard this shrinkage as the main advantage of the reform, a feature not a bug.

sector—for example, the failure of a significant financial firm—MMF shareholders are likely to believe that there is a first-mover advantage to immediate redemption. Redemption at today's higher stale NAV will further reduce tomorrow's asset values, meaning that the appropriate protective strategy is to run.[24] Third, the very strategies designed to control runs—gates and fees—may well be destabilizing. As funds approach the triggering liquidity thresholds, investors are likely to redeem in anticipation—which will create the triggering event. By comparison, US banks have discretionary capacity to suspend withdrawals from corporate transaction accounts—to impose gates—but no bank ever adopted such an approach during the financial crisis, presumably because of the regulators' concerns about triggering a massive run throughout the banking system.

Putting aside issues of regulatory path-dependence and political economy, the logic behind MMFs suggests that they should be regulated as specialized 'narrow banks'. Like banks, they engage in all three elements of credit intermediation. Even if, by design, the portfolio credit and liquidity risks of MMFs are low, the users are looking for absolute safety and liquidity. This would argue for an appropriate level of capital, either to cover losses or to provide collateral in connection with LOLR support. The capital could be sponsor provided, user provided, or supplied by third parties. This is the route to stability in an innovative financial intermediary with trillions in assets.

In addressing European MMFs,[25] the European Commission initially took a 'capital' approach, proposing that MMFs which chose to operate as fixed-NAV funds (this would not be obligatory) would be required to hold 3 per cent of their assets in a 'cash buffer'.[26] This would be supplied typically by the sponsor of the fund but would be held outside the fund by a custodian. Cash would flow out of or into the buffer as the value of the MMF's assets fell below or exceeded par.[27] If the cash buffer were exhausted, the MMF would be required to convert to a variable-NAV fund. However, the Commission proposal would not give MMFs access to deposit insurance or LOLR facilities (though Member States could decide to provide these). Strenuous objections from the European money market fund industry to the idea of a sponsor-provided capital buffer produced a backlash to the Commission's proposal. In response the European Parliament has proposed to shape European MMFs on the US pattern: retail MMFs and government MMFs (holding EU government debt) will be able to remain as 'constant' (fixed) NAV funds; institutional prime funds will become 'variable' (floating) NAV

---

[24] Gordon and Gandia, n 15.

[25] European MMFs are less important as financial intermediaries than in the US, an institutional not a retail product, often operating to service US multinationals that do not want to repatriate surplus cash.

[26] This is a low capital requirement, compared to that now required for banks (see Chapter 14), but it could be said to reflect the lower level of risk attached to MMF assets.

[27] European Commission, Proposal for a Regulation on Money Market Funds, COM (2013) 615 final, September 2013. The cash buffer is to this extent unlike bank capital, which is simply a particular source of funding and is held within the institution and can be used to fund the bank's ordinary activities, such as term lending. The strict capital approach cannot work in relation to a fund because the unit/shareholders are entitled to the value of the fund. The cash buffer would replace the explicit or implicit promise of sponsor support which helped some MMFs in the crisis. Under the EU proposal, any other form of sponsor support would normally be prohibited—in the interests of transparency.

funds—although there may be a long transition period.[28] Other regulatory features are likely to be similar.

The reforms are constrained by the current economic environment rather than by long-term logic. With short-term interest rates at rock bottom, there is simply no margin for sponsors to charge fees that would support the economics of sponsor capital. As a stability matter, we are left in a halfway house. This may be regarded as a 'MacroPru' cost of the central banks' low interest rate policies.

22.2.2 Hedge funds

In the wake of the financial crisis, the regulation of hedge funds became a very controversial issue. In Continental Europe some politicians, who had prior objections to the hedge fund model, wished to use the financial crisis to regulate these funds extensively for reasons unconnected with the crisis.[29] This was a piece of political opportunism, since hedge funds neither made a significant contribution to the events which led to the crisis nor were any such funds bailed out with government money after the crisis—even though a number failed and most saw their assets under management reduced. However, these facts do not mean that hedge funds pose no systemic threat; if they do, it is surely better to address it now rather than when it emerges. Thus, Title IV of the Dodd–Frank Act adds modestly to the regulation of hedge funds in the US, even though the political tides flowed less strongly against the funds in that country than in Continental Europe.

In looking at the regulation of hedge funds from a systemic point of view, one needs to identify first what the benefits of hedge funds might be. If there are no benefits, then regulation to reduce the systemic risks has an easier passage, since no trade-off between the systemic costs and benefits of hedge funds is required. Arguably, hedge funds provide four key benefits.[30] First, they add to market liquidity. This is not simply because of the volume of funds channelled into the market by hedge funds, but because hedge funds (funded by sophisticated investors subject to partial lock-ins) are better able to hold illiquid assets than banks funded by deposits or mutual funds which offer investors immediate redemption rights. So, hedge funds provide liquidity to the market, notably to institutions whose investors are not locked in. Second, because some hedge fund strategies are 'contrarian'—that is, they involve betting against the market—such funds reduce market volatility, counteract bubbles, and, sometimes, correct mispricing.

---

[28] The European Parliament, as part of the co-decision process, rejected the Commission's 3 per cent proposal (http://www.europarl.europa.eu/sides/getDoc.do?type=TA&reference=P8-TA-2015-0170&language=EN). The ultimate 'trilogue' negotiation among the Council of Member States, the Commission, and the Parliament has yet to occur.

[29] D Awrey, 'The Limits of EU Hedge Fund Regulation' (2011) 5 *Law and Financial Markets Review* 119; E Ferran, 'After the Crisis: the Regulation of Hedge Funds and Private Equity in the EU' (2011) 12 *European Business Organization Law Review* 379.

[30] RM Stulz, 'Hedge Funds: Past, Present, and Future' (2007) 21 *Journal of Economic Perspectives* 175; SJ Brown, M Kacperczyk, A Ljungqvist, AW Lynch, LH Pedersen, and M Richardson, 'Hedge Funds in the Aftermath of the Financial Crisis', in VV Acharya and M Richardson (eds), *Restoring Financial Stability* (Hoboken, NJ: Wiley, 2009), 161.

Third, hedge funds now do things which, if done by other institutions, would be regarded as obviously beneficial; for example, they provide credit for business projects. To be sure, the risks of maturity, liquidity, and credit transformation cannot be ignored because the process is carried out by a non-bank financial intermediary—a 'shadow bank' rather than a bank regulated as such—but this type of activity does give the shadow bank a claim to be performing a socially useful function. Fourth, hedge funds provide investors, at least sophisticated ones, with an additional range of potential investment strategies to take up, thus allowing the unused resources of society to be more effectively deployed and contributing to the diversity and completeness of financial markets.

Despite the controversy over the regulation of hedge funds, everyone agrees on one thing: they engage in a wide variety of different investment activities.[31] The wide variety of activity that is assembled under the label 'hedge fund' is reflected in the curious way hedge funds are defined in legislation. This definition is essentially negative, by reference to what they are not, as opposed to what they are. Thus, the EU Alternative Investment Funds Directive speaks of 'alternative investment funds' ('AIFs') defined as funds which do not qualify as UCITS (retail funds) under the associated legislation;[32] and Title IV of the Dodd–Frank Act speaks of 'private funds', defined as funds that are exempted from registration under the Investment Company Act 1940 because they offer their securities to qualifying purchasers only.[33] Their very diversity means that defining what hedge funds actually do seems to have been beyond the capacity of the drafters. This situation means it is very difficult to quantify the aggregate benefits of hedge fund activity, just alluded to, or their systemic risks, to which we will turn. A related regulatory policy question indeed is whether it is wise to trigger regulatory intervention by reference to a residual category, thus defined. Or should the focus be on certain *activities* of hedge funds—especially as those activities may also be undertaken by institutions which are not, on any definition, hedge funds?[34] The very variety of activity carried on by hedge funds certainly suggests caution in applying the same rule to all hedge funds, regardless of their trading strategies.

Nevertheless, there is a convincing argument for applying at least an information-based regulatory strategy to hedge funds, no matter what they do, and this features as a core requirement of both the AIFM Directive and Title IV of Dodd–Frank. Reporting of significant features of their market positions to regulators, such as asset size, leverage, illiquid positions, and risk concentration, may help guide the development of future substantive regulation.[35] Given the importance of the hedge funds' investments, at least in certain markets, regulators also need a good understanding of those

---

[31] For details, see Stulz, n 30.

[32] AIFM Directive, 2011/61/EU [2011] OJ L174/1, Art 4(1).

[33] Investment Companies Act of 1940 (as modified by Dodd–Frank Act), §§3(c)(1), 3(c)(7); Investment Advisors Act of 1940 (as modified by Dodd–Frank Act), §202(a)(29).

[34] Most notably, the proprietary trading desks of financial conglomerates. See further on this, Chapter 23.

[35] AIFM Directive, Art 24; Investment Advisors Act of 1940 (as amended), §204(b). For regulatory response to the information disclosed see eg Mary Jo White, 'Five Years On: Regulation of Private Fund Advisers after Dodd–Frank', speech on 16 October 2015, available at http://www.sec.gov/news/speeches.

positions for macroprudential oversight purposes. They may also need these data when responding to crises in the market. As with OTC derivatives,[36] a major limitation on effective regulatory action—other than bail-out—may be lack of knowledge of the exposures that exist in the market.[37]

Apart from contributing to regulators' understanding of the markets, hedge fund regulation could address the channels by which contagion might spread in the case of the collapse of a single large hedge fund or a number of medium-sized funds. The systemic risks arise here in two ways, the first of which is through interconnections between hedge funds and other, systematically important, institutions. The most obvious concern here relates to investment banks providing prime brokerage services to hedge funds. The second channel for systemic risk is the possibility of asset fire sales upon rapid unwinding of hedge funds' positions, either defensively or upon failure.[38] In the first case, the goal of regulation is to protect for society the benefits of the non-hedge fund institution that has contractual relations with the fund, rather than the benefits of the fund itself. The core example of this relationship is the investment bank that acts as prime broker to the hedge fund and, in that capacity, has funded it via short-term repos and entered into various other financial contracts. A large hit to the bank on its hedge-fund exposures could conceivably put the bank's position in question. Fear of contagion to bank counterparties appears to have been the rationale for the assembling by the Fed of a 'lifeboat' for the Long-Term Capital Management hedge fund in 1998.[39]

However, it is not obvious that this problem is best addressed by regulation of hedge funds. It could equally be addressed by regulation of the banks, for example, by setting capital requirements or exposure limits for bank lending to highly leveraged institutions. Indeed, the issue is probably better addressed in this way, since not all hedge funds are leveraged and not all highly leveraged institutions are hedge funds. Such regulation is sometimes called 'indirect' regulation of hedge funds. Special treatment of loans to highly leveraged institutions has been part of the Basel framework since the beginning of the century.[40]

---

[36] See Chapter 21, section 21.4.

[37] On the other hand, the case for mandatory disclosure to investors or the public (probably much the same thing) on grounds of systemic risk mitigation is much weaker. The intellectual property of the hedge fund is its trading strategy. If data from which that strategy can be inferred in detail is made public, the incentives to hedge fund activity—and its benefits—could be substantially reduced.

[38] FSA, *Hedge Funds: A Discussion of Risk and Regulatory Engagement*, DP 05/04 (2005); T Garbaravius and F Dierick, 'Hedge Funds and their Implications for Financial Stability', ECB Occasional Paper No 34 (2005).

[39] LTCM was a highly leveraged (30:1) hedge fund whose investment model was defeated by the South East Asia financial crisis beginning in 1997. It was rescued by a consortium of its creditor banks and brokers which, under the urging of the Federal Reserve Bank of New York, put in $3.6bn to obtain 90 per cent of the ownership of the firm. This enabled the fund to be wound down in an orderly way, the creditors got their investment back, and the fund's partners and other investors suffered very substantial losses. See M Fleming and W Liu, *Near Failure of Long-Term Capital Management* (available at http://www.federalreservehistory. org/Events/DetailView/52).

[40] BCBS, *Banks' Interactions with Highly Leveraged Institutions, and Sound Practices for Banks' Interactions with Highly Leveraged Institutions* (1999). For current policy developments over these issues see bcbs246 and 257.

The fire-sale risk arises most acutely where the hedge fund is highly leveraged and invested in illiquid or semi-liquid assets. A relatively small shift in asset prices may require it to put up additional collateral and, in the absence of adequate liquidity reserves, the fund may have to engage in a sale of difficult-to-sell assets. If the sale attempts lead to a further decline in asset prices, a spiral of margin requirements and declines in asset prices may occur. Investors observing this may seek to withdraw, thus putting further liquidity pressures on the fund. As the value of the assets held by the fund declines, this may affect the viability of other holders of those assets, in particular banks.[41] This is the second channel of contagion, via market prices rather than counterparty risk.

This description is beginning to build a picture of a hedge fund as a fragile institution in need of regulation in order to avoid systemic risk, along the lines of a bank. However, not all hedge funds are leveraged and it appears that hedge funds are, overall, less leveraged than banks. Furthermore, hedge funds protect themselves from withdrawal demands by stipulating lock-up periods, requiring notice of withdrawal to be given and by allowing withdrawal only at certain times of the year. Hedge funds also commonly contract for the right to put certain illiquid assets in a 'side pocket', which can further limit investors' withdrawal rights. In this way, hedge fund runs are slowed down (though not eliminated). So, it is not clear what the level of fragility of the hedge-fund model is, especially given the variety of trading strategies they pursue. In the wake of the financial crisis, it is perhaps not surprising that regulators were unwilling to take the self-protection measures of hedge funds on trust and wished to put in place at least back-up regulation. On the other hand, it is far from clear what regulatory strategy, beyond disclosure, will effectively address systemic risk without costly trade-offs.

To date, only the European Union has ventured beyond reporting requirements to regulators when addressing (directly) the systemic risks of hedge funds. Besides imposing a modest initial and continuing capital requirement and requiring fund managers to have an adequate liquidity strategy in place,[42] the Directive's main focus is on leverage. Member States are given a backstop power to impose a leverage restriction on funds which, they estimate, pose a threat to financial stability—with the European Securities and Markets Authority (ESMA) having a significant power to lean on Member States which, in its view, are not taking appropriate action.[43] The Directive also imposes restrictions on hedge fund manager compensation, which can be understood as an oblique way of combating systemic risk through reducing firm-level incentives for risk-taking.[44]

The most likely area for the development of an international consensus on hedge fund regulation beyond disclosure is under the rubric of 'shadow banking'. The FSB launched a major initiative on the systemic risks of shadow banking in the wake of the

---

[41] The same impact on non-hedge funds might occur if, without any hedge fund failure, a group of funds following the same strategy decide simultaneously to sell off a particular class of asset. See M Brunnermeier, A Crockett, C Goodhart, A Persaud, and H Shin, *Fundamental Principles of Financial Regulation* (Geneva: ICMB, 2009), 25–6.

[42] AIFM Directive, Arts 9 and 16.

[43] Ibid, Art 25.

[44] Ibid, Art 13 and Annex II. On remuneration controls in fragile firms generally, see Chapter 17.

financial crisis. Although not focused on hedge funds, collective investment funds (including hedge funds) appeared as the fifth (of five) work-streams devoted to shadow banking, under the category of 'other shadow banking entities and activities'.[45] Within hedge funds, only credit hedge funds—that is, hedge funds engaged in credit intermediation—attracted attention. The particular risk of credit hedge funds identified as systemic was the possibility of a run, which might directly disrupt the provision of credit to the real economy and generate a fire sale of assets which would impact on other holders of the assets whose value was impaired.[46]

The FSB's approach, supported by peer review, is to recommend that national policy makers and regulators mount an intensive effort to collect data on the possible financial stability risks of shadow banking, and then to obtain a wide range of policy tools that could be used to address any risks that might emerge. In relation to run risk, the FSB identifies tools such as controls over redemptions by investors, liquidity regulation such as restricting investment in illiquid assets or requiring funds to hold liquidity buffers, leverage ratios, and restrictions on the maturity of assets.[47] This list comes close to the full suite of regulatory tools that might be used to regulate run risk in banks—with the major exception of a guarantee of the value of the investments in the fund and access to LOLR facilities at the central bank. But it is wholly unclear whether the recommended data collection will lead to the adoption of all or any elements of the remedial toolkit in respect of hedge funds. The extent of the maturity, liquidity, and credit transformation activity of credit hedge funds is unclear, as is their leverage. Some of the remedial tools already exist by contract in industry practice, such as restrictions on redemptions. Unsurprisingly, the response to the FSB reports from the hedge fund sector has been to argue that their systemic risks are small, because they have only a small share of the market in credit intermediation, and that the proposed toolkit is disproportionate because funds are already incentivized to manage the risks identified.[48]

22.2.3 Private equity funds

Private equity funds also engage in a range of investment activities, but a much narrower one than hedge funds. Their focus is on investment in the equity of companies. With private equity, the variation consists in the stage of a company's life when the investment occurs. Private equity investment ranges from start-up companies (where it is usually called 'venture capital') to very large publicly traded companies (where it might be called a 'buy-out fund'). If there is any systemic risk in the activities of private equity funds, it is likely to reside at the upper end of the investment scale and this section will therefore focus on private equity and publicly traded companies.

---

[45] FSB, *Strengthening Regulation and Oversight of Shadow Banking: An Overview of Policy Recommendations* (2013).

[46] FSB, *Strengthening Regulation and Oversight of Shadow Banking: Policy Framework for Strengthening Oversight and Regulation of Shadow Banking Entities* (2013), 5.

[47] Ibid, Annex 2.

[48] Hedge Fund Standards Board, *Response to the FSB Consultative Document* (2013). This was a response to the consultation document which preceded the final FSB report.

Private equity funds usually buy out the existing shareholders of target companies, taking the firms private if they are initially publicly held.[49] The fund managers then work with corporate management—who are given 'high-powered' incentive compensation— to improve the performance of the company, over a period of up to a decade.[50] Then, the company is typically sold, either through a return to the public equity market, or to a trade buyer. Most of the reward to the fund is realized through this exit. Funds are normally raised for a fixed period of about ten years. The first years are spent finding targets and making investments; the middle years improving performance; and the final years finding exit opportunities. As well as the performance incentives to corporate management in the individual targets, the fund managers are also strongly incentivized, partly by their fee structure and partly by the opportunities to co-invest with the fund. The funding of the acquisition of each target is usually leveraged, sometimes highly so. The cost of acquiring the target is thus funded in substantial part by multi-layered debt, the top layers of which, after acquisition, are secured on the assets of the target company.

What, if any, are the systemic risks of this type of fund? The risk of a run, which featured large in our previous discussion of systemic risks in MMFs and credit hedge funds, is not present. An investor in a private equity fund is typically locked in for the duration of the fund.[51] The highly leveraged nature of the buy-out creates risk, but this is hardly systemic. The risk is of bankruptcy of the target and the loss of the fund's investment. If the target were a systemically risky company, such as a bank, its failure would obviously raise systemic concerns, but regulators have long had power to control bank acquisitions. Moreover, capital and leverage ratio requirements for banks make a highly leveraged acquisition of a bank improbable. Where the target is not systemically important, the creditors (or some subset of them) will seize control of the failing company from the fund and, eventually, sell it on in a way which likely mirrors the exit route envisaged by the fund. There may be some loss of value in the bankruptcy process, but no systemic risk emerges.

Another possible source of systemic risk might be thought to lie in the use of securitized debt to finance acquisitions. There was a perception in the period leading up to the financial crisis that private equity firms, fuelled by cheap credit, were overpaying for target companies.[52] This credit was facilitated in many cases using securitization—in the form of collateralized loan obligations ('CLOs')—of syndicated loans used to finance the deal. Yet, in contrast to securitization of home mortgage

---

[49] Most buyouts worldwide are of private, rather than publicly traded, firms: Per Strömberg, 'The New Demography of Private Equity', Working Paper Swedish Institute for Financial Research (2007).

[50] Ibid (median holding period of sample of private equity funds worldwide is nine years). See also V Acharya, M Hahn, and C Kehoe, 'Corporate Governance and Value Creation: Evidence from Private Equity' (2013) *Review of Financial Studies* 368 (documenting improvements in performance in investee companies).

[51] There is a limited secondary market in private equity fund participations and, of course, all fund members and the manager could agree to earlier (or indeed later) termination of the fund.

[52] See VV Acharya, J Franks, and H Servaes, 'Private Equity: Boom and Bust?' (2007) 19 *Journal of Applied Corporate Finance* 44; BR Cheffins and J Armour, 'The Eclipse of Private Equity' (2008) 33 *Delaware Journal of Corporate Law* 1.

loans, CLOs ultimately paid out to investors very much as promised.[53] Moreover, it seems easier to control the risks of securitization by regulating the systemically important parties at the nodes of the process—originating banks and dealers.[54]

Despite the difficulty of identifying systemic risk in the operations of private equity funds, there is a case to be made for reporting fund positions to macroprudential authorities, so their view of the market is complete. Both Title IV of Dodd–Frank and the AIFM Directive bring private equity fund managers within their scope in this regard.[55] However, the AIFM Directive goes further, imposing public disclosure and regulatory reporting obligations on the fund manager, not only in relation to the fund, but also in relation to the investee companies—including disclosures to their employees. These requirements are driven by corporate governance rather than systemic risk concerns.[56] It seems likely that the financial crisis was used to provide an opportunity to regulate private equity funds for reasons unrelated to financial stability.[57]

22.3 Insurance

22.3.1 The business model of insurance companies

When we discussed the theory of banking in Chapter 13, we saw that the rationale for regulation of banks derived from a combination of (a) the importance of banking services to the 'real' economy, (b) the fragility of the banks' business model, and (c) the externalities associated with bank failure, so that leaving risk precaution to the banks alone was unlikely to be an appropriate strategy. To what extent do these arguments apply to insurance companies? If they do not, are there other arguments for the regulation of insurance companies along the lines we have identified in relation to banks?

Although possibly less important than the provision of credit, there are good grounds for thinking that the availability of insurance is central to the operation of modern economies. Insurance encourages economic actors to engage in activities that

---

[53] E Benmelech, J Dlugosz, and V Ivashina, 'Securitization without Adverse Selection: The Case of CLOs' (2012) 106 *Journal of Financial Economics* 91.

[54] See Chapter 21, section 21.3.3.   [55] See nn 32–5.

[56] Improving the performance of the company often involves some pain for the company's employees. It is often alleged that the gains to the shareholders of the target company are the result of wealth transfers from employees and other stakeholders to shareholders rather than an increase in the value of the company. Although the empirical literature does not support this assertion (see eg L Renneboog, T Simons, and M Wright, 'Why Do Public Firms Go Private in the UK? The Impact of Private Equity Investors, Incentive Realignment and Undervaluation' (2007) 13 *Journal of Applied Corporate Finance* 591), this 'asset stripping' analysis seems to underlie the EU AIFM Directive's regulation of private equity funds. The Directive imposes additional obligations on funds which acquire control of companies, in particular requiring disclosure of the fund's intentions towards the company, and constraints over distributions to shareholders in the two years following the acquisition of control: AIFM Directive, Arts 28 and 30. See also E Ferran, n 29, 404. For discussion of employment effects that distinguishes between 'public to private' transactions and 'independent to private', see SJ Davis, J Haltiwanger, K Handley, R Jarmin, J Lerner, and J Miranda, 'Private Equity, Jobs, and Productivity' (2014) 104 *American Economic Review* 3956.

[57] See 'Payback Time: The European Union Lashes out at Hedge Funds and Private Equity', *The Economist*, 19 November 2009 ('When a fight breaks out in a bar, you don't hit the man who started it. You clobber the person you don't like instead').

they might otherwise regard as too risky because it enables them to pool some of the risks associated with that activity rather than bear the risk individually—for example, the loss of crucial business assets. Insurance facilitates acceptance by society of risky activities because it provides compensation for those injured by them, often through compulsory insurance—for example, for those who drive automobiles or install machinery in factories or give professional advice. It increases the welfare of individuals by enabling them to plan for old age (for example, via life insurance and annuities) or to insure major assets (such as houses) against loss.

Insurance companies also perform an important role in financial intermediation, as a corollary to their primary activities. Since the business model of insurance companies involves the acceptance of premiums now in exchange for promises to make contingent payments in the future, an important part of their operation involves investing premium income against future payouts. Insurers' ability to make profits is therefore a function of both the accuracy of their estimation of the contingencies associated with their payout obligations and the extent of the returns they generate on their investment portfolio.

Consequently, conditions (a) and (c) appear to be satisfied in relation to insurance companies, as they are for banks. The real economy is promoted by the availability of a deep insurance market and it is unlikely that the shareholders and managers of insurance companies fully price in losses the real economy will suffer from a withdrawal of insurance capacity when setting the risk profile of their insurance company. However, what about condition (b)? Do insurers suffer from a similar level of fragility to banks?

The core insurance company model does not involve the maturity, liquidity, or credit transformation of the bank model. Whereas at the core of banks' business model is borrowing cheap short-term funds to finance expensive long-term but illiquid loans, the insurance company takes in non-returnable premiums to finance the risks it assumes. There is no liquidity transformation in this model, and it is easier for the insurance company to match the maturity of the assets it acquires on the back of the premiums with its liabilities to policyholders. Because the insurance company model does not turn on short-term funding, there is little risk of a run by such funders. The insured's claim against the insurer is to receive the contingent pay-out, not a claim to have a deposit returned on demand or at short notice, and insurers normally have little incentive to raise money in the short-term wholesale market. Certainly, an insurer which acquires a reputation for financial weakness may suffer a significant downturn in new business, including non-renewal of existing policies, but the insurer should be able to manage its existing liabilities on the basis of its existing assets through a 'run off'.

Insurers' risks are also less correlated to the business cycle than those of banks. Banks' credit risk on loans—the core asset class—rises and falls with the economic cycle. Hence, there is both a concern that regulation may reinforce the cyclicality of bank lending (discussed in Chapter 14) and a role for macroprudential policy in ironing out the peaks and troughs in lending (Chapter 19). While correlation with the business cycle is a feature of some lines of insurance (for example, trade credit insurance), much insurance activity is unaffected or only marginally affected by it. Rather, it is a characteristic of most of the risks taken on by insurers that they are uncorrelated and idiosyncratic. The fact that my house burns down is not normally associated with any change in the risk of your house, situated in a different town, burning down. This non-correlation with the general business cycle is reinforced by a fundamental principle of the law of insurance: namely, that the insured must have an 'insurable interest' in the matter covered, such that a pay out under the policy indemnifies them against an actual loss suffered.[58] This principle imposes an inherent limitation on the use of insurance policies for speculative purposes.

22.3.2 Insurers and systemic risk

Although an insurance company's business model may be less risky than that of a bank, it is not riskless and insurance companies do fail because of management mistakes—or worse. The two most common forms of mismanagement are the under-pricing of the premiums necessary to support the risks taken on (for example, in order to obtain a foothold in a competitive market) and failing to set enough aside (inadequate 'provisions') to cover potential claims, perhaps in order to distribute more to shareholders, senior managers, or policy holders (in mutuals). Moreover, insurance companies engaging in inadequate provisioning may gain a (temporary) competitive advantage over those which provision properly, thus driving down standards across the industry. As we saw in Chapter 12, this does create a potential role for regulation, in essence to lend credibility to the insurer's promise—for the benefit of both well-conducted insurers and the insured.

The question for this chapter, however, is whether there is a case for additional regulation of insurers on systemic risk grounds. The fact that insurance is a less risky business than banking implies insurers are less likely than banks to get into financial difficulties. This is obviously an important argument, although not necessarily conclusive, against systemic risk regulation. Perhaps at least as important is that financial distress is less costly for an insurer than for a bank. Should financial difficulties occur, there is generally more time to handle them at an insurer than at a bank, whose funding is likely to disappear at the first hint of trouble. Troubled insurers can go into 'run off'—that is, close to new business and handle future claims on the basis of existing assets and premiums from existing business—or find a solvent insurer to acquire portfolios of policies.[59]

Perhaps most important of all, the failure of an insurer is unlikely to generate contagion. Except in the case of a failure of a reinsurance company or an insurance company forming part of a banking group, the failure of an insurer is unlikely to have

---

[58] This principle is said to originate in two eighteenth-century English statues, the Marine Insurance Act 1745 and the Life Assurance Act 1774. Its primary purpose was to avoid perverse incentives to bring about the event insured against. See KS Abraham, *Insurance Law and Regulation: Cases and Materials*, 4th ed (New York, NY: Foundation Press, 2005), 201–2.

[59] See the account of the wind-down of Equitable Life (a UK insurer) and HIH (an Australian one) in Geneva Association, *Systemic Risk in Insurance* (2010), Appendix D. This is not to deny that existing policyholders suffer in this process, but that is a consumer protection, rather than a systemic matter.

an adverse effect on the viability of another financial institution. In the absence of 'insurer runs' the collapse of one insurer is unlikely to lead to a substantial reduction of insurance capacity in the real economy. Competitors will step into the gap, though there may be transitional difficulties for particular lines of insurance.[60]

If this analysis is correct, why did the US authorities see fit to bail out the insurer AIG—then the world's largest insurer—during the financial crisis? The answer, in short, is that AIG had diversified its business model into running what we have characterized as a 'dealer' operation in relation to credit default swaps ('CDS')—and a very significant one, at that. That is to say, the systemic risk did not arise from its insurance business. AIG's problems stemmed in the main from the CDS it had written on asset-backed securities ('ABS') and collateralized debt obligations ('CDOs') providing structured finance for US subprime home mortgages. These CDS contracts provided credit enhancement for the ABS and CDO securities. AIG sold credit protection against default on the underlying mortgage loans to the special purpose vehicles (SPVs and CDO managers) that issued the securities, thus reducing the risks borne by the end-investors who purchased the securities. Under the terms of the CDS contracts, AIG had to post additional liquid collateral ('variation margin') if the value of the ABS and CDO securities, or AIG's own credit rating, declined. In the financial crisis, both these events occurred, the second a consequence of the first.[61] Since AIG had an enormous CDS book, it ultimately could not meet its collateral calls and would have succumbed to a liquidity crisis, had it not been bailed out. A consequence of the bailout was to avert further pressure on the CDS counterparties, which were large international banks whose finances may well have been incapable of dealing with a default by AIG on the CDS it had written.[62]

In looking for sources of systemic risk, two features stand out from the sorry tale of AIG. First, CDS writing is not a traditional insurance activity. In fact, though akin to insurance in the sense that credit protection involves a payment contingent on an event, the conventional analysis of the law of credit derivatives is that these are *not* contracts of insurance.[63] Consequently, credit protection buyers do not need to have an 'insurable interest': they do not need to have suffered any loss as a result of the default by the reference entity. Thus CDS contracts may be used for speculative purposes: the total amount of credit protection written in fact often exceeds the value of the reference

[60] See the analysis of the failure of HIH in IAIS, *Insurance and Financial Stability* (2011), Appendix 9.

[61] The market for ABS had completely dried up, so the value of these assets had to be estimated. Ironically, this was in some cases done using a benchmark index of the cost of CDS protection for these securities, the ABX.HE index: see Goldman Sachs, 'Valuation and Pricing Related to Transactions with AIG', Memorandum Submitted to the Financial Crisis Inquiry Commission (2010). Because AIG was such a large player in that market, using the index of CDS prices to trigger margin calls on those same CDS—which would in turn drive up prices—appears to have created a feedback loop. The value of the index skyrocketed far beyond 'any reasonable assumption' regarding default rates in the underlying subprime loans: R Stanton and N Wallace, 'The Bear's Lair: Index Credit Default Swaps and the Subprime Mortgage Crisis' (2011) 24 *Review of Financial Studies* 3250.

[62] Settlements on the CDS made after the bail-out included $11bn to Société Générale, $8.1bn to Goldman Sachs, $5.4bn to Deutsche Bank, and $4.9bn to Merrill Lynch (Geneva Association, n 59, Exhibit 50).

[63] See J-P Castignino, *Derivatives: The Key Principles*, 3rd ed (Oxford: OUP, 2009), §4.8; MT Henderson, 'Credit Derivatives are not "Insurance"' (2009) 16 *Connecticut Insurance Law Journal* 1.

debt.[64] Although the CDS market may seem like insurance, it is consequently far more risky, and one for which the ordinary risk management practices of an insurance company may well be inadequate.[65]

Second, the writing of the CDS generated an interconnectedness between the insurance company and other financial institutions whose systemic risks were substantial. AIG's position in the CDS market for ABS and CDOs was so extensive that it had in effect become a sort of lender of last resort for the financial institutions which had distributed these securities, and who remained liable to the end-investors under 'liquidity puts'.[66] Bailing out the insurance company appeared to the US government to be a lesser evil than the arguably more expensive action of bailing out all the (systemically important) counterparties who depended on it.[67]

22.3.3 Identifying systemically important insurers

This analysis gives us some clues about identifying systemically important insurers and distinguishing them from insurers which, however large their businesses, do not present systemic risk. We might focus on two things: the extent to which the insurer engages in non-traditional or non-insurance activities ('NTNI') and the extent of its interconnectedness with other systemically important financial institutions. AIG was an example of an insurer engaging in *non-insurance* activities which exposed systemically important counterparties to contagion from the potential failure of the insurer. *Non-traditional insurance activities* are more difficult to define, but essentially encompass insurance contracts containing features that expose the insurer to risks from which the core model of insurance business protects the insurer. For example, life insurance contracts, when used as savings vehicles for retirement and which guarantee particular annuity rates on the maturity of the policy, create interest rate risk for the insurer,[68] while such contracts guaranteeing returns on investments made by the

---

[64] For example, at the end of 2012, the total notional amounts outstanding in OTC credit default swaps was $25tn, as compared with total issuance of international debt securities, public and private, of just under $22tn (BIS Statistics, Tables 11A and 19).

[65] In effect AIG was leveraging its balance sheet as insurer, fortified to meet regulatory requirements for the protection of policyholders, to generate extra fee income from the writing of CDS. It believed that the risk of loss on the 'super-senior' securitization tranches for which it wrote protection was very small, but in agreeing to variation margin requirements, it did not take account of the possibility that market perceptions (and thus valuations) might become more pessimistic than the actual default risk. Nor did it take account of the correlations among diversified ABS, meaning, if adverse market conditions threatened the creditworthiness of one diversified ABS, other diversified ABS would also be threatened. In effect, AIG had written flood insurance on all the housing on the Florida coast, thinking it was diversified because each house was separately exposed to a hurricane.

[66] See Chapter 21, section 21.3.

[67] Financial Crisis Inquiry Commission, *The Financial Crisis Inquiry Report* (New York, NY: PublicAffairs, 2011), 347–8. The US Government actors stoutly maintain that failure of a major insurer like AIG would have had systemic effects in the insurance market, including policyholder 'runs' based on extractable cash values of life insurance policies, and would have magnified the unsettled economic conditions in fall 2008. For example, at the time of the rescue, AIG had $20 billion in commercial paper outstanding. As a point of comparison, Lehman Brothers had $5.7 billion in outstanding commercial paper, default on which all but brought down the money market fund sector. See R McDonald and A Paulson, 'AIG in Hindsight' (2015) 29 *Journal of Economic Perspectives* 81.

[68] Life insurance contracts often pay an annuity to the assured on retirement or to the surviving spouse of the insured life, calculated as a percentage of the notional sum insured. If this interest rate is floating, then the insured bears all the interest rate risk; if it is fixed, some of the risk is transferred to the insurer.

insurer likewise shift investment risk onto the insurer. While it is bad news for insureds if an insurer cannot meet its promises, does this amount to a systemic risk? It may well if the insureds are themselves systemically important. Even if they are not, a channel of contagion could be that the insurer engages in a fire sale of its assets in an attempt to meet its promises but, in so doing, drives down their market price to the detriment of all holders of those assets. If the insurer is large enough or enough insurers take this action, there emerges a systemic event which is not dissimilar to the collapse of ABS and CDO prices in course of the subprime crisis. Thus, if AIG had been able to meet its collateral calls through a fire sale of its assets, the investment banking counterparties might not have been at risk of default on those contracts but might have suffered extensively via a decline in the price of the assets they held in common with the insurer.

Following this line of thinking, the International Association of Insurance Supervisors ('IAIS'), operating within the framework set by the Financial Stability Board ('FSB') for identifying global systemically important financial institutions,[69] assigned weights of 40 per cent to interconnectedness and 45 per cent to NTNI in its methodology for identifying global systemically important insurers ('G-SIIs'). The other three factors (size, global activity, and substitutability) were assigned only 5 per cent each.[70]

In addition to the identification of global systemically important insurers, national regulators may identify insurers which they regard as systemically important at the national level. For example, the US FSOC has the power to designate as systemically important any non-bank financial company, including insurers.[71] As of the time of writing the FSOC has designated all three US insurers which appear on the IAIS list—AIG, Prudential Financial, and MetLife—on the basis that financial distress of the insurer could pose a threat to the financial stability of the United States. The decisions in relation to the Prudential and MetLife were controversial,[72] though in fact the FSOC seems to have adopted criteria similar to those advocated by the IAIS. For example, the Prudential has a high degree of interconnectedness with global banks because of its derivatives and credit facility arrangements, and its life insurance liabilities had a non-traditional feature which made insureds less locked-in than in traditional life insurance arrangements. This feature was that, 'a substantial portion of the liabilities in the US general account are available for discretionary withdrawal with little or no penalty and therefore could, in practice, have characteristics of short term liabilities'.[73] If these liabilities were cashed in on a large scale, the insurer might have to engage in a fire-sale of its assets which would affect the value of those assets across the market as a whole.

---

[69] The role of these institutions is analysed further in Chapter 29.

[70] IAIS, *Global Systematically Important Insurers: Initial Assessment Methodology*, July 2013, II.B(A). The 2015 list produced by the FSB on the basis of this approach contained nine insurers: Aegon, Allianz SE, American International Group Inc, Aviva plc, Axa SA, MetLife Inc, Ping An Insurance (Group) Company of China Ltd, Prudential Financial Inc, and Prudential plc.

[71] Dodd–Frank Act (US), §113.

[72] Two of the seven members of the council voted against the designations, including a state insurance commissioner. MetLife has brought a court challenge to its designation. See Box below and n.79.

[73] The FSOC's designation decisions in relation to Prudential and MetLife are available at http://www.treasury.gov/initiatives/fsoc/designations/Pages/default.aspx.

The MetLife Designation

The FSOC's designation of two life insurance companies—Prudential and MetLife—as 'systemically important' has seen strenuous pushback from the sector. The criteria FSOC must use in making a designation are: (i) whether the material financial distress of the firm could pose a threat to US financial stability; or (ii) whether the nature, scope, size, scale, concentration, interconnectedness, or mix of activities at the firm could itself (even absent financial distress) pose such a threat.[74] In considering the effects of MetLife's material financial distress, FSOC examined three transmission channels: *exposures* of other financial sector participants to the firm that might significantly impair their functioning should it fail; the *assets* of the firm are such that if put into a *fire sale* on its distress, losses would be suffered by other financial firms holding such assets; and that the firm's distress would impair its ability to provide a *critical function or service* relied upon by market participants, for which there is no ready substitute.[75]

Section 113 of the Dodd–Frank Act of 2010 sets out a list of factors the FSOC must take into account when making such a decision. These consist of: (i) the firm's leverage; (ii) the nature and extent of its off-balance-sheet exposures; (iii) the nature and extent of its transactions with other significant financial firms; (iv) its importance as a source of credit and liquidity in the US economy; (v) its importance as a source of credit, in particular for low-income and minority communities; (vi) the extent to which assets are owned or managed by the company; (vii) the nature, size, scope, scale, concentration, interconnectedness, and mix of activities of the firm; (viii) the degree to which the firm is already regulated by one or more primary financial regulatory agencies; (ix) the amount and nature of any financial assets; (x) the amount and types of any liabilities; and (xi) any other risk-related factors FSOC deems appropriate.[76]

FSOC identified a number of aspects of MetLife's business that might give rise to vulnerabilities if it became financially distressed.[77] For example, it uses short-term wholesale debt markets as a significant source of funding, which might become sharply more expensive should it become financially distressed. Moreover, it runs a large securities lending programme, as part of which it uses cash collateral provided by securities borrowers to invest in other securities. However, the securities in which it invests are significantly less liquid than the cash collateral, which its securities borrower clients may demand back at any time. This might expose it to liquidity risk in the event of financial distress. (Indeed, AIG had suffered large losses in this way.) MetLife's size and interconnectedness with systemically important institutions meant that, in FSOC's view, its distress would be capable of causing a threat to financial stability. A designation that the firm was systemically important would make it subject to 'enhanced prudential supervision' by the Federal Reserve and a ready candidate for Orderly Liquidation Authority (OLA) resolution, meaning that an anticipatory resolution plan would be drawn up that would mitigate the impact of financial distress. The absence of any consolidated supervision of this international insurance company—which was rather subject to piecemeal oversight by fifty different state-level insurance regulators in the US as well as by other sovereign regulators—was also a contributing concern.

---

[74] Dodd–Frank Act of 2010, §113(a)(1).

[75] FSOC, Basis for the Financial Stability Oversight Council's Final Determination Regarding MetLife, Inc (18 December 2014).

[76] These are elaborated upon in the FSOC's rule and guidance: FSOC, 'Authority to Require Supervision and Regulation of Certain Nonbank Financial Companies', 12 CFR Part 1310, (2012) 77 *Federal Register* 21637.

[77] Ibid.

This designation provoked a strident dissent from FSOC's independent member with insurance industry expertise, who objected to reliance on the first criterion (contagion following financial distress) on the basis that this assumes distress, which for an insurance company is far less likely than for other financial institutions.[78] MetLife subsequently obtained judicial review of the FSOC's determination, arguing that the decision was flawed for that reason, and for underestimating the efficacy of the existing insurance regulatory regime.[79]

22.3.4 Regulating systemically important insurers

As we have seen, it is possible to identify a systemic risk rationale for regulation of a subset of insurance companies, which goes beyond the consumer-protection rationale for regulation applicable to all insurers. The actual content of the additional regulation that has been imposed on this basis is not novel. We have analysed its principal elements already in Part D, in relation to banks. Thus, the IAIS standards for global systemically important insurers embrace (a) closer supervision, (b) more effective resolution mechanisms, and (c) higher loss-absorbing capacity than is the case with non-systemic insurers.[80] Equally, the EU-level insurance rules, known as 'Solvency II', mimic the structure and requirements of the Basel II requirements for banks;[81] and the FSB's Key Attributes in relation to resolution concern the resolution of all systemically important financial institutions, not just banks.[82] Because these strategies have been discussed already in this book, they need only brief mention here.

Supervision of G-SIIs, according to the IAIS, should focus on group-wide supervision (so that non-insurance activities do not escape consideration), which implies a high degree of cooperation among parent company and subsidiary regulators, especially on a cross-national basis. The group-wide supervisor should have a 'full suite' of supervisory powers, including the power to require members of the group to hold larger amounts of liquidity, to increase reserves, impose dividend restrictions, and conduct stress tests.[83] The G-SII itself should be required to produce a Systemic Risk Management Plan ('SRMP') containing its strategies for managing and possibly reducing systemic risk, so that risk management is not a purely regulator-led exercise.

Among other things, effective resolution could require G-SIIs to produce recovery and resolution plans ('RRPs'), on the same lines as banks,[84] and provisions for early intervention by regulators. At the time of writing the precise level of additional capital to be required from G-SIIs and the definition of 'high-quality capital', that is, whether it

---

[78] SR Woodall, 'Views of the Council's Independent Member Having Insurance Expertise' (18 December 2014).

[79] But the Treasury is to appeal the district court's decision: 'US government to challenge MetLife "too big to fail" decision', *Financial Times*, 8 April 2016.

[80] IAIS, *Global Systemically Important Insurers: Policy Measures*, July 2013, §3. The powers of the US regulators are similar once a financial institution has been designated as systemically important: Dodd–Frank Act §115. The calculation of required capital in insurance companies is a somewhat different exercise as compared to banks. See n 85.

[81] Directive 2009/138/EC, OJ [2009] L335/1. The Solvency II regime (which came into force at the start of 2016) does not explicitly distinguish between systemic and non-systemic insurers. It does exclude small insurers from its scope (Art 4), but as we have seen, size is unlikely to be a good indicator of systemic status.

[82] Discussed in Chapter 16.   [83] IAIS, n 80.

[84] See Chapter 16, section 16.4.1.

will embrace anything other than equity, which are to be operative from 2019, had not been fully defined by IAIS.[85]

Built into the IAIS's standards is a significant incentive for insurers to ring-fence their NTNI activities. Ring-fencing in this context involves the NTNI entity (i) being capitalized on a stand-alone basis and not being dependent on intra-group financing, (ii) being capable of being resolved without generating a drain on the resources of other group companies, (iii) having operational independence with independent directors on its board, (iv) transactions with the rest of the group being at arm's length, (v) the ring-fenced entity not posing a reputational risk to the rest of the group so that other group entities feel commercial pressure to intervene to save a failing NTNI company, and (vi) the ring-fenced entity not becoming an unregulated operation.[86] A group with a ring-fenced NTNI entity will have its higher reserve requirements calculated on the basis of the assets of that entity alone and any special restrictions imposed by the regulator under its group supervision powers may also be so confined.

An alternative approach would be to prohibit insurers from carrying on the activities which generate systemic risk. The approach in fact adopted, by focusing on activities rather than institutions, allows insurers (or, more accurately, insurance groups) to engage in a wide range of activities, where there is a business case for doing so, but seeks to reduce the opportunities for regulatory arbitrage which might present themselves if an activity carried on by, for example, a bank or broker-dealer would be regulated but the same activity would not be if carried on by an insurance company.

22.4 Pension Schemes

Even more than the traditional insurance company business, the business model of pension schemes generates little in the way of systemic risk. Contributions to pension schemes are traditionally impossible to withdraw. Not only would the tax reliefs applied to the original contributions normally now be removed, but public policy strongly encourages private provision for old age and so is reluctant to facilitate withdrawal of contributions. Pension contributions may often be transferred to an alternative provider, but in that case the transferor is relieved from the obligation to provide the pension as well. A 'run' on a pension scheme is thus difficult to envisage (which is not to say that it is incapable of defaulting on its obligations). Nor is a pension fund likely to need to engage in a fire-sale of its assets. Even in a defined benefit scheme, where the pensioners, actual and prospective, bear no investment risk, there is normally a long time to adjust to any developments which present a threat to the ability of the fund to meet its promises. The scheme is normally carefully drafted so as to make such adjustments possible, if the pension fund trustees, after consultation with employees, think this wise. Contributions, from employers and employees, can be adjusted

---

[85] For current progress see *IAIS, Capital Requirements for Global Systemically Important Insurers (G-SIIs) Basic Capital Requirements (BCR) and Higher Loss Absorbency (HLA)*, October 2015.

[86] IAIS, n 80, para 3.3.4. The comparison with the ring-fencing of banks is close. See Chapter 22. Note that 'ring-fencing' would probably have meant that AIG would never have gone into the CDS-writing business, since the financial capacity of the swaps-writing subsidiary depended upon an explicit AIG-parent guarantee.

upwards; the terms of the pension promise can be revised downwards; and, as increasingly often happens, the fund can be closed to new members or even to new contributions, thus minimizing the deficit which has to be covered. Once the scheme is closed, the investment policy of the fund can be adjusted accordingly.

These developments—or poor investment decisions in defined benefit schemes—may be disastrous for actual and prospective scheme members (and we have examined the consumer protection aspects of pension schemes in Chapter 12) but they pose no risks to financial stability. Nevertheless, there is a systemic risk attached to defined benefit schemes which arises, ironically, not from the business model of the fund itself but from the regulations applied to the fund in the name of consumer protection. These risks are normally considered under the heading of 'procyclicality'. They apply, it should be noted, to the regulation of insurance companies in the name of consumer protection as well.

The principal example of this issue arises in relation to the repair of pension deficits. Pension-fund regulation in most jurisdictions gives pension regulators the power to require defined benefit funds to increase their 'capital', that is, the surplus of its assets over its liabilities, actual and predicted, if it seems likely that the current surplus is insufficient to meet the scheme's promises in the future. If the need for an injection of assets arises from a market-wide collapse in the value of one or more important asset classes in a general economic crisis, it is conceivable that all sponsors of defined benefit funds will be required to inject assets at precisely the time they are least well able to do so.[87] The systemic risk is, in other words, that the real economy is adversely affected by the requirement that large manufacturing or services companies repair their pension fund deficits within the same short timetable. As has been said, the danger of such regulation is that it transforms companies from operating companies with a manageable pension fund attached into pension funds with a small operating business attached. Possible policy tools for dealing with the procyclicality of funding requirements include: the use of buffers in good times which can be drawn on in bad times; a supervisory discretion to lengthen recovery periods in times of economic crisis;[88] as well as a general requirement for consumer-protection regulators to take the systemic effects of their decisions into account.[89]

It is conceivable that unthinking regulation will also produce systemic risks of a type which do not threaten financial stability but which nevertheless threaten the efficient functioning of markets (as well as reducing the wealth of scheme members). Thus, it

---

[87] Note that monetary policy strategies that central banks have used to hold down long-term interest rates may affect the capacity of pension funds to add assets that match their payment obligations. This could well incline pension funds to 'reach for yield' with assets of greater default risk. Securitization flourished in the 2000s because of the demand for higher-yielding assets with low apparent risk, as reflected in credit ratings.

[88] This would make most sense if implemented via a power for macroprudential regulators to give instructions to pension regulators if they deem it necessary. See further Chapter 19.

[89] EIOPA, *EIOPA's Advice to the European Commission on the Review of the IORP Directive* (2012), Ch 12; OECD, 'The Impact of the Financial Crisis on Defined Benefit Plans and the Need for Counter-Cyclical Funding Regulation', Working Paper, July 2010. An implication of this approach is that, while 'mark-to-market' valuation techniques might be used to reveal the size of the deficit, they should not be used uncritically to determine remedial measures.

has been suggested that fiduciary-style regulation of pension funds generates incentives for them (or asset managers acting on their behalf) to follow conventional and short-term investment policies rather than to aim for the long-term results which would seem to be most in line with the liability maturities of the scheme.[90] Both cases represent a warning to the promoters of consumer protection regulation that the possible systemic impact of such regulation should be considered at the design stage.

22.5 Conclusion

The fundamental issue raised in this chapter has been, what do we mean by 'systemic' risk? In the case of banks (see Chapter 13), the analysis of systemic risk is well developed. It is essentially the loss of capacity to provide credit to the 'real' economy, brought about as a result of the fragility of the banks' business model and ease with which contagion spreads from one bank to banks more generally. The business models of the institutions discussed in this chapter do not have the same level of fragility (mainly because the risk of fluctuations in asset values is borne by end investors), nor does the failure of one institution carry the same contagion risks (in some cases investors are locked into the investment). Consequently, wholesale loss of the services these institutions provided to society is a more remote possibility. As has been said, '[t]he good news here is that, unlike in banking, history is not littered with examples of failing funds wreaking havoc in financial markets'.[91]

Nevertheless, a robust business model does not by any means ensure immunity from failure and in this chapter, we have identified ways in which the failure of one of the institutions considered in this chapter might have what could be categorized as systemic consequences. Contagion might spread from failed asset managers (using the term broadly to cover all the institutions considered in this chapter) to the wider economy in at least four ways: through linkages to institutions whose systemic import-ance is clear (notably banks); linkages to markets; linkages to the economy as a whole; and linkages to the corporate governance system.

In the first case (exemplified by the public bail-out of the insurance company, AIG, and the private bail-out of the hedge fund, Long-Term Capital Markets) the concern is that failure of an asset manager will trigger failure in the banking sector (including the shadow-banks). This is really protection of fragile banks (including fragile shadow-banks) at one remove. The ultimate concern about harm to the real economy is *through* harm caused to banks, which in turn would cause harm to the economy at large. The existence of this type of linkage does not constitute a strong argument for regulation of the industry as a whole but rather of transactions (or particular classes of transaction) between asset managers and banks.

Linkages via markets occur when asset managers all respond in a similar way to an adverse financial development, typically by selling securities, perhaps in a fire sale. This

---

[90] K Otjes and F de Graaf, 'Pension Funds and Herding Behavior', Working Paper (2012) (available at http://ssrn.com/abstract=2084725).
[91] A Haldane, 'The Age of Asset Management?', Bank of England Speech 723 (2014) (Speech given at London Business School, 4 April 2014).

may be driven by the demands of the end users for exit or by regulatory rules which encourage such sales (such as the sale of assets which have unexpectedly lost value in order to 'de-risk' the portfolio and reduce regulatory capital requirements). Although a rational way of securing the safety of a particular asset manager, such herd behaviour may make it more difficult for other asset managers *and* all holders of the relevant asset class (including, again, notably banks) to deal with the adverse development.

It is only a small extension of the second linkage (and possibly a more plausible version of it) to see it as operating on the economy as a whole—namely, that there are market and regulatory incentives for herd behaviour on the part of asset managers which increase risk-taking in an economic upturn beyond what is optimal and depress it below what is optimal in an economic downturn.[92] In other words, the problem here is one of procyclicality of asset managers' behaviour and the appropriate response lies with macroprudential regulation (discussed in Chapter 19).[93]

Finally, we come back to the impact of asset managers on the financing of the real economy, this time not predominantly debt finance (as with banks) but equity financing. Some argue that market and regulatory developments have made it less attractive for institutions to hold equity in companies at all or to hold it over sustained periods of time (that is, to act as 'patient' capital).[94] This has been argued, especially in the UK, to be an important factor constraining economic growth and has led to proposals to remove or tone down the disincentives to equity investment. At this point we reach a very broad definition of systemic risk. This last category of risk arises not from the failure of an asset management institution or from its reaction to adverse market developments, but from its steady-state operation; and risks in question are not risks of financial instability but of suboptimal economic growth.

Although the risks noted here have been identified, their quantification is still a work in progress. While the financial crisis demonstrated the first linkage was significant, the evidence in relation to the others is as yet inconclusive. However, this is not an answer to the question whether regulation should address them: an army trained and equipped to fight the last war is rarely successful in the war it actually has to fight. Some lawmakers have jumped in with extensive regulation before the quantification task had been completed, but the international community as a whole has been more cautious. The tentative, largely information-gathering work of the FSB in this area is eloquent testimony to the preliminary state of our understanding of the extent of systemic risks associated with asset managers.

---

[92] See M Feroli, A Kashyap, K Schoenholtz, and H Shin, 'Market Tantrums', Chicago Booth Business School Working Paper No 14-09 (2014).

[93] This type of contagion is stressed in particular by Haldane, n 91.

[94] J Kay, *Final Report of the Kay Review of UK Equity Markets and Long-Term Decision Making* (July 2012, URN 12917), esp Ch 5.

23

Structural Regulation

23.1 Introduction

'Structural regulation' refers to measures designed to limit the range of activities that may be carried on by a banking firm. The popular idea is to reduce the risk of bank failure by prohibiting banks from getting involved in activities that are judged by policymakers to be 'too risky'. Bank failure gives rise to significant externalities; hence, society has an interest in reducing its probability below that which private parties running the bank might want. Moreover, the provision of deposit insurance tends to exacerbate these problems, by creating moral hazard for those running the bank.

Structural regulation of the financial sector is a tremendously controversial topic. The merits of such separation are hotly debated, as we shall see. And lurking in the background is the problem that implementing structural separation imposes particularly large costs on the financial sector, because it requires wholesale reorganization of corporate structures. Thus, even if introducing structural regulation has net benefits, there remains a question whether the benefits are sufficient to overcome the costs of switching. Against this background, it should come as no surprise that structural separation has been implemented only at times when it was possible for legislators to harness widespread popular demand for reform of the banking sector.

Structural regulation has a long history in the US, dating back to the National Bank Acts of the 1860s, which limited the activities in which national bank entities could engage. Separation was extended under the Banking Act of 1933—better known as the Glass–Steagall Act—which prohibited combinations of deposit-taking and investment banks within the same group. However, by the end of the twentieth century, investment–commercial bank combinations were seen as a desirable advance for the industry, and the 'old-fashioned' Glass–Steagall restrictions an unwelcome hindrance. Comparisons were drawn with the position in Europe, where structural regulations had never hindered the operation of universal banks. Following extensive administrative relaxation, the provisions requiring structural separation at the group level were formally eliminated by the Gramm–Leach–Bliley Act of 1999. However, entity-level restrictions remained in place.

Given how soon the financial crisis came after the formal end of group-level separation in the US, it is unsurprising that many saw this step as a contributing cause. This led to what might be thought of as partial re-enactment of Glass–Steagall, the so-called 'Volcker Rule', proposed by the former Fed Chairman to separate proprietary trading activity from banking groups. This proposal was adopted by the Dodd–Frank Act of 2010, and the final rules came into force in April 2014.[1]

---

[1] Note that the Volcker Rule did not purport to restrict a banking group's underwriting of securities or its market-making.

Principles of Financial Regulation. First Edition. John Armour, Dan Awrey, Paul Davies, Luca Enriques, Jeffrey N. Gordon, Colin Mayer, and Jennifer Payne. © John Armour, Dan Awrey, Paul Davies, Luca Enriques, Jeffrey N. Gordon, Colin Mayer, and Jennifer Payne 2016. Published 2016 by Oxford University Press.

For Europe, where the universal banking tradition has long been strong, structural separation is a novel and controversial idea. However, in the aftermath of the financial crisis, the UK government established an Independent Commission on Banking ('ICB'), chaired by the Oxford economist Sir John Vickers, to explore whether some form of structural separation might be a desirable way to reduce the systemic risks associated with very large universal banks. The ICB recommended, amongst other things, that 'retail banking' activities—that is, deposit-taking, payments, and lending from and to individuals and small businesses—be structurally separated at the entity level from investment banking activities. These proposals were slightly adjusted following a further review by the UK's influential cross-party Parliamentary Committee on Banking Standards, and then enacted as the Financial Services (Banking Reform) Act of 2013. They are due to be implemented by 2019.

While the UK proposals were undergoing domestic debate, the European Commission also became interested in the idea of structural regulation. A 2012 report by a High-Level Expert Group chaired by Erkki Liikanen, Governor of the Bank of Finland, recommended EU legislation mandating structural separation of investment and retail banking activity for banks in the Single Supervisory Mechanism. Like the Vickers proposals, Liikanen recommended separation at the entity, rather than the group, level. The European Commission consulted further on this report and produced legislative proposals in 2014, which—to the surprise of many—added a further requirement of group-level separation of proprietary trading activity from banking groups.[2] This proposal, which bears some similarities to the Volcker rule, appears to have been inspired by a desire to ensure that the EU's regime is equivalent in effect to that of the US, so as to mitigate the effects of extraterritoriality.

Perhaps more than any other measure, it is necessary to see the implementation of structural separation in the macro context—that is, as part of a composite bundle of measures. Its usefulness is, in our view, contingent on other key aspects of financial regulation being complementary to—that is, reinforcing—its operation, and vice versa. The case of Lehman Brothers can be seen as a cautionary tale in this regard. Lehman was a 'pure-play' investment bank: it had no deposit-taking activity. As such, it was an artefact of the Glass–Steagall Act's mandated structural separation of commercial and investment banks. As we have seen in Chapter 21, however, it took to raising finance on the wholesale markets that had many of the characteristics of deposit-taking. The fact that these creditors were not, and were not permitted to be, insured by the Federal Deposit Insurance Corporation ('FDIC') arguably exacerbated their tendency to 'run'. And the fact that investment banks were not overseen by the banking regulators, who were concerned with stability of banking institutions, but by the Securities and Exchange Commission ('SEC'), which was principally concerned with investor protection, did not help either.

The rest of this chapter is structured as follows. Section 23.2 considers the policy case for structural partition of commercial banking and investment banking activities. The

---

[2] At the time of writing, the proposal is still working its way through the European legislative process, and it is uncertain whether the idea of a group-level proprietary trading ban will be retained. See nn 50–52 and text thereto.

rest of the chapter examines the way in which three of the structural separation regimes announced—those of the US, the UK, and the EU—are designed. Section 23.3 looks at the strength of the separation—that is, whether it is at the entity level or the group level. Section 23.4 considers which activities are restricted. Section 23.5 discusses common exceptions, and section 23.6 reflects on links to other aspects of prudential regulation. By the end of this chapter you should have an understanding of why structural regulations have been implemented or proposed on both sides of the Atlantic, how they (would) work in the US, the UK, and the rest of the EU, and how effective they can be in their chief goal of enhancing financial stability.

23.2 The Rationale(s) for Structural Regulation

23.2.1 Financial stability

The principal rationale for structural separation has been understood in terms of financial stability. The leading modern account of the case for structural separation is the report of the UK's ICB, which recommended this approach.[3] The concepts were further considered by the High-Level Expert Group chaired by Erkki Liikanen,[4] and by the UK's influential Parliamentary Commission on Banking Standards ('PCBS').[5] Of course, the idea has a much longer history in the US, where the Report of the Pecora Commission, which preceded the Glass–Steagall Act of 1933, contains a very influential case for structural separation.[6]

The central idea behind structural separation is to ensure that the assets and business of financial firms that engage in activities deserving of 'protection' are insulated from risks associated with other activities.[7] The need for such protection is understood in terms of externalities, so that activities merit protection if their failure would impose negative externalities on society. Of course, it does not follow that structural separation is an appropriate form for such protection unless such separation reduces the expected costs of these externalities by more than the new costs it engenders.

This then focuses attention on the ways in which structural separation operates to reduce expected externalities. A naïve understanding is that structural separation serves to partition supposedly 'high-risk' activities (such as investment banking activities) from supposedly 'low-risk' activities (such as commercial banking). Say a firm carries on two activities, A and B. If activity A has low volatility, and activity B has high

---

[3] Independent Commission on Banking ('ICB'), *Final Report: Recommendations* (London: ICB, 2011) ('ICB Report'); J Vickers, 'Banking Reform in Britain and Europe', Paper prepared for IMF Conference on 'Rethinking Macro Policy II: First Steps and Early Lessons' (2013).

[4] High-Level Expert Group on Reforming the Structure of the EU Banking Sector, *Final Report* (2012) ('Liikanen Report').

[5] Parliamentary Commission on Banking Standards ('PCBS'), *First Report: First Report of Session 2012–13*, HL Paper 98; HC 848 (London: HMSO, 2012). See also the PCBS' response to the UK government's legislative proposals on structural separation: PCBS, *Banking Reform—Towards the Right Structure: Second Report of Session 2012–13*, HL Paper 126; HC 1012 (London: HMSO, 2013).

[6] US Senate Commission on Banking and Currency, *The Pecora Commission's Final Report* (Washington DC: USGPO, 1934) ('Pecora Report').

[7] ICB, *Final Report*, 25, 35–6; Liikanen Report, 100.

volatility, then prohibiting the firm from carrying on activity B can in principle reduce the overall volatility of the firm's cash flows. However, this depends on the extent of the difference in volatility, and whether or not the returns to activities A and B are correlated. If the returns are uncorrelated (or *a fortiori*, negatively correlated), then combining the two activities can *reduce* overall volatility, through diversification.

Commercial banking activities—domestic business and residential property lending—are likely to be highly correlated with the business cycle. So too are many investment banking activities, such as underwriting, and market-making. As it happened, many of the US investment–commercial bank combinations around the turn of the century had been driven by a desire to secure a supply of mortgage loans to feed demand for mortgage-backed securities, in which combination the risks of the two sides were, unfortunately, positively correlated. Firms that had undergone such combinations suffered greater losses in the crisis than those that had not.[8]

However, there is no necessary correlation between investment and commercial banking activities. It is possible that risk management and proprietary trading activities in investment banks might be uncorrelated with the business cycle, or even capable of hedging its risks.[9] Interestingly, a study of US banks prior to the enactment of the Glass–Steagall Act in 1933 suggests that banks with securities affiliates were, holding other things constant, *less* likely to fail than those without.[10] The affiliates' operations were more risky than those of the banks, but there is little evidence of correlation, suggesting that they may have helped the commercial banks to diversify.[11]

Nor is it obvious *a priori* that commercial banking is necessarily less volatile than investment banking. Rather, much depends on the way in which risks in each segment are managed. This begins to suggest more nuanced insights into how structural separation may reduce externalities. The first is through interaction between risk management practices. Commercial banking is about long-term risks—it relies on holding assets to term. In contrast, investment banking is more about short-term risks—it relies on market liquidity to be able to sell assets. In commercial banking, risk management is about avoiding default. Whereas in investment banking, the degree of 'liquidity' the firm experiences is in part a function of the effectiveness of the firm's sales team. This leads to different priorities in risk management and compensation, which may generate negative synergies when combined.[12] If these two activities are combined, in many circumstances the traders will produce high profits and thus will be rewarded with managerial decision-making authority for the firm as a whole. Concern about undermining commercial bank risk management by the 'subtle hazard' of sales-

---

[8] A Goldstein and N Fligstein, 'The Transformation of Mortgage Finance and the Industrial Roots of the Mortgage Meltdown', Working Paper, UC Berkeley (2014).

[9] Thus Goldman Sachs famously recouped much of the losses it would otherwise have suffered on subprime mortgage securitization by taking out a large short position on the index of subprime asset-backed securities ('ABS'). See eg G Morgenson and L Story, 'Banks Bundled Bad Debt, Bet Against It and Won', *New York Times*, 23 December 2009.

[10] EN White, 'Before the Glass–Steagall Act: An Analysis of the Investment Banking Activities of National Banks' (1986) 23 *Explorations in Economic History* 33, 41.

[11] Ibid, 43–4.   [12] Liikanen Report, 99.

oriented pressure from an investment banking function was one of the rationales said to underpin the Glass–Steagall Act in the US.[13]

Of course, there need not be 'seepage' from risk-management practices in one area into another if—and it is a big 'if'—regulators are able to oversee activity effectively. This in turn points to a second benefit of structural separation, namely making it easier for regulators to monitor which risks a banking group is taking on, how they are being managed, and how they are faring.[14] The vast disparity in resources between regulators and global banking groups we described in Chapter 4 suggests that measures that serve to reduce the complexity of banks will assist regulators in their ongoing supervision of large banking groups.[15]

Complexity-reducing structural reform will also yield a third benefit—facilitating resolution in times of distress. If firms are organized in legally distinct and functionally self-sufficient units, resolution will be more straightforward; similarly so if socially valuable components are separated from those that are not.[16] Thus structural separation can be seen as a form of 'hard' rescue and recovery plan, in which the rescued part of the firm could be readily hived off from the rest, and transferred under a purchase and assumption-type resolution process.[17] However, this purported advantage of structural separation should not be overstated. Recent thinking about resolution through bail-in advocates a single point of entry ('SPOE') approach. Under SPOE, the financial firm's external finance is organized through as few entities as possible—ideally just a single holding company which raises group finances. As a consequence, it is necessary to put only that 'topco' entity into resolution and restructure its debts, and all the operating subsidiaries are able to continue activity without any events of default.[18] It is possible that structural regulation requiring subsidiaries to be separately capitalized from the rest of the group may hinder this process. It is important that resolution planning and structural separation proceed in tandem: another illustration of the 'macro' nature of this topic.

Perhaps the most important benefit of structural separation, however, is that of reducing distortions generated by other strategies employed to reduce the social costs of failure of financial institutions. This can be seen most obviously with regulatory insurance strategies. If commercial banking activity is backstopped by the provision of deposit insurance, then a banking firm, because of this insurance, obtains a subsidy for engaging in activities that increase its overall risk of default.[19] Insuring some of the firm's creditors means that they will not adjust their terms of lending following the

---

[13] See *Investment Co. Inst. v Camp* 401 US 617 (1971), 630–1. Indeed, Paul Volcker's justification for his 'Rule' is to erase that 'subtle hazard': to avoid contaminating the cautious approach to risk-taking commonly associated with a commercial bank (in which the risk is one way) with the more aggressive approach associated with proprietary trading (in which the risk is two-way). See n 107.

[14] Liikanen Report, 99.   [15] Chapter 4, section 4.2. See also Chapter 24, section 24.2.2.

[16] ICB, *Final Report*, 24–5.   [17] See Chapter 16, section 16.3.

[18] See Chapter 16, section 16.6.

[19] See X Freixas, G Lóránth, and A Morrison, 'Regulating Financial Conglomerates' (2007) 16 *Journal of Financial Intermediation* 479.

firm's entry into these activities.[20] At this point, we need not be agnostic about the effect on the firm's aggregate risk profile of the additional activity. The firm maximizes the value of the 'subsidy' it receives from incomplete risk-adjustment by pursuing the most risky activities it can. The incentives become far worse if the firm expects not just deposit insurance but a complete bail-out, on the basis that it is 'too big to fail'. In this case, none of the firm's creditors may be expected to price in fully the riskiness of its activities.[21]

As we have seen, structural separation is best understood as one element of a composite package of regulatory measures that include prudential, governance, and insurance strategies. As part of such a package, it can be useful in two ways: it can enhance the usefulness of the other components, by ensuring they are targeted at appropriate activities; and it helps avoid the subsidization of inappropriate activities.

At the same time, structural separation will entail very significant costs. The one-off costs of mandatory separation will be considerable, because it will require a complete reorganization of the financial sector.[22] There will also be ongoing costs for financial institutions. These will come primarily from the withdrawal of implicit government guarantees for a portion of their business. To the extent that these guarantees have in the past provided inappropriate subsidies, the increased pricing of risk for these activities, while a private cost for the financial institutions, will not be a social cost. However, there will also be genuine social costs associated with the ongoing costs of compliance with the structural regulations. These will encompass the need to operate separate management for the separated functions and requirements for documenting and classifying transactions to ensure compliance. As we shall see, the structural separation rules are extremely complex, which implies that ongoing compliance costs will be high. The ICB tentatively suggested an approximate annual ongoing *social* cost for the UK in the range of £1bn to 3bn, or around 0.1–0.2 per cent of GDP.[23]

23.2.2 Which activities should be separated?

All this in turn begs the question as to which activities should be able to benefit from 'protection'. The UK's ICB focused on deposit-taking, the payments system, and

---

[20] The regulator managing the deposit insurance fund could, in principle, adjust the premium according to the firm's risk. For the reasons given in text to nn 14–15, structural separation would facilitate this too.

[21] Moreover, capital adequacy requirements can exacerbate such risk-substitution. This is because, to the extent that the firm is required to maintain more capital for its activities than the market would otherwise find necessary, the firm can only achieve an inferior rate of return for funds invested. This can give a regulated firm the incentive to push its activities into higher-yielding—and more volatile—sectors and puts additional pressure on regulators to take forestalling steps. See M Harris, CC Opp, and MM Opp, 'Macroprudential Bank Capital Regulation in a Competitive Financial System', Working Paper (2014).

[22] These will include the costs associated with lobbying efforts by the financial sector to resist such regulation, which—given the size of the stakes—could be very significant.

[23] ICB, *Final Report*, 144. See also European Commission, *Impact Assessment Accompanying the Proposed Structural Measures Regulation: Part 1*, SWD (2014) 30 final, 41–2 (discussing social costs without attempting to quantify them); JC Coates IV, 'Cost-Benefit Analysis of Financial Regulation: Case Studies and Implications' (2015) 124 *Yale Law Journal* 824, 974–8 (critical discussion of cost-benefit analyses of Volcker Rule).

lending to small businesses.[24] These are core to the mobilization of savings, facilitation of payments, and the provision of funding to small business projects.[25] Moreover, they are fragile to contagion, and consequently protected by a range of other measures, as we have discussed in Part D. Based on this, the UK's approach to structural regulation involves requiring the separation of these 'core' features from the other activities of large financial institutions.[26]

However, it is clear that many investment-banking activities are also socially valuable.[27] Underwriters screen and monitor their clients, pledging their reputation when they bring the firm to market.[28] This closely parallels the way in which commercial banks are thought to act as delegated monitors, overcoming information asymmetries in screening and monitoring their borrowers. Consistently with this, the underwriting clients of Lehman Brothers suffered significant reductions in their market valuations following the firm's collapse, reflecting the costs of loss of their relationships with the firm,[29] and this translated into longer-term reductions in financing and, in turn, real investment by these firms.[30] Market-based credit intermediation is frequently a lower-cost way for investment grade companies to obtain credit than a bank loan; moreover, the underwriting process can readily transport this risk outside the financial sector, unlike loans on the bank balance sheet. Similarly, the provision of market-making and prime brokerage services helps facilitate liquidity in the relevant markets.[31] Hence, Continental European and US policymakers have instead advocated a model of structural separation that focuses on 'pushing out' a more limited subset of investment banking activities, namely proprietary trading. The thinking is that there is no particular social value in this activity being carried on by a large complex financial institution, as opposed to a stand-alone firm such as a hedge fund. However, even this view may be open to question, as expertise developed in own-account trading is likely to be useful in providing market-making, underwriting, and similar services.[32]

The narrower UK focus, excluding activities such as market-making and underwriting from the 'protected' sector, may be explained by the more parochial nature of retail deposit-taking and commercial lending. A large firm, which raises funds via the stock market using an investment bank as an intermediary, is able to access international markets for investment banking services. Conversely, small firms, which raise funds

---

[24] ICB, *Final Report*, 36–40.   [25] See generally Chapter 13.
[26] See section 23.4.1.   [27] See Chapter 2, section 2.3.3.
[28] A Morrison and W Wilhelm, Jr, *Investment Banking: Institutions, Politics, and Law* (Oxford: OUP, 2007), 75–81.
[29] CS Fernando, AD May, and WL Megginson, 'The Value of Investment Banking Relationships: Evidence from the Collapse of Lehman Brothers' (2012) 67 *Journal of Finance* 235.
[30] D Oesch, D Schuette, and I Walter, 'Real Effects of Investment Banking Relationships: Evidence from the Financial Crisis', Working Paper, University of St Gallen/NYU Stern School of Business (2013) (averaging 13.4 per cent reduction in financing and 5.9 per cent reduction in investment spending).
[31] See D Duffie, N Gârlenau, and LH Pederson, 'Over-the-Counter Markets' (2005) 73 *Economica* 1815; AG Atkeson, AL Eisfeldt, and P-O Weill, 'Entry and Exit in OTC Derivatives Markets', NBER Working Paper 20416 (2014) (social benefits of market-making functions in OTC markets); GO Aragon and PE Strahan, 'Hedge Funds as Liquidity Providers: Evidence from the Lehman Bankruptcy' (2012) 103 *Journal of Financial Economics* 570 (demonstrating link between prime brokerage services and liquidity in markets in which prime brokerage clients trade).
[32] CW Calomiris, 'Panel Discussion on the Volcker Rule', in PH Schultz, *Perspectives on Dodd–Frank and Finance* (Cambridge, MA: MIT Press, 2014), 115, 122–6. See also Morrison and Wilhelm, n 28, 71–5.

from commercial banks, are far less likely to be able to access finance from international lenders; similarly, domestic depositors may be unable to get ready access to a substitute. It follows that the cost to the real economy of closure of domestic commercial banks is likely to be greater than of domestic investment banks. The same dynamic also affects the ability of regulators to impose prudential measures on financial firms. Additional capital requirements can, policymakers reasoned, be imposed on domestic retail banks without triggering too great a risk of regulatory arbitrage. Matters are different, however, for investment banks, which are usually global in their operations and client base. A unilateral domestic imposition of higher capital requirements on investment banking operations might counterproductively result in such banks either shifting assets offshore, or withdrawing from domestic markets—itself imposing costs on the real economy.[33]

23.2.3 Other rationales for structural separation

Interestingly, financial stability was not a mainstay of the arguments for the Glass–Steagall Act of 1933, which many view as the precursor for the current crop of reforms. To the extent that prudential concerns featured in the rationale for that Act, these mainly took the form of suggestions that commercial banks had been induced to make unsound margin loans to their customers by the lure of brokerage revenues for their investment banking affiliates.[34] There was only a passing mention of the notion that proprietary trading by banks had led to losses,[35] and it was not clear to what extent the concern was that their involvement in securities markets fanned the flames of speculation or had led to instability on the part of commercial banks.

A distinct rationale for structural separation has to do with concerns about conflicts of interest between banks and their clients. In terms of our categorization of regulatory objectives, we can understand this as being concerned with 'customer protection'.[36] Concern with conflicts of interest was one of the original rationales underpinning the Glass–Steagall Act, in particular, advisory conflicts of interest in the run-up to the 1929 stock market crash. Banks had directed their customers, seeking investment advice, to their investment affiliates, who touted the stocks that they were underwriting.[37] There was a strong inference that investment banking compensation patterns, which offered upside-only returns, had led management to push poor underwritings upon their unsuspecting customers.[38] And investment bank affiliates returned the favour for commercial banks by organizing stock pools to support the latter's stock prices, and maintain their soundness in the eyes of investors.[39]

During the period leading up to the financial crisis of 2007–9, there was concern, especially in the US, about the way in which conflicts of interest had returned to the banking sector. These conflicts were of a different variety. The major change in investment banking business during the 1990s was the rise of proprietary trading.[40]

---

[33] PCBS, *Final Report*, 23.   [34] Pecora Report, 156.   [35] Ibid, 183–4.
[36] See Chapter 3, section 3.4.1.   [37] Pecora Report, 163–6.   [38] Ibid, 206–7.
[39] Ibid, 168.   [40] Morrison and Wilhelm, n 28, 26–9.

This put the *investment* banks into conflict with the interests of their clients who relied on them for brokerage and market-making services. Concern about this kind of activity formed part of the original impetus for the Volcker Rule introduced in the US.[41] It is, however, highly doubtful whether customer protection concerns would justify the costs associated with implementing structural regulation, particularly given the sophistication of the institutional clients exposed to the conflict. Hence, a convincing case for doing so must surely be based primarily on financial stability.

23.3 The Strength of the Partition

Structural separation is about partitioning assets related to different types of activity. This partition can be achieved in two ways: either by prohibiting the combination of activities within the same entity ('entity-level separation') or by prohibiting their combination within the same group ('group-level separation'). As a matter of theory, entity-level partitioning might be thought sufficient to avoid any contamination of claims against a firm's assets from activities carried on in other firms.[42] However, it is possible that a parent might cause a controlled subsidiary to circumvent restrictions in subtle ways. Anti-circumvention measures, in particular relating to intra-group transactions, can be used to control such impulses. But if these do not work, then group-level restrictions can be understood as a reinforced form of separation, which is less susceptible to circumvention.

Structural separation in the US began at the entity level, with the National Bank Acts of 1863 and 1864. As part of the price for permitting national banking firms to be established, this statute imposed restrictions on the activities in which these entities were permitted to engage. As financial markets developed in the US during the early twentieth century, large banking firms opened separate investment banking affiliates to conduct market-facing business. This was compatible with the National Banking Act because these were separate entities. However, there were many related party transactions and much inter-linking of business affairs.

Following the 1929 stock market crash, the US went significantly further with structural regulation, further indeed than any of the measures currently being deployed that we analyse in this chapter. The Glass–Steagall Act of 1933 added to the existing restrictions a group-level separation between activities of commercial and investment banks.[43] The resulting regime consisted of (entity-level) restrictions on entities carrying on commercial or investment banking business, restrictions on intra-group transactions for such firms, and (group-level) restrictions on affiliation between entities engaged in these activities.

---

[41] See Group of Thirty Working Group on Financial Reform, *Financial Reform: A Framework for Financial Stability* (Washington DC: The Group of Thirty, 2009), 27 ('Complex and unavoidable conflicts of interest among clients and investors can be acute').

[42] See eg H Hansmann and R Kraakman, 'The Essential Role of Organizational Law' (2000) 110 *Yale Law Journal* 387.

[43] The Glass–Steagall Act's original separation regime was amended and enhanced by the Bank Holding Company Act of 1956. We refer to these provisions together as the 'Glass–Steagall' regime.

The group-level affiliation restrictions imposed by Glass–Steagall were gradually hollowed out through a series of exceptions and reinterpretations during the 1980s and 1990s, and finally repealed with the Gramm–Leach–Bliley Act of 1999. The primary rationale was to permit synergies to be captured from combinations between investment and commercial banks. Commercial banks could thus offer their clients access to financial markets, and the investment banking arm could leverage the commercial bank's client portfolio to generate business. Gramm–Leach–Bliley did not amount to a complete abandonment of structural separation in the US, however. An important part of the case for relaxation at the group level was that entity-level activity restrictions and intra-group restrictions remained in force.[44]

This structure—entity-level activity restrictions combined with intra-group restrictions—is very similar to that which has been adopted by the UK under its 'ring-fencing' proposals. The UK's structural separation regime imposes no restrictions on the activities of a group that includes a commercial bank.[45] However, it does extensively restrict the conduct of intra-group affairs so as to avoid undermining structural separation. By keeping structural separation to the entity level, UK policy-makers sought to preserve some of the benefits of diversification at the group level.[46] The idea is that while intra-group restrictions will prevent core banking subsidiaries from being used to cross-subsidize ailing investment banking subsidiaries, there is nothing to prevent cross-subsidization going in the opposite direction. That is, the UK regime leaves financial conglomerate groups free to use surplus profits from investment banking entities to support a distressed banking entity.

The UK regime is thus *not* the analogue of the Glass–Steagall Act in the US, but rather is closer to that of the post Gramm–Leach–Bliley regime which was in force at the time of the financial crisis. Meanwhile, the US has reinstated a limited set of group-level affiliation restrictions, in the form of the Volcker Rule. This prohibits any member of a group that includes a commercial banking entity from engaging in proprietary trading or participating in hedge funds or private equity funds. Does this imply that the UK's restriction of its regime to the entity level is a mistake? While it is too soon to say, we should bear in mind that the structure of banking activity in the UK is very different, as are other components of financial regulation. In particular, the UK regime is imposing additional capital requirements on retail banking entities, a policy not adopted in the US.[47]

The EU's structural regulation proposals would involve a combination of measures implemented in both the UK and the US. Their announcement came as something of a surprise, as the Liikanen Report had initially proposed measures that echoed those of the UK's Independent Commission on Banking, save that it suggested trading activity, rather than retail banking activity, should be spun out into separate entities from universal banks.[48] The measures proposed by Liikanen were modified significantly by the European Commission, whose proposed Structural Measures Regulation ('SMR')—

---

[44] ST Omarova, 'From Gramm–Leach–Bliley to Dodd–Frank: The Unfulfilled Promise of Section 23A of the Federal Reserve Act' (2010) 89 *North Carolina Law Review* 1683, 1689.

[45] This may change if the proposed EU regime comes into force.

[46] ICB, *Final Report*, 26.   [47] Discussed in section 23.6.   [48] Liikanen Report, 99–103.

announced in January 2014—would add in group-level restrictions as well.[49] However, across other dimensions, it is less demanding than either the US or the UK schema. On the one hand, the group-level restrictions proposed for proprietary trading would be narrower in scope than the Volcker Rule. On the other hand, the entity-level restrictions would only be applicable on a targeted basis to entities assessed as necessitating such measures for the sake of financial stability on a case-by-case basis.

The SMR proposal came in for heavy criticism from European financial sector lobbyists.[50] As a consequence, the status of the proprietary trading ban in particular is uncertain. The Council's general approach, released in June 2015, dropped the group-level ban on proprietary trading in favour of a less invasive entity-level restriction.[51] However, the group-level ban was retained in a text subsequently agreed by the Parliament's Economic and Monetary Affairs Committee.[52]

Several EU Member States—not only the UK but also Germany and France—had already announced structural separation schemes prior to the Commission's SMR. The SMR proposal would permit Member States to obtain a derogation from its application where they have legislated a domestic separation regime that is comparable to the SMR scheme, provided that the relevant national legislation was passed before 29 January 2014, which would permit the UK to apply for such a derogation as regards the Financial Services (Banking Reform) Act 2013.

23.4 The Activities Restricted

We now turn to the scope of the restrictions imposed by the various structural separation regimes. Presumably because a group-level restriction is more invasive than an entity-level restriction, the entity-level restrictions are generally broader in their scope.

23.4.1 Entity-level restrictions

The US Glass–Steagall Act prohibits entities engaged in the securities business from undertaking the core banking activity of taking deposits.[53] US national banks and state

---

[49] European Commission, Proposal for a Regulation of the European Parliament and of the Council on structural measures improving the resilience of EU credit institutions ('Proposed SMR'), Brussels, 29.01.2014 COM (2014) 43 final.

[50] See eg European Banking Federation ('EBF'), The European Commission's proposal for a regulation on structural measures improving the resilience of EU credit institutions: A critical assessment of the EBF Banking Structural Reform Expert Group, November 2014; PwC, Report Commissioned for Association of Financial Markets in Europe ('AFME') on Impact of Bank Structural Reforms in Europe, November 2014 (both suggesting implementation of SMR proposals would lead to higher costs of debt finance for European firms and little benefits in terms of increased stability).

[51] Council of the European Union, Proposal for a Regulation of the European Parliament and of the Council on structural measures improving the resilience of EU credit institutions: General Approach ('Council General Approach'), 2014/0020 (COD), June 2015.

[52] European Parliament Committee on Economic and Monetary Affairs, Compromise Text on Bank Structural Reform Regulation (the 'Hökmark/Weizsäcker Compromise Text'), October 2015; see also J Brunsden, 'Banks Fume at EU Move to Strengthen Break-Up Powers', *Financial Times*, 29 October 2015.

[53] Glass–Steagall Act §21; 12 USC §378. Gramm–Leach–Bliley repealed only the anti-affiliation provisions of the original Act, §20, formerly codified at 12 USC §377, not the provisions that prohibit a securities firm broker-dealer from taking deposits and a bank from underwriting private entity securities.

banks that are members of the Federal Reserve have power to take deposits and make loans, but they (and their subsidiaries) are prohibited from engaging in almost all investment banking activities, including underwriting, market-making, and proprietary trading.[54] In addition, the Dodd–Frank Act has introduced a new prohibition on banks engaging in derivatives transactions other than for hedging purposes.[55] Such banks remain free to engage in brokerage on behalf of customers, provided they engage no more than 10 per cent of their capital.[56]

The UK structural separation regime, which applies at the entity level, has a similar scope. It prohibits 'core activities' (retail banking) from being undertaken other than by a 'ring-fenced body' ('RFB'),[57] which is subject to extensive activity restrictions and higher capital standards. 'Core activities' consist of core deposit-taking, payments, and associated services.[58] 'Core deposits' are those from retail investors or small businesses.[59] These are targeted on the theory that such parties would face the greatest disruption were a bank to fail and thus are most deserving of protection.[60] This rationale does not extend to deposits from foreign nationals, who are presumed to be able to get access to banks in their own countries and rely on own-country safety nets. Yet the scope of implementation includes all deposits from such persons who are within the European Economic Area ('EEA'). This was necessary because to exclude non-UK EEA depositors would have contravened EU Treaty freedoms.

Curiously, lending to small and medium-sized enterprises ('SMEs') is not within the definition of 'core activities', meaning non-RFBs will also be permitted to lend to SMEs. This seems odd, given that loss of credit from domestic banks to SMEs was thought to be one of the greatest externalities of failure of the banking system. Yet, the likely impact of permitting credit to be supplied to the SME sector from non-RFBs is ambiguous. RFBs are likely to face a higher cost of capital, given their additional capital requirements. A pessimist might infer from this that SMEs will obtain finance more cheaply from non-RFBs. Consequently, failures of non-RFBs might significantly impact the availability of credit for SMEs, cutting against the policy rationale for separation. A more sanguine perspective points to the fact that RFBs will have a

---

[54] Specifically, they may not buy and sell securities save on behalf of their customers, or purchase for their own account any corporate shares: Glass–Steagall Act §16; 12 USC §§24 (Seventh), 335. Similarly, FDIC-insured state non-member banks are also subject to activity restrictions defined by reference to those imposed on national banks: 12 USC §1831a. Most of these entity-level restrictions preceded the Glass–Steagall Act. The prohibition on buying and selling securities does not apply to US and municipal government debt.

[55] Dodd–Frank Act of 2010 §716. However, this was amended in December 2014 to permit banks to continue to engage in all except 'structured finance swaps'.

[56] 'Customers' do not have to be *pre-existing* banking customers; that is, the bank may run a brokerage business independently of its banking business: *Securities Industry Association v Comptroller of the Currency* 577 F Supp 252 (DDC 1983).

[57] Financial Services and Markets Act 2000 (UK) ('FSMA 2000') (as amended), s 142B.

[58] Ibid, s 142C.

[59] There is a financial condition in each case. To count as core deposits, they must be held in EEA accounts from natural persons who have less than £250,000 in free assets (net assets excluding domestic residence, insurance policies, and pension entitlements), or from corporate persons with less than £6.5m annual turnover, which are not financial institutions: Financial Services and Markets Act 2000 (Ring-Fenced Bodies and Core Activities) Order 2014, SI 2014/1960.

[60] See section 23.2.2.

monopoly over core deposit-taking, so they will be able to pass costs on to core depositors. As a result, their SME lending need not be more expensive than non-RFB credit. Moreover, they will need to earn a return on the deposit funds raised, and SME lending will be one of the ways they can do this. Consequently, they are unlikely to offer uncompetitive loan rates to SME borrowers. On this view, the domestic SME sector would be insulated against the risk of failure of a non-RFB. On the other hand, it is possible that their access to investment banking functions will mean that non-RFBs will be able to securitize loans more effectively than RFBs, which could lower their costs for certain SME financing. As now, a sudden collapse in such securitization markets would damage many SMEs.

The foregoing suggests a crucial factor for the RFB's success will be core depositors' willingness to shoulder the extra costs of RFBs. If non-RFB vehicles can offer core depositors functionally similar investments to compete with RFB deposit accounts, then RFBs will be rendered uncompetitive. On this, the story of money market funds in the US from the early 1970s onwards is a cautionary tale regarding the willingness of retail customers to switch away from banks in pursuit of functionally equivalent (but economically more attractive) non-bank transaction accounts.[61] RFBs face competitive threats from at least two other sources. The first is through the entry of smaller banks. Only banks with very large core deposits will be required to establish RFBs.[62] Smaller institutions with less than £25 billion of core deposits will be able to operate without ring-fencing and thus the attendant costs. A second concern might be the entry of 'direct lending' platforms. These match consumer lenders and borrowers via a web platform, using algorithms to select a portfolio of loans into which a saver's funds are placed. These do not offer the same liquidity as a deposit account, but offer much higher rates of return. For consumers who do not value liquidity particularly highly, these are becoming an attractive alternative.[63]

Similarly to the US restrictions on banks, the UK regime prevents RFBs from engaging in almost all investment banking activities, through the exclusion of 'dealing in investments [or commodities] as principal'.[64] This prohibits RFBs from engaging in proprietary trading, market-making, underwriting, and derivatives transactions, although it does not prohibit brokerage services. As an anti-circumvention measure, the regime will also prohibit RFBs from having exposures to other non-RFB financial institutions.[65] This will prevent circumvention by exposure to the balance sheet of a 'risky' financial institution.

However, UK RFBs will be permitted to engage in a range of activities that policy-makers deemed to be subsidiary to, and desirable for the successful execution of, core activities. Thus, they may acquire shares under debt-equity swaps (to facilitate corporate restructurings). They are also permitted to have exposures to non-RFB financial

---

[61] See Chapter 22, section 22.2.1.   [62] See section 23.5.3.

[63] See the discussion in Chapter 12, section 12.2.5.

[64] FSMA 2000 (as amended) s 142D. The exclusion of commodities is added by secondary legislation: Financial Services and Markets Act 2000 (Excluded Activities and Prohibitions) Order 2014 (the 'Excluded Activities Order'), SI 2014/2080, Art 5.

[65] The legislation permits the Treasury to impose restrictions on RFBs' transactions with categories of persons or from opening branches or subsidiaries in certain jurisdictions: FSMA 2000 s 142E.

institutions for the purposes of issuing documentary letters of credit, the provision of overdraft facilities to customers, or providing guarantees for customers. Finally, and perhaps less obviously, RFBs may engage in securitizations of their own assets,[66] and enter into repo transactions with other financial institutions.[67] These last two exemptions raise the prospect that UK RFBs may engage in activities that were associated with instability during the crisis—securitization (albeit only of their own loan assets) and repo financing.[68]

In addition to these measures intended to focus RFBs' activities on retail banking, the legislation imposes geographic restrictions intended to minimize the international scope of the organizations, so as to facilitate resolution.[69] These will prohibit RFBs from having operations (branches or subsidiaries) outside the EEA. However, why geographic restrictions should *a priori* reduce risk, rather than increase it, is unclear. The US banking sector experience with such restrictions before Congress abolished them in 1994 illustrates this: it is generally believed that state-level geographic constraints made US banks weaker, because it deprived them of geographic diversity in their loan-making.

The UK's entity-level partition will also impose specific corporate governance requirements. RFBs must be able to ensure as far as practicable that they are able to take decisions independently of the other members of their group.[70] Specifically, no more than one-third of a RFB's board members may overlap with boards of non-RFB entities in the group, and none of its executive directors may hold executive positions at non-RFB group entities.[71]

Finally, the European Commission's proposed Structural Measures Regulation will require Member States' national competent authorities ('NCAs') (or, for the Eurozone's largest banks, the ECB[72]) to review large deposit-taking banks subject to their supervision,[73] with a view to determining whether entity-level structural separation—with ongoing activity restrictions—should be imposed. Domestic banking supervisors must determine whether banks' 'trading activities' constitute a threat to the stability of the bank or to the EU financial system as a whole, using guidance to be supplied by the European Banking Authority ('EBA'). 'Trading activities' are defined very broadly to cover all activities *other* than insured deposit-taking, lending, and retail payment

---

[66] That is, securitizations where the entirety of the assets held by the SPV come from the RFB (Excluded Activities Order, rr 7, 16). This means that any liability the RFB incurs—whether explicit or implicit—to guarantee SPV returns is determined simply by reference to assets the RFB was originally permitted to acquire.

[67] Excluded Activities Order, r 18. Where the other financial institution advances the repo asset to the RFB, it must be a liquid asset.

[68] See Chapter 21, section 21.2.

[69] The UK government would have preferred to prohibit any international activity by RFBs, but this would potentially have contravened the EU Treaty's grant of freedom of establishment to UK banks.

[70] FSMA 2000 s 142H(4).

[71] PRA, 'The Implementation of Ring-Fencing: Prudential Requirements, Intragroup Arrangements and Use of Financial Market Infrastructures', CP37/15 (2015), Appendix 1: PRA Draft Rules on Ring-Fenced Bodies, rr 4.5, 4.7.

[72] See Chapter 24, section 24.3.4.

[73] The current thinking is to exempt banks or parents with less than €35bn of insured deposits within the EU: Council General Approach, n 51, Art 4; Hökmark/Weizsäcker Compromise Text, n 52, Art 4.

services.[74] However, the NCA review is to focus in particular on three types of trading activity thought to be particularly risky, namely market-making, investing in and sponsoring securitizations, and trading in derivatives.[75] If the authorities conclude that some or all of a bank's trading activities do constitute a threat to stability, they will then restrict the bank from carrying on such trading accordingly: this will necessitate structural separation of these activities. The SMR thus contemplates a range of possible activity restrictions being imposed at the entity level across the EU, depending on NCAs' assessments of need. The SMR specifies a maximum permissible restriction— which looks quite similar to the US/UK framework—but gives NCAs a steer towards a lesser level of restriction, simply pushing out 'riskier' activities as described, and does not mandate any separation at all at the entity level, should NCAs conclude that it is unnecessary to preserve financial stability.[76]

If a separation order is made, then it will be permissible for the activities in question to continue to be carried on by a separate entity within the same group as the banking entity, provided that the credit institution does not hold shares in the trading entity.[77] At the same time, the trading entity must not take deposit guarantee scheme ('DGS') eligible deposits or provide retail payment services.[78] The banking entity will, however, be permitted to offer basic risk management services to their clients.[79]

23.4.2 Anti-evasion: intra-group restrictions

Entity-level restrictions are in each instance combined with rules restricting the types of intra-group transactions into which a relevant banking entity may enter. In the US, the key provisions are sections 23A and 23B of the Federal Reserve Act of 1913.[80] Section 23B is the most general in scope, requiring that all transactions between deposit-taking banks and their affiliates, or with third parties for the benefit of affiliates, must be on 'arm's length terms'.[81] In contrast, section 23A imposes a range of restrictions on a hotlist of particular inter-affiliate transactions, known as 'covered transactions'. These include *advances of credit* by the bank to or for (including a

---

[74] Proposed SMR, Art 8.   [75] Ibid, Art 9.

[76] This is more lenient than the recommendations of the Liikanen Group, which considered the option of separation conditional on NCA assessment, but ultimately concluded it was necessary to mandate push-out of 'risky' activities at the entity level: see Liikanen Report, 99–100.

[77] Proposed SMR, Art 13.   [78] Ibid, Art 20.   [79] Ibid, Art 12.

[80] Section 23A in fact dates from the Glass–Steagall Act (§13). This was supplemented in 1987 by §23B. See 12 USC §§371c, 371c-1. These restrictions are extended to all FDIC-insured banks, even if they are not Federal Reserve members: 12 USC §1828(j). Sections 23A and 23B are implemented by detailed regulations promulgated by the Federal Reserve Board, so-called 'Regulation W'. These provisions were enhanced by the Dodd–Frank Act, §608. For a sceptical view of the ring-fencing capacity of these provisions, see Omarova, n 44 (during the financial crisis, exemptions granted by the Federal Reserve permitted banks to support their securities affiliates).

[81] 'Affiliates' are members of the same group, including parents, subsidiaries, and sister companies; they also include investment funds advised by the bank or another affiliate (added by the Dodd–Frank Act). However, operating subsidiaries are treated in effect as extensions of the parent company.

guarantee of) an affiliate;[82] *purchases of assets* from the affiliate (including repos);[83] investing in, or accepting as collateral from anyone, *securities issued by the affiliate*; and *derivative transactions*, to the extent that they give the bank a credit exposure to an affiliate.[84] The bank's total exposure under covered transactions may not exceed 20 per cent of its capital, with a single-party limit of 10 per cent for any particular affiliate. Most of these restrictions may be exempted as between two FDIC-insured banks in the same group ('sister banks'). They are all exempt as regards transactions in US Treasuries, and those in securities traded in public markets at market price, the rationale presumably being that the price in these cases is sufficiently transparent as not to pose a risk of manipulation.

The UK regime will likewise contain restrictions on intra-group activity.[85] In particular, the prohibition on exposures to financial institutions will be expected to do a lot of work in the intra-group context.[86] For intra-group transactions, the restriction is attenuated to permit within-group exposures that are at 'arm's length'. The details of this are developed in Prudential Regulation Authority ('PRA') rules, which will require RFBs to establish procedures for identifying and monitoring intra-group transactions and determining their pricing on an 'arm's length' basis.[87] Moreover, the payment of upstream dividends by the RFB to its parent company must be preceded by notification of the PRA along with an explanation of the payment's impact on the RFB's capital levels.[88] If the PRA is concerned about anticipated consequences for the RFB's capital adequacy, it will be able to restrict the payment of dividends.

Similarly, under the EU's proposed SMR, a series of restrictions will come into play regarding intra-group dealings following entity-level structural separation within a group. Contracts between the credit institution and the trading entity must be on a 'most favoured counterparty' basis; that is, they must be on terms at least as favourable to the credit institution as are comparable contracts or transactions with or involving entities not belonging to the same sub-group.[89] There will also be corporate governance separation: only a minority of the boards of the two entities may overlap.

At present, the details of the EU intra-group restrictions have yet to be spelled out. The US experience does not give grounds for optimism that they will retain the brevity of their current formulations. Nor, for that matter, does the US experience suggest that this sort of intra-group restriction will be particularly effective at controlling manipulation.[90] There is a large volume of complex case law testifying to the ingenuity of legal advisers' attempts to circumvent them. More generally, this strategy of seeking to regulate intra-group activities may be compared to the attempts to restrict within-

---

[82] These must be fully secured with a specified margin of sufficient-quality collateral.

[83] Such assets must not include 'impaired' credits.

[84] This was also introduced by the Dodd–Frank Act. Derivatives had not previously been covered by Reg W, the FRB's implementing rules issued in 2002. The basis for this was that such transactions between banks and affiliates were thought to be for risk management, not for funding purposes: Omarova, n 44, 1764–5.

[85] Excluded Activities Order, r 14(4).   [86] See n 65 and text thereto.

[87] PRA Draft Rules on Ring-Fenced Bodies, n 71, r 12.

[88] See PRA, n 71, 21–2; PRA Draft Rules on Ring-Fenced Bodies, n 71, r 11.

[89] Proposed SMR, Art 13(7).   [90] See Omarova, n 44.

group 'transfer pricing' for the purposes of calculating corporation tax liability, which are thought to be distortive.[91]

23.4.3 Group-level restrictions

Group-level activity restrictions were first introduced by the Glass–Steagall Act of 1933. It supplemented the US entity-level restrictions with a ban on commercial banks being affiliated with any company 'engaged principally' in the core investment banking activities of proprietary trading, underwriting, or dealing in securities,[92] and a prohibition on management and director interlocks between such firms.[93] These were very invasive provisions, which required the break-up of the US banking groups of the time. As might be expected, the banking sector expressed very strong opposition, at least at first. However, the Pecora Commission's inquiry and report into the practices of the financial sector revealed a litany of abuses.[94] That generated such intense public outcry that the financial sector sought to distance itself from the bank-securities nexus.[95] A number of banking firms took the initiative of voluntary divestment of their securities affiliates, and opposition faded from view.

From the early 1970s, US commercial banks found themselves exposed to intense competitive pressure from capital markets as regards corporate financing activity and deposits. The travails of the commercial-investment banking boundary over the next thirty years are a story of how this competitive pressure spurred banks to increasingly far-reaching applications of the maxim 'if you can't beat them, join them', seeking to move into capital markets work of various hues.[96] This involved repeated testing of the boundaries of the Glass–Steagall partition. Over time, bank regulators' ideology shifted, from being one of seeking to restrain this in line with the spirit of the legislation, to one of seeking to facilitate it, in order to protect the survival of the industry against external competition.

Notwithstanding the affiliation restriction, bank holding companies ('BHCs') or their non-bank subsidiaries were permitted to engage in non-banking activities, provided that the Federal Reserve considered these sufficiently 'closely related' to banking. From 1987, the Federal Reserve regularized the practice of permitting BHCs to have subsidiaries carrying on underwriting and dealing in bank-related securities: municipal bonds, mortgage-backed securities ('MBS'), consumer receivable securities, and commercial paper, relying on language in the anti-affiliation provision that spoke in terms of an 'organization engaged *principally*' in the prohibited securities activities. A limit was imposed on the proportion of the revenue of the subsidiary that could come from these technically ineligible activities, which was gradually raised over a ten-year period

---

[91] See C Keuschnigg and MP Devereux, 'The Arm's Length Principle and Distortions to Multinational Firm Organization' (2013) 89 *Journal of International Economics* 432.

[92] Glass–Steagall Act, §20, formerly codified at 12 U.S.C §377.

[93] Ibid, §32.   [94] Pecora Report, 163–200.

[95] JM Hendrickson, 'The Long and Bumpy Road to Glass–Steagall Reform: A Historical and Evolutionary Analysis of Banking Legislation' (2001) 60 *American Journal of Economics and Sociology* 849, 858–60.

[96] JR Macey, 'The Business of Banking: Before and After Gramm–Leach–Bliley' (1999) 25 *Journal of Corporation Law* 691.

so as to undo Glass–Steagall's separation.[97] The Gramm–Leach–Bliley Act of 1999 largely eliminated these restrictions.[98]

The ideological shift away from structural regulation that had taken place in the US during the 1980s and 1990s was partially reversed after the financial crisis. The result was section 619 of the Dodd–Frank Act of 2010, the 'Volcker Rule', which reinstates some group-level restrictions on banks.[99] However, the Volcker Rule does not go anywhere near the extent of the restrictions under Glass–Steagall. Rather, it simply prohibits groups that include FDIC-insured banks from engaging in proprietary trading. The US Congress defined the prohibition broadly, with a series of express exemptions for permitted activities. Thus 'proprietary trading' is defined to mean the *acquisition or disposal* of 'securities',[100] 'principally for the purpose' of selling in order to benefit from 'short-term price movements'.[101] The ban is also expressly extended to doing this through investment in a fund, also prohibiting taking an equity interest in, or sponsoring,[102] private equity or hedge funds.[103]

The Volcker Rule's principal rationale is to mitigate systemic risk.[104] However, this argument has never been very strong. There is no evidence that proprietary trading activity had any destabilizing effect during or before the financial crisis, and removing it from banking groups may simply reduce the extent to which they are able to diversify.[105] Indeed, the Volcker rule would have had no impact on the activities of Bear Stearns or Lehman Brothers, because these were pure investment banks with no FDIC-insured deposit-taking affiliate. Moreover, pushing proprietary trading out from banking groups into hedge funds or 'pure' investment banks is, according

[97] Glass–Steagall prohibited a bank from affiliation with a company that engaged 'principally' in underwriting activities of restricted securities, which did not include US Government and certain municipal securities. Thus in computing 'principally', as the firm's government securities underwriting grew, the underwriting of restricted securities was permitted to grow as well, especially as the regulators increased the 'fraction' that would qualify as not 'principally'.

[98] The Act made it permissible for 'Financial Holding Companies' to own controlling stakes in both FDIC-insured depositary institutions and investment banking entities.

[99] Non-bank financial companies designated for supervision by the Fed by the FSOC are not subject to this restriction. But they might be subject to additional capital requirements and quantitative restrictions with respect to these activities.

[100] Dodd–Frank Act §619(h)(4). These include derivatives, commodity contracts, futures, options, and any other securities.

[101] See Treasury/Federal Reserve/FDIC/SEC, 'Prohibitions and Restrictions on Proprietary Trading and Certain Interests in, and Relationships with, Hedge Fund and Private Equity Funds' (2014) 79 *Federal Register* 5536, 5546–9.

[102] To 'sponsor' a fund means to be general partner, or manager, to select or control the fund's managers, or to share a name with the fund for marketing or trading purposes.

[103] That is, 'private funds' exempted from the Investment Companies Act of 1940: see Chapter 22, sections 22.2.2–22.2.3. There is a *de minimis* exception for small value investments (Dodd–Frank Act §619(d)(4)).

[104] Some have sought to combine this with concerns about conflicts of interest: see eg Group of Thirty Working Group on Financial Reform, n 41; SEC Commissioner KM Stein, 'The Volcker Rule: Observations on Systemic Resiliency, Competition, and Implementation', Speech given in Tokyo, Japan, 9 February 2015. However, this justification is even less convincing: see text to n 41.

[105] On the other hand, an event like the 'London Whale' episode, discussed in section 23.5, in which purported hedging activity gone awry cost JP Morgan approximately $6.2 billion, suggests the possible risk of proprietary trading in a future crisis. See D Kopecki, 'JP Morgan Pays $920 Million to Settle London Whale Probes', *Bloomberg*, 20 September 2013.

to some critics, likely to result in the same risks being run within the system, with less oversight.[106]

An alternative justification suggests that bank proprietary trading receives an implicit subsidy, in the form of access to deposit insurance and the Fed's discount window through the bank affiliate, which is inappropriate. Sections 23A and 23B do not prohibit the bank from funding the transaction at 'arm's length', so in theory, without subsidy, yet the bank is exposed to losses if the affiliate is unable to pay. In the financial crisis, the Federal Reserve apparently granted many exemptions to sections 23A–23B in order to protect securities affiliates from collapse.

Finally, as we have argued, it may be that the attitudes towards risk-taking in proprietary trading are at such variance with the desirable attitudes towards risk-taking in commercial banking that to combine them within a single entity poses particular risks to the banking side of the house. In good times the proprietary traders may earn large profits for the entity, which puts them in a position to have more say-so in formulating the bank's risk appetite. This 'cultural' justification for separating-out proprietary trading is said to be a particular favourite of Paul Volcker.[107]

The activities expressly excluded from the Volcker Rule's prohibition encompass most of the categories of investment banking activity discussed in Chapters 2 and 21. These include: (i) *brokerage* transactions as agent for customers; (ii) *market-making*, to the extent that such activities 'are designed not to exceed the near term demands of clients, customers and counterparties'; and (iii) *underwriting*, insofar as securities are bought and sold 'in connection with underwriting...activities'. Of these, the scope of the exemption for market-making generated the most debate. Early drafts provoked concern that the Volcker Rule would impact adversely market-making activity.[108] For example, Darrell Duffie argued that market-making and proprietary trading could not meaningfully be distinguished.[109] A market-maker is buying securities from market participants with a view to selling them on again later at a higher price, hence the spread. The market-maker's willingness to match a client's demand for liquidity is a function of the degree of liquidity in the market generally, and their capacity to warehouse securities on their own balance sheet. The greater the restrictions on the amount of balance sheet risk market-makers can aggregate in their positions, the more

---

[106] CK Whitehead, 'The Volcker Rule and Evolving Financial Markets' (2011) 1 *Harvard Business Law Review* 39.

[107] PA Volcker, 'Commentary on the Restrictions on Proprietary Trading by Insured Depositary Institutions', attached to Letter to financial regulatory agencies, 13 February 2012, available at http://tinyurl.com/qanzy6d ('The need to restrict proprietary trading is not only, or perhaps most importantly, a matter of the immediate market risks involved. It is the seemingly inevitable implication for the culture of the commercial banking institutions involved, manifested in the huge incentives to take risk inherent in the compensation practices for the traders. Can one group of employees be so richly rewarded, the traders, for essentially speculative, impersonal, short-term trading activities while professional commercial bankers providing essential commercial banking services to customers, and properly imbued with fiduciary values, be confined to a much more modest structure of compensation?').

[108] There was fierce industry lobbying, well documented in KD Krawiec and G Liu, 'The Volcker Rule: A Brief Political History' (2015) 10 *Capital Markets Law Journal* 507.

[109] D Duffie, 'Market Making Under the Proposed Volcker Rule', Stanford University Rock Center for Corporate Governance Working Paper No 106 (2012); AV Thakor, 'The Economic Consequences of the Volcker Rule', US Chamber of Commerce Center for Capital Markets Competitiveness Report (2012).

difficult it will be for them to continue to provide market-making services. In the short term, this might have had an adverse impact on market liquidity, price discovery, and cost of capital, because as we saw in Chapter 21, market-makers handle the vast majority of all trades in OTC markets. In the medium to long term it could result in the movement of market-making activity to non-banks, moving it outside the perimeter of appropriate prudential regulation.[110] The final wording of the Volker Rule's exemption for market-making was widened significantly as a result of this critique. Against it, however, we might note our observations from Chapter 21—that market-making generates distinct risks to stability from banking, and demands prudential regulation that is tailored to this (and not to banking) and targeted by reference to the activity rather than the characterization of the firm.

The EU's proposed SMR would also introduce a group-level restriction that would, put crudely, mirror the Volcker rule.[111] It would prohibit any entity in the same group as a credit institution from engaging in proprietary trading or holding equity positions in alternative investment funds. Despite the superficial similarity, the scope of this proposed prohibition is actually rather narrower than the Volcker Rule. The preamble to the SMR proposal notes the difficulties in distinguishing between market-making and proprietary trading, which bogged down the final rule-making in the US for so long.[112] The Commission's proposed solution, however, is to adopt only a narrow definition of proprietary trading, so that market-making will clearly not be caught. The SMR provision defines 'proprietary trading' as trading 'for the *sole purpose* of making a profit for own account, without any connection to client activity, through use of a specifically dedicated desk' (emphasis added).[113] The language of 'sole purpose' would render unnecessary a series of express exemptions, in contrast to the much broader language of 'principal purpose' under the Volcker Rule.[114] Thus, where trading activity has overlapping purposes—for example, market-making—it requires clarification under the Volcker Rule but would fall clearly outside the EU proposal. The final Volcker Rule, for this reason, is highly prolix, running to over a thousand pages. The narrower scope of the EU proposal would make it easier to implement, but also to evade, than the Volcker Rule.[115] Indeed, one wonders how much activity would actually end up being caught by such a narrowly drafted restriction.[116]

---

[110] See eg R Copeland, 'Citadel is Back and in No Mood to Take It Slow', *Wall Street Journal*, 4 August 2015, A1 (hedge fund that almost failed during the financial crisis now handles nearly one-third of market-making by volume for individual investors).

[111] It is, however, uncertain whether this aspect of the proposal in particular will survive into legislation: see nn 50–52 and text thereto.

[112] SMR Proposal, recital 16.

[113] SMR Proposal, Art 5(4).

[114] See nn 100–108 and text thereto.

[115] Further, the SMR's prohibition would not encompass trading in EU sovereign bonds and cash management through trading cash assets, and investments in UCITS, other retail funds, and unlevered or closed-ended hedge funds: SMR Proposal, Arts 6(3) and 6(4).

[116] A partial explanation might be that the European Commission floated the measure in order to try to negotiate a reciprocal exemption from compliance with the extraterritorial effect of the Volcker Rule, on the basis that the EU rules would thus be equivalent. Yet it is hard to see how the Commission could have imagined the US would view the proposal as equivalent, given its manifestly narrower scope.

23.5 Exemptions

Each of the regimes contains a series of discrete exemptions from the scope of the various activity restrictions. These can be categorized thematically into three types.[117] The first type of exemption is concerned with management of the banking firm's own business risks through hedging positions. The second type exempts classes of investment deemed sufficiently 'safe' for a banking firm to be permitted to invest in them as principal. The third encompasses exemptions based on the size of the banking firm.

23.5.1 Hedging (risk management)

Each activity restriction we have considered contains exemptions to permit the use of derivatives by banking entities and/or groups for risk-management purposes. This is related to the concern that structural separation reduces the ability of firms to diversify their risks. Diversification—or lack of it—in lines of business matters less if firms are able to engage in effective risk management.

In the US, there are exemptions from both the entity-level activity restrictions on banks and the Volcker Rule to permit banking firms to enter into risk-mitigating hedging positions in relation to assets of the bank. Similarly, the UK's provisions permit RFBs to hedge their exposure to interest rate, exchange rate, commodity prices, or credit risk,[118] and the EU's proposed SMR regime also mandates specific exceptions for risk-management activities by entities that have been subjected to entity-level separation.[119] These may be carried on using interest rate, foreign exchange, and credit derivatives that are eligible for clearing through a central counterparty.

A central challenge for the regulator is to strike a balance between facilitating the legitimate goal of risk management, yet constraining the evasion of structural

---

What is a Proprietary Trade and What is a Hedge?

In April 2012 it was reported that JP Morgan had incurred a massive loss on a portfolio of so-called 'London Whale' positions entered into by traders in JP Morgan Chase's London office. The nickname was because the positions were so large they shook the world's markets. Closing out the positions lost the bank more than $6.2 billion.

The positions in question were taken on by the bank's Chief Investment Office, which was a division tasked with earning a return on the bank's excess deposits. Part of its activities involved trading in credit derivatives, which it called its 'Synthetic Credit Portfolio' ('SCP'). This was originally envisaged as a way of hedging against risks in the bank's credit portfolio. The SCP began with primarily short credit derivatives, which paid out if the debtors defaulted on the underlying loans. However, over time the SCP expanded dramatically in

---

[117] In terms of legislative drafting, market-making, underwriting, and brokerage activity are technically exemptions from the US Volcker Rule, although for expositional purposes we treat their non-inclusion as part of the scope of the Rule itself.

[118] These are defined as transactions or financial institution exposures, for which the 'main reason' is limiting the relevant type of hedging.

[119] Proposed SMR, Art 11.

size and began to comprise both long and short credit derivative positions, which supposedly offset one another.

The SCP started to lose large amounts of money on its bets in the first quarter of 2012. Following media speculation in April of that year about the size of JP Morgan's losses, the firm's Communications Officer claimed in an analyst call that the SCP was simply a form of hedging activity, of which regulators were fully aware, and which would be consistent with the Volcker Rule. None of this was true.

The bank's principal regulator, the Office of the Comptroller of the Currency ('OCC'), had been provided with no real information about the SCP, such that the media reports were news to it.

The US Senate Subcommittee on Investigations conducted an inquiry into the affair and concluded by recommending, among other things, that regulators should require any positions described as 'hedges' to be substantiated by detailed documentation establishing which assets are hedged, how the hedge lowers the risk associated with these assets, and how it can be tested for effectiveness and unwound. Regulators should also be able to require banks to undergo periodic testing of the effectiveness of their hedges.

Source: US Senate Permanent Subcommittee on Investigations, *Staff Report on JP Morgan Chase Whale Trades: A Case History of Derivatives Risks and Abuses* (15 March 2013).

---

separation by the same techniques. The box text describes an example where this was not done. The key technique now employed to deliver this balance is to require firms to identify, for each transaction described as a hedge, the specific risks that it is designed to reduce, and how it does this.[120] Conceptually, this is a reasonably straightforward test—more so, for example, than distinguishing between market-making and proprietary trading.[121] Nevertheless, considerable implementation costs will be generated by the associated paper trails.

23.5.2 Permitted investment

The structural separation regimes also contain a series of specific exemptions for asset classes in which banking firms are permitted to invest for their own account. Such investments would ordinarily be for the purpose of liquidity management—that is, a liquid asset class into which the firm could put funds likely to be needed at short notice. The selection of the list of assets is contentious, because national governments are keen to ensure that their bonds are included. For example, the EU's SMR provides that, even under the maximum degree of separation contemplated, banking entities will still be permitted to purchase EU sovereign bonds for their own account.[122] Unfortunately, the Eurozone crisis has made painfully clear that such bonds are not risk-free, and inclusion in a list of 'safe' assets creates a risk of distortions. The shorter the list of permitted investments, the more the inclusion of national bonds will stoke demand from banking

---

[120] Eg Proposed SMR, Art 11(1).
[121] There is complexity nevertheless. Presumably it would be inefficient to hedge individual loans, so banks will engage in portfolio hedging. Suppose the bank perceives the risks of a particular set of loans decreasing and thus wants to reduce the hedge. Unwinding a hedge involves buying an offsetting derivatives position. Is taking a directional bet on the need for hedging (and unwinding it) proprietary trading?
[122] Proposed SMR, Art 8.

firms. This obviously helps governments to market their debt, but could amount to an interest rate subsidy that could exacerbate moral hazard for sovereign debtors.

In the US, there are exemptions from both entity and group-level restrictions for debt issued by the US Government or any of the States and securities issued by government-sponsored entities including Fannie Mae or Freddie Mac. Banking groups are also permitted to make own-account investments in small business investment companies and insurance companies. Similarly, UK RFBs are permitted to buy and sell 'liquid securities' for the purpose of liquidity management,[123] and may enter into transactions with the central bank.

23.5.3 Size-based exemptions

The UK regime will apply only to very large banks. Entities with less than £25 billion of core deposits will be permitted to carry on core activities without being ring-fenced.[124] Although this is described as a '*de minimis* exception', such institutions are in international terms very large. However, the British high street lending market is very concentrated, and an estimated 90 per cent of UK core deposits are held with firms exceeding this size threshold.[125] Similarly, the SMR regime will only apply to the very largest European banks; namely those designated by the FSB as G-SIBs, or those having consolidated assets of more than €30 billion and trading activity of more than €70 billion.[126]

23.6 Linkage to Other Stability Measures

As we have argued, the implications of structural separation vary considerably depending on the way in which it interacts with other stability measures implemented in a system of financial regulation. In this section, we consider two of these.

First, structural separation can be used as a way of imposing enhanced capital adequacy requirements on deposit-taking institutions. Under the UK scheme, large RFBs will be subject, on an entity basis, to an additional core equity tier 1 ('CET1') capital requirement, known as the 'systemic risk buffer' ('SRB').[127] This is an example of what we have termed a 'microprudential plus' approach to the control of cross-

---

[123] Although they may not incur financial institution exposures for this purpose. This is intuitive: it would make the RFB's liquidity dependent on the balance sheet of the non-RFB financial institution and thereby undermine structural separation.

[124] Financial Services and Markets Act 2000 (Ring-Fenced Bodies and Core Activities) Order 2014, SI 2014/1960, Art 12.

[125] HM Treasury/BIS, *Banking Reform: Draft Secondary Legislation*, Cm 8660 July 2013, 11.

[126] SMR Proposal, Art 3(1). Even amongst this group, it is proposed that those with less than €35 billion of insured deposits will be exempted from the possibility of entity-level restrictions being imposed by NCAs: see Council General Approach, n 51, Art 4; Hökmark/Weizsäcker Compromise Text, n 52, Art 4.

[127] Capital Requirements (Capital Buffers and Macroprudential Measures) Regulations 2014, SI 2014/894, as amended by SI 2015/19, Part 5A. This implements, in the UK, the Basel III framework requiring an additional capital buffer for domestically systemically important banks ('D-SIBs'), via Art 133 of the Capital Requirements Directive IV (Directive 2013/36/EU [2013] OJ L176/338). On capital buffers, see Chapter 14, section 14.5.2. Depending on the group structure, the SRB may be imposed on a 'sub-consolidated' basis, including subsidiaries of the RFB. See PRA, n 71, 16.

sectional systemic risk: a traditional microprudential tool such as capital adequacy requirements is deployed in a differential way depending on the systemic importance of the firms in question.[128]

A second point of intersection concerns bank resolution. The case for structural separation, as put by the UK's ICB, turns in part on its ability to facilitate resolution. Having core activities in a separate entity, with limited intra-group liabilities, means that they can readily be slotted into a 'good bank / bad bank' resolution. Indeed, one might go so far as to characterize separation as a form of generalized resolution planning. Whether this is necessary or desirable in addition to firm-specific rescue and recovery plans depends on how firms and regulators go about implementing them.

However, it is conceivable that structural separation might actually impede resolution, if implemented rigidly. For example, overzealous application of heightened capital requirements to banking subsidiaries might make it more difficult to apply an SPOE model of bank resolution via recapitalizing a parent company. The EU's proposed SMR recognizes this potential conflict and provides that in cases where separation is required at the entity level, the credit institution and the trading entity are to be separately capitalized, except insofar as this would run contrary to any resolution plan agreed by the resolution authorities under the Bank Recovery and Resolution Directive ('BRRD').[129] This is a welcome acknowledgement of the need to dovetail the two processes.

The interlinkage between these various measures is further illustrated by a recent controversy over the application of the SRB. The ICB originally envisaged that 'large' RFBs for these purposes would include all those with assets exceeding 1 per cent of UK GDP (£18.6 billion in 2015).[130] However, the Financial Policy Committee ('FPC') decided in early 2016 to apply the SRB only to RFBs with assets of more than £175 billion, or nearly 10 per cent of UK GDP.[131] The FPC suggested, amongst other things, that developments in bank resolution mechanisms since the ICB reported in 2011 meant that significantly less equity capital was required than would previously have been the case.[132] This position has rightly been criticized by John Vickers, who chaired the ICB, on the basis that the ICB assumed the introduction of bail-in powers in setting their framework, and that the *existence* of these powers is a far cry from their trouble-free *deployment*.[133] The extent to which bank resolution can be relied upon is very much a function of the quality of resolution plans, the contents of which are not publicly available and the success of which is as yet untested.[134]

---

[128] See Chapter 19, section 19.3.1.

[129] Proposed SMR, Art 13(6). The BRRD is discussed in Chapter 16.

[130] ICB, *Final Report*, 91–3. UK GDP in 2015 was £1.86 trillion (Office for National Statistics).

[131] Bank of England, 'The Financial Policy Committee's Framework for the Systemic Risk Buffer: A Consultation Paper', January 2016, 13.

[132] Ibid, 16.

[133] See J Vickers, 'The Bank of England Must Think Again On Systemic Risk', *Financial Times*, 14 February 2016; A Bailey and J Cunliffe, 'Proposals Designed to Fulfil BoE's Core Mission', *Financial Times*, 16 February 2016; J Vickers, 'Equity Buffers Are In the Public Interest', *Financial Times*, 17 February 2016.

[134] See Chapter 16, sections 16.4.1 and 16.6.

23.7 Conclusion

The story of structural regulation of banking is a remarkable ideological roller-coaster. First introduced in the 1930s in response to the US experience of bank failures, it gradually fell out of favour in the last quarter of the twentieth century, on grounds that it failed to reflect fully the changing nature of the financial system. After the near collapse of financial systems in 2008–9, the idea of structural regulation has come back into vogue. The new measures seek to carve out a protected space for core activities, and to push activities deemed 'too risky' outside the banking entity, and even in some cases outside the banking group altogether.

Perhaps the most remarkable thing about the current measures is that they will, when implemented, achieve a very high level of convergence on this issue across both sides of the Atlantic. For many years, US banking regulation has been an outlier in that it applied structural regulation in ways that Europeans did not comprehend. A combination of the UK's ring-fencing scheme, and the EU's Structural Measures Regulation—if implemented—would (to the extent that NCAs assess separation is necessary) cause large European banks to be subject to broadly similar restrictions to the entity-level and intra-group restrictions which have remained in force throughout in the US. The SMR may also impose convergence on the separation of commercial banking from proprietary trading.

PART F

THE MIX OF INSTITUTIONS

24

From Principles to Practice

24.1 Introduction

So far, we have considered the objectives of financial regulation, the options open to policymakers, and the trade-offs inherent in regulatory choices. In Part A, we outlined an analytic framework for understanding and evaluating the regulation of the financial system; Parts B to E then applied this to the substantive rules governing different aspects of the financial system. In order to keep the analysis as tractable as possible, these parts have largely ignored two very important processes that connect these substantive rules to real-world actors.[1] These are the processes by which the rules are made and applied.

The operation of each of these processes very much affects the feasibility of putting regulation into action. Put another way, weaknesses in these processes can greatly reduce financial regulation's capacity to improve the financial system. It is sometimes argued that regulatory failure in trying to correct market failures can be as great as or greater than the market failures themselves, thereby negating the case for government intervention to correct them. Worse, it may cause as much or more damage than it mitigates.

Whether this is the case hinges critically on the institutions involved—the legislative bodies and administrative agencies tasked with making and applying financial regulation. In the stylized world of textbook analysis, these institutions might act as perfect mechanisms for the design, implementation, and application of whatever rules the substantive analysis suggests are best. Of course, in the real world, these institutions are not passive conduits, but collections of individual actors—politicians, regulators, and others—who come together to perform their tasks. These individuals do not act solely for the greater good of society, but, like almost everyone, also pursue their own self-interest. How effectively these institutions operate depends on the way in which the pursuit of individual self-interest is managed. And this, in turn, is greatly affected by the design and structure of the relevant institutions—what we term 'institutional architecture'. This institutional architecture is what Part F is about. Some aspects of this material were introduced at the outset in Chapter 4. Part F amplifies and extends this in light of our intervening consideration of the substantive problems.

The institutional architecture of financial regulation encompasses a number of cross-cutting and related aspects of the operation of regulatory agencies. This makes it difficult usefully to describe any single aspect independently of the others. More so perhaps than any other section of the book, Part F therefore should be read as a whole. The rest of this chapter serves as an introduction to the four chapters that follow. Section 24.2 provides a roadmap of how the various components of institutional

---

[1] The exception is Chapter 4, which gives an overview of many of the topics discussed in Part F.

Principles of Financial Regulation. First Edition. John Armour, Dan Awrey, Paul Davies, Luca Enriques, Jeffrey N. Gordon, Colin Mayer, and Jennifer Payne. © John Armour, Dan Awrey, Paul Davies, Luca Enriques, Jeffrey N. Gordon, Colin Mayer, and Jennifer Payne 2016. Published 2016 by Oxford University Press.

architecture discussed in Part F fit together. To give the reader sufficient context to make sense of the more analytic discussions that follow in the rest of Part F, section 24.3 then describes the agencies responsible for financial regulation in the US, the EU, and the UK. Section 24.4 considers a final preparatory topic for Part F, namely the role of market participants in designing and implementing financial regulation.

24.2 Design Choices in Institutional Architecture

We introduce the idea of institutional architecture in financial regulation by reflecting on a number of design choices that would be involved in building from scratch a set of institutions tasked with implementing financial regulation.[2] These choices include: the configuration of regulators' jurisdiction; the resourcing of regulators; regulators' susceptibility to influence; supervision and enforcement powers; and international coordination among regulators.[3]

24.2.1 The allocation of regulatory jurisdiction

In establishing a system of financial regulation, it is necessary to delineate the *jurisdiction* of regulatory agencies—that is, the scope of their rule-making and enforcement powers. We can understand this allocation of jurisdiction as having a vertical and a horizontal dimension. The horizontal dimension denotes the scope of subject-matter jurisdiction, while the vertical dimension denotes hierarchical relationships. Table 24.1 summarizes these dimensions and the choices within them. In section 24.3, we describe the present allocation of regulatory jurisdiction in the UK, the US, and the EU. We return to the question of regulatory jurisdiction in Chapter 27, which takes a more overtly normative perspective.

The choices over (horizontal) allocation of subject-matter jurisdiction, previewed in Chapter 4, section 4.4, are generally seen as being between:[4]

- An *institutional* model, allocating regulatory responsibility on the basis of the legal category into which a firm has been allotted—that is, 'banks', 'securities dealers', or 'insurance companies'—which generally also determines the scope of the firm's permissible activities.

---

[2] This is an expositional device to introduce the subject-matter. Although we speak of 'choices', in some cases observed structures do not so much represent the result of conscious construction as a gradual accretion over time of small changes. To the extent that there is a conscious choice, it is simply *not* to impose anything more ordered than that which has emerged through such a process.

[3] See R Abrams and M Taylor, 'Issues in the Unification of Financial Sector Supervision', International Monetary Fund (IMF) Working Paper WP 00/213 (2000).

[4] There is some variance in terminology between authors, so the categorization offered here is intended to be representative rather than definitive. See ibid; M Čihák and R Podpiera, 'Is One Watchdog Better Than Three? International Experience with Integrated Financial Sector Supervision', IMF Working Paper, March 2006; DT Llewellyn, 'Institutional Structure of Financial Regulation and Supervision: The Basics', paper presented at World Bank seminar, 'Aligning Supervisory Structures with Country Needs', June 2006; Group of Thirty, *The Structure of Financial Supervision: Approaches and Challenges in a Global Marketplace* (Washington DC: Group of Thirty, 2008), 23–5; E Ferran, 'Institutional Design: The Choices for National Systems', in N Moloney, E Ferran, and J Payne (eds), *The Oxford Handbook of Financial Regulation* (Oxford: OUP, 2015), 97.

Table 24.1 Dimensions of regulatory jurisdiction in financial regulation

	Jurisdictions	Agencies	Public/Private	Horizontal (subject-matter)			
Vertical (hierarchy)	Federal/Regional	Senior	Regulators	*Institutional*	Banks	Broker-dealers	Insurers
	State/National	Junior		*Functional*	Banking	Securities	Insurance
			Firms/Networks	*Objectives*	Stability	Market efficiency	Consumer protection
				Unified	All of the above		

- A *functional* model, allocating responsibility on the basis of the type of business activity, regardless of the legal category of institution.[5]
- An *objectives-based* model, allocating responsibility to separate agencies tasked with pursuing the various goals of financial regulation: one for market efficiency, another for consumer protection, another for conduct of business regulation, another for financial stability, and so forth.[6]
- A *unified or integrated* model, allocating jurisdiction to a single regulator responsible for overseeing the entire financial sector, well exemplified by the UK's former Financial Services Authority ('FSA') or Germany's Bundesanstalt für Finanzdienstleistungsaufsicht ('BaFin').[7]

The vertical dimension of regulatory structure reflects the hierarchy between regulators within a given system, or 'agency hierarchy'. This is obviously relevant if there are multiple regulators: it speaks to how potential conflicts between their agendas should be resolved. Since the financial crisis, there is an increasing awareness of the need to make the agency responsible for macroprudential oversight 'senior' to the others, so that if there is a conflict, the measures necessary to ensure stability should prevail.

A second aspect of the vertical dimension relates to hierarchy within a federal or multi-layer legal system, or 'jurisdictional hierarchy'. In the US, federal regulators were gradually introduced to cover most relevant sectors (except, so far, insurance); the financial crisis has provoked the EU to introduce European-level agencies for the first time.

A third and often-overlooked aspect of hierarchy in financial regulation is the role of market participants, widely relied upon in the financial sector to assist with the design,

---

[5] This is clearly a 'line of business' model rather than a 'functional' one as we use the latter term throughout this book (see especially Chapter 1, section 1.4). Yet, we conform here to how this model is most commonly described in the literature on financial architecture. See eg Group of Thirty, n 4, 24–5.

[6] This model was originally suggested by Michael Taylor in a version known as 'twin peaks', under which there were only two objective-based agencies: one responsible for financial stability, and one for consumer protection: MW Taylor, *Twin Peaks: A Regulatory Structure for the New Century* (Centre for Study of Financial Innovation, 1995). See now MW Taylor, 'Regulatory Reform after the Financial Crisis: *Twin Peaks* Revisited', in RH Huang and D Schoenmaker (eds), *Institutional Structure of Financial Regulation: Theories and International Experiences* (Routledge: Abingdon, 2015), 9.

[7] While many authors use the terms 'unified' and 'integrated' as synonyms in this context, some draw a distinction, taking an 'integrated' regulator to be one combining all prudential supervision activity in a single agency, whereas a 'unified' regulator combines the pursuit of other regulatory goals such as market efficiency and consumer protection: see eg Čihák and Podpiera, n 4, 3; Llewellyn, n 4, 3.

implementation, and enforcement of regulation. This can be termed the 'public/private' aspect of the vertical dimension of the allocation of regulatory jurisdiction. Market participants create groups or networks for the purpose of resolving common problems and, in some instances, even establish more formal self-regulatory frameworks, whether with regard to financial activities that are not subject to regulation or as a complement to existing regulations. These activities can often be seen as advancing the objectives of financial regulation. Where the outcome of this activity is sufficient to resolve market failures—or more modestly, where it makes a better job of it than would a regulatory agency—then it is desirable, consistently with our framework, to 'delegate' the regulatory function (or part of it) to such bodies. We describe this aspect of regulatory hierarchy in more detail in section 24.4.

24.2.2 Regulators' resources

It is obvious that the resources available to regulators will affect the effectiveness with which they are able to perform their functions. Regulators' human resources are a function of their ability to attract qualified personnel and pay competitive salaries, the quality of the institutional culture, and the significance of their responsibilities. And regulators' financial resources—that is, their budgets—affect not only their ability to recruit good people, but also the level of expenditure they can sustain in ongoing rule-making, supervision, and enforcement activity.

We presented summary data on national regulatory budgets and financial system depth in Chapter 4, section 4.2. In Table 24.2 we present some of this data differently, to show variation in regulatory budgets and regulatory headcount (a crude measure of human resources), scaled for domestic financial system depth, for certain jurisdictions. Thus, amongst these four countries with significant domestic financial systems, the US allocates the greatest relative level of resources, and Switzerland the least.

There is some evidence that the level of resources directed at financial regulation makes a difference to the functioning of the financial system. For example, Howell Jackson and Mark Roe report a correlation between the resources of securities regulators—scaled for market capitalization—and the depth and liquidity of these markets.[8] However, the policy

Table 24.2 Variations in financial regulators' resources, 2011

Country Variable	UK	US	Germany	Switzerland
Financial system depth/$tn	8.4	42.0	7.3	4.0
Financial regulators' budget/$bn	0.8	6.5	0.2	0.1
Financial regulators' employees	3,439	22,027	2,151	396
Regulators' budget, as percentage of financial system depth	9.5%	15.6%	2.7%	2.5%
Notional value of claims overseen per employee/$bn	2.4	1.9	3.4	10.1

Sources: Financial regulators' annual reports for 2011/12; World Bank, *Global Financial Development 2010*. For details of regulatory agencies included in each country, see Table 4.1 in Chapter 4.

---

[8] H Jackson and M Roe, 'Public and Private Enforcement of Securities Laws: Resource-Based Evidence' (2009) 93 *Journal of Financial Economics* 279.

implication is not quite as straightforward as it might seem. While inadequate resources can constrain regulatory performance, throwing more resources at regulators will not necessarily bring about commensurate improvements. Resources are a necessary, but not sufficient, condition for effective regulation. What matters is the way in which available resources get used, which is a function of the other dimensions of institutional architecture. We therefore focus on these other dimensions in the remainder of Part F.

24.2.3 Regulators' susceptibility to influence

Financial regulators are subject to a range of influences that may deflect them from the discharge of their responsibilities. Some such influences are internal: individuals working at regulatory authorities may intend to advance public-minded objectives, but be distracted by their narrow self-interest. Many other influences are external: the financial services industry, consumers, elected officials, and other constituencies all compete with one another to shape the regulatory process in pursuit of their respective interests. Importantly, these external influences are not always evenly matched in terms of their access to financial, political, relationship, and human capital. Collectively, these influences can result in regulatory capture and forbearance. Chapter 25 examines these internal and external influences on regulatory decision-making, how they can result in regulatory failure, and how we might go about better aligning the private incentives of regulatory authorities with public regulatory objectives. Together, they comprise what is known as the 'political economy' of financial regulation.

24.2.4 Supervision and enforcement

Chapter 26 turns to the strategies regulatory authorities use to influence the incentive structures of the market participants they regulate. Even the most well-designed regulation is unlikely to advance its objectives unless compliance by regulated parties is effectively monitored and enforced. This is especially true of financial regulation, where the complexity of financial markets and institutions—and the resulting asymmetries of information and expertise between regulators and market participants—can make it especially difficult to uncover wrongdoing or identify socially excessive risk-taking. Faced with this challenge, regulatory authorities must confront difficult questions about how best to allocate their finite resources. They must also attempt to strike a balance between the use of strategies designed to bridge the informational gap by fostering deeper, more meaningful cooperation between regulators and market participants, and those designed to generate a credible deterrent, punish wrongdoing, or compensate injured parties. Chapter 26 also examines the role of monitoring and enforcement in the pursuit of regulatory objectives, and how differences in the intensity of monitoring and enforcement can be the source of significant functional divergence across jurisdictions. In particular, it points to a distinction between public enforcement in providing investor protection against contracting failures due to information asymmetries and limited liability and supervision in avoiding systemic failures.

24.2.5 International regulatory coordination

Chapter 28 concludes our exploration of the institutional environment within which financial regulation is written, monitored, and enforced by examining the dynamics of international regulatory coordination.[9] The financial crisis demonstrated how easily financial instability within one market, institution, or jurisdiction can spill over into others. Minimizing the prospect of such negative spillovers requires a high level of international regulatory coordination in several respects, including *ex ante* standard setting to control risk-taking by systemically important financial institutions, supervision that is consistent across regulators to assure adherence to common standards seeking to promote stability, cross-border information flow that facilitates supervision as well as the monitoring of the potential build-up of systemic risk, and agreement on the approach to resolving systemically important financial firms.

When banking and sovereign debt crises have previously become entangled, institutions such as the International Monetary Fund and World Bank traditionally played an important role in restabilizing national banking systems. The financial crisis of 2007–9 energized a latent network of international financial regulatory coordination, which has resulted in new standards in systemic risk control and a commitment to cross-monitoring to enhance common compliance. The challenge will come in times of financial distress, in which the spillovers that provide the impetus for international coordination may also drive a wedge between national interests. Thus, one of the major post-crisis efforts at regulatory coordination relates to the resolution of systemically important financial firms. Without these efforts, international coordination could well break down precisely when it is most clearly and urgently needed. Chapter 28 examines the importance of international regulatory coordination, the frictions threatening to undermine it, and how we might further strengthen the global regulatory architecture.

24.3 An Overview of Regulatory Architecture

In this section, we briefly describe the allocation of regulatory responsibility in the US and the UK, and at EU level. In Chapter 27, we will return to look at this architecture from a critical perspective, to reflect on the most desirable allocation of such responsibility.

24.3.1 The US

At the federal level, the US combines a mix of different models for allocating regulatory jurisdiction.[10] The institutional model is reflected most clearly in the separation between banking, securities, and insurance regulators. However, even within the

---

[9] The phrase 'regulatory coordination' is not casual, since in the absence of sustained international law-making through treaty, 'coordination' is the operative term.

[10] See generally EJ Pan, 'Organizing Regional Systems: The US Example', in N Moloney, E Ferran, and J Payne (eds), *The Oxford Handbook of Financial Regulation* (Oxford: OUP, 2015), 188. The significant US regulators are federal; there are in many cases also state regulators, but we do not refer to them in detail here.

domain of banking regulation, the US has three federal agencies. First, the Federal Reserve (the 'Fed', established in 1914) is the primary prudential regulator for bank holding companies, US branches of foreign banks, foreign branches of US banks, and state chartered banks that are members of the Federal Reserve System. Since the Dodd–Frank Act of 2010, the Fed also has responsibility for regulating non-bank financial institutions that have been determined to be systemically important. Second, there is the Office of the Comptroller of the Currency ('OCC', established in 1863), which is the primary prudential regulator for federally chartered banks and federally chartered branches of foreign banks. And third, there is the Federal Deposit Insurance Corporation ('FDIC', established in 1933), which administers the federal deposit insurance fund and plays a key role in the resolution of banks and, since the introduction of the Dodd–Frank Act, other systemically important financial institutions.

As respects securities, the Securities and Exchange Commission ('SEC') is responsible for regulating the capital-raising, trading, and other activities of issuers, broker-dealers, stock exchanges, and investment funds. The SEC also splits responsibility with the Commodity Futures Trading Commission ('CFTC') for regulating the activities of market participants within both exchange-traded and, since the introduction of the Dodd–Frank Act, OTC derivatives markets. And as regards insurance, the Federal Insurance Office ('FIO'), established by the Dodd–Frank Act, enables the Federal Reserve to monitor the industry, although regulatory authority remains at the state level.[11]

The post-crisis reforms, however, injected an element of objectives-based allocation of regulatory responsibility into the US system. This is most apparent in two new objective-based bodies created under the Dodd–Frank Act: the Financial Stability Oversight Council ('FSOC') and the Consumer Financial Protection Bureau ('CFPB').

The FSOC's objective is to promote financial stability, through interagency coordination and information-sharing amongst US regulatory authorities. It is required to collect information from regulatory authorities, monitor the financial services marketplace in order to identify potential threats to financial stability, identify gaps in regulation that could pose risks to financial stability, and make recommendations to the US Congress, the Fed, and other agencies on various matters. It is also designed to act as a forum for the resolution of jurisdictional disputes among FSOC members. While the FSOC does not have direct responsibility for the oversight of regulated firms, it is responsible for designating systemically important financial institutions, financial market utilities, and payment, clearing, and settlement activities.[12] Supporting the activities of the FSOC is the new Office of Financial Research ('OFR'). The mandate of the OFR is to collect financial market data, conduct research and analysis, and develop tools for the measurement and monitoring of systemic risks.

The CFPB, established as an independent bureau within the US Treasury, is charged with implementing, monitoring, and enforcing compliance with federal consumer financial protection laws. Its statutory objectives include ensuring that consumers of

---

[11] See Dodd–Frank Act of 2010 (US) §502; FIO, *How to Modernize and Improve the System of Insurance Regulation in the United States* (2013).

[12] A financial firm designated as 'systemic' then becomes subject to prudential oversight by the Federal Reserve.

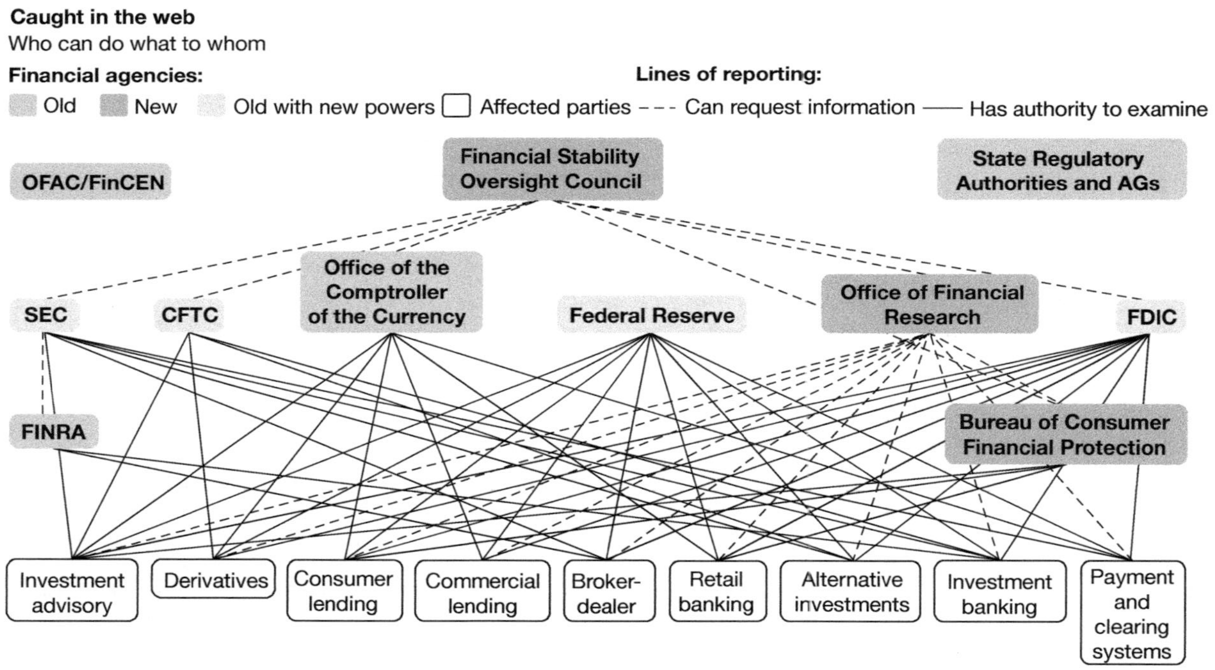

Caught in the web
Who can do what to whom

Financial agencies:
Old | New | Old with new powers | Affected parties

Lines of reporting:
Affected parties — – – Can request information ——— Has authority to examine

OFAC/FinCEN

Financial Stability Oversight Council

State Regulatory Authorities and AGs

Office of the Comptroller of the Currency

Office of Financial Research

CFTC

Federal Reserve

FDIC

SEC

FINRA

Bureau of Consumer Financial Protection

Investment advisory | Derivatives | Consumer lending | Commercial lending | Broker-dealer | Retail banking | Alternative investments | Investment banking | Payment and clearing systems

Fig. 24.1 The Allocation of Regulatory Authority in the US

Source: 'The Dodd–Frank Act: Too Big Not to Fail', *The Economist*, 18 February 2012.

financial products and services are provided with timely, accurate, and understandable information and adequately protected from unfair, deceptive, or abusive practices. Its mandate also extends to monitoring market developments and consumer behaviour, evaluating access and affordability, and promoting consumer protection and awareness. The CFPB's authority extends over a wide range of consumer financial products and services, from savings products, mortgages, credit cards, and payday loans, to the collection of consumer data, debt collection, real estate settlement, and money transfers.[13]

24.3.2 The UK

The UK's current allocation of regulatory responsibility, which was established by the Financial Services Act of 2012,[14] is best described as applying an objectives-based model. There are three principal authorities, two of which are affiliated with, or part of, the Bank of England.

Stylised diagram of the new regulatory framework

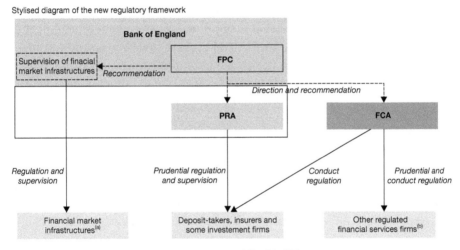

(a) Excludes regulation of trading platforms, which is the responsibility of the FCA.
(b) Includes asset managers, hedge funds, exchanges, insurance brokers and financial advisers.

Fig. 24.2 The Allocation of Regulatory Responsibility in the UK

Source: A Bailey, 'The Prudential Regulation Authority' (2012) *Bank of England Quarterly Bulletin* 354, 355.[15]

---

[13] The scope of this authority, however, varies with the size and nature of the regulated firm. The Dodd–Frank Act also exempts a number of different firms and activities from the CFPB's supervisory and enforcement authority, including real estate brokers and agents, firms registered with the SEC or CFTC, and deposit-taking institutions with less than $10 billion in assets.

[14] It became effective from the beginning of 2013.

[15] While not reflected in Figure 24.2, the FCA is also responsible for certain aspects of the regulation and supervision of financial market infrastructure. There is a memorandum of understanding, reviewed annually, between the Bank of England and FCA governing information sharing and policy coordination in this area: Bank of England and FCA, *Memorandum of Understanding between the Financial Conduct Authority and the Bank of England, including the Prudential Regulation Authority* (2013).

The Prudential Regulation Authority ('PRA')—a subsidiary of the Bank of England—is responsible for the microprudential regulation of banks, insurance companies, and other complex investment firms.[16] At the same time, the Financial Policy Committee ('FPC'), a senior committee of the Bank of England, is responsible for macroprudential oversight. The Financial Conduct Authority ('FCA') then has responsibility for conduct of business regulation—including market integrity and consumer protection—across all regulated firms.[17] This institutional structure means that many financial firms are regulated by both the PRA and FCA, but with different objectives in mind.

24.3.3 EU-level: the European system of financial supervision

Responsibility for financial regulation in the EU has changed very rapidly since the financial crisis, and it is unlikely that the end-point has yet been reached. The current structure is best understood as two concentric layers of regulation—an EU-wide set of common rule-making agencies, and a banking union currently extending only to the Eurozone.[18]

The current EU-level regulatory architecture—the European System of Financial Supervision ('ESFS')—began operation in 2011, the product of a review immediately following the financial crisis.[19] The EU-level agencies follow a largely institutional division of responsibility, shared among the European Securities and Markets Authority ('ESMA'), European Banking Authority ('EBA'), and European Insurance and Occupational Pension Authority ('EIOPA'). These authorities have powers to articulate non-binding guidelines and recommendations, promote coordination and convergence among the regulatory authorities of Member States, conduct peer reviews, collect information, and monitor new market developments. They also have power to write legally binding technical standards in several areas.[20] Once endorsed by the European Commission, these standards have the status of regulations or decisions under EU law. Crucially, however, these agencies do not generally have power to supervise regulated firms, responsibility for which remains largely with national competent authorities

---

[16] The allocation of jurisdiction to the PRA is in part based on an institutional determination of firm type (in the case of deposit takers and insurance companies) and in part on a firm-level determination of stability risk (in the case of investment firms). See Financial Services and Markets Act 2000 (PRA-Regulated Activities) Order 2013, SI 2013/556, Arts 2–4.

[17] It is also responsible for the prudential regulation of firms not regulated by the PRA and, since 2015, has concurrent powers (with the Competition and Markets Authority) to enforce anti-trust rules in the financial services sector. Unlike the PRA, the FCA is not a subsidiary of the Bank of England.

[18] See generally, B Haar, 'Organizing Regional Systems: The EU Example', in N Moloney, E Ferran, and J Payne (eds), n 4, 158.

[19] See High-Level Group on Financial Supervision in the EU, *Report of the High Level Group on Financial Supervision in the EU* (the 'de Larosière Report') (2009).

[20] The three authorities also have the power to recommend to national authorities that they remedy violations of applicable EU law. If these recommendations are not acted upon then, following an opinion from the European Commission, the relevant authority may make decisions that are binding on national authorities and individual firms. Simultaneously, there are important safeguards constraining the use of these powers.

('NCAs'). As exceptions to this general principle, ESMA has been given direct super-visory responsibility for credit rating agencies (CRAs) and trade repositories for OTC derivatives.[21]

Nevertheless, the EU's division of regulatory labour also has an objective-based aspect. This is most pronounced in the role of the European Systemic Risk Board ('ESRB').[22] The ESRB is responsible for macroprudential oversight of the European financial system and, in this capacity, for identifying, monitoring, and assessing potential systemic risks. An objective-based orientation also emerges from the focus of activities of the nominally institutional-based agencies. Thus, the EBA focuses primarily on prudential regulation, ESMA focuses primarily on market efficiency and conduct of business, and EIOPA appears to have taken on the role of the champion of consumers amongst the ESFS agencies.

24.3.4 Eurozone: the European Banking Union

The EU's regulatory structure is greatly complicated, however, by the European Banking Union (the 'Banking Union'), a concentric initiative of the Eurozone Member States. This began life as a response to the Eurozone crisis of 2010–12, in which banking crises and sovereign borrowing crises became intertwined and threatened the viability of the single currency. Policymakers felt it was necessary to go beyond a single rule-book for banking (as exemplified by the activities of the EBA) and introduce a trinity of single *supervisor*, single *resolution mechanism*, and single *deposit guarantee scheme*, at least for systemically important banks. This was an attempt to avoid negative feedback effects between troubled banks and sovereign balance sheets. Domestic bail-outs for failing banks undermine the creditworthiness of their home states; these states' deteriorating creditworthiness, in turn, undermines the health of domestic banks that rely on states for support during periods of instability and typically hold large volumes of domestic sovereign debt. Compounding matters, national supervisory authorities faced with this challenge will be strongly tempted to grant forbearance to struggling banks.

In an attempt to break this pernicious cycle, Eurozone members signed an inter-governmental treaty in February 2012 creating a funding facility known as the European Stability Mechanism ('ESM').[23] Funded by Eurozone members, the ESM is available for use in directly recapitalizing failing Eurozone banks.[24] In order to address the resulting moral hazard problem, however, the need was identified to tighten the framework for banking regulation, supervision, and resolution within the Eurozone.[25] This created an awkward tension: the newly established EBA had been conceived as an EU-wide banking authority, but had no supervisory or resolution powers. What is

---

[21] As described in Chapter 9 section 9.6.2, ESMA has also been granted certain powers in relation to the regulation of short selling.

[22] The ESRB is also part of the ESFS.

[23] See Treaty Establishing the European Stability Mechanism, available at http://www.esm.europa.eu.

[24] The ESM is also authorized to provide loans as part of macroeconomic adjustment programmes and to purchase the sovereign debt of members in both the primary and secondary markets.

[25] See E Wymeersch, 'The Single Supervisory Mechanism: Institutional Aspects', in D Busch and G Ferrarini (eds), *European Banking Union* (Oxford: OUP, 2015), Ch 2; E Ferran, 'European Banking Union: Imperfect, But It Can Work', in D Busch and G Ferrarini, ibid, Ch 3.

more, non-Eurozone states (notably, the UK) wished to retain their own domestic supervisors. The way forward was to establish a new mechanism—the Banking Union—for Eurozone states, while offering non-Eurozone Member States the *option* to participate if they wished. As we write, Denmark is the only non-Eurozone Member State to have signalled that it may in future join the Banking Union.

The Banking Union consists of three closely related mechanisms, each at different stages of development and implementation.[26] The first is the Single Supervisory Mechanism ('SSM'), which transferred certain responsibilities for the prudential super-vision of Eurozone banks from national supervisory authorities to the European Central Bank ('ECB').[27] The SSM envisions a dual track—or 'differentiated'—super-visory system. In all cases, the ECB is responsible for setting the supervisory rules articulating a common approach towards banking supervision.[28] The ECB also has exclusive responsibility for the authorization and licensing of Eurozone banks, moni-toring compliance with capital, liquidity, leverage, governance, risk management, remuneration, and other requirements, evaluating acquisitions and dispositions, and carrying out supervisory reviews and stress tests.[29] Under the SSM, the ECB is then *directly* responsible for the prudential supervision of a relatively small number (as we write, 129) of Eurozone banks deemed to be systemically important.[30] Eurozone banks falling into this category include those with total assets exceeding €30 billion, or 20 per cent of the GDP of their participating state of establishment, or which are identified by the relevant NCAs as being of significant relevance to the domestic economy.[31] Moreover, the ECB also has the power to apply the Basel III macroprudential tools (discussed in Chapter 19, section 19.3.1)—with direct application to all Eurozone banks, notwithstanding the objections of NCAs.[32]

For banks not falling under its direct prudential oversight, the ECB is responsible for overseeing the application of the single handbook by NCAs that, in turn, will maintain day-to-day supervisory responsibility. Moreover, it is empowered to assume at any time, and on its own initiative, responsibility for the direct prudential supervision of non-systemically important banks where it considers this necessary in order to ensure the consistent application of high supervisory standards.

A challenge in establishing the Banking Union was that the ECB's powers under existing European treaties did not support their extension beyond the SSM to

---

[26] See generally D Busch and G Ferrarini (eds), *European Banking Union* (Oxford: OUP, 2015).

[27] Council Regulation (EU) No 1024/2013 conferring specific tasks on the European Central Bank concerning the policies relating to the prudential supervision of credit institutions (the 'SSM Regulation') [2013] OJ L287/63.

[28] Confusingly, while the ECB's manual contains binding requirements, a non-binding Supervisory Handbook is to be issued by the EBA, which is otherwise in charge of issuing implementing regulations in the banking sector. See E Ferran, 'The Existential Search of the European Banking Authority', ECGI Working Paper No 297 (2015), 9.

[29] Simultaneously, however, the ECB is required to coordinate these activities with both the EBA and national supervisory authorities.

[30] See https://www.bankingsupervision.europa.eu/about/thessm/html/index.en.html (last accessed 31 December 2015). The 129 directly supervised banks hold approximately 82 per cent of banking assets in the Eurozone.

[31] The ECB also directly supervises the three most significant banks in each participating Member State.

[32] Regulation (EU) 1024/2013, Art 5.

encompass either the resolution of Eurozone banks or the administration of a pan-European deposit insurance scheme.[33] These functions, in turn, will ultimately be performed by the two other mechanisms at the heart of the European Banking Union: the Single Resolution Mechanism ('SRM') and the European Deposit Insurance Scheme ('EDIS').

The SRM, which establishes a common framework for the resolution of Eurozone banks consistent with the Bank Recovery and Resolution Directive (discussed in Chapter 16),[34] became operative in early 2016. It consists of a Single Resolution Fund, designed to mutualize part of the costs of resolution amongst Eurozone states, and a Single Resolution Board ('SRB') which, in addition to being in charge of the Fund, has the power to commence and execute resolution procedures over banks directly supervised by the ECB.

Progress with the third pillar of the Banking Union, EDIS, has to date been slowest. The European Commission announced a detailed proposal late in 2015, which would proceed in three stages from a currently anticipated start date in 2017.[35] An EDIS fund would be established immediately, under the supervision of the SRB, which would be reconstituted as the 'Single Resolution and Deposit Insurance Board'. The EDIS fund would be accessible in principle to cover deposits for any bank within the Banking Union. During the first transitional stage (lasting three years), EDIS would offer a re-insurance scheme for national deposit guarantee schemes ('DGS', discussed in Chapter 15, section 15.5). That is, national DGS coverage would need to be exhausted before EDIS would contribute. In the second transitional stage, lasting a further four years, EDIS would co-insure alongside national DGS. In the third and final phase (from 2024 on the initial projection), it would then operate as the single deposit insurer for the Eurozone.[36]

24.4 Regulatory Delegation to Market Participants

As discussed in Chapter 4, section 4.2, the information gap between industry participants and regulators may be very large. By delegating rule production and sometimes enforcement to industry associations, the size of the gap can be reduced. Indeed,

---

[33] The legal basis for the SSM is Art 127(6) of the Treaty on the Functioning of the European Union [2012] OJ C326/47, which permits the European Council, acting unanimously, to confer specific tasks on the ECB concerning policies relating to the *prudential supervision* of credit institutions. The prevailing view is that the concept of 'prudential supervision' in this context is not broad enough to include either resolution or the administration of a DGS. See eg E Ferran and VSG Babis, 'The European Single Supervisory Mechanism' (2013) 13 *Journal of Corporate Law Studies* 255.

[34] Regulation (EU) No 806/2014 establishing uniform rules and a uniform procedure for the resolution of credit institutions and certain investment firms in the framework of a Single Resolution Mechanism and a Single Resolution Fund and amending Regulation (EU) No 1093/2010, [2014] OJ L225/1.

[35] European Commission, Proposal for a Regulation of the European Parliament and of the Council amending Regulation (EU) 806/2014 in order to establish a European Deposit Insurance Scheme, COM (2015) 586 final, Strasbourg 24.11.2015.

[36] The EDIS would be funded by levies on banks subject to the SSM. However, contributions to EDIS would count towards banks' obligations to contribute to national DGS under the DGS Directive (2014/49/EU, discussed in Chapter 15, section 15.5). National DGS would only be permitted to access the EDIS under the transitional phases where they meet their funding obligations under that Directive.

market participants may not only be better informed, but also more responsive to change, than regulators. Delegation of this sort—through self-regulation and, to a lesser degree, 'principles-based' regulation—is common in many countries. This section briefly reviews the relevant mechanisms, to complete our introduction to Part F.

In section 24.2.1 we already hinted at how self-regulation can provide meaningful solutions to market failures. Of course, private parties can only be relied on to further regulatory objectives where doing so happens to coincide with their self-interest. They will not expend resources to resolve market failures to any greater extent than they can recoup benefits. While market actors generally have stronger incentives than do regulators to become informed about, and respond to, new developments, their incentives regarding how best to respond may be less well aligned with society's interests. Moreover, their capacity to enforce breaches of the rules is likely to be weaker than that of state agencies, because it is likely to be harder for them to gather evidence of non-compliance and impossible to impose sufficiently harsh penalties. Most obviously, only public authorities are able to impose criminal sanctions.

The capabilities of market actors can be usefully harnessed in the pursuit of regulatory goals by establishing a hierarchical relationship between self-regulatory bodies and initiatives and public regulatory agencies. In essence, the agency sets the general direction, but delegates matters of detail in rule-production to market participants, keeping a close eye on how these are implemented. If the regulator forms the view that the implementation is deficient, then it can take control more directly, pre-empting market participants.

This sort of structure is often observed where market participants have established formal self-regulatory organizations ('SROs') such as the Financial Industry Regulatory Authority ('FINRA') in the US. Public oversight and pre-emptive intervention powers vis-à-vis an SRO respond to the limitations of self-regulatory models of regulation in two important ways. Most fundamentally, they improve SROs' incentives as regards the pursuit of the public interest. Market participants, wishing to avoid pre-emption of their rule-making or enforcement capacity by the regulatory agency, have a powerful incentive *ex ante* to ensure that their implementation will be consistent with the agency's goals.[37]

Second, the regulator can also lend its enforcement capacity to SROs' rules, giving them greater credibility than they would otherwise have in the marketplace. Within such a hierarchical framework, the delegation of rule-making to market participants can harness their superior access to information and responsiveness to new developments, thereby helping regulators to overcome the information gap they otherwise face. Indeed, the threat of intervention by regulatory agencies can be seen as placing competitive pressure on market participants and SROs to design more effective

---

[37] I Ayres and J Braithwaite, *Responsive Regulation: Transcending the Deregulation Debate* (Oxford: OUP, 1992). However, these improvements are harder to achieve as regards international SROs, which may weaken the credibility of oversight by playing nation states off against one another. See generally T Büthe and W Mattli, *The New Global Rulers: The Privatization of Regulation in the World Economy* (Princeton, NJ: Princeton UP, 2012).

regulation—essentially making public and private actors intellectual competitors in the policy domain.[38]

The hierarchical allocation of jurisdiction between market participants and regulatory agencies can be illustrated with two examples: so-called 'enforced' or 'coerced' self-regulation; and so-called 'principles-based' regulation. The difference between the two is really just a matter of degree: 'enforced' self-regulation entails the delegation of responsibility for regulating an entire area of activity to one or more SROs, but with a credible threat in the background that if the matter is not handled adequately, formal regulation will be imposed.[39] In contrast, 'principles-based' regulation refers to a framework in which the regulatory agency prescribes general norms, but their detailed design and implementation is left to market actors under the regulator's supervision.

24.4.1 'Enforced' self-regulation: the case of LIBOR

Recent reforms to the regulation of the London Interbank Offered Rate—better known as 'LIBOR'—provide a salient illustration of how enforced self-regulation works. Created in 1986, LIBOR is a series of indicative interest rates, intended to reflect the rates at which a panel of banks are able to raise funds from one another in the London money market. LIBOR rates have come to be used as benchmark indicators in an extremely wide range of financial contracts.[40] This ubiquity prompted observers to dub LIBOR 'the most important figure in finance'.[41]

LIBOR was developed and, until recently, administered by the British Bankers Association ('BBA'), a UK trade association representing approximately 200 member banks. It is calculated across ten different currencies (including US dollars, pounds, and euros) and fifteen different maturities (ranging from overnight to twelve months).[42] Historically, every business day at approximately 11 a.m. London time, panel banks were asked the following question: 'At what rate could you borrow funds, were you to do so by asking for them and then accepting interbank offers in a reasonable market size just prior to 11 a.m.?' These banks would then be required to submit their responses to Thomson Reuters, which collected the submissions on behalf of the BBA. Once it had received the submissions of all panel banks, Thomson Reuters would discard the highest and lowest quartiles of the responses, and take the arithmetic mean of those remaining to give the official LIBOR rate for each currency and maturity. The official rates, along with the submissions of panel members, were then made public at around 11.45 a.m. each business day.

---

[38] D Esty and D Geradin, 'Regulatory Co-opetition' (2000) 3 *Journal of International Economic Law* 235; M Roe, 'Delaware's Competition' (2003) 117 *Harvard Law Review* 588.

[39] R Baldwin and M Cave, *Understanding Regulation: Theory, Strategy and Practice* (Oxford: OUP, 1999).

[40] It has been estimated, for example, that as of 2012 approximately $165–230 trillion in interest rate swaps, $30 trillion in exchange-traded futures and options, $25–30 trillion in forward rate agreements, $10 trillion in syndicated loans, and $3 trillion in floating rate notes utilized LIBOR as a benchmark: *The Wheatley Review of LIBOR: Final Report* (2012), available at http://www.hm-treasury.gov.uk.

[41] 'The LIBOR Scandal: The Rotten Heart of Finance', *The Economist*, 7 July 2012.

[42] Accordingly, while it is not uncommon for LIBOR to be quoted as a single figure—typically three-month US-dollar LIBOR—there were in fact 150 different LIBOR rates.

In June 2012, the US Department of Justice ('DOJ'), the CFTC, and the UK FSA announced that they had entered into settlement agreements with Barclays Bank plc, a long-standing LIBOR panel member, in connection with the manipulation of LIBOR.[43] The Barclays settlement documents revealed hundreds of attempts by the bank's employees to manipulate LIBOR with a view to generating trading profits for the firm and its clients, and to avoiding media scrutiny regarding Barclays' financial health during the financial crisis. This announcement was followed by a series of further settlements regarding allegations and admissions of criminal misconduct by eleven large banks and brokers, spanning multiple jurisdictions worldwide and by mid-2015 totalling more than $9 billion in fines.[44]

At the heart of the LIBOR scandal was the failure of the BBA to monitor vigorously and enforce compliance with the rate-setting process. Most importantly, the BBA failed to verify the accuracy and independence of the rates submitted by panel banks.[45] This failure spurred public regulatory authorities in several jurisdictions to rethink whether, and if so how, to regulate financial benchmarks. In the UK, for example, following the recommendations of a review commissioned soon after the scandal broke,[46] LIBOR rate-setting now bears all the hallmarks of enforced self-regulation. First, the administration of LIBOR and the submission of LIBOR rates have become 'regulated activities' under the Financial Services and Markets Act 2000,[47] thus formally bringing these activities under the umbrella of public financial regulation. Second, day-to-day governance and oversight of LIBOR has been taken away from the BBA and, following a tender process, given to an independent private administrator.[48] This new administrator is responsible for, amongst other matters, compiling submissions, verifying their accuracy against actual interbank transactions, and publishing official LIBOR rates. It is also responsible for producing a code of conduct for panel banks governing the use of transaction data, recordkeeping, internal systems and controls, and external audit requirements. Finally, new civil and criminal penalties have been introduced for intentionally or recklessly making false or misleading statements in connection with the setting of a benchmark.

---

[43] See DOJ, 'Barclays Bank PLC Admits Misconduct Related to Submissions for the London Interbank Offered Rate and the Euro Interbank Offered Rate and Agrees to Pay $160 Million Penalty' (27 June 2012), available at http://www.justice.gov; CFTC, *In the Matter of Barclays PLC, Barclays Bank PLC and Barclays Capital Inc.*, CFTC Docket No. 12-25 (27 June 2012), available at http://www.cftc.gov, and FSA, *Final Notice of Settlement re Barclays Bank Plc* (27 June 2012), available at http://www.fsa.gov.uk.

[44] See X Huan, A Parbonetti, and G Previts, 'Understanding the LIBOR Scandal: The Historical, the Ethical, and the Technological', Working Paper (2015), available at http://www.ssrn.com, Table 1.

[45] The BBA's failure to provide meaningful oversight continued even after independent observers produced evidence suggestive of widespread rate fiddling: see BBA, 'BBA LIBOR Consultation Feedback Statement' (5 August 2008), 3, available at http://www.bba.org.uk.

[46] *The Wheatley Review*, n 40.

[47] s 22(6), inserted by Financial Services Act 2012. These activities have also been designated 'controlled functions', with the individuals responsible for overseeing them subject to the FCA's approved persons regime.

[48] See Press Release, 'BBA to hand over administration of LIBOR to NYSE Euronext Rate Administration Limited' (9 July 2013), available at http://www.bbatrent.com. *The Wheatley Review* also recommended the creation of an independent oversight committee comprised of LIBOR stakeholders—including, importantly, market participants other than panel banks.

The UK's pivot to enforced self-regulation is an acknowledgement of the relative strengths and weaknesses of public and private actors in this context. There can be little doubt that panel banks are best positioned to *produce*—if not necessarily *verify*—information about their own borrowing costs. Private actors such as the BBA or LIBOR's new independent administrator may also be more responsive than regulators to the evolving demands of market participants.[49] At the same time, however, as the LIBOR scandal amply demonstrates, these private actors may be poorly incentivized to provide meaningful *ex ante* oversight of the rate-setting process or, where necessary, engage in vigorous *ex post* enforcement in pursuit of the broader public interest. By bringing these activities within the scope of a formal regulatory framework, introducing new civil and criminal offences, and bonding the reputation of the administrator to the integrity of the benchmark, these reforms can thus be understood as attempting to improve the alignment of these private actors' incentives with regulatory objectives.

It is clear that the success of enforced self-regulation is contingent on the credibility of the threat of regulatory intervention, whether in the form of individual enforcement actions or wholesale regime change. If regulators fail to acquire the necessary information, expertise, or other resources—or if they lack the will to act—then the threat will not be credible and enforced self-regulation may become little more than a perfunctory validation mechanism for the activities of market participants.

24.4.2 Principles-based regulation

During the decade prior to the financial crisis, one of the most significant developments in financial regulation was the rise to prominence of 'principles-based' regulation. Many hailed principles-based regulation as a key to effective public oversight of financial markets and institutions—with both the UK's FSA and the Australian Securities and Investment Commission ('ASIC') adopting principles-based regimes. After the financial crisis, however, principles-based regulation became a lightning rod for criticism, stemming mainly from a perception that it had institutionalized the FSA's allegedly 'light touch' approach towards public supervision and enforcement. Yet despite this criticism, many regulatory regimes continue to utilize what is essentially a principles-based approach.[50]

So what exactly is principles-based regulation? Principles-based regulation is often framed as embodying a preference for abstract regulatory principles as opposed to detailed prescriptive rules.[51] This is, on one level, correct.[52] On a more fundamental level, however, what defines principles-based regulation is how these principles are employed within the regulatory regime and, ultimately, the relationship between

---

[49] *Wheatley Review*, n 40, 13. Although it is worth pointing out that the BBA was not particularly responsive in this regard during its tenure as LIBOR administrator.

[50] J Black, 'The Rise, Fall and Fate of Principles-Based Regulation', in K Alexander and N Moloney (eds), *Law Reform and Financial Markets* (Cheltenham: Edward Elgar, 2011).

[51] J Black, 'Forms and Paradoxes of Principles-Based Regulation' (2008) 3 *Capital Markets Law Journal* 425; L Cunningham, 'A Prescription to Retire the Rhetoric of Principles-Based Systems in Corporate Law, Securities Regulation and Accounting' (2007) 60 *Vanderbilt Law Review* 1411.

[52] Julia Black characterizes this narrow definition as 'formal' principles-based regulation: Black, n 51.

regulators and market participants. In this respect, principles-based regulation falls under the umbrella of a diverse collection of regulatory techniques often referred to as 'process-oriented' or 'management-based' regulation.[53] These techniques share several traits.[54] First, regulators use high-level *principles* to guide both their own actions and those of regulated market participants. Second, these principles identify the *outcomes* regulators hope to achieve, rather than prescribing the detailed processes for achieving them.[55] Principle 6 of the FCA Handbook, for example, states simply that, 'a firm must pay due regard to the interests of customers and treat them fairly'.[56] Third, regulated market participants—and potentially other stakeholders—are expected to engage in meaningful and ongoing *dialogue* with regulators about what these outcome-oriented principles mean and how best to achieve the desired outcomes. This dialogue can manifest itself in many forms: ranging from informal feedback in the context of day-to-day supervisory interactions, through industry consultation exercises, to the provision of formal guidance by regulators. Finally, on the basis of this dialogue, market participants are expected to use their judgement in designing firm-specific processes, systems, and controls capable of achieving these outcomes. In this respect, principles-based regulation delegates at least some of the responsibility for achieving regulatory objectives from regulators to regulated market participants.

Principles-based regulation is born of the recognition of the information gap between regulators and market participants, and the need for regulation to respond rapidly to emerging developments.[57] The hallmark of process-oriented strategies such as principles-based regulation is that they seek to leverage the superior information and expertise of market participants by granting them the discretion to design bespoke processes, systems, and controls within the confines of a framework of broad public regulatory objectives.[58] Through dialogue, principles-based regulation also seeks to compel market participants to share this information and expertise with public regulators. This dialogue, in turn, becomes the basis for creating, updating, and disseminating regulation on a dynamic basis in response to new market and regulatory developments.

By granting market participants discretion, of course, principles-based regulation opens the door to potential abuse. Crucially, however, the use of outcome-oriented principles can play an important role in constraining such behaviour. As Julia Black explains, qualitative or behavioural outcomes—such as the requirement to 'treat customers fairly'—are inherently difficult to game.[59] Put differently, the ability of

---

[53] S Gilad, 'Institutionalizing Fairness in Financial Markets: Mission Impossible?' (2010) 5 *Regulation and Governance* 309; C Coglianese and D Lazer, 'Management-Based Regulation: Prescribing Private Management to Achieve Public Goals' (2003) 37 *Law and Society Review* 691.

[54] Although these traits need not all be present for a strategy to qualify as process-oriented.

[55] FSA, 'Principles-Based Regulation: Focusing on Outcomes that Matter' (2007); Black, n 51.

[56] For a description and assessment of how the FSA approaches the supervision and enforcement of compliance with this principle, see Gilad, n 53.

[57] J Black, *Rules and Regulators* (Oxford: OUP, 1997); C Sunstein, 'The Problems with Rules' (1995) 83 *California Law Review* 953.

[58] C Parker, 'Meta-Regulation: Legal Accountability for Corporate Social Responsibility', in D McBarnet, A Voiculescu, and T Campbell (eds), *The New Corporate Accountability: Corporate Social Responsibility and the Law* (Cambridge: CUP, 2009).

[59] Black, n 51.

principles-based regulation to respond organically to new developments, new situations, and new practices without modification to its outcome-oriented principles reduces the prospect that market participants will be able to evade the spirit of regulation, while still complying with its technical letter.[60]

Principles-based regulation thus holds out considerable promise. That said, regulators looking to deploy it effectively must overcome several challenges. First, they must establish the mutual trust necessary to build and maintain truly dialogic relationships. If market participants do not trust the regulator to refrain from using the information they provide as a basis for future enforcement action, they will be less forthcoming. Conversely, if regulators do not trust market participants to be honest and forthright, they will be less likely to grant the flexibility needed to design and implement bespoke systems and controls, and may be more willing to resort to formal enforcement in response to perceived non-compliance. Black has characterized this as the 'trust paradox' of principles-based regulation.[61] Resolving this challenge requires regulators to be transparent, predictable, and restrained in their resort to enforcement. Yet the threat of enforcement must somehow be sufficiently credible to align market participants' incentives with regulatory objectives.

A second challenge is that a lack of detailed specification by the regulator of 'rules' can be a source of uncertainty for market participants: there is a risk that the two sides fail to arrive at shared understandings about what giving effect to a principle necessitates. Against this background, market participants will manage compliance risk by adopting interpretations of principles towards the more conservative end of the spectrum.[62] Regulators can address this challenge by issuing regular formal and informal guidance via their relationships with market participants. Moreover, they can once again signal a philosophy of transparency, predictability, and restraint in the use of enforcement.

The final challenge arises from the prospect of regulatory capture. As described here, principles-based regulation envisions frequent contact and close collaboration between market participants and regulators in the context of day-to-day supervision, industry consultations, and other interactions. This proximity has many benefits. Intensive supervision, for example, places regulators closer to the heart of the action: granting them better access to the complex inner workings of the markets and institutions that they oversee. The frequency and intensity of these interactions, however, also place market participants in an advantageous position to influence—over the long term and in potentially very subtle and sophisticated ways—the attitudes and perspectives of regulators.[63] The channels through which such 'soft capture' takes place are examined in greater detail in Chapter 25.

---

[60] J Black, M Hopper, and C Band, 'Making a Success of Principles-Based Regulation' (2007) 1 *Law and Financial Markets Review* 191; and Black, n 51.

[61] Black, n 51.

[62] See SL Schwarcz, 'The "Principles" Paradox' (2009) 10 *European Business Organization Law Review* 175. Black has characterized this as the 'compliance paradox' of principles-based regulation: n 51.

[63] S Johnson and J Kwak, *13 Bankers: The Wall Street Takeover and the Next Financial Meltdown* (New York, NY: Random House, 2010).

24.5 Conclusion

In this chapter we have covered three important topics, by way of introduction to Part F. First, we have reviewed the principal challenges associated with putting regulatory principles into action—that is, the challenges of the institutional architecture of regulatory agencies. Second, we have outlined the architecture of the principal agencies responsible for governing the financial system in the US and the UK, and at EU level. Third, we have explored the role of delegation to private actors in implementing effective regulation. Together, these provide a solid foundation for consideration of the remaining topics in Part F: political economy in Chapter 25, supervision and enforcement in Chapter 26, how regulatory architecture *ought* to be designed in Chapter 27, and international coordination in Chapter 28.

25

The Political Economy of Financial Regulation

25.1 Introduction

In the aftermath of the global financial crisis, a broad consensus has emerged amongst financial policymakers that some form of public regulatory oversight of over-the-counter ('OTC') derivatives markets is desirable.[1] Less than twenty years ago, however, the prevailing consensus was very different indeed. Just how different is perhaps best illustrated by the response to a concept release (consultation paper) issued in May 1998 by the US Commodity Futures Trading Commission ('CFTC'), then under the stewardship of its Chair, Brooksley Born. The concept release sought comment on the question of whether the CFTC should expand its oversight to include the burgeoning markets for many OTC derivatives and, specifically, swaps. The motivations for the proposal were the dramatic growth of these markets over the preceding decade, the potentially significant and difficult to detect risks they generated for both individual firms and the broader financial system, and a series of high-profile derivatives mis-selling scandals.

The response from both the US financial services industry and senior policymakers was immediate and unequivocal. On the same day the concept release was published, Treasury Secretary Robert Rubin, Federal Reserve Board Chair Alan Greenspan, and Securities and Exchange Commission ('SEC') Chair Arthur Levitt issued a joint statement airing their 'grave concerns' about the prospect of public regulatory intervention and questioning the CFTC's authority.[2] Within weeks, draft legislation was introduced imposing a moratorium on further CFTC action. In little more than a year, Born was out as CFTC Chair. Her successor, William Rainer, had co-authored a report under the auspices of the President's Working Group on Financial Markets which recommended what amounted to the complete public *deregulation* of OTC derivatives markets.[3] The report echoed industry concerns—voiced by interest groups such as the International Swaps and Derivatives Association ('ISDA')—that any new regulation would create legal uncertainty, thereby increasing costs for market participants, threatening the US's leadership in financial services, and spurring a flight of derivatives business to other jurisdictions. The report was also heavily influenced by the prevailing belief, held by Greenspan and others, that free and unfettered markets were socially desirable and that private market participants were highly incentivized to manage the

---

[1] Although the form this oversight should take is still very much in dispute.
[2] US Treasury Department, Press Release, 'Joint Statement by Treasury Secretary Robert Rubin, Federal Reserve Board Chairman Alan Greenspan and Securities and Exchange Commissioner Arthur Levitt' (7 May 1998), available at http://www.treasury.gov.
[3] President's Working Group on Financial Markets, 'Over-the-Counter Derivatives Markets and Commodity Exchange Act' (9 November 1999), available at http://www.treasury.gov.

attendant risks.[4] These recommendations would ultimately become enshrined in the Commodities Futures Modernization Act 2000,[5] which exempted OTC derivatives from regulatory oversight by the CFTC, the SEC, and state regulators.

This story illustrates how politics—in this case, industry lobbying during a period of benign economic circumstances—can undermine the implementation of regulation that is in the public interest. A review of the history of financial regulation reveals that these problems of *political economy* are widespread. The response to the recent crisis is another good illustration. The financial crisis raised public awareness, catalysed widespread political support, and spurred politicians to propose new regulation. This enabled industry opposition to be overcome, at least at first. However, measures calculated to appeal to an outraged general public are unlikely to be the best solutions, raising the prospect of poorly crafted regulation. The financial services industry then responded with intensive lobbying efforts designed to highlight the costs the new regulation imposes on market participants and its deleterious impact on international competitiveness and economic growth. As the memory of the crisis begins to fade, the political consensus may be expected to weaken, and the industry to reassert its influence over the policymaking process. Understanding what drives this pattern—along with the other dynamics of financial regulation outlined in Chapter 4—demands that we understand the institutional environment in which decisions about financial regulation are made. This environment, its frictions, and the ways we might better shape it in order to advance regulatory objectives are the focus of this chapter.

Section 25.2 begins by examining the private incentives of the politicians, their appointees sitting at the top of public regulatory agencies, and these agencies' personnel, to whom we delegate responsibility for the production and application of financial regulation.[6] As is well known, while the 'public interest' perspective views such agents as motivated (by their altruism, public service ethos, and the like) to make decisions according to social welfare, the 'public choice' perspective, in contrast, views them as pursuing their private self-interest and therefore as likely to deviate from this objective. While neither perspective is universally accurate, the second is a useful heuristic for identifying potential frictions—or 'regulatory failures'—in financial policymaking, and designing institutional arrangements to minimize them.

Section 25.3 looks at external influences on financial policymakers. Their decisions often have distributional implications, creating winners and losers both in the financial services industry and broader society. This generates pressure for or against regulation on the part of constituencies affected by these decisions and spawns interest groups dedicated to lobbying on their behalf. In addition, electoral concerns may prompt politicians and their appointees to sacrifice long-term financial stability to short-term goals such as credit expansion to spur growth and subsidize home ownership.

---

[4] See A Greenspan, 'The Role of Capital in Optimal Banking Supervision and Regulation' (1998) *Federal Reserve Bank of New York Policy Review* 163.

[5] Pub Law No 106-554, 114 Stat 2763 (2000).

[6] Except as otherwise indicated, we use the generic term 'policymaker' to encompass elected and unelected officials and the personnel employed by specialist regulatory agencies, such as the CFTC and SEC.

Sections 25.4 highlights some important drivers of regulatory failures, while section 25.5 considers a range of institutional arrangements designed to minimize the scope of these failures by holding policymakers more *accountable* for their decisions.

This chapter is not about the substantive merits of various policy alternatives; rather, it is about the *processes* that govern how decisions between these policy alternatives are made. There are three principal takeaways. First, like the rest of us, policymakers tend to respond rationally to the incentives they face. Second, where these incentives are not aligned with regulatory objectives, we can expect policy decisions to deviate from both these objectives and broader social welfare.[7] Third, once we understand the nature of this (agency) problem, we can start to think more constructively about how to design institutional arrangements which harness the private incentives of policymakers in pursuit of regulatory objectives. In the end, of course, there is no silver bullet—no costless and faultless means of holding policymakers to account. Yet it seems reasonable to suggest that better regulation is likely to emerge from institutions that are designed with sensitivity to these issues.

25.2 The Internal Motivations of Financial Policymakers

To this point, we have largely assumed that public policymakers share the objective of designing a financial system which, to the fullest extent possible, maximizes social welfare. This assumption is consistent with the 'helping hand' perspective of policy-making, that views policymakers as, in effect, perfect rule-makers: driven by their altruism and public service ethos to identify and correct market failures.[8] It is also consistent with stewardship theory, which views individuals as gaining greater utility from other-regarding—as opposed to self-interested—behaviour.[9] Pursuant to this perspective, the central problem for society becomes one of simply identifying the most qualified, benevolent policymakers and giving them a wide berth to design and implement socially desirable policy.

In reality, of course, policymakers may eschew such public-minded objectives in favour of their narrow self-interest. This second—'grabbing hand'—perspective views policymakers as rational, utility-maximizing actors who make decisions on the basis of their private interests and existing incentive constraints.[10] First and foremost, self-interested politicians may use their powers over the financial system to boost short-term growth with a view to gaining re-election. They may fuel booms by expanding credit, especially in the politically sensitive housing sector, via government-owned or government-sponsored financial institutions, implicit or explicit guarantees, the

[7] Of course, even where these incentives are aligned, there is no guarantee that the decisions of financial policymakers will be welfare-maximizing. Good governance does not preclude the possibility of poor decision-making.

[8] See A Atkinson and J Stiglitz, *Lectures on Public Economics* (New York, NY: McGraw-Hill, 1980), and P Samuelson, *Foundations of Economic Analysis* (Cambridge, MA: Harvard University Press, 1947).

[9] See eg L Donaldson, 'The Ethereal Hand: Organizational Economics and Management Theory' (1990) 15 *Academy of Management Review* 369.

[10] A Shleifer and R Vishny, *The Grabbing Hand: Government Pathologies and Their Cures* (Cambridge, MA: Harvard University Press, 1998).

promotion of competition in the finance sector, and the relaxation of prudential regulation.[11]

Self-interested unelected officials, in turn, may exploit their delegated discretion with a view to seeking re-appointment, enhancing their current or future career prospects (whether in the public or in the private sector), expanding their power base, procuring additional human and financial resources for their agencies, pursuing pet projects, avoiding disputes with their political masters or the industries they regulate, shielding themselves from political and liability risks, or simply economizing on effort. While these private interests may not always be at odds with broader social welfare, this perspective thus introduces the distinct possibility that the decisions of policymakers may deviate from it.

Acknowledging that the grabbing hand perspective has at least some traction in the context of real-world policymaking allows us to view the relationship between society and policymakers as the source of potentially significant agency problems.[12] Viewed from this perspective, the institutional environment within which policymakers exercise their delegated discretion thus becomes an important determinant of whether, and to what extent, they are able to further their private interests at the expense of society.[13] Section 25.5 examines how we might design institutional arrangements so as to minimize these agency costs and hold delegated policymakers accountable for their decisions.

The takeaway from this section is not that policymakers *never* act in the public interest. Rather, it is simply that they may be no more or no less motivated to do so than other members of the society from which they are drawn.[14] At the same time, these policymakers are likely to face significant external pressures—from politicians, industry, and other constituencies—to make decisions on the basis of interests other than social welfare. These external influences on policymakers are examined in greater detail in the next section.

25.3 The External Influences on Financial Policymakers

The decisions of financial policymakers affect the lives and livelihoods of almost everyone in society. These decisions often have significant distributional implications. Regulation designed to enhance consumer or investor protection, for example, may impose non-recoverable costs on the financial intermediaries who offer savings,

---

[11] See VV Acharya, 'Governments as Shadow Banks: The Looming Threat to Financial Stability' (2012) 90 *Texas Law Review* 1745.

[12] A Dixit, 'The Power of Incentives in Public and Private Organizations' (1997) 87 *American Economic Review (Papers and Proceedings)* 378; T Besley, *Principled Agents? The Political Economy of Good Government* (Oxford: OUP, 2006). Of course, this perspective is further complicated by the fact that society does not act as a single, homogeneous principal.

[13] O Williamson, *The Economic Institutions of Capitalism* (New York, NY: Free Press, 1985).

[14] See J Buchanan and G Tullock, *The Calculus of Consent: The Logical Foundations of Constitutional Democracy* (Ann Arbor: University of Michigan Press, 1965); E Kane, 'How Market Forces Influence the Structure of Financial Regulation', in W Haraf and RM Kushmeider (eds), *Restructuring Banking and Financial Services in America* (Washington DC: American Enterprise Institute, 1988); E Kane, 'Financial Regulation and Market Forces' (1991) 127 *Swiss Journal of Economics and Statistics* 325.

lending, and other financial products. Stricter micro- or macroprudential requirements intended to promote individual banks' safety and soundness, or broader financial stability, may have an adverse impact on bank profitability and curb lending to the real economy. Other regulatory measures may unduly raise barriers to entry into the financial services industry, thereby raising incumbents' rents at the expense of consumers. Explicit and implicit public guarantees for systemically important financial institutions, meanwhile, benefit the creditors and shareholders of these institutions at the expense of taxpayers.

The distributional implications of financial policy decisions understandably generate a demand for regulation that advances the private interests of different constituencies. These constituencies include the financial services industry, providers of services related to financial regulation such as specialized lawyers and consultants, the consumers of financial products and services, and taxpayers.

On one level, of course, the interests *within* these constituencies are unlikely to be entirely homogeneous. The compositions of these groups also overlap, making it difficult to get a clear picture of where interests ultimately reside. On another level, however, the core interests of the members of each of these constituencies can often be seen as broadly aligned. The interests of members of the financial services industry, for example, are generally aligned in terms of their opposition to public regulatory intervention in areas such as capital structure, leverage, executive compensation, and risk management.[15] More importantly for our present purposes, where interests diverge *between* these constituencies, they can be understood as competing with one another to influence the decisions of financial policymakers.[16]

What shapes the dynamics of this competition is that the various constituencies differ in terms of the means available for influencing policy decisions and their effectiveness in reaching preferred outcomes. Taxpayers and consumers, for example, influence the policy process primarily through their participation—as *voters*—in elections. Elections, however, are relatively infrequent events contemplating (near) universal participation.[17] They also distil the complex and potentially contradictory preferences of voters across a broad spectrum of issues into a single, inevitably noisy, signal. Moreover, voters are relatively numerous, dispersed, and often possess heterogeneous interests.[18] At the same time, the costs of evaluating the merits of various policy alternatives are high in comparison to the marginal value of any single vote. Compounding matters, financial policy decisions are likely to have low salience to many voters, except in the wake of financial scandals or crises.[19] The resulting information, coordination, and collective action problems combine to dull the incentives of voters to invest

---

[15] F Heinemann and M Schüler, 'A Stiglerian View of Banking Supervision' (2004) 121 *Public Choice* 99; JC Coffee, 'The Political Economy of Dodd–Frank: Why Financial Reforms Tend to be Frustrated and Systemic Risk Perpetuated' (2012) 97 *Cornell Law Review* 1019.

[16] G Stigler, 'The Theory of Economic Regulation' (1971) 2 *Bell Journal of Economics and Management Science* 3, and Kane, 'Financial Regulation and Market Forces', n 14.

[17] As a result, a voter with an intense interest in a particular policy has precisely the same influence on the policy process as a voter with no interest whatsoever.

[18] Stigler, n 16.

[19] See generally PD Culpepper, *Quiet Politics and Business Power: Corporate Control in Europe and Japan* (Cambridge: CUP, 2011).

their time and energy in attempting to understand financial policy or participating in the policy process. Accordingly, unless a sufficiently large coalition of voters can be mobilized in support of—or opposition to—a given policy, we would expect voting to represent an ineffective means of influencing financial policymakers.

The financial services industry, in contrast, is able to influence the policy process by a number of different means, using a number of different forms of capital.[20] First, and perhaps most obviously, the financial services industry possesses a relatively ample supply of *financial capital*. This capital can be used to contribute to political campaigns, fund special interest groups, provide financial support for academic research, and hire lobbyists with a view to either directly influencing policymakers or indirectly shaping the policy debate.[21] It can also be used to entice policymakers with the prospect of a lucrative career in the private sector. Second, the financial services industry possesses significant *relationship capital* acquired through regular and direct access to policymakers in the context of day-to-day supervisory relationships, its role in various hybrid forms of regulation, and its participation in the broader policy process via mechanisms such as industry consultations. Finally, it possesses significant *human capital*—the information and expertise policymakers need to make informed policy decisions. Indeed, as the financial services industry has grown more complex, this last form of capital has become increasingly important. As described in greater detail in section 25.4.1, these endowments combine to give the financial services industry significant political capital which it can wield to influence the decisions of financial policymakers.

The financial services industry can also be understood as possessing a comparative *organizational* advantage. As a preliminary matter, the decisions of financial policymakers are—for obvious reasons—highly salient to members of the financial services industry. This gives them powerful incentives to participate in the policy process and, importantly, to coordinate their policy positions and activities.[22] At the same time, the financial services industry in many jurisdictions—or at least specific segments of it—is relatively concentrated. As of 2010, for example, the top four UK retail banks collectively enjoyed a 77 per cent market share in personal current accounts and an 85 per cent market share in business accounts.[23] As we saw in Chapter 21, the so-called 'G14' group of derivatives dealers were, similarly, counterparties to swaps representing approximately 82 per cent of the global notional amount outstanding.[24] This concentration makes it relatively easy for the financial services industry to acquire and share

---

[20] R Kroszner, 'The Political Economy of Banking and Financial Regulatory Reform in Emerging Markets' (1998) 10 *Research in Financial Services* 33; R Kroszner and T Stratmann, 'Interest Group Competition and the Organization of Congress: Theory and Evidence from Financial Services' Political Action Committees' (1998) 88 *American Economic Review* 1163; S Johnson and J Kwak, *13 Bankers: The Wall Street Takeover and the Next Financial Meltdown* (New York, NY: Pantheon Books, 2010); J Barth, G Caprio, and R Levine, *Guardians of Finance: Making Regulators Work for Us* (Cambridge, MA: MIT Press, 2012).

[21] See M Olson, *The Logic of Collective Action: Public Goods and the Theory of Groups* (Cambridge, MA: Harvard University Press, 1965), and G Becker, 'A Theory of Competition Among Pressure Groups for Political Influence' (1983) 98 *Quarterly Journal of Economics* 371.

[22] See generally, Olson, n 21.

[23] UK Independent Commission on Banking, *Final Report* (2011) ('ICB Report').

[24] As of 2010, see ISDA, 'Concentration of OTC Derivatives Among Major Dealers', ISDA Research Note, Issue 4 (2010).

information, to coordinate the lobbying activities of its members and, ultimately, to bring its considerable financial, relationship, and human capital to bear on financial law and policy.[25]

Unelected regulators are subject not only to the influence of industry participants and other private parties, but also of elected politicians.[26] Elected politicians typically appoint the people at the top of supervisory agencies and often decide upon those agencies' powers and budget. Similarly, there is no policy upon which regulators have the last word, because politicians can overturn them by legislation. In short, regulators and supervisors generally can only go as far in pursuing their institutional goals as elected politicians will let them.

This only reinforces the room for distortions in the regulatory and supervisory process. First, elected politicians may receive financial contributions from the financial industry—whether directly or indirectly—and act as its appeals forum whenever regulators resist industry pressures. Second, and more importantly, politicians are likely to oppose any measure (potentially) having a negative macroeconomic impact—such as, for example, stricter capital requirements or loan-to-value limits—as it would harm their re-election chances. In fact, political actors come to have a stake in the very behaviour that increases systemic risk, so long as it also spurs economic growth in the short term. In addition, politicians have the power and, in dire circumstances, the incentives to renege on any promise of letting financial institutions fail. When push comes to shove, no matter what legislation and supervisory policies say about the consequences of a systemically important bank's insolvency, politicians will have powerful incentives to bail it out, making moral hazard an intractable problem in financial regulation.

There are three important takeaways from this section. First, different constituencies can be understood as competing with one another to influence the decisions of policymakers. Second, this competition is unlikely to take place on a level playing field. The financial services industry is typically highly motivated, well organized, and possesses enormous reserves of financial, relationship, human, and political capital. Many other constituencies, meanwhile—including taxpayers and consumers of financial products and services—often have relatively weak incentives, heterogeneous interests, and few means of influencing the policy process. Even more fundamentally, society as a whole would seem to possess no natural constituency to champion its interests.[27] Third, a key constraint for regulators comes from elected politicians, who have the means and the incentives to affect their action. Other than in the wake of

---

[25] D Masciandaro and M Quintyn, 'Helping Hand or Grabbing Hand? Supervisory Architecture, Financial Structure and Market View', IMF Working Paper WP/08/47 (2008); see also Stigler, n 16 and Olson, n 21. The importance of industry concentration can arguably be observed in the influence of organizations such as the British Bankers' Association and ISDA on the policymaking process in areas of importance to their core constituencies.

[26] Elected officials can thus be understood as performing a dual role: participating in the policy process as both lawmakers (*supplying* financial regulation) and as important constituents of regulatory agencies (*demanding* regulation which furthers their private interests—eg re-election).

[27] A problem compounded by the fact that concepts such as 'systemic risk' and 'financial stability' are often viewed as amorphous and esoteric—traits which can make it difficult to generate public support in favour of policies designed to promote these objectives. See Chapter 19, section 19.4 and Coffee, n 15.

financial crises, when the harm that a badly regulated financial system can bring to society is conspicuous even to the median voter, politicians will tend to support industry's calls for looser rules and favour procyclical policies that increase their re-election chances. In the next section, we examine in greater detail how these dynamics play out in the real world.

25.4 Regulatory Failures

The combination of self-interested policymakers, special interest group pressures, and re-election-seeking politicians pursuing pro-growth policies naturally leads to frictions in the design, implementation, monitoring, and enforcement of financial regulation. These frictions—or *regulatory failures*—can be understood as driving a wedge between the decisions of financial policymakers and the pursuit of regulatory objectives or broader social welfare. This section examines the potential impact of four different regulatory failures: 'hard' and 'soft' regulatory capture, the regulatory sine curve, regulatory forbearance, and welfare-reducing regulatory competition/arbitrage.

25.4.1 Regulatory capture

In very broad terms, regulatory capture refers to the process by which a regulated industry influences the incentives of policymakers in pursuit of its own self-interest.[28] The concept of regulatory capture proceeds from the view that regulation is a valuable service—imposing various costs (such as direct and indirect taxes) and conferring various benefits (in the form of implicit and explicit subsidies), which regulated industries can acquire for their private benefit. In effect, the idea is that 'captured' regulators cease to be agents for society at large and rather become faithful agents for the industries they regulate.[29]

Regulatory capture can take place through a number of different channels. One involves the transformation of financial capital into political capital. Between 1998 and 2008, for example, the US financial services industry is estimated to have spent approximately $5.1 billion on political campaign contributions and lobbying expenses.[30] Chris Dodd, former Chairman of the Senate Banking Committee and co-sponsor of the eponymous reform legislation, received $2.9 million from the securities industry in 2007–8.[31] The securities industry was also the largest contributor to Barney Frank, Dodd's co-sponsor and former Chairman of the House Financial Services Committee.[32] Ultimately, of course, it is impossible to know whether such contributions are designed to influence the decisions of policymakers or simply to support the political aspirations of those who hold pre-existing policy positions consistent with the interests of the financial services industry. Intuitively, however, the importance of

---

[28] Stigler, n 16.   [29] Kane, 'Financial Regulation and Market Forces', n 14; Stigler, n 16.
[30] Johnson and Kwak, n 20, 91.   [31] Ibid.
[32] Ibid. Despite the fragile financial position of many institutions in the wake of the crisis, the financial services industry actually *increased* its aggregate lobbying expenditures in response to proposed regulatory reforms such as the Dodd–Frank Act: ibid, 179.

financial capital to political campaigns—and the concomitant threat that it might be withheld or, worse, diverted into the campaign war chests of competitors more sympathetic to industry concerns—gives the financial services industry significant leverage in its relationship with elected policymakers. As a corollary, we would expect this form of 'hard' capture to be more pronounced in jurisdictions—such as the US— where aspiring politicians require relatively high levels of financial capital to mount successful campaigns.

A second channel through which the financial services industry can capture policy-makers is a function of their often unparalleled *access* to them. Market participants interact with regulators in the context of both hybrid systems of regulation (such as principles-based regulation and self-regulation, discussed in Chapter 24) and the broader policy process (for example, in public consultations). As we will see in Chapter 26, many also engage with regulators on a more or less continuous basis in the context of day-to-day supervisory relationships. These relationships are often reinforced by the movement of personnel between positions in the financial services industry and the public sector.[33] Perhaps the most prominent example of this so-called 'revolving door' phenomenon is Robert Rubin, who left his position as co-chair of Goldman Sachs to become an economic adviser to President Clinton, was subsequently appointed US Treasury Secretary, and then returned to the private sector as a director and senior executive at Citigroup. Such wide-ranging, sustained, and high-level access enables the financial services industry to build significant relationships with policy-makers and, ultimately, to shape financial law and policy from the inside.[34]

Finally, the financial services industry can capture policymakers by shaping the intellectual environment within which policy decisions are made. As a preliminary matter, market participants control much of the information policymakers need to identify potential risks and assess the desirability of different policy alternatives. While regulators can often compel production of this information, its volume and complexity often mean that they must still rely on market participants to collect, aggregate, and present it in a clear and comprehensive manner. At the same time, market participants possess a comparative advantage in terms of the human capital necessary to analyse this information, identify potential risks, and evaluate their probability and impact.

Together, these asymmetries of information and expertise generate opportunities for market participants to control information flow and frame information in ways designed to advance their narrow self-interest. These asymmetries also allow the financial services industry to advance empirically contestable claims with the knowledge that it will be difficult, if not impossible, for other constituencies to challenge

---

[33] They are also augmented by consulting arrangements with the private sector. The US Treasury Department and Federal Reserve Bank of New York, for example, hired Morgan Stanley to advise them on matters pertaining to the publicly funded bail-outs of both government-sponsored entities and insurance giant AIG: ibid, 185.

[34] At the same time, the strength of the relationships between industry and policymakers may be a function of the broader institutional structure of the political system. The standing committee system in the US, for example, where elected officials are permitted to retain their membership for as long as they continue to achieve re-election, facilitates long-term interactions between the industry and a small subset of elected officials: Kroszner and Stratmann, n 20. In the UK, by contrast, periodic cabinet reshuffles can make it harder for the industry to develop and sustain such relationships.

them effectively. These claims are often designed to make policymakers—and the general public—associate free and unfettered markets with economic *growth*, and regulation with economic *stagnation*.[35] Johnson and Kwak, for example, provide a compelling account of how the US financial services industry fostered a widespread belief, prior to the crisis, that a large and sophisticated financial services sector was in the best interests of all Americans.[36] Ultimately, this form of 'soft' capture helps explain the heavy-handed response to Brooksley Born's concept release on OTC derivatives regulation described in the introduction to this chapter.

Collectively, these channels provide the financial services industry with powerful means of influencing the decisions of financial policymakers. At the same time, of course, this does not necessarily mean that industry concerns *always* dominate the policy process. Rather, it means that in order to effectively neutralize this influence, policymakers must find support from other constituencies. The regulatory failures associated with the (often cyclical) process by which these constituencies gain and lose influence are explored in the next section.

25.4.2 The 'Regulatory Sine Curve'

The influence of the financial services industry over the decisions of policymakers is often disrupted by financial crises or scandals. These recurrent events can be understood as highlighting the social costs of (badly regulated) financial products and services, thereby enhancing the salience of financial law and policy to the general public and generating a demand amongst otherwise dispersed and heterogeneous constituencies for regulatory reform. The demand for regulatory reform, in turn, often leads to the emergence of policymakers seeking to capitalize on prevailing public sentiment in order to advance either a particular policy agenda or their own political aspirations.[37] Where successful, the political capital—that is, potential votes— mobilized by these policymakers can become an effective counterweight to the financial, relationship, and human capital wielded by the financial services industry.

Inevitably, however, even the most damaging crises and scandals fade from the headlines and, ultimately, the public's collective consciousness. This may be because society has started to recover from their harmful effects, because the public's focus has shifted from constraining risk to promoting economic growth, or simply owing to the passage of time. At this point, we would expect financial regulation to become inconspicuous again to both the general public and elected policymakers. Where the effects of a crisis or scandal linger, meanwhile, regulatory reforms could come to be viewed as a potential drag on economic growth. The financial services industry is likely

---

[35] As Jack Coffee has observed: 'Time and again, this is the key move: to blame economic stagnation and job loss, not on a crash or a bubble, but on the regulation that follows it' (Coffee, n 15, 1078).

[36] Johnson and Kwak, n 20.

[37] Roberta Romano, 'Regulating in the Dark' (2013) 1 *Journal of Financial Perspectives* 23; Coffee, n 15. In effect, the prospect of electoral success can be understood as generating high-powered incentives for these policymakers to overcome the information, coordination, and collective action problems which might otherwise make it unlikely that these constituencies would organize their activities in an attempt to influence the policy process. Simultaneously, of course, these 'political entrepreneurs' may also seek to *manufacture* this demand to further their personal aspirations.

to view these developments as an opportunity to reassert its influence over the policy process. This resurgent influence, in turn, can lead to the erosion of post-crisis regulatory reforms—often at the level of technical rule-making and implementation.[38] The evolution of measures for structural regulation of banking, described in Chapter 23, is a good example of how the substance of regulatory reforms can be hollowed out in this way.

Jack Coffee has labelled this crisis-driven, reactive, and ultimately cyclical process the 'regulatory sine curve'.[39] It can lead to a number of potential regulatory failures. As a preliminary matter, there is no guarantee that regulatory reforms introduced in the wake of a crisis or scandal will advance sound regulatory objectives and/or broader social welfare. Indeed, there is little reason to believe that regulation inspired by other constituencies, such as providers of financial regulation-related services, or adopted, often hastily, in response to outcries from the general public, will be any more or less desirable from a broader societal perspective than that adopted in response to lobbying by the financial services industry. Second, and relatedly, policymakers may seek to satisfy the demand for regulatory reform at the leading edge of the curve by undertaking highly visible but ultimately superficial or even counterproductive reforms designed simply to showcase the fact that they are doing *something* to address the problems exposed by the crisis or scandal.[40] Third, even where post-crisis reforms effectively respond to these problems, their design and implementation can divert regulatory attention and resources away from identifying, monitoring, and responding to new risks. As a matter of fact, it is often regulatory reforms themselves that drive structural changes to how financial markets work and risks materialize. At the same time, a return to economic growth, if not the political need for it, may lead policymakers to discount the likely impact of both old and new risks.[41] As a result, the regulatory sine curve can be seen as playing a potentially important role in setting the stage for future crises.

25.4.3 Regulatory forbearance

On 25 September 2008, the US Office of Thrift Supervision ('OTS') placed Washington Mutual—then the country's largest savings and loan association with over $300 billion in assets—into receivership. Yet for much of the period leading up to its collapse, the OTS had given the bank the second highest rating under its qualitative risk assessment framework: in effect declaring it to be 'fundamentally sound'.[42] So what happened? The failure in this case was not one of inadequate information or resources: the OTS had spent over 62,000 person-hours examining the bank's assets and operations in 2007

---

[38] Coffee, n 15.   [39] Ibid.

[40] Romano, n 37. This helps to explain, for example, why one of the most common responses to financial crises is to tinker with the institutional structure of financial regulators: see Chapter 27, section 27.2.5.

[41] Coffee, n 15.

[42] Offices of the Inspector General of the US Treasury Department and Federal Deposit Insurance Corporation, 'Evaluation of Federal Regulatory Oversight of Washington Mutual Bank' (2010) ('FDIC Report'), 16. Washington Mutual's CAMELS rating was downgraded to the third highest rating in February 2008, and the fourth highest in September 2008: ibid.

alone.[43] Nor was it one of competence or communication: the OTS correctly identified the potential risks associated with Washington Mutual's underwriting standards, asset quality, and internal controls, brought these risks to the attention of the bank's senior management, and put forward recommendations regarding how the bank could improve risk management.[44] Rather, the regulatory failure at the heart of Washington Mutual's collapse was one of *inaction*. Specifically, the OTS failed to verify that the bank had implemented these recommendations and to take more aggressive action when it became clear that the bank had failed to do so.[45]

The collapse of Washington Mutual stands out as the largest failure of a deposit-taking institution in US history. The inaction—or *forbearance*—exhibited by the bank's regulators, however, was far less remarkable. Indeed, looking back, regulatory forbearance in some form or another has played an important role in many crises: from the US savings and loan crisis of the 1980s and early 1990s, to the Japanese banking crisis of 1991–2.[46] More recently, meanwhile, forbearance could arguably be observed in the relatively lenient approach adopted by banking regulators towards European banks' sovereign risk-weightings, asset quality, liquidity, and stress testing in the immediate wake of the crisis.[47] This forbearance is made possible by the enormous discretion conferred upon regulators under systems of risk-based prudential supervision (see Chapter 26), combined with the high costs of monitoring the effort and judgement of regulators.

Regulators engage in forbearance for a number of different reasons. First, they may legitimately believe that—given additional time—a distressed financial institution will be able to resolve its problems without resort to public regulatory intervention. Second, they may be of the view that the present value of the social costs stemming from regulatory intervention to resolve a distressed institution will exceed the attendant benefits. Indeed, in at least some cases, we would expect forbearance to represent the socially optimal regulatory strategy.[48] At the same time, however, regulators may use forbearance for self-serving reasons. Consider that bank resolutions reveal, or can be perceived as evidence of, supervisory failures. Because resolution authorities often also have supervisory powers, the blame will easily fall upon their agents. Such agents will thus have a preference for letting distressed—or 'zombie'—institutions continue to

---

[43] Ibid, 17.   [44] Ibid, 19–28.

[45] T Henderson and F Tung, 'Pay for Regulator Performance' (2011) 85 *Southern California Law Review* 1003, and FDIC Report, n 42.

[46] E Kane, 'The Dangers of Capital Forbearance: The Case of the FSLIC and "Zombie" S&Ls' (1987) 5 *Contemporary Policy Issues* 77; Kane, 'Financial Regulation and Market Forces', n 14; C Goodhart, 'An Incentive Structure for Financial Regulation', LSE Financial Markets Group Special Paper No 88 (1996).

[47] Especially in comparison with the US. Notably, EU officials have signalled that this approach is likely to change following the establishment of the Single Supervisory Mechanism: see Chapter 28.

[48] Morrison and White, for example, explore the circumstances in which forbearance may be desirable as a means of avoiding potential reputational contagion (eg where the failure of one bank can undermine the public's confidence in the competence of the relevant banking regulator and, thus, other banks supervised by the same regulator): A Morrison and L White, 'Reputational Contagion and Optimal Regulatory Forbearance' (2013) 110 *Journal of Financial Economics* 642. Forbearance may also be desirable where there is no mechanism in place to resolve a distressed institution without exacerbating financial instability. This may help explain, for example, the forbearance exhibited by EU banking regulators in the wake of the crisis.

operate, in the hope that these institutions will survive until they have moved to a different job or macroeconomic conditions bring those institutions back to health.[49] Along the same vein, supervisors may delay intervention to avoid confrontations not only with zombie institutions' senior managers but also with the powerful politicians those senior managers may have generously bankrolled. Crucially, as the problems within distressed institutions continue to build, so often do the incentives of regulators to postpone the day of reckoning. Forbearance can thus be understood as contributing to the build-up of risk at both the individual bank and systemic levels.

25.4.4 Regulatory competition/arbitrage

In a world where capital and risk did not flow freely across borders, the decisions of financial policymakers would have little impact on constituencies located in other jurisdictions. If domestic policymakers increased capital or liquidity requirements for commercial and investment banks, for example, it would be domestic constituencies that would enjoy any resulting benefits in terms of greater institutional or broader financial stability. Domestic constituencies would, similarly, bear any attendant costs in terms of reduced competition within the banking sector or lower economic growth. As we have seen, these constituencies have a range of means at their disposal with which to influence the decisions of self-interested policymakers.

In a world characterized by regionally or globally interconnected financial markets and institutions, however, the decisions of domestic policymakers can have significant cross-border implications. Perhaps most importantly, their decisions may be the source of externalities: with some jurisdictions becoming net importers of risk, others net exporters. Thus, for example, the decision to decrease capital or liquidity requirements in one jurisdiction may undermine financial stability or harm competitors in other jurisdictions. Hence the incentives of domestic policymakers may diverge from global social welfare. Indeed, these policymakers can arguably be understood as possessing powerful incentives to pursue policies which generate benefits for domestic constituencies but which, wherever possible, externalize the resulting costs to market participants, consumers, and taxpayers in other jurisdictions. These incentives are a product of the fact that, unlike domestic constituencies, these groups often possess few means of influencing the domestic policy process.

At the same time, the free flow of capital and risk across borders can been seen as creating the conditions necessary for the emergence of international *regulatory competition*. Domestic policymakers may thus compete with one another on the basis of substantive regulation, the intensity of supervision and enforcement, and/or the broader investment climate in order to attract market participants and their business from other jurisdictions. Market participants, in turn, may take advantage of this competition by engaging in *regulatory arbitrage*: seeking to do business in those jurisdictions that offer the friendliest regulatory environment.[50]

---

[49] Kane, 'Financial Regulation and Market Forces', n 14.   [50] See Chapter 28, section 28.7.

The prospect of international regulatory competition and arbitrage can be understood as influencing the decisions of domestic policymakers in at least three ways.[51] First, policymakers—viewing regulatory competition as an *opportunity* to enhance their international standing, increase tax revenues, boost domestic growth, or capture other benefits—may seek to win this competition.[52] Second, viewing regulatory arbitrage as a *threat*, they may be reluctant to step out of line with prevailing international regulatory standards. The UK Independent Commission on Banking, for example, felt constrained by the Basel capital adequacy requirements in making its recommendation regarding the appropriate level of core equity for wholesale/investment banking businesses.[53] Third, and in a similar vein, policymakers may proactively seek to influence prevailing international regulatory standards in order to advance domestic interests.

Like regulatory forbearance, regulatory competition and arbitrage are not inherently undesirable. In fact, they may hold out important benefits in terms of facilitating regulatory diversity and experimentation, thereby sending policymakers valuable signals about which policy alternatives work and—crucially—which do not, under different conditions. In addition, when market participants have the right incentives, regulatory arbitrage may allow players in markets with bad or insufficiently enforced regulation to signal their higher quality by choosing a better (stricter) regulatory environment. Simultaneously, however, regulatory competition and arbitrage may in certain circumstances—and especially where the relevant regulation is designed to constrain negative externalities—trigger a welfare-reducing race to the bottom in regulatory standards. Ultimately, the question of whether regulatory competition and arbitrage are socially desirable is an important one, explored in greater detail in Chapter 28. For present purposes, however, the important thing to understand is simply that they also represent significant potential sources of regulatory failure.

25.5　Constraining Regulatory Failure: Holding Policymakers to Account

In light of the regulatory failures described in the preceding section, the salient question becomes: how can we better align the incentives of financial policymakers with both regulatory objectives and broader social welfare? Put differently: how can we hold policymakers accountable for their decisions? Democracies hold elected policymakers to account through the imposition of constitutional constraints interpreted and enforced by independent judiciaries and, ultimately, by holding periodic elections. As we have seen, however, such constraints are mostly ineffective—and in some cases downright counterproductive—as a means of ensuring the quality of financial regulation.

---

[51] In reality, of course, there are two other potential responses: do nothing, or take steps to withdraw from the global financial system.

[52] In effect, policymakers pursuing this strategy can be understood as acknowledging foreign market participants as an important constituency. In this important respect, not all foreign constituencies are created equal: the international mobility of market participants gives them influence which most other constituencies do not enjoy.

[53] ICB Report, n 23, 28.

And what about the unelected bureaucrats, agencies, and agency personnel to whom these policymakers delegate responsibility for large swaths of financial policymaking?

On the one hand, this delegation of responsibility and discretion can be understood as an attempt to ensure that decisions are made by those with both sufficient subject-matter expertise and sufficient autonomy from the vicissitudes of elected politics. On the other hand, however, we would expect the delegation of this decision-making power to result in regulatory failure in the absence of institutional constraints designed to ensure sufficient accountability. At the same time, there exists an obvious tension between regulators' autonomy and their accountability. Indeed, autonomy and accountability can be viewed as residing at opposite ends of a spectrum: too much of the former generates opportunities for regulators to abuse their delegated discretion, while too much of the latter undermines their expertise and political independence.[54] How to balance these competing considerations is thus an important threshold question when designing institutional arrangements with the objective of ensuring the accountability of financial regulators.

This section examines the potential benefits and limitations of five institutional arrangements and two strategies that can be used to constrain regulatory failure. The institutional arrangements are transparency requirements, independent oversight, pre-commitment mechanisms, compensation, and liability. As we will show, none of these five mechanisms is foolproof. Even when effectively designed and deployed, they are perhaps best viewed as useful but insufficient building blocks of an institutional environment that effectively curbs regulators' discretion. Without such mechanisms, regulators bear virtually no risk of meaningful sanctions for misbehaviour. But, as this section concludes, for their joint use to be effective, two additional strategies should be pursued. The first is to harness the relevant agents' concern for their reputation within the community of those who genuinely care about the quality of financial regulation—be they market participants focused on the long term, disinterested observers, or public-interest-minded policymakers. The second is to ensure supervisory agents' substantive independence from politics.

25.5.1 Transparency requirements

In governance terms, transparency refers to the degree to which the activities of an agent are observable by the agent's principal. Viewed from this perspective, promoting transparency in financial policymaking necessarily starts with the articulation of a set of clearly defined objectives against which the performance of regulatory agencies and their personnel can be measured. Next, because regulatory objectives can be overly broad and regulators' resources are inevitably constrained, transparency also requires that regulators spell out their priorities. Further, transparency requires that they

---

[54] As Lastra and Shams have observed, the tension between regulatory independence and accountability thus shares many similarities with the broader tension between freedom and responsibility: R Lastra and H Shams, 'Public Accountability in the Financial Sector', in E Ferran and C Goodhart (eds), *Regulating Financial Services and Markets in the 21st Century* (Oxford: Hart Publishing, 2001).

disclose information about the substantive content of policy decisions, the rationales which underpin them, and, ultimately, how these decisions are expected to advance these regulatory objectives. Finally, *ex post* disclosures about the impact of these decisions, along with the performance of regulators in achieving regulatory objectives, should complete the picture.

Simultaneously, however, the desirability of transparency as a means of holding regulators to account is complicated by the fact that—in at least some circumstances— timely disclosure of information may *undermine* regulatory objectives. Disclosure of the fact that a bank is experiencing financial distress, for example, may trigger a destabilizing run by its depositors and other creditors. Policymakers must therefore attempt to strike a balance between transparency and the need for commercial confidentiality in certain contexts. Striking this balance often requires the use of mechanisms such as lagged disclosure which, if properly designed, avoid the destabilizing impact of timely disclosure but nevertheless facilitate *ex post* scrutiny of regulatory decisions. At the same time, however, there is no clearly optimal balance between these competing imperatives.

There exists no shortage of mechanisms to promote transparency in the design, implementation, monitoring, and enforcement of financial regulation. These mechanisms include requiring regulators to publish periodic reports, appear before congressional or parliamentary committees to answer questions, conduct internal investigations, and submit to external audits of their performance.[55]

Yet, transparency is a double-edged sword: the additional information that financial regulators may disclose will be primarily used by the financial industry itself, which may then more swiftly react to it, for example by urging politicians to curb any attempt to improve the regulatory framework or clamp down on overly risky behaviour. To come back to our initial illustration, suppose that Brooksley Born's CFTC had not been required to conduct a public consultation before enacting new restrictions on OTC derivatives and had in fact been able to issue final rules overnight. It would have arguably been harder for the industry and other policymakers to revert to the status quo.

25.5.2 Independent oversight

Making the policy process more transparent is likely to have little impact if nobody is watching. As we have already observed, however, the constituencies paying the closest attention to the decisions of financial regulators may not be concerned with the pursuit of either regulatory objectives or broader social welfare.[56] In theory at least, this points to the desirability of some form of *independent* oversight as a means of holding regulators accountable for their decisions.

At first glance, there might appear to be a number of different parties to whom this responsibility could be delegated. Thus, for example, we might look to elected

---

[55] L Enriques and G Hertig, 'Improving the Governance of Financial Supervisors' (2011) 12 *European Business Organization Law Review* 357, 372–8.
[56] Barth, Caprio, and Levine, n 20.

politicians, internal or external auditors, or the non-executive directors of regulatory agencies as potential sources of independent oversight. We might also look to the courts responsible for judicial review of administrative decision-making. Casting the net more broadly, meanwhile, we might view an independent media sector as performing a *de facto* oversight function: investigating the impact of policy decisions and bringing them to the public's attention. We might also view regulatory competition as revealing valuable information about the desirability of regulatory decisions and—via the process of regulatory arbitrage—holding regulators to account.[57]

Upon closer inspection, however, each of these potential sources of regulatory oversight has significant drawbacks. Elected politicians, of course, will be driven by political motives. In many cases, they may also lack the expertise needed to effectively challenge the decisions of specialist regulators. We might also question the independence and expertise of internal auditors and non-executive directors of regulatory agencies[58]—although, simultaneously, we must acknowledge that they have often been the source of vigorous (albeit typically *ex post*) oversight.[59] The independence of mainstream media is, similarly, open to question given that major market data and news providers such as Bloomberg and Thompson Reuters derive a significant proportion of their revenues from the financial services industry. They also possess their own commercial, political, and editorial agendas. Moreover, the media does not possess any direct means of holding regulators to account, relying instead on the initiative of others to dole out sanctions and rewards on the basis of the information they produce. Finally, as described in greater detail in Chapter 28, regulatory arbitrage and competition may generate significant negative externalities, thereby driving a wedge between the incentives of self-interested regulators and broader social welfare.

The judiciary may perhaps be viewed as a promising source of independent regulatory oversight. In practice, however, we would expect courts generally to possess considerably less information and expertise than specialist regulators. This, in turn, is reflected in the fact that, in many jurisdictions, the standard of review applied by courts to the decisions of specialist regulators often accords them considerable deference.[60] It follows that we would expect courts only to constrain regulatory failures which manifested themselves in the form of fraud, corruption, bad faith, abuse of process, or other actions outside the lawful scope of the regulator's authority.[61] Put differently: judicial review is designed to constrain *unlawful* decisions, but not *bad* ones. Viewed from this perspective, there exist a number of significant—and justifiable—limits on the ability of the judiciary to provide effective independent oversight.

---

[57] Conversely, we might view international standard and agenda setters such as the Basel Committee on Banking Supervision or the Financial Stability Board, along with so-called 'colleges' of regulators, as coordinating oversight of compliance with common standards at the international level; see Chapter 28.

[58] Especially in the case of non-executive directors with significant industry ties.

[59] See eg the internal audit reports of the UK Financial Services Authority's supervision of both Northern Rock and Royal Bank of Scotland (RBS); Financial Services Authority, *Report into the Failure of Royal Bank of Scotland* (2012) and Financial Services Authority, *Lessons Learned: Review of the Supervision of Northern Rock plc During the Period 1 January 2005 to 9 August 2007* (2008).

[60] Although courts in the UK are perhaps less likely to acknowledge the existence of this deference than courts in many other jurisdictions: see T Endicott, *Administrative Law*, 2nd ed (Oxford: OUP, 2011), Ch 7.

[61] Ibid.

Acknowledging the limits of existing sources of independent oversight, Barth, Caprio, and Levine have advanced the proposal of a regulators' 'Sentinel'.[62] The Sentinel's sole responsibility would be to evaluate financial policy on a continuous basis and deliver periodic reports to policymakers on its current and long-run implications. Its sole power, meanwhile, would be to obtain any information it deems necessary for this purpose. The Sentinel would be comprised of individuals with high levels of expertise and experience in the financial services industry and financial policy. In order to attract qualified personnel, these individuals would receive market-based compensation. They would also be prohibited from receiving compensation from the financial services industry for a period of time after their tenure.

Barth et al envisage a high-profile and credible source of independent information and analysis about the impact of financial policy on society, which would force regulators to defend their decisions and provide a potential counterweight to the influence of the financial services industry. At the same time, however, there remain a number of unanswered questions about the design and likely effectiveness of their proposal. It would be difficult, for example, to completely insulate the process of appointing the Sentinel's personnel from political control and, thus, potential interference. It is also unclear how the Sentinel would make financial policy more salient to the public. More broadly, the Sentinel is ultimately vulnerable to the same criticism that, in one way or another, applies to all sources of independent oversight: *quis custodiet ipsos custodes?* Who will watch over the Sentinel?

25.5.3 Constraining discretion

Another, more invasive, way of ensuring that the decisions of regulators reflect public regulatory objectives is to impose explicit constraints on their delegated discretion. More specifically, policymakers can articulate hard and fast rules requiring regulators to take specified actions upon the occurrence of predetermined trigger events. Where such pre-commitment mechanisms are credible, they can be understood as minimizing the prospect that self-interested motives will influence regulatory decision-making: removing discretion in cases where regulators possess the necessary tools to act, but lack the will to do so. Such mechanisms can also provide regulated actors with additional certainty regarding the nature and timing of regulatory intervention. Indeed, even where these mechanisms are not entirely credible, they can still provide regulators with a 'plausible excuse' for resisting pressure from the financial services industry or elected officials.[63] Clear rules demarcating the boundaries of a regulator's legal authority may also enhance judicial review as a form of independent regulatory oversight.

The 'prompt corrective action' provisions of the US Federal Deposit Insurance Act are often held out as a good example of how such pre-commitment mechanisms

---

[62] Barth, Caprio, and Levine, n 20.

[63] L Enriques and G Hertig, 'The Governance of Financial Supervisors: Improving Responsiveness to Market Developments' (2010), 28–40, available at http://ssrn.com/abstract=1711230.

work.[64] Prompt corrective action requires bank supervisors to act promptly to inter-vene to resolve problems at distressed banks, thereby protecting the Federal Deposit Insurance Corporation's ('FDIC') deposit insurance fund—and taxpayers—from potential losses. It does so by articulating a mandatory, graduated ladder of regulatory actions and business restrictions as the capital position of a bank deteriorates.[65] Where a bank is 'undercapitalized',[66] for example, prompt corrective action requires it to suspend payment of all dividends and management fees and prepare a capital restor-ation plan.[67] Where a bank is 'significantly undercapitalized',[68] meanwhile, regulators are required to take one or more of a range of potential actions. These actions include requiring the bank to recapitalize, imposing restrictions on transactions with the bank's affiliates, capping deposit rates, and subjecting the compensation of senior executive officers to regulatory pre-approval.[69] Prompt corrective action is then coupled with *ex post* oversight: requiring a review of the relevant regulator's supervision of a bank wherever the deposit insurance fund suffers a material loss.[70]

Ultimately, requiring that decisions be based on transparent, consistent, compre-hensible criteria can be understood as reducing the scope for regulatory forbearance. At the same time, however, defining the entire spectrum of problems which regulators are likely to encounter on an *ex ante* basis is extremely difficult. Indeed, prompt corrective action focuses on a bank's capital position not because it is a reliable indicator of distress, but rather because it is readily observable. Moreover, limiting the discretion of regulators may also be problematic in times of crisis—where all options need to be on the table. For this reason, pre-commitment mechanisms are typically softened by the inclusion of override provisions enabling regulators to deviate from ostensibly man-datory requirements. This, however, undermines the *ex ante* credibility of these mechanisms. More broadly, given the enormously high stakes involved in something like the failure of a systemically important financial institution, pre-commitment mechanisms are unlikely to ever be completely credible.

25.5.4 High-powered incentives: compensation

Ultimately, if we are unable to effectively monitor the activities of financial regulators, we need to find other ways of aligning their incentives with regulatory objectives. One way is to link regulatory pay with performance. Historically, performance-based pay has not figured prominently in regulatory compensation practices. This has been

---

[64] Federal Deposit Insurance Act of 1950 (US) ('FDIA'), as amended by Federal Deposit Insurance Corporation Improvement Act of 1991 ('FDICIA'), Pub L 81–797, 64 Stat 873, §38.

[65] At the same time, prompt corrective action also contemplates that supervisors may take certain discretionary action in response to the erosion of a bank's capital position. Conversely, it also contemplates the waiver of some of the mandatory provisions in certain prescribed circumstances.

[66] Defined as failing to meet the required minimum capital level for any relevant capital measure (ie total risk-weighted capital, tier 1 risk-weighted capital, or tier 1 leverage): FDIA, §38(b)(C).

[67] FDIA, §38(e).

[68] Defined as falling significantly below the minimum level for any relevant capital measure; FDIA, §38 (b)(D). The FDIC has historically articulated a more precise level for each measure below which a bank will be deemed to be 'significantly undercapitalized'.

[69] FDIA, §38(f).   [70] FDIA, §38(k).

justified on the grounds that fixed and relatively low levels of explicit pay attract candidates who value public service.[71] Together with guaranteed job security, it also helps insulate regulators from political interference and regulatory capture.[72] Simultaneously, however, fixed pay and job security generate perverse incentives insofar as they make regulators less sensitive to the real-world effects of their performance. They may also make it more difficult for regulatory agencies to attract and retain highly qualified personnel.

While the prospective benefits of performance-based compensation arrangements are relatively straightforward, designing these arrangements proves extremely difficult. As a preliminary matter, financial regulation is a complex activity. This makes it difficult to identify clear, reliable, and objective measures of performance or desired regulatory outcomes—giving rise to a 'multi-dimensional tasking' problem. Focusing on the most observable measures of performance—such as the number of visits to regulated firms or correctly filling out reports—may lead regulators to focus on *processes* which may in fact have little relationship with regulatory *objectives* or *outcomes*.[73] At the same time, it is also often difficult to isolate the effect of an individual regulator's decisions on the realization of these outcomes. Compounding matters, many ostensibly useful measures of performance are, upon closer inspection, ambiguous. If the number of regulatory enforcement actions decreases, for example, should we attribute this to more effective deterrence or more laxity on the part of regulators? Finally, performance-based compensation arrangements encounter conceptual problems where regulators are required to strike a trade-off between competing regulatory objectives. Clearly, then, the extent to which performance-based compensation arrangements align the interests of regulators with regulatory objectives will be a function of how well the objectives themselves are designed.

A recent proposal put forward by Todd Henderson and Frederick Tung illustrates just how difficult it can be to design effective performance-based compensation arrangements for regulators.[74] Their two-pronged proposal focuses specifically on the incentives of bank supervisors in two contexts: day-to-day supervision and decisions about whether to intervene to resolve a failing bank. First, in order to align incentives in the context of day-to-day supervision, Henderson and Tung propose that a component of supervisors' compensation be based on a debt-heavy mix of phantom equity and debt in the banks they supervise.[75] By making the compensation of supervisors more sensitive to bank performance, they argue, this first prong generates

---

[71] Viewed from a slightly different perspective, however, regulatory personnel can be understood as often receiving relatively high levels of *implicit* pay in terms of, for example, the non-pecuniary benefits of public office and enhanced future career prospects.

[72] Although, on another level, it may *increase* the likelihood of capture insofar as regulators' decisions may be influenced by their desire to transition into a more lucrative career in the financial services industry.

[73] C Goodhart, 'Regulating the Regulator—An Economist's Perspective on Accountability and Control', in Ferran and Goodhart, n 54.

[74] Henderson and Tung, n 45.

[75] Henderson and Tung suggest the mix should be heavily weighted towards debt in order to ensure that supervisors focus more on potential losses. They also suggest that the performance-based component should be up to 25 per cent of total compensation so as to provide a meaningful incentive, but not to swamp the fixed-pay component: ibid.

better incentives for supervisors to improve regulatory efficiency (because they participate on the upside) and to intervene to constrain excessive risk-taking (because they participate on the downside).

Second, Henderson and Tung propose a contingent payment linked to the timing of a supervisor's decision to shut down a failing bank. This bonus would be calculated on the basis of a comparison between the costs imposed on the deposit insurance fund stemming from the actual intervention and those which would have incurred had the supervisor intervened at a different—and presumably optimal—point in time. So, for example, if a supervisor intervened at time T and as a result the deposit insurance fund experienced a loss of £100 million, the supervisor would be entitled to a bonus if her superiors determined that, had the intervention taken place at $T+1$, the fund would have lost £200 million.[76] This second prong of the proposal is designed to minimize the prospect of regulatory forbearance. As the authors concede, however, this prong of their proposal is rife with conceptual challenges. How do you construct the necessary counterfactual? How do you deal with the fact that different counterfactuals may lead to very different results? And is it fair to make this determination with the benefit of hindsight? In attempting to answer these questions, what becomes clear is that this process is vulnerable to both biases and manipulation.

Once again, therefore, we find that there is no silver bullet when attempting to align the incentives of self-interested regulators with public regulatory objectives. At the same time, older, more conventional practices at well-regarded supervisory agencies may provide useful insights into how problems can at least be mitigated. High fixed salaries, especially if combined with the advantages of job security and of a generous early retirement scheme acting as a retention bonus, may help reduce the risk of capture.

25.5.5 Institutional and personal liability

The final and, in some respects, extreme means of holding regulators accountable for their decisions is the imposition of institutional or personal liability. Some jurisdictions, including the Netherlands and France, subject financial regulators to tort liability rules under domestic private law,[77] while others grant regulators broad immunity from such liability. In the UK, for example, the Financial Services and Markets Act 2000 stipulates that the Financial Conduct Authority and Prudential Regulatory Authority are only liable for acts or omissions exhibiting bad faith or that are incompatible with the European Convention on Human Rights.[78]

In theory, imposing liability on regulators may help incentivize them to pursue regulatory objectives with greater diligence and care. In practice, however, potential plaintiffs typically face a range of obstacles including evidential problems in establishing

---

[76] As Henderson and Tung suggest, the bonus must be large enough that the supervisor completely discounts the prospect of the bank's recovery in the absence of regulatory intervention: ibid.

[77] R Dijkstra, 'Liability of Financial Regulators: Defensive Conduct or Careful Supervision?' (2009) 10 *Journal of Banking Regulation* 269.

[78] FSMA 2000 (UK), Sch 1, para 19.

fault, and causation and conceptual problems relating to the nature of the loss, liability for omissions, and the deliberate acts of third parties.[79] More importantly, however, there is little reason to think that the motives of plaintiffs in bringing such actions will necessarily reflect regulatory objectives or broader social welfare. Moreover, exposing regulators to liability might have an unintended chilling effect. Financial regulators are required to make difficult judgements on the basis of imperfect information on an almost daily basis. Many of these judgements must strike a balance between competing societal interests. Where these decisions are made in the shadow of potential *ex post* legal action from affected constituencies, we might expect this to translate into an overly cautious approach towards regulatory intervention.[80] We might also expect it to divert regulators' time and attention away from the pursuit of regulatory objectives and towards limiting their potential liability.

25.5.6 Reputational concerns and enhanced independence

The institutional arrangements examined so far in this section should not be viewed as alternatives, but as complements. While each on its own is unlikely to be effective in constraining regulatory failure, together—if properly designed—these mechanisms may at least *help* align the incentives of regulators with regulatory objectives. And yet, even so combined, they will not achieve much unless two further mechanisms are in place: first, delegated policymakers must be chosen and bred that respond to the low-powered incentives of reputational concerns; and second, independence safeguards must be in place to prevent grabbing-hand, re-election-focused politicians from having the upper hand on regulatory and supervisory matters.

Policymakers' concerns about potential negative consequences for their reputation stemming from any perceived misbehaviour may be a powerful constraint on their discretion. While this mechanism, unlike the ones discussed so far, is not legal in nature, some legal provisions aiming to hold policymakers to account do rely on such concerns rather than on any formal legal sanction for failure to comply. For example, the Dodd–Frank Act of 2010 requires that each member of the Financial Stability Oversight Council (the US macroprudential authority) certify that the Council, the Government, and the private sector 'are taking all reasonable steps to ensure financial stability and to mitigate systemic risk that would negatively affect the economy', and if not, to identify what actions should be taken.[81] Clearly, this certification requirement is not meant to rule out the occurrence of tail events, but rather to focus Council members' minds on their institutional tasks: anticipating a rebuke from the media if things go wrong having made such a certification, policymakers will act more diligently in identifying and reviewing systemic risks.[82]

---

[79] D Nolan, 'The Liability of Financial Supervisory Authorities' (2013) 4 *Journal of European Tort Law* 190.

[80] Especially if regulators believe that members of the financial services industry are more likely to bring suit than, for example, consumers: see section 25.3.

[81] Dodd–Frank Act of 2010, §112(b).

[82] Of course, one may wonder how fair it is to expect that these officials, no matter how well educated and technically skilled, will anticipate and gauge the multiple factors and the tail events that usually need to converge before a full-blown financial crisis materializes.

Reputational concerns may play an important role more generally in guiding agents' behaviour. But the real question is the approval of which circle(s) of people policy-makers will care about obtaining and preserving. If they only worry about their standing among elected politicians and/or financial industry leaders, reputational concerns can only make matters worse. Rather, financial policymakers' reputational concerns should extend to a community comprising long-term focused market parti-cipants, disinterested observers, and public-minded policymakers: those, in short, who genuinely care about the quality of financial regulation and supervision. But that is just another way to describe what collectively goes under the label of a strong civil service tradition.

Finally, we have seen throughout this chapter how elected politicians have ultimate control over financial regulation and regulators' actions. While that is inevitable, the degree to which delegated policymakers will let politicians' short-term interests guide their action will vary significantly as a function of the former's independence from the latter.

Key to that is, first, budgetary independence for the relevant agencies. Few would question that the higher degree of independence from politics displayed by the US Fed compared to other agencies, such as the SEC and the CFTC, also reflects the fact that the Fed has a long-standing tradition of self-funding, while the latter are subject to the annual budgetary decisions of the relevant US Congressional Committees.

Second, independence of mind, whether based on the intrinsic motivation to pursue institutional objectives or on the right reputational concerns, should be a key feature of those appointed to top positions within supervisory agencies. Unfortunately, spelling out such a requirement is enough to highlight its inherent instability. It is generally true that politicians can hardly commit to ensuring regulators' substantive independence. Much as they can overturn any regulatory policy, so will they be able to renege on any previously articulated commitment to independence. One relatively inconspicuous way to do that is in fact by simply appointing top agency officials who can be expected to be amenable to political pressures.

25.6 Conclusion

Financial regulation is not independent of the process by which it is made. This process is often characterized by self-interested regulators whose decisions are influ-enced by politicians, on the one hand, and competing constituencies with little regard for either regulatory objectives or broader social welfare, on the other. Politicians worrying about re-election may have a preference for forfeiting financial stability in favour of credit expansion and short-term growth. They often have strong levers to prevent delegated policymakers from getting in their way. They may also be captured by special interests. The result, rather predictably, is regulatory failure. Examining these regulatory failures has provided us with potentially useful insights into how we might contain them.

We have shown how accountability mechanisms are often double-edged swords and argued that the right reputational concerns and institutional arrangements ensuring substantial independence atop of, and within, supervisory agencies are preconditions to ensuring that regulators do not deviate from regulatory objectives. At the same time, there can be no guarantee that politicians will not renege on any prior commitment to a sound and independent supervisory framework, if only by appointing the wrong individuals to key positions. But inscribing such arrangements into 'hard' laws, for example by providing for appointment terms longer than one electoral cycle, will make them harder to unravel.

26

Supervision and Enforcement of Financial Regulation

26.1 Introduction

For perhaps half a century, Bernard 'Bernie' Madoff was able to perpetrate one of the largest and most audacious frauds in the history of finance. Madoff's fraud was a classic 'Ponzi' scheme: extracting billions of dollars from unwitting investors with the promise of high returns, only to use those funds to pay fictitious returns to other, earlier stage investors. On 12 March 2009, Madoff pled guilty to criminal fraud charges and offences under the Securities Act of 1933, Securities Exchange Act of 1934, and Investment Advisers Act of 1940. By this stage, however, investor losses were estimated to be in the range of $18 billion.[1] Apart from the sheer scale of the fraud, what makes the Madoff scandal stand out is the fact that the US regulators responsible for supervising Madoff's activities discounted or altogether ignored numerous warning signs which, if properly investigated, might have uncovered the fraud at a far earlier stage.[2]

To this point, our attention has focused largely on the substantive rules that policymakers adopt in pursuit of the goals of financial regulation identified in Chapter 3. Also important, however, is how compliance with these rules is supervised and enforced.[3] Effective supervision increases the likelihood that activities such as Madoff's Ponzi scheme, excessive risk-taking within financial institutions, or potential threats to financial stability will be brought to light. It can also reduce the likelihood that market participants will violate substantive rules or otherwise engage in socially undesirable activities. Effective enforcement, meanwhile, ensures that the sanctions imposed on those found to have violated substantive rules serve to advance regulatory objectives: whether they be to protect consumers or investors, deter and punish improper conduct, or ensure that market participants internalize the externalities generated by their activities. The effectiveness—or intensity—of supervision and enforcement can thus be understood as a function of two variables: the *probability* of undesirable activities being detected, and the nature and quantum of the *sanctions* imposed on those who engage in these activities.[4]

---

[1] As of December 2015, the total value of allowed claims under the liquidation process stood at $14.89 billion; see I Picard, IPA Trustee for Bernard L Madoff Investment Securities LLC, available at http://www. madofftrustee.com.

[2] See Securities and Exchange Commission (SEC) Office of Investigations, *Investigation of the Failure of the SEC to Uncover Bernard Madoff's Ponzi Scheme*, Report OIG-509 (2009).

[3] R Pound, 'Law in Books and Law in Action' (1910) 44 *American Law Review* 12; G Becker, 'Crime and Punishment: An Economic Approach' (1968) 76 *Journal of Political Economy* 169; J Armour, H Hansmann, and R Kraakman, 'Agency Problems, Legal Strategies and Enforcement', in R Kraakman, J Armour, P Davies, L Enriques, H Hansmann, G Hertig, K Hopt, H Kanda, and E Rock, *The Anatomy of Corporate Law*, 2nd ed (Oxford: OUP, 2009), 45–9.

[4] Becker, n 3.

Principles of Financial Regulation. First Edition. John Armour, Dan Awrey, Paul Davies, Luca Enriques, Jeffrey N. Gordon, Colin Mayer, and Jennifer Payne. © John Armour, Dan Awrey, Paul Davies, Luca Enriques, Jeffrey N. Gordon, Colin Mayer, and Jennifer Payne 2016. Published 2016 by Oxford University Press.

Intuitively, we would expect the intensity of supervision and enforcement to play a particularly important role in the delivery of effective financial regulation. The size and complexity of many financial markets and institutions make it relatively costly to detect undesirable conduct and practices, monitor institutional risk-taking, or identify potential systemic risks. These costs are compounded by the entrenched asymmetries of information and expertise that often pervade relationships between regulators and market participants. Constrained by these costs, regulators must inevitably confront difficult questions about how best to allocate their finite resources in pursuit of different regulatory objectives.

Section 26.2 considers supervision in financial regulation. The term 'supervision' is most frequently used to refer to the role played by regulators in monitoring the activities of commercial and investment banks, insurance companies, and other financial services firms. This form of *institutional* supervision involves: the collection of information about a firm's business model, financial position, and internal systems, processes, and controls; the evaluation of this information in order to determine whether the firm is in compliance with substantive rules and able to effectively manage the risks embedded within its business model; and, lastly, the provision of guidance regarding the ways in which it might—or must—improve how it manages these risks.

'Supervision' can also be used to refer to the role played by regulators in policing activities within financial markets (often referred to as market 'surveillance'). This form of *market* supervision, which is not the primary focus of this chapter, includes efforts to detect unusual trading patterns and price movements that might be indicative, for example, of insider trading or market manipulation. The principal objective of both institutional and market supervision is to identify violations of substantive rules and other socially undesirable activities as a first step towards eliminating them.[5] This section explores the relationship between the intensity of supervision and the pursuit of the regulatory objectives, using the risk-based supervision of banks as an illustrative case study.

In section 26.3, we turn to enforcement. We often think of enforcement as involving the imposition of formal legal sanctions—such as monetary damages, fines, or imprisonment—in the context of administrative, civil, or criminal proceedings. In many areas of financial regulation, however, these 'legal' tools are supplemented by a broader range of (often informal) sanctions: from moral suasion and warning letters, to heightened regulatory scrutiny, business restrictions, and, ultimately, the suspension and revocation of regulatory licences.[6] As we shall see, the rationales underpinning the use of sanctions vary from context to context. In some contexts, the primary objective is to generate a credible deterrent, punish wrongdoing, or ensure that injured parties are provided with adequate compensation. In others, the objective is to promote effective risk management and constrain socially excessive risk-taking. This section explores some of the key dimensions of enforcement—the identity of the enforcers, the

---

[5] Although, as we shall see, insofar as institutional supervision can be understood as influencing the behaviour of market participants, it can also play an important quasi-remedial role.

[6] I Ayres and J Braithwaite, *Responsive Regulation: Transcending the Deregulation Debate* (Oxford: OUP, 1992).

nature of the sanctions they employ, and the targets of enforcement action—with a view to better understanding the relationship between enforcement and the pursuit of regulatory objectives.

What is the relationship between supervision and enforcement? We turn to this question in section 26.4. Up to a point, supervision and enforcement can be seen as *substitutes*. Specifically, policymakers can calibrate the risk-adjusted costs of non-compliance by altering the intensity of either supervision or enforcement—whichever is less costly.[7] Viewed from another perspective, however, supervision and enforcement can be seen as *complements*. Effective supervision, for example, will in many contexts rely on the credible background threat of vigorous enforcement to elicit meaningful cooperation and compliance from market participants. Successful enforcement, meanwhile, is predicated on the existence of highly expert and well-informed regulators—endowments often acquired through their interactions with regulated market participants in the context of day-to-day supervisory relationships. This section also examines the relationship between substantive policy choices and the intensity of supervision and enforcement. More specifically, it explores how moral hazard and other problems generated by these choices might be offset by increasing the intensity of supervision and/or enforcement. It also explores how structural regulation designed to dictate the size and shape of regulated firms may have second-order effects in terms of the costs of supervision and enforcement. Understanding the dynamics of these relationships is important if we are to design effective supervisory and enforcement strategies.

There are three principal takeaways from this chapter. First, the intensity of supervision and enforcement are important determinants of how successful regulators are in advancing regulatory objectives. Second, understanding the relationship between substantive policy choices, supervision, and enforcement in different contexts can pay dividends in terms of the design of effective supervisory and enforcement strategies. Third, designing effective supervisory and enforcement strategies is only the first step; the second, and in many respects more challenging, step is to execute these strategies successfully.

26.2 The Dimensions of Supervision

We might expect that regulation—regardless of its substance—is unlikely to exert a powerful influence on the activities of regulated market participants if nobody is watching. Indeed, intensive supervision can be seen as playing a particularly important role in financial regulation, given the complexity of many financial markets and institutions,[8]

---

[7] Note, however, that relying exclusively on enforcement will not yield the same results, in terms of deterrence, as relying exclusively on supervision: while supervision without enforcement still can be effective, because supervisors have the tools to induce compliance (eg by refusing authorizations to grow via mergers and acquisitions, suspending dividend payments, and sending on-site inspections that will cost the supervised entity time and money), enforcement without supervision is much less likely to punish misbehaviour, given the greater difficulty of detecting and proving wrongdoing.

[8] For a discussion of the complexity of banks, see H Mehran, A Morrison, and J Shapiro, 'Corporate Governance and Banks: What Have We Learned from the Financial Crisis?', in M Dewatripont and X Freixas (eds), *The Crisis Aftermath: New Regulatory Paradigms* (London: CEPR, 2012), 11; R Herring and J Carmassi, 'The Corporate Structure of International Financial Conglomerates—Complexity and Its

the likelihood of imperfect market-based monitoring,[9] and the entrenched asymmetries of information and expertise between regulators and market participants. The resulting information problems make it relatively costly for regulators to detect malfeasance, negligence, or other socially undesirable activities. They also make it relatively easy for regulated actors to obscure the nature and extent of these activities.

The prudential supervision of banks and other large, complex financial institutions offers a compelling illustration of both the importance and challenges of intensive supervision.[10] As Eric Pan observes, the central role of prudential supervision as a means of ensuring the safety and soundness of financial institutions is a relatively recent development.[11] Indeed, until the mid-1990s, prudential supervision by the US Federal Reserve Board consisted primarily of periodic examinations to determine whether banks had complied with applicable regulatory requirements governing, for example, balance sheet composition and regulatory capital.[12] Over time, however, this 'traditional' approach towards prudential supervision—emphasizing as it did technical compliance with prescriptive rules—was undermined by the emergence of new financial markets and instruments (that is, structured finance, swaps, and other derivatives) which enabled financial institutions to engage in regulatory arbitrage: skirting the substantive spirit of these rules, while complying with their technical letter.[13] At the same time, institutional developments such as the gradual dilution and ultimate repeal of the Glass–Steagall Act in the US, so-called 'Big Bang' in the UK (see Chapter 7), and the single market for financial services in the EU, facilitated an increase in the size, international reach, and complexity of many financial services firms.

Predictably, these developments led to a corresponding increase in the costs of monitoring these large, complex, and constantly evolving institutions. Compounding matters, these institutions were viewed by regulators as the most likely sources and conduits for the transmission of systemic risk. Constrained by limited financial and human resources, regulators were thus forced to shift their focus from ensuring technical compliance to evaluating the risks generated by a firm's activities and prioritizing them against regulatory objectives. Pursuant to this new 'risk-based' approach to prudential supervision, firms and activities deemed to pose the greatest

---

Implications for Safety and Soundness', in A Berger, P Molyneux, and J Wilson (eds), *Oxford Handbook of Banking* (Oxford: OUP, 2012). For a discussion of the complexity of modern financial markets, see D Awrey, 'Complexity, Innovation and the Regulation of Modern Financial Markets' (2012) 2 *Harvard Business Law Review* 235.

[9] Owing to high information costs, collective action/free-rider problems, moral hazard, or the fact that financial stability is a public good.

[10] In addition to capital and liquidity (often referred to as 'Pillar 1'), the Basel rules also include a set of high-level principles and other guidance regarding effective supervisory processes (so-called 'Pillar 2').

[11] E Pan, 'Understanding Financial Regulation' [2012] *Utah Law Review* 1897, 1911.

[12] Ibid. See also L DeFerrari and D Palmer, 'Supervision of Large Complex Banking Organizations' (2001) 87 *Federal Reserve Bulletin* 47.

[13] See eg F Mishkin, 'Prudential Supervision: What is it and Why is it Important?', NBER Working Paper No 7926 (2001); D Jones, 'Emerging Problems with the Basel Capital Accord: Regulatory Capital Arbitrage and Related Issues' (2000) 24 *Journal of Money, Banking and Finance* 35.

risks—as measured by both their probability and likely impact—would then receive the highest level of supervisory scrutiny.[14]

There are three key elements of risk-based supervision.[15] First, regulators must *collect* information about regulated firms: their business lines, operations, assets, liabilities, governance, personnel, and internal processes, systems, and controls. This information can be extracted from publicly available information or periodic reports filed with regulators. It can also be obtained via requests for specific information, examinations, and on-site inspections conducted by supervisory personnel. Second, regulators must evaluate this information with a view to both identifying the risks generated by a firm's business model and, importantly, assessing the ability of its internal risk management systems to identify, measure, and manage these risks effectively. Third, where deficiencies in a firm's ability to manage these risks are identified, regulators must work with firms—principally through the provision of formal and informal guidance—to address these deficiencies.[16] In this context, risk-based supervision can be viewed as an *ex ante* strategy for identifying and addressing potential risks to institutional (microprudential) stability before they materialize.

Importantly, risk-based prudential supervision is characterized by the exercise of discretion and judgement by supervisory personnel. Supervisors must use their judgement in deciding what information to collect and evaluate. These judgements must be informed by—and, importantly, inform—their assessment of the risks posed by a firm's business model and whether or not it is able to effectively manage these risks. Supervisors must then use their judgement in prioritizing these risks and, consequently, allocating scarce supervisory resources. Supervisors are also frequently called upon to use their judgement in the context of decisions regarding, for example, the provision of substantive guidance to regulated firms, the imposition of the counter-cyclical capital buffer under Basel capital adequacy rules (discussed in Chapter 14), and the timing and execution of the resolution of a firm in financial distress (discussed in Chapter 16). The effective exercise of this discretion necessitates that supervisory personnel possess strong analytical skills and relevant experience, that they maintain close and continuous contact with regulated firms while preserving their objectivity and independence, and that they be willing to utilize their expertise and available information to second-guess and—where warranted—challenge firms' internal business judgements.

The exercise of discretion by supervisory personnel inevitably leads to concerns that their decisions may be biased, unpredictable, inconsistent, or simply wrong. It also raises the prospect of regulatory forbearance and, especially where supervisors are

---

[14] Such risk-based approaches are not confined to prudential supervision. The SEC, for example, employs a risk-based framework in connection with the conduct of business supervision of broker-dealers: see S Gadinis, 'The SEC and the Financial Industry: Evidence from Enforcement Against Broker Dealers' (2012) 67 *Business Lawyer* 679. For a discussion of risk-based regulation more generally, see R Baldwin and J Black, 'Really Responsive Risk-Based Regulation' (2010) 32 *Law and Policy* 181.

[15] Pan, n 11, 1913–14.

[16] Ibid; I van Lelyveld and A Schilder, *Risk in Financial Conglomerates: Management and Supervision*, Brookings-Wharton Papers on Financial Services (2003).

required to maintain close and continuous contact, regulatory capture.[17] Ultimately, however, the importance of discretion and judgement in risk-based prudential supervision is a reflection of both the resource constraints faced by regulators and the reality that it is simply unrealistic to expect them to write—or, crucially, update on a timely basis—a prudential rulebook capable of prescribing the most desirable course of action in every potential future state of the world in which market participants may find themselves.

The most important question, of course, is whether risk-based prudential supervision supports the advancement of regulatory objectives. Unfortunately, there is relatively little research on this topic, partly because it is difficult to identify both independent and outcome variables. Most of the work that has been done has used institutional characteristics of supervisors (that is, their structure, independence from and accountability to elected officials, and formal legal powers) to construct indices of supervisory 'quality'. For example, looking at bank supervisors in 107 jurisdictions, Barth, Caprio, and Levine find no statistically significant relationship between such measures of bank supervisor quality and financial development.[18] It is unclear, though, whether measures of bank profitability—a key dependent variable in Barth et al's study—are the best way to test for achievement of banking supervisory objectives. In the case of bank supervisors, the key objective will be financial stability, and the most profitable banks in good times might also be highly unstable. Barth et al also report similar results with 'number of financial crises' as a dependent variable, but a binary measure like this may be highly sensitive to the period studied. In contrast, Das, Quintyn, and Chenard report a positive correlation between indices of the quality of bank supervisors and continuous measures of financial stability based on capital adequacy ratios and the quality of banks' assets.[19]

A limitation of most of these studies is their focus solely on formal institutional factors to define regulatory 'quality'—as opposed to seeking to measure the actual intensity of risk-based supervision. In a notable exception, a recent study by Delis and Staikouras measures supervisory intensity by reference to number of on-site audits.[20] They report an inverse-U-shaped relationship between this measure and bank risk in subsequent years, suggesting that more intensive supervision is associated with reductions in risk-taking. Although this result is reassuringly consistent with intuition, even

---

[17] See Chapter 25 (esp section 25.4.1) for further discussion of capture, along with some of the governance strategies which might be employed to minimize it.

[18] J Barth, G Caprio, and R Levine, 'Bank Supervision and Regulation: What Works Best?' (2002) 13 *Journal of Financial Intermediation* 205. The authors' measures of supervisory authority included whether the relevant regulatory regime conferred upon supervisors the ability to, for example, take prompt corrective action, restructure distressed firms or declare them insolvent, or exercise a high degree of supervisory discretion. The authors' proxies for financial development, meanwhile, included credit receivables, bank profitability, and the number of financial crises. Similarly, Barth, Nolle, Phumiwasana, and Yago find no meaningful relationship between the structure, scope, and independence of bank supervisors and bank profitability: J Barth, D Nolle, T Phumiwasana, and G Yago, 'A Cross-Country Analysis of Bank Supervisory Framework and Bank Performance' (2003) 12 *Financial Markets, Institutions & Instruments* 67.

[19] U Das, M Quintyn, and K Chenard, 'Does Regulatory Governance Matter for Financial System Stability?: An Empirical Analysis', International Monetary Fund (IMF) Working Paper 04/89 (2004).

[20] M Delis and P Staikouras, 'Supervisory Effectiveness and Bank Risk' (2011) 15 *Review of Finance* 511.

these authors base their measure of supervisory intensity on a single, and therefore partial and arguably far from perfect, proxy—the number of on-site audits.

Another way to explore the relationship between supervisory intensity and regulatory outcomes is by looking at case studies. The failure of Northern Rock makes a potentially illuminating one. As we saw in Chapter 15, the proximate cause of Northern Rock's failure was a run on its wholesale funding during the early months of the global financial crisis. But why was Northern Rock so exposed to a disruption within wholesale funding markets? As described in a subsequent internal audit report by the UK Financial Services Authority ('FSA'), at least part of the answer to this question resides in the FSA's deficient supervisory strategy.[21] Between January 2005 and its failure in September 2007, responsibility for supervising the activities of Northern Rock was transferred amongst three different FSA departments, under the oversight of three different department heads.[22] Over this same period, FSA supervisory personnel met with the bank's management on a relatively infrequent basis. In fact, they met with management only eight times between January 2005 and August 2007—compared with an average of seventy-four times for other comparable firms over the same period.[23] More importantly, the FSA's internal audit report found that its supervisory personnel failed to conduct any in-depth financial analysis which might have uncovered the risks inherent to Northern Rock's business model and, specifically, its heavy reliance on short-term wholesale funding. The report was also highly critical of the levels of engagement, oversight, and challenge exhibited by front-line supervisors, their lack of expertise in prudential supervision and financial analysis, and the poor internal information flow between front-line supervisors and the FSA's senior management. The result was a supervisory strategy which deemed it a 'low' probability that Northern Rock would pose a risk to the statutory objectives under the FSA's risk-based prudential framework.[24]

The FSA's approach towards the supervision of Northern Rock was ultimately symptomatic of broader shortcomings in its risk-based supervisory strategy. As described in the Turner Review and the FSA's internal audit reports of the supervision of both Northern Rock and Royal Bank of Scotland ('RBS'), this strategy was characterized by the prioritization of conduct of business over prudential risks.[25] More specifically, the FSA was found to have devoted insufficient resources to monitoring and evaluating the capital, liquidity, asset quality, and leverage of investment banks and other systemically important institutions. At the same time, the FSA placed undue reliance on the senior management, internal audit, compliance, and risk management

---

[21] FSA, *Lessons Learned Review of the Supervision of Northern Rock plc during the Period 1 January 2005 to 9 August 2007* (2008). See, similarly, in relation to HBOS plc, PRA/FCA, *The Failure of HBOS plc (HBOS): A Report by the Financial Conduct Authority (FCA) and the Prudential Regulation Authority (PRA)*, November 2015, 247–78.

[22] Ibid. Indeed, between January 2005 and February 2007, Northern Rock was supervised by departments whose primary responsibility was for insurance—not banking—groups.

[23] Ibid.

[24] Ibid, 30. Of course, the fact that the risk actually materialized does not *in itself* mean that the FSA was not correct in assigning it a low probability.

[25] Ibid; FSA, *The Turner Review: A Regulatory Response to the Global Banking Crisis* (2009); FSA, *The Failure of Royal Bank of Scotland* (2012).

functions of regulated firms. It also relied on the flawed concept of a 'regulatory dividend' whereby firms were rewarded with less intensive supervision simply for achieving minimum standards of cooperation and regulatory compliance. All this raises an important question: could the failure of Northern Rock or RBS—or any of the other calamities which befell the UK financial sector between 2007 and 2009—have been prevented had the FSA pursued a different supervisory strategy?

Many of the deficiencies in the FSA's supervisory strategy were of course only apparent with the benefit of hindsight. This, in turn, highlights a crucial tension— and limit—at the heart of risk-based supervision. To take one example, the FSA's judgement that Northern Rock posed minimal risk to its statutory objectives resulted in a decrease in the resources allocated to the supervision of the firm's activities. This, however, undermined the ability of the FSA to detect any subsequent *changes* to the firm's business model—such as rapid loan growth, increased reliance on wholesale funding, and so forth—or risk profile—such as greater susceptibility to runs—which these changes might precipitate.

This has two important implications. First, there is a threshold level of intensity below which risk-based supervision will fail to successfully identify *new* risks. In at least some circumstances, however, we would expect the total costs associated with ensuring this threshold level of supervision across all regulated markets and institutions to exceed the financial and human resources of the relevant supervisors. As a result, supervisors will almost inevitably be called upon to make judgements about the probability and impact of potential risks armed with imperfect information. Second, and relatedly, it is unrealistic to expect that risk-based supervision can or should identify the build-up—let alone prevent the crystallization—of all the potential risks residing within the financial system.

A second potentially illuminating case study is the role of national supervisors in overseeing the implementation of, and ongoing compliance with, the international capital adequacy standards articulated by the Basel Committee on Banking Supervision. As described in Chapter 14, one of the most important determinants of whether these standards enhance institutional stability is the methodology used to calculate risk-weighted assets ('RWAs'). The Basel rules identify two alternative approaches: the *standardized* approach and the *internal ratings-based* ('IRB') approach. The standardized approach assigns predetermined risk weights on the basis of specified asset classes (or 'buckets'). The IRB approach, in contrast, permits firms to utilize their own internal quantitative models to classify and measure the key drivers of credit risk, subject to supervisors' approval and oversight.[26] The IRB approach is thus premised on the idea that firms with sufficiently robust risk management systems possess both the capacity and incentives to effectively measure and manage credit risk.

The IRB approach demands the exercise of considerable judgement and discretion by national supervisors. As a preliminary matter, supervisors must exercise good judgement in deciding which firms should be permitted to use the IRB approach. They must also make complex judgements in the context of evaluating and approving

---

[26] See Chapter 14, section 14.4.

the internal models employed by firms and ensuring that the RWAs that these models generate are consistent with regulatory objectives. In so doing, supervisors must be prepared to issue guidance to firms about the robustness of their models based on historical experience, vigorous stress testing, and more subjective assessments of the risks generated by a firm's business model. As is true of risk-based supervision more generally, the effective exercise of this judgement and discretion requires that supervisory personnel possess strong quantitative skills, relevant experience, and the institutional support to challenge regulated firms' internal risk assessments.

In evaluating the exercise of discretion by supervisors under the IRB approach, it is worthwhile observing that there often exist wide variations in the calculation of RWAs across firms. In 2009, for example, the FSA conducted a benchmarking exercise using a hypothetical portfolio of assets including fifty sovereign issuers, 100 banks, and 200 other large public companies.[27] Thirteen UK banks were asked to run the hypothetical portfolio through their internal models used to estimate probability of default—one of three key inputs in the calculation of RWAs. These banks were then required to report their probability of default for each asset to which they had an exposure. Using a sample of banks with overlapping exposures, the FSA found a large dispersion in estimated probabilities of default: with some banks' estimates three to six times higher than those of their peers.

In a 2012 study, the International Monetary Fund (IMF) similarly found significant variation in the calculation of RWAs across jurisdictions.[28] This variance may reflect differences in national regulatory regimes, accounting frameworks, firms' business models, and/or their lending, valuation, or provisioning practices.[29] As the IMF points out, however, one potentially important source of this variance may be national supervisory strategies.[30] It appears that differences in the financial and human resources of supervisors—or their subjective evaluation and prioritization of risks— may translate into material differences in their approaches towards the implementation and oversight of the IRB approach: that is, the level of scrutiny applied to the initial screening and ongoing monitoring, validation, and stress testing of firms' internal models. The same can equally be said of their approaches towards the implementation and ongoing monitoring of compliance with the Basel rules more generally. Put simply, differences in RWAs—and ultimately the amount of capital held by firms—may be driven, at least in part, by differences in the intensity of supervision.

It is impossible to explore all the dimensions of risk-based supervision in this chapter. What these two case studies illustrate, however, is the potential impact of effective supervision—or lack thereof—in terms of the advancement of regulatory objectives. Perhaps most importantly, the subjective judgements at the core of risk-

[27] FSA, 'Results of 2009 Hypothetical Portfolio Exercise for Sovereigns, Banks and Large Corporations' (2010).

[28] V La Leslé and S Avramova, 'Revisiting Risk-Weighted Assets: Why Do RWAs Differ Across Countries and What Can Be Done About It?' IMF Working Paper (March 2012). Unlike the FSA exercise, the IMF study did not focus solely on variations within the population of firms employing the IRB approach but also on firms employing the standardized approach. As a result, the relative propensity of supervisors in different jurisdictions to permit firms to use the IRB approach might itself be an important source of variance.

[29] Ibid.   [30] Ibid.

based supervision—about material risks, regulatory priorities, and the allocation of supervisory resources—can be important determinants of the effectiveness of substantive rules and, *in extremis*, even contribute to institutional instability and failure. As a corollary, differences in the intensity of supervision can be the source of significant functional divergence between national regulatory regimes. Moreover, these differences are often difficult to identify or measure objectively, thus complicating the already formidable challenge of making functional comparisons across jurisdictions.

Finally, it is worth briefly examining the evolving role of banking supervision in recent years. Two developments in particular stand out. The first is the increasing emphasis on so-called 'stress tests' as an integral part of the supervisory process.[31] Stress tests involve the construction of hypothetical scenarios which reflect a set of adverse circumstances—such as high market volatility, GDP and employment shocks, and sharp increases in bank funding costs—which fall *outside* the scenarios contemplated by banks' normal risk models. The balance sheets of banks are then subjected to simulations designed to assess their likely resilience in the event that these scenarios were to take place. Until recently, most stress tests were designed and conducted by banks themselves.[32] In the wake of the financial crisis, however, supervisors such as the US Federal Reserve Board, the UK Prudential Regulation Authority, and the European Central Bank have taken a more proactive role in the design and conduct of stress tests.[33] These tests have then been used as a basis for identifying potential capital shortfalls. Similar tests have also been used by macroprudential regulators to assess the resilience of broader banking systems.

Second, the information-gathering exercise at the heart of risk-based supervision plays an important role in ensuring the microprudential stability of banks and other financial institutions. It can also be a useful mechanism for uncovering undesirable conduct and practices. Increasingly, however, these same information-gathering exercises are playing an important role in the collection of data for the purposes of *macroprudential* supervision (see Chapter 19). Thus, for example, information gathered as part of the supervisory process regarding a bank's assets and liabilities, investment activities, and interconnections with other banks and markets can be aggregated with the same information for other banks to construct a more complete and accurate picture of the amount of leverage within the banking system, the asset classes into which banks are directing investment, and the potential channels for the transmission of systemic risk. This information can then be used by policy-makers to make more informed decisions about the use of various macroprudential policy tools.

---

[31] Stress tests are discussed further in Chapter 19, section 19.6.

[32] Indeed, the Market Risk Amendment to Basel I identified stress testing as an important part of effective internal risk management.

[33] See eg Federal Reserve Board, 'Stress Tests and Capital Planning', available at http://www.federalreserve. gov/bankinforeg/dfa-stress-tests.htm; Bank of England, 'Stress Testing', available at http://www. bankofengland.co.uk/financialstability/pages/fpc/stresstest.aspx, and European Central Bank, Aggregate Report on the Comprehensive Assessment (October 2014), available at https://www.bankingsupervision. europa.eu/banking/comprehensive/html/index.en.html.

26.3 The Dimensions of Enforcement

As with supervision, we might expect the intensity of enforcement to play an important role in the pursuit of regulatory objectives. Where the probability of successful enforcement is relatively low, or the sanctions imposed are not meaningful, regulation will be unlikely to generate a credible deterrent against undesirable conduct and practices or excessive risk-taking.[34] This, in turn, can undermine the goals of investor and consumer protection, the prevention of financial crime, or the maintenance of financial stability. But who are the parties best positioned to enforce financial regulation? What are the most effective sanctions and how should they be employed? Who should be the targets of enforcement action? And what are the differences in enforcement strategy across jurisdictions?

In order to address these important questions, we must first define what we mean by 'enforcement'. If we restrict our definition to formal legal enforcement, then our primary tools become administrative, criminal, or civil proceedings under the jurisdiction of a court or other tribunal.[35] One of the benefits of this narrow definition is that it enables us to draw a clear distinction between public and private enforcement. Public enforcement is initiated by organs of the state—for example, public regulatory authorities[36]—which are subject to both direct and indirect control by elected officials.[37] In theory, the potential advantages of enforcement undertaken by these public regulatory authorities flow from their mandated focus on the pursuit of regulatory objectives, their ability to coordinate their actions and compel information from regulated actors, and the fact that their enforcement arsenals often include powerful sanctions such as fines, disgorgement, de-licensing, and imprisonment.[38] In reality, however, public authorities can often be seen as possessing, at best, mixed incentives. These incentives may be the product of political interference, other political economy problems, or the fact that the compensation of enforcement personnel is often insensitive to the outcome of enforcement actions. Public authorities may also struggle with asymmetries of information vis-à-vis the regulated actors which their enforcement efforts target.

Private enforcement, in contrast, is initiated by plaintiffs—that is, investors or counterparties—suing under private rights of action. The potential benefits of private enforcement flow from the fact that it is undertaken by parties who are highly motivated by the prospect of compensation contingent upon either a successful verdict

---

[34] See sources cited in n 3. In many cases, high information costs combined with constraints on available regulatory resources will mean that the probability of detection and successful enforcement is relatively low—thus putting the burden on the nature and quantum of applicable sanctions.

[35] J Armour, 'Enforcement Strategies in UK Corporate Governance: A Roadmap and Empirical Assessment', in J Armour and J Payne (eds), *Rationality in Company Law* (Oxford: Hart Publishing, 2009), 71.

[36] Other modalities of public enforcement, broadly construed, may also include self-regulatory organizations such as FINRA, where these organizations are able to compel compliance with their rules *ex ante* or impose sanctions for violations of these rules *ex post*; Armour, Hansmann, and Kraakman, n 3.

[37] 'Direct' control in this context proceeds from the authority of elected officials as *lawmakers*, along with any governance mechanisms designed to ensure the accountability of regulators to these officials. 'Indirect' control, meanwhile, proceeds primarily from the power to control the *budgets* of regulators.

[38] This last advantage may be particularly important if we anticipate a low probability of detection and, as a result, a corresponding need to increase the expected penalty upon successful enforcement.

or settlement.[39] Moreover, insofar as we would expect these parties to be more sensitive than public regulatory authorities to the costs of enforcement, we would also expect any decrease in these costs to translate into an increase in the intensity of private, relative to public, enforcement.[40] In this respect, private enforcement can be understood as a potentially useful means of enhancing the resources that are brought to bear on ensuring vigorous enforcement of financial regulation.

Simultaneously, where the costs of enforcement are relatively high, we would expect this to be reflected in relatively low levels of private enforcement activity. Along this same vein, private enforcement may be hamstrung by collective action/free-rider problems amongst dispersed plaintiffs. In the US, plaintiff-side class action lawyers often play an important role in helping to ameliorate these problems. This, however, leaves the process susceptible to rent-seeking, as these lawyers often stand to receive a sizeable portion of any judgement or settlement. This may result in vexatious litigation—in effect the overproduction of private enforcement—rendering it less likely that regulated actors will voluntarily report potential violations.[41] Collectively, these problems may thus drive a wedge between private enforcement and the pursuit of public regulatory objectives.

Several empirical studies have attempted to measure the impact of both public and private enforcement on market outcomes. A 2006 study by La Porta, Lopez-de-Silanes, and Shleifer examining the impact of securities laws in forty-nine countries found a strong relationship between their proxies for private enforcement—such as mandatory disclosure requirements, liability rules, and the applicable burden of proof—and measures of stock market development.[42] Simultaneously, however, they found little evidence of a significant relationship between their proxies for public enforcement and these same measures. The authors interpret this evidence as supporting the hypothesis that disclosure requirements are efficient because issuers of securities and their advisors are the lowest cost producers of information. When coupled with liability rules and a burden of proof that make it less costly for investors to recover damages for misreporting, these requirements can thus be understood as enhancing the intensity of private enforcement: generating a more credible deterrent and, thereby, supporting market development.[43] A similar study by Djankov et al examining rules against self-dealing found a strong relationship between private—but not public—enforcement mechanisms and market development.[44] Viewed in isolation, these studies suggest that

---

[39] See eg JR Hay and A Shleifer, 'Private Enforcement of Public Laws: A Theory of Legal Reform' (1998) 88 *American Economic Review* 398.

[40] Armour, Hansmann, and Kraakman, n 3.

[41] Insofar as the quest for compensation also drives plaintiffs and their attorneys to focus on deep-pocketed defendants, it also skews the population of likely targets of private enforcement action.

[42] R La Porta, F Lopez-de-Silanes, and A Shleifer, 'What Works in Securities Laws?' (2006) 61 *Journal of Finance* 1.

[43] Supporting this interpretation, Hail and Leuz report that firms from countries with more extensive disclosure requirements, stronger securities laws, and stricter enforcement appear to enjoy a lower cost of equity capital; L Hail and C Leuz, 'International Differences in the Cost of Equity Capital: Do Legal Institutions and Securities Laws Matter?' (2005) 44 *Journal of Accounting Research* 485. Notably, Hail and Leuz use essentially the same proxies as La Porta, Lopez-de-Silanes, and Shleifer, n 42.

[44] S Djankov, R La Porta, F Lopez-de-Silanes, and A Shleifer, 'The Law and Economics of Self-Dealing' (2008) 88 *Journal of Financial Economics* 430. The variables Djankov et al use to measure private

the most constructive role for public regulatory authorities is to ensure that the relevant legal and regulatory frameworks support effective private enforcement.

A criticism of these and other similar studies is that they focus on formal legal mechanisms such as disclosure, liability rules, and available sanctions, along with the governance—that is, independence and accountability—of public regulatory authorities.[45] Indeed, while these proxies may represent a useful starting point, they fail to take into account other important determinants of the intensity of enforcement. The legal authority to impose wide-ranging and powerful sanctions, for example, is unlikely to matter if regulators do not also possess the human or financial resources necessary to uncover and successfully prosecute violations. Simultaneously, we might expect there to be some violations—such as insider trading and (trade-based) market manipulation— where the costs of monitoring and enforcement will discourage private litigation.[46] In such cases, we might thus envision an important role for public monitoring and enforcement. Finally, effective private enforcement may enhance public enforcement. James Cox and Randall Thomas, for example, find that the launch of an SEC enforcement action significantly increases the likelihood of subsequent private enforcement.[47]

For the most part, these and other similar studies examine the impact of enforcement in the context of substantive rules designed to promote investor protection. Clearly, however, we can ask similar questions about the role of enforcement in advancing other regulatory objectives. Take consumer protection, for example. Historically, rules designed to promote consumer protection have been enforced via a number of different channels, ranging from purely private rights of action for breach of contract, misrepresentation, and fraud; to consumer advocacy groups, self-regulatory organizations, and public regulatory authorities.[48] Intuitively, however, there are a number of reasons to think that private rights of action may be particularly ineffective in the consumer setting.

As a preliminary matter, the costs of private enforcement are often substantial in relation to both the extent of an individual consumer's loss and the resources available to them to pursue redress. As a result, effective private enforcement may be impeded by significant collective action and free-rider problems. Second, given that one of the objectives of consumer protection rules is to protect consumers from financial products

---

enforcement include disclosure and approval requirements, directors' and officers' duties, available causes of action, and access to information and discovery. The variables used to measure public enforcement, meanwhile, focus primarily on the range of sanctions available to public regulatory authorities.

[45] See eg J Armour, S Deakin, P Sarkar, M Siems, and A Singh, 'Shareholder Protection and Stock Market Development: An Empirical Test of the Legal Origins Hypothesis' (2009) 6 *Journal of Empirical Legal Studies* 343; H Spamann, 'The "Anti-Directors Rights Index" Revisited' (2010) 23 *Review of Financial Studies* 467. Crucially, these studies also do not establish a *causal* relationship between private enforcement and stock market development. It may be the case, for example, that robust stock markets give rise to powerful constituencies which demand stronger legal protections.

[46] M Polinsky and S Shavell, 'The Economic Theory of Public Enforcement of Law' (2000) 38 *Journal of Economic Literature* 45; U Bhattacharya and H Daouk, 'The World Price of Insider Trading' (2002) 57 *Journal of Finance* 75; L Beny, 'Do Insider Trading Laws Matter? Some Preliminary Comparative Evidence' (2005) 7 *American Law and Economics Review* 144.

[47] J Cox and R Thomas, 'SEC Enforcement Heuristics: An Empirical Inquiry' (2003) 53 *Duke Law Journal* 737.

[48] See eg S Bright, 'Winning the Battle Against Unfair Contract Terms' (2000) 20 *Legal Studies* 331.

and services designed to exploit their decision-making biases and lack of sophistication (discussed in Chapter 10), we also might expect them not to fully understand the protections that may be available to them. Indeed, they might not even understand that they are being exploited. While financial education and consumer advocacy groups can in some cases help tackle these problems, the effectiveness of these mechanisms is itself reliant on consumers being aware of their own biases and lack of sophistication, and thus of their need to seek out further information and advice. All this suggests that there may be some scope for public enforcement of consumer protection rules. It also helps frame the rationale for the creation of regulatory authorities such as the US Consumer Financial Protection Bureau ('CFPB'), designed to promote financial education, conduct research into consumer biases and how market participants attempt to exploit them, and enforce compliance with consumer protection rules.[49]

Ultimately, there is very little empirical work examining the relationship between the *intensity* of public enforcement of financial regulation and market outcomes. One relatively straightforward, albeit imperfect, way to measure intensity is to look at the budget and staffing levels of regulators.[50] In theory, higher budget and staffing levels should enable regulators to build expertise and dedicate more resources to monitoring and enforcement.[51] Using these variables as proxies, Jackson and Roe find a statistically significant relationship between public enforcement and market capitalization, trading volumes, and the number of initial public offerings.[52] Moreover, in a horse race between public and private enforcement, the authors find that public enforcement is at least as important as disclosure requirements and more important than liability rules in explaining market outcomes.[53]

Understanding the impact of public enforcement becomes even more challenging if we expand our definition of 'enforcement' to include the entire range of potential sanctions available to regulators. These sanctions typically include formal administrative sanctions such as business restrictions and the suspension and revocation of regulatory licences. They also include less invasive, more informal sanctions such as moral suasion, guidance, warning letters, and heightened regulatory scrutiny. For the most part, these sanctions are imposed outside the context of formal legal proceedings.[54] When combined with formal legal sanctions, the existence of this broader universe of potential sanctions thus raises at least two important questions. First, how should we conceptualize the relationship between the various sanctions in the regulatory toolkit? Second, when should regulators adopt an accommodative or

---

[49] On the CFPB's approach, see LJ Kennedy, PA McCoy, and E Bernstein, 'The Consumer Financial Protection Bureau: Financial Regulation for the Twenty-First Century' (2012) 97 *Cornell Law Review* 1141.

[50] For a recent study employing this approach, see T Loshse, R Pascalau, and C Thomann, 'Public Enforcement of Securities Market Rules: Resource-Based Evidence from the Securities and Exchange Commission' (2014) 106 *Journal of Economic Behavior and Organization* 197.

[51] See H Jackson, 'Variation in the Intensity of Finance Regulation: Preliminary Evidence and Potential Implications' (2007) 24 *Yale Journal on Regulation* 101. Of course, such 'resource-based' variables manifest their own shortcomings.

[52] H Jackson and M Roe, 'Public and Private Enforcement of Securities Laws: Resource-Based Evidence' (2009) 93 *Journal of Financial Economics* 279.

[53] As with La Porta, Lopez-de-Silanes, and Shleifer, n 42, Jackson and Roe's study does not establish a *causal* relationship between the intensity of public enforcement and market outcomes.

[54] It is here that the overlap between supervision and enforcement is perhaps most readily apparent.

cooperative approach towards encouraging regulatory compliance, and when should they bare their teeth?[55]

Ian Ayres and John Braithwaite, for example, advocate a tit-for-tat enforcement strategy characterized by the incremental escalation of regulatory sanctions.[56] At the core of this strategy is a clearly defined hierarchy—or pyramid—of sanctions: starting at the base with informal persuasion and education; moving up to more formal warning letters; followed by civil and then criminal penalties; and, at the apex, the suspension and revocation of regulatory licences. Pursuant to this strategy, regulators would respond to inadvertent, less serious, or first-time violations with sanctions at the base of the pyramid designed to promote long-term compliance and cooperation. As violations become more wilful, serious, or frequent, however, regulators would shift focus from these compliance-oriented sanctions towards more severe, legalistic sanctions designed to punish violators and generate a credible deterrent. As Ayres and Braithwaite point out, the success of this strategy thus hinges on regulators striking a delicate balance between encouraging voluntary compliance and sending a credible signal that they are willing and able, if necessary, to take more aggressive enforcement action.[57] Insofar as this or other similar strategies are not reflected in our measures of the intensity of enforcement, we may fail to capture a potentially important part of the broader enforcement picture.

Expanding our definition of enforcement even further, we might also consider the role of market-based reputational sanctions. In theory, the revelation that market participants have violated regulatory rules, exploited their customers or clients, or engaged in excessive risk-taking may make others less likely to do business with them in the future. In practice, however, the existence and extent of such reputational sanctions are often obscured by the presence of confounding factors that make it difficult to disentangle reputational from other losses. Armour, Mayer, and Polo examine the impact of the announcement of enforcement actions by the London Stock Exchange (LSE) and FSA on the market price of penalized firms.[58] The authors find that these announcements generate significant reputational sanctions: with the average stock price impact almost nine times larger than the relevant financial penalties. The authors also find that reputational sanctions are confined to misconduct that harms parties who traded with the penalized firm.[59] Conversely, the announcement of sanctions for conduct that harmed third parties had a weakly positive effect.[60] More broadly, the existence and potential welfare implications of reputational sanctions are still somewhat controversial. Some see these market-based sanctions as magnifying the

---

[55] Or as Ayres and Braithwaite characterize this question: 'When to punish; when to persuade?': n 6.
[56] Ibid.   [57] Ibid.
[58] J Armour, C Mayer, and A Polo, 'Regulatory Sanctions and Reputational Damage in Financial Markets' (forthcoming 2016) 51 *Journal of Financial and Quantitative Analysis*. These announcements provide an exceptionally clear signal because the FSA and LSE only announce the existence of an investigation once they have established a violation and imposed financial and other penalties.
[59] The authors also find that the failure rate of unlisted firms sanctioned by the FSA was higher than a sample of firms which were not subject to sanctions; ibid.
[60] As the authors note, one implication of this is that financial penalties should be much larger for misconduct which harms third parties; ibid.

deterrent effect of formal legal enforcement. Others, however, doubt their existence or, alternatively, see them as a source of deadweight losses, as they reduce the capacity of the firm to pay compensation to injured parties.

Ultimately, of course, it is not just the sources of enforcement activity that matter. The targets of enforcement action are also important. In a perfect world, individuals would be held directly responsible for their actions, thus ensuring that the costs of their misconduct were fully internalized.[61] In the real world, however, enforcement action is often targeted at regulated firms.[62] Such firm-level enforcement is important insofar as it generates incentives for the firm to put in place effective processes, systems, and controls designed to ensure regulatory compliance. Firms also often have deep pockets out of which to pay fines or compensate injured parties. At the same time, however, we might expect firm-level enforcement to be a relatively ineffective way of deterring misconduct such as fraud which is both privately motivated and relatively difficult to detect.[63] Moreover, especially in the context of private enforcement, the costs of imposing firm-level liability will often be borne by diversified shareholders.[64]

Crucially, these costs include the premiums paid by firms for directors' and officers' (D&O) insurance, the net effect of which is typically to insulate senior management from personal liability.[65] This, in turn, can be seen as generating moral hazard. While D&O insurance policies often provide a carve-out for violations of applicable securities laws, these carve-outs do not generally apply unless the defendant expressly admits liability.[66] Perversely, this makes it in both sides' interest to settle without admission of liability.[67] Some have suggested that addressing this problem—for example, by insisting on admissions of liability in conjunction with settlement agreements[68]—would

---

[61] J Coffee, 'Reforming the Securities Class Action: An Essay on Deterrence and Its Implementation' (2006) 106 *Columbia Law Review* 1534; J Armour and JN Gordon, 'Systemic Harms and Shareholder Value' (2014) 6 *Journal of Legal Analysis* 35, 61–76.

[62] We might expect this to be especially true of enforcement actions against larger firms, where disentangling proportional responsibility may be very difficult. In a study of SEC enforcement actions against investment banks and other broker-dealers, for example, Gadinis finds that as the size of the defendant firm *increases*, the likelihood that the SEC will also bring an action against individual employees *decreases*; Gadinis, n 14.

[63] Coffee, n 61.

[64] Ibid. As Coffee explains, diversified shareholders will often belong to both the plaintiff class and the class of shareholders who must pay the costs of mounting the defence (essentially because they purchased stock both inside and outside the relevant class period). As a result, private enforcement can result in pocket-to-pocket transfers. Importantly, we would expect these transfers to result in deadweight losses after accounting for legal fees, business interruption, adverse publicity, and increased D&O insurance premiums.

[65] Examining 3,239 federal securities class actions filed between 1991 and 2004, for example, Black, Cheffins, and Klausner identified only thirteen settlements in which outside directors made out-of-pocket payments; B Black, B Cheffins, and M Klausner, 'Outside Director Liability' (2006) 58 *Stanford Law Review* 1055. Karpoff et al, in contrast, find that managers suffer significant personal consequences—eg through job loss, restrictions on future employment, reductions in the market value of their shares, fines, and criminal penalties—following enforcement actions by the SEC or US Department of Justice for accounting related offences; J Karpoff, S Lee, and G Martin, 'The Consequences to Managers of Financial Misrepresentation' (2008) 88 *Journal of Financial Economics* 193.

[66] Coffee, n 61.

[67] See generally, T Baker and SJ Griffith, *Ensuring Corporate Misconduct: How Liability Insurance Undermines Shareholder Litigation* (Chicago: University of Chicago Press, 2010), Chs 7–8.

[68] Notably, the SEC in 2013 announced a shift in its settlement policy pursuant to which it now requires an admission of liability from defendants in certain circumstances; see B Carton, 'SEC to Require Admissions of Wrongdoing in Settlements of Most Egregious Cases', *Compliance Week* (19 June 2013).

Table 26.1 Measures of securities' regulators inputs (by jurisdiction)

Jurisdiction	Securities budget/ market cap ($/bn)	Securities budget/ GDP ($/bn)	Staffing/ million population
Australia	$279,587	$89,217	34.44
Canada	$220,515	$82,706	38.93
United Kingdom	$138,159	$80,902	19.04
United States	$83,943	$83,232	23.75
Hong Kong	$73,317	$320,531	59.59
France	$19,041	$28,852	5.91
Germany	$8,896	$12,903	4.43

Sources: Jackson, n 51, 269 (securities budgets/market capitalization, data from 2004) and Jackson and Roe, n 52, 214–15 (securities budgets/GDP and staffing/millions of population, data from 2006–7).

Table 26.2 Measures of regulatory outputs (aggregate figures for 2002–4)

Jurisdiction	Number of public actions	Public actions: Sanctions ($m)	Private lawsuits: Sanctions ($m)
United States	3,624	$5,287	$3,499
United Kingdom	72	$27	n/a

Source: Jackson, n 51, 280, 283.

discourage highly qualified individuals from standing as directors or officers. Ultimately, however, there is little reliable evidence against which to evaluate whether or not this is likely to be the case. The broader point here is that, intuitively, we would expect the impact of enforcement as both a credible deterrent and source of compensation to depend, at least in part, on the identity of parties against whom enforcement is sought.

Having examined various dimensions of public and private enforcement, an interesting and important question becomes whether we observe significant differences in the intensity of enforcement across jurisdictions. Once again, our ability to answer this question with any certainty is undermined by limitations on available data. Nevertheless, Table 26.1 presents summary measures of the regulatory resources—or 'inputs'—available to securities regulators in several jurisdictions. While crude (and now quite dated), these measures provide us with a potentially useful snapshot of the relative differences between these regulators in terms of the financial and human resources which might be devoted to ensuring effective enforcement.

Another potentially useful set of proxies for measuring the intensity of enforcement are 'outputs' such as the number of enforcement actions brought by regulators and the quantum of financial penalties imposed on regulated actors.[69] Table 26.2 presents measures of regulatory outputs for the US and the UK.

---

[69] JC Coffee, Jr, 'Law and the Market: The Impact of Enforcement' (2007) 156 *University of Pennsylvania Law Review* 229.

How should we interpret these measures? As a preliminary matter, we need to acknowledge the limits of what they can tell us. In terms of resource-based measures, the fact that regulators possess ample resources does not guarantee that they will be deployed towards vigorous monitoring and enforcement.[70] It is also difficult to make apples-to-apples comparisons given the wide variance between jurisdictions in terms of both the structure of domestic financial services sectors (such as the extent to which finance is intermediated through financial markets versus institutions) and the institutional structure of banking, securities, and insurance regulation (see Chapter 24).[71] Output-based measures, on the other hand, can be understood as sending something of an ambiguous signal: with low output levels potentially reflecting either poor enforcement or effective deterrence. Finally, we cannot rule out the possibility that differences in these measures across jurisdictions reflect underlying differences in the optimal policy response given local market conditions.

On a more substantive level, the first thing one is likely to notice is that while private enforcement plays a significant role in the US, it is essentially non-existent in the UK.[72] Second, at least on the basis of outputs, the intensity of public enforcement has historically been far higher in the US than in the UK. Indeed, even after adjusting for market size, the number of public regulatory actions brought and the quantum of monetary sanctions imposed remained several times higher.[73] One explanation for this divergence is that these output-based measures fail to capture important differences in regulatory strategy.[74] Over the relevant period, for example, many have pointed out that the FSA pursued a deliberate policy of attempting to resolve matters within the context of day-to-day supervisory relationships wherever possible—resorting to formal enforcement action in response to only the most egregious violations.[75] Viewed from this perspective, low levels of formal enforcement might thus reflect a broader strategic decision to focus on promoting voluntary compliance and engagement with regulated actors and may tell us less than they appear to about overall effectiveness.

Two observations cut against this view. First, the internal audit reports into the failures of Northern Rock and RBS were highly critical of the FSA's *lack* of engagement. Second, if this was indeed the FSA's strategy, it appears to have abandoned it in the wake of the crisis. Whereas the FSA levied sanctions amounting to $27 million between 2002 and 2004, its successor—the Financial Conduct Authority (FCA)—levied £425 million in

---

[70] Conversely, a poorly resourced but highly motivated regulator may make good use of the resources it has at its disposal: Jackson and Roe, n 52.

[71] Along the same vein, the data in Table 26.1 relate only to securities regulators—not banking or insurance regulators.

[72] In reality, the US is a global outlier in this regard: see Coffee, n 69. Empirical research conducted by John Armour corroborates the data in Table 26.2: while private rights of action against a firm's directors for making false or misleading statements exist in the UK, Armour finds only two instances of actions being brought between 1990 and 2006: see Armour, n 35. This is likely due to differences in both substantive law and litigation funding rules.

[73] Jackson, n 51.

[74] K Cearns and E Ferran, 'Non-Enforcement Led Public Oversight of Financial and Corporate Governance Disclosure of Auditors' (2008) 8 *Journal of Corporate Law Studies* 191; Coffee, n 69.

[75] Cearns and Ferran, n 74.

2013/14, and over £1.4 *billion* in 2014/15.[76] Of course, it remains to be seen whether this dramatic change in the intensity of enforcement will be sustained over the longer term.

A second explanation is that these measures fail to reflect differences in the use of market-based reputational sanctions. Specifically, it may be the case that regulators that impose fewer or smaller financial penalties rely more heavily on reputational sanctions.[77] Ultimately, however, the key takeaway is that while the law on the books may be converging in many areas, the intensity with which those laws are enforced may still vary significantly across jurisdictions. This, in turn, has important implications in terms of the effective equivalence of financial regulation in different countries.

26.4 The Relationship between Regulation, Supervision, and Enforcement

Clearly, supervision and enforcement do not exist independently of one another. The precise nature of their relationship, however, depends somewhat on one's perspective. Viewed solely from the perspective of generating a credible deterrent, for example, supervision and enforcement are effectively *substitutes*. Generating a credible deterrent necessitates simply that the expected costs of undesirable conduct and practices exceed the expected benefits. As we have seen, the relevant costs are a function of the probability that supervision will uncover misconduct, the likelihood that enforcement action will be brought and successfully prosecuted, and the quantum of the penalties thereby imposed. Theoretically, then, policymakers can increase the risk-adjusted costs of engaging in undesirable activities by ratcheting up the intensity of either supervision or enforcement. Like all substitutes, we would expect policymakers to decide which of the two to adjust on the basis of their relative costs.

Viewed from a different and perhaps more nuanced perspective, however, supervision and enforcement can be understood as potential *complements*. Effective supervision, for example, will in many contexts rely on the credible background threat of formal enforcement. Indeed, the success of both Ayres' and Braithwaite's enforcement pyramid and principles-based regulation (discussed in Chapter 24) implicitly relies on a measured, predictable, and credible enforcement threat to promote meaningful engagement, cooperation, and dialogue on the part of regulated actors. Successful enforcement, meanwhile, is often predicated on the existence of highly expert and well-informed regulatory personnel. In many cases, this information and expertise are acquired through interactions with regulated actors in the context of day-to-day supervisory relationships.

Lastly, let us briefly explore the relationship between the intensity of supervision and enforcement and substantive policy choices. While there are many facets to this relationship, there are two in particular that warrant our attention. First, as we have seen, an unfortunate by-product of substantive policy choices such as the provision of

---

[76] See *FCA Annual Report 2013/14*, and *FCA Annual Report 2014/15*, all available at http://www.fca.org. uk.

[77] Armour, Mayer, and Polo, n 58. These regulators could, for example, dedicate resources towards ensuring that news of violations is widely disseminated within the marketplace.

deposit guarantee schemes, mandatory central clearing of OTC derivatives, and bail-outs for systemically important financial institutions is the generation of moral hazard. In such circumstances, increasing the intensity of supervision can play an important role in curbing any socially excessive risk-taking engendered by these policies. Conversely, however, the expectation that systemically important financial institutions will inevitably be bailed out may also lead to moral hazard on the part of regulators, thereby undermining their incentives to engage in intensive supervision. Second, policy choices designed to constrain the size and shape of regulated firms—such as the measures for structural reform of the banking sector discussed in Chapter 23—may have a positive impact on the intensity of supervision and enforcement. Specifically, insofar as these structural policies reduce the complexity of these firms, and thus the costs of effectively monitoring their activities, they may make it easier for regulators to identify undesirable conduct and practices. Ultimately, understanding the dynamics of the multifaceted relationship between substantive policy choices, supervision, and enforcement is important if we are to design effective supervisory and enforcement strategies.

26.5 Conclusion

This chapter has examined the role that supervision and enforcement play in financial regulation. It has shown how the intensity of supervision and enforcement are important determinants of whether substantive policy choices are able to advance regulatory objectives. It has also demonstrated how differences in the intensity of supervision or enforcement can be the source of significant divergence between national regulatory regimes despite the convergence in the law on-the-books. Finally, it has explored the relationship between substantive policy choices, supervision, and enforcement, along with how understanding this relationship can pay dividends in terms of the design of effective supervisory and enforcement strategies.

27

Regulatory Architecture:

What Matters?

27.1 Introduction

In Chapter 24, we introduced Part F with a review of the way in which the architecture of financial regulation—that is, the way in which regulatory power is allocated as between one or more agencies—is set up in the US, the UK, and the EU. As part of that scene-setting exercise, we described the current institutional structures in these jurisdictions. In Chapters 25 and 26, respectively, we then reviewed the challenges faced by regulators from a political economy perspective, and the design choices over strategies of supervision and enforcement. We now consider questions of regulatory architecture from a normative perspective in light of these issues.

A central idea in this chapter is that the way in which we think about regulatory architecture has changed significantly in response to the financial crisis. This emerges in two steps. The first is in section 27.2, where we consider the debate, dating from before the financial crisis, about the respective merits of various horizontal models of regulatory architecture—institutional, functional,[1] integrated, objective-based, and so forth. However, none of the various models of regulatory architecture fared particularly well in the financial crisis. We review why this was the case. It is hard to resist the inference that the choice of regulatory architecture, at least insofar as the question was framed before the crisis, made little difference for financial stability.

Of course, the strength of this inference should not be overstated. It can only be drawn as respects models that were actually in operation prior to the crisis.[2] As we have noted at various points so far, one of the big changes in regulation spurred by the crisis has been the advent of macroprudential oversight. For a macroprudential authority ('MPA') to operate effectively, it must be able to prioritize financial stability over other regulatory goals when necessary. This implies a hierarchical regulatory structure. In contrast, pre-crisis regulatory models differed largely over the horizontal allocation of subject-matter jurisdiction, and had little difference along the vertical—hierarchical—dimension we argue is important for an MPA. We suggest that the way choices across this dimension are implemented, in contrast, may have the potential to make a significant difference to outcomes.

The second step is therefore to consider choices regarding the vertical allocation of jurisdiction, and in particular, responsibility for macroprudential oversight, in section 27.3. Although the US, the UK, and the EU have each sought to create a new MPA with

---

[1] For the use of the word 'functional' in this context, see n 4 and Chapter 24, section 24.2.1.
[2] Moreover, it implicitly assumes that the level of resources invested in executing these approaches was equivalent. Chapter 24, section 24.2.2 casts doubt on this.

Principles of Financial Regulation. First Edition. John Armour, Dan Awrey, Paul Davies, Luca Enriques, Jeffrey N. Gordon, Colin Mayer, and Jennifer Payne. © John Armour, Dan Awrey, Paul Davies, Luca Enriques, Jeffrey N. Gordon, Colin Mayer, and Jennifer Payne 2016. Published 2016 by Oxford University Press.

responsibility for 'MacroPru' oversight, the scope of these new agencies' oversight, and the extent to which their relationship with other regulators is hierarchical, differ considerably. This clearly points to the possibility that some may be better placed to preserve financial stability than others. Nevertheless, we note that, notwithstanding these formal differences as regards MPAs, central banks are probably the primary actors in MacroPru oversight in each of these systems. What is more, this seems appropriate: central banks appear best placed of any agency to manage the analysis of complex intersecting issues that MacroPru entails.

27.2　The Horizontal Allocation of Subject-Matter Jurisdiction

27.2.1　The pre-crisis debate

We reviewed various models for the allocation of subject-matter jurisdiction in Chapter 24, section 24.2.1. Historically, the organizational structure of financial regulation in many jurisdictions reflected the fragmented structure of the domestic financial services industry.[3] This typically resulted in either an *institutional* or a *functional* model of regulatory architecture, or some mixture of both.[4] As such, the division of regulatory jurisdiction was largely horizontal—different regulators covering different parts of the financial system. Because these parts were thought to be largely independent of one another, there was little perceived need to consider whether the goals of these regulators might conflict with one another, or to establish some element of vertical allocation of jurisdiction, or hierarchy (beyond the standard idea about the relationship between public regulatory agencies and self-regulatory organizations).[5]

To be sure, dividing regulatory responsibility amongst multiple agencies gives each agency the opportunity to develop specialist subject-matter expertise. But the more agencies there are, the greater the costs of sharing information between them and coordinating their activities. These problems are exacerbated by the increasing interconnection of the financial system and the emergence of mammoth financial conglomerates.[6]

An alternative model is an *objectives*- or *goal-based* institutional architecture, allocating responsibility according to regulatory objectives. This model responds to the challenge of interconnection by explicitly acknowledging that particular firms and activities might be supervised by more than one agency, but with differing agendas determined by the agencies' respective goals. As initially conceived, it was described as a 'twin peaks' model, envisaging two agencies, one responsible for prudential supervision

---

[3]　HM Schooner and M Taylor, *Global Bank Regulation: Principles and Policies* (London: Elsevier, 2010).

[4]　See Chapter 24, section 24.2. The institutional model allocates regulatory responsibility on the basis of distinctions between different types of regulated *financial institutions*—that is, banks, securities dealers, or insurance companies—irrespective of the nature of the activities actually undertaken by these firms. The functional model, conversely, contemplates the allocation of responsibility on the basis of the nature of the *financial activity*, regardless of institutional type.

[5]　Discussed in Chapter 24, section 24.4.

[6]　See eg C Briault, 'The Rationale for a Single National Financial Services Regulator', FSA Occasional Paper No 2 (1999), 12–17.

and stability and the other for consumer protection.[7] However, there is no inherent limit to two objectives: Charles Goodhart and co-authors, for example, advanced a version of this model structured around six objectives.[8]

Although the objective-based model was adopted by some jurisdictions, including Australia and the Netherlands,[9] it was initially eclipsed by a yet more radical innovation—the so-called *unified* or *integrated* model, under which a single 'mega-agency' is responsible for covering all sectors, and all goals, of financial regulation. Proponents argued that this not only responded to the challenge of interconnection, but also avoided the duplication of oversight costs that would be necessitated by the twin peaks model.[10] This model was adopted in a number of other jurisdictions, such as the UK, Germany, Japan, Ireland, and Iceland.[11]

27.2.2 The complex US system

The US system is instructive as a case study, because perhaps nowhere else have the challenges of dividing regulatory responsibility between multiple specialist agencies been more clearly evident. Prior to the financial crisis, the US regulatory architecture reflected a history-dependent mixture of both the functional and institutional models.[12] Responsibility for various aspects of the regulation of banking activities was shared between no less than four federal agencies: the Federal Reserve (the 'Fed'), the Office of the Comptroller of the Currency ('OCC'), the Federal Deposit Insurance Corporation ('FDIC'), and the Office of Thrift Supervision ('OTS')—not to mention state banking regulators. The Securities and Exchange Commission ('SEC') and the Commodity Futures Trading Commission ('CFTC'), meanwhile, split responsibility for most financial markets, although the regulation of over-the-counter ('OTC') derivatives markets fell largely under the jurisdiction of the Fed and the OCC.

Unsurprisingly, this complex system was characterized by mismatches of regulatory responsibilities. In some instances, institutional allocation of jurisdiction led to oversight by agencies that did not have the requisite competencies. For example, in 2004 the

---

[7] MW Taylor, *Twin Peaks: A Regulatory Structure for the New Century* (London: Centre for the Study of Financial Innovation, 1995).

[8] C Goodhart, P Hartmann, D Llewellyn, L Rojas-Suarez, and S Weisbrod, *Financial Regulation: Why, How, and Where Now?* (London: Routledge, 1998). Their list was as follows: systemic risk, non-systemic prudential, retail conduct of business, wholesale conduct of business, financial exchange, and competition regulation.

[9] See Group of 30, *The Structure of Financial Supervision: Approaches and Challenges in a Global Marketplace* (Group of Thirty: Washington DC, 2008), 30–1.

[10] Briault, n 6.

[11] M Čihák and R Podpiera, 'Is One Watchdog Better Than Three? International Experience with Integrated Financial Sector Supervision', IMF Working Paper 06/57 (2006), http://www.imf.org. Inevitably, institutional frameworks based on the integrated model vary significantly across jurisdictions. One important dimension across which variance can be observed was the relationship between integrated regulators and central banks. In some jurisdictions (eg Ireland), the regulator was subsumed within the organizational structure of the central bank. In others (eg the UK prior to the crisis), the two were legally and functionally independent.

[12] See discussion in E Murphy, Congressional Research Service, 'Who Regulates Whom and How? An Overview of US Financial Regulatory Policy for Banking and Securities Markets', CRS Report 7-5700 (2013); compare GAO, *Financial Regulation: Industry Changes Prompt Need to Reconsider US Regulatory Structure*, GAO-05-61 (2004), 5.

SEC assumed responsibility for the consolidated prudential supervision of certain large investment banking conglomerates—including any affiliates undertaking banking, derivatives, or other activities—under the Consolidated Supervised Entities ('CSE') Program.[13] These firms were not deposit-taking banks, nor were they part of banking groups (that is, owned by bank holding companies). As a result, they did not fall within the prudential bailiwick of any of the banking regulators. The SEC agreed to take on their prudential oversight because these firms were subject to its regulation as regards their market activities as broker-dealers. At the same time, the investment banks ultimately subject to the CSE Program were eager not to fall under the supervisory jurisdiction of the Fed. Unfortunately, the issues of systemic risk raised by their activities were not something in which SEC officials had much background.[14]

Under an institutional or functional model, various regulators may be pursuing a similar list of goals, but using different tactics to implement them. This creates particular problems for coordination in cases of regulatory overlap, a frequent occurrence in the US. Despite the existence of several formal and informal mechanisms intended to promote information flow and interagency coordination,[15] US regulators did not always work well together. For example, even within the banking sector, the OTS and FDIC failed to coordinate their supervisory approaches in connection with the oversight of Superior Bank FSB, which failed in July 2001 with approximately $1.6 billion in insured deposits.[16]

On other occasions, the multiplicity of specialist agencies resulted in pronounced gaps (or 'underlaps') in regulation. The lack of clear regulatory authority over OTC derivatives markets prior to the enactment of the Commodity Futures Modernization Act 2000 is one prominent example. Between 1974 and 2000, neither the SEC nor the CFTC had clear authority to regulate the growing markets for OTC derivatives. At the same time, neither agency wanted the other to assume authority, resulting in an interagency turf war. Complicating matters further, the so-called 'Treasury Amendment' to the Commodity Futures Trading Commission Act of 1974, which created the CFTC, was thought by many to grant the Federal Reserve and OCC authority over the regulation of OTC derivatives.[17] The Commodity Futures Modernization Act 2000 effectively prohibited the SEC and CFTC from intervening to regulate these new markets, thus leaving the field entirely to the Fed and OCC. However, neither of these agencies took a proactive approach to identifying or monitoring the build-up of risk within OTC derivatives markets.

---

[13] Amongst the firms subject to consolidated supervision by the SEC under the CSE Program were Bear Stearns and Lehman Brothers. For a critical evaluation of this program, see SEC Office of the Inspector General, 'SEC's Oversight of Bear Stearns and Related Entities: The Consolidated Supervised Entities Program' (2008). The CSE Program was abolished in 2008: see SEC, 'Chairman Cox Announces End of Consolidated Supervised Entities Program', SEC Press Release 2008-230 (26 September 2008).

[14] See K Judge, 'The First Year: The Role of a Modern Lender of Last Resort' (forthcoming 2016) 116 *Columbia Law Review.*

[15] These mechanisms included, for example, the Federal Financial Institutions Examination Council, created in 1979 in order to coordinate federal regulation of lending activities.

[16] Remarkably, the OTS (as lead supervisor) refused to permit the FDIC (as deposit insurer) to participate in examinations; see GAO, n 12, 15.

[17] See D Awrey, 'The FSA, Integrated Regulation and the Curious Case of OTC Derivatives' (2010) 13 *University of Pennsylvania Journal of Business Law* 101.

Perhaps more importantly, prior to the financial crisis, no single agency was responsible for identifying, monitoring, or taking action to address risks to the financial system as a whole. Indeed, the growth of market-based credit intermediation, which we described in Chapter 20, was in part the result of a particular sort of regulatory competition, described as 'regulatory clientelism', as the bank regulators and the SEC each fostered regulatory changes that favoured their client regulatees.[18] The SEC's regulatory exemption that gave rise to money market funds favoured securities firms at the expense of banks. No umbrella regulator considered the systemic consequences of these far-reaching changes.[19]

27.2.3 The unified UK system

The division of regulatory responsibilities in the US prior to the financial crisis had emerged from historical distinctions between the banking, financial markets, and insurance industries. By the end of the twentieth century, this looked increasingly cumbersome in light of the growing interconnections within the financial system. This stimulated innovation in regulatory architecture. One such innovation was the unified or integrated approach, the standard-bearer for which was in most people's eyes the UK's Financial Services Authority ('FSA').

The FSA came into being in June 2000 following the enactment of the Financial Services and Markets Act 2000. It unified a fragmented institutional structure under which responsibilities had been divided between the Bank of England (for the prudential supervision of deposit-taking institutions) and a two-tiered system of designated agencies and self-regulatory organizations (responsible for consumer and investor protection, market conduct, and other regulation governing the securities, futures, investment management, and insurance industries).[20] The FSA was responsible for writing, monitoring, and enforcing compliance with prudential, conduct of business, and other rules across the banking, securities, and insurance industries. Responsibility for financial stability was shared between the FSA (as prudential regulator), the Bank of England (as lender of last resort—'LOLR'), and the Treasury (as overseer of the regulatory structure and source of any implicit state guarantee).[21]

---

[18] D Langevoort, 'Statutory Obsolescence and the Judicial Process: The Revisionist Role of the Courts in Federal Banking Regulation' (1987) 85 *Michigan Law Review* 672.

[19] See JN Gordon, 'The Empty Call for Benefit-Cost Analysis' (2014) 43 *Journal of Legal Studies* S351, S361–S364.

[20] This two-tier system proceeded from the delegation of powers by the (then) Department of Trade and Industry to private sector designated agencies such as the Securities and Investment Board ('SIB') (the first tier). Under the authorization and oversight of the SIB, day-to-day regulatory responsibility then fell to authorized self-regulatory organizations. See generally, E Ferran, 'Examining the UK's Experience in Adopting the Single Financial Regulator Model' (2003) 28 *Brooklyn Journal of International Law* 257; MW Taylor, 'The Road from "Twin Peaks"—and the Way Back' (2010) 16 *Connecticut Insurance Law Journal* 61, 65–72.

[21] This division of labour was articulated in the Tripartite Memorandum of Understanding between HM Treasury, the Bank of England, and the FSA, available at http://www.fsa.gov.uk/pubs/mou/fsa_hmt_boe.pdf.

The pre-crisis shift towards unified regulation took place within an environment characterized by two related trends. The first was the rise to prominence of large financial conglomerates in jurisdictions such as the US, the UK, Germany, France, and Switzerland.[22] The second was the increasing integration of banking, securities, derivatives, and insurance markets (described in Chapters 20 and 21).[23] These trends generated complex interconnections between various industry segments. They also blurred historical distinctions between many financial markets and institutions. The widespread utilization of structured finance, for example, both strengthened and rendered more complex the relationships between 'traditional' retail and commercial banking and capital markets. Many credit derivatives, meanwhile, simultaneously exhibited characteristics of securities, insurance, and debt instruments. Collectively, these and other similar developments made the gathering and analysis of information by, and coordination amongst, regulatory agencies more vital to the pursuit of regulatory objectives.

Against this backdrop, it is easy to see the benefits of a unified supervisory agency. Bringing management functions together within a single agency could eliminate interagency barriers to effective information flow and coordination and facilitate integration of systems for registration, reporting, disclosure, market surveillance, and so forth, thereby allowing for the aggregation of information across the broadest possible range of markets and institutions.[24] As a result, unified regulators could take a holistic approach to activities such as risk assessment, policymaking, supervision, and enforcement, and identify and respond more effectively to the emergence of new regulatory challenges and potential systemic risks.[25]

Unified regulators might also enjoy an advantage regarding the supervision of large, complex financial services firms. Unified regulators are well positioned to monitor such firms' wide-ranging activities, and ensure they have in place robust organization-wide risk management systems and are adequately capitalized across their various lines of business.[26] Similarly, unified regulators may be better able to address industry-wide issues such as money laundering, terrorist financing, and financial education across the entire spectrum of regulated firms. Perhaps most importantly, however, unified regulators are theoretically best positioned to monitor the nature and extent of regulatory arbitrage activities and, where warranted, take steps to close the regulatory gaps and inconsistencies that these activities seek to exploit.

A unified regulator also eliminates the prospect of costly interagency turf wars, such as that which waged between the SEC and CFTC over OTC derivatives.[27] Integration can also be understood as increasing regulators' *de facto* accountability. Specifically, compared to models based on multiple specialist agencies, integrated regulators have little opportunity to shift blame for regulatory failures. As a result, it generates powerful

---

[22] See eg Chapter 4, Table 4.1.

[23] Briault, n 6; Čihák and Podpiera, n 11; Goodhart, Hartmann, Llewellyn, Rojas-Suarez, and Weisbrod, n 8.

[24] R Abrams and M Taylor, 'Issues in the Unification of Financial Sector Supervision', International Monetary Fund (IMF) Working Paper WP/00213 (2000).

[25] Ferran, n 20; Čihák and Podpiera, n 11; Briault, n 6.

[26] Abrams and Taylor, n 24; Briault, n 6.   [27] Discussed in Chapter 25, section 25.1.

incentives to articulate clear mandates, pursue these mandates vigorously, and set clear expectations for market participants about their obligations and the nature of the available regulatory protection.[28]

Regrettably, the theoretical benefits of unified regulators proved elusive in practice. Three key points emerge from the history of the FSA. The first is that bringing regulatory authority under a single roof does not make questions about the appropriate allocation of regulatory responsibility and resources—across institutional or objective (or indeed other) lines—magically disappear. Rather, these questions are in effect delegated by policymakers to the regulator itself. Consequently, problems of incomplete oversight, or of conflict between objectives, may still arise within a unified regulator.[29] It is widely thought, for instance, that the FSA focused on conduct of business concerns at the expense of prudential oversight. Concomitantly, a unified regulator makes the formal designation of the agency's jurisdictional scope and objectives particularly important, as these are likely to guide the regulator's setting of internal priorities. Notably, 'financial stability' did not feature amongst the list of objectives set for the FSA by the Financial Services and Markets Act 2000 as enacted.[30]

Nor, second, does having only a single agency make coordination problems go away. Just as with objective definition questions, coordination problems become problems *within* the agency, rather than *between* agencies. Solving them requires senior management to foster a healthy and functioning management structure, robust decision-making processes, and a shared organizational culture.[31] Fostering these organizational traits, however, may be amongst the most difficult challenges confronting management of an integrated regulator—especially where 'integration' is achieved, as it was in the case of the FSA, by way of the merger of multiple specialist agencies.[32] Thus, an internal report on the FSA's handling of Equitable Life Assurance Company, a failing insurance company the agency had inherited from its predecessors, identified poor internal communication as a deficiency in the FSA's regulatory approach during the first year of its operation. More recently, the internal audit report into the FSA's supervision of Northern Rock, the UK bank that experienced a fatal run in 2007, identified poor internal communication and information flow, along with inconsistent implementation of rules and procedures, as contributing to an anaemic supervisory strategy which allowed warning signs of the pending crisis at the bank to go undetected.[33]

Third, if—as was the case with the FSA—the unified authority is not situated within the relevant central bank, this creates a particular challenge for the management of

---

[28] Ferran, n 20.   [29] Awrey, n 17; Taylor, n 7.

[30] These originally included the following: (i) maintaining market confidence; (ii) promoting public awareness; (iii) consumer protection; and (iv) the reduction of financial crime: FSMA 2000, s 2(2) (as enacted). 'Financial stability' was subsequently added as a goal by the Financial Services Act 2010.

[31] Abrams and Taylor, n 24.

[32] See Ferran, n 20.

[33] See Financial Services Authority, *Lessons Learned: Review of the Supervision of Northern Rock plc During the Period 1 January 2005 to 9 August 2007* (2008), 5–8.

financial stability.[34] The central bank will remain the LOLR, and so will necessarily still have an important role to play in overseeing the maintenance of financial stability. The Bank of England was thus tasked with overseeing payments systems and 'maintaining a broad overview of the system as a whole'.[35] This meant that the supposedly unified system was not in fact integrated over arguably its most crucial dimension. For the Bank to be able to maintain this overview required it to have access to high-quality information about what banks were actually doing, which was now available primarily to the FSA as prudential supervisor. This necessitated very careful interagency coordination with the FSA, which the House of Commons' Treasury Committee's enquiry into the failure of Northern Rock concluded had not been successfully achieved.[36]

27.2.4 Challenges of interstate coordination: the EU

Within multi-state legal systems such as the US and the EU, another architectural question concerns the appropriate level at which financial regulators should be positioned. In the US, as we have seen, regulation of significant financial firms and markets has been at the federal level in all sectors (save for insurance) since the early twentieth century. The EU, of course, has had a very different trajectory as a legal order. Before the financial crisis, the principal strategy was to pursue harmonization of substantive regulation through a series of Directives, but to leave implementation—in terms of the domestic rulebook—to the domestic regulators, who had direct supervisory contact with local firms.

This process had proved unwieldy by the end of the twentieth century, as the technicality of financial regulatory measures made them inappropriate for detailed provision through the EU's legislative process. In the early 2000s, the EU moved to a model whereby the primary legislation was simply to set out a general framework (so-called 'Level 1') Directive, with the rules then being fleshed out in more detailed ('Level 2') implementing measures.[37] The next stage was performed by three 'Level 3' committees, each of which consisted of a college of domestic regulators: the Committee of European Securities Regulators, Committee of European Banking Supervisors, and Committee of European Insurance and Occupational Pensions Supervisors.[38] The Level 3 committees advised the European Commission on policy and the preparation

---

[34] MW Taylor, 'Regulatory Reform After the Financial Crisis: *Twin Peaks* Revisited', in RH Huang and D Schoenmaker (eds), *Institutional Structure of Financial Regulation: Theories and International Experiences* (London and New York, NY: Routledge, 2015), 9, 19.

[35] Tripartite Memorandum, n 21, para 2(iii).

[36] House of Commons Treasury Committee, *The Run on the Rock: Fifth Report of Session 2007-08*, *Volume I*, HC 56-I (2008), 104–15.

[37] This multilevel process was adopted following the recommendations of the Lamfalussy Report (*Final Report of the Committee of Wise Men on the Regulation of European Securities Markets*, 2001), and was consequently known as the 'Lamfalussy Process', available at http://www.ec.europa.eu. See generally, E Ferran, *Building an EU Securities Market* (Cambridge: CUP, 2004), 58–126.

[38] The horizontal division of responsibilities amongst the Level 3 committees thus largely reflected the 'institutional' model.

of implementing measures,[39] issued non-binding interpretive guidance, and sought to coordinate practices amongst national authorities. However, they did not have the authority to issue binding rules; nor did they possess any direct supervisory authority.[40] These functions were performed at 'Level 4'—the transposition of the EU legislation into the laws of Member States and their enforcement—and generally left to domestic financial regulators.

The former Level 3 committees were exposed as fundamentally inoperable under the strains of the financial crisis.[41] As documented in the de Larosière Report, the EU's regulatory response to the crisis was hampered by lack of coordination amongst domestic regulatory authorities, inconsistent supervisory powers across Member States, inadequate macroprudential oversight, insufficient competence and resources, and, crucially, the absence of a centralized decision-making mechanism.[42]

To address these deficiencies, the EU implemented a fundamental overhaul of the institutional structure of European financial regulation, which involved moving power to write binding rules to the three new EU-level agencies described in Chapter 24, section 24.3.3 and the creation of the European Systemic Risk Board ('ESRB'), the EU MPA. In addition, the EU sovereign debt crisis gave impetus to the creation of the European Banking Union ('Banking Union'), which is geographically limited to the Eurozone and consists of the Single Supervisory Mechanism and the Single Resolution Mechanism (and will also include the proposed European Deposit Insurance Scheme).

The current EU architecture thus comprises:[43] three sectoral regulatory agencies primarily in charge of rule-making; dozens of national competent authorities ('NCAs'), each the product of the almost unfettered discretion of individual Member States in designing their domestic institutional architecture, and each with its own seat on the supervisory boards of the relevant EU authorities:[44] the European Central Bank ('ECB'), the Single Resolution Board ('SRB'), and the ESRB.

As we write, the new multilevel and concentric EU supervisory architecture is still basically untested. Moreover, it has many moving parts and a large number of

---

[39] For a more detailed account of the various roles of the Level 3 committees see eg E Ferran, 'Understanding the New Institutional Architecture of EU Financial Market Supervision', Cambridge Legal Studies Research Paper No 29/2011 (May 2011).

[40] See Chapter 26 for a discussion of the distinction between *supervisory* and other regulatory powers.

[41] Indeed, the efficacy of the Level 3 committee structure had been questioned even before the crisis. Specifically, both the IMF and the European Commission had expressed concerns that the Lamfalussy framework was too slow and lacked sufficient institutional structure and capacity to engage in effective crisis response: IMF, *Euro Area Policies: Staff Report for the 2007 Article IV Consultation with Member Countries* (2007), 15–16; European Commission Communication, 'Review of the Lamfalussy Process—Strengthening Supervisory Convergence,' COM(2007) 727 final, 4–13.

[42] High-Level Group on Financial Supervision in the EU, *Report of the High Level Group on Financial Supervision in the EU* (the 'de Larosière Report') (2009), 39–42, available at http://www.ec.europa.eu. See also Chapter 28 for specific examples of some of the coordination problems which arose during the crisis.

[43] See Chapter 24, section 24.3.3.

[44] In the securities and insurance sectors, the NCAs retain virtually all of the supervisory powers, with the relevant European Supervisory Authorities having little, if any, supervisory powers. NCAs of Member States outside the Eurozone also retain full supervisory authority for banks and, even within the Eurozone, NCAs still play an important role in the day-to-day supervision of banks subject to ECB oversight under the Single Supervision Mechanism. See Chapter 24, section 24.3.3.

interagency relationships that could potentially go awry. First of all, the European Banking Authority ('EBA') will have to tread carefully to maintain its role as the rulemaker for banking regulation within the EU without falling out with either with UK national supervisors or the ECB, which will oversee the bulk of the European banking system outside the UK and formally does not even have a vote on the EBA's supervisory board.[45] Second, while the SRB and ECB must coordinate closely to determine whether an ECB-supervised bank is failing, the SRB has the exclusive power to determine whether the public interest merits opening a resolution proceeding, which could lead to tensions with the ECB.[46] Finally, internal coordination problems may well arise within the Banking Union, given the NCAs' continuing role in day-to-day supervision and in the management of resolution proceedings.[47]

27.2.5 Lessons learned?

The problem for the pre-crisis debate about regulatory architecture is that the regulatory failures that came to light in the crisis occurred almost everywhere. This implies no victor in the debate about which is to be preferred. Notwithstanding the phalanx of US regulators responsible for overseeing the domestic mortgage lending market, for example, no federal agency stepped up to take responsibility for reining in the dubious and often predatory lending practices at the heart of the subprime boom and bust.[48] The competition between banking and securities regulators to increase the market shares of their respective regulatees meant that there was insufficient focus on the corresponding growth of systemic risk within this market. In the UK, the FSA was roundly criticized for focusing on conduct of business as opposed to prudential regulation[49] and, more broadly, for subordinating other regulatory objectives to the promotion of internationally competitive financial markets.[50] Perhaps most importantly, regulators on both sides of the Atlantic failed to adopt a coordinated approach towards monitoring the build-up of potential systemic risks.

A potential lesson from this common failure might be that allocation of responsibility as between regulatory agencies is, by itself, a second-order question for financial

---

[45] See V Colaerts, 'European Banking, Securities and Insurance Law: Cutting through Sectoral Lines?' (2015) 52 *Common Market Law Review* 1579, 1584–94; E Ferran, 'The Existential Search of the European Banking Authority', ECGI Law Working Paper 297 (2015); TH Tröger, 'The Single Supervisory Mechanism—Panacea or Quack Banking Regulation? Preliminary Assessment of the New Regime for the Prudential Supervision of Banks with ECB Involvement' (2014) 15 *European Business Organization Law Review* 449, 484–9.

[46] C Hadjiemmanuil, 'Financial Stability and Integration in the Banking Union', in F Allen, E Carletti, and J Gray (eds), *The New Financial Architecture in the Eurozone* (Florence: European University Institute, 2015) 55, 72–3. See Regulation (EU) No 806/2014 establishing uniform rules and a uniform procedure for the resolution of credit institutions and certain investment firms in the framework of a Single Resolution Mechanism and a Single Resolution Fund [2014] OJ L225/1, Art 18(1).

[47] Tröger, n 45, 470–1 and 473–80.

[48] Financial Crisis Inquiry Commission, *Final Report of the National Commission on the Causes of the Financial and Economic Crisis in the United States* (US Government Printing Office, 2011).

[49] FSA, *The Turner Review: A Regulatory Response to the Global Banking Crisis* (2009), 87.

[50] Awrey, n 17.

stability.[51] Nevertheless, policymakers engaged in widespread reform of regulatory architecture shortly after the financial crisis. The US introduced two new objective-oriented agencies, the Financial Stability Oversight Council ('FSOC') and the Consumer Financial Protection Bureau ('CFPB'). The UK abandoned its integrated regulatory model in favour of an objective-based division between the Prudential Regulation Authority ('PRA') and the Financial Conduct Authority ('FCA'). And the EU moved responsibility for rule-making from national authorities to new European-level agencies, with jurisdiction seemingly divided largely on institutional lines. One interpretation is that such 'regulatory reshuffling' represents simply politicians' desire to be seen to be doing *something* in response to a populist post-crisis surge in the salience of financial regulation.[52]

Others, however, take the view that regulatory architecture is not irrelevant to outcomes.[53] For example, proponents of the objectives-based model argue that a twin peaks approach has been vindicated by the financial crisis.[54] In principle, this approach can mitigate failings of each of the institutional, functional, and integrated models. On the one hand, coordination is easier than under a more fragmented system. At the same time, it may be easier to keep sight of the importance of financial stability if a separate agency is specifically tasked with maintaining it, rather than just being one goal amongst many for an integrated agency. On this view, the UK's new regulatory architecture is a significant improvement, but the corresponding reforms have been woefully incomplete in the US and in the EU. The regulatory architecture in both systems, discussed in Chapter 24, section 24.3, still largely reflects institutional or functional allocations of responsibility. This raises the prospect of regulatory 'gaps' as new markets and institutions emerge and evolve over time, along with the concomitant threat of costly interagency turf wars.[55] It is worth pausing to note, however, that the adoption of a 'twin peaks' (objective-based) model of regulatory architecture in the Netherlands in the late 1990s did not prevent that country from suffering major bank failures during the financial crisis.[56]

Each of the foregoing perspectives has an element of truth. The general failure of regulators to prevent and contain the financial crisis does make it hard to argue

---

[51] See E Ferran, 'Institutional Design: The Choices for National Systems', in N Moloney, E Ferran, and J Payne (eds), *The Oxford Handbook of Financial Regulation* (Oxford: OUP, 2015), 97, 98–9.

[52] See R Romano, 'Further Assessment of the Iron Law of Financial Regulation: A Postscript to Regulating in the Dark', ECGI Law WP 273/2014 (2014), 27–45.

[53] This is not necessarily inconsistent with the previous interpretation. While populism certainly seems plausible as a causal mechanism, it does not necessarily follow that the changes adopted do not improve outcomes—simply that they are less likely to do so than ordinary legislative endeavour.

[54] Taylor, n 34, 20–1. See also J Hill, 'Why Did Australia Fare So Well in the Global Financial Crisis?', in E Ferran, N Moloney, JG Hill, and JC Coffee (eds), *The Regulatory Aftermath of the Global Financial Crisis* (Cambridge: CUP, 2012), 203 (arguing that the mild impact of financial crisis on Australia was in part due to objectives-based regulatory architecture).

[55] While a joint committee has been established by the three agencies in the EU to take forward cross-sectoral work and resolve disputes, it is unclear that this will be enough to avoid the same type of information, coordination, and agency problems that have plagued regulators in the US.

[56] See J Kremers and D Schoenmaker, 'Twin Peaks: Experiences in the Netherlands', LSE Financial Markets Group Special Paper 196 (2010).

strongly in favour of any particular model then implemented. However, one idea derived from the objectives-based model has been significantly developed since the financial crisis, in all the systems we have studied. This is the idea that a particular objective—financial stability—should be accorded priority within the regulatory objective function, and that this is best achieved through the designation of a distinct authority charged with preserving it. The idea of macroprudential oversight was not reflected in any of the pre-crisis regulatory systems; rather, it is a potential solution that has come to prominence in response to the failings of those systems. What distinguishes this idea from those discussed so far is that it emphasizes a vertical, or hierarchical, division of responsibility, rather than the horizontal allocations discussed in this section. In the next section, we consider how successfully this idea has been implemented.

27.3 Regulatory Hierarchy: The Primacy of Financial Stability

Chapter 19 documented the emerging consensus regarding the significance of MacroPru as a means of helping to ensure financial stability. This implies an evolution of the objective-based approach to the allocation of regulatory responsibility.[57] Implementation of MacroPru requires an agency—an MPA—whose task it is to identify systemic risk and invoke or coordinate the use of macroprudential tools. In order for an MPA to work effectively, it should have access to as rich a set of information about the financial system as possible.

However, the nature of MacroPru implies that the MPA is not simply tasked with implementing a particular goal within a horizontal allocation of responsibility. Rather, it is better to think of it as an agency sitting at the apex of a hierarchical relationship with other regulatory agencies beneath it. To see this, consider that because the measures used to control macroprudential risks are general, the MPA needs to be able to impose controls on any regulated firm in the financial sector.[58] Yet a single agency cannot develop thick relationships with a sufficient number of market participants. Rather, it will need to route the implementation of its controls via the relationships and existing frameworks established by other agencies. Moreover, the efforts of other financial regulators to pursue their own regulatory objectives may sometimes lead to a conflict with what the MPA deems necessary from a systemic perspective to maintain stability. The MPA should therefore have power to issue directions or recommendations to the other agencies regarding their rulemaking or policies, in order to ensure financial stability. That is to say, we should think of the MPA as the 'senior' regulator.

This configuration can be seen as an extension of the objectives-based model, whereby one of the objectives—financial stability—is understood to be capable of

---

[57] See eg D Schoenmaker and J Kremers, 'Financial Stability and Proper Business Conduct: Can Supervisory Structure Help to Achieve These Objectives?' in RH Huang and D Schoenmaker (eds), *Institutional Structure of Financial Regulation: Theories and International Experiences* (London and New York, NY: Routledge, 2015), 29, 32–4.

[58] See eg de Larosière Report, n 42, 44–6.

taking precedence over the others, and this is reflected in a hierarchical relationship between the MPA and other agencies.[59] However, the idea of MPA seniority is independent of any particular horizontal allocation of responsibility. Thus a senior MPA could be added to either an institutional or a goal-based model, which is in fact what we see to some degree in the US and in the EU.[60] On this view, the various institutional aspects of the allocation of regulatory responsibility within these systems will be less problematic if the MPA can exercise effective senior oversight.

The need for information and seniority imply that central banks may be well placed to house an MPA, owing to their status both as LOLR and as setters of monetary policy. Given this combination, there is much also to be said—from the standpoint of coordination—if responsibility for attainment of the goal of prudential regulation should also fall under the remit of the central bank. It therefore seems desirable for the regulatory architecture to feature a higher 'peak' as respects financial stability, even if we are agnostic about the merits of different ways of parcelling up the remaining regulatory responsibilities. With this in mind, we now consider critically the allocation of responsibility for MacroPru in the US, the UK, and the EU. While there is an agency designated as being responsible for 'macroprudential' oversight in each system, there are differences in the functions they are each expected to perform.

27.3.1 The US

The mandate of the US FSOC relates primarily to reviewing cross-sectional aspects of systemic risk. It has two components: first, the FSOC must focus on threats posed to stability by systemically important financial institutions ('SIFIs'); and second, it must respond to 'emerging threats' to the stability of the US financial system.[61] 'Systemically important' is a category that automatically includes all large banking groups (bank holding companies having more than $50 billion in assets), but the FSOC can also designate other firms for which it considers the status appropriate. To date, it has designated eight financial market utilities (clearing, payment and settlement systems, and custodians),[62] and four non-bank financial companies as systemically important.[63] Such non-bank SIFIs then become subject to enhanced prudential oversight by the Federal Reserve, along with all the systemically important banks.

---

[59] Taylor, n 34, 24–6.

[60] It could of course also be implemented within an integrated regulator, provided the regulator was willing to give such primacy to stability.

[61] Dodd–Frank Act of 2010, §112(a)(1). The FSOC is also required to promote market discipline by eliminating expectations on the part of investors in, and counterparties to, systemically important financial institutions that the US Government will shield them from losses.

[62] These consist of: the Clearing House Interbank Payments System; CLS Bank International (a foreign exchange clearing and settlement system); the Chicago Mercantile Exchange; the Depository Trust Company; the Fixed Income Clearing Corporation; ICE Clear Credit; the National Securities Clearing Corporation and the Options Clearing Corporation. See FSOC, *Annual Report 2012*, Appendix A.

[63] These are three insurers—AIG, Prudential Financial, and MetLife—and General Electric's finance subsidiary, GE Capital Corporation. See http://www.treasury.gov/initiatives/fsoc/designations/Pages/default.aspx#nonbank.

The MetLife Designation (Again)

As discussed in Chapter 21, section 21.3.3, the FSOC in December 2014 designated life insurance company MetLife as 'systemically important'. As detailed there, MetLife challenged this decision in court.[64] In addition to the substantive issues we already discussed, the litigation raises an equally important procedural question about the regulatory architecture. Who actually *makes* the decision that a firm is systemically important? On the face of things, the FSOC makes the decision, in accordance with a list of relevant criteria set out in the Dodd–Frank Act.[65] But what if the Council makes a decision based on entirely irrelevant considerations? To guard against this, judicial review is available from the FSOC's decisions.[66] However, the problem now is that firms determined by the FSOC to be systemically important may be able to shift the locus of decision-making away from the FSOC and into a courtroom. No firm wishes to be designated as systemically important, as this brings with it increased regulatory costs. And the possibility of court challenge can impede agency decision-making, depending on how the judicial review is conducted. The FSOC's designations are only reviewable on the basis that they are 'arbitrary and capricious', which is a standard very deferential to the agency's decision-making process. An amicus brief submitted in the *MetLife* case argued that given the technical, highly complex subject matter, and the predictive nature of the decision (that is, *could* be a threat, rather than *is*), the court should be especially deferential to the FSOC's own decision-making process.[67]

Understanding the FSOC as primarily oriented towards cross-sectional issues helps to explain other aspects of its structure. Its composition, including the heads of all major financial regulators plus the Secretary of the Treasury, makes sense if it is borne in mind that a primary function is to encourage their cooperation in plugging gaps in the control of cross-sectional systemic risk as these emerge or are discovered.[68] Similarly, the FSOC has no powers to impose regulations or undertake MacroPru measures, nor can it oblige any 'primary' financial regulatory agency (not) to implement any microprudential or MacroPru measures. While the FSOC generally is only able to achieve change through the cooperation of its members, it has the power to call public attention to emerging threats and even to make explicit recommendations for regulatory action by the other regulatory agencies.[69] For example, FSOC prodding led to significant money market fund reform by the SEC and has spurred deeper SEC engagement with asset managers.[70] To guard against the threat of inaction, the FSOC is required to submit an annual report to Congress on systemic stability, and each member is required to certify that the Council, the Government, and the private sector, 'are taking all reasonable steps to ensure financial stability and to mitigate systemic risk that would negatively affect the economy', and if not, what actions should be taken.[71]

---

[64] See *MetLife v FSOC*, Complaint, US District Court for the District of Colombia, 13 January 2015; see also Chapter 21, sections 21.3.2–21.3.3.

[65] Dodd–Frank Act §113(a)(2), discussed in Chapter 23, section 23.3.3.

[66] Dodd–Frank Act, §113(h).

[67] *MetLife v FSOC*, Brief of Professors of Law and Finance as *Amici Curiae* Supporting Defendant, US District Court for the District of Colombia, Civil Action No, 15-cv-00045 (RMC), 22 May 2015, 10–12.

[68] The FSOC's voting members consist of the Secretary of the Treasury, the Chairperson of each of the Federal Reserve Board of Governors, SEC, FDIC, OCC, CFTC and the National Credit Union Administration (NCUA), the directors of the CFPB and the Federal Housing Finance Agency (FHFA), and an independent member with insurance expertise. It is required to meet not less than quarterly, and in practice meets monthly by conference call.

[69] Moreover, the FSOC does have power to require the CFPB to set aside any of its regulations if it deems they pose a threat to US financial stability: Dodd–Frank Act of 2010, §1023.

[70] See eg FSOC, 'Proposed Recommendations Regarding Money Market Mutual Fund Reform' (2012).

[71] Dodd–Frank Act of 2010, §112(b).

In contrast, the application of time-series MacroPru measures, at least those contained in Basel III (such as the counter-cyclical capital buffer), has been left to be implemented not by the FSOC, but by the Federal Reserve, the OCC, and the FDIC acting together.[72] This reflects the overlap between micro- and macroprudential measures in Basel III itself. The application of any other time-varying capital controls to banks would also be a matter for these agencies. More generally, it is the Federal Reserve—not the FSOC—that is tasked with prudential supervisory authority over the financial activities of non-bank financial companies designated as systemically significant by the FSOC, bank holding companies with total consolidated assets of $50 billion or more,[73] and as authority with respect to payment, clearing, and settlement activity designated by the FSOC as systemically important.[74] The FSOC, in other words, reviews cross-sectional risk and determines where the perimeter of enhanced (macro) prudential supervision should lie; the Fed then performs that supervision.

Seen in this light, responsibility for MPA in the US is divided between the cross-sectional work carried out by the FSOC and the time-varying measures that remain the preserve of the traditional banking regulators. Concomitantly, the Fed has responsibility for 'enhanced prudential supervision' over a large swath of US banks, since $50 billion is a relatively low threshold. This raises an important question: is there sufficiently tight coordination for MacroPru policy to function effectively? Prior experience of interagency coordination over financial stability has not been a happy one. A plausible response is that the highly fragmented structure of US financial regulation makes the cross-sectional aspect of MacroPru unusually difficult to implement; on this view, the FSOC's structure is a response to the US-specific challenge it faces. At the same time, because time-varying MacroPru measures have implications for monetary policy, their application is best managed by the central bank. In this respect, the US approach ultimately looks similar to the other two systems we consider.

27.3.2 The UK

The mandate of the UK's Financial Policy Committee ('FPC') clearly encompasses both time-series and cross-sectional dimensions of systemic risk.[75] This is reflected in its organizational positioning. Because the time-series aspects of MacroPru interact with monetary policy, the FPC was established as a separate committee within the Bank of England.[76] Its structure was clearly modelled on the existing Monetary Policy Committee ('MPC'), which has responsibility for setting interest rates. The FPC has ten voting members, consisting not only of representatives from the UK's two 'primary' financial regulators, but also independent outside experts.[77] However, it draws on the

---

[72] See OCC/Federal Reserve, 'Regulatory Capital Rules: Regulatory Capital, Implementation of Basel III, Capital Adequacy, Transition Provisions, Prompt Corrective Action, Standardized Approach for Risk-Weighted Assets, Market Discipline and Disclosure Requirements, Advanced Approaches Risk-Based Capital Rule, and Market Risk Capital Rule', (2013) 78 *Federal Register* 62018, 62038.

[73] Dodd–Frank Act of 2010, §§161, 163, 165.   [74] Ibid, §805.

[75] The FPC has responsibility for 'the identification of and monitoring of, and taking action to remove or reduce, systemic risks with a view to protecting and enhancing the resilience of the UK financial system': Bank of England Act 1998 s 9C.

[76] The FPC was formally established on 1 April 2013 with statutory powers conferred by the Financial Services Act 2012 (modifying the Bank of England Act 1998). However, the Bank had established an interim FPC from February 2011 with a view to undertaking, as far as possible, the future role of the statutory FPC.

[77] Its voting members consist of the Governor and three Deputy Governors of the Bank of England (one of whom is the Chief Executive of the PRA, the UK's banking regulator), the Chief Executive of the FCA, the UK's markets and consumer financial product regulator, a representative of the Treasury, an appointee of

expertise of the Bank of England (through the Governor and Deputy Governors) as well as the expert external members in formulating and setting policy. Although—again unlike the FSOC—senior politicians do not themselves sit on the FPC, the FPC must in its decision-making, as a subordinate goal to achieving financial stability, take into account the government's economic policy; the terms of which are specified by the Chancellor of the Exchequer in a public 'remit letter' to the Governor of the Bank of England.[78]

The broader mandate of the FPC is also reflected in its powers: unlike the FSOC, the FPC is an 'action' agency. For example, it has been granted powers to impose various time-varying MacroPru measures,[79] and to issue directions to the UK's primary regulators—the PRA and FCA—regarding the implementation of MacroPru measures in relation to regulated persons.[80] It may also make relevant recommendations to any other person, including the Treasury and the Bank of England. The FPC is therefore set up to be a more direct macroprudential actor. Because the PRA is itself a subsidiary of the Bank of England, the FPC is well placed to coordinate the intersection between macro- and microprudential issues.

The work of the FPC to date has focused largely on seeking to identify systemic risks, both cross-sectional and time-series. In so doing, it is able to draw on the research capability of the Bank. It has interpreted its mandate broadly, and although it has paid particularly close attention to stress testing the UK banking system and to systemic risks associated with the UK housing market,[81] it has also explored a wide range of emerging risks including, in particular, risks associated with climate change,[82] and the resilience of the system to cyber-attack.[83]

27.3.3 The EU

Like the FPC, but unlike the FSOC, the ESRB also has a broad mandate to cover all aspects of systemic risk.[84] However, its nature as an EU-level authority in an

the Governor of the Bank with executive responsibility for financial stability, and four external members with relevant knowledge and expertise, selected by the Chancellor of the Exchequer (Bank of England Act 1998 s 9B). The four initial external members were Donald Kohn, a former Vice Chairman of the Federal Reserve in the US, Clara Furse, former CEO of the London Stock Exchange, Richard Sharp, an investment banker formerly at Goldman Sachs, and Martin Taylor, former CEO of Barclays and a member of the UK's Independent Commission on Banking. The FPC meets quarterly.

[78] Bank of England Act 1998 ss 9C 1(b), 9D(1).

[79] These include powers to impose (i) higher sectoral capital requirements for banks, or higher capital charges for high-risk mortgage lending (Bank of England Act 1998 (Macroprudential Measures) Order 2013, SI 2013/644); (ii) the Basel III capital conservation buffer (Capital Requirements (Capital Buffers and Macroprudential Measures) Regulations 2014, SI 894/2014), and more recently, (iii) caps on the proportion of bank lending which are at high loan-to-value and debt-to-income ratios (Bank of England Act 1998 (Macroprudential Measures) Order 2015, SI 2015/909).

[80] Bank of England Act 1998 s 9H.

[81] See eg FPC, *Financial Stability Report June 2014* (2014), 22–6.

[82] See eg FPC, Record of the Financial Policy Committee Meeting, 24 March 2015, paras 24–5.

[83] See eg FPC, *Financial Stability Report July 2015* (2015), 31–3.

[84] The ESRB is tasked with 'macro-prudential oversight of the financial system within the [European] Union in order to contribute to the prevention or mitigation of systemic risks to financial stability in the Union that arise from developments with the financial system' (Regulation (EU) 1092/2010, Art 3(1)).

international system necessitates that its configuration look very different from the other two MPAs we have considered. First, the ESRB's decision-making body, its General Board, has representatives from all the Member States as well as the ECB and other EU-level agencies within the European System of Financial Supervision ('ESFS').[85] This brings its voting members to an unwieldy total of thirty-eight,[86] as compared with ten each for the FPC and the FSOC. However, much of the preparation for its meetings and monitoring of progress is carried out by the ESRB's thirteen-member Steering Committee.

Second, like the FSOC—but unlike the FPC—the ESRB is not an action agency. Rather, it produces an annual report that highlights emerging risks to financial stability and analyses measures undertaken by EU Member States in an effort to coordinate them. For example, it produces a 'Handbook on Operationalizing Macroprudential Policy in the Banking Sector' that purports to 'guide' MPAs in the EU, but such guidance is not 'binding' and would yield to 'national flexibility'.[87] Perhaps slightly more effective is the ESRB's power to issue warnings and recommendations to the EU, Member States, and European and national supervisory authorities.[88]

However—in a pattern that resonates with the US—the ECB also plays a very important role in European macroprudential policy. First, the ECB provides structural and institutional support for the unwieldy ESRB. The ECB's President is Chair of the ESRB,[89] meaning that the ECB hosts the ESRB's meetings and puts its reputation behind the ESRB's activities.[90] The ECB also provides the ESRB with all relevant data and analysis for use in its meetings, the ESRB having no data-gathering capacity in its own right. It consequently seems likely that the ECB will play an important role in setting the agenda for meetings of the thirty-eight-member ESRB.

Yet the most significant role of the ECB in MacroPru probably comes not through its influence via the ESRB, but rather in its responsibility for bank oversight under the SSM. The ECB takes responsibility for direct supervision of large Eurozone banks under the SSM, and also has power (analogously with the FSOC) to shift the perimeter of this supervision by taking responsibility for smaller banks that it deems pose a threat to systemic stability.[91] Moreover, following the advent of the SSM, the ECB was given

---

[85] Ibid, Arts 4 and 11. The voting members of the ESRB's General Board are comprised of the President and Vice-President of the ECB, the Governors of EU Member State central banks, a member of the European Commission, the Chairs respectively of the European Banking, Securities and Markets, and Insurance and Occupational Pension Authorities, and representatives from the ESRB's two Advisory Committees (ibid, Art 6). The ESRB's Steering Committee is comprised of the Chair and first Vice-Chair of the ESRB, the Vice-President of the ECB, four other members of the ESRB's General Board who are also members of the ECB's General Council, a Member of the European Commission, the Chairs of the three European financial regulatory authorities (ESMA, EBA, and EIOPA), the President of the Economic and Finance Committee, and the Chairs of the ESRB's two Advisory Committees (ibid, Art 11).

[86] Including non-voting members, the total is sixty-five!

[87] See ESRB, Handbook on Operationalizing Macroprudential Policy in the Banking Sector, Addendum: Macroprudential Leverage Ratios (2015).

[88] Regulation (EU) 1092/2010, Art 16.

[89] Ibid, Art 5(1). This was renewed after the initial term of five years.

[90] European Commission, Report from the Commission to the European Parliament and the Council on the Mission and Organization of the ESRB, COM (2014) 508 final.

[91] See Chapter 24, section 24.3.4.

powers to exercise the Basel III time-series MacroPru measures (such as the counter-cyclical buffer) directly in respect of Eurozone banks.[92]

27.3.4 Assessment: the architecture for MacroPru

At a high level of generality, all the systems we have studied have taken to heart the lesson that financial stability should be prioritized through a hierarchical regulatory architecture. What seems troubling, however, is that the transfer of power to a senior agency may, in the US and the EU, have been insufficiently comprehensive to permit it to function effectively in overseeing financial stability. In the US, for example, although the FSOC is given explicit responsibility for maintaining financial stability, and has access to its own stream of information and research through the OFR, its mandate is limited to cross-sectional measures. It must coordinate with the Fed regarding the supervision of systemically important institutions, and with all three federal banking regulators regarding the imposition of time-varying macroprudential tools. Matters are even worse in Europe, where the ESRB is hampered by its unwieldy size and lack of incisive powers. The ECB has supervisory responsibility for significant banking institutions, and the power to implement the Basel III time-varying macroprudential measures. However, it does not have power to designate any non-bank financial institution or utility as systemically important, in what appears to be a potentially important lacuna. Nor does it have power to implement any time-varying macroprudential measures beyond those in Basel III, this being a matter left to national authorities with loose coordination from the ESRB.[93]

27.4 Conclusion

Does the structure of financial regulation matter? Based on the case studies examined in this chapter, the answer would appear to be 'yes'—but only to a point. In theory, a well-designed institutional structure can help lower information, coordination, and agency costs within the regulatory community. In practice, however, institutional structure is only one of many variables which determine whether and to what extent regulators are able to achieve regulatory objectives. In part this is because functionally equivalent financial products and activities may emerge from diverse sorts of financial institutions. Ultimately, where regulatory structure would seem likely to make the most difference is in the identification, monitoring, and response to potential threats to financial stability. There is a strong argument for allocating this important responsibility to a single regulatory authority and for positioning this authority at the apex of the regulatory community. In short, from the perspective of financial stability, the vertical structure of financial regulation matters much more than the horizontal structure.

---

[92] Regulation (EU) 1024/2013, Art 5.
[93] To some degree, these limitations reflect the inherent challenges of achieving effective legislative outcomes in large federal systems, as opposed to the more streamlined structure a smaller domestic system such as the UK may be able to lay out.

The UK, the US, and the EU have all made significant strides towards the implementation of this lesson in their post-crisis regulatory architecture. However, as we have seen, there are limitations in the way they have done so. In particular, problems of coordination and incomplete transfer of power may continue to impede efforts to preserve financial stability, especially in the EU. Be that as it may, a student of *Realpolitik* may draw comfort from the significant role played by central banks in each of the systems. Although in the US and the EU other agencies—the FSOC and ESRB—are formally tasked with responsibility for macroprudential coordination, the reality on the ground is likely to be that the central bank will be the organization driving the agenda in each case. This seems largely desirable given that, owing to their roles in setting monetary policy and acting as LOLR, central banks probably have more relevant expertise and information for MacroPru than any other agency. As we shall see in the next chapter, the concentration of power in central banks in this way also offers benefits for international coordination.

28

International Regulatory Coordination

28.1 Introduction

One of this book's central themes is that financial stability is a first order financial regulatory concern because it is a public good, meaning (among other things) that market pricing will be insufficient to induce private parties to undertake the costly measures necessary to ensure its protection. This gives rise to a dilemma that this chapter explores: the maintenance of financial stability is an *international* public good (meaning that all nations and all private parties benefit), yet there is no international financial regulator; nor has any single domestic financial regulator the capacity to govern the international financial system. While capital might flow relatively freely across national borders, domestic authorities face inherent jurisdictional constraints and are often hamstrung by both their incomplete access to information and their finite financial, political, and human resources.[1] One cause of the financial crisis of 2007–9 and the subsequent Eurozone crisis of 2010–12 was the mismatch between the scope of global financial activity and the capacity for global financial monitoring and regulation. In the post-crisis period, despite the absence of new formal international law-making (treaty commitments, for example), a global financial regulatory order has emerged— rather remarkably—through the concerted action of states' executive leadership, financial regulatory agencies, central banks, international institutions, and private actors. This new order can be characterized as a regime of 'international financial *regulatory coordination*' rather than '*regulation*' because it is sustained through the determination to cooperate rather than the force of international law. The question over time will be whether this new regime will prove durable and flexible, or whether it will succumb to mercantilist behaviour by nation states and the power of global financial firms.

Financial stability is necessarily an international problem for many reasons. First, with the success of regional and global trade and investment regimes, economic activity has become increasingly global, firms have become increasing multinational, and banks and other financial institutions have followed. Worldwide trade in goods and services grew from approximately $2.2 trillion in 2003 to approximately $23.3 trillion in 2013, a tenfold increase.[2] Trade is funnelled through a relatively small number of large firms.[3] Most are multinationals, which commonly grow through developing networks of

---

[1] S Choi and A Guzman, 'National Laws, International Money: Regulation in a Global Capital Market' (1997) 65 *Fordham Law Review* 1855; H Jackson, 'Centralization, Competition, and Privatization in Financial Regulation' (2001) 2 *Theoretical Inquiries in Law* 649.

[2] UNCTAD statistics on world trade, http://unctadstat.unctad.org/wds/TableViewer/tableView.aspx?ReportId=25116 (last visited 27 November 2015).

[3] AB Bernard, JB Bensen, SJ Redding, and PK Schott, 'Firms in International Trade' (2007) 21 *Journal of Economic Perspectives* 106, 108–9, 117.

Principles of Financial Regulation. First Edition. John Armour, Dan Awrey, Paul Davies, Luca Enriques, Jeffrey N. Gordon, Colin Mayer, and Jennifer Payne. © John Armour, Dan Awrey, Paul Davies, Luca Enriques, Jeffrey N. Gordon, Colin Mayer, and Jennifer Payne 2016. Published 2016 by Oxford University Press.

foreign affiliates.[4] Banks and other financial services firms have become large and global in part to follow their clients, supplying payment systems, foreign exchange services, and trade finance but then leveraging such basic financial services into the full range of capital markets activities. In Chapter 4 (Table 4.1), we described the size and global reach of four international financial institutions. Citigroup, for example, has thousands of subsidiaries[5] operating in 101 countries across almost every conceivable segment of the financial services industry.[6]

Second, capital markets have become global, and large financial firms have become both the conduits for large-scale financial flows as well as the producers of financial products that intermediate between worldwide capital providers (savers) and users (households, firms, and governments). This point was developed by former Fed Chairman Ben Bernanke both before[7] and after the financial crisis,[8] in describing how savers in emerging markets and Europe piled into financial instruments linked to US residential mortgages created by a small number of global financial institutions because they were purportedly 'safe'.

Third, as described in Chapter 21, the vast majority of 'swaps' and other over-the-counter derivatives, for example, are intermediated by just 14 global dealers—the so-called 'G14'—and are entered into under the laws of one of two jurisdictions: New York and the UK. And as described in Chapter 18, a relatively small group of payment and settlement systems, clearinghouses, and custodians are, likewise, responsible for the clearing and settlement of an increasingly large proportion of global currency, equity, and derivatives trades. These financial utilities also are governed by the laws of a small number of jurisdictions. The upshot is that core international financial activities are concentrated within a limited number of firms, subject to the regulation of a limited set of national regulators.

Finally, financial stability is also an international problem because the forces of regulatory arbitrage undermine the capacity of a single regulator to enforce a tough-minded stability regime. In Chapter 4, we said that one possible response to cost-imposing regulation was for a firm to modify the activity so as to take it outside the ambit of the regulatory regime. The firm can also shift the locus of the activity outside of the jurisdiction of the regulator. If such a shift would mean the relocation of highly compensated workers, which would also eliminate support jobs for local workers and reduce income tax receipts, the mere threat of such a move may lead a domestic

---

[4] McKinsey Global Institute, 'Growth and Competitiveness in the United States: The Role of Its Multinational Companies' (2010), 6, 37–8.

[5] See J Carmassi and R Herring, 'Living Wills and Cross-Border Resolution of Systemically Important Banks' (2013) 5 *Journal of Financial Economic Policy* 361, 375 (reporting that Citigroup had 2,319 subsidiaries as of 30 June 2012).

[6] See https://www.citibank.com/tts/global_network/index.html.

[7] BS Bernanke, 'The Global Savings Glut and the US Current Account Deficit' (Federal Reserve Board, 2005), remarks delivered at the Sandridge Lecture, Virginia Association of Economists, 10 March 2005; see also BS Bernanke, 'Global Imbalances: Recent Developments and Prospects' (Federal Reserve Board, September 2007); speech delivered at the Bundesbank Lecture, Berlin, Germany, 1 September 2007.

[8] BS Bernanke, C Bertaut, LP DeMarco and S Kamin, 'International Capital Flows and the Returns of Safe Assets in the United States, 2003–2007', Federal Reserve Board International Finance Discussion Paper No 1014 (2011).

regulator to produce a suboptimal regime from the perspective of international financial stability.

This chapter covers the emergence, catalysed by the financial crisis, of a regime of international financial regulatory coordination, which aims to protect international financial stability. Section 28.2 sketches the institutions and mechanisms of international financial regulatory coordination. Section 28.3 describes the concerted international activity triggered by the crisis, in which previously moribund institutions provided a useful structure for galvanizing a far-reaching regulatory agenda. The post-crisis activity of these energized international institutions can be roughly divided into standard setting and compliance monitoring for important balance sheet requirements (regulatory capital ratios, including leverage, and liquidity). Section 28.4 describes how the follow-on Eurozone crisis triggered the formation of the European Banking Union, which converted a relatively weak regime of regulatory coordination among autonomous financial regulators into a (broadly) uniform regulatory regime with centralized oversight. The 'hard law' regime of the European Banking Union is important because, if effectively implemented, it is bound to reduce the number of governmental actors whose actions must be coordinated at the global level to contain financial crises.

Section 28.5 addresses the specific problem of cross-border supervision, the 'home'/'host' dilemma. The 'Single Supervisory Mechanism' (SSM) of the European Banking Union should help in this regard, and cooperation among key financial regulators including the Fed, the Bank of England, and the European Central Bank ('ECB'), as well as the central banks of other major financial jurisdictions, should also mitigate some of these problems. Section 28.6 discusses cross-border resolution, especially of a globally systemically important bank ('G-SIB'). We outline four strategies that have been employed to attempt to facilitate such coordination. We believe that a network of memorandums of understanding ('MOUs') among key regulatory authorities over home/host responsibility issues is an essential part of the resolution planning process, and that the bail-in approach facilitates this.

Section 28.7 steps back to ask whether regulatory convergence, much less harmonization, is desirable, either because of the inefficiencies of a centrally prescribed regime or because of the potential for systemic regulatory failure. In areas where the risk exists of large externalities from regulatory arbitrage (the flipside of regulatory competition), the pressure for convergent regimes is justified. Section 28.8 asks whether any regime of 'coordination' is sustainable, particularly since it relies mainly upon the 'soft law' of voluntary cooperation rather than the 'hard law' of specific treaty obligations backed by a formal enforcement mechanism. Should power be delegated to a supranational financial regulator—a global regulator to match global systemic risk? A more modest treaty may be in reach that would strengthen cross-border information sharing that would better equip regulators for supervision and timely, effective intervention as a crisis unfolds.

The key question this chapter tries to answer is whether the international financial regulatory coordination system emerging from post-crisis global reforms will succeed in maintaining financial stability. There are reasons to be cautiously optimistic that this will be the case at least over the medium term: chief among them are the concentration of financial activities in jurisdictions where financial supervisors and central banks display a strong inclination to cooperate so as to avoid another financial crisis and the greater integration of supervision in the Eurozone. The risks to the unravelling of the post-crisis regime are likely to arise from financial activity outside the regulatory perimeter and from new financial centres.

28.2 The Institutions of International Regulatory Coordination

Chris Brummer offers a helpful taxonomy for understanding the role of international organizations in financial law—distinguishing among international financial institutions, international agenda setters, and international financial standard setters.[9] International *financial institutions* include post-war organizations such as the International Monetary Fund (IMF) and the World Bank. Although not expressly tasked with responsibility for financial regulation, the mandates of these institutions have evolved over time to encompass monitoring and compliance with various international financial standards.[10] This monitoring takes place as part of the IMF's regular consultations with Member States under Article IV of its articles of agreement.[11] It also takes place under the auspices of initiatives such as the Financial Sector Assistance Program ('FSAP'), jointly administered by the IMF and the World Bank. FSAP assessments seek to identify the developmental and technical assistance needs of Member States, evaluate risks to financial stability, and coordinate policy development with national regulators.[12] These assessments include Reports on Observance of Standards and Codes, which evaluate Member States' adherence to international standards in areas such as banking supervision, securities regulation, accounting, and money-laundering.[13] Importantly, these international financial institutions are the only players within the global regulatory architecture whose constituting documents are formally recognized under international law.

International *agenda setters* are organizations that facilitate coordination amongst states with a view to articulating high-level policy objectives. In the wake of the crisis, the two most influential agenda setters have been the G20 and the Financial Stability Board ('FSB'). The G20 is a forum for the twenty largest advanced and emerging economies—nineteen countries and the EU—to discuss and coordinate economic, financial, and monetary policy.[14] As of January 2014, G20 Member States represented approximately 85 per cent of global GDP, 75 per cent of world trade, and roughly two-thirds of the world's population. The principal outputs of the G20 are public

---

[9] C Brummer, *Soft Law and the Global Financial System: Rule Making in the 21st Century* (New York, NY: Cambridge University Press, 2012).

[10] Ibid. As evidenced by its role in the European debt crisis, the IMF also plays an important role as international lender (to sovereigns) of last resort.

[11] For an evaluation of the effectiveness of IMF monitoring, see D Lombardi and N Woods, 'The Politics of Influence: An Analysis of IMF Surveillance' (2008) 15 *Review of International Political Economy* 711; B Bossone, 'IMF Surveillance: A Case Study on IMF Governance' IMF Independent Evaluation Office Background Paper No BP/08/10 (2008).

[12] For an overview, see A Clark and J Drage, 'International Standards and Codes', Bank of England Financial Stability Review (December 2000).

[13] Ibid.

[14] Listed in Table 28.1. Senior members of both the IMF and World Bank also participate on an *ex officio* basis.

statements—in the form of communiqués and declarations—which set out common policy priorities, objectives, and prescriptions. In response to the crisis, for example, the G20 has issued statements regarding the importance of more robust and globally consistent regulation and oversight of banks, credit rating agencies (CRAs), hedge funds, the shadow banking system, and OTC derivatives markets.[15]

Sitting alongside the G20 is the FSB, consisting of representatives of G20 governments and central banks (plus five others), as well as representatives from international standard-setters.[16] Formerly the Financial Stability Forum, the post-crisis mandate of the FSB has been expanded to include the evaluation of vulnerabilities within the global financial system, monitoring market developments, articulating policy priorities and objectives, and ensuring compliance with Member States' international commitments. The FSB is also responsible for cross-border contingency planning in connection with the failure of systemically important financial institutions.[17] Notably, FSB Member States must submit themselves to periodic peer reviews. They must also commit to pursuing financial stability, maintaining open and transparent financial services sectors, and implementing international financial standards.[18] Unlike the IMF and World Bank, however, both the G20 and FSB operate without a formal legal mandate and, formally at least, arrive at decisions on the basis of consensus.

International *financial standard setters*, meanwhile, are interagency forums that facilitate information sharing, coordinate the design and implementation of common policy approaches, and articulate international financial standards.[19] Arguably the most influential of these institutions is the Basel Committee on Banking Supervision ('BCBS'). Created in 1974 in response to the Herstatt failure described in Chapter 18,[20] members of the BCBS include the central bank governors and national bank supervisors of G20 Member States.[21] The BCBS's stated objective is to enhance understanding of key supervisory issues and improve the quality of banking supervision worldwide. Its principal outputs include the *Concordat on Cross-Border Banking Supervision*, the *Core Principles for Effective Banking Supervision*, and the *Basel Accords* on capital and liquidity adequacy (see Chapters 14 and 15). Despite its influence, however, the BCBS has no formal rule-making or supervisory authority. The BCBS is administratively situated within the Bank for International Settlements ('BIS'), an

---

[15] For a full list of statements, see 'Library', available at http://www.g20.org.

[16] See S Gadinis, 'The Financial Stability Board: The New Politics of International Financial Regulation' (2013) 48 *Texas Journal of International Law* 157. FSB Member States are listed in Table 28.1.

[17] FSB Charter, Art 2(1).

[18] The FSB has since 2010 also pursued an initiative on cooperation and information exchange that has encompassed, in addition to its member countries, a further thirty-six countries that rank highly in financial importance: see FSB, 'Global adherence to regulatory and supervisory standards on international cooperation and information exchange: status update', 18 December 2013.

[19] H Evans, 'Plumbers and Architects: A Supervisory Perspective on International Financial Architecture', FSA Occasional Paper No 4 (2000). On the conditions for success in standard-setting of different types of networks, see S Gadinis, 'Three Pathways to Global Standards: Private, Regulator, and Ministry Networks' (2015) 109:1 *American Journal of International Law* 1.

[20] Chapter 18, section 18.2.3.

[21] Listed in Table 28.1. The BCBS also encourages contact and cooperation between its members and other banking supervisory authorities in non-Member States. For more on the origins of the Basel Committee, see C Goodhart, *The Basel Committee on Banking Supervision: A History of the Early Years, 1974–1997* (Cambridge: CUP, 2011).

organization owned by central banks whose main function is to 'foster international monetary and financial cooperation'.[22]

Another important international standard setter is the International Organization of Securities Commissions ('IOSCO'). The membership of IOSCO is comprised of securities regulators from over 120 countries. Together, these regulators are responsible for the oversight of over 95 per cent of global securities markets.[23] Despite this broad and diverse membership, however, the majority of IOSCO policy is coordinated through its thirty-two-member board and eight technical committees. IOSCO's mission is to develop, implement, and promote adherence to internationally recognized standards for securities regulation. Its key outputs include the Objectives and Principles of Securities Regulation—a set of thirty principles outlining IOSCO's position regarding what constitutes high-quality securities regulation.[24] IOSCO has also been responsible for the development of a multilateral agreement designed to promote information sharing and cooperation amongst national securities regulators.[25] Like the BCBS, IOSCO arrives at its decisions on the basis of consensus.

Other significant international standard-setters include the International Accounting Standards Board ('IASB'), International Association of Insurance Supervisors ('IAIS'), and Committee on Payment and Market Infrastructures ('CPMI').[26] Table 28.1 summarizes the membership and stated objectives of some of the key players within the global regulatory architecture.

With the exception of international financial institutions such as the IMF—which can make compliance with international financial standards a condition for receiving loans and whose Member States are legally obligated to submit to assessments—the global regulatory architecture is structured through informal, non-binding agreements often referred to as 'soft law'.[27] Soft law—as opposed to formal treaties—is often chosen as a means of making progress in international initiatives where the subject-matter is fast developing. It permits delegation of rule production to a specialist organization, facilitating greater responsiveness than would be feasible if a treaty had to be renegotiated.[28] Moreover, the non-binding nature of these agreements facilitates consensus in a world characterized by divergent national interests—enabling international institutions to articulate 'off the rack' standards, which can be tailored to reflect domestic circumstances.[29] As Anne-Marie Slaughter explains, soft law can thus be understood as

---

[22] The BIS, although initially established in connection with the administration of post First World War German reparations, took on its full role in the post Second World War international financial architecture as a bank for central banks, a global financial monitor, a monetary and financial policy research organization, and an international financial regulatory facilitator.

[23] IOSCO's membership also includes approximately eighty other regional and international organizations: see 'About IOSCO', available at http://www.iosco.org.

[24] See IOSCO, *Objectives and Principles of Securities Regulation* (2003).

[25] See IOSCO, *Multilateral Memorandum of Understanding Concerning Consultation and Cooperation and the Exchange of Information* (2002).

[26] The CPMI was, until 1 September 2014, known as the Committee on Payment and Settlement Systems ('CPSS').

[27] Brummer, n 9.

[28] AT Guzman and TL Meyer, 'International Soft Law' (2010) 2 *Journal of Legal Analysis* 171, 197–201.

[29] Brummer, n 9.

providing a focal point for policy convergence.[30] Consistent with this view, international institutions such as the G20, FSB, and BCBS have played an increasingly prominent role in the formulation of high-level policy initiatives in the wake of the global financial crisis.[31]

Table 28.1 Key players in the global financial regulatory architecture

Institution	Est.	Membership	Stated Objectives
IMF	1945	188 Member States.	Promoting world trade, stable exchange rates and orderly international payment systems; conducting FSAP and other assessments; acting as international lender of last resort.
G20	1999	19 Member States (Argentina, Australia, Brazil, Canada, China, France, Germany, India, Indonesia, Italy, Japan, the Republic of Korea, Mexico, Russia, Saudi Arabia, South Africa, Turkey, the UK, and the USA) and the EU.	Promoting discussion and coordination on matters pertaining to economic, financial, and monetary policy.
FSB	2009[32]	Regulators from 24 Member States (G20 Member States plus Hong Kong, the Netherlands, Singapore, Spain, and Switzerland) and international organizations such as the BIS, IMF, World Bank, and OECD; international standard setters such as the BCBS, IOSCO, IASB, and CPMI.	Coordinating the work of national financial authorities and international standard setting bodies and developing and promoting the implementation of effective regulatory, supervisory, and other financial sector policies.
BCBS	1974	Central bank governors and national banking supervisors from 27 Member States (FSB Member States plus Belgium, Luxembourg, and Sweden).	Enhancing the understanding of key supervisory issues and improving the quality of banking supervision worldwide.
IOSCO	1983	Securities regulators from approximately 120 countries; approximately 80 other members.	Promoting high standards of securities regulation; facilitating the exchange of information; establishing standards for international securities transactions; and promoting enforcement of standards.
IASB	2001	16 individual members.	Developing high-quality and enforceable global accounting standards.
CPMI	1990	Central banks from 25 Member States.	Strengthening financial market infrastructure through the promotion of sound and efficient payment and settlement systems.

---

[30] AM Slaughter, *A New World Order* (Princeton: Princeton UP, 2004).

[31] At least within the G20 and other developed economies. The influence of these institutions within emerging economies is less clear.

[32] The FSB's limited predecessor, the Financial Stability Forum, was established in 1999.

28.3 The Post-Crisis Response of International Organizations

The mere cataloguing of international financial institutions, standard setters, and agenda setters does not do justice to the wave governance reforms undertaken through this global financial regulatory architecture in the wake of the financial crisis. An unprecedented series of G20 Leaders' Summits catalysed an outpouring of regulatory guidance from international organizations that had previously been moribund, ignored, or hampered by the difficulty in obtaining consensus.[33] Moreover, international standard and agenda setters undertook monitoring of national adoption of the agreed-upon regulatory measures and of uniform implementation of agreed-upon standards. This close monitoring prepares the way for the implicit threat that dealings with non-compliant institutions will carry a penalty. In this way, the shock of crisis-related fallout has begun to harden the soft law of international financial regulatory coordination. Moreover, the financial crisis showed the value of international financial coordinating bodies, even purportedly ineffectual ones, because they offered a pre-existing structure for collaboration.

The simmering financial crisis exploded after the Lehman bankruptcy in September 2008. Shortly thereafter, President Bush convened a Leaders' Summit of the G20.[34] Beginning with the initial November 2008 Summit, and continuing through nine successive Leaders' Summits over seven years, the G20 has played a major role in driving global financial reform. The G20 transformed the toothless Financial Stability Forum into the FSB and tasked it with a major agenda-setting role.[35] The BCBS, which had previously laboured for six years to produce the Basel II accords,[36] quickly produced a revision, Basel 2.5, to control risk-taking in banks' trading books, and then, in December 2010, Basel III, which provided for comprehensive strengthening of banks' balance sheets as described in Chapters 14 and 15.[37]

To ensure uniform adoption of and adherence to the Basel standards, the FSB and the BCBS created four parallel work streams. First, the BCBS undertook systematic

[33] These were: Washington (November 2008), London (April 2009), Pittsburgh (September 2009), Toronto (June 2010), Seoul (November 2010), Cannes (November 2011), Los Cabos (June 2012), and St Petersburg (September 2013): see University of Toronto G20 Information Centre, 'G20 Summits' (http://www.g20.utoronto.ca/summits/index.html). Summits since 2013 have not focused on the reform of international financial regulation.

[34] See CI Bradford, JF Linn, and P Martin, 'Global Governance Breakthrough: The G20 Summit and the Future Agenda', Brookings Policy Brief No 168 (2008).

[35] See JR Barth, C Brummer, T Li, and DE Nolle, 'Systemically Important Banks (SIBs) in the Post-Crisis Era: "The" Global Response and Reponses Around the Globe for 135 Countries', in AN Berger, P Molyneux, and J Wilson (eds), *The Oxford Handbook of Banking*, 2nd ed (Oxford: OUP, 2015), Ch 26 (describing G20–FSB interaction and initiatives); DE Nolle, 'Who's in Charge of Fixing the World's Financial System? The Under-Appreciated Lead Role of the G20 and the FSB' (2015) 24 *Financial Markets, Institutions & Instruments* 1.

[36] DK Tarullo, *Banking on Basel: The Future of International Banking Regulation* (Washington DC: The Peterson Institute for International Economics, 2008).

[37] For general summaries of the post-crisis regulatory reform agenda, see M Carney, 'The Future of Financial Reform', speech at the 2014 Monetary Authority of Singapore Lecture, 17 November 2014; P Tucker, 'Regulatory Reform, Stability, and Central Banking', Hutchins Center of Fiscal and Monetary Policy at Brookings, 16 January 2014; J Caruana, 'Building a Resilient Financial System', keynote speech, 2012 ADB Financial Sector Forum on 'Enhancing Financial Stability—Issues and Challenges', Manila, 7 February 2012.

monitoring of the extent to which particular nations had adopted the agreed-upon Basel III standards. These monitoring results were formally reported so that the laggards could be publicly targeted, albeit through 'naming and shaming' rather than through hard-law mechanisms. Second, the BCBS undertook to provide more granular guidance as to interpretive questions that would arise under Basel III, so as to facilitate uniform application. For example, the Basel standards require 'risk-weighting' of particular assets as the basis for capital charges, as we discussed in Chapter 14. The BCBS has produced detailed guidance for the application of these standards by domestic regulators, through a 'consultative' or 'notice and comment' process that an administrative lawyer would find very familiar.[38]

Third, the BCBS has monitored the extent to which the standards have been *consistently* applied in the cross-national setting. For example, one important early study showed the extent to which 'risk-weighting' for similar assets varied across jurisdictions, as a way of stimulating greater efforts towards consistency of applica-tion.[39] Fourth, in its 'Regulatory Consistency Assessment Programme' the BCBS has undertaken country-level reviews of compliance with the Basel III regime.[40]

The BCBS has attempted to buttress the authoritativeness of the Basel III standards by bringing them within the G20 process, thus strengthening the legitimacy by which this network of central banks and financial supervisors is imposing a particular vision of international financial regulation. The G20 specifically endorsed the Basel III programme at the November 2010 Seoul summit.[41] In turn, the Committee has sought to retain the G20's engagement:

> The Committee regularly updates the G20 on member jurisdictions' progress towards implementing the Basel III standards. These reports include information on the Committee's efforts to improve consistency in reported prudential capital ratios across banks and jurisdictions, the harmonisation of regulations across member jurisdictions, finalisation of remaining post-crisis reforms that form part of the Basel regulatory framework and steps being taken to reduce variance in implementa-tion practices.[42]

Once again, the main 'enforcement' mechanism, at least at this stage, is informal/ reputational. It is easy to imagine how the Basel process could 'harden', however. For example, an amendment to the Basel III standards could provide for a higher risk weight—or an additional liquidity requirement—in respect of dealings with a party based in a jurisdiction that was found not to be in substantial compliance with the

---

[38] See eg BCBS, 'Revisions to the Standardised Approach for Credit Risk—Second Consultative Docu-ment' (2015).

[39] See eg BCBS, 'Regulatory Consistency Assessment Program: Analysis of Risk-Weighted Assets for Credit Risk in the Banking Book' (2013), bcbs256 (reporting on inter-bank variations in risk-weighting). For the series of regulatory consistency reports, see BCBS, 'Assessing the Consistency of Regulatory Outcomes', available at http://www.bis.org/bcbs/implementation/l3.htm.

[40] See eg BCBS, 'Assessing Consistency of Implementation of Basel Standards (as of June 2015)', available at http://www.bis.org/bcbs/implementation/l2.htm.

[41] See G20, 'The Seoul Summit Document' (2010), para 29.

[42] BCBS, 'Reports to the G20 on Implementation Monitoring,' available at http://www.bis.org/bcbs/impl_moni_g20.htm.

standards, on the view that such a counterparty relationship created special risk factors. The threat of a higher funding cost on international banking markets seems credible so long as the complying institutions are the dominant players in the world financial system.

In addition to the Basel III metrics, the BCBS has re-emphasized the importance of consistent supervisory standards, since supervision and regulation are complements as well as substitutes.[43] This has led to the promulgation of the *Core Principles for Effective Banking Supervision* in September 2012, reflecting a post-crisis re-evaluation of principles first issued in 1997 and most recently revised in 2006. The revised Core Principles include a focus on a bank's risk management and governance, greater attention to systemically important banks, and the importance of applying a system-wide macroprudential perspective to microprudential supervision. Additional Core Principles address greater public disclosure and transparency, as well as enhanced financial reporting and public audit.[44] These supervisory standards have been bolstered by the statement of *Principles for Effective Risk Data Aggregation and Risky Reporting*,[45] which are specifically aimed at G-SIBs and then later to be applied to domestic systemically important banks ('D-SIBs').

Post-crisis supervision efforts illustrate the point made by Anne-Marie Slaughter that an important measure of international regulation comes through networks of national supervisors.[46] For example, in their efforts to supervise large institutions on the dimensions of risk management, the national supervisors and the BCBS 'agreed to monitor and assess banks' progress through the Basel Committee's Supervision and Implementation Group'.[47] This has led, in early stages, to self-assessments by banks with plans for follow-up.[48] This seems plainly an effort by national supervisors to use the international network to present a united front against potentially resistant (and locally powerful) institutions.[49]

28.4 One Hard Law Post-Crisis Response: The European Banking Union

One of the major obstacles to international financial regulatory coordination is regulatory fragmentation, that is, the presence of multiple jurisdictions imposing divergent regulation and supervisory practices. The Basel III regime is obviously an effort to set

---

[43] Supervision has long been regarded as the second 'pillar' of the Basel framework. Disclosure is the third.

[44] See BCBS, *Core Principles for Effective Banking Supervision* (2012), bcbs230.

[45] See BCBS, *Principles for Effective Risk Data Aggregation and Risk Reporting* (2013), bcbs239.

[46] See n 30.

[47] BCBS, *Progress in Adopting the Principles for Effective Risk Data Aggregation and Risk Reporting* (2015), bcbs2684, 1.

[48] Ibid.

[49] Cross-country comparative assessments by expert academics may also help with convergence toward high-quality supervision regimes. See eg JR Barth, G Caprio, Jr, and R Levine, 'Bank Regulation and Supervision in 180 Countries from 1999 to 2011' (2013) 5 *Journal of Financial Economic Policy* 111 (database based on World Bank surveys).

higher standards that will be broadly adhered to, but as we have noted, it is a soft law regime whose staying power may wane as crisis memories fade. Another post-crisis approach was the creation within the EU of hard law regimes of regulatory coordination for banks. As Chapter 24 explains, two sets of regimes were sequentially set up.[50] The first, established in January 2011, created the European Banking Authority ('EBA'), as part of an overall 'European System of Financial Supervision'. The goal of the EBA was to strengthen the traditional EU model of 'coordination' among national regulators by working towards a European 'Single Rulebook' in banking with the objective of providing 'a single set of harmonized prudential rules for financial institutions throughout the EU' and by 'promoting' convergence in supervisory standards.[51] The EBA can adopt mandatory 'technical standards', but its authority over Member State financial regulators is limited.

This 'thin' EU-wide regulatory regime was clearly insufficient to deal with the interlinked sovereign debt and banking crises in the Eurozone over the 2010–12 period that threatened the stability of the euro itself. This crucible overcame nationalist obstacles and led to the creation of the European Banking Union ('Banking Union'). The result was a second, overlapping, and much more robust regime of centralized supervision and solvency monitoring over all banks in the Eurozone (and those of any other EU Member State choosing to opt in). The critical elements were the Single Supervisory Mechanism ('SSM'), which tasked the ECB with supervision of all significant Eurozone banks, and the Single Resolution Mechanism ('SRM'), which gave a new Single Resolution Board ('SRB') the power to put a significant Eurozone bank into resolution.[52]

The impact of these European regimes, especially the Banking Union, for international financial regulatory coordination is to significantly reduce the number of critical players whose actions must be coordinated, especially in a crisis situation.[53] Since post-crisis legislation tended to consolidate prudential oversight of systemically important financial institutions in central banks, this means that, in meaningful respects, the critical decision-makers in the countries primarily involved in a financial crisis like the 2007–9 one are now only three: the Federal Reserve, the Bank of England, and the ECB.[54]

---

[50] Chapter 24, sections 24.3.3–24.3.4.

[51] http://www.eba.europa.eu/about-us/missions-and-tasks.

[52] For more detail, see Chapter 16, section 16.6 and Chapter 24, section 24.3.4. See also JN Gordon and WG Ringe, 'Bank Resolution in the European Banking Union: A Transatlantic Perspective on What It Would Take' (2015) 115 *Columbia Law Review* 1297, 1303–10.

[53] Yet, the internal coordination challenges of the Banking Union, which critically relies on the loyal cooperation of national supervisory authorities with the ECB and the smooth interaction between the ECB and the SRB, will prove crucial to its success. See Chapter 27, section 27.2.3.

[54] Of course, we are not assuming here that the next crisis will be similar to the last one. Whatever the dynamics of the next crisis, given their centrality, the US, the UK, and the EU financial systems will play a role in either containing or propagating it. Intuitively, it should be easier for the relevant decision-makers to coordinate so as to contain a financial crisis under the framework of the European Banking Union than without it.

28.5 International Financial Regulatory
Coordination: The Problem of Supervision

Before the crisis it was of course recognized that effective cross-border supervision of financial institutions was increasingly important. The impact of globalization, concentration, and interconnectedness made large international banking groups and financial conglomerates one of the most likely sources and conduits for the transmission of systemic risk, making them both potentially 'too big' and 'too interconnected' to fail. Indeed, large, internationally active financial institutions were at the epicentre of the global financial crisis.

The crisis revealed many gaps in cross-border supervision. Effective cross-border supervision of these institutions poses a number of challenges. Supervisors in the ('home') jurisdiction in which a parent institution is licensed and authorized will often find it costly to monitor the activities of the institution and its affiliates in other ('host') jurisdictions.[55] They may also find it difficult to evaluate the quality and intensity of supervision in these jurisdictions. Supervisors in the host jurisdictions, conversely, may have little information about the activities or financial health of a parent, or the quality and intensity of supervision in the home jurisdiction.[56] While the obvious solution is for home and host supervisors to coordinate their activities, such coordination is often hampered by asymmetric endowments of information, expertise, and other resources, the absence of clearly defined supervisory responsibilities and, perhaps most importantly, divergent incentives.[57] Effective cross-border supervision is thus both very important and very difficult.[58]

The BCBS has developed a framework for the supervision of international banking groups. This framework has evolved over time in response to both changes in the

---

[55] See F Mishkin and S Eakins, *Financial Markets and Institutions*, 8th ed (Pearson: Harlow, 2014). We would expect these information problems to be compounded by the complexity of these groups and their interconnections: see H Mehran, A Morrison, and J Shapiro, 'Corporate Governance and Banks: What Have We Learned from the Financial Crisis?' in M Dewatripont and X Freixas (eds), *The Crisis Aftermath: New Regulatory Paradigms* (London: CEPR, 2012), 11; R Herring and J Carmassi, 'The Corporate Structure of International Financial Conglomerates—Complexity and Its Implications for Safety and Soundness', in A Berger, P Molyneux, and J Wilson (eds), *Oxford Handbook of Banking* (Oxford: OUP, 2012).

[56] See K Pistor, 'Host's Dilemma: Rethinking EU Banking Regulation in Light of the Global Crisis', ECGI Working Paper No 286/2010 (2010).

[57] Coordination may also be hampered by legal obstacles to cross-border information flow.

[58] A special problem is supervision of financial conglomerates, especially those unaffiliated with a major bank and thus outside of the BCBS regime. In the run-up to the financial crisis, the SEC took on 'consolidated' (that is, worldwide) supervision of the major US investment banks—including Bear Stearns and Lehman Brothers—in response to the EU's Financial Conglomerates Directive (Directive 2002/87/EC [2002] OJ L35/1, now amended by Directive 2011/89/EU [2011] OJ L326/113). The SEC's supervisory efforts were thinly staffed and significantly relied on internal monitoring. This supervisory undertaking did not end well. See US SEC, 'SEC's Oversight of Bear Stearns and Related Entities: The Consolidated Supervised Entity Program' (2008). In the post-crisis period, the BCBS, IOSCO, and the International Association of Insurance Supervisors collaborated on the 'Principles for the Supervision of Financial Conglomerates' (2012), available at http://www.bis.org/publ/joint29.pdf. With the end of large US investment banks as free-standing financial intermediaries, extra-banking group supervision has become less critical to international financial regulation, at least for now.

structure and activities of these groups and various bank failures.[59] This framework calls for the consolidated supervision of an international banking group's worldwide operations under the oversight of a single home supervisor with the power to collect information from host supervisors.[60] In practice, this typically means that home supervisors are responsible for the consolidated supervision of both the parent and the wider group, including any foreign branches and subsidiaries.[61] Thus, for example, if UK-headquartered Barclays or HSBC were to open a branch in Japan, the UK Prudential Regulation Authority would be the consolidated prudential supervisor. Host supervisors would still be responsible for the prudential supervision of domestic subsidiaries and branches of foreign banking groups. Importantly, where a host supervisor determines that a home supervisor is not adequately performing its obligations as consolidated supervisor, it may restrict or altogether prohibit the activities of an international banking group in the host jurisdiction.

A distinction that may be relevant for the allocation of responsibility between home and host supervisors is whether an international banking group elects to conduct its foreign operations through *branches* or *subsidiaries*. Branches have no separate legal personality: they lend and trade using the same capital as their parent, and are jointly liable for all liabilities.[62] Subsidiaries, in contrast, are legally separate entities incorporated in the jurisdiction in which they carry on their operations. They thus possess their own assets and liabilities separate and apart from those of their parent. In the presence of international arrangements for the coordination of bank supervision, such as within the EU, prudential oversight of cross-border branches will primarily fall to the consolidated home supervisor. Host supervisors will have a greater role in the oversight of subsidiaries and will focus only on liquidity with respect to branches.

The framework developed by the BCBS is often augmented by so-called 'colleges' of supervisors. Supervisory colleges are comprised of representatives from both the home and host supervisors of a given international banking group. The primary objective of these colleges is to facilitate the exchange of information between supervisors, ultimately with a view to identifying potential cross-border risks.[63] This exchange of information typically takes place on a voluntary and confidential basis. While the structure of supervisory colleges varies widely in practice, they are generally not

---

[59] The first framework dates back to the mid-1970s in response to the Herstatt failure: see BCBS, *Report on the Supervision of Banks' Foreign Establishments* (1975) (the 'Concordat'). The Concordat was supplemented in 1983 by the BCBS's *Principles for the Supervision of Banks' Foreign Establishments*, and in 1992 by the *Minimum Standards for the Supervision of International Banking Groups and their Cross-Border Establishments* (the latter spurred by the failure of BCCI in 1991). A number of high-level principles relating to cross-border supervision are also articulated in the BCBS *Core Principles*, n 44.

[60] See Principles 24 and 25 of the BCBS *Core Principles*, n 44.

[61] See K D'Hulster, 'Cross Border Banking Supervision: Incentive Conflicts in Supervisory Information Sharing between Home and Host Supervisors' (2012) 13 *Journal of Banking Regulation* 300. The EU 'passport' system, which enables an institution licensed and authorized in one Member State to offer financial services and establish branches in other Member States without also seeking separate authorization in the host jurisdiction, is thus a reflection of this framework.

[62] Branch structures are also often characterized by the centralization of key functions like strategy, operations, and treasury at the parent level.

[63] D'Hulster, n 61.

designed as a forum for substantive decision-making.[64] As a result, participation in these colleges does not restrict the powers of either home or host supervisors to take unilateral action in response to emerging risks. Supervisory colleges have been used as a mechanism for coordinating cross-border supervision for decades. Nevertheless, in the wake of the global financial crisis, there have been renewed calls for the expanded use—and strengthening—of the college system.[65] These calls have resulted in the establishment of supervisory colleges for all global systemically important financial institutions.

The current framework for cross-border supervision suffers from a number of significant structural weaknesses. As a preliminary matter, there is little reason to think that the division of responsibilities between home and host supervisors will necessarily reflect the location, nature, or extent of potential risks.[66] Indeed, this division may actually generate opportunities for regulatory arbitrage, as banking groups structure their operations so as to take advantage of perceived differences in supervisory intensity across jurisdictions. Effective oversight of subsidiaries by host supervisors may, similarly, be undermined by groups channelling capital through non-deposit-taking institutions (such as finance or leasing companies) or by providing services directly to customers in foreign markets.[67]

Further, there is the issue of how to ensure effective, reliable cross-border information flow among supervisors. Historically cross-border information flows have been structured by bilateral or multilateral MOUs entered into by national regulators. Such MOUs ultimately rely on reputational sanctions, which may be insufficient to ensure seamless information sharing when the stakes are high, ie when a cross-border bank is on the verge of insolvency and a full-blown banking crisis may be looming.[68]

In the aftermath of the crisis, there has accordingly been a redoubling of efforts—spearheaded by the FSB—to establish more robust mechanisms for ensuring timely and comprehensive cross-border information flow.[69] These efforts include the proposed global Legal Entity Identifier ('LEI') system. The global LEI system would require the registration of each legal entity within the financial system. Each registrant would be assigned an LEI carrying an increasing amount of reference information. The next, and in many respects more important, phase would be to develop unique product identifiers ('PIs') for each and every species of financial claim—from basic equity and debt, to derivatives, and other more exotic instruments. LEIs and PIs would then work in tandem: with the former capturing information about the counterparties to each

---

[64] Perhaps unsurprisingly, the EU framework for cross-border supervision and supervisory colleges is in many respects more robust than those between other jurisdictions. This framework mandates not only the exchange of information, but also consultation on supervisory action, joint model validation, and written coordination agreements. Colleges of supervisors are also *mandatory* for international banking groups with significant cross-border branches or subsidiaries. Even in the EU, however, where supervisors are unable to reach a consensus, the consolidated home supervisor is still entitled to take unilateral action. Within the Eurozone, after the creation of the European Banking Union, the SSM resolves this problem through the ECB's role.

[65] See eg G20, 'Summit Declaration on Financial Markets and the World Economy' (15 November 2008).

[66] Along a similar vein, fragmenting responsibility for the solvency and liquidity of branches would seem likely to generate coordination problems—especially given how quickly liquidity problems can become solvency problems.

[67] Pistor, n 56.   [68] See section 28.8.

[69] See FSB, 'A Global Legal Entity Identifier for Financial Markets' (2012).

financial transaction, and the latter the salient details of the transactions themselves. Together, LEIs and PIs can thus be understood as the building blocks for a more accurate and complete map of the complex interconnections between financial markets and institutions and, thus, the potential risks residing within the global financial system. At present, however, we are still some distance away from the implementation of a global LEI/PI system.

Perhaps the most significant weakness of the current framework stems from potential conflicts of interest between home and host supervisors.[70] Such conflicts may manifest themselves in a number of ways. Take, for example, the case of a parent of an international banking group that has encountered liquidity problems in its home jurisdiction. Were the consolidated home supervisor to inform host supervisors of these problems, host supervisors might respond by geographically 'ring-fencing' the assets of domestic branches in order to protect local depositors. This ring-fencing could take several forms: from the imposition of higher capital and liquidity requirements, to dividend restrictions, to constraints on intragroup transactions and forced subsidiarization.[71] Geographical ring-fencing, in turn, would serve to exacerbate the parent's liquidity problems. Anticipating this response, the consolidated home supervisor may pre-emptively seek to delay disclosure of the problem to host supervisors or otherwise downplay its significance. The BCBS framework and supervisory colleges are ultimately poorly equipped to address this problem.

This example exposes a broader conflict of interest. Specifically, in the absence of mechanisms enabling supervisors to commit credibly to intensive supervision, timely and comprehensive information flow, and burden sharing, both home and host supervisors possess powerful incentives to pursue strategies designed to ensure that the largest possible pool of *group* assets is available to satisfy the claims of *domestic* depositors, counterparties, and other creditors in the event of insolvency or resolution. The resulting zero-sum game can be seen as driving, for example, recent measures by the US Federal Reserve Board to enhance prudential standards for foreign banking operations.[72] The UK's PRA has also recently announced its intention to force domestic branches of some foreign banking groups to reorganize as subsidiaries.[73] Going forward, these and other similar moves may increase funding costs for international

[70] See R Herring, 'Conflicts Between Home and Host Country Prudential Supervisors', in D Evanoff, R LaBrosse, and G Kaufman (eds), *International Financial Stability: Global Banking and National Regulation* (World Scientific Publishing: Singapore, 2007).

[71] See E Cerutti, A Ilyina, Y Makarova, and C Schmieder, 'Banking Without Borders? Implications of Ring-Fencing for European Cross Border Banks', IMF Working Paper No 10/247 (2010); D'Hulster, n 61; K D'Hulster and I Otker-Robe, 'Ring-Fencing Cross-Border Banks: An Effective Supervisory Response?' (2015) 16 *Journal of Banking Regulation* 169.

[72] See Federal Reserve System, Enhanced Prudential Standards for Bank Holding Companies and Foreign Banking Organizations, 12 CFR Part 252 (27 March 2014). The Fed's position reflected its concern that capital-lite non-bank subsidiaries of European banking groups, funded by wholesale short-term creditors, would compete in the US market on an uneven playing field. The Fed was also mindful that its rescue of AIG had provided massive solvency support for European banks over which it had no regulatory oversight.

[73] See PRA, 'Supervising International Banks: The Prudential Regulation Authority's Approach to Branch Supervision', Policy Statement PS8/14 (2014).

banking groups as capital and liquidity become 'trapped' in different jurisdictions.[74] It may also make these groups less resilient, as excess liquidity in one part of the group will be unavailable to address shortfalls elsewhere.[75] Over the long term, meanwhile, such geographic ring-fencing may even result in global retrenchment as groups withdraw from host jurisdictions. Ultimately, perhaps the only way to deter this type of non-cooperative behaviour is to develop more credible and effective cross-border crisis response and resolution mechanisms.[76] It is to this dimension of international coordination that we now turn.

28.6 Post-Crisis Response: Cross-Border Resolution

Regulatory coordination with respect to internationally active financial institutions in ordinary times is one thing, but at times of financial distress such coordination is much more challenging. Coordination (and cooperation) breaks down because of (i) the divergent national effects, (ii) the manifest failure of *ex ante* regulatory coordination, and (iii) the sense that some *other* national regulator has failed in its responsibility. Yet the inability to coordinate at the moment of failure can be extremely costly, since national ring-fencing and asset-grabbing can disrupt international finance and multiply the damage to the real economy. The limitations of the pre-crisis regime were made abundantly clear by crisis responses that demonstrated that 'banks are global in life and national in death', as it was memorably put by Bank of England Governor Mervyn King.[77] This is interpreted to mean that 'when crises occur, it is national central banks which have to provide lender of last resort ('LOLR') support and national governments that provide fiscal support, and that if there is a failure, bankruptcy procedures are national and it matters with which specific legal entity a creditor has their claim'.[78] During the 2007–9 financial crisis, a number of large, complex financial institutions with extensive cross-border operations were resolved in a disorderly way, often along national lines, including Lehman Brothers and Fortis Bank.[79] At the same time, national resolution regimes were exposed as not fit for purpose. In the US, the Federal Deposit Insurance Corporation's ('FDIC') resolution regime was available only to insured deposit-taking institutions. In the UK, meanwhile, there was no permanent

---

[74] See J Fiechter, I Okter-Robe, A Ilyina, M Hsu, A Santos, and J Surti, 'Subsidiaries or Branches: Does One Size Fit All?', IMF Staff Discussion Note SDN/11/04 (2011) for a general overview of the relevant advantages and disadvantages of different organizational models; see also D'Hulster and Otker-Robe, n 71, for an overview of similar moves in other jurisdictions.

[75] Yet, ring-fencing may also make firms more resolvable insofar as it makes carving out and selling off financially viable parts of the group less complex and costly.

[76] Fiechter, Otker-Robe, Ilyina, Hsu, Santos, and Surti, n 74; D'Hulster and Otker-Robe, n 71; D'Hulster, n 61.

[77] As quoted in A Turner, *The Turner Review: A Regulatory Response to the Global Financial Crisis* (London: FSA, 2009), 36.

[78] Ibid.

[79] Fortis Bank had operations in Belgium, Luxembourg, and the Netherlands. The problems that arose from the inconsistent objectives of the national regulators are described in Z Kudrna, 'Cross-Border Resolution of Failed Banks in the European Union After the Crisis: Business As Usual' (2012) 50 *Journal of Common Market Studies* 283, 288–90. See also S Claessens, R Herring, and D Schoenmaker, *A Safer World Financial System: Improving the Resolution of Systemic Institutions* (Geneva: International Center for Monetary and Banking Studies, 2010).

special resolution regime for financial institutions prior to the reforms introduced under the Banking Act of 2009.

Thus, the capacity to take timely, decisive, and coordinated action to avoid (or contain) a developing crisis has been a major post-crisis objective of international financial regulatory coordination. The crystallization of systemic risk within a large and interconnected economy—precipitated by, for example, the failure of a large, complex financial institution—would almost certainly generate significant cross-border externalities. There is, accordingly, a manifest need for cross-border contingency plans designed to minimize these externalities by providing for the orderly recovery and resolution of systemically important financial institutions. The financial crisis drove home the importance of such contingency planning. Just as clearly, it also drove home the challenges of trying to create such a regime. What stands in the way? First, national regulators invariably face political, fiscal, and institutional pressures to prioritize the interests of domestic constituencies: the financial services industry, depositors, tax-payers, and other economic stakeholders.[80] These pressures encourage national regulators to discount the impact of their decisions on other jurisdictions.[81] Second, and relatedly, the constructive use of resolution tools, such as bail-in, in one jurisdiction can have a deleterious impact on financial stability in other jurisdictions—for example, by undermining the solvency of bailed-in creditors domiciled in these jurisdictions.[82] Finally, national regulators may face different constraints on their legal authority, financial resources, and institutional capacity which effectively limit the range of available policy options. Together, these factors can drive a wedge between the most desirable—or possible—courses of action from the perspective of different jurisdictions.

Four strategies have emerged in the post-crisis era to facilitate cross-border coordination in the resolution context. The first is reflected in the FSB's framework document entitled 'Key Attributes of Effective Resolution Regimes for Financial Institutions', which provides soft law guidance on best practices for resolution.[83] These Key Attributes recommend, *inter alia*, that the scope of national resolution regimes should extend to all financial institutions whose failure could have systemic consequences, that national regulators should wield broad resolution powers, including transfer powers, explicit bail-in powers to write down debt and to convert it to equity and the power to

---

[80] Herring, n 70. Relatedly, national regulators may also be subject to legal regimes which prioritize domestic interests. In the US, for example, national depositor preference is enshrined in the Federal Deposit Insurance Act.

[81] Todorov, Beck, and Wagner, for example, predict that the incentives of domestic regulators to intervene to resolve a cross-border financial institution will (1) *increase* (decrease) with the proportion of the institution's foreign (domestic) equity and (2) *decrease* (increase) with the proportion of its foreign (domestic) assets and deposits: R Todorov, T Beck, and W Wagner, 'Supervising Cross-Border Banks' (2013) 28 *Economic Policy* 5. This prediction proceeds from the intuition that the benefits of regulatory forbearance will accrue mainly to equity-holders, while the costs will fall mainly to debtholders and other economic stakeholders.

[82] This, in turn, serves to underscore the potential benefits of a global tracking system, as discussed at n 69.

[83] FSB, 'Key Attributes of Effective Resolution Regimes for Financial Institutions' (rev 2014). The FSB followed up with additional guidance regarding recovery and resolution planning: FSB, 'Recovery and Resolution Planning: Making the Key Attributes Requirements Operational', Consultative Document (2012).

impose a temporary stay on contractual termination rights, and that resolution funding should come from deposit guarantee scheme ('DGS') funds or separate resolution funds. By facilitating orderly resolution, these tools are designed to reduce the likelihood of a taxpayer-funded bail-out.[84] Addressing the international dimension of bank failures, the Key Attributes recommend an approach to cross-border resolution based on 'modified universalism', with a presumption of cooperation between home authorities, who would take the lead, and host authorities—but host authorities would be in a fallback position to take independent action if necessary to protect financial stability in their jurisdiction. The Key Attributes have received endorsement through formal declaration at the 2011 G20 Summit in Cannes.[85]

The second strategy is the hard-law international coordination achieved through the EU and then the European Banking Union. The EU adopted the Bank Recovery and Resolution Directive, which picks up many of the FSB's Key Attributes,[86] and thus harmonized the national resolution regimes throughout the EU, including the emphasis on bail-in as a regulatory tool. More significant in addressing intra-EU cross-border issues was creation of the European Banking Union, which introduces an SRM for members of the Eurozone. As discussed in section 28.4, this put a single authority, the SRB, in charge of initiating and managing bank resolutions, with a decision procedure that tries to address the possibly diverging national interests.[87] Such a hard law approach would presumably avoid the value-destruction associated with the resolution of Fortis Bank. As we have noted, the Banking Union provides a mandatory regulatory coordination mechanism for Eurozone countries in resolution as well as standard-setting and supervision.

A third strategy to address cross-border coordination problems has been the negotiation of a series of MOUs between regulators in which the 'home' regulator articulates some degree of commitment to ensuring the solvency and liquidity of a foreign branch or subsidiary of a systemically important institution that has been put into resolution. The most important example of this is the MOU negotiated in December 2012 between the FDIC and the Bank of England, in which the regulators have undertaken to conduct resolutions that would:

ensure continuity of all critical services performed by the operating firm(s), thereby reducing risks to financial stability [and] ensure [that] activities of the firms in the

---

[84] See J Armour, 'Making Bank Resolution Credible', in N Moloney, E Ferran, and J Payne (eds), *The Oxford Handbook of Financial Regulation* (Oxford: OUP, 2015), 453, 467–76.

[85] G20, 'Cannes Summit Final Declaration—Building Our Common Future: Renewed Collective Action for the Benefit of All', para 28 (2011). The FSB's November 2015 report on the 'Resolvability Assessment Process' presents a mixed picture of the reception of the Key Attributes: G-SIB home jurisdictions have bank resolution regimes 'with a range of powers that are broadly in line with the *Key Attributes*'; other jurisdictions, not so much. Moreover, 'reforms to resolution regimes and resolution planning are less advanced for insurers and financial market infrastructures than for banks'. FSB, 'Removing Remaining Obstacles to Resolvability' (2015).

[86] Directive 2014/59 of the European Parliament and of the Council of 15 May 2014 Establishing a Framework for the Recovery and Resolution of Credit Institutions and Investment Firms and Amending Council Directive 82/891/EEC, and Directives 2001/24/EC, 2002/47/EC, 2004/25/EC, 2005/56/EC, 2007/36/EC, 2011/35/EU, 2012/30/EU, and 2013/36/EU, and Regulations (EU) No 1093/2010 and (EU) No 648/2012, of the European Parliament and of the Council ('the BRRD') [2014] OJ L173/190.

[87] See Gordon and Ringe, n 52, 1347–8.

foreign jurisdictions in which [the failed parent firm operates] are unaffected, thereby minimizing risks to cross-border implementation.[88]

This approach is easiest to achieve using a Single Point of Entry (SPE) resolution scheme as discussed in Chapter 16, section 16.6, in which the only entity put into resolution is a holding company parent whose only assets are shares in subsidiaries. The SPE strategy entails writing off and converting unsecured term debt as necessary to recapitalize the failed parent institution while at the same time putting none of the operating subsidiaries, including foreign subsidiaries, through any sort of resolution procedure. Such an approach would have avoided the highly disruptive Lehman UK administration proceedings in 2008. Under the Orderly Liquidation Authority created under the Dodd–Frank Act, the FDIC has the authority to supply liquidity to the resolved entity, including its foreign subsidiaries. This approach is not as extraordinary as it seems. In the bankruptcy of non-financial firms with foreign subsidiaries, it is commonplace to structure debtor-in-possession financing so as to avoid bankruptcy of the foreign subsidiaries, precisely to avoid the lost value from possibly conflicting bankruptcy regimes. In the absence of a 'universalist' hard law regime, if the home country regulator (like a funded debtor in possession) can credibly undertake to protect the host's interest, then why would the host's regulator interfere?

Thus, home-country responsibility as reflected in agreements among regulators exercising local statutory authority may go a long way to solve the cross-border resolution problem in those cases. The missing piece is the risk that contracts entered into outside the 'home' jurisdiction may confound the home regulator's capacity to avoid triggering resolution of the subsidiaries, especially foreign subsidiaries. This is particularly a concern with financial contracts, such as derivatives, swaps, and other financing agreements that may contain clauses that provide for acceleration, collateral seizure, set-off, and other remedies upon a resolution of any affiliate. If entered into under the law of another jurisdiction, conceivably these contractual rights would not be stayed by the home (or host's) law. Prodded by their regulators, the large banks are working with the International Swaps and Derivatives Association ('ISDA') to obtain a private ordering solution: mandatory uniform clauses in which counterparties accede in advance to a stay of their acceleration rights in the event of a resolution that will protect their economic interests.

A fourth strategy is reflected in the strengthened resolution cost internalization regime outlined in the FSB's recent definition of a global standard for minimum amounts of Total Loss Absorbency Capacity ('TLAC') to be held by G-SIBs.[89] The goal is to ensure that even after write-downs in a resolution proceeding, a bank would be adequately capitalized so as to continue to provide banking services to the real economy without additional taxpayer support. As described in Chapter 16, section 16.6, the standard would require banks to hold regulatory capital and long-term unsecured debt that would at least double the required risk-weighted capital ratio of

---

[88] FDIC and Bank of England, 'Resolving Globally Active, Systemically Important, Financial Institutions' (2012).

[89] FSB, 'Principles on Loss-Absorbing and Recapitalisation Capacity of G-SIBs in Resolution: Total Loss Absorbing Capacity (TLAC) Term Sheet' (2015).

8 per cent and, separately, also double the required leverage ratio of 3 per cent. The self-insurance of a robust TLAC scheme should make it easier for regulatory authorities to credibly commit to 'home' responsibility, and thus for the spread of MOUs among regulators. Nevertheless, the FSB scheme also contemplates the 'pre-positioning' of 'internal TLAC' on the balance sheet of 'material' foreign subsidiaries, which appears to contemplate that hosts could decide to resolve the subsidiary by imposing write-downs on the upstream parent.

From a systemic risk perspective, what's important is the emergence of a network of MOUs between the regulatory authorities with resolution authority over the G-SIBs and the various jurisdictions in which the G-SIBs have significant activity, giving home regulators responsibility over the process. It might be that the stresses of crisis-time domestic considerations will make it hard for hosts to rely on home regulators, but the ammunition of TLAC provides a basis for home regulator credibility. The testing case would be presented by an instance in which the losses at the foreign subsidiary exceed the prepositioned TLAC, or in general are so large as to require resolution of the parent, if, as per the SPE model, all losses are upstreamed. This would mean imposing losses on the parent's shareholders and long-term debtholders (perhaps local parties) so as to protect depositors and other creditors of the foreign subsidiary. That's what best-case international financial regulatory coordination would require. So there is room for scepticism as well as hope regarding our ability to ensure the orderly resolution of a global systemically important financial institution.

28.7 Is International Financial Regulatory Convergence, or Harmonization, Desirable?

The preceding sections have relied on the unexamined assumption that regulatory convergence is a desirable, perhaps necessary, element of international financial regulatory coordination, and that harmonization would proceed not just through substantive law but also through common approaches to supervision and enforcement. The monitoring regimes of the BCBS, the FSB, and IOSCO focus on adoption and adherence to a common set of standards and behaviours.

Is the push for substantial uniformity justified in light of the arguments made forcefully in other domains about the value of diversity generally and regulatory competition, rather than regulatory fiat, as the mechanism for the emergence of the 'best' regime? The pith of this argument is that the regulated entities have better information about what would make for a 'good' regulatory regime than the regulators. In a competitive environment, in which regulatees can choose among regimes,[90] regulators will be strongly incentivized to design and implement regulatory regimes that take on board this superior information about the 'best' regulatory responses. This information then spurs a process of regulatory experimentation and updating, resulting in progressively more desirable regulatory regimes. Predictably, proponents of regulatory competition tend to view harmonization

---

[90] Either because they can choose the *jurisdiction(s)* in which they carry out their business activities or their *business structure* (where different jurisdictions and/or structures are subject to different regulatory regimes).

as an inherently undesirable suppression of this market mechanism. Some also view it as a source of potential systemic instability.[91] As Roberta Romano has observed, harmonization can amplify the systemic impact of (inevitable) regulatory failures—in effect by incentivizing regulated actors in different jurisdictions to pursue homogeneous business strategies.[92] Viewed from this perspective, regulatory competition and diversity can be understood as representing a potentially valuable hedge against systemic regulatory miscalculation.[93]

There is certainly no guarantee that the regulatory convergence guided by centralized actors will produce the most socially desirable regulatory regimes. Indeed, the most desirable regimes would seem likely to change over time (as new crises will show), yet such change may be harder to obtain in a system of harmonized rules, given the greater complexity of negotiation at the international level and the likely difficulties in achieving consensus.[94] There is also no denying the fact that harmonization can generate significant unintended consequences—especially where regulators have been captured by regulated constituencies. Each of these factors arguably bolsters the case for some degree of regulatory diversity. Nevertheless, the rationale for unconstrained regulatory competition in the field of financial regulation is shortsighted in two important respects. First, supporters of regulatory competition discount the potential negative externalities generated by the pervasive regulatory arbitrage on which it implicitly relies. Second, and perhaps even more importantly, they fail to appreciate how ostensibly 'successful' regulatory experiments can change the flow of capital and risk in ways which put pressure on fragile parts of the financial system, leading to the build-up and crystallization of systemic risk.

Whether regulatory competition promotes the development of socially desirable regulatory regimes ultimately depends on the equilibrium reached in what is, in effect, a joint maximization problem. This problem is typically framed as stemming from a perceived conflict of interest between firms and investors with respect to the costs and benefits of, for example, investor protection mechanisms. As Stephen Choi explains, we would expect firms to institute credible investor protection mechanisms where the costs of doing so are less than the corresponding benefits in terms of the firms' cost of capital.[95] Where firms have the ability to select the regulatory regime which best satisfies this requirement, competition can thus be understood as potentially enhancing the welfare of both firms and their investors.[96] But this logic breaks down in the presence of externalities—that is, where firms and investors do not internalize the full

---

[91] R Romano, 'For Diversity in the International Regulation of Financial Institutions: Critiquing and Recalibrating the Basel Architecture' (2014) 31 *Yale Journal on Regulation* 1. Indeed, this view is not restricted to regulatory competition theorists: see J Gordon and C Mayer, 'The Micro, Macro and International Design of Financial Regulation', Columbia Law & Economics Working Paper No 422 (2012).

[92] Romano, n 91.   [93] Ibid.

[94] R Herring and R Litan, *Financial Regulation in the Global Economy* (Washington DC: Brookings, 1995).

[95] S Choi, 'Channeling Competition in the Global Securities Market' (2002) 16 *Transnational Lawyer* 211. This joint maximization problem also underpins John Coffee's 'bonding' hypothesis: see JC Coffee, Jr, 'The Future as History: The Prospect for Global Convergence in Corporate Governance and Its Implications' (1999) 93 *Northwestern University Law Review* 641.

[96] Choi, n 95.

costs of their decisions; indeed, where firms and investors may seek a regulatory regime that generates benefits for them by *shifting* costs to third parties. Moreover, there are many areas of financial regulation where no such joint maximization problem exists. In these circumstances, the potential welfare effects of regulatory competition must be subjected to closer scrutiny.

Two examples will help illustrate the potential limits of regulatory competition. The first involves the availability of statutory bail-in mechanisms and the unavailability of bail-outs in the context of the resolution of a systemically important financial institution. As described here and in Chapter 16, bail-in mechanisms give domestic resolution authorities the ability to write down the claims of certain classes of creditors of distressed financial institutions. Where the prospect of bail-in and correspondingly no prospect of bail-out exist under a given resolution regime, we would expect a higher cost of debt capital for financial institutions. This means that the *absence* of a bail-in mechanism (or material constraints on its use) and the expectation of a government bail-out in a particular jurisdiction would confer a benefit on domestic financial institutions, their creditors,[97] and their shareholders, since the government protection is likely to translate into higher leverage and thus higher return on equity. Banks within that jurisdiction may expand their balance sheet more rapidly and gain a larger percentage of the global financial business. That, in turn, will put pressure on other jurisdictions not to commit to yes-bail-in/no-bail-out policies, given the competitive disadvantages that would entail for domestic banks. As an outcome, the international financial system will be dominated by too-big-to-fail banks exporting their fragility to other jurisdictions both directly and because their presence is an obstacle to sounder domestic policies abroad.

The second example involves the nascent regulatory regimes governing OTC derivatives markets and, specifically, clearinghouses. As described in Chapter 21, Title VII of the Dodd–Frank Act and the European Market Infrastructure Regulation mandate that certain classes of standardized OTC derivatives be cleared and settled through clearinghouses. These regimes then impose capital, margin, collateral, and other requirements in order to manage the resulting concentration of market, counterparty credit, and other risks. Importantly, however, these requirements impose opportunity and other costs on dealers and end users of OTC derivatives. Insofar as they are for-profit enterprises owned by dealers, we would expect clearinghouses to be sensitive to these costs in the context of their decisions regarding how to operationalize these requirements. Over the longer term, these regulatory costs are likely to have an impact on who emerges as global players in the clearinghouse business. At least so long as there is no credible commitment in place against a government bail-out in the event of clearinghouse insolvency, clearinghouses, dealers, and end users all arguably share a community of interest with regard to the imposition of the least onerous capital, margin, collateral, and other requirements.[98] In an environment of regulatory competition, we

---

[97] Essentially because it increases the expected payouts for these creditors in the resolution context (especially in the presence of a 'too big to fail' subsidy).

[98] Cf S Griffith, 'Governing Systemic Risk: Towards a Governance Structure for Derivatives Clearinghouses' (2012) 61 *Emory Law Review* 1153.

would thus expect to observe an equilibrium characterized by a concentration of market activity in jurisdictions with relatively lax regulation of clearinghouses. Given the systemic importance of major clearinghouses, this equilibrium would manifest potentially significant negative externalities.

The limits of regulatory competition provide us with some insight into the circumstances in which pressure for guided convergence and functional similarity, if not uniformity, is desirable: specifically, where the market for regulation is unlikely to reflect the full social costs of either regulated activities or pervasive regulatory arbitrage—namely, in the presence of negative externalities. Thus, the FSB's post-crisis emphasis on harmonizing domestic regulatory regimes governing clearinghouses and the resolution of systemically important financial institutions, for example, seem broadly justified.[99] Conversely, where the threat of negative externalities is *de minimis*, harmonization will be more difficult to justify. In both cases, of course, the prospective benefits of guided convergence and harmonization must still be weighed against the risks stemming from regulatory miscalculation and forced homogeneity in the business strategies of regulated actors as well as the costs of international harmonization, including those stemming from the reduced timeliness of regulation and hence its lower adaptability to change in financial markets.

28.8 Why Not an International Regulator?

The salient question thus becomes: what tools might we utilize to promote international regulatory coordination? There is no shortage of potential options. At one end of the spectrum is a wide range of soft law tools used extensively within the current global regulatory architecture. At the other end are international treaties and, going further, broad delegation of regulatory, supervisory, and enforcement authority to supranational institutions. This section explores the rationales underpinning the utilization of each of these tools, along with their prospective benefits and drawbacks as mechanisms for promoting cross-border information flow, supervision, crisis response, and at least functional convergence and perhaps harmonization.[100]

As described in section 28.2, international bodies such as the G20, FSB, BCBS, and IOSCO rely predominantly on soft law to promote international coordination. Soft law mechanisms seek to leverage informal peer pressure—often buttressed by more formal peer review, 'name and shame', or 'comply or explain' strategies—to bring national regulators to the table and, ultimately, to ensure compliance with their international commitments. In principle, the effectiveness of these mechanisms depends on a credible threat of reputational sanctions. In practice, however, there are at least three reasons to doubt the credibility of this threat.

---

[99] If not particularly well designed or implemented.

[100] Consistent with the functional orientation of this book, this section does not examine issues surrounding, for example, democratic accountability or legitimacy which might be seen as stemming from the delegation of national rule-making authority to international institutions. However, insofar as these issues can be understood as essentially agency cost problems, they are canvassed in Chapter 25.

First, monitoring compliance with international commitments—especially in the field of financial regulation—can be an extremely costly and complex undertaking. While it may be relatively straightforward to verify whether a jurisdiction has *incorporated* the BCBS's Core Principles for Effective Banking Regulation into domestic law, it is far more difficult to determine whether the relevant regulatory authorities possess the requisite capacity and incentives to effectively comply with these principles. Conversely, it may be difficult to evaluate whether two ostensibly divergent regulatory regimes in fact perform an equivalent economic function, respond to the same problem, or advance the same objective. Articulated in more general terms: it is far easier to monitor compliance with the law on the books than with the law in practice, but it is only the latter that really counts.[101] This injects a degree of uncertainty into the process of determining whether and to what extent a jurisdiction has complied with its international commitments, thereby diluting the force of any reputational sanctions. While that may be true for a hard law mechanism as well, a soft law regime almost invariably relies on the *voluntary* provision of information by national regulators.[102] This, in turn, enables regulators to control the flow and framing of information so as to minimize any reputational consequences. As a result, we might predict that the threat of reputational sanctions would likely not represent a powerful constraint on the behaviour of national regulators in the international arena.

Second, and more importantly, decisions about the function, substance, and application of financial regulation often generate important distributional consequences for domestic constituencies. They may also reflect deeply engrained views regarding the role of the financial sector within the broader economy. Viewed from a public choice perspective, we would expect national regulators to deviate from their international soft law commitments wherever these distributional consequences exceed the reputational costs of non-compliance.[103] Moreover, we might expect these consequences to be most acute where the relevant decisions hold out the potential to generate significant externalities—in the context of a systemic crisis. As a result, soft law mechanisms seem destined to be (most) ineffectual as a means of promoting international regulatory coordination in the precise circumstances when such coordination is most urgently required.

Finally, adopting a *Realpolitik* view of the world, we might expect the jurisdictions that wield the most power within the financial system to be largely insulated from any reputational sanctions stemming from their failure to comply with soft law commitments. Given the size, importance, and global interconnectedness of their domestic financial services sectors—along with the importance of their economies to global growth—it is virtually inconceivable that jurisdictions such as the US, the EU, and

---

[101] This is not to underestimate the costs associated with evaluating compliance with its technical letter. The BCBS Core Principles (n 44), for example, are framed largely as a set of broad principles, requiring national regulators to flesh out and codify numerous technical regulations. Insofar as these regulations may find different expression in the context of different domestic regulatory regimes, it may be costly to evaluate formal compliance.

[102] Both in the sense that they (1) are responsible for collecting this information and providing it to soft law institutions and (2) must consent to any disclosure of information to third parties.

[103] Or where, alternatively, these commitments—given context by the then prevailing circumstances—dictated action which was somehow inconsistent with deeply engrained views.

China, for example, would not continue to exert enormous influence over the global regulatory agenda. Indeed, given their importance, it is hard to envision any meaningful conversation about how to address systemic risks without these jurisdictions imposing their views at the negotiating table. Viewed in this light, soft law mechanisms are likely to elicit the least credible commitments from the jurisdictions most likely to be the source of significant negative externalities.

Given these manifest drawbacks, one might reasonably ask why soft law is utilized so extensively within the current global regulatory architecture. Proponents of soft law identify a number of benefits. These benefits flow primarily from soft law's ability to generate *ex ante* consensus under conditions of uncertainty and in the face of divergent national interests.[104] Ultimately, however, this rationale must be put to one side on the basis that consensus—in and of itself—is at best peripheral to any of the objectives of financial regulation identified in Chapter 3. What is more, *ex ante* consensus is of little value if it does not also generate credible *ex post* commitments. A more compelling explanation for the dominance of soft law is that it is simply a reflection of the prevailing political landscape: a pragmatic response to the fact that, while the problems may be increasingly *global* in nature, the legal and political authority to address these problems resides predominantly at the *national* level. This begs one important question: how might we expand the geopolitical footprint of financial regulation to reflect the globalization, concentration, and interconnectedness of the financial system itself?

One way to expand the global footprint of financial regulation would be through a legally binding treaty. Barry Eichengreen, for example, has proposed a treaty-based World Financial Organization analogous to the existing World Trade Organization.[105] Under Eichengreen's proposal, jurisdictions seeking to secure access to foreign markets for their domestic financial services industry would be required to become a signatory to the treaty and, thereafter, comply with its obligations in terms of the substantive content of regulation and the quality of supervision and enforcement. Disputes as to whether a jurisdiction had complied with these obligations would then be subject to adjudication by a panel of independent experts with the power to levy sanctions including, but not limited to, expulsion from the organization. In effect, market access would represent both a carrot and stick to compel participation and ongoing compliance.

There is no doubt that a treaty-based World Financial Organization would put international commitments in areas such as cross-border information sharing, supervision, crisis response, and functional harmonization on more solid legal footing. This, in turn, might be expected to improve marginally the probability of compliance—in effect by making the threat of sanctions more credible. However, this and other similar proposals have significant drawbacks.[106] As a preliminary matter, the time-consuming and politically delicate process of negotiating (and periodically *renegotiating*) multilateral treaties would seem to be fundamentally at odds with the often frenetic pace of

---

[104] Brummer, n 9.

[105] B Eichengreen, 'Not a New Bretton Woods but a New Bretton Woods Process', in B Eichengreen and R Baldwin, *What G20 Leaders Must Do to Stabilise Our Economy and Fix the Financial System* (London: CEPR, 2008), 25.

[106] In addition to having to overcome pronounced network effects in order to attract a critical mass of signatories.

change within the financial system and the corresponding need to continually update both substantive regulation and approaches towards supervision and enforcement.[107] Moreover, it is not entirely clear how non-financial sanctions—including, theoretically, the withdrawal of market access—could be imposed without generating potentially significant knock-on effects.[108] Finally, using market access as leverage to compel compliance could conceivably give larger and more systemically important jurisdictions a *de facto* veto over both the substantive content and enforcement of treaty obligations.

An even more radical option would be the formal delegation of power to a supranational regulatory authority. Among others, John Eatwell and Lance Taylor have argued that good governance of a globally integrated financial system necessitates a global regulator with responsibility, amongst other things, for supervising systemically important financial institutions.[109] This would be a global extension of the regulatory hierarchy that has emerged more clearly within the US, the UK, and the EU since the financial crisis.[110] However, the challenges for this proposal are heroic. Perhaps most importantly, it raises a series of thorny questions surrounding domestic burden sharing—especially where a global regulator was responsible for decisions regarding the resolution of systemically important financial institutions. Precisely these issues have proved extremely difficult in connection with the creation of the European Banking Union, a far less ambitious project. Such proposals also raise important questions regarding democratic legitimacy and the prospect of regulatory capture.[111] The decisions of a global regulator could have significant distributional consequences, which could vary from country to country. As a result, such proposals are—at least for the foreseeable future—politically unfeasible. However, if the European Banking Union flourishes, it may provide a template for addressing such issues amongst a broader group of countries.

On the basis of this analysis, we might reasonably ask if we find ourselves caught between Scylla and Charybdis—between the relative impotence of soft law and the intractable obstacles to the emergence of more credible and effective international commitments. However, there is perhaps room to work constructively between these two extremes. First, as Brummer observes, the 'compliance pull' of soft law mechanisms is often undermined by structural flaws—eg the confidentiality of peer reviews and legal restrictions on information sharing—which impede the dissemination of information necessary to generate a credible threat of reputational sanctions.[112] By

---

[107] C Reinhart and K Rogoff, 'Regulation Should be International', *Financial Times* (18 November 2008). While Eichengreen (n 105) envisions that the implementation of technical regulation in furtherance of treaty obligations would be the responsibility of individual signatories, this would seem to raise many of the same monitoring issues encountered in connection with the use of soft law mechanisms.

[108] How, for example, could you impose restrictions on the US without precipitating massive and potentially destabilizing international capital flows?

[109] J Eatwell and L Taylor, *Global Finance at Risk: The Case for International Regulation* (New York, NY: WW Norton & Co, 2000).

[110] See Chapter 24, section 24.3.3, Chapter 27, section 27.3.3, and section 28.4.

[111] See N Woods (ed), *The Political Economy of Globalization* (New York, NY: Palgrave MacMillan, 2000).

[112] Brummer, n 9.

taking steps to address these flaws, it might be possible to give these sanctions some real teeth.[113] Second, while comprehensive global treaties and regulators may be politically quixotic, this does not preclude the pursuit of legally binding international commitments on a more incremental scale. The obvious place to start would be cross-border information flow. Leveraging the common infrastructure of the global LEI/PI system,[114] for example, it might be possible to enshrine multilateral information-sharing arrangements within the framework of a formal treaty.[115] This treaty might also envision the aggregation of this information in a 'global information repository'. These proposals would provide national regulators with a common informational foundation from which to engage in enhanced cross-border dialogue. They would also lower the information and coordination costs of mounting effective international policy responses to both new market developments and emerging crises. Yet, a comprehensive system of information sharing about individual transactions would still require a high degree of trust among national governments and supervisors: unless governments can confidently rule out that supervisors in other jurisdictions, no matter how formally independent, will share information with their governments—who could then use it for tax purposes or, worse, political reprisal—even this seemingly technical and incremental step will face high political hurdles.

28.9 Conclusion

The global financial crisis has powerfully illustrated how the forces of globalization, concentration, and interconnectedness can become catalysts of systemic risk. The crisis has also illustrated how these forces can undermine both the capacity and the incentives of national regulators to identify, monitor, and effectively respond to these risks. In other words, the disconnect between an increasingly global and interconnected financial system, on the one hand, and the predominantly domestic and fragmented regulatory regimes and regulators which govern it, on the other, has emerged as a key obstacle to the effective prevention of financial crises. As an outcome, international regulatory coordination in areas such as cross-border information flow, prudential regulation and supervision, and crisis response has been at the top of the post-crisis reform agenda and this chapter has described the progress made.

While most measures were in the domain of soft law or regional in character, there is reason to be cautiously optimistic about the current state of the art in international financial regulatory coordination. The positive factors for financial stability at least over the medium term include the centrality of the US and the UK to global financial

---

[113] Although, in the process, this may have an adverse impact on the incentives of national regulators (or other domestic constituencies) to commit to these mechanisms *ex ante*.

[114] See section 28.5.

[115] Of course, this treaty would potentially still be vulnerable to the problems identified earlier in the chapter—especially in terms of the need for periodic renegotiation. However, given that the substance of this treaty would be restricted to the sharing of information between national regulators, it would be possible to frame the treaty's obligations in such a way as to minimize this prospect (eg by stipulating these obligations at a sufficiently high level of generality and then specifying more granular information requirements outside the formal confines of the treaty).

activity, given their current commitment to high standards,[116] the 'hard law' of an important transnational regulatory regime, the European Banking Union, and the strong inclination of the most powerful central banks to cooperate, so as to avoid another financial crisis. The risks to the unravelling of the post-crisis regime probably arise from financial activity outside the regulatory perimeter, most likely of US origin. Competition from new financial centres—including international regulatory arbitrage— is also a potential threat. Finally, the sine curve dynamic of regulation we described in Chapter 25, section 25.4.2 equally applies to international financial coordination, making the current post-crisis framework less steady and less necessarily an intermediate step to future enhanced cooperation than it may look.

---

[116] Despite the sinister echo of a global financial crisis that propagated from these two countries, their (persistent) centrality can be viewed as a positive for three reasons: first, these two jurisdictions are now committed to high standards; second, two-party cross-monitoring is easier than multi-party monitoring; third, the Fed and the Bank of England have entered into an MOU that would facilitate resolution of a large financial firm domiciled in either the US or the UK.

29

Conclusion—Designing Tomorrow's Financial System Today

> Risks are usually the greatest when they appear the least; and financial market participants the most vulnerable when they think they know all the answers. In a dynamic financial system, all participants need to focus continually on identifying vulnerabilities and improving resilience. Our work has just begun.
>
> (Mark Carney, speech in Geneva, 9 November 2010)

29.1 Gains from Translation

This book's goal is to provide a framework for the analysis of financial regulation. As the first chapter states, it is a topic that has been lent particular relevance by the financial crisis of 2007–9. The book articulates a set of principles around which to frame financial regulation. Financial regulation is concerned with improving the operation of the financial system. So the book's starting principle is that to understand financial regulation, we need to understand the financial system—what it does, and how it is structured.

The financial system is an economic system. Because of this, the book emphasizes the importance of understanding the regulation of the financial system in economic terms. It rationalizes regulation in relation to the correction of market failures and promotes evidence-based analysis to evaluate the efficacy of different remedies.

The financial system is also a dynamic system, subject to continual change as a result of the evolving needs of global commerce and the innovative offerings of technology. The book consequently also emphasizes dynamism in our presentation of regulation and builds it into the structure, with the development from markets to consumers to banks to the messy and contested space in which they all interact.

But the regulatory system is a legal system. While the policies underpinning it may be derived from economics, the content of the regulatory norms is legal. The disjoint between the economic underpinning and the legal superstructure creates a barrier to understanding. Lawyers, regulators, and market actors advised by them understand the system in terms of the legal sources—the legislative pronouncements that give normative force to the regulatory superstructure. These legal sources represent frozen policy moments, capturing how legislators thought about regulation at a particular point in time. To seek to understand the goals of financial regulation as immanent to—that is, inhering within—its legal norms is to understand its functions in a historic, rather than a contemporary, way. Originalism is not a good basis for engineering.

We see this problem of legal framing in the way in which most lawyers working in financial regulation see themselves as 'banking' or 'securities' lawyers. This self-identification derives not from the underlying financial system—global 'banking organizations' cover most of the terrain—but rather from the partition of legal norms.

Principles of Financial Regulation. First Edition. John Armour, Dan Awrey, Paul Davies, Luca Enriques, Jeffrey N. Gordon, Colin Mayer, and Jennifer Payne. © John Armour, Dan Awrey, Paul Davies, Luca Enriques, Jeffrey N. Gordon, Colin Mayer, and Jennifer Payne 2016. Published 2016 by Oxford University Press.

On the other side of the divide, economists make a different mistake. They pay insufficient attention to the detail of the legal framework that defines the operation of financial markets. This leads them to neglect the potentially perverse consequences of overlooked regulatory constraints and to overestimate the extent to which the behaviour of market actors is efficiency-seeking rather than driven by the effort to evade regulation.

To overcome this disjoint, financial lawyers need to have a sense of the economic foundations of financial regulation, and financial economists need to have a better understanding of the legal and institutional superstructure. Lawyers will then be better placed to understand the evolving nature of financial regulation, and economists will be more aware of the significance of institutional constraints and regulatory history.

This book has sought to provide such a translation, by working with a limited set of regulatory goals grounded in responses to market failures. The market failures are economic; the legal goals are interpreted in the light of the necessary policy responses. This approach points to the complexities of addressing the multiple objectives of financial regulation and reveals the contradictions and dilemmas that arise from their parallel pursuit without regard to their interaction.

For example, the use of microprudential rules, designed to protect retail investors who purchase financial products from insurance companies or investment funds, stimulates demand for these products. This increases levels of correlation in the system as a whole, which may render it more fragile to systemic risk. Trade-offs exist almost everywhere, necessitating the application of evidence-based assessments of the merits of particular regulatory policies.

These issues have been made even more significant by disintermediation and the emergence of new forms of intermediaries that have blurred the boundaries amongst different types of financial institutions. For example, investment banks used securities markets to distribute debt securities that substitute for bank loans without the prudential oversight that seeks to stabilize the banking system. These developments were both effects and causes of regulation. They were effects insofar as they reflected arbitrage between existing rules, and they were causes in that regulation has been a response to problems created by financial innovations.

The final part of the book reveals that matters are even messier than the interface between law and economics suggests. The neatness of our stylized analysis of the substance of financial regulation is in practice exposed to the institutional and political realities of regulatory architecture and implementation. What is right in principle frequently fails in practice, and regulatory failures can be at least as great as the market failures that they are designed to address.

29.2 What Have We Learned?

What are the lessons to be learnt from this exercise? Some of the most important insights are: (i) the primacy of institutional and regulatory purpose; (ii) the relevance of function over form; (iii) the significance of a dynamic versus a static framework; (iv) the tendency of yesterday's solutions to frame tomorrow's problems; (v) the dominance of macro over micro considerations; and (vi) the need for an international as well as a domestic approach to regulation. We shall briefly consider each of these in turn.

29.2.1 The primacy of purpose

The framing of regulation has to take as its starting point what it is trying to achieve. For financial regulation, this means trying to improve the functioning of the financial system through avoiding market failures. This presupposes an understanding of regulatory norms in terms of these market failures and it involves trade-offs amongst specific regulatory goals. An overall regulatory objective function is required that specifies how these trade-offs should be made, and who should make them.

These trade-offs have not gone away; only their form will be different in the future from the past. Just as work was completed to reduce the 'hardwiring' of demand for 'low risk' securities into the prudential rules of investment funds, a new offering emerged that creates its own risks: total loss-absorbing capacity claims issued by banks. These must to be sold to the private sector if they are to be used to make bank bail-in feasible. But who will buy them? From a consumer protection perspective, these seem to be a potentially disastrous investment—they look like 'safe' fixed income securities yielding a higher-than-average return, but in some states of the world their capital claims are wiped out.[1] This almost exactly fits the description of the kind of 'low quality' structured product regulators are trying to eliminate.[2] Yet they are suitable as part of the diversified holdings of a pension fund or an insurer.

This has implications for the ranking of regulatory goals, and for the institutional structure of regulators. At present, financial instability is the largest potential source of costs to the financial system, and should be given priority. There should be an 'apex agency'—a microprudential authority—whose task it is to review the state of the financial system and the ordering of goals of financial regulators.

29.2.2 Function not form

Regulation is designed around institutions. It distinguishes between banks and securities markets and between different types of banks and other financial institutions. There are historical reasons why regulation evolved in this way, and it was an acceptable approach during periods in which the functions of institutions were clearly delineated. But that is no longer the case.

One of the primary causes of the financial crisis described in this book was the emergence of different institutions performing functionally equivalent activities. To

---

[1] For example, in December 2015, a bail-in of four regional Italian banks exposed retail customers who had been persuaded by the promise of a high coupon rate to invest in bail-inable bonds in their banks, to heavy losses: see J Politi, 'Italy Bank Rescues Spark Bail-in Debate as Anger at Renzi Grows', *Financial Times*, 22 December 2015. See also Chapter 12, section 12.2.5.

[2] Bail-inable bank bonds were one of the first financial products that the UK's Financial Conduct Authority ('FCA') used new product regulation powers (see Chapter 12, section 12.3.2) to ban from sale to retail investors: see FCA, 'Restrictions on the Retail Distribution of Regulatory Capital Instruments', PS 15/14 (2015).

build different regulations around essentially similar institutions is equivalent to taxing identical products and services in different ways. There are two consequences: first, highly regulated and taxed institutions, products, and services will be displaced in favour of the lightly taxed and regulated ones; and second, incumbent institutions seek regulatory relaxation to compete with new entrants. These problems are exacerbated when financial institutions performing functionally equivalent activities are governed by different regulations and overseen by different regulatory agencies.

That has been the history of regulation and taxation since time immemorial, but what has changed is the speed and ease with which innovation to avoid regulation and taxation is now emerging. Even if an institutional approach did have a rationale, it no longer does, and it makes no sense to regulate financial markets and institutions on anything other than the basis of their functions rather than their form. Similar regulation for functionally equivalent activities and institutions should be the mantra of regulation today.

Applying this instruction, of course, requires us to keep in mind the primacy of regulatory purpose. Should we care if non-bank financial intermediaries are performing bank-like functions? The answer is yes if the reasons for bank regulation carry across when their functions are performed by non-banks. By considering the economic basis for banking fragility,[3] we can—as we have done in Chapters 20–22—explore the extent to which non-bank financial institutions raise similar problems for stability as banks.

29.2.3 Dynamic not static

What of tomorrow's problems? The shape of the financial system is subject to continual change, the pace of which will in all probability accelerate with advancing technology. While it is impossible to predict how risks will change in the future, having the analytic tools to understand the linkages between them allows us to gain a better appreciation of their systemic consequences.

Technological advances, new arbitrage opportunities, shifting financial imbalances across nations and continents, evolving patterns of savings and investment, and demographic changes mean that the financial system is never static. As a consequence, regulation is almost always solving yesterday's problems.

Regulation should be at least as dynamic as the industry it is regulating and aim to anticipate where the next crisis is going to occur, not just react to the last one. That is easier said than done, given how the very enactment of new rules and supervisory tools prompts changes in market dynamics that are hard for anyone (regulators, market participants, or academics) to predict. Conversely, an overzealousness on the part of regulators to overlay new products with extensive regulation risks provoking accusations that they are suffocating innovation before it has been allowed to breathe. It is a difficult balance to strike, but thus far regulators have if anything erred in the direction of being unduly flat-footed rather than agile.

---

[3] See Chapter 13.

We have identified several important ways in which regulators have become more dynamic in their responses in recent years. Done properly, macroprudential oversight brings with it the potential to inject dynamism into the regulatory regime in two ways: first, through the use of time-varying instruments—most obviously but not limited to capital controls—which respond to the build-up of excess credit risk in the economy at large; and second, through cross-sectional reviews of the allocation of regulatory perimeters.[4] The US Financial Stability Oversight Council acts as a referee of whether a firm's activity has taken on systemic importance and it has nudged the Securities and Exchange Commission ('SEC') into more direct regulation of money market funds and asset managers. The UK's Financial Policy Committee has prescribed measures that other UK regulators have implemented. These changes illustrate not only shifting firms within existing perimeters, but also the capacity to redraw the perimeters themselves.

A third source of dynamism in regulatory responses—on a more micro level—is the advent of product governance as a strategy in consumer financial regulation,[5] which paves the way for more dynamic oversight of financial firms' product development processes. Rather than pushing against the grain of market dynamism, product governance seeks to harness it for the good.

29.2.4 Yesterday's solutions: tomorrow's problems?

We may worry that today's solutions are fixing yesterday's problems. A more serious concern, linked to the way in which regulation shapes the structure of the financial system, is that in the near future these solutions will themselves sow the seeds of future problems.

For example, we have seen how the Glass–Steagall Act's separation of investment and commercial banks helped restrict the growth of commercial banking in the US—relative to elsewhere—and promoted the development of the 'dealer banks'—market-based intermediaries that operated outside the banking safety net but undertook functionally equivalent activity without equivalent prudential oversight.[6] Similarly, we saw how Regulation Q, which restricted the interest rates US banks could offer to consumers, promoted the growth of the money market fund sector.[7] Both of these trajectories were harmful for stability.

Should we now pause for thought and reflect on what consequences today's solutions may pose for tomorrow's stability? Take the imposition of dramatically higher capital requirements on large banks.[8] The banks have responded in part by cutting back their lending. This retreat by the banks has been associated with the efflorescence of a host of new forms of lending—from the less appealing (payday lending) to the more 'hyped', such as 'peer-to-peer' lending.[9] Peer-to-peer lending lies outside the bank regulatory system, but from the consumer's perspective, it is much the same: it engages in similar credit scoring and it imposes equivalent conditions to bank loans. But it is not 'banking' in the regulatory sense.

---

[4] See Chapter 19 and Chapter 27, section 27.3.   [5] See Chapter 12, section 12.3.3.
[6] See Chapter 20, section 20.2.   [7] See Chapter 22, section 22.2.1.
[8] See Chapter 14, section 14.5.   [9] See Chapter 12, section 12.2.5.

So, there is one form of lending that is subject to stringent rules about conduct of business, capital requirements, and liquidity, and there is another that is not. Regulation thereby risks recognizing new forms of banking only after the moment of their collapse. More generally, regulation has an uneasy relationship with financial innovation. Early on, few innovations have significant impact on the financial system, but as the innovation disseminates, at critical points in the dissemination curve, the principal effects may switch from the local to the systemic.

Similarly, restrictions on the banking sector imposed by the Volcker Rule in the US and Vickers' ring-fencing in the UK may lead to the creation of a new category of freewheeling asset managers, who buy and sell assets, own exchange infrastructure, and perform investment bank-type functions.[10] Likewise, the mandatory clearing of derivatives markets across clearing houses may create new sources of systemic risk.[11] There is a concern, especially in the Eurozone, that such firms are not yet subject to many of the controls put in place for banks and a concern in the US that they will become the next candidates for bail-out.

Measures to resolve failing banks—the 'bail in' tool and the single point of entry mechanisms—may themselves create fundamental risks depending on who buys the new claims.[12] These are supposed to represent the privatization of losses from failed banks. But if banks are allowed to issue them to one another, then they will become channels for the inter-linkage of contagion. The banking sector may welcome this if it triggers 'too big to fail' rescues and bank regulators will need to be alert to this possibility.[13]

29.2.5 Macro not micro

One of the main messages of the book has been that the most significant aspect of market failure relates to systemic rather than individual institutional failure. It is at the systemic level where the substantial externalities that market participants fail to internalize lie. That is where markets do not have the capability or resources to correct failures. There are problems of information asymmetries and contractual failure at the micro level of institutions, but there are relatively clear ways of addressing them through, for example, disclosure, insurance, and custodianship. Systemic effects are different. Where a firm's conduct has significant systemic consequences, the parties in privity with the firm will not internalize the costs, and a simple restructuring of those private relationships will not provide a solution.

The biggest problems are macro, whereas the main regulatory interventions until recently have been micro. The financial crisis revealed the gaping hole in macroprudential policy that this had left, which regulators have been rushing to fill ever since. This, in turn, leads to the next issue.

---

[10] See Chapter 23.   [11] See Chapter 21, section 21.4.   [12] See Chapter 16, section 16.5.

[13] It is worth noting that recent research suggests that, as of 2012, the debt of large US financial institutions exhibits less price sensitivity to default risk than that of smaller banks, suggesting the market continues to price in an expectation of government support in the event of failure: see VV Acharya, D Anginer, and AJ Warburton, 'The End of Market Discipline? Investor Expectations of Implicit Government Guarantees', Working Paper NYU Stern School of Business (2016).

29.2.6 International not domestic

Financial markets and many of the most significant financial institutions are international. Financial regulation is generally national with a steadily expanding overlay of international integration. The financial crisis revealed how important this international aspect was for the supervision and resolution of international banking behemoths. It has provoked important developments in two places.

First, at the European level, the subprime crisis and then the Euro sovereign debt crisis have provided the kind of aggressive stimulus necessary to forge an international system of bank supervision, resolution, and, it is hoped, deposit insurance.[14] Second, at the international level, the G20's inauguration of the Financial Stability Board has set the scene for a more comprehensive and rapid promulgation of standards and peer reviews.[15]

Although there is now much more awareness of the importance of international cooperation than there was before the financial crisis, the political economy of international coordination remains particularly prone to failure.[16] Accountability issues are more serious and market participant pressures no less relevant internationally than they are domestically. In addition, problems of finding international regulatory solutions are even greater given the serious difficulties of reaching consensus on any effective solution.

29.3 Emerging Issues

At this point, it is appropriate to introduce some humility to the discussion. This is not a short book, but it is far shorter than the range of potentially relevant issues. Some of the omissions are as follows.

29.3.1 Geography

Our project has been explicitly North Atlantic in its orientation. This reflects both our expertise and the interactive role of the US and Europe in the global financial crisis. The US financial system produced the flawed securitization products that damaged the balance sheets of many European banks; the Federal Reserve bailed out European banks that held swaps issued by AIG and provided hundreds of billions of dollars of swap line credit to support European financial banks at the outset of the global financial and the Eurozone crises. This transatlantic focus does not, however, reflect the global financial system, which has been growing more rapidly in Asia in recent years. Incorporating an Asian perspective is an important challenge for future work.

---

[14] See Chapter 24, section 24.3.3; Chapter 27, section 27.2.4; and Chapter 28, section 28.4.
[15] See Chapter 28, section 28.2.   [16] See Chapter 28, section 28.8.

29.3.2 Culture

Second, we have not engaged with questions of changing culture within financial firms, arguably one of the most significant items on the political agenda. A focus on rules, compliance, and enforcement may serve to promote adoption of the letter rather than the spirit of the law. A framework of compliance encourages a mindset of avoidance—trading off penalties and probabilities of detection against the profitability of violations that remain undetected.

To date, regulation has often been seen as a game between regulator and regulated in which the regulator sets the rules and institutions respond to them with strategies that minimize their impact and effectiveness. This puts regulator and regulated in conflict with each other. Regulators are the guardians of the public interest; financial institutions pursue their private purposes.

Even a dynamic regulator will struggle against the well-resourced titans we discussed in Chapter 4.[17] Could a cultural change be brought about inside financial sector firms, such that they recognize the importance of public purpose as well as private profits? This would be a much tougher call for regulators and industry leaders than legislation and enforcement. It requires a rethinking of the way in which financial institutions and market participants perceive their role in the financial system and society.

A number of elements of the new regulatory acquis could, however, help to provoke cultural shifts inside financial firms. We highlight three here. First, the push to product governance in relation to consumer products will put the onus on firms to show how their products are designed and marketed in ways that seek to benefit, rather than bilk, consumers.[18] Although the technique is as yet largely untested, one can imagine that, in the hands of a suitably assertive conduct regulator, this could have a potentially wide-ranging impact on internal culture. It is not inconceivable that commissions led by sales could be replaced by commissions based on medium-term consumer satisfaction scores. Such sales practices are common in other sectors—premium cars, for example—and there is no fundamental barrier to their utilization in the financial sector.

Second, the banishment of proprietary traders from US banks, and the institutional separation of retail and wholesale banks in the UK (and in parts of the EU) will affect the internal culture of these organizations.[19] As Paul Volcker has argued, this cultural change—removing the 'trader-led' mentality in the boardroom—can have a subtle impact on firm culture.

Closely linked to this is the third factor, the regulation (in the EU) of financial firm pay.[20] The dramatic curtailment of variable pay for material risk-takers in EU financial institutions could have a similar cultural impact.

29.3.3 Technology

Technological change is sweeping through the financial system at an ever-increasing pace. Algorithmic active trading has been with us for a number of years, and has been

---

[17] See Chapter 4, section 4.2.   [18] See Chapter 12, section 12.3.3.
[19] See Chapter 23, section 23.2.1.   [20] See Chapter 17, section 17.4.2.

blamed for increasing volatility in public markets.[21] On the horizon are algorithmic asset managers, promising further reduction of management fees, 'robo-advisors', promising cheap access to advice about trading or investment strategies. All these products could come with automated execution, with payments routed through bitcoin or similar algorithmic units of exchange.

At the same time, the burgeoning business of cyber-crime attests to the vulnerability of many bank systems to unauthorized entrants. The growth of algorithmic inter-actions puts a premium on the security of the system as a whole. The deliberate introduction of 'malgorithms' could easily be a major source of systemic risk. Man-aging these structural concerns suggests that those engineering financial regulation in the future will likely need to translate some principles of computer science, as well as economics.

The book has not attempted to answer all these questions, but it is clearly important to pose them. Matters of geography, culture, and technology focus on where the financial system is heading rather than where it has come from. The principles we distilled from the book in the preceding section are well suited to addressing 'whither' questions as well. Given the imperfect and uncertain world in which we live, we nourish no hope of prescribing a formula to prevent the next crisis. Our more modest hope is that we have set out a framework that will allow future policymakers, super-visors, and scholars to better understand the impact, challenges, and risks of financial regulation.

---

[21] See Chapter 7, section 7.5.

Index